SECOND CANADIAN EDITION

BEHAVIOUR IN ORGANIZATIONS

Understanding and Managing the Human Side of Work

Jerald Greenberg
The Ohio State University

Robert A. Baron
Rensselaer Polytechnic Institute

Carol A. Sales
Brock University

Frances A. Owen
Niagara University

Prentice Hall Canada Inc.
Scarborough, Ontario

Canadian Cataloguing in Publication Data

Behaviour in organizations: understanding and managing the human side of work

2nd Canadian ed.
Includes bibliographical references and index.
ISBN 0-13-083672-9

1. Organizational behaviour.   2. Personnel management.   I. Greenberg, Jerald.

HD58.7.B44   2000   658.3   C00-930270-1

Prentice-Hall, Inc., Upper Saddle River, New Jersey
Prentice-Hall International (UK) Limited, London
Prentice-Hall of Australia, Pty. Limited, Sydney
Prentice-Hall Hispanoamericana, S.A., Mexico City
Prentice-Hall of India Private Limited, New Delhi
Prentice-Hall of Japan, Inc., Tokyo
Simon & Schuster Southeast Asia Private Limited, Singapore
Editora Prentice-Hall do Brasil, Ltda., Rio de Janeiro

ISBN 0-13-083672-9

Vice President and Editorial Director: Pat Ferrier
Acquisitions Editor: Mike Ryan
Developmental Editor: Amber Wallace
Senior Marketing Manager: Ann Byford
Copy Editor: Linda Cahill
Production Editor: Mary Ann McCutcheon
Production Coordinator: Deborah Starks
Permissions/Photo Research: Karen Becker
Art Director: Mary Opper
Cover Design: Alex Li
Cover Image: © Susan Leopold/Masterfile
Design: Alex Li
Page Layout: Joan M. Wilson

Original English Language edition published by Prentice-Hall, Inc.,
Upper Saddle River, New Jersey
Copyright © 1997, 1995

1 2 3 4 5   04 03 02 01 00

Printed and bound in the United States of America.

Visit the Prentice Hall Canada Web site! Send us your comments, browse our catalogues, and more. **www.phcanada.com** Or reach us through e-mail at **phcinfo_pubcanada@prenhall.com**.

To my best pal, for giving me strength, serenity, and sustenance.

J.G.

To three of the people who truly matter in my life:
Jessica—who shares my optimism
Richard—who shares my love of good food, and
Randy—who shares so many of my views

R.A.B.

To the memory of Betty C. Sales
and
To Betty Jean and Jane Lavallee

C.A.S.

To F. George-Ann Owen
and
To the memory of John V. Owen

F.A.O.

CONTENTS

Preface   xi

Acknowledgments   xvii

PART 1
Organizational Behaviour: An Introduction

CHAPTER 1
The Nature and Study of Organizations   1

Case Preview: Randy Powell: Managing People, Not Projects   2

Organizational Behaviour: A Working Definition   3
OB Applies the Scientific Method to Practical Managerial Problems   4
OB Focuses on Three Levels of Analysis: Individuals, Groups, and Organizations   5

Organizational Behaviour Today: Characteristics of the Field   6
OB Seeks to Improve People's Quality of Life at Work   6
OB Recognizes the Dynamic Nature of Organizations   7
OB Assumes There Is No "One Best" Approach   8
OB Confronts Challenges Created by the Changing Nature of Work   9

Organizational Behaviour: A Capsule History of the Field   10
Scientific Management: The Roots of Organizational Behaviour   10
The Human Relations Movement: Elton Mayo and the Hawthorne Studies   11
Classical Organizational Theory   14
Organizational Behaviour in the Modern Era   14

Theory and Research: Tools for Learning about Behaviour in Organizations   16
Isn't It All Just Common Sense?   16
Theory: An Indispensable Guide to Organizational Research   17
Survey Research: The Correlational Method   19
Experimental Research: The Logic of Cause and Effect   22
Qualitative Research: Naturalistic Observation and the Case Method   25

Summary and Review   27

Case Preview Questions for Discussion   27

Chapter Questions for Discussion   27

Case in Point: Roots Canada: From Algonquin Park to Nagano   28

Skills Portfolio
Experiencing Organizational Behaviour: Testing Your Assumptions about People at Work   29
Working in Groups: Common Sense about Behaviour in Organizations: Putting It to the Test   29
Take It to the Net   **30**

CHAPTER 2
Work in the Twenty-First Century: The Changing World of People and Organizations   31

Case Preview: Babine Forest Products: Modelling Diversity as a Strategic Advantage   32

Globalization and Culture: Today's International Organizations   33
Organizations in the Global Arena   33
Culture and Its Impact   36
Hofstede's Dimensions of Culture   38

The Shifting Demographics of the Workforce: Trends toward Diversity   40
Two Philosophies of Diversity: Mosaic and Melting Pot   40
Today's—and Tomorrow's—Highly Diverse Workforce   41
Celebrating Diversity   42

Trends in Working Arrangements: New Organizational Forms and Jobs   45
Leaner Organizations: Downsizing and Outsourcing   45
The Contingent Workforce: "Permanent Temporary" Employees   47
The Virtual Corporation: A Network of Temporary Organizations   49
Telecommuting: The Demise of the Office   49

The Quality Revolution: Total Quality Management and Reengineering   50
Total Quality Management: A Commitment to Customers   51
Reengineering: Starting All Over   52

Corporate Social Responsibility: The Ethical Organization   54
Why Does Unethical Organizational Behaviour Occur?   55
What Can Be Done to Promote Ethical Behaviour in Organizations?   56

Summary and Review   58

Case Preview Questions for Discussion   58

Chapter Questions for Discussion   59

Case in Point: ING Direct: A Virtual Arrow to the Heart of Canadian Banks   59

Skills Portfolio
Experiencing Organizational Behaviour: Are You More Ethical Than the Average Manager? Don't Be So Sure!   60
Working in Groups: Canada Awards for Excellence (CAE) Winners: What Makes Them So Special?   61
Take It to the Net   **61**
Cumulative Case Part 1: Keith Kocho: The Renaissance Man and His Company   **62**
CBC ⊕ Video Case Part 1: Vertically Inclined Rock Gym: Climbing the Walls with Virgil   64

PART 2
Basic Human Processes

CHAPTER 3
Perception and Learning: Understanding and Adapting to the Work Environment   65

Case Preview: Nortel Networks: A "Cool Place" to Work   66

Social Perception: The Process of Understanding Others   67

The Attribution Process: Judging the Causes of Others' Behaviour   68

Making Correspondent Inferences: Using Acts to Judge
Dispositions 68
Causal Attribution of Responsibility: Answering the Question
"Why?" 69

The Imperfect Nature of Social Perception: Bias and How to
Overcome It 71
Perceptual Biases: Systematic Errors in Perceiving Others 71
Stereotypes: Fitting Others into Categories 74
Overcoming Bias in Social Perception: Some Guidelines 75

Perceiving Others: Organizational Applications 76
Performance Appraisals: Making Formal Judgments about
Others 76
Impression Management in the Employment Interview:
Looking Good to Prospective Employers 77
Corporate Image: Impression Management by
Organizations 78

Learning: Adapting to the World around Us 80
Operant Conditioning: Learning through Rewards and
Punishments 81
Observational Learning: Learning by Imitating Others 85

Applications of Learning in Organizations 86
Training: Learning and Developing Job Skills 86
Organizational Behaviour Management: Positively Reinforcing
Desirable Organizational Behaviours 88
Discipline: Eliminating Undesirable Organizational
Behaviours 92

Summary and Review 95

Case Preview Questions for Discussion 96

Chapter Questions for Discussion 96

Case in Point: CIBC's Leadership Centre: Employee
Education as a Survival Imperative 97

Skills Portfolio

Experiencing Organizational Behaviour: Identifying
Occupational Stereotypes 97

Working in Groups: Role Play: The Disciplinary
Interview 98

Take It to the Net 99

SPECIAL SECTIONS

Globalization in Today's Organizations: Saving Face
in Japan, Where Renting Acquaintances Is Big Business 80

The Quest for Quality: Corporate Goliaths Training
Corporate Davids 90

The Ethics Angle: Coverups in the Military: Do Sexual
Harassment and Sexual Assault Go Unpunished? 93

CHAPTER 4
**Individual Differences: Personality and
Abilities** 100

Case Preview: Christine Silverberg: The Force Behind
the Force in Calgary 101

Personality: Its Basic Nature and Role in Organizational
Behaviour 102
Is Personality Real? The Person-Situation Controversy 103

Work-Related Aspects of Personality 104
The "Big Five" Dimensions of Personality and Organizational
Behaviour 104
Positive and Negative Affectivity: Stable Tendencies to Feel
Good or Bad at Work 106
The Type A Behaviour Pattern: Why Being in a Hurry Can
Be Costly to Your Health 106

The Proactive Personality: People Who Shape Their
Environments 108
Self-Efficacy: The "Can Do" Facet of Personality 110
Self-Monitoring: Self-Image versus Private Reality 111
Machiavellianism: Using Others to Get Ahead 113
Work-Related Motives: Achievement, Power, and Affiliation 115
Morning Persons and Evening Persons 117

Abilities: Having What It Takes 120
Intellectual Abilities 120
Physical Abilities 122

Measuring Individual Differences: Some Basic Methods 122
Objective and Projective Tests 123
Reliability and Validity: Essential Requirements 123

Summary and Review 125

Case Preview Questions for Discussion 126

Chapter Questions for Discussion 126

Case in Point: Edgar Bronfman Jr.: Through the
Distillery and Back to Hollywood 127

Skills Portfolio

Experiencing Organizational Behaviour: Measuring
Your Own Self-Monitoring 128

Working in Groups: Machiavellianism in Action: The
$10 Game 129

Take It to the Net 130

SPECIAL SECTIONS

Organizational Trends: The Potential Benefits of Boosting
Self-Efficacy: Helping People Help Themselves 112

Globalization in Today's Organizations: Achievement
Motivation and Economic Growth 118

The Ethics Angle: Can Tests Have an Adverse Impact? 124

Cumulative Case Part 2: The Digital Renaissance
Learning Community 130

CBC Video Case Part 2: Stephen Hawking: Of Humour,
Black Holes, and Life in the Present 132

Part 3
The Individual in the Organization

CHAPTER 5
Motivation in Organizations 133

Case Preview: At Husky, Employees Are #1—Really! 134

Motivation in Organizations: Its Basic Nature 135

Need Theories of Motivation 136
Need Hierarchy Theories 136
Managerial Applications of Need Theories 139

Goal-Setting Theory 140
Locke and Latham's Goal-Setting Theory 140
Managers' Guidelines for Setting Effective Performance
Goals 142

Equity Theory 144
Adams's Equity Theory 145
Applying Equity Theory: Some Motivational Tips for
Managers 147

Expectancy Theory 149
Basic Elements of Expectancy Theory 149
Managerial Applications of Expectancy Theory 151

Job Design: Structuring Tasks for High Motivation 153

Job Enlargement and Job Enrichment 153
The Job Characteristics Model 155
Techniques for Designing Jobs That Motivate: Some
Managerial Guidelines 158

Summary and Review 160

Case Preview Questions for Discussion 161

Chapter Questions for Discussion 161

Case in Point: Marine Atlantic: A Drifting Crew
Finds an Anchor 161

Skills Portfolio

Experiencing Organizational Behaviour: Assessing
the Work Rewards You Value 162

Working in Groups: Does Goal Setting Really Work?
Demonstrate It for Yourself 163

Take It to the Net 164

SPECIAL SECTIONS

The Quest for Quality: Sabbaticals: Time Off Satisfies
Many Needs Simultaneously 141

Organizational Trends: Confronting the
Challenge of Paying for Performance at the Top 154

CHAPTER 6
Work-Related Attitudes: Feelings about Jobs, Organizations, and People 165

Case Preview: Workplace Equality Yields High Interest
at the Bank of Montreal 166

Attitudes: What Are They? 167

Job Satisfaction: Attitudes toward One's Job 168
Are People Generally Satisfied with Their Jobs? 169
Measuring Job Satisfaction: Assessing Reactions to Work 170
Theories of Job Satisfaction 172
Consequences of Job Dissatisfaction 175
Promoting Job Satisfaction: Some Guidelines 177

Organizational Commitment: Feelings of Attachment
toward Organizations 178
Organizational Commitment: Its Basic Dimensions 178
Consequences of Low Organizational Commitment 181
Suggestions for Enhancing Organizational Commitment 181

Prejudice: Negative Attitudes toward Others 183
Diversity versus Prejudice: Competing Organizational
Realities 184
Various "Groupisms": Manifestations of Prejudicial
Attitudes in the Workplace 184
Valuing and Managing a Diverse Workforce: Current
Practices 188

Summary and Review 192

Case Preview Questions for Discussion 193

Chapter Questions for Discussion 193

Case in Point: Cultural Diversity at Exxon Chemical 193

Skills Portfolio

Experiencing Organizational Behaviour: Are You
Committed to Your Job? 194

Working in Groups: Recognizing Differences in
Cultural Values on the Job 195

Take It to the Net 195

SPECIAL SECTIONS

The Quest for Quality: The "Happiness Index": Assessing
Job Satisfaction at Wild Oats Market 171

The Ethics Angle: "Automakers Boys' Club"
Is Very Slow to Change 188

Diversity in Today's Organizations: Valuing Diversity:
Taking the Pulse of Canadian Companies 191

CHAPTER 7
Career Development and Work Stress 196

Case Preview: Back from the Brink—The Fall and Rise of
Sergio Zyman 197

Organizational Socialization: The Process of Joining Up 198
The Nature of Organizational Socialization 199

Mentoring: One-on-One Socialization 200
What Do Mentors Do? 201
How Mentoring Relationships Form and Change 202
Gender, Race, and Mentoring 203

Careers: New Forms, New Strategies 203
Choosing a Job: Making Vocational Choices 204
Career Planning: Charting Your Future 204
Current Practice: Signs of Trouble in Your Career 207
Gender and Careers: Do Females and Males Have
Different Experiences? 208

Stress: Its Basic Nature 210

Stress: Its Major Causes 210
Work-Related Causes of Stress 211
Causes of Stress Outside Work 213

Stress: Its Major Effects 215
Stress and Task Performance 215
Stress and Psychological Well-being: Burnout 216
Stress and Health: The Silent Killer 217

Managing Stress: Some Effective Techniques 218
Personal Approaches to Stress Management 218
Organization-Based Strategies for Managing Stress 219

Summary and Review 222

Case Preview Questions for Discussion 223

Chapter Questions for Discussion 223

Case in Point: Toronto Dominion Bank: How Ruth
Getter Cracked the Bank's Glass Ceiling 223

Skills Portfolio
Experiencing Organizational Behaviour:
Developing a Personal Career Plan 224
Working in Groups: The Worry Exercise 225

Take It to the Net 225

SPECIAL SECTIONS

Organizational Trends: The Hottest Careers
of the Twenty-First Century 205

The Ethics Angle: Fear as a Management Tool 220

Cumulative Case Part 3: Digital Renaissance's
"Hip, Hot, Happening" Work Space 226

CBC ⊕ **Video Case Part 3:** Kevin McCarthy:
When a MUT Is Not a Dog 227

Part 4
Group Processes

CHAPTER 8
Group Dynamics and Teamwork 228

Case Preview: Honeywell Ltd.: Teaming Up for Quality 229

Groups at Work: Their Basic Nature 230
What Is a Group? A Working Definition 230
Types of Groups 231
Why Do People Join Groups? 233
Stages in the Development of Groups 233
The Structure of Work Groups 235

The Dynamics of Individual Performance in Groups 240
*Social Facilitation: Individual Performance in the Presence
of Others* 241
Performance in Culturally Diverse Groups 244
Social Loafing: "Free Riding" When Working with Others 246

Teams: Special Kinds of Groups 249
Defining Teams and Distinguishing Them from Groups 249
Types of Teams 251
Managers' Guidelines for Creating Teams 253

Effective Team Performance 255
How Successful Are Teams? A Look at the Evidence 255
Potential Obstacles to Success: Why Do Some Teams Fail? 257
Building High-Performance Teams: Some Tips 259

Summary and Review 261

Case Preview Questions for Discussion 261

Chapter Questions for Discussion 261

Case in Point: XEL: The Little Telecommunications
Company That Could 262

Skills Portfolio
Experiencing Organizational Behaviour: Why Do
You Join Groups? 263
Working in Groups: Demonstrating the Social
Loafing Effect 263

Take It to the Net 264

SPECIAL SECTIONS

The Ethics Angle: The Norm for Punishing Unethical
Behaviour at IBM 238

Organizational Trends: Videoconferencing: Groups
in Cyberspace 244

Globalization in Today's Organizations: Comparing
Team Effectiveness in Japan, the United States,
and Great Britain 258

CHAPTER 9
Interpersonal Communication in
Organizations 265

Case Preview: General Electric Canada: Mining
Employees for Ideas 266

Communication: Its Basic Nature 267
*Communication: A Working Definition and Description
of the Process* 267
The Fundamental Role of Communication in Organizations 269

Verbal Communication: The Written and Spoken Word 269
Varieties of Verbal Media in Organizations 270
*Uses of Oral and Written Communication: Matching
the Medium to the Message* 271
*When Words Go High-Tech: Special Issues of Electronic
Media* 272

Nonverbal Communication: Speaking without Words 274
Style of Dress: Communicating by Appearance 274
Time: The Waiting Game 275
The Use of Space: What Does It Say about You? 275

Individual Differences in Communication 276

Personal Communication Style 276
*Gender Differences in Communication: Do Women and Men
Communicate Differently?* 278
Cross-Cultural Differences in Communication 278

Communication Networks: Formal Channels of
Information in Groups 279
Varieties of Formal Communication Networks 279
Formal Communication Networks and Task Performance 281

Informal Communication Networks: Behind the
Organizational Chart 283
Organizations' Hidden Pathways 283
The Grapevine and the Rumour Mill 284

Organizational Structure: Directing the Flow of Messages 285
Organizational Structure: Its Impact on Communication 286
*Communicating Up, Down, and Across the Organizational
Chart* 287
Communicating Inside versus Outside the Organization 290

Overcoming Communication Barriers: Techniques for
Enhancing the Flow of Information 291
Keep Language Simple 291
Be an Active, Attentive Listener 292
Gauge the Flow of Information: Avoiding Overload 294
*Obtain Feedback: Opening Upward Channels of
Communication* 295

Summary and Review 297

Case Preview Questions for Discussion 298

Chapter Questions for Discussion 298

Case in Point: Tackling Communication Barriers at
General Motors 299

Skills Portfolio
Experiencing Organizational Behaviour: Assessing
Your Personal Communication Style 300
Working in Groups: Sharpening Your Listening Skills 301

Take It to the Net 301

SPECIAL SECTIONS

Globalization in Today's Organizations: Breaking
Down the Barriers to Cross-Cultural Communication 280

The Quest for Quality: "You're Fired!": Tips for
Humanely Communicating the Bad News 288

The Ethics Angle: Sears Installs the "Ethics Assist" Line 296

CHAPTER 10
Decision Making in Organizations 302

Case Preview: Yogen Früz World-Wide Inc.:
Decisions on the Road to Hot Frozen Assets 303

Decision Making: Its Basic Nature 305
A General, Analytical Model of Decision Making 305
Decision Style: Individual Differences in Decision Making 307
Cultural Differences in Decision Making 308

The Broad Spectrum of Decisions in Organizations 309
Programmed versus Nonprogrammed Decisions 309
Certain versus Uncertain Decisions 310
Top-Down versus Empowered Decisions 312

Individual Decisions: How Are They Made? 312
*The Rational-Economic Model: In Search of the Ideal
Decision* 312
*The Administrative Model: Exploring the Limits of Human
Rationality* 314
Image Theory: An Intuitive Approach to Decision Making 315

Individual Decisions: What Makes Them Imperfect? 316

Framing Effects 316
Reliance on Heuristics 317
Bias toward Implicit Favourites 318
Escalation of Commitment: Throwing Good Money after Bad 319
Organizational Barriers to Effective Decisions 320

Group Decisions: Do Too Many Cooks Spoil the Broth? 321
The Pros and Cons of Group Decisions 321
When Are Groups Superior to Individuals? 322
When Are Individuals Superior to Groups? 323

Groupthink: Too Much Cohesiveness Can Be a Dangerous Thing 324
The Nature of Groupthink 325
Strategies for Avoiding Groupthink 326

Improving the Effectiveness of Group Decisions: Some Techniques 327
Training Individuals to Improve Group Performance 327
The Delphi Technique: Decisions by Expert Consensus 328
The Nominal Group Technique: A Structured Group Meeting 330
The Stepladder Technique: Systematically Incorporating New Members 331

Summary and Review 333
Case Preview Questions for Discussion 334
Chapter Questions for Discussion 334
Case in Point: The Classic Case of Coke Classic: Fizzled Decision Making 334
Skills Portfolio
  Experiencing Organizational Behaviour: What Is Your Personal Decision Style? 335
  Working in Groups: Running a Nominal Group: Try It Yourself 336
Take It to the Net 336

SPECIAL SECTIONS
The Ethics Angle: Guidelines for Making Ethical Decisions 313
Organizational Trends: Decisions at 30 000 Feet: Technology Helps Pilots Avoid Fatal Errors 329

CHAPTER 11
Helping, Cooperation, and Conflict in Organizations 337

Case Preview: Saskatoon Chemicals: Truce Tames Chemical Warfare 338
Prosocial Behaviour: Helping Others at Work 339
Organizational Citizenship Behaviour: Some Basic Forms 340
Organizational Citizenship Behaviour: Factors Affecting Its Occurrence 341
Effects of OCB: Does It Really Matter? 341
Whistle-Blowing: Helping an Organization by Dissenting with It 342
Cooperation: Mutual Assistance in Work Settings 343
Individual Factors and Cooperation 344
Organizational Factors and Cooperation 347
Cooperation across Organizations 347
Conflict: Its Nature, Causes, and Effects 349
Integration and Distribution: Basic Dimensions of Conflict 349
Major Causes of Conflict 350
The Effects of Conflict: Definitely a Mixed Bag 352
Conflict Management: Increasing the Benefits and Minimizing the Costs 353
Bargaining: The Universal Process 353

Third-Party Intervention: Mediation and Arbitration 355
The Induction of Superordinate Goals 356
Workplace Violence and Workplace Aggression 357
Workplace Violence: The Tip of the Iceberg? 358
The Causes of Workplace Aggression 359
The Prevention and Control of Workplace Aggression 359
Summary and Review 360
Case Preview Questions for Discussion 361
Chapter Questions for Discussion 361
Case in Point: Revenge by Terror: Valery Fabrikant's Rampage at Concordia University 362
Skills Portfolio
  Experiencing Organizational Behaviour: Personal Styles of Conflict Management 362
  Working in Groups: The Good Mood–Helping Effect: One Reason Why "Wining and Dining" Others Often Works 363
Take It to the Net 364

SPECIAL SECTIONS
The Ethics Angle: Energy Giants Learn to Trade the Right to Spew 348
The Quest for Quality: When Suppliers Become Partners —Not Adversaries 357

Cumulative Case Part 4: Only Team Players Need Apply at Digital Renaissance 365
CBC Video Case Part 4: Spar Aerospace Ltd.: A Business or a Government-Sponsored Lab? 366

Part 5
Influencing Others

CHAPTER 12
Influence, Power, and Politics in Organizations 367

Case Preview: Petro-Canada: Bill Hopper's Power Play in the Oil Patch 368
Organizational Influence, Power, and Politics: Some Key Distinctions 369
Social Influence: Having an Impact on Others 370
Tactics of Social Influence 371
Putting Influence Tactics to Work 371
Individual Power: A Basis for Influence 372
Position Power: Influence That Comes with the Office 372
Personal Power: Influence That Comes from the Individual 373
Power: How Is It Used? 375
Empowerment: The Shifting Bases of Power in Today's Organizations 377
Group or Subunit Power: Structural Determinants 378
The Resource-Dependency Model: Controlling Critical Resources 378
The Strategic Contingencies Model: Power through Dependence 379
Organizational Politics: Power in Action 381
Political Tactics: What Forms Does It Take? 381
When Does Political Action Occur? 384
Organizational Politics: Where in the Organization Does It Occur? 385
Political Behaviour: Is It Ethical? 386

Summary and Review 390
Case Preview Questions for Discussion 391
Chapter Questions for Discussion 391
Case in Point: Chrysler's Battle for the Boardroom 392
Skills Portfolio
    Experiencing Organizational Behaviour: What Kinds of Power Does Your Supervisor Use? 392
    Working in Groups: Recognizing Organizational Politics When You See It 393
Take It to the Net 394

SPECIAL SECTIONS

The Ethics Angle: The Prescription for a Chronic Power Abuser 377
The Quest for Quality: Coping with Organizational Politics: Some Techniques 390

CHAPTER 13
Leadership: Its Nature and Impact in Organizations   395

Case Preview: Maureen Kempston Darkes: A New Kind of Auto Exec 396
Leadership: Its Basic Nature 397
    Leadership: A Working Definition 397
    Leaders versus Managers: A Key Distinction 398
    Canada's Most Respected Corporations and Their Leaders 399
Leader Traits and Behaviours 399
    The Trait Approach: Having "The Right Stuff" 400
    Permissive versus Autocratic Leadership Behaviours 402
    People-Oriented versus Production-Oriented Leaders 403
    Developing Successful Leader Behaviours: Grid Training 405
    Artists, Craftsmen, and Technocrats 406
Leaders and Followers 407
    The Leader-Member Exchange (LMX) Model: The Importance of Being in the "In-Group" 407
    The Attribution Approach: Leaders' Explanations of Followers' Behaviour 408
    Charismatic Leaders: That "Something Special" 409
    Transformational Leadership: Beyond Charisma 411
    Leading Teams: Special Considerations 412
Contingency Theories of Leader Effectiveness 414
    LPC Contingency Theory: Matching Leaders and Tasks 414
    Situational Leadership Theory: Adjusting Leadership Style to the Situation 416
    Path-Goal Theory: Leaders as Guides to Valued Goals 418
    Normative Decision Theory: The Right Time for Employee Participation 419
    Substitutes for Leadership: When Leaders Are Superfluous 422
Summary and Review 423
Case Preview Questions for Discussion 424
Chapter Questions for Discussion 424
Case in Point: When Will Avon Call a Woman CEO? 425
Skills Portfolio
    Experiencing Organizational Behaviour: Determining Your Leadership Style 425
    Working in Groups: Identifying Great Leaders in All Walks of Life 426
Take It to the Net 427

SPECIAL SECTIONS

The Quest for Quality: John Cleghorn: Respected Banker at the Centre of Power 400

Diversity in Today's Organizations: Men and Women: Comparing Their Leadership Styles 404
The Ethics Angle: The Two Faces of Charismatic Leaders 411
Cumulative Case Part 5: Keith Kocho: Visionary, Missionary and Master Storyteller 428
CBC ● Video Case Part 5: Richard Branson: The Fearless CEO 429

Part 6
Organizational Processes

CHAPTER 14
The Work Environment: Culture and Technology   430

Case Preview: The Clash of the Retailing Titans 431
Organizational Culture: Its Basic Nature 432
    Organizational Culture: A Definition 432
    Culture's Role in Organizations 434
    Cultures within Organizations: One or Many? 434
    Types of Organizational Culture 435
The Formation and Maintenance of Organizational Culture 436
    How Is Organizational Culture Created? 436
    Tools for Transmitting Culture 438
Organizational Culture: Its Consequences and Capacity to Change 439
    The Effects of Organizational Culture 439
    Why and How Does Organizational Culture Change? 441
Technology: Its Role in Organizations 445
    Classifying Technology's Basic Dimensions 445
    Automation in Today's Organizations 447
    Human Responses to Technology 447
Using Technology in Modern Organizations 449
    Assistive Technology: Helping People with Disabilities Work Productively 449
    Computerized Performance Monitoring: Management by Remote Control 451
    Technological Aids to Customer Service 453
    Environmentally Friendly Technology: Design for Disassembly 454
Summary and Review 455
Case Preview Questions for Discussion 456
Chapter Questions for Discussion 456
Case in Point: Putting the "Service" Back into United Parcel Service 456
Skills Portfolio
    Experiencing Organizational Behaviour: What Is Your Customer Service Orientation? 457
    Working in Groups: Assessing Organizational Culture 458
Take It to the Net 459

SPECIAL SECTIONS

Organizational Trends: Blending Spirituality into the Workplace Culture: CHOW's Sunrise Ceremony 442
The Quest for Quality: Canadian Companies in Search of a Safety-Conscious Culture 444

CHAPTER 15
Organizational Structure and Design   460

Case Preview: NOVA Reconfigures Itself 461

Organizational Structure: The Basic Dimensions of
Organizations 462
*Hierarchy of Authority: Up and Down the Organizational
Ladder* 463
Division of Labour: Carving Up the Jobs Done 463
Span of Control: Breadth of Responsibility 464
Line versus Staff Positions: Decision Makers versus Advisers 466
Decentralization: Delegating Power Downward 467

Departmentalization: Ways of Structuring Organizations 468
Functional Organizations: Departmentalization by Task 468
*Product Organizations: Departmentalization by Type of
Output* 469
*Matrix Organizations: Departmentalization by Both
Function and Product* 471
*The Boundaryless Organization: A New Corporate
Architecture* 473

Organizational Design: Coordinating the Structural
Elements of Organizations 476
*Classical and Neoclassical Approaches: The Quest for the
One Best Design* 476
*The Contingency Approach: The Impact of Environmental
Conditions on Organizational Design* 477
Mintzberg's Framework: Five Organizational Forms 479

Interorganizational Designs: Going Beyond the Single
Organization 482
Conglomerates: Diversified "Megacorporations" 482
Strategic Alliances: Joining Forces for Mutual Benefit 483

Technology and Organizational Design 485
*Technology and Structure in Manufacturing Companies:
The Woodward Studies* 485
Workflow Integration: The Aston Studies 488
Technology and Interdependence: Thompson's Framework 489

Summary and Review 491

Case Preview Questions for Discussion 492

Chapter Questions for Discussion 492

Case in Point: "Do You, Volvo, Take Thee, Renault...?":
An Alliance Doomed to Divorce 493

Skills Portfolio
Experiencing Organizational Behaviour: Which Do
You Prefer—Mechanistic or Organic Organizations? 493
Working in Groups: Comparing Organizational
Structure and Design 494

Take It to the Net 495

SPECIAL SECTIONS

The Ethics Angle: Doing Business with a Conscience 465
The Quest for Quality: The Sweet Taste of Success 484

CHAPTER 16
Organizational Change and Development 496

Case Preview: Times Certainly Have Changed
at Eaton's 497

Organizational Change: An Ongoing Process 498
Change Is a Global Phenomenon 498
The Message Is Clear: Change or Disappear! 499
The Learning Organization: Benefiting from Change 499

Forces Behind Change in Organizations 502
Planned Change 502
Unplanned Change 505

The Process of Organizational Change: Some Basic Issues 506
Targets of Organizational Change: What Is Changed? 506
*Readiness for Change: When Will Organizational Change
Occur?* 509

Resistance to Change: Will Organizational Change Be
Accepted? 510
Individual Barriers to Change 510
Organizational Barriers to Change 510
*Overcoming Resistance to Organizational Change: Some
Guidelines* 511

Organizational Development: The Implementation
of Planned Organizational Change 512
Survey Feedback: Inducing Change by Sharing Information 513
Sensitivity Training: Developing Personal Insight 514
Team Building: Creating Effective Work Groups 514
Quality of Work Life Programs: Humanizing the Workplace 516
Management by Objectives: Clarifying Organizational Goals 517

Critical Issues in Organizational Development 518
*The Effectiveness of Organizational Development:
Does It Really Work?* 518
What Should Be the Main Focus of OD: Process or Results? 519
*Is Organizational Development Inherently Unethical?
A Debate* 521

Summary and Review 523

Case Preview Questions for Discussion 523

Chapter Questions for Discussion 523

Case in Point: Browns Shoe Shops Inc.: A Montreal
Tradition That Grew 524

Skills Portfolio
Experiencing Organizational Behaviour: Are You
Prepared for Downsizing? 525
Working in Groups: Recognizing Impediments to
Change—and How to Overcome Them 525

Take It to the Net 526

SPECIAL SECTIONS

The Quest for Quality: Competitive Intelligence:
Planning Change by Learning about the Competition 505

Globalization in Today's Organizations: Is OD
Universally Effective? Cultural Barriers to Effective
OD Interventions 520

The Ethics Angle: OD Strategies or Psychological
Abuse? 522

Cumulative Case Part 6: Digital Renaissance:
Leading the Cyber Pack Into the Future 526

CBC ⊕ Video Case Part 6: MacMillan Bloedel:
The Axeman Cometh—But Can He Cut It? 528

Notes 529

Glossary/Subject Index 558

Name Index 568

Company Index 570

Photo Credits 572

PREFACE

Organizational Behaviour in a Changing World

Our goal in preparing this Second Canadian Edition has been to stay at the cutting edge of the field by highlighting the ever-changing nature of organizations and people's involvement in them, with a particular focus on the Canadian scene. These are dynamic times in Canadian business and we have attempted to capture the flavour of this rapidly changing world by presenting a fresh look at the field of organizational behaviour.

One thing that has remained unchanged in this edition is the emphasis on both research and practice. We have continued the research focus and, in fact, used many new studies to broaden the book's research base. At the same time, we continue to augment our coverage of the practical, applications-oriented side of OB—that is, the many ways in which its findings and principles are put to use in organizations across North America and around the world. We have widened our quest to provide up-to-date examples that show how OB practices and principles are used in today's organizations. Not surprisingly, our Company Index is brimming with many new entries. To give readers a good sense of the wide variety of organizations that exist, we purposely refer to a broad range of real companies, both large and small, some offering products and others providing services.

In recent years, the balance between OB research and practice has been brought to the forefront by rapid changes in the nature of organizations and their relationships with the people who work within them. As a result, many new topics have become the focus of systematic study, and many well-established ones have received increased attention. We have carefully monitored these changes and have tailored our coverage accordingly. The result, we believe, is a book that closely reflects the state of OB as it is studied and practised today. We will now point out some of the specific improvements that can be found in this Second Canadian Edition of *Behaviour in Organizations*.

Special New and Revised Features

We have included several new features in this edition that, we believe, will make it a very interesting and useful book.

"You Be the Consultant" Sections

The matter of how organizational research can be applied to solving organizational problems is a special concern in the field of OB. Our new feature, **You Be The Consultant,** provides students with opportunities to make these connections. Brief sections inserted within each chapter ask students questions that require them to apply creatively the material covered to a typical organizational problem. These exercises are designed to help students sharpen their analytical skills while appreciating the complexities involved in making the leap from theory to application.

"Skills Portfolio" Sections

We now include a special section at the end of each chapter in which various types of exercises are provided to help develop students' managerial skills and their appreciation of OB phenomena. They are called the **Skills Portfolio.** Two types of exercises are included in each portfolio.

1. ***Experiencing Organizational Behaviour*** exercises are designed to help students learn about themselves as individuals. Some examples include:

   - Measuring Your Own Self-Monitoring (Chapter 4)
   - Are You Committed to Your Job? (Chapter 6)
   - What is Your Personal Decision Style? (Chapter 10)
   - Personal Styles of Conflict Management (Chapter 11)

2. ***Working in Groups*** exercises are designed to help students learn about group and organizational phenomena by working together with others. Some examples include:

   - Role Play: The Disciplinary Interview (Chapter 3)
   - Recognizing Organizational Politics When You See It (Chapter 12)
   - Identifying Great Leaders in All Walks of Life (Chapter 13)
   - Recognizing Impediments to Change—And How to Overcome Them (Chapter 16)

"Take It to the Net" Sections

Readers will find a **Take It to the Net** section at the end of each chapter that serves as a reminder about the online study materials and research resources available in the text's Companion Website **www.prenticehall.ca/greenberg.**

Cross-References to Other Material

Too often, when people study new material they fail to recognize the connections between concepts. This problem can be quite serious in the case of OB, where many concepts are interrelated and do not fit into unique categories. To overcome the appearance that key concepts are really as isolated as any textbook structure suggests, each chapter contains several references to other places in the text where related material may be found. These cross-references, appearing in marginal annotations, are designed to highlight the connections between various OB concepts and to identify the several major categories of knowledge into which they belong.

Easier Access to Key Terms

Our students tell us that learning definitions is an important way in which they use the text to study the material. With this in mind, we have changed in two ways the manner in which we present definitions. First, we now provide formal definitions of key terms in the margins, next to where they are introduced in the text. Second, we now have a master Glossary included in the index to provide ready access to definitions. To make them especially useful, the definitions appearing in the glossary include the page numbers in the text where they may be found.

More, and New, Cases

In our quest to highlight the involvement of OB in the latest business activities, we have revised all of the chapter-opening **Case Previews,** and chapter-summarizing **Case in Point** sections. Both the Case Previews and the Case in Point sections include discussion questions to elicit critical thinking on the part of students. Some examples of new cases are:

- Randy Powell: Managing People Not Projects (Chapter 1)
- Roots Canada: From Algonquin Park to Nagano (Chapter 1)
- Babine Forest Products: Modelling Diversity as a Strategic Advantage (Chapter 2)
- ING Direct: A Virtual Arrow to the Heart of Canadian Banks (Chapter 2)
- Nortel Networks: A "Cool Place" to Work (Chapter 3)
- CIBC's Leadership Centre: Employee Education as a Survival Imperative (Chapter 3)
- Christine Silverberg: The Force Behind the Force in Calgary (Chapter 4)
- Yogen Früz World-Wide Inc.: Decisions on the Road to Hot Frozen Assets (Chapter 10)
- NOVA Reconfigures Itself (Chapter 15)
- Times Certainly Have Changed at Eaton's (Chapter 16)
- Browns Shoe Shops Inc.: A Montreal Tradition that Grew (Chapter 16)

 At the end of each of the six parts of the book are new **CBC Video Cases** based on segments from the CBC series *Venture* and *The National*. These exciting video segments include documentaries and interviews with business leaders.

Also included at the end of each part is a **Cumulative Case** featuring Keith Kocho, founder of the successful Canadian multimedia company Digital Renaissance. This feature illustrates chapter topics and issues through the experiences of a manager in the twenty-first century.

Enhanced Attention to Major Themes

We have made every effort to highlight the major themes cutting across various aspects of the field of organizational behaviour and to incorporate these throughout the text. This mission begins in a new **Chapter 2, Work in the Twenty-First Century: The Changing World of People and Organizations,** in which we identify five key themes that have had profound effects on OB in recent years. These are:

- Globalization and Culture: Today's International Organizations
- The Shifting Demographics of the Workforce: Trends Toward Diversity
- Trends in Working Arrangements: New Organizational Forms and Jobs
- The Quality Revolution: Total Quality Management and Reengineering
- Corporate Social Responsibility: The Ethical Organization

We pay attention to these themes throughout this book, both in the text itself, and in five different kinds of special boxed sections appearing in the chapters.

Globalization in Today's Organizations

 Many of the most pressing issues faced by organizations today centre around the growing internationalization of all business activities. To reflect this focus we have included a special section called **Globalization in Today's Organizations,** which includes topics such as:

- Saving Face in Japan: Where Renting Acquaintances is Big Business (Chapter 3)
- Comparing Team Effectiveness in Japan, the United States, and Great Britain (Chapter 8)
- Breaking Down the Barriers to Cross-Cultural Communication (Chapter 9)

- Is OD Universally Effective? Cultural Barriers to Effective OD Interventions (Chapter 16)

Diversity in Today's Organizations

The increasing cultural diversity in today's workforce is an area with which OB, as a field, is deeply concerned. This focus is reflected in the special section called **Diversity in Today's Organizations**, which includes:

- Valuing Diversity: Taking the Pulse of Canadian Companies (Chapter 6)
- Men and Women: Comparing their Leadership Styles (Chapter 13)

Organizational Trends

Now that we are beginning the twenty-first century, it is tempting to consider what organizational life might be like in the years to come. Our special section, **Organizational Trends,** focuses on trends in technology and the nature of organizations themselves that are beginning to influence the practice of OB. Some examples:

- The Hottest Careers of the Twenty-First Century (Chapter 7)
- Videoconferencing: Groups in Cyberspace (Chapter 8)
- Decisions at 30 000 Feet: Technology Helps Pilots Avoid Fatal Errors (Chapter 10)
- Blending Spirituality into the Workplace Culture: CHOW's Sunrise Ceremony (Chapter 14)

The Quest for Quality

Whether it's part of a strategic commitment to a *total quality management* philosophy, or simply an effort to gain a competitive edge, many of today's organizations are more committed than ever to improving the quality of their products, services, and the lives of their employees. Because these efforts are such an important part of organizational life today, we have highlighted them in special sections called **The Quest for Quality.** Some examples include:

- Sabbaticals: Time Off Satisfies Many Needs Simultaneously (Chapter 5)
- John Cleghorn: Respected Banker at the Centre of Power (Chapter 13)
- Canadian Companies in Search of a Safety-Conscious Culture (Chapter 14)
- Competitive Intelligence: Planning Change by Learning About the Competition (Chapter 16)

The Ethics Angle

As in previous editions, we continue to highlight the growing concern over matters of ethical behaviour that have permeated the workplace in recent years. Brief sections in each chapter, entitled **The Ethics Angle,** highlight ethical practices and controversies that are relevant to OB. Some of these include:

- Coverups in the Military: Do Sexual Harassment and Sexual Assault Go Unpunished? (Chapter 3)
- Can Tests Have an Adverse Impact? (Chapter 4)
- "Automakers' Boys' Club" Is Very Slow to Change (Chapter 6)
- Energy Giants Learn to Trade the Right to Spew (Chapter 11)
- The Two Faces of Charismatic Leaders (Chapter 13)

Coverage of New Topics

In our quest to stay at the cutting edge of the field of OB, we have updated many sections of the text. As a result, dozens of new topics are now covered. Here is just a partial listing of these topics.

- Hofstede's cultural dimensions (Chapter 2)
- Canadian mosaic versus the melting pot (Chapter 2)
- contingent workforce (Chapter 2)
- expatriates and culture shock (Chapter 2)
- telecommuting (Chapter 2)
- voluntary reduced work-time (V-time) programs (Chapter 2)
- corporate image (Chapter 3)
- first-impression error (Chapter 3)
- selective perception (Chapter 3)
- 360° feedback (Chapter 3)
- morning versus evening persons (Chapter 4)
- proactive personality (Chapter 4)
- intellectual and physical abilities (Chapter 4)
- goal commitment (Chapter 5)
- procedural justice (Chapter 5)
- outplacement services (Chapter 5)
- employee withdrawal (Chapter 6)
- mission statements (Chapter 6)
- skill-based and awareness-based diversity training (Chapter 6)
- careers: new forms and strategies (Chapter 7)
- signs of trouble in a career (Chapter 7)
- cross-functional teams (Chapter 8)
- high-performance teams (Chapter 8)
- shared-screen conferencing and videoconferencing (Chapter 8)
- personal communication style (Chapter 9)
- gender differences in communication (Chapter 9)
- cross-cultural differences in communication (Chapter 9)
- personal decision styles (Chapter 10)
- empowered decision making (Chapter 10)
- implicit favourites (Chapter 10)
- electronic meeting systems (Chapter 10)
- interorganizational coordination (Chapter 11)
- workplace violence and aggression (Chapter 11)
- gender differences in leadership style (Chapter 13)
- leading teams (Chapter 13)
- flexible manufacturing systems (Chapter 14)
- design for disassembly (Chapter 14)
- typology of organizational culture (Chapter 14)
- boundaryless organizations (Chapter 15)
- modular organization (Chapter 15)
- mutual service consortia (Chapter 15)
- value-chain partnerships (Chapter 15)
- virtual organization (Chapter 15)
- competitive intelligence (Chapter 16)
- the learning organization (Chapter 16)

Updated Supplements Package

The changes outlined above constitute the key alterations we have made in the text itself. Other changes, however, involve the materials that accompany **_Behaviour in Organizations_, 2nd Canadian edition**. Foremost among these are the following:

Companion Website with Online Study Guide Our exciting new Website offers students a comprehensive online study guide with 20 multiple-choice and 15 true/false review questions per chapter, experiential exercises, essay questions, Internet exercises, updated Internet destinations and search tools, CBC video case updates, and more. Instructors will be interested in our online syllabus builder and the password-protected Instructors' area containing electronic versions of key supplements and updates to the text. (To obtain your password, please contact your Prentice Hall sales representative.) See **www.prenticehall.ca/greenberg** and explore!

www.prenticehall.ca/ greenberg

Instructor's Manual with Video Guide (013-083673-7) This comprehensive Instructor's Manual contains a variety of helpful features for instructors. Among these are: chapter outlines, chapter synopses, suggestions for the **You Be The Consultant** exercises, answers/suggestions for **Case Preview** discussion questions, answers/suggestions for the **Chapter** discussion questions, answers/suggestions for **Case in Point** critical thinking questions, answer/suggestions for **Skills Portfolio** exercises as well as synopses for **Video** programs and answers/suggestions for the **Video Case** discussion questions.

The Test Item File (013-083677-X) The Test Item File contains over 1500 multiple-choice, fill-in-the-blank, and essay questions. Answers, with page references, are given for all objective questions and suggested answers are provided for essay questions. All questions are rated by level of difficulty. The Test Item File is available in both printed and electronic formats.

PH Test Manager (013-083674-5) Utilizing our new Test Manager program, the computerized test bank for _Behaviour in Organizations_ offers a comprehensive suite of tools for testing and assessment. Test Manager allows educators to easily create and distribute tests for their courses, either by printing and distributing through traditional methods or by on-line delivery via a Local Area Network (LAN) server. Once you have opened Test Manager, you'll advance effortlessly through a series of folders allowing you to quickly access all available areas of the program. Test Manager has removed the guesswork from your next move by incorporating Screen Wizards that assist you with such tasks as managing question content, managing a portfolio of tests, testing students, and analyzing test results. In addition, this all-new testing package is backed with full technical support, telephone "request a test" service, comprehensive on-line help files, a guided tour, and complete written documents. It is available as a CD-ROM for Windows 95.

Transparency Resource Package (013-083678-8) More than 100 transparencies in PowerPoint 7.0 have been created for the text, reproducing figures and illustrating important concepts. This package is available in printed and electronic formats.

CD-ROM Each copy of _Behaviour in Organizations_, 2/C/e includes a _free_ **CD-ROM** containing CBC video case material.

Prentice Hall Canada/CBC Video Library In an exclusive partnership, Prentice Hall Canada and the CBC have worked together to bring you six segments from the CBC series _Venture_ and _The National_. Designed specifically to complement the text, this case collection is an excellent tool for bringing students in contact with the world outside the classroom. These programs have extremely high production quality and have been chosen to relate directly to chapter content. Teaching notes are provided in the *Instructor's Resource Manual with Video Guide*. Please contact your Prentice Hall Canada sales representative for details. The following is the list of Video Cases for this book:

- Part 1: Vertically Inclined Rock Gym: Climbing the Walls with Virgil
- Part 2: Stephen Hawking: Of Humour, Black Holes, and Life in the Present
- Part 3: Kevin McCarthy: When a MUT Is Not a Dog.
- Part 4: Spar Aerospace Limited: A Business or a Government-Sponsored Lab?
- Part 5: Richard Branson: The Fearless CEO
- Part 6: MacMillan Bloedel: The Axeman Cometh—But Can He Cut It?

In Conclusion

Our goal is to present a book that reflects the current character of the field of OB with respect to both scientific inquiry and practical application from a Canadian perspective. The field of OB is truly dynamic and exciting. We hope that our enthusiasm for the material comes through in our presentation of the theory and in the case examples we have used to illustrate it.

ACKNOWLEDGMENT: SOME WORDS OF THANKS

We have thoroughly enjoyed our work with the Prentice Hall Canada team and are grateful to Mike Ryan, Melanie Meharchand, and Linda Cahill for their encouragement and support. We are especially indebted to Amber Wallace for her good humour, patience, and professional guidance.

We would also like to thank the reviewers for their comments: Glenn D. Coltman, Acadia University; Dale Dilamarter, Sir Sandford Fleming College; Susan FitzRandolph, Ryerson Polytechnic University; Beverly Linnell, SAIT; Albert J. Mills, Saint Mary's University.

Thank you to everyone at Digital Renaissance for helping us pull together the Cumulative Case: Keith Kocho, Isolde O'Neill, Graham Ross, and Ellen Durrant.

There are many people to whom we owe a debt of gratitude, some who helped directly with the preparation of this Canadian edition and others who supported us personally. Rosalie Velicevic's skill, good humour, and dedication made the completion of this project much more enjoyable than it would otherwise

have been. We are particularly indebted to our friends Joel J. and Frank B. Samuels for their caring and inspiration.

Carol Sales wishes to thank her colleagues at Brock University, especially: Dean Martin Kusy, Ronald McTavish, Mark Thomas, Eli Levanoni, Margot Adams-Webber, Sharon Broderick, John Barr, Jila Boal, Mary Ann Lesperance, Marshall Angle, Ravi Sodi, Lisa Carson, Bonnie Moyer, and Rosalie Velicevic.

Frances Owen wishes to thank her colleagues at Niagara University: Rev. Daniel O'Leary, O.M.I., Salvatore Pappalardo, Deborah Erickson, Paul Vermette, Robin Erwin, Thomas Sheeran, Frank Calzi, Carmelo Sapone, Jacqueline MacFarland, Chandra Foote, Rita Moretti, Alice Blake-Stalker, Jennifer Wilson-Bridgman, Delar Singh, and Mary Anne Brown for their support. Special thanks to Nancy Johnston for many years' encouragement and mentoring, and to Sheila Moores, Victor Owen, and Jim, Julie, and Evan Owen for caring.

The Prentice Hall Canada

companion Website...

Your Internet companion to the most exciting, state-of-the-art educational tools on the Web!

The Prentice Hall Canada Companion Website is easy to navigate and is organized to correspond to the chapters in this textbook. The Companion Website consists of four distinct, functional features:

1) **Customized Online Resources**

2) **Online Study Guide**

3) **Reference Material**

4) **Communication**

Explore the four areas in this Companion Website. Students and distance learners will discover resources for indepth study, research and communication, which will empower them in their quest for greater knowledge and will maximize their potential for success in the course.

A NEW WAY TO DELIVER EDUCATIONAL CONTENT

1) Customized Online Resources

Our Companion Websites provide instructors and students with a range of options to access, view, and exchange content.

- **Syllabus Builder** provides *instructors* with the option to create online classes and to construct an online syllabus linked to specific modules in the Companion Website.

- **Mailing lists** enable *instructors* and *students* to receive customized promotional literature.

- **Preferences** enable *students* to customize the sending of results to various recipients, and also to customize how the material is sent, e.g., as html, text, or as an attachment.

- **Help** includes an evaluation of the user's system and a tune-up area that makes updating browsers and plug-ins easier. This new feature will enhance the user's experience with Companion Websites.

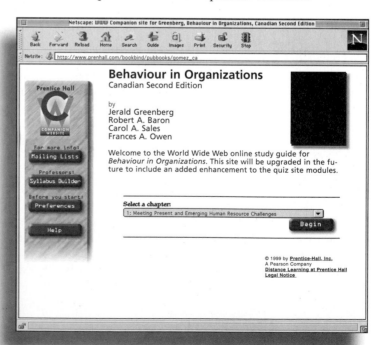

2) Online Study Guide

Interactive Study Guide modules form the core of the student learning experience in the Companion Website. These modules are categorized according to their functionality:

- True-False
- Multiple Choice

The True-False, Multiple Choice, Essay and Experiential Exercise modules provide students with the ability to send answers to our grader and receive instant feedback on their progress through our Results Reporter. Coaching comments and references back to the textbook ensure that students take advantage of all resources available to enhance their learning experience.

3) Reference Material

Reference material broadens text coverage with up-to-date resources for learning. **Web Destinations** provides a directory of Websites relevant to the subject matter in each chapter. **NetNews (Internet Newsgroups)** is a fundamental source of information about a discipline, containing a wealth of brief, opinionated postings. **NetSearch** simplifies key term search using Internet search engines.

4) Communication

Companion Websites contain the communication tools necessary to deliver courses in a **Distance Learning** environment. **Message Board** allows users to post messages and check back periodically for responses. **Live Chat** allows users to discuss course topics in real time, and enables professors to host online classes.

Communication facilities of Companion Websites provide a key element for distributed learning environments. There are two types of communication facilities currently in use in Companion Websites:

- **Message Board** – this module takes advantage of browser technology providing the users of each Companion Website with a national newsgroup to post and reply to relevant course topics.

- **Live Chat** – enables instructor-led group activities in real time. Using our chat client, instructors can display Website content while students participate in the discussion.

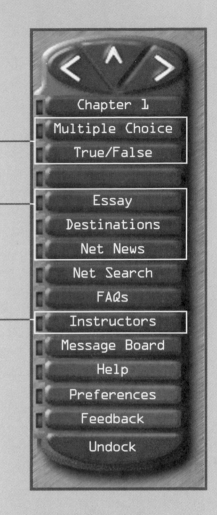

Companion Websites are currently available for:
- Starke: Contemporary Management in Canada
- Robbins: Organizational Behaviour
- Dessler: Human Resource Management in Canada
Note: CW '99 content will vary slightly from site to site depending on discipline requirements.

The Companion Websites can be found at:

PRENTICE HALL CANADA

1870 Birchmount Road
Scarborough, Ontario M1P 2J7

To order:
Call: 1-800-567-3800
Fax: 1-800-263-7733

For samples:
Call: 1-800-850-5813
Fax: (416) 299-2539
E-mail: phcinfo_pubcanada@prenhall.com

CHAPTER 1
The Nature and Study of Organizations

LEARNING OBJECTIVES

After reading this chapter you should be able to:

1. Describe the major focus of the field of *organizational behaviour,* including the three basic units of analysis used.

2. Characterize the major areas of focus of the field of organizational behaviour today.

3. Explain how the study of organizational behaviour relies upon a *contingency approach.*

4. Trace the historical developments and schools of thought leading up to the field of organizational behaviour today.

5. Explain the importance of the *scientific method* in learning about behaviour in organizations.

6. Describe the role of *theory* in the pursuit of knowledge about organizational behaviour.

7. Characterize the major approaches to conducting research in the field of organizational behaviour and compare the relative advantages and disadvantages of each.

Randy Powell: Managing People, Not Projects

Randy Powell has always known what he wanted. He set his sights on becoming the president of a major company and he has done just that—twice![1]

At age 36, Powell left the presidency of S. C. Johnson & Son, Limited to become president of Second Cup Canada. Second Cup kiosks are a familiar feature of malls across Canada and the company's reach is growing. It is the second largest retailer of specialty coffee in North America.[2]

Powell (see Figure 1-1) knew he had to be well focused and well prepared to stay on the rigorous career path he had chosen. Higher education was part of that preparation. He achieved a diploma in business from Sheridan College and then attended night classes at York University to earn his BBA.[3] Two additional weapons in his talent arsenal were his effective use of mentors and his ability to network through the Young President's Organization, Junior Achievement, and other organizations.[4]

Powell, who lives in Oakville, Ontario with his wife, Tina, and their two children, has a clear commitment to his employees."[5] I believe in the power of people. The commitment you give to people comes back," says Powell.[6] Powell has developed his leadership style based on this philosophy. "I create teams that people want to be a part of. I realized early that you move from managing projects to managing people." Powell gets bottom line results by setting a clear course, providing his employees with the resources they need to get the job done, removing obstacles that impede the work of the team, and giving his employees the freedom they need to accomplish their team's goals.[7]

Powell's approach works. While he was at S. C. Johnson in Brantford, Ontario, a survey showed that 97 percent of employees were proud and happy to work for the company.[8] During his time in Brantford, Powell played sports, such as floor hockey, with his employees twice a week. He was also known to cook steak dinners as a reward for employees who excelled in production challenges.[9]

Powell's courage of his convictions has made him a standout among his peers. Before joining S. C. Johnson & Son Ltd., Powell worked at Campbell Soup Co. Ltd. A month after he was hired he found himself in a meeting with the company's senior executives. The company's CEO, David Clark, gave his analysis of why Powell's division was underperforming in the market. Powell disagreed and said so. This earned him the respect of his supervisor and many of his colleagues. Powell credits his "managerial courage" for his success.[10]

FIGURE 1-1   A Commitment to People Is His Strength

At age 33, Randy Powell was named president of S. C. Johnson and Son Ltd., a privately owned Canadian subsidiary of a large U.S. corporation. His commitment to his employees helped to create a working environment that an overwhelming majority of Johnson employees enjoyed. Powell has now taken his people-oriented presidential style to Second Cup Canada.[11]

Second Cup Canada
www.secondcup.com

S. C. Johnson & Son Limited
www.scjohnsonwax.com

There are doubtless many factors responsible for Randy Powell's success. What stands out most is Randy Powell's commitment to his employees. He is keenly aware of one essential fact: People are the key to success! There can be no organizations without people. No matter how healthy an organization's financial status, people problems can bring it down very quickly. Thus it makes sense to realize that "the human side of work" (not coincidentally part of the subtitle of this book) is a critical element in the effective functioning—and basic existence—of organizations. This people-centred orientation is the focus of *organizational behaviour* (*OB* for short)—the field specializing in the study of human behaviour in organizations.

OB scientists and practitioners study and attempt to solve problems by using knowledge derived from research in the **behavioural sciences**, such as psychology and sociology. In other words, the field of OB is firmly rooted in science. It relies on research to derive valuable information about organizations and the complex processes operating within them. Such knowledge is used as the basis for helping to solve a wide range of organizational problems. For example, what can be done to make people more productive and more satisfied on their jobs (see Figure 1-2)? When and how should people be organized into teams? How should jobs and organizations be designed so that people best adapt to changes in the environment? These are just a few of the many important questions that are addressed by the field of organizational behaviour.

As you read this text, it will become very clear that OB specialists have attempted to learn about a large variety of issues involving people in organizations. In fact, over the past few decades, OB has developed into a field so diverse that its scientists have examined just about every conceivable aspect of behaviour in organizations.[12] The fruits of this labour already have been enjoyed by people interested in making organizations not only more productive, but also more pleasant for those working in them.

In the remainder of this chapter, we will give you the background information you will need to understand the scope of OB and its potential value. With this in mind, this first chapter is designed to introduce you formally to the field of OB—its characteristics, its history, and the tools it uses to learn about the behaviour of people in organizations. We will begin by formally defining OB and by describing exactly what it is and what it seeks to accomplish. Following this, we will summarize the history of the field, tracing its roots from its origins to its emergence as a modern science. Finally, we will discuss the research methods OB scientists use to carry out one of OB's major tasks—adding to basic knowledge about the behaviour of people in organizations. After this is accomplished, we will be ready to face our primary task in the rest of the book: enhancing your understanding of the human side of work by giving you a comprehensive overview of the field of organizational behaviour.

behavioural sciences Fields such as psychology and sociology that seek knowledge of human behaviour and society through the use of the scientific method.

organizational behaviour The field that seeks increased knowledge of all aspects of behaviour in organizational settings through the use of the scientific method.

THE FAR SIDE   By GARY LARSON

© 1985 FarWorks, Inc./Dist. by Universal Press Syndicate

8-2

"Excuse me, sir, but Shinkowsky keeps stepping on my sandal."

FIGURE 1-2   Enhancing Employee Performance and Satisfaction: An Important Organizational Issue

Although the scientific study of behaviour in organizations doesn't go back as far as the era depicted here, concerns about enhancing performance and satisfaction have long been quite prevalent in organizations.

(Source: THE FAR SIDE © 1985 FarWorks, Inc. Distributed by Universal Press Syndicate. Reprinted with permission. All rights reserved.)

Organizational Behaviour: A Working Definition

Having just informally described what the topic of organizational behaviour is all about, we are now prepared to define the field more formally and to describe its basic characteristics. Specifically, **organizational behaviour** is the field that seeks knowledge of behaviour in organizational settings by systematically studying individual, group, and organizational processes. This knowledge is used both as an end in itself by scientists who are interested in basic human behaviour and by practitioners interested in enhancing organizational effectiveness and individual well-being. Before beginning our examination of this field, it would be useful to describe further some of the key aspects referred to in our definition.

OB Applies the Scientific Method to Practical Managerial Problems

Our definition of OB refers both to seeking knowledge and to studying behavioural processes. This should not be surprising because, as we noted earlier, OB knowledge is based on the behavioural sciences. Although not yet as advanced as the study of physics or chemistry, the orientation of the field of OB is still scientific in nature. Thus, like other scientific fields, OB seeks to develop a base of knowledge by using an empirical, research-based approach. That is, it is based on systematic observation and measurement of the phenomena of interest. As we will describe later in this chapter—and as you will see for yourself as you read this book—organizational research is neither easy nor foolproof. Yet it is widely agreed that the scientific method is the best way to learn about behaviour in organizations. For this reason, the scientific orientation should be acknowledged as a hallmark of the field of OB.

Why is it so important to learn about behaviour in organizational settings? The answer varies with the different people you ask. To social scientists, learning about human behaviour on the job—"what makes people tick" in organizations—is valuable for its own sake. After all, scientists are interested in the generation of knowledge—in this case, insight into the effects of organizations on people and the effects of people on organizations. This is not to say, however, that such knowledge has no value outside of scientific circles. Far from it! OB specialists also work hard at applying knowledge from scientific studies—putting it to good practical use. As they seek to improve organizational functioning and the quality of life of people working in organizations, they rely heavily on knowledge derived from OB research. For example, researchers have shed light on such practical questions as:

- How can goals be set to enhance people's job performance?

- How may jobs be designed so as to enhance employees' feelings of satisfaction?

- Under what conditions do individuals make better decisions than groups?

- What can be done to improve the quality of organizational communication?

- What steps can be taken to alleviate work-related stress?

- What do leaders do to enhance the effectiveness of their groups?

We will explain scientific research and theory bearing on the answers to these and dozens of other practical questions throughout this book. It is safe to say that the scientific and applied facets of OB not only coexist, but complement each other. Indeed, just as knowledge about the properties of physics may be put to use by engineers, and engineering data can be used to test theories of basic physics, so too are knowledge and practical applications closely intertwined in the field of OB.

Not only may OB specialists use their knowledge about behaviour in organizations to help suggest ways of improving organizational problems in general, but they also may conduct research designed specifically to solve problems in a particular organization. In other words, OB specialists use the scientific method to derive both general knowledge about behaviour in organizations (referred to as *normal science research*) and specific knowledge used to solve problems in a particular organization (referred to as *action research*).[13] Although the underlying reason for conducting the research may be different in each case, both approaches have something in common—namely, their reliance on the scientific method. So, regardless of one's goals for learning about behaviour in organizations—be it deriving theoretical or practical knowledge of organizational behaviour in general or insight into a specific organization—it's safe to say that the scientific approach is a central defining characteristic of modern OB.

OB Focuses on Three Levels of Analysis: Individuals, Groups, and Organizations

To best appreciate behaviour in organizations, OB specialists cannot focus exclusively on individuals acting alone. After all, in organizational settings people frequently work together in groups. Furthermore, people—alone and in groups—both influence and are influenced by their work environments. Considering this fact, it should not be surprising to learn that the field of OB focuses on three distinct levels of analysis: individuals, groups, and organizations.

The field of OB recognizes that *all three levels of analysis* must be used to comprehend fully the complex dynamics of behaviour in organizations (see Figure 1-3). Careful attention to all three levels of analysis is a central theme in modern OB and will be fully reflected throughout this book. For example, at the individual level, we will be describing how OB specialists are concerned with individual perceptions, attitudes, and motives. At the group level, we will be describing how people communicate with each other and coordinate their activities among themselves in work groups. Finally, at the organizational level, we will examine organizations as a whole—the way they are structured and operate in their environments, and the effects of their operations on the individuals and groups within them. We're optimistic that you will come to appreciate the value of all three approaches long before you finish reading this book.

FIGURE 1-3 The Three Levels of Analysis Used in Organizational Behaviour

To understand behaviour in organizations fully, we must consider three levels of analysis: processes occurring within individuals, groups, and organizations.

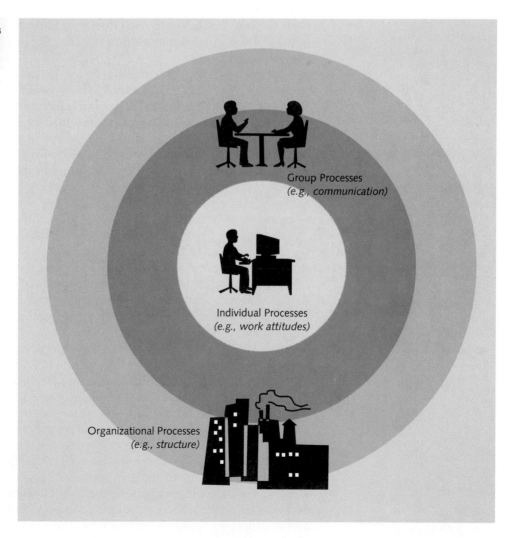

Group Processes
(e.g., *communication*)

Individual Processes
(e.g., *work attitudes*)

Organizational Processes
(e.g., *structure*)

Organizational Behaviour Today: Characteristics of the Field

Now that we have defined what is meant by organizational behaviour, we believe it is useful and important to summarize some of the major characteristics of the field as it exists today. This overview will prepare you for appreciating our presentation of the work of OB scientists in the chapters ahead.

OB Seeks to Improve People's Quality of Life at Work

In the early part of the twentieth century, as railroads opened up the western portion of Canada and the country's population grew rapidly, the demand for manufactured products was great. New manufacturing plants were built, attracting waves of new immigrants in search of a living wage and labourers lured off farms by the employment prospects that factory work offered. These men and women found that factories were gigantic, noisy, hot, and highly regimented—in short, brutal places in which to work. Bosses demanded more and more of their employees and treated them like disposable machines.

Obviously, the managers of 100 years ago held very negative views of employees. They assumed that people were basically lazy and irresponsible and treated them with disrespect. This negativistic approach, which has been with us for many years, reflects the traditional view of management—what Douglas McGregor called a **Theory X** orientation.[14] This philosophy of management assumes that people are basically lazy, dislike work, need direction, and will only work hard when they are being pushed, goaded into performing (i.e., because there is a carrot at the end of the stick).

Today, however, if you asked a diverse group of corporate officials to describe their basic views of human nature, you'd probably find some more optimistic thoughts. Although some of today's managers still believe that people are basically lazy, many others would disagree, arguing that it's not that simple. They would claim that most individuals are at least as capable of working hard as they are of "goofing off." If employees are recognized for their efforts (such as by being appropriately paid) and are given an opportunity to succeed (such as by being well trained), they may be expected to work very hard without being pushed. Thus, employees may put forth a great deal of effort simply because they want to. Management's job, then, is to create those conditions that make people want to perform as desired.

The approach which assumes that people are willing to work hard when the right conditions prevail is known as the **Theory Y** orientation. This philosophy assumes that people have a psychological need to work and seek achievement and responsibility. In contrast to the Theory X philosophy of management, which essentially demonstrates distrust for people on the job, the Theory Y approach is strongly associated with promoting the betterment of human resources (for a summary of the differences, see Figure 1-4).

As you might suspect, the Theory Y perspective currently prevails among those interested in organizational behaviour. This approach assumes that people are highly responsive to their work environments and that how they are treated will influence how they will act. OB scientists are very interested in learning exactly what conditions will lead people to behave in the most positive ways. As you will learn in reading this book, conditions in which employees are treated favourably will help them become more committed to their organizations. In contrary fashion, those who are exploited will act more negatively—slacking off, behaving antisocially (e.g., stealing), or eventually quitting. In short, modern OB assumes that there are no intrinsic reasons why work settings cannot be made both pleasant and productive. Figure 1-5 shows a view of the work space at the headquarters of high-powered ad agency Cossette Communication Marketing in Montreal. The space was designed to unify the multidisciplinary team-based company and to promote creativity.[15]

Theory X A traditional philosophy of management suggesting that most people are lazy and irresponsible and will work hard only when forced to do so.

Theory Y A philosophy of management suggesting that under the right circumstances, people are fully capable of working productively and accepting responsibility for their work.

☛ *As we will see in Chapter 15, Theory X and Theory Y philosophies are reflected in the way organizations are designed.*

Cossette Communication Marketing
www.cossette.com

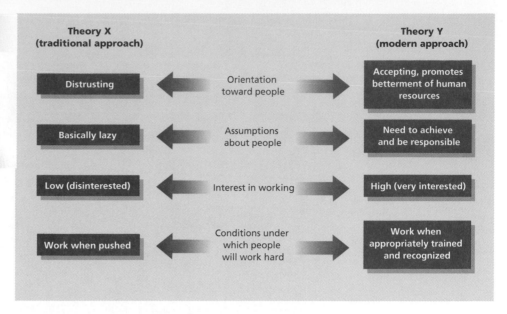

FIGURE 1-4 Theory X versus Theory Y: A Summary

The traditional *Theory X* orientation toward people is far more negativistic than the more contemporary *Theory Y* approach that is widely accepted today. Some of the key differences between these management philosophies are summarized here.

Theory X (traditional approach)		Theory Y (modern approach)
Distrusting	Orientation toward people	Accepting, promotes betterment of human resources
Basically lazy	Assumptions about people	Need to achieve and be responsible
Low (disinterested)	Interest in working	High (very interested)
Work when pushed	Conditions under which people will work hard	Work when appropriately trained and recognized

OB Recognizes the Dynamic Nature of Organizations

Thus far, our characterization of the field of OB has focused more on behaviour than on organizations. Nonetheless, it is important to point out that both OB scientists and practitioners *do* pay a great deal of attention to the nature of organizations themselves. Under what conditions will organizations change? How are organizations structured? How do organizations interact with their environments? Questions such as these are of major interest to specialists in OB. But before we can consider them—as we will later in this book—we must first clarify exactly what we mean by an "organization."

Although you probably have a very good idea of what an organization is, you might find it difficult to define. Thus we offer the following definition. An **organization** is a structured social system consisting of groups and individuals working together to meet some agreed-upon objectives. In other words, organizations consist of structured social units, such as individuals and/or work groups, that strive to attain a common goal, such as to produce and sell a product at a profit.

In studying organizations, OB scientists recognize that organizations are not static; rather, they are dynamic and ever-changing entities. In other words, they recognize that organizations are **open systems**—that is, self-sustaining systems that use energy to transform resources from the environment (such as raw materials) into some form of output (for example, a finished product).[17] Figure 1-6 summarizes some of the key properties of open systems. As this diagram makes clear, organizations receive input from their environments and continuously transform it into output. This output is transformed back to input, and the cyclical operation continues.

Consider, for example, how organizations may tap the human resources of the community by hiring and training people to do jobs. These individuals may work to provide a product in exchange for wages. They then spend these wages, putting money back into the community, allowing more people to afford the

organization A structured social system consisting of groups and individuals working together to meet some agreed-upon objectives.

open systems Self-sustaining systems that transform input from the external environment into output, which the system then returns to the environment.

Figure 1-5 Work Environment Can Enhance Creativity

The headquarters of Cossette Communication Marketing on Drummond Street in Montreal includes areas known as "idea accelerators." These spaces are welcoming and comfortable—ideal for ad hoc meetings and brainstorming with colleagues.[16]

FIGURE 1-6 Organizations as Open Systems

The *open systems* approach assumes that organizations are self-sustaining—that is, they transform inputs into outputs in a continuous fashion.

(Source: Based on suggestions by Katz & Kahn, 1978; see Note 17.)

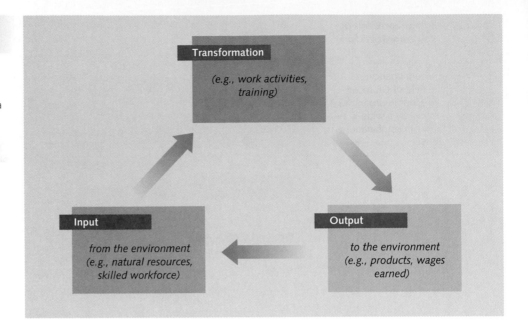

company's products. In turn, this exchange creates the need for still more employees, and so on. If you think about it this way, it's easy to realize that organizations are dynamic and constantly changing. In a sense, then, they are like the operations of the human body. As people breathe, they take in oxygen and transform it into carbon dioxide. This, in turn, sustains the life of green plants, which, in turn, emit oxygen for people to breathe. The continuous nature of the open system characterizes not only human life, but the existence of organizations as well.

OB Assumes There Is No "One Best" Approach

What's the most effective way to motivate people? What style of leadership works best? Should teams be used to make important organizational decisions? Although questions such as these appear to be quite reasonable, there is a basic problem with all of them: They all assume that there is one simple answer. That is, they suggest that there is one best approach—one best way to motivate, to lead, and to make decisions.

Specialists in the field of OB today agree that there is no one best approach when it comes to such complex phenomena. To assume otherwise is not only overly simplistic and naive, but, as you will see, grossly inaccurate. When it comes to studying human behaviour in organizations, there are no simple answers. The processes involved are too complex. Instead, OB scholars accept that behaviour in work settings is the result of many interacting forces. This fact is recognized in what is known as the **contingency approach**, an orientation that is a hallmark of modern OB.[18]

Consider, for example, the broad array of factors that may determine how productive someone is on the job. Clearly important are various personal characteristics, such as an individual's work values, skills, and motives to work hard. But these factors alone tell only part of the story. We also must consider various situational factors, such as the nature of the organization (e.g., the social relations between co-workers). As if all these considerations are not enough, we also need to take into account numerous characteristics of the environmental context in which work is done. For example, how strong is the economy? How competitive is the industry in which the organization operates? Not only may all these variables play separate roles when it comes to influencing how a particular individual is likely to behave on the job, but they may combine to paint a very complicated picture. It is such complexities that come to the forefront in the contingency approach to OB (see Figure 1-7).

When we teach OB to our students, we often find ourselves answering their questions by saying, "It depends." As our knowledge of behaviour on the job becomes

contingency approach A perspective suggesting that organizational behaviour is affected by a large number of interacting factors. How someone will behave is said to be contingent upon many different variables at once.

☞ A popular theory of leadership presented in Chapter 13 explicitly uses a contingency approach to identify the conditions under which certain styles of leadership bring about the best group performance.

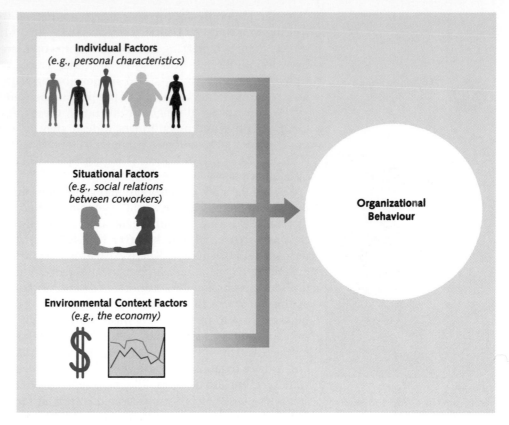

FIGURE 1-7 The Contingency Approach to Organizational Behaviour

By adopting a *contingency approach,* the field of OB recognizes that behaviour in organizations is influenced by a wide variety of factors in combination with each other.

more and more complex, it becomes difficult, if not impossible, to give "straight answers." Rather, it is usually necessary to report that people will do certain things "under some conditions" or "when all other factors are equal." Such phrases provide a clear indication that the contingency approach is being used. They tell us that a certain behaviour is *contingent upon* the existence of certain conditions.

Although this approach may frustrate and disappoint some people because it makes the use of simple cookbook formulas impossible to predict and explain behaviour, we believe that such a complaint is unjustified. After all, *accuracy*, and not simplicity, is the ultimate goal of our studies of behaviour in organizations. In the chapters that follow, you will see how this approach prevails. In presenting this material to you, we will attempt to walk the fine line between being so complex as to be incomprehensible and so simplistic as to be misleading.

OB Confronts Challenges Created by the Changing Nature of Work

It's no secret that the world is constantly changing, and this phenomenon includes the world of work. Consider, for example, the dynamic nature of the workforce itself. In fact, if we had to characterize today's labour force using only one word, it would be *diversity*. The demographic characteristics of the workforce have been changing over the past few decades, and such shifts have not gone unnoticed in the field of OB.[19]

For example, there are more women working today than ever before, and they are more highly educated and better trained for a wider variety of positions. In addition to gender diversity, racial and cultural diversity are other potent demographic trends in the workforce. StatsCan census figures show that 11.2 percent of the population in Canada reports belonging to a visible minority. In this group there are growing numbers of people who identify themselves as Chinese, South Asian, and Black. Over half of the people identifying themselves as members of visible minority groups live in Ontario.[20] Many Canadian companies have distinguished themselves by their exemplary relationship with Native peoples across the country.

Statistics Canada
www.statcan.ca/english/
census 96/list.htm

FIGURE 1-8 Diversity: An Important Trend in the Workplace

Consultant Trevor Wilson, author of *Diversity at Work: The Business Case for Diversity*, is working with a group of 15 companies that is known as the Trinity Group. The group is developing a standardized method for evaluating the responsiveness of organizations to diversity issues.[24]

"Aboriginal people are the fastest-growing part of the Canadian population," according to a study by Hill Sloan Associates.[21] In addition to cultural and racial diversity, there is increasing awareness in the workplace of the needs of workers who have disabilities and workers who are older. Trevor Wilson (see Figure 1-8) and his colleagues in the Trinity Group are developing ways that organizations can assess how responsive they are to all of the people they employ.

As you will see throughout this book, these trends are of considerable interest to OB scientists and practitioners. Indeed, they are closely connected to such topics as prejudice and stereotypes (Chapter 6), organizational culture (Chapter 14), stress (Chapter 7), communication (Chapter 9), conflict (Chapter 11), and career development (Chapter 7).

When the study of behaviour in organizations first emerged, it was a time in which the United States was the world's predominant economic power. As a result, much of what was learned about organizations came from a uniquely American middle-class perspective.[22] Today, however, it is clear that the economy is much more global in scope and orientation. There exist strong economic forces all over the world and organizations operating within many different cultures. Even formerly communist nations are developing into economic powers. Moreover, many organizations have operations in several different countries. Considering these trends, it would be seriously limiting—not to mention very misleading—to ignore the possibility that behaviour in organizations is affected by cultural differences. Indeed, the field of OB is becoming increasingly international in its approach to the study of organizations.[23]

Today's organizations confront challenges related not only to the nature of the workforce, but also to the rapidly changing nature of the work that people do—changes stemming largely from sophisticated computer technology. For example, advances in automation and computers have to a great extent been responsible for eliminating many jobs and creating others. As we will see later in this book (Chapters 2 and 14), jobs that used to take many people to complete may now take only a few—if people are needed at all. And the work people are doing in those new jobs is generally cleaner, safer, and more high-tech. Computer technology has made it possible for people to do more work with less effort, and with greater flexibility, than ever before.

In summary, the world of work is constantly changing in many ways. With these changes come a variety of interesting issues and special challenges for the field of organizational behaviour.

Organizational Behaviour: A Capsule History of the Field

Although today we take for granted the importance of understanding the functioning of organizations and the behaviour of people at work, this was not always the case. In fact, it was not until the early part of the twentieth century that the idea first developed—and only during the last few decades that it gained widespread acceptance.[25] So that we can appreciate how the field of OB got to where it is today, we will now briefly outline its history and describe some of the most influential forces in its development.

Scientific Management: The Roots of Organizational Behaviour

The earliest attempts to study behaviour in organizations came out of a desire by industrial efficiency experts to improve worker productivity. Their central question was straightforward: What could be done to get people to do more work in less time? It's not particularly surprising that attempts to answer this question were made at the turn of the century. After all, this was a period of rapid industrialization and technological change in North America. As engineers attempted to make machines more efficient, it was a natural extension of their efforts to work on the human side of the equation—making people more productive, too. Given this history, it should not be too surprising that the earliest people we now credit for their contributions to OB were actually industrial engineers.

American Frederick Winslow Taylor worked most of his life in steel mills, starting as a labourer and working his way up to the position of chief engineer.[26] In the 1880s, while a foreman at Philadelphia's Midvale Steel Company, Taylor became aware of some of the inefficient practices of the employees. Noticing, for example, that labourers wasted movements when shifting pigiron, Taylor studied the individual components of this task and established what he believed was the best way—motion by motion—to perform it. A few years later, while a consulting engineer at Pittsburgh's Bethlehem Steel, Taylor similarly redesigned the jobs of loading and unloading rail cars so they, too, could be done as efficiently as possible. On the heels of these experiences, Taylor published his groundbreaking book *Scientific Management*. In this work, Taylor argued that the objective of management is "to secure the maximum prosperity for the employer, coupled with the maximum prosperity of each employee."[27]

scientific management
An early approach to management and organizational behaviour emphasizing the importance of designing jobs as efficiently as possible.

Beyond identifying ways in which manual labour jobs can be performed more efficiently, Taylor's **scientific management** approach was unique in its focus on the role of employees as individuals. Taylor advocated two ideas that hardly seem special today but were quite new 85 years ago. First, he recommended that employees be carefully selected and trained to perform their jobs—helping them become, in his own words, "first-class" at some task. Second, he believed that increasing workers' wages would raise their motivation and make them more productive. Although this idea is unsophisticated by today's standards—and not completely accurate—Taylor may be credited with recognizing the important role of motivation in job performance. It was contributions like these that stimulated further study of behaviour in organizations and created an intellectual climate that eventually paved the way for the development of the field of OB. Acknowledging these contributions, management theorist Peter Drucker has described Taylor as, "the first man in history who did not take work for granted, but who looked at it and studied it."[28]

☞ As we will describe in Chapter 5, different theories suggest different ideas about the role of money as a motivator in the workplace.

The publication of *Scientific Management* stimulated several other scientists to pick up on and expand Taylor's ideas. For example, the psychologist Hugo Münsterberg worked to "humanize" the jobs of people by explaining how the concepts of learning and motivation are relevant to the behaviour of people at work.[29] Similarly, management writer Mary Parker Follet claimed that organizations could benefit by attempting to recognize the needs of employees.[30] However, the scientists most closely influenced by Taylor were the industrial psychologists Frank and Lillian Gilbreth. This husband-and-wife team pioneered an approach known as **time-and-motion study**, a type of applied research designed to classify and streamline the individual movements needed to perform jobs, with the intent of finding the most efficient way of doing them.[31] Although this approach appears to be highly mechanical and dehumanizing, the Gilbreths, parents of 12 children, practised Taylorism with a human face in their personal lives. In fact, you may even recall the story of how the Gilbreths applied the principles of scientific management to the operation of their household as told in the classic book and film *Cheaper by the Dozen*.

time-and-motion study A type of applied research designed to classify and streamline the individual movements needed to perform jobs with the intent of finding the most efficient way of doing them.

The Human Relations Movement: Elton Mayo and the Hawthorne Studies

Despite the important contributions of scientific management, this approach did not go far enough in directing our attention to the wide variety of factors that might influence behaviour in work settings. To be sure, the efficient performance of jobs and monetary incentives are very important. Emphasizing these factors, however, tends to make people feel like cogs in a machine. In fact, many employees and theorists alike rejected Taylorism, favouring instead an approach that focused on employees' own views and emphasized respect for individuals.

At the forefront of this orientation was Elton W. Mayo, an American organizational scientist and consultant widely regarded as the founder of what is called the

human relations movement A perspective on organizational behaviour that recognizes the importance of social processes in work settings.

human relations movement.[32] This brand of management philosophy rejects the primarily economic orientation of scientific management and focuses instead on noneconomic, social factors operating in the workplace. Mayo and other proponents of the human relations movement *were* concerned with task performance, but they realized that it was greatly influenced by the social conditions which existed in organizations—the way employees were treated by management and the relationships they had with each other.

The original study. In 1927, a series of studies was begun at the Western Electric's Hawthorne Works near Chicago. Inspired by scientific management, the researchers were interested in determining, among other things, the effects of illumination on work productivity. How brightly or dimly lit should the work environment be for people to produce at their maximum level? Two groups of female employees took part in the study. One group, the *control room* condition, did their jobs without any changes in lighting; the other group, the *test room* condition, worked while the lighting was systematically varied, sometimes getting brighter, sometimes dimmer. The results were baffling: Productivity increased in *both* locations. Just as surprising, there was no clear connection between illumination and performance. In fact, output in the test room remained high even when the level of illumination was so low that workers could barely see what they were doing!

Relay room studies. In response to these puzzling findings, Western Electric officials called in a team of experts headed by Elton Mayo. Attempting to replicate these results, Mayo and his colleagues examined the effects of a wide variety of different variables on productivity. Among these were the length of rest pauses, the duration of the workday and workweek, and the presence or absence of a free midmorning lunch. How would these factors influence the amount of work performed? To answer this question, Mayo and his colleagues studied female employees working in the company's Relay Room. As shown in Figure 1-9, the results were once again quite surprising: Productivity improved following almost every change in working conditions.[33] In fact, performance remained extremely high even when conditions were returned to normal, the way they were before the study began.

FIGURE 1-9 The Hawthorne Studies: Some Puzzling Results

In one part of the Hawthorne studies, female employees were exposed to several changes in working conditions. Surprisingly, almost every one of these alterations produced an increase in productivity.

(Source: Based on data from Roethlisberger & Dickson, 1939; see Note 33.)

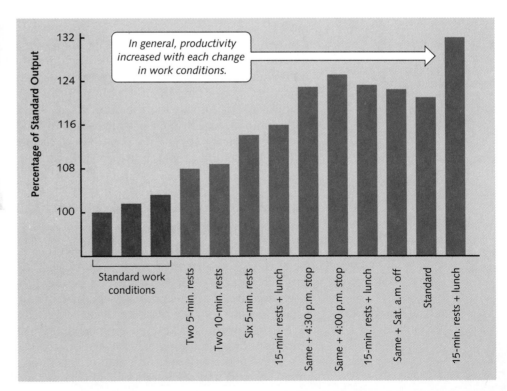

Bank wiring room study. Not all of Mayo's studies showed that Hawthorne employees were highly productive, however. In fact, in another study conducted at the company's Bank Wiring Room, male members of various work groups were observed during regular working conditions and then interviewed at length after work. In this investigation, no attempts were made to alter the work environment. What Mayo found here was also surprising: Instead of improving their performance, employees deliberately restricted their output. Not only did the researchers actually see the men stopping work long before quitting time, but in interviews the men admitted that they easily could do more if they desired.

Why did this occur, especially in view of the increased performance noted in the Relay Room studies? Eventually, Mayo and his associates recognized that the answer resided in the fact that organizations are *social systems*. How effectively people worked depended, in great part, not only on the physical aspects of their working conditions, but also on the social conditions that prevailed. In the Relay Room studies, Mayo noted, productivity rose simply because people responded favourably to the special attention they received. Knowing they were being studied made them feel special and motivated them to do their best. Thus, it was these social factors, more than the physical factors, that had such profound effects on job performance. The same explanation applied in the Bank Wiring Room study. Here, the employees feared that because they were being studied, the company was eventually going to raise the amount of work they were expected to do each day. To guard against the imposition of unreasonable standards (and, hopefully, to keep their jobs), the men agreed among themselves to keep output low. In other words, informal rules were established about what constituted acceptable levels of job performance. These social forces at work in this setting proved to be much more potent determinants of job performance than the physical factors being studied.

☞ *These informal social rules, known as* norms, *play an important role in shaping the behaviour of people in work groups, as we will describe in Chapter 8.*

The legacy of the Hawthorne studies. The conclusion, based on the surprising findings of the Hawthorne studies, is important because it ushered in a whole new way of thinking about behaviour at work. It suggests that to understand behaviour on the job, we must fully appreciate people's attitudes and the processes by which they communicate with each other. This way of thinking, so fundamental to modern OB, may be traced back to Elton Mayo's pioneering Hawthorne studies. In contrast with the scientific management views that prevailed at the time, this perspective was quite novel.

This is not to say, however, that the Hawthorne studies were by any means perfect. Indeed, by modern standards, the research was seriously flawed. As we will describe later in this chapter, the research violated several important rules. For example, no effort was made to assure that the rooms used in the study were identical in every way except for the variables studied (i.e., the level of illumination and the scheduling and duration of the rest pauses), making it possible for factors other than those being studied to influence the results. (Interestingly, research on the topic of illumination is still being done today, although it is far more sophisticated and carefully conducted.[34]) Furthermore, because no attempt was made to assure that the employees chosen for study were representative of all those in their factory (or all manufacturing personnel generally), it is difficult to generalize the results of the study beyond those individuals studied.

Clearly, although the Hawthorne studies are imperfect, their impact on the field of OB is considerable. This contribution lies *not* in what the research tells us about the effects of illumination, but what it reveals indirectly about the importance of human needs, attitudes, motives, and relationships in the workplace. In this respect, the work established a close link between the newly emerging field of OB and the behavioural sciences of psychology and sociology—a connection that persists today. Although the human relations approach was gradually replaced by more sophisticated views, several of its ideas and concepts contributed greatly to the development of the field of OB. Little would those workers in that long-vanished plant outside of Chicago have guessed that their contribution to the social science of organizational behaviour would have been so enduring.

Classical Organizational Theory

classical organizational theory
An early approach to the study of management that focused on the most efficient way of structuring organizations.

During the same time that proponents of scientific management got people to begin thinking about the interrelationships between people and their jobs, another approach to managing people emerged. This perspective, known as **classical organizational theory**, focused on the efficient structuring of overall organizations. This is in contrast, of course, to scientific management, which sought to organize effectively the work of individuals.

Several different theorists are identified with classical organizational theory. Among the first was Henri Fayol, a French industrialist who attributed his managerial success to various principles he developed.[35] Among these are the following:

- A *division of labour* should be used because it allows people to specialize, doing only what they do best.

- Managers should have *authority* over their subordinates, the right to order them to do what's necessary for the organization.

- Lines of authority should be uninterrupted; that is, a *scalar chain* should exist that connects the top management to the lower-level employees.

- There should exist a clearly defined *unity of command*, so that employees receive directions from only one other person so as to avoid confusion.

- Subordinates should be given *initiative* to formulate and implement their plans.

Although many of these principles are still well accepted today, it is widely recognized that they should not always be applied in exactly the same way. For example, whereas some organizations thrive on being structured according to a unity of command, still others require that some employees take directions from several different superiors. We will have more to say about this subject when we discuss various types of organizational structures in Chapter 15. For now, let's say that current organizational theorists owe a debt of gratitude to Fayol for his pioneering and far-reaching ideas.

Probably the best-known classical organizational theorist is the German sociologist Max Weber.[36] Among other things, Weber is known for proposing a form of organizational structure well known today—the **bureaucracy**. This is a way to design organizations in a way that makes them efficient by having a clear hierarchy of authority in which people are required to perform well-defined jobs. Weber's idea was that the bureaucracy is the one best way to organize work in all organizations—much as proponents of scientific management searched for the ideal way to perform a job. The elements of an ideal bureaucracy are summarized in Table 1-1.

bureaucracy An organizational design developed by Max Weber that attempts to make organizations operate efficiently by having a clear hierarchy of authority in which people are required to perform well-defined jobs.

When you think about bureaucracies, negative images probably come to mind of lots of inflexible people getting bogged down in lots of red tape. (By the way, the phrase "red tape" is said to have become popular during World War I, when red tape was used on documents from the British government. Given the tendency for national governments to be bureaucratic in structure, it is not surprising that the term *red tape* came to refer to bureaucracies of all types.[37]) Weber's "universal" view of bureaucratic structure contrasts with the more modern approaches (see Chapter 15) in which it is recognized that different forms of organizational structure may be more or less appropriate under different situations. Although the bureaucracy may not have proven to be a perfect structure for organizing all work, organizational theorists owe a great deal to Weber, many of whose ideas are still considered viable today.

Organizational Behaviour in the Modern Era

Based on the pioneering contributions noted thus far, the realization that behaviour in work settings is shaped by a wide range of individual, group, and organizational factors set the stage for the emergence of the science of organizational behaviour. By the 1940s, clear signs appeared that an independent field had emerged. For

TABLE 1-1 Characteristics of an Ideal Bureaucracy

According to Max Weber, bureaucracies must possess certain characteristics. Here is a summary of the major defining characteristics of bureaucratic organizations.

Characteristic	Description
Formal rules and regulations	Written guidelines are used to control all employees' behaviours.
Impersonal treatment	Favouritism is to be avoided, and all work relationships are to be based on objective standards.
Division of labour	All duties are divided into specialized tasks and are performed by individuals with the appropriate skills.
Hierarchical structure	Positions are ranked by authority level in clear fashion from lower-level to upper-level ones.
Authority structure	The making of decisions is determined by one's position in the hierarchy; people have authority over those in lower-ranking positions.
Lifelong career commitment	Employment is viewed as a permanent, lifelong obligation on the part of the organization and its employees.
Rationality	The organization is committed to achieving its ends (e.g., profitability) in the most efficient manner possible.

example, in 1941 the first doctoral degree in OB was granted (to George Lombard at the Harvard Business School).[38] Only four years later, the first textbook in the field appeared.[39] By the late 1950s and early 1960s, OB was clearly a going concern. By that time, active programs of research were proceeding—research into such key processes as motivation and leadership and the impact of organizational structure.[40]

Latter-day Canadian industrial psychology and research in organizational behaviour have been heavily influenced by these developments in American research. Nevertheless, the field has clearly definable Canadian roots. The first professional reference to "personnel" (the term used before "industrial psychology") in Canada was in 1928. At that time, psychologist Dr. Gerald P. Cosgrave was appointed supervisor of personnel at Sun Life Assurance Company's head office. While a psychologist was hired as an assistant employment manager by the Robert Simpson Company in 1937, this was certainly not the norm at that time.

McGill University engaged in research in issues related to employment through most of the 1930s and had graduates who worked as industrial psychologists before World War II. But it was the war that gave Canadian psychology a more central role—the Canadian army created the Directorate of Personnel Selection. After the war some of the people who had worked for this unit went to the University of Toronto to study industrial psychology and to work in the field of personnel. By 1949 McGill had established masters and doctoral degree programs in industrial-vocational psychology.[41] Over the years, Canadian researchers working at home and abroad have made major contributions to the field of industrial/organizational psychology.[42]

The field of OB has rapidly grown into one that has borrowed heavily from other disciplines. In fact, the field of OB as we know it today may be characterized as a hybrid science that draws from many social science fields. For example, studies of personality, learning, and perception draw on psychology. Similarly, the study of group dynamics and leadership relies heavily on sociology. The topic of organizational communication networks obviously draws on research in the field of communication. Power and politics is studied by political scientists. Anthropologists study cross-cultural themes. And OB scientists look to the field of management science to understand ways to manage quality in organizations. Taken together, it is clear that modern OB is truly a multifaceted field (see Figure 1-10).

In recent years, the study of OB has added new areas of focus. Although there are too many new developments to mention, a few current trends deserve to be pointed out:

- the cross-cultural aspects of business
- (un)ethical behaviour in organizations
- the impact of the external environment on organizational behaviour

FIGURE 1-10 OB: A Hybrid Science

The field of OB may be characterized by the fact that it draws upon several different social science disciplines.

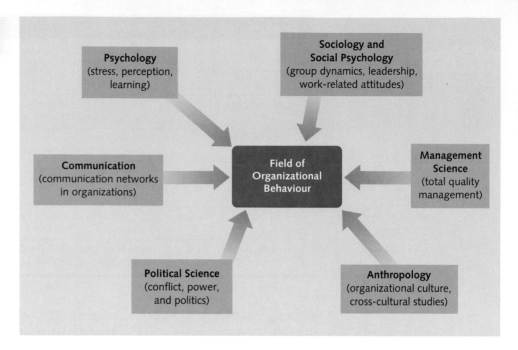

• the impact of service and information sectors on business

• the impact of advances in technology on organizational behaviour and on business in general.

As you read this book, you will learn more not only about the traditional interdisciplinary nature of OB, but also about these rapidly developing topics.

Theory and Research: Tools for Learning about Behaviour in Organizations

Because organizational behaviour is a science, it should not be surprising to learn that the field relies heavily upon the scientific method. As in the case of other scientific fields, OB uses the tools of science to achieve its goals—in this case, to learn about organizations and the behaviour of people working in them. With this in mind, it is essential to understand the basic tools scientists use to learn about behaviour in organizations. In this section, we will briefly describe some of these techniques. Our goal here is not to make you an expert in scientific methodology, but to give you a solid understanding of the techniques you will be encountering as you venture further into this book.

Isn't It All Just Common Sense?

Maybe you're not a top executive of a large business firm with decades of experience in the work world (or, at least, not yet!). Still, you no doubt know *something* about the behaviour of people on the job. After all, you may already have learned quite a bit from whatever jobs you have had yourself or from talking to other people about their experiences. This isn't surprising, given that we can all observe a great deal about people's behaviour in organizational settings just by paying casual attention. So, whether you're the CEO of a *Globe and Mail* 1000 firm or a part-time pizza-delivery driver, you probably have a few ideas about how people behave on the job. Besides, there are probably some things about behaviour in organizations that you take for granted.

For example, would you say that happier employees tend to be more productive? If you're like most people, you would probably say, "Yes, of course." It's logical, right? Well, despite what you may believe, this is generally *not* true. In fact, as we will see in Chapter 6, people who are satisfied with their jobs are generally no more productive than those who are dissatisfied with their jobs. This contradiction of common sense is not an isolated example. This book is full of examples of findings in the field of OB that you might find surprising. To see how good you may be at predicting human behaviour in organizations, we invite you to take the brief quiz appearing in the EXPERIENCING ORGANIZATIONAL BEHAVIOUR section at the end of this chapter (see p. 29). If you don't do very well, don't despair. It's just our way of demonstrating that there's more to understanding the complexities of behaviour in organizations than meets the eye.

If we can't trust our common sense, then on what can we rely? This is where the scientific method enters the picture. Although social science research is far from perfect, the techniques used to study behaviour in organizations can tell us a great deal. Naturally, not everything scientific research reveals contradicts common sense. In fact, a considerable amount of research confirms things we already believe to be true. Is research therefore useless? The answer is emphatically no! After all, scientific evidence often provides a great deal of insight into the subtle conditions under which various events occur. Such complexities would not have been apparent from only casual, unsystematic observation and common sense. In other words, the field of OB is solidly based on carefully conducted and logically analyzed research. Although common sense may provide a useful starting point for getting us to think about behaviour in organizations, there's no substitute for scientific research when it comes to really understanding what happens and why.

Now that you understand the important role of the scientific method in the field of OB, you are prepared to appreciate the specific approaches used to conduct scientific research in this field. We will begin our presentation of these techniques with a discussion of one of the best-accepted sources of ideas for OB research—*theory*.

Theory: An Indispensable Guide to Organizational Research

What image comes to mind when you think of a scientist at work? Someone wearing a white lab coat surrounded by microscopes and test tubes busily testing theories? Although OB scientists typically don't wear lab coats or use microscopes and test tubes, it *is* true that they make use of theories. This is the case despite the fact that OB is, in part, an *applied* science. Simply because a field is characterized as being "theoretical," it does not follow that it is impractical and out of touch with reality. To the contrary, a theory is simply a way of describing the relationship between concepts. Thus, theories help, not hinder, our understanding of practical situations.

theory Efforts by scientists to explain why various events occur as they do. Theories consist of basic concepts and assertions regarding the relationship between them.

Formally, a **theory** is a set of statements about the interrelationships between concepts that allow us to predict and explain various processes and events. As you might imagine, such statements may be of interest to both practitioners and scientists alike. We're certain that as you read this book, you will come to appreciate the valuable role that theories play when it comes to understanding behaviour in organizations—and putting that knowledge to practical use.

Demonstrating the value of theory in OB. To demonstrate the value of theory in OB, let's consider an example based on a phenomenon we'll describe in more detail in Chapter 5—the effects of task goals on performance. Imagine observing that word processing operators type faster when they are given a specific goal (e.g., 75 words per minute) than when they are told to try to do their best. Imagine also observing that salespeople make more sales when they are given quotas than when they are not given any quotas. By themselves, these are useful observations: They allow us to predict what will happen when goals are introduced. In addition, they suggests ways to change conditions so as to improve performance among people in these groups. These two accomplishments—*prediction* and *control*—are major goals of science.

Yet there's something missing—namely, knowing that specific goals improve performance fails to tell us anything about *why* this is so. What is going on here? After all, a phenomenon was observed in two different settings and among two different groups of people. Why is it that people are so productive in response to specific goals? This is where theory enters the picture. In contrast to some fields, such as physics and chemistry, where theories often take the form of mathematical equations, theories in OB generally involve verbal assumptions. In the present case, for example, we might theorize as follows:

- When people are given specific goals, they know exactly what's expected of them.

- When people know what's expected of them, they are motivated to work hard to find ways to succeed.

- When people work hard to succeed, they perform at high levels.

This simple theory, like all others, consists of two basic elements: concepts (in this case goals and motives) and assertions about how they are related.

The research process. In science, the formation of a theory is only the beginning of a sequence of events followed to understand behaviour. Once a theory is proposed, it is used to introduce *hypotheses*—logically derived statements that follow from the theory. In our example, it may be hypothesized that specific goals will only improve performance when they are not so difficult that they cannot be attained. Next, such predictions need to be tested in actual research to see if they are confirmed. If research confirms our hypotheses, we can be more confident about the accuracy of the theory. However, if they are not confirmed after several well-conducted studies, our confidence in the theory is weakened. When this happens, it's time to revise the theory and generate new, testable hypotheses from it. As you might imagine, given the complexities of human behaviour in organizations, theories are rarely—if ever—fully confirmed. In fact, many of the field's most popular and useful theories are constantly being refined and tested. We have summarized the cyclical nature of the scientific endeavour in Figure 1-11.

It will probably come as no surprise to you to learn that the process of theory development and testing we have been describing is very laborious. In view of this fact, why do scientists bother constantly to fine-tune their theories? The answer lies in the very useful purposes that theories serve. Specifically, theories serve three important functions—organizing, summarizing, and guiding. First, given the complexities of human behaviour, theories provide a way of *organizing* large amounts

FIGURE 1-11 Theory Testing: The Research Process

Once a theory has been formulated, hypotheses derived from it are tested through direct research. If these are confirmed, confidence in the theory is increased. If they are disconfirmed, confidence is diminished. At this point, the theory is either modified and retested or completely rejected.

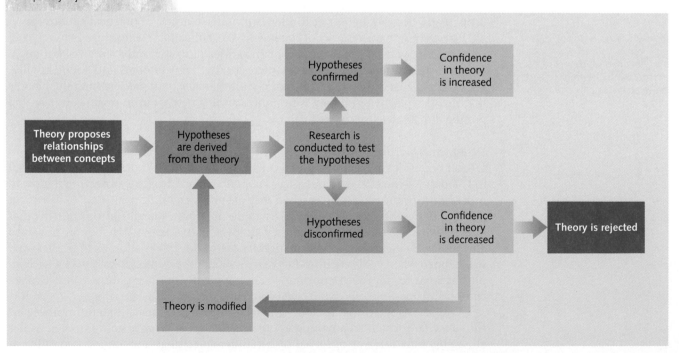

of data into meaningful propositions. In other words, they help us combine information so diverse that it might be difficult to grasp without the help of a theory. Second, theories help us to *summarize* this knowledge by making it possible to make sense out of bits and pieces of information that otherwise would be difficult—if not impossible—to understand. Finally, theories provide an important *guiding* function. That is, they help scientists identify important areas of needed research that would not have been apparent without theories to guide their thinking.

As you read this book, you will come across many different theories attempting to explain various aspects of behaviour in organizations. When you do, we think you will appreciate the useful organizing, summarizing, and guiding roles they play— in short, how theories help provide meaningful explanations of behaviour. In all cases, the usefulness of any theory is based on the extent to which it can be confirmed or disconfirmed. In other words, theories must be *testable*. A theory that cannot be tested serves no real purpose to scientists. Once it's tested, a theory—or at least part of it—must be confirmed if it is to be considered an accurate account of human behaviour. And of course, that's what the field of OB is all about.

How are theories tested? The answer is by conducting *research*. Unless we do research, we cannot test theories, and unless we test theories, we are greatly limited in what we can learn about behaviour in organizations.[43] This is why research is such a major concern of specialists in OB. Thus in order for you to fully appreciate the field of OB, it's critical for you to understand something about the techniques it uses—that is, how we come to know about the behaviour of people at work. As a result, throughout this book, we will not only be explaining *what* is known about OB, but in many cases also *how* that knowledge was derived. We are confident that the better you understand OB's "tools of the trade," the more you will come to appreciate its value as a field. With this in mind, we will now describe some of the major research techniques used to learn about organizational behaviour.

Survey Research: The Correlational Method

surveys Questionnaires designed to measure people's perceptions of some aspect of organizational behaviour.

The most popular approach to conducting research in OB involves giving people questionnaires in which they are asked to report how they feel about various aspects of themselves, their jobs, and their organizations. Such questionnaires, also known as **surveys**, make it possible for organizational scientists to delve into a broad range of issues. This research technique is so very popular because it is applicable to studying a wide variety of topics. After all, you can learn a great deal about how people feel by asking them a systematic series of carefully worded questions. Moreover, questionnaires are relatively easy to administer (be it by mail, by phone, or in person), and—as we will note shortly—they are readily quantifiable and lend themselves to powerful statistical analyses. These features make survey research a very appealing option to OB scientists. Not surprisingly, we will be describing quite a few survey studies throughout this book. The survey approach consists of three major steps.

- First, the researcher must identify the variables in which she or he is interested. These may be various aspects of people (e.g., their attitudes toward work), organizations (e.g., the pay plans they use), or the environment in general (e.g., how competitive the industry is). They may be suggested from many different sources, such as a theory, previous research, or even hunches based on casual observations.

- Second, these variables are measured as precisely as possible. As you might imagine, it isn't always easy to tap precisely people's feelings about things. As a result, researchers must pay close attention to the way they word the questions they use (for examples of questions designed to measure various work-related attitudes, see Table 1-2).

- Third, after the variables of interest have been identified and measured, scientists must determine how—if at all—they are related to each other. With this in mind, scientists analyze their survey findings using a variety of different statistical procedures.

TABLE 1-2 Survey Questions Designed to Measure Work Attitudes

Items such as these might be used to measure attitudes toward various aspects of work.

- Overall, how fairly are you paid?

  Not at all fairly   1   2   3   4   5   6   7   Extremely fairly

- Imagine that one of your office-mates needs to stay late to complete an important project. How likely or unlikely would you be to volunteer to help that person, even if you would not receive any special recognition for your efforts?

  Not at all likely   1   2   3   4   5   6   7   Extremely likely

- How interested are you in quitting your present job?

  Not at all interested   1   2   3   4   5   6   7   Extremely interested

correlational research An empirical research technique in which variables of interest are identified and carefully measured. These measures are then analyzed statistically to determine the extent to which they are related to one another.

hypothesis An unverified prediction concerning the relationships between variables. These propositions may be derived from previous research, existing theory, or informal observation.

☛ *The theories and research to which we allude here are described in Chapters 5 and 6.*

positive correlation A relationship between variables such that more of one variable is associated with more of another.

negative correlation A relationship between variables such that more of one variable is associated with less of another.

correlation coefficient A statistical index indicating the degree to which two or more variables are related.

Scientists conducting surveys typically are interested in determining how variables are interrelated—or, put differently, how changes in one variable are associated with changes in another. This approach is known as **correlational research**. This is an empirical research technique in which the variables of interest are identified and carefully measured. These measures are then analyzed statistically to determine the extent to which the variables are interrelated.

Let's consider an example. Suppose that a researcher is interested in learning the relationship between how fairly people believe they are paid and various work-related attitudes, such as their willingness to help their coworkers and their interest in quitting. Based on various theories and previous research, a researcher may suspect that the more people believe they are unfairly paid, the less likely they will be to help their coworkers and the more likely they will be to desire new jobs. These predictions constitute the researcher's **hypothesis**—the untested prediction the researcher wishes to investigate. After devising an appropriate questionnaire measuring these variables, the researcher would have to administer it to a large number of people so that the hypothesis can be tested.

Once the data are collected, the investigator must analyze them statistically and compare the results to the hypothesis. Suppose a researcher obtains results like those shown in the left side of Figure 1-12. In this case, the more fairly employees believe they are paid, the more willing they are to help their coworkers. In other words, the variables are related to each other such that the more one variable increases, the more the other also increases. Any variables described in this way are said to have a **positive correlation**. Now, imagine what will be found when the researcher compares the workers' perceptions of pay fairness with their interest in quitting their jobs. If the experimenter's hypothesis is correct, the results will look like those shown on the right side of Figure 1-12. In other words, the more people believe their pay is fair, the less interested they are in looking for a new job. Any such case—in which the more one variable increases, the more another decreases—is said to have a **negative correlation**.

OB scientists are not only interested in the direction of the relationship between variables—that is, whether the association is positive or negative—but also in how strong that relationship is. To gauge this, researchers rely on a statistic known as the **correlation coefficient**. This is a number between -1.00 and $+1.00$ used to express the strength of the relationship between the variables studied. The closer this number is to 1.00 (either -1.00 or $+1.00$), the stronger the relationship—that is, the more closely the variables are related to each other. However, the closer the correlation coefficient is to 0, the weaker the relationship between the variables—that is, the less strongly they are associated.

When interpreting correlation coefficients, therefore, there are two things to keep in mind: its *sign* (in keeping with algebraic traditions, positive correlations are usually expressed without any sign) and its *absolute value* (that is, the size of the number without respect to its sign). For example, a correlation coefficient of $-.92$ reflects a much stronger relationship between variables than one of $.22$. The minus sign simply reveals that the relationship between the variables being described is negative (more of one variable is associated with less of another variable). The fact that the absolute value of this correlation coefficient is greater tells us that the relationship between the variables is stronger.

FIGURE 1-12 Positive and Negative Correlations: What They Mean

Positive correlations, such as the one shown on the left, exist when more of one variable is associated with more of another variable. Negative correlations, such as the one on the right, exist when more of one variable is associated with less of another variable.

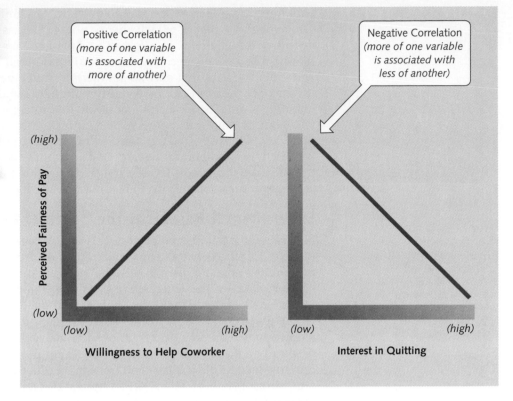

multiple regression A statistical technique indicating the extent to which each of several variables contributes to accurate predictions of another variable.

When variables are strongly correlated, scientists can make more accurate predictions about how they are related to each other. Using our example, in which there is a negative correlation between perceptions of pay fairness and intent to quit, we may expect that, in general, those who believe they are unfairly paid will be more likely to quit their jobs than those who believe they are fairly paid. If the correlation coefficient were high, (say, over −.80) we would be more confident that this would occur than if the correlation were low (say, under −.20). In fact, as correlation coefficients approach 0, it's impossible to make any accurate predictions whatsoever. In such a case, knowing one variable would not allow us to predict anything about the other. As you might imagine, organizational scientists are extremely interested in discovering the relationships between variables and rely on correlation coefficients to tell them a great deal.

Although the examples we've been using involve the relationship between only two variables at a time, organizational researchers are frequently interested in the interrelationships between many different variables at once. For example, an employee's intent to quit may be related to several variables besides the perceived fairness of pay—such as satisfaction with the job itself or liking for one's immediate supervisor. Researchers may make predictions using several different variables at once, using a technique known as **multiple regression**. Using this approach, researchers may be able to tell the extent to which each of several different variables contributes to predicting the behaviour in question. In our example, they would be able to learn the degree to which the several variables studied, both together and individually, are related to the intent to quit one's job. Given the complex nature of human behaviour on the job, and the wide range of variables likely to influence it, it should not be surprising to learn that OB researchers use the multiple regression technique a great deal in their work.

Even though the analysis of surveys using correlational techniques like multiple regression can be valuable, conclusions drawn from correlations are limited in a very important way. Namely, *correlations do not reveal anything about causation.* In other words, although correlations tell us about how variables are related to each other, they don't provide any insight into their cause-and-effect relationships. So, in our example, although we may learn that the less employees feel they are fairly paid the more interested they are in quitting, we cannot tell *why* this is the case. In other words, we cannot tell whether or not employees want to quit *because* they believe they are unfairly paid. Might this be the case? Yes, but it also might be the case that people who believe they are unfairly paid tend to dislike the work they do, and it is this factor that encourages them to find a new job. Another possibility is that people believe they are unfairly paid because their supervisors are too demanding—and it is this factor that raises their interest in quitting (see Figure 1-13). Our point is simple: Although all these possibilities are reasonable, knowing only that variables are correlated does *not* permit us to determine what causes what. Because it is important for researchers to establish the causal relationships between the variables they study, OB researchers frequently turn to another technique that *does* permit such conclusions to be drawn—the experiment.

Experimental Research: The Logic of Cause and Effect

Because both scientists and practitioners want to know not only the degree to which variables are related, but also how much one variable causes another, the **experimental method** is sometimes used in OB. The more we know about the causal connections between variables, the better we can explain the underlying causes of behaviour—and this, after all, is one of the major goals of OB.

To illustrate how experiments work, let's consider an example. Suppose we're interested in determining the effects of social density (the number of people per unit of space) on the job performance of clerical employees—that is, the degree to which the crowdedness of working conditions in an office influences how accurately word processing operators do their jobs. Although this topic might be studied in many different ways, imagine that we do the following. First, we select at random a large group of word processing operators working in a variety of different organizations—the participants in our study. Then, we prepare a specially designed office, the setting for the experiment. Throughout the study, we would keep the design of the office and

experimental method An empirical research method in which one or more variables are systematically varied (the *independent variables*) to determine if such changes have any impact on the behaviour of interest (the *dependent variables*).

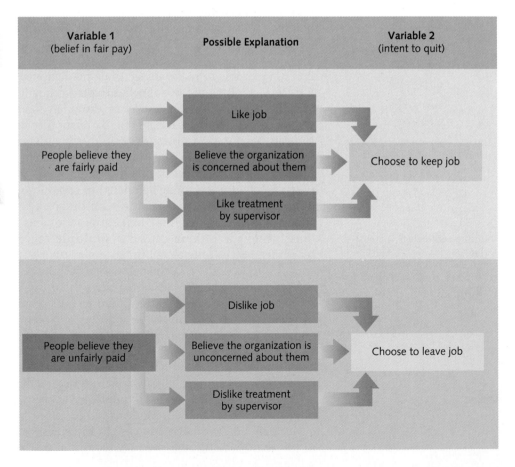

FIGURE 1-13 Correlations: What They Don't Reveal about Causation

Just because there may be a strong negative correlation between pay fairness and the desire to leave one's job, we cannot tell *why* this relationship exists. As shown here, there are many possible underlying reasons that are not identified by knowledge of the correlation alone.

all the working conditions (e.g., temperature, light, and noise levels) alike with one exception—we would systematically vary the number of people working in the office at any given time.

For example, we could have one condition—which we could call the "high-density" condition—in which 50 people are put into a 50-square-metre room at once (allowing 1 square metre per person). In another condition—the "low-density" condition—we could put 5 people into a 50-square-metre room at once (allowing 10 square metres per person). Finally, we can have a "moderate-density" condition in which we put 25 people into a 50-square-metre room (allowing 2 square metres per person). Say that we have several hundred people participating in the study and that we assign them at random to each of these three conditions. Each word processing operator is then given the same passage of text to type over two hours. After this period, the typists are dismissed, and the researcher counts the number of words accurately typed by each typist, noting any possible differences between performance in the various conditions. Suppose that we obtain the results summarized in Figure 1-14.

Let's analyze what was done in this simple hypothetical experiment to help explain the basic elements of the experimental method and its underlying logic. First, recall that we selected participants from the population of interest and assigned them to conditions on a *random* basis. This means that each of the participants had an equal chance of being assigned to any one of the three conditions. This is critical because it is possible that differences between conditions could result from having many very good operators in one condition and many unproductive ones in another. To safeguard against this possibility, it is important to assign people to conditions at random. When this is done, we can assume that the effects of any possible differences between people would equalize over conditions.

Thus, by assigning people to conditions at random, we can be assured that there will be just as many fast operators and slow operators in each. As a result, there is no reason to believe that any differences in productivity that may be noted between conditions can be attributed to systematic differences in the skills of the participants. Given "the luck of the draw," such differences can be discounted, thereby enhancing our confidence that differences are solely the result of the social density of the rooms. This is the logic behind *random assignment*. Although it is not always feasible to use random assignment when conducting experiments in organizations, it is highly desirable whenever possible.

FIGURE 1-14 Example of Simple Experimental Results

In our hypothetical example, word processing operators were put into rooms that differed with respect to only one variable—social density (i.e., the number of people per unit of space). The results summarized here show that people performed best under conditions of lowest density, and worst under conditions of highest density.

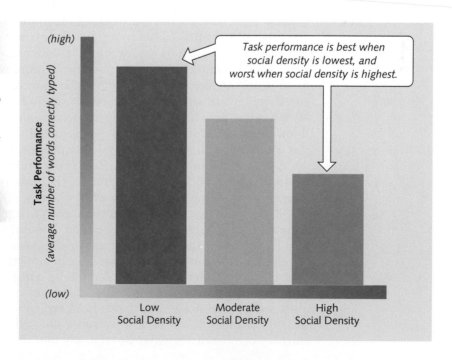

Task performance is best when social density is lowest, and worst when social density is highest.

independent variable The factor in an experiment that is systematically varied by the experimenter to determine its impact on behaviour (the dependent variable).

dependent variable The variable in an experiment that is measured, affected by the impact of the independent variable.

Recall that word processing operators were assigned to conditions that differed with respect to only the variable of interest—in this case, social density. We can say that the experimenter *manipulated* this aspect of the work environment, systematically changing it from one condition to another. A variable altered in this way is called an **independent variable**. An independent variable is a variable that is systematically manipulated by the experimenter so as to determine its effects on the behaviour of interest. In our example, the independent variable is social density. Specifically, it may be said to have three different *levels*—that is, degrees of the independent variable: high, moderate, and low.

The variable that is measured, the one influenced by the independent variable, is known as the **dependent variable**. A dependent variable is the behaviour of interest that is being measured—the behaviour that is dependent upon the independent variable. In this case, the dependent variable was word processing performance, the quantity of words accurately typed. Besides studying this variable, we could have studied other dependent variables, such as satisfaction with the work or the perceived level of stress encountered. In fact, it would be quite likely for OB researchers to study several dependent variables in one experiment. By the same token, researchers also frequently consider the effects of several different independent variables in a given experiment. The matter of which particular independent and dependent variables are being studied is one of the most important judgments researchers make. Often, they base these decisions on suggestions from previous research (other experiments suggesting that certain variables are important) and existing theory (conceptualizations suggesting that certain variables may be important).

The basic logic behind the experimental method is quite simple. In fact, it involves only two major steps. First, some variable of interest (the independent variable) must be systematically varied. Second, the effects, if any, of such variations must be measured. The underlying idea is that if the independent variable does indeed influence behaviour, then people exposed to different amounts of it should behave differently. In our example, we can be certain that social density caused differences in word processing performance because when all other factors were held constant, different amounts of density led to different levels of performance. Our experiment thus follows the same basic logic of all experiments—namely, it is designed to reveal the effects of the independent variables on the dependent variables.

For the conclusions of experiments to be valid, it is critical for them to hold constant all factors other than the independent variable. Then, if there are differences in the dependent variable, we can assume that they are the result of the effects of the independent variable. By assigning participants to conditions at random, we already took an important step to ensure that one key factor—differences in the ability levels of the participants—would be equalized. But there are other possible factors that also may affect the results. For example, it would be essential to hold constant environmental conditions that might influence word processing speed. In this case, more people would generate more heat, so to make sure that the results are influenced only by density—and not heat—it would be necessary to air-condition the work room so as to keep it the same temperature in all conditions at all times. If you think about it, our simple experiment is really not that simple at all—especially if it is conducted with all the care needed to permit valid conclusions to be drawn.

As you might imagine, this is often easier said than done. How simple it is to control the effects of extraneous variables (i.e., factors not of interest to the experimenter) depends, in large part, on where the experiment is conducted. In the field of OB, there are generally two options available: Experiments can be conducted in naturalistic organizational settings, referred to as the *field*, or in settings specially created for the study itself, referred to as the *laboratory* (or, *lab* for short).

The study in our example was a lab experiment. It was conducted in carefully controlled conditions specially created for the research. The great amount of control possible in such settings improves the chances of creating the conditions needed to allow valid conclusions to be drawn from experiments. At the same time, however, lab studies suffer from a lack of realism. Although the working conditions can be carefully controlled, they may be relatively unrealistic, not carefully simulating the conditions found in actual organizations. As a result, it may be difficult to generalize the findings of lab studies to settings outside the lab, such as the workplace.

However, if we conducted our study in actual organizations, there would be many unknowns, many uncontrollable factors at work. To conduct such a study, we would have to distinguish between those who worked in offices differing with respect to social density and later compare people's performance. If we did this, we would be sure that the conditions studied were realistic. However, there would be so little control over the setting that many different factors could be operating. For example, because people would not be assigned to conditions at random, it might be the case that people work in those settings they most desire. Furthermore, there would be no control over such factors as distractions and differences in environmental conditions (e.g., noise and temperature).

In short, field studies, although strong in the level of realism they offer, are weak with respect to the level of control they provide. By contrast, lab experiments permit a great deal of control, but tend to be unrealistic. In view of these complementary strengths and weaknesses, it should be clear that experiments should be conducted in *both* types of sites. As researchers do so, our confidence can be increased that valid conclusions will be drawn about behaviour in organizations. Figure 1-15 summarizes the trade-offs involved in conducting research in each setting.

Qualitative Research: Naturalistic Observation and the Case Method

In contrast to the highly quantitative approaches to research we have been describing thus far, we should also note that OB researchers sometimes use a less quantitative approach. After all, probably the most obvious ways of learning about behaviour in organizations are to observe it firsthand and to describe it after it occurs. Organizational scientists have a long tradition of studying behaviour using these nonempirical, descriptive techniques, relying on what is known as *qualitative research*.[44] The qualitative approach to research relies on preserving the natural

FIGURE 1-15 Trade-offs between Lab and Field Experimentation

Organizational behaviour researchers may conduct experiments in laboratory or field settings, each of which has its own relative advantages and disadvantages. Generally, the lab offers more control but less realism, whereas the field offers less control but more realism.

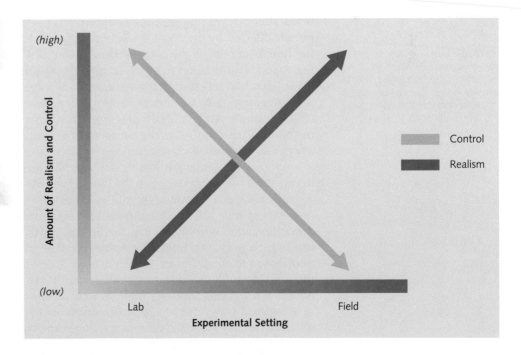

qualities of the situation being studied, attempting to capture the richness of the context while disturbing naturalistic conditions only minimally, if at all. The two major qualitative methods used by OB scientists are *naturalistic observation* and the *case method*.

Naturalistic observation. There's probably no more fundamental way of learning about how people act in organizations than simply to observe them—a research technique known as **naturalistic observation**. Suppose, for example, that you wanted to learn how employees behave in response to layoffs. One thing you could do would be to visit an organization in which layoffs will be occurring and systematically observe what the employees do and say both before and after the layoffs occur. Making comparisons of this type may provide very useful insights into what's going on. As a variation of this technique, you could take a job in the organization and make your observations as an insider actually working there—giving you a perspective you might not otherwise gain. This technique, often used by anthropologists, is known as **participant observation**.

It's not too difficult to think of the advantages and disadvantages of observational research. Its major advantage is that it can be used without disrupting normal routines, allowing behaviour to be studied in its natural state. Moreover, almost anyone—including people already working in the host organization—can be trained to use it. However, observational research also suffers from several important limitations. First, the potential for subjectivity among researchers is considerable. Even among the most diligent of researchers, it's inevitable that different people will make different observations of the same events. Second, being involved in the daily functioning of an organization will make it difficult for observers to be impartial. Researchers interpreting organizational events may be subject to bias due to their feelings about the people involved. Finally, because most of what goes on in an organization is fairly dull and routine, it's very easy for researchers to place a great deal of emphasis on unusual or unexpected events, possibly leading to inaccurate conclusions. Given these limitations, most OB scientists consider observational research to be more useful as a starting point for providing basic insight into behaviour than as a tool for acquiring definitive knowledge about behaviour.

The case method. Suppose that we conducted our hypothetical study of reactions to layoffs differently. Instead of observing behaviour directly, we might fully describe the company's history leading up to the event and some statistics summarizing its aftermath (e.g., how long people were unemployed, how the company was restructured after downsizing, and the like). We might even include some interviews with people affected by the event, and quote them directly. The approach we are describing here is known as the **case method**. More often than not, the rationale behind the case method is *not* to teach us about a specific organization as such, but to learn what happened in that organization as a means of providing cues as to what may be going on in other organizations. The case method is similar to naturalistic observation in that it relies on descriptive accounts of events. However, it is different in that it often involves using subsequent accounts of events from those involved as opposed to firsthand observations by scientists.

As you might imagine, a great deal can be learned by detailed accounts of events in organizations summarized in the form of written cases. Especially when these cases are supplemented by careful interviews, cases can paint a particularly detailed picture of events as they unfolded in a particular organization. Of course, to the extent that the organization is unique, it may not be possible to generalize what is learned to others. To get around this limitation, some researchers have recommended that multiple, as opposed to single, cases should be used to test theories.[45] Another problem with the case method—a limitation it shares with naturalistic observation—is that the potential for bias is relatively high. As a result, many scientists believe that while the case method may serve as a valuable source of hypotheses about behaviour on the job, fully testing those hypotheses requires more rigorous research methods.[46]

naturalistic observation A qualitative research technique in which an investigator observes events occurring in an organization while attempting not to affect those events by being present.

participant observation
Naturalistic observations of an organization made by individuals who have been hired as employees.

case method A qualitative research method in which a particular organization is studied in detail, usually in the hopes of being able to learn about organizational functioning in general.

SUMMARY AND REVIEW

The Field of Organizational Behaviour

Organizational behaviour (OB) seeks knowledge of all aspects of behaviour in organizational settings through the systematic study of individual, group, and organizational processes. It uses this knowledge to promote basic understanding of human behaviour and to enhance the effectiveness of organizations and the well-being of individuals working in them. Because it relies on scientific methods, the field of OB provides much more accurate knowledge about work behaviour than simply relying on common sense.

In contrast to the traditional view that people are basically lazy and uninterested in working (the **Theory X** approach), modern OB is characterized by the belief that under the right combination of conditions people are responsive to their work environments and are highly committed to work (the **Theory Y** approach). The field also recognizes that organizations are dynamic, self-sustaining units known as **open systems**. In view of the complex nature of human behaviour at work, OB generally takes a **contingency approach**, recognizing that behaviour depends on the complex interaction of many different variables. OB also confronts various challenges brought on by the changing nature of work, such as growing diversity in the workforce, globalization, and rapidly advancing technology.

Historical Development of the Field of Organizational Behaviour

The roots of OB can be traced back to the early twentieth century work of Frederick W. Taylor on **scientific management**—a management philosophy that attempted to find the most efficient ways for people to perform their jobs. Around this same time, **classical organizational theory** attempted to discover the most effective ways of designing organizations. Among these was the **bureaucracy**—a form of organization identified by Max Weber that advocated clear organizational hierarchies and well-defined jobs. The field was also greatly influenced by the **human relations approach**, an orientation highlighting the impact of complex social systems on job performance. Elton Mayo's Hawthorne studies represented the pioneering efforts in this area. In the second half of the twentieth century, the field of OB grew dramatically to become the diverse, multidisciplinary field it is today.

Research Methods in Organizational Behaviour

Although much of what OB studies appears to be commonsensical, casual observations are often misleading and fail to reveal the complex nature of behaviour. Accordingly, the field of OB is based on knowledge derived from scientific research. Research is often guided by **theories**, testable explanations as to why various events occur as they do.

Correlational research is among the most popularly used techniques in the field. In this approach potentially important variables are identified and then systematically measured using **surveys** to determine how they are related to one another. The **correlation coefficient** is the statistic used to summarize the degree and direction of the relationship between variables.

Because the correlational method does not allow us to draw conclusions about cause and effect, researchers often rely on the **experimental method**. Using this approach, researchers systematically vary one or more variables (**independent variables**) while holding other factors constant so as to determine the effects on the behaviour of interest (**dependent variables**).

In contrast to these empirical techniques, OB researchers often rely on qualitative approaches, such as **naturalistic observation**, in which trained observers make systematic observations of behaviour in an organization, and the **case method**, in which detailed accounts are given of events that occurred in a particular organization.

CASE PREVIEW QUESTIONS FOR DISCUSSION

1. What advice do you think Randy Powell would offer to Canadian students interested in climbing the corporate ladder? How unusual is Randy Powell's rapid ascent up the corporate ladder in these times in Canada?

2. What does Randy Powell mean by "you move from managing projects to managing people"?

3. What do you learn about Randy Powell's management style in the case? Would you like to work for him? Explain your answer.

CHAPTER QUESTIONS FOR DISCUSSION

1. How can the field of organizational behaviour contribute both to the effective functioning of organizations *and* to the well-being of individuals? Are these goals inconsistent? Why or why not?

2. Explain the following statement: "People influence organizations, and organizations influence people."

3. What is the "contingency approach" and why is it so popular in the field of OB today?

4. Explain how the field of organizational behaviour stands to benefit by taking a global perspective. What would you say are the major challenges associated with such a perspective?

5. Kurt Lewin, a famous social scientist once said, "There is nothing as applied as a good theory." Explain how this statement is applicable to the study of organizational behaviour.

6. Under what conditions would it be advisable to learn about organizational behaviour by using survey research as opposed to experimental research?

7. The Hawthorne studies inadvertently revealed a great deal about behaviour in organizations despite flaws in the way the research was conducted. Using your knowledge of the experimental method, describe some of the weaknesses of the Hawthorne studies and ways they may have been alleviated.

CASE IN POINT

Roots Canada: From Algonquin Park to Nagano

As the Canadian Olympic Team entered the opening ceremonies of the 1998 Winter Olympics in Nagano, surely no two people were more proud than Michael Budman and Don Green, the camp buddies behind Roots Canada. With every athlete resplendent in Roots hat, jacket, pants, and boots, there could be no more powerful exposure for their company. "This is the finest Olympic clothing ever made.... The way they felt in their clothes was part of the success of the Canadian Team. This hat is a unifying piece of Canada," enthused Michael Budman.

Budman and Green met as children at Camp Tamakwa in Ontario's Algonquin Park and, in some ways, they have never left. "Roots is less a company than a summer camp. Don and Michael...are its codirectors, sans whistles, but always enthusiastic, energetic, focused on positives."[47] The founders' inspiration comes from the Algonquin wilderness they experienced as children and is reflected today in the company's commitment to environmental issues. The Roots factory "makes a conscious effort to recycle as much as possible with policies such as making scraps of leather into small leather goods and using only environmentally friendly tanneries."[48]

Founded in 1973, Roots Canada manufactures and retails leather products, such as shoes and jackets, casual clothing for adults and children and, more recently, watches and eye wear. From the "earth" shoe and one store in Toronto, Roots has grown to include 95 stores in Canada, 6 in the United States, and 13 in Japan, Hong Kong, Taiwan, and Korea. Throughout its history, Roots Canada "has adhered to a motto of Quality and Integrity and a vision based on health, family, and the environment."[49]

Budman and Green, who share an office that doubles as a showroom, push their workers to achieve. Green describes their vision of the company as a hockey team. "We have our diggers, our grinders, our utility players, and our all-stars. We try to have the right people in the right positions."[50] But not all their "players" are comfortable with the 60-hour work weeks and the perceived lack of personal recognition. Kathy Wong, former Roots product develop-

ment director, could relate to the sports metaphor but, while she felt she could play her position on the team, she alleged that Budman and Green always wanted to take the credit for the big scores.[51]

Roots' trail to profitability has not always been smooth. The recession of the early 1990s hit Roots hard. The partners had developed some casual work habits that seemed to be catching up with them. Don's father, Irwin Green, reviewed Roots' operation and told the "boys" to get to work. Gone were the morning hockey games. They had to change their work habits, make major personnel alterations, and review their operation from production to retail. The lesson that Don Green took from this time of upheaval was that business results relate directly to the time managers invest in their company.

Their new work plan paid off. Roots came through the recession restructured and reinvigorated.[52] Today Roots clothes are appearing in newspapers and on television worn by everyone from Prince William to James Cameron and Sarah McLachlan to Quincy Jones.[53]

Critical Thinking Questions

1. Would you say Don Green and Michael Budman are using a Theory X or Theory Y approach to managing at Roots? Explain.

2. Discuss the statement, "Roots is less a company than a summer camp." Speculate on the long-term effectiveness of such a management philosophy for Roots Canada.

3. What is Kathy Wong trying to tell Budman and Green about managing people at Roots Canada?

4. Discuss the impact that the changing environment has had on Roots Canada and the approach that Budman and Green have taken to managing the company.

5. What advice would you offer Budman and Green about managing Roots Canada over the next five to ten years?

Roots Canada
www.roots.com

SKILLS PORTFOLIO

Experiencing Organizational Behaviour

Testing Your Assumptions about People at Work

What assumptions do you make about human nature? Are you inclined to think of people as primarily lazy and disinterested in working (a Theory X approach) or as willing to work hard under the right conditions (a Theory Y approach)? This exercise is designed to give you some insight into this question.

Directions

For each of the eight pairs of statements below, select the one that best reflects your feelings by marking the letter that corresponds to it.

1. **(a)** If you give people what they need to do their jobs, they will act very responsibly.
   (b) Giving people more information than they need will lead them to misuse it.
2. **(c)** People naturally want to get away with doing as little work as possible.
   (d) When people avoid working, it's probably because the work itself has been stripped of its meaning.
3. **(e)** It's not surprising to find that employees don't demonstrate much creativity on the job because people tend not to have much of it to begin with.
   (f) Although many people are by nature very creative, they don't show it on the job because they aren't given a chance.
4. **(g)** It doesn't pay to ask employees for their ideas because their perspective is generally too limited to be of value.
   (h) When you ask employees for ideas, you are likely to get some useful suggestions.
5. **(i)** The more information people have about their jobs, the more closely their supervisors have to keep them in line.
   (j) The more information people have about their jobs, the less closely they have to be supervised.
6. **(k)** Once people are paid enough, the less they tend to care about being recognized for a job well done.
   (l) The more interesting the work people do, the less likely they care about their pay.
7. **(m)** Supervisors lose prestige when they admit that their subordinates may have been right while they were wrong.
   (n) Supervisors gain prestige when they admit that their subordinates may have been right while they were wrong.
8. **(o)** When people are held accountable for their mistakes, they raise their standards.
   (p) Unless people are punished for their mistakes, they will lower their standards.

Scoring

1. Give yourself 1 point for having selected b, c, e, g, i, k, m, and p. The sum of these points is your Theory X score.
2. Give yourself 1 point for having selected a, d, f, h, j, l, n, and o. The sum of these points is your Theory Y score.

Questions for Discussion

1. Which perspective did this questionnaire indicate that you endorsed more strongly, Theory X or Theory Y? Is this consistent with your own intuitive conclusion?
2. Do you tend to manage others in ways consistent with Theory X or Theory Y ideas?
3. Can you recall any experiences that may have been crucial in defining or reinforcing your Theory X or Theory Y philosophy?

Working in Groups

Common Sense about Behaviour in Organizations: Putting It to the Test

Even if you already have a good intuitive sense about behaviour in organizations, some of what you think may be inconsistent with established research findings (many of which are noted in this book). So that you don't have to rely on your own judgments (which may be idiosyncratic), working with others in this exercise will give you a good sense of what our collective common sense has to say about behaviour in organizations. You just may be enlightened.

Directions

Divide the class into groups of about five. Within these groups, discuss the following statements, reaching a consensus as to whether each is true or false. Spend approximately 30 minutes on the entire discussion.

1. People who are satisfied with one job tend to be satisfied with other jobs, too.
2. Because "two heads are better than one," groups make better decisions than individuals.
3. The best leaders always act the same, regardless of the situations they face.
4. Specific goals make people nervous; people work better when asked to do their best.
5. People get bored easily, leading them to welcome organizational change.
6. Money is the best motivator.
7. Today's organizations are more rigidly structured than ever before.
8. People generally shy away from challenges on the job.
9. Using multiple communication channels (e.g., written/spoken) tends to add confusion.
10. Conflict in organizations is always highly disruptive.

Scoring

Give your group one point for each item you scored as follows: 1 = True, 2 = False, 3 = False, 4 = False, 5 = False, 6 = False, 7 = False, 8 = False, 9 = False, and 10 = False. (Should you have questions about these answers, information bearing on them appears in this book as follows: 1 = Chapter 6, 2 = Chapter 8, 3 = Chapter 13, 4 = Chapter 5, 5 = Chapter 16, 6 = Chapter 5, 7 = Chapter 15, 8 = Chapter 5, 9 = Chapter 9, 10 = Chapter 11.)

Questions for Discussion

1. How well did your group do? Were you stumped on a few?
2. Comparing your experiences to those of other groups, did you find that there were some questions that proved trickier than others (i.e., ones where the scientific findings were more counterintuitive)? If you did poorly, don't be frustrated. These statements are a bit simplistic and need to be qualified to be fully understood. Have your instructor explain the statements that the class found most challenging.
3. Did this exercise give you a better understanding of the sometimes surprising (and complex) nature of behaviour in organizations?

TAKE IT TO THE NET

Prentice Hall

COMPANION WEBSITE

We invite you to visit the *Greenberg/Baron/Sales/Owen Companion Website* at *www.prenticehall.ca/greenberg* for this chapter's Internet resources.

CHAPTER 2
Work in the Twenty-First Century:
The Changing World of People and Organizations

LEARNING OBJECTIVES

After reading this chapter you should be able to:

1. Describe the impact of *globalization* of the economy on the operation of organizations.

2. Explain how cultural differences between people from various nations may account for different organizational behaviours.

3. Understand the nature and realities of *diversity* in today's organizations.

4. Appreciate the impact of various trends in working arrangements, including *downsizing, outsourcing*, the *contingent workforce, virtual corporations,* and *telecommuting*.

5. Describe various approaches that today's organizations are taking to improve the quality of their goods and services, such as *total quality management,* and *reengineering*.

6. Explain why unethical behaviour occurs in organizations and what can be done to prevent it.

Babine Forest Products: Modelling Diversity as a Strategic Advantage

Burns Lake, British Columbia is a community that many across Canada may envy. "Natives and non-Natives attend school together, alongside each other and relax in the same watering holes. It's not perfect . . . but few dispute that Burns Lake has largely escaped the historic woes of deprivation and bigotry found elsewhere in B.C."[1] Burns Lake is the home of Babine Forest Products, a joint venture of Weldwood of Canada and Burns Lake First Nations which began in the mid-1970s.[2]

Babine Forest Products is the longest-lived joint venture of its kind in Canada. The company, which converts timber into boards and chips, employs 268 workers of whom about 34 percent are Native (see Figure 2-1). This ratio reflects the percentage of Native people living in the region around Burns Lake. Ten percent of Babine Forest Products Ltd. is owned by the Burns Lake Native Development Corporation (BLNDC) with Weldwood of Canada owning 58 percent and West Fraser Timber Co. owning 32 percent. The

Figure 2-1 Strength in Diversity

Babine Forest Products credits its harmonious and unique management-employee relations for its exceptional cost effectiveness.[6]

BLNDC is comprised of five First Nations bands. Former BLNDC chair, Wilf Adam, is enthusiastic about the progress that the corporation has made in furthering Native interests. "We now have financial resources and environmental controls....Before 1974 there was damage to trap lines, berry picking sites, and archaeological grounds. Now that we're in the boardroom, this no longer happens."[3]

Babine has achieved harmony in the relationship between Native and non-Native employees in several ways. For example, the company employs a Native liaison officer and, while it expects the same level of productivity from all employees, it does respect the need to recognize Native holiday celebrations. In fact, there have been times when the mill has been shut down for Native ceremonial days.

Relations between racial groups have not always been smooth. One issue of concern for Native leaders has been the tendency for Native youth to neglect their education in favour of taking a high-paying Babine job. The company responded to this concern by requiring a minimum of a grade 12 education for all employees. In addition, there is concern that more whites than Natives are promoted to managerial ranks. However, despite these concerns, the partnership has been a financial success for the company, the BLNDC, and the Burns Lake community. "This is not like other mills where the union calls a walkout every time management makes a mistake. Burns Lake is unique," says the company's Native liaison officer.[4] With increasing interaction among the peoples of the world in shared business and industrial ventures, Babine Forest Products offers a model for a constructive and mutually respectful partnership. Babine Forest Products has shown "how diversity can work to strategic advantage."[5]

Babine Forest Products is clearly a company that has gone out of its way to capitalize on the strengths of its diverse workforce and to be a pleasant and productive place in which to work. As reasonable as this strategy would appear to be, it represents a departure from the ways many people have been treated in organizations in the past.

Living at the close of the twentieth century, we have seen more changes in our daily lives than people at any earlier times. If what the experts are saying is correct, this is only the beginning. The twenty-first century promises to be even more complex and to bring change at an even more rapid pace.[7] As you might imagine, this state of affairs has important implications for the study of behaviour in organizations. After all, as the world changes, so too does the nature of work. In this chapter we will describe some of the major forces bringing change to the world of organizations. As you will realize after reading this chapter, understanding such trends provides crucial insight into the dynamic nature of the field of organizational behaviour.

Specifically, in this chapter we will focus on several major themes that will be reflected throughout this book—both in the main text and in various *special sections*. To begin, we will examine the rapidly growing trend toward *globalization*—the highly international nature of today's organizations. Then, we will describe changes in the composition of the workforce—the trend toward *diversity*. These themes, focusing as they do on cultural differences between and within organizations, will be highlighted in special sections called GLOBALIZATION IN TODAY'S ORGANIZATIONS and DIVERSITY IN TODAY'S ORGANIZATIONS.

We also will describe various trends in the basic nature of the way work is conducted. Such changes stem primarily from rapid advances in the development of *technology*, which affect the design of jobs and organizations. Throughout this text we will focus on changes in technology and work itself in a special section called ORGANIZATIONAL TRENDS. As the name implies, we will describe the latest trends in the world of work and what the experts predict as they look into their crystal balls.

Third, we will examine the strong *emphasis on quality* that has permeated many of today's organizations. We are thinking not only of improvements in the quality of goods and services that organizations offer, but enhancements in the quality of people's work lives as well. After providing essential background on this trend in this chapter, we will showcase some of these developments throughout this book in special sections called THE QUEST FOR QUALITY.

Finally, we will pay attention to the ethical aspects of behaviour in organizations. Given that the headlines of our newspapers frequently contain stories about scandals in organizations, it is easy to appreciate the importance of studying the ethical and unethical aspects of people's behaviour. We will highlight the determinants of ethical behaviour in this chapter. Then, throughout the text we will provide examples of ethical issues tackled by organizations in special sections called THE ETHICS ANGLE.

In short, this chapter will focus on several key aspects of the changing nature of the world of work, themes that also will be highlighted throughout this book. For a summary of these various topics and the special sections to which they are linked, see Figure 2-2.

Globalization and Culture: Today's International Organizations

Chances are good that the car you drive is constructed of parts made in various countries and may even be assembled in several of them. The bank on the nearest corner may be owned by a large conglomerate headquartered halfway around the world. Your personal computer with the well-known nameplate may be assembled in Mexico using chips made in Korea. Your clothes may be sewn by people in Taiwan using fabric woven in India. We could go on, but by now our point should be clear: The world of business is an international world. As you might imagine, this fact has important implications for the study of organizational behaviour.

Organizations in the Global Arena

To understand behaviour in organizations fully we must appreciate the fact that organizations operate within an economic system in which resources such as

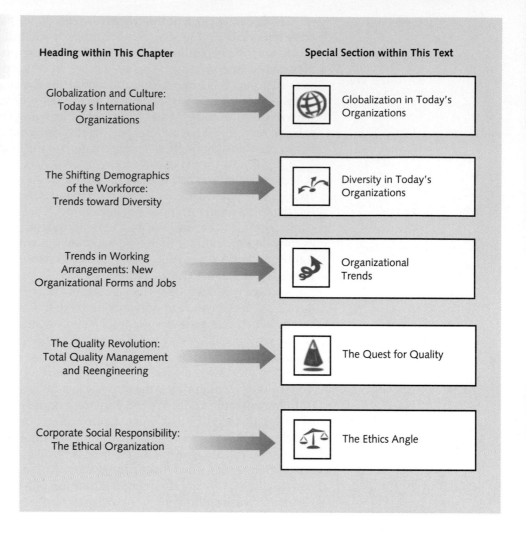

Heading within This Chapter	Special Section within This Text
Globalization and Culture: Today's International Organizations	Globalization in Today's Organizations
The Shifting Demographics of the Workforce: Trends toward Diversity	Diversity in Today's Organizations
Trends in Working Arrangements: New Organizational Forms and Jobs	Organizational Trends
The Quality Revolution: Total Quality Management and Reengineering	The Quest for Quality
Corporate Social Responsibility: The Ethical Organization	The Ethics Angle

information, goods, and money are constantly flowing. In recent decades, economic transactions have not been restricted to those occurring within countries, but with growing frequency, between countries as well. As one expert has put it, "By a wide margin . . . global competition is the single most powerful economic fact of life in the 1990s."[8] Consider these facts:

- Whereas in 1960 foreign investment in Canada was $13.6 billion by 1996 it was $180.4 billion.[9]

- In 1960 Canadian investment abroad was $2.6 billion while it had risen to $170.8 billion by 1996.[10]

International trade. Commerce between nations of the world has grown from U.S.$308 billion in 1950 to U.S.$3.8 trillion in 1993.[11] Several factors account for such dramatic growth. First, technology has drastically lowered the cost of transportation and communication, thereby enhancing opportunities for international commerce. Second, laws regulating trade have generally become less restrictive throughout the world (e.g., in Canada and other heavily industrialized countries, free trade policies have been advocated by many). Third, developing nations have sought to expand their economies by promoting exports and opening their doors to foreign companies seeking investments. This trend has expanded opportunities for economic growth and competition throughout the world. The impact of such worldwide trade can be seen in the rapid growth of international lending. For example, whereas banks loaned companies in other countries U.S.$324 billion in 1980, the figure rose to

U.S.$7.5 trillion in 1991.[12] Money flows rapidly into and out of nations, creating a situation in which the countries of the world are highly interdependent on each other economically and politically. This is part of the growing trend toward **globalization**— the process of interconnecting the world's people with respect to the cultural, economic, political, technological, and environmental aspects of their lives.[13]

globalization The process of interconnecting the world's people with respect to the cultural, economic, political, technological, and environmental aspects of their lives.

Multinational corporations. If international trade is the major driver of globalization, then the primary vehicles are **multinational corporations (MNCs)**—organizations that have significant operations spread throughout various nations but are headquartered in a single nation. MNCs are greatly responsible for direct investment in foreign nations: The 300 largest MNCs account for a quarter of the world's productive assets, with the 100 largest valued at U.S.$3.1 trillion. There are now more than 35 000 MNCs throughout the world.[14] Canada has a growing number of multinational corporations including Seagram Co. Ltd., Alcan Aluminum Ltd., Bombardier Inc., Power Financial Corp, EdperBrascan Corp., and McCain Foods Ltd. among many others.[15]

multinational corporations (MNCs) Organizations that have significant operations spread throughout various nations but are headquartered in a single nation.

Bombardier Inc.
www.bombardier.com

McCain Foods Ltd.
www.mccain.com

MNCs generally have very large proportions of their total assets invested in foreign countries (over 50 percent is not uncommon). This applies as well to the distribution of human resources within MNCs. For example, at Matsushita Electric, the large Japan-based MNC, over half of the employees live and work in other countries.[16] People who are citizens of one country, but who are living in another country, are known as **expatriates**. With today's MNCs having over 170 000 foreign affiliates (including branch offices or other companies owned by the parent company), MNCs are greatly responsible for the existence of expatriates throughout the world.

expatriates People who are citizens of one country but who are living in another country.

Economic interdependence. The major result of large investments in foreign countries is a high degree of financial interdependence. That is, the more a given nation's companies make investments in other countries, the more dependent those other countries' economies become on the foreign companies. In the present economy it is almost impossible for countries to stand alone financially in the world.

Economic interdependence is especially likely among neighbouring countries with peaceful political and social relations. In a move to eliminate trade barriers among Canada, the United States, and Mexico, on new year's day of 1994 these countries ratified the **North American Free Trade Agreement (NAFTA)**. This treaty eliminated tariffs among these three nations, formally acknowledging the highly interdependent nature of their economies. Despite different cultural histories and political systems, the geographic closeness of these three nations encouraged them to cooperate with each other so that they could compete more effectively in the world market. There can be no mistaking the fact that much of the world's business occurs at the international level, and that what happens in one nation can have a major impact on what happens elsewhere. Canada has been involved in other trade agreements in addition to NAFTA including the 1997 agreement with Chile[17] and the negotiations concerning the Multilateral Agreement on Investment (MAI).[18]

North American Free Trade Agreement (NAFTA) An agreement among Canada, the United States, and Mexico, ratified on January 1, 1994, which eliminates tariffs among these nations.

Cultural homogenization. One result of this interdependence is a growing potential for **cultural homogenization**—the tendency for people throughout the world to become culturally similar. As pressures toward cultural uniformity increase throughout the world, some loss of cultural uniqueness is bound to result (see Figure 2-3). This trend has led to social movements throughout the world to strengthen local cultures and to protect them from foreign influences (e.g., movements toward the "Asianization of Japan" and the "re-Islamization of the Middle East").[19] Concern over defining and maintaining our cultural identity is a constant theme for Canadians especially living, as we do, next to the most powerful country in the world. Indeed, the economic integration that has strengthened some nations' economies has come at the expense of cultural uniqueness, contributing to ethnic and religious tensions in various places throughout the world.

cultural homogenization The tendency for people throughout the world to become culturally similar.

FIGURE 2-3 Is the World Becoming Culturally Uniform?

As suggested by this scene, the world is moving in the direction of cultural uniformity. The global nature of today's economy is in large part responsible for this trend.

(Source: Cartoon by Ed Fisher. © 1992, Harvard Business Review. Reprinted by permission of Ed Fisher.)

"Make a left at the Coca-Cola bottling plant, then go about two miles past Apple Computer."

In conclusion, the trend toward globalization has complex and widespread effects on the lives of people all over the world. As we will see throughout this book, this fact has not escaped the attention of specialists in the field of organizational behaviour. In fact, it is widely acknowledged that the management of human resources is an integral aspect of competitiveness in the global arena. As one expert has put it:

> Virtually any type of international problem, in the final analysis, is either created by people or must be solved by people. Hence, having the right people in the right place or the right time emerges as the key to a company's international growth.[20]

Culture and Its Impact

☛ *As with national cultures, organizations are also likely to have various subcultures operating within them, as we note in Chapter 14.*

When it comes to the globalization of organizations, the field of OB is primarily interested in the influence of culture on people's attitudes and behaviours at work.[21] The general question of interest is: Do people in various cultures behave similarly or differently with respect to their behaviour in organizations?

culture The set of values, customs, and beliefs that people have in common with other members of a social unit (e.g., a nation).

To examine this question we must first clarify what is meant by culture. Most social scientists agree that **culture** may be defined as the set of values, customs, and beliefs that people have in common with other members of a social unit (e.g., a nation).[22] For example, to the extent that the citizens of a specific country share a set of values, customs, and beliefs, they may be said to have a distinct culture. However, as we in Canada are aware, it would be erroneous to assume that a country has a single culture shared by everyone. Indeed, Canada, like most other

multicultural society A society within which there are many racial, ethnic, socioeconomic, and generational groups, each with its own culture.

subculture Smaller cultural groups operating within larger, primary cultural groups, each of which may have its own highly defined culture.

culture shock The tendency for people to become confused and disoriented as they find it difficult to adjust to a new culture.

repatriation The process or readjustment associated with returning to one's native culture after spending time away from it.

countries, is a **multicultural society**—one within which there are many different racial, ethnic, socioeconomic, and generational groups, each with its own culture. Recognizing this, scientists use the term **subculture** to describe smaller cultural groups operating within larger, primary cultural groups, each of which may have its own well-defined culture.

Culture shock and adjustment. The effect of culture on people often occurs without their awareness. People often have to be confronted with different cultures before they become conscious of their own culture. In fact, when people—such as expatriates working for MNCs—are faced with new cultures, it is not unusual for them to become confused and disoriented—a phenomenon known as **culture shock**.[23] People also experience culture shock when they return to their native culture after spending time away from it—a process of readjustment known as **repatriation**. In general, the phenomenon of culture shock results from people's recognition of the fact that others may be different from them in ways that they never imagined, and this takes some getting used to.

Specifically, scientists have observed that the process of adjusting to a foreign culture generally follows a U-shaped curve (see Figure 2-4).[24] That is, at first, people are optimistic and excited about learning a new culture. This usually lasts about a month or so. Then, for the next several months, they become frustrated and confused as they struggle to learn the new culture (i.e., culture shock occurs). Finally,

FIGURE 2-4 Adjusting to Foreign Culture: The General Stages

People's adjustment to new cultures generally follows the U-shaped curve illustrated here. After an initial period of excitement, *culture shock* often sets in. Then, after this period of adjustment (about 6 months), the more time spent in the new culture, the better it is accepted.

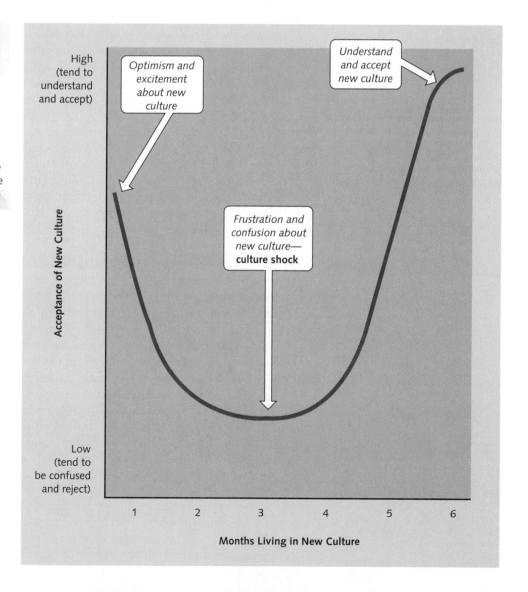

after about six months, people adjust to their new cultures and become more accepting of them and satisfied with them. These observations imply that feelings of culture shock are inevitable. Although some degree of frustration may be expected when you first enter a new country, the more time you spend learning its ways, the better you will come to be understanding and accepting of it.[25]

In general, culture shock results from the tendency for people to be highly *parochial* in their assumptions about others, taking a narrow view of the world by believing that there is one best way of doing things. They also tend to be highly *ethnocentric*, believing that their way of doing things is the best way. As we just explained, over time, exposure to other cultures teaches people that there may be many different ways of doing the same thing (making them less parochial), and that these may be equally good, if not better (making them less ethnocentric). Indeed, because the world's economy is global in nature, highly parochial and ethnocentric views cannot be tolerated.

Convergence versus divergence. Analogously, it may be said that highly narrow and biased views about the management of people in organizations may severely limit our understanding of behaviour in organizations. During the 1950s and 1960s, management scholars tended to overlook the importance of cultural differences in organizations. They made two key assumptions: (1) the principles of good management are universal, and (2) the best management practices are ones that work well in the United States.[26] This highly inflexible approach is known as the **convergence hypothesis**. Such a biased orientation reflects the fact that the study of behaviour in organizations first emerged in the United States.

With the ever-growing global economy, it has become clear that an American-oriented approach may be highly misleading when it comes to understanding the practices that work best in various countries. In fact, there may be many possible ways to manage effectively, and these will depend greatly on the individual culture in which people live. This alternative approach, which is widely accepted today, is known as the **divergence hypothesis**. Following this orientation, understanding the behaviour of people at work requires carefully appreciating the cultural context within which they operate. For example, whereas Canadian and American cultural norms suggest that it would not be inappropriate for an employee to question his or her superior, it would be taboo for a worker in Japan to do the same thing. Thus, today's organizational scholars are becoming increasingly sensitive to the ways in which culture influences organizational behaviour.

Hofstede's Dimensions of Culture

Intuitively, you probably believe that English-speaking Canadians and Americans have more in common with each other culturally than people from a very different and faraway place—say, Zaire. However, such an observation is highly casual, to say the least. To be more scientific, we would have to know exactly what factors distinguish various cultures. Fortunately, theorists have examined this issue. The most comprehensive and best-accepted framework for explaining cultural differences between nations has been proposed by Hofstede.[27] After systematically surveying 160 000 IBM employees in over 60 countries (unfortunately, Canada was not included in this sample), Hofstede found that national culture was a much more important determinant of work attitudes and behaviour than other variables, such as one's organizational position or personal characteristics. Specifically, he found that employees in various countries differed along four separate dimensions: *individualism/collectivism, power distance, uncertainty avoidance,* and *masculinity/femininity.*

Individualism versus collectivism. The distinction between individualism and collectivism is based on the extent to which members of a culture primarily define themselves as individuals as opposed to members of groups. **Individualism** is a characteristic of cultures in which people emphasize taking care of themselves and

convergence hypothesis The biased assumption that principles of good management are universal and that the best management practices are ones that work well in the United States.

divergence hypothesis The assumption that there may be many possible ways to manage effectively and that these will depend greatly on the individual culture in which people live.

individualism According to Hofstede, a characteristic of cultures in which people emphasize taking care of themselves and members of their immediate families.

collectivism According to Hofstede, a characteristic of a culture that orients people toward the good of the group.

members of their immediate families. By contrast, **collectivism** is a characteristic of a culture that orients people toward the good of the group. In highly collectivist cultures, people take care of others in their groups and expect others to take care of them.

People in the United States generally believe that they determine their own fates and need to look out for themselves. However, in more collectivist countries such as Colombia and Pakistan, people are generally concerned with fitting in with others. In fact, in Japan—a relatively collectivist nation—there is an old saying that translates as "the nail that sticks out will be pounded down." Clearly, a highly collectivist orientation is expressed by this phrase. (For a summary of some of the countries that score highest and lowest on this dimension, as well as Hofstede's three other dimensions of culture, see Figure 2-5.)

Power distance. It is typically the case throughout the world that some individuals have more wealth and power than others. However, people from various countries are not equally accepting of such inequalities. **Power distance** is the term Hofstede uses to distinguish between countries in terms of the degree to which the unequal distribution of power is accepted or rejected.

power distance According to Hofstede, the degree to which the unequal distribution of power is accepted by people in a culture (high power distance) or rejected by them (low power distance).

People in high power distance countries, such as the Philippines, Mexico, and India, would not think of bypassing their superiors in order to get their jobs done. In these nations employees show a great deal of respect for authority figures and give considerable weight to symbols of rank and status, such as titles. However, people in low power distance countries, such as Austria, Israel, and Denmark, are readily willing to bypass their superiors in the course of doing their jobs. In these nations, although superiors still have authority, they are not held in awe by subordinates.

Uncertainty avoidance. If there is any one thing for certain it is that the world is full of uncertainty. Whereas this fact is readily accepted by people in some societies, it is highly disquieting to others. This distinction is the basis for Hofstede's third dimension of culture, **uncertainty avoidance**—the degree to which people feel threatened by, and attempt to avoid, ambiguous situations.

uncertainty avoidance According to Hofstede, the degree to which people in a culture feel threatened by, and attempt to avoid, ambiguous situations.

In countries that are high in uncertainty avoidance, such as Greece, Portugal, and Japan, people welcome the stability found in the use of rigid rules and prospects for lifetime employment. By contrast, in the low uncertainty avoidance countries of Singapore, Hong Kong, and Denmark, people tend to be more mobile and change jobs more frequently.

FIGURE 2-5 Hofstede's Four Dimensions of Culture: A Summary

In his framework, Hofstede categorized 60 different countries with respect to the four dimensions of culture shown here. Three countries anchoring each end of these dimensions are identified.

(Source: Based on information reported by Hofstede, 1980; see Note 27.)

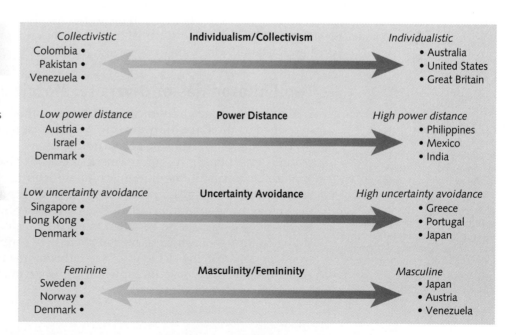

masculine culture According to Hofstede, cultures in which people are highly materialistic and value assertiveness and the acquisition of money.

feminine culture According to Hofstede, the cultural orientation in which people emphasize concern for others and the relationships among people.

Masculinity/femininity. Hofstede found that people in some countries, such as Japan, Austria, and Venezuela, were highly materialistic. They value assertiveness and the acquisition of money. Such nations are referred to as having a **masculine culture**. By contrast, in other countries, such as the Scandinavian nations, the predominant cultural value emphasizes concern for others and the relationships among people. This orientation Hofstede refers to as a **feminine culture.** (It is important to acknowledge that it was *not* Hofstede's intent to suggest that males and females possess or lack certain characteristics. Although you may feel uneasy with the stereotypical images evoked by Hofstede's terminology, his distinction is an important one and should not be dismissed.)

In "masculine" cultures people tend to define sex roles rigidly and reject the practice of performing jobs outside of one's gender-based stereotype. For example, in Japan there are very few female executives. However, in "feminine" cultures, such as Sweden, women and men may be found doing a wide variety of jobs. Moreover, Swedish businesspeople tend to demonstrate very high degrees of concern for their families. For example, whereas Americans (whose culture is considered relatively "masculine") may work all night on an important project, Swedes would be inclined to stop work at 5:00 P.M. and return to their families. Although Americans may mistake the Swedes' behaviour as demonstrating a lack of commitment to their work, the Swedes simply may be demonstrating their cherished cultural value of commitment to the quality of their lives. This is an excellent example of the types of culture clashes that may be expected to arise in a global economy.

The Shifting Demographics of the Workforce: Trends toward Diversity

Thus far, we have been discussing cultural differences between people from companies in different nations. However, widespread cultural differences also may be found *within* organizations. A broad range of people from both sexes, different races, ethnic groups, nationalities, and ages can be found throughout Canadian organizations. In fact, it has been said that today's workplace contains the most highly diverse group of people ever.[28] The implications of this state of affairs will be discussed throughout this book, including in the special sections called **DIVERSITY IN TODAY'S ORGANIZATIONS.** Here, we will chronicle the highly diverse nature of today's workforce and share experts' projections about diversity in the future. We will also outline some of the things modern organizations are doing to accommodate—and capitalize on—growing levels of diversity within the workforce. Before getting to these matters, however, we will begin by distinguishing between two approaches to diversity that have been taken in North American society.

Two Philosophies of Diversity: Mosaic and Melting Pot

Canadian mosaic (cultural pluralism) The idea that people's separate cultural identities should be maintained and accepted by others as they work alongside each other.

melting pot The principle that people from different racial, ethnic, and religious backgrounds are transformed into a common culture.

Traditionally, Canada has functioned from a culturally pluralistic perspective often described as the **Canadian mosaic**. In contrast to the early U.S. **melting pot**, which attempted to assimilate people from different racial, ethnic, and religious backgrounds into a larger, common American culture, Canada's approach has emphasized the maintenance of differing cultural identities within confederation. As the Canadian cultural landscape broadened with increased immigration at the beginning of the twentieth century, then Prime Minister Sir Wilfrid Laurier expressed his vision of what was later to be called multiculturalism. He likened his vision of the young country to a cathedral he had visited on a trip to Britain. Made of granite, wood, and marble, the elements of the cathedral maintained their integrity but together they created a magnificent whole. "It is the image of the nation I would like to see Canada become," he said.[29]

Later prime ministers have built on this vision, and have added their own perspectives (some of which have been enshrined in legislation). Pierre Trudeau made multiculturalism a government policy in 1971 and ensured that it was guaranteed in the Canadian Charter of Rights and Freedoms in 1982. "Mr. Trudeau said multiculturalism meant '...encouraging cultural diversification within a bilingual framework.'"[30] Canada passed the Multiculturalism Act in 1988, the first country in the world to do so. The three principles underlying the Act emphasize the central role of multiculturalism in Canadian citizenship, the freedom of all Canadians to enhance, enjoy, and share their cultural heritage, and the responsibility of the federal government to promote multiculturalism in all government bodies.[31]

Since the growth of the civil rights movement in the 1960s, the U.S. melting pot philosophy has fallen into disrepute and has been replaced with a growing commitment to cultural pluralism. This approach is frequently reflected in terms of the movement toward **valuing diversity**—that is, encouraging awareness of and respect for all people in the workplace. In Chapter 6 we will examine the factors affecting attitudes toward other people and ways to manage diversity in the workforce effectively. Here, however, we will focus on the demographic trends themselves.

valuing diversity Encouraging awareness of and respect for different people in the workplace.

☛ *The nature and impact of negative sex-role stereotypes is discussed in Chapters 3 and 6.*

Statistics Canada
www.statcan.ca/english/
Pgdb/stats.htm

Today's—and Tomorrow's—Highly Diverse Workforce

During the late 1950s and early 1960s, several popular TV situation comedies portrayed the typical North American family in which a middle-aged white male head of the household worked from 9:00 to 5:00 each day and earned enough money to support several children and a wife who stayed at home and took care of the household. However, this picture is very far from today's reality in three key respects. First, with huge numbers of women in the workforce, the distinction between the male "breadwinner" and the female "caregiver" has all but vanished. Second, with shifts in immigration patterns in recent years, the proportion of people of European descent within the workforce is lower than ever before. Third, large numbers of people in the workforce are growing older. We will now examine these three trends.

Women in the workforce. There can be no mistaking the widespread—and ever-growing—presence of women in today's workforce. Statistics Canada figures show that, in 1966, 43 percent of women in Canada had full-time or part-time jobs. This figure grew to 65 percent by 1976 and to 78 percent by 1986. In 1979 the number of women in the Canadian workforce was 4.9 million, compared to 2.5 million a decade earlier. In contrast, the proportion of males in the Canadian workforce decreased from 70 percent in 1960 to 54 percent in 1990.[32]

It is not difficult to find the roots of this massive gender shift in the workplace.[33] The women's movement that began in the mid-1960s challenged stereotypes that had kept women from pursuing work outside the home. As this occurred, social norms followed suit, making it not only acceptable, but commonplace, for women to combine a career and a family (see Figure 2-6).

In addition, economic changes made it both feasible and desirable—if not also necessary—for women to hold jobs outside the home. As the real incomes of single-wage-earner families declined in the 1970s, growing numbers of women took jobs to reduce their families' financial burden. In addition, as the divorce rate rose and the number of single mothers increased, women went to work outside the home as their families' sole financial support.

FIGURE 2-6 Women in the Workplace

BC Bearing Engineers Ltd.'s Chairman and CEO Wendy McDonald has survived the deaths of three husbands, raised ten children, and built BC Bearing into a multinational company. The company has operations in Singapore, Chile, Mexico, and the United States. At age 75 she was part of a Canadian trade mission to Latin America.[34]

Racial and ethnic groups. Throughout its history, Canada has opened its doors to immigrants, although earlier immigration laws did place restrictions on immigration by members of certain groups. People who were non-white were excluded until immigration regulations were changed in 1962.[35] Of course, all Canadians, except aboriginal peoples, are immigrants or descendants of immigrants to Canada.

In their examination of demographic trends in Canada entitled *Boom, Bust and Echo*, David Foot and Daniel Stoffman have suggested that people in their 20s are at a prime age to migrate since they are usually at a point in their lives when they have been educated but have not yet established a career, are strong enough and flexible enough to cope with the rigours of adapting to a new culture, are able to take entry-level positions in the workforce, and have their whole lives to benefit from their move.[36] Based on this analysis, Foot and Stoffman project that Canada's immigration pattern in the new century will shift away from Asia, where there will be fewer people in the high-migration 20s. The next wave of immigrants, they predict, will come from Latin America and from Africa.[37]

Canada is an ethnically and linguistically diverse country. After English and French, Italian, German, and Chinese are the next most frequently spoken languages across the country.[38] Canada is becoming more racially and culturally diverse as well. The 1996 Census showed that 11.2 percent of Canadians were neither aboriginal nor white.[39]

baby boom generation The large group of people born in the years following World War II.

Older workers. As sociologists tell us, the population grows unevenly over time. It rises and falls with changes in social and economic conditions. For example, in the years following World War II Canada's population increased as military and support personnel returned from overseas and began families. The generation of children born during this period is widely referred to as the **baby boom generation**. "Canada's was the loudest baby boom in the industrialized world,"[40] due to increased immigration in combination with an increased birth rate. The baby boom period in Canada extended from 1947 to 1966. The impact of the baby boom generation has been significant. By 1996, baby boomers constituted one-third of the Canadian population.[41] Baby boomers are living longer than the generations before them. By 2002, the first Canadian baby boomers will turn 55 and will be counted as "older workers" by labour economists.[42]

The fact that people are living longer is creating an interesting phenomenon. As people get older, they are likely to suffer from ailments that lead them to require assistance in their daily lives. Needing help, the elderly often move in with their children, who are likely to be raising their own children, creating a *multigenerational household*. This situation often creates a financial strain on the caretakers, who may be forced to choose between such major expenses as college and university for their children and health care for their elderly parents. Because they are "squeezed" between the demands of the young and old within their households, the middle members of multigenerational households have been referred to as the **sandwich generation.**

sandwich generation The generation of people who face economic pressures associated with taking care of their own children and their elderly parents, both of whom live with them.

Given the aging of the large baby boom segment of the population, today's young people are expected to become members of the sandwich generation. After all, by 2031, the whole Canadian baby boom generation will be 65 years of age or older. Not surprisingly, experts predict that the sandwich will gain even more layers in the years ahead, and that families with four generations under one roof (great-grandparents, grandparents, parents, and children) will not be uncommon.[43] When this occurs, the sandwich may be squeezed even harder than it is today.

Celebrating Diversity

Many of today's organizations (such as Babine Forest Products, as described in our CASE PREVIEW) have recognized that the diversity within its workforce can be a source of strategic advantage *if* it is properly valued and managed. After all, a culturally diverse workforce can bring broad perspectives to organizational issues, allowing problems to be approached from a wider variety of angles than might otherwise occur within a more homogeneous workforce. Several approaches have been taken in contemporary organizations.

diversity training The process of training employees not only to recognize and accept others who are different from themselves, but also to value these differences.

Caribou Systems Inc.
www.caribou-systems.com

Canadian Imperial Bank of Commerce
www.cibc.com

☞ *Two major approaches to diversity training are described in Chapter 6—awareness-based training and skill-based training.*

flextime programs Policies that give employees some discretion over when they can arrive and leave work, thereby making it easier to adapt their work schedules to the demands of their personal lives.

Bank of Montreal
www.bmo.com

compressed workweeks Scheduling workweeks such that people are permitted to work fewer, but longer, days (e.g., four ten-hour days), instead of five days of eight hours each.

job sharing A form of regular part-time work in which pairs of employees assume the duties of a single job, splitting its responsibilities, salary, and benefits in proportion to the time worked.

Diversity training.   A growing number of companies have instituted specific programs, known as **diversity training**, designed to get all employees not only to recognize and accept people who are different from themselves, but to value these differences. These are usually sessions lasting from several hours to several days in which employees participate in exercises typically designed to get them to recognize the prejudices they may have and how to overcome them. Sessions may focus on any number of prejudicial beliefs, including those held toward people of different races and ethnic groups, ages, genders, physical conditions, sexual orientations, and so on. Several Canadian companies, including Caribou Systems Corp., Nortel Networks, Union Gas Limited, and CIBC have been at the forefront of diversity training efforts.

Because we will describe diversity training techniques more fully in Chapter 6, in the context of prejudicial attitudes, we will not elaborate on them here. However, we cannot end this discussion without underscoring a crucial point: Diversity training by itself may be a waste of time unless it is part of a concerted effort to recognize and accept diversity throughout the organization. Lip service alone will not do. For organizations to reap the benefits of diversity in their workforces, the celebration of diversity must be integrated into the core values of the organization (much as with profitability).[44] Formal and informal policies, and actions by everyone from the CEO down, must recognize pluralism in the organization. When this occurs, diversity training programs can be a valuable part of the total effort to manage diversity in an organization.

Flexible work arrangements.   Four decades ago, when husbands worked outside the home and wives stayed at home with the children, the standard 9-to-5 working hours worked out fine. Today, however, with two-income families, single-parent households, and people taking care of elderly relatives, greater flexibility is needed. Fortunately, several practices have gained popularity in recent years.

- **Flextime programs** give employees some discretion over when they can arrive and leave work, thereby making it easier to adapt their work schedules to the demands of their personal lives. Typically, employees must work a common core of hours, such as 9:00 A.M. to 12 noon and 1:00 P.M. to 3:00 P.M. Scheduling of the remaining hours, within certain spans (such as 6:00 to 9:00 A.M. and 3:00 to 6:00 P.M.), is then left up to the employees themselves. Generally, such programs have been well received and have been linked to improvements in performance and job satisfaction, as well as drops in employee turnover and absenteeism.[45] In recent years, companies such as Levi Strauss & Co. (Canada), Pacific Bell, Duke Power Company, and the Bank of Montreal have found that flexible work scheduling has helped their employees meet the demands of juggling work and family lives.[46]

- **Compressed workweeks** are programs that allow people to work fewer days but longer hours each day (e.g., four ten-hour days) instead of working five days of eight hours each. The popular practice among firefighters of being on duty for 24 hours, and then off duty for 48 hours is a good example of the compressed workweek. Shell Canada has found that compressed workweek schedules have helped it make more efficient use of its manufacturing plant in Sarnia, Ontario. The Royal Bank of Canada, headquartered in Montreal, has found that compressed-workweek options greatly help its recruitment efforts by offering prospective employees the choice of schedules based on either compressed workweeks (four 9.5-hour days) or standard five-day workweeks.[47]

- **Job sharing** is a form of regular part-time work in which pairs of employees assume the duties of a single job, splitting its responsibilities, salary, and benefits in proportion to the time worked. Job sharing is rapidly growing in popularity as people enjoy the kind of work that full-time jobs allow, but require the flexibility of part-time work. Often, job sharing arrangements are temporary. For example, at Xerox several sets of employees share jobs, including two female

Royal Bank of Canada
www.royalbank.com

voluntary reduced work time (V-time) programs Programs that allow employees to reduce the amount of time they work by a certain amount (typically 10 or 20 percent), with a proportional reduction in pay.

flexplace policies Policies that allow employees to spend part of their regular working hours performing their jobs while at home (see *telecommuting*).

Xerox Canada
www.xerox.com

child-care facilities Sites at or near company locations where parents can leave their children while they are working.

Ontario Hydro
www.hydro.on.ca

elder-care facilities Sites at or near company locations where, while working, employees can leave their elderly relatives (e.g., parents and grandparents) for whom they may serve as caretakers.

Victorian Order of Nurses
www.von.ca

employees who once were sales rivals, but who joined forces to share one job when both faced the need to reduce their working hours so they could devote time to their new families.[48] Pella (the Iowa-based manufacturer of windows) has found that job sharing has been successful in reducing absenteeism among its production and clerical employees.[49] At the Royal Bank of Canada employees can use a self-assessment form to determine if their work habits match those of a potential job sharing partner. "It covers issues such as whether an employee tends to carry information in his [or her] head or prefers to write it down—an obvious source of conflict between job sharers."[50] In Canada, 84 percent of job sharing arrangements involve women. Job sharers tend to be university trained, hold a professional position (40 percent), and have children.[51]

- **Voluntary reduced work time (V-time) programs** allow employees to reduce the amount of time they work by a certain amount, with a proportional reduction in pay. Data from a Statistics Canada survey suggests that, while two-thirds of respondents would prefer to continue working the same hours for the same pay, 6 percent would prefer the V-time option. There are differences among the regions with only 3 percent of Atlantic Canadian respondents indicating a preference for V-time compared with just over 7 percent in Quebec and approximately 6 percent in Ontario, the Prairie provinces, and B.C.[52]

- **Flexplace policies** allow employees to spend part of their regular working hours performing their jobs while at home. Flexplace—used at such companies as Xerox Canada—makes it possible for employees to avoid the hassle of daily commuting.[53] Because flexplace frequently involves the use of computers and telephone lines connecting people to their offices, it is also referred to as *telecommuting* and *telework*. We will describe this innovative work method more fully later in this chapter.

Support facilities. With increasing frequency, companies are taking proactive steps to help employees meet their personal needs and family obligations. In so doing, they make it possible for employees to satisfy the demands imposed by their non-work lives. And this allows companies to draw on the resources of a diverse group of prospective employees who otherwise might not be able to lend their talents to the organization. Three practices have proven especially useful in this regard.

- **Child-care facilities** are sites at or near company locations where parents can leave their children while they are working. Ontario Hydro started Hydrokids, a non-profit day care to serve the children of its head office employees. The day care is now operated separately from Hydro although the utility has representation on its board of directors. Despite this separation, the presence of the day care has an impact on the company. "The kids are very visible. They've been known to tromp through the halls when they can't get outside because of bad weather or they parade through dressed in Halloween costumes. It brings to our head office complex a sense of community we wouldn't otherwise have," says Ontario Hydro's senior communications advisor, Kim Taylor.[54]

- **Elder-care facilities** are provisions made to take care of employees' elderly relatives, such as parents and grandparents, for whom they are responsible.[55] As the mean age of Canada's population increases with the aging of the baby boom, it is likely that the pressure for elder-care facilities will grow. In response to this need, the Victorian Order of Nurses (VON) created the Mildly Ill Child/Eldercare program. The CIBC in eastern Ontario was the first business to use the program. Marilyn Petrie, a CIBC administrative assistant in the St. Lawrence Valley District, reported that the company was planning to continue paying for the program since, in its first phase, it had had a positive impact on both absenteeism and company morale.[56] Further, in the United States, Lancaster Laboratories provides a place where its employees can bring adult family members who are in need of care during working hours.[57] The *St. Petersburg Times* advises its employees about ways to help meet the problems of elderly family members.[58]

personal support policies Widely varied practices (e.g., helping with transportation to and from the job) that assist employees in meeting the demands of their family lives, freeing them to concentrate on their work.

- **Personal support policies** are widely varied practices that help employees meet the demands of their family lives, freeing them to concentrate on their work. In Canada, Husky Injection Molding Systems' employees are given an annual allowance to cover the cost of vitamins. In addition, they benefit from the services of an on-site massage therapist, nurse, physician, and naturopathic doctor. (See CASE PREVIEW for Chapter 5.)[59] In the United States, the SAS Institute (Cary, North Carolina) not only offers its employees free, on-site Montessori child care, but also nutritious take-home dinners. Wilton Connor Packaging (Charlotte, North Carolina) provides even more unusual forms of support, such as an on-site laundry, high school equivalency classes, door-to-door transportation, and a children's clothing swap centre.[60]

Although these practices may be costly, the organizations that use them are generally convinced that they are wise investments. First, they help retain highly valued employees—not only keeping them from competitors, but also saving the costs of having to replace them. In fact, officials at AT&T found that the average cost of letting new parents take up to a year of unpaid parental leave was only 32 percent of an employee's annual salary, compared with the 150 percent cost of replacing that person permanently.[61] Second, by alleviating the distractions of nonwork issues, employees are freed to concentrate on their jobs and to be their most creative. Research has found that people who use the support systems their employers provide are not only more active in team problem-solving activities, but also almost twice as likely to submit useful suggestions for improvement. Commenting on such findings, Ellen Galinsky, co-president of the Families & Work Institute, said, "There's a cost to *not* providing work and family assistance."[62] A third benefit—and an important one, at that— is that such policies help attract the most qualified human resources, giving companies that use them a competitive edge over those that do not.[63]

Trends in Working Arrangements: New Organizational Forms and Jobs

Ever since the industrial revolution people performed carefully prescribed sets of tasks—known as *jobs*—within large networks of people who answered to those above them—hierarchical arrangements known as *organizations*. This picture, although highly simplistic, does a good job of characterizing the working arrangements that most people had during much of the twentieth century. Now, as this era is drawing to a close, however, we are finding that the essential nature of jobs and organizations as we have known them is changing. Although there are certainly many factors responsible for such change, experts agree that the major catalyst is rapidly advancing computer technology. Currently, the computing power of microprocessors doubles approximately every 18 months. And, as more work is shifted to digital brains, some work that was once performed by human brains becomes obsolete. At the same time, new opportunities arise as people scurry to find their footing amidst the shifting terrain of the high-tech revolution.

As you might imagine, this state of affairs has important implications for the field of OB, many of which will be described throughout this text—and highlighted in special sections called **ORGANIZATIONAL TRENDS**. In this part of the chapter we will set the stage for these discussions by focusing on some of the most prominent trends in the world of work that have been identified in recent years.

Leaner Organizations: Downsizing and Outsourcing

Technology has made it possible for fewer people to do more work than ever before. *Automation*, the process of replacing people with machines is not new, of course; it has gone on, slowly and steadily, for centuries. Today, however, because it is not large mechanical devices, but the manipulation of digital data that is responsible,

informate The process by which workers manipulate products by "inserting data" between themselves and those objects instead of doing so physically.

We discuss the general topic of workplace technology in Chapters 14 and 15.

downsizing The process of adjusting downward the number of employees required to perform jobs in newly designed organizations.

rightsizing See *downsizing*.

The motivational problems created by losing one's coworkers as a result of downsizing are identified in Chapter 5.

outsourcing The practice of eliminating nonessential aspects of business operations by hiring other companies to perform these tasks.

core competency The main things that an organization does best; those activities most central to its mission.

ServiceMaster Canada Ltd.
www.servicemaster.ca

scientists have referred instead to the *informating* of the workplace. The term **informate** describes the process by which workers manipulate products by "inserting data" between themselves and those objects.[64] When jobs are informated, information technology is used to change a formerly physical task into one that involves manipulating a sequence of digital commands. So, for example, a modern factory worker can move around large sheets of steel by pressing a few buttons on a keypad. Likewise, with the right programming, an order entered into a salesperson's laptop computer can trigger a chain of events involving everything associated with the job: placing an order for supplies, manufacturing the product to exact specifications, delivering the final product, sending out the bill, and even crediting the proper commission to the salesperson's payroll cheque.

Unlike the gradual process of automation, today's technology—and the process of informating—is occurring so rapidly that the very nature of work is changing as fast as we can keep up. With this, many jobs are disappearing, leaving organizations (at least the most successful ones) smaller than before.[65] For example, whereas Ford employs some 400 people in its accounts payable department, Mazda's highly computerized system does the same work with only 5 people. Although Mazda is considerably smaller, this difference is still quite striking.

In addition to services, product manufacturing also has been informated. At GE's Faunc Automation plant in Charlottesville, Virginia, for example, circuitboards are manufactured by half as many employees as required before informating the facility.[66] It is not only blue-collar, manual-labour jobs that are eliminated, but white-collar, mental-labour jobs as well. In many places, middle managers are no longer needed to make decisions that can now be made by computers.

Indeed, organizations have been rapidly reducing the number of employees needed to operate effectively—a process known as **downsizing**.[67] Typically, this process involves more than just laying off people in a move to save money. It is directed at adjusting the number of employees needed to work in newly designed organizations and is therefore also known as **rightsizing**.[68] Whatever you call it, the bottom line is clear: Many organizations need fewer people to operate today than in the past—sometimes, far fewer.

Another way organizations are restructuring is by completely eliminating those parts of themselves that focus on non-core sectors of the business (i.e., tasks that are peripheral to the organization), and hiring outside firms to perform these functions instead—a practice known as **outsourcing**.[69] By outsourcing secondary activities, an organization can focus on what it does best, what is known as its **core competency**. Companies like ServiceMaster Canada Ltd., which provides janitorial management services to the Halifax District School Board's schools, make it possible for organizations to concentrate on the business functions most central to their mission, thereby freeing them from these peripheral support functions. ServiceMaster has guaranteed the Halifax board a minimum $500 000 annual saving in its property services budget.[70] "Clearly Canadian Sparkling Water" is produced by a company that employs about 40 people, but about 12 000 are involved in the product's bottling, transportation, distribution, and retailing. Clearly Canadian is directly involved only in the source of the water and in its marketing. The rest is outsourced.[71]

In some cases, the only way people can tell that their part of the organization no longer exists is that they receive paycheques from someone else. For example, Xerox has taken over all the internal service functions of Bankers Trust (e.g., mailroom, print shop, employee recordkeeping, payroll, telephone switchboard), employing in many cases, the same individuals who used to perform these functions while working for Bankers Trust.[72] Ironically, some businesses providing outsourcing services, such as EDS, a data processing firm with U.S.$8.2 billion in annual sales, have become so large that they may outsource some services themselves while providing outsourcing services to their clients.[73]

Some critics fear that outsourcing represents a "hollowing out" of companies—a reduction of functions that weakens organizations by making them more dependent on others.[74] Others counter that outsourcing makes sense when the outsourced work is not highly critical to competitive success (e.g., janitorial services), or when it is so highly critical that it only can succeed by seeking outside assistance.[75] For example, when Apple Computer introduced its first notebook computer, the Macintosh Powerbook 100, it subcontracted its manufacturing to Sony, enabling it to speed entry into the market.[76] While outsourcing in Canada is growing more slowly than it is in the rest of the world it is, nonetheless, significant. According to research figures from Dun & Bradstreet, "Canada's outsourcing market is estimated to be about $15 billion to $20 billion and is growing at a rate of 14 percent annually."[77]

Dun & Bradstreet
www.dnb.com

The Contingent Workforce: "Permanent Temporary" Employees

Sometimes, instead of eliminating entire organizational functions and buying them back through outside service providers, organizations are eliminating individual jobs and hiring people to perform them on an as-needed basis. Such individuals comprise what has been referred to as the **contingent workforce**—people hired by organizations temporarily, to work as needed for finite periods of time.[78] The contingent workforce includes not only the traditional part-time employees, such as department store Santas, but also freelancers, subcontractors, and independent professionals. Such highly flexible arrangements make it possible for organizations to grow or shrink as needed and to have access to experts with specialized knowledge when these are required.

contingent workforce People hired by organizations temporarily to work as needed for finite periods of time.

In view of this trend, it should not be surprising that the greatest growth in jobs in recent years has been seen in "a category Statistics Canada refers to as 'nonstandard' work: part-time or temporary jobs, and the fastest-growing category of all, self-employed workers with no employees."[79] According to an analysis by well-known pollster Angus Reid, during the decade of the 1990s, the number of full-time jobs in Canada decreased by 130 000. In his book *Shakedown: How the New Economy is Changing Our Lives,* Reid reported that "non-standard" work had increased from representing 28 percent of the Canadian workforce in 1989 to 33 percent in 1994.[80]

The trend toward corporate restructuring has caused many companies to keep their staff sizes so small that they must frequently draw on the services of temporary employment firms for help. British consultant Charles Handy has described the organization of the future as being more like an apartment than a home for life, "an association of temporary residents gathered together for mutual convenience."[81] Although others believe this prospect is far-fetched, it is clear that a growing number of people are seeking the freedom and variety of temporary employment rather than facing repeated layoffs from ever-downsizing corporations.

There are, of course, downsides to temporary employment, both for employees and employers.[82] Benefits for temporary employees, which make up about 30 percent of a full-time employee's wages, are typically lacking, and wages are often lower. Moreover, some "unwilling contingent workers" consider their temporary work too stressful and would prefer full-time employment—*if* they could find it.

Many corporate officials strongly adhere to the belief that quality performance depends on the kind of skill and commitment to the organization that temporaries cannot offer. Indeed, several corporate officials have complained that contingent workers are not as good as permanent ones. Furthermore, some have complained that because they are unpractised, temporary workers lack basic job skills and are inclined to perform poorly.[83]

These are important considerations when you take into account the fact that the trend toward hiring contingent workers is fueled by employers' beliefs that temporary workers can help save money. However, as these examples suggest—and as human resource managers have found—there are hidden costs associated with using large numbers of contingent workers.[84] In view of these considerations, it may be said that the flexibility of contingent labour comes at a price. Accordingly, although the size of the permanent workforce may be dwindling, it does not appear that the permanent employee faces any immediate danger of extinction.

However, there is certainly no status quo when it comes to employment these days. Those employees who are finding work are likely to be ones who are highly educated and bring the greatest variety of skills to their employers. With the end of the Cold War, the defense industry, and its boom in manufacturing, has all but come to an end. Add to this the shifting of manufacturing jobs overseas, and it's easy to see how factory work has slowed dramatically. Considerable growth, however, may be seen among **knowledge workers**: professionals, engineers, and scientists—people whose technical skills can contribute to the explosion in high-tech fields.

The individuals who will be most successful at finding work in the years ahead will be those whose training, both academic and technical, makes them most qualified for the kinds of jobs likely to be found in the years ahead. The companies that will predominate in the world market will be those whose workers can contribute the most. And, it will be these individuals who will be the best paid, as opposed to simply those who have hung around the longest. More than ever, the key to success lies in training. But people throughout the world are not equally well trained to face the challenges of doing technical work. In what nations are the most qualified workforces to be found these days? As Figure 2-7 shows, the best-trained employees (with respect to public education, on-the-job training, and computer literacy) may be found in several nations throughout Europe and Asia; Canada ranks seventeenth overall.[85]

knowledge workers Professional people, such as scientists and engineers, whose technical skills can contribute to the explosion in high-tech fields.

☞ A discussion of the basic approaches to job training appears in Chapter 3.

FIGURE 2-7 Where in the World Are the Best-Trained Workers?

The most qualified employees in the world (with respect to quality of public education, on-the-job training, and computer literacy) may be found in the countries of western Europe and eastern Asia. The Figure shows rankings of the top 20 countries.

(Source: Based on data reported by Sasseen, Neff, Hattangadi, & Sasoni, 1994; see Note 85.)

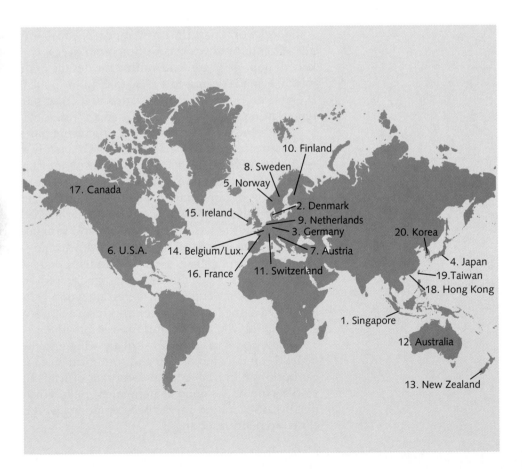

The Virtual Corporation: A Network of Temporary Organizations

virtual corporation A highly flexible, temporary organization formed by a group of companies that join forces to exploit a specific opportunity.

As more and more companies are outsourcing various organizational functions and paring down to their core competencies, they might not be able to perform all the tasks required to complete a project. However, they can certainly perform their own highly specialized part of it very well. Now, if you put together several organizations whose competencies complement each other and have them work together on a special project, you'd have a very strong group of collaborators. This is the idea behind an organizational arrangement that is growing in popularity—the **virtual corporation**. A virtual corporation is a highly flexible, temporary organization formed by a group of companies that join forces to exploit a specific opportunity.[86]

For example, various companies often come together to work on special projects in the entertainment industry (e.g., to produce a motion picture) and in the field of construction (e.g., to build a shopping centre). After all, technologies are changing so rapidly and skills are becoming so specialized these days that no one company can do everything by itself. So, they join forces temporarily to form virtual corporations—not permanent organizations, but temporary ones without their own offices or organization charts. If you think about it, the term makes sense. When you use your personal computer's virtual memory, you are relying on memory that isn't a permanent part of its memory chips, but created temporarily (by allocating a portion of your hard drive to RAM). When the computer is turned off, virtual memory is gone. Likewise, when the project is over, the virtual corporation vanishes as well.

☞ *More permanent organizational alliances are identified as a popular form of organizational design in Chapter 15.*

Virtual organizations may be created where you least expect them. For example, the Rolling Stones' 1994–1995 *Voodoo Lounge* world tour may be considered a virtual corporation.[87] Although you may think of it as "only rock 'n' roll," the 65-site international tour was a business—and with worldwide revenues of over U.S.$300 million, a very big one at that. Despite its mammoth size, the tour was very much a virtual corporation. Its head was Michael Cohl, who coordinated the tour's operations out of a crate of files, a laptop computer, and a fax machine that he moved from hotel room to hotel room as the tour moved along. One company set up the lighting, another coordinated the stagehands, and another handled the logistics of moving sets that filled 56 trucks from city to city. And after the last date, the Voodoo Lounge virtual corporation disbanded as quickly as it formed. Its various participating organizations joined up with new ones on other projects.

Although virtual corporations are not yet common, experts expect them to grow in popularity in the years ahead.[88] As one consultant has put it, "It's not just a good idea; it's inevitable."[89]

Telecommuting: The Demise of the Office

Question: What current organizational activity simultaneously helps alleviate child-care problems, reduces traffic jams, and cuts air pollution and fuel consumption, while also saving millions of dollars on office space? The answer is **telecommuting**—the practice of using communications technology to enable work to be performed from remote locations, such as the home.

telecommuting The practice of using communications technology so as to enable work to be performed from remote locations, such as the home. (see *flexplace*)

Advanced technology and enlightened attitudes toward work have made it possible for today's employees to be freed from traditional offices. (This is the practice of *flexplace* described earlier.) They can work from their homes, cars, or the decks of their yachts—virtually anywhere they can plug in a computer and phone line. In fact, as wireless communications become more advanced, workers can be completely untethered and hide away with their laptops on a desert island, if they so desire. Statistics reveal that telecommuting is in full swing today. In 1996, Canada had approximately 400 000 teleworkers, a figure that is expected to grow to one million by the year 2000.[90]

For some, telecommuting can open a whole new world of employee recruitment. The Bank of Montreal's Liz Codling created the bank's Learning for Success system. She was employed in the company's Institute for Learning in Toronto when she and her husband decided to return to Britain. Naturally, Codling thought this would mean she would have to leave her job with the bank. Her boss, Malcolm Roberts, had another idea. He suggested Codling telecommute. Armed with her computer, fax, modem, e-mail, and Internet access she became the bank's first transatlantic telecommuter. There have been challenges. She had to adjust her workday to close the gap caused by the five-hour difference in time between Britain and Toronto, and she had to learn to sense what was going on in a teleconference meeting without being able to see the reactions of participants. However, despite the challenges, transatlantic telecommuting has worked well for Codling and for BMO. In fact she has been promoted and now works out of Chicago. Now she is a cross-border telecommuter.[91]

Despite the success of Liz Codling, telecommuting is not for everyone; it also has its limitations.[92] Notably, when employees do not come into contact with each other, it is difficult to build the team spirit that is needed to produce quality goods and services in some organizations. Additionally, telecommuting does not lend itself to all jobs. It works best for jobs that involve information handling, significant amounts of automation, and relatively little face-to-face contact. Sales representatives, computer programmers, word processing technicians, insurance agents, and securities traders are all good candidates for telecommuting.

This is not to say that all individuals performing these jobs should be issued a laptop and sent packing. Good candidates for telecommuting must have the emotional maturity and self-discipline to work without direct supervision. To assist those who have difficulty adjusting to telecommuting, IBM carefully monitors the work of its telecommuters and offers counselling to those who appear to be having trouble.

To function effectively, workers who telecommute must be thoroughly trained in the use of the technologies that are required for them to do their work off-site, as well as the proper conditions for working safely (e.g., avoiding physical problems resulting from staring into video terminals for hours on end and from overusing wrist muscles). They also must be trained in ways to function independently, such as how to manage their time effectively and how to avoid interference from their families while working.

Companies also face the issue of establishing fair wages for telecommuters. For workers who are paid by the amount of work produced, such as the number of insurance claims processed, this is not a problem. Clear criteria for measuring performance (e.g., specific quantity and quality goals) are enormously helpful when paying telecommuters. However, for salaried employees doing jobs for which clear performance criteria are difficult to come by, policies need to be established regarding what telecommuters should do when, for instance, they complete their work in less than the allotted time. At the office, they probably would pitch in and help others, but away from the office they may be tempted to goof off. The key task is to resolve all potentially thorny policy issues regarding pay and performance expectations *before* employees begin telecommuting—and ensuring that they are clearly understood and accepted.

[You Be The Consultant]

A small manufacturing company has had difficulty attracting and retaining sales associates. To turn things around, it is now considering ways of changing the job to make it more attractive to prospective employees who are highly qualified, but whose personal obligations do not permit them to spend 40 hours a week at the office.

1. How can telecommuting be used to help solve this problem? What potential benefits and problems may be expected by using this practice?

2. What other types of "flexible working arrangements" or "support facilities" may help? Why?

The Quality Revolution: Total Quality Management and Reengineering

For many years, people complained but could do little when the goods they purchased fell apart, or the service they received was second-rate. After all, if everything in the market is shoddy, there are few alternatives.

Today's companies operate quite differently from those of the past. For them, the watchword is not "getting by," but "making things better," which has been referred to as *the quality revolution*. The best organizations are ones that strive to deliver better goods and services at lower prices than ever before. Those that do so flourish, and those that do not tend to fade away. Throughout this text, in special sections called **THE QUEST FOR QUALITY,** we will be highlighting organizational practices that have been effective at improving quality, either with respect to organizational performance or employees' work lives. Here, however, we will review two approaches to improving quality that have been used in recent years—*total quality management* and *reengineering*.

Total Quality Management: A Commitment to Customers

total quality management (TQM) An organizational strategy of commitment to improving customer satisfaction by developing techniques to carefully manage output quality.

One of the preferred approaches to establishing quality is known as **total quality management (TQM)**—an organizational strategy of commitment to improving customer satisfaction by developing techniques to manage output quality carefully. TQM is not so much a special technique as a well-ingrained set of corporate values—a way of life demonstrating a strong commitment to improving quality in everything that is done.

According to W. Edwards Deming, the best-known advocate of TQM, successful TQM requires that everyone in the organization—from the lowest-level employee to the CEO—must be committed fully to making whatever innovations are necessary to improve quality. This involves both carefully measuring quality (through elaborate statistical procedures) and taking whatever steps are necessary to improve it. Typically, this requires continuously improving the manufacturing process in ways that make it possible for higher quality to result.

For example, in developing its Lexus LS 400, Toyota purchased competing cars from Mercedes and BMW, disassembled them, examined the parts, and developed ways of building an even better car. Spending some U.S.$500 million in this process, Toyota was clearly dedicated to creating a superior product. And, given the recognition that Lexus has received among customers for its high quality, it appears as if Toyota's TQM efforts have paid off. The process of comparing one's own products or services with the best from other firms is known as **benchmarking**.

benchmarking The process of seeking to improve quality by comparing one's own products or services with the best products or services of others.

Another key ingredient of TQM is incorporating concern for quality into all aspects of organizational culture (a concept we will discuss more fully in Chapter 14).[93] At Rubbermaid, for example, concern for quality is emphasized not only in the company's manufacturing process but also in its concern for cost, service, speed, and innovation. To ensure that it is meeting quality standards, many companies conduct **quality control audits**—careful examinations of how well they are meeting its standards. For example, companies such as Pepsi Cola and FedEx regularly interview their clients to find out what problems they may be having. These responses are then taken very seriously in making whatever improvements are necessary to avoid problems in the future. Countless companies in Canada have reported success with TQM such as management consultants Ernst & Young,[94] Hydro Quebec,[95] J. M. Schneider Inc.,[96] the Chrysler minivan plant in Windsor, Ontario,[97] and Xerox Canada.[98]

quality control audits Careful examinations of how well a company is meeting the standards of quality toward which it is striving.

A quality designation increasingly sought by a variety of work settings around the world is ISO, which was developed by the **International Organization for Standardization.** ISO was derived from the Greek word *isos*, which means equal. KPMG's Mark O'Sullivan explains the 9000 standards series that is applied to management systems "What ISO does is say these are the things that ought to be in place in a well-run organization. Whether a company produces a product at the end of an assembly line or provides a service really doesn't matter."[99] Saskatoon's Merlin Motors was the first North American Ford dealership to achieve ISO 9002 certification. Merlin's Al Elsasser credited the ISO system with helping the dealership to organize its management system and focus its employees on customer service.

International Organization for Standardization An organization that has established international standards for quality in its ISO 9000 certification and for protecting the environment in its ISO 14000 certification.

In addition to the 9000 quality designation, ISO also has a 14000 series focusing on environmental management. There is some indication that the 9000 and 14000 systems will eventually merge.[100]

International Organization for Standardization
www.iso.ch

To achieve the coveted ISO certification, organizations must pass an audit and must be successful in review audits conducted every 6–12 months. Large organizations and small, some with as few as three employees, can be and have been successful in achieving the designation. It takes time, commitment, and money to prepare for the audit. However, the rewards can be worth the effort. Paul Smith, whose Toronto real estate firm is preparing for its audit, expects that the ISO process will save his company money in reduced mistakes, and being one of the first in his business sector to achieve the designation will give him a marketing edge over his competitors.[101] As the proliferation of ISO banners testifies, there is a growing number of Canadian organizations achieving the designation. Included in this number in New Brunswick alone are Maritime Paper Products Limited, the Wood Science & Technology Centre at the University of New Brunswick, and Acadie Presse Ltée.[102]

Six Sigma A measure of quality at which there are only 3.4 defects per million (99.9997 percent perfection).

Yet another quality system that is gaining a following is **Six Sigma**. The system allows organizations to assess their current level of production quality and to set a clear performance objective. "TQM sounds like fluff and we had seen lots of companies pursue TQM and get nowhere.... Six Sigma is attractive because you know whether you are making progress or not. It isn't anecdotal. It is quantitative," says Gary Reiner of General Electric.[103]

Sigma refers to a measure of the degree to which a process deviates from perfection. Six Sigma is the level at which there are only 3.4 defects per million (99.9997 percent perfection), while One Sigma represents 690 000 defects per million. The system not only measures an organization's approximation to perfection, it also offers a methodology, known as Design of Experiments (DOE), that guides people looking for alternatives to reduce process defects.

For example, Camco Inc., a Canadian appliance company owned by General Electric, used DOE to determine what aspect of its cooktop manufacturing process could be altered to reduce its high scrap rate. The DOE process allowed Camco employees to develop equations to test various possible processes without actually undertaking them in a trial-and-error manner. The problem was found and solved. This resulted in a more than $500 000 reduction in costs to the company. A major requirement for organizations committing to the system is to have Six Sigma–trained "Black Belts" on staff who work full time on quality related projects, and "Green Belts" who devote part of their workday to quality projects.[104]

Some companies have been so successful at achieving high quality in all respects that they have been honoured for their accomplishments. The Canada Awards for Excellence (CAE) recognize achievement in a wide variety of areas including entrepreneurship, innovation, manufacturing, service, education, health care, and government.[105] "The criteria for all Quality categories are rigorous. Organizations considered for an award must show outstanding continuous achievement in seven key areas: Leadership, Customer Focus, Planning for Improvement, People Focus, Process Optimization, Supplier Focus, and Organizational Performance."[106]

Organizations interested in being considered for the award complete a detailed application in which they thoroughly document their quality achievements. They also pay a fee. The applications are screened and those rated as most promising receive a site visit. All applicants are given comprehensive feedback on their application. Winners are selected by a jury in each category (see Table 2-1).[107]

Reengineering: Starting All Over

reengineering The fundamental rethinking and radical redesign of business processes to achieve drastic improvements in performance.

Pioneered by consultants Michael Hammer and James Champy, **reengineering** is defined as the fundamental rethinking and radical redesign of business processes to achieve drastic improvements in performance. Reengineering does not involve fixing anything—rather, as the term implies, it means starting over from scratch about the fundamental way things are done. Organizations that use reengineering forget all about how work was performed in the past and start anew with a clean sheet of paper, thinking about how things can be done best right now—hence the term "radical" in the definition.

The main focus of reengineering is the customer. Everything that is done starts with the idea of adding value for the customer: improving service, raising quality, lowering costs. Practices that are traditional or convenient for the company are eradicated if they don't otherwise help the customer. Doing this involves organizing

TABLE 2-1 The Canada Awards for Excellence: 1997 Winners

The Canada Awards for Excellence were first awarded in 1983. Since that time, more than 300 organizations have been recognized for outstanding achievement in their field of endeavour.[108]

Source: Recipients 97, see Note 109.

Category	Winners
Innovation—Trophy	Quartz Imaging Corporation Vancouver, BC Research in Motion Kitchener, ON
Innovation—Certificate of Merit	E.Q.U.I.P. International Inc. Baie D'Urfé, QC Sierra Wireless Inc. Richmond, BC
Entrepreneurship—Trophy	Lorraine Lush The Career Academy St. John's, NF
Small Service—Trophy	B.C. Tel Education Burnaby, BC
Large Service—Trophy	Dominion Directory Information Services Burnaby, BC
Health Care—Trophy	Orillia Soldiers Memorial Hospital Orillia, ON
Large Manufacturing—Trophy	Brock Telecom Brockville, ON
Education—Certificate of Merit	Glen Park Public School North York, ON

☛ *We discuss various organizational design strategies more fully in Chapter 15.*

around process rather than function. That is, work is arranged according to the processes needed to get the job done most effectively (for this reason, reengineering is also known as *process innovation*). For example, in many companies the simple process of filling orders is frequently chopped up into single tasks performed by people in many different departments although customers may be better served by assigning it to a single unit responsible for the entire process.

As an example of reengineering in action, consider changes made at IBM Credit Corp., a subsidiary responsible for financing IBM's hardware and software. Before reengineering, the task of processing a credit application was cumbersome and very slow—so slow, in fact, that it frequently cost the company sales. A credit request would come in by phone and would be logged on a piece of paper. The paper then went on a long journey from credit checkers, to "pricers" (who determined what interest rate to charge), to many others who also performed single, specialized functions. Often, applications were bounced back and forth between departments before they were properly completed. Total processing time ranged from six days to two weeks.

Out of curiosity, some IBM senior managers decided one day to walk a financing request through the process, taking it from department to department and asking personnel in each office to put aside whatever they were doing and process this request in the normal fashion, only without the delay. What they found was quite an eye-opener: The actual process took only *90 minutes*; the remaining time was consumed by handing the form off between departments. Enlightened by this demonstration, IBM Credit reengineered its operations by replacing a series of specialists with generalists. Now, one person processes an entire application from beginning to end without handing it off to others.

Did it work? In the newly reengineered jobs, credit approval takes only about four hours (much closer to the 90-minute minimum time needed to do the job). Furthermore, the number of applications processed has increased 100-fold—and, using *fewer* employees than before. Other companies, such as Petro-Canada, Novacor Chemicals, Hallmark (see Figure 2-8), Ford, Taco Bell, and Kodak have all used reengineering successfully. Union Carbide claims to have reduced its fixed costs by U.S.$400 million in just three years by using reengineering. Don't let all these big names mislead you; small companies also have been using reengineering to achieve success.

FIGURE 2-8 A Reengineering Success Story at Hallmark Cards

These employees of Hallmark Cards have seen their company remain the dominant player in the greeting card industry in large part because of reengineering. For example, by bringing together people from various departments, such as writers, artists, and designers (specialists who previously were separated by great distances), to work on developing new greeting cards, Hallmark has been successful in reducing the time needed to bring new products to market. This has helped the company stay ahead of the competition.

Corporate Social Responsibility: The Ethical Organization

The history of North American business is riddled with sordid tales of those who would go to any lengths in their quest for success, destroying in the process not only natural resources and the public's trust, but also the hopes and dreams of millions of people.

For example, in recent years, incidents of insider trading have brought down one of the world's most powerful brokerage firms, Drexel Burhnam Lambert. Accusations of fraudulent practices in its auto repair business have tarnished the reputation of venerable retailing giant Sears.[110] Further, the Bre-X saga has riveted Canadians, from the alleged discovery of the largest gold find in the world to the painful revelations as the myth exploded. It is not clear who salted the Busang core samples and who perpetrated such fraud on hopeful investors who went from riches to rags after the revelations of Freeport McMoRan Copper & Gold Inc. shattered their golden dreams.[111]

Clearly, human greed has not faded from the business scene. However, something *has* changed—namely, the public's acceptance of unethical behaviour on the part of organizations. Consider this statement by a leading expert on business ethics:

> Ethical standards, whether formal or informal, have changed tremendously in the last century. Boldly stated, no one can make the case that ethical standards have fallen in the latter decades of the twentieth century. The reverse is true. Standards are considerably higher. Business-people themselves, as well as the public, expect more sensitive behavior in the conduct of economic enterprise. The issue is not just having the standards, however. It is living up to them.[112]

To the extent that people are increasingly intolerant of unethical business activity, it makes sense for the field of OB to examine the factors that encourage unethical practices. Even more importantly, we need to develop strategies for promoting ethical conduct. Here, we will turn our attention to these matters. But, this is only the beginning. Throughout this book, we will take close-up looks at the ethical aspects of various organizational decisions in special sections named THE ETHICS ANGLE.

Why Does Unethical Organizational Behaviour Occur?

Unethical organizational practices are embarrassingly commonplace. It is easy to define practices such as dumping chemical wastes into rivers, insider trading, and overcharging the government for health services as morally wrong. Yet these and many other unethical practices occur almost routinely in many organizations. Why is this so? In other words, what accounts for the unethical actions of people within organizations?

One answer to this question is based on the idea that *organizations often reward behaviours that violate ethical standards*. Consider, for example, how many business executives are expected to deal in bribes and payoffs and how good corporate citizens blowing the whistle on organizational wrongdoings may fear being punished for their actions. Organizations tend to develop *counternorms*—accepted organizational practices that are contrary to prevailing ethical standards.[113] Some of these are summarized in Figure 2-9.

The top of Figure 2-9 identifies being "open and honest" as a prevailing ethical norm. Indeed, governmental regulations requiring full disclosure and freedom of information reinforce society's values toward openness and honesty. Within organizations, however, it is often considered not only acceptable, but desirable, to be much more secretive and deceitful. The practice of *stonewalling*—willingly hiding relevant information—is quite common. One reason for this is that organizations may actually punish those who are too open and honest. Consider, for example, the disclosure that B. F. Goodrich rewarded employees who falsified and withheld data on the quality of aircraft brakes to win certification. Similarly, it has been reported that executives at Metropolitan Edison encouraged employees to withhold information from the press about the Three Mile Island nuclear accident in the United States. In both incidents, the counternorms of secrecy and deceitfulness were accepted and supported by the organization.

☞ For a discussion of the topic of whistle-blowing in organizations, see Chapter 11. For more on norms, see Chapter 8.

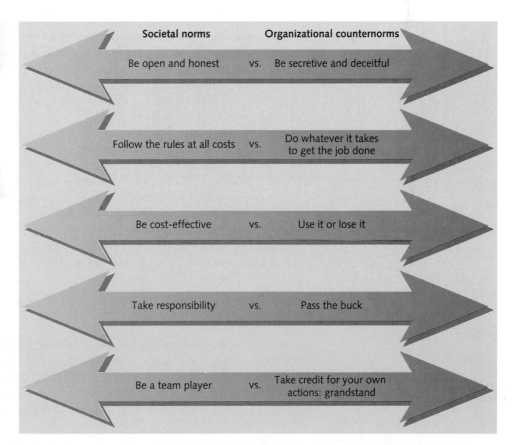

FIGURE 2-9 Societal Norms vs. Organizational Counternorms

Although societal standards of ethics dictate the appropriateness of certain actions, *counternorms* that encourage and support opposite practices often develop within organizations.

(Source: Based on suggestions by Jansen & Von Glinow, 1985; see Note 113.)

Societal norms | Organizational counternorms

Be open and honest — vs. — Be secretive and deceitful

Follow the rules at all costs — vs. — Do whatever it takes to get the job done

Be cost-effective — vs. — Use it or lose it

Take responsibility — vs. — Pass the buck

Be a team player — vs. — Take credit for your own actions: grandstand

As you can see from Figure 2-9, many other organizational counternorms promote ethically questionable practices. That these practices are commonly rewarded and accepted suggests that organizations may be operating within a world that dictates its own set of accepted rules. This reasoning leads to a second explanation as to why organizations act unethically—namely, that certain *managerial values undermine integrity*. In an analysis of executive integrity, Professor Donald M. Wolfe explains that managers have developed some ways of thinking (of which they may be quite unaware) that foster unethical behaviour.[114]

One culprit is referred to as the **bottom-line mentality**. This way of thinking supports financial success as the only value to be considered. It promotes short-term solutions that are immediately financially sound even if they cause problems for others within the organization or for the organization as a whole. It promotes the unrealistic belief that everything boils down to a monetary game. As such, rules of morality are merely obstacles, impediments along the way to bottom-line financial success.

Wolfe also notes that managers tend to rely on an **exploitative mentality**—the view that encourages "using" people in a way that promotes stereotypes and undermines empathy and compassion. This highly selfish perspective sacrifices concern for others in favour of benefits to one's own immediate interests.

In addition, there is a **Madison Avenue mentality**—a perspective suggesting that anything is right if the public can be convinced that it's right. The idea is that executives may be more concerned about their actions *appearing* to be ethical than about their legitimate morality—a public relations–guided mentality. This kind of thinking leads some companies to hide their unethical actions (e.g., by dumping their toxic wastes under cover of night) or to justify them by attempting to explain them as acceptable.

Recognizing the problems associated with these various orientations is not difficult. Their overemphasis on short-term monetary gain may lead to decisions that not only hurt individuals in the long run, but also threaten the very existence of organizations themselves. Although an organization may make an immediate profit by cutting corners, exploiting people, and convincing others that they have behaved appropriately, it is unlikely that such practices are in the long-term best interest of organizations. Just as people are learning that they cannot continue to exploit their natural environments forever without paying a cost (e.g., depletion of natural resources, hazards allegedly caused by openings in the earth's ozone layer), the same may apply to business environments as well. Indeed, society appears to be increasingly intolerant of organizations that continue to violate moral standards in the name of short-term profit.

It even has been argued that when organizations continue to behave unethically, they may find that doing so is unprofitable in the long run. Consumers who find the well-publicized unethical actions of various companies objectionable may cast their votes for greater social responsibility by not patronizing those organizations. In contrast, a growing number of organizations—such as the Celestial Seasonings and Patagonia, to name only two—have long engaged in highly ethical practices with respect to the treatment of living beings and the environment and have prospered in great part because of consumers' appreciation of these policies.[115]

What Can Be Done to Promote Ethical Behaviour in Organizations?

As you might imagine, getting people to behave ethically isn't a simple matter. Yet, to the extent that "good ethics" may in fact be "good business," as they say, it is worth considering tactics for discouraging unethical behaviour.

The first thing that should be done is to *test the ethics of any decision you are contemplating*. In this regard, there are four main questions you should ask yourself:[116]

- *Is it right?* Although it is not always easy to judge whether a certain action is right, there are certain universally accepted principles of right and wrong that should not be violated. For example, it is widely considered wrong to steal.

- *Is it fair?* Fairness demands treating likes as likes. So, for example, two equally qualified people should be paid the same wages for doing the same job.

- *Is it purely selfish?* If your actions benefit only yourself, then they may be unethical. Morally acceptable behaviours are ones that benefit the greatest number and harm the fewest.

- *How would you feel if others found out?* If you think you might be embarrassed by having your actions described on the front page of your local newspaper, then those actions may be ethically dubious.

codes of ethics Documents describing what an organization stands for and the general rules of conduct expected of employees (e.g., to avoid conflicts of interest, to be honest, etc.).

A second step that can be taken to promote ethical behaviour (and one that many organizations, such as Nortel, Shell Canada, Bell Mobility, and Placer Dome have been using) is to develop a **code of ethics**. These are documents describing what the organization stands for and the general rules of conduct expected of employees (e.g., to avoid conflicts of interest, to be honest).[117] Some codes are highly specific, stating, for example, the maximum size of gifts that can be accepted and exactly how people will be punished for violating the rules. Research has shown that codes of ethics are especially effective when they are used in conjunction with training programs that reinforce the company's values.[118] In the absence of such training, too many codes are seen as "window dressing" and are ignored—if they are even read at all.

ethics audit The practice of regularly assessing the morality of a company's employees' behaviour so as to identify incidents of dubious ethical value.

Third, conduct an **ethics audit**. Just as companies regularly audit their books to check on irregularities in their finances, it is advised that they regularly assess the morality of their employees' behaviour so as to identify irregularities in this realm as well. Specifically, an ethics audit involves actively investigating and documenting incidents of dubious ethical value. Then, these unethical practices should be discussed in an open and honest fashion, and a concrete plan should be developed to avoid such actions in the future.

Our fourth recommendation involves something you can do as an individual: *Challenge your rationalizations about ethical behaviour.* We all tend to rationalize the things we do so we can convince ourselves that they are right although they really may be wrong. Some of the most common rationalizations are as follows:

- *Convincing yourself that something is morally acceptable just because it is legally acceptable.* Think of the law as the minimum standard of acceptable behaviour, and strive for higher moral standards.

- *Convincing yourself that something is right just because it benefits you.* It may be easy to talk yourself into accepting a bribe because you feel underpaid. Regardless, it is still wrong.

- *Convincing yourself that something is right because you will never get caught.* What's wrong is wrong—even if you don't stand a chance of getting caught.

- *Convincing yourself that something is right because it helps the company.* Don't expect the company to condone your immoral actions, even if doing so gives it an edge. The best companies want to succeed because they have taken the moral high road, not because of the unacceptable practices of their employees.

It isn't always easy to avoid these rationalizations. Still, do your best to catch yourself in the act of rationalizing your actions. To the extent that you are rationalizing, you may be covering up unethical behaviour.

SUMMARY AND REVIEW

Globalization and Culture

International trade and commerce is becoming increasingly commonplace in the world of business. Companies with operations throughout the world, **multinational corporations (MNCs)**, are becomingly increasingly common. As tariffs are eliminated, world markets grow and countries become financially interdependent. One result of this is **cultural homogenization,** the tendency for people throughout the world to become culturally similar.

People living in other countries, or returning home after long visits abroad, often experience feelings of disorientation and confusion known as **culture shock.** However, these feelings tend to disappear as people spend more time in their new surroundings.

In contrast to traditional approaches to management which assume that there is one best way to manage people—the North American way—today's scientists recognize that different approaches may operate effectively in different cultures—the **divergence hypothesis.** In fact, Hofstede's framework organizes several important dimensions of culture that distinguish people in various nations with respect to the way they are likely to behave in organizations. These dimensions are **individualism/collectivism, power distance, uncertainty avoidance,** and **masculinity/femininity.**

Diversity in the Workplace

Today's organizations may be characterized not only by cultural differences between them, but within them as well. In fact, a popular philosophy today is cultural pluralism—the idea that people's unique identities should be maintained and accepted by others. This is in contrast to the traditional, **melting pot,** philosophy, according to which people blend their cultures, creating a new culture. Cultural pluralism is at the root of the **Canadian mosaic** and is embraced by organizations who make efforts to **value diversity** among their employees.

The North American workforce may be characterized as growing in the numbers of women, minorities, and older people. Recognizing these trends, organizations have implemented **diversity training** programs, flexible work arrangements (e.g., **flextime programs, compressed workweeks,** and **job sharing**), and support facilities (e.g., **child-care** and **elder-care**).

Trends in Working Arrangements

Rapid advances in technology have made it possible for organizations to do more work with fewer employees than before. As a result they **downsize,** laying off employees who are no longer needed. They also eliminate non-core functions (e.g., janitorial services, duplication services, payroll processing) by purchasing them from other companies who specialize in these tasks—a popular process known as **outsourcing.** Also adding flexibility in the numbers of employees needed, many companies are simply hiring people on an as-needed basis, creating a **contingent workforce.**

As organizations are growing smaller, they sometimes find it impossible to tackle large projects themselves. Instead, they join forces temporarily with other companies to form temporary companies known as **virtual organizations.** Today, as technology makes it possible for employees to do more work from outside the office, to which they are connected by computers and telephone lines, the practice of **telecommuting** has grown in popularity.

The Quality Revolution

To stay competitive in the world marketplace, today's organizations are more concerned than ever with producing high quality goods and services. An approach known as **total quality management (TQM)** has been popular in recent years. It refers to an organizational strategy of commitment to improving customer satisfaction by developing techniques to manage output quality carefully. Companies that have met rigorous quality standards may be recognized by the Canada Awards For Excellence program. Companies also attempt to improve the quality of their work by **reengineering.** This involves radically redesigning the way organizational processes are performed, with the ultimate goal of better serving customers.

Ethical and Unethical Behaviour in Organizations

Corporate scandals have become commonplace in recent years. These appear to be due, in large part, to the fact that organizations sometimes reward behaviours that violate ethical standards, and some managerial values undermine integrity. For example, the **bottom-line mentality** encourages people to seek short-term profit at all costs.

Ethical behaviour in organizations may be fostered by encouraging people to test the morality of the decisions they are contemplating, developing a **code of ethics,** conducting an **ethics audit,** and challenging rationalizations about ethical behaviour.

CASE PREVIEW QUESTIONS FOR DISCUSSION

1. Explain how valuing diversity could lead to strategic advantage for companies in Canada in the twenty-first century such as Babine Forest Products.

2. What special challenges do you expect would confront the managers of Babine Forest Products given their diverse workforce?

3. What other Canadian companies besides Babine Forest Products have achieved a good working relationship between Native and non-Native employees? How have such good working relationships been achieved?

CHAPTER QUESTIONS FOR DISCUSSION

1. Based on the material in this chapter, argue for or against the following statement: "Technology has made the world smaller culturally." Explain your answer.

2. In what ways can we expect the demographics of the workforce to change in the years ahead?

3. In what ways can training help people who are looking to become successful in leaner organizations?

4. How has technology created flexibility in the workplace?

5. What steps are organizations taking to eliminate mediocrity and to become as quality-minded as possible?

6. If someone said, "Some people are unethical and there's nothing you can do to change them," what would you say? Do you agree or disagree with this statement as it applies to behaviour in organizations? Why or why not?

CASE IN POINT

ING Direct: A Virtual Arrow to the Heart of Canadian Banks

What will financial institutions look like in the next century? Mergers, globalization, smart cards, electronic banking, decreasing numbers of local branches all point to revolutionary changes in how we manage our money. Standing at the threshold of a brave new world of banking, Matthew Barrett, former Chairman and CEO of the Bank of Montreal Group of Companies is far from blasé about the revolution ahead: "We need to face as squarely as we can the new realities that are transforming banking so swiftly that to analyze them is like trying to map the clouds."[119]

A major factor contributing to this banking revolution is technological innovation, which allows people to have access to their money any time of the day or night and from any location. Virtual banking has grown by leaps and bounds in the 1990s and will continue to grow in the years ahead as consumers demand convenient, customized banking services provided through a variety of delivery channels.[120]

The no-frills approach has grown in popularity in grocery stores and in retailing establishments such as Wal-Mart and beyond. But would it work for banking?[121] International Nederlanden Groep NV launched its branchless bank, ING Direct in Canada in 1997.[122] "What's missing in Canadian banking is discounters," said ING's chief executive Arkadi Kuhlmann at the time of the launch.[123]

ING was not the first virtual bank in Canada. The Bank of Montreal launched its mbanx in October 1996 while the Royal Bank and CIBC have had remote-access banking for some time.[124] For ING marketers, Toronto-based Garneau Würstlin Philp Brand Engineering, such increased focus on virtual banking was a boon. "So ... we sat back and said, 'Wow —the six most credible marketing institutions in the country have just told Canadians at great expense that it's okay to bank from home.' We just crossed that challenge off the list and focused on more specific things, like promoting value."[125]

Although ING's parent company is not new in this country, ING Direct is, however, the first all-electronic foreign bank in Canada. ING Groep NV's Canadian roots date back to the 1950s through its various subsidiaries, including Halifax Insurance Co., Belair Direct, Western Union Insurance, Baring Asset Management, and NN Life Insurance Co. of Canada. ING's focus on entering the Canadian market is to offer a single product: a high-interest savings account with no service charges. The company brings with it prodigious assets of U.S.$350 billion.

ING's Canadian operation is based in its North York, Ontario 3345-square-metre call centre. "Even a virtual bank needs a physical presence." In fact, the ING Direct café, on the ground floor of the call centre, has helped to put a human face on this virtual business for many clients and potential clients.[126] For those potential clients who may still be nervous about who receives those electronic deposits, the company has installed a Web cam in its offices. If they want to see ING employees slaving away at their computers—and many do—they just need to check out the ING Website, **www.ingdirect.ca**. At any given time, net surfers can get a very good look at several employees who are sitting close to the camera and a fuzzier look at those in more distant locations. Annette Borger, a company spokesperson, says in defense of the camera, "While it's not exactly Melrose Place... This is a way of helping educate the Canadian population as to what a call centre is and what ING looks like."[127]

ING Direct's approach to customer service has extended to an innovative partnership with Canadian Tire Corporation, Limited to test a new service known as Canadian Tire Direct. This partnership allows Canadian Tire, Options, or MasterCard holders to undertake various banking functions without fees through automated banking machines located in Canadian Tire stores. Customers can print statements, pay accounts, and get account balance information seven days a week. Arkadi Kuhlmann is enthusiastic about his company's new venture: "Canadian Tire and ING Direct share the same business goal of giving Canadians high value and exceptional service. Service, convenience, and value are what make Canadian Tire Direct a unique experience for both organizations' customers—and marks a new level of innovation in the retail banking marketplace."[128]

The future of banking is closely tied to developments in technology. Companies like ING Direct are strategically positioned to take advantage of every innovation. Canada's Big Six bankers are well aware of the challenge ING poses. "ING aims to shake up the comfortable world of Canadian banking." In the words of one banker, "If we aren't scared of it [ING], we should be taken out and shot."

Critical Thinking Questions

1. Explain what Matthew Barrett meant by "new realities that are transforming banking so swiftly that to analyze them is like trying to map the clouds."

2. Discuss the advantages and disadvantages of using a Web cam in virtual organizations in general and in a bank in particular. Be sure to visit ING's Website as you answer this question.

3. Which of the major topics discussed in this chapter are particularly salient for ING's Canadian operations?

SKILLS PORTFOLIO

Experiencing Organizational Behaviour

Are You More Ethical Than the Average Manager? Don't Be So Sure!

"The world is full of unethical people," you say—adding, "but I'm not one of them." If we all believe we're ethical, we will be predisposed to trust our own judgments but to question others. This perceptual bias can have major implications for the way we act and how we respond to others. This exercise is designed to demonstrate this phenomenon.

Directions

1. Prepare two versions of the following questionnaire, in one using the phrases "you/your job" and in the other, "most managers/their jobs" in the spaces indicated. To tell them apart, print each version on a different-coloured paper.

2. Divide a group of people (e.g., another class) into two groups and ask them to complete the questionnaire following the directions.

Instrument

For each of the following statements indicate, by using the scale below, how willing [you/most managers] would be to perform the action indicated if it were necessary to protect [your job/their jobs].

0 = Always, 1 = Usually, 2 = Sometimes, 3 = Rarely, 4 = Never

____ **1.** Keep negative information from a superior.

____ **2.** Lie about facts in a performance report.

____ **3.** Distort information in a financial statement.

____ **4.** Blame a subordinate for one's own mistake.

____ **5.** Break union rules so as to cut costs.

____ **6.** Authorize the use of deceptive marketing techniques.

____ **7.** Exaggerate figures on an expense report.

____ **8.** Pay off an inspector to avoid making costly repairs to already safe equipment.

Scoring

Compute the average scores for each of the two groups. The higher the score, the more it is believed that the focal person ("you" or "the average manager") will be ethical.

Questions for Discussion

1. We would expect that the "you" group would have higher scores than the "average manager" group. Is this what you found?
2. Were there some people in the group who consistently responded more extremely than others? If so, ask them to explain what they were thinking.
3. What are the implications of this exercise? What did you learn about yourself, and how can you put it to use?

Working in Groups

Canada Awards for Excellence (CAE) Winners: What Makes Them So Special?

One of the best ways to come to appreciate the things that companies are doing to promote quality is to study their practices carefully. Among the most quality-conscious companies to be found are those that have won a CAE award. This exercise is designed to help you learn about the things that these successful companies are doing—and that separate the best from the rest.

Directions

1. Divide the class into small groups and assign each group one of the CAE winners in Table 2-1.
2. For each of the companies prepare a profile of the company's activities, especially its quality-fostering practices. In other words, working in groups, research and prepare a report on what these companies are doing that makes them so quality-minded. Your school's librarians should be able to help you search through computerized databases to find information about the companies.
3. Your group's report should attempt to answer the following basic questions:
   (a) What are the company's core business activities?
   (b) What has the company done to improve the quality of its goods or services?
   (c) What has the company done to improve relations with its employees?
   (d) What has the company done to promote customer satisfaction?
4. After all the reports have been prepared, members of each group should take turns reporting their findings to the class.

Questions for Discussion

1. Were there any common practices followed by all award winners? Explain.
2. Did the winners in the various categories do things that were very different from each other? Explain.
3. What ideas did you get with respect to how quality may be fostered in the organization within which you work?
4. What general value do you think the CAE program has in promoting quality in Canadian organizations?

TAKE IT TO THE NET

Prentice Hall

COMPANION WEBSITE

We invite you to visit the *Greenberg/Baron/Sales/Owen Companion Website* at *www.prenticehall.ca/greenberg* for this chapter's Internet resources.

Keith Kocho: The Renaissance Man and His Company

Whom would you pick as your Web surfing guide? How about the founder of one of Canada's hottest young multimedia companies? Keith Kocho's favourite sites include Microsoft's travel site (www.expedia.com) for daydreaming, Excite (www.excite.com) for searching, and Sympatico (www.sympatico.ca) for keeping up with Canadian content while he is travelling—something he does a lot as his business grows.[1]

Kocho is well aware of what's hot and what's not in all things high tech. In January 1991 Keith Kocho, a 22-year-old recent graduate of Ryerson Polytechnic University's Radio and Television Arts program, founded Digital Renaissance, a venture he describes as "a new media engineering company." By 1999, with offices in Toronto, Ottawa, and San Francisco; a staff of 150; an eye-popping list of heavyweight clients, strategic partners and investors; and an annual sales level of $15 million, Digital Renaissance had established itself as a national and international force to be reckoned with in the nascent multimedia industry.[2] No wonder Ryerson chose Keith Kocho, along with his Ryerson contemporary, Perry Keller, another of Digital Renaissance's founding members, as co-recipients of its first Outstanding Recent Graduate Award.

Even in a world of "colourful" characters, Kocho is a standout. "He's brilliant, and he's sometimes crazy," says computer science graduate, Amy Kovarick, another of Digital Renaissance's co-founders. Others have described him as "a child prodigy,"[3] "a shrewd capitalist,"[4] "massively ambitous, yet so egoless,"[5] "renaissance man,"[6] and, yes, even "a geek."[7]

Kocho grew up in Oshawa, Ontario, with a talent for sports and no interest in computers. Now he runs one of Canada's fastest-growing companies and is writing a sci-fi novel in the few off-hours he can put together.

Kocho wears shorts and a T-shirt when he and his ever-present canine partner, Scout, meet with power-brokers such as Jean Monty of BCE. With the leading edge technology his company is developing, the corridors of power are wide open for Keith Kocho.[8]

Kocho's career path to date has been neither smooth nor predictable. Instead, a series of what proved to be fortunate misadventures put him on the road to success. Since Kocho grew up in Oshawa, Ontario, a GM town, it might have seemed logical that he would end up in the auto industry. However, a bad back set him on a different course. He decided to enter Ryerson Polytechnic University as a journalism major. It turned out he unwittingly registered for the wrong program. "I thought Radio and Television was journalism, but it wasn't," he says.[9] This apparently false start turned out to be an inspiration for Kocho, who became fascinated with how the technology in the Radio and Television program worked, and just how much more it could do.

In fact, even before his founding of Digital Renaissance, Kocho's road took many twists and turns. In 1989, to help pay for his education, he took a part-time secretarial job at Humanagement, a Toronto-based human resources consulting firm. As it happened, the job was pivotal in his multimedia career.[10] When one of the company's clients asked for a video as part of a training program, Kocho initiated the company's multimedia division to design innovative computer video technology to meet the client's needs. However, since this innovation was not a core function of his employer's business, he was soon told to return to his secretarial duties. One of the company's senior partners, recognizing the promise displayed by the young man, urged him to go out on his own. Kocho heeded the advice and[11] founded Digital Renaissance at a time when the term "multimedia" did not even exist.

To be precise, Kocho started his company in his bedroom with no help from banks, which were, at the time, less than keen on backing small businesses at all, much less media companies. In the earliest days, Kocho chose a "two-pronged approach," i.e., his new company offered both services and software products to corporate clients seeking assistance with multimedia presentations. With his own money and a $100 000 loan from his father, an engineer with General Motors, Kocho started Digital Renaissance with the vision of Toronto's becoming the world's next Silicon Valley. Keith was convinced that "the new media business . . . translated to economics, revitalized by 'technology and the digitalization of various forms of communications and commerce and content.'" One of the first business decisions Kocho, Kovarick, and Keller made was to rent a "massive 2100-square-foot warehouse space" in downtown Toronto. Kovarick recalls the uncertainty of those early days: "We'd sit around tossing a Nerf football around this gigantic space, and going, 'What next?'"[12]

Then came a big break. Kocho landed a $200 000 project for the CRB Foundation, managed by the Bronfman family, "to create interactive kiosks based on the foundation's . . . 'Canadian Heritage Moments.' "[13] A prominent entertainment lawyer employed by the CRB Foundation was so impressed with Kocho and his "pitch," he explained: "He was totally fledgling, but he had this enormous presence. . . . He really sensed before us that interactive was going to be big."[14]

As the World Wide Web grew, Digital Renaissance focused more on newer modalities such as WebTV and on "developing network applications, helping companies to define their goals and pick the best platform on which to convey an application or message." From the outset, Kocho's philosophy was to provide value for his customers. " 'Sometimes it's just computing platforms, so Macs, PCs. Increasingly, it's WebTV platforms, it's kiosks, television, print,' says Kocho."[15]

On Digital Renaissance's Website, Keith Kocho announces "OUR WORLD is built on the foundations of STORYTELLING:

"This is the future for Digital Renaissance. We will pursue the development of tools, technologies and the stories to empower the storyteller in all of us. We will create the models and platforms to allow businesses to utilize stories to capture knowledge, increase efficiency and conduct commerce. We will continue to evolve new classes of tools to enable today's master storytellers to engage the audiences of the future. And we will join the ranks of the storytellers by driving the forefront of the new form, the new story, our story."[16]

With enormous pride, the staff at Digital Renaissance offer browsers, and better still, potential new clients, an opportunity to see samples of the projects they have completed for such well-known clients as Bank of Montreal, Bell Canada, NBTel, Rogers Communications, Royal Bank of Canada, Science Alberta, Pelmorex/The Weather Channel, McMichael Canadian Art Collection, National Aviation Museum, and many others.[17]

So far, in its young life, Digital Renaissance has deservedly gained a lot of attention in the media, trade publications, and professional organizations in the field for reaching some very impressive milestones including many "firsts" such as: resellers of the first Canadian Digital Video technology (with Intel and IBM), deployment of the first digital video server application for video-on-demand over a local area network, deployment of the first public-access interactive kiosk network in North America using a central digital video server, deployment of the first North American inter-city live access of multimedia content from a remote digital video server (with Stentor Resource Centre), and deployment of the first interactive application delivered from a digital video server to a remote city using cable modem technology (with Rogers Communications).[18]

Further, in 1996, Digital Renaissance's Product Group released its revolutionary media annotation technology software called T.A.G. (Temporal Annotation Generator). This product immediately caught the eye of Bill Gates. T.A.G. became "the first third-party technology to be featured in a Microsoft product release."[19] "The software creates interactive hyperlinks to time-based media sources such as video, audio and animation— for example, someone looking at a video clip on a Web site could retrieve more detailed information about something that interests them in the clip, by clicking an icon, or links that appear alongside the video."[20]

And the awards and honours keep on pouring in! Here is just a sampling: named best "Small Haven" employer in the high-tech field by *The Globe and Mail Report on Business*, named one of the top companies to watch in the future by *Upside*, named Young Entrepreneur of the Year by the Business Development Bank of Canada for 1998, winner of two Product of the Year awards from the Ontario Society for Training and Development, listed as number 174 of the top 4000 growth companies in Canada in recognition of its 486 percent growth in 1995–1998, and numerous awards for its Internet-based designs completed for clients.

All of these milestones and awards, as you might imagine, have turned the heads of some notable corporations eager to invest in technology of the future. As one writer put it: By 1997 when Keith Kocho and his company had "become a fixture" at Canadian multimedia and Internet conferences, "a pre-apocalyptic panic had set in among businesses confronted by new communication media, and they were desperate for someone to make sense of it all."[21] (The biggest investors so far are Bell Canada, Arthurs-Jones, and Alliance/Atlantis Communications.)

From its humble beginnings, Digital Renaissance has truly taken off. The remarkable story of this company's development as a powerful force in Canada's burgeoning multimedia industry reflects changes in the way Canadians, especially the 20- and 30-somethings, are working together in organizations to accomplish personal and organizational goals simultaneously.

At the end of each of the five remaining Parts of this book, we will revisit Digital Renaissance and show you more of organizational behaviour in action.

Discussion Questions

1. Put yourself in Keith's place as founder and CEO of a rapidly growing Canadian high-tech company. How would you expect your knowledge of organizational behaviour to help you advance the interests and effectiveness of your company?

2. Why do you think Digital Renaissance was chosen over all other Canadian companies as the Cumulative Case for this book?

3. Speculate on what it would be like to work at Digital Renaissance as the company races into the twenty-first century.

4. What is meant by the term "renaissance man"? What does this term tell you about Keith Kocho?

Vertically Inclined Rock Gym: Climbing the Walls with Virgil

It looks like every climber's dream come true. Build a mountain, an indoor mountain, and they will come. Or at least that was the dream of Jake Kreutzer and his partners when they opened Edmonton's Vertically Inclined Rock Gym in 1996. The company's Web page (**www.verticallyinclined.com**) features VIRGIL the climbing frog. If you click on VIRGIL you will find the company's mission statement: "Our mission is to be Edmonton's premiere climbing facility, supplying active human beings with an exhilarating visual and physical adventure-experience."

Sport climbing has become very popular, in part because of the increase in indoor climbing gyms such as Vertically Inclined. Kreutzer emphasizes that, for those interested in developing skills for all kinds of climbing, "... an indoor climbing gym is an excellent place where that base of experience can start." Vertically Inclined's advertising focuses on the fun and fitness aspects of indoor climbing in a safe environment. "We have taken the challenge and fitness of rock climbing and removed the unpredictable nature of the mountain environment to offer a truly alternative form of active recreation."

Kreutzer and his partners are living through the infamous challenges of starting and growing a new business. Armed with his University of Calgary M.B.A., Kreutzer felt he was ready for what lay ahead. But he soon discovered just how tough the real world of entrepreneurship can be.

Today, Jake talks to business undergraduates about his experiences. He tells them how important it is to pay close attention, especially to their course in organizational behaviour. "Take as much OB [as you can] and really take it because it's the real stuff," he emphasizes.

As the business has developed he has found that 90 percent of the problems he faces as a manager are people problems. He struggles with the best way to communicate to staff the importance of the business' making money without demotivating them as keen climbing instructors. He has come to realize the fundamental importance of the hiring and training processes. Kreutzer holds training seminars for groups of up to 20 applicants. On the first day of the interview process, they are asked a series of questions and are asked to participate in team development activities. They are also given an assignment to perform in front of a group by singing a song or telling a joke. Those applicants who wish to continue to compete for a position after their experience on the first day are assessed and those who are considered as possible candidates attend six more training seminars.

From the initial gym construction stage, through financial strains and staffing challenges, Kreutzer has worked long hours to make the business a success. He now spends over 60 hours a week at the climbing gym while his wife attends medical school. Their twin daughters are growing into active youngsters demanding increasing amounts of their parents' energy.

The original partnership has changed. Although Kreutzer and his major financial backer remain, Brendan Waye, who helped to start the gym, has left. Brendan admitted that he was not comfortable dealing with the myriad of human resources issues he was surprised to find were a major part of running the business. Troy Nixon has joined as operations manager and shareholder.

The business remains all consuming for Kreutzer and Nixon. As Jake points out, "If it was easy, everyone would own their own business."

Video Case Discussion Questions

1. Imagine that you and a friend have decided to start a small business together. What decisions do you anticipate in your first six months in business? In your first two years in business?

2. What does Jake mean when he says, "If it was easy, everyone would own their own business"?

3. Why did Brendan Waye leave the business?

4. Why do you think Jake advises business undergraduates to "Take as much OB [as you can] and really take it because it's the real stuff"?

CBC Source: Mountain Men, *Venture* #625 (July 13, 1997).

Video Case Sources: Kreutzer, J. (1998, July 24). All climbing lumped into dangerous type. *The Edmonton Journal*, p. A15; Vertically Inclined Rock Gym, www.verticallyinclined.com; Kreutzer, J. (1998, November 2). Personal Communication.

CHAPTER 3

Perception and Learning:

Understanding and Adapting to the Work Environment

LEARNING OBJECTIVES

After reading this chapter you should be able to:

1. Define *social perception* and indicate its relevance to organizational behaviour.

2. Explain how the *attribution* process helps us understand the causes of others' behaviour.

3. Appreciate the various sources of bias in social perception and how they may be overcome.

4. Understand how the process of social perception operates in the context of performance appraisals, employment interviews, and the cultivation of corporate images.

5. Explain the concept of learning and describe how it operates in organizations.

6. Describe the concepts of *operant conditioning* and *observational learning*.

7. Appreciate how principles of learning are involved in organizational programs involving training, organizational behaviour management, and discipline.

Nortel Networks: A "Cool Place" to Work

The demand for computer science and engineering graduates is increasing steadily in "Silicon Valley North" and Canada's high-tech industry is competing for the best and the brightest. " 'The competition for talent is fierce,' says [Nortel's president and CEO, John] Roth."[1] Ottawa-based Software Human Resource Council has estimated that 50 000 information technology jobs will be open by the end of the century.[2] Money is not enough to attract highly skilled technology professionals. Companies are now packaging themselves as "cool" places to work.[3]

Nortel takes no chances in getting its share of Canada's human resources.[4] The company offers some employees the opportunity to telecommute[5] (see Figure 3-1) and provides a giant gym with squash courts, weights, and health food. There are softball teams and a company arts club. These efforts, and others, seem to be paying off. Nortel's turnover rate is a lot lower than those found in the real Silicon Valley in California.[6]

At Nortel, the search for talent begins in-house with the opportunity for employees to be trained in new skills. The company's commitment to training begins even before many employees are hired. As Canada's largest supporter of co-op and internship placements for university students, Nortel reaches out to potential employees before they graduate. To attract students, Nortel uses strategies such as a $500 000 job fair attended by 1000 invited engineering and computer science students. They are housed in some of Ottawa's best hotels and regaled with descriptions of the company's career opportunities. In many cases, students are hired by the company before graduation.

Nortel's commitment to training does not end with the hiring process. "Training, Nortel managers say, is a crucial part of keeping employees content."[7] Not surprisingly, Nortel's approach to training is high tech all the way. According to Nortel's senior manager of the virtual-reality-applications design unit, Darrell Ferris, "We've found that the virtual-reality approach reaches all kinds of learners—visual, trial-and-error, audio, and detail-based—to boost retention from 12 to 15 percent to 20 to 30 percent."[8] Participants, including Nortel's operators, technicians, and customers, can use one CD-ROM course to replace a three-day training program. The ease of access and flexibility of this three-dimensional virtual-reality program saves participants five days of lost work time getting to and from and attending a traditional familiarization course.[9]

Nortel's commitment to training and keeping its employees is a critical factor in its continued success in the rapidly changing high-tech world.

Figure 3-1 Creative Strategies Lead to Satisfied Employees

Brenda Pavlovic is convinced that Nortel is a cool place to work—she works from her home. Pavlovic is employed in the company's employee satisfaction program.[10]

Nortel Networks
www.nortelnetworks.com

Software Human Resource Council
www.shrc.ca

eading this case, you probably cannot help but consider how these educational experiences have enriched the lives of so many Nortel interns and employees. By acquiring new skills, the people who work at Nortel enjoy opportunities for advancement in the company. By making these educational opportunities available to its employees, Nortel has enhanced its image among university students and in the community.

What is responsible for the way we come to view other people and the companies in which they work? Clearly, there is an active and complex process going on, a mechanism through which people are able to make sense out of the things they confront in the world around them—the process of *perception*.

Although it may sound mysterious, perception is a fundamental process, and one that explains many different types of situations in organizations. For example, think about what goes on when you apply for a job. Your prospective employer attempts to learn about you—based, most likely, on an interview and your résumé—and makes a judgment about what you'd be like as an employee. Will you be lazy or hard-working? Do you know how to do the job? At the same time, you are attempting to figure out what it would be like to work for that company. Will the boss be pleasant? Will the work be challenging? If hired, you'll be sizing up your new co-workers (who's nice and who's going to stab me in the back?) while they do the same to you (what's the new person like?). Then, as time goes on, you'll be evaluated by your superior (how well is this person doing?). Obviously, there's a lot of perceiving going on here. Understanding the complex nature of perceptual processes, basic as they are to human behaviour in organizations, is critical to our understanding of OB, and so it will be one of the key themes of this chapter.

Equally fundamental is another basic psychological process that is highlighted in this case—*learning*. The broad array of training modalities at Nortel provides exceptional opportunities for its employees to add important new capabilities to their repertoires of job skills. However, learning may involve much more than formally training people in the classroom. The process of learning is also involved in such everyday activities as attaining information about who holds the power in an organization, how to get things done most effectively, who to talk to in the event of a problem, and even what to eat or avoid at the company cafeteria. Principles of learning are also applied in ways designed to help improve the functioning of organizations by systematically doing things that help maintain desirable employee behaviours and reduce undesirable behaviours. In this chapter, we will explain not only the psychological processes responsible for learning—that is, how it occurs—but also ways in which these processes are used to improve organizational functioning.

Social Perception: The Process of Understanding Others

There can be no doubt about it: The world around us is a very complex place. At any given moment we are flooded with input from our various senses. Yet we do not respond to the world as a random collection of sights, sounds, smells, and tastes. Rather, we notice order and pattern everywhere. This process of making sense out of the vast array of sensory inputs involves the active processing of information, and is known as the process of **perception**. Formally, we may define perception as the process through which people select, organize, and interpret information.[11]

To illustrate this process, let's consider an example. Suppose that you meet your new boss. You know her general reputation as a manager, and you see the way she looks, hear the words she says, and read the memos she writes. In no time at all, you're trying to figure her out. Will she be easy to work with? Will she like me? Will she do a good job for the company? On the basis of whatever information you have available to you (even if it's very little), you will try to understand her and

perception The process through which we select, organize, and interpret information gathered by our senses in order to understand the world around us.

how you will be affected by her. In other words, you will attempt to combine the various things you learn about her into a meaningful picture. Interestingly, this process is so automatic that we are almost never aware of it. Yet it goes on all the time. Clearly, when it comes to understanding the objects and people in our environment, there's a lot more going on than may be obvious.

The process of perception is especially important in the field of OB. Indeed, other people—whether they're bosses, coworkers, subordinates, family, or friends—can have profound effects on us. To understand the people around us—to figure out who they are and why they do what they do—may be very helpful to us. After all, you wouldn't want to ask your boss for a raise when you believe he or she is in a bad mood. Clearly, **social perception**—the task of combining, integrating, and interpreting information about others to gain an accurate understanding of them—is very important, especially in organizations.[12]

social perception The process through which individuals attempt to combine, integrate, and interpret information about others.

We will explore various aspects of the social perception process in the sections that follow. To begin, we will summarize the *attribution* process—the way people come to judge the underlying causes of others' behaviour. Then, we will note various imperfections of this process—errors and sources of bias that contribute to inaccurate judgments of others—as well as ways of overcoming them. Finally, we will present specific ways in which the attribution process is used in organizations.

The Attribution Process: Judging the Causes of Others' Behaviour

A question we often ask about others is "why?" Why did Kim goof up the order? Why did the company president make the policy she did? When we ask such questions, we are attempting to get at two different types of information: (1) what someone is really like (that is, what traits and characteristics does he or she possess?) and (2) what made the person behave as he or she did (that is, what accounted for his or her actions?). People attempt to answer these questions in different ways through the process of **attribution**.[13]

attribution The process through which individuals attempt to determine the causes of others' behaviour.

Making Correspondent Inferences: Using Acts to Judge Dispositions

Situations frequently arise in organizations in which we want to know what someone is like. Is your opponent a tough negotiator? Are your coworkers prone to be punctual? The more you know about what people are like, the better equipped you are to know what to expect and how to deal with them. How, precisely, do we go about identifying other people's traits? Generally speaking, we do so by observing their behaviour and then inferring their traits from this information. The judgments we make about what someone is like based on what we have observed about him or her are known as **correspondent inferences**.[14] Simply put, correspondent inferences are judgments about people's dispositions—their traits and characteristics—that correspond to what we have observed of their actions (see Figure 3-2).

correspondent inferences Judgments made about what someone is like based on observations of his or her behaviour.

At first blush, it would appear to be a simple matter to infer what people are like based on their behaviour. A person with a disorganized desk may be thought of as sloppy. Someone who slips on the shop floor may be considered clumsy. Such judgments might be accurate—but not necessarily. After all, the messy desk actually may be the result of a coworker rummaging through it to find an important report. Similarly, the person who slipped could have encountered oily conditions under which anyone, even the least clumsy individual, would have fallen. In other words, it is important to recognize that the judgments we may make about someone may be inaccurate because there are many possible causes of behaviour. Someone's underlying characteristics certainly may play a large role in determining what they do, but as we will explain in the next section, it is also possible for behaviour to be shaped

Figure 3-2 Correspondent Inferences: Judging Dispositions Based on Behaviour

One of the ways in which we come to judge what others are like is by making inferences about them that follow from what we have observed of their behaviour. Such judgments, known as *correspondent inferences*, are frequently misleading. How might your inferences in this example be inaccurate?

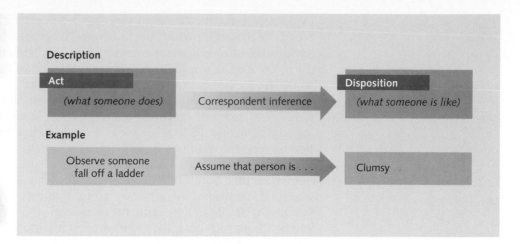

by external forces (in our examples, the coworker's actions and the oil on the floor). For this reason, correspondent inferences may not always be accurate.

Another reason why this is so has to do with the tendency for people to conceal some of their traits—especially when they may be viewed as negative. So, for example, a sloppy individual may work hard in public to appear to be organized. Likewise, the unprincipled person may talk a good show about the importance of being ethical. In other words, people often do their best to disguise some of their basic traits. In summary, then, due to two basic facts, the making of correspondent inferences is a risky business: (1) behaviour is complex and has many different causes and (2) people sometimes purposely disguise their true characteristics.

Despite such difficulties, we can use several techniques to help make more accurate correspondent inferences. First, we can focus on others' behaviour in situations in which they do not *have* to behave in a pleasant or socially acceptable manner. For example, anyone would behave in a courteous manner toward the president of the company, so when people do so, we don't learn too much about them. However, only those who are *really* courteous would be expected to behave politely toward someone of much lower rank—that is, someone toward whom they don't have to behave politely. In other words, someone who is polite toward the company president but condescending toward a secretary is probably really arrogant. The way people behave in situations in which a certain behaviour is not clearly expected of them may reveal a great deal about their basic traits and motives.

Similarly, we can learn a great deal about someone by focusing on behaviour for which there appears to be only one explanation. For example, imagine finding out that your friend accepts a new job. Upon questioning him, you learn that the position is very high-paying, involves interesting work, and is in a desirable location. What have you learned about what's important to your friend? The answer is "not too much." After all, any of these are good reasons to consider taking a position. Now, imagine finding out that the work is very demanding and that the job is in an undesirable location but that it pays very well. In this case, you're more prone to learn something about your friend—namely, that he highly values money. Clearly, the opportunity to make accurate correspondent inferences about people is far greater in situations in which there is only one plausible explanation for their behaviour.

Causal Attribution of Responsibility: Answering the Question "Why?"

Imagine finding out that your boss just fired one of your fellow employees. Naturally, you'd ask yourself, "Why did he do that?" Was it because your coworker violated the company's code of conduct? Or was it because the boss is a cruel and heartless person? These two answers to the question "why?" represent two major classes of explanations for the causes of someone's behaviour: *internal* causes, explanations based on actions for which the individual is responsible, and *external* causes, explanations based on situations over which the individual has no control. In this case, the internal cause would be the person's violation of the rules, and the external cause would be the boss's cruel and arbitrary behaviour.

Generally speaking, it is very important to be able to determine whether an internal or an external cause was responsible for someone's behaviour. Knowing why something happened to someone else might help you prepare for what might happen to you. For example, in this case, if you believe that your colleague was fired because of something for which she was responsible herself, such as violating a company rule, then you might not feel as vulnerable as you would if you thought she was fired because of the arbitrary, spiteful nature of your boss. In the latter case, you might decide to take some precautionary actions—to do something to protect yourself from your boss, such as staying on his good side or even giving up and finding a new job before you are forced to. The key question of interest to social scientists is: How do people go about judging whether someone's actions were caused by internal or external causes?

An answer to this question is provided by **Kelley's theory of causal attribution**. According to this conceptualization, we base our judgments of internal and external causality on three types of information:[15]

1. *Consensus:* the extent to which other people behave in the same manner as the person we're judging. If others do behave similarly, consensus is considered high; if they do not, consensus is considered low.

2. *Consistency:* the extent to which the person we're judging acts the same way at other times when he or she is in the same situation. If the person acts the same at other times, consistency is high; if he or she does not, then consistency is low.

3. *Distinctiveness:* the extent to which this person behaves in the same manner in other contexts. If he or she behaves the same way in other situations, distinctiveness is low; if he or she behaves differently, distinctiveness is high.

According to the theory, after collecting this information, we combine what we have learned to make our attributions of causality. Here's how. If we learn that other people act like this one (consensus is high), that this person behaves in the same manner at other times (consistency is high), and that this person does not act in the same manner in other situations (distinctiveness is high), we are likely to conclude that this person's behaviour stemmed from *external* causes. In contrast, imagine learning that other people do *not* act like this one (consensus is low), that this person behaves in the same manner at other times (consistency is high), and that this person acts in the same manner in other situations (distinctiveness is low). In this case, we will probably conclude that this person's behaviour stemmed from *internal* causes.

Because this explanation is highly abstract, let's consider an example that helps illustrate how the process works. Imagine that you're at a business lunch with several of your company's sales representatives when the sales manager makes some critical remarks about the restaurant's food and service. Further imagine that no one else in your party acts this way (consensus is low), that you have heard her say the same things during other visits to the restaurant (consistency is high), and that you have seen her acting critically in other settings, such as the regional sales meeting (distinctiveness is low). What would you conclude in this situation? Probably that her behaviour stems from *internal* causes. In other words, she is a "picky" person, someone who is difficult to please.

Now, imagine the same setting but with different observations. Suppose that several other members of your group also complain about the restaurant (consensus is high), that you have seen this person complain in the same restaurant at other times (consistency is high), but that you have never seen her complain about anything else before (distinctiveness is high). In this case, then you would probably conclude that the sales manager's behaviour stems from *external* causes: The restaurant really *is* inferior. For a summary of these contrasting conclusions, see Figure 3-3.

Kelley's theory of causal attribution The approach suggesting that people will believe others' actions to be caused by internal or external factors based on three types of information: consensus, consistency, and distinctiveness.

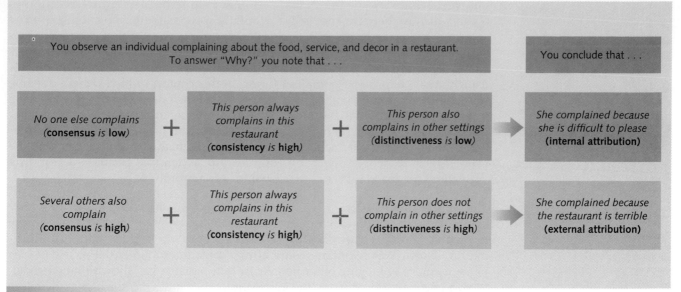

You observe an individual complaining about the food, service, and decor in a restaurant. To answer "Why?" you note that . . .

You conclude that . . .

| No one else complains (**consensus** is **low**) | + | This person always complains in this restaurant (**consistency** is **high**) | + | This person also complains in other settings (**distinctiveness** is **low**) | → | She complained because she is difficult to please (**internal attribution**) |

| Several others also complain (**consensus** is **high**) | + | This person always complains in this restaurant (**consistency** is **high**) | + | This person does not complain in other settings (**distinctiveness** is **high**) | → | She complained because the restaurant is terrible (**external attribution**) |

Figure 3-3 Kelley's Theory of Causal Attribution: A Summary

In determining whether others' behaviour stems mainly from internal or external causes, we focus on the three types of information illustrated here.

The Imperfect Nature of Social Perception: Bias and How to Overcome It

As you might imagine, people are far from perfect when it comes to making judgments of others. In fact, researchers have noted that there are several important types of biases that interfere with making completely accurate judgments of others. In this section, we will describe some of these errors and ways of overcoming them.

Perceptual Biases: Systematic Errors in Perceiving Others

Some of the errors people make in judging others reflect systematic biases in the ways we think about others in general. These are referred to as **perceptual biases**. We will consider five such biases—the *fundamental attribution error*, the *halo effect*, the *similar-to-me-effect*, *first-impression error*, and *selective perception*.

perceptual biases Predispositions that people have to misperceive others in various systematic ways.

The fundamental attribution error. Despite what Kelley's theory says, people are not equally predisposed to reach judgments regarding internal and external causality. Rather, they are more likely to explain others' actions in terms of internal rather than external causes. In other words, we are prone to assume that others' behaviour is due to the way they are, their traits and dispositions (e.g., "she's that kind of person"). So, for example, we are more likely to assume that someone who shows up for work late does so because she is lazy rather than because she got caught in traffic. This tendency is so strong that it has been referred to as the **fundamental attribution error**.[16]

fundamental attribution error The tendency to attribute others' actions to internal causes (e.g., their traits) while largely ignoring external factors that also may have influenced their behaviour.

This phenomenon stems from the fact that it is far easier to explain someone's actions in terms of his or her traits than to recognize the complex pattern of situational factors that may have affected his or her actions. As you might imagine, this tendency can be quite damaging in organizations. Specifically, it leads us to assume prematurely that people are responsible for the negative things that happen to them (e.g., "he wrecked the company car because he is careless"), without considering external alternatives, ones that may be less damning (e.g., "another driver hit the car"). This tendency can lead to inaccurate judgments about people.

halo effect The tendency for our overall impressions of others to affect objective evaluations of their specific traits; perceiving high correlations between characteristics that may be unrelated.

The halo effect: Keeping perceptions consistent. Have you ever heard someone say something like, "She's very smart, so she must also be hardworking"? Or, "He's not too bright, so I guess he's lazy"? If so, then you are already aware of a common perceptual bias known as the **halo effect**.[17] Once we form a positive impression of someone, we tend to view the things that person does in favourable terms—even things about which we have no knowledge. Similarly, a generally negative impression of someone is likely to be associated with negative evaluations of that person's behaviour. Both of these tendencies are referred to as halo effects—even the negative case.

In organizations, the halo effect often occurs when superiors rate subordinates using formal performance appraisal forms. In this context (which we will describe more fully later in this chapter), a manager evaluating one of his employees highly on some dimensions may assume that someone so good must also be good at other things and rate that person highly on other dimensions (see Figure 3-4). Put differently, the halo effect may be responsible for finding high correlations between the ratings given to people on various dimensions. When this occurs, the resulting evaluations are inaccurate, and their quality is compromised.

The similar-to-me effect: "If you're like me, you must be pretty good." Another common type of perceptual bias involves the tendency for people to perceive more favourably others who are like themselves than those who are dissimilar. This inclination, known as the **similar-to-me effect**, constitutes a potential source of bias when it comes to judging other people. In fact, research has shown that when superiors rate their subordinates, the more similar the parties are, the higher the rating the superior tends to give.[18] This tendency applies with respect to several different dimensions of similarity—similarity of work values and habits, similarity of beliefs about the way things should be at work, and similarity with respect to demographic variables (such as age, race, gender, and work experience).

This effect appears to be partly the result of the tendency for people to be able to empathize and relate better to similar others and to be more lenient toward them. However, it also appears that subordinates tend to be more trusting and confident in supervisors whom they perceive as similar than in those they perceive as dissimilar.[19] As a result, they may have a more positive relationship, and this may lead superiors to judge similar subordinates in a more favourable light. Regardless of the underlying explanation for the similar-to-me effect, it is important to recognize its important implications: Differences in the way people are perceived are based in large part on the similarities between the perceiver and the individual being perceived.

similar-to-me effect The tendency for people to perceive in a positive light others who are believed to be similar to themselves in any of several different ways.

Figure 3-4 The Halo Effect: A Demonstration

One manifestation of *the halo effect* is the tendency for people rating others to give either consistently high ratings (if the individual is generally perceived in a positive manner), or low ratings (if the individual is generally perceived in a negative manner). Because each rating dimension is not considered independently, inaccurate evaluations may result.

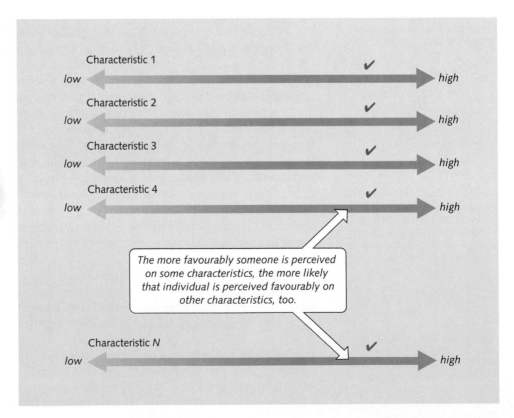

The more favourably someone is perceived on some characteristics, the more likely that individual is perceived favourably on other characteristics, too.

first-impression error The tendency to base our judgments of others on our earlier impressions of them.

First-impression error: Confirming one's expectations. Often, the way we judge someone is not based solely on how well that person performs now, but rather on our initial judgments of that individual—that is, our *first impressions*. To the extent that our initial impressions guide our subsequent impressions, we have been victimized by **first-impression error**. As you might imagine, this error can be especially problematic in organizations, where accurately judging others' performance is a crucial managerial task. When a subordinate's performance has improved, that needs to be recognized, but to the extent that current evaluations are based on poor first impressions, recognizing such improvement is impossible. Likewise, inaccurate assessments of performance will result when initially good performers leave positive impressions that linger on even when a manager is confronted with evidence suggesting that one's performance has dropped (for a summary of this process, see Figure 3-5).

Recent evidence by Dougherty, Turban, and Callender suggests that the first-impression error takes very subtle forms.[20] Participants in their study were corporate interviewers who evaluated the application forms and test scores of prospective employees. These researchers found that the more highly interviewers judged these applicants based on these two criteria alone, the more positively the applicants were treated during the interview process. Analyses made of audiotaped interviews showed that candidates who made initially positive impressions were treated more positively: They were spoken to in a more pleasant interpersonal style and were more likely to be told about the good features of the company. In other words, instead of using the interviews to gather additional unbiased information, the recruiters used them to confirm the first impressions they developed on the basis of the test scores and application forms. This study provides clear evidence of the first-impression error in action.

selective perception The tendency to focus on some aspects of the environment while ignoring others.

Selective perception: Focusing on some things while ignoring others. A fifth perceptual bias, known as **selective perception** refers to the tendency for individuals to focus on certain aspects of the environment while ignoring others.[21] Insofar as people operate in complex environments in which there are many stimuli that demand our attention, it makes sense that we tend to be selective, narrowing our perceptual fields. This practice constitutes a bias insofar as it limits our attention to some stimuli while heightening our attention to other stimuli.

Recent research has shown that this process operates in organizations. Waller, Huber, and Glick surveyed a large number of top executives from numerous

Figure 3-5 First-Impression Error: A Summary

When a *first-impression error* is made, the way we evaluate someone is more highly influenced by our initial impressions of that person than by his or her current performance. In this example, someone who was initially perceived as performing well continues to be rated highly despite a downturn in performance.

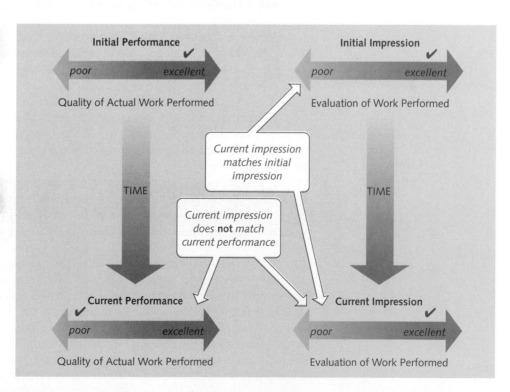

organizations about various aspects of their organizations that contribute to organizational effectiveness.[22] In general, they found that the executives attended most to those aspects of the work environments that matched their backgrounds in various functional areas. For example, executives whose backgrounds were in sales and marketing perceived changes in a company's line of products and services as being most important. Similarly, those who worked previously in research and development focused more on product designs in their perceptions of the business environment than on other issues.

In other words, executives tend to be affected by selective perception: They give greatest attention to those aspects of the business environment that match their background experiences. This finding underscores our point that the process of social perception is greatly affected by perceiver variables such as one's personal history. That is why different people tend to perceive the same situations very differently.

Stereotypes: Fitting Others into Categories

What comes to mind when you think about people who wear glasses? Are they studious? Shy? Lacklustre? Although there is no evidence of such connections, it is interesting to note that for many people, such images linger in their minds. Of course, this is only one example. You can probably think of many other commonly held beliefs about the characteristics of people belonging to specific groups. Such statements usually take the form: "People from group *X* possess characteristic *Y*." In most cases, the characteristics described tend to be negative. Assumptions of this type are referred to as **stereotypes**—beliefs that all members of specific groups share similar traits and behaviours.

Deep down inside, many of us know, of course, that not all people from a specific group possess the negative characteristics with which we associate them. In other words, most of us accept that the stereotypes we use are at least partially inaccurate. After all, not *all* *X*s are *Y*; there are exceptions (maybe even quite a few). If so, then why are stereotypes so prevalent? Why do we use them?

Why do we rely on stereotypes? To a great extent, the answer resides in the fact that people tend to do as little cognitive work as possible when it comes to thinking about others.[23] That is, we tend to rely on mental shortcuts. If assigning people to groups allows us to assume that we know what they are like and how they may act, then we can save the tedious work of learning about them as individuals. After all, we come into contact with so many people that it's impractical—if not impossible—to learn everything about them we need to know. So, we rely on readily available information—such as someone's age, race, gender, or job type—as the basis for organizing our perceptions in a coherent way. If you believe that members of group *X* tend to have trait *Y*, then simply observing that someone falls into group *X* becomes the basis for your believing that he or she possesses *Y*. To the extent that the stereotype applies in this case, then the perception will be accurate. However, such mental shorthand often leads us to make inaccurate judgments about people—the price we pay for using stereotypes.

The problem with our tendency to rely on stereotypes, of course, is that it leads us to judge people prematurely, without the benefit of learning more about them than just the categories into which they fit (see Figure 3-6). Still, we all rely on stereotypes at least sometimes; the temptation is far too great to resist.

Using stereotypes in organizations. It is easy to imagine how the use of stereotypes can have powerful effects on the kinds of judgments people make in organizations. For example, if a human resource manager believes that members of certain groups are lazy, then she purposely may avoid hiring or promoting individuals who belong to those groups. The manager may firmly believe that she is using good judgment—gathering all the necessary information and listening to the candidate carefully. Still, without being aware of it, the stereotypes she holds may influence the way she judges that person. The result, of course, is that the fate of the individual in question

stereotypes Beliefs that all members of specific groups share similar traits and behaviours.

☞ *The stereotypes we use contribute to the attitudes we hold toward various groups. Thus, the topic of stereotypes will be reintroduced in Chapter 6, where we discuss attitudes toward coworkers.*

Figure 3-6 What Are These People Like?

If you have formed some image of what these individuals are like just from this photograph, you may be relying on *stereotypes*—judgments of others based on their membership in various groups. Stereotypes may lead to inaccurate judgments, ones that might differ if we took the time to learn about the people we're perceiving.

is sealed in advance—not necessarily because of anything he or she may have done or said, but by the mere fact that he or she belongs to a certain group. In other words, even people who are not being intentionally bigoted still may be influenced by the stereotypes they hold.

We realize, of course, that the effects of stereotyping others are not always as profound as they are in our example (in which someone was not hired or promoted). Referring to accountants as "bean counters" and professors as "absent-minded" are observations that also reflect stereotypes—ones that appear to be only mildly negative. Still, it must be cautioned that holding stereotypes of people in various groups runs the risk of causing miscommunication and conflict between them.

☛ *The ways in which stereotypes contribute to problems associated with interpersonal communication and conflict are discussed in Chapters 9 and 11, respectively.*

Overcoming Bias in Social Perception: Some Guidelines

For the most part, people's biased perceptions of others are not the result of any malicious intent to inflict harm. Instead, biases in social perception tend to occur because we, as perceivers, are imperfect processors of information. We assume that people are internally responsible for their behaviour because we cannot be aware of all the possible situational factors that may be involved. Thus, we make the fundamental attribution error. Further, it is highly impractical to be able to learn everything about someone that may guide our reactions. As a result, we use stereotypes. This does not mean, however, that we cannot minimize the impact of these and other biases. Indeed, there are several steps that can be taken to help promote the accurate perception of others in the workplace:

1. ***Do not overlook the external causes of others' behaviour.*** The fundamental attribution error leads us to discount the possibility that people's poor performance may be due to conditions beyond their control. As a result, we may ignore legitimate explanations for poor performance. Ask yourself if anyone else may have performed just as poorly under the same conditions. If the answer is yes, then you should not automatically assume that the poor performer is to blame. Good managers need to make such judgments accurately so that they can decide whether to focus their efforts on developing employees or changing work conditions.

2. **_Identify and confront your stereotypes._** Let's face it, we all rely on stereotypes—especially when it comes to dealing with new people. Although this tendency is natural, erroneous perceptions are bound to result—and quite possibly, at the expense of someone else. For this reason, it's good to identify the stereotypes you hold. Doing so will help you become more aware of them, taking a giant step toward minimizing their impact on your behaviour. After all, unless you are aware of your stereotypes, you may never be able to counter them.

3. **_Evaluate people based on objective factors._** The more objective the information you use to judge others, the less your judgments will be subjected to perceptual distortion. People tend to bias subjective judgments in ways that are self-serving (such as positively evaluating the work of those we like and negatively evaluating the work of those we dislike). To the extent that evaluations are based on objective information, this error is less likely to occur.

4. **_Avoid making rash judgments._** It is human nature to jump to conclusions about what people are like, even when we know very little about them. Take the time to get to know people better before convincing yourself that you already know all you need to know about them. What you learn just may make a big difference in your opinion.

We realize that many of these tactics are far easier to extol than to practise. However, to the extent that we conscientiously try to apply these suggestions to our everyday interactions with others in the workplace, we stand a good chance of perceiving people more accurately. And this is a fundamental ingredient in the recipe for managerial success.

Perceiving Others: Organizational Applications

Thus far, we have identified some of the basic processes of social perception and have alluded to ways in which they are involved in organizational behaviour. Now, in this section we will make these connections more explicit. Specifically, we will describe the role of perception in three organizational activities: employee performance appraisal, the employment interview, and the organization's development of its corporate image.

Performance Appraisals: Making Formal Judgments about Others

performance appraisal The process of evaluating employees on various work-related dimensions.

One of the most obvious instances in which social perception occurs is when someone formally evaluates the job performance of another. This process, known as **performance appraisal**, occurs in organizations—often on an annual or semiannual basis—for purposes of determining raises, promotions, and training needs.[24] Ideally, this process should be completely rational, leading to unbiased and objective judgments about exactly how well each employee has performed and how he or she should be treated. However, based on what we have said about perception thus far, you're probably not surprised to learn that the performance evaluation process is far from objective. Indeed, people have a limited capacity to process, store, and retrieve information, making them prone to bias when it comes to evaluating others (see Figure 3-7).[25]

Several such biases have been observed by researchers. For example, it has been shown that people's ratings of other's performance depends on the extent to which that performance is consistent with their expectations. Specifically, in one study Hogan asked bank managers to indicate how well they expected their newest tellers to perform their jobs.[26] Four months later, they were asked to rate the tellers' actual job performance. It was found that managers gave higher ratings to those tellers whose performance matched their earlier expectations than to those who did either better

"Beats the hell out of performance reviews."

Figure 3-7 Performance Appraisals: Subject to Bias

The process of evaluating others' job performance, so vital to making important organizational decisions, such as pay raises, is subject to several sources of error and bias. Acknowledging this, the men shown here appear to be using quite another basis for determining pay raises.

(Copyright © 1991, 1994 by Andrew Toos. Reprinted by permission.)

or worse than predicted. These effects are unsettling insofar as they suggest that the improved performance of some employees may go unrecognized—or, worse yet, be downgraded. Of course, to the extent that human resource management decisions are made on the basis of several sources of information, not merely judgments by single superiors, it is unlikely that such biased judgments may go uncorrected. Nonetheless, these findings clearly underscore a key point: Perceptions are based on the characteristics not only of the person being perceived, but of the perceiver as well.

This conclusion is supported by research showing several different attribution biases in evaluations of job performance. We can illustrate just one of these if we recall our earlier discussion of the similar-to-me effect, showing that people tend to perceive more positively those who are similar to themselves than those who are dissimilar. A recent study by Wayne and Liden has demonstrated this effect in the context of performance appraisals.[27] Studying 111 pairs of superiors who were rating their subordinates in performing a variety of different jobs, they found that the more employees did things to cultivate positive impressions on their superiors (e.g., do favours for them, agree with their opinions), the more their superiors viewed them as being similar to themselves. And the more their superiors judged them to be similar to themselves, the more highly the superiors evaluated their work.

Employees often attempt to make themselves look good to superiors by sharing explanations for their work that focus on the internal reasons underlying good performance and the external reasons underlying poor performance. Indeed, it has been shown that two equally good performers are unlikely to receive the same performance ratings when different attributions are made about the underlying causes of their performance. Managers tend to give higher ratings to individuals whose poor performance is attributed to factors outside the individual's control (e.g., someone who is trying hard but is too inexperienced to succeed) than to those whose poor performance they attribute to internal factors (e.g., those who are believed to be capable but who are just lazy and holding back). In other words, our evaluations of others' performance are qualified by the nature of the attributions we make about that performance.

Findings such as these illustrate our point that organizational performance evaluations are far from the unbiased, rational procedures one would hope to find. Instead, they represent a complex mix of perceptual biases—effects that must be appreciated and well understood if we are to have any chance of ultimately improving the accuracy of the performance evaluation process.

Impression Management in the Employment Interview: Looking Good to Prospective Employers

The desire to make a favourable impression on others is universal. In one way or another, we all do things to control how other people see us, often attempting to get them to think of us in the best light possible. This process is known as **impression management**.[28] Generally, individuals devote considerable attention to the impressions they create in the eyes of others—especially when these others are important, such as prospective employers.

impression management Efforts by individuals to improve how they appear to others.

The impressions that prospective employers form of us may be based on subtle behaviours, such as how we dress and speak, or more elaborate acts, such as announcing our accomplishments.[29] They may be the result of calculated efforts to get others to think of us in a certain way or be the passive, unintended effects of our actions. When it comes to the employment interview, there are several things job candidates commonly do to enhance the impressions they make. In a recent study Stevens and Kristof audiotaped the interviews between college students looking for jobs and representatives of companies that posted openings at the campus job placement centre.[30] The various statements made by the candidates were categorized with respect to the impression management techniques they used. Several tactics were commonly observed. Table 3-1 lists these specific tactics, gives an example of each, and shows the percentage of candidates who used these techniques. Interestingly, the most common technique was *self-promotion*—flatly asserting that one has desirable characteristics. In this case, candidates commonly described themselves as being hardworking, interpersonally skilled, and goal-oriented, as well as effective leaders.

Importantly, the study also found that candidates used these impression management techniques with great success. The more they relied on these tactics, the more positively they were viewed by the interviewer along several important dimensions (e.g., fit with the organization). This study not only confirms that job candidates do indeed rely on impression management techniques during job interviews, but also that these tend to cultivate the positive impressions desired. With this in mind, the job interview may be seen as an ongoing effort on behalf of candidates to present themselves as favourably as possible and for interviewers to try to see through those attempts, trying to judge candidates accurately. As the evidence suggests, this task may be considered far from simple.

[You Be The Consultant]

A car dealership has been having problems retaining its new salespeople. The general manager suspects that the problem rests in the selection process: Candidates for sales positions are so convincing that they are selling themselves, making it hard for the company to accurately assess the candidates' shortcomings.

1. What interview questions might be asked that will help "cut through" the smoke created by these expert salespeople?

2. What biases might the dealership face when it comes to accurately assessing these individuals? How might these be overcome?

Corporate Image: Impression Management by Organizations

corporate image The impressions that people have of an organization.

It is not only individuals who desire to cultivate positive impressions of themselves, but entire organizations, too—what has been termed **corporate image**.[31] As described in the CASE PREVIEW for this chapter, Nortel is working to show prospective employees that it is a cool place to work. A factor that contributes to this image is the company's global headquarters. Nortel Brampton Centre near Toronto is described as an indoor "cityscape." Work spaces are grouped into "neighbourhoods" and the complex contains a wide variety of services including a travel agency, a bank, and sandwich and cappuccino stores. The complex has 19 skylights bringing daylight into the converted factory space. Nortel Vice-Chairman and CEO Jean Monty is understandably proud of his company's headquarters, which he describes as, "a dynamic, unique work environment where employee innovation and creativity can flourish."[32]

As you might imagine, the impression an organization makes on people can have a considerable effect on the way these individuals relate to it. Extending our discussion of the job recruitment setting, not only do individual candidates want to make good impressions on prospective employers, but employers want their job offers to be accepted by the best candidates.

The importance of a corporate image in this context has been demonstrated in a study by Gatewood, Gowan, and Lautenschlager.[33] These researchers found that a company's image is strongly related to people's interest in seeking employment with it. Specifically, the more favourably a company's reputation was rated, the more interested a group of college seniors was in working there. This is important insofar as organizations must recruit prospective employees to function effectively. Given this important point, it seems worthwhile to consider exactly what factors contribute to a corporate image.

Impression Management Technique	Description (Example)	Frequency of Use
Self-promotion	Directly describing oneself in a positive manner for the situation at hand (e.g., "I am a hard worker").	100%
Personal stories	Describing past events that make oneself look good (e.g., "In my old job, I worked late anytime it was needed").	96%
Opinion conformity	Expressing beliefs that can be assumed to be held by the target (e.g., agreeing with something the interviewer says).	54%
Entitlements	Claiming responsibility for successful past events (e.g., "I was responsible for the 90% sales increase that resulted").	50%
Other enhancement	Making statements that flatter, praise, or compliment the target (e.g., "I am very impressed with your company's growth in recent years").	46%
Enhancements	Claiming that a positive event was more positive than it really was (e.g., "Not only did our department improve, but it was the best in the entire company").	42%
Overcoming obstacles	Describing how one succeeded in the face of obstacles that would have lowered performance (e.g., "I managed to get a 3.8 average although I worked two part-time jobs").	33%
Justifications	Accepting responsibility for one's poor performance but denying the negative implications of it (e.g., "Our team didn't win a lot, but it's just how you play the game that really matters").	17%
Excuses	Denying responsibility for one's actions (e.g., "I didn't complete the application form because the placement centre ran out of them").	13%

Interestingly, Gatewood and his colleagues found that a company's image was positively correlated with the amount of information people had about it (such as from previous work experiences and recruitment ads in college placement guides). In general, longer ads were associated with more positive images. This finding is likely the result of not only what is in the ad, but the mere length of the ad itself. Specifically, because recruitment ads emphasize the benefits of employment with a firm, longer ads describe more benefits than shorter ones, thereby creating even stronger positive images. Moreover, to the extent that people believe that longer ads reflect a company's commitment to obtaining good employees (by their willingness to invest in a large ad), they may be more impressed with a company as a prospective place to work.

Another mechanism that organizations use to promote their corporate images is their *annual reports*—a company's official statement to its stockholders on its activities and financial well-being. Traditionally, these are strikingly beautiful glossy booklets with elaborate photography and glitzy images, trappings of success designed to instill confidence in the minds of investors. In recent years, however, many companies have spared such expenses, issuing bare-bones annual reports.[34] They have done so to promote an image of austerity. As today's investors are looking for value, companies are going out of their way to cultivate the impression that they're not wasting money. So, whether these publications are elaborate or just plain vanilla, the conclusion is the same: Annual reports are designed to cultivate "the right" corporate image, whatever that may be. Our overall conclusion is clear: Organizations, just like individuals, stand to benefit by making positive impressions on others, and work hard at doing so.

As you might imagine, it is not only in organizations that people seek to make positive impressions, but in other walks of life too. For a look at a fascinating business that has developed recently in Japan from the great concern that the Japanese people have for being perceived positively by others, see the GLOBALIZATION IN TODAY'S ORGANIZATIONS section.

Learning: Adapting to the World around Us

Recall our CASE PREVIEW about Nortel, the company that made a big investment in developing the skills of its employees. Thus far, we have focused on one of the basic human processes involved in this case—perception. Now, we will turn our attention to the other basic psychological process involved in this case—*learning*.

Globalization in Today's Organizations

Saving Face in Japan, Where Renting Acquaintances Is Big Business

Generally, we think of the need to make positive impressions on others as a universal phenomenon: We all wish to be highly regarded by others. To be thought of in a negative manner is shameful. However, it appears that people in some nations are more sensitive to shame than others. Among present-day Japanese, the concern over shame is so great that a big business has grown out of the need to avoid shame. Agencies called *benriya* have sprung up to help people avoid the loss of face they would suffer by not having their social events go just right.[35] In general, these agencies provide stand-ins at various functions. These "rented acquaintances" are, in reality, strangers, but no one except the customer ever knows that.

One bride, fearing that a small turnout at her wedding would embarrass her family, paid Kazushi Ookunitani's "All Purpose Company" $10 000 to rent 40 fake friends. To avoid arousing suspicion, the actors were all thoroughly briefed on the bride's background. So convincing was the charade that some even rose to give speeches at the reception. Another bride hired all her guests, except for her parents and one friend, for fear that real friends would get talking and divulge

that she was divorced, a status that holds a social stigma in Japan. Men use stand-ins at their weddings too, usually distinguished-looking gentlemen posing as the grooms' bosses, whose attendance at one's wedding reception is seen as a sign of honour. For one's boss not to attend would be embarrassing, but it must never come to pass—at least not if a groom can get an actor to play the part. And during the busy autumn wedding season, such accomplices may be hard to come by.

But these agencies don't limit their business to weddings. *Benriya* employees also have been sent to funerals so that the requisite number of mourners would be present. They've even been hired at welcome-home parties for people just released from prison. Some young men have gone so far as to hire actors posing as thugs to stage unsuccessful muggings just so they could impress their girlfriends with their bravery. Again, these are not the plots of bad situation comedies, but real-life events that have been occurring in Japan.

To understand these activities is to understand the importance of saving face in modern-day Japanese culture. "It has a lot to do with keeping up appearances," says Ookunitani. Indeed, the entire *benriya* industry is designed to help cultivate whatever image one wishes to convey. And, when this task cannot be performed alone, Mr. Ookunitani and his colleagues stand ready to help (for a fee, of course).

The process of learning is heavily involved in the way new-comers to organizations learn the ropes (known as socialization). We will pay special attention to this process in Chapter 7.

learning A relatively permanent change in behaviour occurring as a result of experience.

Whether we're talking about how a person develops new job skills, social skills, or general life skills, many of the same basic processes are involved. Clearly, learning is a fundamental process in organizational behaviour. In fact, the more a company fosters an environment in which employees are able to learn, the more productive and profitable it is likely to be.[36] Naturally, scientists in the field of OB are extremely interested in understanding the process of learning—both how it occurs, and how it may be applied to the effective functioning of organizations.

Before we turn our attention to these matters, we should first explain exactly what we mean by learning. Specifically, we define **learning** as a relatively permanent change in behaviour occurring as a result of experience.[37] Despite its simplicity, several aspects of this definition bear pointing out. First, it's clear that learning requires that some kind of *change* occurs. Second, this change must be more than just temporary. Finally, it must be the result of *experience*—that is, continued contact with the world around us. Given this definition, we cannot say that short-lived performance changes on the job, such as those due to illness or fatigue, are the result of learning. Learning is a difficult concept for scientists to study because it cannot be directly observed. Instead, it must be inferred on the basis of relatively permanent changes in behaviour.

We will now consider two of the most prevalent forms of learning that occur in organizations—*operant conditioning* and *observational learning*.

Operant Conditioning: Learning through Rewards and Punishments

Imagine you are a chef working at a catering company where you are planning a special menu for a fussy client. If your dinner menu is accepted and the meal is a hit, the company stands a good chance of adding a huge new account. You work hard at doing the best job possible and present your culinary creations to the skeptical client. Now, how does the story end? If the client loves your meal, your grateful boss gives you a huge raise and a promotion. However, if the client hates it, your boss asks you to turn in your chef's hat. Regardless of which of these outcomes occurs, one thing is certain: Whatever you did in this situation, you will be sure to do it again *if* it was successful and avoid doing it again *if* it failed.

operant conditioning (or instrumental conditioning) The form of learning in which people associate the consequences of their actions with the actions themselves. Behaviours with positive consequences are acquired; behaviours with negative consequences tend to be eliminated.

This situation nicely illustrates an important principle of **operant conditioning** (also known as **instrumental conditioning**)—namely, that our behaviour produces consequences and the way we behave in the future will depend on what those consequences are. If our actions have pleasant effects, then we will be more likely to repeat them in the future. If, however, our actions have unpleasant effects, we are less likely to repeat them in the future. This phenomenon, known as the **Law of Effect**, is fundamental to operant conditioning. Our knowledge of this phenomenon comes from the work of the famous social scientist B. F. Skinner.[38] Skinner's research has shown us that it is through the connections between our actions and their consequences that we learn to behave in certain ways. We summarize this process in Figure 3-8.

Law of Effect The tendency for behaviours leading to desirable consequences to be strengthened and those leading to undesirable consequences to be weakened.

Reinforcement contingencies. Operant conditioning is based on the idea that our behaviour is learned because of the positive outcomes that we associate with it. In organizations, for example, people usually find it pleasant and desirable to receive monetary bonuses, paid vacations, and various forms of recognition. The process by which people learn to perform acts leading to such desirable outcomes is known as **positive reinforcement**. The behaviour that led to the positive outcomes is likely to occur again, thereby strengthening that behaviour. For a reward to serve as a positive reinforcer, it must be made contingent on the specific behaviour sought. So, for example, if a sales representative is given a bonus after landing a huge account, that bonus will only reinforce the person's actions *if* he or she associates it with the landing of the account. When this occurs, the individual will be more inclined in the future to do whatever it was that helped get the account.

positive reinforcement The process by which people learn to perform behaviours that lead to the presentation of desired outcomes.

Sometimes we also learn to perform acts because they permit us to avoid undesirable consequences. Unpleasant events, such as reprimands, rejection, probation,

Figure 3-8 The Operant Conditioning Process: An Overview

The basic premise of *operant conditioning* is that people learn by connecting the consequences of their behaviour with the behaviour itself. In this example, the manager's praise increases the subordinate's tendency to perform the job properly in the future. Learning occurs by providing the appropriate antecedents and consequences.

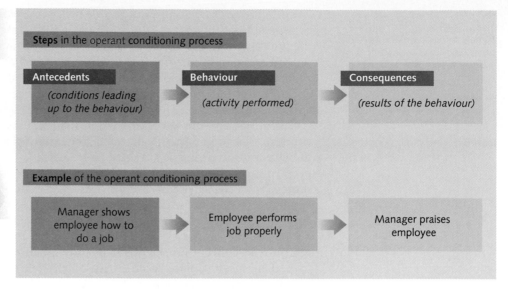

Steps in the operant conditioning process

Antecedents	Behaviour	Consequences
(conditions leading up to the behaviour)	*(activity performed)*	*(results of the behaviour)*

Example of the operant conditioning process

| Manager shows employee how to do a job | Employee performs job properly | Manager praises employee |

negative reinforcement (or avoidance) The process by which people learn to perform acts that lead to the removal of undesired events.

and termination are some of the consequences faced for certain negative actions in the workplace. The process by which people learn to perform acts leading to the avoidance of such undesirable consequences is known as **negative reinforcement**, or **avoidance**. Whatever response led to the termination of these undesirable events is likely to occur again, thereby strengthening that response. For example, you may stay late at the office one evening to revise a sales presentation because you believe that the boss will "chew you out" if it's not ready in the morning. You learned how to avoid this type of aversive situation and behave accordingly.

Thus far, we have identified responses that are strengthened—either because they lead to positive consequences, or the termination of negative consequences. However, the connection between a behaviour and its consequences is not always strengthened; such links also may be weakened. This is what happens in the case of **punishment**. Punishment involves presenting an undesirable or aversive consequence in response to an unwanted behaviour. A behaviour accompanied by an undesirable outcome is less likely to recur if the person associates the negative consequences with the behaviour. For example, if you are chastised by your boss for taking excessively long coffee breaks, you may be considered punished for this action. As a result, you will be less likely to take long breaks again in the future.

punishment Decreasing undesirable behaviour by following it with undesirable consequences.

The link between a behaviour and its consequences also may be weakened by withholding reward—a process known as **extinction**. When a response that was once rewarded is no longer rewarded, it tends to weaken and eventually die out—to be *extinguished*. Let's consider an example. Suppose for many months you brought boxes of doughnuts to your weekly staff meetings. Your colleagues always thanked you as they gobbled them down. You were positively reinforced by their approval, so you continued bringing the doughnuts. Now, after several months of eating doughnuts, your colleagues have begun dieting. So, although tempting, your doughnuts go un-eaten. After several months of no longer being praised for your generosity, you will be unlikely to continue bringing doughnuts. Your once-rewarded behaviour will no doubt cease; it will be extinguished.

extinction The process through which responses that are no longer reinforced tend to gradually diminish in strength.

contingencies of reinforcement The various relationships between one's behaviour and the consequences of that behaviour—positive reinforcement, negative reinforcement, punishment, and extinction.

The various relationships between a person's behaviour and the consequences resulting from it—*positive reinforcement, negative reinforcement, punishment,* and *extinction*—are known collectively as **contingencies of reinforcement**. They represent the conditions under which rewards and punishments will either be given or taken away. The four contingencies we discussed are summarized in Table 3-2. As we will see later in this chapter, administering these contingencies can be an effective tool for managing behaviour in organizations.

TABLE 3-2 Contingencies of Reinforcement: A Summary

The four reinforcement contingencies may be defined in terms of the presentation or withdrawal of a pleasant or unpleasant stimulus. Positively or negatively reinforced behaviours are strengthened; punished or extinguished behaviours are weakened.

Stimulus Presented or Withdrawn	Desirability of Stimulus	Name of Contingency	Strength of Response	Example
Presented	Pleasant	Positive reinforcement	Increases	Praise from a supervisor encourages continuing the praised behaviour
	Unpleasant	Punishment	Decreases	Criticism from a supervisor discourages enacting the punished behaviour
Withdrawn	Pleasant	Extinction	Decreases	Failing to praise a helpful act reduces the odds of helping in the future
	Unpleasant	Negative reinforcement	Increases	Future criticism is avoided by doing whatever the supervisor wants

continuous reinforcement A schedule of reinforcement in which all desired behaviours are reinforced.

partial (or intermittent) reinforcement A schedule of reinforcement in which only some desired behaviours are reinforced. Types include: fixed interval, variable interval, fixed ratio, and variable ratio.

fixed interval schedules Schedules of reinforcement in which a fixed period of time must elapse between the administration of reinforcements.

variable interval schedules Schedules of reinforcement in which a variable period of time (based on some average) must elapse between the administration of reinforcements.

fixed ratio schedules Schedules of reinforcement in which a fixed number of responses must occur between the administration of reinforcements.

Schedules of reinforcement: Patterns of administering rewards. Thus far, our discussion of whether a reward will be presented or withdrawn has assumed that presentation or withdrawal will follow *each* occurrence of behaviour. However, it is not always practical (or, as we will see, advisable) to do this. Rewarding *every* desired response made is called **continuous reinforcement**. Unlike animals performing tricks in a circus, however, people on the job are rarely reinforced continuously. Instead, organizational rewards tend to be administered following **partial** (or **intermittent**) **reinforcement** schedules: That is, rewards are administered intermittently, with some desired responses reinforced and others not. Four varieties of partial reinforcement schedules have direct application to organizations.[39]

1. **Fixed interval schedules** are those in which reinforcement is administered the first time the desired behaviour occurs after a specific amount of time has passed. For example, the practice of issuing paycheques each Friday at 3:00 P.M. is an example of a fixed interval schedule insofar as the rewards are administered at regular times. Fixed interval schedules are not especially effective in maintaining desired behaviour. For example, employees who know that their boss will pass by their desks every day at 11:30 A.M. will make sure they are working hard at that time. However, without the boss around to praise them, they may take an early lunch or otherwise work less hard because they know that they will not be positively reinforced for their efforts or punished for not working.

2. **Variable interval schedules** are those in which a variable amount of time (based on some average amount) must elapse between the administration of reinforcements. For example, consider a bank auditor who pays surprise visits to the branch offices an average of once every six weeks (e.g., visits may be four weeks apart one time and eight weeks apart another time). The auditor may be said to be using a variable interval schedule. Because the bank managers cannot tell exactly when their branch may be audited, they cannot afford to slack off. Not surprisingly, variable interval schedules tend to be more effective than fixed interval schedules.

3. **Fixed ratio schedules** are those in which reinforcement is administered the first time the desired behaviour occurs after a specified number of such actions have been performed. For example, suppose members of a sales staff know that they will receive a bonus for each $1000 worth of goods they sell. Immediately after receiving the first reward, performance may slack off. But as their sales begin to approach $2000, the next level at which reward is expected, performance will once again improve.

variable ratio schedules
Schedules of reinforcement in which a variable number of responses (based on some average) must occur between the administration of reinforcements.

4. **Variable ratio schedules** are those in which a variable number of desired responses (based on some average amount) must elapse between the administration of reinforcements. A classic example may be seen in the behaviour of people playing slot machines. Most of the time when people put a coin into the slot they lose. But after some unknown number of plays, the machine will pay off. Because gamblers can never tell which pull of the handle will win the jackpot, they are likely to keep on playing for a long time. As you might imagine, variable ratio schedules tend to be more effective than fixed ratio schedules.

The various patterns described are known as **schedules of reinforcement**—rules governing the timing and frequency of the administration of reinforcement. We have summarized these schedules in Figure 3-9. As you review this figure, keep in

schedules of reinforcement Rules governing the timing and frequency of the administration of reinforcement.

Figure 3-9 Schedules of Reinforcement: A Summary

The four schedules of reinforcement summarized here represent different ways of administering rewards intermittently.

Fixed Interval

Rewards are given after a constant amount of time has passed.

Boss gives out paycheques at the same exact time each week.

Variable Interval

Rewards are given after a variable amount of time has passed.

Teacher gives a pop quiz an average of once a week, but not always on the same day.

Fixed Ratio

Rewards are given after a constant number of actions are performed.

A farm hand is paid $1 for every box of fruit picked and packed.

Variable Ratio

Rewards are given after a variable number of actions are performed.

A slot machine pays a large jackpot on the average of once per million plays.

mind that these schedules represent "pure" forms. Used in practice, several different reinforcement schedules may be combined, making complex new schedules. Still, whether they operate separately or in conjunction with one another, it is important to recognize the strong influences that schedules of reinforcement can have on people's behaviour in organizations.

Observational Learning: Learning by Imitating Others

Although operant conditioning is based on the idea that we engage in behaviours for which we are directly reinforced, many of the things we learn on the job are *not* directly reinforced. Suppose, for example, that on your new job you see many of your co-workers complimenting your boss on his attire. Each time someone says something flattering, the boss stops at his or her desk, smiles, and acts friendly. By complimenting the boss, they are reinforced by being granted his social approval. Chances are, after observing this several times, you too will eventually learn to say something nice to the boss. Although you may not have directly experienced the boss's approval, you would expect to receive it based on what you have observed from others. This is an example of a kind of learning known as **observational learning**, or **modelling**.[40] It occurs when someone acquires new knowledge *vicariously*—that is, by observing what happens to others. The person whose behaviour is imitated is referred to as the *model*.

For someone to learn by observing a model, several processes must occur.

observational learning (or modelling) The form of learning in which people acquire new behaviours by systematically observing the rewards and punishments given to others.

1. The learner must pay careful *attention* to the model: The greater the attention, the more effective the learning will be. To facilitate learning, models sometimes call attention to themselves. This is what happens when supervisors admonish their subordinates to "pay close attention" to what they're doing.

2. People must have good *retention* of the model's behaviour. It helps to be able to develop a verbal description or a mental image of someone's actions in order to remember them. After all, we cannot learn from observing behaviour we cannot remember.

3. There must be some *behavioural reproduction* of the model's behaviour. Unless people are capable of doing exactly what the models do, they will not be able to learn from observing them. Naturally, this ability may be limited at first but improve with practice.

4. People must have some *motivation* to learn from the model. Of course, we don't emulate every behaviour we see but focus on those we have some reason or incentive to match—such as actions for which others are rewarded. For a summary of these processes, see Figure 3-10.

A great deal of what is learned about how to behave in organizations is the result of the process of observational learning.[41] On the job, observational learning is a key part of many formal job-instruction training programs.[42] As we will explain in the next section, trainees given a chance to observe experts doing their jobs, followed by an opportunity to practise the desired skills and receive feedback on their work, tend to learn new job skills quite effectively. Observational learning also occurs in a very informal, uncalculated manner. For example, people who experience the norms and traditions of their organizations and who subsequently incorporate these into their own behaviour may be recognized as having learned through observation. It is important to note that people learn not only what to do by observing others, but also what *not* to do. Specifically, research has shown that people observing their co-workers getting punished for behaving inappropriately on the job tend to refrain from engaging in those same actions themselves.[43] As you might imagine, this is a very effective way for people to learn how to behave—and, without ever experiencing any displeasure themselves.

Figure 3-10 Observational Learning: An Overview

The process of observational learning requires that an observer pay attention to and remember a model's behaviour. By observing what the model did and rehearsing those actions, the observer may learn to imitate the model, but only if the observer is motivated to do so (i.e., if the model was rewarded for behaving as observed).

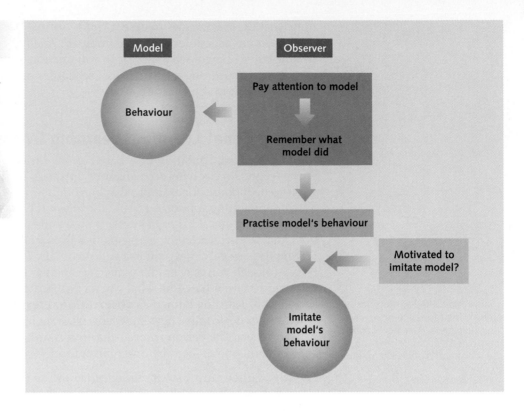

Applications of Learning in Organizations

The principles of learning we have discussed thus far are used in organizations in many different ways. We will now discuss three systematic approaches to incorporating learning in organizations: *training, organizational behaviour management,* and *discipline*.

Training: Learning and Developing Job Skills

training The process of systematically teaching employees to acquire and improve job-related skills and knowledge.

Probably the most obvious use to which principles of learning may be applied in organizations is **training**—that is, the process through which people systematically acquire and improve the skills and knowledge needed to better job performances. Just as students learn basic educational skills in the classroom, employees must learn job skills. Training is used not only to prepare new employees to meet the challenges of the jobs they will face, but also to upgrade and refine the skills of existing employees.

Training takes many forms. For example, growing in popularity are *apprenticeship* and *co-op programs*, in which classroom training is systematically combined with on-the-job instruction. Furthermore, learning does not end with the completion of initial training. Rapid change makes lifelong learning necessary and new technologies make it practical. A major force is *computer-based training (CBT)* programs, which are flexible and, in keeping with the principles of adult learning, allow participants to direct their own rate of training.[44]

☞ *Many executive training sessions focus on the development of leadership skills. Our discussion of leadership in Chapter 13 highlights some of these approaches.*

Also currently popular are *executive training programs*—sessions in which companies systematically attempt to develop the skills of their top managers, such as how to use computer software,[45] or how to get along with others.[46] This is accomplished either by bringing in outside experts to train personnel in-house, or by sending them to specialized programs conducted by private consulting firms or by colleges and universities.[47]

In fact, some companies (e.g., Canadian Tire Acceptance Ltd., Apple Computer, Motorola, McDonald's, and Sprint), are so serious about training that they have developed their own *corporate universities*—centres devoted to handling a company's training needs on a full-time basis. Canadian banks are known for their learning centres such as the CIBC Leadership Centre (see Figure 3-11 and the CASE IN POINT for this chapter) and the Bank of Montreal's Institute for Learning.

**Figure 3-11 CIBC's Leadership
Centre: Training Bank
Employees**

CIBC's Leadership Centre north of Toronto is designed to provide intensive training to prepare the bank's employees to meet the rigours of a rapidly changing banking environment. Here the bank's former chairman and CEO, Al Flood, leads a seminar.[48]

It is important to note that most organizational training is not as formal as the approaches we have been describing. Still, training is involved in everyday job instruction in which employees simply are told about the job, shown how to do it, and allowed to practise as a more experienced coworker watches and offers suggestions. Informal though it may be, this is also training, and it requires every bit as much attention to the principles of learning for it to be successful as any more formal method.

As you might imagine, no one approach to training is ideal. Some techniques are better suited to learning certain skills because they incorporate more principles of learning. Not surprisingly, the best training programs often use many different approaches, thereby assuring that several different learning principles may be incorporated into training.[49] If you recall some of the ways you learned skills such as how to study, drive, or use a word processor, you probably can appreciate some of the principles that help make training effective. Four major principles are most relevant.

participation Active involvement in the process of learning; more active participation leads to more effective learning.

1. **Participation.** People not only learn more quickly, but also retain the skills longer when they have actively participated in the learning process. This applies to the learning of both motor tasks as well as cognitive skills. For example, when learning to swim, there's no substitute for actually getting in the water and moving your arms and legs. In the classroom, students who listen attentively to lectures, think about the material, and get involved in discussions tend to learn more effectively than those who just sit passively.

repetition The process of repeatedly performing a task so that it may be learned.

2. **Repetition.** If you know the old adage "Practice makes perfect," you are already aware of the benefits of repetition for learning. Perhaps you learned the multiplication table, or a poem, or a foreign-language phrase by going over it repeatedly. Indeed, mentally "rehearsing" such cognitive tasks has been shown to increase our effectiveness at performing them.[50] Scientists have established not only the beneficial effects of repetition on learning, but have shown that these effects are even greater when practice is spread out over time than when it is lumped together. After all, when practice periods are too long, learners can suffer from fatigue, whereas learning a little bit at a time allows the material to sink in.

transfer of training The degree to which the skills learned during training sessions may be applied to performance of one's job.

3. **Transfer of training.** As you might imagine, for training to be most effective, what is learned during training sessions must be applied on the job. In general, the more closely a training program matches the demands and conditions faced on a job, the more effective that training will be. A good example is the elaborate simulation devices used to train pilots and astronauts. More down to earth is the equipment used in many technical schools for people to learn skilled trades

such as welding, computer repair, and radiation technology. By closely simulating actual job conditions, training skills are expected to transfer to the job.

The same may be said of training in supervisory skills. In this context, research has shown that the benefits of training are best realized when the trainees attempt to apply their newly learned skills in organizations that accept the forms of supervision they learned.[51] However, learning to supervise others in ways that may be resisted back on the job may be not only a waste of time, but potentially disruptive as well.

feedback Knowledge of the results of one's behaviour.

4. **Feedback.** It is extremely difficult for learning to occur in the absence of feedback—that is, knowledge of the results of one's actions. Feedback provides information about the effectiveness of one's training.[52] Of course, unless you learn what you already are doing well and what behaviours you need to correct, you probably will be unable to improve your skills. For example, it is critical for people being trained as word processing operators to know exactly how many words they correctly entered per minute if they are to be able to gauge their improvement.

360° feedback The practice of collecting performance feedback from multiple sources at a variety of organizational levels.

☞ *Because 360° feedback also helps assess the performance of an organization as a whole, it is often used in conjunction with* organizational development *efforts. Such practices are presented in Chapter 16.*

One type of feedback that has become popular in recent years is known as **360° feedback**—the process of using multiple sources from around the organization to evaluate the work of a single individual. This goes beyond simply collecting feedback from superiors, as is customary, but extends to the gathering of feedback from other sources, such as one's peers, direct reports (i.e., immediate subordinates), and customers—even oneself (see Figure 3-12).[53] Many companies—General Electric, AT&T, Digital Equipment Corporation, Nabisco, and Warner-Lambert among them—have used 360° feedback to give more complete performance information to their employees, greatly improving not only their own work but overall corporate productivity as well.

In sum, these four principles—*participation, repetition, transfer of training*, and *feedback*—are key to the effectiveness of any training program. The most effective training programs are those that incorporate as many of these principles as possible. In recent years, large organizations have found it worthwhile not only to train their own employees, as we have been discussing, but also to train the employees of other companies with which they do business. For a closer look at this unusual practice, see The Quest for Quality section on page 90.

Organizational Behaviour Management: Positively Reinforcing Desirable Organizational Behaviours

Earlier, in describing operant conditioning, we noted that the consequences of our behaviour determine whether we repeat it or abandon it. Behaviours that are rewarded tend to be strengthened and repeated in the future. With this in mind, it is possible to administer rewards selectively to help reinforce behaviours that we wish repeated in the future. This is the basic principle behind **organizational behaviour management** (also known as **organizational behaviour modification**, or more simply, **OB Mod**). Organizational behaviour management may be defined as the systematic application of positive reinforcement principles in organizational settings for the purpose of raising the incidence of desirable organizational behaviours.

organizational behaviour management (also known as **organizational behaviour modification** or **OB Mod**) The practice of altering behaviour in organizations by systematically administering rewards.

To be effective in using organizational behaviour management programs, managers should follow the steps outlined as follows:[54]

1. *Pinpoint the desired behaviours.* That is, specify exactly what you want done differently (e.g., saying that you want to answer customers' inquiries 50 percent quicker, instead of saying that you want to improve customer service).

2. *Perform a baseline audit.* In other words, determine exactly how well people perform the behaviour they wish to change (e.g., how quickly do they currently answer calls?).

3. *Define a criterion standard.* Determine exactly what performance goal is being sought. For example, should all calls be answered within the first 30 seconds?

Figure 3-12 360° Feedback: An Overview

Many of today's companies have begun using *360° feedback*, the process of using multiple sources of feedback to improve performance.

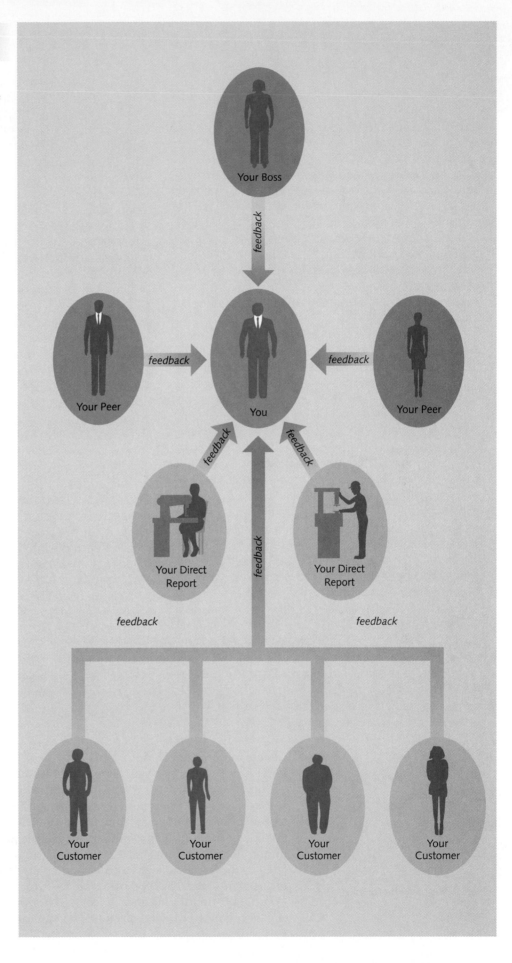

Corporate Goliaths Training Corporate Davids

Almost all companies purchase goods from outside suppliers. Frequently, these vendors are very small companies that are so inefficiently run that they are forced to charge high prices just to stay afloat. This situation, in combination with the uneven quality and availability of their products, can spell serious problems for corporations that are dependent on them. Several of today's larger companies have taken an ingenious step to combat this problem: They are training employees of those companies with which they do business.[55]

GE Capital, for example, has opened a "Small Business College" inside its Stamford, Connecticut, headquarters. It offers classroom training and on-site counselling to small businesses in urban areas, focusing on all the business basics from accounting to human resources management. As you might imagine, GE's interests are far from altruistic. The more they can get small business owners to understand what it takes to operate profitably, the more appreciative they will become of the company's line of small business loans (and, of course, the more confident they can be that these will be repaid). By helping small businesses grow and prosper, GE Capital is doing much to develop its own business. Canadian Imperial Bank of Commerce (CIBC) is taking the same approach. The bank's *Managing and Financing Independent Business Seminar* is designed to help franchisees to be successful.[56] The bank also has a support network to assist aboriginal entrepreneurs.[57]By training entrepreneurs in various financial skills, it is helping to develop more knowledgeable companies with which to do business.

Other large companies have trained their suppliers in different ways, such as focusing on ways of getting these vendors to operate more effectively so that they could reap the benefits (such as lower prices, consistent quality, and availability). For example, about a third of Allied Signal's suppliers are small companies (annual sales under $10 million). To improve their manufacturing quality and efficiency, Allied Signal provides practical training in ways for these suppliers to improve the quality and efficiency of their manufacturing processes. Kodak has taken another approach to accomplishing the same goal. It has formed joint teams—some 500 of them—composed of Kodak managers and suppliers who work together to find ways those vendors might improve the quality, design, and cost of their products. To provide an incentive, half of whatever Kodak saves as a result of this process is returned to the suppliers.

Still other companies are working with their suppliers on a one-on-one basis. Notably, Honda of America sends technicians to its suppliers' plants to teach their employees ways of improving efficiency, cutting waste, reducing inventory, and trimming downtime. At Northrop/Grumman, engineers pay regular monthly visits to key suppliers to monitor the quality of their manufacturing processes. They also share the company's advanced computer technology to help suppliers design better parts. At Hughes Electronics, a mentorship program is used to develop the expertise of small companies owned by members of minority groups so that these individuals can become eligible for government contracts—including, of course, ones involving Hughes (we will describe mentorship more fully in Chapter 7).

Despite their different approaches, these big companies are all doing essentially the same thing: building their own businesses by developing the skills of those other smaller companies with which they do business. Just as companies invest in their own employees, they are finding it beneficial to invest in their own suppliers. The improvements in quality that result are shared by both the Davids and the Goliaths alike.

---

4. ***Choose a reinforcer.*** Decide exactly how the desired behaviour will be rewarded. Will service agents be given a bonus for answering all calls received in a month within 30 seconds? If so, what form will the bonus take? Many of today's companies have been using nonmonetary incentives, in part because they serve as reminders of one's accomplishments (a $100 cheque can be gone in no time flat, but the reward value of a trophy on the mantle persists for a long time).[58] Some nonmonetary incentives have been quite exotic, such as Caribbean cruises offered by the Royal Bank of Canada,[59] and balloon trips over the Napa Valley and mountain-climbing expeditions to the Swiss Alps offered by MCI Communications.[60] But incentives need not be so elaborate: Praise is a highly effective reinforcer in organizations, and an inexpensive one at that.

MCI WorldCom Inc.
www.mciworldcom.com

5. ***Selectively reward desired behaviours that approximate the criterion standard.*** In other words, the learning process may be facilitated by rewarding behaviours that come close to the desired level. So, for example, if agents are answering calls within 60 seconds, their progress should be rewarded. But after a while, reward should only be given after the 50-second level is reached, then the 40-second level, and so on. The process of selectively reinforcing a behaviour that approaches a goal is known as **shaping**. This technique, frequently used in training animals to perform tricks, applies equally well to teaching human beings to perform a desired behaviour.

6. ***Periodically reevaluate the program.*** Is the goal behaviour still performed? Are the rewards still working? Changes in these events over time should be expected. As a result, administrators of behaviour management programs must carefully monitor the behaviours they worked so hard to develop.

Organizational behaviour management programs have been used successfully to stimulate a variety of behaviours in many different organizations (see summary in Table 3-3).[61] For example, a particularly interesting and effective program has been used in recent years at Diamond International, a U.S. company of 325 employees that manufactures Styrofoam egg cartons. In response to sluggish productivity, a simple but elegant reinforcement was put into place. Any employee working for a full year without an industrial accident is given 20 points. Perfect attendance is given 25 points. Once a year, the points are totalled. When employees reach 100 points, they get a blue nylon jacket with the company's logo on it and a patch identifying their membership in the "100 Club." Those earning still more points receive extra awards. For example, at 500 points, employees can select any of a number of small household appliances. These inexpensive prizes go a long way toward symbolizing to employees the company's appreciation for their good work.

This program has helped improve productivity dramatically at Diamond International. After the inauguration of the OB Mod program, output improved 16.5 percent, quality-related errors dropped 40 percent, grievances decreased 72 percent, and time lost due to accidents was lowered by 43.7 percent. The result of all of this has been over U.S.$1 million in gross financial benefits to the company—and a much happier workforce. Although not all such programs are equally successful, evidence suggests that they are generally quite beneficial.

TABLE 3-3 Organizational Behaviour Management Programs: Some Success Stories

Although not all organizational behaviour management programs are as successful as the ones summarized here, many have been extremely effective in bringing about improvements in desired behaviours.

Source: Based on material appearing in Frederiksen, 1982 and, Cox, 1993, see Note 61.

Company	Reinforcers Used	Results
Marine Atlantic	Praise and recognition	Consumer satisfaction increased from 72 percent to 95 percent in three years, cost savings resulted
General Electric	Praise and constructive reinforcement	Productivity increased, cost savings resulted
Weyerhaeuser	Contingent pay, and praise or recognition	Productivity increased in mostwork groups (by 18–33 percent)
B. F. Goodrich Chemical	Praise and recognition	Production increased more than 300 percent
Connecticut General Life Insurance	Time off based on performance	Chronic absenteeism and lateness were drastically reduced
General Mills	Praise and feedback for meeting objectives	Sales increased

Discipline: Eliminating Undesirable Organizational Behaviours

discipline The process of systematically administering punishments.

Just as organizations systematically use rewards to encourage desirable behaviour, they also use punishment to discourage undesirable behaviour. Problems such as absenteeism, lateness, theft, and substance abuse cost companies vast sums of money, situations many companies attempt to manage by using **discipline**—the systematic administration of punishment.

By administering an unpleasant outcome (e.g., suspension without pay) in response to an undesirable behaviour (e.g., excessive tardiness), companies seek to minimize that behaviour. In one form or another, using discipline is a relatively common practice. Survey research has shown, in fact, that 83 percent of companies use some form of discipline, or at least the threat of discipline, in response to undesirable behaviours.[62] But, as you might imagine, disciplinary actions taken in organizations vary greatly. At one extreme, they may be very formal, such as written warnings that become part of the employee's permanent record. At the other extreme, they may be informal and low-key, such as friendly reminders and off-the-record discussions between supervisors and their problem subordinates. In a recent study, Trahan and Steiner asked a sample of nursing supervisors to list the disciplinary actions they most used.[63] They found that a broad range of disciplinary measures was used, including giving warnings (both oral and written), counselling the employee, putting the employee on probation, and termination. Although these responses come from a limited sample, we suspect that these results are fairly typical of what would be found across a wide variety of jobs.

progressive discipline The practice of gradually increasing the severity of punishments for employees who exhibit unacceptable job behaviour.

One very common practice involves using punishment *progressively*—that is, starting mildly and then increasing in severity with each successive infraction. This is the idea behind **progressive discipline**—the practice of basing punishment on the frequency and severity of the infraction.[64] Let's consider an example of how progressive discipline might work for a common problem such as chronic absenteeism or tardiness. First, the supervisor may give the employee an informal oral warning. Then, if the problem persists, there would be an official meeting with the supervisor, during which time a formal warning would be issued. The next offence would result in a formal written warning that becomes part of the employee's personnel record. Subsequent offences would lead to suspension without pay. And finally, if all this fails, the employee would be terminated. In the case of more serious offences—such as gambling, for example—some of the preliminary steps would be dropped, and a formal written warning would be given. For the most serious offences, such as stealing or intentionally damaging company property, officials would move immediately to the most severe step, immediate dismissal.

Companies with the most effective disciplinary programs tend to make the contingencies clear, such as by publicizing punishment rules in the company handbook. When this is done, employees know exactly what kind of behaviours the company will not tolerate, often minimizing the need to actually use discipline at all.

It probably comes as no surprise to you that supervisors do not always punish all inappropriate behaviours they encounter.[65] A key reason for this is that supervisors may feel constrained by limitations imposed by labour unions or by their own lack of formal authority. Also, in the absence of a clear company policy about how to use discipline, individuals may fear strong negative emotional reactions from the punished individual, if not also revenge and retaliation. As a result, many supervisors may turn the other way and simply do nothing when employees behave inappropriately. Although doing nothing may be easy in the short run, ignoring chronic problems is a way of informally approving of them, leading to increasingly serious problems in the future. For a discussion of this phenomenon, see **THE ETHICS ANGLE**.

With this in mind, companies with the best disciplinary programs make it a practice to take immediate action. At Honda of America, for example, human resource specialist Tim Garrett notes that the company pays very close attention to all infractions of the rules, including ones "that other companies wouldn't think of paying attention to," adding, "if there's a problem, we'll pay attention to it right away."[66]

Coverups in the Military: Do Sexual Harassment and Sexual Assault Go Unpunished?

In 1992, several hundred men in the U.S. navy were accused of sexually harassing some 90 U.S. navy women while attending a meeting at a Las Vegas hotel. The specific accusations are too distasteful to recount, but suffice it to say that the infractions were not only serious but quite widespread. In fact, such incidents of harassment had been going on regularly during these meetings for several years—rituals that the male sailors regarded as fun, rewards associated with attending.

When complaints were issued in the past, navy brass simply turned a blind eye to the incidents, suggesting that "boys will be boys." In 1992, however, the outcries went public, resulting in the resignation of the secretary of the navy. But still, not much else happened. The navy's highest-ranking admiral was asked to resign, but he later received a reprieve from the secretary of defense. And of the hundreds of men alleged to have been involved, only a handful were disciplined at all—and only very slightly. Two years later, the woman who filed the initial complaint, Lt. Paula Coughlin, was forced to resign from the navy, explaining that the hateful treatment she received following the incident limited her ability to serve. Bottom line: 90 women were assaulted, but not one of the men responsible ever faced a court-martial or any other serious disciplinary action.

Some have questioned whether this response sends the message that at least some degree of sexual harassment is permitted in the U.S. navy—unofficially, of course.[67] When undesirable behaviour is left unpunished, the message is sent that such behaviour is condoned.

The Canadian military has been facing similar charges. Articles in *Maclean's*, arising from interviews with women in the Canadian forces who reported being sexually assaulted, "...reveal a culture—particularly in the navy and combat units—of unbridled promiscuity, where harassment is common, heavy drinking is a way of life, and women...are often little more than game for sexual predators."[68] In the wake of these unwanted behaviours, the Ministry of Defence has instituted strategies including anti-harassment programs, a grievance board, and a military investigation unit in response to the growing public awareness of this issue. While some women who are members of the Canadian forces vehemently disagreed with the notion that sexual harassment pervades the Canadian military, they did not deny the plausibility of the reports on which the *Maclean's* articles were based.[69] Further, the *Maclean's* reports suggest that the roots of sexual harassment in the Canadian military are deep and have been supported passively and, in some cases, actively by some officers.[70] The message that is learned by observing such tolerant reactions to such profoundly unethical behaviour must be considered carefully by any organization desiring to curb this behaviour.

Maclean's
www.macleans.ca

Obviously, it isn't easy to know exactly when and how to administer punishment, and how it can be done in a way that is considered fair and reasonable. Fortunately, research and theory have pointed to some effective principles that may be followed to maximize the effectiveness of discipline in organizations.[71] We will now consider several of these key principles.

1. ***Deliver punishment immediately after the undesirable response occurs.*** The less time that passes between the occurrence of an undesirable behaviour and the administration of a negative consequence, the more likely people are to make the connection between them. When people make this association, the consequence is likely to serve as a punishment, thereby reducing the probability of the unwanted behaviour. With this principle in mind, it is best for managers to talk to their subordinates about their undesirable behaviours immediately after committing them (or, at least as soon thereafter as may be practical). Expressing disapproval after several days or weeks have gone by will be less effective because the passage of time will weaken the association between behaviour and its consequences.

2. ***Give moderate levels of punishment—nothing too high or too low.*** If the consequences for performing an undesirable action are not very severe (e.g.,

rolling one's eyes as a show of disapproval), then it is unlikely to operate as a punishment. After all, it is quite easy to live with such a mild response. In contrast, consequences that are overly severe might be perceived as unfair and inhumane.[72] When this occurs, not only might the individual resign, but a strong signal will also be sent to others about the unreasonableness of the company's actions. In either case, the company risks losing its most valuable assets—its human resources.

3. ***Punish the undesirable behaviour, not the person.*** Good punishment is impersonal in nature and focuses on the individual's actions rather than his or her personality. So, for example, when addressing an employee who is repeatedly caught taking excessively long breaks it is unwise to say, "You're lazy and have a bad attitude." Instead, it would be better to say, "By not being at your desk when expected, you're making it more difficult for all of us to get our work done on time." Responding in this manner will be less humiliating for the individual, making the discussion far less unpleasant. Additionally, focusing on exactly what people can do to avoid such disapproval (taking shorter breaks, in this case) increases the likelihood that they will attempt to alter their behaviour in the desired fashion. By contrast, the person who feels personally attacked might not only "tune out" the message, but not know exactly how to improve.

4. ***Use punishment consistently—all the time, for all employees.*** Sometimes, managers attempting to be lenient turn a blind eye to infractions of company rules. Doing this may cause more harm than good insofar as it inadvertently reinforces the undesirable behaviour (by demonstrating that one can get away with breaking the rules). As a result, it is considered most effective to administer punishment after each occurrence of an undesirable behaviour. Similarly, it is important to show consistency in the treatment of all employees. In other words, everyone who commits the same infraction should be punished the same way, regardless of the person administering the punishment. When this occurs, supervisors are unlikely to be accused of showing favouritism. Also, if one supervisor is perceived to be very lenient and another very harsh, subordinates may learn to avoid the harsh supervisor rather than the undesirable behaviour.

5. ***Clearly communicate the reasons for the punishment given.*** Making clear exactly what behaviours lead to what disciplinary actions greatly facilitates the effectiveness of punishment. Clearly communicated expectations help strengthen the perceived connection between behaviour and its consequences. Wise managers use their opportunities to communicate with subordinates to make clear that the punishment being given does not constitute revenge, but an attempt to eliminate an unwanted behaviour (which, of course, it is). Communicating information about poor performance in a personal interview is a good idea, but doing so isn't easy. To make such interviews as effective as possible, managers should conduct them systematically, following the steps outlined in Figure 3-13.[73]

6. ***Do not follow punishment with noncontingent rewards.*** Imagine that you are a supervisor who has just written a formal letter of discipline in reaction to a serious infraction of the rules by a particular subordinate. The disciplined employee is feeling very low, which makes you feel remorseful. Feeling bad, you reduce your guilt by telling the employee that he can take the rest of the day off with pay. Although this may make you feel better, it poses a serious problem: You inadvertently rewarded the person for the unwanted behaviour. The serious infraction was punished by the letter but rewarded by the time off. Consequently, the effect of the punishment may be greatly diminished. More seriously, such an action sends the wrong message to the other employees. Soon, they too may learn that you will give them time off if they display the proper degree of dejection. The advice is clear: For punishment to be most effective, supervisors should refrain from inadvertently rewarding undesirable behaviours.

Figure 3-13 Conducting a Disciplinary Interview: Some Key Steps

It is never easy to communicate a performance problem. Following the steps listed here will help ensure that the problem is identified and that the consequences for failing to improve are made clear.

(Source: Based on suggestions by Lussier, 1990; see Note 73.)

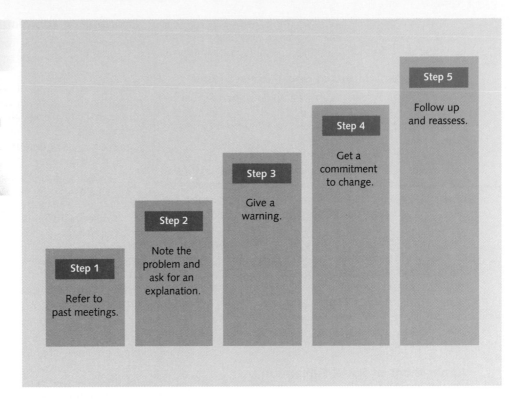

As obvious as this suggestion may be, it is not always followed.[74] In fact, a recent survey has revealed that top executives recognize that today's organizations frequently reward behaviours *opposite* to those they really desire.[75] For example, although they tend to hope for teamwork and collaboration, they tend to reward the best individual team member. Similarly, although we tend to hope for high achievement, we tend to reward merely putting in another year of service. Thus, it cannot be said that organizations do a good job of rewarding desirable behaviours. In fact, many times they do just the opposite.

If, after reading all this, you are thinking that it is truly difficult to properly administer rewards and punishments in organizations, you have reached the same conclusion as experts in the field of organizational behaviour. Indeed, one of the key skills that makes some managers so effective is their ability to influence others by properly administering rewards and punishments.

SUMMARY AND REVIEW

The Processes of Social Perception and Attribution

Perception is the process through which people select, organize, and interpret the information around them. When this process focuses on the interpretation of information about people, it is referred to as **social perception**.

The process of **attribution** involves judging the underlying reasons for people's behaviour. Some of our judgments are based on inferences made on the basis of

observing others' behaviour. These judgments, known as **correspondent inferences**, are often inaccurate. Our search for explanations about the causes of others' behaviour leads us to make either judgments of *internal causality* (the individual is responsible for his or her own actions) or *external causality* (someone or something else is responsible). **Kelley's theory of causal attribution** explains that such judgments will be based on three types of information: *consensus* (whether others act in a similar manner), *consistency* (whether the individual previously acted this way in the same situation), and *distinctiveness* (whether this person acted similarly in different situations).

The Imperfect Nature of Social Perception

Several types of systematic errors, known as **perceptual biases**, limit the accuracy of social perception. These include the **fundamental attribution error** (the tendency to attribute others' actions to internal causes), the **halo effect** (the tendency to perceive others in either consistently positive or negative terms), the **similar-to-me effect** (the tendency to perceive similar others in a favourable light), **first impression error** (the tendency for initial impressions to guide subsequent ones), and **selective perception** (the tendency for people to focus on only certain aspects of the environment). Perceptual inaccuracies also result from the tendency for people to rely on the use of **stereotypes** (the judgments of others based on the categories to which they belong).

Perceptual biases are not easily overcome, although attempts at doing so can be made by considering the external causes of others' behaviour, identifying and confronting one's stereotypes, evaluating others objectively, and avoiding rash judgments.

Applications of Social Perception in Organizations

Biased judgments about others sometimes occur during the process of **performance appraisal**. In this context, research has shown that people judge as superior those individuals whose performance matches their expectations, and those whose good performance is attributed to internal sources and whose poor performance is attributed to external sources.

People are generally interested in getting others to perceive them favourably, and their efforts in this regard are referred to as **impression management**. This process is particularly important in **employment interviews**, although it sometimes interferes with the accuracy of information presented about individuals or companies. An organization's overall impression on people, its **corporate image**, is a determinant of its ability to attract qualified job applicants.

Principles of Learning

Learning refers to relatively permanent changes in behaviour occurring as a result of experience. In organizations, two approaches are most common. In the **operant conditioning** approach, individuals learn to behave certain ways based on the consequences of those actions. Stimuli that increase the probability of the behaviours preceding it are known as **reinforcers**. Reinforcement may be either *positive*, if it is based on the presentation of a desirable outcome, or *negative*, if it is based on the withdrawal of an unwanted outcome. The probability of certain responses can be decreased if an unpleasant outcome results (**punishment**), or if a pleasant outcome is withdrawn (**extinction**).

Observational learning involves learning by modelling the behaviour of others. By paying attention to and rehearsing the behaviour of others, we can learn vicariously, that is, through the model's experiences.

Applications of Learning Principles in Organizations

Learning is directly involved in efforts to teach people to acquire new job skills, the process of **training**. Training is most effective when people can actively participate in the learning process, repeat the desired behaviours, receive feedback on their performance, and learn under conditions closely resembling those found on the job (i.e., *transfer of training*).

Organizational behaviour management is a systematic attempt to apply principles of reinforcement to the workplace in order to improve organizational functioning. Studies have shown that reinforcing desired behaviours can greatly improve organizational functioning.

In contrast to applications of reinforcement, **discipline** is the systematic application of punishments to minimize undesirable organizational behaviours. The effects of discipline are most effective when punishment is applied immediately after the undesirable activity, moderately severe, focused on the activity rather than the individual, applied consistently over time, and for all employees, clearly explained and communicated, and not weakened by the use of inadvertent rewards.

CASE PREVIEW QUESTIONS FOR DISCUSSION

1. What do you think might be gained and lost in the effectiveness of Nortel's training process as it moves to more virtual-reality training formats?

2. Do you agree that Nortel is a "cool company to work for"? Explain.

3. What could the company do to make itself even more appealing to new graduates in the twenty-first century?

CHAPTER QUESTIONS FOR DISCUSSION

1. Describe an organizational situation in which it would be important to judge whether someone's behaviour stems primarily from internal or external causes.

2. How do stereotypes influence the way we judge others in organizations? How may stereotypical judgments be overcome?

3. What kinds of things might people do to be able to enhance the impressions they leave on others in organizations?

4. Identify an organizational event in which operant conditioning is used and one in which observational learning is used.

5. Name four different schedules of reinforcement and describe how each may be used in organizations.

6. Describe how principles of reinforcement and punishment are used in organizational behaviour management programs and disciplinary programs.

CASE IN POINT

CIBC's Leadership Centre: Employee Education As a Survival Imperative

North of Toronto, in what was a spa, is CIBC's Leadership Centre, an innovative facility dedicated to a different kind of learning. Ongoing employee education here is seen as a survival imperative for the twenty-first century.[76] While businesses have traditionally measured their success through the accumulation of financial capital and other more tangible assets, in the new millennium the focus is shifting to the development of human capital.

CIBC has focused on the formation of its corporation's intellectual capital and has committed significant resources to this endeavour. "In CIBC's approach, the bank's intellectual capital is divided into the individual skills needed to meet customers' needs (human capital), the organizational capital demanded by the market (structural capital), and the strength of its franchise (customer capital)."[77]

CIBC's Leadership Centre was started by Hubert St. Onge, the bank's former vice-president, learning organization and development. He differentiated between "how-to" learning that could take place close to the work site, and "mind set" knowledge that focuses on employees' beliefs. The Leadership Centre is a place where employees can learn about the bank's shared vision.[78] St. Onge rejected the notion of training as something that is done to employees in favour of a self-actualization approach to learning. While at CIBC, he emphasized that "for learning to really take place, individual employees have to have full ownership of their learning and full responsibility and accountability for their performance."[79] To achieve this, CIBC offers employees a variety of ways to engage in learning including the support provided by their 14 learning centres across Canada and job-opportunity information online.[80] St. Onge emphasized that there is nothing "magic" about building intellectual capital, "All we're doing is opening new windows on how we define good, effective, value-adding organizations."[81]

During his tenure at CIBC, his emphasis on training bankers to be "apostles of teamwork, leadership, and empowerment"[82] was more than a commitment to a philosophical ideal. St. Onge and others have sought ways to measure intellectual capital and its relationship to an organization's financial performance. CIBC employees receive "competency models" that detail their skills and those they need to target for development. However, measurement of a company's intellectual capital will go further than detailing individual competencies. Systemic analysis of intellectual capital will likely include reports on the number of new ideas produced or new products developed in a fiscal year. However, there is no question that developing a reliable and functional system of intellectual capital accounting remains a challenge.[83]

Building intellectual capital means unleashing a company's full capacity for development. From new hires to burned-out middle managers, St. Onge's vision of self-directed learning can help CIBC employees to realize their full potential.

Critical Thinking Questions

1. If you were a trainer in a private Canadian company, would you "benchmark" Mr. St. Onge's training methods and adopt his philosophy of training? Explain.

2. How can managers measure human capital, structural capital, and customer capital?

3. What differences would you expect to see between a traditional classroom-style training session and sessions based on the CIBC Leadership Centre's self-actualization approach to learning?

SKILLS PORTFOLIO

Experiencing Organizational Behaviour

Identifying Occupational Stereotypes

Although we usually focus our concern over stereotypes on women and members of racial and ethnic minorities, the simple truth is that people can hold stereotypes toward members of just about *any* group. In organizations, people are likely to hold stereotypes about people based on a variable whose importance cannot be overstated—the occupational groups to which they belong. What we expect of people, and the way we treat them, is likely to be affected by stereotypes about their professions. This exercise will help you better understand this phenomenon.

Directions

Using the scale below, rate each of the following occupational groups with respect to how much of the characteristics listed members of these groups tend to show.

1 = not at all
2 = a slight amount
3 = a moderate amount
4 = a great amount
5 = an extreme amount

- Accountants
____ interesting
____ generous
____ intelligent
____ conservative

- Professors
____ interesting
____ generous
____ intelligent
____ conservative

- Lawyers
____ interesting
____ generous
____ intelligent
____ conservative

- Clergy
____ interesting
____ generous
____ intelligent
____ conservative

- Physicians
____ interesting
____ generous
____ intelligent
____ conservative

- Plumbers
____ interesting
____ generous
____ intelligent
____ conservative

Questions for Discussion

1. Did your ratings of the various groups differ? If so, which were perceived most positively and which were perceived most negatively?
2. To what extent did your ratings agree with those of others? In other words, was there general agreement about the stereotypical nature of people in various occupational groups?
3. To what extent were your responses based on specific people you know? How did knowledge, or lack of knowledge, of members of the various occupational groups influence your ratings?
4. Do you believe that by becoming aware of these stereotypes you will perpetuate them in the future or refrain from behaving in accord with them? Explain.

Working in Groups

Role Play: The Disciplinary Interview

Knowing how to discipline employees who behave inappropriately is an important managerial skill. The trick is to change the bad behaviour into good behaviour permanently, getting people to accept their mistakes and understand how to correct them. As you might imagine, this is often far more difficult than it sounds. After all, people are generally reluctant to admit their errors and may have developed bad work habits that must be overcome. In addition, they tend to resist being chastised and don't like listening to criticism. Thus disciplining others represents quite a challenge for managers, making it a skill worth developing.

Directions

1. Select four students from the class and divide them into two pairs. One person from each pair should read only the role sheet below for Chris F., machine operator, and the other person from each pair should read only the role sheet for Ravi B., his supervisor. Send both pairs outside the room until called upon.
2. Members of the class will serve as observers and should read both role sheets.
3. Call in the first pair of role players and ask them to spend about 10–15 minutes playing their roles—that is, acting as they would if they were the characters about whom they just read in the role sheets. They should feel free to assume any additional facts not described in these sheets.

4. Members of the class should observe the role play, taking careful notes. The class should *not* get involved in what the actors are saying, but pay close attention to it.
5. Repeat steps 3 and 4 with the second pair of role players.

Role Sheets

CHRIS F., MACHINE OPERATOR:

You have worked at Acme Manufacturing for six years now, and have had a good record. Because you do your job so well, you sometimes take liberties and horse around with your buddies. For example, one Friday afternoon you were caught dancing around the shop floor when a good song came on the radio. Ravi B., your supervisor, called you on the carpet for leaving your station. You think he has it in for you and is trying to run you off the job. Although you were acting silly, you are convinced that it doesn't matter since you were getting your job done. Now, he has called you in to see him to discuss the situation.

RAVI B., SUPERVISOR:

After several years of experience in other shops, you were hired by Acme Manufacturing to be its new shop supervisor, a job you've had for only four months. Things have gone well during that time, but you've been having trouble with one machine operator, Chris F. Chris seems to do an acceptable job, but is not giving it his all. Part of the problem is that he goofs around a lot. You have spoken to him about this informally a few times on the floor, but to no avail. One Friday afternoon you caught him away from his station, dancing around the shop floor. Not only wasn't he doing his own job, but he was distracting the others. You have just called Chris in to see you to discuss the situation.

Questions for Discussion

1. Did the supervisor, Ravi B., define the problem in a nonthreatening way?
2. Did each party listen to the other, or did they shut each other out, merely explaining their own sides of the story?
3. Did Ravi B. suggest specific things that Chris F. could do to improve? Were the specific punishments associated with future bad acts spelled out explicitly?
4. Were the discussions impersonal in nature or did the parties focus on each other's personalities?
5. Considering all these questions, which supervisor would you say did a better job of administering discipline? What could be done to improve the way each supervisor conducted the disciplinary meeting?

TAKE IT TO THE NET

Prentice Hall
COMPANION WEBSITE

We invite you to visit the *Greenberg/Baron/Sales/Owen Companion Website* at *www.prenticehall.ca/greenberg* for this chapter's Internet resources.

CHAPTER 4

Individual Differences:
Personality and Abilities

LEARNING OBJECTIVES

After reading this chapter you should be able to:

1. Define personality and comment on the question of whether it is stable and real.

2. Identify the "big five" dimensions of personality and explain how they are related to organizational behaviour.

3. Explain what is meant by negative affectivity and the Type A behaviour pattern.

4. Explain what is meant by the proactive personality and indicate its effects on organizational behaviour.

5. Describe the Machiavellian personality and steps you can take to protect against persons showing this trait.

6. Distinguish between the work-related motives of achievement, power, and affiliation.

7. Describe the differences between morning and evening persons and the relevance of these individual differences to on-the-job behaviour.

8. Describe the major intellectual and physical abilities.

9. Distinguish between a test's reliability and its validity.

Christine Silverberg: The Force Behind the Force in Calgary

"I had never grown up thinking that girls did certain things and boys did certain things....My mother always told me I could do whatever I wanted to do." Calgary Police Chief Christine Silverberg listened to her mother and became the first woman to head one of Canada's major police forces (see Figure 4-1).[1]

Getting there has not been an easy road. From the Mississauga police superintendent who made her wait eight hours just to get an application for a police job to the commander who told her she was a success in policing because her hormones were not like those of other women, Silverberg has faced challenges not encountered by her male counterparts. To Silverberg, however, the gender issue is irrelevant.[2]

Christine Silverberg describes herself as determined and others agree. Lenna Bradburn, Canada's first woman police chief, confirmed Silverberg's determination and said, "You can get kind of exhausted trying to keep up with her sometimes."[3] This determination gave her the strength to wait the eight hours in Mississauga and it paid off. She was hired as the second woman on the force.[4]

Silverberg graduated from York University in 1970 with a bachelor's degree in sociology. Following graduation she worked as a correctional

officer in Brampton, Ontario before starting her police career working in the Mississauga, Ontario department's youth bureau where she dealt with issues such as child abuse and juvenile crime. When the Mississauga department became part of the Peel Regional Police Service in 1974, Silverberg set up the new department's public relations department and went on to hold a variety of administrative positions. However, at the time she joined the police service, women did not work on uniformed patrol duty. Concerned that this was a liability for future promotions, Silverberg decided to pursue a master's degree in criminology, which she earned in 1983. She felt this might help to compensate for her lack of patrol experience. Silverberg's final job in the Peel department was, in fact, in a uniformed position as an inspector taking responsibility for traffic management. She left the police force in 1990 and joined the Ontario Ministry of the Solicitor General.[5] In 1992 she became deputy chief of administration with the Hamilton-Wentworth (Ontario) Regional Police Service. Her appointment as chief in Calgary came in 1995.

Her rise to the top has been earned through hard work and a clear focus. It is not unusual for her to arrive at work or, for that matter, leave the office at 4:00 A.M.[6] On the job, a lot of her hard work focuses on people. In Calgary, Silverberg is working to give "beat cops" a voice. She is well aware that they are the people who know what is going on in Calgary's streets. According to her deputy chief, Jim Mathews, "She's a people person. . . . When she first arrived, she spent a lot of time talking to us one-to-one to find out what we thought was right and what was wrong, what could be improved and what was fine as it is. It didn't matter what level you were."[7] Her quest for front-line information extends to the streets where she has been known to find officers on duty and invite them to coffee to discuss their concerns. Silverberg's commitment to including all ranks in decision making is exemplified in her use of cross-rank "issue teams" such as the one that wrote a report for the force on promotion policy.[8] "From an internal point of view, people wanted greater communication. There needed to be better

Figure 4-1 Chief Christine Silverberg Stresses People Skills
Despite initial controversy over her salary and other compensation, Christine Silverberg still feels welcome in Calgary. Silverberg is the first woman to become chief of a major metropolitan police force in Canada.[9]

communication, both up and down as well as across the organization," she said.[10]

She has been described sensitive but with the ability to be tough.[11] (She has a copy of Machiavelli's writings on the bookshelf in her office.)[12] Soon after arriving in Calgary, Silverberg made good on wishes expressed by the front-line officers who looked for a reduction in what they saw as a top-heavy bureaucracy. She wiped out an entire level of the force's bureaucracy by offering half its senior officers a retirement package.[13]

Her approachability has made Christine Silverberg a favourite of both the press and the public in Calgary. A *Calgary Herald* columnist credited Silverberg with being open and truly human in her dealings with members of the press. It is clear that this humanity extends to the members of her force. Silverberg has expressed a commitment to encouraging wide participation from police officers at all levels in her drive for all police forces to become "learning organizations."[14]

Calgary Police Service
www.gov.calgary.ab.ca/
police

It is obvious that Chief Christine Silverberg has already followed an amazing career path. The question of *why* she has achieved so much so quickly, however, is much more open to debate. Was it a sea change in law enforcement, simple good luck (being in the right place at the right time), or something about Silverberg herself that put her on the road to such success? The answer certainly involves many different factors, for achievements like Silverberg's are too complex in nature to stem from one or even a few causes.

Having said that, though, we wish to add that it seems clear that Silverberg's success has stemmed, to an important extent, from her own *personality*—her unique set of traits and characteristics. In other words, it took a special kind of person with an unusual combination of personal traits to work her way up the leadership ladder in law enforcement. This suggestion, in turn, points to another that is the underlying theme of this chapter: Personal characteristics (sometimes described as *individual differences*) play a key role in many aspects of organizational behaviour. To provide you with an overview of what we know about the impact of such factors, we'll proceed as follows.

First, we'll define *personality* more precisely and examine contrasting views concerning its relative importance in human behaviour. Next, we'll consider several specific aspects of personality—those that have been found to play an important role in key aspects of organizational behaviour. Third, we'll turn briefly to *abilities*—mental and physical capacities to perform various tasks, and the role of such abilities in work-related behaviour. Finally, we'll examine various methods used to measure personality and abilities. These measurement techniques are essential if we wish to compare individuals with respect to various traits or abilities and to use this information for making practical decisions, such as whom to hire for a specific job or whom to promote.

Personality: Its Basic Nature and Role in Organizational Behaviour

If we learn anything from our experiences with other people it is this: They are all, in some ways, *unique* and all, to a degree, *consistent* in their behaviour. That is, all human beings possess a distinct pattern of traits and characteristics not fully duplicated in any other person; furthermore, many of these characteristics are quite stable over time. Thus, if you know someone who is optimistic, confident, and friendly today, the chances are good that he or she also showed the same traits in the past and will continue to show them in the future, too. Moreover, this person will probably also demonstrate such traits in many different situations. The person will be optimistic, friendly, and confident when making a presentation at work and may also show the same style when meeting people for the first time in a local night spot (see Figure 4-2). Together, these two features form the basis for a useful working defini-

Figure 4-2 Consistency in Individual Behaviour

People often show a considerable amount of consistency in their behaviour both across situations and over time. Such consistency is a central aspect of personality.

personality The unique and relatively stable patterns of behaviour, thoughts, and emotions shown by individuals.

tion of **personality**, which we'll define as the unique and relatively stable pattern of behaviour, thoughts, and emotions shown by individuals.[15] In contrast, *abilities* refer to the capacity to perform various tasks or cognitive activities.[16]

Is Personality Real? The Person-Situation Controversy

Because we often think of behaviour as resulting from stable personal traits, you may find it surprising to learn that some social scientists have rejected the notion of personality, arguing instead that how we behave is mainly determined by the external conditions we face.[17] Indeed, several have gone so far as to claim that what we often describe as personality is really an illusion stemming from the fact that we *want* to perceive consistency in others' behaviour. Why? Because it makes predicting what they will say or do easier.

On the opposite side of this controversy are social scientists who have argued, just as strongly, that stable traits *do* exist and that these lead people to behave consistently across time and in different settings. In support of their claims, they point to the findings of research in which individuals are studied over extended periods of time. The research does indeed show a fair amount of consistency with respect to many aspects of their behaviour.[18] Further support for the reality of personality is provided by research comparing the personalities of identical twins who have been raised together (the usual state of affairs) or, after being separated early in life, in different homes. The findings of such studies indicate that even when raised in sharply different environments, the twins show remarkable similarity in many aspects of their personalities.[19] This evidence, too, supports the view that personality is real—that people *do* show a notable degree of consistency in their behaviour. Moreover, these studies also indicate that genetic factors may well play a role in certain aspects of personality.

Now for another question: If, as growing evidence indicates, personality is indeed much more than an illusion, to what extent is it responsible for how we behave? In other words, do we behave the way we do in a given situation because of personality, because of situational pressures, or both? The answer suggested by careful research on this topic is both. In other words, behaviour in many situations is the result of both an individual's personality and the nature of the situation. For example, consider an individual who is known to all his acquaintances as having a very short fuse; he loses his temper frequently in response to fairly mild provocations.

Now, imagine that one day, this person is stopped for speeding by a state trooper. Will he "blow up" when the officer approaches his car? Perhaps; but it is more likely that he will restrain this tendency and behave in a more polite manner. After all, the costs of losing one's temper in *this* situation are both high and obvious! So, in general, we can say that our behaviour is determined by a complex interaction between our personality traits and the external environment; both are important and can affect what we do or say. Almost all social scientists accept this view—known as the **interactionist perspective**—and it is the dominant position in organizational behaviour, too.

An interesting implication of the interactionist perspective—and one with important implications for organizational behaviour—is that a given work setting may "fit" with the personalities (and abilities) of specific persons to varying degrees. In other words, some persons may find that their traits and abilities closely match those required by a given job, while others find that their traits and abilities do *not* match these requirements. The degree to which there is a "match" between employees' characteristics and their jobs is known as **person-job fit**, and it has recently been the subject of a considerable amount of research.[20] The basic findings of this work are that people are more productive and satisfied when there is a close match between their personal traits and the demands of the job than when this match is less optimal (see Figure 4-3 for an amusing illustration of this fact).[21]

These findings offer support for the importance of considering individual difference variables in efforts to enhance both productivity and job satisfaction. The closer the fit between individuals' personal traits and the requirements of their jobs, the more positive are the results. In view of this fact, it seems worthwhile to consider potential person-job fit in many organizational contexts—for instance, when individuals are hired or considered for promotion.

Work-Related Aspects of Personality

Now that we have established that personality is indeed real and called attention to its potentially important effects, we'll turn to another task: examining several aspects of personality that appear to influence important aspects of organizational behaviour.

The "Big Five" Dimensions of Personality and Organizational Behaviour

How many different words can you think of that describe others' personalities? Would you believe *17 953*? That's the number of personality-related words found in a search of an English language dictionary in a study conducted more than 60 years ago.[22] Even after combining words with similar meanings, the list still contained 171 distinct traits. Does this mean that we must consider a huge list of characteristics to understand fully the role of personality in organizational behaviour? Fortunately, the answer appears to be no. A growing body of evidence points to the conclusion that, in fact, there may be only five key dimensions to consider.

Because these same five dimensions have emerged in so many different studies conducted in so many different ways, they are often referred to as the **"big five" dimensions of personality**.[23] These dimensions can be described as follows:

1. *Conscientiousness:* a dimension ranging from careful, thorough, responsible, organized, self-disciplined, and scrupulous at one end to irresponsible, disorganized, lacking in self-discipline, and unscrupulous at the other.

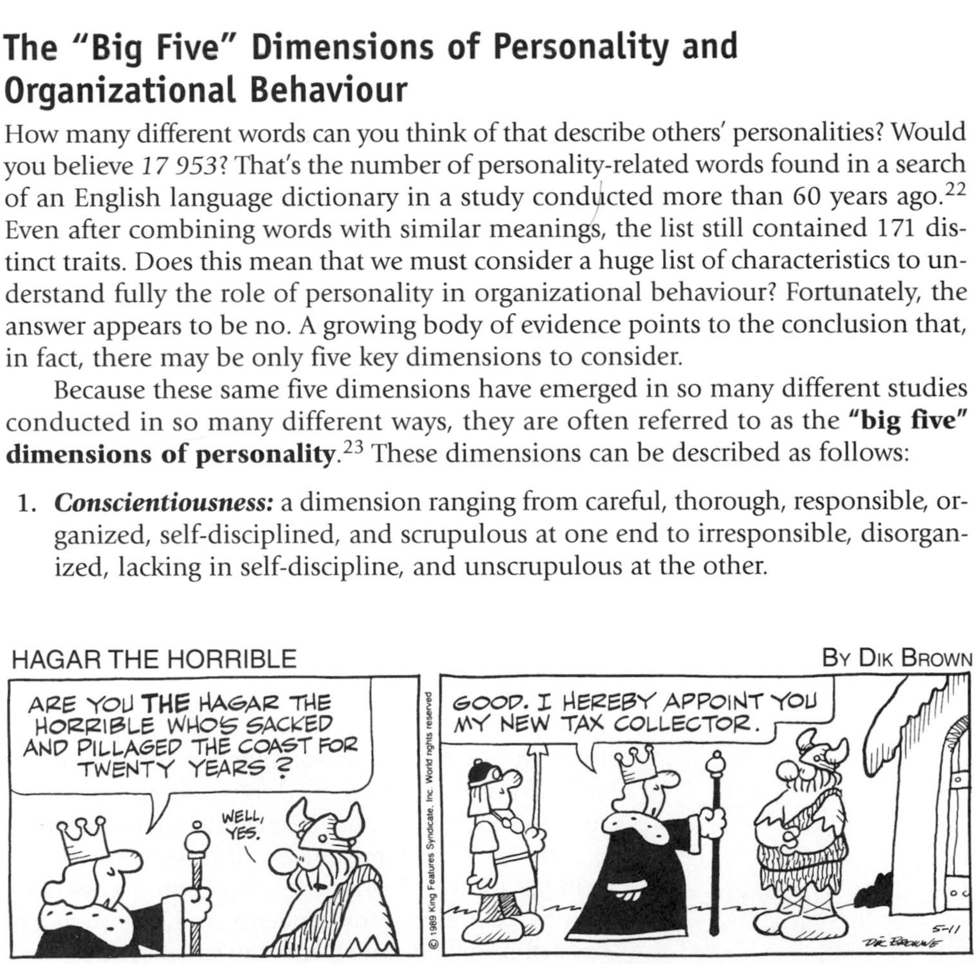

Figure 4-3 Person-Job Fit: An Example

As you can readily see, Hagar's personality traits make him especially well-suited for this particular job. In other words, the person-job fit is high!

(Source: Copyright © 1989. Reprinted with special permission of King Features Syndicate.)

HAGAR THE HORRIBLE   BY DIK BROWN

2. ***Extroversion-Introversion:*** a dimension ranging from sociable, talkative, assertive, and active at one end to retiring, sober, reserved, and cautious at the other.

3. ***Agreeableness:*** a dimension ranging from good-natured, gentle, cooperative, forgiving, and hopeful at one end to irritable, ruthless, suspicious, uncooperative, and inflexible at the other.

4. ***Emotional Stability:*** a dimension ranging from anxious, depressed, angry, emotional, insecure, and excitable at one end to calm, enthusiastic, poised, and secure at the other.

5. ***Openness to Experience:*** a dimension ranging from imaginative, sensitive, intellectual, and polished at one end, to down-to-earth, insensitive, narrow, crude, and simple at the other.

Sample items similar to those used to assess individuals' standing on each of these dimensions are presented in Table 4-1. By completing them, you may be able to gain some insight into just where *you* stand with respect to these traits.

How basic, and therefore important, are the big five dimensions? Many researchers believe that the answer is *very* basic. This is indicated, in part, by the fact that these dimensions are ones to which most people in many different cultures refer in describing themselves.[24] In addition, these dimensions are often readily apparent to total strangers even in very brief meetings.[25]

That these dimensions also play an important role in organizational behaviour is suggested by the findings of many recent studies.[26,27] For example, in one large-scale study, Barrick and Mount examined the results of over 200 separate studies in which at least one of these dimensions was related to job performance.[28] Several interesting findings were uncovered. First, conscientiousness was found to be a good predictor of performance for all types of jobs. As you might expect, highly conscientious employees were generally more productive than unconscientious ones. However, contrary to the researchers' predictions, emotional stability was not found to be related to performance. This may well be because those who are least stable tend to quit their jobs, leaving a restricted sample of relatively stable individuals behind.

Another interesting finding was that for people in managerial and sales positions extroversion was highly related to job success. This is consistent with the popular image of successful salespersons, who are generally viewed as being sociable and outgoing. Another interesting—and perhaps more surprising—finding was that agreeableness was not related to performance across many different jobs. Why? Perhaps, again, because only persons who are at least moderate on this dimension remain on the job; the others are simply too uncooperative and too difficult to last.[29]

TABLE 4-1 The "Big Five" Dimensions of Personality

The items shown here are similar to ones used to measure each of the "big five" dimensions. Does answering them give you insight into your own personality?

Instructions: Indicate the extent to which you agree with each of the items below by entering a NUMBER in the space next to that item. Enter 5 if you strongly agree with the item; 4 if you agree; 3 if you are neutral; 2 if you disagree; and 1 if you strongly disagree.

Conscientiousness:
_____I keep my room neat and clean.
_____I'm not as reliable as I should be.

Extroversion:
_____I like lots of excitement.
_____I'm usually cheerful.

Agreeableness:
_____I'm generally courteous to other people.
_____Some people think I'm cold and sly.

Emotional Stability:
_____I worry a lot.
_____I'm rarely sad or "down."

Openness to Experience:
_____I have a lot of curiosity.
_____I don't like change.

Positive and Negative Affectivity: Stable Tendencies to Feel Good or Bad at Work

Moods fluctuate rapidly, and often widely, during the course of a single day. An e-mail message containing good news may leave us smiling, while an unpleasant conversation with a coworker may leave us feeling "down." Such temporary shifts are only part of the total picture where our affective states—the way we feel at work—are concerned. Superimposed over these rapidly changing reactions are more stable *traits*—consistent differences in the overall tendency to experience positive or negative affect.[30] Some people tend to be "up" most of the time, while others tend to be more subdued or even depressed.

These tendencies are apparent in a wide range of contexts. People who are high in the trait of **positive affectivity** tend to have an overall sense of well-being, see people and events in a positive light, and tend to experience positive emotional states. In contrast, those high in the trait of **negative affectivity** tend to hold negative views of themselves and others, interpret ambiguous situations in a negative manner, and frequently experience negative emotional states.[31] Note, by the way, that these are relatively independent dimensions; they are *not* opposite ends of a single trait.

Do such differences in people's characteristic mood play any role in organizational behaviour? Recent findings suggest that they do. For instance, in one revealing study on this topic, Staw and Barsade assessed the positive and negative affectivity of MBA students who participated in a series of exercises simulating business decision making.[32] Several different measures of performance on this important task were gathered—accuracy (the number of decisions that were correct), rankings of overall performance by other students, and ratings of managerial potential (ratings by experts of the degree to which participants could succeed as a manager). The results were clear: For each of these criteria, people showing positive affectivity were superior to those showing negative affectivity.

Other research indicates that affectivity influences group as well as individual performance. Work groups that have a positive affective tone (that is, the average level of positive affectivity is high) function more effectively than groups that have a negative affective tone (the average level of negative affectivity is high).[33] In sum, a growing body of evidence suggests that stable tendencies to experience positive or negative moods at work have important implications not only for personal happiness and well-being of the individuals involved, but for their organizations as well.

positive affectivity The tendency to experience positive moods and feelings in a wide range of settings and under many different conditions.

negative affectivity The tendency to experience negative moods in a wide range of settings and under many different conditions.

[You Be The Consultant]

A department store has recently noted a sharp increase in customer complaints about one of its departments. These complaints focus on the fact that customers feel they are being ignored by a sales staff that seems completely uninterested in helping them.

1. Could this be due to high levels of negative affectivity among the persons working in the department?

2. If so, what could be done to improve the moods of these persons—and so their level of service to customers?

The Type A Behaviour Pattern: Why Being in a Hurry Can Be Costly to Your Health

Think about the people you know. Can you name one who always seems to be in a hurry, is extremely competitive, and is often irritable? Now, try to name one who shows the opposite pattern—someone who is usually relaxed, not very competitive, and easygoing. The people you have in mind represent extremes on one key dimension of personality. The first person shows signs of what is termed the **Type A behaviour pattern**, while the second shows what is usually termed the **Type B behaviour pattern**.[34] People in the first group—known as Type A's—show high levels of competitiveness, irritability, and time urgency—they are always in a hurry. In contrast, people classified as Type B show the opposite pattern: They are much calmer and laid-back. There are several different techniques for classifying people as Type A's or Type B's, including short questionnaires and special structured interviews.

Type A behaviour pattern A pattern of behaviour involving high levels of competitiveness, time urgency, and irritability.

Type B behaviour pattern A pattern of behaviour characterized by a casual, laid-back style; the opposite of the Type A behaviour pattern.

As you can probably guess, the differences between Type A's and Type B's have vital implications for their behaviour in work settings. The most important of these involve differences in personal health, in task performance, and in relations with others.[35,36] Because we will consider the impact of the Type A behaviour pattern on health later in this book (in connection with our discussion of stress in Chapter 7), we'll focus here on the remaining two issues.

Type A's and performance.   First, do people who are Type A's and Type B's differ with respect to job performance? Given their high level of competitiveness it seems reasonable to expect that Type A's will work harder at various tasks than Type B's and, as a result, will perform at higher levels. In fact, however, the situation turns out to be more complex than this. Type A's *do* tend to work faster on many tasks than Type B's, even when no pressure or deadline is involved. Similarly, they are able to get more done in the presence of distractions.[37] In addition, Type A's often seek more challenges in their work than Type B's: Given a choice, they tend to select more difficult or complex tasks.[38]

But Type A's don't *always* perform better than Type B's. For example, Type A's frequently do poorly on tasks requiring patience or careful judgment. They are simply in too much of a hurry to complete such work effectively.[39] Consistent with this idea are surveys revealing that most top executives are Type B's rather than Type A's.[40] Several factors probably contribute to this pattern. First, it is possible that Type A's simply don't last long enough to rise to the highest management levels; as we'll see in Chapter 7, the health risks of their "always-in-a-hurry" lifestyle are too great! Second, the irritability or hostility often shown by Type A's may have negative effects on their careers, preventing them from rising to the top of their organizations. In fact, Type A's do appear to have very "short fuses"—they often become angry and behave aggressively in situations that other persons tend to ignore.[41] Finally, their impatience is often incompatible with the deliberate, carefully considered decisions required of top-level managers (see Figure 4-4).

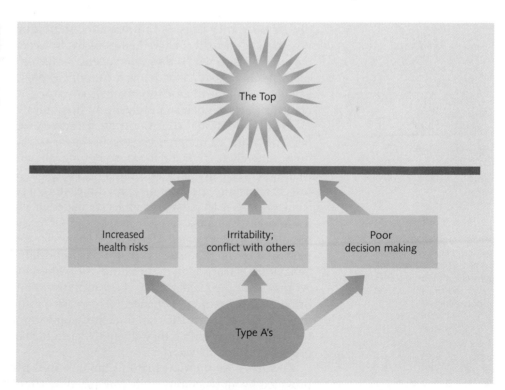

Figure 4-4 Why Type A's Don't Make It to the Top

Research findings indicate that, contrary to what you might guess, most top executives are more Type B than Type A. The factors shown here may provide an explanation for this finding.

Taken together, these findings suggest that neither pattern has an overall edge when it comes to task performance. Although Type A's may excel on tasks involving time pressure or solitary work, Type B's have the advantage when it comes to tasks involving complex judgments and accuracy as opposed to speed. So, the question of whether Type A's or Type B's make more productive employees boils down to the issue of *person-job fit*: The closer the match between job requirements and this aspect of personality, the better performance tends to be. As you'll soon see, the same principle applies to many aspects of personality examined in this chapter.

Type A's and interpersonal relations. What about relations with others? Intuition suggests that here Type B's might well have an edge, and this prediction has been confirmed by research findings. Because of their impatience and irritability, Type A's do tend to annoy their coworkers. Moreover, they are also more likely to lose their tempers and lash out at others. Type A's tend to become involved in more conflicts at work than Type B's.[42] And very recent evidence collected by Baron and Neuman suggests that they may also be more likely to engage in various acts of *workplace aggression* than Type B's.[43] Note that we said *aggression*, not *violence*. As we'll see in Chapter 11, there are many ways in which individuals can seek to harm coworkers other than direct violence against them.

In sum, while Type A's often seem to be cyclones of activity and do tend to move large amounts of work across their desks very quickly, there is definitely a downside to this pattern, both for Type A's themselves and for other members of their organizations. Fortunately, Type A behaviour is not set in stone: It can be modified so that such persons retain the "pluses" of being active, committed, and energetic, while eliminating, or at least reducing, the "minuses" associated with impatience, irritability, and hostility.[44]

☞ We will examine the role of the Type A behaviour pattern in reactions to stress in Chapter 7.

The Proactive Personality: People Who Shape Their Environments

Earlier, we noted that behaviour is often the result of a complex interplay between personal traits on the one hand and situational factors on the other. Put very simply, because they possess various traits, individuals prefer to act in certain ways. Whether they actually behave in these ways, however, depends on the extent to which the situations in which they operate encourage or discourage such behaviours. For example, an individual with a very humorous personality may well make jokes and behave in an amusing or silly manner at parties. In contrast, she or he will probably *not* show such behaviour during an interview for an important job.

While situational constraints often exert powerful effects on the expression of personal traits or preferences, it is also clear that the opposite is also true: People do not merely react to situations; sometimes they take active steps to shape them as well. Recently, Bateman and Crant have suggested that individual differences in this respect constitute another important dimension of personality.[45] They note that while some persons react passively to the external environment, adapting to the conditions it imposes, others take a more active approach, seeking to influence their environment and bend it to *their* preferences. They refer to this dimension as the **proactive personality** trait and suggest that it has important implications for organizational behaviour. Persons high on this dimension, they suggest, identify opportunities and act on them; they take action, show initiative, and persevere until they manage to bring about meaningful change. In contrast, persons low on this dimension show the opposite pattern: They fail to identify opportunities and make little or no effort to change things; rather, they accept the current state of affairs and try to "make the best of things as they are."

Evidence for the view that this dimension is both measurable and important is provided by an ingenious study conducted by Crant.[46] In this investigation, real estate agents completed a measure of the proactive personality trait and measures of two of the big five dimensions of personality we discussed earlier—conscientiousness

proactive personality A personality trait reflecting the extent to which individuals seek to change the environment to suit their purposes and to capitalize on various opportunities.

and extroversion. Their scores on these scales were then related to several measures of job performance: The number of houses they sold, the number of listings they generated, and their commission income. Crant predicted that job performance would be related to the proactive personality trait even when the effects of the big five factors were held constant (i.e., removed statistically). Results confirmed this finding. As shown in Figure 4-5, the higher the real estate agents scored in terms of the proactive personality dimension, the more houses they sold, the larger commissions they earned, and the larger the number of listings they obtained.

How could having a proactive personality lead to such effects? As suggested by Crant, it leads the real estate agents to engage in various proactive behaviours—for instance, advertising their services or visiting persons trying to sell their homes themselves and convincing them to list with the agent. Clearly, the tendency to engage in proactive ways—to seek opportunities and develop them, and, more generally, "to make things happen,"—may also be related to performance of many other jobs and to the success of entire organizations.

Growing awareness of this basic fact has led many companies to concentrate on "growing" their *change agents*—people who get results when they are needed most. Such persons seem to combine proactive attitudes—the belief that things *can* get better—with the ability to motivate others. They persuade and cajole the people around them into doing more than they did before, and often, more than they thought they *could* do. Perhaps most of all, these change agents are flexible: If a method or technique works, they'll adopt it.

According to John R. Katzenbach, who has studied such persons extensively, change agents are crucial for organizational success. They are the ones who translate

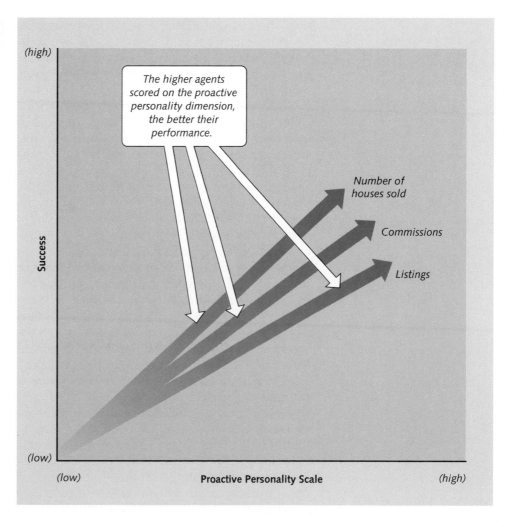

Figure 4-5 The Proactive Personality and Success

The higher real estate agents scored on a measure of the proactive personality dimension, the more successful they were at their jobs.

(Source: Based on data from Crant, 1995, see Note 46.)

new strategies outlined by top management into reality. As Katzenbach notes, it was a shortage of such persons that derailed John Akers's plan to transform IBM in the 1990s. The plan was good, but there were simply not enough change agents in his company to make it happen.[47] To the extent this conclusion is accurate, attracting and retaining such persons is indeed a crucial ingredient in corporate success.

Self-Efficacy: The "Can Do" Facet of Personality

Suppose that two individuals are assigned the same task by their supervisor, and that one is confident of her ability to carry it out successfully, whereas the other has some serious doubts on this score. Which person is more likely to succeed? Assuming that all other factors (for instance, differences in their ability and motivation) are held constant, it is reasonable to predict that the first will do better. Such an individual is higher in **self-efficacy**—the belief in one's own capacity to perform a specific task.[48,49] When considered in the context of a given task, self-efficacy is not, strictly speaking, an aspect of personality. However, people also seem to acquire general expectations about their ability to perform a wide range of tasks in many different contexts. Such generalized beliefs about their task-related capabilities are stable over time, and these can be viewed as an important aspect of personality.

How do beliefs about self-efficacy develop? Existing evidence indicates that there are two major factors involved: *direct experience*—feedback from performing similar tasks in the past—and *vicarious experience*—observations of others' performance on these tasks.[50] On the basis of information from these sources, individuals reach initial conclusions about the skills and abilities required to succeed on the task, whether they possess these, whether there are factors or conditions that may interfere with their performance, and so on. Together, these conclusions shape their current beliefs of self-efficacy. These beliefs, in turn, are then adjusted in the light of new information—for example, further experience with actually performing the task.

Interestingly, recent findings reported by Mitchell and his colleagues suggest that initially, when individuals are acquiring the skills for performing a new task, they devote a great deal of cognitive effort to forming self-efficacy beliefs. They think about many factors that might potentially influence their ability to perform the task—for instance, their alertness, their previous experience, complexity of the task—and exert considerable effort to formulate self-efficacy beliefs. With continued practice, however, they seem to shift to a more *automatic* and less effortful mode of reaching such judgments—one in which they simply consider their previous performance.

Evidence for this kind of shift is provided by an ingenious study conducted by Mitchell and others.[51] In this study, undergraduate students performed a complex air traffic controller task, in which they had to learn a number of different rules in order to perform the task of landing planes safely. The game occurred in discrete trials or sessions and, before several of these trials, participants reported on their self-efficacy and how they reached such judgments. Specifically, they indicated their self-efficacy by reporting their confidence that they could achieve various levels of performance. They also rated the extent to which they considered nine different factors in reaching such judgments: their current alertness, desire to do well, level of effort, current mood, task difficulty, task complexity, task novelty, work disturbances, and past experience with similar tasks. Results indicated that as they gained increasing experience with the tasks, they made such judgments more quickly, and also devoted less attention to many of these factors (see Figure 4-6).

These findings suggest that, as is true with many other tasks we perform, we shift from making self-efficacy judgments in a conscious and careful manner to making such judgments in a faster and more automatic manner. This has important implications for viewing self-efficacy as a personality dimension, because other research indicates that once people have shifted to the automatic mode, they are less likely to change such judgments.[52] Thus, once individuals have concluded that they are relatively high or low in the capacity to perform various tasks, these perceptions become quite resistant to change—with tragic consequences for persons whose conclusion is "I am generally low in self-efficacy." Fortunately, however, such

self-efficacy Individuals' beliefs concerning their ability to perform specific tasks successfully.

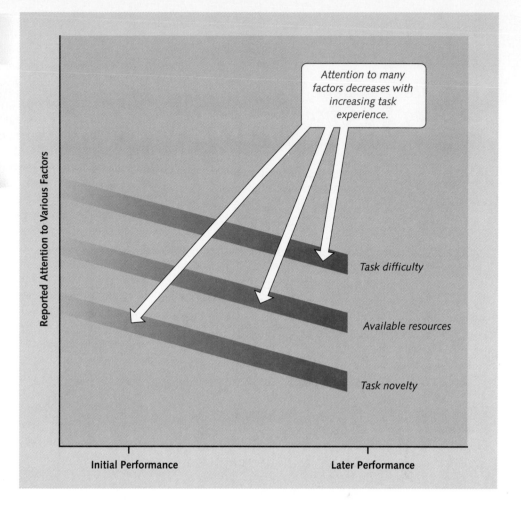

perceptions *can* be altered under appropriate conditions. For some encouraging evidence on this score, please see the **ORGANIZATIONAL TRENDS** section.

Self-Monitoring: Self-Image versus Private Reality

Imagine that you are a first-level supervisor. Will you behave differently when interacting with your subordinates than with your boss or with your boss's boss? Interestingly, research findings indicate that there are large individual differences in this respect. Some people readily change their behaviour so that it matches the specific situation and so that they can make the best possible impression on others. They adopt one style when dealing with their subordinates and another—perhaps more respectful and tentative—when dealing with their boss.

In contrast, other individuals are less willing to change their personal "style" in this manner; with them, "what you see is what you get," across a wide range of contexts. Thus, such persons are less likely to behave differently toward different groups with whom they come into contact. This aspect of personality is known as **self-monitoring**, and it, too, has been found to have important implications for organizational behaviour.[53]

Self-monitoring and performance. First, and perhaps most important, self-monitoring has been found to be related to several aspects of performance. For instance, high self-monitors tend to do better than low self-monitors in jobs requiring what are known as *boundary spanning* activities. These involve communicating and interacting with different groups of people from contrasting professional or occupational groups.[54] Since they can readily adjust their actions to the normal expectations and

self-monitoring A personality trait involving the extent to which individuals adapt their behaviour to the demands of specific situations, primarily to make the best possible impression on others.

☞ *Self-monitoring also plays an important role in conflict; we'll examine this relationship in Chapter 11.*

The Potential Benefits of Boosting Self-Efficacy: Helping People Help Themselves

What makes the difference between winning the Stanley Cup and starting the golf season early? For the 1990 Edmonton Oilers, it may have been the self-efficacy training the team was given by Lou Tice, founder of the Pacific Institute in Seattle. And Tice was so confident his methods would work that he took half his fee after the training session and the other half only after the Oilers had the Stanley Cup firmly in their hands.[55] The members of the Oilers' organization believed they could win the Cup and that may have been just the edge they needed to achieve their goal.

Because so much of our self-concept is tied to our job, whether, for hockey players, it is to win the Stanley Cup or, for blue-collar workers, it is to assemble GM vans, losing a job can be a devastating blow, raising serious doubts about how good we really are at what we do.[56] When such thoughts occur, people might be reluctant to look for new jobs, thinking that they don't stand a chance of succeeding. This can be the start of a vicious cycle: Job loss reduces self-efficacy, which reduces one's effort at searching for a new job, which lowers self-efficacy further, and so on.

Realizing the devastating personal toll that this cycle takes on people, Eden and Aviram[57] developed a technique designed to help people who are unemployed to break the cycle and seek reemployment. They reasoned that self-efficacy could be rebuilt in two ways. First, they had to teach people how to be effective as job seekers—for instance, how to make a convincing presentation of their job skills during an interview. Second, they had to expose their clients to models of people who searched for and found a good job; remember, self-efficacy derives from vicarious as well as direct experiences.

To accomplish these goals, they worked with a group of unemployed Israeli vocational workers (unemployed between 2 and 18 weeks) who enrolled in a special workshop conducted to help them seek reemployment. The workshop, conducted over the two-and-a-half-week period, began with the presentation of four-to-five-minute videotapes showing people successfully performing various job-searching behaviours. These behaviours were then discussed by the group, and reinforced by role-playing sessions in which participants rehearsed the behaviour they saw on the tape. Feedback was provided about how effectively the individual practised the behaviours, and strong verbal encouragement was provided. To determine the effectiveness of the workshops, the investigators compared workshop participants with a similar group of Israeli vocational workers who did not participate.

Some intriguing results were obtained. First, the workshops did raise levels of self-efficacy among the participants. Second, and perhaps even more important, these gains in self-efficacy helped these people in getting a new job. The training received by persons who scored relatively low in self-efficacy at the start of the workshops helped them to conduct more active job searches; in fact, after the workshop they conducted job searches that were just as active as for those who started with high self-efficacy.

These changes in job search paid off in very practical terms. Not only did self-efficacy training get people to engage in more active job searches, but these active searches also increased their chances of obtaining another job (see Figure 4-7).

These findings point to two important conclusions. First self-efficacy is definitely *not* an unchangeable characteristic; rather, it can be significantly raised even by short-term interventions. Second, providing persons who have lost their jobs with self-efficacy-boosting experiences can be highly beneficial: It can help them to conduct better job searches and so increase their chances of obtaining another job.

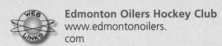

Edmonton Oilers Hockey Club
www.edmontonoilers.com

styles of each group, high self-monitors are more successful in dealing with them, and this improves their performance. Boundary-spanning roles are very important in most organizations, so it makes good sense to consider assigning people high in self-monitoring to such positions.

Self-monitoring and career success. Second, self-monitoring has important effects upon success in one's career. High self-monitors tend to obtain more promotions than low self-monitors, especially when these involve movement from one company to another.[58] Why are high self-monitors more successful in getting ahead than low self-monitors? Perhaps because their greater willingness to adapt their behaviour to each situation they encounter, and to act in ways that please others, helps them to get over the all-important first round of promotion contests.[59] High self-monitors seem to approach various situation by asking, "What kind of person does this situation require, and how can I best be that person?" In contrast, low self-monitors ask, "How can I best be *me* in this situation?" The result is that high self-monitors make a better impression on others and so get the early promotions. Once they do, they are on the "high road" to success, and their careers prosper.

Another reason behind the success of many high self-monitors may be their ability to empathize with others—to "walk around inside their shoes" or see the world through their eyes. Many observers attribute high self-monitoring to the outstanding success of Orit Gadiesh, head of Bain & Co., a highly successful management consulting firm in Boston.[60] Gadiesh is often noticed first for her flamboyant personal style: Her hair sports several different colours, and her skirts start about eight inches above the knee. It is her ability to look at things from others' perspective, however, that truly impresses her clients. It is this high degree of empathy—a characteristic of high self-monitors—that keeps her clients impressed and coming back for more. Interestingly, many studies indicate that women may have an important edge in this respect: They tend to be higher in empathy than men. We'll return to the potential value of empathy in a later discussion of an important form of intelligence.

Self-monitoring and impression management. From our comments so far, you can probably already guess another way in which high and low self-monitors differ: High self-monitors have a distinct edge where the important process of *impression management* is concerned. Since they are willing to change their behaviour or style across situations, they are more effective at doing whatever it takes to generate positive reactions from others. And as we saw in Chapter 3, this can yield many important benefits.

Self-monitoring and mentoring. A fourth effect of self-monitoring on organizational behaviour involves its role in the *mentoring* process—a topic we'll examine in detail in Chapter 7. In mentoring relationships, younger, less experienced employees receive help and guidance from older, more experienced ones, and often this provides an important boost to their careers.[61] Recent findings reported by Turban and Dougherty indicate that high self-monitors are more likely than low self-monitors to initiate mentoring relationships. Specifically, they are more likely to seek to become acquainted with higher-level managers, to make personal efforts to make their work visible to higher-level managers, and to seek counselling and advice from such persons. The result is that they are more successful in obtaining mentors than low self-monitors, with all the benefits this confers.[62]

The potential downside of self-monitoring. Before you conclude that being high in self-monitoring is an unmixed blessing, we should quickly add that there is a downside to this trait, too. Because they are so changeable—some researchers refer to high self-monitors as "social chameleons"—they run the risk of being viewed as unreliable, inconsistent, or even manipulative by others.[63] Similarly, research findings indicate that high self-monitors may tend to form less stable and less deep personal relationships than low self-monitors.[64] Since high self-monitors change their style and behaviour across situations, they may seek different friends for each context. In contrast, low self-monitors remain much the same, so they form fewer—but deeper—relationships. In short, self-monitoring, like most other dimensions of personality, has complex effects, and any assessment of the relative costs and benefits of being high or low on this dimension must take careful account of such complexity.

Machiavellianism: Using Others to Get Ahead

In 1513, the Italian philosopher Niccolo Machiavelli published a book entitled *The Prince*. In it, he outlined a ruthless strategy for seizing and holding political power.

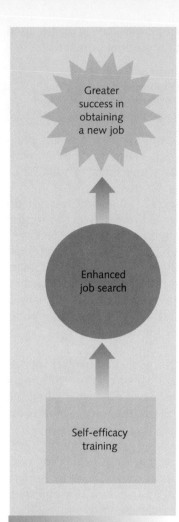

Figure 4-7 The Benefits of Self-Efficacy Training

Individuals who received training designed to boost their self-efficacy conducted more effective job searches and were more successful in obtaining new jobs than those who did not receive such training.

(Source: Based on findings reported by Eden & Aviram, 1993.)

The essence of his approach was straightforward: Other people can be readily used or manipulated by sticking to a few basic rules. Among the guiding principles he recommended were the following:

> Never show humility; arrogance is far more effective when dealing with others. Morality and ethics are for the weak; powerful people feel free to lie, cheat, and deceive whenever it suits their purpose. It is much better to be feared than loved.

In general, Machiavelli urged those who desired power to adopt a totally pragmatic approach. Let others be swayed by friendship, loyalty, or beliefs about fair play; a truly successful leader, he suggested, should always be above those factors. He or she should be willing to do *whatever it takes to get his or her own way.*

Clearly, most people don't adopt Machiavelli's philosophy. But some, at least, do seem to operate according to these principles. This fact led researchers to propose that acceptance of this ruthless creed involves yet another dimension of personality—one known, appropriately, as **Machiavellianism**. Persons high on this dimension (high Machs, as they are termed) accept Machiavelli's suggestions and seek to manipulate others in a ruthless manner.[65] In contrast, persons low on this dimension (low Machs), reject this approach, and *do* care about fair play, loyalty, and other principles Machiavelli rejected. Machiavellianism is measured by means of a relatively brief questionnaire. Sample items similar to ones on the *Mach Scale* are shown in Table 4-2.

Machiavellianism and success.   If high Machs are willing to do whatever it takes to succeed, you might expect that they would tend to be rather successful. The answer seems to be that they are, but primarily in *loosely structured situations*—where there are few established rules.[66] In tightly structured situations, where the rules regarding expected behaviour are clearly stated, high Machs do not appear to have an edge.

Dealing with high Machs.   Because of their merciless approach to dealing with others, high Machs can be difficult to have around in one's work environment. Because they are attracted to situations in which they can use their devious skills and show little concern for the welfare of others, they can be tough adversaries. Although you cannot always restructure work situations so as to block high Machs, there are several steps you can take to protect yourself from them. Here are a few that may prove effective:

1. ***Expose them to others.***   One reason high Machs so often get away with breaking promises, lying, and using "dirty tricks" (see Chapter 12) is that in many cases their victims choose to remain silent. This is hardly surprising because few people wish to call attention to the fact that they have been cheated or manipulated. This understandable desire to protect one's ego, however, plays directly into the

---

Machiavellianism A personality trait involving willingness to manipulate others for one's own purposes.

☛ *Many of the tactics adopted by persons high in Machiavellianism fall under the heading of organizational politics—a topic we'll examine in detail in Chapter 12.*

TABLE 4-2 Measuring Machiavellianism

The items shown here are similar to those contained on one measure of Machiavellianism. Persons who are high Machs tend to agree strongly with items 1, 3, 4, 5, and 8; persons who are low Machs tend to disagree with these items, and to strongly agree with items 2, 6, and 7.

Instructions: Enter a number next to each item. If you disagree strongly enter 1; if you disagree, enter 2; if you are neutral, enter 3; if you agree enter 4; if you strongly agree, enter 5.

_____ **1.** The best way to handle people is to tell them what they want to hear.

_____ **2.** When you ask someone to do something for you, it is best to give the real reasons for wanting it rather than giving reasons which might carry more weight.

_____ **3.** Anyone who completely trusts anyone else is asking for trouble.

_____ **4.** It is hard to get ahead without cutting corners and bending the rules.

_____ **5.** It is safest to assume that all people have a vicious streak and that it will come out when they are given a chance.

_____ **6.** It is never right to lie to someone else.

_____ **7.** Most people are basically good and kind.

_____ **8.** Most people will work hard only when they are forced to do so.

hands of high Machs, leaving them free to repeat such actions. One means of blocking them is to make their actions public. This warns others and puts them on guard, making it harder for high Machs to get away with their manipulative games.

2. **Pay attention to what others do, not what they say.** High Machs are often masters of deception. They convince other people that they have the others' interests at heart, and they are often at their most persuasive when they are busily cutting the ground out from under their unsuspecting victims. How can you protect yourself against such tactics? In part, by focusing on what others *do* rather than what they say. If their actions suggest that they are cold-bloodedly manipulating the people around them, disregard even fervent claims about commitment to principles of loyalty and fair play: These are just camouflage, designed to mislead you.

3. **Avoid situations that give high Machs an edge.** To assure their success, high Machs prefer to operate in certain types of situations—ones in which others' emotions run high and in which others are unsure about how to proceed. The reason for this preference is simple: High Machs realize that under such conditions many people will be distracted and less likely to recognize that they are being manipulated. It is usually wise, therefore, to avoid such situations. If this is not possible, you should at least refrain from making important decisions or commitments in them. Such restraint may make it harder for high Machs to use you for their own benefit.

Together, these suggestions may help you to avoid falling under the spell—and into the clutches—of unprincipled high Machs. Given the presence of at least some high Machs in most organizations and the dangers they pose to the unwary, it is worth keeping these suggestions and the existence of this unsettling aspect of personality firmly in mind.

Work-Related Motives: Achievement, Power, and Affiliation

Do you remember the person in your high-school class who was named "Most likely to succeed"? If so, you probably recall that this individual was truly achievement-oriented: This person wanted to succeed in every situation—or at least in all the important ones. (Recall Christine Silverberg from our CASE PREVIEW; she certainly seems to fit this description.) Can you remember someone else you've known who was interested not so much in success, but in *power*—in being in charge? And how about the person who was chosen "most popular"; what was his or her central motive? Probably, to be liked by others. In short, if you search your own memory, you'll soon find evidence suggesting that people differ with respect to several basic motives. Not surprisingly, these motives—which focus, respectively, on *achievement*, *power*, and *affiliation*—have been found to exert important effects on organizational behaviour. As such, they are certainly worthy of our careful attention here.

achievement motivation The strength of an individual's desire to excel—to succeed at difficult tasks and to do them better than other persons.

Achievement motivation: The quest for excellence. As its name suggests, **achievement motivation** (sometimes termed the *need for achievement*) refers to the strength of an individual's desire to excel—to succeed at difficult tasks and to do them better than other persons. People high in achievement motivation may be characterized as having a highly task-oriented outlook: They are more concerned with getting things done than they are with having good relationships with others. Also, because they are so interested in achieving success, people who have a high amount of achievement motivation tend to seek tasks that are moderately difficult and challenging.[67] Why not tasks that are extremely difficult and challenging? Because the chances of failing on such tasks is too high.

Similarly, such persons reject tasks that are too easy; succeeding on such tasks doesn't constitute "real" achievement. So, for these reasons, persons high in achievement motivation seek and prefer tasks that are moderate in difficulty. In contrast, people low in achievement motivation prefer either extremely difficult or extremely easy tasks. This is because success is almost guaranteed on easy tasks, while failure on extremely difficult ones can be attributed to external causes.

Another characteristic of people high in achievement motivation is a strong desire for feedback on performance: They want to know how well they are doing so they can adjust their goals to make these challenging—but not impossible (we'll consider the topic of goal setting in detail in Chapter 5). Evidence for this preference on the part of persons high in achievement motivation is provided by research conducted by Turban and Keon.[68] They asked management students to read descriptions of companies in which pay and promotions were based entirely on the quality of performance (a *merit-based* pay system) or in which these rewards were based on seniority (a *seniority-based* pay system). Participants—whose achievement motivation had previously been measured—indicated their preferences for working in each company. As shown in Figure 4-8, results indicated that all participants preferred to work for companies with merit-based pay systems. However, this tendency was stronger among people high in achievement motivation. This is not surprising: Such people, after all, are the ones most interested in gaining recognition for their accomplishments.

Given their strong desire to excel, it seems reasonable to expect that people high in achievement motivation will attain greater success in their careers than others. To some extent, this is true. People high in achievement motivation tend to gain

Figure 4-8 Achievement Motivation and Attraction to Organizations

People were more strongly attracted to organizations that used merit-based pay systems. However, this attraction was much stronger among individuals who scored high in achievement motivation than among those who scored low in achievement motivation.

(Source: Based on data from Turban & Keon, 1993.)

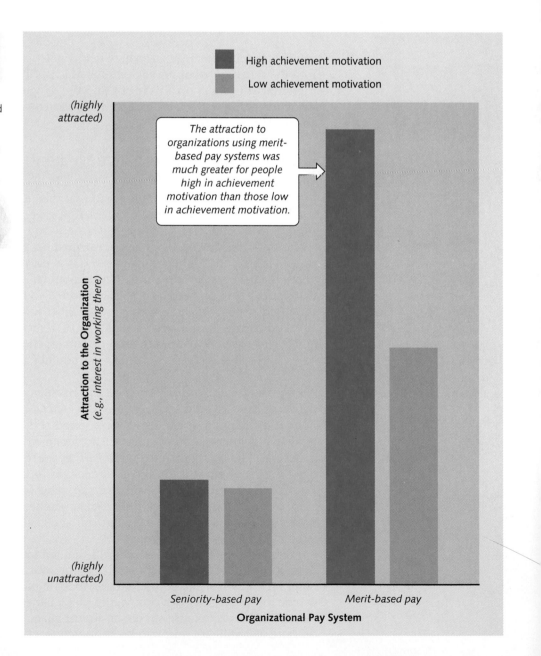

promotions more rapidly than those who are low in achievement motivation, at least early in their careers.[69] However, people who are high in achievement motivation are not necessarily superior managers. For example, recent findings indicate that CEOs who are high in achievement motivation are more likely to centralize power—to keep it in the hands of just a few—than are CEOs who are low on achievement motivation.[70] Such conditions are not always appropriate, and they sometimes generate negative reactions among employees—especially in these days of increasing *empowerment*. In short, while high achievement motivation may contribute to individual success, it is not always a "plus" from the point of view of effective management or organizational performance. (For a discussion of the effects of achievement motivation on the economic fortunes of entire nations, please see the GLOBALIZATION IN TODAY'S ORGANIZATIONS section.)

Affiliation and power motivation: Two sides of the same coin?   At first glance, the desire to be in charge—known as **power motivation**—and the desire to have close, friendly relations with others—known as **affiliation motivation**—appear to be unrelated. It is possible to imagine people high on both dimensions, people who are low on both, and people who are high on one and low on the other. Research findings suggest, however, that the two are often linked.

power motivation The strength of an individual's desire to be in charge, to be able to exercise control over others.

affiliation motivation The strength of an individual's desire to have close, friendly relations with others.

First, consider the matter of managerial success. What kind of individuals are most successful as managers? One possibility, suggested by McClelland and Boyatzis, is that persons most likely to succeed in this role are high in power motivation but low in affiliation motivation.[71] Such individuals will focus on gaining influence over others while at the same time avoiding the trap of being unduly concerned about being liked by them. In other words, they will seek power and influence but won't shy away from the tough decisions and actions often required by this quest.

Are individuals who possess this combination of traits—known as the **leadership motivation pattern (LMP)**—actually more effective than those who do not? Some research findings suggest that this is so. However, in addition to high power motivation and low affiliation motivation, existing evidence indicates that to be successful, managers need another characteristic, too: what McClelland and Boyatzis term a high degree of *self-control*. This refers to the ability to keep firm control over one's own behaviour—for example, holding one's temper in check even in the face of provocation. When this trait is coupled with the leadership motivation pattern, a high level of success often results. For instance, persons showing this pattern tend to receive more promotions than ones who do not.[72]

leadership motivation pattern (LMP) A pattern of personality traits involving high power motivation, low affiliation motivation, and a high degree of self-control.

In sum, it appears that individual differences with respect to several motives are closely linked to important aspects of organizational behaviour. However, the nature of this relationship is far from simple. To understand how individuals' motives influence their job performance or careers, we must take careful account not only of the motives themselves, but also of the combinations or patterns in which they occur, the specific jobs being performed, and the organizational context in which these motives operate. In other words, once again we come face-to-face with the essential accuracy of the interactionist perspective and the complex interplay between personality and situational factors and constraints.

Morning Persons and Evening Persons

The growth in shift work may have its advantages for companies that need to produce goods around the clock. Unfortunately, there appear to be significant costs to this trend: Working at night and especially rotating shifts seem to adversely affect the health and well-being of persons exposed to them.[73] Yet, there are some persons who seem to thrive on "the graveyard shift," and actually prefer it. This fact suggests that there may be large individual differences in what is known as *circadian rhythm*—the times of day at which people feel most alert and energetic.

In fact, growing evidence suggests that such differences exist and that they are stable over time. In other words, they may constitute yet another important individual difference factor relevant to organizational behaviour. More specifically, it

Achievement Motivation and Economic Growth

That the economic fortunes of nations rise and fall with the passage of time is obvious. When students took high school economics in the late 1950s, the teacher showed many graphs suggesting that the United States was truly the dominant economic power in the world: It accounted for a majority of the world's output of steel, automobiles, and electricity, to name just a few important items. Today, of course, such graphs tell a very different story. The United States no longer accounts for most of the world's production in these areas, and in recent years, its rate of growth has been much lower than that of several Asian countries. What factors contribute to such trends? Most persons (including trained economists) would quickly list such variables as the price and availability of natural resources, labour costs, and government policies that encourage or discourage growth. To this list we'd add another factor, closely related to the content of the present chapter: national differences in achievement motivation.

While achievement motivation is a dimension of personality, and as such relates primarily to differences between individuals, considerable evidence suggests that it also varies across different cultures. For example, in classic research on this topic, McClelland analyzed children's stories in 22 different cultures with respect to the degree to which they contained themes of achievement motivation (e.g., the story "The Little Engine That Could," which was read by millions of children in North America, reflected a great deal of achievement motivation).[74] McClelland then related these levels of achievement motivation to two measures of economic development: per capita income and production per capita. The major finding was clear: Achievement motivation scores were highly correlated with economic growth. In other words, the greater the emphasis placed on achievement in the stories told to children in various nations, the more rapid the economic growth in these nations as the children grew up.

While you may find these results surprising, they have been confirmed repeatedly.[75] For example, a massive study was conducted by Furnham, Kirkcaldy, and Lynn (1994), involving more than 12 000 participants in 41 different countries.[76] These researchers examined the relationship between a wide range of attitudes that are closely related to achievement motivation—for instance, attitudes toward work, achievement, competitiveness, money, and saving—and two economic indicators: gross domestic product (the amount of income per person in the country) and growth rate (the percent of increase in economic output from year to year). Results indicated the existence of significant relationships between several of these achievement-related attitudes and economic growth. For instance, across all countries, attitudes toward competitiveness were a significant predictor of economic growth: The stronger these attitudes, and therefore the higher the achievement motivation, the greater the rate of growth. Similarly, attitudes about the importance of money or personal wealth were a significant predictor of gross domestic product: The stronger these attitudes, the greater the wealth in the countries studied.

These findings, and those reported in several earlier studies, lend support to McClelland's claim that a nation's economic success is critically related to the achievement motivation of its people. A very clear example of this relationship is provided by Japan, where in modern times there has existed "a pervasive preoccupation with achievement and accomplishment."[77] Such motivation, in turn, is reflected in what is known as *kaizen* (pronounced *ky'zen*)—an emphasis on continuous, ongoing improvement for everyone in an organization, which is the direct opposite of the philosophy so prevalent in many North American companies, at least in the past: "If it ain't broke, don't fix it!"[78]

Many experts believe that the *kaizen* philosophy is one factor responsible for the great success of many Japanese companies. This philosophy—which is a traditional value in Japan—gives cultural expression and support to the essence of achievement motivation. And as we have already noted, considerable evidence indicates that such motivation may be closely linked to the economic fortunes of nations.

But how, you may be wondering, can this be so? How can the achievement motivation, which is a characteristic of individuals, influence economic activity? Perhaps the answer lies in the following fact: In the final analysis, economic trends are the reflection of actions by large numbers of individuals. To the extent this is so, it is not really very surprising that factors such as achievement motivation might well play a role in shaping the destiny of national economies. The economic whole, after all, is indeed the sum of its parts—and these "parts" consist of thinking, feeling, behaving human beings.

morning persons Individuals who feel most energetic and alert early in the day.

evening persons Individuals who feel most energetic and alert late in the day.

appears that most people fall into one of two categories—either they are **morning persons**, who feel most energetic early in the day, or they are **evening persons**, who feel most energetic at night. Presumably, evening persons would find the task of adapting to night work less stressful than morning persons and would, consequently, do better work when exposed to such conditions. Growing evidence indicates that this is indeed the case. For example, in a recent study, Guthrie, Ash, and Bandapudi[79] asked college students to keep diaries in which they reported on the times each day when they slept and the times each day when they studied. In addition, information was obtained from university records concerning the students' class schedules and their academic performance. All participants also completed a brief questionnaire designed to measure the tendency to be a morning or evening person.

Results revealed intriguing differences between participants who were classified as being high in the tendency to be a morning person or high in the tendency to be an evening person. As might be expected, morning persons reported sleeping primarily at night and studying in the morning, while evening persons reported the opposite pattern. Similarly, class schedules for the two groups also indicated interesting differences: Students classified as morning persons tended to schedule their classes earlier in the day than those classified as evening persons. Perhaps most interesting of all, morning persons did better in their early classes than they did in their later ones, while the opposite was true for students who were classified as being evening persons (see Figure 4-9).

Figure 4-9 Circadian Rhythm and Performance

Students who felt most alert and energetic early in the day (morning persons) did better in early classes than in late classes. In contrast, students who felt most alert and energetic late in the day (evening persons) did better in late classes.

(Source: Based on data from Guthrie, Ash, & Bandapudi, 1995.)

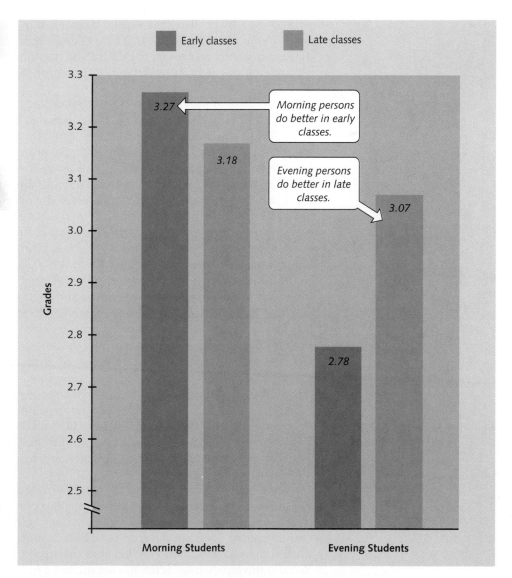

These findings, and those of many other studies,[80] suggest that individual differences in circadian rhythms are indeed important from the point of view of job performance. Ideally, only individuals who are at their best late in the day would be assigned to night work. The results of following such a policy might well be better performance, better health, and fewer accidents for employees—outcomes beneficial both to them and their organizations.

Abilities: Having What It Takes

abilities Mental and physical capacities to perform various tasks.

It is clear that human beings possess a very large number of **abilities**—the capacity to perform various tasks—and that they also differ tremendously with respect to many of these. While the number of different abilities is very large, it is also clear that most fall into two categories: *intellectual abilities*, which refer to the capacity to perform various cognitive tasks, and *physical abilities*, which refer to the capacity to perform various physical actions. We'll now consider both types briefly.

Intellectual Abilities

Different jobs clearly make different intellectual demands on the persons who hold them. Some require high levels of *information processing*—cognitive effort involving the combination, integration, and use of complex information. For example, top-level executives who must plan the long-term strategies of their companies must engage in such activities on a regular basis. Clearly, such persons need considerable cognitive ability to perform their jobs effectively. In contrast, other jobs are far less demanding with respect to such abilities; they are largely routine and do not require careful thought or analysis of information.

The many faces of intelligence. Many tests exist to measure various aspects of human mental abilities. For instance, *IQ tests* are designed to measure *intelligence*—which is generally defined as the ability to think abstractly and to learn readily from experience.[81] Intelligence, however, is not a single, unitary ability. On the contrary, it is best viewed as a multifaceted process—or jewel, if you will! For example, one recent theory of human intelligence suggests that it actually involves three distinct aspects.[82] The first—known as *componential intelligence*—involves the abilities to think critically and analytically. A high level of such intelligence is necessary for jobs involving complex decision making and detailed analysis of financial data, to mention just two.

A second type of intelligence is known as *experiential intelligence*. It involves the ability to pull seemingly unrelated information together so as to formulate new ideas. In other words, such intelligence is closely related to *creativity* and is necessary for jobs such as new product development and marketing. Finally, there is *contextual intelligence*. This is the practical side of intelligence; persons high in such intelligence are, in a sense, "streetwise": They can quickly size up a situation and adapt to it. A high level of contextual intelligence might be especially useful in such jobs as direct sales and in serving as a "troubleshooter" with respect to production equipment.

All of these aspects of intelligence relate to what might be termed the *cognitive side* of intelligence—the ability to work with various forms of information. According to Daniel Goleman, however, there is another important kind of intelligence—one he describes as **emotional intelligence** (**EQ** for short).[83] This refers to the ability to both perceive and control emotions—our own and those of other people. Growing evidence indicates that this type of intelligence, too, is important from the point of view of career success.

emotional intelligence The ability to perceive and control emotions.

For example, in one recent study, new life-insurance salespersons who scored high in optimism—one aspect of emotional intelligence—sold 37 percent more insurance than their lower-scoring counterparts.[84] Similarly, scientists who are adept at accurately "reading others," and so who tend to be liked by their colleagues, tend to be more productive than scientists who are lower in this aspect of emotional intelligence. Why? Because the highly liked scientists are included in informal e-mail networks and get the latest word on what's happening in the field; their less-liked and less emotionally intelligent associates are cut out of such networks. In short, there's more to intelligence than just being able to mentally manipulate information or mental symbols.

In fact, Goleman argues that there are at least five different components of emotional intelligence and that all can influence our effectiveness on the job: knowing our own emotions, controlling them, recognizing the emotions of others, controlling them, and self-motivation. He views empathy, which we discussed earlier in this chapter, as a key skill in several of these tasks.

Multi-Health Systems
www.mhs.com

Canadian publisher MHS Inc. published what it describes as "the first scientifically valid measure of a person's emotional health."[85] Developed by Israeli clinical psychologist, Dr. Reuven Bar-On, the 152-item questionnaire, the EQ-i, examines 15 factors related to emotional "well-being."[86]

One final point about intelligence: Until recently, the only measures of this central aspect of mental abilities involved paper-and-pencil tests. Recently, however, intelligence has been linked to underlying neural activity in the brain. For example, it has been found that persons who score high on standard tests of intelligence actually show more rapid conduction of neural impulses in certain portions of their brains than other persons.[87] Such findings open up new possibilities for measuring intelligence in relatively direct, biological terms.

Cognitive abilities and memory. While intelligence is important, it is not the entire story where cognitive abilities are concerned. In addition, there are more specific aspects to cognitive functioning that are related to the performance of various kinds of jobs. Among these, the most important appear to be *perceptual speed*—the ability to recognize similarities and differences in visual stimuli quickly—*number aptitude*—the ability to work with numbers in a quick and accurate manner, and *spatial visualization*—the ability to imagine how various objects will look when rotated or moved in space. As you can readily see, persons scoring high or low on each of these abilities may well be especially suited—or unsuited—for specific jobs. For instance, number aptitude is important for such jobs as accounting and financial analysis; perceptual speed is essential for jobs such as air traffic controller or nuclear power plant inspectors, while spatial visualization is important for many kinds of engineering and architecture.

Another cognitive ability—perhaps one of the most important—is memory—the ability to store and later retrieve various forms of information.[88] While we generally think of memory as a single system, careful research actually suggests that there are several different forms of memory. These include (1) *semantic memory*—the capacity to store abstract, general knowledge; (2) *implicit memory*—the ability to retain information that can't be put into words, such as motor skills like riding a bicycle; and (3) *working* or *short-term memory*—the memory system that lets us retain information for very short periods of time, as, for example, when dialling a telephone number. Table 4-3 provides an overview of these and other types of memory.

Memory and aging: Do we really "lose it" as we grow older? Do you ever forget where you have put something down, such as your glasses, a pen, or a book? Do you ever come out of a large shopping mall only to discover that you can't remember where you left your car? Everyone has experiences like these but there is a widespread belief that they become more common as we grow older. In other words, many people believe that memory decreases with age. Is this true? If it is, there is an important implication for organizational behaviour: Replace older employees with younger ones in jobs requiring extensive use of memory—that is, most high-level jobs.

Before you jump to this conclusion, however, we should quickly note that research on how memory changes over the course of our lives doesn't actually support such a strategy. Some aspects of memory do seem to decrease with age—especially working memory. In other words, as people grow older, they find it increasingly difficult to hold onto large amounts of information very briefly or to keep several tasks going simultaneously (an action that requires effective working memory).[89] Similarly, *prospective memory*—remembering to perform various

TABLE 4-3 Memory Systems: An Overview

As shown here, we actually possess several different kinds of memory, each specialized for performing different tasks.

Memory System	Function
Semantic memory	Holds general, abstract knowledge—for example, the meaning of words
Implicit memory	Stores information that cannot be expressed verbally—for example, how to ride a bicycle
Working or short-term memory	Holds a small amount of information for very brief periods of time—for example, a telephone number you have just found in the directory as you dial it
Episodic memory	Stores memories for events we have experienced personally
Prospective memory	Holds information about actions we should perform at specific times
Long-term memory	A permanent storage system that holds large amounts of information for very long periods of time—perhaps indefinitely

actions at specific times—also seems to decline with age.[90] But other kinds of memory—for instance, semantic and implicit memory—remain largely unchanged until well into our 70s and beyond. When the benefits of growing experience are added to this picture, it becomes clear that there are no grounds for assuming that younger employees will always be superior to older ones; on the contrary, the total pattern with respect to memory and other cognitive abilities is quite mixed.

Physical Abilities

While many jobs require a high level of cognitive ability, others do not. Yet, such jobs often require considerable physical ability. Many different physical abilities exist, but from the point of view of job performance, the most important are those involving *strength*—the capacity to exert muscular force against various objects—and *flexibility*—the capacity to engage in bodily movements. The importance of such abilities is obvious with respect to many jobs—for example, construction work, production-line jobs, working on the loading dock, and so on. However, physical abilities are also important for jobs that, at first glance, do not appear to involve large physical components. For instance, secretaries must often sit in specific postures or bend over files for hours at a stretch. Considerable flexibility is needed for such jobs. So, in sum, physical abilities play a key role in many jobs and should be carefully considered both by individuals seeking to fill these jobs and the organizations that hire them.

Measuring Individual Differences: Some Basic Methods

Physical traits such as height and weight can be measured readily by means of simple tools. Various aspects of personality and intellectual abilities, however, cannot be assessed quite so simply. There are no rulers for measuring self-monitoring and no thermometers for assessing achievement motivation or intelligence. How, then, can we quantify differences between individuals with respect to the various personality characteristics or intellectual abilities we've described? Several methods exist for accomplishing this task. In this section, we'll describe the two that are most important and will then consider some of the essential requirements of all procedures for measuring individual differences.

Objective and Projective Tests

While many different procedures for measuring personality and other individual differences exist, most fall into two major categories, often described by the terms *objective* and *projective*, respectively.

Objective tests, such as *inventories* and *questionnaires*, are the most widely used method for measuring personality and many intellectual abilities. In the case of personality, these consist of a series of questions or statements to which individuals respond in various ways. For example, a questionnaire may ask respondents to indicate whether each of a set of statements is true or false about themselves, the extent to which they agree or disagree with various sentences, or to indicate which of a pair of named activities they prefer (see Table 4.1 on p. 105 and the EXPERIENCING ORGANIZATIONAL BEHAVIOUR section at the end of this chapter for some examples). With respect to intellectual abilities, such tests often include problems—both verbal and numerical—that test-takers must complete or solve.

Answers to the questions on objective tests are then scored by means of special keys. The score obtained by a specific person is then compared with those obtained by hundreds or even thousands of other people who have taken the test previously. In this way, an individual's relative standing on the trait or ability being measured can be determined. Because such tests can be scored directly, without requiring any special interpretation of the responses (beyond counting them), they are described as being *objective* in nature.

Projective tests, in contrast, adopt another approach. They are used primarily to measure various aspects of personality and attempt to do so by presenting individuals with ambiguous stimuli such as the drawing in Figure 4-10. Persons taking such tests are then asked to indicate what they see. Since the stimuli are ambiguous in nature, it is assumed that the answers given by respondents reflect various aspects of their personality. In other words, different persons "see" different things in these ambiguous stimuli because they differ from one another in terms of various traits.

The illustration in Figure 4-10 is similar to ones contained in a widely used test designed to measure achievement motivation—the *Thematic Apperception Test*.[91] This test consists of a series of ambiguous drawings, and people completing it are asked to make up a story about each one. These are then carefully analyzed for basic themes, according to highly specific scoring procedures. For instance, if you interpret Figure 4-10 as someone who is saddened by learning that she or he didn't pass a test, this may be an indication that you are worried about failing—a sign that you are relatively high in achievement motivation. It is important to note that the task of scoring and interpreting projective tests is complex and should only be performed by people who have had extensive training in such procedures. Administering such tests and then interpreting them on the basis of intuition or "common sense" would probably lead to false conclusions, and would be unethical, too. However, when projective tests are administered and scored by trained professionals, they can provide valuable information about many different aspects of personality.

Reliability and Validity: Essential Requirements

Regardless of whether they are objective or projective in nature, all measures of personality and intellectual abilities must meet two basic requirements: They must be *reliable* and they must be *valid*. **Reliability** refers to the extent to which a test yields stable, consistent scores over time. For example, consider how useless a tailor's measurements of your waist would be if she or he used an elastic tape measure. Each time a measurement was taken, it would be different from the previous occasion—not because your weight had changed, but because the measuring instrument itself is unreliable. In a similar manner, measures of personality must yield consistent scores if they are to be useful.

---

objective tests Questionnaires and inventories designed to measure various aspects of personality.

☞ *Objective tests are used to measure many other aspects of organizational behaviour. As we will see in Chapter 6, such tests are often used to measure work-related attitudes.*

projective tests Methods for measuring personality in which individuals respond to ambiguous stimuli. Their responses provide insights into their personality traits.

Figure 4-10 Projective Tests: An Example

The drawing shown here is similar to those contained in one famous projective test of personality—the Thematic Apperception Test. This test is used to measure individual differences in achievement motivation. Persons taking the test make up a story about each drawing. The contents of these stories is then used to assess the person's achievement motivation and several other motives as well.

(Source: From Robert J. Gregory, Behaviour in Organizations, 2nd ed. Copyright © 1996 by Allyn & Bacon. Reprinted with permission.)

reliability The extent to which a test yields consistent scores on various occasions, and the extent to which all of its items measure the same underlying construct.

validity The extent to which a test actually measures what it claims to measure.

How is such reliability established? In several different ways. One that is commonly used in the field of organizational behaviour involves statistical procedures that provide an index of *internal consistency*—the extent to which all items on the test are measuring the same thing. Another involves the kind of consistency to which we referred earlier—consistency across time, or *test-retest reliability*. When such reliability is high, individuals obtain highly similar scores each time they complete the test (please see top portion of Figure 4-11).

Another basic requirement for all tests of personality is that they be valid. **Validity** refers to the extent to which a test measures what it actually claims to measure. Interestingly, a test can be high in reliability but low in validity. For example, suppose that to measure intelligence, we recorded the dimensions of your skull and then used this to estimate the size of your brain. Such measurements could be highly reliable—each time we took them, we'd get very much the same physical readings. But would they actually tell us anything about your intelligence? Definitely not; the notion that brain size is directly linked to intelligence has been thoroughly discredited through scientific research.

In a corresponding manner, no test of personality or intellectual abilities is useful unless it actually measures what it claims to measure. But how do we establish such validity? This is a difficult task, requiring many separate steps, but, generally, validity is established by relating scores on the test to various outcomes or aspects of behaviour assumed to reflect the trait being measured; this is known as *criterion-related validity*. For example, if scores on a test of intelligence are closely related to grades in school or scores on tests like the GMAT (the General Management Aptitude Test, used by many schools in selecting MBA students), this would provide some evidence for its validity. Other means for establishing the validity of a test exist, but, in several respects, this is the most straightforward and convincing. (Please see the bottom portion of Figure 4-11).

Before concluding, we should note that all of the traits and abilities considered in this chapter are measured by tests known to be both reliable and valid. Thus, you can be confident that the findings we have discussed do in fact relate to important aspects of personality—ones that have significant implications for various forms of organizational behaviour. See **THE ETHICS ANGLE** for a discussion of the dangers inherent in invalid or biased tests.

The Ethics Angle

Can Tests Have an Adverse Impact?

What if tests to measure individual differences—used for making important decisions concerning a specific persons—are invalid or misused? Serious problems with important legal ramifications may result. For instance, if scores on a test are not closely related to performance of a specific job, using the test to select job applicants for that position is not only on shaky ground from the point of view of ethics, it is illegal in many countries.

For example, 35 Ottawa bus drivers were fired "when they failed psychological tests required by their new employer."[92] Their union settled the issue for the drivers. The federal privacy commissioner's office is concerned about the use of this kind of testing. "Eugene Oscapella, a policy advisor for the commission, believes such tests reinforce the need for stricter laws protecting the privacy rights of employees."[93]

In addition to the concern about privacy, there is the potential that a test used for choosing job applicants may be biased so that a smaller proportion of minority applicants than nonminority applicants are hired. The rejected employees in this type of situation can file suit based on the fact that use of this test harms the careers of minority applicants to a greater extent than those of nonminority applicants. Clearly, such issues must be carefully considered whenever tests designed to measure individual differences are used as a basis for making hiring or promotional decisions.

Figure 4-11 Reliability and Validity: An Overview

Reliability (top) refers to the extent to which scores on a test are consistent over time. *Validity* (bottom) refers to the extent to which a test actually measures what it claims to measure. Both reliability and validity are measured in several different ways.

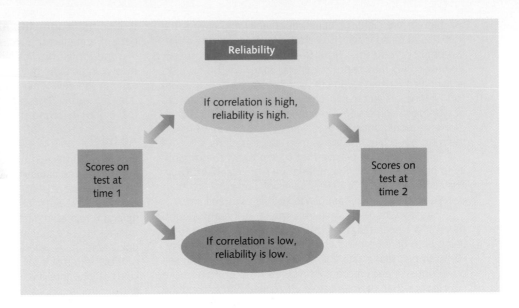

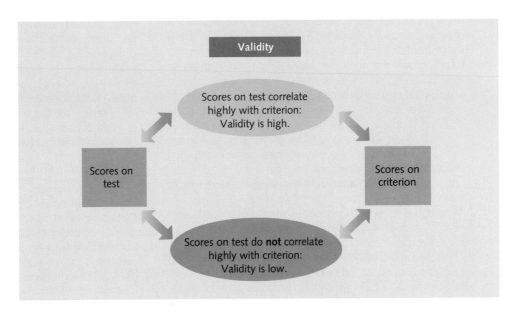

SUMMARY AND REVIEW

The Nature of Personality and Abilities

Personality is the unique and relatively stable pattern of behaviour, thoughts, and emotions shown by individuals. In contrast, **abilities** refer to the capacity to perform various tasks or cognitive activities. Organizational behaviour is often the result of a complex interplay between *individual difference* factors, such as personality and abilities, and situational factors. This fact is recognized in the **interactionist perspective** that is widely accepted in the field of organizational behaviour. Because of this interaction between personal and situational factors, work-related outcomes are usually most positive when there is a close match between people's personalities and the requirements of their jobs (known as **person-job fit**).

Work-Related Aspects of Personality

Several aspects of personality are related to important forms of organizational behaviour. The **"big five" dimensions of personality**—so named because they appear to be very basic aspects of personality—appear to play a role in successful performance of many jobs. In particular, two of these dimensions, *conscientiousness* and *extroversion*, are good predictors of success in many different jobs. **Positive affectivity** and **negative affectivity**—stable tendencies to experience positive or negative moods at work—are related to the quality of individual decision making and willingness to help others.

Another personality factor related to organizational behaviour is the **Type A behaviour pattern**. Persons showing this pattern are highly competitive, irritable, and always in a hurry. Such persons tend to perform better than those with the opposite pattern—**Type B**—on tasks requiring speed. However, they may perform less well than Type B's on tasks requiring considered judgment. Type A's experience more conflict with others and may become involved in more instances of workplace aggression. They also experience serious health problems more frequently than Type B's, and this may prevent them from reaching the top in many organizations.

Individuals who believe that they possess the capability to perform many different tasks are high in **self-efficacy**. They often do achieve higher levels of performance than people who lack such confidence in their own abilities.

Persons who seek to change the environment around them and to capitalize on opportunities are described as being high on a trait known as the **proactive personality**. For example, real estate agents high on this dimension sell more houses, earn more commissions, and bring in more new listings than persons low on this dimension. Among the most important aspects of personality from the point of view of organizational behaviour is **self-monitoring**. High self-monitors are concerned with making good impressions on others and readily adapt their behaviour to match the requirements of a given situation. In contrast, low self-monitors remain much the same person across many different contexts. High self-monitors are more effective *boundary-spanners* than low self-monitors, and are better at *impression management*. High self-monitors also obtain more promotions, and are better at acquiring mentors.

Individuals who adopt a manipulative approach to their relations with others are described as being high in **Machiavellianism**. They are not influenced by considerations of loyalty, friendship, or ethics. Instead, they simply do whatever is needed to get their own way.

People differ with respect to several important *work-related motives*. **Achievement motivation** is the desire to excel. People high in achievement motivation seek situations of moderate difficulty because they are challenging enough to master, but not so difficult as to make failure certain. Such persons prefer jobs in which their accomplishments are recognized on an individual basis—for instance, jobs using merit-based pay. People who are high on **power motivation**—the desire to be in charge, and low on **affiliation motivation**—the desire to have friendly relations with others, and also possess a high degree of self-control, show what is termed the **leadership motivation pattern (LMP)**. This pattern is related to success in managerial jobs.

Individuals also differ with respect to when they feel most alert and energetic. **Morning persons** are at their best early in the day, while **evening persons** are at their best late in the day. These differences can play an important role in jobs involving shift work.

Abilities

Individuals differ with respect to many abilities. These fall into two major categories: intellectual abilities and physical abilities. Intellectual abilities refer to the capacity to perform cognitive tasks. *Intelligence* is one important intellectual ability and is related to success in many different fields. Recent findings indicate that intelligence is multifaceted rather than unidimensional—several different kinds appear to exist. Each of these forms of intelligence is related to success in various kinds of jobs. Intelligence also involves the ability to perceive and control emotions (**emotional intelligence**). In addition to intelligence, individuals also vary with respect to specific intellectual abilities such as *perceptual speed*, *number aptitude*, and *spatial visualization*. Memory, the ability to store and later retrieve information, is another important aspect of intellectual abilities. Several kinds of memory exist, including semantic memory, implicit memory, and working memory. Contrary to popular belief, most aspects of memory do not decrease sharply as people age.

Physical abilities refer to the capacity to perform various physical actions. Two important components of such abilities are *strength* and *flexibility*.

Measuring Individual Differences

Individual differences in personality and abilities are generally assessed either by objective tests or projective tests. **Objective tests**, used for measuring personality and intellectual abilities, involve questionnaires that are scored using established keys. In contrast, **projective tests** are used exclusively for measuring personality. Such tests expose individuals to ambiguous stimuli and use their interpretations of these stimuli to reach conclusions about important aspects of personality. To be useful, any measure of individual differences must be **reliable**—it must yield consistent measurements over time. In addition, all such tests must be **valid**—they must measure what they claim to measure.

CASE PREVIEW QUESTIONS FOR DISCUSSION

1. In what ways, if any, would you expect a female chief of police to be different from her male counterparts?

2. How would you describe Silverberg's personality and leadership style?

3. Is Christine Silverberg's personality a match for the job? Please explain your answer.

CHAPTER QUESTIONS FOR DISCUSSION

1. Why might two individuals whose personalities are very similar behave differently in a given situation?

2. How does a close *person-job fit* contribute to good performance?

3. What is the difference between being in a good mood and having the characteristic of positive affectivity?

4. Suppose that you were hiring someone to perform a job that required very fast performance. Would you prefer to hire a Type A or Type B person? Why?

5. In what fields do you think individuals high on the *proactive personality* dimension would excel? Why?

6. How does having low self-efficacy interfere with task performance?

7. Why are persons high in self-monitoring so effective in *boundary-spanning positions*? Can you think of jobs that they would *not* do very well?

8. If you suspect that someone with whom you are dealing is high in Machiavellianism, what steps should you take to protect yourself from this person?

9. Can you think of cultures that induce a low level of need for achievement among persons living in them? Are these cultures high or low in economic development?

10. Suppose that you are a *morning person*—you feel most alert and energetic early in the day. What steps can you take to make this characteristic a "plus" for your personal productivity?

11. As they get older, many people seem to become more "absent-minded." Does this mean that their memory abilities are decreasing? If not, then what accounts for this change?

12. Is it ever appropriate to use personality tests as a hiring tool—a technique for deciding which persons to hire for a specific job? What are the potential dangers of using personality tests in this way?

CASE IN POINT

Edgar Bronfman, Jr.: Through the Distillery and Back to Hollywood

He leads a charmed life, or so it would seem to many. Young, handsome, wealthy, the heir to a Canadian business dynasty, Edgar Bronfman, Jr. is making his own mark as the third generation of Bronfmans at the helm of Seagram.

Edgar Bronfman, Jr. is certainly raising eyebrows with his acquisitions in the entertainment industry. First he set his sights on buying a 15 percent stake in Time Warner. He sold Seagram's share of E. I. du Pont de Nemours and Company (more commonly known as Du Pont) and acquired 80 percent of the Hollywood entertainment conglomerate MCA from Matsushita Electric Industrial Company of Japan. The MCA deal included such assets as Universal Pictures, Universal Television, MCA Records, G .P. Putnam, Berkeley Publishing, and Universal theme parks.[94] Later, Bronfman renamed the business Universal Studios.

In October 1997 Bronfman sold most of Universal's television assets to Barry Diller of HSN Inc. Universal received a stake in the new company, which Diller named USA Networks. While Bronfman was delighted with the deal, many felt it was a bad move for Universal. "The taking of Edgar is now a cottage industry," said one Hollywood insider.[95] In 1998 Bronfman acquired the largest music company in the world, PolyGram NV. The deal, with others he has made in the entertainment industry, leaves Seagram with two-thirds of its revenue coming from entertainment. In 1993 that figure was zero.[96]

His radical reengineering, his deals, and his hiring practices have raised eyebrows among Hollywood power brokers. As things have become tougher for Bronfman he has not looked for a way out of his entertainment holdings as some speculated he might. " 'He would not do that—it would be an admission of failure.' His instinct, rather, seems to be to dig deeper, and to prove to his family and to the world that he can do it after all."[97]

In the 1960s, Edgar Sr., young Edgar's father, acquired 15 percent of Metro-Goldwyn-Mayer. He later created a Broadway production company. Edgar Jr. has had a clear interest in show business ever since he produced his first movie while he was still in high school. He went straight from high school to Hollywood, where he was involved in producing an unsuccessful movie in 1982. He even tried his hand at song writing,[98] a passion that he continues today under the pen name "Sam Roman."[99]

From the beginning, young Edgar has been his own man, a trait his father has apparently found both irksome and admirable.[100] It may be this that prompted the elder Bronfman to select his younger son as his successor. Edgar Jr. joined the family business in 1982 after discussing the move with his older brother, Samuel (now "relegated to overseeing the Seagram Classics Wine Company in San Mateo, California").[101]

After a brief apprenticeship, Edgar Jr. was sent to Europe to help clean up Seagram's troubled operations there. In this venture, he demonstrated his ability to learn and to make difficult decisions in the best interests of the company. In 1984, he moved back to the United States where he spearheaded a major restructuring initiative which resulted in cutting the company's staff by 55 percent. Edgar Jr. became president and chief operating officer of Seagram in 1989. In June 1994, he succeeded his father as CEO of the company.[102]

Just who is this American-born heir to a powerful Canadian dynasty? Tall, slight, quiet, he is described as, "soft-spoken and extremely precise, even formal, in conversation."[103] There are rumours that some executives find him intimidating and distant, but this view is not universally shared.[104] The fear some of his employees experience may be caused by Bronfman's perfectionism about even the smallest details.[105] For his part, Bronfman describes himself as not the typical CEO. "I think I have parts of an artistic temperament and parts that are more consonant with a traditional business temperament. And I think the mix is valuable." He emphasizes his belief that, with an increasing emphasis on service, "people become a major part of the product."[106]

"Bronfman says he believes in setting goals, motivating his people, and then delegating authority. He describes his own management style as 'a very light grip on the throat.' "[107] With this orientation, he brought his own style to the Seagram executive offices. In late 1993, when he was working on acquiring the rights to distribute Absolut vodka, he taught his conservative management team to sing "Together Wherever We Go" for the Swedish executives.[108]

As anyone can imagine, there is considerable pressure on Edgar Bronfman, Jr. to make his mark as his father and grandfather have done before him.[109] He continues to face considerable, but by no means universal, criticism for his entertainment focus. "I think it's been remarkable that he's been as tame as he has been under the barrage that's hit

him," says Edgar Sr., his son's biggest supporter. "He's fairly sensitive personally, but he's got a thick enough skin to run this company, and to make the hard and tough decisions."[110]

Critical Thinking Questions

1. How would you characterize Bronfman with respect to the "big five" personality dimensions?

2. Do you think Bronfman has a Type A or a Type B personality? What leads you to this assessment?

3. Does Bronfman demonstrate high or low self-efficacy? What experiences might have led to the development of his self-efficacy?

4. Describe Bronfman's achievement, power, and affiliation motives.

MCA
www.mca.com

Seagram
www.seagram.com

SKILLS PORTFOLIO

Experiencing Organizational Behaviour

Measuring Your Own Self-Monitoring

As we noted earlier in this chapter, one important dimension of personality is *self-monitoring*. Persons high on this dimension are, in a sense, capable of being very different people in different situations or contexts. This is very useful in several respects; for instance, persons high in self-monitoring are more successful in obtaining mentors than persons low in self-monitoring and report having fewer and less intense conflicts with others at work. Where do you stand on this dimension? To get some idea, please follow the directions below.

Directions

Please indicate whether each of the statements below is true (or mostly true) or false (or mostly false) about yourself. If a statement is true (or mostly true) enter the letter *T* in the blank space. If it is false (or mostly false) enter the letter *F*.

_F_ **1.** It is difficult for me to imitate the actions of other people.

_F_ **2.** My behaviour usually reflects my true feelings, attitude, or beliefs.

_T_ **3.** At parties and social gatherings, I always try to say and do things others will like.

_T_ **4.** I can give a speech on almost any topic—even ones about which I know very little.

_F_ **5.** I would probably make a very poor actor.

_T_ **6.** Sometimes I put on a show to impress or entertain people.

_T_ **7.** I find it difficult to argue for ideas that I don't believe in.

_T_ **8.** In different situations and with different people I often act in very different ways.

_F_ **9.** I would not change my attitudes or my actions in order to please other people or win their approval.

_F_ **10.** Sometimes other people think I'm experiencing stronger emotions than I really am.

_T_11. I'm not especially good at making other people like me.

_T_12. If I have a strong reason for doing so, I can look others in the eye and lie with a straight face.

_T_13. I make up my own mind about movies, books, or music; I don't rely on the advice of my friends in these respects.

_T_14. At a party, I usually let others keep the jokes and stories going.

_T_15. I'm not always the person I seem to be.

Scoring

To obtain your score, use the following key. Give yourself one point for each of your answers that agrees with the key:

1. F, 2. F, 3. T, 4. T, 5. F, 6. T, 7. F, 8. T, 9. F, 10. T, 11. F, 12. T, 13. F, 14. F, 15. T

Questions for Discussion

1. How did you score? If your total was eight or higher, you are probably high in self-monitoring. If it was four or lower, you are relatively low on this dimension.

2. Is being a high self-monitor always a "plus"? Or can you think of situations in which being high on this trait might have a negative impact on one's career or performance?

3. Suppose you were hiring employees for the following jobs. Would you prefer people who are high or low in self-monitoring for each position?

   • salesperson
   • engineer
   • accountant
   • human resource manager

Working in Groups

Machiavellianism in Action: The $10 Game

As we noted earlier, persons high in Machiavellianism often come out ahead in dealing with others, because they are true pragmatists: They are willing to do or say whatever it takes to win or get their way. Several questionnaires exist for measuring Machiavellianism as a personality trait. However, tendencies in this direction can also be observed in many face-to-face situations. The exercise below offers one useful means for observing individual differences along this dimension.

Directions

1. The class is divided into groups of three persons.
2. These three persons are handed a sheet with the following instructions:

   "Imagine that I have placed a stack of ten loonies on the table in front of you. This money will belong to any two of you who can decide on how to divide it."

3. Groups are then allowed up to ten minutes to reach a decision. At the end of ten minutes, the instructor announces: "Time is up."

4. Each group is then asked whether they reached a decision, and what it was. In each group, it will probably be found that two persons agreed on how to divide the money and left the third "out in the cold."

Questions for Discussion

1. How did the coalitions of two persons form? Was there a particular person in each group who was largely responsible for the formation of the winning coalition?

2. Why did the third person get left out of the agreement? What did this person say or do—or fail to say or do—that led to his or her being omitted from the two-person coalition that divided the money?

3. Do you think that actions in this situation are related to Machiavellianism? How?

4. How can people low in Machiavellianism protect themselves from being left "out in the cold" in such situations?

Prentice Hall

COMPANION WEBSITE

We invite you to visit the *Greenberg/Baron/Sales/Owen Companion Website* at *www.prenticehall.ca/greenberg* for this chapter's Internet resources.

CUMULATIVE CASE - PART 2

The Digital Renaissance Learning Community

In the spring of 1998, *The Globe and Mail Report on Business Magazine* identified Digital Renaissance as the number one small high-tech company that "geeks love" to work for.[1] As he reflects on the company's short history, Keith Kocho admits that, when Digital Renaissance started back in 1991, its open work space, lack of job titles, and relaxed culture "were way out there." Now these are "de rigueur."

People working in this field have come to expect the beer fridge, pool table, and casual dress. He points out that the twenty-first century "knowledge workers" have a higher degree of mobility than workers in other, more traditional sectors of the economy. They are in high demand and can pick and choose from among abundant employment opportunities. Kocho cautions that, in this kind of climate, a top-down, hierarchical, authoritarian style is not effective.[2]

Keith Kocho seems to be a natural at meeting the challenges of the people side of management at Digital Renaissance. He describes himself as "open, honest, direct, and curious." He likes to be involved with all aspects of the operation and prefers to take a broad focus. His desk sits in an open area under the mezzanine (and on the much-travelled pathway to the company's kitchen!) where anyone and everyone can talk with him at any time. In keeping with Digital Renaissance's culture of interdependence and teamwork, he expects those who stop by his work area not just to bring him a problem but to bring a suggested solution as well. He explains that he is "not there just to take flak." He sees himself as working for his colleagues within the company as a "servant leader" who facilitates teams in their work accomplishments.[3]

With a company that is growing as rapidly as Digital Renaissance, a constant influx of new employees is the norm. Kocho looks for individuals who have more than just the requisite technical skills. He says those who are chosen to work at Digital Renaissance must be "good team players" and have "the ability to communicate both what is working and what needs fixing." While Kocho does expect his people to be well trained with respect to computers, he also expects them to take a multidisciplinary perspective on their work and to have a variety of interests and training. He adds, "It helps if you are a philosopher as well."

Introducing a high volume of new hires at Digital Renaissance requires a special kind of training process. Kocho explains that people in the organization fall into two broad categories: (1) "specialists," who have a particular career-track focus stemming from a set of skills, e.g., animators; and (2) "mentors," who possess a set of skills that they contribute to the company and who are responsible for transferring such skills to other organizational members. At Digital Renaissance, employees are expected and encouraged to continuously advance their knowledge base and skill set. Those who take college and university courses and/or attend conferences or skill seminars are supported by the company. Kocho adds, "If you don't treat employees with respect, it won't work. Their development is the company's development."[4]

Beyond Digital Renaissance's own commitment to keeping its people up to date and well trained, this fledgling company designs innovative and dynamic training programs for many of its clients. In fact, many

Canadians have encountered the company's technology without realizing it. When Sunnybrook Health Science Centre in Toronto needed a program in customer-service training, it turned to Digital Renaissance. Digital Renaissance had worked previously with Sunnybrook in the areas of desktop publishing and audio-visual production. This background proved to be useful in the training project. The project manager from Digital Renaissance described Sunnybrook's move to multimedia training as a "paradigm shift towards customer service in a situation where classroom training was not appropriate."[5] The resulting program, the Sunnybrook Customer Connection series, used "full motion digital video, narration, animation, still photography and morphing to teach staff at Sunnybrook the relationship between good customer service and high quality patient care."[6]

Digital Renaissance's multimedia technology was also used to develop the "Heritage Minutes" seen in movie theatres and on television. The prototype for these one-minute reenactments of Canadian historical events was produced by Digital Renaissance in cooperation with Simon Fraser University's EXCITE Centre. This was Digital Renaissance's first big project and a turning point for the company as it strengthened ". . . its consulting and systems integration business as well as in the development of the content of custom multimedia applications. 'From there' says Kocho, 'we entered every vertical market—education, health care, government, retail, industrial, banks, insurance companies.' "[7]

The advantage of Digital Renaissance's CD-ROM training programs is that employees can use them for self-directed learning.[8] With multimedia applications, self-directed learning is anything but boring. A program Digital Renaissance helped London Life to develop included an animated game-show host as a guide in the learning process. "Our business is serious and a little boring. To read a paper-based procedural manual, there is nothing more boring," said a London Life project leader. "With the Game of London Life, employees were trained faster, more cheaply and in a more enjoyable way. . . ."[9]

Discussion Questions

1. What is meant by the term "geek"? What purpose is served by such judgments? What danger lurks in making such judgments?

2. What makes the twenty-first century knowledge worker such an interesting challenge for managers?

3. What does Keith Kocho mean when he says he is a "servant leader"?

4. What is Digital Renaissance's corporate image? What are the ways in which an organization such as Digital Renaissance communicates this image?

5. In what ways is Keith Kocho's and his company's philosophy of training and development on the leading edge of change when it comes to educating adults in the workplace?

Stephen Hawking: Of Humour, Black Holes, and Life in the Present

"I have faith in reason, even though there is not much around." If there is little reason around, Stephen Hawking certainly has more than his fair share of this rare commodity. He is in the best position to make this judgment, as he did in an interview with Hana Gartner in April of 1998. Dr. Hawking's extraordinary contributions to science through his research in theoretical physics are all the more amazing considering the challenges he faces daily as a person living with amyotropic lateral sclerosis (ALS, also known as "Lou Gehrig's Disease").

Stephen Hawking has degrees from both Oxford and Cambridge, and is Lucasian Professor of Mathematics at Cambridge University, a chair previously held by Sir Isaac Newton. Among the many honours and awards that have been bestowed on him are: election to the Royal Society in 1974 making him one of the youngest members of this august body, 12 honourary degrees, Commander of the British Empire, and a Companion of Honour.

Hawking was born in Oxfordshire, England in 1942. Hawking's parents had originally lived in London but had moved to Oxford to avoid the terrors of the blitz (German bombing of Britain during World War II) at the time of Stephen's birth. He grew up in St. Albans, a town north of London. While his father, also a graduate of Oxford University, would have preferred him to study medicine, Stephen was interested in mathematics and physics. Indeed, his research has pushed the boundaries of scientific knowledge to the edges of the universe. In actual fact, after extensive research, he has concluded that the universe does not have edges at all. His work on black holes suggests that they are not black but emit radiation which evaporates.

His work is impressive even without factoring in his personal challenges. As an undergraduate at Oxford, Hawking began to notice that he was becoming more clumsy. He even fell over for no apparent reason. He ignored these symptoms, but when he entered doctoral training at Cambridge, his father noticed his problem and took him to see the family doctor. At the age of 21, he was diagnosed with a degenerative condition that later proved to be ALS. His doctors did not tell him very much about their findings and Hawking did not ask for the grim details. The doctors told him to go back to work, so he did, feeling as if he had been given a reprieve. Hawking says of that time in his life, "I found to my surprise, that I was enjoying life in the present more than before." His research was progressing and he became engaged to, and subsequently married, Jane Wilde. The couple has three children.

While his degenerating physical condition has necessitated changes in his family's housing arrangements and increased nursing care, Hawking has continued to work. He was able to speak, but with deteriorating clarity, until a bout with pneumonia in 1985 caused him to need a tracheostomy. He now uses a sophisticated voice simulator with which he has been very pleased, except that it gives him an American accent. With his now legendary wit, he confides that he is waiting for a British version of the program.

Stephen Hawking's world has no limits. Undaunted, he continues his gruelling regimen of research, writing, and lecturing around the world. When asked about the impact that ALS has had on his celebrity status, Hawking has said, "People are fascinated by the contrast between my very limited physical powers, and the vast nature of the universe I deal with."

Video Case Discussion Questions

1. How would you describe Stephen Hawking's personality?

2. What motivates Stephen Hawking?

3. Describe how someone who did not know Stephen Hawking and his work might stereotype him.

4. What lessons can Stephen Hawking teach a Canadian manager?

CBC Source: Stephen Hawking Interview, CBC *The National*, (April 27, 1998).

Video Case Sources: Hawking, Stephen L. *Britannica*, www.eb.com:180/cgi-bin/g?DocF=micro/262/63.html; A Brief History of Mine, www.damtp.cam.ac.uk/user/hawking/history.html; Disability advice: My Experience with ALS, www.damtp.cam.ac.uk/user/hawking/disability.html; Questions and Answers to Professor Hawking, www.damtp.cam.ac.uk/user/hawking/QA.html.

CHAPTER 5
Motivation in Organizations

LEARNING OBJECTIVES

After reading this chapter you should be able to:

1. Define *motivation* and explain its importance in the field of organizational behaviour.

2. Describe *need hierarchy theory* and what it recommends about improving motivation in organizations.

3. Identify and explain the conditions through which *goal setting* can be used to improve job performance.

4. Explain *equity theory* and describe some of the research designed to test its basic tenets.

5. Describe *expectancy theory* and how it may be applied in organizations.

6. Distinguish between *job enlargement* and *job enrichment* as techniques for motivating employees.

7. Describe the *job characteristics model* and its implications for redesigning jobs to enhance motivation.

At Husky, Employees Are #1—Really!

Imagine your ideal workplace. Would this workplace be located in the Canadian manufacturing industry? Would it include on-site wellness services with a fitness centre, a massage therapist, nurse, physician, and naturopathic doctor? How about a well-equipped learning centre for the children of employees?[1] Imagine that this workplace also has a demonstrated commitment to lifelong learning and that it has been built on a foundation of such strong values as: "uncompromising honesty; genuine care for all who are affected by what we do; proactive environment[al] responsibility; and a drive to do things better." Maybe your ideal company is Husky Injection Molding Systems.[2]

Not surprisingly, Husky has been identified as one of the 100 best companies to work for in Canada.[3] It sounds like a company in Silicon Valley North rather than a manufacturer of injection molding machines that produce everything from sandwich containers to car bumpers.[4] Based in Bolton, Ontario, Husky has operations in Dudelange, Luxembourg; Milton, Vermont; and Pittsfield, Massachusetts;[5] and Technical Centres in Europe, Japan, and the Americas.[6]

Husky's founder and president, Robert Schad (Figure 5-1), lives by his values. Colorado-based author and management consultant Jim Collins is impressed by both Schad and his company, "The real source of Husky's success is the fact that Schad's value system is authentic....It's not cynical in the least."[7] Schad's commitment to the wellness of his employees and their families and to environmental responsibility[8] is reflected in the company-subsidized cafeteria's vegetarian meals, the no-smoking policy (instituted before it was fashionable), the $500 annual vitamin allowance, and the 100 percent coverage of costs for tuition and books for workers who attend college or university.[9]

Ties, titles, and time clocks are out at Husky. Open communication without hierarchical barriers is in. Employees lead the agenda at Employee Council Meetings, which include representatives from all business sectors, as well as Schad and other senior leadership personnel. These are not simple gripe sessions. Schad is committed to act on issues arising from these discussions.[10]

At Husky Injection Molding Systems, values are central. "I think you build something to last if you treat workers well," insists Schad.[11] And he has built something to last. As of year-end 1997, the company reported a return on investment of 25.3 percent, revenue of U.S.$646.4 million, and profit of U.S.$34.9 million.[12] Husky ranks third in the world in its sector. In addition, it has been reported that Husky has lower-than-average drug costs for its employees, lower employee absenteeism, more accident-free days, and that it earns $200 000 per year by recycling its waste.[13]

Figure 5-1 Authentic Values Lead to Attractive Workplace

Injection Molding Systems' Robert Schad believes, "Whoever has the best people will win." His commitment to providing his employees with a wide range of benefits, combined with an egalitarian management style, has made Husky a very attractive place to work.[14]

Husky Injection Molding Systems
www.service.com/com/husky

The success enjoyed at Husky Injection Molding Systems is certainly impressive. But, it is by no means accidental. In fact, it can be traced to several important things that Robert Schad does to get Husky employees to work as hard as they do. He makes sure that Husky employees have ample opportunity to communicate their concerns, and he is committed to addressing them. He also makes it interesting to work at the company. The bottom line: Working hard at Husky not only puts cash in your pockets but is enjoyable. It is clear that Schad has addressed the question: How do you go about motivating people to work? We will examine the process of *motivation* in this chapter (see Figure 5-2).

Although people in business may have lots of interesting ideas about how to go about motivating employees, OB's approach is based on science. This is not to say that we are only interested in research and theory—far from it. We are also extremely interested in what these efforts tell us about ways to motivate real people performing real jobs. The point is that our approach, in keeping with the orientation of the field of OB, is based on conducting and applying sound scientific research. Nowhere in the field are these dual interests more clearly realized than in the study of motivation. Indeed, we are interested in asking both theoretical questions, such as *"What* motivates people, and *why?"* and applied questions, such as *"How* can this knowledge be put to practical use?" Hence, our focus in this chapter will be both on theories of motivation and on their practical application.

The theories we will consider represent the major approaches to the topic of motivation as currently studied.[15] Our look at each major approach to motivation will focus on what the theory says, the research bearing on it, and its practical implications. However, before turning to these theories and applications, we will begin by taking a closer look at the concept of motivation itself.

Motivation in Organizations: Its Basic Nature

Although motivation is a broad and complex concept, organizational scientists have agreed on its basic characteristics.[16] We define **motivation** as the set of processes that arouse, direct, and maintain human behaviour toward attaining some goal. The diagram in Figure 5-3 will guide our explanation as we elaborate on this definition.

The first part of our definition deals with *arousal*. This has to do with the drive, or energy, behind our actions. For example, people may be guided by their interest in making a good impression on others, doing interesting work, being successful at what they do, and so on. Their interest in fulfilling these motives stimulates them to engage in behaviours designed to fulfill them.

But, what will people do to satisfy their motives? Motivation is also concerned with the choices people make, the *direction* their behaviour takes. For example, employees interested in cultivating a favourable impression on their supervisors may do many different things: compliment them on their good work, do them special favours, work extra hard on an important project, and the like. Each of these options may be recognized as a path toward meeting the person's goal.

The final part of our definition deals with *maintaining* behaviour. How long will people persist at attempting to meet their goal? To give up in advance of goal attainment means not to satisfy the need that stimulated their behaviour in the first

Figure 5-2 What Motivates These People?

Peek into the windows of this Tokyo office building and you see people working late into the night. The question of what motivates these and other people to work so hard is one of the most important ones raised in the field of OB.

motivation The set of processes that arouse, direct, and maintain human behaviour toward attaining some goal.

Figure 5-3 Motivation: Its Basic Components

Motivation involves the arousal, direction, and maintenance of behaviour toward a goal. An example of this process is shown here.

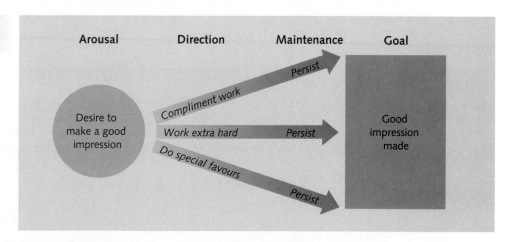

place. Obviously, people who do not persist at meeting their goals (e.g., salespeople who give up before reaching their quotas) cannot be said to be highly motivated.

To summarize, motivation requires all three components: the arousal, direction, and maintenance of goal-directed behaviour. An analogy may help tie these components together. Imagine that you are driving down a road on your way home. The arousal part of motivation is like the energy created by the car's engine. The direction component is like the steering wheel, taking you along your chosen path. Finally, the maintenance aspect of the definition is the persistence that keeps you going until you arrive home, reaching your goal.

Now that we have defined motivation, it is time to bring up two important points. First, motivation cannot be seen, but only inferred on the basis of performance. However, *motivation and job performance are not synonymous*. Just because someone performs at a task well does not mean that he or she is highly motivated. This person actually may be very skillful but not putting forth much effort at all. If you're a mathematical genius, for example, you may breeze through your calculus class without hardly trying. By contrast, someone who performs poorly may be putting forth a great deal of effort but still be falling short of a desired goal because he or she lacks the skill needed to succeed. If you've ever tried to learn a new sport but found that you couldn't get the hang of it no matter how hard you tried, you know what we mean.

A second key point is that *motivation is multifaceted*. By this we mean that people may have several different motives operating at once. Sometimes, these may conflict. For example, a word processing operator might be motivated to please his boss by being as productive as possible. However, being too productive may antagonize one's coworkers, who fear that they're being made to look bad. The result is that the two motives may pull the individual in different directions, and the one that wins out is the one that's strongest in that situation.

These examples clearly show that motivation is a complex and important concept in the field of organizational behaviour. In fact, many observers of North American business trends have attributed problems of sagging production to a general lack of motivation within the workforce.[17] However, to claim that today's employees are poorly motivated would be misleading. After all, surveys show that most North Americans would continue to work even if they didn't need the money.[18] Although money is certainly important to people, they are motivated to attain many other goals as well. Because of technological advances that took the drudgery out of many jobs, today's workers are motivated by the prospect of performing jobs that are interesting and challenging—not just jobs that pay well (see Figure 5-4). The field of OB considers a wide variety of factors that motivate people on the job. Our discussion of the various theories will highlight these variables.

"I'll quit when it stops being fun."

Figure 5-4 The Quest for Interesting Work: A Key Motivator

Surveys showing that people are highly motivated by interesting work suggest that this ant may be speaking for all of us.

(Source: Drawing by M. Twohy, © 1994 The New Yorker Magazine, Inc.)

Need Theories of Motivation

The first approach to motivation we will consider is the most basic: theories that explain motivation in terms of the satisfaction of basic human needs. Indeed, organizational scholars have paid a great deal of attention to the idea that people are motivated to use their jobs as mechanisms for satisfying their needs.

Need Hierarchy Theories

Probably the best-known concept of human needs in organizations has been proposed by Abraham Maslow.[19] Maslow was a clinical psychologist who introduced a theory of personal adjustment, known as **need hierarchy theory**, based on his observations of patients throughout the years. His premise was that if people grow up in an environment in which their needs are not met, they will be unlikely to function as healthy, well-adjusted individuals. Much of the popularity of Maslow's approach is based on applying the same idea in organizations: That is, unless people get their needs met on the job, they will not function as effectively as possible.

Specifically, Maslow theorized that people have five types of needs and that these are activated in a *hierarchical* manner. This means that the needs are aroused in a specific order from lowest to highest, and that the lowest-order need must be fulfilled before the next-highest-order need is triggered, and so on. The five major categories of needs are listed on the left side of Figure 5-5. Please refer to this diagram for a summary of the needs as we describe them here.

1. *Physiological needs* are the lowest-order, most basic needs specified by Maslow. These refer to satisfying fundamental biological drives, such as the need for food, air, water, and shelter. To satisfy such needs, organizations must provide employees with a salary that allows them to afford adequate living conditions. Similarly, sufficient opportunities to rest (e.g., coffee breaks) and to engage in physical activity (e.g., fitness and exercise facilities) are also important for people to meet their physiological needs. With increasing frequency, companies are providing exercise and physical fitness programs for their employees to help them stay healthy.[20] The rationale is quite simple: People who are too hungry or too ill to work will hardly be able to make much of a contribution to their companies.

2. *Safety needs*, the second level of need in Maslow's hierarchy, are activated after physiological needs are met. Safety needs refer to the need for a secure environment, free from threats of physical or psychological harm. Organizations can do many things to help satisfy safety needs. For example, they may provide employees with safety equipment (e.g., hard hats and goggles), life and health insurance plans, and security forces (e.g., police and fire protection). Similarly, jobs that

Figure 5-5 Need Theories: A Comparison

The five needs identified by Maslow's *need hierarchy theory* (shown at left) correspond to the three needs of Alderfer's *ERG theory* (shown at right). Whereas Maslow's theory specifies that these needs are activated in order from lowest level to highest level, Alderfer's theory specifies that needs can be activated in any order.

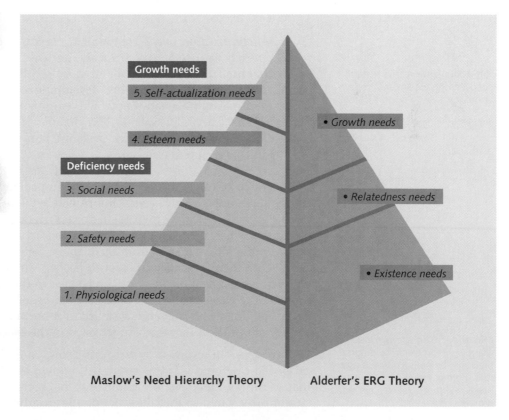

provide tenure (such as teaching) and no-layoff agreements provide a psychological security blanket that helps satisfy safety needs. All of these practices enable people to do their jobs without fear of harm and in a safe and secure atmosphere.

3. **Social needs**, Maslow's third level of needs, are activated after safety needs have been met. Social needs refer to the need to be affiliative—to have friends, to be loved and accepted by other people. To help meet social needs, organizations may encourage participation in social events, such as office picnics or parties. Company bowling or softball leagues, as well as country club memberships, also provide good opportunities for meeting social needs. Not only do such activities help promote physical fitness—helping satisfy physiological needs, as we noted above—but they also give employees a chance to socialize and develop friendships.

Taken together as a group, physiological needs, safety needs, and social needs are known as *deficiency needs*. Maslow's idea was that if these needs are not met, an individual will fail to develop into a healthy person—both physically and psychologically. In contrast, the next two highest-order needs, the ones at the top of the hierarchy, are known as *growth needs*. Gratification of these needs is said to help a person grow and to develop to his or her full potential.

4. **Esteem needs** are the fourth level of needs. These refer to a person's need to develop self-respect and to gain the approval of others. The desires to achieve success, have prestige, and be recognized by others all fall into this category. Companies do many things to satisfy their employees' esteem needs. They may, for example, have awards banquets to recognize distinguished achievements. Giving monetary bonuses—even small ones—in recognition of employees' suggestions for improvement helps promote their esteem. Nonmonetary awards, such as trophies and plaques, provide reminders of an employee's important contributions, continuously fulfilling esteem needs.[21] Including articles in company newsletters describing an employee's success, giving keys to the executive washroom, assigning private parking spaces, and posting signs identifying the "employee of the month" are also examples of things that can be done to satisfy esteem needs.

5. **Self-actualization needs** are found at the top of Maslow's hierarchy. These are the needs aroused only after all the lower-order needs have been met. **Self-actualization** refers to the need for self-fulfillment—the desire to become all that one is capable of being, developing to one's full potential. By working at their maximum creative potential, employees who are self-actualized can be extremely valuable assets to their organizations. Individuals who have self-actualized are working at their peak and represent the most effective use of an organization's human resources.

Research testing Maslow's theory has supported the distinction between deficiency needs and growth needs. Unfortunately the research has shown that not all people are able to satisfy their higher-order needs on the job. For example, Porter found that whereas lower-level managers were able to satisfy only their deficiency needs on the job, managers from the higher echelons of organizations were able to satisfy both their deficiency and growth needs.[22] In general, Maslow's theory has not received a great deal of support with respect to the specific notions it proposes—namely, the exact needs that exist and the order in which they are activated.[23] Specifically, many researchers have failed to confirm that there are only five basic categories of need and that they are activated in the exact order specified by Maslow.

ERG theory.   In response to these criticisms, an alternative formulation has been proposed by Alderfer.[24] His approach, known as **ERG theory**, is much simpler than Maslow's. Alderfer specifies not only that there are only three types of needs instead of five, but also that these are not necessarily activated in any specific order.

self-actualization The need to discover who we are and to develop ourselves to our full potential.

ERG theory An alternative to Maslow's *need hierarchy theory* proposed by Alderfer, which asserts that there are three basic human needs: existence, relatedness, and growth.

In fact, Alderfer postulates that any need may be activated at any time. The three needs specified by ERG theory are the needs for *existence*, *relatedness*, and *growth*. *Existence* needs correspond to Maslow's physiological needs and safety needs. *Relatedness* needs correspond to Maslow's social needs, the need for meaningful social relationships. Finally, *growth* needs correspond to the esteem needs and self-actualization needs in Maslow's theory—the need for developing one's potential. A summary of Alderfer's ERG theory is shown on the right side of Figure 5-5.

Clearly, ERG theory is much less restrictive than Maslow's need hierarchy theory. Its advantage is that it fits better with research evidence suggesting that although basic needs exist, they are not exactly as specified by Maslow.[25] Despite the fact that need theories are not in complete agreement about the precise number of needs and the relationships among them, they do agree that satisfying human needs is an important part of motivating behaviour on the job.

Managerial Applications of Need Theories

Probably the greatest value of need theories lies in the practical implications they have for management. In particular, the theories are important insofar as they suggest specific things that managers can do to help their subordinates become self-actualized. Because self-actualized employees are likely to work at their maximum creative potential, it makes sense to help people attain this state by helping them meet their needs. With this in mind, it is worthwhile to consider what organizations may do to help satisfy their employees' needs.

1. ***Promote a healthy workforce***. Some companies are helping satisfy their employees' physiological needs by providing incentives to keep them healthy. You will recall from the CASE PREVIEW for this chapter that Husky Injection Molding Systems subsidizes vegetarian meals in its cafeteria, provides an annual $500 allowance for employees to purchase vitamins, and has an on-site fitness centre—all designed to promote employee well-being.[26] Further, Hershey Foods Corporation, and Southern California Edison Company, among others, give insurance rebates to employees with healthy lifestyles, while charging extra premiums to those whose habits (e.g., smoking) put them at greater risk for health problems.[27] To the extent that these incentives encourage employees to adopt healthier lifestyles, the likelihood of satisfying their physiological needs is increased. For a summary of some of the creative ways today's companies are promoting healthy lifestyles—and the resulting benefits—see Table 5-1.[28]

2. ***Provide financial security***. Financial security is an important type of safety need. In this regard, some companies are going beyond the more traditional forms of payroll savings and profit-sharing plans. Notably, Barrick Gold Corp., in addition

TABLE 5-1 Companies Promoting Healthy Lifestyles

Here are some examples of companies whose wellness programs have benefited both their employees and themselves.

Source: Tully, 1995 and Waymen, 1998; see Note 29.)

Aetna Canada
www.aetna.ca

Company	Program Highlight	Payoff
Nortel Networks	Nortel's Alralia Centre offers comprehensive health education, fitness and wellness promotion programs, including weight issues, asthma management, and ulcer care	Positive correlation between employee satisfaction and customer satisfaction
L. L. Bean	U.S.$200 paid to each employee whose families quit smoking	Annual insurance premiums are half the U.S. national average
Coors	Employees with healthy habits receive awards used to buy extra days off or financial planning services	Fewer absences
Aetna	7600 employees enrolled in five state-of-the-art fitness centres	U.S.$282 per year saved for each employee who exercises

to giving employees stock options, also has a scholarship fund that pays approximately $3000 per year to academically qualified children of Barrick employees. This helps cover the students' expenses at accredited postsecondary institutions. Not only does this relieve some of the financial burden faced by Barrick employees who are shouldering the cost of their children's education, it also encourages employees to stay with the company until their children graduate.[30]

Financial security is a key aspect of job security, particularly in troubled economic times, when layoffs are inevitable. To help soften the blow of layoffs, more and more organizations are providing **outplacement services**—assistance in securing new employment. Although it is certainly more desirable not to be laid off at all, knowing that such assistance is available, if needed, helps reduce the negative emotional aspects of job insecurity. Companies such as Alcan, PetroCanada, Exxon, Brenda Mines (owned by Noranda), General Electric, AT&T, Wang, and Novacor offer outplacement programs for their employees who are laid off.[31]

3. *Provide opportunities to socialize*. To help satisfy its employees' social needs, IBM each spring holds a "Family Day" picnic near its Armonk, New York headquarters.[32] Some other companies have incorporated social activities deep into the fabric of their cultures. For example, Odetics Inc. (the Anaheim, California, manufacturer of intelligent machine systems) not only has its own repertory theatre troupe, but also regular "theme" days (e.g., a "sock hop" in the company's cafeteria), and a standing "fun committee," which organized such events as a lunch-hour employee olympics complete with goofy games.[33]

4. *Recognize employees' accomplishments*. Recognizing employees' accomplishments is an important way to satisfy their esteem needs. In this connection, Avon Canada, based in Pointe-Claire, Quebec,[34] offers its successful "independent Avon representatives" a variety of rewards for performance. Wilma Snipe of St. Catharines, Ontario is an eight-time Albee award winner. The award is named for the first "Avon Lady" and is given to the company's top earners. "A lot of ladies work just for that," says Snipe. Snipe also earned a three-day trip to the Bahamas and is a member of the prestigious President's Council, consisting of the ten top producers in each of the 11 Avon Canada districts that has at least $50 000 annual wholesale earnings.[35]

Whatever form they take, it is important to caution that awards are only effective at enhancing esteem when they are clearly linked to desired behaviours. Awards that are too general (e.g., a trophy for "best attitude") may not only fail to satisfy esteem needs, but also may minimize the impact of awards that are truly deserved. However, several of today's companies have recognized that one particular reward—time off the job—can be valuable for all employees because it helps satisfy a variety of different needs. For a closer look at this practice, see **THE QUEST FOR QUALITY** section.

Goal-Setting Theory

Just as people are motivated to satisfy their needs on the job, they are also motivated to strive for and attain goals. In fact, the process of setting goals is one of the most important motivational forces operating on people in organizations.[36] We will describe a prominent theory of **goal setting** and then identify some practical suggestions for setting goals effectively.

Locke and Latham's Goal-Setting Theory

Suppose that you are doing a task, such as word processing, when a performance goal is assigned. You are now expected, for example, to type 70 words per minute (wpm) instead of the 60 wpm you've been doing all along. Would you work hard to

outplacement services Assistance in finding new jobs, which companies provide to employees they lay off.

Avon Canada
www.avon.ca

goal setting The process of determining specific levels of performance for workers to attain.

The Quest for Quality

Sabbaticals: Time Off Satisfies Many Needs Simultaneously

In addition to doing things to satisfy employees' needs on the job, many companies have been satisfying their employees' needs by giving them time *off*—leaves known as *sabbaticals*. Once reserved for university professors who were given time to pursue their research, the concept of sabbaticals has found its way into growing numbers of private companies—among them, such companies as Toronto-based Alias/Wavefront (whose parent company is California-based Silicon Graphics Inc.),[37] DuPont, McDonald's, and Xerox.[38]

Proponents of such programs have argued that sabbaticals yield several benefits. First, sabbaticals help satisfy employees' basic physiological needs by giving them a chance to earn a well-deserved rest. Franca Miraglia, Alias/Wavefront's PR director, used her sabbatical to produce a play she had written, *Life on a Diet*, and to start work on another. Alias/Wavefront employees are given the opportunity to take a six-week sabbatical once every four years. The company wants employees to return from sabbatical "energized and creatively stimulated." Franca Miraglia is enthusiastic about her experience. "It's like doing any kind of fantastic travel," she says. "Just when you're starting to have enough of it, that's the time to go back to work." The goal of the sabbatical program is to reduce employee turnover related to burnout.[39]

Sabbaticals provide yet another important benefit: They reward faithful service, thereby satisfying esteem needs. This important source of recognition is offered by Wells Fargo Bank in the U.S. This company's leave program encourages sabbaticals taken for purposes of personal growth (e.g., one employee trained for the Master's World Swimming Championships) and those taken to perform social service (e.g., one executive went to Lithuania to help its transition from communism to capitalism). A Wells Fargo manager referred to the sabbatical as "one way we recognize the contributions that long-term employees have made."[40]

Experts caution that sabbaticals can be problematic in organizations in which those who take them are seen as weak and not dedicated to the company. To the contrary, organizations with effective sabbatical programs require employees to take leaves without fear of reprisals or damage to their reputations so that both the individual and the company benefit. Indeed, as consultant Joan Kofodimos explains, "growing people is good for the company. Companies have to say, 'Go get a life. That's what we reward around here.'"[41] Indeed, as companies take steps to satisfy their employees' needs, such as by offering sabbaticals, need theories lead us to expect that both employees and their organizations will reap the benefits.

Alias/Wavefront
www.aw.sgi.com

☞ *A complete description of self-efficacy and a general discussion of the important role it plays in OB appears in Chapter 3.*

meet this goal, or would you simply give up? Some insight into the question of how people respond to assigned goals is provided by a model proposed by Locke and Latham.[42] These theorists claim that an assigned goal influences people's beliefs about being able to perform the task in question (i.e., *self-efficacy*) and their personal goals. Both of these factors, in turn, influence performance.

The basic idea behind Locke and Latham's theory is that a goal serves as a motivator because it causes people to compare their present capacity to perform with that required to succeed at the goal. To the extent that people believe they will fall short of a goal, they will feel dissatisfied and work harder to attain it—so long as they believe it is possible for them to do so. When they succeed at meeting a goal, they feel competent and successful.[43] Having a goal enhances performance in large part because the goal makes clear exactly what type and level of performance is expected. Goals also help improve performance because they provide information about how well one is performing a task.

The model also claims that assigned goals will lead to the acceptance of those goals as *personal* goals. In other words, they will be accepted as one's own. This is the idea of **goal commitment**—the extent to which people invest themselves in meeting a goal.[44] Indeed, it has been shown that people will become more committed to a goal to the extent that they desire to attain that goal and believe they have a reasonable chance of doing so.[45] Likewise, the more strongly people believe they are capable of meeting a goal, the more strongly they will accept it as their own. By contrast, workers who

goal commitment The degree to which people accept and strive to attain goals.

perceive themselves as being physically incapable of meeting performance goals, for example, are generally not committed to meeting them, and do not strive to do so.[46]

Finally, the model claims that beliefs about both self-efficacy and personal goals influence task performance. This makes sense insofar as people are willing to exert greater effort when they believe they will succeed than when they believe their efforts will be in vain.[47] Moreover, goals that are not personally accepted will have little capacity to guide behaviour. In fact, research has shown that the more strongly people are committed to meeting goals, the better they will perform.[48] In general, Locke and Latham's model of goal setting has been supported by several studies, suggesting that it is a valuable source of insight into how the goal-setting process works.[49]

Managers' Guidelines for Setting Effective Performance Goals

Because researchers have been actively involved in studying the goal-setting process for many years, it is possible to summarize their findings in the form of principles. These represent very practical suggestions that practising managers can use to enhance motivation.

Assign specific goals. Probably the best-established finding of research on goal setting is that *people perform at higher levels when asked to meet a specific high-performance goal than when simply asked to "do their best" or when no goal at all is assigned.*[50] People tend to find specific goals quite challenging and are motivated to try to meet them—not only to fulfill management's expectations, but also to convince themselves that they have performed well.

A classic study by Latham and Baldes conducted at an Oklahoma lumber camp provides a particularly dramatic demonstration of this principle.[51] The participants in this research were lumber-camp crews who hauled logs from forests to their company's nearby sawmill. Over a three-month period before the study began, it was found that the crew loaded trucks to only about 60 percent of their legal capacity, wasting trips that cost the company money. Then, a specific goal was set, challenging the loggers to load the trucks to 94 percent of their capacity before returning to the mill. How effective was this goal in raising performance? The results, summarized in Figure 5-6, show that the goal was extremely effective. In fact, not only was the specific goal effective in raising performance to the goal level in just a few weeks, but the effects were long-lasting as well. In fact, the loggers were found to sustain this level of performance as long as seven years later. The resulting savings for the company were considerable.

This is just one of many studies that clearly demonstrate the effectiveness of setting specific, challenging performance goals. Other research has found that specific goals are also helpful in bringing about other desirable organizational goals, such as reducing absenteeism and industrial accidents.[52] Naturally, to reap such beneficial effects, goals must be not only highly specific, but challenging as well.

Assign difficult but acceptable performance goals. The goal set at the logging camp was successful not only because it was specific, but because it pushed crew members to a higher standard. Obviously, a goal that is too easy to attain will *not* bring about the desired increments in performance. For example, if you already type at 70 wpm, a goal of 60 wpm—although specific—would probably *lower* your performance. The key point is that *a goal must be difficult as well as specific for it to raise performance.* At the same time, however, people will work hard to reach challenging goals so long as these are within the limits of their capability. As goals become too difficult, performance suffers because people reject the goals as unrealistic and unattainable.[53]

For example, you may work much harder as a student in a class that challenges your ability than in one that is very easy. At the same time, you would probably give up trying if the only way of passing was to get perfect scores on all exams—a standard you would reject as being unacceptable. In short, specific goals are most effective if they are set neither too low nor too high.

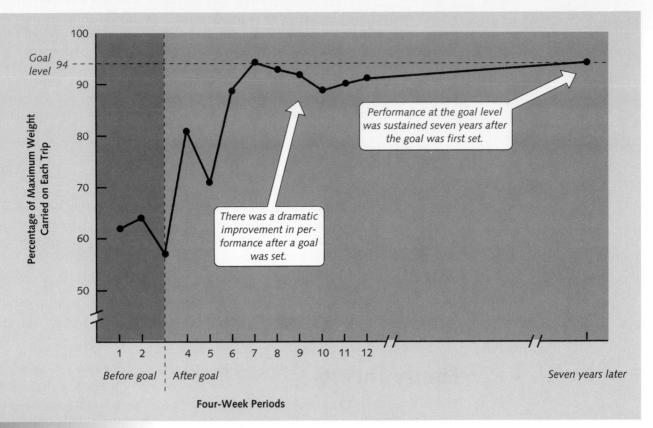

Figure 5-6 Goal Setting: Some Impressive Effects

The performance of loggers loading timber onto trucks markedly improved after a specific, difficult goal was set. The percentage of the maximum weight of timber loaded onto trucks rose from approximately 60 percent before any goal was set, to approximately 94 percent—the goal level—after the goal was set. Performance remained at this level for as long as seven years later.

(Source: Adapted from Latham & Baldes, 1975; see Note 51.)

☞ *Feedback is not only important in gauging one's progress toward meeting goals, but as detailed in Chapter 3, is key to the overall process of learning.*

The same phenomenon occurs in organizations. For example, Bell Canada's telephone operators are required to handle calls within 23 seconds, and FedEx's customer service agents are expected to answer customers' questions within 140 seconds.[54] Although both goals were initially considered difficult when they were imposed, the employees of both companies eventually met—or exceeded—these goals, and enjoyed the satisfaction of knowing they succeeded at this task. At a General Electric manufacturing plant, specific goals were set for productivity and cost reduction. Those goals that were perceived as challenging but possible led to improved performance, whereas those thought to be unattainable led to decreased performance.[55] How, then, should goals be set in a manner that strengthens employees' commitment to them?

One obvious way of enhancing goal acceptance is to *involve employees in the goal-setting process.* Research on workers' participation in goal setting has demonstrated that people accept goals that they have been involved in setting better than goals that have been assigned by their supervisors—and they work harder as a result.[56] In other words, participation in the goal-setting process tends to enhance goal commitment. Not only does participation help people better understand and appreciate goals they had a hand in setting, but it also helps ensure that the goals set are not unreasonable.

Provide feedback concerning goal attainment. The final principle of goal setting appears to be glaringly obvious, although in practice it is often not followed: Feedback helps people attain their performance goals. Just as golfers interested in improving their swings need feedback about where their balls are going, so do workers need feedback about how closely they are approaching their performance goals in order to meet them.

The importance of using feedback in conjunction with goal setting has been demonstrated in an ambitious study comparing the performance of work crews in the U.S. Air Force.[57] A standardized index of job performance was used to measure five different groups repeatedly over a two-year period. During the first nine months, a baseline measure of effectiveness was taken that was used to compare the relative impact of feedback and goal setting. Then the groups received feedback for five months (reports detailing how well they performed on various performance measures). After five months of feedback, the goal-setting phase of the study was begun. During this period, the crew members set goals for themselves with respect to their performance on various measures. Then, for the final five months, in addition to the feedback and goal setting, an incentive (time off from work) was made available to crew members who met their goals. The effectiveness of the crews during each phase of the study is summarized in Figure 5-7.

As Figure 5-7 clearly shows, feedback and goal setting dramatically increased group effectiveness. Group feedback improved performance approximately 50 percent over the baseline level. The addition of group goal setting improved it 75 percent over baseline. These findings show that the combination of goal setting and feedback helps raise the effectiveness of group performance. Groups that know how well they're doing and have a target goal to shoot for tend to perform very well. Providing incentives, however, improved performance only negligibly. The real incentive seems to be meeting the challenge of performing up to the level of the goal.

In sum, goal setting is a very effective tool managers can use to motivate people. Setting a specific, acceptably difficult goal and providing feedback about progress toward that goal greatly enhances job performance.

Equity Theory

The theories we've described thus far are based on the operation of completely individual processes—the activation of needs and the responses to goals. The next approach to motivation we will consider, **equity theory**, is also an individual-based theory, but one that adds a social component. Specifically, equity theory views motivation from the perspective of the *social comparisons* people make—that is, what they see when they compare themselves to others.[58] It proposes that individuals are motivated to maintain fair, or *equitable*, relationships among themselves and to avoid those relationships that are unfair, or *inequitable*.[59] The ways in which this is done has been a topic of considerable interest in the field of organizational behaviour.

equity theory The theory stating that people strive to maintain ratios of their own outcomes (rewards) to their own inputs (contributions) that are equal to the outcome/input ratios of others with whom they compare themselves.

Figure 5-7 Feedback: An Essential Aspect of Goal Setting

Research on U.S. Air Force crews over a two-year period showed that feedback enhanced performance and that the addition of goal setting enhanced it even more.

(Source: Based on data reported by Pritchard, Jones, Roth, Steubing, & Ekberg, 1988; see Note 57.)

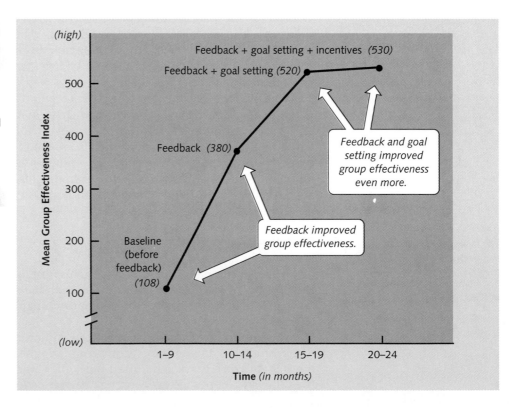

Adams's Equity Theory

outcomes The rewards employees receive from their jobs, such as salary and recognition.

inputs People's contributions to their jobs, such as their experience, qualifications, or the amount of time worked.

Equity theory, introduced by J. Stacy Adams, proposes that people comparing themselves to others focus on two variables, *outcomes* and *inputs*.[60] **Outcomes** are what we get out of our jobs, including pay, fringe benefits, and prestige. **Inputs** refer to the contributions made, such as the amount of time worked, the amount of effort expended, the number of units produced, and the qualifications brought to the job. Equity theory is concerned with outcomes and inputs as they are *perceived* by the people involved, not necessarily what they might actually be based on any objective standards. Not surprisingly, therefore, people sometimes disagree about what constitutes equitable treatment on the job.

Equity theory states that people compare their outcomes and inputs to those of others and judge the equitableness of these relationships in the form of ratios—that is, relationships of *equal to*, *greater than*, or *less than*. Specifically, they compare the ratios of their own outcomes/inputs to the ratios of other's outcomes/inputs. This "other" that serves as the basis of comparison may be someone else in one's work group, another employee in the organization, an individual working in the same field, or even oneself at an earlier point in time—in short, almost anyone against whom we compare ourselves. As shown in Figure 5-8, these comparisons can result in any of three different states: *overpayment inequity, underpayment inequity*, or *equitable payment*.

overpayment inequity The condition, resulting in feelings of guilt, in which the ratio of one's outcomes to inputs is more than the corresponding ratio of another person with whom that person compares himself or herself.

underpayment inequity The condition, resulting in feelings of anger, in which the ratio of one's outcomes to inputs is less than the corresponding ratio of another person with whom that person compares himself or herself.

equitable payment The state in which one person's outcome/input ratio is equivalent to that of another person with whom this individual compares himself or herself.

To illustrate these concepts, let's consider an example. Imagine that Sanjay and Rafaat work alongside each other on an assembly line doing the same job. Both workers have equal amounts of experience, training, and education, and work equally long and hard at their jobs—in other words, their inputs are equivalent. But, suppose Sanjay is paid a salary of $500 per week while Rafaat is paid only $350 per week. In this case, Sanjay's ratio of outcomes/inputs is higher than Rafaat's, creating a state of **overpayment inequity** for Sanjay and **underpayment inequity** for Rafaat (since the ratio of his outcomes/inputs is lower). According to equity theory, Sanjay, realizing that he is paid more than an equally qualified person doing the same work, will feel *guilty* in response to his overpayment. By contrast, Rafaat, realizing that he is paid less than an equally qualified person for doing the same work, will feel *angry* in response to his underpayment. Feeling guilty or angry are negative emotional states that people are motivated to change. Specifically, they will seek to create a state of **equitable payment** in which their outcome/input ratios are equal, leading them to feel *satisfied*.

How can people change inequitable states to equitable ones? Equity theory suggests several possible courses of action (see Table 5-2). In general, people who are underpaid may either lower their inputs or raise their outcomes. Either action would effectively bring the underpaid individual's outcome/input ratio into line with that of the comparison person. In our example, the underpaid Rafaat might lower his

TABLE 5-2 Possible Reactions to Inequity: A Summary

People can respond to overpayment and underpayment inequities in behavioural and/or psychological ways. A few of these are summarized here. These reactions help change the perceived inequities into a state of perceived equity.

Type of Inequity	Type of Reaction	
	Behavioural (What you can do is . . .)	Psychological (What you can think is . . .)
Overpayment inequity	Raise your inputs (e.g., work harder), or lower your outcomes (e.g., work through a paid vacation).	Convince yourself that your outcomes are deserved based on your inputs (e.g., rationalize that you work harder than others and so you deserve more pay).
Underpayment inequity	Lower your inputs (e.g., reduce effort), or raise your outcomes (e.g., get a raise in pay).	Convince yourself that others' inputs are really higher than your own (e.g., rationalize that the comparison worker is really more qualified and so deserves higher outcomes).

Figure 5-8 Equity Theory: An Overview

To judge equity or inequity, people compare the ratios of their own outcomes/inputs to the corresponding ratios of others (or themselves at earlier points in time). The resulting states—*overpayment inequity, underpayment inequity,* and *equitable payment*—and their associated emotional responses are summarize here.

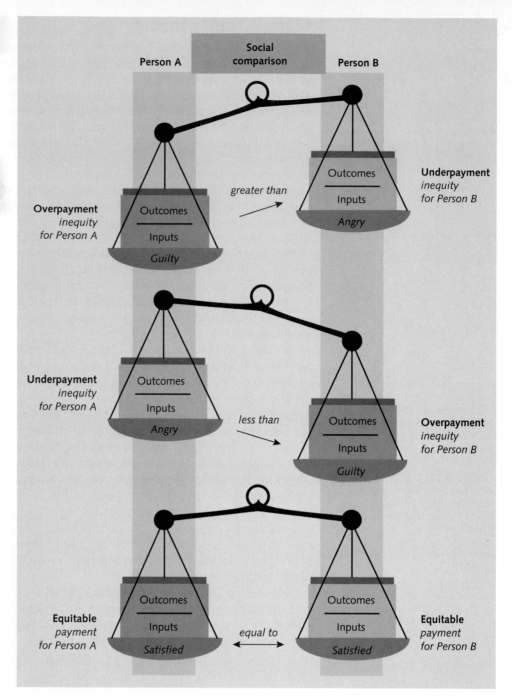

inputs—say, by slacking off, arriving at work late, leaving early, taking longer breaks, doing less work, or lowering work quality. In an extreme case, he may quit his job. He also may attempt to raise his outcomes, such as by asking for a raise, or even taking home company property, such as tools or office supplies. By contrast, the overpaid person, Sanjay, may do the opposite—raise his inputs or lower his outcomes. For example, he might put forth much more effort, work longer hours, and try to make a greater contribution to the company. He also might lower his outcomes, such as by working through a paid vacation, or not taking advantage of fringe benefits the company offers. These are all specific *behavioural* reactions to inequitable conditions—that is, things people *do* by way of attempting to change inequitable states to equitable ones.

As you might imagine, people may be unwilling to do some of the things necessary to respond behaviourally to inequities. In particular, they may be unwilling to restrict their productivity (in fear of getting caught "goofing off"), or uncomfortable asking their bosses for raises. As a result, they may resort to resolving the inequity not by changing their behaviour, but by changing the way they think about the situation. Because equity theory deals with perceptions of fairness or unfairness, it is reasonable to expect that inequitable states may be redressed by merely altering one's thinking about the circumstances. For example, underpaid people may rationalize that others' inputs are really higher than their own (e.g., "I suppose she really *is* more qualified than me"), thereby convincing themselves that the other person's higher outcomes are justified. Similarly, overpaid people may convince themselves that they really *are* better and really do deserve their relatively higher pay. So, by changing the way they see things, people can come to perceive inequitable situations as equitable, thereby effectively reducing their inequity distress.[61]

There is a great deal of evidence to suggest that people are motivated to redress inequities at work and that they respond much as equity theory suggests. For example, research has shown that professional basketball players who are underpaid (i.e., ones who are paid less than others who perform as well or better) score fewer points than those who are equitably paid.[62] That is, they lowered their inputs.

We also know that underpaid workers attempt to raise their outcomes. One way they might do this, although it is unethical, is by stealing from their employers. That this occurs was demonstrated in an organization studied by one of the authors (J. G.). Due to a financial crisis, workers at two manufacturing plants suffered an underpayment inequity created by the introduction of a temporary pay cut of 15 percent.[63] During the ten-week period under which workers received lower pay, company officials noticed that theft of company property increased dramatically. However, in another factory in which comparable work was done by workers paid at their normal rates (the control group), the theft rate remained low (see Figure 5-9). This pattern suggests that employees may have stolen property in order to compensate for reduced pay. Consistent with this possibility, it was found that when the normal rate of pay was reinstated in the two factories, the theft rate returned to its normal (pre-pay cut), low level.

Applying Equity Theory: Some Motivational Tips for Managers

Equity theory has some important implications for ways of motivating people. We will highlight several of these here.

1. **Underpayment should be avoided.** Companies that attempt to save money by reducing employees' salaries may find that employees respond in many different ways to even the score. For example, they may steal, shave a few minutes off their work days, or otherwise withhold production.

   In recent years, a particularly unsettling form of institutionalizing underpayment has materialized in the form of **two-tier wage structures**—payment systems in which newer employees are paid less than those hired to do the same work at an earlier point in time. Not surprisingly, such systems are considered to be highly unfair, particularly by those in the lower tier.[64] When such a plan was instituted at the Giant Food supermarket chain, two-thirds of the lower-tier employees quit their jobs in the first three months. "It stinks," said a clerk at one Giant store in Los Angeles, "They're paying us lower wages for the same work."[65]

   A proposal to institute a two-tier wage system at United Airlines in the mid-1980s led its pilots to go on strike (see Figure 5-10).[66] And, who can blame them? The plan would have virtually cut in half the amount new DC-10 pilots would be earning when they reached the top of their careers—an annual difference of over U.S.$64 000 compared to the earlier hired pilots. Clearly, the negative reactions to such forms of inequities should make employers think twice before introducing any plan that would compensate employees unfairly.

2. **Overpayment should be avoided.** You may think that because overpaid employees work hard to deserve their pay, it would be a useful motivational technique to pay people more than they merit. There are several reasons why this

two-tier wage structures
Payment systems in which newer employees are paid less than employees hired at earlier times to do the same work.

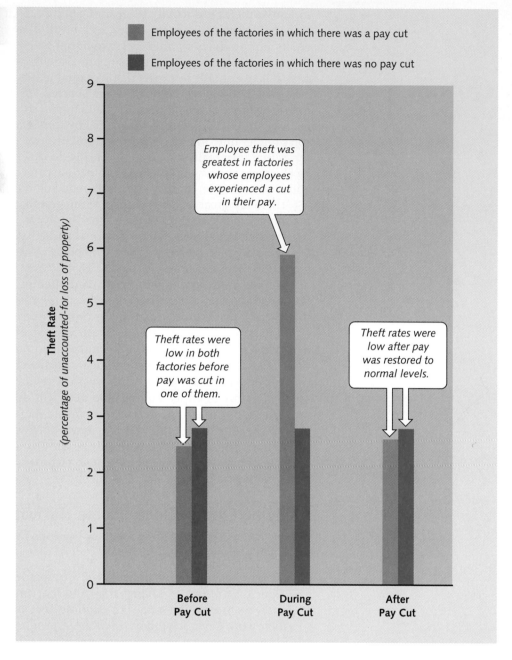

would not work. First, the increases in performance shown in response to over-payment inequity tend to be only temporary. As time goes on, people begin to believe that they actually deserve the higher pay they're getting and bring their work level down to normal. A second reason why it is unwise to overpay employees is that when you overpay one employee, you are underpaying all the others. When the majority of the employees feel underpaid, they will lower their performance, resulting in a net *decrease* in productivity—and widespread dissatisfaction. Hence, the conclusion is clear: *Managers should strive to treat all employees equitably.*

We realize, of course, that this may be easier said than done. Part of the difficulty resides in the fact that feelings of equity and inequity are based on perceptions, and these perceptions aren't always easy to control. One approach that may help is to *be open and honest about outcomes and inputs.* People tend to overestimate how much their superiors are paid and therefore tend to feel that their own pay is not as high as it should be.[67] However, if information about pay is shared, inequitable feelings may not result.

☞ *For a general discussion of the distortions associated with the process of perception, see Chapter 3.*

Figure 5-10 Striking: A Response to Feelings of Inequity
In the mid-1980s, pilots from United Airlines went on strike to protest a proposed *two-tier wage system* that would have paid new pilots considerably less than those who were already employed. Their strike was a potent response to their feelings of inequity.

3. *Managers should present information about outcomes in a thorough and socially sensitive manner*. This suggestion follows from research showing that people's assessments of fairness on the job go beyond merely what their outcomes and inputs are to their knowledge of *how* these were determined—that is, to their sense of **procedural justice**. For example, it has been found that even negative outcomes such as layoffs and pay cuts can be accepted and recognized as fair to the extent that people understand the procedures that brought them about. Such information, particularly when presented in a highly sensitive and caring manner, tends to take some of the sting out of those undesirable outcomes.[68]

To live through a pay freeze is painful, of course, but people are more likely to accept it as fair if a good explanation for it has been provided. Schaubroeck, May, and Brown demonstrated this in their recent study of manufacturing workers' reactions to a pay freeze.[69] Comparisons were made between two groups: one that received a thorough explanation of the conditions

procedural justice Perceptions of the fairness of the procedures used to determine outcomes.

necessitating the pay freeze (e.g., information about the organization's economic problems) and one that received no such information. Although all workers were adversely affected by the freeze, those receiving the explanation better accepted it. In particular, it reduced their interest in looking for a new job. These findings suggest that even if managers cannot do anything to eliminate workplace inequities, they may be able to take some of the sting out of them by providing explanations as to why these unfortunate conditions are necessary.

Expectancy Theory

expectancy theory The theory that asserts that motivation is based on people's beliefs about the probability that effort will lead to performance (*expectancy*), multiplied by the probability that performance will lead to reward (*instrumentality*), multiplied by the perceived value of the reward (*valence*).

Instead of focusing on individual needs, goals, or social comparisons, **expectancy theory** takes a broader approach: It looks at the role of motivation in the overall work environment. In essence, the theory asserts that people are motivated to work when they *expect* that they will be able to achieve the things they want from their jobs. Expectancy theory characterizes people as rational beings who think about what they have to do in order to be rewarded and how much the reward means to them before they perform their jobs. But, as we will see, the theory doesn't focus only on what people think. It also recognizes that these thoughts combine with other aspects of the organizational environment to influence job performance.

Basic Elements of Expectancy Theory

Although slightly different versions of expectancy theory have been proposed—including popular ones by Vroom and by Porter and Lawler—expectancy theorists agree that motivation is the result of three different types of beliefs that people have.[70,71] These are as follows:

expectancy The belief that one's efforts will positively influence one's performance.

- **expectancy**—the belief that one's effort will result in effective performance
- **instrumentality**—the belief that one's performance will be rewarded
- **valence**—the perceived value of the rewards to the recipient.

instrumentality An individual's beliefs regarding the likelihood of being rewarded in accord with his or her own level of performance.

Sometimes people believe that putting forth a great deal of effort means that they will get a lot accomplished. However, in other cases, people do not expect that their efforts will have much effect on how well they do. For example, an employee operating a faulty piece of equipment may have a very low *expectancy* that his or her efforts will lead to high levels of performance. Naturally, someone working under such conditions probably would not continue to exert much effort.

valence The value a person places on the rewards he or she receives from an organization.

Even *if* an employee works hard and performs at a high level, motivation may falter if that performance is not suitably rewarded—that is, if the performance is not perceived as *instrumental* in bringing about the rewards. So, for example, a worker who is extremely productive may be poorly motivated to perform if he or she has already reached the top level of pay given by the company.

Finally, even *if* employees believe that hard work will lead to good performance *and* that they will be rewarded commensurate with their performance, they still may be poorly motivated *if* those so-called rewards have a low *valence* to them. In other words, someone who doesn't value the rewards offered by the organization is not motivated to attain them. As an example, a reward of $100 would not be likely to motivate a multimillionaire, whereas it may be a very desirable reward for someone of more modest means. Only those rewards that have a high positive valence to their recipients will motivate behaviour.

Expectancy theory claims that motivation is a multiplicative function of all three components. This means that higher levels of motivation will result when expectancy, instrumentality, and valence are *all* high than when they are all low. The multiplicative assumption also implies that if any one of these three components is zero, the overall level of motivation will be zero. So, for example, even if an employee believes that his or her effort will result in performance, which will result in reward, motivation will be zero if the valence of the reward he or she expects to receive is zero. Figure 5-11 summarizes the definitions of expectancy theory components and shows their relationships.

Figure 5-11 also highlights a point we made in our opening remarks about motivation: Motivation is not equivalent to job performance. Expectancy theory recognizes that motivation is one of several important determinants of job performance. In particular, the theory assumes that *skills and abilities* also contribute to a person's job performance. It's no secret that some people are better suited to performing their jobs than others by virtue of their unique characteristics and special skills and abilities. For example, a tall, strong, well-coordinated person is likely to make a better professional basketball player than a very short, weak, uncoordinated one—even if the shorter person is highly motivated to succeed.

Expectancy theory also recognizes that job performance will be influenced by people's *role perceptions*—in other words, what they believe is expected of them on the job. To the extent that there are disagreements about what one's job duties are, performance may suffer. For example, an assistant manager who believes her primary job duty is to train new employees may find that her performance is downgraded by a supervisor who believes she should be spending more time doing routine paperwork instead. In this case, the person's performance wouldn't suffer as a result of any deficit in motivation, but simply because of misunderstandings about what the job entails.

Figure 5-11 Expectancy Theory: An Overview

According to *expectancy theory,* motivation is the product of three types of beliefs: *expectancy* (the belief that one's effort will influence performance), *instrumentality* (the belief that one will be rewarded for one's performance), and *valence* (the perceived value of the rewards expected). The theory also recognizes that motivation is only one of several factors responsible for job performance.

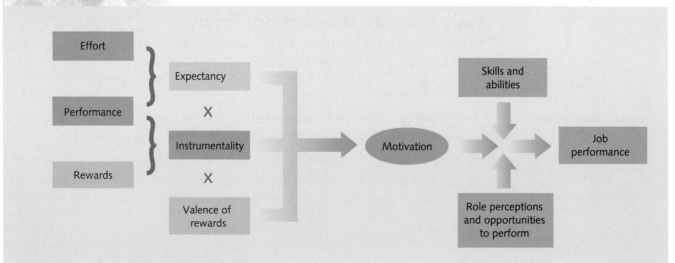

Finally, expectancy theory also recognizes the role of *opportunities to perform* one's job. Even the best employees may perform at low levels if their opportunities are limited. For example, a highly motivated salesperson may perform poorly if opportunities are restricted (say, the territory is having a financial downturn or available inventory is limited).

It is important to recognize that expectancy theory views motivation as just one of several determinants of job performance. Motivation, combined with a person's skills and abilities, role perceptions, and opportunities, influences job performance.

Expectancy theory has generated a great deal of research and has been successfully applied to understanding behaviour in many different organizational settings.[72] Although the theory has received only mixed support about some of its specific aspects (e.g., the multiplicative assumption), it is still one of the dominant approaches to the study of motivation in organizations. Probably the primary reason for expectancy theory's popularity is the many useful suggestions it makes for practising managers. We will now describe some of the most essential applications of expectancy theory, giving examples from organizations in which they have been implemented.

Managerial Applications of Expectancy Theory

Expectancy theory has several important implications for ways of motivating employees.

1. ***Clarify people's expectancies that their effort will lead to performance.*** Motivation may be enhanced by training employees to do their jobs more efficiently and so achieve higher levels of performance from their efforts. It also may be possible to enhance effort-performance expectancies by following employees' suggestions about ways to change their jobs. To the extent that employees are aware of problems in their jobs that interfere with their performance, attempting to alleviate these problems may help them perform more effectively. In essence, what we are saying is: *Make the desired performance attainable.* Good supervisors not only make it clear to people what is expected of them, but they also help them attain that level of performance.

☞ As discussed in Chapter 3, training can be accomplished in many different ways and can serve many different purposes.

2. ***Administer rewards that are positively valent to employees.*** In other words, the carrot at the end of the stick must be tasty for it to have potential as a motivator. These days, with a highly diverse workforce, it would be misleading to assume that all employees care about having the same rewards. Whereas some might recognize the incentive value of a pay raise, others might prefer additional vacation days, improved insurance benefits, day-care, or elder-care facilities. "There's nothing wrong with a cash award, but then it's spent. Seemingly small gestures—a parking spot, a plaque, bulletin boards with pictures of employees—can be as effective as banquets and travel," said Donald Gagnon, training coordinator at Brunswick Mining and Smelting in Bathurst, New Brunswick.[73] With this in mind, many companies have introduced **cafeteria-style benefit plans**—incentive systems allowing employees to select their fringe benefits from a menu of available alternatives. Given that fringe benefits represent almost 40 percent of payroll costs, more and more companies are recognizing the value of administering them flexibly.[74] For example, Primerica has had a flexible benefit plan in use since 1978—one that almost 95 percent of the company's 8000 salaried employees believe is extremely beneficial to them.[75] Today's companies are doing many creative things to help ensure that their employees can achieve rewards that have value to them (see Table 5-3).[76]

cafeteria-style benefit plans
Incentive systems in which employees have an opportunity to select the fringe benefits they want from a menu of available alternatives.

3. ***Clearly link valued rewards and performance.*** In other words, managers should enhance their subordinates' beliefs about instrumentality by specifying exactly what job behaviours will lead to what rewards. To the extent that it is possible for employees to be paid in ways directly linked to their performance—such as through piece-rate incentive systems, sales commission plans, or bonuses—

TABLE 5-3 Ensuring Positively Valent Rewards: What Some Companies Are Doing	Company	Practice
All companies pay their employees, but a few also provide more creative incentives that help ensure that employees receive rewards that have value to them.	Cynamid Canada Winnipeg, Manitoba	Key to Innovation Program rewards employees who are frequent innovators. If their ideas improve productivity, employees receive points that can be exchanged for items such as appliances or trips.
(Source: Based on Nelson and Human Resources Development Canada; see Note 77.)	Meloche Monnex Montreal, Quebec	Employees with top performance records receive a letter of congratulations from the president of the insurance banking company, are given double the annual rate of increase, and are given the privilege of choosing training opportunities and new responsibilities in the company.
	Precision Metalcraft Winnipeg, Manitoba	Daily work assignments are distributed at a "Huddle" every morning. Senior executives in the sheet metal company now work from the shop floor to emphasize the sense of teamwork.
	AGT Ltd. Edmonton, Alberta	Employees receive variable pay above their annual salary depending on the company's profits.

pay-for-performance plan A payment system in which employees are paid differentially, based on the quantity and quality of their performance. Pay-for-performance plans strengthen *instrumentality* beliefs.

Canadian Tire Acceptance Ltd.
www.canadiantire.ca

expectancy theory specifies that it would be effective to do so. Indeed, a great deal of research has shown that performance increases can result from carefully implemented merit systems—frequently referred to as **pay-for-performance plans**.[78] For employees of Canadian Tire Acceptance Ltd. in Welland, Ontario, compensation is tied to performance, with the pay range being determined by the "pay band" of the organizational level to which the employee is assigned. The "pay band" or range is based on a yearly assessment of each employee's Current Actual Capacity (how complex the job is and to what extent the employee has mastered the necessary skills).[79]

It is important to caution that such systems are usually so highly effective that it is crucial for organizations to consider exactly what employees might do to perform at high levels. For example, in 1992 Sears auto mechanics were paid in proportion to the volume of their repairs. This policy appears to have encouraged the mechanics to make repairs that weren't necessary—or so it was alleged in 1992.[80] (To avoid such problems Sears has since eliminated this method of paying its auto mechanics.) Following from this example, our advice is clear: When you pay people for their performance, be sure you know exactly what performance you're buying.

To further illustrate the importance of selecting only the most desired performance to reward, let's consider IBM's newly instituted pay plan for its 30 000 sales representatives. Previously, most of the pay these reps received was based on flat salary; their compensation was not linked to how well they did. Now, however, their pay is carefully tied to two factors that are essential to the company's success—profitability and customer satisfaction. So, instead of receiving commissions on the amount of the sale, as so many salespeople do, 60 percent of IBMers' commissions are tied to the company's profit on that sale. As a result, the more the company makes, the more the reps make. And to make sure that the reps don't push only high-profit items that customers might not need, the remaining 40 percent of their commissions are based on customer satisfaction. Customers are regularly surveyed about the extent to which their sales representatives helped them meet their business objectives. The better the reps have done in this regard, the greater their commissions. Since introducing this plan in late 1993, IBM has been effective in reversing its unprofitable trend. Although there are certainly many factors responsible for this turnaround, experts are confident that this practice of clearly linking desired performance to individual rewards is a key factor.

Of course, the rewards need not be monetary in nature; even verbal recognition for a job well done can be very effective. In some extreme cases, good performance is rewarded with shares of ownership in the company.[81] Unfortunately, not all incentive plans do as good a job as they should in rewarding desired performance. A recent survey found that only 25 percent of employees see a clear link between good job performance and their pay raises. Obviously many organizations have a long 2ay to go in raising their employees' instrumentality beliefs.[83] However, experts believe that pay–for–performance will constitute a key part of the pay for top managers and executives in the future. For a closer look at the way this practice is expected to operate, see the **ORGANIZATIONAL TRENDS** section.

Job Design: Structuring Tasks for High Motivation

job design An approach to motivation suggesting that jobs can be created so as to enhance people's interest in doing them (see *job enlargement, job enrichment* and the *job characteristics model*).

☞ *In Chapter 1 we described the highly influential nature of Taylor's now-rejected "classical" approach to the study of organizations.*

The final approach to motivation we will consider is the largest in scope because it is directed at improving the nature of the work performed. The idea behind **job design** is that motivation can be enhanced by making jobs more appealing to people. As you may recall from Chapter 1, Frederick W. Taylor's principle of *scientific management* attempted to stimulate performance by designing jobs in the most efficient fashion. However, treating people like machines often meant having them engage in repetitive movements which they found highly routine and monotonous. Not surprisingly, people became bored with such jobs and frequently quit.[83] Fortunately, today's organizational scientists have found several ways of designing jobs that can not only be performed very efficiently, but also are highly pleasant and enjoyable.

Job Enlargement and Job Enrichment

job enlargement The practice of expanding the content of a job to include more variety and a greater number of tasks at the same level.

Imagine that you have a highly routine job, such as tightening the lugs on the left rear wheel of a car as it rolls down the assembly line. Naturally, such a highly repetitive task would be monotonous and not very pleasant. One of the first modern approaches to redesigning jobs suggested that such consequences could be minimized by having people perform an increased number of different tasks all at the same level. This approach is known as **job enlargement.** To enlarge the jobs in our example, workers could be required to tighten the lugs on all four wheels. As a result of such an action, employees have no more responsibility nor use any greater skills, but they perform a wider variety of different tasks at the same level. Adding tasks in this fashion is said to increase the *horizontal job loading* of the position.

A few years ago, American Greetings Corp. enlarged some 400 jobs in its creative division.[84] Now, rather than always working exclusively on Christmas cards, for example, employees will be able to move back and forth between different teams, such as those working on birthday ribbons, humorous mugs, and Valentine's Day gift bags. Employees at American Greetings reportedly enjoy the variety, as do those at RJR Nabisco, Corning, and Eastman Kodak, other companies that have recently allowed employees to make such lateral moves.

Although most reports of the effectiveness of job enlargement have been anecdotal, carefully conducted empirical studies also have examined their impact. For example, Campion and McClelland studied the effects of a job enlargement program instituted at a large financial services company.[85] The unenlarged jobs had different employees perform separate paperwork tasks such as preparing, sorting, coding, and keypunching various forms. The enlarged jobs combined these various functions into larger jobs performed by the same people. Although it was more difficult and expensive to train people to perform the enlarged jobs than the separate jobs, important benefits resulted as well. In particular, employees expressed greater job satisfaction and less boredom. And because one person followed the whole job all the way through, greater opportunities to correct errors existed. Not surprisingly, customers were satisfied with the result.

Confronting the Challenge of Paying for Performance at the Top

You see it quite often in the popular press: Someone exclaiming that many of today's executives are grossly overpaid—especially when they receive millions of dollars in compensation despite the poor performance of their companies.[86] For most executives the big bucks come not only in the form of regular salaries, but also stock options.[87] But when stock exchanges are enjoying a bull market, many stocks rise simply because the market is rising, and not because of anything the executives themselves might have done to enhance their companies' values. As a result, they are reaping unearned benefits and are not necessarily paid in proportion to their contributions to their companies' successes.

In this era, in which shareholders are clamouring for value, such a practice is clearly unacceptable. With this foundation in mind, futurist and management consultant Barry Minkin has predicted that the days of relying on short-term measures of executive performance (such as quarterly performance) are coming to a close.[88] Replacing them will be longer-term measures, such as how well the company has reached biannual goals. Longer-term approaches may lead to lower pay for executives, especially if their base pay also shrinks, as it is expected to do.

Part of the problem in establishing pay-for-performance plans for top executives is that the nature of their work doesn't immediately lend itself to quantification. By contrast, paying salespeople or production workers for their performance is a relatively straightforward matter. Yet, there has been, and will continue to be, a shift toward pay-for-performance plans among people in higher-level jobs.

Experts believe that the time is approaching when people will no longer receive raises just for showing up. If you—and your company—perform well, you may receive a tidy sum. Conversely, if your company performs poorly, you will be penalized. This was the case at Spar Aerospace Ltd. When the company did not do well in 1997 its president and CEO, Colin Watson, took a major cut in compensation receiving no bonus and no raise. His bonus the previous year had been $300 000.[89]

This gamble paid off for managers who work for the Yoplait yogurt division of General Mills, several of whom have enjoyed bonuses as high as 50 percent above their salaries in exchange for exceeding the company's performance goals. Such rewards not only keep Yoplait managers motivated, but keep them on the job. In the words of product manager Kim Nelson, "I get calls from headhunters talking about bigger salaries. But I'm not interested. Here, if you do a great job, you get a bigger reward."[90] The pay-for-performance system at Taco Bell rewards real estate managers (people who find sites for new restaurants) so lavishly that one such individual, 36-year-old Amy McConnell, recently earned eight times her base pay in bonuses.

It would be misleading to suggest that such bonuses—or any pay-for-performance plans, for that matter—work because they opulently reward employees. To the contrary, they provide incentives for employees to work extremely hard. If they are paid highly, it is because they made great contributions to the company's success. Ms. McConnell secured a whopping 45 new sites for Taco Bell. And those Yoplait managers beat company performance goals by 250 percent.

The bottom line is this: Pay-for-performance plans motivate workers and help companies succeed because they align the interests of the employees with the interests of the company. When the company thrives, so do its employees. Although implementing pay-for-performance plans creates special challenges when it comes to paying executives, you can expect to see such problems addressed in the years to come. From all appearances, it looks as if there's just no turning back: Pay–for–performance is here to stay.

Spar Aerospace Ltd.
www.spar.ca

Unfortunately, in a follow-up investigation of the same company conducted two years later, Campion and McClelland found that not all the beneficial effects continued.[91] Notably, employee satisfaction levelled off and the rate of errors went up, suggesting that as employees got used to their enlarged jobs they found them less interesting and stopped paying attention to all the details. Hence, although job enlargement may help improve job performance, its effects may not be long-lasting.

In contrast to job enlargement, **job enrichment** gives employees not only more jobs to do, but more tasks to perform at a higher level of skill and responsibility (see Figure 5-12). Job enrichment gives employees the opportunity to take greater control over how they do their jobs. Because people performing enriched jobs have increased opportunities to work at higher levels, the job enrichment process is said to increase a job's *vertical job loading*.

Probably the most carefully studied job enrichment program was the one developed by Volvo, the Swedish auto manufacturer. In response to serious dissension within its workforce in the late 1960s, the company's then-president, Pehr Gyllenhammar, introduced job enrichment in its Kalmar assembly plant.[92] Cars are assembled by 25 groups of approximately 20 workers, each of whom is responsible for one part of the car's assembly (e.g., engine, electrical system). In contrast to the usual assembly-line method of manufacturing cars, Volvo's work groups are set up so they can freely plan, organize, and inspect their own work. In time, the workers became more satisfied with their jobs and the plant experienced a significant reduction in turnover and absenteeism.

Although evidence suggests that job enrichment programs have also been successful at other organizations, several factors limit their popularity.[93] Most obvious is the *difficulty of implementation*. To redesign existing facilities so that jobs can be enriched is often prohibitively expensive. Besides, the technology needed to perform certain jobs makes it impractical for them to be redesigned. Another impediment is the *lack of employee acceptance*. Although many relish it, some people do *not* desire the additional responsibility associated with performing enriched jobs. In particular, individuals low in achievement motivation are especially frustrated with enriched jobs.[94] Similarly, people may get used to doing their jobs in certain ways and don't like having to change. In fact, when a group of American auto workers was sent to Sweden to work in a Saab engine assembly plant where jobs were highly enriched, five out of six indicated that they preferred their traditional assembly-line jobs.[95] Clearly, enriched jobs are not for everyone.

☞ The underlying reasons why people are resistant to change, as well as ways of overcoming such resistance, are discussed in Chapter 16.

Thus far, we have failed to specify precisely *how* to enrich a job. *What* elements of a job need to be enriched for it to be effective? An attempt to expand the idea of job enrichment, known as the *job characteristics model*, provides an answer to this important question.

The Job Characteristics Model

This approach assumes that jobs can be designed to help people get enjoyment out of their jobs and care about the work they do. The **job characteristics model** identifies how jobs can be designed to help people feel that they are doing meaningful and valuable work. In particular, the model proposed by Hackman and Oldham specifies that enriching certain elements of jobs alters people's psychological states in a manner that enhances their work effectiveness.[96] Specifically, the model identifies five *core job dimensions* that help create three *critical psychological states*, leading, in turn, to several beneficial *personal and work outcomes* (see Figure 5-13).

The five critical job dimensions are *skill variety, task identity, task significance, autonomy*, and *feedback*. Let's take a closer look at these.

1. **Skill variety** refers to the extent to which a job requires a number of different activities using several of the employee's skills and talents. For example, an office manager with high skill variety may have to perform many different tasks (e.g., word processing, answering the telephone, greeting visitors, and filing records).

2. **Task identity** refers to the extent to which a job requires completing a whole piece of work from beginning to end. For example, tailors will have high task identity if they do everything related to making a whole suit (e.g., measuring the client, selecting the fabric, cutting and sewing it, and altering the suit to fit).

3. **Task significance** refers to the degree of impact the job is believed to have on others. For example, medical researchers working on a cure for a deadly disease

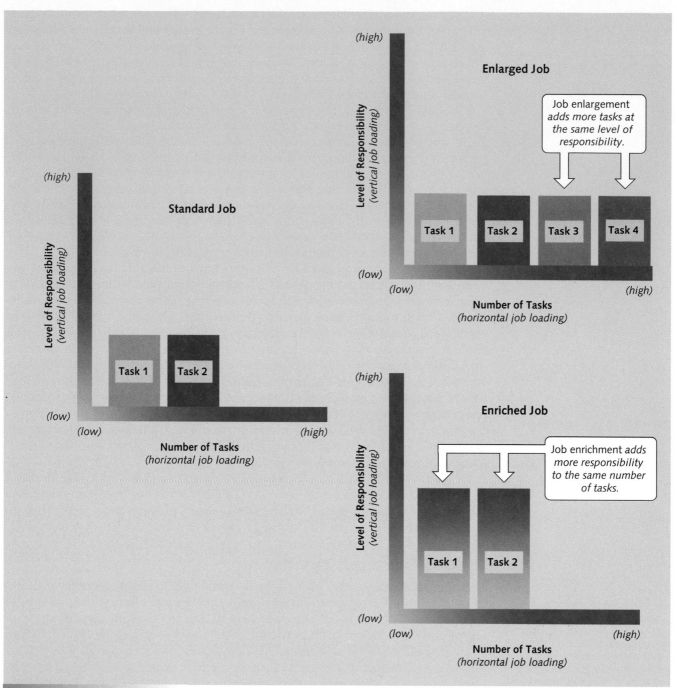

Figure 5-12 Job Enlargement and Job Enrichment: A Comparison

Designing jobs by increasing the number of tasks performed at the same level (*horizontal job loading*) is referred to as *job enlargement*. Designing jobs by increasing employees' level of responsibility and control (*vertical job loading*) is referred to as *job enrichment*.

probably recognize the importance of their work to the world at large. However, more modest contributions to a company can be recognized as significant to the extent that employees understand the role of their jobs in the overall mission of the organization.

4. ***Autonomy*** refers to the extent to which employees have the freedom and discretion to plan, schedule, and carry out their jobs as desired. For example, a furniture-repair person may act highly autonomously by freely scheduling his or her day's work and by freely deciding how to tackle each repair job confronted.

5. ***Feedback*** refers to the extent to which the job allows people to have information about the effectiveness of their performances. For example, telemarketing representatives regularly receive information about how many calls they make per day and the number and values of the sales made.

Absenteeism has been so chronically high at a manufacturing plant that on many days, there is not enough crew present at the start of a shift to staff all stations of the assembly line. The company is suffering as a result and turns to you for advice.

1. How can the job be made more interesting to encourage employees to show up for work?

2. How can rewards be used to help alleviate the problem? What are the theoretical bases for these suggestions?

The model specifies that these various job dimensions have important effects on various critical psychological states. For example, skill variety, task identity, and task significance jointly contribute to a task's *experienced meaningfulness*: A task is considered to be meaningful to the extent that it is experienced as being highly important, valuable, and worthwhile. Jobs that provide a great deal of autonomy are said to make people feel *personally responsible and accountable for their work*. When they are free to decide what to do and how to do it, they feel more responsible for the results, whether good or bad. Finally, effective feedback is said to give employees *knowledge of the results of their work*. When a job is designed to provide people with information about the effects of their actions, they are better able to develop an understanding of how effectively they have performed—and, such knowledge improves their effectiveness.

The job characteristics model specifies that the three critical psychological states affect various personal and work outcomes—namely, people's feelings of motivation, the quality of work performed, satisfaction with work, absenteeism, and turnover. The higher the experienced meaningfulness of work, responsibility for the work performed, and knowledge of results, the more positive the personal and work benefits will be. When they perform jobs that incorporate high levels of the five core job dimensions, people should feel highly motivated, perform high-quality work, be highly satisfied with their jobs, be absent infrequently, and be unlikely to resign from their jobs.

We should also note that the model is theorized to be especially effective in describing the behaviour of individuals who are high in *growth need strength*—that is, people who have a high need for personal growth and development. People not

Figure 5-13 The Job Characteristics Model: Its Basic Components

The *job characteristics model* stipulates that certain *core job dimensions* lead to certain *critical psychological states*, which in turn lead to several beneficial *personal and work outcomes*. This model recognizes that these relationships are strongest among individuals who have high levels of *growth need strength*.

(Source: Adapted from Hackman & Oldham, 1980; see Note 96.)

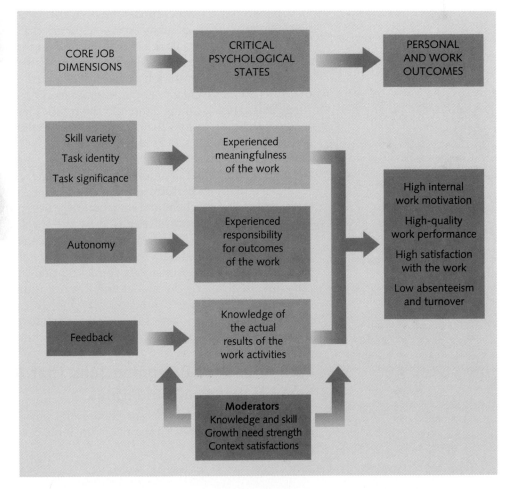

particularly interested in improving themselves on the job are not expected to experience the theorized psychological reactions to the core job dimensions, nor consequently, to enjoy the beneficial personal and work outcomes predicted by the model.[97] This concept of growth need strength is known as a *moderator variable*, that is, a factor that moderates or changes the impact of the core job dimensions on the critical psychological states and the impact of the critical psychological states on the personal and work outcomes. Other moderator variables, in addition to growth need strength, are the satisfaction a person feels with the job context and the person's knowledge and skills in performing the job tasks. Job context includes such factors as administrative policies, nature of supervision, pay, and working conditions. By introducing the moderator variable, the job characteristics model recognizes the important limitation of job enrichment noted earlier—not everyone wants and benefits from enriched jobs.

Based on the proposed relationship between the core job dimensions and their associated psychological reactions, the model claims that job motivation will be highest when the jobs performed rate high on the various dimensions. To assess this relationship, a questionnaire known as the Job Diagnostic Survey (JDS) has been developed to measure the degree to which various job characteristics are present in a particular job.[98] Based on responses to the JDS, we can make predictions about the degree to which a job motivates people who perform it. This is done by using an index known as the **motivating potential score (MPS)**, computed as follows:

$$MPS = \frac{Skill\ variety\ +\ Task\ identity\ +\ Task\ significance}{3} \times Autonomy \times Feedback$$

The MPS is a summary index of a job's potential for motivating people. The higher the score for a given job, the greater the likelihood of experiencing the personal and work outcomes specified by the model. Knowing a job's MPS helps one identify jobs that might benefit by being redesigned.

The job characteristics model has been the focus of many empirical tests, most of which are supportive of many aspects of the model.[99] One study conducted among a group of South African clerical workers found particularly strong support.[100] The jobs of employees in some of the offices in this company were enriched in accordance with techniques specified by the job characteristics model. Specifically, employees performing the enriched jobs were given opportunities to choose the kinds of tasks they perform (high skill variety), do the entire job (high task identity), receive instructions regarding how their job fit into the organization as a whole (high task significance), freely set their own schedules and inspect their own work (high autonomy), and keep records of their daily productivity (high feedback). Another group of employees, equivalent in all respects except that their jobs were not enriched, served as a control group.

After employees performed the newly designed jobs for six months, comparisons were made between them and their counterparts in the control group. With respect to most of the outcomes specified by the model, individuals performing redesigned jobs showed superior results. Specifically, they reported feeling more internally motivated and more satisfied with their jobs. There were also lower rates of absenteeism and turnover among employees performing the enriched jobs. The only outcome predicted by the model that was not found to differ was actual work performance: People performed equally well in enriched and unenriched jobs. Considering the many factors that are responsible for job performance (as discussed in connection with expectancy theory), this finding should not be too surprising.

Techniques for Designing Jobs That Motivate: Some Managerial Guidelines

The job characteristics model specifies several ways in which jobs can be designed to enhance their motivating potential.[101] In Table 5-4 we present these in the form of general principles.

motivating potential score (MPS) A mathematical index describing the degree to which a job is designed so as to motivate people, as suggested by the *job characteristics model*. It is computed on the basis of a questionnaire known as the Job Diagnostic Survey (JDS).

	Core Job Dimensions
Principles of Job Design	**Incorporated**
1. Combine jobs, enabling workers to perform the entire job	Skill variety Task identity
2. Open feedback channels, giving workers knowledge of the results of their work	Feedback
3. Establish client relationships, allowing providers of a service to meet the recipients	Skill variety Autonomy Feedback
4. Load jobs vertically, allowing greater responsibility and control over work	Autonomy

TABLE 5-4 Enriching Jobs: Some Suggestions from the Job Characteristics Model

The job characteristics model specifies several ways jobs can be designed to incorporate the core job dimensions responsible for enhancing motivation and performance. A few are listed here.

(Source: Based on information in Hackman, 1976; see Note 102.)

1. ***Combine tasks***. Instead of having several workers each performing a separate part of a whole job, it would be better to have each person perform the entire job. Doing so helps provide greater skill variety and task identity. For example, Corning Glass Works in Medford, Massachusetts, redesigned jobs so that people who assembled laboratory hot plates put together entire units instead of contributing a single part to the assembly process.[102]

2. ***Open feedback channels***. Jobs should be designed to give employees as much feedback as possible. The more people know how well they're doing (be it from customers, supervisors, or coworkers), the better equipped they are to take appropriate corrective action (we already noted the importance of feedback in the learning process in Chapter 3). Sometimes, cues about job performance can be clearly identified as people perform their jobs (as we noted in conjunction with goal setting). In the best cases, open lines of communication between employees and managers are so strongly incorporated into the corporate culture—as has been reported to exist at Husky Injection Molding Systems—that feedback flows without hesitation (see the CASE PREVIEW for this chapter). The company's rotating Employee Council gives head office employees at all levels the chance to meet with company president Schad on a monthly basis.[103]

☛ *Once again, the topic of feedback, introduced in Chapter 3, is identified as a key determinant of behaviour in organizations.*

3. ***Establish client relationships***. The job characteristic model suggests that jobs should be set up so that the person performing a service (such as an auto mechanic) comes into contact with the recipient of the service. Jobs designed in this manner will not only help the employee by providing feedback, but also provide skill variety (e.g., talking to customers in addition to fixing cars), and enhance autonomy (by giving people the freedom to manage their own relationships with clients).

   This suggestion has been implemented at Sea-Land Service, the large containerized ocean-shipping company.[104] Once this company's mechanics, clerks, and crane operators started meeting with customers, they became much more productive. Having faces to associate with the once-abstract jobs they did clearly helped these employees take their jobs more seriously.

4. ***Load jobs vertically***. As we described earlier, loading a job vertically involves giving people greater responsibility for their jobs. Taking responsibility and control over performance away from managers and giving it to their subordinates increases the level of autonomy the jobs offer these lower-level employees. According to a recent poll, autonomy is among the most important things people look for in their jobs—even more important than high pay.[105] In view of this, a growing number of companies are yielding control and giving employees increasing freedom to do their jobs as they wish (within limits, at least).

   Consider, for example, Childress Buick Co., a Phoenix, Arizona auto dealership. This company suffered serious customer dissatisfaction and employee retention problems before owner Rusty Childress began encouraging his employees to use their own judgment and initiative. Sometimes, previously autocratic managers are shocked when they see how hard people work when they are allowed to make their own decisions. Bob Freese, CEO of Alphatronix Inc., in Research Triangle Park, North Carolina, is among the newly converted. "We let employees tell us when they can accomplish a project and what resources they need," he says. "Virtually always they set higher goals than we would ever set for them."[106]

Naturally, autonomy is not a cure-all. If it were *always* effective, all companies would be using it all the time. There are, however, some commonalities between organizations in which it works. For one, companies that have successfully given employees autonomy tend to invest a lot of time and effort in making sure they hire people who can do their jobs properly without close supervision. Second, autonomy works in organizations in which high-quality performance is always expected—and in which it is the performance itself, and not the process, that matters. This is not to say that there are never any boundaries to restrict employees. Indeed, companies that successfully grant autonomy usually provide some guidelines within which employees must operate. But, within these boundaries, it's clear that new levels of motivation—and performance—can be evidenced.

SUMMARY AND REVIEW

The Nature of Motivation

Motivation is concerned with the set of processes that arouse, direct, and maintain behaviour toward a goal. It is not equivalent to job performance but is one of several determinants of job performance. Today's work ethic motivates people to seek interesting and challenging jobs, instead of just money.

Need Theories

Maslow's **need hierarchy theory** postulates that people have five types of needs, activated in a specific order from the most basic, lowest-level need (physiological needs) to the highest-level need (need for self-actualization). Although this theory has not been supported by rigorous research studies, it has been quite useful in suggesting several ways of satisfying employees' needs on the job. A less restrictive conceptualization, Alderfer's **ERG theory** proposes that people have only three basic needs: existence, relatedness, and growth.

Following from these theories, companies are encouraged to do several things to motivate their employees. Notably, they should promote a healthy workforce, provide financial security, provide opportunities to socialize, and recognize employees' accomplishments.

Goal-Setting Theory

Locke and Latham's **goal-setting theory** claims that an assigned goal influences a person's beliefs about being able to perform a task (referred to as *self-efficacy*) and his or her personal goals. Both of these factors, in turn, influence performance. Research has shown that people will improve their performance when specific, acceptably difficult goals are set and feedback about task performance is provided. The task of selecting goals that are acceptable to employees is facilitated by allowing employees to participate in the goal-setting process.

Equity Theory

Adams's **equity theory** claims that people desire to attain an equitable balance between the ratios of their work rewards (outcomes) and their job contributions (inputs) and the corresponding ratios of comparison to others. Inequitable states of *overpayment* and *underpayment* are undesirable, motivating people to try to attain equitable conditions. Responses to inequity may be either behavioural (e.g., raising or lowering one's performance) or psychological (e.g., thinking differently about work contributions). Research supports equity theory's claim that people lower their inputs in response to perceived underpayment and raise their inputs in response to perceived overpayment. Equity theory suggests that companies should avoid intentionally underpaying or overpaying employees and that managers should thoroughly explain the basis for outcomes in a socially sensitive manner.

Expectancy Theory

Expectancy theory recognizes that motivation is the product of a person's beliefs about **expectancy** (effort will lead to performance), **instrumentality** (performance will result in reward), and **valence** (the perceived value of the rewards). In conjunction with skills, abilities, role perceptions, and opportunities, motivation contributes to job performance. Expectancy theory suggests that motivation may be enhanced by linking rewards to performance (as in **pay-for-performance plans**) and by administering rewards that are highly valued (as may be done using **cafeteria-style benefit plans**).

Job Design

An effective organizational-level technique for motivating people is the designing or redesigning of jobs. **Job design** techniques include **job enlargement** (performing more tasks at the same level) and **job enrichment** (giving people greater responsibility and control over their jobs). The **job characteristics model**, a currently popular approach to enriching jobs, identifies the specific job dimensions that should be enriched (skill variety, task identity, task signifi-cance, autonomy, and feedback), and relates these to the critical psychological states influenced by including these dimensions on a job. These psychological states will, in turn, lead to certain beneficial outcomes for both individual employees (e.g., job satisfaction) and the organization (e.g., reduced absenteeism and turnover). Jobs may be designed to enhance motivation by combining tasks, opening feedback channels, establishing client relationships, and loading jobs vertically (i.e., enhancing responsibility for one's work).

CASE PREVIEW QUESTIONS FOR DISCUSSION

1. a) Would you like to work in the Canadian manufacturing industry? Please explain your answer.

   b) Would you like to work for Husky Injection Molding Systems? Please explain your answer.

2. Do you agree with Schad that, "You build something to last if you treat workers well"? Please explain your answer.

3. Speculate on Schad's leadership style.

CHAPTER QUESTIONS FOR DISCUSSION

1. Based on Maslow's need hierarchy theory, what specific things can be done to enhance an employee's motivation?

2. Why might setting goals be an effective way of motivating people on the job? What steps can be taken to ensure the effectiveness of goal setting in practice?

3. Suppose an employee feels underpaid relative to his or her coworkers. What conditions may have led to these feelings, and how might you expect such an individual to behave on the job?

4. Consider a poorly performing employee who explains to his boss that he is trying very hard. According to expectancy theory, what factors would contribute to such effort? What additional factors, besides motivation, contribute to task performance?

5. According to the job characteristics model, what steps might be taken to enhance the motivation of someone performing a sales job?

6. Explain the role that money plays as a motivator in all five of the theories of motivation presented in this chapter.

CASE IN POINT

Marine Atlantic: A Drifting Crew Finds an Anchor

Marine Atlantic's ferry service in Atlantic Canada marked its 100th anniversary in June of 1998. The 50 passenger steamer *SS Bruce* was the company's first ferry, plying the route from Newfoundland to Cape Breton. Today, the company operates the *MV Caribou* and the *MV Joseph and Clara Smallwood* on the same route. These are the largest superferries in Canada accommodating 1200 passengers and 300 automobiles each.[107]

There have been many other changes at Marine Atlantic over the years. Gone are the days when the employees of this Crown corporation were secure in the knowledge that they had a monopoly on the ferry business between Prince Edward Island and the New Brunswick mainland. With the completion of the Confederation Bridge, the ferry service's rule ended. As the plans for the bridge developed and the recession of the early 1990s hit Atlantic Canada, Marine Atlantic realized it would have to live in a radically changed business environment.

In the early 1990s, a survey found that only 72 percent of the more than two million ferry passengers a year were satisfied with its service. Travellers complained of things like long waits, unkempt washroom conditions, and poor food. The first move toward the improvement of the ferry system was to cut the workforce by about 585 people through severance and retirement packages. Some employees left because they feared the next move planned by the company's management—the introduction of a system of monitoring, measurement, recognition, and reward. Then-president Terry Ivany and his assistant, Richard McConnell (both of whom later moved to VIA Rail), preached the gospel of performance management with religious fervour, demanding employees take responsibility for their jobs and be accountable on a regular basis for the tasks they performed.

At first, some leaders among Marine Atlantic's unions rejected the plan, insisting management would now be watching every move employees made. They scoffed at the idea of deck hands or engineers being marked by supervisors on their jobs, and mocked the charts that began popping up on the company's vessels and in its terminals. "I guess I had to use a two-by-four to kick-start this," Mr. Ivany said at the time. "I really had to be aggressive, holding people accountable, insisting things be done a different way. I had to shock people into realizing we had to be attuned to what was going on in the real world."

The company made it clear that every person's performance would be measured and recognized and that no one would be punished for poor "marks." "Once people realize they aren't going to be punished, this becomes fun," Mr. Ivany said. "I think all employees want to know where they stand and how well they are doing their jobs." The plan worked, and the company and its employees found ways to both save money and improve the quality of the service on the ferries. The engine-room crew on one ferry found a way to save $600 000 in annual fuel costs. These workers received commemorative key chains at the company's head office. "Everybody was elated to get the key chains because they were earned—they were recognition

from the headquarters of the company," said the senior chief engineer.

Among the first changes was a doubling of the employee training budget with half being spent on customer service. Chefs aboard the ferries started planning menus based on graphs that charted sales. By keeping track of sales, the galley staff could see how much it cost to run a cafeteria, and then investigate ways of reducing waste. One ferry's galley crew was able to cut costs by $1000 a month. Washrooms were inspected and rated for cleanliness. But the most telling feedback for this program came from the passengers. When surveyed after the new program was instituted, 95 percent were satisfied with the services they were receiving on the ferries.[108]

Critical Thinking Questions

1. Evaluate the reward system in practice at Marine Atlantic.
2. Compare Marine Atlantic's "performance management" program with OB Mod introduced in Chapter 3 of this book.
3. Why would employees be motivated more by praise and reinforcement for good work, as they were at Marine Atlantic, than by traditional financial rewards?

Marine Atlantic
www.marine-atlantic.ca

SKILLS PORTFOLIO

Experiencing Organizational Behaviour

Assessing the Work Rewards You Value

According to expectancy theory, one thing companies can do to motivate employees is to give rewards with positive valence. What work-related rewards have the greatest value to you? Completing this questionnaire will help you answer this question.

Directions

Below are ten work-related rewards. For each, circle the number that best describes the value that a particular reward has for you personally. Use the following scale to express your feelings: 1 = no value at all, 2 = slight value, 3 = moderate value, 4 = great value, 5 = extremely great value.

Reward	Personal value				
Good pay	1	2	3	4	5
Prestigious title	1	2	3	4	5
Vacation time	1	2	3	4	5
Job security	1	2	3	4	5
Recognition	1	2	3	4	5
Interesting work	1	2	3	4	5
Pleasant conditions	1	2	3	4	5

Chances to advance	1	2	3	4	5
Flexible schedule	1	2	3	4	5
Friendly coworkers	1	2	3	4	5

Questions for Discussion

1. Based on your answers, which rewards do you value most? Which do you value least? Do you think these preferences will change as you get older and perform different jobs? If so, how?
2. To what extent do you believe that you will be able to attain each of these rewards on your job? Do you expect that the chances of receiving these rewards will improve in the future? Why or why not?
3. Do you believe that the rewards you value most are also the ones valued by other people? Are these reward preferences likely to be the same for all people everywhere, or at least for all workers performing the same job in the same company?
4. Do you ever find yourself thinking about these rewards while on the job? Are you aware of these rewards most of the time, or do they only come to your attention when they are not received?

Working in Groups

Does Goal Setting Really Work? Demonstrate It for Yourself

The tendency for specific, difficult goals to enhance task performance is very well established. The following exercise is designed to help you demonstrate this effect yourself. All you need is a class of students willing to participate and a few simple supplies.

Directions

1. Select a page of text from a book and make several photocopies. (Your instructor will advise you on obtaining prior permission from the book's publisher.) Then, carefully count the words, and number each word on one of the copies. This will be your score sheet.
2. Find another class of 30 or more students who don't know anything about goal setting. (We don't want their knowledge of the phenomenon to bias the results.) On a random basis, divide the students into three equal-sized groups.
3. Ask the students in the first group ("baseline" group) to copy as much of the text as they can onto another piece of paper, giving them exactly one minute to do so. Direct them to work at a fast pace. Using the score sheet created in step 1, identify the highest number of words copied by any one of the students. Then, multiply this number by 1.5. This will be the specific, difficult goal level.
4. Ask the students in another group ("specific goal" group) to copy the words on the same printed page for exactly one minute. Tell them to try to reach the specific goal number identified in step 3.
5. Repeat this process with the third group ("do your best" group) but instead of giving them a specific goal, direct them to "try to do your best at this task."
6. Compute the average number of words copied in the "difficult goal" group and the "do your best" group. Have your instructor compute the appropriate statistical test (a *t*-test, in this case) to determine the statistical significance of the difference between the performance levels of the groups.

Questions for Discussion

1. Was there, in fact, a statistically significant difference between the performance levels of the two groups? If so, did students in the "specific goal" group outperform those in the "do your best" group, as expected? What does this reveal about the effectiveness of goal setting?
2. If the predicted findings were not supported, why do you suppose this happened? What was it about the procedure that may have led to this failure? Was the specific goal (1.5 times the fastest speed in the "baseline" group) too high, making the goal unreachable? Or, was it too low, making the specific goal too easy?

3. What do you think would happen if the goal was lowered, making it easier, or raised, making it more difficult?
4. Do you think it would have helped to provide feedback about goal attainment (e.g., someone counting the number of words copied, and calling this out to the performers as they worked)?
5. For what other kinds of tasks do you believe goal setting may be effective? Specifically, do you believe that you can use goal setting to improve your own performance on something you do? Explain this possibility.

TAKE IT TO THE NET

We invite you to visit the *Greenberg/Baron/Sales/Owen Companion Website* at *www.prenticehall.ca/greenberg* for this chapter's Internet resources.

CHAPTER 6

Work-Related Attitudes:

Feelings about Jobs, Organizations, and People

LEARNING OBJECTIVES

After reading this chapter you should be able to:

1. Define *attitudes* and understand their basic components.

2. Identify and describe the major theories of *job satisfaction* and the techniques used to measure it.

3. Explain the major causes and consequences of job satisfaction.

4. Describe the major dimensions of *organizational commitment,* including its foci and bases.

5. Describe the major causes and consequences of organizational commitment.

6. Distinguish between *prejudice* and *discrimination,* and describe various types of prejudice in organizations.

7. Describe some of the steps being taken by organizations today to value and manage *diversity* in the workforce.

CASE PREVIEW

Workplace Equality Yields High Interest at the Bank of Montreal

When you're Canada's oldest bank, people probably assume that you're going to be stodgy and conservative. However, Chairman Matthew Barrett and President Tony Comper knew that getting an edge up on the competition (and there's lots of it these days) required incorporating new perspectives into the Bank of Montreal's traditional corporate structure. This meant capitalizing on the rich diversity of its workforce. But opportunities for advancement were far from equal. Although women held 91 percent of the bank's nonmanagerial jobs, they accounted for only 9 percent of executive jobs.

Something had to be done to achieve equality, and Barrett and Comper sprang into action. They formed the Task Force on the Advancement of Women and charged it with the responsibility for identifying barriers to advancement for women and specific plans for breaking them down. The Task Force conducted extensive research and reported that the major barrier to advancement was a series of widely held myths about women executives that held them back. For example, survey findings revealed that women were assumed to be less committed to their companies because they quit their jobs to raise children. However, the reality is that for most jobs at the bank, women actually had *longer* service records than men—a direct contradiction of conventional wisdom.

Johanne M. Totta, senior vice-president and chief auditor (see Figure 6-1), reasoned that one of the keys to turning the situation around was to speak the language best understood within the bank—numbers. Typically, managers were used to getting quarterly reports assessing the impact of their work on the bank's financial picture. Now, in addition, managers receive quarterly feedback telling them how well they're doing with respect to meeting equality goals, such as hiring women and helping those already working for the bank learn new skills and advance through the ranks. And, managers' own performance evaluations—and their pay—carefully reflect attainment of these goals.

As a further measure, Advisory Councils have been set up in which a diverse sample of employees at various levels meet quarterly with bank officials to discuss progress and problems with respect to achieving equality. These sessions provide useful feedback to be channelled to Totta's office. More importantly, perhaps, they provide people with helpful ideas for promoting equality that they can take back to their workplaces.

The Bank of Montreal has received several awards for its Workplace Equality Program, including the Distinction Award from the YWCA, and the Mercury Award from the International Communications Academy of Arts and Sciences. For bank officials, however, the highest accolade will come from overcoming the barriers to developing human potential that not only hold back the bank's female employees, but keep it from better serving its customers. With thousands of branches internationally, there are surely a lot of customers to serve. Thus far, it looks as if the Bank of Montreal's Workplace Equality Program promises to be a high-yield investment.[1]

Figure 6-1 Bank of Montreal Staff Help Remove Barriers

Johanne Totta is a senior vice-president and the chief auditor at the Bank of Montreal. She is understandably proud of the Bank's awards for promoting female employees. "By removing barriers for our employees," says Totta, "...we are removing barriers for our customers. There's a definite link."[2]

hat is behind this systematic effort by the Bank of Montreal to promote equality in the workplace? Primarily, it's the belief that its employees have a great deal to offer and that by giving them equal opportunities, the bank will be able to draw on this human capital to improve its performance. This, in turn, will keep the bank's employees feeling good about working there, keeping them on the job. Obviously, such reactions can have a strong impact on the way we behave in organizations. Indeed, such feelings—*attitudes* as they are called—represent an important part of people's lives, particularly on the job. Our attitudes toward our jobs or organizations—referred to as *work-related attitudes*—may have profound effects not only on the way we perform but also on the quality of life we experience while at work. We will carefully examine these effects in this chapter.

We will begin by describing the general nature of attitudes. With this background behind us, we will take a closer look at several specific types of work-related attitudes. We'll start with *job satisfaction*—essentially, people's positive or negative feelings about their jobs.[3] Specifically, we will describe some of the major factors contributing to feelings of satisfaction and dissatisfaction with one's work, and then consider the consequences of such reactions on organizational behaviour.

Building on this, we will turn to another important work-related attitude—*organizational commitment*. This has to do with people's feelings about the organizations for which they work—the degree to which they identify with the organizations that employ them.[4] Finally, we will turn to a special type of attitude with which you are probably already somewhat familiar (unfortunately)—*prejudice*. This involves negative views about others who fall into certain categories, such as women and ethnic minorities, to mention just a few.[5] As we will see, such attitudes can have a seriously disruptive impact on the lives of individuals and the effective functioning of the organizations in which they are employed.

Attitudes: What Are They?

If we asked you how you feel about your job, we'd probably find you to be full of reactions. You might say, for example, that you really like it and think it's very interesting. Or perhaps, you may complain about it bitterly and feel bored out of your mind. Maybe, you'd hold views that are more complex, liking some things (e.g., "my boss is great") and disliking others (e.g., "the pay is terrible"). Regardless of exactly how you might feel, the attitudes you express may be recognized as consisting of three major components: an evaluative component, a cognitive component, and a behavioural component.[6] Because these represent the basic building blocks of our definition of attitudes, it will be useful for us to take a closer look at them (see Figure 6-2).

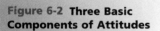

Figure 6-2 Three Basic Components of Attitudes

Attitudes are made up of the three fundamental components shown here: the *evaluative* component, the *cognitive* component, and the *behavioural* component.

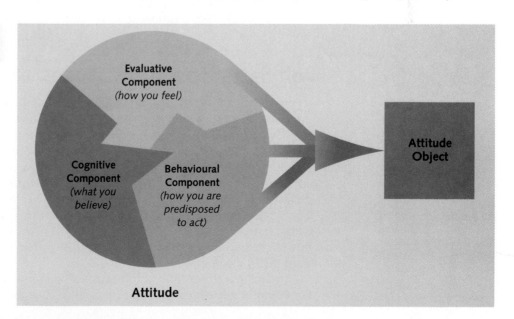

So far, we've been suggesting that attitudes have a great deal to do with how we feel about something. Indeed, this aspect of an attitude, its *evaluative component*, refers to our liking or disliking of any particular person, item, or event (what might be called the *attitude object*, the focus of our attitude). You may, for example, feel positively or negatively toward your boss, the sculpture in the lobby, or the fact that your company just landed a large contract.

Attitudes involve more than feelings; they also involve knowledge—that is, what you believe to be the case about an attitude object. For example, you might believe that one of your coworkers is paid much more than you, or that your supervisor doesn't know too much about the job. These beliefs, whether they're completely accurate or totally false, comprise the *cognitive component* of attitudes.

As you might imagine, the things you believe about something (e.g., "my boss is embezzling company funds") and the way you feel about it (e.g., "I can't stand working for him") may have some effect on the way you are predisposed to behave (e.g., "I think I'm going to look for a new job"). In other words, attitudes also involve a *behavioural component*—a predisposition to act in a certain way. It is important to note that such a predisposition may not actually be predictive of one's behaviour. For example, although you may be interested in taking a new job, you might not actually take one if a better position isn't available, or if there are other aspects of the job you like enough to compensate for the negative feelings. In other words, your intention to behave a certain way may or may not dictate how you will actually behave.

attitudes Stable clusters of feelings, beliefs, and behavioural intentions toward specific objects, people, or institutions.

Combining these various components we can define **attitudes** as relatively stable clusters of feelings, beliefs, and behavioural predispositions (i.e., intentions toward some specific object). By including the phrase "relatively stable" in the definition, we are referring to something that is not fleeting and that, once formed, tends to persist. Indeed, as we will explain in the next section, changing attitudes may require considerable effort.

work-related attitudes Attitudes relating to any aspect of work or work settings.

When we speak about **work-related attitudes**, we are talking about those lasting feelings, beliefs, and behavioural tendencies toward various aspects of the job itself, the setting in which the work is conducted, and/or the people involved. As you will discover as you read this chapter, work-related attitudes are associated with many important aspects of organizational behaviour, including job performance, absence from work, and voluntary turnover. Such relationships are often very complex, varying across different situations and different people, and are not understandable without a great deal of carefully conducted systematic research.

Now that we have identified the basic nature of attitudes, and the mechanisms by which they are changed, we are prepared to turn our attention to specific work-related attitudes. We will begin by describing a very fundamental work-related attitude—*job satisfaction*, attitudes toward one's job.

Job Satisfaction: Attitudes toward One's Job

If you were to ask people about their jobs, you would likely find that they have strong opinions about how they feel (e.g., "I really dislike what I do"), what they believe (e.g., "we provide important services to the community"), and how they intend to behave (e.g., "I am going to look for a new position"). When you consider that people spend roughly one-third of their lives at work, and that what we do to earn a living represents a central aspect of how we think of ourselves as individuals, such strong feelings should not be surprising. The various attitudes people hold toward their jobs are referred to as **job satisfaction**, one of the most widely studied work-related attitudes, and the topic we will now consider. Formally, we may define job satisfaction as individuals' cognitive, affective, and evaluative reactions toward their jobs.[7]

job satisfaction People's cognitive, affective, and evaluative reactions toward their jobs.

In taking a closer look at job satisfaction, we will address several major issues. For example, we will consider how job satisfaction is measured, a key issue involved in assessing this concept. We also will describe various theories of job satisfaction, systematic attempts to address how the process of job satisfaction works. Following this, we will review the major factors that are responsible for making people satisfied or dissatisfied with their jobs. Then, finally, we will consider the principal effects of job satisfaction on various aspects of organizational behaviour. Before considering these topics, however, we will begin by addressing a very basic question: Are people generally satisfied with their jobs?

Are People Generally Satisfied with Their Jobs?

Angus Reid
www.angusreid.com

If you were to make assumptions about people's general levels of job satisfaction from stories you read in the newspaper about disgruntled workers going on strike or even killing their supervisors, you would probably think that people are generally very dissatisfied at work.[8] However, according to an Angus Reid poll, 87 percent of Canadian respondents to a telephone survey were satisfied with their job. Despite this positive response, the answer to this one question does not tell the whole story. While most (66.67 percent) wanted to stay with their present employer for the majority of their career, only a little more than half felt that their boss cared about employees. Of the respondents to this survey, only 58 percent "thought they mattered in their workplace." Twenty-five percent reported that employees do not benefit when the company makes money. In this poll, workers in the Prairies were the most happy with their jobs while Quebeckers reported the lowest job satisfaction.[9]

Not everyone doing every type of job is equally satisfied. There exist certain groups for whom specific patterns of job satisfaction or dissatisfaction have been clearly established. So then, who tends to be most satisfied with their jobs? Here are some key findings:

- White-collar personnel (e.g., managerial and professional people) tend to be more satisfied than blue-collar personnel (e.g., physical labourers, factory workers).[10]

- Older people are generally more satisfied with their jobs than younger people. Interestingly, satisfaction does not increase at an even pace. People become more satisfied with their jobs in their 30s (as they become more successful). Satisfaction levels off in the 40s (as people become disenchanted). Finally, people become more satisfied again in their late 50s (as they resign themselves to their lot in life).[11]

- People who are more experienced on their jobs are more highly satisfied than those who are less experienced.[12] This shouldn't be too surprising since people who are highly dissatisfied with their jobs may be expected to find new jobs when they can.

- Women and members of minority groups tend to be more dissatisfied with their jobs than men and members of majority groups. This appears to be due to the tendency for victims of employment discrimination to be channelled into lower-level jobs and positions with limited opportunities for advancement.[13]

Not only may certain groups of people be more satisfied with their jobs than others, but in addition some individuals are likely to be either consistently satisfied or dissatisfied with their jobs. The main idea is that job satisfaction is a relatively stable *disposition*, a characteristic of individuals that stays with them across situations.

Evidence of this effect was provided in a fascinating study by Staw and Ross.[14] Their survey of over 5000 men who changed jobs between 1969 and 1971 found that expressions of job satisfaction were relatively stable. In other words, despite the fact that they had different jobs, men who were satisfied or dissatisfied in 1969 were equally satisfied or dissatisfied in 1971. Although some scientists have challenged claims regarding the dispositional stability of job satisfaction, a considerable amount of follow-up research supports Staw and Ross's findings, strengthening the possibility that the tendency to be satisfied or dissatisfied with one's job is a stable disposition.[15]

☛ *The idea that some people, by nature, may be predisposed to being either satisfied or dissatisfied with their jobs is in keeping with the concept of positive and negative affect discussed in Chapter 4.*

Measuring Job Satisfaction: Assessing Reactions to Work

Although people have many different attitudes toward various aspects of their jobs, these are not as easy to assess as you might think. Not only can't you directly observe an attitude, but, as we noted, you cannot accurately infer its existence on the basis of people's behaviour. So, for the most part, we have to rely on what people tell us to determine their attitudes. However, people are generally not entirely open about their attitudes and keep much of what they feel to themselves. Moreover, sometimes our attitudes are so complex that it's difficult to express them in any coherent fashion—even if we are willing to do so.

In view of these challenges, social scientists have worked hard over the years to develop reliable and valid instruments designed to systematically measure job satisfaction.[16] Several useful techniques have been developed, including *rating scales* or *questionnaires*, *critical incidents*, and *interviews*.

Rating scales and questionnaires.   The most common approach to measuring job satisfaction involves the use of questionnaires in which highly specialized rating scales are completed. Using this method, people answer questions allowing them to report their reactions to their jobs. Several different scales have been developed for this purpose, and these vary greatly in form and scope (see Table 6-1).

One of the most popular instruments is the **Job Descriptive Index (JDI),** a questionnaire in which people indicate whether or not each of several adjectives describes a particular aspect of their work.[17] Questions on the JDI deal with five distinct aspects of jobs: the work itself, pay, promotional opportunities, supervision, and people (coworkers).

Another widely used measure, the **Minnesota Satisfaction Questionnaire (MSQ)** uses a different approach.[18] People completing this scale rate the extent to which they are satisfied or dissatisfied with various aspects of their jobs (e.g., their pay, chances for advancement). Higher scores reflect higher degrees of job satisfaction.

Although the JDI and the MSQ measure many different aspects of job satisfaction, other scales focus more narrowly on specific facets of satisfaction. For example, as its name suggests, the **Pay Satisfaction Questionnaire (PSQ)** is primarily concerned with attitudes toward various aspects of pay.[19] The PSQ provides valid measures of such critical aspects as satisfaction with pay level, pay raises, fringe benefits, and the structure and administration of the pay system.[20]

An important advantage of rating scales—these and others—is that they can be completed quickly and efficiently by large numbers of people. Another benefit is that when the same questionnaire already has been administered to many thousands of

Job Descriptive Index (JDI) A rating scale for assessing job satisfaction. Individuals respond to this questionnaire by indicating whether or not various adjectives describe aspects of their work.

Minnesota Satisfaction Questionnaire (MSQ) A rating scale for assessing job satisfaction in which people indicate the extent to which they are satisfied with various aspects of their jobs.

Pay Satisfaction Questionnaire (PSQ) A questionnaire designed to assess employees' level of satisfaction with various aspects of their pay (e.g., its overall level, raises, benefits).

TABLE 6-1 Measures of Job Satisfaction: Some Widely Used Scales

The items shown here are similar to those used in three popular measures of job satisfaction.

Source: Based on items from the JDI, MSQ, and PSQ; see Notes 17, 18, and 19.

Job Descriptive Index (JDI)	Minnesota Satisfaction Questionnaire (MSQ)	Pay Satisfaction Questionnaire (PSQ)
Enter "Yes," "No," or "?" for each description or word below.	Indicate the extent to which you are satisfied with each aspect of your present job. Enter one number next to each aspect.	Indicate the extent to which you are satisfied with each aspect of present pay. Enter one number next to each aspect.
Work itself: ___ Routine ___ Satisfactory ___ Good	1 = Extremely dissatisfied 2 = Not satisfied 3 = Neither satisfied nor dissatisfied 4 = Satisfied 5 = Extremely satisfied	1 = Extremely dissatisfied 2 = Not satisfied 3 = Neither satisfied nor dissatisfied 4 = Satisfied 5 = Extremely satisfied
Promotions: ___ Dead-end job ___ Few promotions ___ Good opportunity for promotion	___ Utilization of your abilities ___ Authority ___ Company policies and practices ___ Independence ___ Supervision–human relations	**Satisfaction with pay level:** ___ My current pay ___ Size of my salary **Satisfaction with raises:** ___ Typical raises ___ How raises are determined

individuals, average scores for people in many kinds of jobs and many types of organizations are available. This makes it possible to compare the scores of people in a given company with these averages and obtain measures of *relative* satisfaction. This may be useful information not only for scientists interested in studying job satisfaction, but also for companies interested in learning about trends in the feelings of its employees. Although most companies that conduct attitude surveys use relatively traditional rating scales such as those noted here, some do things a bit differently. For a look at one company that assesses its employees' attitudes in a rather offbeat way, see THE QUEST FOR QUALITY section.

critical incidents technique A procedure for measuring job satisfaction in which employees describe incidents relating to their work that they have found especially satisfying or dissatisfying.

Critical incidents. A second procedure for assessing job satisfaction is the **critical incident technique**. Here, individuals describe events relating to their work that they have found especially satisfying or dissatisfying. Their replies are then examined to uncover underlying themes. For example, if many employees mentioned on-the-job situations in which they were treated rudely by their supervisors, or praised supervisors for sensitivity they showed in a difficult period, this would suggest that supervisory style plays an important role in their job satisfaction.

The Quest for Quality

The "Happiness Index": Assessing Job Satisfaction at Wild Oats Market

In 1984, when Libby Cook, Michael Gilliland, and Randy Clapp opened their tiny grocery store, the Wild Oats Market, in Boulder, Colorado, they always knew how their employees felt. Working with them shoulder to shoulder, they had no difficulty getting feedback. By 1988 their business had grown to a dozen stores in three states, and the owners found themselves looking more at spreadsheets than at people. As a result, it became impossible for them to keep in touch with their employees' feelings about their jobs and their suggestions for improvement. To help, Gilliland and his management team developed the company's "Happiness Index," a friendly, unintimidating way of assessing job satisfaction.[21]

In their words, the purpose of the survey is to determine "if morale is giddy or suicidal," so that better working conditions could be created. To keep things from getting boring and to maintain the playful atmosphere that the company promotes, the language is purposely kept unintimidating. None of the other rating instruments you'll come across use labels such as "ecstatic," "awful," "remarkably bad," or "wonderful," but Wild Oats' semiannual survey does just that. The friendliness of it all keeps 90 percent of employees completing the voluntary, two-page survey (composed of ten rating scales and six open-ended questions).

Besides being fun, one sure reason why employees accept the survey is that they know that the owners pay careful attention to the results, trying to be as responsive as possible. For example, when the employees indicated that they wanted more varied benefits, management responded by giving each employee a $200 annual "wellness allowance" to help cover uninsured expenses such as acupuncture and health club memberships.

In 1994, after employees expressed interest in getting in on the company's success, stock options were added to the list of benefits. For a long time, one of the biggest gripes was that performance reviews were often delayed (because managers were so very busy), causing delays in the raises that stemmed from them. In response to such criticism, the company now makes raises retroactive to the scheduled date of the performance review, regardless of when it actually took place.

Gilliland notes that turnover at Wild Oats stores has steadily decreased since the company started using the survey. Not only does he cite its "therapeutic benefits," but also the useful ways of improving working conditions that have been generated. In fact, he claims that each round of surveys yields some 20 good ideas.

As Wild Oats has grown in the past decade, Cook, Gilliland, and Clapp, no longer stocking shelves with their hourly employees, have found a useful way of keeping in touch with the front lines. Although formal employee surveys are commonly used in large companies, the Wild Oats experience shows us that even small companies—and their employees—stand to benefit from using (and responding to) attitude surveys. The Happiness Index appears to have helped make Wild Oats Market a happy place to work.

Interviews and confrontation meetings. A third procedure for assessing job satisfaction involves carefully interviewing employees in face-to-face sessions. By questioning people in person about their attitudes, it is often possible to explore them more deeply than by using highly structured questionnaires. By carefully posing questions to employees and systematically recording their answers, it is possible to learn about the causes of various work-related attitudes. For example, one team of researchers relied on face-to-face meetings with employees to learn their feelings about their company's recent bankruptcy filing.[22] The highly personal approach to data collection was particularly effective in gathering reactions to such a complex and difficult situation.

Sometimes, interviews are designed to have employees "lay it on the line," and discuss their major complaints and concerns. Interviews of this type are known as *confrontation meetings*. If such sessions are conducted skillfully, in an environment in which employees feel free to speak out without retaliation, serious problems that adversely affect job satisfaction but might otherwise remain hidden can be brought out into the open. This may be a crucial first step toward correcting or eliminating the problems.

As you might imagine, confrontation meetings—or any type of self-report measure, for that matter—are only successful to the extent that people respond honestly and are capable of accurately reporting their feelings. An important key is gaining people's cooperation. With this in mind, it is important for researchers collecting information about job satisfaction to keep all individuals' responses completely confidential and to assure them of this clearly. In fact, it is also useful to keep respondents' identities anonymous so that it is impossible to identify anything that any one respondent may have said. In short, it is essential for measures of job satisfaction—or any work-related attitudes, for that matter—to protect respondents' rights to privacy, not only because doing so helps safeguard the validity of the measures, but also because it is unethical to do otherwise.

Theories of Job Satisfaction

What makes some people more satisfied with their jobs than others? What underlying processes account for people's feelings of job satisfaction? Insight into these important questions is provided by various theories of job satisfaction. We will describe two of the most influential approaches—Herzberg's *two-factor theory* and Locke's *value theory*.

Herzberg's two-factor theory. Think about something that may have happened on your job that made you feel especially satisfied or dissatisfied. What were these events? (This is an example of the description of the *critical incident technique* described above.) Over 30 years ago Frederick Herzberg posed this question to more than 200 accountants and engineers and carefully analyzed their responses.[23] What he found was somewhat surprising: Different factors accounted for job satisfaction and dissatisfaction.

Although you might expect that certain factors lead to satisfaction when they are present and dissatisfaction when they are absent, this was *not* the case. Job satisfaction and dissatisfaction were found to stem from different sources (see Figure 6-3). In particular, dissatisfaction was associated with conditions surrounding the jobs (e.g., working conditions, pay, security, quality of supervision, relations with others) rather than the work itself. Because these factors prevent negative reactions, Herzberg referred to them as *hygiene* (or *maintenance*) *factors*. By contrast, satisfaction was associated with factors associated with the work itself or to outcomes directly derived from it, such as the nature of their jobs, achievement in the work, promotion opportunities, and chances for personal growth and recognition. Because such factors were associated with high levels of job satisfaction, Herzberg called them *motivators*.

two-factor theory (of job satisfaction) A theory, devised by Herzberg, suggesting that satisfaction and dissatisfaction stem from different groups of variables (*motivators* and *hygienes*, respectively).

Concerned, as it is, with both motivators and hygiene factors, Herzberg's theory is referred to as **two-factor theory**. Research testing this theory has yielded mixed results. Some studies have found that job satisfaction and dissatisfaction were based on different factors and that these are in keeping with the distinction made by Herzberg.[24] Other studies, however, have found that factors labelled as hygienes and

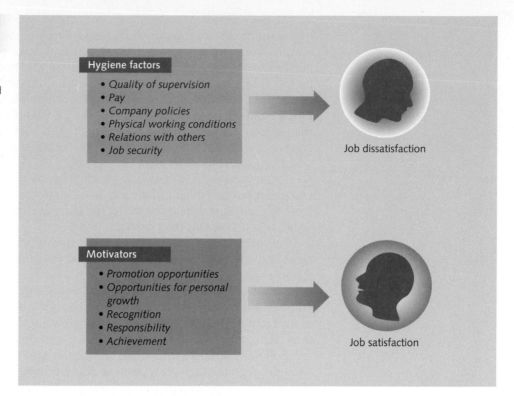

Hygiene factors
- *Quality of supervision*
- *Pay*
- *Company policies*
- *Physical working conditions*
- *Relations with others*
- *Job security*

Job dissatisfaction

Motivators
- *Promotion opportunities*
- *Opportunities for personal growth*
- *Recognition*
- *Responsibility*
- *Achievement*

Job satisfaction

motivators exerted strong effects on both satisfaction and dissatisfaction, thereby casting doubt on two-factor theory.[25] In view of such equivocal evidence, we must label Herzberg's theory as an intriguing but unverified framework for understanding job satisfaction.

Still, this theory has important implications for managing organizations. Specifically, managers would be well advised to focus their attention on factors known to promote job satisfaction, such as opportunities for personal growth. Indeed, several of today's companies have realized that satisfaction within their workforces is enhanced when they provide opportunities for their employees to develop their repertoire of professional skills on the job. For example, front-line service workers at Marriott Hotels, known as "guest services associates," are hired to perform a variety of tasks, including checking guests in and out, carrying their bags, and so on.[26] Instead of doing just one job, this approach enables Marriott employees to call upon and develop many of their talents, thereby adding to their level of job satisfaction.

Two-factor theory also implies that steps should be taken to create conditions that help avoid dissatisfaction—and, it specifies the kinds of variables required to do so (i.e., hygiene factors). For example, creating pleasant working conditions may be quite helpful in getting people to avoid being dissatisfied with their jobs. Specifically, research has shown that dissatisfaction is great under conditions that are highly overcrowded, dark, noisy, have extreme temperatures, and poor air quality.[27] These factors, associated with the conditions under which work is performed, but not directly linked to the work itself, contribute much to the levels of job dissatisfaction encountered.

☞ *If you are thinking that this sounds like an example of* job enrichment, *described in Chapter 5, you are correct. Indeed, two-factor theory was greatly responsible for the development of the job enrichment approach to motivation.*

value theory (of job satisfaction) A theory, devised by Locke, suggesting that job satisfaction depends primarily on the match between the outcomes individuals value in their jobs and their perceptions about the availability of such outcomes.

Locke's value theory. A second important theory of job satisfaction is Locke's **value theory**.[28] This conceptualization claims that job satisfaction exists to the extent that the job outcomes (such as rewards) an individual receives match those outcomes that are desired. The more people receive outcomes they value, the more satisfied they will be; the less they receive outcomes they value, the less satisfied they will be. Locke's approach focuses on *any* outcomes that people value, regardless of what they are. The key to satisfaction in Locke's theory is the *discrepancy* between those aspects of the job one has and those one wants; the greater the discrepancy, the less people are satisfied.

Recent research provides good support for value theory. Using a questionnaire, one team of investigators measured how much of various job facets—such as freedom to work one's own way, learning opportunities, promotion opportunities, and pay level—a diverse group of workers wanted, and how much they felt they already had.[29] They also measured how satisfied the respondents were with each of these facets and how important each facet was to them. As shown in Figure 6-4, an interesting trend emerged: Those aspects of the job about which respondents experienced the greatest discrepancies were the ones with which they were most dissatisfied, and those with which they experienced the smallest discrepancies were the ones with which they were most satisfied. Interestingly, the researchers also found that this relationship was greater among individuals who placed a high amount of importance on a particular facet of the job. In other words, the more important a particular facet of the job was believed to be, the less satisfied people were when they failed to get as much of this facet as they wanted.

An interesting implication of value theory is that it calls attention to the aspects of the job that need to be changed for job satisfaction to result. Specifically, the theory suggests that these aspects might not be the same ones for all people, but any valued aspects of the job about which people perceive serious discrepancies. By emphasizing values, Locke's theory suggests that job satisfaction may be derived from many factors. Thus, an effective way to satisfy employees would be to find out what they want and, to the extent possible, give it to them.

Believe it or not, this is sometimes easier said than done. In fact, organizations sometimes go through great pains to find out how to satisfy their employees. With this in mind, a growing number of companies, particularly big ones, have been systematically surveying their employees. For example, FedEx has been so interested in tracking the attitudes of its employees that it has started using a fully automated online survey. The company relies on information gained from surveys as the key to identifying sources of employee dissatisfaction.

Figure 6-4 Job Satisfaction: The Result of Getting What We Want

Research has shown that the larger a discrepancy that exists between what people have and what they want with respect to various facets of their jobs (e.g., pay, learning opportunities), the more dissatisfied they are with their jobs. This relationship is greater among those who place a great deal of importance on that facet than among those who consider it less important.

(Source: Adapted from McFarlin & Rice, 1992; see Note 29.)

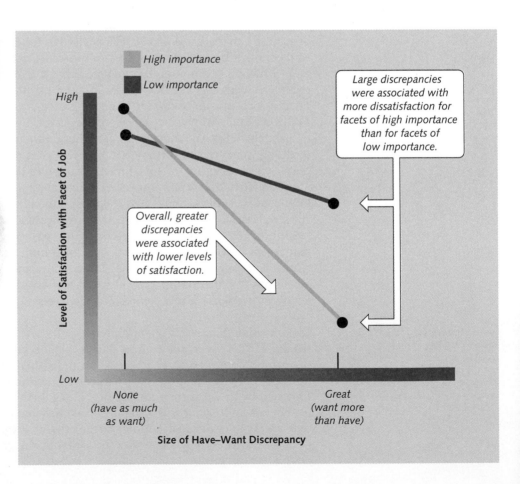

Consequences of Job Dissatisfaction

People talk a great deal about the importance of building employee satisfaction, assuming that morale is critical to the functioning of organizations. As we will see, although job satisfaction does indeed influence organizations, its impact is not always as strong as one might expect. Thus, we might ask: What are the consequences of job dissatisfaction? Our summary will focus on two main variables—employee withdrawal (i.e., absenteeism and turnover) and job performance.

employee withdrawal
Actions, such as chronic absenteeism and voluntary turnover (i.e., quitting one's job), that enable employees to escape from adverse organizational situations.

Job satisfaction and employee withdrawal. When employees are dissatisfied with their jobs, they try to find ways of reducing their exposure to them. That is, they stay away from their jobs—behaviour known as **employee withdrawal**. Two main forms of employee withdrawal are absenteeism and voluntary turnover.[30] By not showing up to work and/or by quitting to take a new job, people may be expressing their dissatisfaction with their jobs, or attempting to escape from the unpleasant aspects of them they may be experiencing.

With respect to absenteeism, research has shown that the lower individuals' satisfaction with their jobs, the more likely they are to be absent from work.[31] The strength of this relationship, however, is only modest. The reason is that dissatisfaction with one's job is likely to be just one of many factors influencing people's decisions to report or not report to work. For example, even someone who really dislikes her job may not be absent if she believes her presence is necessary to complete an important project. However, another employee might dislike her job so much that she will "play hooky" without showing any concern over how the company will be affected. Thus, although it's not a perfectly reliable reaction to job dissatisfaction, absenteeism is one of its most important consequences.

Another costly form of withdrawal related to job satisfaction is voluntary turnover. The lower people's levels of satisfaction with their jobs, the more likely they are to consider resigning and actually to do so. As in the case of absenteeism, this relationship is modest, for similar reasons.[32] Many factors relating to the individuals, their jobs, and economic conditions shape decisions to move from one job to another. As you might imagine, there are many more variables involved in making turnover decisions. Many of these are described in a model of the voluntary turnover process described by Mobley (see Figure 6-5).[33] According to this conceptualization, job dissatisfaction leads employees to think about the possibility of

Figure 6-5 Voluntary Turnover: A Model

According to Mobley and his associates, voluntary turnover is a complex process triggered by low levels of job satisfaction. This leads people to think about quitting and then to search for another job. Finally, they form intentions to quit or to remain on their present jobs. At several steps in this process, the probability of finding an acceptable alternative plays a role.

(Source: Based on suggestions by Mobley, Horner, & Hollingsworth, 1978; see Note 33.)

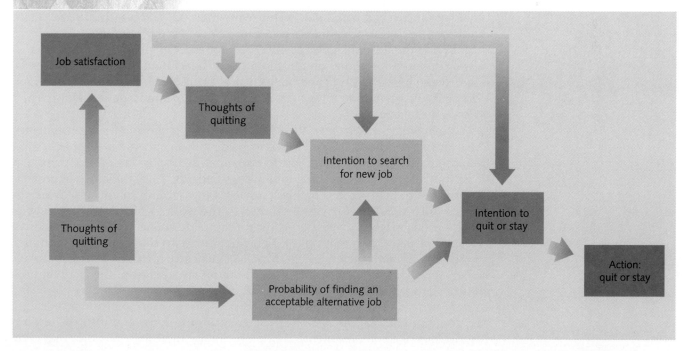

quitting. This, in turn, leads to the decision to search for another job. Then, if the search is successful, the individual will develop definite intentions either to quit or to remain on the job. Finally, these intentions are reflected in concrete actions.

Mobley's suggestion that economic conditions, and hence the success of an initial search for alternative jobs, exert a strong impact on voluntary turnover is supported by the findings of an interesting study by Carsten and Spector.[34] These researchers examined the results of a large number of previous studies concerned with turnover. For each, they contacted the people who had conducted the study and determined the precise dates during which their data had been collected. Then, Carsten and Spector obtained data on the unemployment rates prevailing at those times. They predicted that the relationship between job satisfaction and turnover would be stronger at times when unemployment was low than when it was high. When unemployment was low, they reasoned, people would recognize that they have many other job opportunities and would be prone to take one when they are highly dissatisfied with their present jobs. By contrast, conditions of high unemployment would limit alternative job options, leading people to stay with their present jobs despite their dissatisfaction with them. This is precisely what they found: The higher the unemployment rates were, the lower was the correlation between job satisfaction and turnover.

Organizations are highly concerned about withdrawal insofar as it is generally very costly. The expenses involved in selecting and training employees to replace those who have resigned can be considerable. Even unscheduled absences can be expensive. The Conference Board of Canada has estimated that the cost to Canadian employers of unplanned absences is approximately $12 billion per year.[35] Although voluntary turnover is permanent, whereas absenteeism is a short-term reaction, both are effective ways of withdrawing from dissatisfying jobs.

The Conference Board of Canada
www.conferenceboard.ca

As an example, consider the reactions of the highly dissatisfied bakery workers at the Safeway market in Clackamas, Oregon. So upset with their jobs (particularly the treatment they received from management) were the bakery's 130 employees, that they frequently were absent, quit, and had on-the-job accidents. And these were no minor problems. In one year alone, accidents resulted in 1740 lost work days—a very expensive problem. Accidents only occurred, of course, when employees showed up. At unpopular times, such as Saturday nights, it was not unusual for as many as 8 percent of the workers to call in sick. Almost no one stayed on the job for more than a year. Clearly, withdrawal was a very disruptive response to dissatisfaction in this organization.

Job satisfaction and task performance. Many people believe that "happy workers are productive workers." But, is this really the case? *Is* job satisfaction, in fact, directly linked to task performance or organizational productivity? Overall, research suggests that the relationship is positive, but not especially strong. In fact, after reviewing hundreds of studies on this topic, researchers found that the mean correlation between job satisfaction and performance is considerably smaller, only 0.17.[36] Why does job satisfaction have such a limited relationship to performance? There are several explanations.

First, in many work settings, there is little room for large changes in performance. Some jobs are structured so that the people holding them *must* maintain at least some minimum level of performance just to remain at their jobs. For others, there may be very little leeway for exceeding minimum standards. Thus, the range of possible performance in many jobs is highly restricted. Moreover, for many employees, the rate at which they work is closely linked to the work of others or the speed at which various machines operate. As such, their performance may have such little room to fluctuate that it may not be highly responsive to changes in their attitudes.

Second, job satisfaction and performance may actually not be directly linked. Rather, any apparent relationship between them may stem from the fact that both are related to a third factor—receipt of various rewards. As suggested by Porter and Lawler, the relationship may work as follows.[37] Past levels of performance lead to the receipt of both extrinsic rewards (e.g., pay, promotions) and intrinsic rewards (e.g., feelings of accomplishment). If employees judge these to be fair, they may eventually recognize a link between their performance and these outcomes. This, in turn, may have two effects. First, it may encourage high levels of effort, and thus, good performance. Second, it may lead to high levels of job satisfaction. In short, high productivity and high satisfaction may both stem from the same conditions. These two factors, themselves, however, may not be directly linked. For these and other reasons, job satisfaction may not be directly related to performance in many contexts.

Promoting Job Satisfaction: Some Guidelines

In view of the negative consequences of dissatisfaction just discussed, it makes sense to consider ways of raising satisfaction and preventing dissatisfaction on the job. Although an employee's dissatisfaction might not account for all aspects of his or her performance, it is important to try to promote satisfaction if for no other reason than to make people happy. After all, satisfaction is a desirable end in itself. With this in mind, we now turn to an important question: What can be done to promote job satisfaction? Based on what scientists know about this, we offer several suggestions.

1. ***Pay people fairly.*** People who believe that their organizations' pay systems are inherently unfair tend to be dissatisfied with their jobs. This applies not only to salary and hourly pay, but also to fringe benefits. In fact, when people are given opportunities to select the fringe benefits they most desire, their job satisfaction tends to rise. This idea is consistent with value theory. After all, given the opportunity to receive the fringe benefits they most desire, employees may have little or no discrepancies between those they want and those they actually have.

   One of the clauses in the Employee's Charter at Magna International Inc. is a commitment to providing employees with competitive wages and benefits. Magna supplies its employees with information about the compensation packages earned by employees working in competing firms. Magna promises to alter the wages of its employees if they do not compare favourably with those being paid in other companies in the community.[38]

2. ***Improve the quality of supervision.*** Satisfaction tends to be highest among those who believe that their supervisors are competent, treat them with respect, and have their best interests in mind. Similarly, job satisfaction is enhanced when employees believe that they have open lines of communication with their superiors.

   For example, in response to the dissatisfaction problems that plagued the Safeway bakery employees described earlier, company officials responded by completely changing their management style. Traditionally, they were highly intimidating and controlling, leaving employees feeling powerless and discouraged. Realizing the problems caused by this iron-fisted style, they began loosening their highly autocratic way, replacing it with a new openness and freedom. Employees were allowed to work together toward solving problems of sanitation and safety and were encouraged to make suggestions about ways to improve things. The results were dramatic: Work days lost due to accidents dropped from 1740 a year down to 2, absenteeism fell from 8 percent to 0.2 percent, and voluntary turnover was reduced from almost 100 percent annually to less than 10 percent. Clearly, improving the quality of supervision went a long way toward reversing the negative effects of dissatisfaction at this Safeway bakery.

3. ***Decentralize the control of organizational power.*** Decentralization is the degree to which the capacity to make decisions resides in several people, as opposed to one or just a handful. When power is decentralized, people are allowed to participate freely in the process of decision making. This arrangement contributes to their feelings of satisfaction because it leads them to believe that they can have some impact on their organizations. By contrast, when the power to make decisions is concentrated in the hands of just a few, employees are likely to feel powerless and ineffective, thereby contributing to their feelings of dissatisfaction.

☞ *Beliefs about the perceived relationships between performance and reward are basic to expectancy theory, discussed in Chapter 5.*

☞ *As we discussed in Chapter 5, equity theory recognizes that people also perceive their pay to be fair to the extent that they recognize that they are rewarded in a manner that recognizes their relative performance contributions.*

Magna International Inc.
www.MagnaInt.com

☞ The concept of centralization and decentralization of power is also discussed in conjunction with the topics of communication (Chapter 9), social influence (Chapter 12), and organizational structure (Chapter 15).

The changes in supervision made at the Safeway bakery provide a good illustration of moving from a highly centralized style to a highly decentralized style. The power to make certain important decisions was shifted into the hands of those who were most affected by them. Because decentralizing power gives people greater opportunities to control aspects of the workplace that affect them, it makes it possible for employees to receive the outcomes they most desire, thereby enhancing their satisfaction.

Magna International Inc. includes in its Operating Principles the commitment to maintain a decentralized operating structure. This principle states that "Magna's manufacturing divisions operate as independent profit centres. This decentralized structure prevents bureaucracy and makes the Company more responsive to customer needs and the changing industry."[39]

4. **Match people to jobs that are congruent with their interests.** People have many interests, and these are only sometimes satisfied on the job. However, the more people find that they are able to fulfill their interests while on the job, the more satisfied they will be with those jobs. For example, a recent study found that college graduates were more satisfied with their jobs when these were consistent with their college majors than when these fell outside their fields of interest.

It is, no doubt, with this in mind that career counsellors frequently find it useful to identify people's nonvocational interests. For example, several companies, such as AT&T, IBM, Ford Motor Company, Shell Oil, and Kodak, systematically test and counsel their employees so they can effectively match their skills and interests to those positions to which they are best suited. Some, including Coca Cola, and Disneyland, go so far as to offer individualized counselling to employees so that their personal and professional interests can be identified and matched.

In conclusion, there is good news for managers interested in promoting satisfaction (and avoiding dissatisfaction) among employees. Although it might not always be easy to make a special effort to promote job satisfaction, especially amidst the hectic pace of everyday work, what we know about the benefits of keeping employees satisfied with their jobs suggests that the effort may be worthwhile.

Organizational Commitment: Feelings of Attachment toward Organizations

Suppose you really enjoy the work you do and are very satisfied with your job. This doesn't necessarily mean that you will feel positively toward your company as well. In fact, you may even despise it and hope to get out as soon as possible. Similarly, it's possible for you to think your company is a wonderful place to work, although you might be terribly displeased about the job you do. The point we are making is that to understand people's work-related attitudes fully we must go beyond the concept of job satisfaction and also consider people's feelings toward their organizations.[40]

organizational commitment
The extent to which an individual identifies and is involved with his or her organization and/or is unwilling to leave it.

Such attitudes, referred to as **organizational commitment**, reflect the extent to which people identify with and are involved with their organizations and are unwilling to leave them. As you might imagine, many factors are responsible for organizational commitment, and the impact of such attitudes may be quite serious. Before we consider these various consequences of organizational commitment and ways to increase commitment, we will take a closer look at its basic dimensions.

Organizational Commitment: Its Basic Dimensions

To help understand the complex nature of organizational commitment, theorists have broken it down to its basic components. Notably, a distinction has been made between the *foci of commitment*—the particular entity, such as the group or individual to which a person is committed—and the *bases of commitment*—the underlying reasons why the commitment occurs. We will discuss each of these basic dimensions.

Foci of commitment. It is important to note that people can be committed to various entities in their organizations. For example, they may have varying degrees of commitment to their coworkers, subordinates, superiors, customers, the union, or top management—in short, any particular individual or group target. In an attempt to categorize some of these various foci, Becker and Billings distinguished between those whose commitment is concentrated at lower organizational levels, such as one's immediate work group and supervisor, and those who are primarily focused on higher levels, such as top management and the organization as a whole.[41] By combining high and low levels of each of these, they identified the four distinct *commitment profiles* summarized in Table 6-2.

First, individuals who are low in commitment to both their work groups and supervisors as well as low in commitment to top management and the organization are labelled *uncommitted*. By contrast, individuals who are high in commitment to both sets of foci are labelled *committed*. In between are two groups: those who are highly committed to their supervisor and work group but not to top management and the organization—known as *locally committed*; and those who are highly committed to top management and the organization, but not to their supervisor and work group—known as *globally committed*.

In a study conducted at a large military supply organization, Becker and Billings found that employees' attitudes differed in ways consistent with their profiles. For example, individuals falling into the uncommitted category (based on their responses to various questionnaire items) were more interested in quitting their jobs and less interested in helping others than those who were in the committed category. Those who were globally committed and locally committed scored in between these two extremes. In conclusion, although this method of distinguishing between various foci of commitment is still new, it appears to hold a great deal of promise as a tool for understanding a key dimension of organizational commitment.

Bases of commitment. To understand the concept of commitment fully, we must look at not only various foci, but also their bases—that is, the motives that people have for being committed. Historically, two different approaches to understanding these bases have dominated—the *side-bets orientation* and the individual-organizational *goal-congruence orientation*.[42]

Becker's **side-bets orientation** focuses on the accumulated investments an individual stands to lose if he or she leaves the organization.[43] The idea is that over time, leaving an organization becomes more costly because people fear losing what they have invested in the organization and become concerned that they cannot replace these things. For example, people may be unwilling to leave their jobs because they are concerned about being perceived as "job hoppers" and stake their reputation for stability on remaining in their present jobs (i.e., they make a "side bet" on some aspect of themselves on continued organizational membership).

The individual-organizational **goal-congruence orientation** focuses on the extent to which people identifying with an organization have personal goals that are in keeping with those of the organization. This approach, popularized by Porter and his associates, reflects people's willingness to accept and work toward attaining organizational goals.[44] It views organizational commitment as the result of three fac-

side-bets orientation The view of organizational commitment that focuses on the accumulated investments an individual stands to lose if he or she leaves the organization.

goal-congruence orientation An approach to organizational commitment according to which the degree of agreement between an individual's personal goals and those of the organization is a determinant of organizational commitment.

TABLE 6-2 Four Different Commitment Profiles

Becker and Billings have distinguished between two major foci of commitment: the supervisor and the work group, and top management and the organization. By combining low and high levels of each, the four *commitment profiles* shown here emerge.

Source: Based on information in Becker & Billings, 1993; see Note 41.

Attachment to Top Management and Organization	Attachment to Supervisor and Work Group	
	Low	High
Low	Uncommitted	Locally committed
High	Globally committed	Committed

tors: (1) acceptance of the organization's goals and values, (2) willingness to help the organization achieve its goals, and (3) the desire to remain within the organization.

As researchers began to study organizational commitment from each of these two perspectives, it became clear that both approaches were useful for understanding organizational commitment—and that a third was necessary.[45] With this in mind, three distinct bases of organizational commitment have been identified—*continuance commitment*, *affective commitment* and *normative commitment*.[46]

Continuance commitment, related to the side-bets approach, refers to the strength of a person's tendency to continue working for an organization because he or she cannot afford to do otherwise. **Affective commitment**, suggested by the goal congruence approach, refers to the strength of a person's desire to continue working for an organization because he or she agrees with it and wants to do so. After researching these two forms of commitment it became apparent that a third type also existed—**normative commitment**.[47] This kind of commitment refers to employees' feelings of obligation to stay with the organization because of pressures from others. For a summary of these three bases of commitment, see Figure 6-6.

Questionnaires measuring these three bases of commitment have been developed, and research using them has confirmed that the three different forms are, in fact, distinct from each other.[48] By looking at items similar to those used to measure each kind of commitment, shown in the EXPERIENCING ORGANIZATIONAL BEHAVIOUR exercise on pages 194–195, you will be able to recognize the distinction between the three different forms. By using questionnaires such as this,

continuance commitment The strength of a person's desire to continue working for an organization because he or she needs to do so and cannot afford to do otherwise.

affective commitment The strength of a person's desire to work for an organization because he or she agrees with it and wants to do so.

normative commitment The strength of a person's desire to continue working for an organization because he or she feels obligations from others to remain there.

Figure 6-6 Organizational Commitment: Three Types

Organizational commitment consists of the three facets shown here: *continuance commitment, normative commitment,* and *affective commitment.*

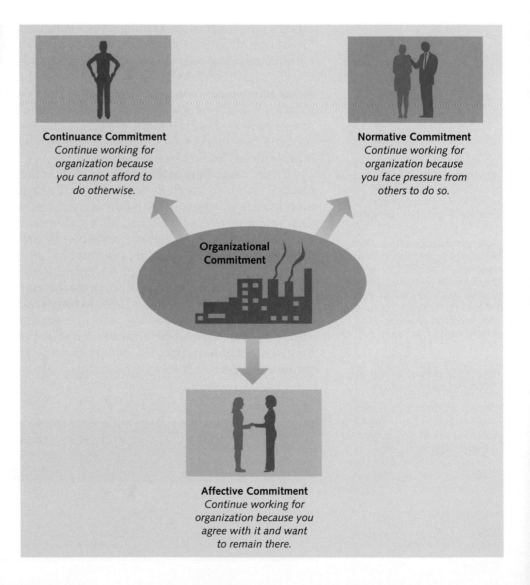

Continuance Commitment
Continue working for organization because you cannot afford to do otherwise.

Normative Commitment
Continue working for organization because you face pressure from others to do so.

Organizational Commitment

Affective Commitment
Continue working for organization because you agree with it and want to remain there.

scientists have been able to identify people's level of commitment to their organizations and link these to various consequences.[49] As you might imagine, the problems associated with low levels of commitment can be quite severe. We will now summarize these.

Consequences of Low Organizational Commitment

The prediction that people who feel deeply committed to their organizations will behave differently from those who do not seems reasonable. Despite very complex findings, considerable evidence supports this suggestion.[50] Organizational commitment greatly affects several key aspects of work behaviour.

First, generally speaking, low levels of organizational commitment tend to be associated with *high levels of absenteeism and voluntary turnover.*[51] In most cases, more committed individuals are less likely to look for new jobs than less committed ones. Interestingly, it appears that people enter jobs with a predisposition toward commitment, and this influences their tendency to stick with their organizations.

Second, low organizational commitment is associated with *unwillingness to share and make sacrifices.*[52] It should not be surprising that these types of voluntary acts are related to commitment inasmuch as we can expect those who are most committed to their organizations to be those who give most generously of themselves. People who are uncommitted to their organizations will certainly have little motivation to go out of their way to do any more than they absolutely must on behalf of the organization.[53] In fact, they may be outright selfish and try to get away with doing as little as possible.

Finally, low organizational commitment has *negative personal consequences.* Although one might expect commitment to an organization to detract from one's personal life (based on the idea that it would be costly in terms of time and emotional investment), research suggests otherwise. In a survey of work attitudes among public employees, it was found that those who were most strongly attached to their organizations enjoyed highly successful careers and pleasant nonwork lives.[54] To the extent that work is an important part of people's lives, it makes sense that feeling uncommitted to one's company would contribute to one's feelings of discontent with life in general.

Taking all these findings into account, steps designed to generate high levels of organizational commitment among employees seem worthwhile. A committed work force, it appears, is indeed beneficial to both individuals and organizations.

Suggestions for Enhancing Organizational Commitment

Some determinants of organizational commitment fall outside of managers' spheres of control, giving them few opportunities to enhance these feelings. For example, commitment tends to be lower when the economy is such that employment opportunities are plentiful. An abundance of job options will surely lower continuance commitment, and there's not too much a company can do about it.[55] However, although managers cannot control the economy, they can do several things to make employees want to stay working for the company—that is, to enhance affective commitment.

☞ *Chapter 5 presents theories that explain the underlying reasons why enriching jobs may enhance organizational commitment, and describes specific methods for making jobs more enriched.*

1. ***Enrich jobs.*** People tend to be highly committed to their organizations to the extent that they have a good chance to take control over the way they do their jobs and are recognized for making important contributions.[56]

    This approach worked well for the Ford Motor Company. In the early 1980s, Ford confronted a crisis of organizational commitment in the face of budget cuts, layoffs, plant closings, lowered product quality, and other threats. In the words of Ernest J. Savoie, the director of Ford's Employee Development Office:

    > The only solution for Ford, we determined was a total transformation of our company…to accomplish it, we had to earn the commitment of all Ford people. And to acquire that commitment, we had to change the way we managed people.[57]

With this in mind, Ford instituted its *Employee Involvement* program, a systematic way of involving employees in many aspects of corporate decision making. They not only got to perform a wide variety of tasks, but also enjoyed considerable autonomy in doing them (e.g., freedom to schedule work and to stop the assembly line if needed). By 1985, Ford employees were more committed to their jobs—so much so, in fact, that the acrimony that usually resulted at contract renewal time had all but vanished. Although employee involvement may not be the cure for all commitment ills, it was clearly highly effective in this case.

2. ***Align the interests of the employees with those of the company.*** It only makes sense that employees will remain committed to working in organizations when those employees and the company have the same interests in mind—that is, when what benefits one also benefits the other. This is certainly the case among companies that use *profit-sharing plans*—incentive programs in which employees receive bonuses in proportion to the company's profitability. Such plans are often quite effective in enhancing organizational commitment, especially when they are perceived to be administered fairly.[58]

For example, Barrick Gold gives all of its employees stock options, not just senior management. By staggering the rate at which employees can liquidate these assets the company encourages its employees to plan for a long-term commitment to the organization. The company's philosophy is reflected in one of its objectives, to "continue to develop the Company's human resources, through the conviction ... that involved, well-treated employees will work with skill and extra dedication to achieve Barrick's goals."[59] The rationale for such actions is obvious: By letting employees share in the company's profits, they are more likely to see their own interests as consistent with those of their company. When these interests are aligned, commitment is high.

3. ***Recruit and select newcomers whose values closely match those of the organization.*** Just as individuals have certain things they value (e.g., preserving the natural environment, respect for law and order), so, too, do organizations. In fact, organizations frequently declare their values in documents known as **mission statements**—documents in which organizations formally state their basic values and purpose. For example, Canadian National Railways' mission statement includes the following: "Safety is critically important and will never be compromised. CN intends to be the safest railway, for the benefit of its employees, customers, and the communities it serves."[60]

As you might imagine, the more closely the values of an organization match the values of the individuals employed in them, the more strongly those employees will be committed to the organizations.[61] For example, someone who finds environmental pollution unacceptable probably would be unwilling to work in a factory that emits hazardous chemicals into the air. Our advice is clear: Both organizations and prospective new employees should pay close attention to the extent to which their values closely mesh (such as by carefully reviewing the company's mission statement during the interview process). Failure to do so may lead to a very brief—and potentially unsettling—association.

The recruitment process is important not only insofar as it provides opportunities to find people whose values fit those of the organization, but also because of the dynamics of the recruitment process itself. In this connection, the more an organization invests in someone by working hard to lure him or her to the company, the more that individual is likely to return the same investment of energy by expressing commitment toward the organization.[62] In other words, companies that show their employees they care enough to work hard to attract them are likely to find strong commitment among those who are so actively courted.

In conclusion, it is useful to think of organizational commitment as an attitude that may be influenced by managerial actions. Not only might people be

mission statements Documents in which organizations formally state their basic values and purpose.

Canadian National Railway Company
www.cn.ca

☞ *Organizations do many things to help ensure that newcomers "learn the ropes" in their new organizations. This process, known as socialization is described in Chapter 7.*

selected who are predisposed to be committed to the organization, but also various measures can be taken to enhance commitment in the face of indications that it is suffering. Given the problems associated with having an uncommitted workforce, it would appear wise to consider such efforts carefully.

Prejudice: Negative Attitudes toward Others

"Don't jump to conclusions." That's advice we often hear. But, when it comes to forming attitudes toward others, it is often ignored. Instead, people frequently *do* jump to conclusions about others—and on the basis of very limited information. If you have ever made a judgment about someone else on the basis of his or her ethnic background, age, gender, sexual orientation, or physical condition, then you are well aware of this tendency. As we discussed in conjunction with the topic of *stereotypes* (see Chapter 3), such judgments are frequently negative in nature.

A negative attitude we hold toward another based on his or her membership in a particular group is referred to as **prejudice**.[63] Not only might people holding prejudicial attitudes have negative beliefs and feelings, but these may predispose people to behave in ways consistent with these attitudes. For example, it would not be surprising to find that an employment interviewer who holds negative stereotypes toward members of a certain minority group evaluates negatively a candidate belonging to that group and is disinterested in hiring such an individual. Then, if this prejudicial attitude actually leads the interviewer not to hire the candidate, this may be said to be an act of **discrimination**. That is, the interviewer acted consistently with his or her negative attitude, not giving the candidate a fair chance, treating different people in different ways. The key thing to keep in mind is this: Prejudice is a negative attitude, whereas discrimination is the behaviour that follows from it (the behavioural expression of that attitude). For a summary of this idea, see Figure 6-7.

prejudice Negative attitudes toward the members of specific groups, based solely on the fact that they are members of those groups (e.g., age, race, sexual orientation).

discrimination The behaviour consistent with a prejudicial attitude; the act of treating someone negatively because of his or her membership in a specific group.

Figure 6-7 Prejudice vs. Discrimination: A Key Distinction

Prejudice is an attitude and, as such, consists of the three basic components of attitudes. *Discrimination* refers to behaviour based on that attitude. The example presented here illustrates this important distinction.

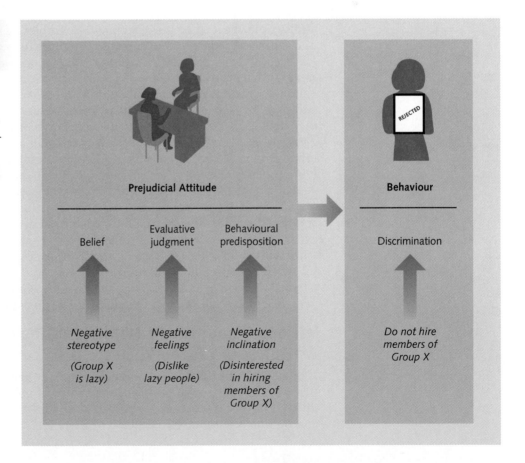

Prejudicial Attitude → Behaviour

Belief — Evaluative judgment — Behavioural predisposition → Discrimination

Negative stereotype (Group X is lazy) — Negative feelings (Dislike lazy people) — Negative inclination (Disinterested in hiring members of Group X) — Do not hire members of Group X

Diversity versus Prejudice: Competing Organizational Realities

There can be no mistaking the fact that Canada is an ethnically diverse nation—and that it is becoming more so. The Ministry of Culture and Citizenship has projected that the proportion of people from visible minorities in Canada would be 15 percent by the start of the new millennium.[64] It has also been estimated that, by the year 2003, more than 80 percent of the Ontario workforce will be made up of women, Native people, people with various kinds of disabling conditions, and people from ethnic minority groups.[65]

The trend toward increasing diversity in the American workforce is just as strong. For example, it has been estimated that by the year 2004, half of the U.S. population will be composed of people of African, Latin, Native American, and/or Asian descent. In addition, women—who, for many years only infrequently worked outside the home—are currently filling 65 percent of all new jobs, and in just a few years about half of the civilian workforce will be composed of women.[66] For some companies, diversity is already a reality. For example, at the Solectron Corporation, a computer-assembly company in California, 30 nationalities can be found speaking 40 different languages and dialects among the company's 3200 employees.[67]

Interestingly, as this picture of the highly diverse North American workforce unfolds, equally real is the unfortunate fact that prejudice against various groups still exists, and that these prejudices are likely to have serious consequences. Before describing the nature of such prejudicial attitudes, we will first outline some of the general problems that they create.

☞ For a discussion of the general nature of organizational conflict, see Chapter 11.

First, prejudice can be a *source of serious friction or conflict* between people. Although a highly diverse workforce can potentially bring the advantage of differing opinions and perspectives, this may turn into a disadvantage among individuals who hold prejudicial attitudes. Indeed, if one's group membership causes an underlying current of distrust, then the conflict that results may be disruptive to the organization as people fail to cooperate with each other to get their jobs done. In extreme cases, the discriminatory actions that follow from prejudicial attitudes culminate in legal action—be it employees charging their employers with unfair discrimination,[68] or customers charging companies with discriminatory actions.[69]

Second, prejudice may have *adverse effects on the careers of people who are the targets of such attitudes*. Affected individuals may encounter various forms of discrimination—some very subtle, but others quite overt—with respect to hiring, promotion, and pay. For example, although there are more women than ever in the workforce, they are highly underrepresented in the upper echelons of organizations—in fact, only 2 percent of CEOs in Canada's top 500 companies and 9 percent of corporate directors are women.[70] Because the discrimination is quite real, but not openly admitted, it is frequently referred to as the *glass ceiling* (i.e., a barrier that cannot be seen).

☞ We will discuss the impact of the glass ceiling more thoroughly in Chapter 7.

Third, we cannot overlook the devastating psychological impact of prejudice on victims of discrimination. Not only is the victim penalized, but so, too, are others who share the same background, what has been called *covictimization*.[71] To the extent that talented individuals are passed over because of their membership in certain groups, individuals suffer an affront to their self-esteem that can be quite harmful. This, of course, is in addition to the loss to the organization of overlooking talented individuals simply because they are not white males. In today's highly competitive global economy, this is a mistake that no companies can afford.

Various "Groupisms": Manifestations of Prejudicial Attitudes in the Workplace

If there is any one truly "equal opportunity" for people in today's workplace, it is that we *all* stand a chance of being the victim of prejudice. Indeed, there are many different forms of *groupism*—prejudices based on membership in certain groups—and no one is immune (see Figure 6-8).[72]

"Well, sir, then I take it you would vote for any cat in preference to a capable dog."

Figure 6-8 Prejudice Is All Around Us

As suggested here, prejudicial attitudes toward members of various groups may be even more widespread than we might think.

(Source: Drawing by Drucker; © 1980 The New Yorker Magazine, Inc.)

Generation X The generation of people born at the end of the baby boom, 1960–1966.

Generation Y The generation of people born between 1967 and 1979.[77]

☛ *We will describe the trend toward relying on teams in Chapter 8.*

Prejudice based on age. We're all going to get older (if we're lucky). People are living longer and the median age of Canadians is rising as the huge baby boom generation ages. The baby boom generation, born between 1947 and 1966, makes up approximately a third of the Canadian population.[73] In 1951, 7.75 percent of Canadians were in the over-65 age range, while 8.09 percent were in this range in 1971, and 11.61 percent in 1991.[74] As the leading edge of the baby boomers reaches age 65 in 2012 this percentage will rise dramatically. Despite this trend, it is clear that prejudice based on age is all too common. Although legal guarantees, such as the Canadian Charter of Rights and Freedoms and legislation in other countries, have done much to counter employment discrimination against older workers, prejudices continue to exist.

Part of the problem resides in stereotypes people have that older workers are too set in their ways to train, and that they will tend to be sick or accident-prone. As in the case of many attitudes, these prejudices are not founded on accurate information. Recent survey findings paint just the opposite picture of older workers. Namely, organizations tend to have extremely positive experiences with older workers: They have good skills, are highly committed to doing their jobs well, and have outstanding safety records.[75]

It is not just older workers who find themselves victims of prejudice but younger ones, too. For them, part of the problem is that as the average age of the workforce advances there develops a gap in expectations between the more experienced older workers who are in charge and the younger employees just entering the workforce. Specifically, compared to older workers, who grew up in a different time, today's under-40 employees view the world differently. These are **Generation X**, born at the end of the baby boom between 1960 and 1966, and the so-called baby bust generation often known as **Generation Y**, born between 1967 and 1979.[76] They are more prone to question the way things are done, not to see the government as an ally, and not to expect loyalty. They are likely to consider self-development to be their main interest and are willing to learn whatever skills are necessary to make them marketable. These differing perspectives may lead older employees, who are likely to be their superiors, to feel uncomfortable with their younger colleagues. This is especially problematic as the nature of work shifts so that people with different skills are brought together to work in teams.

However, a recent study brings encouraging news. In a survey of employees' attitudes toward older workers, it has been found that even younger workers hold generally positive views of older workers—although these were not quite as positive as older workers' views of themselves.[78] Interestingly, the same study found that the more time younger people spent working with their older colleagues, the more positive (and less stereotypical) their attitudes were toward them. The implications of this are that simply bringing younger and older workers together may be an effective means of chipping away at age-based stereotypes.

Prejudice based on physical condition. If you think about it, every one of us has one physical feature or another that keeps us from doing a certain kind of work. Some people are not strong enough to load heavy packages onto trucks, others are not athletic enough to play professional sports, and still others might lack the agility and stamina needed to be a firefighter. Thus, although we all may be disabled in some way, certain physical conditions tend to be the focus of widely held prejudicial attitudes. Such conditions (e.g., blindness, disfigurement, physical paralysis) are said to have *stigmas* attached to them—that is, negative aspects of one's identity.[79]

☞ *This idea of designing work so that it may be performed by people with physical disabilities is not new. In fact, as noted in Chapter 1, it dates back to the work of the Gilbreths over 80 years ago.*

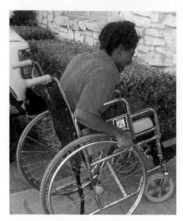

Figure 6-9 Accommodating People with Physical Disabilities: An Effective Way of Avoiding Discrimination

Companies are finding simple ways of accommodating employees who have physical disabilities. Doing so not only avoids discrimination, but enables companies to take full advantage of their human resources.

Bell Canada
www.bell.ca

Section 15 of the Canadian Charter of Rights and Freedoms (1982) specifies that "Every individual is equal before and under the law and has the right to the equal protection and equal benefit of the law without discrimination and, in particular, without discrimination based on race, national or ethnic origin, colour, religion, sex, age, or mental or physical disability (see Figure 6-9)."[80]

Many companies are finding that it is possible for them to meet the needs of disabled employees quite easily and with little expense. For example, Greiner Engineering, Inc., in Irving, Texas, was able to accommodate its employees in wheelchairs by simply substituting a lighter-weight door on its restrooms, and raising a drafting table by putting bricks under its legs.[81] Although not all accommodations are as easily made, companies are more aware than ever before of the need for them.[82]

Prejudice based on sexual orientation. Unlike people with physical disabilities, who are protected from discrimination by the Charter, no such protection exists (yet, at least) for another group whose members are frequently victims of prejudice—gay men and lesbian women. Unfortunately, although more people than ever are tolerant of nontraditional sexual orientations, antihomosexual prejudice still exists in the workplace. Indeed, about two-thirds of CEOs from major companies note that they are reluctant to put a homosexual on a top management committee.[83] Not surprisingly, without the law to protect them, and widespread prejudices against them, many gays and lesbians are reluctant to openly make their sexual orientations known.[84]

Fears of being "discovered," exposed as a homosexual, represent a considerable source of stress among such individuals. For example, a gay vice-president of a large office equipment manufacturer in Chicago admitted in a magazine interview that he'd like to become the company's CEO, but fears that his chances would be ruined if his sexual orientation became known.[85] Although the pressure of having to go through life (or, at least, an important part of it) with a disguised identity must be extreme, imagine the cumulative effect of such efforts on organizations in which several employees are homosexual. Such misdirection of energy can become quite a serious productivity issue. In the words of consultant Mark Kaplan, "gay and lesbian employees use a lot of time and stress trying to conceal a big part of their identity."[86] To work in an organization with a homophobic culture and to have to endure jokes slurring gays and lesbians can easily distract even the most highly focused employees.

To help avoid these problems—and, out of respect for diverse sexual orientations—many organizations have adopted internal fair-employment policies that include sexual orientation. In addition, some companies are actively working to prohibit discrimination on the basis of sexual orientation. In Canada, increasing numbers of companies are offering benefits to employees and their domestic partners, regardless of whether they are of the opposite sex or the same sex. Recognizing diversity in sexual orientation has helped many companies attract and retain personnel in companies such as London Life Insurance Co., Shoppers Drug Mart Ltd., NOVA Corp., Dow Chemical, Bell Canada, Toronto Dominion Bank, Sun Life Assurance Co. of Canada, and Nortel Networks.[87] Clearly, although some companies are passively discouraging diversity with respect to sexual orientation, others, by encouraging diversity, are using it to their own—and their employees'—advantage.

Prejudice based on race and national origin. As mentioned earlier in this chapter, the Canadian Charter of Rights and Freedoms (Section 15) guarantees Canadians freedom from discrimination based on a wide variety of characteristics and circumstances. While the Charter pertains only to direct government action, it has been used as a basis for various discrimination cases. Nevertheless, discrimination is far from eradicated.[88] Racial harassment is prohibited by law in Canada. Employers are liable for the discriminatory behaviour of anyone they employ, and employees who experience discrimination can pursue a number of legal remedies.[89]

Some companies are taking concrete steps to minimize discrimination. For example, the Canadian Imperial Bank of Commerce held a one-month diversity awareness event. One person who helped to organize the event was Holly Payton, an Ojibway student at Hamilton, Ontario's McMaster University. Holger Kluge, CIBC's president of the personal and commercial bank division, reflects the company's stated commitment to diversity: "We as a business have to reflect the make-up of our community and the customers we serve...if you want to be an employer of choice, you have to respect the individuals you have in the organization, and their viewpoints and their differences."[90]

Other examples include, AT&T Bell Labs in Murray Hill, New Jersey, which is working with managers to find ways of helping the company's many ethnic minority employees get promoted more rapidly. Similarly, Hughes Aircraft Co. of Los Angeles has been assigning mentors to minority group employees to help teach them about the company's culture and the skills needed to succeed.[91] Although these examples are only modest steps, they represent very encouraging trends intended to help reduce a long-standing problem (see Figure 6-10).

Prejudice against women.   Equality for women in the workplace is improving, although it is a slow victory, to be sure (see **THE ETHICS ANGLE**). As discussed in Chapter 2 and earlier in this chapter, there can be no mistaking the widespread—and ever-growing—presence of women in today's workforce. However, very few top executive jobs and corporate directorships are held by women.[92] Why is this the case? Although some argue that sufficient time may not have passed to allow more women to work their way into the top echelons of organizations, there appear to be more formidable barriers. Most notably, it is clear that powerful *sex role stereotypes* persist, narrow-minded beliefs about the kinds of tasks for which women are most appropriately suited. Such stereotypes have kept women from important organizational positions.

Judith McBride-King co-authored the first systematic Canadian study examining the role of women in senior management positions from the perspectives of both women and men. Her conclusion is that "Although many barriers to women are unintentional, 'there are only slight cracks in the glass ceiling.' "[93] The study, entitled *Closing the Gap*, was conducted by the Conference Board of Canada and a New York–based group known as Catalyst. Four hundred women and 159 men, all in very senior positions with their organizations, answered questionnaires and some were also interviewed. Overall, the women in the study blamed male stereotyping for locking them out of the country's top jobs, while the male respondents said women did not have enough experience. Of the male respondents in the corporate sector, all of whom were CEOs, 62 percent said that the advancement of women was very important. Less than half of their counterparts in the professional sector felt the same way. "Women in the study reported that to get ahead they had to consistently exceed expectations, seek out difficult or highly visible assignments, and develop a style with which male managers were comfortable."[94]

☞ *A discussion of the many valuable roles played by mentors, and the nature of the mentorship process, appears in Chapter 7.*

☞ *The process of stereotyping is more fully discussed in Chapter 3.*

Figure 6-10 Targeting Ethnic Markets

IBM Canada's Yang-Hai Wang is head of the company's ethnocultural business unit which is focusing on targeting ethnic markets. CEO John Wetmore says the company recognizes the size and importance of the Chinese market. The company planned to start its ethnic marketing focus with the Chinese and Italian communities and then expand to include other ethnic groups such as aboriginals.[95]

IBM Canada Ltd.
www.can.ibm.com

"Automakers' Boys' Club" Is Very Slow to Change

The progress toward full acceptance of diversity in some work settings is slow and can be very difficult. The auto industry is one area that has a reputation for being clearly male dominated and at times uncomfortable for women. For example, auto parts manufacturer Magna International Inc. was sued for alleged sexual discrimination by a female employee in suburban Detroit. Included as evidence in the suit were admissions by male employees at Magna that they entertained potential customers at strip clubs.[96] This suit is significant not only for Magna but for the industry which has been trying to clean up its act in light of the fact that women make half of all vehicle purchasing decisions.[97]

Ford Canada president Bobby Gaunt knows what it is like to deal with the automaker "boys' club." "When I look back at 25 years I've certainly seen significant changes," she says. "But as with anything that I think is as huge as this industry, and as old as this industry is, we're really talking about cultural change. And changing cultures and changing behaviours takes a very long time."[98]

Maureen Kempston-Darkes, GM Canada's CEO, emphasizes that she does not handle her job differently simply because she is a woman. "The challenges that confront chief executives are the same whether they are men or women,"she says. "Once you get to the CEO spot, you're focused on the same kinds of issues that men would focus on. That's why you're in the job." She urges women trying to work their way up the ladder to persevere, to have a clear sense of purpose, and to maintain a sense of balance.[99]

Valuing and Managing a Diverse Workforce: Current Practices

There can be little doubt that many organizations have taken steps to bring women and members of minority groups into the workforce. However, many of today's organizations are interested in not just hiring a wider variety of different people, but also creating an atmosphere in which diverse groups can flourish. They are attempting not merely to be socially responsible, but to recognize that diversity is a business issue.

diversity management programs Programs in which employees are taught to celebrate the differences between people and in which organizations create supportive work environments for women and minorities.

As one consultant put it, "A corporation's success will increasingly be determined by its managers' ability to naturally tap the full potential of a diverse workforce."[100] It is with this goal in mind that many organizations are adapting **diversity management programs**—efforts to celebrate diversity by creating supportive, not just neutral, work environments for women and minorities.[101] Simply put, the underlying philosophy of diversity management programs is that cracking the glass ceiling requires that women and minorities are not just tolerated, but valued.[102] In this section of the chapter we will identify various types of diversity management programs and then describe some examples of successful diversity management efforts.

Varieties of diversity management programs. In general, diversity management programs fall into two categories: *awareness-based diversity training* and *skill-based diversity training*.[103] Specifically, **awareness-based diversity training** is designed to raise people's awareness of diversity issues in the workplace and to get them to recognize the underlying assumptions they make about people. It is a very basic orientation, a starting point—one that takes a cognitive approach. Typically, it involves teaching people about the business necessity of valuing diversity, and makes them sensitive to their own cultural assumptions and biases. This may involve using various experiential exercises that help people view others as individuals as opposed to stereotyped members of groups.

awareness-based diversity training A type of diversity management program designed to make people more aware of diversity issues in the workplace and to get them to recognize the underlying assumptions they make about people.

skills-based diversity training An approach to diversity management that goes beyond *awareness-based diversity training* and is designed to develop people's skills with respect to managing diversity.

Building on the awareness approach is **skills-based diversity training**. This orientation is designed to develop people's skills with respect to managing diversity. As such, it goes beyond raising awareness to developing the tools needed to interact effectively with others. There are four main tools involved in this process.[104] These include:

1. ***Cross-cultural understanding:*** understanding the cultural differences responsible for why different coworkers behave differently on the job.

2. ***Intercultural communication:*** learning to ensure that verbal and nonverbal barriers to communication across cultures are overcome.

3. ***Facilitation skills:*** training in how to help others alleviate misunderstanding that may result from cultural differences.

4. ***Flexibility and adaptability:*** cultivating the ability to patiently take new and different approaches when dealing with others who are different.

Both approaches to diversity training have the same long-term goals. They strive to make interaction between diverse groups of people easier and more effective. Then, once people are paying attention to each other, the road is paved for morale to improve, for productivity to be enhanced, and for people to be able to focus their creative energies. With all of these benefits, organizations are positioned to attain their ultimate goal—to improve their economic position in the marketplace. (For a summary of these approaches, see Figure 6-11.)

Recent evidence paints a very convincing picture of the ultimate effectiveness of diversity management efforts. Wright, Ferris, Hiller, and Kroll reasoned that when companies effectively use their human resources they can lower their costs and thereby perform better than their competition.[105] To test this notion they compared two groups of companies from 1986 through 1992. One group was composed of organizations that had received awards for their exemplary efforts at managing diversity. The other group was composed of companies that had settled large claims against them for employment discrimination. To compare the performance of these organizations, the researchers relied on a key index of economic success—stock returns. Their findings were striking: Companies that made special efforts to use their diverse human resources were considerably more profitable than those that

Figure 6-11 Diversity Management: Two Major Approaches to Training

Skills-based diversity training builds on the approach taken by *awareness-based diversity training.* However, both approaches strive toward achieving the same goals.

(Source: Adapted from material in Carnevale & Stone, 1995; see Note 103.)

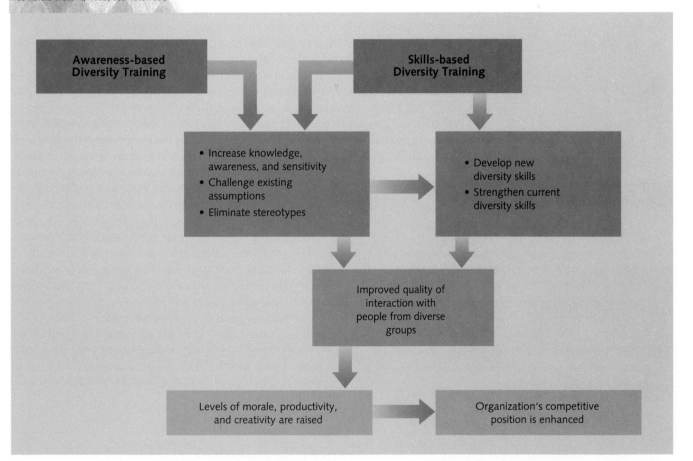

discriminated against their employees. Wright and his associates explain that the organizations that capitalized on the diversity of their workforces were better able to attract and maintain the talented people needed for organizations to thrive. Clearly, managing diversity makes sense not only because it is the right way to treat people, but also because it is good business.

DEC is one company that has recognized the benefits of managing diversity. However, it has not been alone. Pepsi Cola, American Express Travel Related Services, and the accounting firm Coopers & Lybrand also have been actively engaged in diversity management efforts.[106] Several companies have gone beyond simply embracing the differences between people by creating opportunities for diverse groups of people within organizations. For example, Xerox's "Step-Up" program, in existence for some 30 years, has been one of the most thorough and sustained efforts to hire minority group members and train them to succeed.[107] Although we have been listing the diversity management efforts of several organizations, it would be misleading to imply that these are representative of what most organizations are doing. Accordingly, in the DIVERSITY IN TODAY'S ORGANIZATIONS section we ask: How actively involved in diversity management efforts are today's organizations?

A note of caution.   Although most companies have been pleased with the ways their diversity management efforts have promoted harmony among employees, some have encountered problems. In the most serious cases, diversity management efforts have backfired, leaving race and gender divisions even greater.[108] The most serious problems have stemmed from the practice of focusing on stereotypes, even positive ones. Thinking of people in stereotypical ways can create barriers that interfere with looking at people as individuals. So, instead of looking at the *average* differences between people (which may reinforce stereotypes), experts recommend that managing diversity demands accepting a *range* of differences between people (a range that promises to become even greater in the years ahead).[109]

With this in mind, managers are advised not to treat someone as special because he or she is a member of a certain group, but because of the unique skills or abilities he or she brings to the job. To the extent that managers are trained to seek, recognize, and develop the talents of their employees regardless of the groups to which they belong, they will help break down the barriers that made diversity training necessary in the first place. In fact, several important notes of caution may be identified, caveats that need to be carefully considered when it comes to conducting diversity training successfully.[110] For a summary of several such concerns, see Table 6-3.

Perhaps the main key to the effectiveness of diversity management is *complete managerial support*. Indeed, you cannot do something as complex as celebrate diversity with a one-time effort. Successful diversity management requires sustained attention to diversity in all organizational activities. For example, it has been shown that companies that have successful diversity management training programs also tend to require everyone to be trained, define diversity very broadly (i.e., they do not limit it to only one or two groups), and reward managers for their special efforts at increasing diversity.[111] Without "going the extra mile," by completely supporting diversity activities, organizations may find themselves quite disappointed with their efforts.

In conclusion, although mistakes have been made in the way some diversity management programs have been implemented, diversity management programs have, in many cases, greatly helped organizations find ways of tapping the rich pool of talent found in a highly diverse workforce.

[**You Be The Consultant**]

The president of a large manufacturing company is concerned about racial tension that has been building among employees in the plant. The workforce includes large numbers of people from racial and ethnic minorities. A diversity management program is being considered.

1. Do you think a diversity management program would be useful in this case? If not, why? If so, what steps would you take to initiate such a plan?

2. What potential problems and limitations would you expect to find should a diversity management program be started?

TABLE 6-3 Potential Problems in Diversity Training

For diversity training efforts to be successful they must avoid the potential problems outlined here.

(Source: Adapted from Gardenswartz & Rowe, 1994; see Note 110.)

Problem	Description and Solution
Emotional tension is heightened.	Talking about prejudices is likely to make people feel uneasy. Training needs to be conducted in a "safe," comfortable environment.
Possibility of polarization.	Avoid discussions that have yes or no answers (e.g., "should gays be allowed in the military?"). Instead, encourage consideration of a broad range of options.
Some people may have personal "axes to grind."	Training sessions should not provide platforms for people who want to vent about past problems. Facilitators should keep the group on target.
Personal attacks may occur.	Strong opinions on diversity issues may box people into corners. Treat everyone with respect and dignity.
Reactions to training will be varied.	Some may welcome the training whereas others may resent having to go through it. Addressing these feelings should be made a part of training sessions.
White males tend to be blamed.	It is tempting to blame the dominant group, white males, for diversity problems. However, no one group has a monopoly on prejudice and discrimination. White males should discuss their difficulties adjusting to a changing world.
Timing may be problematic.	Avoid adding to stress by not scheduling sessions during periods in which other sensitive events (e.g., layoffs, contract negotiations) are occurring.
Reasons for training may be ingenuine.	Diversity training works best when it is part of a strategic effort on the part of management to change policies so as to make a more "inclusive" organization. However, training conducted because "everyone's doing it" is likely to fail—and maybe even backfire.

Diversity in Today's Organizations

Valuing Diversity: Taking the Pulse of Canadian Companies

Canada's largest private employer of aboriginal people is The North West Company. The company is based in Winnipeg, has 156 Canadian *Northern* stores and 21 *AC Value Center* stores operating in Alaska, and employs 3700 people.[112] The North West Company supplies the North with everything from flour and sugar to boots and outboard motors. It even develops film and cashes cheques.[113]

The North West Company has developed a 120-module training program in an effort to reduce staff turnover and to give all employees the opportunity to develop skills and progress in the company. All the materials used in the program are culturally adapted using aboriginal names and situations that reflect the reality for employees in northern communities.[114] "The company feels that the Stores Training Program has had a significant positive impact in reducing management turnover and increasing the percentage of Aboriginal people in management positions."[115]

Organizations in other parts of Canada are also developing policies and strategies for fostering diversity in the workplace. Pharmaceutical, health-care products, and confectionary producer, Warner-Lambert Canada Inc., based in Scarborough, Ontario, has committed itself to reflecting the diversity of its consumers. "The more our organization reflects the consumer population, the more it will be in sync with what customers want, need, and are looking for."[116] The organization's Diversity Task Force was established with membership from all of the company's functional areas. The Task Force established five employee teams that review the employment systems at Warner-Lambert. Goals and action plans are developed from the results of these reviews. Having a diverse workforce allows Warner-Lambert to match the ethnocultural background of its sales representatives to that of its customers.[117]

Union Gas Limited, employing 2600 people across Ontario, bases its workplace equity programs on its Mutual Respect Policy, which reflects the company's focus on the development of a harassment-free workplace. Union Gas staff have had input into the company's diversity policies through its "diversity teams." The policy states in part: "We are committed to valuing the diversity of our work force by providing an equitable work environment, and hiring and promoting people based on qualifications, to ensure that our work force is reflective of the communities we serve...."[118] Feedback from staff has led to changes in hiring practices in the company. Line managers are now being trained to take over some of the hiring responsibilities from the company's human resources department.[119]

In addition to their focus on in-house diversity management practices, some companies are also finding ways to support diversity initiatives in the community. Weyerhaeuser Canada Ltd. sponsors Diversity Education Awards. The company, which operates in Saskatchewan, Alberta, and British Columbia, believes that "By providing financial assistance to students of a diverse background, Weyerhaeuser is helping these individuals to reach their educational objectives. And, by assisting diverse students to reach their educational goals, Weyerhaeuser will also help to increase the pool of qualified individuals from which to select future employees."[120]

Further, Nortel was one of the sponsors of the fifteenth anniversary Harry Jerome Awards. This award program was established by the Black Business and Professional Association (BBPA) as a way to recognize the excellent achievements of African Canadians.[121]

The efforts of organizations across Canada to support an increasingly diverse workforce reflect the ever-changing nature of our country and the wealth of resources that diversity offers to the development of business.

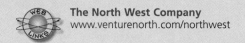

The North West Company
www.venturenorth.com/northwest

SUMMARY AND REVIEW

What Are Attitudes?

Attitudes are stable clusters of feelings, beliefs, and behavioural tendencies directed toward some aspect of the external world. **Work-related attitudes** involve such reactions toward various aspects of work settings or the people in them. All attitudes consist of a *cognitive* component (what you believe), an *evaluative* component (how you feel), and a *behavioural* component (the tendency to behave a certain way).

Job Satisfaction

Job satisfaction involves positive or negative attitudes toward one's work. Such attitudes can be measured by completing *rating scales* (such as the JDI or the MSQ), recounting *critical incidents* (instances found to be especially pleasing or displeasing), and by conducting *interviews* or *confrontation meetings*.

According to Herzberg's **two-factor theory**, job satisfaction and dissatisfaction stem from different factors. Specifically, it claims that factors leading to job satisfaction stem from factors associated with the work itself (known as motivators), and that factors leading to job dissatisfaction are associated with the conditions surrounding jobs (e.g., the work environment). Evidence for the accuracy of this theory has been mixed. Locke's **value theory** suggests that job satisfaction reflects the apparent match between the outcomes individuals desire from their jobs (what they *value*) and what they believe they are actually receiving.

When people are dissatisfied with their jobs they tend to withdraw. That is, they are frequently absent and are likely to quit their jobs. However, evidence suggests that job performance is only very weakly associated with dissatisfaction. Levels of job satisfaction can be raised by paying people fairly, improving the quality of supervision, decentralizing control of organizational power, and matching people to jobs that are congruent with their interests.

Organizational Commitment

Organizational commitment deals with people's attitudes toward their organizations. People can have various targets, or *foci* of commitment, such as top managers, or one's work group. Commitment may be based primarily on three different *bases*. One is **continuance commitment**—the strength of a person's tendency to continue working for an organization because he or she has to and cannot afford to do otherwise. Another is **affective commitment**—the strength of a person's tendency to continue working for an organization because he or she agrees with its goals and values and desires to stay with it. A third is **normative commitment**—commitment to remain in an organization stemming from social obligations to do so.

Low levels of organizational commitment have been linked to high levels of absenteeism and voluntary turnover, the unwillingness to share and make sacrifices for the company, and negative personal consequences for employees. However, organizational commitment may be enhanced by enriching jobs, aligning the interests of employees with those of the company, and recruiting and selecting newcomers whose values closely match those of the organization.

Prejudice in Work Settings

Prejudice refers to negative attitudes toward members of specific groups, and **discrimination** refers to treating people differently because of these prejudices. Today's workforce is characterized by high levels of diversity, with many groups finding themselves victims of prejudicial attitudes and discriminatory behaviours (based on many different factors, including age, sexual orientation, physical condition, racial or ethnic group membership, and gender). Although people are becoming more tolerant of individuals from diverse groups, prejudicial attitudes persist.

To help tap the rich pool of resources available in today's highly diverse workforce, many companies are using **diversity management programs**—techniques for systematically teaching employees to celebrate the differences between people. Typically, these programs go beyond efforts to recruit and hire women and members of minority groups, to creating supportive work environments for them. Although implementing these programs is potentially difficult, experts acknowledge that the benefits, both organizational and personal, are considerable.

CASE PREVIEW QUESTIONS FOR DISCUSSION

1. Compare the stereotype of the 1950s bank manager with today's bank manager. Explain the differences, if any.

2. Examine how the major banks have changed in the last five to ten years. How have changing attitudes toward diversity affected the management and customer service in the banks?

3. Visit several of Canada's major financial institutions on the Web. Profile their various diversity initiatives. How would bank mergers impact diversity initiatives?

CHAPTER QUESTIONS FOR DISCUSSION

1. Someone tells you that people in general don't like their jobs. Would you agree or disagree with this statement? Why?

2. As a manager, you want to enhance job satisfaction among your subordinates. What steps might you take to accomplish this goal?

3. "Happy workers are productive workers." Do you agree or disagree? Why?

4. Absenteeism and voluntary turnover are costly problems for many companies. What specific steps can be taken to reduce the incidence of these forms of employee withdrawal?

5. Suppose an employee is highly dissatisfied with his or her job and organization but remains on the job and does not look for a new one. How would you explain this person's behaviour?

6. "Sexism and racism are a thing of the past." Do you agree or disagree? Why?

7. What steps are today's organizations taking toward valuing diversity in their workforces? Give an example.

CASE IN POINT

Cultural Diversity at Exxon Chemical

With U.S. headquarters in Houston, Texas, and European regional headquarters in Brussels, Belgium, Exxon Chemical is a huge multinational company. You might think that having employees in many different nations on two continents would lead naturally to acceptance of cultural diversity. But, Exxon Chemical officials did not take this for granted. Recognizing that its highly diverse, international workforce was key to improving the company's performance, as well as its reputation as an international organization, Exxon Chemical recently surveyed its employees to see how well the company was doing.

To this end, a team was put together to "take the temperature of the organization" with respect to the matter of diversity. This involved writing questions, training interviewers to ask them, then visiting 25 European cities, and speaking to 973 different people about the company's acceptance of different people.

Among the many findings were several particularly troublesome observations regarding the way employees saw the company. In their eyes, it was a rather elitist organization and did not encourage people to be themselves—especially if that meant being different in some way. Employees also reported a bias against women and a bias against people who did not speak English. These attitudes, it was feared, would not only demotivate the workforce, but would reduce the competitive advantage that the company would otherwise have if it were able to tap its diverse human resources to their fullest potential.

One of the things Exxon Chemical did to help was to introduce its *Choices* program—a series of courses for

European middle managers whose objectives included increasing awareness of the value of diversity within the company. In some of these sessions, managers from Great Britain, Belgium, France, the Netherlands, Germany, Sweden, and the United States were brought together in groups (led by multilingual facilitators) to perform various exercises in which they were required to work cooperatively with each other.

On several occasions these exercises put people in situations in which the dynamics taught a lesson in valuing diversity. For example, some groups were assembled in which a minority of the members spoke a common language that the majority did not speak. As the discussions progressed, an interesting dynamic was observed: Unless conscientious efforts were made to bring the minority group members into the discussions, these individuals tended to talk only to each other and did not make contributions to the group's task. And, on occasions in which these people in the linguistic minority had valuable input to offer, the groups frequently never benefited from hearing from them. As the facilitator later discussed this matter with the group, an important lesson was learned about the importance of tapping the richness of human resources at one's disposal—even if it means going out of one's way to bring someone into the discussion who might otherwise feel left out and unappreciated.

So impressed have Exxon Chemical's managers been with the *Choices* program that it has been expanded to even more locations throughout the company's huge empire. Although the large numbers make the project quite overwhelming, Exxon Chemical's goal is quite simple: to tap the vast array of diverse resources it already has at its disposal.[122]

Critical Thinking Questions

1. What impediments do you believe Exxon Chemical may face on its way to valuing the diversity of its employee base?

2. What steps can the company take to help overcome these barriers?

3. In addition to the *Choices* program, what other measures could Exxon Chemical take to help encourage the acceptance of diversity within its workforce? Do you think it is realistic to expect that such measures will actually help encourage diversity in a multinational workplace?

4. Exxon Chemical officials are assuming that there are advantages to having a highly diverse workforce, if these can only be tapped. What, specifically, would you say these advantages are—especially in a large multinational organization, like Exxon Chemical?

SKILLS PORTFOLIO

Experiencing Organizational Behaviour

Are You Committed to Your Job?

Questionnaires similar to the one presented here (which is based on established instruments) are used to assess three types of organizational commitment—continuance, affective, and normative. Completing this scale (based on Meyer & Allen, 1991; see Note 47) will give you a good feel for your own level of job commitment and how this important construct is measured.

Directions

In the space to the left of each of the 12 statements below write the one number that reflects the extent to which you agree with it personally. Express your answers using the following scale: 1 = not at all; 2 = slightly; 3 = moderately; 4 = a great deal; 5 = extremely.

___ 1. At this point, I stay on my job more because I have to than because I want to.

___ 2. I feel I strongly belong to my organization.

___ 3. I am reluctant to leave a company once I have been working there.

___ 4. Leaving my job would entail a great deal of personal sacrifice.

___ 5. I feel emotionally connected to the company for which I work.

___ 6. My employer would be very disappointed if I left my job.

___ 7. I don't have any other choice but to stay on my present job.

___ 8. I feel like I am part of the family at the company in which I work.

___ 9. I feel a strong obligation to stay on my job.

___ 10. My life would be greatly disrupted if I left my present job.

___ 11. I would be quite pleased to spend the rest of my life working for this organization.

___ 12. I stay on my job because people would think poorly of me for leaving.

Scoring

1. Add the scores for items 1, 4, 7, and 10. This reflects your degree of *continuance commitment.*

2. Add the scores for items 2, 5, 8, and 11. This reflects your degree of *affective commitment*.

3. Add the scores for items 3, 6, 9, and 12. This reflects your degree of *normative commitment*.

Questions for Discussion

1. Which form of commitment does the scale reveal you have most? Which do you have least? Are these differences great, or are they highly similar?

2. Did the scale tell you something you didn't already know about yourself, or did it merely reinforce your intuitive beliefs about your own organizational commitment?

3. To what extent is your organizational commitment, as reflected by this scale, related to your interest in quitting your job and taking a new position?

4. How do your answers to these questions compare to those of your classmates? Are your responses similar to theirs or different from them? Why do you think this is?

Working in Groups

Recognizing Differences in Cultural Values on the Job

One of the major barriers in understanding and appreciating people from other cultures is the fact that they may adopt widely different values—especially when it comes to basic organizational activities, such as hiring. The following exercise (adapted from Gardenswartz & Rowe, 1994; see Note 110) is designed to make you aware of such differences and to sensitize you to their impact on life in organizations.

Directions

1. Divide the class into groups of approximately five to ten students.

2. Review the values differences noted in the chart below.

3. As a group, identify and discuss specific examples of each of the cultural distinctions noted in the chart based on your personal experiences.

4. As a group, discuss the implications of these values differences. Note, for example, specific problems that are likely to arise as a result of such differences.

5. As a class, review the major implications identified by each group in step 4.

In mainstream North American culture . . .	But, in many other cultures . . .
• People's primary obligation is toward their jobs.	• People's primary obligation is toward their family and friends.
• Employment is "at will"; an employee may be terminated at the discretion of the organization.	• Employment is for life.
• Competition is an accepted way of life.	• Cooperation is considered better because it promotes harmony between people.
• People strive for personal achievement.	• Personal ambition is frowned upon; group achievement is highly valued.

Questions for Discussion

1. Was your group, or the class as a whole, generally sensitive to the differences in values noted in this exercise?

2. What were the major organizational implications of the cultural differences in values identified by the class?

3. What do you think could be done to help people recognize and accept these cultural differences in values?

4. Did you come away from this exercise with a better understanding of the way cultural differences between people may impact organizational activities?

TAKE IT TO THE NET

Prentice Hall

We invite you to visit the *Greenberg/Baron/Sales/Owen Companion Website* at *www.prenticehall.ca/greenberg* for this chapter's Internet resources.

CHAPTER 7
Career Development and Work Stress

LEARNING OBJECTIVES

After reading this chapter you should be able to:

1. Understand the concept of *socialization* and identify the stages through which it develops.

2. Explain what *mentors* are, what they do, and both the benefits and costs of mentoring to mentors and their protégés.

3. Describe the process through which people choose their careers, and explain how the nature of careers has changed in recent years.

4. Explain how the careers of women and men may differ, including the impact of the *glass ceiling*.

5. Define *stress* and distinguish between stress and strain.

6. Describe some of the major organizational and personal causes of stress, including conflict between work and family responsibilities.

7. Explain the concept of *burnout,* including its major causes and effects.

8. Describe the adverse effects of stress and explain how individual difference factors play a role in such effects.

9. Describe both individual and organizational techniques for managing stress.

Back from the Brink—The Fall and Rise of Sergio Zyman

Failure. The very word sends chills up and down the spines of most managers. And not surprisingly; after all, it implies the end to all those dreams of glory, as one's career goes down in flames. Amazing as it may seem, though, many top executives have experienced the bitter pain of failure—sometimes on a colossal scale—only to bounce back. One of the most dramatic examples of this kind of "re-ascent from the ashes" is provided by Sergio Zyman (see Figure 7-1).

In 1990, Zyman was head of U.S. marketing for Coca-Cola, giant of the soft-drink industry. Disturbed by the slow erosion of Coke's market share, most of which had been lost to archrival Pepsi-Cola, Zyman decided on a bold move: Coca-Cola would replace the company's mainstay with a new product—New Coke. The result? One of the biggest marketing fiascoes in history. Consumers soundly rejected New Coke and angrily demanded a return to their old favourite. So large and unsettling was the drop in sales that only 79 days later, "old Coke" was back on the shelves—and Sergio Zyman was out of a job.

Does he now describe his decision to pull old Coke from the market as a mistake? "No," he remarked in a recent interview. "Something between a failure and a bust. The strategy didn't work, but the totality of the action ended up being positive." After his blunder with New Coke, Zyman dropped from sight and worked as a consultant for seven years. "That first year I consulted for 7-Eleven, a reengineering company in France, Continental Airlines, and Jones New York," Zyman reports. Working out of his Atlanta home, he soon built a thriving business. "Marketing is marketing," Zyman states, so his services were certainly very much in demand.

And then, the seemingly impossible happened: His old company wanted him back. For two years the suave CEO of Coca-Cola, Roberto Goizueta, tried to rehire him; he wanted Zyman—who is famous in the soft-drink industry for his abrasive personality—to help shake things up. Ultimately, Zyman agreed, but only after winning promises of almost total freedom. So, like the proverbial Phoenix, he rose from the ashes of his previous failure and returned to Coca-Cola as its top marketing executive.[1] David Greising, author of *I'd Like to Buy the World a Coke: The Life and Leadership of Roberto Goizueta*, commented, "Inside and outside the company, Zyman was greeted with a mix of hope, fear, and consternation reminiscent of Napoleon returning from Elba."[2] Goizueta demonstrated that he, "would brook Zyman's [infamous] occasional autocratic excesses in return for the man's marketing genius and ability to get things done."[3] In fact, Goizueta even went so far as to have a T-shirt imprinted with the slogan, "Get Used To Sergio"— GUTS.[4] And although his return was not welcomed by others with as much enthusiasm as it was by Roberto Goizueta, the company did indeed profit from his audacious marketing moves over the next five years.

On March 19, 1998, just months after the untimely death of Roberto Goizueta from lung cancer, the irrepressible Sergio Zyman, 52, decided to resign.[5] Not concerned about his future in the corporate world, Sergio said, "I've always had destinations."[6] In short, he's confident that come what may—even another failure—he'd quickly pick up the pieces and cement them into a new pattern of success.

FIGURE 7-1 Bouncing Back from Failure

Sergio Zyman, the marketing executive behind the disastrous New Coke product launch, was rehired as Coca-Cola's chief global marketer in 1993. According to then-CEO Roberto Goizueta,"We became uncompetitive by not being tolerant of mistakes." Goizueta said that Sergio's return signalled a change in the company's thinking.[7]

Sergio Zyman is not the only executive to have made a career-destroying mistake and then to bounce back. Failure is not a one-way ticket to oblivion where one's career—the sequence of jobs, roles, and positions we hold during our working lives—is concerned.[8] On the contrary, for many it is a learning experience which helps them to shape even greater success. For example, Paul Reichmann describes himself as a "much more cautious developer" after the famous bankruptcy of his Canary Wharf project. He adds, "it would be very sad if I did not learn from my mistakes."[9] As Bill Gates of Microsoft, who likes to hire people who have made mistakes, puts it: "It [failure] shows that they take risks. The way people deal with things that go wrong is an indicator of how they deal with change."

While failure can be a learning experience, and even a boost to one's later career, it is clear that it also involves very high levels of *stress*—emotional and physiological reactions occurring in response to *stressors*, demands from within and outside an organization.[10] In fact, the stress resulting from failure can be so great that it wreaks havoc with personal health. This fact, in turn, suggests that the two topics on which we'll focus in this chapter—*careers* and *stress* are closely related, and they definitely are: Many of the events and processes that shape our careers influence the level of stress we encounter, and high levels of stress and the effects these produce can strongly affect our careers.

To provide you with basic information on these two important topics, we'll proceed as follows. We'll start with a discussion of two topics relating to careers: *organizational socialization*—the process by which new employees become fully members of their organizations[11] and *mentoring*—a process in which younger and less experienced individuals receive help and guidance from older and more experienced ones.[12] Then, we'll turn to the changing nature of careers themselves. In the past, most persons expected their careers to involve a straightforward climb up the organization's ladder, with each new rung involving increased responsibility and rewards. Now, however, this traditional pattern has been largely replaced by a much more complex picture involving many *lateral moves, job rotation,* and similar experiences. We'll consider several of these changes and also examine the effects of *gender* on careers—how the work experiences of women and men differ and the possibility that different factors determine whether they "make it to the top."[13]

After considering the nature of careers, we'll turn to the closely related topic of *stress*. Here, we'll examine the major causes of stress both at work and outside work, and its major effects. Then we'll describe some important techniques for managing stress that can be adopted both by individuals and their organizations. As we'll note repeatedly through our discussion of stress, there are close, two-way links between the experiences individuals have in their careers and the levels of stress they encounter. By considering these two topics in the same chapter, we will be able to emphasize these links and so provide you with a better understanding of both.

Organizational Socialization: The Process of Joining Up

Think back over the jobs you have held in recent years. Can you recall your feelings and reactions during the first few days or weeks on each? If so, you probably remember that these were somewhat uncomfortable periods. As a new employee, you were suddenly confronted with a work environment that was different in many respects from the one you had just left. Most, if not all, of the people around you were strangers, and you had to begin the process of getting to know them—and their personal quirks—from scratch. Unless your job was identical to the one you had before, you also had to learn new procedures, skills, and operations relating to it, as well as policies and practices in force in your new organization. In short, you had to *learn the ropes* so that you could perform your new job effectively.

organizational socialization The process through which newcomers to an organization become full-fledged members who share its major values and understand its policies and procedures.

The process through which you accomplished this task is known as **organizational socialization.** More formally, it can be defined as the process through which individuals are transformed from outsiders to participating, effective members of organizations.[14] In a sense, a career can be viewed as consisting of a series of socialization experiences, as an individual moves into new organizations or new positions. Thus, understanding organizational socialization is important to understanding careers. What happens during organizational socialization? What can organizations do to make this process more efficient? These are the questions on which we'll now focus.

The Nature of Organizational Socialization

Organizational socialization is clearly a continuous process, one that starts before people arrive on the job and continues for weeks or months after they begin working. However, the process can be divided into three basic periods described by one expert on this topic as *getting in, breaking in,* and *settling in* (see Figure 7-2).[15]

Getting in: What happens before people are hired.   Can you think of a specific company in which you'd like to work sometime in the future? Why would you like to work there? What is it about this company that makes it such an attractive choice for you? To the extent you can answer these questions, you already recognize that you know quite a bit about an organization even before you start working there. In other words, people often develop expectations about what an organization is like before actually being hired by it. In a sense, then, organizational socialization starts before people accept and fill a new job—a period described in several models of organizational socialization as the *pre-entry period.*[16]

Several sources of information contribute to beliefs about an organization. First, friends or relatives who work there might tell you about their experiences. Second, you might acquire information about an organization from sources such as professional journals, magazine and newspaper articles about it, and corporate annual reports. While these sources of information about an organization are far from perfect—they may paint a rosier picture than is justified by the facts—they are still useful from the point of view of forming preliminary ideas about what it might be like to work for that organization.

FIGURE 7-2 The Three Stages of Organizational Socialization

Organizational socialization generally involves the three stages summarized here: *getting in, breaking in,* and *settling in.*

(Source: Based on suggestions by Feldman, 1981; see Note 15.)

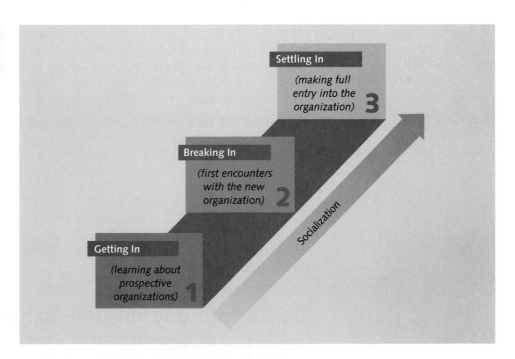

Another source of information is that provided by the organization itself—information supplied by recruiters or interviewers. Unfortunately, such information, too, can be biased. Competition for top-notch employees is fierce, so successful recruitment usually involves a skilled combination of marketing and diplomacy. Recruiters tend to describe their companies in glowing terms, glossing over internal problems and external threats, while emphasizing the positive features. The result is that potential employees often receive unrealistically positive impressions of conditions prevailing in a specific organization. When they arrive on the job and find that their expectations are not met, they experience disappointment, dissatisfaction, and even resentment about being misled. In fact, research findings indicate that the less employees' job expectations are met, the less satisfied and committed they are, and the more likely they are to think about quitting—and to actually do so.[17]

entry shock The confusion and disorientation experienced by many newcomers to an organization.

realistic job previews Accurate information concerning the conditions within an organization or job provided to potential employees prior to their decision to join an organization.

In order to avoid such negative reactions—which are sometimes termed **entry shock**—it is important for organizations to provide job candidates with accurate information about the organization. In other words, prospective employees should be given **realistic job previews**—previews in which they are provided with accurate information about their jobs and the conditions under which they will be performed—so that they can know what to expect if they do enter the organization. Growing evidence indicates that people exposed to realistic job previews later report higher satisfaction and show lower turnover than those who receive glowing, but often misleading, information about their companies.[18] Moreover, having realistic expectations helps to smooth the next period in the socialization process, to which we'll now turn.

Breaking in: The encounter stage. The second stage in organizational socialization begins when individuals actually assume their new duties. During this stage, they face several key tasks. They must master the skills required by their new jobs.[19] They must become oriented to the practices and procedures of the new organization—the way things are done there. In other words, they must learn the organization's *culture*, the shared attitudes, values, and expectations of existing organization members (see Chapter 14). Third, new members must establish good social relations with others and gain their acceptance.

During the encounter stage—sometimes known as *accommodation*—newcomers learn what the organization expects from them and how to be a participating member of their work group. Formal *orientation programs* are conducted, designed to teach new employees formally about their organizations—not only day-do-day operations, but also their histories, missions, and traditions. Without such orientation programs, new employees are likely to find it harder to fit in and to understand what the organization is all about. Although much of what is covered in such programs may be learned informally over time, formal programs, when well conducted, are often more efficient from the point of view of transmitting large amounts of information to new employees in a short amount of time (see Figure 7-3).

Settling in: The metamorphosis stage. Sometime after an individual enters an organization, she or he attains full member status. Depending on the type and length of orientation program used, this entry may be marked by a formal ceremony—a dinner, a graduation exercise—or it may be quite informal. In other cases, especially when training has been short or informal, full acceptance may be signalled through informal actions such as being invited to lunch with "the group."

Whatever form it takes, the settling-in phase of socialization marks important shifts both for individuals and their organizations. Employees make permanent adjustments to their jobs, and organizations now treat them as if they will be long-term members of the work team rather than temporary fill-ins.

Mentoring: One-on-One Socialization

Consider 50 new college or university graduates hired by a large corporation to do pretty much the same job. All start out on fairly equal footing, but if you returned in one year to see how they were doing, you might already notice substantial

FIGURE 7-3 Corporate Orientation Programs: A Vital Aspect of Socialization

As part of its employee orientation efforts, new employees of Canadian Tire Acceptance Ltd. (CTAL) in Welland, Ontario learn about the company and its operations by participating in an organizational scavenger hunt.

mentoring The process of serving as a mentor.

mentor A more experienced employee who offers advice, assistance, and protection to a younger and less experienced one (a *protégé*).

protégé A less experienced (often new) employee whose organizational socialization is facilitated by working with a *mentor*.

differences. Some would be gone, others would be falling behind, and a few would clearly be "leading the pack"—they would already appear to be on the fast track to success. What accounts for these differences? Many factors certainly play a role, but one of the most important of these involves **mentoring**.[20] This is a process in which a more experienced employee—known as a **mentor**—advises, counsels, and otherwise enhances the personal development (and career) of a new employee, known as a **protégé**. If you've ever had an older, more experienced person take you under her or his wing and guide you, then you already know how valuable mentoring can be. In fact, research findings indicate that having a mentor early in one's career is an important predictor of success: The more mentoring people receive, the more promotions they receive and the more highly they are compensated.[21]

Let's now take a closer look at mentoring relationships, examining precisely what mentors do, how mentoring relationships form and change over time, and the role of mentors in career success.

What Do Mentors Do?

Research on the nature of mentor-protégé relationships suggests that mentors do many things for their protégés.[22] For example, they provide much-needed emotional support and confidence for those who are just starting out and are likely to be somewhat insecure. Mentors also help pave the way for their protégés' job success. They nominate them for promotions, provide them with opportunities to demonstrate their competence, and generally bring them to the attention of higher management. Mentors also suggest useful strategies for reaching work goals—often, ones protégés might not generate for themselves. Finally, mentors often protect their protégés from the consequences of errors and help them avoid situations that may prove risky for their careers.

In short, mentors do a number of things designed to help their protégés get ahead. Yet, as beneficial as mentor-protégé relationships may be, not all new employees seek out mentors. Individual difference factors, such as the ones we discussed in Chapter 4 seem to play a role in this process. For instance, as we noted in that chapter, persons high in self-monitoring tend to seek out and obtain mentors to a greater extent than persons low in self-monitoring.[23] Perhaps this is because high self-monitors find it easier to adapt their behaviour to the requirements of new situations, and this fact includes adapting to the requests and style of potential mentors. Similarly, persons high in need for achievement tend to seek mentors more often than persons low in need for achievement.[24]

Because becoming the protégé of a highly successful person is so potentially valuable to one's career, there is often considerable competition among newcomers for available mentors. As a result, such persons are often quite selective—they choose only those newcomers they view as "the cream of the crop" as their protégés. The winners in this kind of competition are not always the persons with the highest level of talent; sometimes, victory goes to those who are especially skilled at the task of *impression management*—looking good to others. In any case, given the benefits of becoming a protégé, seeking a successful mentor is definitely one strategy newcomers should consider when they enter a new organization. The career they boost may well be their own.

☞ *Mentors also act as* models *for their protégés, helping them to learn through the process of* observational learning *we described in Chapter 3.*

How Mentoring Relationships Form and Change

As we have just noted, mentor-protégé relationships do not form at random. Rather, they are often the results of a complex selection process in which both mentors and potential protégés play an active role. Mentors, of course, don't want to waste their time and effort on just anybody. Rather, they seek to choose only the best and most promising newcomers for their protégés. The process by which they do so is not always explicit, but given that potential protégés outnumber potential mentors in most organizations, careful selection of potential protégés does tend to occur.

Protégés, of course, engage in selection, too. They generally seek mentors who are older and more experienced than themselves, and ones who are known to be successful in the organization. Once they identify a potential mentor, they may take active steps to establish a relationship with this person.

How, precisely, do they go about initiating mentor-protégé bonds? Research findings suggest that they tend to rely on certain tactics for building such a relationship.[25] Specifically, would-be protégés seem to focus on such activities as seeking *personal* interactions with their boss, negotiating the terms of their relationships directly (known as *direct* tactics), and expressing willingness to exceed their boss's expectations (*noncontractual* tactics). Persons who do not enter into mentor-protégé relationships, in contrast, tend to use other tactics, such as trying to put themselves in a favourable light (*regulative* tactics) and demonstrating conformity to formal role requirements and the boss's expectations (*contractual* tactics).

But what happens to mentoring relationships once they are established? Do they remain unchanged for long periods of time? Research on this issue indicates that, in fact, most mentor-protégé relationships pass through several distinct phases.[26] The first, known as *initiation*, lasts from six months to a year and represents the period during which the relationship gets started and takes on importance for both parties. The second phase, known as *cultivation*, may last from two to five years. During this time, the bond between mentor and protégé deepens, and the young individual may make rapid career progress because of the skilled assistance she or he is receiving.

The third stage, *separation*, begins when the protégé feels it is time to assert independence and strike out on his or her own, or when there is some externally produced change in their roles—for instance, the protégé is promoted or the mentor is transferred. Separation also can occur if the mentor feels unable to continue providing support and guidance to the protégé (e.g., if the mentor becomes ill). This stage can be quite stressful if the mentor resents the protégé's growing independence, or if the protégé feels that the mentor has withdrawn support prematurely.

If this separation is successful, the relationship may enter a final stage, termed *redefinition*. Here, both persons perceive their bond primarily as one of friendship. They come to treat one another as equals, and the roles of mentor and protégé fade away. However, the mentor may continue to take pride in the accomplishments of her or his former protégé. Likewise, the protégé may continue to feel gratitude toward the former mentor. Although there is bound to be variation in the way mentor-protégé relationships actually develop, it seems safe to conclude that these phases represent a relatively accurate picture of the way in which many of these relationships unfold.

At this point, we should note that many companies do not leave the formation of mentor-protégé relationships to chance. Rather, they have formal programs in which newcomers are assigned to more experienced persons who are expected to serve as their mentors. For a summary of what some companies are doing in this respect, see Table 7-1.

	Company	Description
TABLE 7-1 Mentorship Programs: What Some Companies Are Doing	Colgate-Palmolive	All new white-collar employees are assigned individual higher-ranking employees to serve as mentors.
	The New Brunswick Hospital Association	Trained mentors who are experienced hospital trustees are paired with a hospital board member to carry out an evaluation on the board and facilitate board problem-solving.
	Dow Jones	Groups of four are formed consisting of a high-level mentor and three others: a white male, a woman of any race, and a minority group member of either gender.
	Chubb & Son Insurance	In its Sponsorship Program, three protégés are assigned to each of ten different mentors.

Because the mentoring process is so important, many companies have been unwilling to leave it to chance. Thus, they have developed formal mechanisms for encouraging the formation of mentoring relationships.

Source: Based on information in Granfield, M. (1992, November). "'90s mentoring: Circles and quads." Working Woman, p. 15; and Staff Writer (1990, March/April). "Prepare to meet your mentor." Hospital Trustee, pp. 6–7.

Gender, Race, and Mentoring

It is a basic fact of social relationships that in general, people tend to prefer, like, and feel more comfortable around persons who are similar to themselves than persons who are different.[27] Thus, they tend to form friendships and other personal relationships not with persons who are opposite to themselves in traits, attitudes, or background, but with persons who are generally similar. Does this principle apply to mentoring relationships? Growing evidence suggests that it does. There are exceptions, but it appears that women and minorities are at a distinct disadvantage where obtaining a mentor is concerned.[28] One reason for this state of affairs seems to involve the principle we stated earlier: Even today, most managers in Canada, the United States, and many other countries are white males, and such persons feel most comfortable around persons of similar background.

However, other factors, too, play a role. In recent surveys, women have reported less willingness to serve as mentors than men.[29] Apparently, this is because they have greater concern than men about the potential negative consequences that may follow if they adopt a protégé and this person fails.

On the other side of the coin, many male managers express concerns about serving as a mentor for female employees: They fear that the close relationships that develop may be misperceived as romantic entanglements.[30] Given the fact that having a mentor early in one's career is often highly beneficial, it seems important for organizations to take active steps to reduce these barriers and to increase mentoring opportunities for women and minorities. Failing to do so may deny persons in these groups access to one vital ingredient in career success.

[You Be The Consultant]

Turnover among new female hires at a large life insurance company is high—far higher than among males. In fact, the very best new employees, persons hired at great effort and expense, are the ones who tend to leave. The company is losing many talented persons because of this trend and is beginning to acquire a reputation as a place where women do *not* like to work.

1. Could a program specifically designed to help new female employees obtain a mentor help turn this situation around?

2. How could such a program actually be put into operation?

Careers: New Forms, New Strategies

Where do you want to work when you complete your studies? Common conceptions of what careers will be—or should be—like have altered greatly in recent years, partly as a result of equally sweeping changes in the business world. In other words, if people currently hold different conceptions of what their careers will be like than was true in the past, it is because they are increasingly aware of the tremendous shifts that have occurred in the way many companies do business, including how they hire, train, promote, and retain their employees.

In this section, we'll focus on several important aspects of a **career**—the evolving sequence of a person's work experience over time—and their changing nature. First,

career The evolving sequence of a person's work experience over time.

we'll consider the question of how individuals make vocational choices—why they choose specific jobs. Next, we'll examine some of the major ways in which careers have changed in recent years and how individuals can best react to such changes when planning their careers. Finally, we'll consider the role of gender in careers, addressing the question of whether women and men have different career experiences and if so, why this may be so.

Choosing a Job: Making Vocational Choices

How do people end up in specific jobs? Many different factors play a role in this process, but here, we'll focus on several that appear to be most important.

To understand the first of these factors, ask yourself this question: What kind of person becomes an auto mechanic? A lawyer? An elementary school teacher? Do your descriptions of these persons differ? If so, they reflect your understanding of a basic fact: Persons possessing specific characteristics are attracted to certain kinds of jobs. This is the idea of person-job fit that we discussed in Chapter 4—the suggestion that because of their personal characteristics (traits or abilities), individuals are better suited for performing some jobs than others.

☛ Person-job fit *plays an important role in many aspects of organizational behaviour, including job satisfaction (see Chapter 6) and job performance (see Chapter 4).*

Some researchers who have studied this relationship believe that people generally tend to select jobs that match their personalities, abilities, and values, and findings tend to confirm this idea.[31,32] The closer the person-job fit, the greater individuals' job satisfaction.[33] In fact, many people tend to assign greater importance to this kind of "fit" than to pay or promotional opportunities when choosing a job.[34,35]

Another factor that strongly influences job choices is people's beliefs about the future of these jobs. In other words, we tend to be quite rational in our choice of jobs, focusing on ones we believe will offer growing opportunities, while avoiding ones that seem to be declining in these respects. Most people know that there isn't much call for blacksmiths or train conductors today, so they tend to drop these jobs from consideration, even if they find them personally appealing. In contrast, there are many jobs that can be expected to grow in numbers—and opportunities—in the future. These are the ones that tend to capture individuals' attention when they are considering which jobs to enter. For a closer look at jobs and careers that promise to be "hot" in the future, please see the **ORGANIZATIONAL TRENDS** section.

Career Planning: Charting Your Future

In the closing years of the twentieth century, careers do *not* generally involve a straightforward climb through a successive series of clearly defined steps. On the contrary, they more frequently include lateral moves, rotation through several different jobs, geographic relocations, and—increasingly—periods of time spent as an independent contractor or subcontractor rather than as a regular, full-time employee.

☛ *We will examine several aspects of organizational structure and design in Chapter 15 and organizational change in Chapter 16.*

Why have these shifts in the nature of careers occurred? Mainly because organizations themselves have altered. First, many have adopted a much flatter internal structure. The number of managers—especially middle-level managers—has decreased sharply, and companies have sought to respond to increased global competition by becoming "lean and mean."[36] At the same time, organizations have redrawn their boundaries to focus more directly on their core business and core competencies, while at the same time relying more and more on specialists from outside the company. Instead of maintaining large internal staffs of experts, organizations are, increasingly, turning to external contractors to meet specific needs as they arise. The result of these trends, when coupled with major efforts to restructure or engage in "reengineering," are clear: Traditional career paths, in which someone is hired and then remains with the same company, and even the same unit for years or decades, are vanishing.[37] Given this radically altered set of conditions, what kind of career goals and career paths should individuals seek?

Career goals: What should employees seek in return for their hard work?   Since they can no longer count on job security, employees should focus on using each job

The Hottest Careers of the Twenty-First Century

As the workplace changes, new career options appear and old ones disappear. One of the most important aspects of career planning is to keep abreast of the changing job scene and to prefer work in areas that will grow and prosper. With this in mind, experts have identified several areas in which job growth is expected to be much greater than average in the future.[38]

The first is *information technology*. The digital era has arrived, and jobs related to computers, e.g., *computer programmers* and *systems analysts*, will be at the forefront of career growth in the years ahead. Although this already has been true for a decade, there are no signs of a slowdown. We also can expect lots of new jobs for *database managers*—people responsible for administering the systems controlling the vast amounts of information essential for business operations, *LAN* (local area network) *administrators*—people expert at linking together computer systems, and *telecommunications managers*—specialists in the transfer of information through telephones, modems, voice mail, and other equipment.

Another growth area for jobs, *education and training*, also reflects rapid changes in the ways companies do business. As conditions change, organizations will experience growing needs for specialists who can help them keep their employees up-to-date. Included in this category are *employee trainers*, who will focus on pro-

viding employees with new skills, and *environmental specialists*—people who can help companies deal with a broad range of environmental issues and laws.

Health care, too, is likely to experience major growth. Here, there will be increased need for healthcare providers such as *family physicians, nurse practitioners, in-home nurses, physiotherapists, health-care information specialists*, and *pharmacists*.[39]

To keep organizations at the cutting edge, an increasing number of *managers* will also be needed. These won't be run-of-the-mill generalists, however; rather, they will be highly focused specialists skilled in dealing with specific sets of problems and challenges that organizations are certain to face.

In short, there won't be any shortage of opportunities in the years ahead, but these will occur in new fields and take new forms. For specific predictions on high-growth careers, see Table 7-2. Careers are ranked according to their projected percentage growth between 1995 and 2005. Other data given in the table are: % female (percentage of each occupational group that will be female in 2005); % part-time (percentage of each job category that will be part-time); earnings (approximate comparative salary levels of each job— the more $ signs, the higher the earnings level); stress level (the approximate stress level is shown by an ! symbol—the more ! symbols, the higher the stress level); minimum educational requirements (for entry-level positions); and required on-the-job travel (shown by the letter T—the more Ts, the more travel).[40]

---

developmental opportunities
Jobs or assignments that can contribute to employees' competence and skills.

or assignment as a means of acquiring valuable skills. In short, they should view their careers as a series of **developmental opportunities** for gaining new proficiencies that will increase their value in the job market. The basic idea is simple: As individuals acquire these competencies, they will become more desirable as employees, and so the scope of their future career possibilities, too, will expand. This means that when contemplating a job, it is probably better to ask "What will I learn from this assignment?" than "How long will it last?" or "What are the possibilities of promotion?" When individuals view jobs primarily as learning experiences or environments, they can map out a career strategy that will lead them to where they ultimately want to go: being a highly desirable commodity where employers are concerned.

Career paths: Specific roles in today's organizations. But assuming that individuals focus on their jobs as skill-building opportunities, what specific roles can they expect to fill? According to Frank Walker, President of GTW Corp., a company that sells project-management consulting services to large corporations, there are actually four distinct career tracks available to today's employees.[41] The first is most similar to past conceptions of a straight, upward rise to the top and involves becoming an expert in setting *corporate strategy*. This is the realm of CEOs, presidents, and executive VPs, and, as has always been true, very few people can hope to attain

TABLE 7-2 The Top Ten Best Growth Careers to 2005

As the nature of work continues to change, several new kinds of jobs are developing. Here are a few you are likely to hear about with increasing frequency in the future.

(Source: Feather, Frank [1997]. Canada's Best Careers Guide [1997–1998 edition]. Toronto: Warwick Publishing, p. 77.)

Growth Rank #	Type of Occupation	% Increase Over 1995	% Female	% Part-Time	Earnings ($)	Stress Level (!)	Education	Job Travel (T)
1	In-Home Nurse	76	90	60	$$	!!	Coll	TT
2	Programmer/Analyst	73	40	15	$$$	!!	Coll	
3	Physiotherapist	70	90	40	$$$	!	Univ	T
4	Physician/Surgeon	65	40	15	$$$$$	!!!	Univ	
5	Teacher, Vocational	62	60	25	$$	!	Univ	
6	Psychiatrist/-ologist	61	50	20	$$$$	!!	Univ	
7	Pharmacist	60	70	30	$$$	!	Univ	
8	Radiology Technician	60	90	40	$$	!!	Coll	
9	Teacher, Special Ed.	59	85	25	$$	!!	Univ	T
10	Audio-Therapist	58	90	40	$$$	!	Univ	

these positions. Such persons must have exceptional judgment and decision-making skills, and be able to predict where and how current markets will change. Their key task is that of formulating strategies that will allow their companies to meet these challenges by being there first—or best.

A second career track involves *project managers*. These are persons who oversee and manage important projects. They focus on using financial resources and talent to accomplish goals. The value of such managers—and the success of their careers—lies in the magnitude of the contributions the projects they manage make to their organizations. For instance, Chrysler Corporation now develops new cars by using "platform teams"—teams that are independent of departments within the corporation such as engineering, finance, and marketing. Persons who lead such teams are judged primarily in terms of the success of the new vehicles their teams design.

A third possible career track in today's organizations is that of *resource provider*. These are the persons who develop the talent and money needed by project managers for successful completion of their tasks. Consider Anderson Consulting. At any time, about 80 percent of all employees are busy working on specific projects. Newcomers to the company are assigned to a regional Human Resources group—a resource provider—which has the task of nurturing and developing them—that is, maximizing their talents. These HR groups, in turn, assist project managers by finding the talent they need in this pool of new employees and coordinating the use of these human resources. As corporations shift more and more into a project mode, the need for such coordination will increase; and so, too, will the opportunities for resource providers.

Finally, a fourth career track involves that of providing the *talent* needed by organizations. These are the people who actually "make it happen" by virtue of their technical knowledge, skills, and experience. Financial experts, chemists, engineers, marketing experts—you name it; if an organization needs such skills, it needs such persons. But this doesn't mean that these individuals must work full-time for a single company. On the contrary, an increasing number operate as freelance consultants. Even if they are full-time, regular employees, persons filling the role of *talent* should view themselves as self-employed: They are there not only to do a job for an employer, but also to add to their own skills and experience. Remember: In today's organizations, insiders must compete, more and more, with each other and with outside consultants offering similar skills and expertise. For this reason alone, it's best for all individuals to focus on improving their own skills—thus making themselves

job rotation Lateral transfers of employees between jobs in an organization.

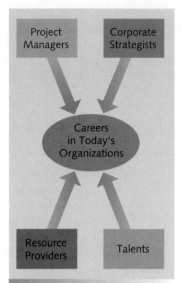

FIGURE 7-4 Career Tracks in Today's Organizations

Among the major types of careers open to individuals in modern organizations are these four: (1) corporate strategists, (2) project managers, (3) resource providers, and (4) talents.

better able to compete and more marketable should they leave the organization. An overview of the four career tracks we have discussed is presented in Figure 7-4.

Job rotation: A key ingredient in career development. It is one thing to recommend that employees view their jobs as learning experiences, and quite another to translate this general principle into concrete steps they can take to reach this goal. How, precisely, can individuals use their jobs as a base for acquiring marketable skills? Fortunately, recent research on this issue offers a clear-cut answer. One important way in which they can accomplish these goals is through judicious use of **job rotation**—lateral transfers of employees between jobs in an organization.[42] Recent findings indicate that job rotation is experienced primarily by high-performing employees relatively early in their careers, and that it is correlated with such positive outcomes as promotion rate and salary growth.[43] In addition, the persons who experience it perceive that job rotation has added to their skills and knowledge (see Figure 7-5). The career implications of these findings are obvious: If you are offered job rotation, don't hesitate to accept it. The benefits of doing so can be substantial.

Current Practice: Signs of Trouble in Your Career

How can you tell if your career is *not* on track—not proceeding along the lines described above? Here are some tips. Everyone—even Ziggy—wants to have a successful career (see Figure 7-6). In the past, it was relatively easy to judge whether a person was on track in this respect. Individuals knew that if their careers were going well, they would move through a regular series of promotions, occurring at fairly predictable times. Now, as we've already noted, such linear career tracks are increasingly rare. Given this fact, how can you determine whether your career is going well—or poorly? Experts on careers suggest paying careful attention to the following points:

- Ask yourself whether you are learning: If you can't state clearly what you've learned during the past six months or what you expect to learn in the next six months, your career may be at a standstill—and in trouble.

- Ask yourself: "If my job were open, would I get it?" If you have doubts on this score, it means that you are falling behind in terms of acquiring new skills.

- Do you know what you are contributing? Today, employees' value is being judged increasingly in terms of what they provide to their organizations, not their seniority or experience. If you can't state clearly what you are contributing, your career may be dead in the water.

- Ask yourself: "What would I do if my job disappeared tomorrow?" If you have done a good job of increasing your skills and knowledge base, you should be able to answer: "I'd be able to get another job at least as good as this one." If you can't answer that way, you are probably not making good personal progress.

FIGURE 7-5 Job Rotation: A Plus for Many Careers

As shown here, job rotation tended to occur early in individuals' careers and to be more common for high-performing than low-performing persons. In addition, it was related to both promotion rate and salary growth.

(Source: Based on findings reported by Campion, Cheraskin, & Stevens, 1994; see Note 41.)

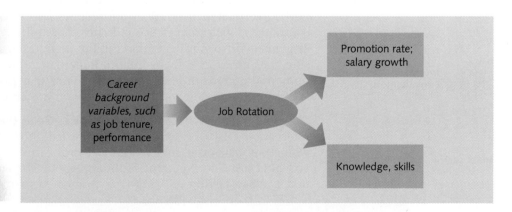

FIGURE 7-6 How NOT to Achieve Success!

Almost everyone wants success, but in today's highly competitive and rapidly changing world, it seems harder to obtain than ever before. Few persons want to find themselves in the situation faced by Ziggy.

(Source: ZIGGY © 1986 Ziggy & Friends, Inc. Reprinted with permission of Universal Press Syndicate. All rights reserved.)

International Labour Organization
www.ilo.org

glass ceiling A barrier preventing females from reaching top positions in many organizations.

- Are you being exploited? If you suspect that you are—that you are being asked to sacrifice your own welfare or personal growth for the good of the company, you should begin to wonder about the value of this particular job for your career.

- Are you worried about your job? If you are, experts agree, you probably should be. People who know what they are contributing and how valuable they are to their companies have few concerns in this regard. If you have such concerns, watch out: They may well be justified.

Gender and Careers: Do Females and Males Have Different Experiences?

In Chapter 6, we noted that despite major changes in recent years, women and minorities are still the victims of lingering prejudice and discrimination in many work settings. The form of such prejudice is often much more subtle than it was in the past, but it is still real—and still damaging. In this section, we'll turn to a related issue: Do the career experiences of women and men differ? If they do, why is this so?

The careers of women and men: Contrasting experiences on the road to success.   The answer to the first question posed above seems to be quite straightforward: For many complex reasons, women and men really *do* seem to have somewhat different career experiences. Such differences take many forms, but perhaps the most important involve what might be termed contrasting formulas for success—somewhat different routes for making it to the top. Research on this issue is complex, but some of its major findings can be readily summarized:[44]

- Increased training leads to managerial advancement for both women and men, but these benefits are greater for men.

- Work experience and education increase training opportunities for both genders, but again, links between these variables are stronger for men than women.

- Having a spouse and dependents at home reduce women's work experience but increase that of men.

- Career encouragement (encouragement for career advancement from colleagues) is more closely related to managerial advancement for women than for men.

In sum, existing evidence indicates that while the same factors play a role in the career success of women and men, these factors operate somewhat differently in shaping the careers of the two genders.

Additional findings suggest that women often have fewer developmental opportunities than men—they are afforded less access to jobs or assignments that can contribute to their competence and skills.[45] Specifically, women are often given fewer assignments involving high responsibility, high stakes, and dealing with external pressure.[46] As noted recently by Ohlott, Ruderman, and McCauley, the reduced developmental opportunities women experience may prevent them from getting key assignments—a result which can severely limit their career opportunities.[47]

The glass ceiling: Why more women don't rise to the top.   A recent report by the International Labour Organization revealed this: Despite growing numbers of women in managerial jobs worldwide, they earn less than men in those positions and hold just 2 to 3 percent of the top spots. The authors of the report conclude that a **glass ceiling** still prevents women from reaching the top jobs.[48] More formally, the glass ceiling may be defined as, "those artificial barriers based on attitudinal or organizational bias that prevent qualified individuals from advancing upward in their organization."[49]

Is this barrier real? If so, why does it occur? Existing evidence on these issues is just beginning to accumulate, so we can't offer any definitive answers here. However, a recent Canadian study called, *Closing The Gap: Women's Advancement in Corporate and Professional Canada*, concludes the following:

☞ *We examined the potential role of prejudice toward females in Chapter 6.*

- A glass ceiling—an invisible barrier of male-dominated networks and prejudices—still prevents women from reaching the top jobs.

- Senior women managers feel the major impediment to corporate advancement is male stereotypes and perceptions; male CEOs believe women's relative inexperience is a key barrier.

- The demographic profile of women senior executives (vice-president or higher), based on the responses of the 417 senior women managers who participated in the study, is as follows:

  30 percent are age 40–44; 22 percent are 35–39

  6 percent are visible minorities

  76 percent are married

  65 percent have children

  54 percent make $100 000 to $200 000; 26 percent make $200 000 to $400 000.[50]

"A key challenge for employers today is to ensure that they have the policies and practices in place to attract, retain, and motivate the top talent—both women and men—they need to help them succeed in the global marketplace. The study and the conference undertaken by the Conference Board and Catalyst provides important insights for leaders and for women aspiring to senior positions," says Jim Nininger, President and Chief Executive Officer of The Conference Board of Canada.[51]

Why some women executives are choosing to leave senior-level jobs. Many women executives have clearly obtained a great deal of success in the Canadian corporate world. Table 7-3 showcases 10 outstanding achievers who have shattered the glass ceiling. According to the *Closing The Gap* study mentioned above, almost two-thirds of the 417 women senior executives who responded said that they were considering leaving their jobs. Some of the reasons given were: increased compensation (40 percent), greater advancement opportunities (34 percent), increased intellectual stimulation (33 percent), desire for compatible organizational values (33 percent), different type of work (31 percent), work environment more supportive of personal commitments

TABLE 7-3 Ten Women Executives in Canada Who Have Shattered the Glass Ceiling

These 10 women have all made it to the top, demonstrating that the glass ceiling can be breached.

(Source: Maley, Dianne [1997, October 20]. Canada's Top Women CEOs. Maclean's, pp. 52–53.)

Kraft Canada
www.kraftfoods.com

Name	Position
Joy Calkin	President and CEO, Extendicare
Sheelagh Whittaker	President and CEO, EDS Canada
Maureen Kempston-Darkes	President and General Manager, General Motors of Canada
Bobbie Gaunt	President and CEO, Ford Motor Co. of Canada
Carol Stephenson	President and CEO, Stentor Resource Centre
Annette Verschuren	President, Home Depot Canada
Janice Tomlinson	President, Chubb Insurance Canada
Irene Rosenfeld	President, Kraft Canada
Colleen Fleming	President, Laura Secord
Dee Parkinson-Marcoux	President, Ensyn Energy Corp.

midlife crisis A period of great emotional turmoil and uncertainty, supposedly experienced by many individuals during middle age.

(21 percent), more flexible work arrangements (20 percent), and family responsibilities that require leaving the workforce (5 percent).[52]

It is interesting to note that of the 417 women respondents, 30 percent were age 40 to 44—the traditional centre of what has been termed the **midlife crisis**—a period in life when many people experience grave doubts and increasing dissatisfaction with the past and future course of their lives.[53]

Women now in the their 40s—the first generation to invade previously male bastions in the business world—were raised in the 1950s and 1960s, a time when traditional roles for women and men were still the norm. Perhaps younger women, raised with greater exposure to models of female achievement, will react differently at midlife; indeed, perhaps they will not experience a midlife crisis at all.

Judging from increased entrepreneurial activity among young women, another possibility is that many will avoid the issue entirely by starting their own businesses. Consider, for example, Lizzie Denis and Louise Kramer, who became unhappy with the slow pace of baking cookies on traditional racks. Their solution: the Double-Decker Baking Rack. With the financial help of their families, they founded a company—L&L Products—and began marketing the rack. To date, thousands have been sold, at large department stores, as well as through catalogues. The company has already become profitable, and customers seem to like the no-nonsense copy placed on the package by the teenaged inventors: "We hope you'll agree that the Double-Decker Baking Rack does make sense and buy it. Then we can go to college or the mall."

Stress: Its Basic Nature

stress The pattern of emotional states, cognitions, and physiological reactions occurring in response to *stressors*.

stressors Various factors in the external environment that induce stress among people exposed to them.

strain Deviations from normal states or functioning resulting from stress.

Have you ever experienced situations in which you felt that you were about to be overwhelmed by your job and pressures relating to it? If so, then you are already familiar with *stress*.[54] What, precisely, is stress? Many definitions exist, but in general, **stress** refers to a complex pattern of emotional states, physiological reactions, and related thoughts occurring in response to external demands (**stressors**). A related term—**strain**—refers to the effects of stress, primarily to deviations from normal states or performance resulting from exposure to stressful events. As we'll soon see, these can involve physical symptoms, reduced performance, and many other changes in behaviour.

A key point to keep in mind with respect to stress is that whether, and to what extent, it occurs in a given situation, depends heavily on people's interpretation of what is happening to them—their *cognitive appraisal* of the stressors they confront.[55] Stress occurs only to the extent people perceive that (1) the situation they face is somehow threatening to them, and (2) they will be unable to cope with these potential dangers or demands—that the situation is, in some sense, beyond their control.[56] The Canadian Mental Health Association has reported that 47 percent of Canadians experience high levels of stress. One indication of the acceleration in stress among Canadian workers is the increase in use of Employee Assistance Program (EAP) counselling services. While only three to four percent of employees used these services in the mid-1980s, by the early 1990s the rate had jumped to between seven and eight percent.[57]

Canadian Mental Health Association www.radiant.net/cmha

Stress: Its Major Causes

What factors contribute to stress in work settings? We called attention to one at the start of this chapter: failure in one's career. Many other factors, too, influence the level of stress individuals experience at work. For purposes of clarity, we'll divide these into two major categories: factors relating to organizations or jobs, and factors relating to other aspects of individuals' lives.

Work-Related Causes of Stress

As anyone who has ever held a job well knows, work settings are often highly stressful environments. Yet, they vary greatly in this respect. Some jobs and organizations expose individuals to high levels of stress while others involve much lower levels of stress. What factors account for these differences?

Occupational demands: Some jobs are more stressful than others. Consider the following jobs: production manager, librarian, emergency room physician, custodian, firefighter, airline pilot. Do they differ in stressfulness? Obviously, they do. Some jobs, such as emergency room physician, firefighter, and airline pilot, expose the people who hold them to high levels of stress. Others, such as custodian or librarian, do not. This basic fact—that some jobs are much more stressful than others—has been confirmed by the results of a survey involving more than 130 different occupations.[58] The results indicated that several jobs —for example, physician, office manager, supervisor, server—are quite high in stress. In contrast, others, such as maid, craft worker, farm labourer, are much lower.

What, precisely, makes some jobs more stressful than others? Apparently, several factors.[59] Jobs become increasingly stressful to the extent that they require (1) making decisions, (2) constant monitoring of devices or materials, (3) repeated exchange of information with others, (4) unpleasant physical conditions, and (5) performing unstructured rather than structured tasks.

Conflict between work and nonwork: Stress from competing demands. When we were children, our mothers did not work outside the home, and neither did those of our friends. Today, of course, the situation is totally different. In a majority of families with children, both spouses work full-time. The result is a constant juggling of work and family responsibilities (known as *work juggling*). Further, incompatibilities between their work and family obligations expose them to what is widely recognized as another important cause of stress: **role conflict**, which is usually defined as incompatibility between the expectations of parties or between aspects of a single role. In this case, the expectations of spouses and children conflict, in many cases, with the expectations of bosses and coworkers.

How stressful is such family–work role conflict? Recent research findings indicate that it is stressful indeed. For example, in recent studies, Williams, Alliger, and their colleagues have employed a novel technique known as *experience sampling* to study this issue.[60,61] In this procedure, individuals wear a watch or other small device that signals them, at either random or prearranged times during the day, to record their current activities, levels of stress, current moods, and other reactions on a special form. Research using such experience-sampling procedures indicates that juggling work and family tasks often causes individuals to experience feelings of distress and other negative mood states.

Fortunately, additional findings indicate that such effects can be lessened by high levels of social support in work settings.[62] And as we'll see in a later section, the level of stress produced by such factors can also be lessened by certain employment policies—for instance, flexible work scheduling and supportive supervisors.[63]

Role ambiguity: Stress from uncertainty. Even if individuals are able to avoid the stress associated with role conflict, they may still encounter another source of job-related stress: **role ambiguity**. This occurs when individuals experience uncertainty about what actions to take to fulfill a job. Most people dislike uncertainty and find it quite stressful, but it is difficult to avoid. In fact, role ambiguity is quite common: 35 to 60 percent of employees surveyed report experiencing it to some degree.[64]

Interestingly, the amount of role ambiguity experienced by employees seems to differ sharply from culture to culture. In a recent study involving participants from 21 different countries, Peterson and his colleagues found that in countries where large differences in status or power between managers and subordinates are the norm (high

role conflict Incompatible demands made on an individual by different groups or persons.

role ambiguity Uncertainty among employees about the key requirements of their jobs.

☞ *Ambiguity concerning one's job responsibilities is also an important cause of job dissatisfaction (see Chapter 6).*

☞ *Power distance was discussed in Chapter 2.*

power distance countries) role ambiguity is relatively low.[65] Similarly, such ambiguity was also found to be relatively low in countries where people prefer to act as members of groups rather than as individuals (low individualism). These are considered to be basic dimensions along which many cultures vary.[66] For example, role ambiguity was found to be low in Asian and African countries (known to be high in power distance but low in individualism); in contrast, role ambiguity was found to be higher in Western countries (known to be low in power distance and high in individualism).[67]

Overload and underload: Doing too much or too little. When the phrase "work-related stress" is mentioned, most people think of scenes in which employees are working frantically, doing more than they can handle. Such images relate to overload, which, in fact, can take two different forms. **Quantitative overload** occurs in situations where individuals are asked to do more work than they can complete in a specific period of time. In contrast, **qualitative overload** refers to employees' beliefs that they lack the required skills or abilities to perform a given job. Both types of overload are unpleasant and can lead to high levels of stress.[68]

Overload is only part of the total picture, however. While being asked to do too much can be stressful, so can being asked to do too little. Here again, there are two types of *under*load: **quantitative underload**, which refers to the boredom that results from having too little to do, and **qualitative underload,** which refers to the lack of mental stimulation that accompanies many routine, repetitive jobs.

Responsibility for others: A heavy burden. Research findings indicate that in general, people who are responsible for others—who must motivate them, reward or punish them, communicate with them—experience higher levels of stress than those who handle other organizational functions.[69] Such people are more likely to report feelings of tension and anxiety, and are actually more likely to show overt symptoms of stress such as ulcers or hypertension.

There are two major reasons for this difference. First, it is managers who must, ultimately, confront the human costs of organizational policies and decisions. For example, they must deliver negative feedback and then witness the distress it generates. Second, it is their task to deal with the many frictions that are a normal part of human relations at work. This involves listening to endless complaints, mediating disputes, promoting cooperation, and exercising leadership. All these tasks are demanding and can contribute to the total burden of stress experienced by managers.

Lack of social support: The costs of isolation. One old saying suggests that "Misery loves company," and existing evidence indicates that it is definitely true where stress is concerned. When confronted with stressful situations, we fare much better when we have a network of friends and associates to whom we can turn for support and counsel. In fact, several studies indicate that managers who believe they have the friendship and support of their immediate supervisors and coworkers report fewer physical symptoms when exposed to high levels of stress than those who do not feel that they enjoy such support. Indeed, in one recent study, Doby and Caplan found that employees were particularly likely to experience adverse effects from exposure to stressors that threatened their relationships or reputation with their supervisor.[70]

Sexual harassment: A pervasive problem in work settings. According to the *Canada Labour Code*, **sexual harassment** in the workplace "may be broadly defined as unwelcome conduct of a sexual nature that detrimentally affects the work environment or leads to adverse job-related consequences for the victims of the harassment."[71]

Maureen Geddes, a diversity management consultant, president of Cangram Inc., and co-organizer of a conference in Chatham, Ontario, in 1996 on the topic of sexual harassment in the workplace, warned: "Sexual harassment is no game....It ruins people's lives and it can even take lives."[72] And that is just what happened on June 2, 1996 in Chatham.

quantitative overload A situation in which individuals are required to do more work than they can actually accomplish in a given period of time.

qualitative overload The belief among employees that they lack the skills or abilities needed to perform their jobs.

quantitative underload A situation in which individuals have so little to do that they spend much of their time doing nothing.

qualitative underload The lack of mental stimulation that accompanies many routine, repetitive jobs.

sexual harassment Unwanted contact or communication of a sexual nature.

Canada Labour Code
labour.hrdc-drhc.gc.ca

Early in 1995, Mrs. Theresa Vince, an employee of the Sears Canada store in Chatham, after repeatedly rejecting unwanted personal attention from her store manager, Russell Davis, complained to a regional manager. Despite the fact that the regional manager did meet with Mrs. Vince and the fact that Sears Canada had a sexual harassment policy in place at the time, the matter was never completely investigated. The unwanted attentions continued and, although fellow workers were aware of the situation, they shrugged it off as infatuation. The regional manager did, however, write a memo suggesting that Mr. Davis be transferred to another store. No action was ever taken on the memo. Further, the regional manager informed Mrs. Vince in the process that Mr. Davis, a married man with children in university, could be terminated by Sears Canada if she took the complaint further. Tragically, on June 2, 1996, Russell Davis, 57, shot Theresa Vince, 58, dead with a handgun and then killed himself.[73]

While this is an extreme case, various forms of sexual harassment are far from rare in today's work settings, and they are certainly an important source of stress for many individuals. Geri Sanson, a human rights lawyer with Sanson & Hunt, reports that different workplaces can and do foster different forms of sexual harassment. For instance, as in the tragic case of Theresa Vince, in environments where most employees are women and the bosses are men, harassment usually "begins with compliments that become too persistent and [lead to] the treatment of women as sex objects or romantic partners when they don't desire it." A second type of harassment, says Ms. Sanson, can arise when women are hired into jobs traditionally held by men. In these situations, "behaviour more likely takes the form of passing around pornographic pictures, leaving anonymous messages, and name-calling to let women know they don't belong."[74] For instance, in a survey conducted by Ontario Hydro of its female engineers, a third responded that they had experienced sexual harassment at work.[75] A third kind of harassment, Ms. Sanson warns, may well be aimed at female supervisors. Sanson suggests the fact that these supervisors have private offices may facilitate harassment.[76]

Alberta Human Rights Commission www.gov.ab.ca/mcd/ citizen/hrc/hrc.htm

According to the Alberta Human Rights Commission, about 70 percent of women—and 15 percent of men—have been subjected to unwanted sexual attention in the workplace.[77] Is such harassment more common today than it was in the past? Statistics suggest that this may be so: The number of complaints filed by U.S. employees rose from 4272 in 1981 to almost 6000 by 1990, and have doubled again since then.[78] Whether this is due to an actual increase in the incidence of sexual harassment or merely to greater reporting of its occurrence is impossible to say. Certainly, media attention to this problem has increased tremendously in recent years. Regardless of any effects of the media, however, it is clear that for every case of sexual harassment reported, many more go unrecorded. Clearly, organizations must take concerted action to protect their employees from this devastating cause of stress. As for complainants, Geri Sanson advises that they view sexual harassment as a workplace danger and thereby invoke health and safety law as well as human rights law.[79]

Unpleasant physical working conditions. Because of legislation aimed at protecting the health and well-being of employees, most work settings today are relatively safe and comfortable. The word *relatively* should be emphasized, however, because even within the limits imposed by law, there is room for a wide range of variation. In fact, many individuals report that the physical conditions under which they work cause them considerable stress. In particular, many employees identify such factors as excessive variations in temperature, inadequate or glaring lighting, dusty or polluted air, and noise as major causes of stress at work.[80] With respect to noise, the sound of human voices, in particular, appears to be stressful and distracting, and interferes greatly with effective performance on many tasks.[81,82]

Causes of Stress Outside Work

Although work is clearly one of the most important activities in many people's lives, it is not the only activity. For this reason, events occurring outside work settings often generate stress that persists and, as we noted earlier, is carried back to work.[83] While many different factors contribute to stress in this manner, most fit under broad categories: *major stressful life events* and *daily hassles*.[84]

Stressful life events.   The death of a spouse, divorce, injury to one's child, a stock market crash, unwanted pregnancy—unless an individual leads a truly charmed life, he or she is likely to experience traumatic events or changes like these at some point. What are the effects of such events? This question was first studied by Holmes and Rahe who asked large groups of people to assign arbitrary points (from 1 to 100) to various life events according to how much readjustment each had required.[85] Holmes and Rahe reasoned that the greater the number of points assigned to a given event, the more stressful it was for people who experienced it.

Some of the values assigned by participants to various stressful life events are shown in Table 7-4. As you can see, the highest numbers were assigned to serious events such as death of a spouse, divorce, and being sent to jail. The results of collecting a high level of such "stress points," as they might be termed, are dramatic: When individuals experience events totalling 300 points or more, they show a much higher incidence of becoming ill during the next several months than persons who score 200 points or lower.[86]

The hassles of daily life.   Traumatic life events are very stressful but they are—thankfully—relatively rare. Many people live for years or even decades without experiencing any of them. Does this mean that such individuals live a totally tranquil life? Hardly. Daily living is filled with countless minor irritations that seem to make

TABLE 7-4 Stressful Life Events

When asked to assign arbitrary points (1 to 100) to various life events according to the degree of readjustment they required, a large group of individuals provided the values shown here. The higher the numbers shown, the more stressful these events were perceived to be.

(Source: Based on data from Holmes & Rahe, 1967; see Note 85.)

Event	Relative Stressfulness
Death of a spouse	100
Divorce	73
Marital separation	65
Jail term	63
Death of a close family member	63
Personal injury or illness	53
Marriage	50
Fired from a job	47
Retirement	45
Pregnancy	40
Death of a close friend	37
Son or daughter leaving home	29
Trouble with in-laws	28
Trouble with boss	23
Change in residence	20
Vacation	13
Christmas	12
Minor violations of the law	11

daily hassles Problems of everyday life that serve as important causes of stress.

up for their low intensity by their high frequency of occurrence. That such **daily hassles**, as they are often termed, are an important cause of stress is suggested by the findings of several studies by Lazarus and his colleagues.[87] These researchers found that the more daily hassles people experience, the greater their levels of self-reported stress. Daily hassles occur in several areas of life: household hassles (e.g., preparing meals, shopping), time-pressure hassles (e.g., too many things to do), and financial hassles (e.g., concerns about owing money).

In sum, although traumatic life events such as the death of a loved one or the loss of one's job are stressful and have adverse effects on health, the minor problems of daily life, too, are important in this respect and should not be overlooked.

Total life stress: The combined picture. In the preceding discussion, we separated stressors related to work and those related to personal life events. This distinction reflects the fact that research on stressors often focuses on one or the other of these two major categories. But from the individual's point of view, work-related stress and life-related stress often combine into a seamless—and potentially overwhelming—pattern of adversity. Is an important project going poorly? Is one's boss "acting up?" Then, it often seems, this is the time for problems with one's children or one's spouse. And it is when one is already feeling overloaded, that the furnace, car, or refrigerator breaks down.

The usefulness of adopting a broad approach in which work-related and personal causes of stress are combined into the construct of *total negative life stress* is suggested by the fact that total stress is a better predictor of negative organizational outcomes—for example, reduced job satisfaction and commitment, increased turnover intentions—than either work-related or life-related stressors alone.[88] And there is considerable spillover—emotional and otherwise—between these two spheres of life.[89] So, where stress as actually experienced by individuals is concerned, it makes sense to view stress from work and stress from life events as two sides of the same coin.

Stress: Its Major Effects

Stress, as we've already noted, is an unavoidable part of working life—and life generally. Does it exert important effects on persons exposed to it? The answer is a definite "Yes." Stress-related problems cost Canadian business $12 billion a year.[90] Further, in the United States, it has been estimated that the costs of adverse effects of stress exceed 10 percent of the gross national product.[91] Much of this amount stems from the health-related effects of stress; however, growing evidence indicates that stress can influence us in other ways, too. Specifically, it can strongly affect our psychological well-being and our performance on many tasks. Let's take a closer look at these effects.

Stress and Task Performance

In the past, it was generally assumed that the relationship between stress and performance on many tasks is *curvilinear* in nature. Low levels of stress were assumed to increase performance, while beyond some point, further increments in stress tended to reduce performance. Although this relationship may hold true under some conditions, recent evidence suggests that stress exerts mainly negative effects on task performance even at relatively low levels.[92]

Why is this so? Shouldn't the activation generated by moderate levels of stress increase performance in many cases? Although this may be true in some situations, there are several reasons for expecting that even moderate levels of stress will interfere with performance. First, even relatively mild stress can be distracting. People experiencing it may focus on the unpleasant feelings and emotions stress involves rather than on the task at hand—with the result that their performance suffers. Second, prolonged or repeated exposure to even mild levels of stress may exert harmful effects on health, and this may interfere with the ability to perform many tasks. Finally, even moderate levels of stress can sometimes generate very high levels of arousal, and these have been found to interfere with performance. Have you ever "choked under pressure?" In such situations, the very high levels of arousal generated by stressful conditions—for example, an audience watching your performance—can interfere with effective performance.[93]

Having said all this, we must note that there are exceptions to the general rule that stress interferes with task performance. Some individuals do seem to "rise to the occasion" and turn in exceptional performance at times of high stress. This may result from the fact that they are truly expert in the tasks being performed. Alternatively, the individuals involved may view stress as a *challenge* rather than as a *threat*. As we noted earlier, such cognitive appraisal plays a key role in determining the level of stress we experience.

Second, large individual differences exist with respect to the impact of stress on task performance. As your own experience may suggest, some individuals—the Type A's we described in Chapter 4, for instance—seem to thrive on stress. They actively seek arousal and high levels of sensation or stimulation. For such people, stress is exhilarating and may improve their performance. In contrast, other people react in an opposite manner. They seek to avoid arousal and high levels of sensation. Such persons find stress upsetting, and it may interfere with their performance on many tasks.

In sum, taking available evidence into account, the most reasonable conclusion seems to be: In many situations, stress interferes with task performance. However, its precise effects depend on the nature of the tasks being performed, the expertise of the persons performing them, and several personality traits. For this reason, generalizations about the impact of stress on task performance should be made with considerable caution.

Stress and Psychological Well-being: Burnout

Most jobs involve some degree of stress. Yet somehow, the people holding them manage to cope. Some individuals, however, are not so fortunate. Over time, they seem to be worn down psychologically by repeated exposure to stress. Such people are often described as suffering from **burnout**—a syndrome involving several kinds of exhaustion coupled with several kinds of negative attitudes.

With respect to exhaustion, victims of burnout often suffer from *physical exhaustion, emotional exhaustion*, and *attitudinal exhaustion*. Physical exhaustion is just what you might expect: reduced energy coupled with symptoms of physical strain such as frequent headaches, nausea, poor sleep, and loss of appetite. Emotional exhaustion involves feelings of depression, helplessness, and being trapped in one's job. Finally, attitudinal exhaustion (often known as *depersonalization*) involves cynical beliefs about others—for instance, the view that they are all incompetent and callous—coupled with negative beliefs about oneself, one's job, one's organization, or even one's entire life. To put it simply, persons experiencing such exhaustion come to view the world around them through dark gray rather than rose-coloured glasses. Finally, victims of burnout often report feelings of *low personal accomplishment*; they feel that they haven't accomplished much in the past and won't succeed in the future, either. Figure 7-7 gives an overview of the major components of burnout.

Burnout: Some major causes. What are the causes of burnout? As we have already noted, the primary factor seems to be prolonged exposure to stress. However, other variables also play a role. A number of conditions within an organization plus several personal characteristics seem to determine whether and to what degree individuals experience burnout.[94] For example, *job conditions* suggesting that one's efforts are useless, ineffective, or unappreciated seem to contribute to burnout.[95] Under such conditions, individuals develop the feelings of low personal accomplishment that are an important part of burnout. Similarly, *poor opportunities for promotion* and the *presence of inflexible rules and procedures* lead

burnout A syndrome resulting from prolonged exposure to stress, consisting of physical, emotional, and mental exhaustion plus feelings of a lack of personal accomplishment.

FIGURE 7-7 Burnout: Its
Major Components

When people are exposed to high
levels of stress over prolonged periods of time, they may experience
burnout. This syndrome involves
physical, mental, and attitudinal
exhaustion, plus feelings of low
personal accomplishment.

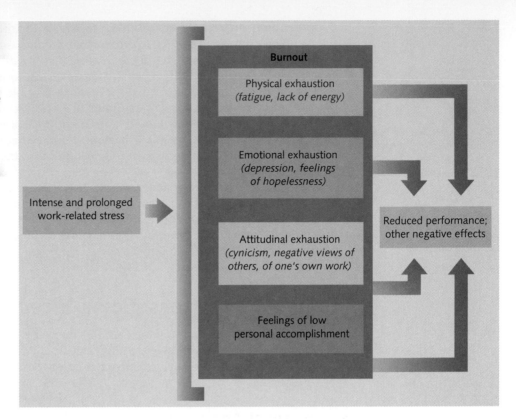

employees to feel that they are trapped in an unfair system and contribute to the
development of negative views about their jobs.[96] Another important factor is the
leadership style used by employees' supervisors. The lower the amount of consideration demonstrated by their supervisors (i.e., the less they are concerned with
employees' welfare or with maintaining good relations with them), the higher employees' reported levels of burnout.[97] (We'll discuss various styles of leadership in
Chapter 13.)

Burnout: Can it be reversed? Before concluding, we should comment briefly on
one final question: Can burnout be reversed? Fortunately, growing evidence suggests that it can. With appropriate help, victims of burnout can recover from their
physical and psychological exhaustion. If ongoing stress is reduced, if burnout victims gain added support from friends and coworkers, and if they cultivate hobbies
and other outside interests, at least some people can escape from the dead-end trap
of burnout. Such results can be attained, however, only through active efforts designed to overcome burnout and to change the conditions that produce it.

Stress and Health: The Silent Killer

How strong is the link between stress and personal health? According to medical experts, very strong indeed. In fact, some authorities estimate that stress plays a role in
anywhere from 50 to 70 percent of all forms of physical illness.[98] Moreover, included
in these figures are some of the most serious and life-threatening ailments known to
medical science: heart disease and stroke, ulcers, headaches, diabetes, cancer.

In addition to its role in such *degenerative diseases*, growing evidence indicates
that stress may also play a key role in *infectious diseases*—diseases that are caused by
infectious agents such as bacteria or viruses. Many studies indicate that exposure to
high levels of stress increases susceptibility to diseases such as upper respiratory infections, herpes virus infections, and various bacterial infections.[99] So, in sum, it
often exerts powerful, adverse effects on personal health.

☞ We examined the nature of the Type A behaviour pattern, and its effects on several forms of organizational behaviour, in Chapter 4.

Individual differences in resistance to stress. Earlier, we noted that while most people are adversely affected by stress, some seem to thrive on such conditions. Here, we want to expand on that point by noting that several personal characteristics seem to play a role in such differences. In other words, to the extent individuals possess certain traits, they may be more—or less—susceptible to the potentially harmful effects of stress. We've already mentioned one of these: the Type A behaviour pattern. While Type A people seem to seek out high levels of stress—for instance, by taking on several jobs at once—this behaviour is somewhat self-destructive: Many studies indicate that Type A persons are more susceptible to the harmful effects of stress than Type B persons.[100,101]

Other personal characteristics, too, have been found to influence the impact of stress on personal health; several of these are summarized in Table 7-5. As you can see, to the extent individuals possess these traits, they appear to be "buffered" or protected against the harmful effects of stress. Thus, these traits appear to be adaptive from this important perspective.

Managing Stress: Some Effective Techniques

Stress itself may be unavoidable, but this doesn't mean that its harmful effects, too, are inescapable. In fact, there are many steps both individuals and organizations can take to minimize the adverse impact of stress. Let's take a closer look at several of these.

Personal Approaches to Stress Management

What can you do as an individual to protect yourself from the serious consequences of stress? Four major strategies appear to be most useful.

Lifestyle management: The effect of diet and exercise. Exercise is a powerful defense against stress—a conclusion that is supported by many research studies. Getting into good physical shape is one of the best ways to increase resistance to stress.[102] Good diet, too, is an integral part of such efforts. As the old saying goes "We are what we eat," and if you eat wisely—and avoid gaining weight—the benefits where stress resistance is concerned are obvious.

Physiological techniques: Relaxation and meditation. When you think of successful executives at work, what picture comes to mind? Someone trying to speak on three phones at once while reading a report and talking to a visitor? That's close to the common conception of how such people live. Definitely *not* part of this image is someone resting calmly in a serene setting. Yet, for a growing number of

TABLE 7-5 Personal Traits and Resistance To Stress

The traits described here have been found to influence the extent to which individuals are susceptible to the harmful effects of stress.

(Source: Based on a review of pertinent literature by R. A. Baron.)

Personal Characteristic	Description; Effects
Type A Behaviour Pattern	Always in a hurry; highly competitive, irritable. Highly susceptible to the adverse effects of stress.
Optimism	Hopeful outlook on life; see situations in a positive light; expect favourable outcomes. These traits lead to problem-focused coping which helps such people deal with stress.
Hardiness	High levels of commitment to their jobs; believe they can control their outcomes; see stress as challenge. Together these traits make them resistant to the adverse effects of stress.
Tension Discharge Rate	Persons high in this trait dissipate job-related tension quickly at the end of the day. This reduces the harmful effects of such stress on them.

today's employees, this picture is quite common. At Symmetric (a Lexington, Massachusetts software developer), for example, many of the company's 125 employees spend as long as 20 minutes a day behind closed office doors quietly meditating.[103] Their company doesn't merely tolerate this practice: It encourages it and has even paid consultants to teach employees how to relax in this manner. Many other organizations, too, have adopted this practice: Marriott, Polaroid, The Boston Co. (an investment firm), to name a few.

What's going on in these companies is an effort to help employees become more productive by providing them with techniques for coping more effectively with stress. One such technique is known as **meditation**, a process in which people learn to clear their minds of external thoughts, often by repeating a single syllable over and over again. Meditation requires sitting quietly in a comfortable position, closing your eyes, relaxing your muscles, and breathing slowly. The trick is to keep other thoughts that would break your restful state from entering your mind. Doing this once or twice a day for 10–20 minutes per session is believed to be an effective way of reducing stress and increasing one's capacity to work and to enjoy life generally.[104]

A related technique is **relaxation training.** In this method, people learn how first to tense and then to relax their muscles.[105] By becoming familiar with the differences between these states, people become able to induce relaxation whenever they feel themselves becoming too tense.

Cognitive techniques: Thinking yourself out of stress. Do you worry too much? Surveys indicate that almost 90 percent of all people answer "Yes."[106] Moreover, many realize that they worry about issues that are either unimportant, outside their control, or both. Clearly, worrying about such matters is a waste of cognitive effort and can contribute to increased stress. By reducing such worrying, many persons can help reduce the stress they experience.

Excessive worrying is not the only thing we do that contributes to our own stress, however. Often, we engage in what have been termed *awfulizing* or *castastrophizing*—patterns of thought in which we magnify the effects of failure, not being perfect, or being rejected by others. Such thinking, too, often adds to our level of stress. Reducing such irrational and self-defeating cognitions, therefore, can be another useful step in combating stress. Clearly, Sergio Zyman, the top executive discussed in our chapter CASE PREVIEW did not fall prey to such thinking; on the contrary, he took crushing failure in stride—and so bounced back without experiencing the devastating effects that such stress could potentially produce.

Perhaps the guiding principle in all cognitive techniques for managing stress is this: We must realize that we can't always change the world around us, but we can change our reactions to it. In other words, we don't have to worry excessively about things we can't change, strive for absolute perfection, or allow irritating but minor situations to drive us up the wall. Instead, we can actively decide to avoid such reactions and in this manner, reduce our own stress.

Organization-Based Strategies for Managing Stress

Can organizations, too, take steps to reduce the level of stress experienced by their employees? Absolutely. (See THE ETHICS ANGLE section for a concrete example.) Several organization-based or organization-initiated tactics can be highly effective in this regard.

Family-supportive practices: Helping to reduce the stress of work-family conflicts. As we noted earlier, the task of juggling work and family obligations is an important source of stress for many persons at the present time. Given this basic fact, it seems reasonable to suggest that organizational policies designed to help lessen such role conflict might also be effective in reducing stress and *strain*—the negative effects resulting from it. Growing evidence indicates that this is, indeed, the case.

For example, in a recent study on this issue, Thomas and Ganster asked nurses and nursing supervisors to complete a questionnaire designed to measure the extent to which their organizations had adopted policies designed to reduce work-family

meditation A technique for inducing relaxation in which individuals clear disturbing thoughts from their minds by repeating a single syllable.

relaxation training Procedures through which individuals learn to relax in order to reduce anxiety or stress.

Fear as a Management Tool

When Ricardo Semler took over his family's manufacturing business in Brazil, *fear* was the dominant management system in place. Armed guards patrolled the factory floor, frisked workers as they left the plant, and timed their trips to the bathroom.[107] If employees broke a piece of equipment, they had to replace it out of their wages. At first Semler went along with this philosophy of "management-through-intimidation," but when he collapsed in exhaustion, and was told by the physician that he was the most "stressed-out" 25-year-old the doctor had ever seen, he decided on major change. Fear was replaced by freedom, as employees were given the right to run their own jobs—and the company. They could wear what they wanted, come and go as they chose, and even set their own salaries. The only hitch: They had to reapply for their jobs every six months. Results have been favourable: Sales and earnings are up. But not everyone agrees with this new approach. Decision making tends to be chaotic, and it's not clear how long-term strategy will be set. But many employees certainly think that their new freedom is far better than their old fear.

conflict (*family-supportive policies*), the amount of work-family conflict they experienced, and psychological, physiological, and behavioural signs of strain.[108] The questionnaire also included a measure of perceived control over work and family life because Thomas and Ganster hypothesized that family-supportive practices would reduce work-family conflict directly, and also through increased feelings of personal control (see Figure 7-8). Among the **family-supportive policies** investigated were information and referral services (e.g., referrals for child care, written materials on parenting), dependent services (e.g., on-site day care, on-site care for sick children), flexible work schedules, and supervisor support (e.g., switching schedules to accommodate family responsibilities).

Results indicated that several family-supportive policies did indeed have beneficial effects. Specifically, policies such as flexible scheduling and supportive supervisor behaviours increased feelings of personal control, reduced work-family conflict, and so reduced several aspects of strain—for example, depression, health complaints, and even blood cholesterol levels. In short, it appeared that when organizations adopted policies designed to reduce the degree of work-family conflict their employees experienced, the stress they experienced was decreased. Since the adverse effects of stress (i.e., strain) have been found to exert negative effects on employee performance, such policies appear to benefit organizations as well as individual employees (see Figure 7-9).

family-supportive policies
Policies adopted by an organization that help reduce the con-flict between family and work obligations.

FIGURE 7-8 Family-Supportive Policies: An Effective Means of Reducing Stress

Several family-supportive policies (e.g., flexible scheduling, supportive supervisor behaviours) increase feelings of personal control among employees and serve to reduce work-family conflict. These effects, in turn, tend to reduce several aspects of strain—for example, depression, health complaints, and even blood cholesterol levels.

(Source: Based on data reported by Thomas & Ganster, 1995; see Note 63.)

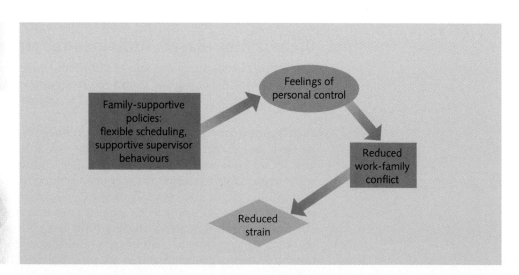

FIGURE 7-9 Helping a Stressed-Out Workforce

Lisa Sladen is a corporate concierge for the 10 000 employees in Toronto's First Canadian Place. Positions such as Lisa's are "taking hold, as employers try to meet the needs of their hard-worked, much-travelled and stressed-out workforces." Concierges help employees with the day-to-day errands that can drain their time and energy. They will arrange for services to take an employee's car to be repaired, pick up laundry, make sure pets are fed, and make dinner reservations.[109]

stress management programs Systematic efforts by organizations designed to help employees reduce and/or prevent stress.

Stress management programs.   Another step organizations can take to help their employees manage stress is **stress management programs**.[110] These involve extensive in-house training that concentrates on many of the techniques described earlier (e.g., meditation, relaxation, lifestyle management), as well as others. For example, the Equitable Life Insurance company's "Emotional Health Program" offers a program in stress management to its employees that relies mostly on the physiological techniques described above. Company officials estimate that each $33 it spends on employees helps relieve symptoms that would have cost the company $100 in lost productivity.[111] Because many companies cannot afford to create their own stress management programs, they often rely on prepackaged programs provided by outside consultants, or on off-the-shelf audiovisual programs on videocassettes.

employee assistance programs (EAPs) Plans that provide employees with assistance in meeting various problems (e.g., substance abuse, career planning, financial and legal problems).

Companies that do not use stress management programs have other systematic ways of helping their employees. Many provide help through their **employee assistance programs (EAPs)**—plans that provide employees with assistance in meeting various problems (e.g., substance abuse, career planning, financial and legal problems). For example, the employee assistance plan at General Motors of Canada Ltd. covers a wide variety of options including legal services, paid educational leave, and a program to ease injured workers back to the job gradually.[112] The Metropolitan Life Insurance Company (MetLife) is another company whose EAP has been actively involved in helping its employees reduce stress.[113] It reaches out to its 42 000 U.S. employees by providing toll-free telephone consultation for those in need of help, as well as access to on-site and external medical and psychological professionals. Although few EAPs are as extensive as MetLife's, the cost-effective nature of such programs is making them an increasingly common form of worker benefit in today's organizations.

SUMMARY AND REVIEW

Organizational Socialization

The process through which newcomers learn the ropes in their organizations and become full-fledged members is known as **organizational socialization**. This process involves three distinct stages: *getting in, breaking in, and settling in*. **Realistic job previews** during the recruitment of newcomers help them avoid unrealistically optimistic or pessimistic expectations, and so **entry shock**. Organiza-tions often expose newcomers to formal *socialization programs*; however, newcomers themselves play an active role in the socialization process through their *information-search* activities.

Mentoring

A one-on-one form of socialization known as **mentoring** occurs when an experienced employee (a **mentor**) advises, counsels, and aids the personal development of a new employee (a **protégé**). Mentors not only pave the way for their protégé's job success, they also provide a source of emotional support to them. Mentoring relationships benefit both parties. Typically, the mentoring relationships move through four phases: *initiation, cultivation, separation*, and *redefinition*. Because of their personal characteristics—for example, being high in self-monitoring or need for achievement—some persons are more successful in obtaining mentors than others.

Research has shown that because individuals are generally more comfortable interacting with persons who are similar to themselves, females and members of various minorities often have fewer opportunities to obtain a mentor than other persons. For this reason, it is important for organizations to take active steps to reduce such barriers and increase mentoring for women and minorities.

Careers

A **career** is the evolving sequence of a person's work experiences over time. Common conceptions of what careers will—or should be—like have altered greatly in recent years, partly as a result of equally sweeping changes in the business world. When people make vocational decisions, they often consider the extent to which their values and attitudes match those of a prospective organization—*person-job fit*. Careers now rarely involve movement through a series of steps up the corporate ladder. On the contrary, they more frequently include lateral moves, rotation through several different jobs, geographic relocations, and—increasingly— periods of time spent as an independent contractor or subcontractor rather than as a regular, full-time employee.

Because individuals can no longer count on job security, most experts on careers agree that they should focus on using each job or assignment as a means for acquiring valuable skills. In short, they should view their careers as a series of opportunities for gaining new proficiencies that will increase their value on the job market. Individuals can fill four distinct roles in today's organizations: planners of *corporate strategy, project managers, resource providers*, who provide the financial and human resources needed by project managers, and *talents*, persons who offer specific technical skills and knowledge. **Job rotation**, lateral transfers of employees between jobs in an organization, is often beneficial for those who experience it. Individuals can tell their careers are in trouble when they feel that they are not acquiring new skills, would not be able to get their job if it were open, are uncertain about what they are contributing, and are worried about their job.

Although the careers of women and men appear to be affected by many of the same factors, some of these operate differently for the two genders. For example, while men's careers are often facilitated by marriage and children, women's careers are sometimes impaired by these factors—because women still take most of the responsibility for household management and child rearing. Women often receive fewer developmental experiences at work, and this can adversely affect their careers. The **glass ceiling** appears to be real—few women are promoted to very high-level jobs.

The Basic Nature of Stress

Stress refers to a complex pattern of emotional states, physiological reactions, and related thoughts occurring in response to external demands (**stressors**). In contrast, **strain** refers to the effects of stress, primarily to deviations from normal states or performance resulting from exposure to stressful events.

Major Causes of Stress

Stress stems from both *work-related* causes and factors outside work. One of the most important work-related causes of stress involves **role conflict** resulting from the competing demands of work and family obligations. Other important work-related causes of stress include occupational demands, **role ambiguity, overload** and **underload**, responsibility for others, lack of social support, and **sexual harassment**. Causes of stress outside work include traumatic life events and the **daily hassles** of everyday life.

Effects of Stress

Stress adversely influences task performance, even at relatively low levels. In addition, it exerts harmful effects on psychological well-being. Prolonged exposure to stress can lead to **burnout**, a syndrome consisting of physical, emotional, and mental exhaustion, plus intense feelings of low personal accomplishment.

Stress also exerts harmful effects on health. It has been linked to various *degenerative diseases* such as heart disease, high blood pressure, ulcers, and diabetes, and to *infectious diseases* as well. Some persons are more resistant to the adverse effects than others. Type B's, for instance, are more resistant to stress than Type A's.

Managing Stress

Techniques for managing stress exist at both the personal and organizational level. Personal techniques include *lifestyle management*, such as good diet and exercise, *physiological* techniques, such as meditation and relaxation, and *cognitive techniques*, which involve changes in the way individuals think about stress and the situations that produce it.

Organization-based tactics for managing stress include the adoption of **family-supportive policies**, such as flexible work schedules and provision of day care for children, and **stress-management programs**, designed to teach employees various techniques for managing stress. **Employee assistance programs**, which assist employees in dealing with important problems (e.g., substance abuse, career planning, financial and legal problems), are yet another organization-based strategy for managing stress.

CASE PREVIEW QUESTIONS FOR DISCUSSION

1. Speculate on the pros and cons of a career as a marketing executive.
2. Is Serge Zyman's personality a good match for the stressors inherent in the position of marketing executive for a large global corporation such as Coca-Cola? Explain.
3. In what ways could large corporations, such as Coca-Cola reduce stress for their employees?

CHAPTER QUESTIONS FOR DISCUSSION

1. What concrete steps can organizations take with respect to new hires to assure that they do not experience *entry shock* upon joining the company?
2. How could you go about increasing the availability of mentors to women and minorities?
3. What are the potential benefits of job rotation? Are there any potential drawbacks to such experience?
4. Do you think that women have more choice with respect to changing their careers at midlife than men? If so, why? If not, why?
5. Why are fewer and fewer graduates of MBA programs choosing to work for large corporations? Do you think their reluctance to accept such jobs is justified?
6. Why are the cognitive appraisals that individuals have about a given situation so important in determining the level of stress they experience in it?
7. Suppose that a female manager made several comments about the physique of a male subordinate: Would this constitute sexual harassment? Explain.
8. Suppose you were faced with the task of choosing employees for a high-stress job. What personal characteristics would you seek in these individuals? What characteristics would you try to avoid?
9. What policies can organizations adopt to reduce stress among their employees resulting from family-work conflicts?
10. What steps can individuals take to effectively manage the stress to which they are exposed?

CASE IN POINT

Toronto Dominion Bank: How Ruth Getter Cracked the Bank's Glass Ceiling

In the spring of 1994, Ruth Getter was appointed by the Toronto Dominion Bank as their first-ever female senior vice-president and chief economist. Indeed, Getter is the first woman to hold both influential positions at any of Canada's big banks. Women had previously progressed to the position of vice-president, but rarely higher, at the banks' Bay Street towers.

Getter acknowledges that she represents a boulder through the industry's glass ceiling. But she describes herself as "the thin edge of the wedge" for a throng of talented women poised to move into top banking positions. "The world is changing," she says matter-of-factly. "There are more and more renegade females out there who are butting their heads against these so-called glass ceilings until they break."

The renegade label is applicable to the "untraditional women's lifestyle" that is the foundation of her accomplishments, she believes. Born in Palestine, now Israel, Getter emigrated to Montreal with her family in 1952. Once there, her father opened a small typewriter-parts factory. As a teenager, Getter worked long, gruelling hours after school and on weekends at her father's factory, while maintaining a straight-A average. She was picked as a prize student by Montreal's McGill University and awarded a full scholarship to complete her Bachelor of Science degree in genetics. "I was a pretty rare sight in the classrooms in those days," she recalls. "But I soon earned the respect of my male peers by getting straight A's."

After she graduated from McGill, Getter married and moved with her husband to the United States, where she gave birth to two children. Around the same time she made the switch to economics. Getter earned her Masters degree from Ohio University and later a Ph.D. in economics from Boston University. "I was, again, quite a rare sight more than 20 years ago, sitting in classrooms, pregnant, and the only woman in the economics program."

Getter divorced while completing her Ph.D. She was obliged to take a job as an economist with a Boston consulting firm, at U.S.$17 000 a year, to support her family. "I was 35, working full time, raising two kids, and working on my doctoral thesis every free waking moment. Those were tough times financially and psychologically and I wouldn't want to repeat them. But I was determined, and my father had taught me to never give up, and fight harder when the going got tough."

In 1987, she developed a longing to return to Canada and decided that then-booming Toronto was the place to be. She packed her belongings into a van and crossed the border into Canada on "Black Monday" in October, 1987,

the day that the markets posted their biggest single-day crash since the start of Depression. "My thoughts that day were, 'Great timing. The market is crashing and I'm heading to Toronto to find a job,' " Getter says. One month after her Toronto job search began she landed a position as the senior economist at TD.

Ruth Getter takes her position as a role model and mentor for both women and men very seriously. She helped to establish the TD Bank's Task Force for the Advancement of Women and sits on one of its subcommittees that has focused on mentoring programs. In 1996, Getter was named Toronto's Woman of the Year by Jewish Women International in recognition of her achievements and the fact she is seen as a role model in advancing women's effectiveness.[114]

Critical Thinking Questions

1. What factors do you believe have most influenced Ruth Getter's career path to date?

2. Outline and discuss the stressors on Ruth Getter before she accepted her current position at the TD Bank.

3. Research the career paths of the women listed in Table 7-3. Identify common themes in these various career histories.

Toronto Dominion Bank
www.tdbank.ca

SKILLS PORTFOLIO

Experiencing Organizational Behaviour

Developing a Personal Career Plan

One of the most important things people can do to fulfill their career goals is to develop a career plan. Overall, there are five steps in this process, the first three of which you can do right now. The final two will have to wait until you're already on the job.

Directions

To complete each of the first three steps in the career-planning process, ask yourself the questions listed below and record your answers. To come up with the most accurate assessment, try to answer the questions as honestly as possible.

Step 1: Personal Assessment

    a. What special skills and aptitudes can you bring to your job?

    b. What are your most serious weaknesses and limitations? (Really try to be honest on this one).

    c. What types of jobs do you like to do?

    d. To what extent do the jobs you've identified in step c require the skills identified in step a? And to what extent might they suffer from the limitations identified in step b?

Step 2: Opportunities Analysis

    a. How has the economy affected various job prospects?

    b. Is there an overabundance or a shortage of people to fill various jobs you might consider?

Step 3: Career Objectives

    a. What are your long-term goals? (5–10 years)?

    b. What are your intermediate goals (3–5 years)?

    c. What are your short-term goals (1–3 years)?

Step 4: Implement Plan

Step 5: Revise Plan as Necessary

(Select a position. Then, after working on it, monitor your progress, solicit feedback, compare the results to your objectives, and revise your plan as needed. Remember: The key to successful career management is *not* necessarily obtaining promotions. Rather it is building your skills base so that you will be a desirable employee for many different companies.)

Working in Groups

The Worry Exercise

Everyone worries, but the trick is to worry *constructively*, not *destructively*. This exercise will help you to move toward this goal, while gaining insight into what other people aside from yourself worry about.

Directions

1. First, all members of the class list the things they worry about. This list of current worries should include as many issues and problems as possible—everything that each person is worrying about at the present time.
2. Next, the class is divided into groups, and each group does the following:

    (a) First, each person, in turn, presents one of her/his worries.

    (b) The group then decides where each of these worries fits in the chart below.

	Important	**Unimportant**
Can Be Controlled		
Can't Be Controlled		

3. After this activity is completed, each group reports on its findings.

Questions for Discussion

1. Did members of the class admit to worrying about issues and problems they could not control and which were unimportant?
2. Why do people worry about such matters?
3. Does worrying about them make any sense? Can it produce harmful effects?
4. How can people who worry about things they can't control and that are unimportant stop doing so?

TAKE IT TO THE NET

We invite you to visit the *Greenberg/Baron/Sales/Owen Companion Website* at *www.prenticehall.ca/greenberg* for this chapter's Internet resources.

Digital Renaissance's "Hip, Hot, Happening" Work Space[1]

"A Great Place To Work." "Do you want: A position that's more than a job? To work on the leading edge of technology? To use computers for human communications? To join a skilled, savvy and enthusiastic team? Then we are interested in hearing from you." So goes the invitation on Digital Renaissance's Website.[2]

Attracting and keeping "digital talent" is no small task for Canadian high-tech companies in today's highly competitive environment. "High-tech companies have always griped about the dearth of freshly minted whiz kids. But it's grown appreciably worse in recent years." The ranks of the science, math, and engineering graduates have not kept pace with the demand generated by burgeoning numbers of computers.[3] Keith Kocho sees recruitment as selling the company to those he wants to hire. Once new recruits have joined the company, he knows they look for a congenial organizational climate that is sensitive to diversity and that provides constant challenge.

In 1996, Digital Renaissance moved to its current location, a 2800-square-metre converted warehouse in downtown Toronto. Some say it looks like it could be "a Manhattan apartment"[4] while others say it looks "more like an art gallery than a tech company."[5] At Digital Renaissance, there are no offices. A canoe hangs from the ceiling. There are big couches, bean-bag chairs, a hammock, two kitchens, a pool table, play stations with Play-Doh, Lego, and Rubik's Cubes, shower facilities, and a children's play area.[6] Staff can bring their dogs to work, hit a punching bag, or even sleep at work.[7] The company has been described as being like Microsoft in its early days, ". . . but without the 'corporate' edge."[8] "All the furniture is on wheels . . . It's totally fluid, which speaks to their culture and their work processes," says Deborah Middleton, a principal of Workspace Dynamics.

Keith Kocho and his colleagues at Digital Renaissance exhibit the strength, energy, and distinctive working style that characterize Generation X, the "Nexus Generation." Generation X has been described as the tail end of the baby boom, those born between 1960 and 1966.[9] A more functional definition offered by one Gen-Xer is this: "If you graduated from university in anything other than computer science without encountering a computer, you're too old; if you can't remember a time when there were no video stores, you're too young."[10]

Appropriately for people who are living in a fast-paced, ever-changing digitally driven world, members of the Nexus Generation tend to have an entrepreneurial spirit. They ". . .are confident in their own ability to pull through"[11] and are comfortable changing jobs to get the kind of challenge and experience they want. They know that the notion of lifetime employment is a thing of the past and they tend to stay ". . . in work relationships only as long as the fit between employee and employer is mutually beneficial."[12] Members of the Nexus Generation are adaptable, craving change in their work. To support their transient lifestyle, they ". . . create temporary support structures through real or virtual communities."[13] What better match could there be for pioneering new technologies?

Digital Renaissance reflects the values of the Nexus generation. At the company's headquarters in Toronto, staff spend long hours working in a highly competitive industry. To compensate, they find ". . . comfort and community wherever they can."[14] Linda Petrin, a usability architect at Digital Renaissance, had worked previously at Revenue Canada and Andersen Consulting. She says, "Honestly, I didn't care if the company was big or small. It was a group of people who had the same values I had." Marc Caron left his higher-paying job at Digital Equipment Corp. to come to Digital Renaissance because "You're closer to the action. . .. You have a greater sense of making a direct contribution to the company's growth. We work crazy hours, but we're working with people we like and doing things we enjoy."[15] Other staff cite "the flattened management structure, employee empowerment, a commitment to ethical business practices."[16]

In the absence of a rigid organizational hierarchy with predictable promotion patterns, employees at Digital Renaissance are presented with flexible career options and are free to make many lateral moves within the company. The staff at Digital Renaissance are offered abundant opportunities to work on many and varied projects. And, oh yes, partying is important! Social events help to support team members in a working environment where a gruelling daily work pace is a given.

Discussion Questions

1. What are the characteristics of the Nexus Generation? Are distinctions such as this valid in your opinion?

2. What impact would the characteristics you mentioned in the first part of Question 1 above have on the way organizations manage their people?

3. Why is Kocho so concerned about "selling the company to those he wants to hire?" Is he justified in his concerns?

4. What methods does Digital Renaissance use to win in the current Canadian high-tech talent wars? Name some high-tech companies in Canada with which he competes for the best talent.

5. What additional methods could you suggest to Keith Kocho for attracting and retaining top knowledge workers?

Kevin McCarthy: When a MUT Is Not a Dog

Bishop's Falls, Newfoundland is justifiably proud of its industrial and commercial heritage. The town manufactures products that are sold around the world. The Bishop's Falls Development Corporation boasts that "products with the 'Made in Bishop's Falls' label can be found across Canada and the United States, and in countries as far away as South America, the Middle East, Russia, Australia, and Japan."

Included among the Bishop's Falls success stories is MUT (Multi Unit Transporter), which was the dream of founder and president Kevin McCarthy, a former worker at General Motors. The MUT "is designed for the venturesome outdoor enthusiast." The original MUT unit is a portable fishing hut that can be towed behind any sort of vehicle, including a skidoo or motorcycle. The collapsible MUT can be assembled in under a minute. "It has two seats, fishing-pole holders, built-in coat hangers, interior 12V light, and a convenient store-away table (hole in ice not included)." The company has come up with variations on the product for use in a variety of situations including in emergency transport situations, and for portable storage.

McCarthy dreamed up the MUT in the summer of 1994. He sought help in the development process through the Canadian Industrial Innovation Centre in Waterloo, Ontario. The Centre gave McCarthy a Critical Factor Analysis (CFA) on his MUT prototype. McCarthy calls the CFA "the motor to make things move." He gave the CFA results to the Atlantic Canada Opportunities Agency (ACOA) and to Enterprise Newfoundland to support his search for funds to underwrite the new project. His pro-ject was accepted and he was able to work on achieving design protection and a patent for the MUT.

In March of 1995, McCarthy hit the road, visiting the Toronto Sportsman's Show. He realized that "you can't just sit at home and expect opportunities to happen." In fact, sitting at home is something McCarthy rarely does. Starting a new venture is tough (to say nothing of growing it). The long hours on the road and at the factory have taken their toll on McCarthy. He says he has experienced burnout on several occasions but works to remedy the situations that have brought him to this point. Above all, he has recognized the need to delegate some responsibilities to other people in his organization.

Video Case Discussion Questions

1. Why do you think an ex–General Motors employee like Kevin McCarthy might want to start up his own business?

2. What were the stressors for Kevin in the early years of his business?

3. What signs in the video do you see of Kevin's burnout?

4. What advice can you offer to Kevin McCarthy now that you have studied seven chapters of this book on organizational behaviour?

CBC Source: MUT, *Venture* #649 (July 6, 1997).

Video Case Sources: Bishop's Falls Manufacturers, www.thezone.net/bfdc./clients.html; This MUT is No Dog! www.innovationcentre.ca/info/eureka/fall95/sec_3.htm; Introducing the MUT, www.exploitschamber.nf.ca/mut.htm.

CHAPTER 8

Group Dynamics and Teamwork

LEARNING OBJECTIVES

After reading this chapter you should be able to:

1. Define what is meant by a *group*, and explain why it is not just a collection of people.

2. Identify different types of groups operating within organizations and understand how they develop.

3. Describe the importance of *norms*, *roles*, *status*, and *cohesiveness* within organizations.

4. Explain how individual performance in groups is affected by the presence of others (*social facilitation*), the cultural diversity of group membership, and the number of others with whom one is working (*social loafing*).

5. Define what *teams* are and how they may be distinguished from groups in general.

6. Describe the various types of teams that exist in organizations and the steps that should be followed in creating them.

7. Understand the evidence regarding the effectiveness of teams in organizations.

8. Explain the factors responsible for the failure of some teams to operate as effectively as possible.

9. Identify things that can be done to build high-performance teams.

CASE PREVIEW

Honeywell Ltd.: Teaming up for Quality

At the Honeywell plant in Scarborough, Ontario, workers are encouraged to shut down the production line. In fact, teams shut down the operation whenever they detect a problem. How can a company stay in business that way?[1]

Not only does Honeywell Ltd. stay in business, but the company's per-person productivity rate nearly doubled in the first five years that the company instituted self-managed work teams (see Figure 8-1).[2] Before the advent of the teams, a group of workers was assigned specifically to rework defects. Under the new team system, such a group is no longer needed. Team members monitor product quality themselves now that they are familiar with all aspects of the work.[3]

Honeywell Limited is Canada's number one producer of controls for electronic equipment such as air conditioners, security systems, and furnaces.[4] The company has over 50 Canadian locations and 2800 employees.[5]

Honeywell's self-managed work team system was initiated in 1991. Before the new system was instituted, the relationship between management and union

FIGURE 8-1 Productivity Rises at Team-Based Plant

Members of the self-managed work teams at Honeywell Ltd.'s Scarborough, Ontario plant set their own agenda. The manufacturer of electronic controls has reaped many benefits from such work teams, such as the elimination of the majority of its quality control inspectors as teams monitor their own work.[10]

had been strained. "We have tried to build an environment where anyone can walk in and you wouldn't know who is a unionized employee and who is management—no reserved parking spaces or suits and ties," says John MacMillan, director of manufacturing at Honeywell Ltd., who spearheaded the team concept. A shared commitment to improving workers' skills has helped the union and management to work together. The "Learning for Life" education program was launched with courses such as computer technology and English as a second language.[6]

For any company, team-based systems yield many benefits and, of course, cause many challenges. On the upside, workers at Honeywell who once performed a single task have become multiskilled and thus perform a variety of tasks, including some management activities.[7] As a result, workers earn higher wages. Further, job rotation, which is part of Honeywell's team-based design, has helped to reduce the incidence of repetitive strain injuries at the plant.[8] In addition, team members enjoy more control over their own work.

However, on the downside, not everyone at Honeywell was thrilled with the switch to teams. Some managers felt understandably threatened as they saw their authority dissipate. And yet, it is well understood by management theorists that support and information sharing by management is key to the success of self-managed work teams. "At Honeywell, 35 teams draw members from various parts of the plant. They include engineers, skilled tradespeople, maintenance workers, electricians, materials planners, purchasing staff, and others. No departmental kahunas required. The old style of supervisor is obsolete—now they are 'coaches' or 'facilitators.' "[9]

Honeywell Ltd.
www.honeywell.com

The practice of relying on teams of people working in concert seems to have been a key to improved efficiency at Honeywell Ltd. The company's employees and management share a strong concern for their work, and they want to produce quality products. What is it that makes groups of employees like those at Honeywell so successful? Are all such work teams effective, or is this case unusual? How should such groups be formed? What problems might be expected and how can they be overcome? These questions are all basic to the topics of *group dynamics* and *teamwork*, the two major foci of this chapter.

Group dynamics focuses on the nature of groups—the variables governing their formation and development, their structure, and their interrelationships with individuals, other groups, and the organizations within which they exist.[11] **Teamwork** refers to the practice of using teams, special kinds of groups in which members are mutually committed to some goal, and share the leadership toward attaining it. Given the prevalence of groups in organizations, and the growing popularity of teams, the importance of these topics in the field of organizational behaviour is easy to appreciate.

Because groups exist in all types of social settings, the study of group dynamics has a long history in the social sciences—including OB.[12] In this chapter we will draw upon this work. Specifically, we will describe the nature of groups by defining what groups are, identifying various types of groups and why they form, explaining the various stages through which groups develop, and describing the dynamics of the way groups are structured. Following this, we will shift our attention to how effectively groups operate. Specifically, we will describe how people are affected by the presence of others, how the cultural makeup of a group affects performance, and the tendency for people to withhold their individual performance under certain conditions. Then, in the second half of the chapter we will describe special kinds of groups known as *teams*. Specifically, we will define teams and distinguish them from groups, describe various types of teams that exist, and identify some basic steps in creating teams. Finally, we will describe the performance of teams, examining the evidence regarding team effectiveness, the obstacles that sometimes lead teams to fail, and tips for making teams reach high levels of performance.

group dynamics The social science field focusing on the nature of groups—the factors governing their formation and development, the elements of their structure, and their interrelationships with individuals, other groups, and organizations.

teamwork The practice of working in teams (see *team*).

Groups at Work: Their Basic Nature

To understand the dynamics of groups and their influence on individual and organizational functioning, we must begin by raising some basic questions—namely, what is a group, what types of groups exist, why do people join groups, how do groups come into being, and how are groups structured? We will now address these questions.

What Is a Group? A Working Definition

Imagine three people waiting in line at the cashier's stand at a supermarket. Now compare them to the board of directors of a large corporation. Which collection would you consider to be a "group"? Although in our everyday language we may refer to the people waiting in line as a group, they are not a group in the same sense as the members of the board. Obviously, a group is more than simply a collection of people. But, what exactly is it that makes a group a group? Social scientists have formally defined a **group** as a collection of two or more interacting individuals with a stable pattern of relationships between them who share common goals and who perceive themselves as being a group.[13] To help us examine this definition more closely, we summarize the four key characteristics of groups in Figure 8-2.

One of the most obvious characteristics of groups is that they are composed of *two or more people in social interaction*. In other words, the members of a group must have some influence on each other. The interaction between the parties may be either verbal (such as sharing strategies for a corporate takeover) or nonverbal (such as exchanging smiles in the hallway), but the parties must have some impact on each other to be considered a group.

group A collection of two or more interacting individuals who maintain stable patterns of relationships, share common goals, and perceive themselves as being a group.

FIGURE 8-2 A Group: Its
Defining Characteristics

To be a group, four different criteria must be met: There must be
two or more people in social interaction, they must also share
common goals, have a stable
group structure, and perceive
themselves as being a group.

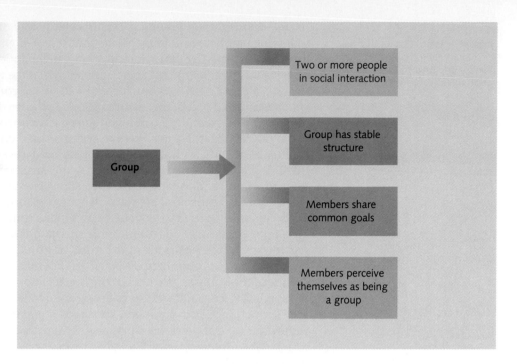

Groups also must possess a *stable structure*. Although groups can change, and
often do, there must be some stable relationships that keep group members together
and functioning as a unit. A collection of individuals that constantly changes (e.g.,
the people inside an office waiting room at any given time) cannot be thought of
as a group. To be a group, a greater level of stability would be required.

A third characteristic of groups is that their *members share common interests or goals*.
For example, members of a stamp collecting club constitute a group that is sustained
by the mutual interest of members. Some groups form because members with
common interests help each other achieve a mutual goal. For example, the owners
and employees of a sewing shop constitute a group formed around a common interest in sewing, and the common goal of making money.

Finally, to be a group, the individuals involved must *perceive themselves as a group*.
Groups are composed of people who recognize each other as members of their group
and can distinguish these individuals from nonmembers. The members of a corporate finance committee or a chess club, for example, know who is in their group and
who is not. In contrast, shoppers in a checkout line probably don't think of each
other as being members of a group. Although they stand physically close to each
other and may have passing conversations, they have little in common (except, perhaps, a shared interest in reaching the end of the line) and fail to identify themselves
with the others in the line.

By defining groups in terms of these four characteristics, we have identified a
group as a very special collection of individuals. As we shall see, these characteristics
are responsible for the important effects groups have on organizational behaviour.
To better understand these effects, we will now review the wide variety of groups that
operate within organizations.

Types of Groups

What do the following have in common: a military combat unit, three couples getting together for dinner, the board of directors of a large corporation, and the
three-person cockpit crew of a commercial airliner? As you probably guessed, the answer is that they are all groups. But, of course, they are very different kinds of groups,
ones people join for different reasons.

formal groups Groups that are created by the organization, intentionally designed to direct its members toward some organizational goal.

Formal and informal groups.   The most basic way of identifying types of groups is to distinguish between *formal groups* and *informal groups* (see Figure 8-3). **Formal groups** are created by the organization and are intentionally designed to direct members toward some important organizational goal. One type of formal group is referred to as a *command group*—a group determined by the connections between individuals who are a formal part of the organization (i.e., those who can legitimately give orders to others). For example, a command group may be formed by the vice-president of marketing who gathers together her regional marketing directors from around the country to hear their ideas about a new national advertising campaign. The point is that command groups are determined by the organization's rules regarding who reports to whom, and usually consist of a supervisor and his or her subordinates.

A formal organizational group also may be formed around some specific task. Such a group is referred to as a *task group*. Unlike command groups, a task group may be composed of individuals with some special interest or expertise in a specific area regardless of their positions in the organizational hierarchy. For example, a company may have a committee on equal employment opportunities whose members monitor the fair hiring practices of the organization. It may be composed of personnel specialists, corporate vice-presidents, and workers from the shop floor. Whether they are permanent committees, known as *standing committees*, or temporary ones formed for special purposes (such as a committee formed to recommend solutions to a parking problem), known as *ad hoc committees* or *task forces*, task groups are common in organizations.

informal groups Groups that develop naturally among people, without any direction from the organization within which they operate.

As you know, not all groups found in organizations are as formal as those we've identified. Many groups are informal in nature. **Informal groups** develop naturally among an organization's personnel without any direction from the management of the organization within which they operate. One key factor in the formation of informal groups is a common interest shared by its members. For example, a group of employees who band together to seek union representation, or who march together to protest their company's pollution of the environment, may be called an *interest group*. The common goal sought by members of an interest group may unite workers at many different organizational levels. The key factor is that membership in an interest group is voluntary—it is not created by the organization, but encouraged by an expression of common interests.

Of course, sometimes the interests that bind individuals together are far more diffuse. Groups may develop out of a common interest in participating in sports, or going to the movies, or just getting together to talk. These kinds of informal groups are known as *friendship groups*. A group of coworkers who hang out together during lunch may also bowl or play cards together after work. Friendship groups extend beyond the workplace because they provide opportunities for satisfying the social needs of workers that are so important to their well-being.

FIGURE 8-3 Varieties of Groups in Organizations

Within organizations one may find formal groups (such as *command groups* and *task groups*) and informal groups (such as *interest groups* and *friendship groups*).

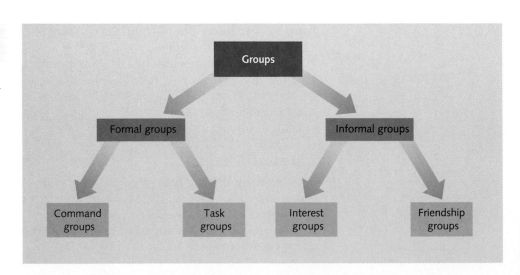

Informal work groups are an important part of life in organizations. Although they develop without direct encouragement from management, friendships often originate out of formal organizational contact. For example, three employees working alongside each other on an assembly line may get to talking and discover their mutual interest in basketball and decide to get together to shoot hoops after work. As we will see, such friendships can bind people together, helping them cooperate with each other, having beneficial effects on organizational functioning.

Why Do People Join Groups?

We have already noted that people often join groups to satisfy their mutual interests and goals. To the extent that getting together with others allows us to achieve ends that would not be possible alone, forming groups makes a great deal of sense. In fact, organizations can be thought of as collections of groups that are focused toward achieving the mutual goal of achieving success for the company. But, this is not the only motivation that people have for joining groups. There are also several additional reasons (see the summary in Table 8-1).

Not only do groups form for purposes of mutually achieving goals, they also frequently form for purposes of seeking protection from other groups. If you've ever heard the phrase, "there's safety in numbers," you are probably already aware that people join groups because they seek the security of group membership. Historically, for example, trade unions, such as CUPE and CAW, have been formed by labour for purposes of seeking protection against abuses by management. Similarly, professional associations, such as the Canadian Medical Association and the Canadian Bar Association were created, in large part, for purposes of protecting their constituents against undesirable governmental legislation.

This is not to say that groups are always designed to promote some instrumental good; indeed, they also exist because they appeal to a basic psychological need to be social. As we already discussed in the context of Maslow's need hierarchy theory (in Chapter 5), people are social animals; they have a basic need to interact with others. Groups provide good opportunities for friendships to develop—hence, for social needs to be fulfilled.

☛ We discussed the importance of social needs and esteem needs in conjunction with our description of Maslow's need hierarchy theory in Chapter 5.

Also as suggested by Maslow, people have a basic desire for their self-esteem to be fulfilled. Group memberships can be a very effective way of nurturing self-esteem. For example, if a group to which one belongs is successful (such as a sales group that meets its quota), the self-esteem of all members (and supporters) may be boosted. Similarly, election to membership in an exclusive group (e.g., a national honour society) will surely raise one's self-esteem.

As we have shown, people are attracted to groups for many different reasons. Despite the fact that people may have different motives for forming groups, it is interesting to note that once formed, groups develop in remarkably similar ways. We will now turn our attention to this issue.

Stages in the Development of Groups

Just as infants develop in certain ways during their first months of life, groups also show relatively stable signs of maturation and development.[14] One popular theory

TABLE 8-1 Why do people join groups? Some major reasons

People become members of groups for a variety of different reasons. Any one or more of the following may explain why people join groups.

Reason	Explanation
• To satisfy mutual interests and goals	By banding together, people can share their interests (e.g., hobbies) and help meet their mutual goals.
• To achieve security	Groups provide safety in numbers, protection against a common enemy.
• To fill social needs	Being in groups helps satisfy people's basic need to be with others.
• To fill need for self-esteem	Membership in certain groups provides people with opportunities to feel good about their accomplishments.

identifies five distinct stages through which groups develop.[15] As we describe these below, you may want to review our summary of the five stages shown in Figure 8-4.

The first stage of group development is known as *forming*. During this stage, the members get acquainted with each other. They establish the ground rules by trying to find out what behaviours are acceptable, with respect to both the job (how productive they are expected to be) and interpersonal relations (who's really in charge). During the *forming* stage, people tend to be a bit confused and uncertain about how to act in the group and how beneficial it will be to become a member of the group. Once the individuals come to think of themselves as members of a group, the forming stage is complete.

The second stage of group development is referred to as *storming*. As the name implies, this stage is characterized by a high degree of conflict within the group. Members often resist the control of the group's leaders and show hostility toward each other. If these conflicts are not resolved and group members withdraw, the group may disband. However, as conflicts are resolved and the group's leadership is accepted, the storming stage is complete.

The third stage of group development is known as *norming*. During this stage, the group becomes more cohesive, and identification as a member of the group becomes greater. Close relationships develop, shared feelings become common, and a keen interest in finding mutually agreeable solutions develops. Feelings of camaraderie and shared responsibility for the group's activities are heightened. The norming stage is complete when the members of the group accept a common set of expectations that constitutes an acceptable way of doing things.

The fourth stage is known as *performing*. By this stage, questions about group relationships and leadership have been resolved and the group is ready to work. Having fully developed, the group may now devote its energy to getting the job done—the group's good relations and acceptance of the leadership helps the group perform well.

Recognizing that not all groups last forever, the final stage is known as *adjourning*. Groups may cease to exist because they have met their goals and are no longer needed (such as an ad hoc group created to raise money for a charity project), in which case the end is abrupt. Other groups may adjourn gradually, as the group disintegrates, either because members leave or because the norms that have developed are no longer effective for the group.

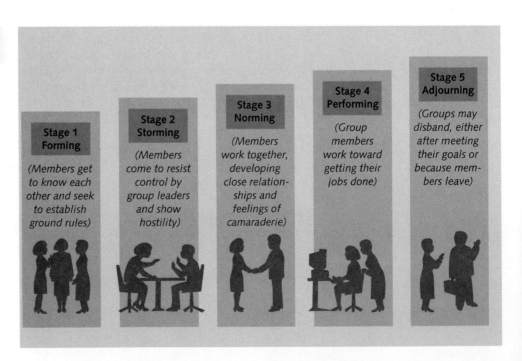

FIGURE 8-4 The Five Stages of Group Development

In general, groups develop according to the five stages summarized here.

(Source: Based on information in Tuckman & Jensen, 1977; see Note 15.)

Stage 1 Forming

(Members get to know each other and seek to establish ground rules)

Stage 2 Storming

(Members come to resist control by group leaders and show hostility)

Stage 3 Norming

(Members work together, developing close relationships and feelings of camaraderie)

Stage 4 Performing

(Group members work toward getting their jobs done)

Stage 5 Adjourning

(Groups may disband, either after meeting their goals or because members leave)

To illustrate these various stages, imagine that you have just joined several of your colleagues on your company's newly created budget committee. At first, you and your associates feel each other out: You watch to see who comes up with the best ideas, whose suggestions are most widely accepted, who seems to take charge, and the like (the forming stage). Then, as members struggle to gain influence over others, you may see a battle over control of the committee (the storming stage). Soon, this will be resolved, and an accepted leader will emerge. At this stage, the group members will become highly cooperative, working together in harmony, and doing things together, such as going out to lunch as a group (the norming stage). Now, it becomes possible for committee members to work together at doing their best, giving it their all (the performing stage). Then, once the budget is created and approved, the group's task is over, and it is disbanded (the adjourning stage).

It is important to keep in mind that groups can be in any one stage of development at any given time. Moreover, the amount of time a group may spend in any given stage is highly variable. In fact, research has revealed that the boundaries between the various stages may not be clearly distinct and that several stages may be combined—especially as deadline pressures force groups to take action.[16] It is best, then, to think of this five-stage model as a general framework of group formation. Although many of the stages may be followed, the dynamic nature of groups makes it unlikely that they will progress through the various stages in a completely predictable order.

The Structure of Work Groups

As noted earlier, one of the key characteristics of a group is its stable structure. When social scientists use the term **group structure**, they are referring to the interrelationships among the individuals constituting a group, the characteristics that make group functioning orderly and predictable. In this section, we will describe four different aspects of group structure: the various parts played by group members (*roles*), the rules and expectations that develop within groups (*norms*), the prestige of group membership (*status*), and the members' sense of belonging (*cohesiveness*).

Roles: The many hats we wear. One of the primary structural elements of groups is members' tendencies to play specific roles in group interaction, often more than one (see Figure 8-5). Social scientists use the term "role" in much the same way as a director of a play would refer to the character who plays a part. Indeed, the part one plays in the overall group structure is what we mean by a role. More formally, we may define a **role** as the typical behaviours that characterize a person in a social context.[17]

In organizations, many roles are assigned by virtue of an individual's position within an organization. For example, a boss may be expected to give orders, and a teacher may be expected to lecture and to give exams. These are behaviours expected of the individual in that role. The person holding the role is known as a **role incumbent**, and the behaviours expected of that person are known as **role expectations**. The person holding the office of the prime minister of Canada (the role incumbent) has certain role expectations simply because he or she currently has that post. When a new prime minister takes office, that person assumes the same role and has the same formal powers as the previous prime minister.

The role incumbent's recognition of the expectations of his or her role helps avoid the social disorganization that surely would result if clear role expectations did not exist. Sometimes, however, workers may be confused about the things that are expected of them on the job, such as their level of authority or their responsibility. Such **role ambiguity**, as it is called, is typically experienced by new members of organizations who have not had much of a chance to "learn the ropes," and often results in job dissatisfaction, a lack of commitment to the organization, and an interest in leaving the job.[18]

As work groups and social groups develop, the various group members come to play different roles in the social structure—a process referred to as **role differentiation**.

☞ The topics of power and leadership in organizations will be discussed in Chapters 12 and 13, respectively.

group structure The pattern of interrelationships among the individuals constituting a group; the guidelines of group behaviour that make group functioning orderly and predictable.

role The typical behaviour that characterizes a person in a specific social context.

role incumbent A person holding a particular role.

role expectations The behaviours expected of someone in a particular role.

☞ We will discuss the topic of formal power more extensively in Chapter 12.

role ambiguity Confusion arising from not knowing what one is expected to do as the holder of a role.

role differentiation The tendency for various specialized roles to emerge as groups develop.

FIGURE 8-5 Playing Roles: Wearing Several Different Hats

The roles people play in organizations represent specific sets of behaviours that characterize their positions. It is not unusual for people to have to play more than one role at a time.

(Source: Copyright © 1992 by Henry R. Martin. Reprinted by permission.)

The emergence of different roles in groups is a naturally occurring process. Think of committees to which you have belonged. Was there someone who joked and made people feel better, and another member who worked hard to get the group to focus on the issue at hand? These examples of differentiated roles are typical of role behaviours that emerge in groups. Organizations, for example, often have their "office comedian" who makes everyone laugh, or the "company gossip" who shares others' secrets, or the "company historian" who tells newcomers the stories about the company's "good old days."

Group researchers long ago found that one person may emerge who, more than anyone else, helps the group reach its goal.[19] Such a person is said to play the *task-oriented role*. In addition, another group member may emerge who is quite supportive and nurturant, someone who makes everyone else feel good. Such a person is said to play a *socioemotional (or relations-oriented) role*. Still others may be recognized for the things they do for themselves, often at the expense of the group—individuals recognized for playing a *self-oriented role*. Many specific role behaviours can fall into one or another of these categories. Some of these more specific subroles are listed in Table 8-2. Although this simple distinction will help us understand some of the roles found in work groups, we should note that more complex conceptualizations have been proposed, including one that identifies as many as 26 different roles.[20] These efforts at understanding role differentiation, regardless of how simple or complex the distinctions may be, help make the point that similarities between groups may be recognized by the common roles members play.

Norms: A group's unspoken rules. One feature of groups that enhances their orderly functioning is the existence of group norms. **Norms** may be defined as generally agreed upon informal rules that guide group members' behaviour.[21] They represent shared ways of viewing the world. Norms differ from organizational rules in that they are not formal and written. In fact, group members may not even be aware of the subtle group norms that exist and regulate their behaviour. Yet, they have profound effects. Norms regulate the behaviour of groups in important ways, such as by fostering workers' honesty and loyalty to the company, establishing appropriate ways to dress, and dictating when it is acceptable to be late for or absent from work.

norms Generally agreed on informal rules that guide group members' behaviour.

TABLE 8-2 Some Roles Commonly Played by Group Members

Organizational roles may be differentiated into task-oriented, relations-oriented (or socioemotional), and self-oriented roles—each of which has several subroles. A number of these are shown here.

(Source: Based on Benne & Sheats, 1948; see Note 19.)

Task-oriented roles	Relations-oriented roles	Self-oriented roles
Initiator-contributors	Harmonizers	Blockers
Recommend new solutions to group problems	*Mediate group conflicts*	*Act stubborn and resistant to the group*
Information seekers	Compromisers	Recognition seekers
Attempt to obtain the necessary facts	*Shift own opinions to create group harmony*	*Call attention to their own achievements*
Opinion givers	Encouragers	Dominators
Share own opinions with others	*Praise and encourage others*	*Assert authority by manipulating the group*
Energizers	Expediters	Avoiders
Stimulate the group into action whenever interest drops	*Suggest ways the group can operate more smoothly*	*Maintain distance, isolate themselves from fellow group members*

If you recall the pressures placed on you by your peers as you grew up to dress or wear your hair in certain styles, you are well aware of the profound normative pressures exerted by groups. Norms can be either *prescriptive*—dictating the behaviours that should be performed—or *proscriptive*—dictating the behaviours that should be avoided. For example, groups may develop prescriptive norms to follow their leader or to help a group member who needs assistance. They also may develop proscriptive norms to avoid absences or to refrain from telling each other's secrets to the boss. Sometimes the pressure to conform to norms is subtle, as in the dirty looks given a manager by his peers for dressing too casually for the job. Other times, normative pressures may be quite severe, such as when one production worker sabotages another's work because he is performing at too high a level, making his coworkers look bad.

The question of how group norms develop has been of considerable interest to organizational researchers.[22] An insightful analysis of this process has been presented by Feldman (see summary in Table 8-3).[23] First, norms develop because of *precedents set over time*. Whatever behaviours emerge at a first group meeting will usually set the standard for how that group is to operate. Initial group patterns of behaviour frequently become normative, such as where people sit and how formal or informal the meeting will be. Such routines help establish a predictable, orderly interaction pattern.

Second, norms develop because of *carryovers from other situations*. Group members usually draw from their previous experiences to guide their behaviours in new situations. The norms governing professional behaviour apply here. For example, the norm for a physician to behave ethically and to exercise a pleasant bedside manner is generalizable from one hospital to another. Such carryover norms can assist in making interaction easier in new social situations.

Third, sometimes norms also develop in *response to an explicit statement by a superior or coworker*. Newcomers to groups quickly "learn the ropes" when someone tells them, "That's the way we do it around here." This explanation is an explicit statement of the norms; it describes what one should do or avoid doing to be accepted by the group. Often, the explicit statement of group norms represents the accepted desires of more powerful or experienced group members.[24]

Fourth and finally, group norms may develop out of *critical events in the group's history*. If an employee releases an important organizational secret to a competitor, causing a loss to the company, a norm to maintain secrecy may develop out of this incident. For an example of this type of norm, see THE ETHICS ANGLE.

Status: The prestige of group membership.   Have you ever been attracted to a group because of the prestige accorded its members? You may have wanted to join a certain fraternity or sorority because it is highly regarded by the students. Students hoping to attend a certain university may look forward to wearing that school's insignia on their clothing. No doubt, members of Grey Cup–winning football teams proudly sport their Grey Cup rings to identify themselves as members of a championship team. Clearly, one potential reward of group membership is the status associated with being in that group. Even within social groups, different members are accorded different levels of prestige. Fraternity and sorority officers, and committee chairpersons, for example, may be recognized as more important members of their

☛ The process of organizational socialization, discussed in Chapter 7, examines how people "learn the ropes" in a new organization.

TABLE 8-3 Norms: How Do They Develop?

This table summarizes four ways in which group norms can develop.

(Source: Based on Feldman, 1984; see Note 23.)

Basis of Norm Development	Example
1. Precedents set over time	Seating location of each group member around a table
2. Carryovers from other situations	Professional standards of conduct
3. Explicit statements from others	Working a certain way because you are told "that's how we do it around here"
4. Critical events in group history	After the organization suffers a loss due to one person's divulging company secrets, a norm develops to maintain secrecy

The Norm for Punishing Unethical Behaviour at IBM

If you're an employee of IBM, even a high-level manager, chances are good that if you get caught violating ethical principles you will not be demoted or transferred, but fired. The norm to take swift and decisive action toward those who break moral rules developed years ago when then-President Thomas J. Watson Jr. learned a hard lesson about the consequences of turning a blind eye to unethical behaviour.[25]

On one occasion, some IBM plant managers started a chain letter—a "pyramid" scam in which they sent U.S. savings bonds to five other employees, who would write to five others, who would send bonds back to the sender, and so on. Such schemes generally only benefit the people at the beginning of the chain. One day, after a recipient of one of the letters complained to Watson, he brought it to the attention of the division head. This individual admitted

that the managers' actions were improper and ordered them to stop. But, he chose not to fire the offenders. Watson didn't agree with that decision but decided to let the matter rest.

Unfortunately, this came back to haunt him. Years later in the same division, a low-level employee was fired after he was caught selling engineering diagrams to a competitor. The employee was outraged and did his best to publicly humiliate Watson. Among the things that angered the fired employee was that years earlier the company had failed to fire the higher-ranking managers for their improper acts. Although two wrongs might not make a right, the employee was indignant about the apparent double standard.

After this incident occurred, Watson was quick to overrule division heads who failed to fire those who violated ethical standards. Following Watson's lead, and the lesson he learned from this critical incident, the norm developed at IBM to fire employees at any level who violate ethical standards—a norm that is said to exist to this day.

---

status The relative prestige, social position, or rank given to groups or individuals by others.

status symbols Objects reflecting the position of any individual within an organization's hierarchy of power.

respective groups. This is the idea behind **status**—the relative social position or rank given to groups or group members by others.[26]

Within most organizations, status may be recognized as both formal and informal in nature. *Formal status* refers to attempts to differentiate between the degrees of formal authority given employees by an organization. This is typically accomplished through the use of **status symbols**—objects reflecting the position of an individual within an organization's hierarchy. Some examples of status symbols include job titles (e.g., Director); perquisites, or perks, (e.g., a reserved parking space); the opportunity to do desirable and highly regarded work (e.g., serving on important committees); and luxurious working conditions (e.g., a large, private office that is lavishly decorated).[27]

Status symbols help groups in many ways.[28] For one, such symbols remind organizational members of their relative roles, thereby reducing uncertainty and providing stability to the social order (e.g., your small desk reminds you of your lower organizational rank). In addition, they provide assurance of the various rewards available to those who perform at a superior level (e.g., "maybe one day I'll have a reserved parking spot"). They also provide a sense of identification by reminding members of the group's values (e.g., a gang's jacket may remind its wearer of his expected loyalty and boldness). It is, therefore, not surprising that organizations do much to reinforce formal status through the use of status symbols.

Symbols of *informal status* within organizations are also widespread. These refer to the prestige accorded individuals with certain characteristics that are not formally dictated by the organization. For example, employees who are older and more experienced may be perceived as higher in status by their coworkers. Those who have special skills (such as the home-run hitters on a baseball team) also may be regarded as having higher status than others. In some organizations, the lower value placed on the work of women and members of minority groups by some individuals also can be considered an example of informal status in operation.[29]

One of the best-established findings in the study of group dynamics is that higher-status people tend to be more influential than lower-status people. This phenomenon may be seen in a classic study of decision making in three-man bomber crews.[30] After the crews had difficulty solving a problem, the experimenter planted clues to the solution with either a low-status group member (the tail gunner) or a high-status group member (the pilot). It was found that the solutions offered by the pilots were far more likely to be adopted than the same solutions presented by the tail gunners. Apparently, the greater status accorded the pilots (because they tended to be more experienced and hold higher military ranks) was responsible for the greater influence they wielded. Similar findings have been obtained in analyses of jury deliberations. Research in this area has shown that members of juries having high-status jobs (such as professional people) tend to exert greater influence over their fellow jurors than others holding lower occupational status.[31]

Cohesiveness: Getting the team spirit.   One obvious determinant of any group's structure is its **cohesiveness**—the strength of group members' desires to remain part of their groups. Highly cohesive work groups are ones in which the members are attracted to each other, accept the group's goals, and work toward meeting them. In very uncohesive groups, the members dislike each other and may even work at cross-purposes.[32] In essence, cohesiveness refers to a "we" feeling, an "esprit de corps," a sense of belonging to a group.

cohesiveness The strength of group members' desires to remain part of their groups.

Several important factors have been shown to influence the extent to which group members tend to "stick together." One such factor involves the severity of initiation into the group. Research has shown that the greater the difficulty people overcome to become a member of a group, the more cohesive the group will be.[33] To understand this, consider how highly cohesive certain groups may be that you have worked hard to join. Was it particularly difficult to "make the cut" on your sports team? The rigorous requirements for gaining entry into elite groups, such as the most prestigious medical schools, may well be responsible for the high degree of camaraderie found in such groups. Having "passed the test" tends to keep individuals together and separates them from those who are unwilling or unable to "pay the price" of admission.

Group cohesion also tends to be strengthened under conditions of high external threat or competition. When workers face a "common enemy," they tend to draw together. Such cohesion not only makes workers feel safer and better protected, but also aids them by encouraging them to work closely together and to coordinate their efforts toward the common enemy. Under such conditions, petty disagreements that may have caused dissension within groups tend to be put aside so that a coordinated attack on the enemy can be mobilized.

Research also has shown that the cohesiveness of groups is established by several additional factors.[34] For one, cohesiveness generally tends to be greater the more time group members spend together. Obviously, limited interaction cannot help but interfere with opportunities to develop bonds between group members. Similarly, cohesiveness tends to be greater in smaller groups. Generally speaking, groups that are too large make it difficult for members to interact and, therefore, for cohesiveness to reach a high level. Finally, because "nothing succeeds like success," groups with a history of success tend to be highly cohesive. It is often said that "everyone loves a winner," and the success of a group tends to help unite its members as they rally around their success. For this reason, employees tend to be loyal to successful companies.

Although we often hear about the benefits of highly cohesive groups, the consequences of cohesiveness are not always positive. In fact, research has shown both positive and negative effects of cohesiveness (see Figure 8-6). On the positive side, people are known to enjoy belonging to highly cohesive groups. Members of closely knit work groups participate more fully in their group's activities, more readily accept their group's goals, and are absent from their jobs less often than members of less cohesive groups.[35] Not surprisingly, cohesive groups tend to work together quite well and are sometimes exceptionally productive. In fact, research has shown that high levels of group cohesiveness tend to be associated with low levels of voluntary turnover.[36]

FIGURE 8-6 Group Cohesiveness: Its Causes and Consequences

As summarized here, several factors contribute to a group's cohesiveness. High levels of cohesiveness may have both positive and negative consequences.

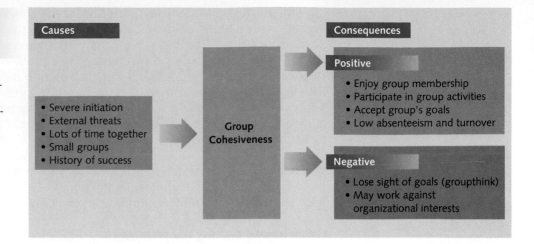

Because of the negative impact of groupthink on the quality of group decisions, we will discuss this phenomenon in greater detail in the context of decision making in Chapter 10.

People's willingness to work together quite well and to conform to the group's norms is often responsible for their success, and their willingness to stay with the group.[37]

However, the tendency for members of highly cohesive groups to go along with their fellow members' wishes sometimes has negative consequences for the ultimate group product. Poor decisions resulting from too high a level of cohesiveness reflect a phenomenon known as *groupthink*. Groupthink occurs when a group is so cohesive that its members potentially lose sight of its ultimate goals for fear of disrupting the group itself.[38] For example, in an impassioned article in the days leading up to a decision on the Meech Lake Accord, Jim Henderson, a Liberal MP from Ontario, wrote, "We need a heightened sense of individual accountability and a pulling away from partisan rhetoric, display, and groupthink. . . . Canadians are timid in this matter of party groupthink. . . . Reasoned voices of constructive dissent are a matter for caucus pride, not for embarrassment."[39] Henderson echoed a finding by the McGrath Special Committee on Reform of Canada's House of Commons, that identified party solidarity as an overly dominant feature of Canadian politics.[40]

Group cohesion can influence productivity in many additional ways. It makes sense that after a group experiences success, its members will feel more committed to each other. Similarly, we might expect a cohesive group to work well together and to achieve a high level of success. However, a work group whose members are strongly committed to each other does not necessarily perform well within an organization.[41] For example, if a group's goals are contrary to the organization's goals, a highly cohesive group may actually do a great deal of harm to an organization, working against its interests. Highly cohesive group members who conspire to sabotage their employers are a good example. Apparently, group cohesiveness can have either positive *or* negative effects on performance.

The Dynamics of Individual Performance in Groups

Now that we have reviewed the basic nature of groups and teams, we will turn to an aspect of group dynamics most relevant to the field of organizational behaviour—the effects of groups on individual performance. Specifically, we will take a look at three different issues in this connection. First, we will consider how people's work performance is affected by the presence of others. Second, we will examine how the composition of groups—in particular, their racial and ethnic diversity—affects performance. Third, we will describe how performance is affected by group size.

Social Facilitation: Individual Performance in the Presence of Others

Imagine that you have been studying drama for five years and you are now ready for your first acting audition in front of some movie producers. You have been rehearsing diligently for several months, getting ready for the part. Now you are no longer alone at home with your script in front of you. Your name is announced and silence fills the auditorium as you walk to the front of the stage. How will you perform now that you are in front of an audience? Will you freeze, forgetting the lines you studied so intensely when you practised alone? Or will the audience spur you on to your best performance yet? In other words, what impact will the presence of the audience have on your behaviour?

After studying this question for a century, using a wide variety of tasks and situations, social scientists found that the answer is not straightforward.[42] Sometimes people were found to perform better in the presence of others than when alone, and sometimes they were found to perform better alone than in the presence of others. This tendency for the presence of others to enhance an individual's performance at times and to impair it at other times is known as **social facilitation**. (Although the word "facilitation" implies improvements in task performance, scientists use the term "social facilitation" to refer to both performance improvements and decrements stemming from the presence of others.) What accounts for these seemingly contradictory findings?

Explaining social facilitation. According to Robert Zajonc, the matter boils down to several basic psychological processes.[43] First, Zajonc explained that social facilitation was the result of the heightened emotional arousal (e.g., feelings of tension and excitement) people experience when in the presence of others. (Wouldn't you feel more tension playing the piano in front of an audience than alone?) Second, when people are aroused, they tend to perform the most dominant response—their most likely behaviour in that setting. (Returning the smile of a smiling coworker may be considered an example of a dominant act; it is a very well learned act to smile at another who smiles at you.) If someone is performing a very well learned act, the dominant response would be a correct one (such as speaking the right lines during your fiftieth performance). However, if the behaviour in question is relatively novel, newly learned, the dominant response would likely be incorrect (such as speaking incorrect lines during an audition). Together, these ideas are known as Zajonc's **drive theory of social facilitation**.[44] According to this theory, the presence of others increases arousal, which increases the tendency to perform the most dominant responses. If these responses are correct, the resulting performance will he enhanced; if they are incorrect, the performance will be impaired. Based on these processes, performance either may be helped (if the task is well learned) or hindered (if the task is not well learned). (For a summary of this process see Figure 8-7.)

A considerable amount of research has shown support for this theory: People perform better on tasks in the presence of others if that task is very well learned, but poorer if it is not well learned. However, it is still unclear exactly *why* this effect occurs. Three positions receive a considerable amount of support. First, according to Zajonc, people become aroused simply because the others are there, what he calls their "mere presence." However, other scientists have modified Zajonc's approach, claiming that the arousal resulting from others is not due to the fact that others are simply there, but that these others can potentially evaluate the person. Their major idea, our second explanation, is that social facilitation results from **evaluation apprehension**—the fear of being evaluated or judged by another person.[45] Indeed, people may be aroused by performing a task in the presence of others because of their concern over what those others might think of them. For example, lower-level employees may suffer evaluation apprehension when they are worried about what their supervisor thinks of their work. Finally, a third explanation, known as the **distraction-conflict model** recognizes that the presence of others creates a conflict between paying attention to others and paying attention to the task at hand.[46]

social facilitation The tendency for the presence of others sometimes to enhance an individual's performance and at other times to impair it.

drive theory of social facilitation The theory according to which the presence of others increases arousal, which increases people's tendencies to perform the dominant response. If that response is well learned, performance will improve. But, if it is novel, performance will be impaired.

evaluation apprehension The fear of being evaluated or judged by another person.

distraction-conflict model A conceptualization explaining social facilitation in terms of the tendency for others' presence to cause a conflict between directing attention to others versus the task at hand.

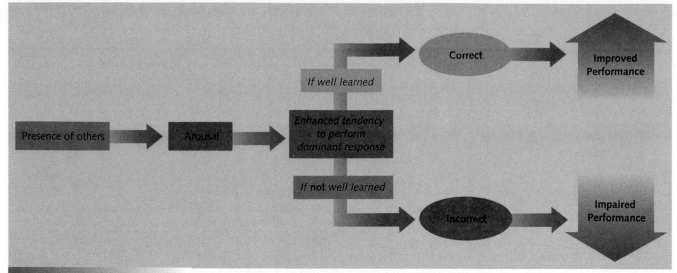

FIGURE 8-7 Social Facilitation: A Drive Theory Approach

Zajonc's *drive theory of social facilitation* states that the presence of others is arousing. This, in turn, enhances the tendency to perform the most dominant (i.e., strongest) responses. If these are correct (such as if the task is well learned), performance will be improved, but if these are incorrect (such as if the task is novel), performance will suffer.

computerized performance monitoring The process of using computers to monitor job performance.

The conflict created by these tendencies leads to increased arousal, which, in turn, leads to social facilitation. If you've ever tried doing a homework assignment while your friends or family watch TV nearby, you're probably already aware of the conflict that competing demands for your attention can create.

Although many researchers currently favour the distraction-conflict explanation of social facilitation, all three explanations provide some important insights into social facilitation. In other words, while the processes underlying social facilitation are somewhat unclear, the effect itself may have a profound influence on organizational behaviour.

Computerized performance monitoring: Social facilitation via an "electronic presence." If you read George Orwell's classic book *1984*, you will recall "Big Brother," the all-knowing power that monitored people's every moves. As often occurs, the science fiction of one era eventually becomes scientific fact in another. In the case of "Big Brother," in the workplace, at least, Orwell wasn't many years off in his predictions. The use of computers to monitor work performance today is becoming increasingly common. **Computerized performance monitoring** is already widely used in the insurance, banking, communications, and transportation industries, and it promises to become even more prevalent in tomorrow's organizations.[47] In view of this, it is important to learn about the effects of monitoring on people's job performance.

One way of understanding how computerized monitoring may influence performance is by extending our thinking about social facilitation. After all, instead of having an individual who is physically present to watch, this technique is akin to doing the same thing indirectly, by computer—an "electronic presence." Imagine, for example, that you are entering data into a computer terminal. You can be monitored in a direct physical way by an individual looking over your shoulder or indirectly by someone checking a computerized record of the speed and accuracy of your every keystroke. If the task being performed is a complex one, social facilitation research suggests that the physical presence of an observer would lead to reduced performance. But would the same thing occur when there is only an electronic presence?

A study by Aiello and Svec provides an answer to this question.[48] Participants in this research were college students who performed complex anagram tasks (unscrambling letters to form words) by entering their responses into a computer terminal. The conditions under which they performed this task were systematically varied by the researchers in several different ways, three of which are relevant here. One group of participants (the "control" condition) performed the task without anyone observing them work in any form. A second group (the "person monitored" condition) was monitored by stationing two female observers immediately behind them as they performed their task in front of the computer. Finally, a third group of subjects (the "computer monitoring" condition) was told that their performance would be monitored by people who could see their work on another computer to which theirs was connected on a network. (To make this convincing, participants were shown the other computer equipment.) Participants performed the task for 10 minutes, after which the researchers counted the number of anagrams solved correctly by people in each condition. A summary of these findings is shown in Figure 8-8.

As these data show, people performed worse when others were physically observing them (person monitored group) than when they performed the task alone (control group). This finding is in keeping with research and theory on social facilitation, according to which performance on complex tasks is expected to suffer when in the presence of others. Even more interesting is the finding that performance also suffered when it was monitored by computer—that is, even when people were not distracted by having others looking over their shoulders. Apparently, performance can suffer even when the presence of another is known to exist, although imperceptible.

These findings support the idea that social facilitation may be due to people's concerns about being evaluated negatively by another—that is, evaluation apprehension. In the case of the task at hand, participants in the study knew that their performance could be just as easily evaluated by watching a remote computer as by watching them directly. Accordingly, opportunities for evaluation existed in both conditions, possibly accounting for the apprehension that led to the performance decrements found.

There is also a very important applied implication of these results—namely, that the act of monitoring job performance to keep levels high may actually backfire. That is, instead of causing people to improve their performance (for fear of being caught doing poorly), monitoring might actually interfere with performance (by providing a distracting source of evaluation). Because participants in Aiello and Svec's study performed their tasks for only brief periods of time, we cannot tell whether people would eventually get used to the monitoring and improve their performance over time. However, until further research addresses this question, we must issue the following caution: Using computers to monitor work performance might impair the very performance monitoring is intended to improve. "Big Brother" just might be defeating his own purposes. (A growing trend in today's organizations involves using computers not only for monitoring performance, but also for bringing groups together electronically when they cannot be together physically. For a closer look at this practice, see the **ORGANIZATIONAL TRENDS** section.)

FIGURE 8-8 Computer Monitoring: Evidence of Its Counterproductive Effects

Participants in a recent study performed complex tasks either alone, or while being monitored by a computer or by two other people who were physically present. Consistent with other research on *social facilitation*, people performed the complex task worse in the presence of others than alone. They also performed more poorly when they were monitored by the "electronic presence" of a computer.

(Source: Based on data reported by Aiello & Svec, 1993; see Note 48.)

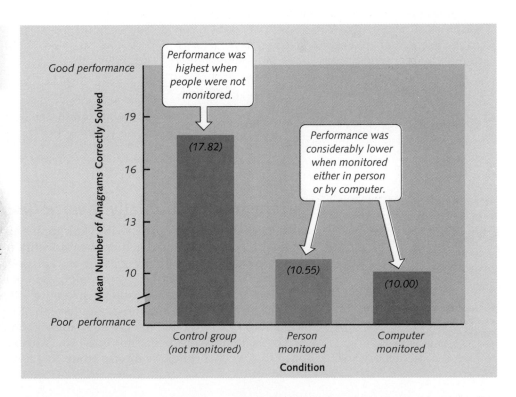

Videoconferencing: Groups in Cyberspace

If you've ever attempted to schedule a group meeting, then you surely know how difficult it can be to find a mutually acceptable time when several busy people can get together. This problem is compounded when the meeting involves people in distant locations. In such cases, we must consider not only the time spent meeting, but also the considerable downtime and expense associated with travel. With an eye toward reducing these obstacles, we are now beginning to see a technological advance that brings people together electronically, in "virtual" space, as opposed to physical space. It's called **videoconferencing**—the practice of using technology to provide audio and video links (either limited or full-motion) between work sites, allowing visual communication between people who are not physically present.

Although videoconferencing is still quite expensive and in limited use today, experts predict that it is likely to become more common in the future. If for no other reason, the savings in travel costs alone may make it cost effective. One company that has made this investment is Noranda Inc. With its staff travel costs at over $1 million per year, not to mention the cost of work time lost to travel, the company realized videoconferencing was a better alternative. Noranda has 25 videoconferencing locations in Canada and the U.S., and is planning to link in many of its worldwide sites. Bob Sayer, president of an Etobicoke, Ontario company that supplies videoconferencing equipment, says, "The only thing videoconferencing can't do is pass a coffee and some Timbits through the wire."[49]

Given the increased ease of coordination gained through videoconferencing, it is no surprise that some companies have used this technology to gain a competitive advantage. For example, Bata Shoes, with operations in 60 countries, has used videoconferencing to reduce its product-development time by some 90 percent.[50]

A more limited form of multimedia conferencing is **shared-screen conferencing**—connecting computer workstations so as to provide concurrent displays of information and interaction among several individuals.[51] Group members using this technology can call up a common document on their desktop computers and work on it at the same time. This might involve something simple, such as drafting a memo, or a more complex process, such as drawing a new design on a blackboard program. It's even possible for some members of the group to send completely private side-messages to each other, without the others knowing it—the high-tech equivalent of whispering something into another's ear.[52]

These emerging technologies are clearly still in their infancy, but they are becoming increasingly popular in many organizations. Although only large businesses may be able to afford the huge investment in videoconferencing equipment, even small companies can rent public videoconferencing facilities for as long as they need them. Several private businesses, such as many Kinko's locations, offer this service. And given how satisfied companies have been with these services, we may expect to see more videoconferencing in the future. As one management consultant put it, "Although the next decade does not promise the total replacement of face-to-face meetings with electronic togetherness, new varieties of computer-mediated interactions among people will nevertheless increase."[53]

Noranda Inc.
www.noranda.com

---

videoconferencing The practice of using technology to provide audio and video links (either limited or full-motion) between work sites, allowing visual communication between people who are not physically present.

shared-screen conferencing The process of connecting computer workstations so as to provide concurrent displays of information and interaction among several individuals.

Performance in Culturally Diverse Groups

For many years, the task of composing work groups involved finding individuals with the right blend of skills and getting them to work together—a task that was challenging enough. Today, however, as the workplace grows increasingly diverse with respect to the racial and ethnic group composition of its members, there's a new consideration. How does a group's cultural diversity affect its task performance? Although attempts to answer this question do not have the long history of research on social facilitation, recent research has provided some good insight.

For example, considering this question, Watson, Kumar, and Michaelsen reasoned that when a culturally diverse group first forms, its members will need time to be able to adjust to the racial and ethnic differences among them.[54] To the extent that people's differing perspectives and styles may interfere with their ability to work together, then task performance may be expected to suffer. As time goes on, however, and group members learn to interact with each other despite their different backgrounds, performance differences should disappear.

The researchers tested these hypotheses by assigning U.S. college students enrolled in a management class to two kinds of four-person groups. *Homogeneous groups* were composed of members from the same racial and ethnic background. *Diverse groups* were created by assembling groups consisting of one white American, one African American, one Hispanic American, and one non American. After being formed, the groups were asked to analyze business cases (a task with which management students were familiar). The groups worked on four occasions scheduled one month apart. Their analyses were then scored (using several different predetermined criteria) by experts who did not know which groups were diverse and which were homogeneous. How did following these two different recipes for group composition influence task performance? The data summarized in Figure 8-9 bear on this question.

As shown in Figure 8-9, the answer depends on the length of time the group had worked together. At first, the homogeneous group did considerably better than the diverse group. Then, during the second session these differences grew smaller. By the third session, the differences had almost completely disappeared, and by the fourth session they were gone (in fact, the diverse group even did slightly better than the homogeneous group). Although all groups improved their performance over time, as you would expect, the initial advantage of homogeneous groups was found to be only a temporary condition found in newly created groups. As group members had more experiences working with each other, the differences between them became less of a source of interference.

Because research on the effects of racial and ethnic group composition on task performance is just beginning, we do not yet know if these same results would hold for different kinds of tasks. We also don't know whether diverse groups would eventually perform even better than homogeneous ones. In fact, on tasks in which differing perspectives might help a group do its job, diverse groups may be expected to have an edge over heterogeneous ones. Although several key questions about the effects of diversity on group performance remain unanswered, the importance of this factor as a variable in group performance is clearly established.

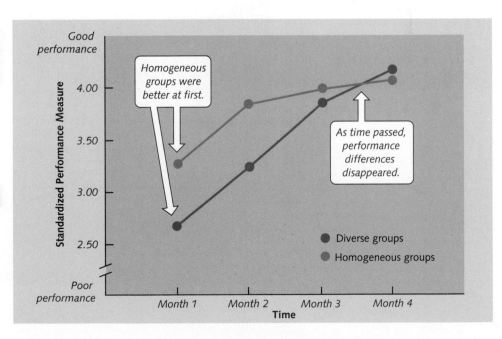

FIGURE 8-9 Task Performance in Culturally Diverse Groups: An Experimental Demonstration

An experiment found that although culturally diverse groups performed worse than homogeneous groups at first, these differences disappeared over time.

(Source: Based on data reported by Watson, Kumar, & Michaelsen, 1993; see Note 54.)

Social Loafing: "Free Riding" When Working with Others

Have you ever worked with several others helping a friend move into a new apartment, each carrying and transporting part of the load from the old place to the new one? Or, how about sitting around a table with others stuffing political campaign letters into envelopes and addressing them to potential donors? Although these tasks may seem quite different, they actually share an important common characteristic: Performing each requires only a single individual, but several people's work can be pooled to yield greater outcomes. Insofar as each person's contributions can be added together with another's, such tasks have been referred to as **additive tasks**.[55]

If you've ever performed additive tasks, such as the ones described here, there's a good chance that you found yourself working not quite as hard as you would have if you did them alone. Does this sound familiar to you? Indeed, a considerable amount of research has found that when several people combine their efforts on additive tasks, each individual contributes less than he or she would when performing the same task alone.[56] As suggested by the old saying "many hands make light the work," a group of people would be expected to be more productive than any one individual. However, when several people combine their efforts on additive tasks, each individual's contribution tends to be less. Five people working together raking leaves will *not* be five times more productive than a single individual working alone; there are always some who go along for a "free ride." In fact, the more individuals who are contributing to an additive task, the less each individual's contribution tends to be—a phenomenon known as **social loafing**.[57]

This effect was first noted almost 70 years ago by a German scientist named Max Ringelmann, who compared the amount of force exerted by different-sized groups of people pulling on a rope.[58] Specifically, he found that one person pulling on a rope alone exerted an average of 63 kilograms of force. However, in groups of three, the per-person force dropped to 53 kilograms, and in groups of eight it was reduced to only 31 kilograms per person—less than half the effort exerted by people working alone. Social loafing effects of this type have been observed in many different studies conducted in recent years.[59] The general form of the social loafing effect is portrayed in Figure 8-10.

additive tasks Types of group tasks in which the individual efforts of several people are added together to form the group's product.

social loafing The tendency for group members to exert less individual effort on an additive task as the size of the group increases.

FIGURE 8-10 Social Loafing: Its General Form

According to the social loafing effect, when individuals work together on an additive task, the more people contributing to the group's task, the less effort each individual exerts.

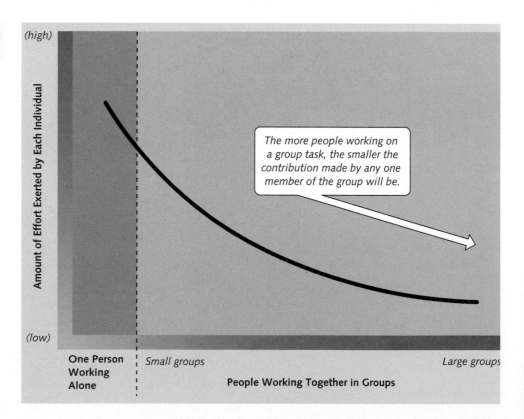

The more people working on a group task, the smaller the contribution made by any one member of the group will be.

social impact theory The theory that explains *social loafing* in terms of the diffused responsibility for doing what is expected of each member of a group. The larger the size of a group, the less each member is influenced by the social forces acting on the group.

The phenomenon of social loafing has been explained by **social impact theory**.[60] According to this theory, the impact of any social force acting on a group is divided equally among its members. The larger the size of the group, the less the impact of the force on any one member. As a result, the more people who might contribute to a group's product, the less pressure each person faces to perform well—that is, the responsibility for doing the job is diffused over more people. As a result, each group member feels less responsible for behaving appropriately, and social loafing occurs.

Although feeling less responsible for an outcome is clearly one possible explanation for the social loafing phenomenon, the effect also may result from other experiences likely to arise among people performing their jobs. For example, people may engage in social loafing because they feel that the presence of others makes their contributions less needed—that is, more dispensable. Demonstrating this phenomenon, Weldon and Mustari had college students perform a judgment task (e.g., assessing the desirability of a job as the basis of describing it to potential applicants) and told them either that they were the only ones performing the task or that their judgments would be one of two or one of sixteen judgments used to make a final assessment.[61] The experimenters reasoned that people who believed their judgments would be one of many would take their jobs less seriously, spending less time on the task and making less complex judgments. In fact, this is exactly what they found. The larger the size of the group, the more dispensable people believed their judgments were, and the less complex these judgments were found to be. These data strongly support the idea that social loafing occurs because people believe that in larger groups their contributions are less necessary than when working alone.

Is social loafing a universal phenomenon? A simple way of understanding social loafing is that it occurs because people are more interested in themselves (getting the most for themselves while doing the least) than their fellow group members (who are forced to do their work for them). That this phenomenon occurs in North America should not be particularly surprising in view of the tendency for our culture to be individualistic (i.e., individual accomplishments and personal success are highly valued). However, people in collectivistic nations, such as Israel and the People's Republic of China, place a high value on shared responsibility and the collective good of all. In collectivistic cultures, people working in groups would not be expected to engage in social loafing because doing so would have them fail in their social responsibility to the group (a responsibility that does not prevail in individualistic cultures). In fact, to the extent that people in collectivistic cultures are strongly motivated to help their fellow group members, they would be expected to be *more* productive in groups than alone. That is, not only wouldn't they loaf, but they would work especially hard.

☞ *The distinction between individualistic and collectivistic cultures is discussed in Chapter 2, in conjunction with Hofstede's cultural framework.*

An experiment by Earley tested these ideas.[62] In this research managers from the United States, Israel, and the People's Republic of China were each asked to complete an "in-basket" exercise. This task simulated the daily activities of managers in all three countries, such as writing memos, filling out forms, and rating job applicants. They were all asked to perform this task as well as they could for a period of one hour, but under one of two different conditions: either *alone*, or as part of a *group* of ten. Research participants who worked alone were simply asked to write their names on each item they completed and to turn it in. In the group condition participants were told that their group's overall performance would be assessed at the end of the performance period. Fellow group members were not physically present but were described as being highly similar to themselves with respect to their family and religious backgrounds as well as their interests. (Earley reasoned that groups of this type would be ones whose members people would be especially reluctant to let down by loafing.) To compare the various groups, Earley scored each participant's in-basket exercises by converting the responses to standardized performance scores. Did social loafing occur, and in which countries? The results are summarized in Figure 8-11.

These data clearly show that social loafing occurred in the United States. That is, individual performance was significantly lower among people working in groups

FIGURE 8-11 Social Loafing: Is It a Universal Phenomenon?

Research compared the group and individual performance of people performing a managerial task in three countries: the People's Republic of China, Israel, and the United States. Although individual performance alone was better than performance as part of a group in the United States (i.e., *social loafing* occurred), the opposite was found in China and Israel. The more *collectivistic* nature of these cultures discouraged people from letting down their fellow group members.

(Source: Based on data reported by Earley, 1993; see Note 62.)

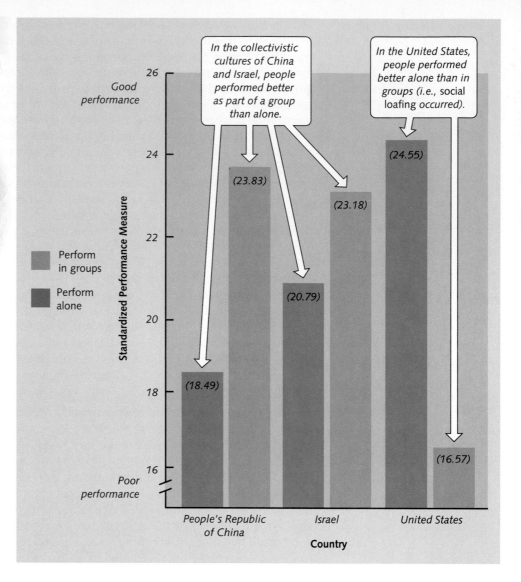

than those working alone. However, the opposite was found in each of the two highly collectivistic cultures, the People's Republic of China and Israel. In both these countries, individuals performed at higher levels when working in groups than when working alone. In these nations, people not only failed to loaf in groups, but they worked *harder* than they did when alone. Because they strongly identified with their groups and were concerned about the welfare of its members, members of collectivistic cultures placed their group's interests ahead of their own. (It is important to note that these findings only occurred when people believed that they had strong ties to the members of their groups.)

Earley's research suggests that culture plays an important part in determining people's tendencies to engage in social loafing. Although it is tempting to think of social loafing as an inevitable aspect of human nature, it appears that the phenomenon is not as universal as you might think. Instead, loafing appears to be a manifestation of cultural values: Among cultural groups in which individualism is stressed, individual interests guide performance, but among groups in which collectivism is stressed, group interests guide performance.

Tips for eliminating social loafing. Obviously, the tendency for people to reduce their effort when working with others could be a serious problem in organizations. Fortunately, research has shown that there are several ways in which social loafing can be overcome. One possible antidote to social loafing is to *make each performer identi-*

fiable. Social loafing may occur when people feel they can get away with "taking it easy"—namely, under conditions in which each individual's contributions cannot be determined. A variety of studies on the practice of "public posting" support this idea.[63] This research has found that when each individual's contribution to a task is displayed where it can be seen by others (e.g., weekly sales figures posted on a chart), people are less likely to slack off than when only overall group (or companywide) performance is made available. In other words, the more one's individual contribution to a group effort is highlighted, the more pressure each person feels to make a group contribution. Thus, social loafing can be overcome if one's contributions to an additive task are identified: Potential loafers are not likely to loaf if they fear getting caught.

Another way to overcome social loafing is to *make work tasks more important and interesting*. Research has revealed that people are unlikely to go along for a free ride when the task they are performing is believed to be vital to the organization.[64] For example, George found that the less meaningful salespeople believed their jobs were, the more they engaged in social loafing—especially when they thought their supervisors knew little about how well they were working.[65] To help in this regard, corporate officials should deliberately attempt to make jobs more intrinsically interesting to employees. To the extent that jobs are interesting, people may be less likely to loaf. It also has been suggested that managers should *reward individuals for contributing to their group's performance*—that is, encourage their interest in their group's performance.[66] Doing this (e.g., giving all salespeople in a territory a bonus if they jointly exceed their sales goal) may help employees focus more on collective concerns and less on individualistic concerns, increasing their obligations to their fellow group members. This is important, of course, in that the success of an organization is more likely to be influenced by the collective efforts of groups than by the individual contributions of any one member.

Another mechanism for overcoming social loafing is to *use punishment threats*. To the extent that performance decrements may be controlled by threatening to punish the individuals slacking off, loafing may be reduced. This effect was demonstrated in an experiment by Miles and Greenberg.[67] The participants in this study were members of high school swim teams who swam either alone or in relay races during practice sessions. In some conditions, the coach threatened the team by saying that everyone would have to swim "penalty laps" if anyone on the team failed to meet a specified difficult time for swimming 100 metres freestyle. In a control group, no punishment threats were issued. How did the punishment threats influence task performance? The researchers found that people swam faster alone than as part of relay teams when no punishment was threatened, thereby confirming the social loafing effect. However, when punishment threats were made, group performance increased, thereby eliminating the social loafing effect.

Together, these findings suggest that social loafing is a potent force—and one that can be a serious threat to organizational performance. But, it can be controlled in several ways that counteract the desire to loaf, such as by making loafing socially embarrassing or harmful to other individual interests.

☞ *As we discussed in Chapter 5, designing jobs so as to make them seem more important and interesting is also an effective way of enhancing motivation.*

Teams: Special Kinds of Groups

Now that you have a clear understanding of groups and how they operate, we can compare them to another type of collection of individuals known as *teams*. In this section we will define what is meant by teams and how they are different from groups. We will then describe various types of teams that may be found in organizations. Finally, we will present guidelines for creating teams in organizations

Defining Teams and Distinguishing Them from Groups

If you think about some of the groups we've described thus far in this chapter, such as the ones in use at Honeywell (in our CASE PREVIEW) and the hypothetical corporate budget committee described earlier, you'll probably realize that they are somehow

team A group whose members have complementary skills and are committed to a common purpose or set of performance goals for which they hold themselves mutually accountable.

different. Although they are each composed of several individuals working together toward common goals, the connections between the employees at Honeywell appear to be much deeper in scope. Although the budget-committee members may be interested in what they're doing, the group members at Honeywell seem more highly committed to their work and are more highly involved in the way their jobs are done. This is not to say that there is necessarily anything wrong with the corporate budget committee; in fact, it would appear to be a rather typical group. The groups at Honeywell, however, are examples of special kinds of groups known as *teams*. A **team** may be defined as a group whose members have complementary skills and are committed to a common purpose or set of performance goals for which they hold themselves mutually accountable.[68]

At this point, it is probably not entirely clear to you exactly how a team is different from an ordinary group. This confusion probably stems in part from the fact that people often refer to their groups as teams, although they are really not teams.[69] Yet, there are several important distinctions between them (see Figure 8-12).

First, in groups, performance typically depends on the work of individual members. The performance of a team, however, depends on both individual contributions and *collective work products*—the joint outcome of team members working in concert.

A second difference has to do with where accountability for the job lies. Typically, members of groups pool their resources to attain a goal, although it is individual performance that is taken into consideration when it comes to issuing rewards. Members of groups usually do not take responsibility for any results other than their own. By contrast, teams focus on both individual and *mutual accountability*. That is, they work together to produce an outcome (e.g., a product, service, or decision) that represents their joint contributions, and each team member shares responsibility for that outcome. The key difference is this: In groups, the supervisor holds individual members accountable for their work, whereas in teams, members hold themselves accountable.

FIGURE 8-12 Groups vs. Teams: A Comparison

Groups may be distinguished from teams in terms of the various characteristics summarized here.

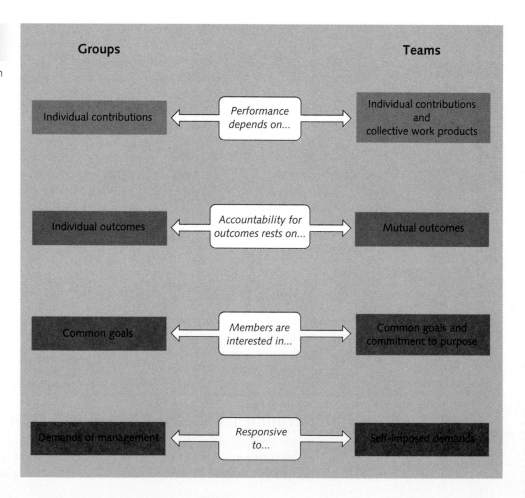

Groups		Teams
Individual contributions	Performance depends on...	Individual contributions and collective work products
Individual outcomes	Accountability for outcomes rests on...	Mutual outcomes
Common goals	Members are interested in...	Common goals and commitment to purpose
Demands of management	Responsive to...	Self-imposed demands

Third, whereas group members may share a common interest goal, team members also share a *common commitment to purpose*. Moreover, these purposes typically are concerned with winning in some way, such as being first or best at something. For example, a work team in a manufacturing plant of a financially troubled company may be highly committed to making the company the top one in its industry. Another team, one in a high school, may be committed to preparing all its graduates for the challenges of the world better than any other school in the area. Team members focusing jointly on such lofty purposes, in conjunction with specific performance goals, become heavily invested in the team's activities. In fact, teams are said to establish "ownership" of their purposes, and usually spend a great deal of time establishing their purposes. Like groups, teams use goals to monitor their progress. Teams, however, also have a broader purpose, which supplies a source of meaning and emotional energy to the activities performed.

Fourth, in organizations, teams differ from groups with respect to the nature of their connections to management. Work groups are typically required to be responsive to demands regularly placed on them by management. By contrast, once management establishes the mission for a team, and sets the challenge for it to achieve, it typically gives the team enough flexibility to do its job without any further interference. In other words, teams are to varying degrees *self-managing*—that is, they are to some extent free to set their own goals, timing, and the approach that they wish to take, usually without management interference. Thus, many teams are described as being *autonomous* or *semiautonomous* in nature. This is not to say that teams are completely independent of corporate management and supervision. They still must be responsive to demands from higher-levels (often, higher-level teams, known as *top management teams*).

Clearly, teams are very special entities. Some teams go beyond the characteristics of teams described here and are known as **high-performance teams**. These are teams whose members are deeply committed to one another's personal growth and success.[70] Such teams are referred to as high-performance teams inasmuch as they tend to perform at much higher levels than ordinary teams (whose members lack this additional commitment to others' growth and success). Indeed, as we will see later in this chapter, the best-performing teams tend to have members who show exceptionally high levels of mutual care, trust, and respect for each other.

high-performance teams Teams whose members are deeply committed to one another's personal growth and success.

Types of Teams

In view of their widespread popularity, it should not be surprising to learn that there are many different kinds of teams. To help make sense out of these, scientists have categorized teams into several different commonly found types which vary along four major dimensions (see Figure 8-13).[71]

The first dimension has to do with their major *purpose or mission*. In this regard, some teams—known as *work teams*—are primarily concerned with the work done by the organization, such as developing and manufacturing new products, providing services for customers, and so on. Their principal focus is on using the organization's resources to effectively create its results (be they goods or services). Other teams—known as *improvement teams*—are primarily oriented toward the mission of increasing the effectiveness of the processes that are used by the organization. For example, Texas Instruments has relied on teams to help improve the quality of operations at its plant in Malaysia.[72]

A second dimension has to do with *time*. Specifically, some teams are only *temporary* and are established for a specific project with a finite life. For example, a team set up to develop a new product would be considered temporary. As soon as its job is done, it disbands. However, other kinds of teams are *permanent* and stay intact as long as the organization is operating. For instance, teams focusing on providing effective customer service tend to be permanent parts of many organizations.

A third distinction has to do with the degree to which teams operate autonomously.[73] At one end of the scale we may have *work groups*, in which leaders make decisions on behalf of group members, whose job it is to follow the leader's orders. This traditional kind of group is becoming less popular as more organiza-

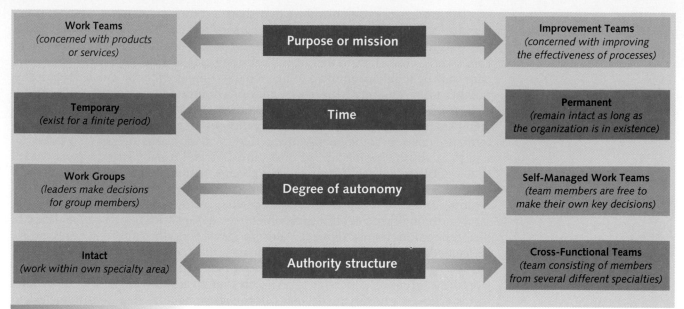

Work Teams *(concerned with products or services)*	**Purpose or mission**	**Improvement Teams** *(concerned with improving the effectiveness of processes)*
Temporary *(exist for a finite period)*	**Time**	**Permanent** *(remain intact as long as the organization is in existence)*
Work Groups *(leaders make decisions for group members)*	**Degree of autonomy**	**Self-Managed Work Teams** *(team members are free to make their own key decisions)*
Intact *(work within own specialty area)*	**Authority structure**	**Cross-Functional Teams** *(team consisting of members from several different specialties)*

FIGURE 8-13 Types of Teams

The teams found in organizations may be distinguished from each other with respect to the four major dimensions identified here.

(Source: Based on suggestions by Mohrman, 1993; see Note 71.)

self-managed work teams Teams whose members are permitted to make key decisions about how their work is done.

Pratt & Whitney Canada
www.pweh.com

☛ *A complete discussion of the structure of authority relations in organizations appears in Chapter 15.*

cross-functional teams Teams represented by people from different specialty areas within organizations.

tions are turning to the opposite end of the scale, where employees are free to make their own key decisions. Such groups are commonly referred to as **self-managed work teams**.

Typically, self-managed work teams consist of small numbers of employees, often around ten, who take on duties that used to be performed by their supervisors. This is likely to include making work assignments, deciding on the pace of work, determining how quality is to be assessed, and even who gets to join the team. In fact, the more self-managed teams do, the less they have to be supervised at all.

Consider these examples of some of the ways members of self-managed work teams are assuming supervisory duties:[74]

- Team members at a Colgate-Palmolive factory in Ohio write their own technical training manuals.

- Work teams at Lake Superior Paper Industries schedule their own work assignments and vacations.

- The Brazilian baking equipment manufacturer, Semco S/A, had team members decide where to locate the company's new plant.

As these examples illustrate, self-managed work teams are given wide latitude over a broad range of important areas of organizational decision making. Self-managed work teams are not only in widespread use today, but they are growing in popularity. The list of companies using teams includes many large corporations, such as Xerox, Hewlett-Packard, Pratt & Whitney Canada, and PepsiCo. In fact, Procter & Gamble and General Motors have used self-managed work teams for over 30 years.[75]

The fourth dimension reflects the team's connection to the organization's overall *authority structure*—that is, the connection between various formal job responsibilities. In some organizations teams remain *intact* with respect to their organizational functions. For example, at Ralston-Purina projects are structured such that people work together on certain products all the time and do not apply their specialty to a wide range of products. Within such organizations, teams can operate without the ambiguities created by straying from one's area of expertise.

However, with growing frequency, we are seeing teams that cross over various functional units (e.g., marketing, finance, human resources, and so on). Such teams are commonly referred to as **cross-functional teams**. These are teams composed of employees at identical organizational levels, but from different specialty areas, to work together on a task. Cross-functional teams represent an effective way of bringing people together from throughout the organization to cooperate with each other on the diverse tasks needed to complete large projects. In organizations using cross-functional teams, the boundaries between all teams must be considered permeable. Indeed, people are frequently members of more than one team—a situation often required for organizations to function effectively. For example, members of an organization's manufacturing team must carefully coordinate their activities with members of its marketing team. To the extent that people are involved in several different kinds of teams, they may gain broader perspectives and make more important contributions to their various teams.

Cross-functional teams have proven to be useful in organizations of all sizes. David Feldberg uses cross-functional teams at his company, Teknion Furniture Systems in Toronto, to reduce production costs and lead time, and to keep up with the unrelenting demand for new products.[76] For over a decade, many automobile manufacturers—including the major North American and Japanese companies—have relied on cross-functional teams to create and manufacture new models. As a case in point, the successful Dodge Neon was completely created by cross-functional teams of experts from throughout Chrysler. Similarly, in the aircraft industry, Boeing created cross-functional teams that designed and manufactured its latest aircraft, the 777 (see Figure 8-14). In these cases, the use of teams has been credited with both the record speed with which the products came to market and their exceptional quality. As you might imagine, cross-functional teams are difficult to manage. It takes time for specialists in different areas to learn to communicate with each other and to coordinate their efforts. It also takes time to develop the mutual trust and acceptance that is required for people to work closely with each other. However, in view of the great successes of cross-functional teams, the effort required to make them work out appears to be worthwhile.

Managers' Guidelines for Creating Teams

As you might imagine, assembling a team is no easy task. Doing so requires not only having the right combination of skilled people, but also individuals who are willing to work together with others as a team. A model proposed by Hackman provides some useful guidance on how to design work teams effectively, suggesting that the process proceeds in four distinct stages.[77] As we present this model, you may find it useful to refer to the summary in Table 8-4.

FIGURE 8-14 The Boeing 777: A Product of Cross-Functional Teams
Large projects, such as the design and production of commercial aircraft, are often aided by the use of cross-functional teams. Such teams of Boeing employees helped produce the company's latest product, the model 777 airliner.

TABLE 8-4 **Stages of Work Team Creation: A Summary**

For teams to function effectively, they must be created properly. The four stages outlined here summarize how this may be accomplished.

(Source: Based on information in Hackman, 1987; see Note 77.)

Stage 1: Do Prework	Stage 2: Create Performance Conditions	Stage 3: Form and Build the Team	Stage 4: Provide Ongoing Assistance
• Decide what work needs to be done.	• Provide all the needed materials and equipment to do the job.	• Establish boundaries—that is, who is and is not in the team.	• Intervene to eliminate team problems (e.g., members not doing their share).
• Determine if a team is necessary to accomplish the task.	• Ensure that the team consists of all personnel necessary to do the job.	• Arrive at an agreement regarding the tasks to be performed.	• Replenish or upgrade material resources.
• Determine what authority the team should have.		• Clarify the behaviours expected of each team member.	• Replace members who leave the team.
• Decide on the team's goals.			

The first stage of creating an effective team is known as *prework*. One of the most important objectives of this phase is to determine whether a team should be created. A manager may decide to have several individuals working alone answer to him, or a team may be created if it is believed that it may develop the most creative and insightful ways to get things done. In considering this, it is important to note exactly what work needs to be done. The team's objectives must be established, and an inventory of the skills needed to do the job should be made. In addition, decisions should be made in advance about what authority the team members should have. They may just be advisory to the manager, or they may be given full responsibility and authority for executing their task (i.e., they may be *self-regulating*).

Building on this, stage two involves *creating performance conditions*. In this stage, organizational officials are to ensure that the team has the proper conditions under which to carry out its work. Resources necessary for the team's success should be provided. This involves both material resources (e.g., tools, equipment, and money), human resources (e.g., the appropriate blend of skilled professionals), and support from the organization (e.g., willingness to let the team do its own work as it sees fit). Unless managers help create the proper conditions for team success, they are contributing to its failure.

Stage three involves *forming and building the team*. Three things can be done to help a team get off to a good start. First, managers should form boundaries—clearly establish who is and who is not a member of the team. Some teams fail simply because membership in it is left unclear. Reducing such ambiguity can help avoid confusion and frustration. Second, members must accept the team's overall mission and purpose. Unless they do, failure is inevitable. Third, organizational officials should clarify the team's mission and responsibilities—make perfectly clear exactly what it is expected to do (but not necessarily *how* to do it). Will team members be responsible for monitoring and planning their own work? If so, such expectations should be spelled out explicitly.

Finally, once a team is functioning, supervisors should *provide ongoing assistance*. Although once teams start operating they often guide themselves, managers may be able to help by providing opportunities for the team to eliminate problems and perform even better. For example, disruptive team members may be either counselled or replaced. Similarly, material resources may have to be replenished or upgraded. Although it may be unwise for a manager to intervene in the successful affairs of a team that has taken on its own life, it also may be unwise to neglect opportunities to help a team do even better.

As you ponder these suggestions, you will doubtlessly recognize the considerable managerial skill and hard work it takes to create and manage teams effectively. However, as managers learn these skills, and as individuals gain successful experiences as members of effective work teams, the deliberate steps outlined above may become second nature to all concerned. As Hackman concludes, "When that stage is reached, the considerable investment required to learn how to use work teams well can pay substantial dividends—in work effectiveness and in the quality of the experience of both managers and [team] members."[78] As we will describe later in this chapter, both the potential pitfalls and benefits of work teams can be considerable.

Effective Team Performance

In recent years, the popular press has been filled with impressive claims about the success of teams in improving quality, customer service, productivity, and the bottom line. Here is just a sampling of the findings cited:

- At one Nortel plant, the switch to teams resulted in improved employee satisfaction, an 83 percent increase in revenue, a 51 percent improvement in quality, and a 93 percent increase earnings for each employee.[79]

- Teams at Corning lowered defect rates from 1800 parts per million to 9 parts per million at its specialty cellular ceramics plant.[80]

- At General Electric's plant in Salisbury, North Carolina, productivity was two and a half times higher than at other plants where people made the same products.[81]

Such reports lead us to believe that teams in general can produce very impressive results. However, it is important to consider whether or not these findings are typical. In this section we will examine evidence bearing on this question. Then, we will focus on some of the obstacles to team success and some of the things that can be done to help promote highly successful teams.

How Successful Are Teams? A Look at the Evidence

Questions regarding the effectiveness of teams in the workplace are not easy to answer. Not only are there many different kinds of teams doing different kinds of jobs operating in organizations, but their effectiveness is influenced by a wide variety of factors that go well beyond any possible benefits of teams, such as managerial support, the economy, available resources, and the like. As a result, understanding the true effectiveness of teams is a tricky business, at best. This difficulty has been fuelled in recent years by cover stories in the top business periodicals touting the success of teams.[82,83] How much of this is hype stemming from the latest management fad, and how much should be accepted as valid evidence for the effectiveness of teams? Fortunately, several types of research investigations have examined this issue.[84]

One of the most direct ways of learning about companies' experiences with work teams is to survey the officials of organizations that use them. In a large-scale study, Lawler, Mohrman, and Ledford did just that.[85] Their sample consisted of several hundred of the 1000 largest companies in the United States. About 47 percent used some work teams, although these were typically in place in only a few selected sites, not throughout the entire organizations. Where they were used, however, they were generally highly regarded. Survey results collected in 1987 and again in 1990 revealed that whereas 53 percent characterized the teams as "successful" or "very successful" in 1987, this figure grew to 60 percent only three years later. For both years, almost all the other responses fell into the "undecided" category; "unsuccessful" or "very unsuccessful" responses occurred in only 1 percent of the cases each year.

These optimistic results are further supported by in-depth case studies of numerous teams in many different organizations.[86] Research of this type, although difficult to quantify and to compare across organizations, provides some interesting insight into what makes teams successful and why. For example, Manz and Sims studied the work teams used in General Motors' battery plant in Fitzgerald, Georgia.[87] The 320 employees at this facility operate in various teams, including managers working together in *support teams*, middle-level teams of *coordinators* (similar to supervisors and technicians), and *employee teams*, natural work units of three to nineteen members performing specific tasks. Although the teams work closely together, coordinating their activities, they function almost as separate businesses. Because plant employees must perform many different tasks in their teams, they are not paid based on their positions, but for their knowledge and competence. In fact, the highest-paid employees are individuals who have demonstrated their competence (usually by highly demanding tests) on all the jobs performed in at least two different teams. This is GM's way of rewarding people for broadening their perspectives, appreciating "the other guy's problems." By many measures, the Fitzgerald plant has been very effective. Its production costs are lower than comparable units in traditionally run plants. Furthermore, employee turnover is also much lower than average. Employee satisfaction surveys also reveal that job satisfaction at this plant is among the highest found at any General Motors facility.

Teams also have been successful in service businesses. For example, consider IDS, the financial services subsidiary of American Express.[88] In response to rapid growth in the mid-1980s, IDS officials realized that their operations were becoming highly inefficient and created several teams to work on reorganizing them. With the help of employee teams, IDS's operations become so efficient that response time improved by 96 percent: from several minutes to only a few seconds. During the stock market crash of October 1987, this quick response capability is credited for saving lots of money for IDS's customers.

These cases are two examples of very different companies that used teams in different ways, but with something in common—high levels of success. And, there are many more.[89] Although there are far too many cases to review here, we think you'll find it fascinating to review the summary of company experiences with teams in Table 8-5.[90,91]

As Table 8-5 makes clear, many companies have reported having successful experiences with teams. The problem with such reports, of course, is that they may not be entirely objective. This is not to say that case studies cannot be trusted. Indeed, when the information is gathered by outside researchers (such as those reported here), the stories they tell about how teams are used and the results of using them can be quite revealing.[92] Still, there is a need for completely objective, empirical studies of team effectiveness.

Research of this type is now just beginning to be done. In one such investigation Pearson compared various aspects of work performance and attitudes of two groups of employees at a railroad-car repair facility in Australia: Those who were assembled into teams that could freely decide how to do their jobs, and those whose work was structured in the more traditional, nonautonomous fashion.[93] After the work teams had been in place for several months, it was found that they had significantly fewer accidents, as well as lower rates of absenteeism and turnover. Unfortunately, not all empirical studies paint such an optimistic picture of the benefits of work teams. For example, Wall, Kemp, Jackson, and Clegg examined the long-term effects of using work teams in an English manufacturing plant.[94] Although they found that employees were more satisfied with their jobs in teams compared to those in conventional work arrangements (in which individuals take orders from a supervisor), they were individually no more productive. However, because the use of teams made it possible for the organization to eliminate several supervisory positions, the company became more profitable.

These two studies do not paint a clear and convincing case for the overall effectiveness of teams. While teams are generally well received—that is, people enjoy working in them—it is not yet apparent that they are responsible for making individuals any more productive. From an organizational perspective, teams appear to be an effective way of eliminating layers of management. When people are highly committed to achieving excellence, it is not surprising that their companies may reap the results. In fact, it is precisely these types of beneficial outcomes that are being reported by the case studies we summarized above. (Researchers are just beginning to understand that team effectiveness is closely related to national culture. For a look at one aspect of this relationship, see the GLOBALIZATION IN TODAY'S ORGANIZATIONS section.)

TABLE 8-5 Teams in Organizations: Some Impressive Results

Case studies have reported many remarkable outcomes stemming from teams. Here is just a sampling of the impressive results.

Sources: Wellins, R. S., Byham, W. C., & Wilson, J. M. (1991). Empowered teams. San Francisco: Jossey-Bass; Katzenbach, J. R., & Smith, D. K. (1993). The wisdom of teams. Boston: Harvard Business School Press; Osburn, J. D., Moran, L., Musselwhite, E., & Zenger, J. H. (1990). Self-directed work teams. Burr Ridge, IL: Irwin; Pritchard, T. (1992, September 22). The solid-state factory. The Globe and Mail, p. B26; Ritchie, S. (1993, June 8). Life in the fast lane. The Globe and Mail, p. B24; List, W. (1992, November 10). Tapping the power of workers' minds. The Globe and Mail, p. B26; Mark, K. (1994, Spring). All in one go. Canadian Business, Special Technology Issue, p. 39.

Company	Result
Federal Express	Reduced errors (e.g., incorrect bills, lost packages) by 13 percent in 1989
Corning	Defects dropped from 1800 parts per million to only 9 parts per million in its cellular ceramics plant
GSW Water Heating Co.	Reduced warranty work and scrap accumulation by 10 percent, increased productivity, and substantially lowered costs because of lower inventory and materials handling costs
Pratt & Whitney Canada	Produced a design for its PW 500 turbofan jet engine in less than 12 months instead of its more usual 18 to 24 months
Xerox	Increased productivity by 30 percent
Exxon	Saved $10 million in 6 months

Potential Obstacles to Success: Why Do Some Teams Fail?

Although we have reported many success stories about teams, we also have hinted at several possible problems and difficulties in implementing them. After all, working in a team demands a great deal, and not everyone may be ready for them. Fortunately, we can learn from these experiences. Analyses of failed attempts at introducing teams into the workplace suggest several obstacles to team success, pitfalls that can be avoided if you know about them.

First, some teams fail because their members are *unwilling to cooperate with each other*. John MacMillan, director of manufacturing at the Honeywell Ltd. plant in Scarborough, Ontario (see the CASE PREVIEW for this chapter), has found that conflict, especially in the early stages of team development, is not unusual. "Anger, stress and conflict are not a downside of teamwork," says MacMillan. "They're perfectly natural by-products."[95] This was illustrated a few years ago at Dow Chemical Company's plastics group in Midland, Michigan, where a team was put into place to create a new plastic resin.[96] Some members (those in the research field) wanted to spend several months developing and testing new options, while others (those on the manufacturing end) wanted to slightly alter existing products and start up production right away. Neither side budged, and the project eventually stalled. By contrast, when team members share a common vision and are committed to attaining it, they are generally very cooperative with each other, leading to success.

A second reason why some teams are not effective is that they *fail to receive support from management*. Consider, for example, the experience at the Lenexa, Kansas, plant of the Puritan-Bennett Corporation, a manufacturer of respiratory equipment.[97] After seven years of working to develop improved software for its respirators, product development teams did not get the job done, despite the fact that the industry average for such tasks is only three years. According to Roger J. Dolida, the company's director of research and development, the problem is that management never made the project a priority, and refused to free up another key person needed to do the job. As he put it, "If top management doesn't buy into the idea . . . teams can go nowhere."[98]

A third obstacle to group success, and a relatively common one, is that *some managers are unwilling to relinquish control*. Good supervisors work their way up from the plant floor by giving orders and having them followed. However, team leaders have to build consensus and must allow team members to make decisions together. As you might expect, letting go of control isn't always easy for some to do. At Black Diamond Cheese, the operations manager had to replace five production supervisors because they were not able to make the change to teamwork.[99] The message sent was clear: Those who cannot adjust to teamwork are unwelcome.

Fourth, teams might fail not only because their members do not cooperate with each other, but also because they *fail to cooperate with other teams*. This problem occurred in General Electric's medical systems division when it assigned two teams of engineers, one in Wisconsin, and another in Japan, the task of creating software for

Comparing Team Effectiveness in Japan, the United States, and Great Britain

When your team confronts a problem that requires it to seek advice, where would it be most likely to turn: a company policy manual, informal policies, advice from superiors, advice from fellow teammates, or your own experience? And, how effective are these various alternatives? Research has shown that the answer to both questions depends on the national culture of the teams in question.

If you recall from Chapter 2 the distinction between highly individualistic cultures (such as the United States and Great Britain) and highly collectivistic cultures (such as Japan), it should not be difficult to envision differences between the ways teams from each culture operate. After all, in individualistic cultures people tend to be self-reliant whereas in collectivistic cultures people tend to be group-oriented. As such, we would expect people from collectivistic cultures to consult their teammates, whereas people from individualistic cultures would rely on their own experiences. A recent study by Smith, Peterson, and Misumi found just this.[100] Specifically, they surveyed team members in the United States, Great Britain, and Japan about how likely they would be to take certain actions in response to problems confronted in their teams. Their findings were clear: In Japan, people were most likely to consult their fellow team members, whereas in the United States and Great Britain, people were most likely to rely on their own previous experience and training. These results suggest that national culture is likely to influence the way team members operate when they face problems.

However, a question remains—which of the various strategies is most effective? To answer this question the researchers examined the association between the various strategies the teams preferred and how productive supervisors rated the teams as being. The results were quite interesting. In general, Japanese teams were regarded as more productive to the extent that they relied on company manuals for help. However, teams from the United States and Great Britain were rated as being more productive to the extent that they relied on their own previous experiences. These findings are in keeping with the tendency for Japanese people to rely closely on formal procedures insofar as they represent the collective wisdom of the past, and the tendency for the more individualistic Americans and British people to put their faith in their individual experiences.[101]

It is important to note that the findings of Smith and his associates need to be interpreted with caution insofar as they relied on supervisors' ratings of team productivity instead of objective measures. The problem is that the results could stem from either of two possibilities: (1) supervisors gave higher ratings to teams because they adhered to culturally endorsed practices, or (2) supervisors gave higher ratings because these practices were, in reality, most effective. Unfortunately, this research does not rule out the first possibility. However, the study does provide very good evidence that the effectiveness of team performance is likely to be closely linked to cultural differences in the way teams operate. For this reason, researchers interested in the matter of team effectiveness would be well advised to consider the influence of national culture in their future studies.

two new ultrasound devices.[102] Shortly, teams pushed features that made their products popular only in their own countries and duplicated each other's efforts. When the teams met, language and cultural barriers separated them, further distancing the teams from each other. Without close cooperation between teams (as well as within them), organizations are not likely to reap the benefits they hoped for when creating teams in the first place.[103]

A fifth reason why teams fail is that *management does not gain the support of the union* from the beginning. Some unions, in fact, have rejected outright the idea of teamwork as proposed by management. For instance, in 1989 the Canadian Auto Workers (CAW) resisted "collaboration with employers for any reorganization of the workplace that would include employee participation in work teams, and in quality-of-work-life programs."[104] In this situation, the CAW saw teams as potentially extending management's power by increasing workers' loyalty to the company and therefore decreasing the employees' loyalty to the union. Management-union agreement on teams has progressed since 1989, according to the 1994 Workplace

Canadian Auto Workers
www.caw.ca

[You Be The Consultant]

In response to sagging productivity among its work crews, a large construction company has been giving serious thought to using self-managed teams. You have been asked to give your advice on this matter.

1. Do you think teams would be effective in this situation? Why or why not?

2. What potential problems do you think would be associated with the move to teams and how might these be overcome?

3. What advice would you give to help the teams work as effectively as possible?

Innovation report by the Bureau of Labour Information.[105] In the final analysis, effective teamwork will be made possible by unions and management working together from the outset.

Building High-Performance Teams: Some Tips

As we just described, making teams work effectively is no easy task. Success is not automatic. Rather, teams need to be carefully cared for and maintained in order for them to accomplish their missions. As one expert expressed it, "Teams are the Ferraris of work design. They're high performance but high maintenance and expensive."[106] What, then, could be done to help make teams as effective as possible? Based on analyses of successful teams, several keys to success may be identified.[107] Here are some tips:

1. *Diversify team membership.* Teams function most effectively when they are composed of highly skilled individuals who can bring a variety of different skills and experiences to the task at hand.[108]

2. *Keep teams small in size.* Effective teams consist of the smallest number of people needed to do the work. Coordination is difficult when teams are too large, and overload is likely when teams are too small. Generally, about 10–12 members is ideal.[109]

3. *Select the right team members.* There are some individuals who enjoy working in teams and others who prefer to work alone. To the extent that it is possible to do so, problems can be eliminated by not forcing loners onto teams. Similarly, it is important to select team members based on their skills or potential skills. Insofar as the success of teams demands that they work together closely on a wide variety of tasks, it is essential for them to have a complementary set of skills. This includes not only job skills but also interpersonal skills (especially since getting along with one's teammates is so very important).

4. *Train, train, train.* For teams to function effectively, members must have all the technical skills needed to do their jobs. This may well involve cross-training on the key aspects of others' specialty areas. It is also essential for them to be well trained in the interpersonal process skills needed for team members to get along with each other. Given the great responsibilities team members have, it also is advised that they be trained in the most effective ways to make decisions.

5. *Clarify goals.* When team members have a well-defined mission, they are likely to all pull in the same direction and attempt to reach the same team goals. It is therefore important that team goals be clearly articulated.

6. *Link individual rewards to team performance.* To the extent that team members are rewarded for their groups' successes by getting to share in the financial rewards, they are likely to be highly committed to striving for success.

7. *Use appropriate performance measures.* Teams work best when they develop their own measures of success. Furthermore, these measures should be based on the processes involved instead of the outcomes. For example, instead of measuring profitability, a traditional measure of success, a manufacturing team may concentrate on measures that have some diagnostic value, such as the average time per service call or the number of late service calls. After all, team members who are aware of these indices may be able to do something in response to them.

8. *Encourage participation.* To the extent that team members are allowed to participate in making decisions, they are more likely to feel committed to those decisions. Thus, for teams to be committed to their work, it is essential for all team members to be involved.

☞ *Recall our discussion of training techniques in Chapter 3.*

9. **Cultivate team spirit and social support.** Teams work most effectively when they have a "can-do" attitude, believing that they can succeed. This is often encouraged when team members lend interpersonal and task support to their teammates. Just as importantly, if not more so, support must come from top management. To the extent that team members suspect that management is not fully behind them, they will be unlikely to dedicate themselves to the task at hand.

10. **Foster communication and cooperation.** Naturally, team members must carefully communicate and cooperate with each other so that they can coordinate their efforts toward their common goal. At the same time, they must communicate and cooperate with other teams. In so doing, the overall success of the organization is fostered.

11. **Emphasize the urgency of the team's task.** Team members are prone to rally around challenges that compel them to meet high performance standards

12. **Clarify the rules of behaviour.** Effective teams have clear rules about what behaviours are and are not expected.

13. **Regularly confront teams with new facts.** Fresh approaches are likely to be prompted by fresh information, and introducing new facts may present the kind of challenges that teams need to stay innovative.

14. **Acknowledge and reward vital contributions to the team**. As indicated in Chapter 3, rewarding desired behaviour is a key way of ensuring that the behaviour will be repeated in the future. Rewards don't have to be large to work.

If after reading this list you are thinking that it is no easy matter to get teams to work effectively, you have reached the same conclusion as countless practising managers. Indeed, you don't just form teams and then sit back and watch the amazing results pour in. Teams can be very useful tools, but using them effectively requires a great deal of work. It is important to caution that although these suggestions are important, they alone do not ensure the success of work teams. Many other factors, such as the economy, the existence of competitors, and the company's financial picture are also important determinants of organizational success. However, in view of the considerable gains that have been found to occur, the effort would appear to be well worthwhile, as in the case of XEL Communications Inc. (see Figure 8-15).

FIGURE 8-15 Self-directed Work Teams Can Lead to Success

Team meetings, such as this one, are critical to the success of XEL Communications (see the Case in Point for this chapter). Its employee recruitment literature emphasizes, "At XEL we maintain a work culture that rewards initiative. Career growth is fostered through such initiatives as self-directed work teams, a 360° peer-review process, and skill-based compensation."[110]

XEL Communications
www.xel.com

SUMMARY AND REVIEW

The Nature of Groups

A **group** is defined as a collection of two or more inter-acting individuals with a stable pattern of relationships between them who share common goals and who perceive themselves as being a group. Within organizations, there are two major classes of groups—*formal groups* and *informal groups*. Groups often develop by going through five principal stages—*forming, storming, norming, performing,* and *adjourning.*

The structure of groups is determined by four key factors: *roles,* the typical pattern of behaviour in a social context; *norms,* generally agreed upon informal rules; *status,* the prestige accorded group members; and *cohesiveness,* the pressures faced by group members to remain in their groups.

Individual Performance In Groups

Individual productivity is influenced by the presence of other group members. Sometimes, a person's performance improves in the presence of others (when the job they are doing is well learned), and sometimes performance declines in the presence of others (when the job is novel). This phenomenon is known as **social facilitation**. Not only is performance influenced by the presence of others, but by the group's racial/ethnic diversity. Performance in diverse groups is initially worse than performance in homogeneous groups, although these differences disappear with repeated involvement with the group.

On *additive tasks,* in which each member's individual contributions are combined, **social loafing** occurs. According to this phenomenon, the more people who work on a task, the less each group member contributes to it. Loafing can be reduced by making workers identifiable, making the work important and interesting, rewarding people for their group contributions, and threatening punishment.

The Nature of Teams

Teams are special kinds of groups, ones whose members focus on collective, rather than individual, work products, are mutually accountable to each other, share a common commitment to purpose, and are usually self-managing. Teams differ with respect to four dimensions: their *purpose* or *mission* (work or improvement), *time* (temporary or permanent), *degree of autonomy* (none or self-managed), and *authority structure* (overlaid or intact). Creating teams involves four steps: prework, creating performance conditions, forming and building a team, and providing ongoing assistance.

Team Performance

In surveys, organizational officials report that teams operating in their organizations have mostly been successful. Comprehensive case studies also have found organizational productivity gains (e.g., increased outcome, improved quality, lowered costs) resulting from the use of teams. However, more objective field research has found that while employees are generally more satisfied in teams than working under traditional management, they tend to be no more productive at the individual level. Many of the organizational benefits resulting from teams appear to come from the elimination of middle-management positions.

Despite some evidence of team successes, teams sometimes fail. This is often because team members are unwilling to cooperate with each other, they fail to receive support from management, some managers are unwilling to relinquish control, and some teams fail to coordinate their efforts effectively with other teams. However, with some effort, teams can bring exceptionally high levels of performance. Among the many key factors contributing to team success are diversity in team membership, small size, effective training, using clear goals, and encouraging participation.

CASE PREVIEW QUESTIONS FOR DISCUSSION

1. What were the benefits to Honeywell of adopting self-managed work teams?

2. In implementing its self-managed work teams, what strategies did Honeywell put in place to overcome the potential barriers to successful teamwork?

3. If you had been a first-line manager with ten years' experience at Honeywell before the advent of self-managed work teams, how would you have reacted initially to the idea of the teams?

CHAPTER QUESTIONS FOR DISCUSSION

1. What is the difference between a collection of individuals and a *group*? Why is a "group" of people waiting in line to see a movie not really a group?

2. Identify the stages of *group development* described in the text and apply them to any group to which you belong. Do all the stages apply?

3. Give examples demonstrating how *norms, roles,* and *status* operate within any groups to which you may belong.

4. Imagine that you are about to go on stage to give a solo piano recital. How would the phenomenon of *social facilitation* account for your performance?

5. Describe an incident of *social loafing* in which you may have been involved (e.g., a class project). What might be done to overcome this effect?

6. What makes a team a special form of group? Is a baseball team really a team or is it just a group?

7. Based on the evidence regarding the effectiveness of teams, would you say that the popularity of teams today is well founded?

8. Suppose you were to compose a work team in your organization. What potential pitfalls would you expect? What might you be able to do to help make that team perform at high levels?

CASE IN POINT

XEL: The Little Telecommunications Company That Could

The telecommunications industry is populated by giants, like AT&T and Nortel Networks. So, when you're a David in an ocean of Goliaths, you have to do something different than the competition—and much better—just to stay afloat. This was the situation Bill Sanko and his partners faced in the mid-1980s when they broke off from GTE and started their own 180-employee telecommunications equipment company, XEL Communications, Inc. Sanko knew that the success of his fledgling operation depended on providing speedy responses to customers' needs at reasonable prices. The custom circuit boards XEL was selling (mostly to its former parent, GTE) were taking about eight weeks to produce. This was much too long, and the company began to struggle. Customers became disgruntled, and too much money was tied up in inventory.

The problem, Sanko realized, was that it took too many individuals to get anything done, and jobs were poorly coordinated. So Sanko and his colleagues decided that the solution to their problem would be to eliminate the many layers of management that were slowing down the process. In its place they would substitute small teams of people responsible for getting their jobs done.

XEL's teams typically are composed of about a dozen members, people with individual responsibilities that are clearly identified and agreed to mutually by all team members. Teams track their own attendance, on-time deliveries, and other aspects of job performance. Regularly each day, team members meet to plan their parts in meeting the company's weekly schedule. All of this goes on without management intervention. In fact, only once each quarter does management get involved—during a meeting in which each team makes a presentation describing what it has accomplished.

By 1993, only five years after the teams began, things had dramatically turned around at XEL. Since introducing teams, the cost of assembly had dropped 25 percent, and inventory had been reduced 50 percent, all while increasing quality levels 30 percent. And, that eight-week production time? It had dropped to only four days—and was still falling. Importantly, sales figures reflected these dramatic improvements: Between 1992 and 1993 sales jumped from U.S.$17 million to U.S.$25 million.

This success hasn't been exactly easy for XEL. Because team members work so closely together, adding new members has been a challenge. Teams are so concerned about getting their jobs done that they are often impatient with newcomers, fearing that their output will suffer. Another problem has been that in some groups, the freedom has proven to be too much. In XEL's stockroom, for example, some employees were abusing the system by cheating on their time cards. At first, problem employees were replaced, but eventually stockroom teams had to be disbanded and replaced by full-time supervisors with disciplinary authority.

As far as Bill Sanko and his colleagues at XEL are concerned, these adjustments are a small price to pay for an approach that has worked so effectively. XEL has been so successful, in fact, that it was chosen to be featured on a video about team-based management produced by the Association for Manufacturing Excellence in the United States.[111]

Critical Thinking Questions

1. What measures could XEL take to help make its teams as effective as possible?

2. What problems are XEL's teams likely to face and how can they be overcome?

SKILLS PORTFOLIO

Experiencing Organizational Behaviour

Why Do You Join Groups?

Groups are important in people's lives, and we join them for several different reasons. However, chances are good that you haven't given too much thought to the matter of why you may have joined certain groups in the first place. So, to identify these reasons, you may find it enlightening to complete the following questionnaire.

Directions

Think of a group you recently joined (e.g., a sports league, a campus club, a sorority or fraternity, a committee in your company). Then, indicate the importance of each of the following reasons for joining by using the following scale: 1 = not at all important; 2 = slightly important; 3 = moderately important; 4 = greatly important; 5 = extremely important.

I joined this group because . . .
___ **1.** I had something important in common with the other members.
___ **2.** By joining the group, I had greater clout.
___ **3.** People in the group shared my interests.
___ **4.** The group helped me feel safe and secure.
___ **5.** I enjoy being with other people.
___ **6.** I thought the people in the group would make me feel good about myself.
___ **7.** I wanted to feel less lonely.
___ **8.** I expected the group members to recognize my accomplishments.

Scoring

1. Add your responses to numbers 1 and 3. This score reflects your interest in joining the group *to seek the satisfaction of mutual interests and goals.*
2. Add your responses to numbers 2 and 4. This score reflects your interest in joining the group *to achieve security.*
3. Add your responses to numbers 5 and 7. This score reflects your interest in joining the group *to fill social needs.*
4. Add your responses to numbers 6 and 8. This score reflects your interest in joining the group *to seek the fulfillment of self-esteem (feeling good about yourself) that others can provide.*

Questions for Discussion

1. What were your strongest (highest score) and weakest (lowest score) reasons for joining this group?
2. Besides the four reasons identified here, what other reasons did you have for joining this group?
3. Would your scores be different if you thought about another group you may have joined? Repeat the questionnaire to find out.

Working in Groups

Demonstrating the Social Loafing Effect

The social loafing effect is quite strong and is likely to occur in many different situations in which people make individual contributions to an additive group task. This exercise is designed to demonstrate the effect firsthand in your own class.

Directions

1. Divide the class into groups of different sizes. Between five and ten people should work alone. In addition, there should be a group of two, a group of three, a group of four, and so on, until all members of the class have been assigned to a group. If the class is small, assign students to groups of vastly different sizes, such as two, seven, and fifteen. Form the groups by putting together at tables people from the same group.

2. Each person should be given a page or two from a telephone directory and a stack of index cards. Then have the individuals and the members of each group perform the same additive task—copying entries from the telephone directory onto index cards. Allow exactly 10 minutes for the task to be performed, and encourage everyone to work as hard as they can.
3. After the time is up, count the number of entries copied.
4. For each group, and for all the individuals, compute the average per person performance by dividing the total number of entries copied by the number of people in the group.
5. At the board, the instructor should graph the results. Along the vertical axis show the average number of entries copied per person. Along the horizontal axis show the size of the work groups—one, two, three, four, and so on. The graph should look like the one in Figure 8-10.

Questions for Discussion

1. Was the social loafing effect demonstrated? What is the basis for this conclusion?
2. If the social loafing effect was not found, why do you think this occurred? Do you think it might have been due to the possibility that your familiarity with the effect led you to avoid it? Test this possibility by replicating the exercise using people who do not know about the phenomenon (e.g., another class), then compare the results.
3. Did members of smaller groups feel more responsible for their group's performance than members of larger groups?
4. What could have been done to counteract any "free riding" that may have occurred in this demonstration?

TAKE IT TO THE NET

Prentice Hall

We invite you to visit the *Greenberg/Baron/Sales/Owen Companion Website* at *www.prenticehall.ca/greenberg* for this chapter's Internet resources.

CHAPTER 9

Interpersonal Communication in Organizations

LEARNING OBJECTIVES

After reading this chapter you should be able to:

1. Describe the process of *communication* and its role in organizations.

2. Identify various forms of verbal media used in organizations and explain which ones are most appropriate for communicating messages of different types.

3. Explain how style of dress and the use of time and space are employed to communicate nonverbally in organizations.

4. Describe various types of individual differences with respect to how people communicate with each other.

5. Distinguish between formal and informal *communication networks,* and explain the influence of each on organizational communication.

6. Describe how the formal structure of an organization influences the nature of the communication that occurs within it.

7. Identify and describe measures that can be taken by both individuals and organizations to improve the effectiveness of organizational communication.

General Electric Canada: Mining Employees for Ideas

From the time he was appointed chairman of General Electric Co. (GE) in 1981, Jack Welch (see Figure 9-1) had started a revolution. "He has taken the established order at GE and thrown it out the window."[1]

Welch saw a company whose systems were becoming outdated, a company that was about to have a lot of trouble keeping up with global competition and fast-paced change.[2] He believed the answer lay in empowering employees and managers to solve local problems themselves. But, to get this done, he had to develop a way to foster open, clear, and honest communication at all levels in the organization.

Jack Welch and his executives, in searching for a vehicle to unleash employees' ideas, hit upon the old-fashioned idea of holding "town hall meetings." Soon after, these meetings, known as Work-Out, evolved into a strategy to improve internal communication and a method to import ideas from outside GE.[3]

Work-Out began with four primary goals. First, the program was designed to build trust at all levels of the organization so that all employees and managers could feel free to speak openly about issues of concern. Second, those most directly engaged in any task were given more power to solve problems themselves, rather than having to rely on higher levels in the organization. Third, unnecessary work was eliminated to increase productivity and to encourage workers who felt overworked. Fourth, Welch hoped that Work-Out would help to break down boundaries within the organization. "In effect, Welch wanted the whole organization to participate in defining itself."[4] GE "mines its employees for ideas in Work-Out sessions" and has made it clear that "blocking a Work-Out session is a 'career-limiting move' for a manager."[5]

While Work-Out may not be the tool to solve the problems of all businesses, it has proven to be a powerful way for GE to get useful problem-solving input from its employees.[6] As Welch explains: "How will we know if Work-Out is successful? We'll know because over time we'll become more productive. Our attitudes will be better, people will be happier, better ideas will flow."[7]

In an effort to import ideas from the outside, GE expanded the Work-Out program to include the notion of GE employees' benchmarking the "Best Practices" of other companies. For example, as part of a "Best Practices" study on product delivery systems, Serge Huot, a Canadian and the manufacturing manager of Camco, GE's appliance subsidiary in Canada, flew to New Zealand to visit a company that had set an enviable record for reducing product cycle time (time from placing the order in a store to delivery of the finished product to the distribution centre). As a result of Huot's research, the "Quick Response" program was introduced throughout GE's operations. One GE executive enthused: "A guy in Canada . . . gets the spirit, finds a company that makes sense to him. . . . He gets on a plane. He absorbs, he brings it back on his own authority. . . . That's boundarylessness, that's speed, that's simplicity, and self-confidence."[8]

General Electric Canada
www.ge.com

FIGURE 9-1 Empowering Employees through Communication

Above all else, Jack Welch, CEO of General Electric Co., is a communicator "par excellence." He communicates enthusiasm and a shared vision that helps the company's 270 000 employees move in the same direction.[9]

Few CEOs—particularly CEOs of very large corporations—go the same lengths as Jack Welch to promote communication within their companies. By ensuring that everyone in the company knows what's going on, Welch has put into action his belief that open communication is vital to organizational success. Given the company's record, it's clear he has been on the right track.

FIGURE 9-2 Communication: An Important Process in Organizations

This man appears to be realizing something that both scientists and practising managers have appreciated for some time—that the process of communication is central to organizational functioning.

(Source: Copyright © 1992, 1994 Leo Cullum.)

Jack Welch is not alone in his beliefs about the importance of communication in organizations. Indeed, experts consider communication to be a key process underlying all aspects of organizational operations.[10] In fact, employees' overall performance is strongly related to their competence as communicators.[11] Contemporary scholars have variously referred to organizational communication as "the social glue . . . that continues to keep the organization tied together,"[12] and "the essence of organization."[13] Writing many years earlier, well-known management theorist Chester Barnard said, "The structure, extensiveness and scope of the organization are almost entirely determined by communication techniques."[14] This strong statement makes sense if you consider that supervisors spend as much as 80 percent of their time engaging in some form of communication, such as speaking or listening to others, or writing to and reading material from others (see Figure 9-2).[15]

Given the importance of communication in organizations, we will closely examine this process in this chapter. To begin, we will define the process of communication and characterize its role in organizations. Following this, we will describe the two basic forms of communication: verbal and nonverbal. Then, we will examine several of the major influences on communication at the individual, group, and organizational levels. These include individual differences, formal and informal communication networks, and organizational structure—aspects of the social and work environments that shape the nature and direction of the flow of information. Finally, we will turn to several barriers to effective communication—both individual and organizational in nature—and examine techniques for overcoming them.

Communication: Its Basic Nature

Before we can fully appreciate the process of organizational communication, we need to address some basic issues. To begin, we will formally define what we mean by *communication* and then elaborate on the process by which it occurs. Following this, we will describe the important role that communication plays in organizations.

Communication: A Working Definition and Description of the Process

What do the following situations have in common?

- The district manager posts a notice stating that smoking is prohibited on company property.

- An executive prepares a report about the financial status of a potential corporate takeover prospect.

- A taxi dispatcher directs Cab 54 to pick up a fare at 1065 Cherry Drive.

The answer, if you haven't already guessed it, is that each of these incidents involves some form of *communication*. Although you probably already have a good idea of what communication entails, we can better understand communication in organizations by defining it precisely and describing the nature of the communication process.

With this in mind, we define **communication** as the process by which a person, group, or organization (the *sender*) transmits some type of information (the *message*) to

communication The process by which a person, group, or organization (the sender) transmits some type of information (the message) to another person, group, or organization (the receiver).

another person, group, or organization (the *receiver*). To clarify this definition, and to further elaborate on how the process works, we have summarized it in Figure 9-3. You may find it helpful to follow along with this diagram as we describe the various steps.

Encoding.   The communication process begins when one party has an idea that it wishes to transmit to another (either party may be an individual, a group, or an entire organization). It is the sender's mission to transform the idea into a form that can be sent to and understood by the receiver. This is what happens in the process of **encoding**—translating an idea into a form, such as written or spoken language, that can be recognized by a receiver. We encode information when we select the words we use to write a letter or speak to someone in person. This process is critical if we are to clearly communicate our ideas. Unfortunately, people are far from perfect when it comes to encoding their ideas (although, as we will note later, this skill can be improved).

Channel of communication.   After a message is encoded, it is ready to be transmitted over one or more *channels of communication*, the pathways along which information travels, to reach the desired receiver. Telephone lines, radio and television signals, fibre-optic cables, mail routes, and even the air waves that carry the vibrations of our voices all represent potential channels of communication. Of course, the form of encoding largely determines the way information may be transmitted. Visual information—such as pictures and written words—may be mailed, delivered in person by a courier, shipped by an express delivery service, or sent electronically, such as via modems, fax machines, and satellite dishes. Oral information may be transmitted over the telephone, via radio and television waves, and, of course, the old-fashioned way, in person. Whatever channel is used, the goal is the same: to send the encoded message accurately to a desired receiver.

Decoding.   Once a message is received, the recipient must begin the process of **decoding**—converting the message back into the sender's original ideas. This can involve many different subprocesses, such as comprehending spoken and written words, interpreting facial expressions, and the like. To the extent that the sender's message is accurately decoded by the receiver, the ideas understood will be the ones intended. Of course, our ability to comprehend and interpret information received from others may be imperfect (e.g., restricted by unclear messages or by our own language skills). Thus, as in the case of encoding, limitations in our ability to decode information represent another potential weakness in the communication process—but, as we will describe later in this chapter, one that can be overcome.

Feedback.   Finally, once a message has been decoded, the process can continue with the receiver transmitting a new message back to the original sender. This part of the

encoding The process by which an idea is transformed so that it can be transmitted to, and recognized by, a receiver (e.g., a written or spoken message).

decoding The process by which a receiver of messages transforms them back into the sender's ideas.

FIGURE 9-3 The Communication Process

Communication generally follows the steps outlined here. Senders *encode* messages and transmit them via one or more communication channels to *receivers*, who then *decode* them. The process continues as the original receiver sends *feedback* to the original sender. Factors distorting or limiting the flow of information, known as *noise*, may enter into the process at any point.

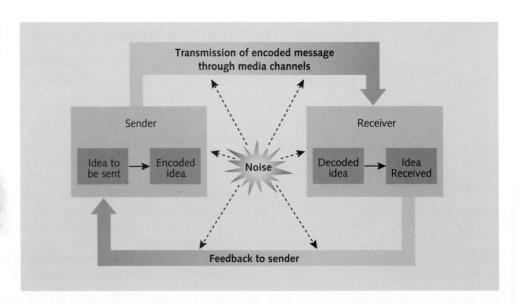

☛ In Chapter 12 we will explain when and why political motives lead to the distortion of information communicated within organizations.

process is known as **feedback**—knowledge about the impact of messages on receivers. Receiving feedback allows senders to determine whether their messages have been understood properly. At the same time, giving feedback can help convince receivers that the sender really cares about what he or she has to say. Once received, feedback can trigger another idea from the sender, and another cycle of transferring information may begin. For this reason, we have characterized the process of communication summarized in Figure 9-3 as continuous.

Noise. Despite the apparent simplicity of the communication process, it rarely operates as flawlessly as we have described it here. As we will see, there are many potential barriers to effective communication. The name given to factors that distort the clarity of a message is **noise**. As we have shown in Figure 9-3, noise can occur at any point along the communication process. For example, messages that are poorly encoded (e.g., written in an unclear way) or poorly decoded (e.g., not comprehended), or channels of communication that are too full of static (e.g., receivers' attentions are diverted from the message) may reduce communication's effectiveness. These factors, and others (e.g., time pressure, organizational politics), may contribute to the distortion of information transmitted from one party to another and to the complexity of the communication process. As you continue reading this chapter, you will come to appreciate many of the factors that make the process of organizational communication so very complex and important.

The Fundamental Role of Communication in Organizations

When you think about people in organizations communicating with each other, what image comes to mind? A typical picture might involve one person telling another what to do. Indeed, one key purpose of organizational communication is to *direct action*, that is, to get others to behave in a desired fashion. However, communication in organizations often involves not only single efforts, but also concerted action. Thus, for an organization to function, individuals and groups must carefully coordinate their efforts and activities.[16] The waiter must take the customer's order and pass it along to the chef. The market researcher must collect information about consumers' needs and share it with the people in charge of manufacturing and advertising. Communication is the key to these attempts at coordination. Without it, people would not know what to do, and organizations would not be able to function effectively—if at all. In other words, it may be said that another key function of communication in organizations is to *achieve coordinated action*.

This function is served by the systematic sharing of information. Indeed, *information*—whether it's data about a product's sales performance, directions to a customer's residence, or instructions on how to perform a task—is the core of all organizational activities. It would be misleading, however, to imply that communication involves only the sharing of facts and data. There is also an *interpersonal* facet of organizational communication, a focus on the social relations between people.[17] For example, communication is also highly involved in such important purposes as *developing friendships* and *building trust and acceptance*. As you know, what you say and how you say it can have profound effects on the extent to which others like you. To the extent that people are interested in creating a pleasant interpersonal atmosphere in the workplace, they must be highly concerned about communication.

Verbal Communication: The Written and Spoken Word

Because you are reading this book, we know you are familiar with **verbal communication**—transmitting and receiving ideas using words. Verbal communication can be either *oral*, using spoken language in forms such as face-to-face talks, telephone conversations, tape recordings, and the like, or *written*, in forms such as memos, letters, order forms, and electronic mail, to name just a few. Because both oral and written communications involve the use of words, they fall under the heading of verbal communication.

Varieties of Verbal Media in Organizations

Verbal media can be distinguished with respect to their capacity to convey information (see Figure 9-4).[18] Some verbal media, such as *face-to-face discussions* are considered especially *rich* insofar as they not only provide vast amounts of information, but are also highly personal in nature and provide opportunities for immediate feedback. A bit less rich are non-face-to-face interactive media, such as the *telephone*. However, not all business communication requires a two-way flow of information. For example, further toward the *lean* end of the continuum are personal, but static media, such as *memos* (written messages used for communication within an organization) and *letters* (written messages used for external communication).[19] This includes one-way communications sent either physically (e.g., by letter), or electronically (e.g., via fax or e-mail). Finally, at the most lean end of the continuum are highly impersonal, static media, such as *flyers* and *bulletins*, written information that is targeted broadly, and not aimed at any one specific individual.

Two types of written media deserve special mention because of the important role they play in organizations—*newsletters* and *employee handbooks*.

Newsletters. Although they are impersonal and aimed at a general audience, **newsletters** serve important functions in organizations. Newsletters are regularly published internal documents describing information of interest to employees regarding an array of business and nonbusiness issues affecting them.[20] Approximately one-third of companies rely on newsletters, typically as a means of supplementing other means of communicating important information, such as group meetings.[21]

McDonnell Aircraft Company, for example, relies on its newsletter as a means of communicating information about its merit pay system, a medium that has been very well received.[22] In fact, research at McDonnell Aircraft has shown that the more time its employees spend examining their company's newsletter, the more satisfied they are with their company's pay policy, and the fairer they believe it to be.[23] Newsletters appear to be effective devices in improving employees' attitudes and morale not only because of the information they provide about matters of interest to them, but also because the mere act of publishing a newsletter sends a message that the company cares enough about its employees to communicate with them.

Employee handbooks. Another important internal publication used in organizations is the **employee handbook**—a document describing to employees basic information about the company. It is a general reference regarding the company's background, the nature of its business, and its rules.[24] Specifically, the major purposes

newsletters Regularly published internal documents describing information of interest to employees regarding an array of business and nonbusiness issues affecting them.

☞ *Recall our discussion of work-related attitudes, such as job satisfaction, in Chapter 6.*

employee handbook A document describing to employees basic information about a company; a general reference regarding a company's background, the nature of its business, and its rules.

FIGURE 9-4 A Continuum of Verbal Communication Media

Verbal communication media may be characterized along a continuum ranging from highly rich, interactive media, such as face-to-face discussions, to lean, static media, such as flyers and bulletins.

(Source: Adapted from Lengel & Daft, 1988; see Note 18.)

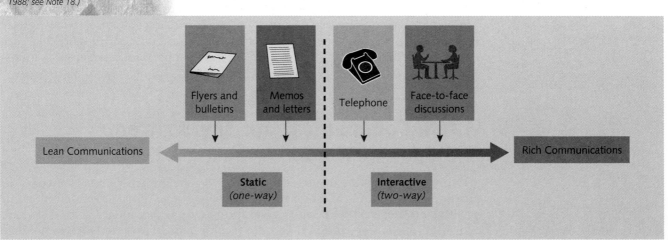

of employee handbooks are (1) to explain key aspects of the company's policies, (2) to clarify the expectations of the company and employees toward each other, and (3) to express the company's philosophy.[25]

Handbooks are more popular today than ever before. This is not only because clarifying company policies may help prevent lawsuits, but also because corporate officials are recognizing that explicit statements about what their company stands for is a useful means of effectively socializing new employees and promoting the company's values. As the major formal means of communicating pertinent company information to employees, employee handbooks are, in the opinion of one expert, "the most important document a company can have."[26]

☞ We discussed the process of socializing new employees, and its importance, in Chapter 7.

Uses of Oral and Written Communication: Matching the Medium to the Message

Now that we have reviewed various types of verbal communication, it makes sense to consider what types are most effective, and when. In this regard, research has shown that *communication is most effective when it uses multiple channels, such as both oral and written messages.*[27] Apparently, oral messages are useful in getting others' immediate attention, and the follow-up written portion helps make the message more permanent, something that can be referred to in the future. Oral messages also have the benefit of allowing for immediate two-way communication between parties, whereas written communiqués are frequently only one-way or take too long for a response.

Not surprisingly, researchers have found that two-way communications (e.g., face-to-face discussions, telephone conversations) are more commonly used in organizations than one-way communications (e.g., memos). For example, Klauss and Bass found that approximately 83 percent of the communications taking place among civilian employees of a U.S. Navy agency used two-way media.[28] In fact, 55 percent of all communications were individual face-to-face interactions. One-way, written communications tended to be reserved for more formal, official messages that needed to be referred to in the future at the receiver's convenience (e.g., official announcements about position openings). Apparently, both written and spoken communications have their place in organizational communication.

Additional research has shown that a medium's effectiveness depends on how appropriate it is for the kind of message being sent. Specifically, Daft, Lengel, and Treviño reasoned that oral media (e.g., telephone conversations, face-to-face meetings) are preferable to written media (e.g., notes, memos) when messages are ambiguous (requiring a great deal of assistance in interpreting them), whereas written media are preferable when messages are clear.[29] The researchers surveyed a sample of managers about the medium they preferred using to communicate messages that differed with respect to their clarity or ambiguity. (For example, "giving a subordinate a set of cost figures" was prejudged to be a very unambiguous type of message, whereas "getting an explanation about a complicated technical matter" was prejudged to be a very ambiguous message.) The results, summarized in Figure 9-5, show that the choice of medium was related to the clarity or ambiguity of the messages.

The data reveal that the more ambiguous the message, the more managers preferred using oral media (such as telephones or face-to-face contact), and also that the clearer the message, the more managers preferred using written media (such as letters or memos). Apparently, most managers were sensitive to the need to use communications media that allowed them to take advantage of the rich avenues for two-way oral communications when necessary, and to use the more efficient one-way, written communications when these were adequate. Note, however, that although many managers selected media based on the pattern described here (people identified as "media-sensitive"), others did not. They made their media choices almost randomly (this group was referred to as "media-insensitive").

Further analysis of the data revealed that these differences were related to the managers' job performance. Those who were media-sensitive were expected to be more effective than those who were media-insensitive. After all, effective communication is an important part of managers' activities, and using the appropriate medium could

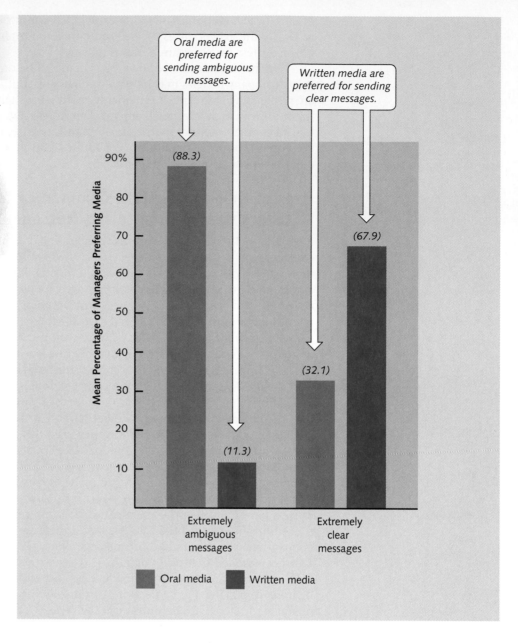

FIGURE 9-5 Oral vs. Written Communication: Preference for Media Depends on the Message

Research has shown that managers' preferences for a communications medium depends on the degree of clarity or ambiguity of the message being sent. Oral media (e.g., telephones or face-to-face contact) are preferred for ambiguous messages. Written media (letters or memos) are preferred for clear messages.

(Source: Based on data reported by Daft, Lengel, & Treviño, 1987; see Note 29.)

enhance their effectiveness. Comparisons of the performance ratings of managers in the media-sensitive and media-insensitive groups supported this hypothesis. Specifically, whereas most of the media-sensitive managers (87 percent) received their company's highest performance ratings, only about half of the media-insensitive managers (47 percent) received equally high evaluations. Apparently, the skill of selecting the appropriate communications medium is an important aspect of a manager's success. Unfortunately, it is difficult to say whether the managers' choices of communications media were directly responsible for their success, or whether their media sensitivity was part of an overall set of managerial skills that together led to their success. Still, these findings highlight the importance of making appropriate media choices in successful managerial communication.

When Words Go High-Tech: Special Issues of Electronic Media

In the past decade or two, advances in technology have transformed the way people engage in verbal communication while on the job. In particular, three forms of technology have revolutionized organizational communication—*video display terminals, electronic mail,* and *voice messaging.*

Video display terminals (VDTs).   In the modern office *video display terminals* (*VDTs*) linked to computers have replaced the paper-cluttered desks of office workers in the past. Although computers vastly improve office productivity, there is a hidden cost in using them.

Clerical employees forced to do their work in the shadow of a computer screen all day may miss human contact, especially when they are encased in cubicles separated from others by tall partitions. In an attempt to escape such isolation, the employees in an office studied by Zuboff mischievously pried open the seam of a metal partition that separated them from their coworkers.[30] People reported feeling isolated and solitary, and longed for the kind of informal contact denied them by the design of their surroundings. When contact between managers and their subordinates is restricted, critical opportunities to identify and solve organizational problems may be lost. Ironically, the same technology that makes people so efficient often makes interpersonal collaboration unnecessary, adding to feelings of isolation, which may undermine some of the productivity gains.

Electronic mail (e-mail).   One of the primary technological advances in organizational communication in recent years has been the use of **electronic mail** (popularly referred to as **e-mail**), a system whereby people use personal computer terminals to send and receive messages between each other. The electronic transmission of messages represents a communication revolution in that it allows for the very rapid transmission of information and the simultaneous sharing of identical information by people regardless of how widely dispersed they may be. What may be lost in terms of depth and richness of communication is more than made up for by high levels of efficiency.[31] The unprecedented access to other people and organizations is revolutionizing the nature of organizational communication.

Unfortunately, as e-mail systems have proliferated, with them have come some age-old problems—most notably, the potential for invasion of privacy. Employers have argued that the practice of electronic surveillance is justified because they need to keep tabs on their employees to ensure that they are doing what they are supposed to do. Because companies own the computer systems, corporate officials feel justified accessing them whenever they wish. Indeed, a recent survey revealed that one out of five supervisors has on at least one occasion examined employees' computer files, e-mail, or voice mail, allegedly for purposes of investigating larceny or measuring performance.[32] Somehow, the remoteness of electronic snooping makes people feel less uncomfortable than they would about breaking into an employee's file drawer.

The proliferation of electronic communication devices and strategies makes the question of privacy a complex one. Products like Investigator (software by WinWhatWhere Corp.) can provide companies with reports on every computer keystroke made by an employee. Companies such as Corel Corp., and many other call-centre operators, use electronic monitoring for quality control. Corel's Christine Bertin "said this is a common practice to ensure customer service employees are meeting an established set of criteria such as etiquette and product knowledge."

Employers are also concerned about how their employees are using the Internet. Whether because of a concern about illegal activity on the Net or because of a desire to insure employees are not frittering away their time, companies are seeking ways to control Internet access. Watts Industries (Canada) Inc. has taken a step toward preventing inappropriate Internet activity by its employees by limiting their Internet access to the company's Website and those of its market competitors. "In cooperation with the Royal Canadian Mounted Police . . . Bell Canada has also compiled a list of websites inaccessible to employees." It is not difficult for employers to track employees' electronic activity, and it can be done overtly or covertly. Some employees may not be aware of how closely their activities are being monitored.[33] The bottom line (today, at least) is clear: Employers *can*, and *do*, examine their employees' communications. So, if as an employee you are concerned about potential invasions of privacy, you may wish to follow the advice of Bill Moroney, executive director of the Electronic Messaging Association: "Don't put anything in writing that you wouldn't want other

Corel Corporation
www.corel.com

Royal Canadian Mounted Police
www.rcmp-grc.gc.ca

☞ *In Chapter 14 we will more fully discuss the feelings of isolation that tend to emerge when people work in highly automated environments.*

electronic mail (e-mail) A system whereby people use personal computer terminals to send and receive messages between each other.

TABLE 9-1 A Model Employee Communication Policy

Because many organizations do not have explicit policies about communication, employees do not know what levels of privacy they can expect. The following points represent what many experts consider the basic features of a good electronic privacy communication policy.

(Source: From "Bosses with X-ray Eyes" by Charles Piller in MACWORLD, July 1993, p. 121. Reprinted courtesy of Macworld Communications, 501 Second St., San Francisco, CA 94107.)

- Employees are entitled to reasonable expectations of personal privacy on the job.
- Employees know what electronic surveillance tools are used, and how management uses the collected data.
- Management uses electronic monitoring or searches of data files, network communications, or electronic mail to the minimum extent possible. Continuous monitoring is not permitted.
- Employees participate in decisions about how and when electronic monitoring or searches take place.
- Data are gathered and used only for clearly defined work-related purposes.
- Management will not engage in secret monitoring or searches, except when credible evidence of criminal activity or other serious wrongdoing comes to light.
- Monitoring data will not be the sole factor in evaluating employee performance.
- Employees can inspect, challenge, and correct electronic records kept on their activities or files captured through electronic means.
- Records no longer relevant to the purposes for which they were collected will be destroyed.
- Monitoring data that identify individual employees will not be released to any third party, except to comply with legal requirements.
- Employees or prospective employees cannot waive privacy rights.
- Managers who violate these privacy principles are subject to discipline or termination.

people to read."[34] Meanwhile, it is widely recommended that companies develop clear policies about the privacy of employee communication.[35] For a summary of points that should be included in such a policy, see Table 9-1.

Voice messaging.   Although e-mail can be very quick and efficient, it lacks the capacity to send a personal message using one's own voice. However, another technology known as **voice messaging** (or **voice mail**) allows for just that. Voice messaging systems use computers to convert human speech into digital information saved on a hard disk for playback any time from any touch-tone telephone.

Because 76 percent of all business calls are nonimmediate in nature (i.e., they do not require instantaneous action), and 56 percent of all calls completed involve one-way communication (i.e., they either give or receive information, but not both), voice messaging is frequently very useful.[36] Voice messaging allows people to avoid wasting time playing "telephone tag" and permits the highly efficient use of voice as an information tool because it precludes the need to translate messages into written characters or keystrokes. Voice messaging systems are so efficient, in fact, that they have been credited with saving an average of U.S.$2000 per employee annually.[37] Given its ease of use, it is not surprising that researchers have found voice mail to be generally well accepted.[38]

voice messaging (voice mail) A system that uses a computer to convert human speech into digital information saved on a hard disk for playback later by the receiver at any time from any touch-tone telephone.

Nonverbal Communication: Speaking without Words

As we noted in Chapter 3, nonverbal cues such as smiles and glances are important sources of information influencing our impressions of people. Here we will describe other vehicles of **nonverbal communication**, the transmission of messages without the use of words. Specifically, some of the most prevalent nonverbal communication cues in organizations have to do with people's manner of dress and their use of time and space.

nonverbal communication The transmission of messages without the use of words (e.g., by gestures, the use of space).

Style of Dress: Communicating by Appearance

If you have ever heard the expression "clothes make the man (or woman)," you are probably already aware of the importance of mode of dress as a communication vehicle. This is especially the case in organizations where, as self-styled "wardrobe engineer" John T. Malloy reminds us, what we wear communicates a great deal about our competence as employees.[39] In fact, research has shown that compared to people dressing inappropriately for job interviews (e.g., T-shirts and jeans), those dressing appropriately (e.g., business suits) feel more confident about themselves and, as a result, ask for higher starting salaries.[40]

Despite what fashion consultants might advise, there does not exist a simple formula for exactly how to "dress for success." As you might imagine, what we communicate about ourselves by the clothing we wear is not a simple matter. Importantly, we cannot make up for the absence of critical job skills simply by putting on the right clothes.

Of course, what is appropriate dress for one kind of job may not be appropriate for another. For example, people working at a small software development firm may be out of place wearing a skirt or a coat and tie, just as bankers would be inappropriately attired in T-shirts and jeans. As Bing Gordon, co-founder of the video game company Electronic Arts, put it, "If somebody wears a suit to work around here, it's a sure sign that he is interviewing."[41] Although the interviewee may feel obligated to dress up for an interview, even in an organization with an informal style, you can be sure that shortly after starting the job he or she will quickly adapt to its customary, informal style of dress.

Time: The Waiting Game

Another important mechanism of nonverbal communication in organizations is the use of time. Have you ever waited in the outer office of a doctor or dentist? Surely you have—after all, they have special "waiting rooms" just for this purpose. Why do you have to wait for such people? Mainly, because they have special skills that create high demands for their services. As a result, their time is organized in a manner that is most efficient *for them*—by keeping others lined up to see them at their convenience.[42]

Medical professionals are not the only ones who make people wait to see them. In fact, individuals in high-status positions often communicate the idea that their time is more valuable than others' (and therefore that they hold higher-status positions) by making others wait to see them. This is a very subtle, but important, form of nonverbal communication. Typically, the longer you have to wait to see someone, the higher the organizational status that person has attained. This has been shown in a study by Greenberg.[43]

The Use of Space: What Does It Say about You?

Like time, space is another important communication vehicle. Research has shown that one's organizational status is communicated by the amount of space at one's disposal. Generally speaking, the more space one commands, the more powerful one is likely to be in an organization. For example, higher-status life insurance underwriters in one organization were found to have larger desks and larger offices than lower-status underwriter trainees.[44] Not only does the amount of space communicate organizational status, but also the way that space is arranged. For example, among faculty members at a small college, senior professors were more likely to arrange their offices so as to separate themselves from visitors with their desks, whereas junior professors were less likely to impose such physical barriers.[45] These various office arrangements systematically communicated different things about the occupants. Specifically, professors who did not distance themselves from their students by use of their desks were seen as more open and unbiased in their dealings with students than those who used their desks as a physical barrier.

The use of space appears to have symbolic value in communicating something about group interaction. Consider, for example, who usually sits at the head of a rectangular table. In most cases, it is the group leader. It is, in fact, traditional for leaders to do so. But at the same time, studies have shown that people emerging as the

FIGURE 9-6 The Head of the Table: A Good Location for Communication

In part because of the ease with which they can see others and be seen by them, people who sit at the heads of rectangular tables enjoy effective communication with others seated at the sides.

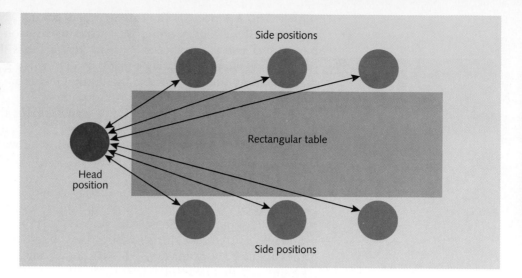

leaders of groups tend to be ones who just happened to be sitting at the table heads.[46] Apparently, *where* a person sits influences the available communication possibilities. Sitting at the head of a rectangular table enables a person to see everyone else and to be seen by them. That leaders tend to emerge from such positions is, therefore, not surprising (see Figure 9-6).

It is not only individuals who communicate something about themselves by the use of space, but organizations as well.[47] For example, according to John Sculley, former president of PepsiCo, his company's world headquarters were designed to communicate to visitors that they were seeing "the most important company in the world."[48] Similarly, by adding a second office tower to its company headquarters in Cincinnati, Procter & Gamble was said to be attempting to create a gateway-like complex that communicated the company's connection to the community.[49] As these examples suggest, organizations, as well as individuals, use space to communicate symbolically certain aspects of their identities.

In concluding this section, we note that the nonverbal mechanisms we have presented here, as important as they are, represent only a single channel of communication. Both verbal and nonverbal channels are important sources of information used in conjunction with each other in the process of communication. Thus, although we separated the various forms of communication for purposes of presenting them to you, it is important to realize that they operate together, complementing each other in complex ways in actual practice.

Individual Differences in Communication

As you know from experience, different people tend to communicate in different ways. Two people saying the same thing might do so very differently and communicate their messages in ways that may have different effects on you. In other words, there seem to be individual differences in the way people communicate. Researchers have verified that such differences are indeed real. We now will examine key individual differences in communication—differences based on personal style, gender, and nationality.

Personal Communication Style

Jila and Zoron are two supervisors who are approached by a subordinate, Roberto, to discuss the possibility of receiving a salary increase. They both think that Roberto is not deserving of the raise he requests. However, Jila and Zoron each go about communicating their feelings quite differently. Jila couldn't have been more direct. "I'll be frank," she said, "a raise is out of the question." Zoron's approach was far more analytical: "Well, Roberto, let's look at the big picture. I see here in your file that we just gave you a raise two months ago, and that you're not scheduled for another salary review for four months. Let me share with you some of the numbers and thoroughly explain why the company will have to stick with that schedule . . . ."

Although the message was the same in both cases, Jila and Zoron presented it quite differently. In other words, they appear to differ with respect to their **personal communication style**—the consistent ways people go about communicating with others. As you might imagine, some personal communication styles may be more effective than others—particularly, depending on the other person involved and the situation they are in. Communication style is learned, and so it can change. But, before we can consider changing how we communicate, we must first recognize the style we use. With this in mind, Linda McCallister has identified six major communication styles, one of which is likely to describe most people.[50]

personal communication style
The consistent ways people go about communicating with others (e.g., the *Noble*, the *Socratic*, the *Reflective*, the *Magistrate*, the *Candidate*, and the *Senator*).

☞ *Personal communication style is not the same as personality, but it is most likely related to several of the personality variables discussed in Chapter 4.*

1. **The Noble**: Such individuals tend not to filter what they are thinking but come right out and say what's on their minds (like Jila, in our example). Nobles use few words to get their messages across. They cut right to the bottom line.

2. **The Socratic**: These are people who believe in carefully discussing things before making decisions. Socratics enjoy the process of arguing their points and are not afraid to engage in long-winded discussions. They have a penchant for details and often "talk in footnotes."

3. **The Reflective**: These individuals are concerned with the interpersonal aspects of communication. They do not wish to offend others, and they are great listeners. Reflectives would sooner say nothing, or tell you what you want to hear (even if it's a "little white lie"), than say something that might cause conflict.

4. **The Magistrate**: A magistrate is a person whose style is a mix of part Noble and part Socratic. Magistrates tell you exactly what they think and make their cases in great detail (such as Zoron, in our example). These individuals tend to have an air of superiority about them as they tend to dominate the discussion.

5. **The Candidate**: Such individuals have a style that is a mix between Socratics and Reflectives. As such, they tend to be warm and supportive, while also being analytical and chatty. They base their interactions on a great deal of information, and do so in a very likable manner.

6. **The Senator**: Senators are individuals who have developed both the Noble style *and* the Reflective style. They do not mix the two styles. Rather, they move back and forth between the two of them as needed.

It is important to keep in mind that we all have the potential to use any of these styles.[51] However, we generally tend to rely on one style more than any other. Each has its strengths and weaknesses, and no one style is better than another. They are simply different. Effective communication begins with understanding your own style (see the Experiencing Organizational Behaviour exercise on p. 300) and that used by others. Then, when you first meet another, it is advisable to attempt to match that person's style. This is because people generally expect others to communicate in the same manner as themselves. However, the better we get to know and accept another's communication style, the better we come to accept how it blends with our own. In either case, the advice is the same: Recognizing and responding to communication styles can enhance the extent to which people are able to communicate effectively with one another (see Figure 9-7).

FIGURE 9-7 Open Communication Important to Public Agency

Lynda Cranston, CEO of the Canadian Blood Services, has committed her agency to open communication. "We are going to let people know why we made decisions. We don't have anything to hide. We're not going to skulk around and shred our documents in the middle of the night." This philosophy is consistent with Cranston's history as an administrator. As president of a major hospital, Cranston issued both a personal apology and a public one at a news conference given to explain the circumstances surrounding the death of a child who had been treated incorrectly at the hospital. Cranston does not believe in coverups.[52]

☞ *Gender differences in communication styles may well be related to sex role stereotypes. These are described in Chapter 6.*

 **Canadian Blood Services**
www.bloodservices.ca

☞ *Communication difficulties are but one manifestation of the growing trend toward globalization of organizations discussed in Chapter 2.*

Gender Differences in Communication: Do Women and Men Communicate Differently?

Recently, Deborah Tannen, a sociolinguist, has explained that men and women frequently miscommunicate with each other because they have learned different ways of using language.[53] In general, what appears "natural" to women doesn't come easily to men, and vice versa.

When it comes to communication, the basic difference between women and men, Tannen argues, is that men emphasize and reinforce their status when they talk, whereas women downplay their status. Rather, women focus on creating positive social connections between themselves and others. Thus, whereas men tend to say "I," women tend to say "we." Similarly, whereas men try to exude confidence and boast, thinking of questions as signs of weakness, women tend to downplay their confidence (even when they are sure they are correct) and are not afraid to ask questions.

This difference in style between women and men explains why they respond differently to problems. Whereas women tend to listen and lend social support, men tend to take control by offering advice. When men do this, they are asserting their power, contributing to a communication barrier between the sexes. Not surprisingly, whereas men may complain that women are "too emotional," women may complain that men "do not listen." Similarly, men tend to be much more direct and confrontative than women. Although a man might come right out and say, "I think your sales figures are inaccurate," a woman might ask, "Have you verified your sales figures by comparing them to this morning's daily report?"

The implications of this set of differences come to the surface once we point out another of Tannen's findings: People in powerful positions tend to reward people whose linguistic styles match their own.[54] As a result, in most organizations, where men tend to be in charge, the contributions of women are often downplayed because the things they say tend to be misinterpreted. The woman who politely defers to a dominant male speaker at a meeting may come across (to men, at least) as being passive. As a result, her contributions may never come to the table. However, the woman who breaks from this pattern and interjects her ideas may come across (again, to men) as being pushy and aggressive. And here too, her contributions may be discounted. In both cases, the communication barrier has caused a situation in which organizations are not only breeding conflict, but also not taking advantage of the skills and abilities of their female employees. The solution, although not easy, lies in appreciating and accepting the different styles that people have. As Tannen put it: "Talk is the lifeblood of managerial work, and understanding that different people have different ways of saying what they mean will make it possible to take advantage of the talents of people with a broad range of linguistic styles."[55]

Cross-Cultural Differences in Communication

In Chapter 2 we noted that the phenomenon of globalization presents many challenges. Clearly, one of the most immediate challenges has to do with communication. When people speak different languages, it makes sense that communication between them may be imperfect.

Part of the problem is that different words may mean different things to different people.[56] For example, as hard as it might be for people from countries with long-standing capitalist economies to realize, Russians have difficulty understanding words such as "efficiency" and "free market," which have no direct translation in their own language. People who have never known a free-market economy while they were

Campus Bookstore
www.campusbookstore.com

Celebrating 90 Years
of
tudents Serving Students

Queen's University Grounds
Kingston, Ontario
Telephone: 613-533-2955
R119390052

ans #15967   MC# 16
d Oct 06 1999, 5:48pm   Temp1

U #9780013083672
HAVIOR IN ORGANIZATIONS200HC   79.46 GST

o Total   79.46 ST
T   5.56 GST
tal   85.02 TL

eb it Card   85.02 Tnd
92970000038344355   EXP: 0110
t# 0065870
ange   0.00
em Count: 1
ANSACTION RECORD 99/10/06 17:30:57
TERAC DIRECT PAYMENT

MPUS BOOKSTORE
EEN UNIVERSITY GR
NGSTON   ONTARIO

_3N6

RM ID: 02322529   OP ID: 016
): 00584177
RD # 5892970000038344355   EXP: 0110
CT TYPE: CHEQUING   PURCHASE

AN REC # 0006578   AMOUNT $85.02

OO)APPROVED = THANK YOU AUTH # 0065870

[You Be The Consultant]

A produce distribution company located in a large city has a highly diverse workforce: There are lots of men and women working there who are new immigrants to this country. Unfortunately, the company is experiencing a serious problem with key jobs either not getting done at all or getting done incorrectly.

1. Explain why this situation might be linked to communication problems within the workforce.

2. What could be done at an individual level to help solve the problem?

3. What advice would you give with respect to changing the nature of the organization so as to help solve the problem?

growing up certainly may find it difficult to grasp the concept. It is therefore not surprising to find that communication barriers have been found to exist when Canadian executives attempt to conduct business in Russia.[57]

In addition to different vocabularies, cross-cultural communication is made difficult by the fact that in different languages even the same word can mean different things. Just imagine, for example, how confused a Canadian executive might become when she speaks to her counterpart in Israel, where the same Hebrew word, *shalom*, means both "hello" and "good-bye" (as well as "peace"). Confusion is bound to arise. The same may be said for cultural differences in the tone of speech used in different settings. Whereas English-speaking Canadians might feel free to say the word "you" in both formal and informal situations, the French have different words in each (*tu* for informal speech, and *vous* for formal speech).

To confuse these may be tantamount to misinterpreting the nature of the social setting, a potentially costly blunder—and all because of a failure to recognize the subtleties of cross-cultural communication. What can be done to eliminate blunders likely to be caused by the barriers inherent in cross-cultural communication? In the **GLOBALIZATION IN TODAY'S ORGANIZATIONS** section we outline several key suggestions.

Communication Networks: Formal Channels of Information in Groups

Imagine two different work groups in the Sales and Marketing Division of a large corporation. One consists of a team of creative writers, artists, and market researchers sitting around a table working together on developing the company's new advertising campaign. Another includes field representatives in various territories who report to regional sales managers throughout the country about consumers' preferences for various products. These people, in turn, analyze this information and report it to the vice-president of sales and marketing. If you think about how these two groups differ, one key variable becomes obvious: The pattern of communication within them is not the same. Members of the creative team working on the advertising campaign can all communicate with each other at once, whereas people in the sales force speak only to those who are immediately above or below them. The patterns determining which organizational units (either people or groups) communicate to which other units are referred to as **communication networks**.

communication networks
Pre-established patterns dictating who may communicate with whom.

Varieties of Formal Communication Networks

As you might imagine, there are many different possible communication networks within organizations. Do such arrangements matter? Do they make any difference in how well groups do their jobs and how satisfied group members feel? A considerable amount of research has shown that the nature of the communication linkages between group members can greatly influence group functioning.[58] So that we can appreciate these research findings, let's first consider some of the possible configurations of connections between people. Some of the most commonly studied possibilities are shown in Figure 9-8. (These various diagrams depict communication networks that have five members, although they can have any number of members from three or more.) In each diagram, the circles represent individual people and the lines connecting them represent two-way lines of communication between them. (Some communication flows only in one direction, but for simplicity's sake only two-way, mutual communication flows will be used in our examples.)

Breaking Down the Barriers to Cross-Cultural Communication

As we have noted, the potential for miscommunication between people from different cultures is considerable. However, short of becoming expert in foreign languages and cultures, there are several steps that can be taken to promote cross-cultural communication.[59]

1. *Observe, but do not evaluate.* Suppose while touring a factory in a foreign country you observe several assembly-line workers sitting down and talking instead of working. Based on your own country's culture, this would be inappropriate, a sure sign of laziness. Fearing what this means about the plant's productivity, you develop second thoughts about doing business with that company. However, as you learn about these workers' national culture, you discover that they were engaging in a traditional work break ritual: resting while remaining on the work site. The people in question were merely doing what was expected of them culturally and may not be lazy after all. The point is that you evaluated the situation by applying your own cultural values, and were misled by them. To avoid such problems, it is advisable in cross-cultural communications to describe what you observe (i.e., the workers are resting) rather than to use these observations as the basis for making evaluations (i.e., the workers are lazy). Doing so can help you avoid serious misinterpretation.

2. *Do not jump to conclusions.* When we perceive various situations, we tend to assume that our judgments are correct. However, experts caution that when it comes to cross-national settings, we should consider our judgments more as educated guesses than as certain conclusions. If you think that something is correct (such as your interpretation of the lazy workers in the above example), it is better to compare your judgments to those of experts in the local culture than to assume you are correct. By confirming the accuracy of your judgments, misinterpretation is less likely.

3. *Assume that people are different from yourself.* Most of us tend to assume that others are similar to ourselves until we learn otherwise. However, such an assumption is likely to lead us down the wrong track. Seasoned international managers know this. They take the opposite stance, assuming that others are different until proven otherwise. Because they "know that they don't know," they are less likely to be surprised by differences they don't expect—but which are inevitable.

4. *Take the other person's perspective.* Try to see the situation through the eyes of your foreign colleague. Consider this individual's values and experiences and ask yourself how he or she might view things differently. To the extent that you can effectively switch roles, you will be able to avoid the narrow-mindedness ("cultural myopia") with which we all tend to make decisions.

Although these measures may be easier said than done, with a little practice they can be mastered. Given that such practices are key to the success of international managers, the effort involved in following them would appear to be well worthwhile.

---

centralization The degree to which information must flow through a specific central member of a communication network.

centralized networks Communication networks that have central members through which all information must pass to reach other members (e.g., the *Y*, the *wheel*, and the *chain*).

decentralized networks Communication networks in which all members play an equal role in the transmittal of information (e.g., the *circle* and the *comcon*).

As Figure 9-8 highlights, communication networks may differ with respect to a key feature: their degree of **centralization.** Briefly, this refers to the degree to which information must flow through a specific member of the network. As you can see in Figure 9-8, communication networks such as the *Y, wheel,* and *chain* are identified as **centralized networks**. For members of centralized networks to communicate with each other, they must go through a central person who is at the "crossroads" of the information flow. In contrast, the *circle* and *comcon* are referred to as **decentralized networks** because information can freely flow between members without going through a central person. People in decentralized networks have equal access to information, whereas those in centralized networks are unequal because the individuals at the centres have access to more information than those at the periphery.

FIGURE 9-8 Communication Networks: Some Basic Types

Some examples of five-person communication networks are shown here. *Decentralized networks*, such as the *circle* and the *comcon*, give all members equal opportunities to communicate with each other. *Centralized networks*, such as the *Y*, *wheel*, and *chain* contain members (marked by a dark gold circle) through whom messages must pass to reach others.

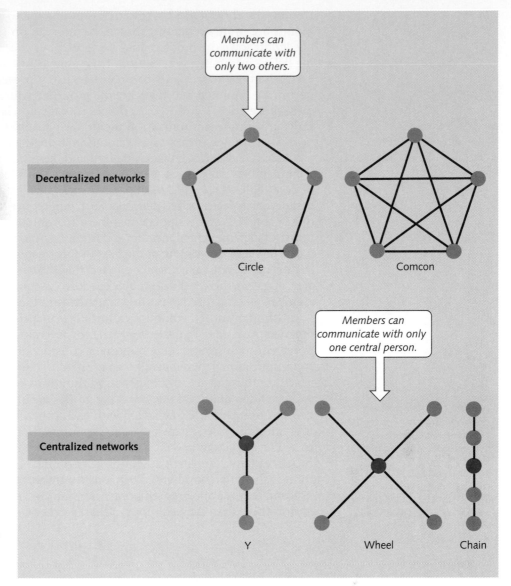

Members can communicate with only two others.

Decentralized networks

Circle

Comcon

Members can communicate with only one central person.

Centralized networks

Y

Wheel

Chain

☛ *The concepts of centralization and decentralization apply not only to groups, but as we will describe in Chapter 15, to the design of organizations as well.*

Formal Communication Networks and Task Performance

Research has shown that these differences in communication networks are responsible for determining how effectively groups will perform various jobs. Generally speaking, it has been found that when the tasks being performed are simple, centralized networks perform better, but when the tasks are complex, decentralized networks perform better.[60] Specifically, comparing these two types of network: *Centralized networks are faster and more accurate on simple tasks, whereas decentralized networks are faster and more accurate on complex tasks.*

Why is this so? The answer has to do with the pressures put on the central member of a centralized network. The more information any one member of a group has to deal with, the greater the degree of **saturation** that person experiences. If you've ever tried working on several homework assignments at the same time, you probably already know how information saturation can cause performance to suffer. This is what happens when a centralized network performs a complex task. The central person becomes so overloaded with information that the group is slowed down and many errors are made. However, when the problem is simple, the central person can easily solve it alone after receiving all the information from the other members.

saturation The amount of information a single member of a communication network must handle.

Decentralized networks have no one central person, so information and work demands are more evenly distributed. As a result, on simple tasks the information needed to solve the problem may be spread out over all the group members, causing delays in coming to a solution. This same feature represents an advantage, however, when tasks are highly complex because it prevents any single member from becoming saturated and lowering the group's performance. (See our summary of these processes in Figure 9-9.) In short, centralization is a double-edged sword. When tasks are simple, centralization facilitates getting the job done. However, when tasks are complex, it may cause saturation, bringing performance to a halt.

Research also shows that centralized and decentralized networks differ in terms of their members' satisfaction. Would you be more satisfied as a member of a centralized or decentralized network? Most people enjoy the greater equality in decision making that occurs in decentralized networks. Such groups give everyone involved an equal status. In contrast, as a peripheral member of a centralized network, you would be less powerful than the central member and left out of the decision-making process. The central member controls more of the flow of information and is clearly more important, leading many peripheral members to feel that their contributions are not fully appreciated. Together, these factors combine to cause lower overall levels of satisfaction among members of centralized networks compared with those in decentralized networks.

Although formal communication networks clearly play an important role in organizations, they represent only one of several factors responsible for organizational communication. One important consideration is that although the lines of communication between people can greatly influence their job performance and satisfaction, the various advantages and limitations of different communication networks tend to disappear the longer the groups are in operation.[61] As group members gain more experience interacting with each other, they may learn to overcome the limitations imposed by their communication networks. (For example, they may learn to send messages to specific individuals who have proven themselves in the past to be particularly competent at solving certain kinds of problems.) In other words, although the differences between various communication networks may be quite significant, they may be only temporary, accounting for the behaviour of newly formed groups more than the behaviour of highly experienced groups.

FIGURE 9-9 Comparing the Performance of Centralized and Decentralized Communication Networks

As shown here, *centralized* networks are superior on simple tasks (top), and *decentralized* networks are superior on complex tasks (bottom).

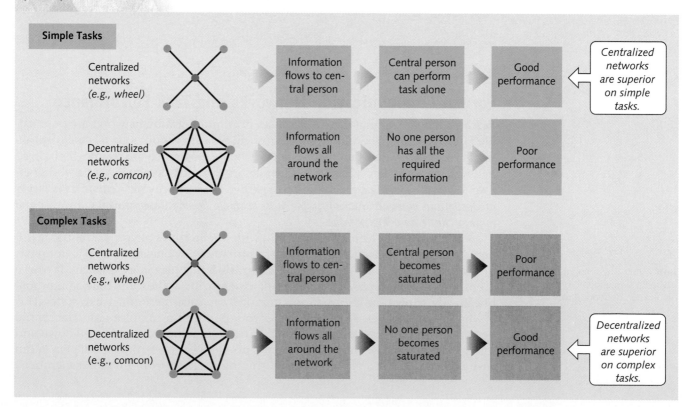

Another important point is that any formal lines of communication operate in organizations in conjunction with widespread informal networks that also may help groups accomplish their goals. Even if formal channels impede the communication of information, informal connections between people—such as friendships or contacts in other departments—may help the communication process. As we will describe next, the informal connections between people are extremely important in organizational communications.

Informal Communication Networks: Behind the Organizational Chart

For a moment, think about the people with whom you communicate during the course of an average day. Friends, family members, classmates, and colleagues at work are among those with whom you may have *informal communication*—information shared without any formally imposed obligations or restrictions. When you think about it carefully, you may be surprised to realize how widespread our informal networks can be. You know someone who knows someone else who knows your best friend—and before long, your informal networks become very far-reaching. Informal communication networks, in part because they are so widespread, constitute an important avenue by which information flows in organizations. In fact, in a recent survey middle managers ranked informal networks as better sources of organizational information than formal networks.[62] Therefore, if an organization's formal communication represents its skeleton, its informal communication constitutes its central nervous system.[63]

Organizations' Hidden Pathways

It is easy to imagine how important the flow of informal information may be within organizations. People transmit information to those with whom they come into contact, thereby providing conduits through which messages can travel. We also tend to communicate most with those who are similar to ourselves on such key variables as age and time working on the job.[64] Because we are more comfortable with similar people than with dissimilar ones, we tend to spend more time with them and, of course, communicate with them more. As a result, many informal gender-segregated networks tend to form in organizations (what among men has been referred to as the *old-boys network*).

To the extent that these associations may isolate people from others in power who may be different from themselves, this practice is limiting.[65] At the same time, however, exposure to similar others with whom people feel comfortable provides valuable sources of information. Further, there is scientific evidence showing that the more involved people are in their organizations' communication networks, the more powerful and influential they become.[66]

☛ For more on this topic, see the discussion of mentoring appearing in Chapter 7.

The idea that people are connected informally also has been used to explain a very important organizational phenomenon—turnover. Do people resign from their jobs in ways that are random and unrelated to each other? A study by Krackhardt and Porter suggests that they do not, but that turnover is related to the informal communication patterns between people.[67] These investigators theorized that voluntary turnover (employees freely electing to resign their jobs) occurs as a result of a *snowball effect*. A snowball does not accumulate snowflakes randomly, but collects those that are in its path. Analogously, it was reasoned, patterns of voluntary turnover may not be independently distributed within a work group, but may be the result of people's influences on each other. Thus, predicting which people will resign from their jobs may be based, in large part, on knowledge of the communication patterns within groups. Someone who leaves her job for a better one in another organization may know someone who has already done so. Krackhardt and Porter found support for this snowball effect among teenagers working in fast-food restaurants. Specifically, turnover tended to be concentrated among groups of people who communicated informally with each other a great deal before they resigned. This study provides an excellent example of the importance of informal patterns of communication in organizations.

Informal communication networks are characterized by the fact that they often are composed of individuals at different organizational levels. People can tell anyone in the network whatever informal information they wish. For example, one investigator found that jokes and funny stories tended to cross organizational boundaries, and were freely shared by those in both the managerial and nonmanagerial ranks of organizations.[68] On the other hand, it would be quite unlikely—and considered "out of line"—for a lower-level employee to communicate something to an upper-level employee about how to do the job. What flows within the pathways of informal communication is informal information, messages not necessarily related to individuals' work.

The Grapevine and the Rumour Mill

When anyone can tell something informal to anyone else, it results in a very rapid flow of information along what is commonly referred to as the **grapevine**—the pathways along which unofficial, informal information travels. In contrast to a formal organizational message, which might take several days to reach its desired audience, information travelling along the organizational grapevine tends to flow very rapidly, often within hours. This is not only because informal communication can cross formal organizational boundaries (e.g., you might be able to tell a good joke to almost anyone, not just your boss or subordinates with whom you are required to communicate), but also because informal information tends to be communicated orally.

grapevine An organization's informal channels of communication, based mainly on friendship or acquaintance.

The problem of inaccuracy. As we noted earlier, oral messages are communicated faster than written ones but may become increasingly inaccurate as they flow from person to person. Because of the confusion grapevines may cause, some people have sought to eliminate them, but they are not necessarily bad. Informally socializing with our coworkers can help make work groups more cohesive, and also may provide excellent opportunities for desired human contact, keeping the work environment stimulating. Grapevines must be considered an inevitable fact of life in organizations.[69]

It is interesting to note that most of the information communicated along the grapevine is accurate. In fact, one study found that 82 percent of the information communicated along a particular company's organizational grapevine on a single occasion was accurate.[70] The problem with interpreting this figure is that the inaccurate portions of some messages may alter their overall meaning. If, for example, a story is going around that someone got passed by for promotion in favour of a lower-ranking employee, it may cause quite a bit of dissension in the workplace. However, suppose everything is true except that the person turned down the promotion because it involved relocating. This important fact completely alters the situation. Only one fact needs to be inaccurate for the accuracy of communication to suffer.

This problem of inaccuracy is clearly responsible for giving the grapevine such a bad reputation. In extreme cases, information may be transmitted that is almost totally without any basis in fact and is usually unverifiable. Such messages are known as **rumours**. Typically, rumours are based on speculation, an overactive imagination, and wishful thinking, rather than on facts. Rumours race like wildfire through organizations because the information they present is so interesting and ambiguous. The ambiguity leaves it open to embellishment as it passes orally from one person to the next. Before you know it, almost everyone in the organization has heard the rumour, and its inaccurate message becomes taken as fact ("It must be true, everyone knows it"). Hence, even if there was, at one point, some truth to a rumour, the message quickly becomes untrue.

rumours Information with little basis in fact, often transmitted through informal channels.

Organizations can be injured by rumours. If you've ever been the victim of a personal rumour, then you know how difficult they can be to crush and how profound their effects can be. This is especially so when organizations are the victims of rumours. Tout Sweet Chocolates in Vancouver was sent into bankruptcy after anonymous letters, alleging some of the company's product was poisoned, were received by a variety of firms that sold the candy. The letters were a hoax.[71] Further, a rumour about the use of worms in McDonald's hamburgers circulated in the Chicago area in the late 1970s. Even though the rumour was completely untrue, sales dropped as much as 30 percent in some restaurants.[72] You may recall that in June 1993 stories appeared in the press stating that people across the United States found syringes in cans of Pepsi-Cola. Although the stories proved to be completely without fact, the hoax cost Pepsi plenty in terms of investigative and advertising expenses.[73]

One of the most persistent nagging corporate rumours has tied the consumer-products giant Procter & Gamble to satanism.[74] Since 1980, rumours have swirled that the company's moon-and-stars trademark was linked to witchcraft. Although the company has emphatically denied the rumour and has won court judgments against various individuals spreading rumours, it has persisted. As recently as 1995 P&G sued an Amway distributor for making false and defamatory statements about the company's links to devil worshipping. This has been the sixth suit P&G filed against an Amway distributor (Amway sells a line of competing products through a network of independent distributors), and its fifteenth suit overall.

Combating rumours: Some suggestions.   What can be done to counter the effects of rumours? Although this is a difficult question to answer, evidence suggests that directly refuting a rumour may not always counter its effects. Although Pepsi officials denied the reports about their tainted product, the rumour was not only implausible, but was also quickly disproven by independent investigators from the U.S. Food and Drug Administration.

Sometimes, however, as the P&G rumour illustrates, rumours are more difficult to disprove and do not die quickly. In such cases, directly refuting the rumours only fuels the fire. When you directly refute a rumour (e.g., "I didn't do it"), you actually may help spread it among those who have not already heard about it ("Oh, I didn't know people thought that") and strengthen it among those who have already heard it ("If it weren't true, they wouldn't be protesting so much"). In the case of P&G, the problem is compounded by the allegation that some parties may be making a concerted effort to keep the rumour alive. In such cases, directing the public's attention away from the rumour may help minimize its adverse impact. For instance, the company can focus its advertising on other positive things the public knows about it. In research studying the McDonald's rumour, for example, it was found that reminding people of other things they thought about McDonald's (e.g., that it is a clean, family-oriented place) helped counter the negative effects of the rumour.[75]

If you should ever become the victim of a rumour, try immediately to refute it with indisputable facts if you can. But, if it lingers on, try directing people's attention to other positive things they already believe about you. Although rumours may be impossible to stop, with some effort their effects can be effectively managed.

Organizational Structure: Directing the Flow of Messages

Although the basic process of communication described thus far is similar in many different contexts, a unique feature of organizations has a profound impact on the communication process—namely, their structure. Organizations are often designed in ways that dictate who may and may not communicate with whom. Given this, we may ask: How is the communication process affected by the structure of an organization? **Organizational structure** refers to the formally prescribed pattern of interrelationships existing among the various units of an organization. Although we will have a great deal more to say about organizational structure in Chapter 15, here we describe the many important ways in which organizational structure influences communication.

organizational structure The formally prescribed pattern of interrelationships existing among the various units of an organization.

Organizational Structure: Its Impact on Communication

organizational chart A diagram showing the formal structure of an organization, indicating who is to communicate with whom.

An organization's structure may be described using a diagram known as an **organizational chart**. Such a diagram provides a graphic representation of an organization's structure. It may be likened to an X-ray showing the organization's skeleton, an outline of the planned, formal connections between its various units.[76] An organizational chart showing the structure of part of a fictitious organization is shown in Figure 9-10. (Keep in mind that this diagram represents only *one* possible way of structuring an organization. Several other possibilities are described in detail in Chapter 15.)

Note the various boxes in the diagram and the lines connecting them. Each box represents a person performing a specific job. The diagram shows the titles of the individuals performing the various jobs and the formally prescribed pattern of communication between them. These are relatively fixed and defined. Each individual is responsible for performing a specified job. Should the people working in the organization leave their jobs, they must be replaced if their jobs are to be done. The key point is that the formal structure of an organization does not change just because the personnel changes. The lines connecting the boxes in the organizational chart are lines of *authority* showing who must answer to whom. Each person is responsible to (or answers to) the person at the next higher level to which he or she is connected. At the same time, people are also responsible for (or give orders to) those who are immediately below them. The boxes and lines form a sort of blueprint of an organization showing not only what people have to do, but with whom they have to communicate for the organization to operate properly.

☞ *We discuss the topic of power more thoroughly in Chapter 12.*

The organizational chart in Figure 9-10 makes it clear that people may be differentiated with respect to their levels in the organization's hierarchy. Some people (e.g., the president) are higher up in terms of the formal organizational power they wield, and others (e.g., department managers) are lower down. Such differences in one's level in an organizational hierarchy may be communicated in various ways. For example, people at higher levels tend to be called by their titles and are usually addressed in a formal manner. Such individuals also may communicate their higher positions by the way they dress (e.g., formal as opposed to informal attire) and by the size and location of their offices.[77]

That individuals are connected to each other by formal lines of communication can have important effects. For example, it has been found that the more employees are integrated into an organization's formal structure, the better they adapt

FIGURE 9-10 The Organizational Chart: An Organization's Formal Communication Network

An organizational chart, such as this simple one, shows the formally prescribed patterns of communication in an organization. Different types of messages typically flow upward, downward, and horizontally throughout organizations.

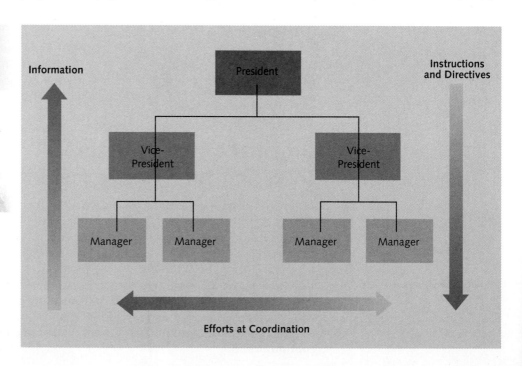

to using new technology.[78] This is not surprising if you consider that "being connected" to others promotes opportunities to learn. However, when formality is so great that individuals are denied opportunities to communicate their desires regarding the organization's operations, they tend to experience negative reactions such as stress, emotional exhaustion, and low levels of job satisfaction and commitment.[79] Such findings do not suggest that formal organizational structures are necessarily problematic—indeed, they are in many ways absolutely necessary for organizations to operate effectively.

Communicating Up, Down, and Across the Organizational Chart

As you might imagine, the nature and form of communication vary greatly as a function of people's relative positions within an organization. Even a quick look at an organizational chart reveals that information may flow up (from lower to higher levels), down (from higher to lower levels), or horizontally (between people at the same level). However, as summarized in Figure 9-10, different types of information typically travel in different directions within a hierarchy.

Downward communication. Imagine that you are a supervisor. What types of messages do you think would characterize communication between you and your subordinates? Typically, *downward communication* consists of instructions, directions, and orders—messages telling subordinates what they should be doing.[80] We also would expect to find feedback on past performance flowing in a downward direction (such as when managers tell subordinates how well they have been working). A sales manager, for example, might direct members of her sales force to promote a certain product and may then congratulate them for being successful.

Despite the fact that superiors mean to communicate certain information to their subordinates, the subordinates do not always accurately perceive their superiors' messages. This phenomenon was demonstrated in a study by Schnake and his associates.[81] These researchers surveyed a large group of managers and their subordinates about the extent to which the managers communicated various things to them (e.g., goals, assignments). The study revealed considerable disagreement between what the managers thought they communicated and what the subordinates thought their managers communicated. In all cases, the managers perceived their own communications as more positive than their subordinates believed them to be. Unfortunately, these discrepancies were associated with low levels of job satisfaction; the less supervisors and subordinates were on the same wavelength, the less satisfied the subordinates were with their jobs. In short, downward communication is not always a simple matter.

Downward communication flows from one level to the next lowest one, slowly trickling down to the bottom. As a message passes through various levels, it often becomes less accurate (especially if the information is spoken). Thus, it is not surprising to find that the most effective downward communication techniques are ones directly aimed at those who are most affected by the messages—namely, small group meetings and organizational publications targeting specific groups.[82] Such methods are being used—and successfully. For example, executives at Tandem Computers hold monthly teleconferences with their employees. Such efforts at improving downward communication have been credited with improving productivity and reducing turnover.[83] One of the most distasteful types of downward communication in which managers engage involves telling employees that they are fired. However, the process of communicating a termination decision can be made less unpleasant by following the suggestions outlined in **THE QUEST FOR QUALITY** section.

Upward communication. Information flowing from lower levels to higher levels within an organization, such as from a subordinate to her supervisor, is referred to as *upward communication*. Messages flowing in this direction tend to contain the information managers need to do their jobs, such as data required for decision making and the status of various projects. In short, upward communication is designed

"You're Fired!": Tips for Humanely Communicating the Bad News

Let's face it, no one likes to tell someone else that he or she is fired. Yet, it's inevitable; supervisors are forced to terminate employees all the time. Fortunately, several steps can be taken that will not only make the distasteful task less unpleasant, but that also will remove some of the sting felt by the terminated worker and the colleagues he or she leaves behind on the job (known as *survivors*). In other words, when a supervisor handles a termination interview properly, it can improve greatly the quality of work life for the supervisor, the fired employee, and the surviving employees. Here are several tips for doing the job more humanely.

1. *Thoroughly explain the reasons for the termination decision.* Too often when people are fired they claim that they had no idea why it happened.[84] However, when it comes to letting people know why they are being terminated, there's no such thing as being too clear. The terminated employee will have a great need to understand the reasons for the decision, and it is in the supervisor's best interest to explain them thoroughly. If a reduction in staff is necessitated by a merger, then the new organizational plan should be described. Likewise, if the termination follows from poor performance or some improper behaviour, these acts should be thoroughly documented in an unbiased manner. In any case, the terminated employee should leave the interview with a clear understanding of exactly why the decision was necessary. To the extent that this occurs, the decision is likely to be better accepted as fair and reasonable.[85]

2. *Be sympathetic to the fired worker's feelings.* Because so much of how we define ourselves is based on the work we do, losing a job is a major threat to one's identity. Naturally, the resulting feelings of uncertainty—both personal and financial—are quite unsettling. Because this is bad enough, it is important that the supervisor doesn't make the situation worse by being insensitive and uncaring. Doing so would only add insult to injury. A supervisor who is made uncomfortable by the situation is likely to want to get it over with and may not take the time needed to demonstrate sympathy and caring for the fired employee. Unfortunately, compassion is just what is needed at such a time. Showing compassion makes the termination interview less anxiety-arousing for both the supervisor and the fired employee. In fact, recent research has shown that the more workers who have been fired believe they were treated in a sensitive and caring manner while they were being terminated, the less likely they were to sue their former employers on the grounds of wrongful termination.[86] Thus, the act of demonstrating sympathy and compassion toward the terminated employee can help him or her accept this unfortunate outcome and move on with life.

3. *Explain that the decision is final.* It is only natural for an employee to feel desperate while in the process of being fired. As a result, he or she might go so far as to beg the boss to reconsider. However, the termination interview is not the place to enter into negotiations about the final decision. Once company officials have jointly decided to terminate someone, that decision needs to be presented—clearly and compassionately—but not negotiated. This is not to say that a poorly performing employee should not be given a second chance. In fact, this is a good idea. Our point is simply that once the decision to terminate has been made, it should not be considered negotiable at the interview. Any such reversal of judgment at this stage would greatly weaken the supervisor's power in the future.

4. *Offer assistance during the transition period.* It is important to explain during the termination interview exactly what arrangements will be made to ease the transition. Will the fired employee receive severance pay? If so, how much, and for how long? How about continuation of insurance benefits? Many companies are offering outplacement services to terminated employees (i.e., assistance in finding a new job, counselling, and so on), especially those who are victimized by restructuring. When outplacement is available, supervisors should make it clear exactly what kind of help is available and how to go about receiving it. Even if no formal outplacement program exists, the supervisor might be able to help by calling other prospective employers and offering to write a letter of recommendation. Again, to the extent that the supervisor can lessen the blow of being fired, the employee is likely to respond much more positively. This makes the interview more pleasant for everyone.

5. *Reassure the surviving employees.* When someone gets fired the word tends to spread quickly. The

☞

surviving employees cannot help but wonder what the future holds for them. Has the boss gone mad? Is the company in financial trouble? To the extent that uncertainty may breed distrust and spin off rumours, people's attentions may be diverted from doing their jobs. Thus, it is wise for supervisors to provide appropriate reassurances about the future. If more terminations are planned, be honest about it. Likewise, if the remaining employees have nothing to fear, such assurances should be provided in a clear and convincing way. It often helps for the "big boss" to be readily available during such times. An "open door" communication policy can greatly help employees attempting to alleviate their uncertainties about the future. When employees' fears about losing their jobs are addressed, and when they understand why previous terminations were necessary, they may feel the reassurance they need to focus on their own jobs.

Although firing someone is never easy, there is good reason to believe that by following the advice outlined here, this task can be made much less distasteful for everyone involved.

to keep managers aware of what is going on. Among the various types of information flowing upward are suggestions for improvement, status reports, reactions to work-related issues, and new ideas.

Upward communication is not simply the reverse of downward communication. The difference in status between the communicating parties makes for some important distinctions. For example, it has been established that upward communication occurs much less frequently than downward communication. In fact, one classic study found that 70 percent of assembly-line workers initiated communication with their supervisors less than once a month.[87] Further research has found that managers direct less than 15 percent of their total communication to their superiors.[88] And, when people do communicate upward, their conversations tend to be shorter than discussions with their peers.[89]

Perhaps more important, upward communication often tends to suffer from serious inaccuracies. For example, subordinates frequently feel they must highlight their accomplishments and downplay their mistakes if they are to be looked on favourably.[90] Similarly, some individuals fear that they will be rebuked by their supervisors if they anticipate that their remarks will be perceived as threatening.[91] As a result, many people frequently avoid communicating bad news to their supervisors, or simply "pass the buck" for doing so to someone else.[92] This general reluctance to transmit bad news is referred to as the **MUM effect**.[93] As you might imagine, because superiors rely on information when making decisions, keeping silent about important news, even if it's bad, may be one of the worst things a subordinate can do. As one executive put it, "All of us have our share of bonehead ideas. Having someone tell you it's a bonehead idea before you do something about it is really a great blessing."[94]

MUM effect The reluctance to transmit bad news, shown either by not transmitting the message at all, or by delegating the task to someone else.

Horizontal communication. Finally, we note the nature of *horizontal communication* within organizations. Messages that flow laterally (at the same organizational level) are characterized by efforts at coordination (attempts to work together). Consider, for example, how a vice-president of marketing would have to coordinate her efforts to initiate an advertising campaign for a new product with information from the vice-president of production about when the first products will be coming off the assembly line. Unlike vertical communication, in which the parties are at different status levels, horizontal communication involves people at the same level, and therefore tends to be easier and friendlier. Communication between peers also tends to be more casual and occurs more quickly because fewer social barriers exist between the parties. Note, however, that even horizontal communication can be problematic. For instance, people in different departments may feel that they are competing against each other for valued organizational resources and may show resentment toward each other, thereby substituting an antagonistic, competitive orientation for the friendlier, cooperative one needed to get things done.[95]

☞ *Horizontal communication is likely to require high amounts of helping coordination, processes discussed in Chapter 11.*

Communicating Inside versus Outside the Organization

All corporate communication can be distinguished with respect to whether it is aimed at other people within the organization (e.g., fellow employees) or outside the organization (e.g., the general public). Do executives say different kinds of things when aiming their remarks inside versus outside the company? A recent study by Fiol comparing the nature of these two types of communications suggests that they do.[96]

Fiol analyzed the comments made by CEOs of ten forest products companies in their letters to shareholders (external communications) over the ten-year period from 1979 to 1988. She also examined various planning documents (internal communications) for these same companies during this same period. Instead of looking at exactly what was said, Fiol categorized these communications with respect to how they were framed. Specifically, she considered whether statements focused on threats the company faced (e.g., the rising cost of materials) or on opportunities (e.g., growth in the housing market).

The results were quite interesting. In general, because the industry improved during the period studied, the proportion of documents framed in terms of threat dropped. However, the mention of threat was not equally likely to occur in both internal and external statements. For each year studied, a greater proportion of internal documents than external documents referred to threats. Likewise, with only few exceptions, a greater proportion of external documents than internal documents focused on opportunities. (For a summary of these results, see Figure 9-11.) Taken together, these findings suggest that executives were attempting to present their companies in a positive light to the public (by focusing on opportunities), but were more willing to address threats internally. They may well have been thinking that whereas it is important not to frighten the investing public, it is important to keep employees appraised of any and all threats the company faces so that it can take proper steps to defend itself.

FIGURE 9-11 Internal vs. External Communications: Is There a Difference?

Research has shown that executives tend to communicate differently when sending messages inside and outside their organizations. Internal communications tend to focus on threats more than opportunities, whereas external communications tend to focus on opportunities more than threats.

(Source: Based on suggestions by Fiol, 1995; see Note 96.)

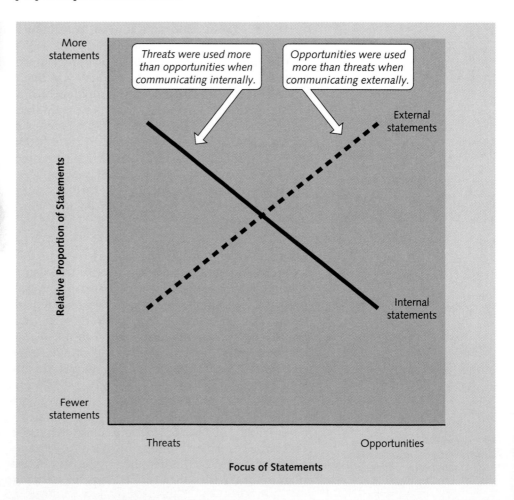

This research raises an important point that is now just beginning to be appreciated by organizational researchers. Namely, the way information is communicated is likely to be quite different depending on where that information is aimed. Insofar as the same information may have different meaning to internal constituents (e.g., employees) and external constituents (e.g., stockholders), it is likely to be framed in a different manner. This is not to say that any of this information is misleading. Far from it. Rather, the nature and focus of the presentation may be altered to suit the audience. Framing messages differently for internal and external audiences is a way of recognizing the different interests these audiences are likely to have.

Overcoming Communication Barriers: Techniques for Enhancing the Flow of Information

Throughout this chapter we have noted the central role of communication in organizational functioning. Given this, it is easy to understand how any efforts at improving the communication process in organizations may have highly desirable payoffs for organizations as well as for the individuals and groups working in them. Several steps can be taken to obtain the benefits of effective communication.[97] In this final section, we will describe some of these techniques, including measures that can be taken by individuals, as well as tactics for improving communication that involve entire organizations.

Keep Language Simple

You've certainly already encountered enough business double-talk without getting any more from us. Fortunately, our point can be stated simply: *Using needlessly formal language may impose a serious barrier to communication.*

Keep in mind that all organizations, fields, social groups, and professions have their **jargon**—their own specialized language. Your own college or university may have a "quad," or, as a student, you may have a "roomie" who is interested in "rushing." These are examples of a college student's jargon. No doubt, you've encountered a lot of language in this book that may at first sound strange to you. Our point is that the use of jargon is inevitable when people within the same fields or social groups communicate with each other. Some degree of highly specialized language may help communication by providing an easy way for people in the same fields to share complex ideas. Jargon also allows professionals to identify unknown others as people in their field because they "speak the same language." For example, management professors would describe this book as dealing with the field of OB, a term that would have a very different meaning to medical doctors (for whom it refers to the field of obstetrics). Obviously, within professions jargon helps communication, but it can lead to confusion when used outside the groups within which it has meaning.

Studying the use of jargon in one large organization, Kanter noted that a COMVOC—itself a jargon term for "common vocabulary"—developed among its members.[98] For example, within some divisions there were "fast-trackers" who "shot from the hip" to go for "the big win." Unfortunately, people in other departments of the corporation who didn't understand this jargon often felt out of place, creating a communication barrier. This happened not only between various departments of the large organization studied by Kanter, but also between various employees and their family members, who, as a result, often had great difficulty understanding what their spouses or parents did on the job. In fact, the wives of male executives identified over 100 unfamiliar work-related terms and phrases that they could not understand. Accordingly, we can safely say that jargon may be an effective communication device between people within one's social or professional group, but it should be avoided when attempting to communicate with outsiders.

In addition to avoiding jargon, the clearest communicators also keep language short, simple, and to the point. Hence, it is wise to adopt the **KISS principle** when

jargon The specialized language used by a particular group (e.g., people within a profession).

KISS principle A basic principle of communication advising that messages should be as short and simple as possible (an acronym for *k*eep *i*t *s*hort and *s*imple).

satisfaction over brief periods of time. **Centralized networks** have certain members through whom messages must travel. In **decentralized networks**, however, all members play an equal role in transmitting information. On simple tasks, centralized networks perform faster and more accurately; on complex tasks, decentralized networks do better. Members of decentralized networks tend to be more satisfied than members of centralized networks.

Informal Communication Networks

Information also flows along *informal communication networks*. These informal connections between people are responsible for spreading information very rapidly because they transcend formal organizational boundaries. Informal pathways known as the **grapevine** are often responsible for the rapid transmission of partially inaccurate information known as **rumours**. Rumours may be costly to organizations as well as individuals. Fortunately, there are several ways they can be combated.

The Influence of Organizational Structure on Communication

Communication also is influenced by **organizational structure**, the formally prescribed pattern of interrelationships between people in organizations. Structure dictates who must communicate with whom (as reflected in an **organizational chart**, a diagram outlining these reporting relationships) and the form that communication takes. Orders

flow down an organizational hierarchy, and information flows upward. However, the upward flow of information is often distorted insofar as people are reluctant to share bad news with their superiors. Attempts at coordination characterize horizontal communication, messages between organizational members at the same level.

Executives tend to communicate differently when sending messages inside and outside their organizations. Internal communications tend to focus on threats more than opportunities, whereas external communications tend to focus on opportunities more than threats.

Overcoming Communication Barriers

People can become better communicators by keeping their messages brief, clear, and avoiding the use of **jargon** when communicating with those who may not be familiar with such specialized terms. They also may improve their *listening* skills, learning to listen actively (thinking about and questioning the speaker) and attentively (without distraction).

The problem of **overload** can be reduced by using *gatekeepers* (individuals who control the flow of information to others) or by *queuing* (the orderly lining up of incoming information). The *distortion* and *omission* of messages can be minimized by making messages *redundant* and by encouraging their *verification*. At the organizational level, communication may be improved by using techniques that open upward channels of communication to employee feedback (e.g., *suggestion systems, corporate hotlines,* and *employee surveys*).

CASE PREVIEW QUESTIONS FOR DISCUSSION

1. If you were Jack Welch, how would you communicate with your tens of thousands of employees around the world? Include a discussion of both verbal and nonverbal methods of communication in your answer.

2. If you were Jack Welch, would you have as strong a passion to communicate with all of your employees worldwide, as he does? Explain.

3. What should a CEO of a global company communicate to his or her employees?

CHAPTER QUESTIONS FOR DISCUSSION

1. Using an example of an everyday communication in an organization (e.g., a supervisor asking her assistant for the month's production schedule), describe how the communication process operates (e.g., how information is encoded, etc.).

2. Imagine that you are a district manager attempting to explain a new corporate policy to a group of plant managers. Should this be accomplished using written or spoken communication, or both? Explain your decision.

3. Suppose you're interviewing for a job. Describe how the way you dress and the interviewer's use of time and space can influence what you communicate to each other.

4. You find yourself having difficulty communicating with a new coworker. Explain the kinds of individual differences that might be responsible for this and what can be done to overcome them.

5. Your company is being victimized by a totally untrue rumour about a pending merger. What steps would you recommend taking to put the story to an end? Explain.

6. In Shakespeare's *Hamlet,* Polonius said, "Give every man thine ear, but few thy voice." Discuss the implications of this advice for being an active listener. What other suggestions should be followed for enhancing the effectiveness of listening?

CASE IN POINT

Tackling Communication Barriers at General Motors

Something was wrong at the Saginaw Division of General Motors. Ron Actis, the facility's director of public affairs, sensed "a lack of trust between management and labour, [and] poor communications throughout the division . . . ." An employee survey confirmed his suspicions, and the problem was taking its toll on both productivity and morale.

Actis knew he had to get "the right message to the right audience at the right time with the right medium." He took a multipronged approach to opening a two-way dialogue between management and labour. Realizing that success depended on management support, he started at the top. He inundated GM's highest-ranking managers with reports from technical journals and popular magazines that demonstrated his point: Effective communication can improve productivity.

But, convincing management was only the beginning. An effective communication system had to be designed. With this in mind, Actis changed the content of the *Daily Newsletter*, a one-page publication distributed throughout the plant. General stories about the auto industry were replaced by stories with greater local interest, the division in particular. Readership increased dramatically; the plant's 20 000 employees became hooked on learning about what was going on under their roof.

This was just one of several publications Actis relied on to keep people informed. He also started a monthly tabloid, the *Steering Column*, mailed to employees' homes and distributed within the Saginaw community. Actis also targeted publications to specific groups. For example, a bimonthly newsletter, *Report to Supervisors*, contained tips for improving communication and advance information about key issues. To improve relations between management and the unions, *Joint Activities* contained features describing ways of reducing costs, improving quality, and staying competitive. A quarterly video magazine, *Perspective*, containing interviews with managers, customers, employees, suppliers, and union officials, did a good job of getting people at all levels talking to each other.

Appreciating that such conversations were too important to leave to chance, Actis also initiated a series of face-to-face meetings between labour and management. These turned into candid, no-holds-barred sessions in which various business issues were intensely discussed. Responses to such meetings have been so positive that as many as 17 different labour-management sessions are regularly held at the plant, some meeting as often as weekly.

Biannual communication audits (surveys assessing communication practices) have revealed that these various efforts have been successful. Before Actis's plan, fewer than half of the Saginaw Division's employees believed anything management said. Four years after the plan, the level of trust had grown dramatically: More than 80 percent of the employees not only believed management, but also were pleased with the effectiveness of the company's various mechanisms in getting information to them.

Although it is difficult to link any single program to a company's bottom-line performance, the Saginaw Division's financial picture dramatically improved during the first seven years in which Mr. Actis's communication plan was in effect. Not only did annual operating costs decrease in the neighbourhood of 5 percent, but sales per employee doubled, and the level of on-time deliveries improved to 100 percent.[117]

Can Maureen Kempston-Darkes, president and general manager of General Motors of Canada, grease the wheels of communication as well as Ron Actis has done at the Saginaw Division? Communication has been one of her greatest challenges in a company "with a history of strained labour-management relations and a productivity rating that is one of the worst in the auto industry."[118] According to her colleagues, she is "a team player who places great store in open communication."[119] Kempston-Darkes admits, "When you work in a rigid, hierarchical structure...that limits opportunities for people to communicate."[120] (See the CASE PREVIEW for Chapter 13 for a closer look at the leadership challenges faced by Maureen Kempston-Darkes at General Motors of Canada.)

 **General Motors of Canada**
www.gm.com

Critical Thinking Questions

1. In what ways did the things that Mr. Actis did at General Motors help overcome the company's communication problems? What made his actions so effective?

2. To what extent do you think that the success enjoyed by General Motors might be generalized to other types of organizations? Would these same actions work just as well in a service business, for example?

3. What additional steps could be taken to enhance communication in this General Motors plant?

SKILLS PORTFOLIO

Experiencing Organizational Behaviour

Assessing Your Personal Communication Style

When you read about the six different personal communication styles on pp. 277, did you have some idea of which one you tend to use? The following test, based on questions similar to those used by scientists to test communication style (McCallister, 1994; see Note 50), will give you a good idea of your own personal communication style.

Directions

Read all 18 of the following statements. For each one, think of how you *actually* communicate (and not what you think you should do). If you believe that the statement describes how you usually communicate, mark a "Y" for "yes." If you believe the statement does not describe how you usually communicate, mark an "N" for "no."

_____ **1.** When I talk to others I tend to be direct and straightforward.
_____ **2.** I am a "tell it like it is" kind of person.
_____ **3.** I freely share my opinions with others.
_____ **4.** I usually say the first thing that comes to my mind.
_____ **5.** I tend to get impatient when others speak.
_____ **6.** I tend to avoid long, detailed discussions.
_____ **7.** I very much enjoy chatting with other people.
_____ **8.** I tend to give very long, exact directions to others.
_____ **9.** I am sometimes accused of being redundant.
_____ **10.** I am prone to explain things by using anecdotes and examples.
_____ **11.** I enjoy arguing and debating things with others.
_____ **12.** I have seen people "tune me out" when I speak.
_____ **13.** People tend to tell me their problems.
_____ **14.** I tend to ignore people who seem angry.
_____ **15.** I tend to be soft-spoken.
_____ **16.** I may tell another person that I agree with him or her, even if I do not.
_____ **17.** People tend to interrupt me when I am speaking to them.
_____ **18.** I tend to be polite and supportive when I talk to people.

Scoring

1. Add the number of Y's in response to items 1 through 6. This is your Noble score.
2. Add the number of Y's in response to items 7 through 12. This is your Socratic score.
3. Add the number of Y's in response to items 13 through 18. This is your Reflective score.
4. To determine your style, compare your scores to each other.
   (a) If your Noble score is higher than the other two, you are a Noble. If your Socratic score is higher than the other two, you are a Socratic. If your Reflective score is much higher than the other two, you are a Reflective. These are the three dominant styles.
   (b) If your Noble and Socratic scores are close to each other, but far from your Reflective score, you are a Magistrate. If your Socratic and Reflective scores are close to each other, but far from your Noble score, you are a Candidate. If your Noble and Reflective scores are close to each other, but far from your Socratic score, you are a Senator.
   (c) If all three of your scores are very close to each other, you might not be aware of how you communicate. Retake the test, concentrating on what you actually do, instead of what you think you should do.

Questions for Discussion

1. What style did the test reveal that you have? How did this compare to the style you thought you had before you took the test?
2. Based on the descriptions of the personal communication styles in the text, were you able to guess in advance which test items were indicative of which styles? What additional items may be added to the test to assess each style?
3. How effective do you think you would be in altering your communication style to match another's?

Working in Groups

Sharpening Your Listening Skills

Are you a good listener, a *really* good listener—one who understands exactly what someone else is saying to you? Most of us tend to think that we are much better than we really are when it comes to this important skill. After all, we've been listening to others our whole lives. And, with that much practice, we must certainly be okay. To gain some insight into your own listening skills, try the following group exercise.

Directions

1. Divide the class into pairs of people who do not already know each other. Arrange the chairs so that the people within each pair are facing one another, but separated from the other pairs.
2. Within each pair, one person should be selected as the speaker, and the other, the listener. The speaker should tell the listener about a specific incident on the job or at school in which he or she was somehow harmed (e.g., disappointed by not getting a raise, being embarrassed by a teacher or boss, losing a battle with a coworker, getting fired, etc.), and how he or she felt about it. The total discussion should last about 10–15 minutes.
3. Listeners should carefully attempt to follow the suggestions for good listening summarized in Figure 9-12. To help, the instructor should discuss these with the class.
4. After the conversations are over, review the suggestions with your partner. Discuss which ones the listener followed and which ones were ignored. Try to be as open and honest as possible about assessing your own, and the other's strengths and weaknesses. Speakers should consider the extent to which they felt the listeners were really paying attention to them.
5. Repeat steps 2 through 4, but change roles. Speakers now become listeners, and listeners now become speakers.
6. As a class, share your experiences as speakers and listeners.

Questions for Discussion

1. What did this exercise teach you about your own skills as a listener? Are you as good as you thought? Do you think you can improve?
2. Was there general agreement or disagreement about each listener's strengths and weaknesses? Explain.
3. After the discussion about the first listener's effectiveness, you might expect the second listener to do a better job. Was this the case in your own group or throughout the class?
4. Which particular listening skills were easiest and most difficult to put into practice? Are there certain conditions under which good listening skills may be difficult to implement?
5. Do you think you will learn something from this exercise that will get you to improve your listening skills in other situations? If so, what? If not, why not?

TAKE IT TO THE NET

Prentice Hall

COMPANION WEBSITE

We invite you to visit the *Greenberg/Baron/Sales/Owen Companion Website* at *www.prenticehall.ca/greenberg* for this chapter's Internet resources.

CHAPTER 10
Decision Making in Organizations

LEARNING OBJECTIVES

After reading this chapter you should be able to:

1. Identify the steps in the *analytical model of decision making.*

2. Describe reliable individual and cultural differences with respect to *decision styles.*

3. Distinguish between *programmed* vs. *nonprogrammed* decisions, *certain* vs. *uncertain* decisions, and *top-down* vs. *empowered* decisions.

4. Understand the *rational-economic model,* the *administrative model,* and *image theory* as approaches to decision making.

5. Describe how *framing* effects, the reliance on *heuristics,* a bias toward *implicit favourites,* and the *escalation of commitment* phenomenon dictate against high-quality decisions in organizations.

6. Compare the advantages and disadvantages of using groups and individuals to make decisions in organizations.

7. Describe the conditions under which groups make better decisions than individuals and the conditions under which individuals make better decisions than groups.

8. Explain *groupthink* and how it may be a barrier to effective group decisions.

9. Describe techniques that can be used to improve the quality of group decisions (e.g., *individual decision training,* the *Delphi technique,* the *nominal group technique,* and the *stepladder technique*).

CASE PREVIEW

Yogen Früz World-Wide Inc.: Decisions on the Road to Hot Frozen Assets

What do you do when you are running low on opportunities to expand your business in Canada? For most companies the logical answer might be to move south of the border into the United States. For Michael, Aaron, and Simon Serruya (see Figure 10-1), the answer was to go global. The young entrepreneurs, who parlayed one frozen yogurt store near Toronto into the 4000-store Yogen Früz World-Wide Inc., reasoned that the U.S. market was already fairly saturated. Their gamble paid off and they now own the largest frozen yogurt franchise company in the world with stores in 82 countries. Currently the company has turned its attention back to North America and is in the process of buying small and midsized companies in the U.S.[1]

Ninety percent of the company's revenue is now from outside Canada. Its rapid expansion is presenting problems as well as opportunities. "One risk as it continues to grow will be managing that growth properly....It needs the infrastructure to look after all its investments."[2] In addition, there are projections that the world market for frozen yogurt may be reaching the saturation point.

Challenges like this are not new for the Serruya brothers. Their venture into frozen yogurt started in 1985 in Miami. Aaron and his uncle were operating a bagel shop when they found their store surrounded by frozen yogurt stores, one on either side. As they witnessed the success of both of the frozen yogurt stores, they became fascinated and tried to get the Canadian franchise rights for TCBY (The Country's Best Yogurt) but, at that time, the company was not ready to venture into Canada. Undeterred, they borrowed $90 000 from their father, Sam, and, combining that amount with the $25 000 Aaron earned from selling his share of the bagel enterprise, they opened their own frozen yogurt store in their hometown of Thornhill, Ontario in 1986. Brother Michael made up the name, Yogen Früz, and it stuck.[3]

Barely three months after this first store opened, Michael and Aaron were offered $200 000 for a 50 percent share in the business. This was a considerable morale boost for these young men in their twenties who had spent far less starting the business! They were tempted by the offer but, just before the papers were to be signed that would seal the deal, Aaron verbalized what they had both been thinking. "It's not right. We can do this on our own."[4] And they have, with a little help from family and friends. As they have worked to build their company, the brothers have had the benefit of both the practical advice of their father and the sound business philosophy of Seymour Schulich, future father-in-law of Simon, and the man after whom York University's school of business is named. Yogen Früz went public in 1994 with its first offering on the Alberta Stock Exchange, followed by its entry into the Toronto Stock Exchange in 1995.

As the success of low-fat yogurt grew, so did the pressure from those wishing to be franchisees. The Serruya brothers' skill at recruiting master franchisees around the world has been a key factor in their international success.[5] Another key factor has been the brothers' choice of mall locations for their stores. As Canadians, they recognized that frozen yogurt and Canadian winters were an un-

FIGURE 10-1 Strategic Decisions Contribute to Brothers' Success

Michael, Aaron, and Simon Serruya, the combined force behind Yogen Früz, continue to face challenges as they supply the world with frozen yogurt. The brothers are recognizing the limits of the frozen yogurt market and are making strategic decisions about diversification.[6]

likely match. The solution was indoor locations, a factor that was overlooked by another frozen yogurt chain that chose street locations and now has only 2 of its 100 stores still operating.[7]

With the popularity of frozen yogurt on the wane in Canada, the brothers Serruya decided to diversify. The company bought I Can't Believe It's Yogurt Ltd. (ICBIY) with its 1200 yogurt franchisees, an ice-cream manufacturing company (Bresler's Industries Inc. in Chicago), another company with a plant to produce hard-packed frozen yogurt (Brice Foods in Dallas), and a specialty coffee chain (Java Coast Fine Coffees). Such diversification ventures may well be the lifeblood of the company for the future.

Meanwhile the brothers continue to be committed to Yogen Früz as a family venture. "We won't fight any McCain fights," says Aaron. "We'll always do something as a group. We're a tight family."[8]

TCBY Enterprises Inc.
www.tcby.com

Yogen Früz World-Wide Inc.
www.yogenfruz.com

You may consider the Yogen Früz tale a success story, and it surely is. But, it's more than that. It's a tale of a string of decisions: deciding to start their own frozen yogurt store when they were refused a franchise licence by another chain, deciding not to bring in an outside partner after their first few months in business, deciding to go global before entering the U.S. market, deciding to locate in malls, deciding to take the company public, and deciding to diversify. Although you might not be making these kinds of decisions (at least not yet), you are no stranger to *decision making*. If you've ever wrestled with decisions about which college or university to attend or which job to take, you probably already have a good idea about how difficult it can be to make the right decision. If you think about the difficulties involved in making decisions in your own life, you can surely appreciate how complicated—and important—the process of decision making can be in organizations, where stakes are often considerable and the impact is widespread. Although we will provide much more detail throughout this chapter, decision making may be defined as the process of making choices from among several alternatives.

decision making The process of making choices from among several alternatives.

might not be making these kinds of decisions (at least yet), you are probably no stranger to decision making. If you've ever wrestled over decisions about what college to attend or what job to take, you probably already have a good idea about how difficult it can be to make the right decision. If you think about the difficulties involved in making decisions in your own life, you can surely appreciate how complicated—and important—the process of decision making can be in organizations, where the stakes are often considerable and the impact is widespread. Although we will provide much more detail throughout this chapter, **decision making** may be defined as the process of making choices from among several alternatives.

According to Canadian researcher Henry Mintzberg, it is safe to say that decision making is one of the most important—if not *the* most important—of all managerial activities.[9] Management theorists and researchers agree that decision making represents one of the most common and most crucial work roles of executives. Every day, people in organizations make decisions about a wide variety of topics ranging from the mundane to the monumental (see Figure 10-2).[10] Understanding how these decisions are made, and how they can be improved, is an important goal of the field of organizational behaviour.

"No decision. They're still sleeping on it"

FIGURE 10-2 Decision Making: A Basic Organizational Process

The making of decisions by both individuals and groups is a fundamental aspect of life in organizations. This particular group, however, appears not to be taking the task as seriously as it might.

(Source: Drawing by Bernard Schoenbaum; © 1988 The New Yorker, Inc.)

This chapter will examine theories, research, and practical managerial techniques concerned with decision making in organizations both by individuals and groups. Beginning with individuals, we will review various perspectives on how people go about making decisions. We then will identify factors that may adversely affect the quality of individual decisions and ways of combating them—that is, techniques for improving the quality of decisions. Then, we will shift our focus to group decisions, focusing on the conditions under which individuals and groups are each better suited to making decisions. Finally, we will describe some of the factors that make group decisions imperfect and various techniques that can be used to improve the quality of group decisions.

Decision Making: Its Basic Nature

We begin by examining the basic nature of the decision-making process itself. With this in mind, we will present a model describing the general steps by which decisions are made. We will then consider the idea that all people don't make decisions in exactly the same manner. Specifically, we will discuss individual differences and cultural differences in the ways people go about making decisions.

A General, Analytical Model of Decision Making

Traditionally, scientists have found it useful to conceptualize the process of decision making as a series of analytical steps that groups or individuals take to solve problems.[11] A general model of the decision-making process can help us understand the complex nature of organizational decision making (see Figure 10-3).[12] This approach highlights two important aspects of decision making: *formulation*, the process of understanding a problem and making a decision about it, and *implementation*, the process of carrying out the decision made.[13] As we present this model, keep in mind that all

FIGURE 10-3 The Traditional, Analytical Model of Decision Making

In general, the process of decision making follows the eight steps outlined here. Note how each step may be applied to a hypothetical organizational problem: having insufficient funds to meet payroll obligations.

(Source: Based on information in Wedley & Field, 1984; see Note 12.)

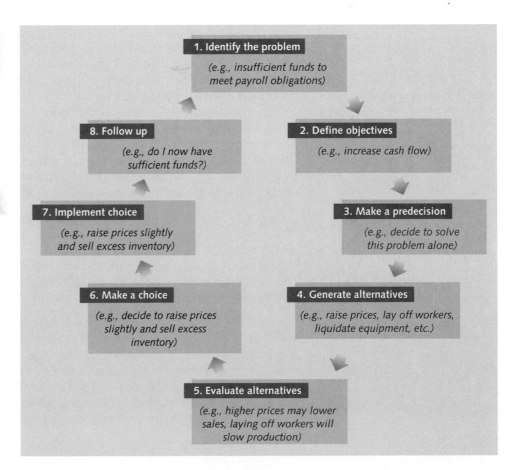

1. **Identify the problem**
   (e.g., insufficient funds to meet payroll obligations)

2. **Define objectives**
   (e.g., increase cash flow)

3. **Make a predecision**
   (e.g., decide to solve this problem alone)

4. **Generate alternatives**
   (e.g., raise prices, lay off workers, liquidate equipment, etc.)

5. **Evaluate alternatives**
   (e.g., higher prices may lower sales, laying off workers will slow production)

6. **Make a choice**
   (e.g., decide to raise prices slightly and sell excess inventory)

7. **Implement choice**
   (e.g., raise prices slightly and sell excess inventory)

8. **Follow up**
   (e.g., do I now have sufficient funds?)

decisions might not fully conform to the neat, eight-step pattern described (e.g., steps may be skipped and/or combined).[14] However, for the purpose of pointing out the general way the decision-making process operates, the model is quite useful.

1. The first step is *problem identification*. To decide how to solve a problem, one must first recognize and identify the problem. For example, an executive may identify as a problem the fact that the company cannot meet its payroll obligations. This step isn't always as easy as it sounds. In fact, research has shown that people often distort, omit, ignore, and/or discount information around them that provides important cues regarding the existence of problems.[15] You may recall from our discussion of the social perception process (see Chapter 3) that people do not always accurately perceive social situations. It is easy to imagine that someone may fail to recognize a problem if doing so makes him or her uncomfortable. Denying a problem may be the first impediment to solving it.

2. After a problem is identified, the next step is to *define the objectives to be met in solving the problem*. It is important to conceive of problems in such a way that possible solutions can be identified. The problem identified in our example may be defined as not having enough money, or in business terms "inadequate cash flow." By looking at the problem in this way, the objective is clear: Increase available cash reserves. Any possible solution to the problem should be evaluated relative to this objective. A good solution is one that meets it.

predecision A decision about what process to follow in making a decision.

3. The third step in the decision-making process is to *make a predecision*. A **predecision** is a decision about how to make a decision. By assessing the type of problem in question and other aspects of the situation, managers may opt to make a decision themselves, delegate the decision to another, or have a group make the decision. Decisions about how to make a decision should be based on research that tells us about the nature of the decisions made under different circumstances, many of which we will review later in this chapter.

   For many years, managers have been relying on their own intuition or empirically based information about organizational behaviour (contained in books like this) for the guidance needed to make predecisions. Recently, however, computer programs have been developed summarizing much of this information in a form that gives managers ready access to a wealth of social science information that may help them decide how to make decisions.[16] Such **decision support systems (DSS)**, as they are called, can only be as good as the social science information that goes into developing them. Research has shown that DSS techniques are effective in helping people make decisions about solving problems.[17] The use of decision-making technology leads to outcomes believed to be better than those made in the absence of such techniques. Moreover, computer-based DSS techniques have been found to be especially helpful in getting people to generate a higher number of alternative solutions.[18]

decision support systems (DSS) Computer programs in which information about organizational behaviour is presented to decision makers in a manner that helps them structure their responses to decisions.

4. The fourth step in the process is *alternative generation*, the stage in which possible solutions to the problem are identified. In attempting to come up with solutions, people tend to rely on previously used approaches that might provide ready-made answers for them.[19] In our example, some possible ways of solving the revenue shortage problem would be to reduce the workforce, sell unnecessary equipment and material, or increase sales.

5. Because all these possibilities may not be equally feasible, the fifth step calls for *evaluating alternative solutions*. Which solution is best? What would be the most effective way of raising the revenue needed to meet the payroll? The various alternatives need to be assessed. Some may be more effective than others, and some may be more difficult to implement than others. For example, although increasing sales would help solve the problem, that is much easier said than done. It is a solution, but not an immediately practical one.

6. Next, in the sixth step, *a choice is made*. After several alternatives are evaluated, one that is considered acceptable is chosen. As we will describe shortly, different approaches to decision making offer different views of how thoroughly people consider alternatives and how optimal their chosen alternatives are. Choosing which course of action to take is the step that most often comes to mind when we think about the decision-making process.

7. The seventh step calls for *implementation of the chosen alternative*. That is, the chosen alternative is carried out.

8. The eighth and final step is *follow-up*. Monitoring the effectiveness of the decisions they put into action is important to the success of organizations. Does the problem still exist? Have any new problems been caused by implementing the solution? In other words, it is important to seek feedback about the effectiveness of any attempted solution. For this reason, the decision-making process is presented as circular in Figure 10-3. If the solution works, the problem may be considered solved. If not, a new solution will have to be attempted.

It is important to reiterate that this is a very general model of the decision-making process. Although it may not be followed exactly as specified in all circumstances, it paints a good picture of the general nature of a complex set of operations.

Decision Style: Individual Differences in Decision Making

Do all individuals go about making decisions the same way, or are there differences in the general approaches people take? In general, research has shown that there are meaningful differences between people with respect to their orientation toward decisions—that is, their **decision style**.

Whereas some people are primarily concerned with achieving success at any cost, others are more concerned about the effects of their decisions on others. Furthermore, some individuals tend to be more logical and analytical in their approach to problems whereas others are more intuitive and creative. Clearly, important differences exist in the approaches decision makers take to problems. The **decision-style model** classifies four major decision styles (see summary in Figure 10-4).[20]

1. The *directive style* is characterized by people who prefer simple, clear solutions to problems. Individuals with this style tend to make decisions rapidly because

decision style Differences between people with respect to their orientations toward decisions.

decision-style model The conceptualization according to which people use one of four predominant decision styles: *directive, analytical, conceptual,* and *behavioural.*

☛ *Compare decision styles to various personality differences between people described in Chapter 4.*

FIGURE 10-4 Decision-Style Model: A Summary

Research has shown that people tend to adhere to one of the four decision styles summarized here.

(Source: Based on information in Rowe, Boulgaides, & McGrath, 1984; see Note 20.)

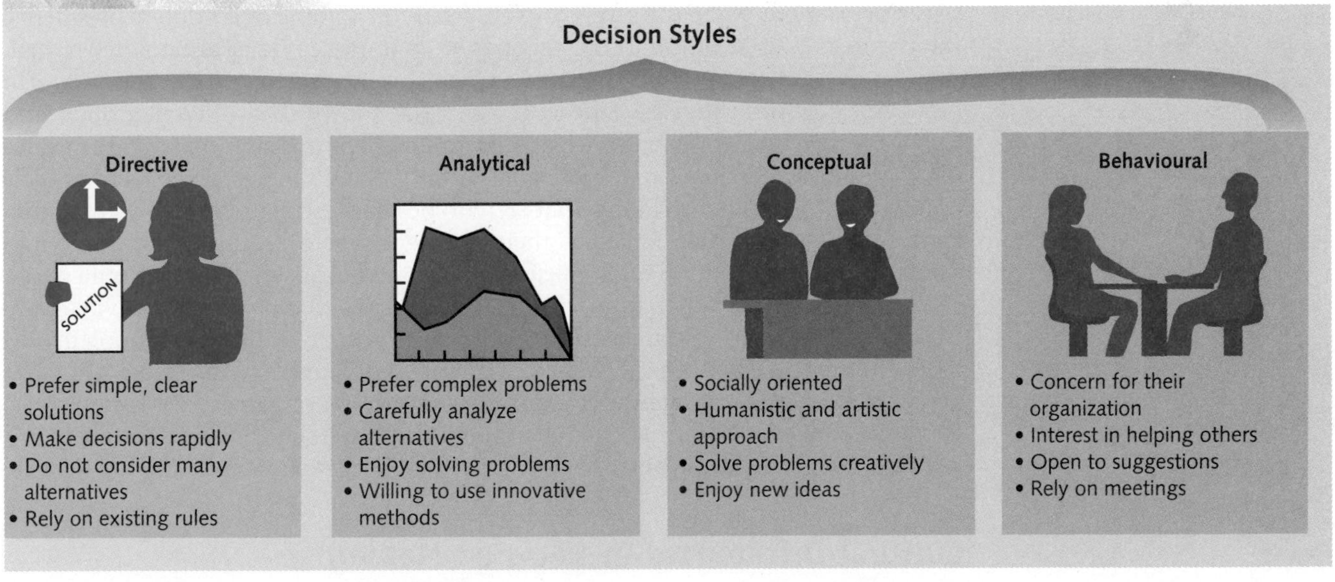

Decision Styles

Directive
- Prefer simple, clear solutions
- Make decisions rapidly
- Do not consider many alternatives
- Rely on existing rules

Analytical
- Prefer complex problems
- Carefully analyze alternatives
- Enjoy solving problems
- Willing to use innovative methods

Conceptual
- Socially oriented
- Humanistic and artistic approach
- Solve problems creatively
- Enjoy new ideas

Behavioural
- Concern for their organization
- Interest in helping others
- Open to suggestions
- Rely on meetings

they use little information and do not consider many alternatives. They tend to rely on existing rules to make their decisions and aggressively use their status to achieve results.

2. By contrast, individuals with the *analytical style* tend to be more willing to consider complex solutions based on ambiguous information. People with this style tend to analyze their decisions carefully using as much data as possible. Such individuals tend to enjoy solving problems. They want the best possible answers and are willing to use innovative methods to achieve them.

3. Compared to the directive and analytical styles, people with the *conceptual style* tend to be more socially oriented in their approach to problems. Their approach is humanistic and artistic. Such individuals tend to consider many broad alternatives when dealing with problems and to solve them creatively. They have a strong future orientation and enjoy initiating new ideas.

4. Individuals with the *behavioural style* may be characterized as having a deep concern for the organizations in which they work and the personal development of their coworkers. They are highly supportive of others and very concerned about others' achievements, frequently helping them meet their goals. Such individuals tend to be open to suggestions from others and, therefore, tend to rely on meetings for making decisions.

It is important to point out that although most managers may have one dominant style, they use many different styles. In fact, those who can shift between styles—that is, those who are most flexible in their approach to decision making—have highly complex, individualistic styles of their own. Despite this, people's dominant styles reveal a great deal about the way they tend to make decisions. Not surprisingly, conflicts often occur between individuals with different styles. For example, a manager with a highly directive style may have a hard time accepting the slow, deliberate actions of a subordinate with an analytical style.

Researchers have argued that being aware of people's decision styles is a potentially useful way of understanding social interactions in organizations. With this in mind, Rowe and his associates have developed an instrument known as the *decision-style inventory*, a questionnaire designed to reveal the relative strength of people's decision styles.[21] The higher an individual scores with respect to a given decision style, the more likely that style is to dominate his or her decision making. (To give you a feel for how the various decision styles are measured, and your own personal decision style, see the EXPERIENCING ORGANIZATIONAL BEHAVIOUR section on pp. 335–336.)

Research using the decision-style inventory has revealed some interesting findings. For example, when the inventory was given to a sample of corporate presidents, their scores on each of the four categories were found to be approximately equal. Apparently, they had no one dominant style but were able to switch back and forth between categories with ease. Further research has shown that different groups tend to have, on average, different styles that dominate their decision making. For example, military leaders tend to have high conceptual-style scores. They were not the highly domineering individuals that stereotypes suggest. Rather, they were highly conceptual and people-oriented in their approach. Such findings paint a far more humanistic and less authoritarian picture of military officers than many would guess.

In conclusion, research on decision styles suggests that people tend to take very different approaches to the decisions they make. Their personalities, coupled with their interpersonal skills, lead them to approach decisions in consistently different ways—that is, using different decision styles. Although research on decision styles is relatively new, it is already clear that understanding such stylistic differences is a key factor in appreciating potential conflicts likely to arise between decision makers.

Cultural Differences in Decision Making

People are people, and the process of decision making is essentially the same all over the world—right? Not exactly. Even if people were to follow the same basic steps when making decisions, there exist widespread differences in the *way* people from various cultures may go about doing so.[22] Because we tend to take for granted the way we do things in our own countries, especially such basic tasks as making decisions, some of these differences may seem quite surprising.

For example, suppose you are managing a large construction project when you discover that one of your most important suppliers will be several months late in delivering the necessary materials. What would you do? You're probably thinking, "This is a silly question; I'd simply try to get another supplier." If you're from Canada, this is probably just what you'd do. But, if you're from Thailand, Indonesia, or Malaysia, chances are good that you'd simply accept the situation as fate and allow the project to be delayed. In other words, to the Canadian or Western European manager, the situation may be perceived as a problem in need of a decision, whereas no such problem would be recognized by Thai, Indonesian, or Malaysian managers. Thus, as basic as it seems that decision making begins with recognizing that a problem exists, it is important to note that not all people are likely to perceive the same situations as problems.

Cultures also differ with respect to the nature of the decision-making unit they typically employ. In the United States, for example, where people tend to be highly individualistic, individual decisions are commonly made. However, in more collectivist cultures, such as Japan, it would be considered inconceivable for someone to make a decision without first gaining the acceptance of his or her immediate colleagues.

☞ *Recall the distinction between individualistic and collectivist cultures described in Chapter 2.*

Similarly, there exist cultural differences with respect to *who* is expected to make decisions. In Sweden, for example, it is traditional for employees at all levels to be involved in the decisions affecting them. However, in India, where autocratic decision making is expected, it would be considered a sign of weakness for a manager to consult a subordinate about a decision.

Another cultural difference in decision making has to do with the amount of time taken to make a decision. For example, in Canada, one mark of a good decision maker is that he or she is "decisive," willing to take on an important decision and make it without delay. However, in some other cultures, time urgency is downplayed. In Egypt, for example, the more important the matter, the more time the decision maker is expected to take in reaching a decision. Throughout the Middle East reaching a decision quickly would be perceived as overly hasty.

☞ *For insight into cultural differences in decision making, see the description of cross-cultural differences appearing in Chapter 2.*

As these examples illustrate, there exist some interesting differences in the ways people from various countries go about formulating and implementing decisions. Understanding such differences is an important first step toward developing appropriate strategies for conducting business at a global level.[23]

The Broad Spectrum of Decisions in Organizations

As you might imagine, because decision making is so fundamental to organizations, decisions themselves tend to be of many different kinds. Understanding the wide variety of decisions that are made in organizations is an important first step toward understanding the nature of the decision-making process. With this in mind, we will distinguish between decisions in three important ways: how routine they are, how much risk is involved, and who in the organization gets to make them.

Programmed versus Nonprogrammed Decisions

Think of a decision that is made repeatedly, according to a preestablished set of alternatives. For example, a word processing operator may decide to make a backup copy of the day's work on disk, or a manager of a fast-food restaurant may decide to order hamburger buns as the supply starts to get low. Decisions such as these are known as **programmed decisions**—routine decisions, made by lower-level personnel, that rely on predetermined courses of action.

programmed decisions Highly routine decisions made according to preestablished organizational routines and procedures.

By contrast, we may identify **nonprogrammed decisions**—ones for which there are no ready-made solutions. The decision maker confronts a unique situation in which the solutions are novel. A research scientist attempting to find a cure for a rare disease faces a problem that is poorly structured. Unlike the order clerk, whose course of action is clear when the supply of paper clips runs low, the scientist in this example must rely on creativity rather than preexisting answers to solve the problem at hand.

Certain types of nonprogrammed decisions are known as **strategic decisions**.[24] These decisions are typically made by coalitions of high-level executives and have important long-term implications for the organization. Strategic decisions reflect a consistent pattern for directing the organization in some specified fashion—that is, according to an underlying organizational philosophy or mission. For example, an organization may make a strategic decision to grow at a specified yearly rate, or to be guided by a certain code of corporate ethics. Both of these decisions are likely to be considered "strategic" because they guide the future direction of the organization.

Table 10-1 summarizes the differences between programmed and nonprogrammed decisions with respect to three important questions. First, *what type of tasks are involved?* Programmed decisions are made on tasks that are common and routine, whereas nonprogrammed decisions are made on unique and novel tasks. Second, *how much reliance is there on organizational policies?* In making programmed decisions, the decision maker can count on guidance from statements of organizational policy and procedure. However, nonprogrammed decisions require the use of creative solutions that are implemented for the first time; past solutions may provide little guidance. Finally, *who makes the decisions?* Not surprisingly, nonprogrammed decisions typically are made by upper-level organizational personnel, whereas the more routine, well-structured decisions are usually relegated to lower-level personnel.[25]

Certain versus Uncertain Decisions

Just think of how easy it would be to make decisions if we knew what the future had in store. Making the best investments in the stock market would simply be a matter of looking up the changes in tomorrow's newspaper. Of course, we never know exactly what the future holds, but we can be more certain at some times than others. Certainty about the factors on which decisions are made is highly desired in organizational decision making.

Degrees of certainty and uncertainty are expressed as statements of *risk*. All organizational decisions involve some degree of risk—ranging from complete certainty (no risk) to complete uncertainty, "a stab in the dark" (high risk). To make the best possible decisions in organizations, people seek to "manage" the risks they take—that is, minimizing the riskiness of a decision by gaining access to information relevant to the decision.[26]

What makes an outcome risky or not is the *probability* of obtaining the desired outcome. Decision makers attempt to obtain information about the probabilities, or odds, of certain events occurring given that other events have occurred. For example, a financial analyst may report that a certain stock has risen 80 percent of the time that the prime rate has dropped, or a meteorologist may report that the precipitation probability is 50 percent (i.e., in the past it rained or snowed half the time

TABLE 10-1 Programmed and Nonprogrammed Decisions: A Comparison

The two major types of organizational decisions—*programmed decisions* and *nonprogrammed decisions*— differ with respect to the types of task on which they are made, the degree to which solutions may be found in existing organizational policies, and the typical decision-making unit.

| Variable | Type of Decision | |
	Programmed Decisions	Nonprogrammed Decisions
Type of task	Simple, routine	Complex, creative
Reliance on organizational policies	Considerable guidance from past decisions	No guidance from past decisions
Typical decision maker	Lower-level workers (usually alone)	Upper-level supervisors (usually in groups)

certain atmospheric conditions existed). These data may be considered reports of *objective probabilities* because they are based on concrete, verifiable data. Many decisions are also based on *subjective probabilities*—personal beliefs or hunches about what will happen (see Figure 10-5). For example, a gambler who bets on a horse because it has a name similar to one of his children's or a person who suspects it's going to rain because he just washed his car is basing these judgments on subjective probabilities.

Obviously, uncertainty is an undesirable characteristic in decision making. We may view much of what decision makers do in organizations as attempting to reduce uncertainty (i.e., putting the odds in their favour) so they can make better decisions. How do organizations respond when faced with highly uncertain conditions? Studies have shown that decision uncertainty can be reduced by *establishing linkages with other organizations*. The more an organization knows about what another organization will do, the greater certainty it will have in making decisions.[27] This is part of a general tendency for organizational decision makers to respond to uncertainty by reducing the unpredictability of other organizations in their business environments. Those outside organizations with which managers have the greatest contact are most likely to be the ones whose actions are copied.[28]

In general, what reduces uncertainty in decision-making situations? The answer is *information*. Knowledge about the past and the present can be used to help make projections about the future. A modern executive's access to data needed to make important decisions may be as close as the nearest computer terminal. Indeed, computer technology has greatly aided managers' ability to make decisions quickly, using the most accurate and thorough information available.[29] A variety of on-line information services are designed to provide organizational decision makers with the latest information relevant to the decisions they are making.

Of course, not all information needed to make decisions comes from computers. Many managerial decisions are also based on the decision maker's past experiences and intuition.[30] This is not to say that top managers rely on subjective information in making decisions (although they might), but that their history of past decisions—both successes and failures—is often given great weight in the decision-making process. In other words, when it comes to making decisions, people often rely on what has worked for them in the past. This strategy is often successful in part because experienced decision makers tend to make better use of information relevant to the decisions they are making.[31] Individuals who have expertise in certain subjects know what information is most relevant and also how to interpret it to make the best decisions. It is therefore not surprising that people seek experienced professionals,

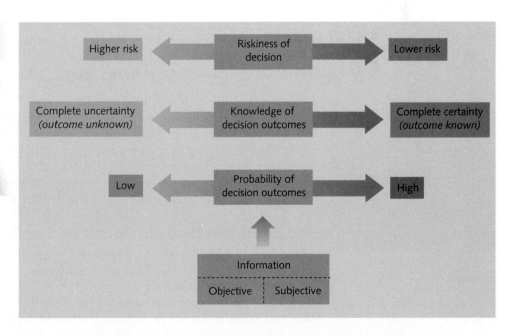

FIGURE 10-5 The Riskiness of a Decision: A Summary

Decisions differ with respect to their degree of riskiness, based on how certain (high probability) or uncertain (low probability) various outcomes may be. Information—both objective and subjective—is used as the basis for estimating the probability of a decision outcome.

such as doctors and lawyers who are seasoned veterans in their fields, when it comes to making important decisions. With high levels of expertise comes information relevant to assessing the riskiness of decision alternatives, and how to reduce it.

Top-Down versus Empowered Decisions

top-down decision making The practice of vesting decision-making power in the hands of superiors as opposed to lower-level employees.

empowered decision making The practice of vesting power for making decisions in the hands of employees themselves.

☛ *The concept of empowerment is also discussed in the context of teams in Chapter 8 and power in Chapter 12.*

Traditionally, in organizations, the job of making all but the most trivial decisions belonged to managers. In fact, organizational scientist Herbert Simon, who won a Nobel prize for his work on the economics of decision making, has gone so far as to describe decision making as synonymous with managing.[32] Subordinates collected information and gave it to superiors, who used it to make decisions. This approach, known as **top-down decision making** puts decision-making power in the hands of managers, leaving lower-level workers little or no opportunities to make decisions. If this sounds familiar to you, it is because it has been the way most organizations have operated.

Today, however, a new approach has come into vogue which is in many ways exactly the opposite. The idea of **empowered decision making** allows employees to make the decisions required to do their jobs without first seeking supervisory approval. As the name implies, it gives them the power to decide what they need to do in order to do their jobs effectively. The rationale for this philosophy of decision making is that the people who do the jobs know what's best, so having someone else make the decisions may not make the most sense. In addition, when people are empowered to make their own decisions they are more likely to accept the consequences of those decisions. If the decision was a good one, they can feel good about it. If not, then they have learned a valuable lesson for the next time. In either case, people are more committed to courses of action based on decisions they have made themselves than ones based on decisions that others have made. And, such commitment can be important to keeping the organization functioning effectively.

Many different companies today are empowering their employees to make a wide variety of decisions. As an example, the Ritz-Carlton hotel chain has empowered each of its employees to spend up to U.S.$2000 of the company's money per day to fix whatever they find that needs to be repaired. No longer would a chambermaid who finds a broken lamp in one of the guest rooms need to fill out a form that gets passed from one person to the next. He or she is empowered to get the right person to get the job done right away. Similarly, employees at Volvo's assembly plant in Kalmar, Sweden, are empowered to make decisions about how to do their work (see Figure 10-6). In fact, this practice has been going on in Sweden for many years.

It is not only individual employees who might be empowered, but work teams as well. Indeed, the concept of self-managed work teams discussed in Chapter 8 involves systematically empowering several individuals working together with the tools needed to make the most effective decisions possible.

FIGURE 10-6 Volvo Employees Make Empowered Decisions

People working at Volvo's assembly plant in Kalmar, Sweden, are empowered to make a wide variety of decisions about how to do their jobs. Work teams themselves, not top management, take responsibility for scheduling tasks and distributing rewards.

Individual Decisions: How Are They Made?

Now that we have identified the types of decisions people make in organizations, we are prepared to consider the matter of how people go about making them. Perhaps you are thinking, "What do you mean, don't you just think things over and do what you think is best?" Although this sometimes may be true, you will see that there's a lot more to decision making than meets the eye. (For a test of the ethics of decisions, see **THE ETHICS ANGLE**.) In fact, scientists have considered several different approaches to how individuals make decisions. Here, we will review three of the most important ones.

The Rational-Economic Model: In Search of the Ideal Decision

rational decisions Decisions that maximize the chance of attaining an individual's, group's, or organization's goals.

We all like to think that we are "rational" people who make the best possible decisions. But what exactly does it mean to make a *rational* decision? Organizational scientists view **rational decisions** as ones that maximize the attainment of goals, whether they are the goals of a person, a group, or an entire organization.[33] What would be the most rational way for an individual to go about making a decision? Economists

Guidelines for Making Ethical Decisions

If you consider all the moral scandals that have made headlines in recent years (e.g., stockbrokers defrauding their customers, religious leaders stealing from their ministries, and politicians misusing their power for personal gain), it's easy to see that people often have difficulty judging what's right and behaving accordingly. Unfortunately, cheating and stealing have become more commonplace than we would like.[34] However, the pursuit of quality in organizations demands that everyone adheres to the highest moral standards.

The problem with this ideal is that even those of us who subscribe to high moral values are sometimes tempted to behave unethically. If you're thinking, "other people act unethically, but not me," then ask yourself: Have you ever taken home small articles of company property (e.g., pencils, tape) for personal use? Or, have you ever made personal copies on the company copier or fudged a little on your expense account?

If the answer is yes, you may be saying, "Sure, but companies *expect* employees to do these things." And, of course, taking home a pencil is not the same as making off with a million-dollar payroll. Although this may be true, we cannot ignore the fact that people often attempt to justify their actions by rationalizing that they are not really unethical. For example, you may find yourself saying something like, "Everybody's doing it, so it must be okay." This kind of rationalization makes it possible for us to talk ourselves into making unethical decisions, thinking that they are really not so bad. To avoid such situations—and, thereby to improve ethical decision making—it may be useful to run your contemplated decisions through an ethics test.[35] To do so, ask yourself the following questions:

1. *Does it violate the obvious "shall-nots"?* Although many people realize that "thou shall not lie, or cheat, or steal," they do it anyway. So, instead of thinking of a way around such prohibitions (e.g., by convincing yourself that "it's acceptable in this situation"), avoid violating these well-established societal rules altogether.

2. *Will anyone get hurt?* Philosophers consider an action to be ethical to the extent that it brings the greatest good to the greatest number. Thus, if someone may be harmed in any way as a result of your actions, you should probably rethink your decision; it's probably unethical.

3. *How would you feel if your decision was reported on the front page of your newspaper?* If your decision is really ethical, you wouldn't have any reason to worry about having it made public. (In fact, you'd probably be pleased to receive the publicity.) However, if you find yourself uneasy about answering this question affirmatively, the decision you are contemplating may be unethical.

4. *What if you did it 100 times?* Sometimes, an unethical action doesn't seem so bad because it's done only once. In such a case, the damage might not be so bad, although the action still might not be ethical. However, if the act you're contemplating appears to be more wrong if it were done 100 times, then it's probably also wrong the first time.

5. *How would you feel if someone did it to you?* If something you are thinking of doing to another really is ethical, you would probably find it acceptable if your situations were reversed. Thus, if you have any doubts as to how you'd feel being the person affected by your decision, you may wish to reconsider.

6. *What's your gut feeling?* Sometimes things just look bad, and probably because they *are*. If your actions are unethical, you probably can tell by listening to that little voice inside your head. The trick is to listen to *that* voice and to silence the one that tells you to do otherwise—although we acknowledge that this may be easier said than done.

To be sure, considering these questions will not transform a devil into an angel. Still, they may be useful for judging the ethicalness of the decisions you may be contemplating. Your answers to these six questions may help you avoid rationalizing that unethical acts are really ethical. And, once we recognize that the decisions we are thinking of making may not be ethical, we are well on the way to behaving in an ethical fashion.

---

rational-economic model The model of decision making according to which decision makers consider all possible alternatives to problems before selecting the optimal solution.

interested in predicting market conditions and prices have relied on a **rational-economic model** of decision making, which assumes that decisions are optimal in every way. An economically rational decision maker will attempt to maximize his or her profits by systematically searching for the *optimum* solution to a problem. For this to occur, the decision maker must have complete and perfect information, and be able to process all this information in an accurate and unbiased fashion.[36]

In many respects, rational-economic decisions follow the same steps outlined in our analytical model of decision making (see Figure 10-3). However, what makes the rational-economic approach special is that it calls for the decision maker to recognize *all* alternative courses of action (step 4) and to evaluate accurately and completely each one (step 5). It views decision makers as attempting to make *optimal* decisions.

Of course, the rational-economic approach to decision making does not fully appreciate the fallibility of the human decision maker. Based on the assumption that people have access to complete and perfect information and use it to make perfect decisions, the model can be considered a *normative* (also called *prescriptive*) approach—one that describes how decision makers ideally ought to behave so as to make the best possible decisions. It does not describe how decision makers actually behave in most circumstances. This task is undertaken by the next major approach to individual decision making, the *administrative model*.

The Administrative Model: Exploring the Limits of Human Rationality

As you know from your own experience, people generally do not act in a completely rational-economic manner. To illustrate this point, consider how a human resources department might select a new receptionist. After several applicants are interviewed, the manager might choose the best candidate seen so far and stop interviewing. Had the manager been following a rational-economic model, he or she would have had to interview all possible candidates before deciding on the best one. However, by ending the search after finding a candidate who was just good enough, the manager is using a much simpler approach.

The process used in this example characterizes an approach to decision making known as the **administrative model**.[37] This conceptualization recognizes that decision makers may have a limited view of the problems confronting them. The number of solutions that can be recognized or implemented is limited by the capabilities of the decision maker and the available resources of the organization. Also, decision makers do not have perfect information about the consequences of their decisions, so they cannot tell which one is best.

How are decisions made according to the administrative model? Instead of considering all possible solutions, decision makers consider solutions as they become available. Then they decide on the first alternative that meets their criteria for acceptability. Thus, the decision maker selects a solution that may be just good enough, although not optimal. Such decisions are referred to as **satisficing decisions**. Of course, a satisficing decision is much easier to make than an optimal decision. In most decision-making situations, satisficing decisions are acceptable and are more likely to be made than optimal ones.[38] The following analogy is used to compare the two types of decisions: making an optimal decision is like searching a haystack for the sharpest needle, but making a satisficing decision is like searching a haystack for a needle just sharp enough with which to sew.

As we have noted, it is often impractical for people to make completely optimal, rational decisions. The administrative model recognizes the **bounded rationality** under which most organizational decision makers must operate. The idea is that people lack the cognitive skills required to formulate and solve highly complex business problems in a completely objective, rational way.[39] It should not be surprising that the administrative model does a better job than the rational-economic model of describing how decision makers actually behave. The approach is said to be *descriptive* (also called *proscriptive*) in nature. This interest in examining the actual, imperfect behaviour of decision makers, rather than specifying the ideal, economically rational behaviours that decision makers ought to engage in, lies at the heart of the distinction between the administrative and rational-economic models. Our point is not that decision makers do not want to behave rationally, but that restrictions posed by the innate capabilities of the decision makers preclude "perfect" decisions.

administrative model A model of decision making that recognizes the *bounded rationality* that limits the making of optimally rational-economic decisions.

satisficing decisions Decisions made by selecting the first minimally acceptable alternative as it becomes available.

bounded rationality The major assumption of the administrative model—that organizational, social, and human limitations lead to the making of *satisficing* rather than optimal decisions.

Image Theory: An Intuitive Approach to Decision Making

If you think about it, you'll probably realize that some, but certainly not all, decisions are made following the logical steps of our general model of decision making. Consider Elizabeth Barrett Browning's poetic question "How do I love thee? Let me count the ways."[40] It's unlikely that anyone would ultimately answer the question by carefully counting what one loves about another (although many such characteristics can be enumerated). Instead, a more intuitive-based decision making is likely, not only for matters of the heart, but for a variety of important organizational decisions as well.[41]

The point is that selecting the best alternative by weighing all the options is not always a major concern when making a decision. People also consider how various decision alternatives fit with their personal standards as well as their personal goals and plans. The best decision for someone might not be the best for someone else. In other words, people may make decisions in a more automatic, *intuitive* fashion than is traditionally recognized. Representative of this approach is Beach and Mitchell's **image theory**.[42] This approach to decision making is summarized in Figure 10-7.

Image theory deals primarily with decisions about adopting a certain course of action (e.g., should the company develop a new product line?) or changing a current course of action (e.g., should the company drop a present product line?). According to the theory, people make adoption decisions on the basis of a simple two-step process. The first step is the *compatibility test*, a comparison of the degree to which a particular course of action is consistent with various images—particularly individual principles, current goals, and plans for the future. If any lack of compatibility exists with respect to these considerations, a rejection decision is made. If the compatibility test is passed, then the *profitability test* is carried out. That is, people consider the extent to which using various alternatives best fits their values, goals, and plans. The decision is then made to accept the best candidate. These tests are used within a certain *decision frame*—that is, with consideration of meaningful information about the decision context (such as past experiences). The basic idea is that we learn from the past and are guided by it when making decisions. The example shown in Figure 10-7 highlights this contemporary approach to decision making.

According to image theory, the decision-making process is very rapid and simple. The theory suggests that people do not ponder and reflect over decisions but make them using a smooth, intuitive process with minimal cognitive processing. If

image theory A theory of decision making that recognizes that decisions are made in an automatic, intuitive fashion. According to the theory, people will adopt a course of action that best fits their individual principles, current goals, and plans for the future.

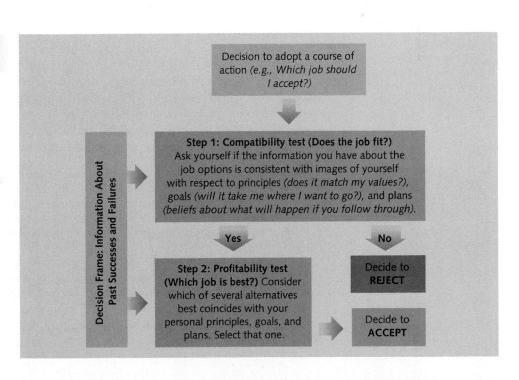

FIGURE 10-7 Image Theory: A Summary and Example

According to *image theory*, decisions are made in a relatively automatic, intuitive fashion following the two steps outlined here.

(Source: Adapted from Mitchell & Beach, 1990; see Note 42.)

you've ever found yourself saying that something "seemed like the right thing to do," or "something doesn't feel right," you're probably well aware of the kind of intuitive thinking that goes on in a great deal of decision making. Recent research suggests that when it comes to making relatively simple decisions, people tend to behave as suggested by image theory.[43] For example, it has been found that people decide against various options when past evidence suggests that these decisions may be incompatible with their images of the future.[44]

To summarize, in contrast with the rational-economic approach, the administrative model and image theory represent ways in which people actually go about making decisions. Both of these approaches have received support, and neither should be seen as a replacement for the other. Instead, several different processes may be involved in decision making. Not all decision making is carried out the same way: Sometimes decision making might be analytical, and sometimes it might be more intuitive. Modern organizational behaviour scholars recognize the value of both approaches. Something both approaches have in common is that they recognize the fallibility of the human decision maker. With this in mind, we will now turn our attention to the imperfect nature of individual decisions.

Individual Decisions: What Makes Them Imperfect?

Let's face it, as a whole, people are less than perfect when it comes to making decisions. Mistakes are made all the time. Obviously, people have limited capacities to process information accurately and thoroughly, like a computer. For example, we often focus on irrelevant information in making decisions.[45] We also fail to use all the information made available to us, in part because we may forget some of it.[46] Beyond these general limitations in human information-processing capacity, we may note several systematic determinants of imperfect decisions, factors that contribute to the imperfect nature of people's decisions. These variables reside not only within individuals themselves (e.g., biases in the way people make decisions) but also the organizations within which we operate. We will now examine five major factors contributing to the imperfect nature of individual decisions.

Framing Effects

framing The presentation of a problem to an individual, either in negative terms (leading to risk-seeking) or positive terms (leading to risk-aversion).

One well-established decision-making bias has to do with the tendency for people to make different decisions based on how the problem is presented to them—that is, the **framing** of a problem. Specifically, Kahneman and Tversky have noted that when problems are framed in a manner that emphasizes the positive gains to be received, people tend to shy away from taking risks and go for the sure thing (i.e., decision makers are said to be *risk-averse*). However, when problems are framed in a manner that emphasizes the potential losses to be suffered, people are more willing to take risks so as to avoid those losses (i.e., decision makers are said to make *risk-seeking* decisions).[47] To illustrate this phenomenon consider the following example:

> The government is preparing to combat a rare disease expected to take 600 lives. Two alternative programs to combat the disease have been proposed, each of which, scientists believe, will have certain consequences. *Program A* will save 200 people, if adopted. *Program B* has a one-third chance of saving all 600 people, but a two-thirds chance of saving no one. Which program do you prefer?

When Kahneman and Tversky presented such a problem to people, 72 percent expressed a preference for Program A, and 28 percent for Program B. In other words, they preferred the "sure thing" of saving 200 people over the one-third possibility of saving them all. However, a curious thing happened when the description of the programs was framed in negative terms. Specifically:

Program C was described as allowing 400 people to die, if adopted. *Program D* was described as allowing a one-third probability that no one would die, and a two-thirds probability that all 600 would die. Now which program would you prefer?

Compare these four programs. Program C is just another way of stating the outcomes of Program A, and Program D is just another way of stating the outcomes of Program B. However, Programs C and D are framed in negative terms, which led to opposite preferences: 22 percent favoured Program C and 78 percent favoured Program D. In other words, people tended to avoid risk when the problem was framed in terms of "lives saved" (i.e., in positive terms) but to seek risk when the problem was framed in terms of "lives lost" (i.e., in negative terms). This classic effect has been replicated in several studies.[48]

Scientists believe that such effects are due to the tendency for people to perceive equivalent situations framed differently as not really equivalent.[49] In other words, focusing on the glass as "half full" leads people to think about it differently than when it is presented as being "half empty," although they might recognize intellectually that the two are really the same. Such findings illustrate our point that people are not completely rational decision makers but are systematically biased by the cognitive distortions created by simple differences in the way situations are framed.

Reliance on Heuristics

Framing effects are not the only cognitive biases to which decision makers are subjected. It also has been established that people often attempt to simplify the complex decisions they face by using **heuristics**—simple rules that guide them through a complex array of decision alternatives.[50] Although heuristics are potentially useful to decision makers, they represent potential impediments to decision making. Two very common types of heuristics may be identified.

heuristics Simple decision rules used to make quick decisions about complex problems.

First, the **availability heuristic** refers to the tendency for people to base their judgments on information that is readily available to them—even though it might not be accurate. Suppose, for example, that an executive needs to know the percentage of entering college students who go on to graduate. There is not enough time to gather the appropriate statistics, so she bases her judgments on her own recollections of when she was a college student. If the percentage she recalls graduating, based on her own experiences, is higher or lower than the usual number, her estimate will be off accordingly. In other words, basing judgments solely on information that is conveniently available increases the possibility of making inaccurate decisions. Yet, the availability heuristic is often used when making decisions.[51]

availability heuristic The tendency for people to base their judgments on information that is readily available to them although it may be potentially inaccurate, thereby adversely affecting decision quality.

Second, the **representativeness heuristic** refers to the tendency to perceive others in stereotypical ways if they appear to be typical representatives of the category to which they belong. For example, suppose you believe that accountants are bright, mild-mannered individuals, whereas salespeople are less intelligent but much more extroverted. Further, imagine that there are twice as many salespeople as accountants at a party. You meet someone at the party who is bright and mild-mannered. Although mathematically the odds are two to one that this person is a salesperson rather than an accountant, chances are you will guess that the individual is an accountant because she possesses the traits you associate with accountants. In other words, you believe this person to be representative of accountants in general—so much so that you would knowingly go against the mathematical odds in making your judgment. Research has consistently found that people tend to make this type of error in judgment, thereby providing good support for the existence of the representativeness heuristic.[52]

representativeness heuristic The tendency to perceive others in stereotypical ways if they appear to be typical representatives of the category to which they belong.

☞ *The powerful effects of stereotypes in organizations are discussed more fully in Chapters 3 and 6.*

It is important to note that heuristics do not *always* interfere with the quality of decisions made. In fact, they can be quite helpful. People often use simple rules to help simplify the complex decisions they face. For example, management scientists employ many useful heuristics to aid decisions regarding such matters as where to locate warehouses or how to compose an investment portfolio.[53] We also use heuristics in our everyday lives, such as when we play chess ("control the centre of the board") or blackjack ("hit on 16, stick on 17"). However, the representativeness heuristic and the availability heuristic may be recognized as impediments to superior decisions because they discourage people from collecting and processing as much information as they should. Making judgments on the basis of only readily available information, or on stereotypical beliefs, although simplifying things for the decision maker, does so at a potentially high cost—poor decisions. Thus, these systematic biases represent potentially serious impediments to individual decision making.

Bias toward Implicit Favourites

Don was about to receive his MBA. This was going to be his big chance to move to Vancouver. Don had long dreamed of living there, and his first "real" job, he hoped, was going to be his ticket. As the corporate recruiters made their annual migration to campus, Don eagerly signed up for several interviews. One of the first was Samuels, Nichol, and Jorena, a medium-sized consulting firm in Vancouver. The salary was right and the people seemed pleasant, a combination that excited Don very much. Apparently the interest was mutual; soon Don was offered a position.

Does the story end here? Not quite. It was only March, and Don felt he shouldn't jump at the first job to come along, even though he really wanted it. So, to do "the sensible thing," he signed up for more interviews. Shortly thereafter, Jefferson, Williams, and Fredrick, a local firm, made Don a more attractive offer. Not only was the salary higher, but, there was every indication that the job promised a much brighter future than the one in Vancouver.

What would he do? Actually, Don didn't consider it much of a dilemma. After thinking it over, he came to the conclusion that the work at Jefferson, Williams, and Fredrick was much too low-level—not enough exciting clients to challenge him. And the starting salary wasn't really all *that* much better than it was at Samuels, Nichol, and Jorena. The day after graduation Don was packing for his new office overlooking the Lions Gate Bridge.

Do you think the way Don made his decision was atypical? He seemed to have his mind made up in advance about the job in Vancouver, and didn't really give the other one a chance. Research suggests that people make decisions in this way all the time. That is, people tend to pick an **implicit favourite** option (i.e., a preferred alternative) very early in the decision-making process.[54] Then, the other options they consider subsequently are not given serious consideration. Rather, they are merely used to convince oneself that the implicit favourite is indeed the best choice. An alternative considered for this purpose is known as a **confirmation candidate**. It is not unusual to find that people psychologically distort their beliefs about confirmation candidates so as to justify selecting their implicit favourites. Don did this when he convinced himself that the job offered by the local firm really wasn't as good as it seemed.

Research has shown that people make decisions very early in the decision process. For example, in one study of the job recruitment process investigators found that they could predict 87 percent of the jobs that students would take as early as two months before the students acknowledged that they actually had made a decision.[55] Apparently, people's decisions are biased by the tendency for them not to consider all the relevant information available to them. In fact, they tend to bias their judgments of the strengths and weaknesses of various alternatives so as to make them fit their already-made decision, their implicit favourite.[56] This phenomenon clearly suggests that people not only fail to consider all possible alternatives when making decisions, but that they even fail to consider all readily available alternatives. Instead, they tend to make up their minds very early and convince themselves that they are right. As you might imagine, this bias toward implicit favourites is likely to limit severely the quality of decisions that are made.

implicit favourite One's preferred decision alternative, selected even before all options have been considered.

confirmation candidate A decision alternative considered only for purposes of convincing oneself of the wisdom of selecting the *implicit favourite*.

Escalation of Commitment: Throwing Good Money after Bad

Because decisions are made all the time in organizations, some of these inevitably will be unsuccessful. What would you say is the rational thing to do when a poor decision has been made? Obviously, the ineffective action should be stopped or reversed. In other words, it would make sense to "cut your losses and run." However, people don't always respond in this manner. In fact, it is not unusual to find that ineffective decisions are sometimes followed up with still further ineffective decisions.

Imagine, for example, that you have invested money in a company, but the company appears to be failing. Rather than lose your initial investment, you may invest still more money in the hope of salvaging your first investment. The more you invest, the more you may be tempted to save those earlier investments by making later investments. That is to say, people sometimes may be found "throwing good money after bad" because they have "too much invested to quit." This is known as the **escalation of commitment phenomenon**—the tendency for people to continue to support previously unsuccessful courses of action because they have sunk costs invested in them.[57]

Although this might not seem like a rational thing to do, this strategy is frequently followed. Consider, for example, how large banks and governments may invest money in foreign governments in the hope of turning them around even though such a result becomes increasingly unlikely. Similarly, the organizers of Expo '86 in British Columbia continued pouring money into the fair long after it became apparent that it would be a big money-losing proposition.[58] Decision-making specialist Glen Whyte has identified the Ontario government's 1986 decision to invest $4 billion in the completion of Ontario Hydro's Darlington Nuclear Station as an example of this kind of problem. The rationale given for the expenditure at the time was the $7 billion that had already been spent on the plant.[59]

Why do people do this? If you think about it, you may realize that the failure to back your own previous courses of action in an organization would be taken as an admission of failure—a politically difficult act in an organization. In other words, people may be very concerned about "saving face"—looking good in the eyes of others and oneself.[60] Staw and his associates have recognized that this tendency for *self-justification* is primarily responsible for people's inclination to protect their beliefs about themselves as rational, competent decision makers by convincing themselves and others that they made the right decision all along, and are willing to back it up.[61] Although there are other possible reasons for the escalation of commitment phenomenon, research supports the self-justification explanation.[62] For a summary of the escalation of commitment phenomenon, see Figure 10-8.

Researchers have noted several conditions under which people will refrain from escalating their commitment to a failing course of action.[63] Notably, it has been found that people will stop making failing investments under conditions in which the *available funds for making further investments are limited* and the *threat of failure is overwhelmingly obvious.*[64]

It also has been found that people will refrain from escalating commitment when they can *diffuse their responsibility for the earlier failing actions.* That is, the more people feel they are just one of several people responsible for a failing course of action, the less likely they are to commit to further failing actions.[65] In other words, the less one is responsible for an earlier failure, the less one may be motivated to justify those earlier failures by making further investments in them.

Finally, it has been found that people are unwilling to escalate commitment to a course of action when it is made clear that the *total amount invested exceeds the amount expected to be gained.*[66] Although people may wish to invest in projects that enable them to recoup their initial investments, there is little reason for them to do so when it is obvious that doing so will be a losing proposition. Under such conditions, it is difficult to justify doing so, even if one "hopes against hope" that it will work out. Indeed, research has shown that decision makers do indeed refrain from escalating commitment to decisions when it is made clear that the overall benefit to be gained

---

escalation of commitment phenomenon The tendency for individuals to continue to support previously unsuccessful courses of action.

Ontario Hydro
www.hydro.on.ca

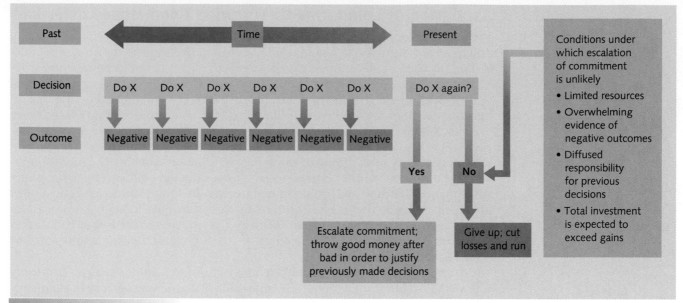

FIGURE 10-8 Escalation of Commitment: An Overview

According to the *escalation of commitment phenomenon,* people who have repeatedly made poor decisions will continue to support those failing courses of action in order to justify their decisions. Under some conditions, summarized here, the effect will not occur.

is less than the overall costs to be borne.[67] This finding was more apparent among students with accounting backgrounds than those without such backgrounds, presumably because their training predisposed them to be more sensitive to these issues.

To conclude, the escalation of commitment phenomenon represents a type of irrational decision making that has the potential to occur. However, whether or not it does occur will depend on the various circumstances that decision makers confront.

Organizational Barriers to Effective Decisions

Thus far we have emphasized the human cognitive shortcomings and biases that limit effective decision making. However, we must not ignore several important organizational factors that also interfere with rational decisions. Indeed, the situations faced by many organizational decision makers cannot help but interfere with their capacity to make decisions.

Time constraints. One obvious factor is *time constraints.* Many important organizational decisions are made under severe time pressure. Under such circumstances, it is often impossible for exhaustive decision making to occur. This is particularly the case when organizations face crisis situations requiring immediate decisions. Under such conditions, when decision makers feel "rushed into" taking action, they frequently restrict their search for information and consideration of alternatives that may otherwise help them make effective decisions.[68]

Political "face-saving" pressure. The quality of many organizational decisions also may be limited by *political "face-saving" pressure.* In other words, decision makers may make decisions that help them look good to others, although the resulting decisions might not be in the best interest of their organizations. Imagine, for example, how an employee might distort the available information needed to make a decision if the correct decision would jeopardize his job. Unfortunately, such misuses of information to support desired decisions are all too common. One study on this topic reported that a group of businesspeople working on a group decision-making problem opted for an adequate—although less than optimal—decision rather than risk generating serious conflicts with their fellow group members.[69] In an actual case, a proponent of medical inoculation for the flu was so interested in advancing his pro-inoculation position that he proceeded with the inoculation program although there was only a 2 percent chance of an epidemic.[70] Apparently, people often make the decisions they need to make to cultivate the best impressions although these may not be the best ones for their organizations.

☞ *Face-saving as a political necessity in organizations is discussed in the context of organizational politics in Chapter 12.*

bounded discretion Limitations imposed on decisions due to moral and ethical constraints.

☛ As indicated in Chapter 2, ethical constraints on behaviour are not always as effective as they should be.

Bounded discretion. Besides the time constraints and political pressures that often limit the quality of organizational decisions, note also the limitations imposed by moral and ethical constraints—what is known as **bounded discretion**.[71] According to this idea, decision makers limit their actions to those that fall within the bounds of current moral and ethical standards.[72] So, although engaging in illegal activities such as stealing may optimize an organization's profits (at least in the short run), ethical considerations strongly discourage such actions.

Group Decisions: Do Too Many Cooks Spoil the Broth?

Decision-making groups are a well-established fact of modern organizational life. Groups such as committees, study teams, task forces, or review panels are often charged with the responsibility for making important business decisions.[73] They are so common, in fact, that it has been said that some administrators spend as much as 80 percent of their time in committee meetings.[74]

The Pros and Cons of Group Decisions

Given this, it is important to consider the strengths and weaknesses of using groups to make organizational decisions. Refer to our summary of these factors in Figure 10-9.

There is little doubt that much can be gained by using decision-making groups. Several potential advantages of this approach may be identified. First, bringing people together may increase the amount of knowledge and information available for making good decisions. In other words, there may be a *pooling of resources*. A related benefit is that in decision-making groups there can be a *specialization of labour*. With enough people around to share the workload, individuals can perform only those tasks at which they are best, thereby potentially improving the quality of the group's efforts. Another benefit is that group decisions are likely to enjoy *greater acceptance* than individual decisions. People involved in making decisions may be expected to understand those decisions better and be more committed to carrying them out than decisions made by someone else.[75]

Of course, there are also some problems associated with using decision-making groups. One obvious drawback is that groups are likely to *waste time*. The time spent socializing before getting down to business may be a drain on the group and be very costly to organizations. Another possible problem is that potential disagreement over important matters may breed ill will and *group conflict*. Although constructive

FIGURE 10-9 Group Decision Making: Advantages and Disadvantages

Should groups be used to make decisions, as opposed to individuals? The answer depends largely on the trade-offs summarized here.

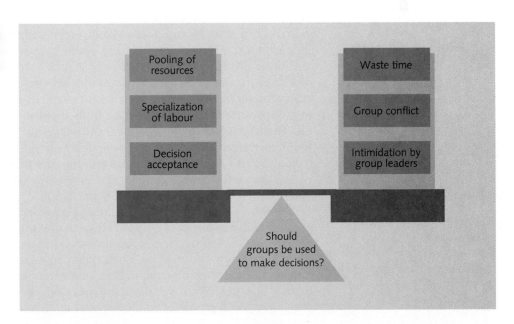

☞ For a discussion of other causes of conflict and the impact of conflict in organizations, see Chapter 11.

disagreement can actually lead to better group outcomes, highly disruptive conflict may interfere with group decisions. Indeed, with corporate power and personal pride at stake, it is not at all surprising to find that lack of agreement can cause bad feelings to develop between group members. Finally, we may expect groups to be ineffective sometimes because of members' *intimidation by group leaders*. A group composed of several "yes" men or women trying to please a dominant leader tends to discourage open and honest discussion of solutions. In view of these problems, it is easy to understand the old adage "a camel is a horse put together by a committee."

Given the several pros and cons of using groups to make decisions, we must conclude that neither groups nor individuals are always superior. Obviously, there are important trade-offs involved in using either one to make decisions. Since there are advantages associated with both group and individual decision makers, a question arises as to *when* each should be used. That is, under what conditions might individuals or groups be expected to make superior decisions? Fortunately, research has addressed this important question.[76]

When Are Groups Superior to Individuals?

Imagine a situation in which an important decision has to be made about a complex problem—such as whether one company should merge with another. This is not the kind of problem about which any one individual working alone would be able to make a good decision. Its highly complex nature may overwhelm even an expert, thereby setting the stage for a group to do a better job.

Whether a group actually will do better than an individual depends on several important considerations. For one, we must consider who is in the group. Successful groups tend to be composed of *heterogeneous group members with complementary skills*. So, for example, a group composed of lawyers, accountants, real estate agents, and other experts may make much better decisions on the merger problem than would a group composed of specialists in only one field. Indeed, research has shown that the diversity of opinions offered by group members is one of the major advantages of using groups to make decisions.[77]

☞ The success of heterogeneous groups is one reason why racially and ethnically diverse groups are considered desirable in organizations, as discussed in Chapter 2.

As you might imagine, it is not enough simply to have skills. For a group to be successful, its members also must be able to communicate their ideas freely to each other in an open, nonhostile manner. Conditions under which one individual (or group) prevents another from contributing his or her expertise can easily negate any potential gain associated with composing groups of heterogeneous experts. After all, *having* expertise and being able to make a contribution by *using* that expertise are two different things. Indeed, research has shown that only when the contributions of the most qualified group members are given the greatest weight does the group derive any benefit from that member's presence.[78] Thus, for groups to be superior to individuals, they must be composed of a heterogeneous collection of experts with complementary skills who can freely and openly contribute to their group's product.

As an example of this, Michaelsen, Watson, and Black studied the performance of 222 groups of approximately six students who worked together extensively on class projects (team learning exercises) over the course of a semester.[79] Assignments to groups were made so as to create units that were as broadly diversified as possible. The teams had to work together on answering exam questions about the material they studied. The questions were generally difficult, some requiring the ability to analyze and synthesize complex concepts. The researchers were interested in comparing the performance of the groups as a whole with that of individual members. Their findings are summarized in Figure 10-10.

As shown in Figure 10-10, the average score on the exams completed jointly by group members was not only higher than that of the average group member, but also higher than that of the best group member. In fact, of the 222 groups studied, 215 (97 percent) outperformed their best member, 4 groups tied their best member, and only 3 groups scored lower than their best member. Clearly, these findings support the idea that *on complex tasks, a benefit is derived from combining individuals into groups that goes beyond the contribution of what the best group member can do*. People can

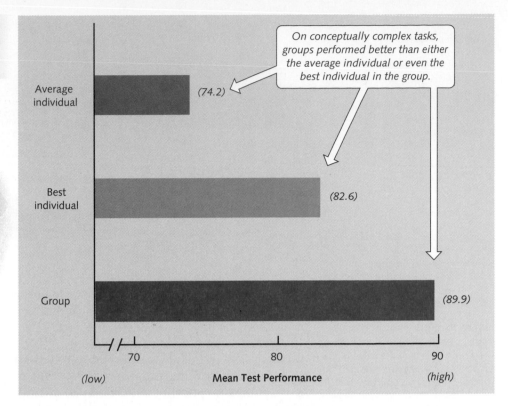

FIGURE 10-10 Group vs. Individual Performance on a Complex Task: Empirical Evidence

Research comparing the performance of groups and individuals on a complex learning task has shown that groups as a whole performed better than either the average individual or even the best individual in the group. Such findings support the idea that the benefit of working in groups goes beyond the simple combination of individual skills.

(Source: Based on data reported by Michaelsen, Watson, & Black, 1989; see Note 79.)

On conceptually complex tasks, groups performed better than either the average individual or even the best individual in the group.

Average individual (74.2)

Best individual (82.6)

Group (89.9)

70   80   90

(low)   **Mean Test Performance**   *(high)*

help each other solve complex problems not only by pooling their resources, but also by correcting each other's answers and assisting each other to come up with ideas. There is also likely to be the intangible *synergy* created when a group of people help each other and create a climate for success.

In contrast to complex decision tasks, imagine a situation in which a judgment is required on a simple problem with a readily verifiable answer. For example, imagine that you are asked to translate a phrase from a relatively obscure language into English. Groups might do better than individuals on such a task, but probably because the odds are increased that someone in the group knows the language and can perform the translation for the group. However, there is no reason to expect that even a large group will be able to perform such a task better than a single individual who has the required expertise. In fact, an expert working alone may do even better than a group. This is because an expert individual performing a simple task may be distracted by others and suffer from having to convince them of the correctness of his or her solution. For this reason, exceptional individuals tend to outperform entire committees on simple tasks.[80] In such cases, for groups to benefit from a pooling of resources, there must be some resources to pool. The pooling of ignorance does not help. In other words, the question "Are two heads better than one?" can be answered this way: *on simple tasks, two heads may be better than one if at least one of those heads has enough of what it takes to succeed.*

In summary, whether groups perform better than individuals depends on the nature of the task performed and the expertise of the people involved. We have summarized some of these key considerations in Figure 10-11.

When Are Individuals Superior to Groups?

As we have described thus far, groups may be expected to perform better than the average or even the exceptional individual under certain conditions. However, there are also conditions under which individuals are superior to groups. Most of the problems faced by organizations require a great deal of creative thinking. For example, a company deciding how to use a newly developed adhesive in its consumer products is facing decisions on a poorly structured task. Although you would expect that the

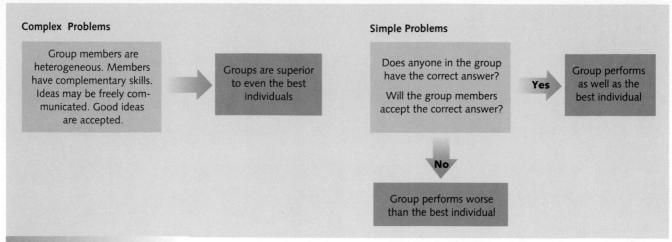

Complex Problems

Group members are heterogeneous. Members have complementary skills. Ideas may be freely communicated. Good ideas are accepted. → Groups are superior to even the best individuals

Simple Problems

Does anyone in the group have the correct answer?

Will the group members accept the correct answer? — **Yes** → Group performs as well as the best individual

No

Group performs worse than the best individual

FIGURE 10-11 Group Decisions: When Are They Superior to Individual Decisions?

When solving complex problems, groups are superior to individuals if certain conditions prevail (e.g., members have heterogeneous, complementary skills, they can freely share ideas, and good ideas are accepted). However, when solving simple problems, groups perform only as well as the best individual in the group, and then only if that person has the correct answer and that response is accepted by the group.

brainstorming A technique designed to foster group productivity by encouraging interacting group members to express their ideas in a noncritical fashion.

complexity of such creative problems would give groups a natural advantage, this is not the case. In fact, research has shown that *on poorly structured, creative tasks, individuals perform better than groups.*[81]

An approach to solving creative problems commonly used by groups is **brainstorming**. This technique was developed by advertising executive Alex Osborn as a tool for coming up with creative, new ideas.[82] The members of brainstorming groups are encouraged to present their ideas in an uncritical way and to discuss freely and openly all ideas on the floor. Specifically, members of brainstorming groups are required to follow four main rules:

1. Avoid criticizing others' ideas.

2. Share even far-out suggestions.

3. Offer as many comments as possible.

4. Build on others' ideas to create your own.

Does brainstorming improve the quality of creative decisions? To answer this question, Bouchard and his associates conducted a study in which they compared the effectiveness of individuals and brainstorming groups working on creative problems.[83] Specifically, participants were given 35 minutes to consider the consequences of situations such as "What if everybody went blind?" or "What if everybody grew an extra thumb on each hand?" Clearly, the novel nature of such problems requires a great deal of creativity. Comparisons were made of the number of solutions generated by groups of four or seven people and a like number of individuals working on the same problems alone. The results were clear: Individuals were significantly more productive than groups.

In summary, groups perform worse than individuals when working on creative tasks. A great part of the problem is that some individuals feel inhibited by the presence of others even though one rule of brainstorming is that even far-out ideas may be shared. To the extent that people wish to avoid feeling foolish as a result of saying silly things, their creativity may be inhibited when in groups. Similarly, groups may inhibit creativity by slowing down the process of bringing ideas to fruition.

Groupthink: Too Much Cohesiveness Can Be a Dangerous Thing

One reason groups may fare so poorly on complex tasks lies in the dynamics of group interaction. As we noted in Chapter 8, when members of a group develop a very strong group spirit—or a high level of *cohesiveness*—they sometimes become so con-

groupthink The tendency for members of highly cohesive groups to conform to group pressures regarding a certain decision so strongly that they fail to think critically, rejecting the potentially correcting influences of outsiders.

cerned about not disrupting the like-mindedness of the group that they may be reluctant to challenge the group's decisions. When this happens, group members tend to isolate themselves from outside information, and the process of critical thinking deteriorates. This phenomenon is referred to as **groupthink**.[84]

The Nature of Groupthink

The concept of groupthink was proposed initially as an attempt to explain ineffective decisions made by U.S. government officials that led to fiascoes such as the Bay of Pigs invasion in Cuba and the Vietnam War.[85] Analyses of each of these cases have revealed that the president's advisers actually *discouraged* more effective decision making. An examination of the conditions under which the decision was made to launch the ill-fated space shuttle *Challenger* in January 1986 revealed that it too resulted from groupthink.[86] Post hoc analyses of conversations between key personnel suggested that the team that made the decision to launch the shuttle under freezing conditions did so while insulating itself from the engineers who knew how the equipment should function. Given that NASA had such a successful history, the decision makers operated with a sense of invulnerability. They also worked so closely together and were under such intense pressure to launch the shuttle without further delay that they all collectively went along with the launch decision, creating the illusion of unanimous agreement.

It appears that the Canadian government is not immune to the groupthink phenomenon. An example reported in the *Calgary Herald* noted that when a Progressive Conservative Member of Parliament publicly opposed the GST, then–Prime Minister Brian Mulroney indicated that he would refuse to sign the member's election candidate form. The writer for the *Calgary Herald* identified this situation as an indication that different political parties in Canada "... cannot tolerate controversy and dissent; there is a party line—obey it or else."[87] Recall as well the comment in Chapter 8 from a Member of Parliament who was deeply concerned about the possibility that groupthink was interfering with the political decision making surrounding the Meech Lake Accord. For a summary of the groupthink phenomenon, including some of its symptoms, see Figure 10-12.

Calgary Herald
www.calgaryherald.com

FIGURE 10-12 Groupthink: An Overview

Groupthink occurs when highly cohesive conditions discourage group members from challenging the group's actions. Poor-quality decisions result.

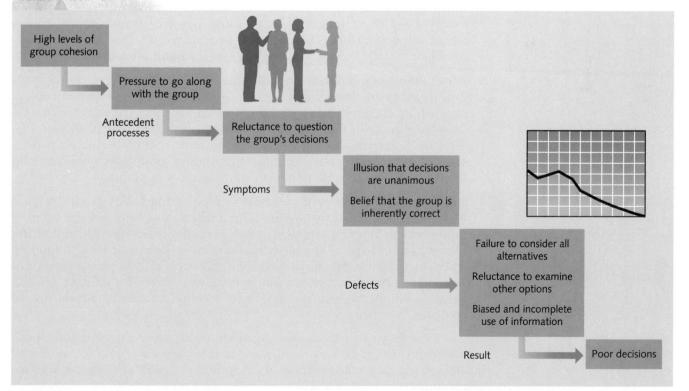

Groupthink doesn't occur only in governmental decision making, of course, but also in the private sector (although the failures may be less well publicized). For example, analyses of the business policies of large corporations such as Lockheed and Chrysler have suggested that it was the failure of top management teams to respond to changing market conditions that at one time led them to the brink of disaster.[88] The problem is that members of very cohesive groups may have considerable confidence in their group's decisions, making them unlikely to raise doubts about these actions (i.e., "the group seems to know what it's doing"). As a result, they may suspend their own critical thinking in favour of conforming to the group. When group members become fiercely loyal to each other, they may ignore potentially useful information from other sources that challenges the group's decisions. The result of this process is that the group's decisions may be completely uninformed, irrational, or even immoral.[89]

Strategies for Avoiding Groupthink

So as not to conclude on an entirely pessimistic note, we point out that several strategies can effectively combat groupthink. Here are a few proven techniques:

1. *Promote open inquiry.* Remember: Groupthink arises in response to group members' reluctance to "rock the boat." Group leaders should encourage members to be skeptical of all solutions and to avoid reaching premature agreements. It sometimes helps to play the role of *devil's advocate*, that is, to find fault intentionally with a proposed solution.[90] Research has shown that when this is done, groups make higher-quality decisions.[91] In fact, some corporate executives use exercises in which conflict is intentionally generated just so the negative aspects of a decision can be identified before it's too late.[92] This is not to say that leaders should be argumentative. Rather, raising a nonthreatening question to force both sides of an issue can be very helpful in improving the quality of decisions. Randy Powell (see CASE PREVIEW for Chapter 1) has learned the value of dissent and has used it effectively. "Groupthink can happen, and what the senior person says tends to rule. I have always believed I should speak for what I believe to be true," says Powell. It is this style of independent thought that leaders can promote if they want to encourage an environment in which inquiry and honest debate are valued.[93]

2. *Use subgroups.* Because the decisions made by any one group may be the result of groupthink, basing decisions on the recommendations of two groups is a useful check. If the two groups disagree, a discussion of their differences is likely to raise important issues. However, if the two groups agree, you can be relatively confident that their conclusions are not *both* the result of groupthink.

3. *Admit shortcomings.* When groupthink occurs, group members feel very confident that they are doing the right thing. Such feelings of perfection discourage people from considering opposing information. However, if group members acknowledge some of the flaws and limitations of their decisions, they may be more open to corrective influences. Keep in mind that no decision is perfect. Asking others to point out their misgivings about a group's decisions may help avoid the illusion of perfection that contributes to groupthink.

4. *Hold second-chance meetings.* Before implementing a decision, it is a good idea to hold a *second-chance meeting* during which group members are asked to express any doubts and propose any new ideas they may have. Alfred P. Sloan, former head of General Motors, is known to have postponed acting on important matters until any group disagreement was resolved.[94] As people get tired of working on problems, they may hastily reach agreement on a solution. Second-chance meetings can be useful devices for seeing if a solution still seems good even after "sleeping on it."

Given the extremely adverse effects groupthink can have on organizations, practising managers would be wise to put these simple suggestions into action. The alternative—facing the consequences of groupthink—clearly suggests the need for serious consideration of this issue.

Improving the Effectiveness of Group Decisions: Some Techniques

As we have made clear in this chapter, certain advantages can be gained from sometimes using individuals and sometimes using groups to make decisions. A decision-making technique that combines the best features of groups and individuals, while minimizing the disadvantages, would be ideal. Several techniques designed to realize the "best of both worlds" have been widely used in organizations. These include techniques that involve the structuring of group discussions in special ways. An even more basic approach to improving the effectiveness of group decisions involves training decision makers in ways of avoiding some of the pitfalls of group decision making. We will begin this section of the chapter with a discussion of this training approach to improving group decisions and then go on to consider various ways of creating specially structured groups.

Training Individuals to Improve Group Performance

As we noted earlier in this chapter, how well groups solve problems depends in part on the composition of those groups. If at least one group member is capable of coming up with a solution, groups may benefit from that individual's expertise. Based on this reasoning, it follows that the more qualified individual group members are to solve problems, the better their groups as a whole will perform.

Researchers Bottger and Yetton found that individuals trained to avoid four common types of errors significantly reduced the number of mistakes made by their groups when attempting to solve a creative problem.[95] Specifically, participants in the study were asked to be aware of and to try to avoid four common problems:

☛ *This is but one of the many possible uses of training in organizations described more fully in Chapter 3.*

1. *Hypervigilance*: This state involves frantically searching for quick solutions to problems, going from one idea to another out of a sense of desperation that one idea isn't working and that another needs to be considered before time runs out. A poor, "last chance" solution may be adopted to relieve anxiety. This problem may be avoided by keeping in mind that it is best to stick with one suggestion and work it out thoroughly, and reassuring the person solving the problem that his or her level of skill and education is adequate to perform the task at hand. In other words, a little reassurance may go a long way toward keeping individuals on the right track and avoiding the problem of hypervigilance.

2. *Unconflicted adherence*: Many decision makers make the mistake of sticking to the first idea that comes into their heads without more deeply evaluating the consequences. As a result, such people are unlikely to become aware of any problems associated with their ideas or to consider other possibilities. To avoid *unconflicted adherence*, decision makers are urged to (1) think about the difficulties associated with their ideas, (2) force themselves to consider different ideas, and (3) consider the special and unique characteristics of the problem they are facing and avoid carrying over assumptions from previous problems.

3. *Unconflicted change*: Sometimes people are too quick to change their minds and adopt the first new idea to come along. To avoid such unconflicted change, decision makers are encouraged to ask themselves about (1) the risks and problems of adopting that solution, (2) the good points of the first idea, and (3) the relative strengths and weaknesses of both ideas.

4. *Defensive avoidance*: Too often decision makers fail to solve problems effectively because they avoid working on the task at hand. To minimize this problem, they should do three things. First, they should attempt to *avoid procrastination*. Don't put off the problem indefinitely just because you cannot come up with a solution right away. Continue to budget some of your time on even the most frustrating problems. Second, *avoid disowning responsibility*. It is easy to minimize the importance of a problem by saying, "It doesn't matter, so who cares?" Avoid giving up so soon. Finally, *don't ignore potentially corrective*

information. It is tempting to put your nagging doubts about the quality of a solution to rest in order to be finished with it. Good decision makers would not do so. Rather, they use their doubts to test and potentially improve the quality of their ideas.

The encouraging aspect of Bottger and Yetton's findings is that merely having members of problem-solving groups consider these four potential pitfalls was an effective way of improving the quality of their groups' solutions. Apparently, how well groups perform depends to a great extent on the problem-solving skills of the individual group members. Attempting to avoid the four major pitfalls described here appears to be an effective method of improving individual decision-making skills—and hence the quality of group decisions. Obviously, this is only one approach that can improve organizational decision making. For a close-up description of how training in decision-making techniques can also be adapted to one highly specialized situation, see the **ORGANIZATIONAL TRENDS** section.

The Delphi Technique: Decisions by Expert Consensus

According to Greek mythology, people interested in seeing what fate the future held for them could seek the counsel of the Delphic oracle. Today's organizational decision makers sometimes consult experts to help them make the best decisions as well. A technique developed by the Rand Corporation, known as the **Delphi technique**, represents a systematic way of collecting and organizing the opinions of several experts into a single decision.[96] The steps in the process are summarized in Figure 10-13.

The Delphi process starts by enlisting the cooperation of experts and presenting the problem to them, usually in a letter. Each expert then proposes what he or she believes is the most appropriate solution. The group leader compiles all of these individual responses and reproduces them so they can be shared with all the other experts in a second mailing. At this point, each expert comments on the others' ideas and proposes another solution. These individual solutions are returned to the leader, who compiles them and looks for a consensus of opinions. If a consensus is reached, the decision is made. If not, the process of sharing reactions with others is repeated until a consensus is eventually obtained.

Delphi technique A method of improving group decisions using the opinions of experts, which are solicited by mail and then compiled. The expert consensus of opinions is used to make a decision.

FIGURE 10-13 The Delphi Technique A Summary

The *Delphi technique* allows decisions to be made by several experts without encountering many of the disadvantages of face-to-face group interaction.

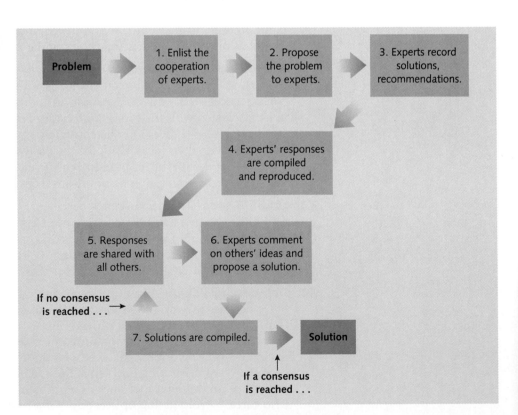

Decisions at 30 000 Feet: Technology Helps Pilots Avoid Fatal Errors

A poor decision by an executive may lead a company down the road to ruin. A poor decision by a physician may lead to the death of a patient. But a poor decision by a commercial airline pilot may take hundreds of lives at once, including his or her own. Indeed, "pilot error" has been cited as the cause of a growing number of commercial airline crashes.[97] To avoid such tragedies, the airline industry has focused on things that can be done to improve the quality of the decisions made by pilots. As you might imagine, such improvements usually involve the use of high-tech instruments—especially devices that warn pilots of unforeseen weather hazards. But, technology itself can be ineffective unless pilots are carefully trained to make decisions about when and how to take appropriate precautionary manoeuvres. Fortunately for the flying public, efforts are presently underway to improve the decision making of tomorrow's commercial aviators.

One of the most vexing problems pilots encounter results from *wind shear*, a condition created when a microburst (a small area of very turbulent wind) causes a sudden downdraft leading to a loss of lift. Reports by investigators have shown that wind shear has been a factor in many accidents or near accidents in the past few decades.[98] Wind shear is not a condition that can be avoided by completely mechanical means; it requires quick action on the part of pilots in response to proper warnings. For example, on July 11, 1988, several pilots flew into an area over Denver reported to have microburst activity because they were not adequately warned in advance. To the extent that pilots can accurately interpret the signals they receive, they are better able to take the correct, timely actions needed to guide their aircraft safely.

What can be done to help in such situations? Specifically, what type of information should be presented to pilots, when, and in what form? This question was considered by Lee in an intensive investigation of 18 experienced commercial air crews (i.e., a captain and a first officer) who were studied in an elaborate flight simulator.[99] After being familiar-ized with the training apparatus, crews were required to fly a simulated round-trip between Salt Lake City and Denver. The flight conditions were made to match closely those over Denver on July 11, 1988. Crews were assigned to one of two groups differing with respect to the nature of the weather-related information they received. In the *control group*, crews received only the standard oral weather briefings given by air traffic control transmissions. In the *experimental* group, this information was supplemented by visual displays (simulated ground-based Doppler radar) that warned pilots of wind shear as they approached the runway. How did these differences influence air crews' decision-making behaviour?

The results revealed some critical differences. Whereas 17 percent of the discussion in the experimental group dealt with wind shear, attention to the topic was virtually nonexistent in the control group. The investigators also analyzed the results with respect to decision time—that is, the average time that elapsed from the alert to the captain's decision about what approach to take in landing. Crews assigned to the experimental group made decisions more quickly than those assigned to the control group. These data reveal that the visual presentation of redundant data allowed airline cockpit crews to make critical decisions about avoiding microbursts much faster. In fact, a mean difference of approximately one minute (and 700–800 feet of additional altitude) was found—margins that may be critical to avoiding potentially dangerous conditions.

Although additional factors may be involved in potentially dangerous air travel situations, these results strongly suggest the need to use redundant visual information to supplement oral information. Given that good information is the key to good decision making, such knowledge about the most effective ways to present critical information may be exceptionally useful. Although such redundant visual displays may be costly to introduce, one must consider these costs relative to the loss of life that might occur when the appropriate visual display technology is not put into place. Findings such as these strongly suggest that, although human decision making is highly imperfect, the use of technology is helping to improve it.

The obvious advantage of using the Delphi technique to make decisions is that it allows for the collection of expert judgments without the great costs and logistical difficulties of bringing many experts together for a face-to-face meeting. However, the technique is not without limitations. As you might imagine, the Delphi process can be very time-consuming. Sending out letters, waiting for everyone to respond, transcribing and disseminating the responses, and repeating the process until a consensus is reached can take quite a long time. Experts have estimated that the minimum time required to use the Delphi technique would be more than 44 days. In one case, the process took five months to complete.[100] Obviously, the Delphi approach would not be appropriate for making decisions in crisis situations or whenever else time is of the essence. However, the approach has been successfully employed to make decisions such as what items to put on a conference agenda and what the potential impact of implementing new land-use policies would be.[101]

The Nominal Group Technique: A Structured Group Meeting

When there are only a few hours available to make a decision, group discussion sessions can be held in which members interact with each other in an orderly, focused fashion aimed at solving problems. The **nominal group technique (NGT)** brings together a small number of individuals (usually about seven to ten) who systematically offer their individual solutions to a problem and share their personal reactions to others' solutions.[102] The technique is referred to as "nominal" because the individuals involved form a group in name only. The participants do not attempt to agree as a group on any solution, but rather vote on all the solutions proposed. For an outline of the steps in the process, see Figure 10-14.

As shown in Figure 10-14, the nominal group process begins by gathering the group members together around a table and identifying the problem at hand. Then each member writes down his or her solutions. Next, one at a time, each member presents his or her solutions to the group and the leader writes these down on a chart. This process continues until all the ideas have been expressed. Following this, each solution is discussed, clarified, and evaluated by the group members. Each member is given a chance to voice his or her reactions to each idea. After all the ideas have been evaluated, the group members privately rank-order their preferred solutions. The idea that receives the highest rank is taken as the group's decision.

nominal group technique (NGT)
A technique for improving group decisions in which small groups of individuals systematically present and discuss their ideas before privately voting on their preferred solution. The most preferred solution is accepted as the group's decision.

FIGURE 10-14 The Nominal Group Technique: An Overview

The *nominal group technique* structures face-to-face meetings in a way that allows for the open expression and evaluation of ideas.

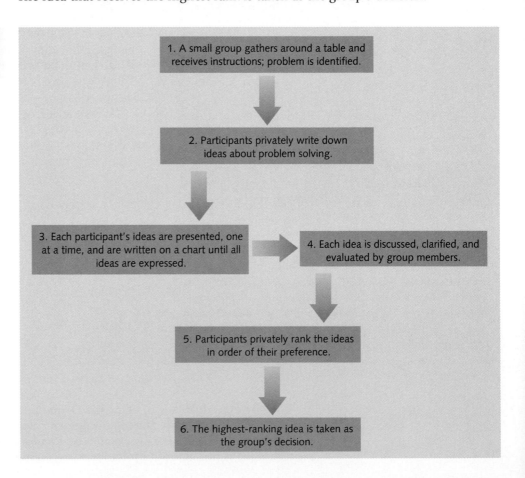

1. A small group gathers around a table and receives instructions; problem is identified.

2. Participants privately write down ideas about problem solving.

3. Each participant's ideas are presented, one at a time, and are written on a chart until all ideas are expressed.

4. Each idea is discussed, clarified, and evaluated by group members.

5. Participants privately rank the ideas in order of their preference.

6. The highest-ranking idea is taken as the group's decision.

The NGT has several advantages and disadvantages.[103] We have already noted that this approach can be used to arrive at group decisions in only a few hours. The benefit of the technique is that it discourages any pressure to conform to the wishes of a high-status group member because all ideas are evaluated and the preferences are expressed in private balloting. The technique must be considered limited, however, in that it requires the use of a trained group leader. In addition, using NGT successfully requires that only one narrowly defined problem be considered at a time. So, for very complex problems, many NGT sessions would have to be run—and only *if* the problem under consideration can be broken down into smaller parts.

Although nominal groups traditionally meet in face-to-face settings, advances in modern technology enable nominal groups to meet even when its members are far away from each other. Specifically, **electronic meeting systems** have been used, in which individuals in different locations participate in group conferences by means of telephone lines or direct satellite transmissions.[104] The messages may be sent either via characters on a computer monitor or images viewed during a teleconference. Despite their high-tech look, automated decision conferences are really just nominal groups meeting in a manner that approximates face-to-face contact. Insofar as electronic meetings allow for groups to assemble more conveniently than face-to-face meetings, they are growing in popularity. Presently, such companies as GE Appliances and Marriott Corp. have relied on electronic meetings.

It is important to consider the relative effectiveness of nominal groups and Delphi groups over face-to-face interacting groups. In general, research has shown the superiority of these special approaches to decision making in many ways on a variety of decision problems.[105] For example, the effectiveness of both techniques has been demonstrated in a study by Van de Ven and Delbecq in which seven-member groups (nominal, Delphi, and interacting) worked on the task of defining the job of a dormitory counsellor.[106] Nominal groups tended to be the most satisfied with their work and made the best-quality judgments. In addition, both nominal groups and Delphi groups were much more productive than interacting groups.

As we noted earlier, however, there is a potential benefit to be derived from face-to-face interaction that cannot be realized in nominal and Delphi groups—that is, acceptance of the decision. Groups are likely to accept their decisions and be committed to them if members have been actively involved in making them. Thus, the more detached and impersonal atmosphere of nominal and Delphi groups sometimes makes their members less likely to accept their groups' decisions. We may conclude, then, that there is no one best type of group that can be used to make decisions. Which type is most appropriate depends on the trade-offs decision makers are willing to make in terms of speed, quality, and commitment.[107]

The Stepladder Technique: Systematically Incorporating New Members

Another way of structuring group interaction known as the **stepladder technique** has been introduced by Rogelberg, Barnes-Farrell, and Lowe.[108] This approach minimizes the tendency for group members to be unwilling to present their ideas by adding new members to a group one at a time and requiring each to present his or her ideas independently to a group that already has discussed the problem at hand. To begin, each of two people works on a problem independently and then they come together to present their ideas and discuss solutions jointly. While the two-person group is working, a third person working alone also considers the problem. Then, this individual presents his or her ideas to the group and joins in a three-person discussion of a possible solution. During this period a fourth person works on the problem alone and then presents his or her ideas to the group and joins in a four-person group discussion. After each new person has been added to the group, the entire group works together at finding a solution. (For a summary of the steps in this technique, see Figure 10-15.)

electronic meeting systems The practice of bringing individuals from different locations together for a meeting via telephone or satellite transmissions, either on television monitors or via shared space on a computer screen.

stepladder technique A technique for improving the quality of group decisions that minimizes the tendency for group members to be unwilling to present their ideas by adding new members to a group one at a time and requiring each to present his or her ideas independently to a group that already has discussed the problem at hand.

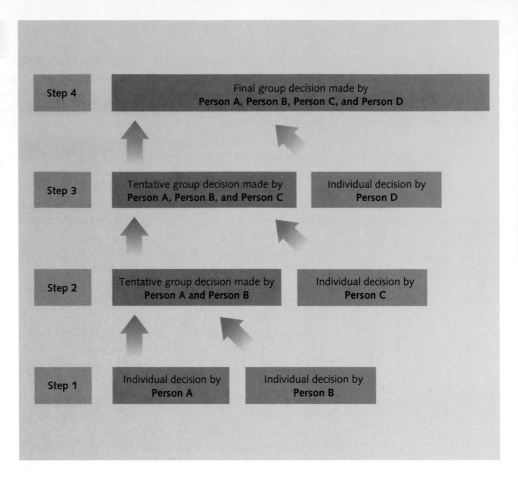

FIGURE 10-15 The Stepladder Technique: A Summary

By systematically adding new individuals into decision-making groups, the *stepladder technique* helps increase the quality of the decisions made.

(Source: Adapted from Rogelberg, Barnes-Farrell, & Lowe, 1992; see Note 108.)

Step 4 — Final group decision made by **Person A, Person B, Person C, and Person D**

Step 3 — Tentative group decision made by **Person A, Person B, and Person C** | Individual decision by **Person D**

Step 2 — Tentative group decision made by **Person A and Person B** | Individual decision by **Person C**

Step 1 — Individual decision by **Person A** | Individual decision by **Person B**

[You Be The Consultant]

A large product-distribution company is having a problem during its group meetings: One department manager is constantly disrupting the meetings while trying to get her ideas across. She has so consistently intimidated her coworkers that they are reluctant to speak up. As a result, their ideas are not coming across.

1. Explain what steps might be taken to avoid this problem.
2. What are the advantages and disadvantages of the tactic you identify?

In following this procedure, it is important for each individual to be given enough time to work on the problem before he or she joins the group. Then, each person must be given enough time to present thoroughly his or her ideas to the group. Groups then must have sufficient time to discuss the problem at hand and reach a preliminary decision before the next person is added. The final decision is then made only after all individuals have been added to the group.

The rationale underlying this procedure is that by forcing each person to present independent ideas without knowing how the rest of the group has decided, the new person will not be influenced by the group, and the group is required to consider a constant infusion of new ideas. If this is so, then groups solving problems using the stepladder technique would be expected to make better decisions than conventional groups meeting all at once to discuss the same problem.

In an experiment comparing both types of groups, this is exactly what Rogelberg and his associates found. Moreover, members of stepladder groups reported feeling generally more positive about their group experiences. Although the stepladder technique is new, this evidence suggests that it holds a great deal of promise as a way of enhancing the decision-making capacity of groups.

SUMMARY AND REVIEW

The Nature of Decision Making

Traditionally, theorists have looked at **decision making** as the multistep process through which a problem is identified, solution objectives are defined, a **predecision** is made (i.e., a decision about how to make a decision), alternatives are generated and evaluated, and an alternative is chosen, implemented, and then followed up.

There are individual differences in the way people make decisions. Generally, individuals have one dominant decision style, either *directive*, *analytical*, *conceptual*, or *behavioural*. Research also has shown that people in different cultures tend to make decisions in different ways.

The Broad Spectrum of Organizational Decisions

Decisions made in organizations can be characterized as being either **programmed**, routine decisions made according to pre-existing guidelines, or **nonprogrammed**, decisions requiring novel and creative solutions. Decisions also differ with respect to the amount of risk involved, ranging from those in which the decision outcomes are relatively *certain* to those in which the outcomes are highly *uncertain*. Uncertain situations are expressed as statements of probability based on either objective or subjective information. Finally, decisions may be differentiated with respect to whether they are made by high-level organizational officials (**top-down decisions**) or by employees themselves (**empowered decisions**).

How Are Individual Decisions Made?

The **rational-economic model** characterizes decision makers as thoroughly searching through perfect information to make an optimal decision. This is a *normative* approach, in that it describes how decision makers ideally ought to behave to make the best possible decisions.

In contrast, the **administrative model** is a *descriptive* approach, which describes how decision makers actually behave. It recognizes that limitations imposed by people's ability to process the information needed to make complex decisions (*bounded rationality*) restrict decision makers to making **satisficing decisions**—solutions that are not optimal, but good enough.

An alternative approach, **image theory**, recognizes that decisions are made in an automatic, intuitive fashion. It claims that people will adopt a course of action that best fits their individual principles, current goals, and plans for the future.

Impediments to Optimal Individual Decisions

People make imperfect decisions due to cognitive biases. One such bias, **framing**, refers to the tendency for people to make different decisions based on how a problem is presented. For example, when a problem is presented in a way that emphasizes positive gains to be received, people tend to make conservative, risk-averse, decisions, whereas when the same problem is presented in a way that emphasizes potential losses to be suffered, people tend to make riskier decisions.

Simple rules, known as **heuristics**, also may bias decisions. For example, according to the **availability heuristic**, people base their judgments on information readily available to them, and according to the **representativeness heuristic**, people are perceived in stereotypical ways if they appear to be representatives of the categories to which they belong. People are biased toward **implicit favourites**, alternatives they prefer in advance of considering all the options. Other alternatives, **confirmation candidates**, are considered for purposes of convincing oneself that one's implicit favourite is the best alternative.

According to the **escalation of commitment phenomenon**, people continue to support previously unsuccessful courses of action because they have sunk costs invested in them. This occurs in large part because people need to justify their previous actions and wish to avoid having to admit that their initial decision was a mistake. Individual decisions are also limited by organizational factors, such as time constraints, political "face-saving" pressure, and **bounded discretion** (moral and ethical restrictions imposed on decisions).

Group Decision Making

Groups are superior to individual members when they are composed of a heterogeneous mix of experts who possess complementary skills. However, groups may not be any better than the best member of the group when performing a task that has a simple, verifiable answer. Compared with individuals, face-to-face **brainstorming** groups tend to make inferior decisions on creative problems.

Groupthink is a major obstacle to effective group decisions. It refers to the tendency for strong conformity pressures within groups to lead to the breakdown of critical thinking and to encourage premature acceptance of potentially questionable solutions.

Techniques for Improving Group Decisions

The quality of group decisions can be enhanced in several different ways. First, the quality of group decisions has been shown to improve following individual training in problem-solving skills. Second, using the **Delphi technique**, the judgments of experts are systematically gathered and used to form a single joint decision. Third, the **nominal group technique** is a method of structuring group meetings so as to elicit and evaluate the opinions of all members. Finally, the **stepladder technique** systematically adds new individuals to decision-making groups one at a time, requiring the presentation and discussion of new ideas.

CASE PREVIEW QUESTIONS FOR DISCUSSION

1. How would the decision-making process at Yogen Früz have been changed if Michael and Aaron Serruya had accepted the offer of an outside partnership early in the company's history?

2. Critique the various decisions the Serruya brothers have made so far.

3. What are the advantages and disadvantages of being in business with siblings?

CHAPTER QUESTIONS FOR DISCUSSION

1. Argue pro or con: "All people make decisions in the same manner."

2. Think of any decision you recently made. Would you characterize it as programmed or nonprogrammed? Highly certain or highly uncertain? Top-down or empowered? Explain your answers.

3. Describe a decision that you are likely to make following the administrative model and one that you are likely to make using the intuitive approach of image theory.

4. Identify ways in which decisions you have made may have been biased by framing, heuristics, the use of implicit favourites, and the escalation of commitment.

5. Imagine that you are a manager facing the problem of not attracting enough high-quality personnel to your organization. Would you attempt to solve this problem alone or by committee? Explain your reasoning.

6. Groupthink is a potentially serious impediment to group decision making. Describe this phenomenon and review some things that can be done to avoid it.

7. Suppose you find out that a certain important organizational decision has to be made by a group, but you suspect that a better decision might be made by an individual. Describe three different ways you could use groups to make a decision while at the same time avoiding many of the problems associated with groups.

CASE IN POINT

The Classic Case of Coke Classic: Fizzled Decision Making

"Don't mess with success," the saying goes. But, on April 23, 1985, Coca-Cola's CEO Roberto Goizueta did just that. In a surprise announcement he declared that the highly successful 99-year-old formula was going to be replaced by a sweeter, "new Coke."

As you might imagine, this decision was not made readily. After spending some U.S.$4 million on market research over four-and-a-half years, it seemed like the new formula would be a hit. After all, 200 000 people were involved in the taste tests. Further, a poll of consumers, ad agency officials, and outside consultants agreed that the new Coke would be a hit.

Soon after the new Coke was introduced, however, complaints started pouring in from the public, and sales nosedived. As time went on, people never accepted the new formula, and cries from pop drinkers got louder. Cases of the original formula Coke were imported from foreign countries and sold on the black market for ten times the normal price. Protest groups formed, and a class action lawsuit was planned to bring back the beloved original formula Coca-Cola.

Needless to say, company officials were caught off guard by the way their decision had backfired. In retrospect, they blame the way the market research was done. Consumers who said they liked the new formula never dreamed that they would be endorsing the elimination of the classic formula Coke. Other company officials said that the poor decision resulted from the fact that a number of top company officials came to their posts from foreign operations and were not com-

pletely familiar with the way North Americans in general viewed Coca-Cola—a cherished icon undeserving of change.

On July 11, 1985, less than three months after Goizueta's announcement, he made another announcement: Original Coke would return under the name "Coca-Cola Classic," and the new product would remain on the market as simply "Coca-Cola." In short order, the newly returned original formula outsold the revised one by at least a two-to-one margin, and as much as nine-to-one in some cities. Together, the overall market share of both "Coca-Cola" and "Coca-Cola Classic" rose to the pre-April 25 level.

Every bad decision has a "heavy." Sergio Zyman, Coke's head of marketing (see CASE PREVIEW for Chapter 7), took the fall in the "New Coke" fiasco but he was able to move past this episode in his life. Nevertheless, the story of "New Coke" has taken on legendary proportions, even in political circles. For example, Quebec Premier Lucien Bouchard compared Jean Charest's entry into Quebec provincial politics with the "New Coke" decision "[s]aying the introduction was well done while the product was flawed...."[109]

Critical Thinking Questions

1. Using the analytical model of decision making, how do you think the process unfolded to decide to change Coca-Cola's formula?

2. What did Coca-Cola Co. do to reduce the uncertainty that surrounded its decision to change the formula?

3. Do you think groupthink may have been involved in the decision? Explain how it may have operated in this context.

SKILLS PORTFOLIO

Experiencing Organizational Behaviour

What Is Your Personal Decision Style?

As you read about the various personal decision styles, did you put yourself into any one of the categories? To get a feel for what the *Decision-Style Inventory* reveals about your personal decision style, complete this exercise. It is based on questions similar to those appearing in the actual instrument (Rowe, Boulgaides, & McGrath, 1984; see Note 20).

Directions

For each of the following questions, select the one alternative that best describes how you see yourself in your typical work situation.

1. When performing my job, I usually look for
   a. practical results
   b. the best solutions to problems
   c. new ideas or approaches
   d. pleasant working conditions
2. When faced with a problem, I usually
   a. use approaches that have worked in the past
   b. analyze it carefully
   c. try to find a creative approach
   d. rely on my feelings
3. When making plans, I usually emphasize
   a. the problems I currently face
   b. attaining objectives
   c. future goals
   d. developing my career
4. The kind of information I usually prefer to use is
   a. specific facts
   b. complete and accurate data
   c. broad information covering many options
   d. data that is limited and simple to understand
5. Whenever I am uncertain about what to do, I
   a. rely on my intuition
   b. look for facts
   c. try to find a compromise
   d. wait, and decide later
6. The people with whom I work best are usually
   a. ambitious and full of energy
   b. self-confident
   c. open-minded
   d. trusting and polite
7. The decisions I make are usually
   a. direct and realistic
   b. abstract or systematic
   c. broad and flexible
   d. sensitive to others' needs

Scoring

1. For each *a* you select, give yourself a point in the *directive* category.
2. For each *b* you select, give yourself a point in the *analytical* category.
3. For each *c* you select, give yourself a point in the *conceptual* category.
4. For each *d* you select, give yourself a point in the *behavioural* category.

The points reflect the relative strength of your preferences for each decision style.

Questions for Discussion

1. What style did the test reveal that you have? How did this compare to the style you thought you had before you took the test?

2. Based on the descriptions of the personal decision styles in the text, were you able to guess in advance which test items were indicative of which styles? What additional items may be added to the test to assess each style?

Working in Groups — Running a Nominal Group: Try It Yourself

A great deal can be learned about nominal groups by running one—or, at least, participating in one—yourself. Doing so will not only help illustrate the procedure, but demonstrate how effectively it works.

Directions

1. Select a topic suitable for discussion in a nominal group composed of students in your class. It should be a topic that is narrowly defined and on which people have many different opinions (these work best in nominal groups). Some possible examples include:
   * What should your school's student leaders be doing for you?
   * What can be done to improve the quality of instruction in your institution?
   * What can be done to improve the quality of jobs your school's students receive when graduating?

2. Divide the class into groups of approximately ten. Arrange each group in a circle, or around a table, if possible. In each group, select one person to serve as the group facilitator.

3. Following the steps outlined in Figure 10-14, facilitators should guide their groups in discussions regarding the focal question identified in step 1, above. Allow approximately 45 minutes to 1 hour to complete this process.

4. If time allows, select a different focal question and a different group leader, and repeat the procedure.

Questions for Discussion

1. Collectively, how did the group answer the question? Do you believe that this answer accurately reflected the feelings of the group?

2. How did the various groups' answers compare? Were they similar or different? Why?

3. What were the major problems, if any, associated with the nominal group experience? For example, were there any group members who were reluctant to wait their turns before speaking up?

4. If you conducted more than one nominal group discussion with different leaders, was the process smoother the second time around, as everyone learned how it works?

5. How do you think your group experiences would have differed had you used a totally unstructured, traditional face-to-face group instead of a nominal group?

TAKE IT TO THE NET

Prentice Hall
COMPANION WEBSITE

We invite you to visit the *Greenberg/Baron/Sales/Owen Companion Website* at *www.prenticehall.ca/greenberg* for this chapter's Internet resources.

CHAPTER 11

Helping, Cooperation, and Conflict in Organizations

LEARNING OBJECTIVES

After reading this chapter you should be able to:

1. Define *prosocial behaviour* and distinguish it from altruism.

2. Describe *organizational citizenship behaviour* and the major forms it often takes.

3. Explain the nature of *whistle-blowing* and describe some of the ethical issues it raises.

4. Explain the basic nature of *cooperation* and describe both individual and organizational factors that influence its occurrence.

5. Define *trust* and explain its relationship to both organizational citizenship behaviour and cooperation.

6. Define *conflict* and indicate how it can produce positive as well as negative effects.

7. Describe various styles of managing conflict and the basic dimensions that underlie them.

8. List several organizational and interpersonal causes of conflict.

9. Describe several effective means for managing conflict.

10. Distinguish between *workplace violence* and *workplace aggression*.

11. Describe causes of workplace aggression and techniques for reducing this harmful form of organizational behaviour.

Saskatoon Chemicals: Truce Tames Chemical Warfare

Once a cauldron of labour unrest, Saskatoon Chemicals Ltd. radically transformed its labour-management relations through a process other companies are now studying. The company is run by 16 union-management committees that deal with everything from pensions to business development. They serve as the heart of a system that allows union and bosses essentially to co-manage the company (see Figure 11-1). "In the traditional system, management decides and union objects," says Mike Haner, vice-president and general manager. "In this system, management and union decide, implement, and correct."

The company, located just north of Saskatoon, grosses about $60 million a year producing chlorine-based chemicals for the pulp and paper industry, water-treatment plants, and swimming pools. But over many years, Saskatoon Chemicals had fought a running battle with its unionized workers, represented now by the Communications, Energy, and Paperworkers Union of Canada (CEP) following a backlog of more than 100 union grievances. "It had deteriorated to the point where we were communicating by letter only," says chemical worker Vern Pura. "The company was posting policies without consultation, whether it went against the collective agreement or not."

Just after Christmas in 1989, the union decided to strike, the first job action in the plant's 33-year history. The sticking point was work scheduling. The strike lasted just ten days, but that was long enough for both sides. Fed up with constant confrontation, they began to explore ways to settle their differences and, eventually, formed a joint standing committee charged with the responsibility for improving relations at the plant.

The committee languished until Mac Roberts, a Toronto industrial relations consultant, came in. Through Mr. Roberts, workers and management discovered they shared common goals. For example, job security, the main union concern, depended on long-term profitability, a company goal. Mr. Roberts helped the parties understand that "we have more to gain helping each other than hurting each other," says organization development manager Richard Rybiak.

But the former combatants had heavy baggage to unload if "the change process"—as the experiment is known—was to work. Managers learned to share confidential financial information with the union and to allow employees unprecedented freedom in their working lives and input into decision making.

Mr. Phillips, the union chief steward, says the Saskatoon workers became believers because the gains were clear. As a result of the process, the company expanded its education program significantly and created a new employee benefit plan. Workers were guaranteed employment security and attended to tasks with a minimum of supervision. Mr. Haner, the general manager, says the new structure boosted productivity, cut costs, and made the plant a safer place. The inventory of grievances dried up and it took only five days to negotiate the collective agreement in 1994, all thanks to the new system.[1]

FIGURE 11-1 Union and Management Work Together at Saskatoon Chemicals

After long periods of management-labour conflict, a new spirit of cooperation was developed at Saskatoon Chemicals Ltd. Union-management committees became the basis for the company's co-management system.[2]

Communications, Energy and Paperworkers Union of Canada
www.cep.ca

cooperation A process in which individuals or groups work together to attain shared goals.

prosocial behaviour Actions that benefit others within an organization.

Air Canada
www.aircanada.ca

FIGURE 11-2 Negative Outcomes of Conflict
The September 1998 Air Canada pilots' strike grounded the 65 000 passengers the airline serves each day on its 600 flights around the world. The strike issues included a conflict between Air Canada and its pilots over wages, pensions, and scheduling.[10]

With the help of Mac Roberts, employees and managers made a key discovery—they shared common goals. Why is it so hard for employees and managers to grasp the idea that they are truly *interdependent*? Saskatoon Chemicals was not alone in its tendency to fall short of the cooperative ideal. After Mac Roberts's intervention, Saskatoon Chemicals' employees and managers exchanged their narrow perspectives for a vision of the common good. This approach was based on **cooperation**—a process in which individuals or organizations seek to coordinate their efforts in order to maximize joint outcomes or reach shared goals.[3]

Instead of benevolent places filled with the spirit of mutual assistance, organizations are just as likely to be places dominated by indifference, needless competition, smouldering feuds, and even open conflict.[4] In many situations, a choice between these contrasting strategies exists. The fact that it does raises an intriguing question: What factors lead individuals, groups, or organizations to choose one approach over the other? This will be one of the key questions on which we will focus in this chapter. In more general terms, we will examine three basic processes relating to the extent to which individuals, groups, or organizations work with—or against—one another. The first of these processes is known as **prosocial behaviour** and involves actions that benefit others within an organization, usually without requiring anything obvious or immediate in return. Growing evidence indicates that prosocial behaviour plays an important role in organizational effectiveness, so it is clearly a topic worthy of careful attention.[5] The second process, *cooperation*, involves mutual, two-way assistance in which individuals, groups, or organizations provide benefits to each other in a reciprocal, joint manner. Many factors influence cooperation, and as we'll soon see, it can occur between as well as within organizations.[6]

The third major topic we'll consider is *conflict*, which is often defined as a process which develops when individuals or groups perceive that actions by others have, or will soon, exert negative effects on their important interests.[7] Such perceptions often trigger a costly spiral that produces negative outcomes for both parties (see Figure 11-2). Indeed, long-standing, bitter conflicts may proceed to the point at which both sides become more concerned with harming their opponents than with maximizing their own outcomes.

Closely related to conflict in several respects, but also distinct from it, is the topic of workplace violence or, more generally, *workplace aggression*—actions through which individuals seek to harm one or more target persons in their organizations.[8] What forms does workplace aggression take? Are these increasing in frequency, and if so, why? These are the questions we'll address with respect to this disturbing form of organizational behaviour.

Prosocial Behaviour: Helping Others at Work

Is there such a thing as pure *altruism*—actions by one person that benefit one or more others under conditions in which the donor expects nothing in return? Philosophers have long puzzled over this question, and more recently, social scientists have entered the debate.[9] Disappointingly, their research casts considerable doubt on the existence of totally selfless helping. It is true: Individuals do sometimes offer help to others—or even risk their lives for them—without expecting anything tangible in return. (Parents who sacrifice their own lives for those of their children provide a dramatic example.) But such actions appear to be quite rare, and, in most instances where individuals help others, they do seem to anticipate *some* form of compensation. This return on their investment can be quite subtle—for example, the warm glow of feeling that one has "done the right thing" or the pleasure of seeing another person's joy or relief. Yet, such gains are certainly real and seem to provide at least a portion of the motivation behind seemingly altruistic acts.

While pure altruism seems to be relatively rare, it is clear that people do frequently engage in prosocial behaviour—actions that help others in various ways. Moreover, such behaviour is quite common in work settings, and may contribute, in important ways, to the success and effectiveness of organizations. While many forms of prosocial behaviour exist in organizations,[11] several of the most important are included within the concept of **organizational citizenship behaviour (OCB)**—actions by organization members that exceed the formal requirements of their job and are, therefore, "above and beyond the call of duty."[12] We'll now examine such behaviour more closely, considering the various forms it takes, factors that influence its occurrence, and the effects it can exert on both individuals and organizations.

Organizational Citizenship Behaviour: Some Basic Forms

According to widely accepted definitions of *organizational citizenship behaviour* (or *OCB* for short), such actions involve three major components. First, they exceed the role requirements (or formal descriptions) of employees' jobs. Second, they are discretionary in nature—individuals decide to perform them in a voluntary manner. Third, they are not generally recognized by the formal reward structure of the organization. While there is general agreement about the first two of these requirements, we should note that experts don't agree about the third: Some believe that certain forms of prosocial behaviour are, indeed, recognized by formal reward structures. Such behaviours are described by the term **organizational spontaneity** to distinguish them from OCB.[13]

Putting such complexities aside, there *is* general agreement on what kinds of behaviour OCB involves. Briefly, these fall into five basic categories:

1. **Altruism**: Have you ever offered to aid a coworker with a difficult project? If so, you have engaged in this type of OCB.

2. **Conscientiousness**: Going well beyond the minimum requirements in such areas as attendance, obeying rules, taking breaks, and so on. If you pride yourself on never missing a day at work, you are engaging in this type of OCB.

3. **Civic virtue**: Participation in and concern about the life of the organization. This behaviour involves such actions as attending voluntary meetings and reading announcements, rather than tossing them into the "circular file."

4. **Being a good sport**: Willingness to tolerate less than ideal circumstances without complaining. If you've followed the dictum "Grin and bear it" at work, then you have engaged in such behaviour.

5. **Courtesy**: Behaviours aimed at preventing interpersonal problems with others. Examples of each of these five types of organizational citizenship behaviour are shown in Table 11-1.[14]

organizational citizenship behaviour (OCB) Actions by organization members that exceed the formal requirements of their job and are, therefore, "above and beyond the call of duty."

organizational spontaneity Prosocial behaviour within an organization that may or may not be recognized by the formal reward system.

TABLE 11-1 Specific Forms of Organizational Citizenship Behaviour

While *organizational citizenship behaviour* (OCB) can take many different forms, most seem to fall into the major categories shown here.

Form of OCB	Examples
Altruism	Helping a coworker with a project; switching vacation dates with another person; volunteering
Conscientiousness	Never missing a day of work; coming to work early if needed; not spending time on personal calls
Civic virtue	Attending voluntary meetings and functions; reading memos; keeping up with new information
Being a good sport	"Grin and bear it"; making do without complaint; not finding fault with the organization
Courtesy	"Turning the other cheek" to avoid problems; not "blowing up" when provoked

Organizational Citizenship Behaviour: Factors Affecting Its Occurrence

☛ Perceptions of procedural and distributive justice also play an important role in motivation, as we saw in Chapter 5.

What factors lead individuals to engage in various forms of OCB? Why, in short, do employees sometimes go well "beyond the call of duty" in performing their jobs? Recent findings indicate that a number of different factors probably play a role. One of the most important of these appears to be *trust*—the belief among employees that they will be treated fairly by their organization and, more specifically, by their immediate supervisor. Briefly, recent findings indicate that to the extent employees believe that their supervisors' decisions follow principles of distributive and procedural fairness, the greater their trust in these persons. And the greater such trust, the greater is employees' willingness to engage in prosocial behaviour (see Figure 11-3).[15]

Trust in one's supervisor is not the only determinant of OCB, however. Additional findings indicate that it is influenced by several other factors, too. One of the most important of these is simply employees' perceptions of the breadth of their jobs—what behaviours are "in-role" and what behaviours are "extra-role" in nature.[16] In other words, the more broadly employees define their jobs, the more likely they are to engage in actions often viewed as involving OCB. In fact, from the employees' point of view, they may simply be doing things that are actually part of their jobs.[17]

☛ The nature of punishment, and its effects upon employees' behaviour, were discussed in detail in Chapter 3.

Finally, employees' willingness to engage in OCB seems to be strongly influenced by their perceptions of any *punishment* they receive. The more employees perceive punishment as fair, and under their control—a process to which they can have input and which they can influence—the greater their tendency to engage in OCB.[18] Overall, then, it appears that many different factors influence employees' tendencies to engage in OCB and "go the extra mile" for their organizations.

Effects of OCB: Does It Really Matter?

More than 30 years ago, one leading organizational theorist suggested that there are three major ingredients in organizational effectiveness: (1) the organization must recruit and retain excellent employees, (2) these employees must carry out the requirements of their jobs, and (3) they must also engage in innovative, spontaneous activity that goes beyond formal job descriptions or role requirements.[19] Despite the tremendous changes that have occurred in the intervening years, these observations still impress us as a sound prescription for organizational excellence. And as you can readily see, the third point relates to organizational citizenship behaviour. We have already described some of the conditions that seem to encourage such behaviour by employees; clearly, organizations wishing to increase the incidence of OCB should pay careful attention to these points. But a basic question remains: Does OCB really enhance organizational performance?

This question is more difficult to answer than it might at first appear, because many aspects of OCB are *not* included in standard measures of individual or group performance. Moreover, organizational citizenship behaviours are, by definition, not generally part of formal reward systems: Individuals perform them for reasons other than the external rewards they hope to receive. Yet, despite these complexities, a growing body of evidence suggests that OCB does indeed contribute to organizational excellence. For instance, willingness to engage in OCB has been found to be related to such factors as organizational commitment and job satisfaction—variables that *do* impinge on the bottom line.[20] In addition, OCB often involves tendencies by employees to make positive statements about their organizations—to praise them to others. This can enhance an organization's reputation and a positive reputation, in turn, has been shown to have many beneficial effects on an organization—for example, increased ease of hiring first-rate employees.[21] For these

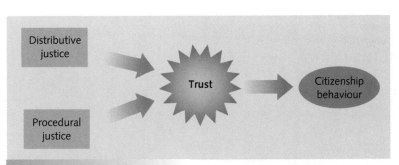

FIGURE 11-3 Procedural Justice, Trust, and OCB

The greater the extent to which employees perceive that their supervisor's decisions follow principles of distributive and procedural justice, the greater their trust in the supervisors, and the greater their tendency to engage in prosocial behaviour.

(Source: Based on findings reported by Konovsky & Pugh, 1994; see Note 15.)

[**You Be The Consultant**]

An organization is having difficulties in recruiting top-notch employees. The Director of Human Resources believes that this may be due to the fact that disgruntled former employees—and even some current employees—are saying negative things about the company, thus harming its reputation.

1. How could the Human Resources Director find out if this is so?

2. If it is the case that the company's reputation is being damaged by disgruntled employees, what steps could be taken to reverse this state of affairs—to increase the likelihood that former and current employees say positive things about the company and boost its reputation?

whistle-blowing Calling attention to actions or practices that are inconsistent with established organizational norms or policies.

Hospital for Sick Children
www.sickkids.on.ca

and other reasons, it seems clear that OCB does indeed contribute to an organization's overall effectiveness. Such contributions may not always be easy to measure, but this in no way implies that they are not real, or are unimportant.

Whistle-Blowing: Helping an Organization by Dissenting with It

Before concluding our discussion of *prosocial behaviour* in work settings, we should call attention to a very different way in which employees sometimes seek to help their organizations. This is known as **whistle-blowing**, which involves disclosure by employees of illegal, immoral, or illegitimate practices by employers to people or organizations able to do something about it.[22] Is whistle-blowing a prosocial action? From the point of view of society, it usually is. In many instances, the actions of whistle-blowers can protect the health, safety, or economic welfare of the general public.

For example, consider the case of Dr. Nancy Olivieri at Toronto's Hospital for Sick Children (see Figure 11-4). Dr. Olivieri's research on a drug to treat thalassemia (a blood disorder) was supported by the drug's manufacturer. Dr. Olivieri faced a very difficult dilemma when her data suggested that the drug actually did more harm than good. The dilemma stemmed from the fact that Dr. Olivieri had signed a confidentiality agreement with the company. Despite this agreement and the pharmaceutical company's threat to sue her, Dr. Olivieri believed she had a responsibility to her patients and her colleagues to inform them of the possibility that the drug could be harmful. Naturally, she believed that the hospital administration would support her in this. She was wrong. When the hospital refused to hire a lawyer for Dr. Olivieri, her colleagues rallied behind her calling for an inquiry. A member of the hospital's administration said that the institution would, in fact, have supplied legal assistance for Dr. Olivieri if the pharmaceutical company had pursued legal action. Even the process the hospital designed to investigate the matter caused controversy.[23]

FIGURE 11-4 The Costs of Whistle-Blowing
Dr. Nancy Olivieri stood up for her belief that a drug she was testing might be harmful. Her "whistle-blowing" prompted a storm of controversy at the world-renowned Hospital for Sick Children.[24]

Dr. Olivieri is not alone as a whistle-blower. Jorma Jyrkkanen brought to public attention the dangers of the use of the herbicide spray Roundup by the government of British Columbia. Ross Gray claimed to have been fired for revealing alleged illegal activities by Standard Trustco. Major Barry Armstrong alleged that senior officers covered up abuse of the Somali people by members of the former Canadian Airborne Regiment.[25]

What happens when someone blows the whistle? Not what you might expect. Instead of being treated like heroes and heroines, whistle-blowers are often punished for their actions. Such persons frequently find themselves facing a long, uphill battle as they attempt to prove the wrongdoing they have reported. They often lose their jobs—their companies are all too quick to find "other" grounds for dismissing them—and then they discover that they have been "blackballed" in their industry or profession and can't find another.

In Canada, only Ontario has legislation protecting whistle-blowers from being fired for their actions,[26] although pressure is building for such legislation in other areas of the country.[27] While there is no federal protection for whistle-blowing, there are pieces of legislation and guidelines that encourage this behaviour. For example, the Canadian Environmental Protection Act encourages the identification of actual or potential release of harmful substances, and protects the reporter from retribution.[28]

Large and small companies are grappling with the whistle-blowing issue. Some are even looking for ways to promote it. In 1995, General Motors of Canada announced the establishment of its "Awareline," which employees quickly dubbed the "snitch line." GM Canada president Maureen Kempston Darkes (see CASE PREVIEW for Chapter 13) wrote to employees to explain that the line is designed to allow "...employees to report anonymously 'concerns of possible criminal wrongdoing by the company, its management, supervisors, employees or agents.' "[29] CAW president Buzz Hargrove responded, saying "the attempt to turn workers on each other with the 'Awareline'... reveals an insulting attitude to the work we do, and an arrogant disregard for the problems workers face."[30]

Does whistle-blowing really qualify as prosocial behaviour? Or are whistle-blowers merely disgruntled employees, looking for a way to "get even" with their organizations? The latter conclusion can be ruled out in most cases. Careful study of whistle-blowing incidents indicates that most whistle-blowers are motivated to correct what they perceive as wrongdoing. Moreover, most have tried to work inside their companies before informing the public or legal authorities about the situation. They "go public" only when these efforts fail.[31]

Yet, despite this fact, the situation remains complex. Whether such actions are or are not prosocial in nature depends on the motivation underlying them. If, in contrast to the conditions described above, a whistle-blower benefits from his or her actions while the organization suffers, or if the whistle-blower's actions are part of a personal quest for vengeance, the actions cannot be viewed as prosocial with respect to the organization. So, before a whistle-blower's actions can be regarded as prosocial in nature, they must be motivated by an underlying desire to help the organization and/or its employees—an assurance it may be difficult to obtain.

Cooperation: Mutual Assistance in Work Settings

Although prosocial behaviour is quite common in work settings, another pattern known as *cooperation* is even more widespread.[32] In cooperation, assistance is mutual, and two or more individuals, groups, or organizations work together toward shared goals and for their mutual benefit.[33] Cooperation is a very common form of coordination in work settings, partly because, by cooperating, the persons or groups involved can often accomplish more than they can by working alone.

Given the obvious benefits that can result from cooperation, a basic question arises: Why, if it is so useful, does cooperation often fail to develop? Why don't people seeking the same (or at least similar) goals always join forces? Although there are many factors involved, the most important reason is that cooperation simply *cannot* develop in some situations, because the goals sought by the individuals or groups involved cannot be shared. Two people seeking the same job or promotion, for instance, cannot join forces to attain it: The reward can go to only one. Similarly, two companies courting the same potential merger candidate cannot cooperate to reach their goal: Only one can conclude the merger.

In cases such as these, an alternative form of behaviour known as **competition** often develops. As we noted previously, this is a pattern in which each person, group, or organization seeks to maximize its own gains, often at the expense of others.[34] In some contexts, competition is both natural and understandable. People and groups do have to compete for scarce resources and rewards. And organizations themselves must compete in the marketplace for supplies, government contracts, customers, and market share. In many instances, however, competition is not dictated by current conditions, and cooperation might well develop. What factors serve to tip the balance toward or away from cooperation in such instances? As we'll soon see, both individual and organization-level factors play a role.

Individual Factors and Cooperation

Several factors affecting the tendency to cooperate function primarily through their impact on individuals. They influence the perceptions and reactions of specific persons and in this manner shape decisions about whether to cooperate or compete with others. Among the most important of these are the principle of *reciprocity*, and several *personal characteristics*.

Reciprocity: The matching game. Throughout life, we are urged to treat others the way we would want to be treated. Despite such appeals, however, we usually behave in a different manner. Most people tend to react to others not as they would prefer to be treated, but rather as they have actually been treated by these persons (or others) in the past. In short, people follow the principle of **reciprocity** much of the time: They return the kind of treatment they have previously received.[35] The choice between cooperation and competition is no exception to this powerful rule. When others act in a competitive manner, we usually respond in the same way. If, in contrast, they behave cooperatively, we usually match *this* pattern.[36]

So, in short, reciprocity appears to be the guiding principle of cooperation. The key task in establishing cooperation in organizations, then, seems to be that of getting it started. Once individuals, groups, or units have begun to cooperate, the process may be largely self-sustaining. To encourage cooperation, therefore, managers should do everything possible to get the process under way. After it begins, the obvious benefits of cooperation, plus powerful tendencies toward reciprocity, may tend to maintain it at high levels.

Trust: A powerful antecedent of cooperation. Earlier, we noted that *trust* is an important determinant of organizational citizenship behaviour: The greater employees' trust in their supervisors, the greater their tendency to engage in OCB.[37] It should not be surprising to learn, therefore, that **trust**—which can be defined, more broadly, as an individual's confidence in the good will of others, and the belief that they will make efforts consistent with the group's goals—also plays an important role in cooperation.[38] Specifically, recent findings indicate that the greater the degree of trust individuals have in their coworkers, the more likely they are to cooperate with them.[39] Moreover, it appears that there are two distinct kinds of trust, and that these may be related in distinct ways to increased cooperation.[40]

The first type of trust is known as *cognition-based trust*, which refers to our beliefs about others' reliability and trustworthiness. It is measured by the extent of agreement with such items as, "Given this person's track record, I see no reason to doubt his/her competence and preparation for the job." The second type of trust is known as *affect-based trust*, which refers to the emotional bond between

competition A process in which individuals or groups seek to attain desired goals at the expense of others seeking the same goals.

reciprocity The tendency to treat others as they have treated us.

trust The belief among employees that they will be treated fairly by their organization and, more specifically, by their immediate supervisor.

individuals—bonds involving genuine care and concern for the welfare of others. It is measured by items such as, "I should say that we have both made considerable emotional investments in our working relationship."

To study the impact of these two kinds of trust on various forms of cooperation, McAllister recently conducted an investigation in which managers completed measures designed to assess both their affect- and cognition-based trust in peers, the antecedents of such trust, and the extent to which they cooperated with these persons. As shown in Figure 11-5, results indicated that affect-based trust was influenced by the frequency with which the managers interacted with their peers and prior helping from these persons. Such trust influenced several forms of helping and cooperation, and, indirectly, both managers' and peers' performance. In contrast, cognition-based trust exerted its effects through affect-based trust. The higher such trust, the higher affect-based trust; however, cognition-based trust did not influence cooperation directly.

Additional findings indicate that trust derives, in part, from perceptions that one's boss or leader has reached decisions through the use of fair procedures (procedural justice).[41] Further, the higher such trust, the greater employees' commitment to their bosses' or leaders' decisions.

In sum, trust is an important determinant of cooperation. Since cooperation, in turn, yields many beneficial effects—increased performance, coordination, and reduced costs (through, for example, reduced cycle time), it appears that efforts to build high levels of trust among persons who work together is an activity well worth the effort involved.

Personal orientations and cooperation. Think about the many people you have known during your life. Can you remember ones who were highly competitive—individuals who viewed most situations as contests in which they, or someone else, would triumph? In contrast, can you recall others who were highly cooperative—people who preferred to minimize differences between their own outcomes and those of others? You probably have little difficulty in bringing examples of both types to mind, for large individual differences in the tendencies to prefer cooperation or competition exist. Such differences, in turn, seem to reflect contrasting perspectives toward working with others—perspectives that individuals carry with them from situation to situation and over relatively long periods of time.[42]

Research on such differences suggests, in fact, that on the basis of their relative preferences for cooperation or competition, individuals can be divided into four distinct groups. A sizable proportion are **competitors**—their primary motive is doing better than others. In fact, extreme competitors prefer negative outcomes that are better than those obtained by other persons to positive ones that are worse than those obtained by their opponents. A second group can be described as **individualists**. These are people who have little interest in the outcomes of others and don't really care whether these persons do better or worse than they do. Their major focus is simply on gaining as much as possible in every situation.

competitors Individuals who are primarily concerned with exceeding the outcomes of others.

individualists People primarily concerned with maximizing their own outcomes.

FIGURE 11-5 Trust, Cooperation, and Job Performance

Managers' affect-based trust in peers is influenced by several different factors, including frequency of interaction between managers and peers and prior helping from these persons. Such trust, in turn, influences several forms of cooperation and helping, and also job performance.

(Source: Based on findings reported by McAllister, 1995; see Note 37.)

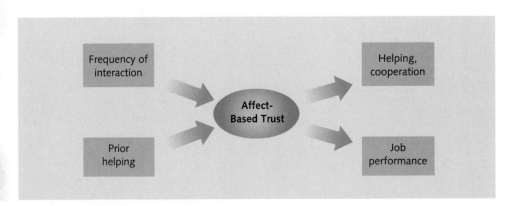

☞ *Recall the distinction between individualistic and collectivistic cultures discussed in Chapter 2.*

A third group can be classified as **cooperators**. They are primarily concerned with maximizing joint outcomes—the total received by themselves and others. They want everyone they work with to be satisfied with their rewards and do not wish to defeat them. Finally, a few people can be described as **equalizers**. Their major goal is minimizing differences between their own performance or outcomes and those of others. In short, they wish to assure that everyone they work with receives the same basic results. Figure 11-6 presents an overview of the motives of these four types of people.[43]

Another, and closely related dimension along which individuals differ, and which is also closely related to cooperation, is one referred to as **individualism-collectivism**.[44] Persons high in individualism attach greater importance to their personal interests than to those of groups to which they belong, and will "take care of #1" if their personal interests and those of the group conflict in any way. In contrast, persons high on collectivism attach more importance to group interests than to their own interests and put those of the group above their own if these conflict. Cultures differ greatly with respect to these dimensions; some—for example, many Asian and African cultures—are high on collectivism, while others—European and North American cultures—are high on individualism. Such differences, in turn, can strongly influence the behaviour of individuals. In fact, it appears that while persons high in collectivism cooperate with others under a wide range of conditions, persons high in individualism are much more selective in terms of such cooperation: They cooperate only when their individual contributions to a team project are readily apparent, and when in small groups (see Figure 11-7).[45]

FIGURE 11-6 Personal Orientations Toward Working with Others

As shown here, individuals with different orientations toward working with others demonstrate sharply contrasting patterns of motives. These differences, in turn, influence their behaviour in a wide range of situations.

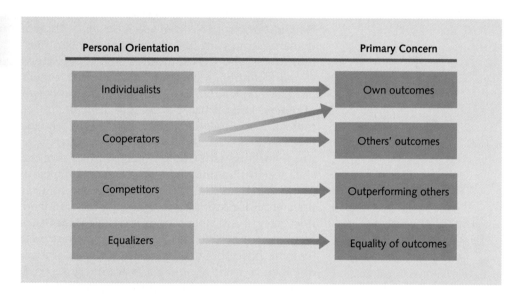

FIGURE 11-7 Collectivism, Individualism, and Cooperation

Persons high in collectivism show a high level of cooperation under a wide range of conditions. In contrast, persons high in individualism show cooperation only under certain conditions.

(Source: Based on findings reported by Wagner, 1995; see Note 45.)

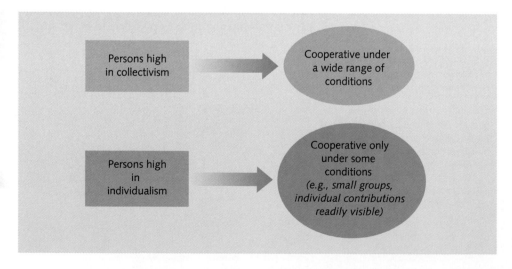

In sum, individual differences do seem to matter to an important degree where cooperation is concerned. Managers should recognize this fact and consider its relevance to several key personnel decisions—hiring, promotion, and work assignments.

Organizational Factors and Cooperation

The fact that organizations differ greatly in their internal levels of cooperation is obvious. Some—typically those that are quite successful—demonstrate a high degree of coordination between their various departments.[46] What accounts for these differences? Individual factors provide only a partial answer. Several factors relating to an organization's internal structure and function also play a role.

Reward systems and organizational structure. Consider the following situation. A large insurance company has two major divisions: Consumer Underwriting (which issues policies for individuals) and Commercial Underwriting (which issues policies for businesses). The company has a bonus system in which annual bonuses are distributed to individuals in the more profitable division. This results in a high degree of competition between the units. At first glance, this might seem beneficial. However, it may lead to situations in which sales personnel from one division actively interfere with efforts of sales personnel from the other division. For example, while working hard to win a multimillion-dollar policy with a large manufacturing concern, agents from the Commercial Underwriting division actually may discourage top managers within this company from seeking individual life and property policies from their own company; after all, this will contribute to the sales of their rival, Consumer Underwriting. And the opposite pattern is true as well. Agents for the consumer division may discourage large clients from seeking policies for their businesses from the commercial division.

Although this might seem to be an extreme case, it reflects conditions that are all too common in many organizations. Reward systems are often "winner-take-all" in form. This fact, coupled with internal differentiation, tends to reduce coordination between units or divisions, as each seeks to maximize its own rewards. This is not to imply that such internal competition is necessarily bad or counterproductive—far from it. Still, managers should ensure that it does not reach a level where it hinders the functioning and success of the entire organization.

Interdependence among employees: The nature of specific jobs. Imagine two organizations. In the first, the major tasks performed by employees can be completed alone; there is no need for individuals to work closely with others. In the second, the tasks performed by employees cannot be completed alone; they must work together closely to do their jobs. In which organization will higher levels of cooperation develop? Obviously, the second. The reason for this difference, too, is apparent. The level of cooperation attained is determined by the nature of the work performed: The greater the degree of interdependence among employees, the higher cooperation among them tends to be. This relationship has been verified in many studies, so it appears to be a strong and general one.[47]

Cooperation across Organizations

When we think about relations between different organizations in the same industry, the first word that comes to mind is *competition*. We tend to concentrate on the ways in which such organizations compete with one another and the strategies they adopt to improve their competitive advantage in the marketplace. Yet, there are also situations in which independent organizations choose to coordinate their actions or efforts to attain mutual gains. In short, there are important instances of what might be termed **interorganizational coordination**. Why would organizations in the same industry ever agree to cooperate with one another? Primarily under three sets of conditions.

interorganizational coordination
Instances or situations in which independent organizations choose to coordinate their actions or efforts to attain mutual gains.

First, such coordination may occur when independent companies conclude that, by joining forces, they can greatly increase their potential gains. A dramatic example of the benefits that can result from "joining forces" in such situations is provided by OPEC, which, during the 1970s and early 1980s, seized worldwide control of the petroleum market.

Second, interorganizational coordination often occurs when one or more new competitors enter a mature and previously stable market. This occurred in North America in the late 1970s and early 1980s, when the sales of Japanese automobiles rose to very high levels. In response to this external threat, the Big Three auto manufacturers joined forces to lobby for government protection. They succeeded and legislation restricting the import of Japanese cars gave them the breathing room they needed to improve their own products.

Third, such coordination sometimes develops as a response to rapidly changing environmental conditions. New patterns of trade, advances in technology, shifts in government policies, and other trends combine to create an environment in which independent organizations find it difficult to continue "business as usual." One response to such conditions is *merger*—becoming part of a larger company. Another is the formation of a **consortium**—a confederation in which organizations maintain their formal independence but agree to coordinate their activities through a central management. By doing so, they are able to control rising costs, provide a better mix of products or services, and avoid duplication of personnel and equipment.

consortium A confederation in which organizations maintain their formal independence but agree to coordinate their activities through a central management.

In some situations, interorganizational cooperation can further the interests of individual companies while, at the same time, serving the greater good. An example is GEMCo (see **THE ETHICS ANGLE** section), a consortium that is looking for a market-driven answer to global warming.

The Ethics Angle

Energy Giants Learn to Trade the Right to Spew

Governments and energy companies are asking themselves: Is there really a market solution to combat global warming? Meet GEMCo (Greenhouse Emissions Management Consortium), a consortium of ten Canadian energy companies that is tackling that very question. The group's membership includes Husky Oil Ltd., British Columbia Hydro and Power Authority, Canadian Utilities Ltd., Epcor Inc., Nova Gas Transmission Ltd., Nova Scotia Power Inc., Ontario Hydro, Saskatchewan Power Corp., TransAlta Corp., and Westcoast Energy Group. GEMCo is a nonprofit group that explores market-economy ways of reducing greenhouse-gas emissions.

"We had to face up to the fact that we will be facing a carbon-constrained future...whether we like it or not," says Aldyen Donnelly, the Vancouver-based president and chief executive officer of GEMCo. The group is also trying to create what Ms. Donnelly calls a new commodity: tradable emissions credits for those who do right by the environment.

Emissions trading is a concept that many people talk about but few can actually define. Perhaps the best analogy comes from urban high-rise development in the 1970s and mid-1980s. Developers would win the right to put up a 40-storey building in a particular zone. But if they only erected 32 storeys, they could sell the remaining eight to someone else. In the case of greenhouse-gas emissions, what would be "sold" is the hot air that has yet to be produced.

GEMCo has set itself up as an internal market to handle the buying and selling of experimental pollution credits among its members as their needs arise. It is also an investor, using half its membership fees to buy into clean-power projects or to scoop up experimental credits anywhere in the world, primarily to see how it's done.

GEMCo is a consortium with attitude. "My members are competitive and they don't like each other very much," Ms. Donnelly reports. "Having built a deal through GEMCo, they just go out and beat each other over the head." But if these companies don't like each other, they fear U.S. competitors even more. Ms. Donnelly suggests the U.S. is likely to develop what amounts to a quota system, perhaps even a mechanism for administering cross-border import charges on natural gas and electricity. Canadian companies had better learn how these quota deals are structured from the ground up if they want to stay in the game, she adds.[48]

Conflict: Its Nature, Causes, and Effects

If prosocial behaviour and cooperation constitute one end of a continuum describing how individuals and groups work together in organizations, then *conflict* certainly lies at or near the other end. This term has many meanings, but in the context of organizational behaviour, it refers primarily to instances in which units or individuals within an organization work *against* rather than with one another.[49] More formally, according to one widely accepted definition, **conflict** is a process in which one party perceives that another party has taken some action that will exert negative effects on its major interest, or is about to take such actions. The key elements in conflict, then, seem to include (1) opposing interests between individuals or groups, (2) recognition of such opposition, (3) the belief by each side that the other will thwart (or has already thwarted) these interests, and (4) actions that actually produce such thwarting.

conflict A process that begins when individuals or groups perceive that others have taken or will soon take actions incompatible with their own major interests.

Unfortunately, conflict, defined in this manner, is all too common in modern organizations. Moreover, its effects are far too costly to ignore. Practising managers report that they spend approximately 20 percent of their time dealing with conflict and its effects.[50] And the smouldering resentment and broken relationships that are the aftermath of many conflicts can persist for months or even years, continuing to exact a major toll in precious human resources long after the situation that initiated the conflict is merely a memory. For these reasons, organizational conflict is an important topic for the field of OB, one deserving of our careful attention. In this section, we will provide an overview of current knowledge about this costly process. First, we will examine two basic dimensions that underlie many forms of conflict. Second, we will consider various causes of conflict. Finally, we'll examine major effects of conflict which, you may be surprised to learn, are sometimes positive as well as negative in nature.

Integration and Distribution: Basic Dimensions of Conflict

Consider this actual incident: Michelle-Élise, a marketing expert for a telephone company, persuaded two of her friends to start a company together. They were good friends, so she was certain they would succeed. Soon, though, it became apparent that her partners had goals that contrasted strikingly with hers. "They wanted the company to pay for their cars and to conduct meetings in the Bahamas," the disillusioned founder notes, "I wanted to plow our money back into the business." Over and over they outvoted her, until, finally, drained of all resources, the company collapsed. Now, Michelle-Élise doesn't even nod to her former partners when she passes them in the street. "I never thought a business relationship could overpower friendship," she notes, "but this one did. Where money's involved, people change."[51]

distribution A basic dimension of conflict situations, referring to the extent to which individuals show concern for their own outcomes.

integration A basic dimension of conflict situations, referring to the extent to which individuals show concern for others' outcomes.

This incident provides a textbook illustration of two basic dimensions that seem to play a role in many conflicts: **distribution**—concern with one's own outcomes, and **integration**—concern with the outcomes of others. Michelle-Élise was clearly concerned with integration—she wanted the company, and therefore both herself and her partners, to thrive. Her friends, however, had different ideas: All they wanted to do was "take care of #1"—themselves. So they outvoted their more conservative partner and stripped the company of all its assets for their own gain.

A large body of research evidence indicates that these two dimensions are important and that, moreover, they are largely independent. Thus, in a given situation, it is possible to pursue actions that are high in both distribution and integration, low in both, or high in one and low in the other.[52] In fact, various combinations of these motives underlie five distinct styles of handling conflict with others when it occurs: *competing, collaborating, avoiding, accommodating,* and *compromising.*[53] The relative positions of each of these styles or approaches in terms of the key dimensions of distribution and integration are shown in Figure 11-8. As you can see, *competition* is high on distribution but low on integration; *compromise* is in the middle on both dimensions; and *avoidance* is low on both. *Accommodation*—giving others what they want—is high on integration but low on distribution. Finally, *collaboration* is high on both dimensions.

FIGURE 11-8 Basic Styles of Resolving Conflict

Different approaches to resolving conflict reflect two underlying dimensions present in most conflict situations: concern with one's own outcomes (*distribution*) and concern with others' outcomes (*integration*). The five major styles of resolving conflict reflect various positions with respect to these two dimensions.

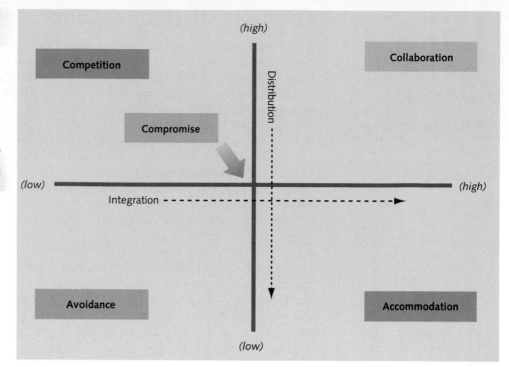

In view of our earlier discussion of individual differences with respect to preferences for cooperation and competition, you will not find it surprising to learn that individuals differ greatly in their tendencies to prefer these various conflict-handling styles.[54] What you may find more unexpected, however, is the fact that cultures differ in this respect, too. In many Western cultures, which, as we saw earlier, are *individualistic* in orientation, there is a strong preference for competition (sometimes known as *dominating*). In contrast, in many African and Asian cultures, which are *collectivistic* in orientation, preferences for accommodating and avoiding are relatively strong.[55] Such differences are worth noting, because they have important implications for conflict management—a topic we'll consider in detail later in this chapter.

Major Causes of Conflict

As we noted before, conflict involves the presence or perceptions of opposing interests. Yet, this condition, by itself, is neither necessary nor sufficient for the occurrence of actual conflict. Open confrontations sometimes fail to develop despite the existence of incompatible interests. Conflict sometimes emerges even when opposing interests are not present. Clearly, then, many factors and conditions contribute to the occurrence of conflict. These can be divided in two major groups: factors relating to organizational structure or functioning, and factors relating to interpersonal relations.

Organizational causes of conflict. Perhaps the most obvious organization-based cause of conflict is *competition over scarce resources*. No organization has unlimited resources, and conflicts often arise over the division or distribution of space, money, equipment, or personnel. Each side tends to overestimate its contribution to the organization and therefore its fair share of available resources. The result can be intense, prolonged conflict.

Two additional, and closely related, causes of conflict are *ambiguity over responsibility* and *ambiguity over jurisdiction*. Groups of individuals within an organization are sometimes uncertain as to who is responsible for performing various tasks or duties. When this occurs, each involved party disclaims responsibility, and conflict can develop over this issue. Similarly, uncertainty frequently exists over who has jurisdiction or authority. Figure 11-9 provides a summary of these and other organization-based causes of conflict.

☛ *As we saw in Chapter 7, uncertainty is also a major cause of stress; in fact, high levels of stress often seem to intensify ongoing conflicts or contribute to the initiation of new ones.*

FIGURE 11-9 Organizational
Causes of Conflict

As shown here, several organization-based factors contribute to
conflict in work settings.

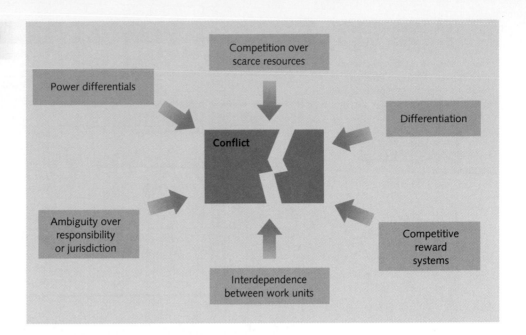

Power differentials

Competition over
scarce resources

Differentiation

Conflict

Ambiguity over
responsibility
or jurisdiction

Interdependence
between work units

Competitive
reward
systems

Interpersonal causes of organizational conflict. Take a look at the cartoon in Figure 11-10. Do you think the person who is saying "It's always nice besting you again" is setting the stage for future conflict with the other character? It seems likely that he is, because no one likes to "lose face," and seeing one's opponent gloat after a victory is one sure way to set strong desire for revenge in operation.[56] This cartoon suggests that conflict often stems from *interpersonal factors*—aspects of relations between individuals, as well as from organizational structure or underlying conflicts of interest, and this conclusion is supported by a growing body of research findings. What are these interpersonal factors? Here is an overview of several of the most important.

The cartoon in Figure 11-10 calls attention to the potential conflict-enhancing effects of *grudges*. People who have lost face while dealing with others often spend a lot of time and energy planning revenge against them. In fact, such grudges can persist for years, with obvious negative effects for organizations or work groups.[57]

Second, conflict often stems from (or is intensified by) *faulty attributions*—errors in judging the causes of others' behaviour. When individuals find that their interests have been thwarted by another person, they generally try to determine why this person acted the way he or she did. Was it malevolence, a desire to harm them? Or did the provoker's actions stem from factors beyond his or her control? A growing body of evidence suggests that when people reach the former conclusion, anger and subsequent conflict are more likely and more intense than when they reach the latter conclusion.[58]

A third interpersonal factor of considerable importance in generating organizational conflict might be termed *faulty communication*. This refers to the fact that individuals often communicate with others in a way that angers or annoys them, even though it is not their intention to do so. In other cases, conflict involves *inappropriate criticism*—negative feedback delivered in a manner that angers the recipient rather than helping this person to do a better job. What makes criticism *constructive* rather than *destructive*? Research findings point to the factors shown in Table 11-2.[59,60]

"Drop back soon, Benzinger. It's always nice besting you again."

FIGURE 11-10 Interpersonal Factors Often Play an Important Role in Conflict

Do you think that the person shown gloating here is setting himself up for further conflict with his defeated opponent?

(Source: Drawing by Lorenz; © 1980 The New Yorker Magazine, Inc.)

TABLE 11-2 Constructive
versus Destructive Criticism

The factors listed here distinguish constructive criticism (negative feedback that may be accepted by the recipient and improve her or his performance) from destructive criticism (negative feedback likely to be rejected by the recipient and unlikely to improve his or her performance).

Constructive Criticism	Destructive Criticism
Considerate—protects self-esteem of recipient	Inconsiderate—harsh, sarcastic, biting
Does not contain threats	Contains threats
Timely—occurs as soon as possible after the substandard performance	Not timely—occurs after an inappropriate delay
Does not attribute poor performance to internal causes	Attributes poor performance to internal causes (e.g., lack of effort, motivation, ability)
Specific—focuses on aspects of performance that were inadequate	General—a sweeping condemnation of performance
Focuses on performance, not on the recipient	Focuses on the recipient—his or her personal characteristics
Motivated by desire to help the recipient improve	Motivated by anger, desire to assert dominance over recipient, desire for revenge
Offers concrete suggestions for improvement	Offers no concrete suggestions for improvement

A fourth interpersonal source of conflict is *distrust*.[61] The more strongly people suspect that someone or some group is out to get them, the more likely they are to have a relationship with that person or group that is riddled with conflict. In general, companies that are considered great places in which to work are characterized by high levels of trust between people at all levels; and as we saw earlier in this chapter, trust is conducive to both cooperation and citizenship behaviour.[62]

Finally, several *personal characteristics*, too, seem to play a role in organizational conflict (see Chapter 4). For example, *Type A* individuals report becoming involved in conflict with others more often than *Type B* persons (see our discussion of this characteristic in Chapter 4). Conversely, people who are high in *self-monitoring*—those who are highly aware of how others are reacting to them—report resolving conflict in relatively productive ways (e.g., through collaboration or compromise) to a greater extent than persons who are low in self-monitoring.[63]

In sum considerable evidence suggests that conflict in work settings often stems from relations between individuals and from their personal traits as well as from underlying structural (organization-based) factors.

The Effects of Conflict: Definitely a Mixed Bag

In everyday speech, the term *conflict* has strong negative connotations. It seems to imply anger, direct confrontations, and harsh, damaging behaviour. In fact, however, conflict in work settings operates like the proverbial "double-edged sword." Depending on why it occurs and how it develops, conflict can yield beneficial as well as harmful effects.

The negative effects of conflict.   Some of the negative effects produced by conflict are too obvious to require much comment. For example, it often yields strong negative emotions and this can be quite stressful. Conflict frequently interferes with communication between individuals, groups, or divisions. In this way, it can all but eliminate coordination between them. Third, it diverts attention and needed energies away from major tasks and efforts to attain key organizational goals. In all these ways, conflict can seriously interfere with organizational effectiveness.

Other effects of conflict are more subtle and are, therefore, sometimes overlooked. First, it has been found that conflict between groups often encourages their leaders to shift from participative to authoritarian styles.[64] The reason for this is that groups experiencing stress require firm direction. Recognizing this fact, their leaders adopt more controlling tactics when conflict develops. As a result of such changes, the group experiencing conflict tends to provide less pleasant work environments than ones not faced with this type of stress.

Second, conflict increases the tendency of both sides to engage in negative stereo-typing. As we noted earlier, the members of opposing groups or units tend to emphasize the differences between them. These differences are interpreted in a negative light, so that each side views the other in increasingly unfavourable terms.

Finally, conflict leads those on each side to close ranks and emphasize loyalty to their own department or group. Anyone who suggests, even tentatively, that the other side's position has some merit is viewed as a traitor and is strongly censured. As a result, it becomes increasingly difficult for opponents to take each other's perspectives—a development that sharply reduces the likelihood of an effective resolution of their differences, and increases the likelihood of *groupthink* (see Chapter 10).

The positive effects of conflict. The picture is not entirely bleak, however. Although conflict often has a disruptive impact on organizations, it can sometimes yield benefits as well. The most important of these are:

As we will see in Chapter 16, change is frequently required for organizational survival.

- Conflict serves to bring problems that have previously been ignored out into the open.

- Conflict motivates people on both sides of an issue to know and understand each others' positions more fully.[65]

- Conflict often encourages the consideration of new ideas and approaches, facilitating innovation and change.[66]

- Conflict can lead to better decisions: When decision makers receive information incompatible with their views—which is often the case when conflict exists—they tend to make better decisions than when controversy does not exist.[67] This only occurs, of course, when the conflict forces people to challenge their assumptions, confront new ideas, and consider new positions. If, however, people resent having to engage in such activities, results may be far more disruptive.[68]

- Conflict enhances group loyalty, increasing motivation and performance within the groups or units involved.

- Conflict, especially *cognitive conflict*, in which opposing views are brought out into the open and fully discussed, can enhance organizational commitment.[69,70]

In sum, conflict can actually contribute to organizational effectiveness. Note, however, that benefits occur only when conflict is carefully managed and does not get out of control. If conflict is permitted to become extreme, rationality—and the potential benefits described above—may vanish in a haze of intense negative emotions.

Conflict Management: Increasing the Benefits and Minimizing the Costs

If conflict can yield benefits as well as costs, the key task organizations face with respect to this process is *managing* its occurrence. In short, the overall goal should not be the elimination of conflict, but rather that of maximizing its potential benefits, while minimizing its potential costs. A number of techniques for reaching this goal exist, and in this section, we will examine several of the most useful.

Bargaining: The Universal Process

bargaining (or **negotiation**) A process in which two or more parties in a dispute exchange offers, counteroffers, and concessions in an effort to attain a mutually acceptable agreement.

By far the most common strategy for resolving organizational conflicts, and therefore for managing them effectively, is **bargaining** (or **negotiation**).[71] In this process, opposing sides exchange offers, counteroffers, and concessions, either directly or through representatives. If the process is successful, a solution acceptable to both parties is attained and the conflict is resolved, perhaps with some "extras," such as enhanced understanding and improved relations between the two sides thrown in as well. If, instead, bargaining is unsuccessful, costly deadlock may result and the conflict may intensify. What factors determine which of these outcomes occurs? Given the importance of bargaining and its occurrence in virtually all spheres of life, this question has been the subject of intensive study for decades.[72] Here, briefly, are some of the key findings of this research.

Specific tactics. One group of factors that strongly affects the outcomes of negotiations involves the specific tactics adopted by bargainers. Many of these are designed to reduce opponents' aspirations—to convince them that they have little chance of reaching their goals and should, instead, accept offers that are actually quite favourable to the sides proposing them. Many strategies can be used for this purpose. For example, one side can suggest that it has other potential partners and will withdraw from the current negotiations if its proposals are not accepted.

Similarly, one party to a dispute can claim that its break-even point is much lower than it really is—a procedure known as the "big lie" technique.[73] If the other side accepts this information, it may make sizable concessions. Third, the course of negotiations and final settlements are often strongly affected by the nature of initial offers. Relatively extreme offers seem to put strong pressure on opponents to make concessions, resulting in settlements favourable to the side adopting such positions.[74] On the other hand, if initial offers are too extreme, opponents may be angered and decide to seek other negotiating partners.

Framing: Cognitive lenses for viewing conflict. A second group of factors that strongly determines the nature and outcomes of bargaining involves what has been termed **framing**—the cognitive set or focus adopted by bargainers.[75] In other words, framing refers to the ways in which bargainers perceive or define the situation. What are such frames like? One important study of this topic indicated that cognitive frames for perceiving conflict situations may vary along three key dimensions.[76] One, the *relationship/task* dimension, refers to whether bargainers are focused on their relationship with opponents or on the task—the material aspects of the dispute (money, property, etc.).

The second dimension, *emotional/intellectual*, reflects the degree to which bargainers direct their attention to affective or emotional components of the dispute (jealousy, hatred, frustration, anger), or to the actions and behaviours that occur quite apart from these emotions. Finally, the third, *cooperate/win*, refers to the extent to which disputants focus on maximizing the benefits to both parties, or, alternatively, on winning—defeating their opponent and maximizing their own gain, even at this person's expense. These three dimensions, which are largely independent, are summarized in Figure 11-11.

A growing body of evidence indicates that framing exerts powerful effects on bargaining.[77,78] Specifically, disputants who adopt task or cooperation-focused frames attain higher personal and joint outcomes in the negotiation than those who adopt a win-focused frame. Similarly, those with intellectual and relationship-focused frames are often more satisfied with the negotiation than those with task or emotion-focused frames.

Perceptions of the situation. A third aspect of negotiations that plays an important role in this process is the perceptions of the persons involved.[79] Studies by Thompson and her colleagues reveal that negotiators often enter bargaining situations with important misperceptions. In particular, they seem to begin with the view that their own interests and those of the other side are entirely incompatible—the **incompatibility error**. This, of course, causes them to overlook interests that are actually compatible. In addition, they tend to begin with the view, often false, that the other party places the same importance or priority that they do on each issue, a tendency known as the **fixed-sum error**. Both of these assumptions are false and often prevent bargainers from obtaining an agreement that is maximally beneficial to both sides.

framing In the context of bargaining, refers to the cognitive set or focus adopted by bargainers.

incompatibility error The perception on the part of bargainers that their own interests and those of the other side are completely incompatible.

fixed-sum error The perception on the part of bargainers that the other party places the same importance or priority as they do on each issue.

FIGURE 11-11 Cognitive
Frames in Bargaining

Bargainers often frame the situation in which they are involved
along the three dimensions shown
here: relationship/task, emotional/
intellectual, cooperative/win. Such
framing exerts strong effects on
their behaviour during negotiations.

*(Source: Based on suggestions by Pinkley,
1990; see Note 76.)*

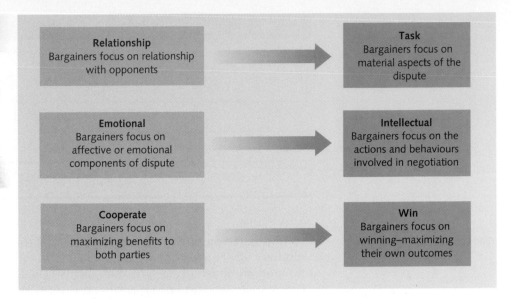

Fortunately, these misperceptions concerning interests and priorities often change
during the course of negotiations, fading over time, often within the first few minutes of negotiations.[80] However, many negotiators retain these false perceptions even
over prolonged periods of bargaining, with the result that both parties experience
lower payoffs than would otherwise be true. As might be expected, the smaller such
errors in perception (i.e., the more accurate the bargainers' perceptions of each others' outcomes are), the higher the joint payoffs obtained by both sides.[81] Clearly,
then, steps designed to improve the accuracy of negotiators' perceptions of the situations they face and each others' interests and priorities can go a long way toward
enhancing the outcomes of this process.

Win-win versus win-lose orientations. Perhaps the single most important factor
determining the success of negotiations in producing settlements satisfactory to both
sides, however, involves participants' overall orientation toward this process. Three
decades ago, Walton and McKersie pointed out that people taking part in negotiations can approach such discussions from either of two distinct perspectives.[82] On
the one hand, they can view negotiations as "win-lose" situations in which gains
by one side are necessarily linked with losses for the other. On the other hand, people can approach negotiations as potential "win-win" situations—ones in which the
interests of the two sides are not necessarily incompatible and in which the potential gains of both can be maximized.[83]

Not all situations offer the potential for such agreements, but many that at
first glance seem to involve simple head-on clashes between the two sides do, in
fact, provide such possibilities. If participants are willing to explore all options
carefully, and exert the effort required to identify creative potential solutions, they
can attain integrative agreements—ones that offer greater joint benefits than
simple compromise (splitting all differences down the middle.)

Table 11-3 summarizes some of the ways in which such *integrative agreements* can
be attained. Examine this table carefully because we are certain that you will find many
situations in your own career when the approaches it describes will come in handy.

Third-Party Intervention: Mediation and Arbitration

Despite the best efforts of both sides, negotiations sometimes deadlock. When they
do, the aid of a third party, someone not directly involved in the dispute, is often
sought. Such third-party intervention can take many forms, but the most common
are known as *mediation* and *arbitration*.[84]

TABLE 11-3 Techniques for Reaching Integrative Agreements

Several strategies can be useful in attaining integrative agreements in bargaining. A few of the major ones are summarized here.

Type of Agreement	Description
Broadening the pie	Available resources are broadened so that both sides can obtain their major goals.
Nonspecific compensation	One side gets what it wants; the other is compensated on an unrelated issue.
Logrolling	Each party makes concessions on low-priority issues in exchange for concessions on issues that it values more highly.
Cost cutting	One party gets what it desires, and the costs to the other party are reduced or eliminated.
Bridging	Neither party gets its initial demands, but a new option that satisfies the major interests of both sides is developed.

mediation A form of third-party intervention in disputes in which the intervenor does not have the authority to dictate an agreement.

In **mediation**, the third party attempts, through various tactics, to facilitate voluntary agreements between the disputants. Mediators have no formal power and cannot impose an agreement on the two sides. Instead, they seek to clarify the issues involved and enhance the communication between the opponents. Mediators sometimes offer specific recommendations for compromise or integrative solutions; in other cases, they merely guide disputants toward developing such solutions themselves. Their role is primarily that of *facilitator*—helping the two sides toward agreements they both find acceptable.[85]

arbitration A form of third-party intervention in disputes in which the intervening person has the power to determine the terms of an agreement.

In contrast, third parties are more powerful during **arbitration**. Specifically, arbitrators do have the power to impose (or at least strongly recommend) the terms of an agreement. In *binding arbitration*, the two sides agree in advance to accept these terms. In *voluntary arbitration*, though, the two sides retain the freedom to reject the recommended agreement (although the personal stature and expertise of the arbitrator may make it difficult for them to do so). In *conventional arbitration*, the arbitrator can offer any package of terms he or she wishes. However, in *final-offer arbitration*, the arbitrator merely chooses between final offers made by the disputants.

Both mediation and arbitration can be helpful in resolving organizational conflicts. However, both suffer from certain drawbacks. Because it requires voluntary compliance by the disputing parties, mediation often proves ineffective. Indeed, it may simply serve to underscore the depth of the differences between the two sides. Arbitration also suffers from several potential problems. First, it may exert a *chilling effect* on negotiations, bringing voluntary progress to a halt. Since both sides know the arbitrator will resolve the dispute for them, they see little point in engaging in serious bargaining, which, after all, is hard work. Second, one or both sides may come to suspect that the arbitrator is biased. The result: Disputants become increasingly reluctant to agree to arbitration. Third, arbitration tends to cost more and take longer than mediation.[86] Finally, there is some indication that commitment to arbitrated settlements is weaker than that to directly negotiated ones.

The Induction of Superordinate Goals

At several points in this chapter, we have noted that individuals often divide the world into two opposing camps: "us" and "them." They perceive members of their own group as quite different from, and usually better than, people belonging to other groups. These dual tendencies to magnify the differences between one's own group and others and to disparage outsiders are very powerful and are as common in organizations as in other settings.[87] Further, they seem to play a central role in many conflicts between various departments, divisions, and work groups. How can they be countered? One answer, suggested by research findings, is through the induction of **superordinate goals**—ones that tie the interests of the two sides together.[88] The basic idea behind this approach is simple: By inducing conflicting parties to focus on and work toward common objectives, the barriers between them—ones that interfere with communication, coordination, and agreement—can be weakened. When this occurs, the chances for cooperation rather than conflict are enhanced. To see how organizations are using both bargaining and superordinate goals to improve their bottom line, see THE QUEST FOR QUALITY section.

superordinate goals Goals shared by the parties in a conflict or dispute.

When Suppliers Become Partners—Not Adversaries

In order to improve the "bottom line," many organizations have adopted stringent cost-cutting measures. They have downsized, replaced full-time employees with contract labour, invested heavily in new, efficient equipment, and even cut travel and other executive perks. The gains from such steps have been significant, but as many organizations have learned, they do have limits.

Another approach to improving the bottom line would be to hammer away at suppliers, beating them down on price as much as possible. But this can backfire. Suppliers can be pushed only so far; and when large companies reduce the profit margins of their suppliers, they reduce the ability of these companies to invest in equipment that would make them more efficient—and so enable them to reduce prices still more.

As we noted in Chapter 3, growing realization of this fact has led some companies to seek a partnership with their suppliers.[89] Rather than treating them as adversaries across the bargaining table, they view them as partners whose outcomes are intimately linked to their own. Thus, not only do they offer them training and assistance, they adopt a win-win approach in which superordinate goals shared by both organizations—greater efficiency and reduced prices— are established. For example, consider the case of Allied Signal, a manufacturer of auto parts and aerospace electronics. To reduce the costs of the components it uses in its operations, it has worked out win-win arrangements with many of its suppliers. For example, in 1993, Allied Signal offered to double its orders from Mech-Tronics, but only if Mech-Tronics would cut its prices 10 percent. These terms initially eliminated Mech-Tronics' profits, but with help from Allied Signal in improving its efficiency, the higher volume soon paid off. The result? Both companies gained.

Here are a few other steps companies are taking in their efforts to reduce the costs of materials and supplies:

1. *Leveraging their buying power:* Companies are centralizing purchasing so that all operations place their orders at once. Larger orders often qualify for lower prices, so the savings can be large.
2. *Committing to a handful of suppliers:* Instead of seeking competitive bids from dozens of suppliers, large companies are working with a few tried-and-trusted suppliers. This helps the suppliers improve their efficiency and, ultimately, to offer lower prices.
3. *Developing internal sources of goods and services:* Some companies—especially very large ones—find that they can supply some of their own needs.

In short, many companies are finding that purchasing—long ignored as being a dull, necessary evil—can be a major contributor to the quest for quality. Yes, it's mundane, but as it is used more effectively, it is beginning to change the way many organizations do business.

Workplace Violence and Workplace Aggression

The people of Yellowknife still grieve, especially the mothers, the wives, the children of the men who were so brutally murdered in the 1992 blast at the Giant Mine's B-Shaft.[90] Roger Warren was on midnight picket duty that September night, walking a line he and his brothers in the Canadian Association of Smelter and Allied Workers (CASAW) had walked for four months.[91] According to reports, he left his post, climbed into the empty mine shaft, and travelled down 230 metres to rig a bomb that was set to detonate when the next mine car ran over it. He claimed that his intention was to blow up an ore car. Instead, he killed nine men.[92] All had been brought in as replacement workers to keep the mine open during the long and bitter strike.[93]

workplace violence Direct physical assaults by present or former employees against other persons in their organizations.

Canadian newspapers and magazines have been filled in recent years with accounts of such **workplace violence**—direct physical assaults by present or former employees against other persons in their organizations. Disturbing statistics seem to suggest that media attention to such events is fully justified. A study conducted by the United Nations Criminal Research Unit found that "Canada ranked fourth out of 32 countries for the number of women who were assaulted in the workplace. Number one was Argentina, followed by France. England and Wales came in third." Canada is faring no better for violence against men. The study placed Canada at number five in this area with France ranked as having the most men reporting assaults, Romania second, Argentina third, and Switzerland fourth. However, the news may not be all bad. Vittorio Di Martina, co-author of the International Victimization Survey, suggested that Canada's high rate of reported violence may reflect that "... the awareness of violence is more in Canada." The study also showed that U.S. workers are statistically more likely than Canadians to be murdered in the workplace, while Canadians are more apt to experience sexual harassment and assault at work than their U.S. counterparts. The Canadian Union of Public Employees (CUPE) has established guidelines for employers to assist in efforts to reduce violence.[94]

Some professions experience a higher rate of violence than others. In law enforcement, "...since 1961 an average of three Canadian police officers have been killed annually."[95] Lawyers are also open to workplace attacks. Toronto lawyer John Rosen cites the particular vulnerability of lawyers working in civil and family law: "Part of it is frustration with the system. Clients take it out on lawyers, the most visible part of the system. They are in the front line."[96] Health workers are also becoming increasingly concerned about workplace violence. The Alberta College of Physicians and Surgeons issued this warning to its membership to be aware of increasing violence in health-care settings: "Recent incidents of violence in Canada and the U.S. toward health-care workers have made professionals, their staff and family members understandably nervous."[97]

While Workers' Compensation Boards across Canada use different methods to track violence, there is an indication that rates have been increasing in some areas. For example, between 1986 and 1996 the number of WCB claims in British Columbia increased from 699 to 1257. In Alberta there were 253 injuries due to violence in 1992, and 286 in 1996. However, not all jurisdictions reported increases. Nova Scotia had 584 violence claims in 1992 and 227 in 1996.

Clearly, workplace violence represents an end point on the continuum of working with or against others we have addressed in this chapter. In this section, we will examine the nature of workplace violence and its relation to other forms of antisocial behaviour at work. Then we'll turn to the causes of such behaviour. Finally, we'll examine several techniques for reducing its occurrence.

Workplace Violence: The Tip of the Iceberg?

Instances of workplace violence are dramatic, to say the least. And given the numbers listed above, many persons have concluded that work settings are dangerous places indeed. Moreover, growing evidence suggests that workplace violence is really only the dramatic and unsettling tip of a broader problem: **workplace aggression**—efforts by individuals to harm others with whom they work, or have worked, or the organizations in which they are presently, or were previously, employed.

Workplace aggression, like aggression in any context, can take many different forms. It can be verbal as well as physical—for example, spreading false, damaging rumours about another person. It can be *passive* as well as active—failing to return phone calls, withholding action on some issue of importance to the target person. It can be *indirect* as well as direct—damaging property belonging to the target person, or failing to speak in defence of the target person when this is necessary. In fact, considerable evidence suggests that in many situations, persons seeking to harm others with whom they work prefer to do this in relatively *covert* ways—they prefer actions that make it difficult for the intended target to identify them as the source of such harm, or even to know whether they are the victim of intentional harm-doing or merely negative circumstances.[98]

Consistent with this pattern, a recent study by Neuman and Baron found that verbal and passive forms of workplace aggression were more frequent in many organizations than physical and active.[99] This in no way implies that instances of workplace violence are unimportant; on the contrary, they are often devastating in their effects. However, it appears that they are relatively rare occurrences in work settings and that other, less dramatic forms of aggression are more prevalent. Since these

Canadian Union of Public Employees
www.solinet.org/cupe.html

College of Physicians and Surgeons of Alberta
www.cpsa.ab.ca

workplace aggression Efforts by individuals to harm other members of their organization, persons with whom they previously worked, or their organization itself.

forms may also cause considerable harm to the intended victims, however, they pose a serious problem for organizations and their employees alike.

The Causes of Workplace Aggression

What are the causes of workplace aggression? In one sense, the same as the causes of aggression in any other context. Modern theories of human aggression suggest that behaviour directed toward the goal of harming others stems from many factors.[100] Most of these, however, fall into four major categories.

First, aggression sometimes stems from the characteristics of individuals. Some people have "shorter fuses," unstable personalities, and specific traits that predispose them toward aggression in any context, including organizations. Such factors include the *Type A behaviour pattern*, which we discussed in Chapter 4, and a trait known as the **hostile attributional bias**.[101] Persons high on this latter characteristic tend to perceive others' actions as stemming from hostile intentions, even when this is not the case. In other words, such persons are very low on trust; and while high levels of trust lead to citizenship and cooperation, low levels seem to promote hostility and aggression.

Second, aggression, like conflict, often stems from interpersonal sources. People who work together do often "rub each other the wrong way"—they annoy, frustrate, and anger each other. Moreover, they often perceive others as having treated them unfairly in some manner. When they do, anger and the desire for revenge may come into play, with the result that workplace aggression, too, increases. This pattern is clearly evident with respect to employee thefts and vandalism. In the past, it was assumed that thefts, at least, stemmed primarily from economic motives—the gains that would result from stealing valuable items. Recent findings, however, indicate that employees often steal from their companies as a way of "evening the scales"—paying them back for perceived injustice.[102]

Third, aggression can stem from environmental conditions that, seemingly, have little or nothing to do with harming others. Unpleasant environmental conditions—uncomfortable temperatures, high levels of noise, polluted air, glaring lights—can induce negative feelings among the persons exposed to them. Such *negative affect*, in turn, has been found to increase aggression in many situations.[103]

Finally, and perhaps most important of all, growing evidence indicates that some of the changes that have occurred recently in many organizations—changes such as increased workforce diversity, downsizing, wage freezes, restructuring—may be contributing to increased aggression among employees.[104] How can such changes produce an increase in workplace aggression? Again, by inducing psychological states among employees that have been found to increase the likelihood of overt aggression. Downsizing and layoffs, for example, have been found to induce anger, anxiety, and frustration among both the persons who are fired and survivors—those who remain.[105]

Similarly, increased workforce diversity sometimes leads to increased interpersonal friction between persons from different cultural backgrounds who, quite literally, don't speak each other's language.[106] We could continue, but the main point should be clear: The wrenching changes that have occurred recently in many organizations may be yet another factor contributing to what appears to be a rising spiral of workplace aggression.

The Prevention and Control of Workplace Aggression

Can anything be done to reduce the incidence of workplace aggression? In other words, can this process be managed effectively? Research on this issue is just beginning, but some steps and techniques do seem useful in this regard. First, efforts can be made to *screen* prospective employees. Those with a history of aggressive behaviour, or those who evidence high levels of traits associated with aggression, may be more prone than other persons to become involved in workplace aggression. Thus, efforts should be made to avoid hiring them whenever possible. As noted recently by Folger and Skarlicki, some persons are more likely to "explode" aggressively

hostile attributional bias A tendency to perceive others' actions as stemming from malevolent intentions, even when this is not the case

☞ We noted in Chapter 7 that unpleasant physical (environmental) conditions are an important cause of work-related stress.

than others when faced with difficult, unpleasant conditions.[107] Thus, developing techniques for accurately identifying such persons has the potential to yield handsome dividends with respect to reducing workplace aggression.

A second approach to reducing workplace aggression involves the establishment of clear disciplinary procedures for such behaviour. Aggression cannot thrive in an environment where it is made clear that such behaviour is viewed as inappropriate and that instances of workplace aggression will be met with swift and certain punishment. Programs of *progressive punishment* have been found to be effective in deterring other forms of behaviour considered inappropriate in work settings, and there is every reason to assume that such procedures can be effective—if used with care—in deterring at least some forms of workplace aggression.[108]

Third, since workplace aggression often stems from anger and feelings of having been treated unfairly, such behaviour may be reduced by assuring high levels of *organizational justice*. In particular, two aspects of such justice—interpersonal justice and informational justice—are especially important.[109] Interpersonal justice refers to demonstrating sensitivity for others, especially in the context of the distribution of outcomes they receive. In contrast, informational justice refers to providing individuals with adequate explanations of, and reasons for, the procedures used to determine those outcomes. To the extent these types of justice are present in a work setting, instances of workplace aggression may be held to a minimum.

Finally, training of employees, too, may be helpful. Although instances of physical violence are relatively rare, they do occur. Thus, employees should be trained in techniques for responding to threats posed by present and previous employees as well as customers. Efforts to develop systematic programs for equipping managers with the skills needed to recognize potentially dangerous situations and, perhaps, to defuse them, are currently underway.[110]

Through these and other steps, the incidence of workplace aggression may be reduced. It is our view that workplace aggression poses a threat not only to the safety and well-being of individual employees, but also to the effectiveness of their organizations as well. Quests for vengeance and personal vendettas tend to drain time and energy away from more productive activities. Thus, we believe that efforts to manage workplace aggression are worthwhile not simply from the standpoint of ethics, but from the perspective of enhanced organizational effectiveness as well.

☞ *The effects of punishment or discipline on employee behaviour were examined in detail in Chapter 3.*

SUMMARY AND REVIEW

Prosocial Behaviour: Helping Others At Work

People often engage in **prosocial behaviour** in work settings, performing actions that benefit others. One important form of prosocial behaviour is **organizational citizenship behaviour (OCB)**, which involves actions by organization members that exceed the formal requirements of their jobs. The incidence of OCB is increased by several factors, including employees' trust in their supervisors, their perceptions of the breadth of their jobs, and their perceptions concerning the fairness of any punishments they have received. **Whistle-blowing**—disclosure by employees of illegal, immoral, or illegitimate practices to others who can right the wrong—may be considered prosocial actions, but they often prove costly to both organizations and the individuals involved.

Cooperation: Mutual Assistance in Organizations

Cooperation involves mutual assistance or coordination between two or more persons or groups. Its occurrence in work settings is affected by factors relating to individuals (e.g., strong tendencies toward reciprocity, personality orientations concerning cooperation), and by several organizational factors (e.g., reward systems, interdependence among employees). **Competition,** a sharply contrasting pattern, develops when individuals, groups, or organizations seek to achieve gains at others' expense. Cooperation sometimes develops between organizations—a process known as **interorganizational coordination**. One important form of such coordination involves the formation of a **consortium**—a confederation in which organizations maintain their formal independence, but agree to coordinate their activities through a central management.

Conflict: Its Nature, Causes, and Effects

Conflict is a process that begins when one person or group perceives that another person or group has taken or is about to take some action inconsistent with the perceiver's major interests. Conflict situations involve two basic dimensions; **distribution**, concern with one's own outcomes, and **integration**, concern with others' outcomes. Contrasting styles or approaches to resolving conflict, such as *competing, collaborating, avoiding, accommodating,* and *compromising,* reflect specific points along these dimensions. Conflict in work settings often stems from organizational factors, such as competition over scarce resources and ambiguity over jurisdiction or responsibility. However, it also stems from interpersonal factors such as *attributional errors, faulty communication,* and personal characteristics such as the Type A behaviour pattern and the **hostile attributional bias**.

Conflict often exerts negative effects on organizations, interfering with communication and coordination. However, it sometimes produces positive results. These include bringing problems out into the open, increased consideration of new ideas, and enhanced organizational commitment.

Conflict Management

A key task with respect to conflict is managing its occurrence—maximizing its benefits while reducing its potential costs. **Bargaining** (or **negotiation**) is the most common procedure for resolving organizational conflicts. Many factors influence the course and outcomes of bargaining, including specific tactics used by participants, their cognitive **frames** with respect to the bargaining situation, their perceptions of each others' interests and priorities, and the overall approach to bargaining—"win-lose" or "win-win."

Third-party interventions such as **mediation** and **arbitration** can also prove helpful in resolving conflicts. Another approach involves the induction of **superordinate goals**—ones shared by both sides. This technique has recently been used by many manufacturing companies in dealings with their suppliers.

Workplace Violence and Workplace Aggression

Dramatic incidents of **workplace violence** have been much in the news recently. Efforts by individuals to harm others with whom they work—**workplace aggression**—can take many forms other than direct physical attacks. Such behaviour may be passive as well as active, and indirect as well as direct. Many factors influence the occurrence of workplace aggression, including personal characteristics, friction in interpersonal relations, and unpleasant physical conditions. In addition, changes that have occurred recently in many workplaces—downsizing, increased workforce diversity, increased use of part-time employees—may contribute to such behaviour.

Efforts to reduce workplace aggression include screening for "high-risk" employees, clear disapproval of such behaviour coupled with appropriate disciplinary procedures, assuring high levels of organizational justice, and training employees on how to deal with such behaviour.

CASE PREVIEW QUESTIONS FOR DISCUSSION

1. Do management and union relations have to be adversarial?
2. What has to change on both sides to achieve successful cooperation between management and unions?
3. What factors prompted the management and union leaders at Saskatoon Chemicals to move from confrontation to cooperation?

CHAPTER QUESTIONS FOR DISCUSSION

1. What kinds of organizational citizenship behaviours have you observed in your own work experience? Why, if individuals receive no direct benefit for engaging in such actions, do they ever perform them?
2. What factors in an organization might lead to high levels of trust between employees? Would it be worthwhile to assure that these factors are present?
3. What are the ethical issues one must consider when deciding whether or not to blow the whistle on an organization suspected of some wrongdoing?
4. What role do cultural factors play in cooperation? In other words, would you expect to observe different levels of cooperation in different cultures? Why?
5. Do you think that individuals differ with respect to their preferred modes of resolving conflicts (e.g., compromise, collaboration, competition)? Would these differences show up in all situations or only under certain circumstances?
6. "Conflict doesn't exist until it is recognized by the parties involved." Do you agree with this statement? Why or why not?
7. Growing evidence indicates that conflict can sometimes produce positive results. Have you ever experienced positive results from a conflict? If so, why do you think such effects occurred?
8. If people in your organization are frequently in conflict with each other, what techniques could you use to reduce the number or intensity of these conflicts?
9. Do you think that workplace violence and workplace aggression are increasing? If so, why? If not, why?

CASE IN POINT

Revenge by Terror: Valery Fabrikant's Rampage at Concordia University

How could it happen at a Canadian university? When 52-year-old associate research professor Valery Fabrikant killed four Concordia University engineering professors and wounded a departmental secretary in August 1992, it was not as unexpected as the shocked Canadian public may have believed.

Fabrikant was hired by Concordia in 1979 as a research assistant. He claimed to be a dissident who had left his native Soviet Union for Israel to escape religious persecution.[111] Fabrikant's conflicts with Concordia crystallized in the fall of 1991. His department recommended against the renewal of his two-year contract. Subsequently, a faculty committee disagreed with that recommendation and, instead, offered him a one-year contract.[112]

Rose Sheinin, Concordia's vice-rector (academic), had had serious misgivings about Fabrikant for some time. Fabrikant had a history of flooding the university's e-mail system with allegations against university personnel at all levels. Sheinin even went so far as to consult with a psychiatrist to get an opinion on how dangerous Fabrikant could be, but was reassured that he would seek attention in any way he could, but that he would not be likely to kill anyone. Nevertheless, the feelings of threat that Fabrikant sparked in his colleagues were deep and widespread.[113]

"He charged that his colleagues enriched themselves on the work of their students and forced professors like him to publish their research under the names of the more established professors."[114] Despite the feelings of threat felt by Concordia University faculty and staff, to the point that some put locks on their doors, Fabrikant could not be fired because no one ever issued a formal complaint against him. "People found his conduct harassing, sometimes intimidating, certainly annoying . . . . But there never were threats that were the object of formal complaints," reported Patrick Kenniff, Concordia's rector.[115] Four deaths, one wounding, ten lawyers, and a turbulent trial later (during which Fabrikant represented himself), Fabrikant was convicted of four counts of first-degree murder and sentenced to life in prison with no possibility of parole for 25 years.[116]

Inquiries conducted at Concordia in the wake of the tragedy found that the three Concordia professors Fabrikant had particularly cited in his allegations were found to have engaged in inappropriate behaviour and misuse of power. After a subsequent audit found that they misused research money, the three key professors discussed in the report agreed to leave Concordia. The university's rector was fired in May 1994. The investigation found that he was ill-informed and too detached from the everyday operations of the university. The vice-rector's term was not renewed after the report accused her of failing to ensure that the allegations made by Fabrikant were inadequately investigated.[117]

Valery Fabrikant is now serving his sentence at Donnacona Prison. In 1995 he launched a suit (which was subsequently dismissed) against Concordia University for $900 000 and legal costs. "In his application, the professor claimed the university was responsible for his actions. He said his murderous rampage was an act of self-defence and that his victims were part of a university-wide plot to deny him tenure."[118]

Critical Thinking Questions

1. What could the university's administration have done to prevent the tragedy at Concordia?

2. What aspects of the university's culture contributed to the conflict within the engineering faculty?

3. If you were responsible for following up on the findings of the inquiries at Concordia, what steps would you take?

Concordia University
www.concordia.ca

SKILLS PORTFOLIO

Experiencing Organizational Behaviour

Personal Styles of Conflict Management

Conflict among people is a common and inescapable part of life. Given this fact, it is important for all of us to *manage* conflict effectively when it arises. How do *you* deal with such situations? What is your preferred mode of handling disagreements and conflicts with others? The following exercise is designed to give you some insights into this important issue.

Directions

First, recall three events in which you have experienced conflict with others. On a sheet of paper, describe each briefly, and then answer each of the five following questions with respect to each. (It may help to make three copies of the questionnaire.)

1. To what extent did you try to resolve this conflict through *avoidance*—sidestepping the issue, withdrawing from the situation?

Did not do this   Did do this
1   2   3   4   5   6   7

2. To what extent did you try to resolve this conflict through *accommodation*—giving in to the other person?

Did not do this   Did do this
1   2   3   4   5   6   7

3. To what extent did you try to resolve this conflict through *competition*—trying to win, standing up for your rights or views?

Did not do this   Did do this
1   2   3   4   5   6   7

4. To what extent did you try to resolve this conflict through *compromise*—finding the middle ground between your position and the other person's?

Did not do this   Did do this
1   2   3   4   5   6   7

5. To what extent did you try to resolve this conflict through *collaboration*—working with the other person to find some solution that would satisfy both of your basic needs or concerns?

Did not do this   Did do this
1   2   3   4   5   6   7

Questions for Discussion

1. Do you notice any consistencies in your responses? Did you prefer one basic mode of resolving conflict over the others?
2. If you did, what effects do you think this will have on your success in handling a wide range of conflicts?
3. Do you think that you would prefer different modes of handling conflicts in different situations—for example, depending on the person with whom you are having the conflict?
4. Do you think you could alter your preferred mode or modes for handling conflicts? If so, how?

Working in Groups The Good Mood–Helping Effect: One Reason Why "Wining and Dining" Others Often Works

What do you do when you want a favour from another person? One strategy is just to come out and ask for what you want. But most people know that asking for help "cold" is not always the best approach. Sometimes, it is useful either to wait until others are in a good mood, or, if you don't care to bide your time, to take steps to put them into such a mood. This can be accomplished in several different ways—through praise, through giving them a small gift, through exposing them to something amusing or funny. As long as their mood is improved, the chances that they will say "yes" are increased. This exercise demonstrates the power of such effects.

Directions

The class is divided into two parts. One half, who will serve as JOB APPLICANTS, reads the following information:

Your task is to play the role of a job candidate during a brief job interview. The job is a general entry-level management position, and you are to do everything you can to come across well and increase the chances that you'll be selected.

The other half, who will play the role of INTERVIEWERS, is divided into two parts. One receives the following information:

Your task is to play the role of an interviewer during a brief job interview. You will ask questions of the candidate (see a list of questions below). Supposedly, you will then evaluate this person's performance. HOWEVER, YOU WILL ACTUALLY PROVIDE A VERY FAVOURABLE EVALUATION NO MATTER WHAT THE OTHER PERSON SAYS OR DOES (see form below). Then, after the demonstration is over, you will ask this person, in a matter-of-fact manner, for a small favour—the loan of their notes from today's class.

The other group receives the same instructions with this exception:

HOWEVER, YOU WILL ACTUALLY PROVIDE AN UNFAVOURABLE EVALUATION NO MATTER WHAT THE OTHER PERSON SAYS OR DOES . . .

Questions to be asked by Interviewers:
1. What is your major?
2. What is your grade point average?
3. What would you say is your best trait?
4. What would you say is your worst trait or failing?
5. How would you describe your work habits?
6. How well do you get along with other people?

Evaluation Form (to be given to job applicants after the interview):
1. Qualifications (check one):
   ____Very Poor   ____Poor   ____Average   ____Good   ____Excellent

2. Motivation (check one):
   ____Very Poor   ____Poor   ____Average   ____Good   ____Excellent

3. Interpersonal skills:
   ____Very Poor   ____Poor   ____Average   ____Good   ____Excellent

4. Probability of being a successful employee:
   ____Very Poor   ____Poor   ____Average   ____Good   ____Excellent

5. Overall rating:
   ____Very Poor   ____Poor   ____Average   ____Good   ____Excellent

Group One (Favourable Evaluation): Check items as follows: Good, Excellent, Excellent, Excellent, Excellent

Group Two (Unfavourable Evaluation): Check items as follows: Poor, Poor, Average, Poor, Average

After students in both groups make their request, a tabulation is made of how many job applicants agreed to the request in each condition (Favourable Evaluation, Unfavourable Evaluation).

Questions for Discussion
1. Did the favourable evaluation improve the mood of persons who received it?
2. Did the unfavourable evaluation decrease the mood of persons who received it?
3. What other techniques could be used to put people in a good mood?
4. Have you ever used this technique yourself or had someone use it on you?

TAKE IT TO THE NET

Prentice Hall

We invite you to visit the *Greenberg/Baron/Sales/Owen Companion Website* at *www.prenticehall.ca/greenberg* for this chapter's Internet resources.

Only Team Players Need Apply at Digital Renaissance

"What makes an organization unique? What makes one organization innovative, dynamic, unrivalled while another is predictable, stagnant and boring?" teases Digital Renaissance in its promotional material. The answer, according to the Digital Renaissance's Services Group, is the people. "Not just the skills, but the experiences, the attitudes, the dedication, creativity, and pride they bring to their work."[1]

Kocho sees his Digital Renaissance colleagues as self-starters, "people who seek greater responsibility and challenge. [They] relish that [and] want to pursue their evolution personally. [They have a] thirst for knowledge."[2] The organization's team-centred design fulfills these needs and more. Rob Martell, director of product development at Digital Renaissance and a 13-year veteran of Northern Telecom, enthuses about the working environment at Digital Renaissance: "The communication is 10 times better here than anywhere else I've seen. And there's lots of empowerment, which breeds people who make decisions and do things. . . . It's a much more conducive environment to creative, intelligent thinking."[3]

Flexibility in team functioning, constant communication, and openness to new ideas are hallmarks of Digital Renaissance's dynamic work environment. For each individual project, the staff, using what they call their "matrix resource management system," assemble a multidisciplinary team of project managers, instructional designers, usability architects, technical architects, software engineers, and graphic designers. "These key members are peers—no one person is the boss. However, the team is jointly accountable to the company and the client for the project's success including balancing the budget, schedule [and] quality requirements." Other staff with different skill sets, such as new media designers, audio-visual experts, animators, writers, software engineers, etc. will be brought in as required. The exact makeup of the team will be dictated by the demands of the particular project.[4]

Key roles within the project teams are those performed by project managers, functional leads, technical leads, and creative leads. The ideal recruits for these positions have a university degree, a minimum of two years' experience working in a related industry, "strong organization and communication skills," "exceptional people skills," a desire to work "in a dynamic team environment (you'd have to see it to believe it)," "a creative and innovative mind," "ability to mentor and guide," and of course, exceptional technical skills.[5]

Individual staff members join specific project teams based on their domain expertise (ability in a specific technical area) and their interest in participating on the project team. A person who wishes to join a particular team expresses his or her interest to the "functional lead" who is in charge of the project team. The functional lead acts as a link between the person and the management group. Thus, the functional lead is in a position to negotiate the team membership with the Human Resources department, the support group that identifies the skills needed for the task and develops work schedules. Team members move onto and away from projects in a dynamic ebb and flow. Generally staff stay with a given project for at least a few months at a time before moving on.[6]

Kocho realizes that communication is the glue of a team-centred organization such as his. In describing his communication style, Kocho explains his penchant for using metaphors to set the context for issues under discussion. According to the ever-forthright Kocho, he is often criticized for overuse of metaphors. He describes his approach to problem solving as "thoughtful" rather than "guns a-blazing." He prefers to listen for "the real problem," take stock, assess each situation individually and not give quick answers. Keith Kocho does not see himself as the final arbiter in all decisions. He describes his approach to decision making as "consultative with a touch of expediency." He says that he does his best to explain the decisions he makes but, in the end, he is acutely aware that the decisions have to be made in a timely fashion.[7]

Open communication is the lifeblood of the company's goal-setting process, a collective process based on "open planning." Everyone at Digital Renaissance has abundant opportunity to contribute his or her ideas. The company's goals and plans develop from the two-way communication that takes place in all meetings, i.e., the monthly company meetings, the weekly "department" meetings, and the weekly management meetings. These company goals cascade to individual staff. One-on-one goal-setting sessions between employees and their managers facilitate the establishment of realistic individual objectives. Compensation systems and peer performance review systems are designed to allow individual staff members input into the setting and measurement of their personal as well as professional goals.[8]

Discussion Questions

1. How and why are teams used at Digital Renaissance?

2. Why would the Nexus Generation be interested in teamwork?

3. Describe Kocho's communication style and decision-making style. Discuss the fit between these styles and the needs of Digital Renaissance at this point in its history.

4. Describe the goal-setting process at Digital Renaissance. How does such a process motivate and enhance the performance of Digital Renaissance's employees?

5. Would you be an ideal candidate for one of Digital Renaissance's "Lead" positions (assuming that you had acceptable educational qualifications and job experience)? Please explain with reference to the skills/competencies expected by this company.

Spar Aerospace Ltd.: A Business or a Government-Sponsored Lab?

The Canadarm. The word conjures up visions of astronauts floating and working in space, pushing the limits of technology and stretching our imagination. Behind the romance and the pride we have felt about our Canadian contribution to the international space program is a company that is struggling to make a turnaround and is faced with making difficult business decisions.

Spar Aerospace Ltd. has produced Canadian dreams. The company traces its roots back to the Special Products and Applied Research division of deHavilland Canada. This division played a major role in the development of the infamous Avro Arrow, the state-of-the-art aircraft project that was cancelled by the government of then prime minister John Diefenbaker. The company is known around the world for the Canadarm and for the Anik E satellite. Spar's operations are located around the world.

However, despite its triumphs, Spar faces severe business challenges. In 1998 its stock was not performing well and management realized that it was time for a sea change. The company's president and CEO, Colin D. Watson, worked to focus the company "on fewer, large, core businesses" rather than continuing to operate a variety of different lines of business. "The result," he emphasized to shareholders, "will be a company that is more manageable and better able to grow profitably, while being easier for the investment community to analyze."

In 1998 the company sold off its communications division. "Once touted as the future of Spar, the unit has been a major disappointment since it was purchased in 1992 for $58.2 million in an effort at diversification." The decision was greeted with approval by analysts, one of whom felt that it ended "... a misbegotten diversification program and [brought] Spar back to where it was years ago."

In explaining the company's position to shareholders shortly before the sale of the communications division, Watson differentiated between the company's lower-risk ventures in aviation and robotics, and its higher-risk endeavours in space communications. He characterized the aviation and robotics divisions as stable moneymakers and the communications venture as more expensive with longer payback periods. Watson announced to shareholders that he and his management team were implementing an elaborate rebalancing plan to correct this situation. The plan included, among many other initiatives, the divestiture of high-risk divisions and the strengthening of Spar's already strong aviation operations.

Spar will be faced with difficult decisions as it implements its restructuring plans. Watson is not alone in the turnaround attempt. He will depend greatly on his management team. He emphasizes that the best strategy is worthless without the right people to implement it: "... what is real are the people who work the long, hard, smart hours in a business that they believe in."

Video Case Discussion Questions

1. **a)** What changes have taken place in the aerospace industry over the last decade?

   b) How have these changes impacted on decision making at companies such as Spar?

2. Was Colin Watson the right choice for CEO of Spar?

3. Critique Watson's decision to focus on "fewer, large, core businesses."

4. What is the significance of one analyst's question: Is Spar a business or a government-sponsored lab?

CBC Source: Spar Turnaround, *Venture* #647 (June 22, 1997).

Video Sources: Spar History, www.spar.ca/corp/history.htm; Spar Aerospace, www.monet.uwaterloo.ca/lite/Companies/SPAR.HTM; Watson, C. (1997, November 18). Thinking global, going global: Myths, realities and lessons from a global player, www.spar.ca/corp/newspch1.htm; Spar Locations, www.spar.ca/corp/location.htm; Watson, C. (1998, May 6). Remarks by Colin D. Watson, President and Chief Executive Officer Spar Aerospace Limited to the 1998 Annual General Meeting of Shareholders, www.spar.ca/corp/colin506.htm; Fitzpatrick, P. (1998, May 7). Spar waits for stock rebound. *Financial Post Daily*, 11, p. 11; Fitzpatrick, P. (1998, August 29/31). Spar unloads troubled ComStream. *Financial Post*, p. 7.

CHAPTER 12
Influence, Power, and Politics in Organizations

LEARNING OBJECTIVES

After reading this chapter you should be able to:

1. Distinguish among *social influence, power,* and *politics* in organizations.

2. Characterize the major varieties of social influence that exist.

3. Describe the conditions under which social influence is used.

4. Identify the major types of individual power in organizations and the conditions under which each is used.

5. Explain the two major approaches to the development of subunit power in organizations (the *resource-dependency model* and the *strategic contingencies model*).

6. Describe when and where *organizational politics* is likely to occur and the forms it is likely to take.

7. Explain the major ethical issues surrounding the use of political behaviour in organizations.

Petro-Canada: Bill Hopper's Power Play in the Oil Patch

For Petro-Canada (PetroCan), the upstart public interloper in the oil patch, it was a long road from its beginnings in a Calgary hotel room in 1976 to its 1988 high-profile, cross-Canada Olympic Torch relay. And Bill Hopper (see Figure 12-1) was seen as just the man to guide the fledgling Crown corporation to success in an industry that did not rejoice at its creation.

Hopper had all the right credentials. A geologist with wanderlust, he had moved from his first foray into the oil industry with Imperial Oil in 1940, to international petroleum consulting. This journey took him to every major oil field in the world. With his family's public service connections in Ottawa as his calling card, Hopper "took control of the company as an executive with solid energy credentials and a personal passport to the exclusive chambers of government."[1] Ironically, this was the same Hopper who, as a consultant hired by the government in 1970, had reported that state oil companies were "ineffective as tools of public policy."[2] Within a few years, this man who was described as "personable and persuasive, irascible, aggressive, and blunt" was assistant deputy minister for energy policy and was working on the creation of PetroCan.[3] Hopper was in an excellent position to dive into the PetroCan pool, since he was part of Donald MacDonald's support team during the evolution of the PetroCan concept between 1972 and 1975.

By October 1990, the Mulroney government had brought forward a bill to privatize Petro-Canada.[4] In November 1990, Hopper appeared before a House of Commons committee arguing for the privatization of the Crown corporation. But privatization proved to be less rosy than Hopper had expected. The company posted a huge loss of $149 million in its first period as a private company.[5] Hopper complained, "Every year labour says that they need another four- or five-percent in-

FIGURE 12-1 Perks Prove Costly to This CEO

Bill Hopper's lavish lifestyle when he was chairman and CEO of Petro-Canada had dramatic repercussions.[12]

crease. Well, you can't sustain all of those higher costs. Eventually you're out of business."[6]

Meanwhile, Hopper reportedly had two private jets and access to company cars and drivers in both Calgary and his home, Ottawa. A leaked in-house letter from a disgruntled employee reported that, in addition to these perks, Hopper also had private chefs and servants. A company spokesperson denied the existence of chefs and servants, but refused to confirm or deny that the company had purchased a $500 000 condominium in Calgary for its CEO. Nevertheless, even this spokesperson had to admit that frustration with Hopper's spending habits was growing.[7]

As the company prepared for its first investors' meeting as a private corporation, a mystery letter-writer urged the 85 percent of Petro-Canada employees who held stock to "go to it and boo Hopper off the stage."[8]

The meeting was as challenging as the internal letter suggested it might be. "Attacked by shareholders, demoralized employees, and human rights activists, PetroCan executives emerged from the company's first annual meeting battered and humbled—and running a much smaller business."[9]

Despite his apparent skill at image management, Bill Hopper was removed from the positions of chairman and chief executive officer of Petro-Canada on January 28, 1993. Reportedly, most oil patch insiders were surprised that Hopper was fired by a board of directors composed of his allies. "Ironically, the day after unceremoniously dumping Hopper, Petro-Canada's board released year-end financial results they claimed showed a 'major improvement' in the company's performance."[10]

Many have asked how Hopper got away with his lavish lifestyle for so long. One writer answered, "Hopper created a web of obligations. He did people favours. He gave old cronies jobs. He got politicians and journalists on his jet. He announced petroleum discoveries when the party nodded. He put the projects in the ridings."[11] In the end it seems that it was the lifestyle that brought down Bill Hopper. "Hopper's lavish corporate lifestyle, tolerated when PetroCan's only shareholder was the free-spending federal government, was apparently no longer suitable after Canada's second-biggest oil and gas company was partially privatized in

1991."[13] Hopper himself said the firing was not a complete surprise to him. "It didn't come out of the blue . . . . Was there a difference of philosophy? Yeah. Can I be more specific? No."[14]

Hopper did not leave empty handed, however. Estimates of Hopper's severance package suggest he may have received $1.2 million in direct severance and $280 000 in annual pension benefits.[15]

Meanwhile, his successor, Jim Stanford, "lives alone in a southwest Calgary townhouse, and spends his vacations on Vancouver Island, where he keeps his sailboat."[16]

Petro-Canada
www.petro-canada.ca

Although Bill Hopper's situation at Petro-Canada was extreme, such apparent abuses of power are not as unusual as you might think. In fact, this case illustrates a basic fact of life in organizations: People seek to control the actions of others and try to influence their behaviour. This occurs when a dispatcher asks the delivery person to complete the route more quickly, or when the board of directors pressures a company president to make the company more profitable. Efforts to get others to behave as desired, known as *social influence*, are commonplace in all social settings, especially organizations. A large part of this process, as illustrated by Hopper's behaviour, is an interest in *power*—the formal capacity to influence others and/or the company. In this case, Hopper was strongly focused on cultivating a grand image of himself and protecting his self-interest, efforts known as *organizational politics*.

Because the processes of influence, power, and politics play key roles in organizational functioning, we will devote this chapter to examining them. Specifically, we will describe the tactics used to influence others in organizations. Then we will examine how power is attained—both by individuals and by organizational subunits—and how that power is used. Following this, we will examine the political mechanisms used to gain power—what they are and when they occur. As part of this discussion, we will also pay special attention to the ethical aspects of organizational politics insofar as activities of this nature may be of questionable morality due to their potentially adverse effects on others. Before turning to these topics, however, we will begin by defining the concepts of influence, power, and politics.

Organizational Influence, Power, and Politics: Some Key Distinctions

Imagine that you are a supervisor heading a group of a dozen staff members working on an important new project for your company. Tomorrow is the day you're supposed to make a big presentation to company officials, but the report isn't quite ready. If only several staff members will work a few hours extra, the job will be done on time. Unfortunately, a company party is scheduled for tonight and nobody wants to work late. Question: What can you do to persuade some of your staff to work late and complete the job? In other words, how will you attempt to influence their behaviour?

social influence Attempts to affect another in a desired fashion.

The concept of **social influence** refers to attempts (whether successful or unsuccessful) to affect another in a desired fashion (see Figure 12–2). It may be said that we have influenced someone to the extent that our behaviour has had an effect—even if unintended—on that person. Although we may attempt to affect another's behaviour in a certain fashion, our attempts may be unsuccessful. This would not mean, however, that we did not influence the person, just that we did not influence him or her successfully.

To illustrate this point, let's return to our example of a boss needing people to work overtime on party night. Imagine that you see the boss coming out of her office, and you expect her to ask you to work overtime. Uninterested in doing so, you walk away from your desk, hoping that the boss has not seen you and will ask someone else instead. In this case, can we say that the boss influenced you? Although she was unsuccessful, she

FIGURE 12-2 Relationship among Social Influence, Power, and Politics

When someone attempts to get another to act in a desired fashion, that person is seeking to *influence* the other. The capacity to exert influence over another is known as *power*. Unofficial uses of power to enhance or protect one's self-interest is known as *organizational politics*.

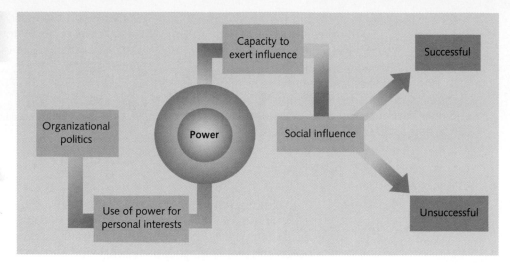

clearly *did* have an effect on you. After all, you ran away from her. Thus, we *can* say that the boss influenced you. However, we *cannot* say that the boss influenced your behaviour as desired. For that to be true, the boss would have to have been successful in bringing about the intended effects—in this case, getting you to stay and work overtime.

Where do power and politics fit in? As illustrated in Figure 12-2, **power** refers to the potential to influence another successfully. More formally, it is the capacity to change the behaviour or attitudes of another in a desired fashion.[17] In contrast with social influence (actions that affect others), the related concept of power refers to the *capacity* to have a desired effect on others. As we will detail in the next section, there are several different sources of such power. For now, however, assume that the boss has power over you by virtue of her access to considerable resources that enable her to reward you with raises (in exchange for being cooperative) or punish you by not supporting your promotion (if you refrain from pitching in). These represent the formal actions the supervisor can take to attempt to influence you successfully. That is, they are the sources of power.

Often, when people exercise their power, they take into account their own individual interests. For example, the supervisor in our story may be motivated by an interest in promoting—or at least saving—her own career by making sure that the report gets done on time. This is not to say that she might not also recognize the value of the report to the company. It's just that her actions are motivated primarily by her own selfish concerns. The actions taken to satisfy these concerns reflect **organizational politics**. This term refers to unauthorized uses of power that enhance or protect one's own or one's group's personal interests.[18] If this kind of behaviour sounds quite negative, it is. In fact, it is technically illegitimate in both its means and ends and, not surprisingly, typically a source of conflict. Later in this chapter we will describe many types of political actions that exist, ways in which people can use their power to promote their personal interests in organizations.

Now that we have clarified the distinctions between social influence, power, and politics, we will focus on each of these concepts separately in the remainder of this chapter. We will begin with the process of social influence.

Social Influence: Having an Impact on Others

By what means do you persuade others to fulfill your wishes? Are you straightforward and tell people what you want them to do, or are you more inclined to emphasize why they should do what you say and what will happen to them if they do not do so (see Figure 12-3)? Is it your style to pressure people, or to convince them to do what you want by getting them to like you? Regardless of your answers, you are confronting the challenge of *social influence*—getting others to do what you want.

power The capacity to change the behaviour or attitudes of others in a desired manner.

organizational politics (or **politics**) Unauthorized uses of power that enhance or protect one's own or one's group's personal interests.

"Terrific, but you're still expected to wear a tie to work like everyone else."

FIGURE 12-3 Social Influence: An Everyday Organizational Phenomenon

Social influence takes many forms in organizations, one of which involves directly telling someone else what you want him or her to do.

(Source: Copyright © 1992, 1994 by Charles Barsotti.)

It is widely acknowledged that successful managers are those who are adept at influencing others.[19] We will summarize the social influence techniques used, and then review when and how people use their influence over others.

Tactics of Social Influence

In recent years, researchers have examined several major techniques that people use to influence each other in organizations.[20] These are as follows.[21]

1. ***Rational persuasion***. Using logical arguments and facts to persuade another that a desired result will occur.

2. ***Inspirational appeal***. Arousing enthusiasm by appealing to one's values and ideals.

3. ***Consultation***. Asking for participation in decision making or planning a change.

4. ***Ingratiation***. Getting people to do what you want by putting them in a good mood or getting them to like you.

5. ***Exchange***. Promising some benefits in exchange for complying with a request.

6. ***Personal appeal***. Appealing to feelings of loyalty and friendship before making a request.

7. ***Coalition building***. Persuading by seeking the assistance of others, or by noting the support of others.

8. ***Legitimating***. Pointing out one's authority to make a request, or verifying that it is consistent with prevailing organizational policies and practices.

9. ***Pressure***. Seeking compliance by using demands, threats, or intimidation.

Research has shown that these various tactics are used differently based on whether one is attempting to influence another who is at a higher, lower, or equivalent organizational level.[22] In general, the most popularly used techniques to influence people at all levels were consultation, inspirational appeal, and rational persuasion.[23] Each one of these techniques involves getting someone else to accept a request as being highly desirable, and each is socially acceptable for influencing people at all levels. It is therefore not surprising that people who use these techniques are believed to be highly effective in carrying out their responsibilities.

By contrast, the more socially undesirable forms of influence, pressure and legitimating, were much less frequently used. In fact, pressure, when it was used, was more likely to be relied on as a follow-up technique than as a tool for one's initial influence attempt—and then, only for subordinates. It is important to note that some techniques, such as ingratiation, coalition, personal appeal, and exchange, are more likely to be used in combination with other techniques than used alone. Clearly, people attempt to influence others using a wide variety of different combinations of techniques. However, as a general rule, more open, consultative techniques are believed to be more appropriate than more coercive techniques.[24]

Putting Influence Tactics to Work

As you might imagine, when people decide to use a certain influence tactic, they take into account the reaction they anticipate from the person being influenced. Specifically, research findings indicate that people attempting to influence their bosses used upward appeals and ingratiation when they believed their bosses were inclined to be highly authoritarian, but used rational persuasion when they believed their bosses were highly participative.[25] This makes sense if you imagine that influence requires a highly coercive action (such as appealing to one's superior) to influence an authoritarian boss, whereas a participative boss might be more amenable to learning about a rational argument. These findings are important because they suggest that people's use of power is a function of not simply their own characteristics, but also their beliefs about the likely effects of their actions.

The social influence tactics we've been discussing can be effective in changing people's behaviour. Typically, we think of such techniques as helpful in bringing about behaviour that is adaptive to oneself and helpful to the organization. Returning to our "overtime" example, it certainly would be helpful to your boss and the organization as a whole for you to work overtime. Doing so also would benefit you to the extent that you are credited for your last-minute contribution; indeed, a good manager would remember and reward you for your good organizational citizenship. However, because people are typically part of many different social groups, they may confront several conflicting sources of social power—including some that may be quite negative.

☞ Recall the discussion of organizational citizenship behaviour appearing in Chapter 11.

Individual Power: A Basis For Influence

As defined earlier, *power* involves the potential to influence others—both the things they do and the ways they feel about something. In this section, we will focus on the individual bases of power—that is, factors that give people the capacity to control others successfully. It is an inevitable fact of organizational life that some individuals can boast a greater capacity to influence people successfully than others. Within organizations, the distribution of power is typically unequal. Why is this so? What sources of power do people have at their disposal? We will consider several specific bases of power falling into two major categories—that which comes with one's office and that which comes from oneself as an individual.

Position Power: Influence That Comes with the Office

A great deal of the power people have in organizations comes from the posts they hold. In other words, they are able to influence others because of the formal power associated with their jobs. This is known as **position power**. For example, there are certain powers that the prime minister of Canada has simply because he or she holds office (e.g., appointing Cabinet ministers, deciding when to call elections, etc.). These formal powers remain vested in the position and are available to anyone who holds that position. When the prime minister's term is up, these powers transfer to the new officeholder. There are four bases of position power: *legitimate power, reward power, coercive power,* and *information power.*

position power Power based on one's formal position in an organization.

Legitimate power. The power that people have because others recognize and accept their authority is known as **legitimate power**. As an example, students recognize that their instructors have the authority to make class policies and to determine grades, giving them legitimate power over the class. If someone were to challenge the teacher's decision, saying, "Who are you to do that?" the answer might be, "I'm the instructor, that's who." This exchange would clarify the legitimacy of the officeholder's behaviour. However, it is important to note that legitimate power covers a relatively narrow range of influence and that it may be inappropriate to overstep these bounds. For example, whereas a boss may require her secretary to type and fax a company document using her legitimate power to do so, it would be an abuse of power to ask that secretary to type her son's homework assignment. This is not to say that the secretary might not take on the task as a favour, but doing so would not be the direct result of the boss's formal authority. Legitimate power applies only to the range of behaviours that are recognized and accepted as appropriate by the parties and institution involved (see Figure 12-4).

legitimate power Power based on the recognition and acceptance of one's authority.

Reward power. Associated with holding certain jobs comes the power to control the rewards others receive—that is, **reward power**. Extending our teacher-student example, instructors have reward power over students insofar as they may reward

reward power The individual power base derived from an individual's capacity to administer valued rewards to others.

FIGURE 12-4 Legitimate Power: Control Based on Formal Authority

Legitimate power is based on the idea that members of an organization recognize and accept the formal authority of individuals who have higher-ranking positions within the organizational hierarchy.[26]

☞ *Keep in mind (based on our discussion of the concepts of reinforcement in Chapter 3 and valence in Chapter 5) that rewards may enhance one's power only to the extent that they are actually desired by the recipients.*

coercive power The individual power base derived from the capacity to administer punishment to others.

☞ *As cautioned in Chapter 3, punishments may have undesirable side effects if they are overly harsh or inconsistently administered.*

information power The extent to which one has access to information that makes one especially influential.

personal power The power that one derives because of one's individual qualities or characteristics.

them with high grades and glowing letters of recommendation. In the case of managers, the rewards available may be either tangible, such as raises and promotions, or intangible, such as praise and recognition. In both cases, access to these desired outcomes gives power to the individuals who control them.

Coercive power. By contrast, power also results from the capacity to control punishments—that is, **coercive power**. Although most managers do not like using the threat of punishments, it is a fact of organizational life that many people rely on coercive power. If any boss has ever directly told you, "Do what I say, or else," or even implied it, you are probably all too familiar with coercive power. Often, people have power simply because others know that they have the opportunity to punish them, even if the threat of doing so is not made explicit. For example, in the military, when your commanding officer asks you to do something, you may comply since that request can turn into an order, with severe consequences for not going along. In private organizations, threats of demotions, suspensions without pay, and assignments to undesirable duties may enhance the coercive power of many managers.

Information power. The fourth source of power available to people by virtue of their positions is based on data and other knowledge—known as **information power**. Traditionally, people in top positions have available to them unique sources of information that are not available to others (e.g., knowledge of company performance, market trends, and so on). As they say, "Knowledge is power," and such information greatly contributes to the power of people in many jobs. Although information power still exists, it is becoming a less potent source of influence in many of today's organizations. The reason is that technology has made it possible for more information to be available to more people than ever before. As a result, information need no longer be the unique property of a few people holding special positions.

Personal Power: Influence That Comes from the Individual

Thus far, all the sources of influence we've discussed have been based on an individual's position in an organization. However, this is not the only way people are able to influence others (for a review, see Figure 12-5). There's also power derived from an individual's own unique qualities or characteristics. This is known as **personal power**. There are four sources of personal power: *rational persuasion, expert power, referent power,* and *charisma.*

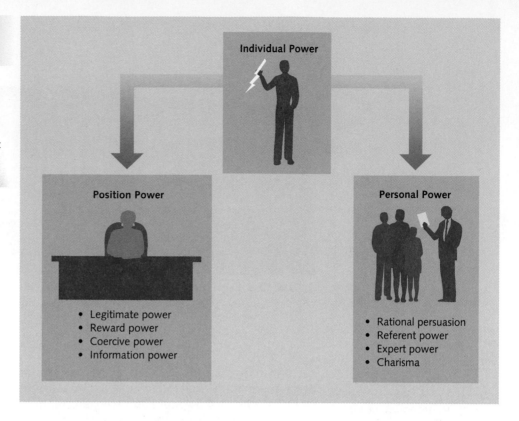

Individual Power

Position Power

- Legitimate power
- Reward power
- Coercive power
- Information power

Personal Power

- Rational persuasion
- Referent power
- Expert power
- Charisma

rational persuasion Using logical arguments and factual evidence to convince others that an idea is acceptable.

Rational persuasion. This approach relies on logical arguments and factual evidence to convince others that a certain idea is acceptable. **Rational persuasion** is highly effective when the parties involved are intelligent enough to make their cases strongly and to understand them clearly. Given that it is based on clear logic, good evidence, and the desire to help the company, rational persuasion tends to be highly effective. Not surprisingly, rational persuasion is among the most popular types of influence used in organizations.

expert power The individual power base derived from an individual's recognized superior skills and abilities in a certain area.

Expert power. This approach consists of power based on superior knowledge of a certain field. A coach has **expert power** over athletes to the extent that he or she is recognized by them as knowing what is best. Once experts have proven themselves, their power over others can be considerable. After all, people will respect and want to follow those in the know.

Should a supervisor's expertise be shown to be lacking, any power he or she may have based on that expertise is threatened. Insofar as no one is expected to be an expert on everything, this is not necessarily problematic. The less-than-expert person can simply admit his or her shortcomings and seek guidance from others. Where problems develop, however, is if someone in a position of power has not yet developed a level of expertise that is acknowledged and respected by lower-ranking persons (especially when these individuals believe they are more expert). Those who have not demonstrated their expertise clearly lack this important source of power. However, people whose expertise is highly regarded are among the most powerful people in organizations.

referent power The individual power base derived from the degree to which one is liked and admired by others.

Referent power. As you surely know, it is not only expertise but personal qualities that form the basis of our admiration for others in organizations. Individuals who are liked and respected by others can get them to alter their actions, a type of influence known as **referent power**. Senior managers who possess desirable qualities and good reputations may find that they have referent power over younger managers who identify with them and wish to emulate them.

charisma An attitude of enthusiasm and optimism that is contagious; an aura of leadership.

☞ *This use of the term* charisma *is similar to the way it will be used to refer to a characteristic of a leader in Chapter 13.*

Charisma. Some people are liked so much by others that they are said to have the quality of **charisma**—an engaging and magnetic personality. There's no ignoring the fact that some people become highly influential because of their highly charismatic ways. What makes such individuals so influential? There appear to be several factors involved. First, highly charismatic people have definite visions of the future of their organizations and how to get there. Second, people with charisma tend to be excellent communicators. They tend to rely on colourful language and exciting metaphors to excite the crowd. They also supplement their words with emotionally expressive and animated gestures. Third, charismatic individuals inspire trust. Their integrity is never challenged, and is a source of their strength. Fourth, people with charisma make others feel good about themselves. They are receptive to others' feelings and acknowledge them readily. "Congratulations on a job well done" is a phrase that may flow freely from a charismatic individual.

To summarize, people may influence others by virtue of both the jobs they have, and their individual characteristics. For a summary of the factors within each category, refer to Figure 12-5. To see how scientists measure different types of social influence, and to make some preliminary judgments about the types of influence your own supervisor uses, see the EXPERIENCING ORGANIZATIONAL BEHAVIOUR section on p. 392–393.

Power: How Is It Used?

As you might imagine, there is widespread overlap in the ways people use power. Only sometimes is a single source of power used; indeed, it is recognized that the various power bases are closely related to each other.[27] For example, the more someone uses coercive power, the less that person is liked, and hence, the lower his or her referent power tends to be. Similarly, managers who have expert power are also likely to have legitimate power because their directing others within the field of expertise is accepted. In addition, the higher someone's organizational position, the more legitimate power that person has, which in turn is usually accompanied by greater opportunities to use reward and coercion.[28] Clearly, then, the various bases of power should not be thought of as completely separate and distinct from each other. It is interesting to speculate about the power bases used by "the most powerful CEOs in Canada" (see Table 12-1).

What bases of power do people prefer to use? Although the answer to this question is quite complex, research has shown that people prefer using expert power most and coercive power least often.[29] These findings are limited to the power bases we've identified thus far. However, when we broaden the question and ask people to report exactly which sources of power they have on their jobs, a fascinating picture emerges. Figure 12-6 depicts the results of a survey in which 216 CEOs of American

TABLE 12-1 The Ten Most Powerful CEOs in Canada

These were the most powerful CEOs in Canada in 1998. What power bases do you suppose each uses?

(Source: Cole, 1998; see Note 30.)

Ford Motor Company of Canada Limited
www.ford.ca

CEO	Company	Birthplace
1. Maureen Kempston Darkes	General Motors of Canada Ltd.	Toronto
2. Jean Monty	BCE Inc.	Montreal
3. Bobbie Gaunt	Ford Motor Co. of Canada Ltd.	Pittsburgh
4. John Roth	Northern Telecom Ltd.	Lethbridge, Alta.
5. Edgar Bronfman, Jr.	Seagram Co. Ltd.	New York
6. John Cleghorn	Royal Bank of Canada	Montreal
7. Al Flood	Canadian Imperial Bank of Commerce	Monkton, Ont.
8. William Glaub	Chrysler Canada Ltd.	Chicago
9. Matthew Barrett	Bank of Montreal	County Meath, Ireland
10. George Watson	TransCanada Pipelines Ltd.	Leamington, Ont.

corporations were asked to rank order the importance of a series of specific sources of power.[31] The figures indicate the percentage of executives who included that source of power among their top three choices. These findings indicate not only that top executives rely on a broad range of powers, but also that they base these powers on support from people located in a host of other places throughout their organizations. Interestingly, when asked about how much power they currently had compared to ten years ago, only 19 percent said they now had more power. Thirty-six percent indicated that they had the same amount of power, and the largest group, 42 percent, indicated that they had less power.

Although many different forms of power tend to be used to influence subordinates, research has shown that expert power is the preferred form used to influence peers and superiors.[32] After all, it is almost always appropriate to try to get others to go along with you if you justify your attempt on the basis of your expertise. In contrast, coercive tactics tend to be frowned on in general and are especially inappropriate when one is attempting to influence a higher-ranking person.[33] Influencing superiors is tricky because of the *counterpower* they have. When attempting to influence another who is believed to have no power at his or her disposal, one doesn't have to worry about fear of retaliation. When dealing with an individual with considerably greater power, however, one can do little other than simply comply with that more powerful person. (For an example of how such power can be abused, see **THE ETHICS ANGLE**.)

However, the situation is complicated by the fact that one party may have higher power on one dimension, and another party may have higher power on another dimension. Consider, for example, the case of some secretaries who have acquired power because they have been with their companies for many years. They know the ropes and can get things done for you if they want, or they can get you hopelessly bogged down in red tape. Their expert knowledge gives them a great sense of power over others. Although they may lack the legitimate power of their executive bosses, secretaries' expertise can be a valuable source of counterpower over those with more formal powers.

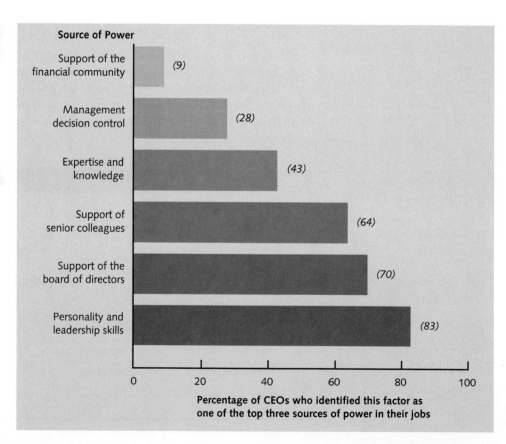

FIGURE 12-6 Power Bases of American CEOs

A survey of more than 200 American CEOs revealed that they obtained their power primarily by cultivating the support of others at different levels throughout the organization.

(Source: Based on data appearing in Stewart, 1989; see Note 31.)

Source of Power

Source	
Support of the financial community	(9)
Management decision control	(28)
Expertise and knowledge	(43)
Support of senior colleagues	(64)
Support of the board of directors	(70)
Personality and leadership skills	(83)

Percentage of CEOs who identified this factor as one of the top three sources of power in their jobs

The Prescription for a Chronic Power Abuser

The problem with power is that it sometimes goes to one's head, leading to ethically dubious behaviour. And when it does, the impact on an organization can be devastating. Toronto-based consultant Marti Smye co-authored a book about corporate bullying entitled *Corporate Abuse: How Lean and Mean Robs People and Profits*. Smye emphasizes the financial as well as the human impact of bullying in the workplace. "Who do you think comes up with the best ideas— people with good self-esteem or poor self-esteem? It's a business case, not just a humane case. When you have a tyrant, everyone shuts down."[34]

Take, for example, the case of Robert Schoellhorn, the former CEO of Abbott Labs (which has offices in Montreal, Mississauga, Ontario, and Freelton, Ontario).[35] After guiding the large pharmaceutical company through some of its best years in the early 1980s, Schoellhorn enjoyed the recognition he received.

By the mid-1980s, however, Schoellhorn had become "drunk with power." He surrounded himself with subordinates who would do whatever he wanted and would never challenge him. Anyone who dared not go along with Schoellhorn was out— including three company presidents in eight years. Schoellhorn spent millions of dollars in company funds on not one, but two corporate jets—one each to usher around himself and his new wife (and former secretary). All that was on his mind was to maintain his image as a leader, even if it meant making short-sighted decisions. When he cut research and development funds to boost short-term corporate earnings, the company went into a tailspin.

By March 1990 the board of directors had had enough and fired Schoellhorn, just months before he was due to retire. However, flexing his muscles to the end, Schoellhorn did not take the ouster lying down. In a rare move for a top executive, he sued his former employer. Eventually he received a U.S.$5.2 million settlement—a lot of money, but an amount the board of directors considered a small price to pay to rid itself of its power-hungry chief executive.[36]

Abbott Laboratories
www.abbott.com

Empowerment: The Shifting Bases of Power in Today's Organizations

A phenomenon is occurring in a growing number of today's organizations: Power is shifting out of the offices of managers and into the hands of employees themselves. Many of today's workers are not being "managed" in the traditional, authoritarian styles that have been used by managers of generations past. Instead, power is often shifted down the ladder to a team of workers allowed to make decisions themselves. This is the idea of **empowerment**—the passing of responsibility and authority from managers to employees. For many years workers have used the excuse, "I did it because my manager told me to." However, as employees become empowered in the workplace, this explanation is no longer likely to be heard. It is important to note that empowerment involves more than simply giving employees leeway in determining how to carry out a leader's stated mission. Beyond autonomy, it also involves sharing the appropriate information and knowledge that allows employees to do what is needed to help the organization meet its goals.

To underscore this point: The key to empowering people successfully is the sharing of expert information (as opposed to the hoarding of information that has been popular in the past). Today's managers are likely to be more open than their predecessors. As such, they are likely to empower employees by widely disseminating information, allowing better decisions to be made. For example, Steven Jobs (best known as one of the cofounders of Apple Computer) strongly believes that employees must be privy to vital information about sales and profits and such for them to appreciate the work they do. In fact, Jobs goes so far as to make available a list of each employee's pay. When questions arise as to why someone else may be getting paid more, Jobs uses that occasion to explain what he sees as the differences in their

empowerment The passing of responsibility and authority from managers to employees.

☞ Naturally, empowerment involves the use of empowered decision making described in Chapter 10.

contributions. Such information, he believes, helps cultivate the impression that company management is being straight with employees and has nothing to hide.

Empowerment programs in Canada have been initiated in a wide range of organizations. The Maritime School of Social Work at Dalhousie University in Halifax has developed a Bachelor of Social Work degree specifically for Native students. Control of the program is shared by the university and the Native community.[37] Giant General Electric and small firms like Oneida Canada Limited, in Niagara Falls, Ontario, and Plymouth Tool and Stamping in Agincourt, Ontario, have all reaped the financial benefits of empowering employees.[38]

As you might imagine, empowerment may be seen as not just a simple yes-or-no option, but a matter of degree.[39] At one end of the scale are companies, such as the traditional assembly lines, in which workers have virtually no power to determine how to do their jobs. At the opposite end are jobs in which employees have complete control over what they do and how they do it. We see this at companies using self-managed work teams, as described in Chapter 8. For example, at Chaparral Steel, managers are free to hire, train, and use new employees however they think best.[40] At W. L. Gore & Associates (manufacturer of Gore-tex, a synthetic material used in camping equipment), the empowerment philosophy is so strongly entrenched that employees work without any fixed, assigned sets of responsibilities.[41] Between these two extremes are companies whose employees have some degree of responsibility for their work and have a voice in important decisions, but are not completely free to work however they see fit. A growing number of companies fall into this category, including the General Motors Saturn plant in Spring Hill, Tennessee.[42]

If the practices we've been describing here don't square with your experiences, don't feel bad. The empowered employee is still in the minority in the vast majority of today's organizations—but, experts predict a change in that direction is coming, and fast.[43] If this prognostication is correct, as we believe it is, we can look forward to significant changes in the way people will use power in organizations.

Group or Subunit Power: Structural Determinants

Thus far, this chapter has examined the uses of power by individuals. However, in organizations, it is not only people acting alone, but also groups, who wield power.[44] Organizations are frequently divided into subunits given responsibility for different functions such as finance, human resource management, marketing, and research and development. The formal departments devoted to these various organizational activities often must direct the activities of other groups, requiring them to have power. What are the sources of such power? By what means do formal organizational groups successfully control the actions of other groups? Two theoretical models have been proposed to answer these questions—the *resource-dependency model* and the *strategic contingencies model*. Our review of these approaches will help identify the factors responsible for subunit power and describe how they operate.

The Resource-Dependency Model: Controlling Critical Resources

It is not difficult to think of an organization as a complex set of subunits that are constantly exchanging resources with each other. By this, we mean that formal organizational departments may be both giving to and receiving from other departments such valued commodities as money, personnel, equipment, supplies, and information. These critical resources are necessary for the successful operation of organizations.

Various subunits often depend on others for such resources. To illustrate this point, imagine a large organization that develops, produces, and sells its products. The Sales Department provides financial resources that enable the Research and

Dalhousie University
www.dal.ca

Development Department to create new products. Of course, it cannot do so effectively without information from the Marketing Department about what consumers are interested in buying and how much they would be willing to pay. The Production Department has to do its part by manufacturing the goods on time, but only if the Purchasing Department can supply the needed raw materials—and at a price the Finance Department accepts as permitting the company to turn a profit.

It is easy to see how the various organizational subunits are involved in a complex set of interrelationships with others. To the extent that one subunit controls the resources on which another subunit depends, it may be said to have power over it. After all, controlling resources allows groups to influence the actions of other groups successfully. Subunits that control more resources than others may be considered more powerful in the organization. Indeed, such imbalances, or *asymmetries*, in the pattern of resource dependencies occur normally in organizations. The more one group depends on another for needed resources, the less power it has (see Figure 12-7).

In proposing their **resource-dependency model**, Pfeffer and Salancik note that a subunit's power is based on the degree to which it controls the resources required by other subunits.[45] Thus, although all subunits may contribute something to an organization, the most powerful ones are those that contribute the most important resources. Controlling the resources other departments need puts a subunit in a better position to bargain for the resources it requires. To illustrate this point, let's consider an important study by Salancik and Pfeffer.[46] Within a university, the various academic departments may be very unequal with respect to the power they possess. For example, some may have more students, be more prestigious in their national reputation, receive greater grant support, and have more representatives on important university committees than others. As such, they would be expected to have greater control over valued resources. This was found to be the case within the large university studied by Salancik and Pfeffer. The more powerful departments proved to be those that were most successful in gaining scarce and valued resources from the university (e.g., funds for graduate student fellowships, and faculty research grants). As a result, they became even more powerful, suggesting that within organizations, the rich subunits get richer.

The resource-dependency model suggests that a key determinant of subunit power is the control of valued resources. However, as we will now illustrate, it is not only control over resources that dictates organizational power, but also control over the activities of other subunits.

The Strategic Contingencies Model: Power through Dependence

The Accounting Department of a company might be expected to have responsibility over the approval or disapproval of funds requested by various departments. If it does, its actions greatly affect the activities of other units, who depend on its decisions—that is, other departments' operations are *contingent* on what the Accounting Department does. To the extent that a department is able to control the relative power of various organizational subunits by virtue of its actions, it is said to have control over *strategic contingencies*. For example, if the Accounting Department consistently approved the budget requests of the Production Department but rejected the budget requests of the Marketing Department, it would be making the Production Department more powerful.

Where do the strategic contingencies lie within organizations? In a classic study, Lawrence and Lorsch found out that power was distributed in different departments in different industries.[47] They found that within successful firms, the strategic contingencies were

resource-dependency model The view according to which power resides within subunits that are able to control the greatest share of valued organizational resources.

FIGURE 12-7 The Resource-Dependency Model: An Example

The *resource-dependency model* of organizational power explains that subunits acquire power when they control critical resources needed by other subunits. In this example, the accounting department would be considered more powerful than either the production department or the marketing department.

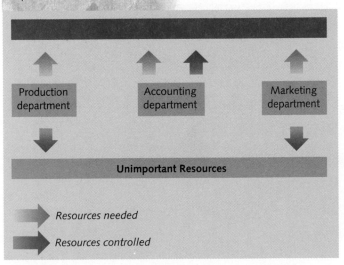

The use of the contingency approach was described in Chapter 1 as one of the major orientations of the modern field of OB. As its name implies, the strategic contingencies model utilizes this approach.

strategic contingencies model
A view explaining power in terms of a subunit's capacity to control the activities of other subunits. A subunit's power is enhanced when (1) it can reduce the level of uncertainty experienced by other subunits, (2) it occupies a central position in the organization, and (3) its activities are highly indispensable to the organization.

controlled by the departments that were most important for organizational success. For example, within the food processing industry, where it was critical for new products to be developed and sold, successful firms had strategic contingencies controlled by the Sales and Research departments. In the container manufacturing field, where the timely delivery of high-quality goods is a critical determinant of organizational success, successful firms placed most of the decision-making power in the Sales and Production departments. Thus, successful firms focused the control over strategic contingencies within the subunits most responsible for their organization's success.

What factors give subunits control over strategic contingencies? The **strategic contingencies model** of Hickson and his associates suggests several key considerations.[48] Refer to the summary of these factors in Figure 12-8.

Power may be enhanced by subunits that can help reduce the levels of uncertainty faced by others. Any department that can shed light on the uncertain situations organizations may face (e.g., those regarding future markets, government regulation, availability of needed supplies, financial security) can be expected to wield the most organizational power. Accordingly, the balance of power within organizations may be expected to change as organizational conditions change. Consider, for example, changes that have taken place over the years in public utility companies. Studying the strategic contingencies in such organizations, Miles noted that a shift has occurred.[49] When public utilities first began, the engineers tended to wield the most power. But now that these companies have matured and face problems of litigation and governmental regulation (particularly over nuclear power), the power has shifted to lawyers. A similar shift toward the power of the Legal Department has occurred in recent years in the area of human resource management, where a complex set of laws and governmental regulations have created a great deal of uncertainty for organizations. Powerful subunits are those that can help reduce organizational uncertainty.

That more powerful subunits are ones that have *a high degree of centrality in the organization* also has been established. Some organizational subunits perform functions that are more central, and others, more peripheral. For example, some departments—such as Accounting—may have to be consulted by most others before any action can be taken, giving them a central position in their organizations. Centrality is also high when a unit's duties have an immediate effect on an organization. For example, the effects would be much more dramatic on an auto manufacturer if the production lines stopped than if market research activities ceased. The central connection of some departments to organizational success dictates the power they wield.

Third, a subunit controls power when its *activities are nonsubstitutable and indispensable*. If any group can perform a certain function, subunits responsible for

FIGURE 12-8 Strategic Contingencies Model: Identifying Sources of Subunit Power

The *strategic contingencies model* explains intraorganizational power in terms of the capacity of some subunits to control the actions of others. Subunit power may be enhanced by the factors shown here.

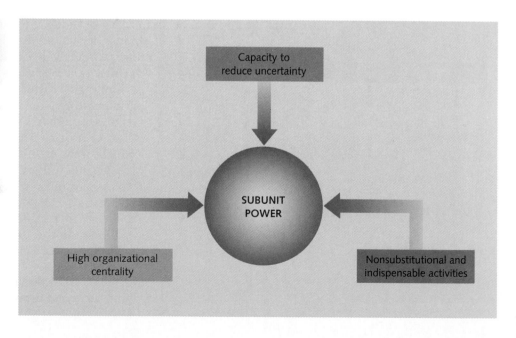

Capacity to reduce uncertainty

SUBUNIT POWER

High organizational centrality

Nonsubstitutional and indispensable activities

380   PART 5   Influencing Others

controlling that function may not be particularly powerful. In a hospital, for example, personnel on surgical teams are certainly more indispensable than personnel in the maintenance department because fewer individuals have the skills needed to perform their unit's duties. Because an organization can easily replace some employees with others either within or outside it, subunits composed of individuals who are most easily replaced tend to wield very little organizational power.

The strategic contingencies model has been tested and supported in organizational studies.[50] For example, one investigation conducted in several companies found that a subunit's power within an organization was higher when it could reduce uncertainty, occupied a central place in the work flow, and performed functions that other subunits could not perform.[51] The strategic contingencies model should be considered a valuable source of information about the factors that influence the power of subunits within organizations.

Organizational Politics: Power in Action

Our discussion of power focused on the potential to influence others successfully. When this potential is realized, put into action to accomplish desired goals, we are no longer talking about power, but *politics*.[52] It is quite easy to imagine situations in which someone does something to accomplish his or her own goals, which do not necessarily agree with the goals of the organization. This is what *organizational politics* is all about—actions not officially approved by an organization taken to influence others to meet one's personal goals.[53]

If you think we're describing something that is a bit selfish and appears to be an abuse of organizational power, you are correct. Organizational politics does involve placing one's self-interests above the interests of the organization. Indeed, this element of using power to foster one's own interests distinguishes organizational politics from uses of power that are approved and accepted by organizations.[54]

Political Tactics: What Forms Does It Take?

To understand organizational politics, one must recognize the various forms political behaviour can take in organizations. In other words, what are the techniques of organizational politics? Six techniques are used most often.[55]

Controlling access to information.   Information is the lifeblood of organizations. Therefore, controlling who knows and doesn't know certain things is one of the most important ways to exercise power in organizations. Although outright lying and falsifying information may be used only rarely in organizations (in part because of the consequences of getting caught), there are other ways of controlling information to enhance one's organizational position. For example, you might (1) withhold information that makes you look bad (e.g., negative sales information), (2) avoid contact with those who may ask for information you would prefer not to disclose, (3) be very selective in the information you disclose, or (4) overwhelm others with information that may not be completely relevant. These are all ways to control the nature and degree of information people have at their disposal. Such information control can be critical.

An analysis of the organizational restructuring of AT&T's Phone Stores revealed that control was transferred through the effective manipulation, distortion, and creation of information.[56] A vice-president's secret plan to feed incomplete and inaccurate information to the CEO was responsible for that vice-president's winning control over the stores.

Cultivating a favourable impression.   People interested in enhancing their organizational control commonly engage in some degree of image building—an attempt to create a good impression on others. Such efforts may take many forms, such as

☞ As we noted in Chapter 10, information is the key to successful decision making in organizations.

(1) "dressing for success," (2) associating oneself with the successful accomplishments of others (or, in extreme cases, taking credit for others' successes), or (3) simply drawing attention to one's own successes and positive characteristics.[57]

With this in mind, Ferris and King identified those individuals who worked hard to fit into their organizations as *organizational chameleons*.[58] Such individuals figure out what behaviours they believe are considered generally appropriate in their organization and then go out of their way to make sure that others are aware that they behaved in such a manner. These are all ways of developing the "right image" to enhance one's individual power in organizations.

☞ Recall from Chapter 3 that impression management involves the processes of social perception and attribution.

Developing a base of support. To influence people successfully it is often useful to gain the support of others within the organization. Managers may, for example, lobby for their ideas before they officially present them at meetings, ensuring that others are committed to them in advance and thereby avoiding the embarrassment of public rejection. They also may "scatter IOUs" throughout the organization by doing favours for others who may feel obligated to repay them in the form of supporting their ideas. The norm of *reciprocity* is very strong in organizations, as evidenced by the popular phrases, "You scratch my back, and I'll scratch yours" and "One good turn deserves another." After all, when someone does a favour for you, you may say, "I owe you one," suggesting that you are aware of the obligation to reciprocate that favour. "Calling in" favours is a well-established and widely used mechanism for developing organizational power.

Blaming and attacking others. One of the most popularly used tactics of organizational politics involves blaming and attacking others when bad things happen. A commonly used political tactic is finding a *scapegoat*, someone who could take the blame for some failure or wrongdoing. A supervisor, for example, may explain that the failure of a sales plan she designed was based on the serious mistakes of one of her subordinates—even if this is not entirely true.

Finding a scapegoat can allow the politically astute individual to avoid (or at least minimize) association with the negative situation. For example, research has found that when corporate performance drops, powerful chief executives often resort to placing the blame onto a lower-ranking individual, protecting themselves from getting fired while their subordinate gets the axe.[59]

Aligning oneself with more powerful others. One of the most direct ways to gain power is by connecting oneself with more powerful others. There are several ways to accomplish this. For example, a lower-power person may become more powerful if she has a very powerful mentor, a more powerful and better-established person who can look out for and protect her interests. As another example, people may also agree in advance to form *coalitions*—groups that band together to achieve some common goal (e.g., overthrowing a current corporate CEO).[60] Research has shown that the banding together of relatively powerless groups is one of the most effective ways they have to gain organizational power.[61] Two relatively powerless individuals or groups may become stronger if they agree to act together, forming a coalition. People may also align themselves with more powerful others by giving them "positive strokes" in the hope of getting more powerful people to like them and help them, a process known as *ingratiation*.[62] Agreeing with someone more powerful may be an effective way of getting that person to consider you an ally. Such an alliance, of course, may prove indispensable when you are looking for support within an organization. To summarize, having a powerful mentor, forming coalitions, and using ingratiation are all potentially effective ways of gaining power by aligning oneself with others.

☞ In Chapter 7 we fully discuss the role of mentorship as a process facilitating career development.

Playing political games. One expert in the field of organizational power and politics, Henry Mintzberg, has suggested that political behaviour is a collection of games going on in a multiring circus.[63] His idea is that many people or groups may be trying to influence many other people or groups simultaneously, as in playing a game. What, then, are the political games that unfold in organizations? Mintzberg has identified four major categories of political games. As we describe them, refer to our summary in Table 12-2.

1. **Authority games**. Some games, known as *insurgency games*, are played to resist authority. Others, known as *counterinsurgency games*, are played to counter such resistance to authority. Insurgency can take forms ranging from quite mild (such as intentionally not doing what is asked) to very severe (such as organizing workers to mutiny or sabotage their workplaces).[64] Companies may try to fight back with counterinsurgency moves. One way they may do so is by invoking stricter authority and control over subordinates. Often unproductive for both sides, such games frequently give way to the more adaptive techniques of bargaining and negotiation.

2. **Power base games**. These games are played to enhance the degree and breadth of one's organizational power. For example, the *sponsorship game* is played with superiors. It involves attaching oneself to a rising or established star in return for a piece of the action. A relatively unpowerful subordinate, for example, may agree to help a more established person (such as his boss) by loyally supporting him in exchange for getting advice and information from him, as well as some of his power and prestige. Both benefit as a result. Similar games may be played among peers, such as the *alliance game*. Here, workers at the same level agree in advance to support each other mutually, gaining strength by increasing their joint size and power. One of the riskiest power base games is known as *empire building*. In this game, an individual or group attempts to become more powerful by gaining responsibility for more and more important organizational decisions. Indeed, a subunit may increase its power by attempting to gain control over budgets, space, equipment, or any other scarce and desired organizational resource.

3. **Rivalry games**. Some political games are designed to weaken one's opponents. For example, in the *line versus staff game* managers on the "line," who are responsible for the operation of an organizational unit, clash with those on "staff," who are supposed to provide needed advice and information. For example, a supervisor on an assembly line may attempt to ignore the advice from a corporate legal specialist about how to treat one of his production workers, thereby rendering the staff specialist less powerful. Another rivalry game is the *rival camps game*, in which groups or individuals with differing points of view attempt to reduce each other's power. For example, an organization's Production Department may favour the goals of stability and efficiency, whereas the Marketing Department may favour the goals

TABLE 12-2 Political Games: A Summary of Some Examples

Many political games are played in organizations, each involving different individuals playing for different political goals.

(Source: Adapted from Mintzberg, 1983: see Note 19.)

Game	Typical Major Players	Purpose
Authority Games		
Insurgency game	Lower-level managers	To resist formal authority
Counterinsurgency game	Upper-level managers	To counter resistance to formal authority
Power Base Games		
Sponsorship game	Any subordinate employee	To enhance base of power with superiors
Alliance game	Line managers	To enhance base of power with peers
Empire building	Line managers	To enhance base of power with subordinates
Rivalry Games		
Line versus staff game	Line managers and staff personnel	To defeat each other in the quest for power
Rival camps game	Any groups at the same level	To defeat each other in the quest for power
Change Games		
Whistle-blowing game	Lower-level managers	To correct organizational wrongdoings
"Young Turks" game	Upper-level managers	To seize control over the organization

of growth and customer service. The result may be that each side attempts to cultivate the favour of those allies who can support it and who are less sensitive to the other side's interests. Of course, because organizational success requires the various organizational subunits to work in concert with each other, such rivalries are considered potentially disruptive to organizational functioning. One side or the other may win from time to time, but the organization loses as a result.

☞ Whistle-blowing is described in Chapter 11, where it is presented as a form of prosocial organizational behaviour.

4. **Change games.** Several different games are played to create organizational change. For example, in the *whistle-blowing game* an organizational member secretly reports some organizational wrongdoing to a higher authority in the hope of righting the wrong and bringing about change. A game played for much higher stakes is known as the *"Young Turks" game.* In it, camps of rebel workers seek to overthrow the existing leadership of an organization—a most extreme form of insurgency. The change sought by people playing this game is not minor, but far-reaching and permanent. In government terms, they are seeking a "coup d'état." Some political activities may readily coexist with organizational interests (e.g., the sponsorship game), whereas others are clearly antagonistic to organizational interests (e.g., the "Young Turks" game). As such games are played out, it becomes apparent that although they may sometimes have little effect on organizations, they also may be quite harmful.[65] Now that we know what types of behaviour reflect political activity in organizations, we are prepared to consider the conditions under which such behaviours occur.

When Does Political Action Occur?

Imagine the following situation. You are the director of a large charitable organization that administers funds supporting many charitable projects (e.g., saving endangered animals, providing shelter to the homeless). A wealthy philanthropist dies, and his will leaves your organization $10 million to be spent in any desired manner. Hearing of this generous bequest, the directors of the various charitable groups are all interested in obtaining as much of this money as possible to support their projects. Several aspects of this situation make it liable to trigger political activity.[66]

Conditions triggering political action. First, this situation is fraught with uncertainty; it is not obvious where the money should be spent. If the organization has no clearly prescribed priorities about how to spend its funds, various groups might very well try to get their share by any means possible. Second, this is clearly a matter in which there is an important decision involving large amounts of scarce resources. If the size of the gift were much smaller, say $500, or if it involved something trivial or readily available, such as paper clips, the incentive for political action would probably be weak.

The different groups in our example each have conflicting goals and interests. The save-our-wildlife group is intent on serving its interests; the shelter-for-the-homeless group has very different interests. These differing goals make political activity likely. Finally, note that the potential for political activity in this situation is great because the different charitable groups are all approximately equal in power. If there were a highly asymmetrical balance of power (with one group having a lot more control over resources than the others), political action would be futile because the most powerful group would simply make the decision.

In summary, political behaviour is likely to occur when: (1) uncertainty exists, (2) large amounts of scarce resources are at stake, (3) organizational units (individuals or groups) have conflicting interests, or (4) the parties involved have approximately equal power.

Politics in human resource management. If you think about these conditions, you won't be surprised that political behaviour often centres on key human resource management activities such as performance appraisal, personnel selection, and compensation decisions.[67] For example, given that there is often a certain amount of ambiguity associated with evaluating another's performance, and that such evaluations might cultivate certain images of oneself, it follows that performance ratings may be recognized as more of a reflection of the rater's interest in promoting a certain image of him or herself than an interest in accurately evaluating another's behaviour.[68] Similarly, when making personnel decisions, people are at least as much concerned about the implications of their hires for their own ideal careers (e.g., will this person support me or make me look bad?) as they are concerned about doing what's best for the organization.[69]

Finally, pay raise decisions have been shown to be politically motivated. Specifically, in a management simulation exercise, Bartol and Martin found that managers gave the highest raises to individuals who threatened to complain if they didn't get a substantial raise, particularly if it were known that these people had political connections within the organization.[70] Taken together, these findings suggest that the very nature of human resource management activities in organizations makes them prime candidates for activities within which organizational politics are likely to be activated.

Politics and the organizational life span. The conditions leading to political activities are likely to differ as a function of the stage of an organization's life. Hence, contrasting degrees and types of political activity are expected. Organizations can be distinguished as those that are just being started by entrepreneurs (the *birth* and *early growth* stage), those that are fully developed (the *maturity* stage), and those that face decline and dissolution (the *decline* or *redevelopment* stage). As Gray and Ariss explain, different types of political activity are likely to occur during these various stages of an organization's life.[71]

When an organization is newly formed, it may have little or no structure and be guided by the philosophy of the founder. During this stage, the entrepreneur gains political power by presenting his or her ideas as rational to the employees, who accept this person's image of the corporate mission. The founder usually has complete access to information and makes decisions based on his or her own values. Explaining these decisions to subordinates is a way of inculcating these values in others in the organization, and thereby exercising power over them. Political activity is not particularly likely during this stage.

However, as organizations mature and become more complex, they tend to grow and to departmentalize, creating conditions in which the vested interests of different groups are likely to conflict. Political means may be used to gain an advantage in such a situation. Indeed, it is likely that the full range of political activities noted earlier will be employed when organizations are mature (e.g., forming coalitions, using information). It is particularly interesting to note that when organizations begin to decline, subunits may be quite insecure and the need for political action may be great as people and groups compete for the power to control (and perhaps turn around) the organization. A period of decline reflects a time of great uncertainty, and thus a period in which political activity is likely to be quite intense. For example, Hannan and Freeman found that staff members employed in school districts experiencing declining enrollments tended to have more intense competitive interactions and were at odds with each other more than members of similar organizations during periods of growth.[72] Clearly, the use of political practices in an organization is likely to be affected by its degree of maturity.

Organizational Politics: Where in the Organization Does It Occur?

Although organizational politics is widespread, political activity is not equally likely to occur throughout all parts of organizations.[73] Specifically, a survey by Gandz and Murray found that the most likely areas of political activity were those in which clear policies were nonexistent or lacking, such as interdepartmental coordination, promotions and transfers, and delegation of authority.[74] However, when it came to organizational activities that had clearly defined rules and regulations, such as hiring and disciplinary policies, political activities were lowest.

A survey of organizational political practices by Allen and his associates revealed similar findings.[75] Specifically, organizational politics was perceived to be greatest in subunits that followed poorly defined policies (such as boards of directors and members of the marketing staff), whereas political activity was perceived to be lowest in areas in which clearly defined policies existed (such as production and accounting). Similarly, because of the inherently high levels of ambiguity associated with human resource management tasks (such as personnel selection and performance appraisal), political behaviour is likely to occur when these functions are being performed.[76] Together, these findings help make an important point: *Political activity is likely to occur in the face of ambiguity.* When there are clear-cut rules about what to do, it is unlikely that people will be able to abuse their power by taking political action. However, when people face highly novel and ambiguous situations in which the rules guiding them are unclear, it is easy to imagine how political behaviour results.

Where in the organization is the political climate most active? In other words, at what organizational levels do people believe the most political activities are likely to occur? As shown in Figure 12-9, Gandz and Murray found that organizations were perceived as more political at the higher levels and less political at the lower managerial and nonmanagerial levels of the organization.[77] Apparently, politics is most likely to occur at the top, where, of course, the stakes are highest and power may corrupt.

Political Behaviour: Is It Ethical?

Probably one of the most important effects of organizational power is that it invites corruption. Indeed, the more power an individual has at his or her disposal, the more tempted that person is to use that power toward some immoral or unethical purpose.[78] Obviously, then, the potential is quite real for powerful individuals and organizations to abuse their power and to behave unethically. Because such behaviours are negatively regarded, the most politically astute individuals—including politicians themselves—often attempt to present themselves in a highly ethical manner.

FIGURE 12-9 Organizational Politics: More Likely at the Top

Survey research has shown that employees believe political activity is more likely to occur at higher organizational levels (where the guiding rules are more ambiguous and the stakes are higher) than at lower levels.

(Source: Based on data reported by Gandz & Murray, 1980; see Note 74.)

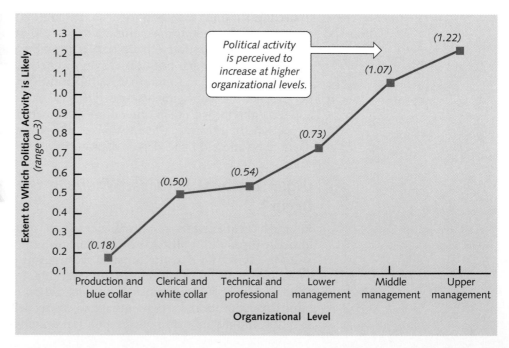

Unfortunately, the potential to behave unethically is too frequently realized. Consider, for example, how greed overtook concerns about human welfare when the Manville Corporation suppressed evidence that asbestos inhalation was killing its employees, or when Ford failed to correct a known defect that made its Pinto vulnerable to gas tank explosions following low-speed rear-end collisions.[79] Companies that dump dangerous medical waste materials into our rivers and oceans also appear to favour their own interests over public safety and welfare. Although these examples are better known than many others, they do not appear to be unusual. In fact, the story they tell may be far more typical than we would like; one expert estimates that about two-thirds of the 500 largest American corporations have been involved in one form of illegal behaviour or another.[80] Given the scope of the problems associated with unethical organizational behaviours, we will focus on the ethical aspects of politics in this final section of this chapter.

☞ *Political behaviour is just one of several forms of organizational behaviour that may be of dubious ethical value. Others are identified in Chapter 2.*

Although there are no clear-cut ways to identify whether a certain organizational action is ethical, Velasquez and his associates suggest some useful guidelines.[81] For a summary of the central questions associated with assessing the ethics of political behaviour, see Figure 12-10.

As a first consideration, we may ask: Will the political tactics promote purely selfish interests, or will they also help meet organizational goals? If only one's personal, selfish interests are nurtured by a political action, it may be considered unethical. Usually, political activity fails to benefit organizational goals, but not always. Suppose, for example, that a group of top corporate executives is consistently making bad decisions that are leading the organization down the road to ruin. Would it be unethical in such a case to use political tactics to try to remove the power holders from their positions? Probably not. In fact, political actions designed to benefit the organization

FIGURE 12-10 Guidelines for Determining Ethical Action

Although assessing the ethicality of a behaviour is a complex matter, answers to the three questions shown here can provide a good indication. This flowchart shows the path that must be taken to achieve ethical action.

(Source: Based on suggestions by Velasquez, Moberg, & Cavanaugh, 1983; see Note 81.)

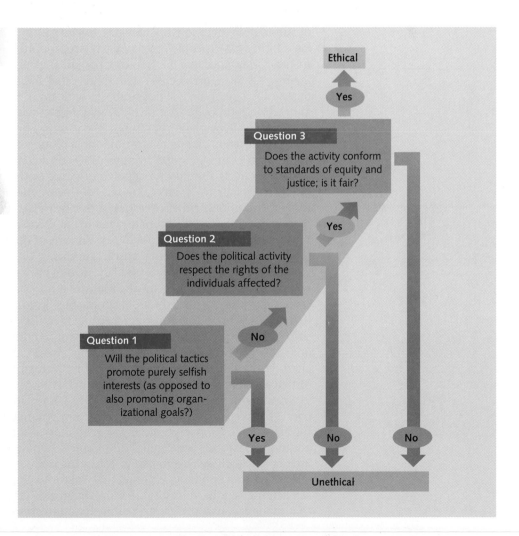

as a whole (as long as they are legal) may be justified as appropriate and highly ethical. After all, they are in the best interest of the entire organization.

A second question in considering the ethics of organizational politics is this: Does the political activity respect the rights of the individuals affected? Generally speaking, actions that violate basic human rights are, of course, considered unethical. For example, dirty political tricks that rely on espionage techniques (such as wiretapping) are not only illegal, but also unethical in that they violate the affected individual's *right to privacy*. However, as you may know, police agencies are sometimes permitted by law to use methods that violate privacy rights under circumstances in which the greater good of the community at large is at stake. It is not easy, of course, to weigh the relative benefits of an individual's right to privacy against the greater societal good. Indeed, making such decisions involves a potential misuse of power in itself. It is because of this that society often entrusts such decisions to high courts charged with the responsibility for considering both individual rights and the rights and benefits of the community at large.

Velasquez and his associates also identified a third consideration in assessing the ethics of political action: Does the activity conform to standards of equity and justice; is it fair? Any political behaviour that unfairly benefits one party over another may be considered unethical. Paying one person more than another similarly qualified person is one example. Standards regarding the fair treatment of individuals are often unclear. Not surprisingly, more powerful individuals often use their power to convince others (and themselves) that they are taking action in the name of justice. That is, they seek to implement seemingly fair rules that benefit themselves at the expense of others.[82] This, of course, represents an abuse of power.

However, we must sometimes consider instances in which violating standards of justice may be considered appropriate. For example, it has been found that managers may sometimes give poorly performing employees higher pay than they deserve in the hope of stimulating them to work at higher levels.[83] Although the principle of equity is violated in this case (people should be paid in proportion to their job contributions), the manager may argue that the employee and the organization benefit as a result. Of course, the result may be considered unfair to the other individuals who are not so generously treated. Obviously, we will not be able to settle this complex issue here. Our point is that although ethical behaviour involves adhering to standards of justice, there may be instances in which violations of these standards may be considered ethically acceptable.

As you can probably tell by now, most matters involving the resolution of moral and ethical issues are quite complex. Each time a political strategy is considered, its potential effects should be evaluated in terms of the questions outlined here. If the practice appears to be ethical based on these considerations, it may be acceptable in that situation. If ethical questions arise, however, alternative actions should be seriously considered. Unfortunately, many unethical political practices are followed in organizations despite their obvious violations of moral standards. We will now consider some of the underlying reasons for this.

More than 1000 professionals in the field of human resources management were surveyed concerning their feelings about the ethics of various managerial practices.[84] Interestingly, among the ethical situations considered most serious were several practices that dealt with political activities reflecting an abuse of power. These included practices such as "making personnel decisions based on favouritism instead of job performance," and "basing differences in pay on friendship." In fact, these were the two most frequently cited types of unethical situations faced by human resource managers (with almost 31 percent of the sample indicating that each was among *the* most serious violations).

Another type of unethical political behaviour (indicated as being most serious by over 23 percent of the sample) was "making arrangements with vendors or consulting agencies leading to personal gain." As shown in Figure 12-11, these actions are in addition to various other types of unethical behaviour that represent bias, but that are not so clearly self-serving as to constitute political acts.

Given that so many critical ethics violations appear to be politically motivated, self-serving actions, it is not surprising that these happened to be the very behaviours that managers had the greatest difficulty addressing. In fact, only about half of the

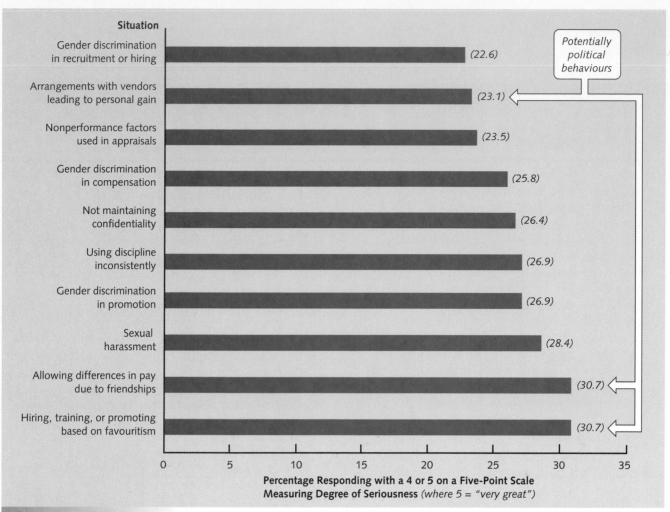

Situation

Gender discrimination in recruitment or hiring	(22.6)
Arrangements with vendors leading to personal gain	(23.1)
Nonperformance factors used in appraisals	(23.5)
Gender discrimination in compensation	(25.8)
Not maintaining confidentiality	(26.4)
Using discipline inconsistently	(26.9)
Gender discrimination in promotion	(26.9)
Sexual harassment	(28.4)
Allowing differences in pay due to friendships	(30.7)
Hiring, training, or promoting based on favouritism	(30.7)

Potentially political behaviours

Percentage Responding with a 4 or 5 on a Five-Point Scale
Measuring Degree of Seriousness *(where 5 = "very great")*

FIGURE 12-11 Political Antics Top the "Most Unethical List": Survey Results

Among the most widely reported sources of unethical behaviours noted in a survey of human resources managers are those dealing with *political behaviours*—actions that benefit oneself as opposed to the organization.

(Source: Based on data reported by the Commerce Clearing House, 1991; see Note 84.)

managers surveyed reported having any success in minimizing a problem such as hiring based on favouritism. The very fact that such behaviours benefit oneself makes them difficult to eliminate. In contrast, it is easier to combat unethical behaviours based on insensitivity (e.g., lack of attention to privacy) because these serve no beneficial functions for the person doing the violating.

Managers tend to be relatively unaware of the political biases underlying their unethical actions, however. Instead, they attribute their actions to the attitudes and behaviours of senior management. Specifically, whereas only 10 percent of the participants attributed unethical behaviours to political pressures, 56 percent attributed unethical behaviours to the attitudes and behaviours of senior management. They blamed top management most frequently for instances of unethical behaviour, but they also recognized that top management of organizations tends to be committed to ethical conduct. Despite such commitment, company officials often overlook the capacity of human resources managers to help promote their company's ethical values. Too often, they tend to concentrate on using human resources managers for maintaining up-to-date legal information about personnel matters. But, ethics goes well beyond mere compliance with the law, and society expects companies to go well beyond the ethical minimums. For these reasons—not to mention the long-term success of companies themselves—it is essential for human resource officials to help institute policies that encourage basing personnel-related decisions on job performance instead of favouritism. In view of the potential problems that may arise in organizations in which the amount of political activity is high, it is necessary to consider ways of curbing such behaviour. For a look at several ways of doing so, see the **THE QUEST FOR QUALITY** section.

Coping with Organizational Politics: Some Techniques

Given how fundamental the need for power appears to be among people, and how differences in power among employees are basic to organizations, it is safe to say that organizational politics is inevitable. This is not good news, however, as many of the effects of organizational politics are quite negative. Indeed, lowered corporate morale and diversion from key organizational goals (as employees pay closer attention to planning their attacks on others than to doing their jobs) are expected to result from political activity. The more organizational politics is recognized as going on, the less trust and more alienation people are likely to feel.[85] And this can only threaten the quality of organizational performance.[86]

In view of this, managers must consider ways to minimize the effects of political behaviour. Although it may be impossible to abolish organizational politics, managers can do several things to limit its effects.

1. **Clarify job expectations**. You will recall that political behaviour is nurtured by highly ambiguous conditions. To the extent that managers help reduce uncertainty, they can minimize the likelihood of political behaviour. For example, managers should give very clear, well-defined work assignments. They should also clearly explain how work will be evaluated. Employees who know precisely what they are supposed to do and what level of performance is acceptable will find political games to assert their power unnecessary. Under such conditions, recognition will come from meeting job expectations, instead of from less acceptable avenues.

2. **Open the communication process**. People have difficulty trying to foster their own goals at the expense of organizational goals when the communication process is open to scrutiny by all. Compare, for example, a department manager who makes budget allocation decisions in a highly open fashion (announced to all) and one who makes the same decisions in secret. When decisions are not openly shared and communicated to all, conditions are ideal for unscrupulous individuals to abuse their power. Decisions that can be monitored by all are unlikely to allow any one individual to gain excessive control over desired resources.

3. **Be a good role model.** It is well established that higher-level personnel set the standards by which lower-level employees operate. As a result, managers who are openly political in their use of power are likely to create a climate in which their subordinates behave the same way. Engaging in dirty political tricks teaches subordinates not only that such tactics are appropriate, but also that they are the desired way of operating within the organization. Managers will certainly find it difficult to constrain the political actions of their subordinates unless they set a clear example of honest and reasonable treatment of others in their own behaviour.

4. **Do not turn a blind eye to game players**. Suppose you see one of your subordinates attempting to gain power over another by taking credit for that individual's work. Immediately confront this individual and do not ignore what he did. If the person believes he can get away with it, he will try to do so. What's worse, if he suspects that you are aware of what he did but didn't do anything about it, you are indirectly reinforcing his unethical political behaviour—showing him that he can get away with it.

In conclusion, it is important for practising managers to realize that because power differences are basic to organizations, attempts to gain power advantages through political manoeuvres are to be expected. However, a critical aspect of a manager's job is to redirect these political activities away from any threats to the integrity of the organization. Although expecting to eliminate dirty political tricks would be unrealistic, we believe the suggestions offered here provide some useful guidelines for minimizing their impact.

SUMMARY AND REVIEW

Social Influence

When someone attempts to affect another in a desired fashion, that person is said to be using **social influence**. People generally prefer to use open, consultative forms of influence (e.g., rational persuasion, inspirational appeal) rather than coercive methods (e.g., pressure, coalition building).

Individual Power

The concept of **power** refers to the capacity to change the behaviour or attitudes of others in a desired manner. One major type of power, known as **position power**, resides within one's formal organizational position. It includes: (1) **reward power** and (2) **coercive power,** the capacity to control valued rewards and punishments, respectively; (3), **legitimate power**, the recognized authority that an individual has by virtue of his or her organizational position; and (4) **information power**, the power that stems from having special data and knowledge.

Another major type of power, known as **personal power**, resides within an individual's own unique qualities or characteristics. It includes: (1) **rational persuasion**, using logical arguments and factual evidence to convince others that an idea is acceptable; (2) **expert power**, the power an individual has because he or she is recognized as having some superior knowledge, skill, or expertise; (3) **referent power**, influence based on the fact that an individual is admired by others; and (4) **charisma**, having an engaging and magnetic personality.

Research has shown that differences in the use of power depend on the specific situations faced (e.g., facing others who have counterpower). For example, people tend to use rational persuasion when communicating with superiors.

There has been a recent trend toward **empowerment**, the shifting of power away from managers and into the hands of subordinates. Empowerment occurs in varying degrees in different organizations.

Group or Subunit Power

Power also may reside within work groups, or subunits. The **resource-dependency model** asserts that power resides within the subunits that control the greatest share of valued organizational resources.

The **strategic contingencies model** explains power in terms of a subunit's capacity to control the activities of other subunits. Such power may be enhanced by the capacity to reduce the level of uncertainty experienced by another unit, having a central position within the organization, or performing functions that other units cannot perform.

Organizational Politics

Behaving in a manner that is not officially approved by an organization to meet one's own goals by influencing others is known as **organizational politics**. Political tactics may include blaming and attacking others, controlling access to information, cultivating a favourable impression, developing an internal base of support, and aligning oneself with more powerful others. This may involve the playing of political games, such as asserting one's authority, enhancing one's power base, attacking one's rivals, and trying to foster organizational change.

Such activities typically occur under ambiguous conditions (such as in areas of organizational functioning in which clear rules are lacking). Furthermore, politics is likely to occur under conditions in which organizational uncertainty exists, important decisions involving large amounts of scarce resources are made, and the groups involved have conflicting interests but are approximately equal in power. Specifically, political activity is expected to be high when it comes to matters of human resource management and during an organization's mature and declining stages of development (as opposed to its early stage).

Although there are exceptions, political behaviour may be considered ethical to the extent that it fosters organizational interests over individual greed, respects the rights of individuals, and conforms to prevailing standards of justice and fair play. The effects of organizational politics can be limited by practices such as clarifying job expectations, opening the communication process, being a good role model, and not turning a blind eye to game players.

CASE PREVIEW QUESTIONS FOR DISCUSSION

1. How did Bill Hopper's skill in organizational politics help him to attain his position at PetroCan and support his lifestyle?

2. Using the Guidelines for Determining Ethical Action (see Figure 12-10), discuss Hopper's rise to power and fall from grace at PetroCan.

3. Identify Hopper's power bases and the use he made of each.

CHAPTER QUESTIONS FOR DISCUSSION

1. Suppose your professor asks you to redo a homework assignment. Explain the various bases of individual social power he or she may use to influence your behaviour in this situation.

2. Using the resource-dependency model and the strategic contingencies model as the basis for your analysis, describe the relative power differences between groups in any organization with which you are familiar.

3. Describe the political tactics and tricks that one person may use to gain a power advantage over another in an organization.

4. Suppose you're the manager of a human resources department. Are political activities more likely or less likely to take place in your department compared to other departments? Why? What form might these actions be expected to take?

5. Argue for or against this statement: "The use of power in organizations is unethical."

6. Although it might not be possible to completely eliminate organizational politics, it might be possible to manage political activity effectively. Describe some of the things that can be done to cope with organizational politics.

Chrysler's Battle for the Boardroom

Few companies have undergone the roller coaster ride that Chrysler has endured during the past two decades. Although twice on the brink of bankruptcy, the venerable automaker became the most profitable of the old "Big Three" automakers. The pressure to keep the company healthy has been understandably intense at times, and everyone has had a different idea about how to go about it. As Chrysler and Daimler-Benz work through the challenges presented by their alliance, announced in 1998, it is interesting to reflect on some of Chrysler's recent history.

Chrysler faced a battle in the early-to-mid 1990s. In the challenger's corner was Las Vegas billionaire Kirk Kerkorian, a corporate raider who owned 9.2 percent of Chrysler's stock. The defender was Chrysler Chairman and CEO Robert J. Eaton, who took over that post in 1992 from Lee Iacocca. Kerkorian's press for control of Chrysler was based on several complaints about Eaton. Claiming he was too bland and indecisive to do the job, and too conservative in his approach to money and expansion into foreign markets, Kerkorian launched a campaign that would land him in Eaton's seat. However, showing that he was not exactly the pushover that Kerkorian made him out to be, Eaton successfully quashed Kerkorian's 1995 U.S.$20.5-billion takeover bid.

Eaton may lack Iacocca's dynamic personality, but he has gained a great deal of support within Chrysler with his warm and unassuming manner. To his credit, soon after taking over as chairman, Eaton built a strong alliance with then-president Robert A. Lutz—this, despite some disappointment on Lutz's part over being passed up for Iacocca's job. Indeed, Eaton and Lutz formed an impressive team that led Chrysler down the road to success. Successful products earned the company high marks with both the buying public and the automotive press. On the strength of such success, Chrysler increased its market share. Eaton had merely to point to results like these to defend himself successfully against Kerkorian, or any other power-hungry foes.

Eaton's admirers have welcomed his open approach to company matters. Witness, for example, Eaton's practice of sharing with top executives reports of talks within the corporate boardroom, a domain with a long history of secretiveness. Also, in contrast to Iacocca's more heavy-handed style, Eaton has not ordered changes within the company but, instead, has suggested them. Eaton has tended to see himself as the coach of a team, along with the company's president, chief financial officer, and administrative officer.

Shifting to this orientation took some doing, but Eaton did it up right: He hosted a retreat for top brass during which he introduced ways of empowering them to do their jobs better. Symbolizing his interest in egalitarianism, Eaton personally greeted the execs as they drove up to the resort, and carried their bags out of their cars for them. Is this any way for a major corporate leader to act? If you're Robert J. Eaton the answer is "definitely, yes."[87]

Eaton is now taking his particular style of leadership to Europe with the merger of Chrysler and Daimler-Benz AG. The automotive behemoth that will result, DaimlerChrysler AG, will be co-led until 2002 by Eaton and Daimler's Jürgen E. Schrempp. This shared governance will offer new leadership challenges for Eaton and his colleagues.[88] Eaton's previous European experience as president of GM Europe before he joined Chrysler will serve him well as DaimlerChrysler's new culture evolves. "Culture clash is the biggest worry. The tone will be set at the top."[89] Eaton and Schrempp have been described as "polar opposites—Eaton is buttoned up, while Schrempp overflows with energy—but their companies fit together like yin and yang." It remains to be seen how well the power of yin and yang mesh in their leadership.[90]

Critical Thinking Questions

1. What political tactics did Eaton use to defend himself against Kerkorian?

2. What bases of individual power does Eaton appear to have at his disposal in his encounters with Kerkorian?

3. Speculate on the "power and politics" issues that faced Eaton and Schrempp as they formed DaimlerChrysler.

Chrysler Canada Ltd.
www.chryslercanada.ca

SKILLS PORTFOLIO

Experiencing Organizational Behaviour **What Kinds of Power Does Your Supervisor Use?**

One of the main ways of learning about social influence in organizations is to use questionnaires in which people are asked to describe the behaviours of their superiors. If a consistent pattern emerges with respect to the way subordinates describe superiors, some very strong clues are provided as to the nature of that superior's influence style. Questionnaires similar to this one are used for this purpose (Schriesheim & Hinkin, 1990; see Note 20). Complete this questionnaire to gain some indication of the types of social influence favoured by your supervisor.

Directions

Indicate how strongly you agree or disagree with each of the following statements as it describes your immediate supervisor. Answer by using the following scale: 1 = strongly disagree; 2 = disagree; 3 = neither agree nor disagree; 4 = agree; 5 = strongly agree. For each statement select the number corresponding to the most appropriate response.

My supervisor can:

____ **1.** Recommend that I receive a raise.
____ **2.** Assign me to jobs I dislike.
____ **3.** See that I get the promotion I desire.
____ **4.** Make my life at work completely unbearable.
____ **5.** Make decisions about how things are done.
____ **6.** Provide useful advice on how to do my job better.
____ **7.** Comprehend the importance of doing things a certain way.
____ **8.** Make me want to look up to him or her.
____ **9.** Share with me the benefit of his or her vast job knowledge.
____ **10.** Get me to admire what he or she stands for.
____ **11.** Find out things that nobody else knows.
____ **12.** Explain things so logically that I want to do them.
____ **13.** Have access to vital data about the company.
____ **14.** Share a clear vision of what the future holds for the company.
____ **15.** Come up with the facts needed to make a convincing case about something.
____ **16.** Put me in a trance when he or she communicates to me.

Scoring

1. Add the numbers assigned to statements 1 and 3. This is the *reward power* score.
2. Add the numbers assigned to statements 2 and 4. This is the *coercive power* score.
3. Add the numbers assigned to statements 5 and 7. This is the *legitimate power* score.
4. Add the numbers assigned to statements 6 and 9. This is the *expert power* score.
5. Add the numbers assigned to statements 8 and 10. This is the *referent power* score.
6. Add the numbers assigned to statements 11 and 13. This is the *information power* score.
7. Add the numbers assigned to statements 12 and 15. This is the *rational persuasion* score.
8. Add the numbers assigned to statements 14 and 16. This is the *charisma* score.

Questions for Discussion

1. With respect to which dimensions did your supervisor score highest and lowest? Are these consistent with what you would have predicted in advance?
2. Does your supervisor behave in ways consistent with the dimension along which you gave him or her the highest score? In other words, does he or she fit the description given in the text?
3. How do you think your own subordinates would answer the various questions with respect to yourself?
4. Which of the eight forms of social influence do you think are most common and least common, and why?

Working in Groups

Recognizing Organizational Politics When You See It

A good way to make sure you understand organizational politics is to practise enacting different political tactics and to attempt to recognize these tactics portrayed by others. This exercise is designed with these objectives in mind. The more practised you are at recognizing political activity when you see it, the better equipped you may be to defend yourself against political adversaries.

Directions

1. Divide the class into groups of approximately four students each.
2. Each group should select at random one of the six major political tactics described on pages 381–383, including any of the political games listed in Table 12-2.
3. Meeting together for about 30 minutes, each group should prepare a brief skit in which the four members enact the particular political tactic selected. These should be as realistic as possible and not written simply to broadcast the answer. That is, the tactic should be presented much as you would expect to see it used in a real organization.

4. Each group should take a turn presenting its skit to the class. Feel free to announce the setting or context in which your portrayal is supposed to occur. Don't worry about giving an award-winning performance; it's okay to keep a script or set of notes in your hand. The important thing is that you attempt to depict the political tactic in a realistic manner.

5. After each group presents its skit, members of the class should attempt to identify the specific political tactic depicted. This should lead to a discussion of the clues that suggested that answer and additional things that could have been done to depict the particular tactic portrayed.

Questions for Discussion

1. How successful was the class in identifying the various political tactics portrayed? Were some tactics more difficult to portray than others?
2. Based on these portrayals, which tactics do you believe are most likely to be used in organizations, and under what circumstances?
3. Which political tactics do you believe are most negative? Why?
4. Using the suggestions in the **QUEST FOR QUALITY** section (p. 390) as a head start, what steps can be taken to combat the effects of the most negative political tactics?

TAKE IT TO THE NET

Prentice Hall

COMPANION WEBSITE

We invite you to visit the *Greenberg/Baron/Sales/Owen Companion Website* at *www.prenticehall.ca/greenberg* for this chapter's Internet resources.

CHAPTER 13
Leadership:
Its Nature and Impact in Organizations

LEARNING OBJECTIVES

After reading this chapter you should be able to:

1. Define *leadership* and indicate why leading and managing are not the same.

2. Describe traits that distinguish leaders from other people.

3. Describe various forms of participative and autocratic leader behaviour.

4. Distinguish between the two basic forms of leader behaviour: *person-oriented* behaviour and *production-oriented* behaviour.

5. Explain what the *leader-member exchange (LMX) model* says about the relationships between leaders and followers.

6. Describe the role of *attribution* in the leadership process.

7. Describe the nature of *charismatic* leadership and how it compares to *transformational* leadership.

8. Appreciate the special considerations involved in leading teams.

9. Explain the general nature of *contingency theories* of leader effectiveness.

10. Summarize the basic nature of five different contingency theories: *LPC contingency theory*, *situational leadership theory*, *path-goal theory*, *normative decision theory*, and the *substitutes for leadership framework*.

Maureen Kempston Darkes: A New Kind of Auto Exec

A lawyer running General Motors of Canada!? Maureen Kempston Darkes (see Figure 13-1) is a far cry from the traditional "boys' club" image of the automobile industry. Yet make no mistake, Kempston Darkes is nothing if not a company person. "We're talking pit bull here. When she's on a cause for GM, she will not let go."[1]

Maureen Kempston Darkes' loyalty to GM is deep and stems from her long association with the company. She was hired by GM in 1975 and was appointed GM Canada's first female president in 1994. (*The Globe and Mail Report on Business Magazine* ranked Maureen Kempston Darkes as number 1 on its list of the most powerful Canadian CEOs in 1998. See Chapter 12.)

Kempston Darkes grew up in Toronto. Educated at the University of Toronto, she received a B.A. in history and later a law degree. Kempston Darkes has certainly proven herself in a variety of jobs, including positions in a law firm for a year, with GM's legal staff (specializing in tax), in New York at GM's treasury office, as head of GM Canada's public affairs branch in Oshawa, as vice-president of corporate affairs, and as a director of GM Canada.[2]

Her focus as president of General Motors of Canada Ltd. is marketing. Kempston Darkes makes it clear that "Everything we do will be focused on the customer."[3] For advice on how to handle marketing challenges, Kempston Darkes turns to her management team at "The Swamp," GM Canada's Oshawa headquarters, which is located in wetlands.[4]

Kempston Darkes has earned her way to the top. She has a reputation as a capable administrator, "a bookish intellectual who admits she works until she doesn't know what time of day it is. 'She's probably the most thoroughly prepared auto executive I've ever met,' says industry analyst Dennis DesRosiers."[5] Her commitment to hard work will stand her in good stead as the company strives to implement its Vision 2000 plan, aimed at improving customer satisfaction.[6]

And what does she do for fun on her days off? Kempston Darkes and her husband Larry (also a lawyer) happily climb into their pickup truck and head for their log cabin in the Haliburton Highlands.[7]

While Kempston Darkes did not set out to be a role model for other women, she does hope that her success will make it easier for others to get ahead, and she has "helped form a company advisory council that visits area schools urging young women to study math and science and pursue non-traditional careers."[8]

Her interest in diversity is significant. Kempston Darkes is committed to having GM Canada maximize the contributions of minority groups of all kinds. Her aim is to develop diversity in the company "that reflects the makeup of the outside world. 'I think diversity is a major strength in a corporation. We have to establish real opportunities for women and others, and that's a culture issue.'"[9] Kempston Darkes believes that "It's good to have different ways of thinking. It's good to have people challenging traditional systems. It can only make everyone grow stronger."[10]

Kempston Darkes certainly does not fit into the stereotypical big business president mould—in more ways than just gender. Her office at GM

FIGURE 13-1 The Qualities of a Successful Leader

Maureen Kempston Darkes, a lawyer by training, was appointed president of General Motors of Canada Ltd. in 1994. She has a reputation as a capable administrator, a "pit bull" when it comes to a cause for General Motors, a firm believer in the strategic advantage of diversity in the workplace, and a "real person."[11]

Canada's headquarters is sparse. Actually, she does not have an office at all, just a desk with a private meeting space nearby. Her friend, Anne Fawcett, a professional CEO recruiter, describes Kempston Darkes as being firmly "connected to the real world. She's about the most real person I've met in the senior executive role."[12]

General Motors of Canada
www.gm.com

Very few people in business in Canada have been as successful as Maureen Kempston Darkes, and few have achieved such a powerful position from which to touch the lives of so many people. Why was she chosen as the successor to George Peaples at General Motors of Canada? Was it because she was a woman? Was it because she was a Canadian? Or was it because she was seen as the best person to lead the company into the twenty-first century? She would certainly hope it was this last.

If you asked 100 executives to name the single most important factor in determining organizational success, chances are good that many would reply "effective leadership." This answer reflects the general belief in the world of business that *leadership* is a key ingredient in corporate effectiveness. And this view is by no means restricted to organizations; leadership also plays a central role in politics, sports, and many other human activities.

Is this view justified? Do leaders really play such a crucial role in shaping the fortunes of organizations? Almost a century of research on this topic suggests that they do.[13] Effective leadership, it appears, is indeed a key factor in organizational success.[14] Given this fact and its relevance to the field of organizational behaviour, it seems appropriate for us to consider the topic of leadership in some detail. In this chapter, therefore, we will summarize current information about this complex process. One review of research on leadership published a few years ago cited more than 10 000 separate articles and books on this topic.[15] Not surprisingly, leadership is considered the most studied concept in the social sciences.[16]

Obviously, there is quite a lot of ground to cover. To make the task of summarizing this wealth of information more manageable, we will proceed as follows. First, we will consider some basic points about leadership—what it is and why being a leader is not necessarily synonymous with being a manager. Second, we will examine views of leadership focusing on the traits of leaders and on their behaviours. Third, we will examine several major theories of leadership that focus on the relationship between leaders and their followers. Finally we will review several contrasting theories dealing with the conditions under which leaders are effective or ineffective in their important role.

Leadership: Its Basic Nature

In a sense, *leadership* resembles love: It is something most people believe they can recognize but often find difficult to define. What, precisely, is it? And how does being a leader differ from being a manager? We will now focus on these questions.

Leadership: A Working Definition

Imagine that you have accepted a new job and entered a new work group. How would you recognize its *leader*? One possibility, of course, is through the formal titles and assigned roles each person in the group holds. In short, the individual designated as department head or project manager would be the one you would identify as the group's leader. But imagine that during several staff meetings, you noticed that this person was really not the most influential. Although she or he held the formal authority, these meetings were actually dominated by another person, who, ostensibly, was the top person's subordinate. What would you conclude about leadership then? Probably that the real leader of the group was the person who actually ran things—not the one with the fancy title and the apparent authority.

In many cases, of course, the disparity we have just described does not exist. The individual possessing the greatest amount of formal authority is also the most influential. In some situations, however, this is not so. And in such cases, we typically identify the person who actually exercises the most influence over the group as its leader. These facts point to the following working definition of leadership—one accepted by many experts on this topic: **Leadership** is the process whereby one individual influences other group members toward the attainment of defined group or organizational goals.[17]

leadership The process whereby one individual influences other group members toward the attainment of defined group or organizational goals.

Note that according to this definition, leadership is primarily a process involving influence—one in which a leader changes the actions or attitudes of several group members or subordinates. As we saw in Chapter 12, many techniques for exerting such influence exist, ranging from relatively coercive ones—the recipient has little choice but to do what is requested—to relatively noncoercive ones—the recipient can choose to accept or reject the influence offered. In general, leadership refers to the use of relatively noncoercive influence techniques. This characteristic distinguishes a leader from a *dictator*. Whereas dictators get others to do what they want by using physical coercion or by threats of physical force, leaders do not.[18] As Mao Zedong (founder of the People's Republic of China) put it, "Power grows out of the barrel of a gun." This may be true with respect to the power of dictators but *not* the power of leaders. The point is that leadership rests, at least in part, on positive feelings between leaders and their subordinates. In other words, subordinates accept influence from leaders because they respect, like, or admire them—not simply because they hold positions of formal authority.[19]

Our definition also suggests that leadership involves the exercise of influence for a purpose—to attain defined group or organizational goals. In other words, leaders focus on altering those actions or attitudes of their subordinates that are related to specific goals; they are far less concerned with altering actions or attitudes that are irrelevant to such goals.

Finally, note that our definition, by emphasizing the central role of influence, implies that leadership is really something of a two-way street. Although leaders do indeed influence subordinates in various ways, leaders are also influenced by their subordinates. In fact, it may be said that leadership exists only in relation to followers. After all, one cannot lead without followers.

Leaders versus Managers: A Key Distinction

In everyday speech, the terms *leader* and *manager* are often used almost interchangeably. Although we understand the temptation to do so, the two terms need to be clearly distinguished. According to Kotter, the primary function of a **leader** is to create the essential purpose or mission of an organization and the strategy for attaining it. By contrast, the job of the *manager* is to implement that vision. He or she is the means of achieving the end, the vision created by the leader. Thus, whereas management is about coping with complexity, leadership is about coping with change. Specifically, managers create plans and monitor results relative to those plans. However, leaders establish direction by creating a vision of the future. Effective leaders then get people to buy into their vision and to go along with it (see Figure 13-2).[20]

leader An individual whose primary function is to create the essential purpose of an organization and the strategy for attaining it.

The confusion between these two terms rests in the fact that the distinction between establishing a mission and implementing it is often blurred in practice. This is because many leaders, such as top corporate executives, are frequently called upon not only to create a vision but also to help implement it. Similarly, managers are often required to lead those who are subordinate to them while at the same time carrying out their leader's mission. Kotter has observed that good leadership is not as common as it should be. Too many so-called leaders get bogged down in the managerial aspects of their job, creating organizations that are overmanaged and underled.

FIGURE 13-2 Leaders and Managers: Distinguishing Their Roles

Whereas *leaders* are primarily responsible for establishing an organizational mission and formulating a strategy for implementing it, *managers* are responsible for the actual implementation of that strategy. In many cases, however, these distinctions are blurred in actual practice.

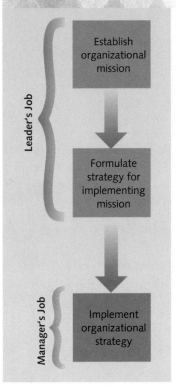

In summary, although some managers are indeed leaders, others are not, making no clear link between these two roles. For this reason, we will distinguish carefully between these two terms throughout this chapter.

Canada's Most Respected Corporations and Their Leaders

In an April 1998 survey, 301 CEOs in Canada rated Canadian corporations in terms of people management, corporate responsibility, innovation, financial performance, and investment value. (See Table 13-1 for the top ten Canadian corporations and their CEOs in the people management and corporate responsibility categories.) The top ranking corporation in all categories except innovation was the Royal Bank of Canada. (For a closer look at John Cleghorn and his leadership of the Royal Bank, see **THE QUEST FOR QUALITY** feature for this chapter.) Not surprisingly, and consistent with their ratings, the 301 CEOs identified that the "most serious issue facing business today" was international competitiveness. The Canadian corporations that were ranked the highest in the survey were companies supplying "products or services with a global market ... Respect is no longer a matter of bowing to some outdated notion of noblesse oblige. CEOs who run these companies must earn admiration of employees, communities, shareholders, and directors if they want their corporations to succeed."[21]

Leader Traits and Behaviours

At one time or another, most people have daydreams about being a leader. They fantasize about taking charge of large groups and being viewed with great awe and respect. Despite the prevalence of such daydreams, however, relatively few individuals convert them into reality by becoming leaders. Further, among these, only a small proportion are considered effective in this role. This fact raises an intriguing question: What sets effective leaders apart from most others? Why, in short, do some people, but not others, become effective leaders? Many answers have been proposed, but two have received the most attention. These perspectives suggest, respectively, that effective leadership is largely a function of either the traits possessed by individuals or the patterns of behaviour they demonstrate.[22]

TABLE 13-1 The Canadian Corporations Most Respected for People Management and Corporate Responsibility

These Canadian corporations and CEOs are recognized by their peers both for their people management skills and their level of corporate responsibility.

Source: Smith (1998); see Note 23.

Company	CEO	People Management Rank	Corporate Responsibility Rank
Royal Bank	John Cleghorn	1	1
Bank of Montreal	Matthew Barrett	2	2
Magna International	Donald Walker	3	10
Northern Telecom	John Roth	4	7
Bombardier Inc.	Laurent Beaudoin	5	*
Dofasco Inc.	John Mayberry	6	*
BCE Inc.	Lynton Wilson	7	3
Cascades Inc.	Laurent Lemaire	8	*
IBM Canada	John Wetmore	9	*
Imperial Oil	R. B. Peterson	10	5

Note: * Denotes the fact that these companies were not ranked in the top ten for corporate responsibility. CIBC, Noranda Inc., Alcan Aluminum Ltd., and DuPont Canada were ranked fourth, sixth, eighth, and ninth respectively on corporate responsibility but were not ranked in the top ten on people management.

Imperial Oil Limited
www.imperialoil.ca

John Cleghorn: Respected Banker at the Centre of Power

How many people, especially those leading major Canadian corporations, are described by friends and acquaintances as taking their jobs seriously but not themselves, and as being "generous, patriotic, and community-minded"?[24] This may not be the stereotypic image of big bankers. Nevertheless, this is how John Cleghorn, chairman and CEO of the Royal Bank, is described by those who know him.

George Cohon, a member of the Royal Bank's board of directors and senior chairman of McDonald's Restaurants of Canada, recognizes Cleghorn's open style: "John has dispelled the myth of the banker being removed....He calls up directors and says, 'Can we have lunch?' And he takes me out to lunch and says, 'George, what can we do better?' John is very hands-on."[25] This sentiment is echoed by management theorist Henry Mintzberg, who has described Cleghorn as "very hands-on. He's amazing for his attention to detail but also his ability to look at it in a very large way." Mintzberg also emphasizes the role of business leaders as diplomats concerned with more than the bottom line and cited Cleghorn as a good example. "John Cleghorn is not just worried about the bank, he's worried about the bank's role in society. Because he has to worry."[26]

Cleghorn's concern about the role of banks in Canadian society will become even more important in the on-again, off-again push for bank mergers. If the Royal Bank does ultimately succeed in merging with the Bank of Montreal, as they proposed in 1998, "Cleghorn [would] represent the greatest source of nongovernmental power in this country."[27] He brings to all his ventures the philosophy that has guided his success at the Royal, the philosophy that is rooted in his experiences as a football centre for the McGill Redmen. Centres "are human missiles who don't admit diversion or defeat. That remains the key to Cleghorn's operational code."[28] It remains to be seen whether this tenacity will ever win him the mega-merger prize.

Cleghorn's down-to-earth approach includes a rejection of the luxurious trappings of his position. He sold the bank's company jet, drives himself to work, and has eliminated "the pretentiously decorated private dining rooms on the top floor of the Royal's headquarters in Toronto."[29] He likes to stay close to the front lines and keeps a time sheet to insure that he spends a quarter of his time with customers and employees.[30]

With this philosophy it is no surprise that the Royal Bank topped the *Globe and Mail Report on Business Magazine's* 1998 list of Canadian Corporations Most Respected for People Management and Corporate Responsibility (see Table 13-1.)

Royal Bank of Canada
www.royalbank.com

The Trait Approach: Having "The Right Stuff"

Are some people born to lead? Common sense suggests that this is so. Great leaders of the past such as Alexander the Great, Queen Elizabeth I, Napoleon, and Abraham Lincoln do seem to differ from ordinary human beings in several respects. For example, they all seem to have possessed high levels of ambition coupled with clear visions of precisely where they wanted to go. To a lesser degree, even leaders lacking in such history-shaping fame seem different from their followers. Top executives, some politicians, and even sports heroes or heroines often seem to possess an aura that sets them apart from others. On the basis of such observations, early researchers interested in leadership formulated a view known as the **great person theory**. According to this approach, great leaders possess key traits that set them apart from most other human beings. Further, the theory contends that these traits remain stable over time and across different groups. Thus, it suggests that all great leaders share these characteristics regardless of when and where they lived or the precise role in history they fulfilled.

Certainly, these are intriguing suggestions and seem to fit quite well with our own informal experience. You will probably be surprised to learn, therefore, that they have not been strongly confirmed. Decades of active research (most conducted prior to 1950) failed to yield a short, agreed-upon list of key traits shared by all leaders.[31] A few consistent findings did emerge (e.g., leaders tend to be slightly taller and more

great person theory The view that leaders possess special traits that set them apart from others and that these traits are responsible for their assuming positions of power and authority.

intelligent than their followers), but these were hardly dramatic in nature or in scope.[32] Indeed, the overall results of this persistent search for traits associated with leadership were so disappointing that most investigators gave up in despair and reached the following conclusion: Leaders simply do not differ from followers in clear and consistent ways.

☞ The idea that personal traits and characteristics play an important role in determining behaviour in organizations is discussed in detail in Chapter 4.

Until quite recently this conclusion was widely accepted as true. Now, however, it has been called into question by a growing body of evidence indicating that leaders *do* actually differ from other people in several important—and measurable—respects.[33] After reviewing a large number of studies on this issue, Kirkpatrick and Locke recently reached the conclusion that traits *do* matter—that certain traits, together with other factors, contribute to leaders' success in business settings.[34] What are these traits? A listing and description of those identified as most important by Kirkpatrick and Locke is presented in Table 13-2. You will readily recognize and understand most of these characteristics (drive, honesty and integrity, self-confidence). However, others seem to require further clarification.

leadership motivation The desire to influence others, especially toward the attainment of shared goals.

Consider, first, what Kirkpatrick and Locke term **leadership motivation**. This refers to leaders' desire to influence others and—in essence—to lead. Such motivation, however, can take two distinct forms. On the one hand, it may cause leaders to seek power as an end in itself. Leaders who demonstrate such *personalized power motivation* wish to dominate others, and their desire to do so is often reflected in an excessive concern with status. In contrast, leadership motivation can cause leaders to seek power as a means to achieve desired, shared goals. Leaders who evidence such *socialized power motivation* cooperate with others, develop networks and coalitions, and generally work with subordinates rather than trying to dominate or control them. Needless to say, this type of leadership motivation is usually far more adaptive for organizations than personalized leadership motivation.

With respect to *cognitive ability*, it appears that effective leaders must be intelligent and capable of integrating and interpreting large amounts of information. However, mental genius does not seem to be necessary and may, in some cases, prove detrimental.[35] A final characteristic, *flexibility*, refers to the ability of leaders to recognize what actions are required in a given situation and then to act accordingly. Evidence suggests that the most effective leaders are not prone to behave in the same ways all the time, but to be adaptive, matching their style to the needs of followers and the demands of the situations they face.[36]

In summary, recent evidence seems to necessitate some revision in the widely accepted view that leaders do not differ from other people with respect to specific traits. As noted by Kirkpatrick and Locke,

> Regardless of whether leaders are born or made . . . it is unequivocally clear that *leaders are not like other people*. Leaders do not have to be great men or women by being intellectual geniuses or omniscient prophets to succeed, but they do need to have

TABLE 13-2 Characteristics of Successful Leaders

Research findings indicate that successful leaders demonstrate the traits listed here.

Trait or Characteristic	Description
Drive	Desire for achievement; ambition; high energy; tenacity; initiative
Honesty and integrity	Trustworthy; reliable; open
Leadership motivation	Desire to exercise influence over others to reach shared goals
Self-confidence	Trust in own abilities
Cognitive ability	Intelligence: ability to integrate and interpret large amounts of information
Knowledge of the business	Knowledge of industry, relevant technical matters
Creativity	Originality
Flexibility	Ability to adapt to needs of followers and requirements of situation

the "right stuff" and this stuff is not equally present in all people. Leadership is a demanding, unrelenting job with enormous pressures and grave responsibilities. It would be a profound disservice to leaders to suggest that they are ordinary people who happened to be in the right place at the right time. . . . In the realm of leadership (and in every other realm), the individual does matter.[37]

Supplementing the idea that various traits distinguish effective leaders from others—that is, *who leaders are*—is the idea that leaders also may be distinctive with respect to the way they behave—in other words, *what leaders do*.

Permissive versus Autocratic Leadership Behaviours

Think about the different bosses you have had in your life or career. Can you remember one who wanted to control virtually everything—someone who made all the decisions, told people precisely what to do, and wanted, quite literally, to run the entire show? In contrast, can you recall a boss or supervisor who allowed employees greater freedom and responsibility—someone who was open to suggestions and allowed them to carry out various tasks in their own way? If so, you already have firsthand experience with two sharply contrasting styles of leadership: **autocratic** and **permissive**.

In the past, these styles were viewed as endpoints along a single continuum. However, as noted by Muczyk and Reimann, they actually seem to involve two separate dimensions.[38] The first is the extent to which leaders permit subordinates to take part in decisions; this is the *autocratic-democratic* dimension. The second involves the extent to which leaders direct the activities of subordinates and tell them how to carry out their jobs; this is the *permissive-directive* dimension. Combining these two variables yields four possible patterns, which Muczyk and Reimann label (1) directive autocrat, (2) permissive autocrat, (3) directive democrat, and (4) permissive democrat. (These patterns are summarized in Table 13-3.) Although any attempt to divide human beings into discrete categories raises thorny issues, these patterns do seem to make good sense; many managers adopt a leadership style that fits, at least roughly, within one.

Given that leaders differ along these two dimensions and can, as a result, be classified as falling into one of the four listed patterns, do any of them have a clear-cut edge? In short, is one pattern superior to the others in many, if not most, situations? Existing evidence suggests that this is doubtful. All four styles seem to involve a mixed pattern of advantages and disadvantages. Moreover—and this is the crucial point—the relative success of each depends heavily on conditions existing within a given organization and its specific stage of development. For example, consider a manager who might be described as a *directive autocrat*. Such a person makes decisions without consulting subordinates and supervises subordinates' work activities very closely. It is tempting to view such a pattern as undesirable (it runs counter to the value of personal freedom), but this approach may actually be highly successful in some settings—such as when employees are inexperienced or underqualified for their jobs or when subordinates adopt an adversarial stance toward management and must be closely supervised.

autocratic (leadership style) A style of leadership in which the leader makes all decisions unilaterally.

permissive (leadership style) A style of leadership in which the leader permits subordinates to take part in decision making and also gives them a considerable degree of autonomy in completing routine work activities.

TABLE 13-3 Contrasting Styles of Leadership

According to Muczyk and Reimann, leaders tend to adopt any of four distinct styles described here.

(Source: Based on suggestions by Muczyk & Reimann, 1987; see Note 38.)

Are subordinates told exactly how to do their jobs?	Are subordinates permitted to participate in making decisions?	
	Yes (democratic)	No (autocratic)
Yes (directive)	**Directive democrat** (*makes decisions participatively; closely supervises subordinates*)	**Directive autocrat** (*makes decisions unilaterally; closely supervises subordinates*)
No (permissive)	**Permissive democrat** (*makes decisions participatively; gives subordinates latitude in carrying out their work*)	**Permissive autocrat** (*makes decisions unilaterally; gives subordinates latitude in carrying out their work*)

In contrast, consider the case of the *permissive autocrat*—a leader who combines permissive supervision with an autocratic style of making decisions. This pattern may be useful in dealing with employees who have a high level of technical skill and want to be left alone to manage their own jobs (e.g., scientists, engineers, computer programmers), but who have little desire to participate in routine decision making. The remaining two patterns (directive democrat and permissive democrat) are also most suited to specific organizational conditions. The key task for leaders, then, is to match their own style to the needs of their organization and to change as these needs shift and evolve. What happens when leaders in organizations lack such flexibility?

Actual events in one former company—People Express Airlines—are instructive.[39] Don Burr, the founder and CEO of this airline, had a very clear managerial style: He was a highly permissive democrat. He involved employees in many aspects of decision making and emphasized autonomy in work activities. Indeed, he felt that everyone at People Express should be viewed as a "manager." This style worked well while the company was young, but as it grew and increased in complexity, such practices created mounting difficulties. New employees were not necessarily as committed as older ones, so permissive supervision was ineffective with them. And as decisions increased in both complexity and number, a participative approach became less and less appropriate. Unfortunately, top management was reluctant to alter its style; after all, it seemed to have been instrumental in the company's early success. This poor match between the style of top leaders and changing external conditions seems to have contributed (along with many other factors) to People Express's mounting problems. Losses rose until finally the company was purchased by Texas Air, whose CEO, Frank Lorenzo, favoured a much more directive leadership style.

To conclude, no single leadership style is best under all conditions and in all situations. However, recognizing the importance of differences in this respect can be a constructive first step toward assuring that the style most suited to a given set of conditions is, in fact, adopted. As you read about these different leadership styles, you may have found yourself wondering if they are equally likely to apply to men and women. For some insight into this question, see the **DIVERSITY IN TODAY'S ORGANIZATIONS** section.

People-Oriented versus Production-Oriented Leaders

Think again about all the bosses you have had in your career. Divide these into two categories: those who were relatively effective and those who were relatively ineffective. How do the two groups differ? If you think about this issue carefully, your answers are likely to take one of two forms. First, you might reply, "My most effective bosses helped me to get the job done. They gave me advice, answered my questions, and let me know exactly what was expected of me. My most ineffective bosses didn't do this." Second, you might answer, "My most effective bosses seemed to care about me as a person. They were friendly, listened to me when I had problems or questions, and seemed to help me toward my personal goals. My ineffective bosses didn't do this."

A large body of research, much of it conducted in the 1950s at the University of Michigan[40] and at the Ohio State University[41] suggests that leaders do differ greatly along these dimensions. Those at the high end of the first dimension, known as **initiating structure**, are mainly concerned with production and focus primarily on getting the job done. They engage in actions such as organizing work, inducing subordinates to follow rules, setting goals, and making leader and subordinate roles explicit. In contrast, other leaders are lower on this dimension and show less tendency to engage in these actions.

Leaders at the high end of the second dimension, known as **consideration**, are primarily concerned with establishing good relations with their subordinates and being liked by them. They engage in actions such as doing favours for subordinates, explaining things to them, and assuring their welfare. Others, in contrast, are low on this dimension and don't really care much about how they get along with subordinates.

initiating structure Activities by a leader designed to enhance productivity or task performance. Leaders who focus primarily on these goals are described as demonstrating a task-oriented style.

consideration Actions by a leader that demonstrate concern with the welfare of subordinates and establish positive relations with them. Leaders who focus primarily on this task are often described as demonstrating a person-oriented style.

Men and Women: Comparing their Leadership Styles

Do men and women lead differently? The many studies that have looked at this question have found that members of the two sexes are more similar than they are different when it comes to leadership.[42] If you think about it, this should not be too surprising. After all, to become a leader, one needs to have the various traits described earlier: leadership motivation, flexibility, and so on. These characteristics are just as important for men as they are for women. And, as a result, the leadership profiles of men and women tend to look remarkably similar.

This is not to say, however, that men and women do not go about the task of leading others in quite different ways. Indeed, there appears to be a consistent difference between men and women with respect to leadership style: Women prefer democratic leadership whereas men prefer directive leadership.[43] Specifically, women are more likely than men to encourage other group members to participate in making the decisions before them. And when they do, they attempt to make these others feel good about their contributions. They tend to influence others by relying on their interpersonal skills. By contrast, men tend to be comfortable using a more controlling style. That is, they are more likely than women to issue direct orders and to rely on the power that comes from their position.[44]

Although these descriptions are good generalizations, they are not, of course, completely accurate in all situations. For example, how effective would a highly democratic female leader be in a situation in which she is expected to be highly autocratic, as would be the case in a male-dominated job, such as a military officer? As you might imagine, the results would be disastrous. In fact, research has shown that women tend to act more like men when they are in such situations.[45] That is, to be effective leaders, they learned to act in ways that overcame their personal preferences.

Interestingly, however, as organizations have become more oriented toward requiring the interpersonal skills needed to make teams work effectively (as discussed in Chapter 8), a high premium is placed on the particular leadership style that women bring to the job. Their greater interpersonal sensitivity and concern for others tends to make women more accepting of different perspectives, better equipping them to work in cross-functional teams. As a result, it appears that when it comes to many of the requirements for successful leadership in today's organizations, the leadership edge goes to women. Although this may not be the case in the traditional, rigid, bureaucratic organization, as organizations are changing, so too are the styles of the individuals who lead them. And not surprisingly, more of these individuals tend to be women than ever before.

At first glance, you might assume that initiating structure and consideration are linked such that people high on one of these dimensions are automatically low on the other. In fact, this is not the case. The two dimensions actually seem to be largely independent.[46] Thus, a leader may be high on both concern with production and concern for people, high on one of these dimensions and low on the other, moderate on one and high on the other, and so on (see Figure 13-3).

Is any one of these possible patterns best? Careful study indicates that this is a complex issue; production-oriented and people-oriented leadership behaviours both offer a mixed pattern of pluses and minuses. With respect to showing consideration (high concern with people and human relations), the major benefits are improved group atmosphere and morale.[47] However, since leaders high on this dimension are reluctant to act in a directive manner toward subordinates and often shy away from presenting them with negative feedback, productivity sometimes suffers. Regarding initiating structure (high concern with production), efficiency and performance are indeed sometimes enhanced by this leadership style. If leaders focus entirely on production, however, employees may soon conclude that no one cares about them or their welfare. Then work-related attitudes such as job satisfaction and organizational commitment may suffer.

Having said all this and pointed out the complexities, we add that one specific pattern may indeed have an edge in many settings. This is a pattern in which lead-

FIGURE 13-3 **Leader Behaviour: Two Basic Dimensions**

Leaders' behaviour can vary from low to high with respect to *consideration* (person orientation) and *initiating structure* (task orientation). Patterns of leader behaviour produced by variations along these two dimensions are illustrated here.

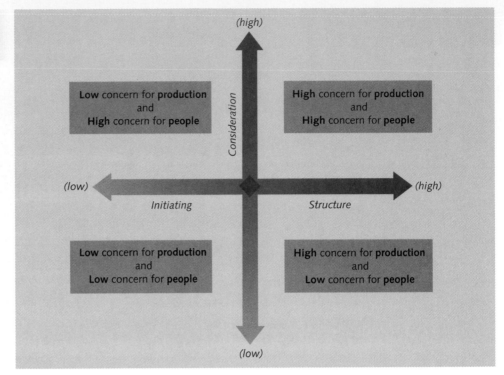

ers demonstrate high concern with both people *and* production.[48]Indeed, research has shown that high amounts of concern with people (showing consideration) and concern with productivity (initiating structure) are not incompatible. Rather, skillful leaders can combine both of these orientations into their overall styles to produce favourable results. Thus, although no one leadership style is best, leaders who combine these two concerns may often have an important edge over leaders who show only one or the other.

Developing Successful Leader Behaviours: Grid Training

grid training A technique designed to strengthen leaders' concerns for people and their concerns for production.

How can one go about developing these two forms of leadership behaviour—demonstrating concern for production and concern for people? A technique known as **grid training** proposes a multistep process designed to cultivate these two important skills.[49]

The initial step consists of a *grid seminar*—a session in which an organization's managers (who have been previously trained in the appropriate theory and skills) help organization members analyze their own management styles. This is done using a specially designed questionnaire that allows managers to determine how they stand with respect to their *concern for production* and their *concern for people*. Each participant's approach on each dimension is scored using a number ranging from 1 (low) to 9 (high).

☞ *Because grid training may be used to change organizational leadership behaviour systematically, it has been considered a technique of organizational development, the focus of Chapter 16.*

Managers who score low on both concern for production and concern for people are scored 1,1—evidence of *impoverished management*. A manager who is highly concerned about production but shows little interest in people, the *task management* style, scores 9,1. In contrast, ones who show the opposite pattern—high concern with people but little concern with production—are described as having a *country club* style of management; they are scored 1,9. Managers scoring moderately on both dimensions, the 5,5 pattern, are said to follow a *middle-of-the-road* management style. Finally, there are individuals who are highly concerned with both production and people, those scoring 9,9. This is the most desirable pattern, representing what is known as *team management*. These various patterns are represented in a diagram like that shown in Figure 13-4, known as the *managerial grid*®.

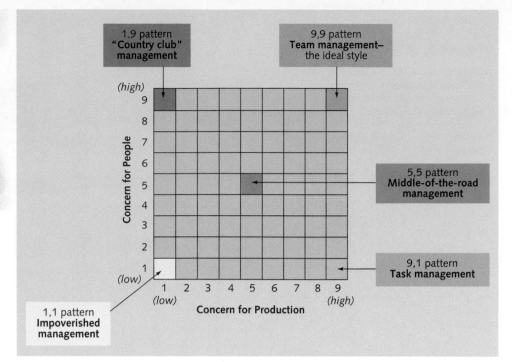

FIGURE 13-4 The Managerial Grid®

A manager's standing allowing two basic dimensions, concern for production and concern for people, can be illustrated by means of a diagram such as this, known as the *managerial grid®*. In *grid training,* people are trained to be effective leaders by demonstrating high amounts of both dimensions.

(Source: Based on dimensions by Blake & Mouton, 1969; see Note 49.)

After a manager's position along the grid is determined, training begins to improve concern over production (planning skills) and concern over people (communication skills) to reach the ideal, *9,9* state. This consists of organization-wide training aimed at helping people interact more effectively with each other. Then, training is expanded to focus on reducing conflict between groups that work with each other. Additional training includes efforts to identify the extent to which the organization is meeting its strategic goals and then comparing this performance to an ideal. Next, plans are made to meet these goals, and these plans are implemented in the organization. Finally, progress toward the goals is continuously assessed and problem areas are identified.

Grid training is widely considered an effective way of improving the leadership behaviours of people in organizations. Indeed, the grid approach has been used to train hundreds of thousands of people in developing the two key forms of leadership behaviour.

Artists, Craftsmen, and Technocrats

Ecole des Hautes Etudes Commerciales
www.hec.unil.ch/english.htm

Patricia Pitcher, a professor of leadership at Ecole des Hautes Etudes Commerciales in Montreal and protégé of Henry Mintzberg, conducted an eight-year study of 15 chief executive officers in a major international financial services organization. Her methodology consisted of (1) the construction of a 60-adjective checklist (ACL), data collection in which she asked ten of each CEO's closest colleagues—"admirers" and "detractors"—to complete the adjective checklist with the particular CEO in mind, (2) the administration of a psychological test known as the Minnesota Multiphasic Personality Inventory (MMPI) to each CEO, (3) the interpretation of the MMPI profiles with the help of a clinical psychologist, (4) research on internal and public documents for the target organization for the years 1960 to 1990, and the (5) completion of two rounds of 60 in-depth interviews with CEOs and board members (in 1986 and again in 1990). The analysis of the data led her to conclude that the 15 CEOs represented three different types of leaders, namely: Artists, Craftsmen , and Technocrats.[50]

According to Pitcher, the Artists are emotional, visionary, entrepreneurial, people-oriented, intuitive, and open-minded. The Craftsmen are "fellow travellers" with the Artists and are described as realistic, stable, honest, responsible, amiable, and wise. In stark contrast to the Artists and Craftsmen, the Technocrats are methodical, intense, hard-headed, fastidious, and difficult.

Pitcher argues for the need to have each of the three types represented in senior management teams. In her view, the key is to have the right balance of the three types and to ensure that the Artists, Craftsmen, and Technocrats are placed in the kinds of jobs that make the best use of their styles. For example, she suggests that the CEO should be a visionary, entrepreneurial Artist, the chief operating officer should be an experienced and wise Craftsman, and the Senior Vice-President of "No" (as she calls the position) should be the logical, conservative Technocrat. While the theoretical stereotypes of these classifications are clear, in reality, few people fall neatly into a single type. More often individuals have characteristics of two or, rarely, all three types.[51]

Leaders and Followers

Thus far in this chapter, we have focused on leaders—their traits and their behaviours. Followers, by and large, have been ignored. But note: In a crucial sense, followers are the essence of leadership. Without them, there really is no such thing as leadership (see Figure 13-5).

The importance of followers, and the complex, reciprocal relationship between leaders and followers, is widely recognized by organizational researchers. Indeed, major theories of leadership, such as those we will consider in this section, note—either explicitly or implicitly—that leadership is really a two-way street. We will now consider four such approaches: the *leader-member exchange model*, the *attribution approach* to leadership, *charismatic leadership*, and *transformational leadership*. After reviewing these approaches we will end this section by discussing the changing nature of the relationship between leaders and followers—special issues involved in the leadership of teams.

The Leader-Member Exchange (LMX) Model: The Importance of Being in the "In-Group"

leader-member exchange (LMX) model A theory suggesting that leaders form different relations with various subordinates and that the nature of such exchanges can exert strong effects on subordinates' performance and satisfaction.

Do leaders treat all their subordinates in the same manner? Informal observation suggests that, clearly, they do not. Yet, many theories of leadership ignore this fact. They discuss leadership behaviour in terms that suggest similar actions toward all subordinates. The importance of potential differences in this respect is brought into sharp focus by the **leader-member exchange (LMX) model** developed by Graen and his associates.[52]

This theory suggests that for various reasons leaders form different kinds of relationships with various groups of subordinates. One group, referred to as the *in-group* is favoured by the leader. Members of in-groups receive considerably more attention from the leader and larger shares of the resources they have to offer (such as time and recognition). By contrast, other subordinates fall into the *out-group*. These individuals are disfavoured by leaders. As such, they receive fewer valued resources from their leaders.

Leaders distinguish between in-group and out-group members very early in their relationships with them—and, on the basis of surprisingly little information. Sometimes, perceived similarity with respect to personal characteristics such as age, gender, or personality, is sufficient to categorize followers into a leader's in-group.[53] Similarly, a particular follower may be granted in-group status if the leader believes that person to be especially competent at performing his or her job.[54]

Research has supported the idea that leaders favour members of their in-groups. For example, one study found that supervisors inflated the ratings they gave poorly performing employees when these

"Naturally, I can't take all the credit. I have a wonderful support group."

FIGURE 13-5 Leaders: Nothing without Followers

Like all leaders, this one probably would be unsuccessful without "support" from his followers. Recognizing this, several theories of leadership have focused on the relationship between leaders and followers.

(Source: Copyright © 1994 by Leo Cullum.)

The LMX model is based on principles of group dynamics discussed in Chapter 8.

individuals were members of the in-group, but not when they were members of the out-group.[55] Given the favouritism shown toward in-group members, it follows that such individuals would perform their jobs better and hold more positive attitudes toward their jobs than members of out-groups. In general, research has supported this prediction. For example, it has been found that in-group members are more satisfied with their jobs and more effective in performing them than out-group members.[56] In-group members are also less likely to resign from their jobs than out-group members.[57] And, as you might imagine, members of in-groups tend to receive more mentoring from their superiors than do members of out-groups, helping them become more successful in their careers.[58]

Together, these studies provide good support for the LMX model. Such findings suggest that attention to the relations between leaders and their followers can be very useful. The nature of such relationships can strongly affect the morale, commitment, and performance of employees. Helping leaders to improve such relations, therefore, can be extremely valuable in several respects.

The Attribution Approach: Leaders' Explanations of Followers' Behaviour

As we have just noted, leaders' relationships with individual subordinates can play an important role in determining the performance and satisfaction of these individuals. One specific aspect of such exchanges serves as focus of another contemporary perspective on leadership—the **attribution approach**.[59] This theory emphasizes the role of leaders' attributions concerning the causes behind followers' behaviour—especially, the causes of their job performance.

attribution approach (to leadership) The approach to leadership that focuses on leaders' attributions of followers' performance—that is, their perceptions of its underlying causes.

The general nature of the attribution process, as it applies to organizations, is considered in depth in Chapter 3.

Leaders observe the performance of their followers and then attempt to understand why this behaviour met, exceeded, or failed to meet their expectations. Since poor performance often poses greater difficulties than effective performance, leaders are more likely to engage in a careful attributional analysis when confronted with the former. When they are, they examine the three kinds of information described in Chapter 3 (consensus, consistency, and distinctiveness), and on the basis of such information form an initial judgment as to whether followers' performance stemmed from internal causes (e.g., low effort, commitment, or ability) or external causes (factors beyond their control, such as faulty equipment, unrealistic deadlines, or illness). Then, on the basis of such attributions, they formulate specific actions designed to change the present situation, and perhaps improve followers' performance. Attribution theory suggests that such actions are determined, at least in part, by leaders' explanations of followers' behaviour. For example, if they perceive poor performance as stemming from a lack of required materials or equipment, they may focus on providing such items. If, instead, they perceive poor performance as stemming mainly from a lack of effort, they may reprimand, transfer, or terminate the person involved (for a summary example, see Figure 13-6).

Evidence for the accuracy of these predictions has been reported in several studies.[60] In perhaps the best known of these, Mitchell and Wood presented nursing supervisors with brief accounts of errors committed by nurses.[61] The incidents suggested that the errors stemmed either from internal causes (lack of effort or ability) or from external causes (e.g., overdemanding work environment). After reading about the incidents, supervisors indicated what kind of action they would be likely to take in each situation. Results showed that they were more likely to direct corrective action toward the nurses when they perceived the errors as stemming from internal causes (e.g., showing them how to do something), but more likely to direct action toward the environment when they perceived the errors as stemming from external factors (e.g., changing schedules or improving facilities).

In summary, the attribution approach suggests that leaders' behaviour often reflects their attributions concerning the actions and performance of followers. Leadership, then, lies as much in the perceptions of the people who exercise such influence as in the perceptions of those who confer the right to wield it over them.

FIGURE 13-6 Leaders' Attributions of Followers' Poor Performance

The way leaders respond to their followers depends on the attributions leaders make regarding the causes of followers' performance. In this example, attributions made about the causes of a subordinate's poor performance directs a leader to take very different courses of action.

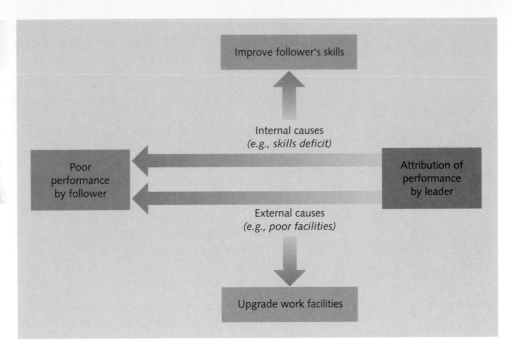

Charismatic Leaders: That "Something Special"

charismatic leaders Leaders who exert especially powerful effects on followers by virtue of the attributions followers make about them. Such individuals have high amounts of self-confidence, present a clearly articulated vision, behave in extraordinary ways, are recognized as change agents, and are sensitive to the environmental constraints they face.

Through the ages, some leaders have had extraordinary success in generating profound changes in the beliefs, perceptions, values, and actions of their followers. Individuals who accomplish such feats have been referred to as **charismatic leaders**.[62] Such individuals seem to possess unusual and special skills that equip them for leading others. (The word *charisma* means "divinely inspired gifts" in Greek.) In Canadian business today, several CEOs may be identified as charismatic leaders. These include: Sheelagh Whittaker, president and CEO of EDS Canada, Matthew Barrett, former chairman and CEO of the Bank of Montreal (see Figure 13-7), and Christina Gold, former chairwoman, president, and CEO of Avon Canada (see the CASE IN POINT for this chapter).

What makes a leader charismatic? Researchers have found that charismatic leaders tend to be special in a number of important ways. Specifically, several factors differentiate charismatic leaders from noncharismatic leaders. These are as follows:

FIGURE 13-7 Matthew Barrett: A Charismatic Leader
Former Bank of Montreal CEO Matthew Barrett has been described as "the country's most charismatic banker."[65]

1. ***Self-confidence:*** Charismatic leaders are highly confident in their ability and judgment. Others readily become aware of this. For example, Diane McGarry, former chairperson, president, and CEO of Xerox Canada and now vice-president and general manager of the colour business unit, Office Products Group at Xerox[63] is widely regarded by company employees as someone who really knows her stuff.

2. ***A vision:*** A leader is said to have vision to the extent that he or she proposes a state of affairs that improves upon the existing conditions. He or she also must be able to clearly articulate that vision, making it understandable to followers. For example, recall the Royal Bank's John Cleghorn (**THE QUEST FOR QUALITY** for this chapter), who was described by Henry Mintzberg as having a concern not only for the bank but for the bank's role as part of society.[64] Charismatic leaders also must demonstrate strong commitments toward their vision, such as by taking on

personal risk or sacrifices to make it come true. For example, to demonstrate his willingness to help Chrysler during its troubled times, Lee Iacocca took only a $1 salary one year.

3. ***Extraordinary behaviour:*** Charismatic leaders are frequently unconventional. Their quirky ways, when successful, elicit admiration. For example, much of the success of Southwest Airlines in the United States is attributed to the zany antics of CEO Herb Kelleher. Likewise, Campbell Soup's David Johnson is frequently remembered by company employees for wearing outrageous costumes in an attempt to fire them up. And then there is Virgin Group's founder and chairman, who is bringing his business and his flamboyant style to Canada. Richard Branson has a penchant for dressing up, or even undressing (he appears naked in an October 1998 *Business Week* article).[66]

4. ***Recognized as change agents:*** The status quo is the enemy of charismatic leaders. They make things happen. This can be said of BCE's Jean Monty, named the *Financial Post Magazine's* CEO of the Year for 1997 after leading a massive turnaround at Nortel.[67]

5. ***Environmental sensitivity:*** Charismatic leaders are highly realistic about the constraints imposed upon them and the resources needed to change things. Consequently, they know what they can and cannot do.

BCE Inc.
www.bce.ca

☞ *In Chapter 16 we consider the role of the environment as a determinant of organizational change.*

At first glance, it is tempting to assume that charismatic leaders are special by virtue of the traits they possess. In other words, such leadership might be understood as an extension of the great person theory described earlier in this chapter.[68] Although traits may play a role in charismatic leadership, there is a growing belief that such leadership involves a special type of relationship between leaders and their followers.[69] Within this framework, charismatic leadership rests more on specific types of reactions by followers than on traits possessed by leaders. That is to say, leaders are considered charismatic by virtue of their effects on followers. Such reactions include: (1) levels of performance beyond those that would normally be expected;[70] (2) high levels of devotion, loyalty, and reverence toward the leader;[71] and (3) enthusiasm for and excitement about the leader and the leader's ideas.[72] In short, charismatic leadership involves a special kind of leader-follower relationship, in which the leader can, in the words of one author, "make ordinary people do extraordinary things in the face of adversity."[73]

The effects of charismatic leadership—both good and bad. As you might imagine, charismatic leaders can have dramatic effects on the behaviour of their followers. Indeed, studies have shown that charismatic leadership is positively correlated with job performance.[74] And, because these leaders are perceived as being so heroic, followers are very pleased with them—satisfaction that generalizes to perceptions of the job itself. In short, people enjoy working for charismatic leaders and do well under their guidance. On a larger scale, research by House and his associates has found that U.S. presidents believed to be highly charismatic (as suggested by biographical accounts of their personalities and their reactions to world crises) received higher ratings by historians of their effectiveness as president.[75] In short, evidence suggests that charismatic leadership can have some very beneficial effects.

It is important to caution, however, that being charismatic does not necessarily imply being virtuous. There appears to be a "dark side" of charisma as well.[76] After all, several of history's most infamous people, dictator Adolph Hitler, as well as cult leaders Luc Joret, leader of the Quebec-based Order of the Solar Temple,[77] David Koresh, and Charles Manson in the United States were very charismatic. Indeed, it was their clear visions of different worlds, misguided though they may have been, that led them to have such profound effects on their followers. (See **THE ETHICS ANGLE** for a closer look at research on the two faces of charisma.)

The Two Faces of Charismatic Leaders

When we think of charismatic leaders we tend to picture larger-than-life *heroes* celebrated for turning around ailing companies and launching new enterprises—dynamic forces for change and improvement. However, as Jane Howell, of the University of Western Ontario, and Bruce Avolio, of the State University of New York at Binghamton, have pointed out, there is also a dark side to some charismatic leaders.[78] Such individuals use their charisma to promote dangerous values, building fanaticism to serve their passions for power.

Based on surveys and firsthand interviews with 150 business leaders from 25 Canadian organizations, as well as analyses of leaders appearing in the popular press, Howell and Avolio distinguished between two groups of charismatic leaders—those who used their charisma to advance ethical ends, and those who did just the opposite. *Ethical charismatics* go out of their way to promote the collective interests of employees by incorporating their followers' hopes and dreams into their visions. By contrast, *unethical charismatics* are primarily interested in pursuing their own personal visions.

According to Howell and Avolio, ethical and unethical charismatics differ in several major dimensions. First, with respect to exercising power, unethical charismatics use power in dominant and authoritarian ways for their personal gain, showing insensitivity to followers' needs. However, ethical charismatics use power to serve others, and show considerable concern for others. Second, charismatic leaders differ with respect to how they create and express their visions. Whereas ethical charismatics align their visions with those of their followers, unethical charismatics promote their own selfish visions. A third difference has to do with the way the leaders communicate with their followers. Ethical charismatics consider their followers' ideas and learn from them, using two-way communication. They stimulate their followers to think independently and to question their leaders' views. In contrast, unethical charismatics censure critical and opposing views, use one-way communication, and demand that their own decisions be accepted without question.

And how can organizations create and sustain ethical charismatic leaders? Howell and Avolio make the following six recommendations:

1. Show commitment to a code of ethics that is continually enforced.
2. Recruit, select, and promote only those individuals with the highest moral standards.
3. Create performance standards that emphasize respect for people.
4. Train leaders how to respect and integrate diverse viewpoints.
5. Train leaders in ethical values and develop their skills in this area.
6. Identify as heroines and heroes individuals who show exemplary moral conduct.[79]

University of Western Ontario
www.uwo.ca

Transformational Leadership: Beyond Charisma

If you're thinking that charismatic leaders are really something special, we're inclined to agree. But being charismatic is only the beginning of doing what it takes to get followers to be their most effective. Theorists have recognized that although charisma is important, the most successful leaders also do things that revitalize and transform their organizations. Accordingly, their orientation is referred to as **transformational leadership**.

Transformational leaders may be described according to several characteristics. First, as we said, they have *charisma*. That is, they provide a strong vision and a sense of mission for the company. As leadership theorist Jay Conger put it, "If you as a leader can make an appealing dream seem like tomorrow's reality, your subordinates will freely choose to follow you."[80] Consider, for example, the great vision expressed by one highly charismatic leader, Dr. Martin Luther King Jr., when he shared his vision of world peace in his "I have a dream" speech.

But charisma alone is insufficient for changing the way an organization operates. For this to occur, transformational leaders also must provide *intellectual stimu-*

transformational leadership
Leadership in which leaders have charisma and provide intellectual stimulation, individualized consideration, and inspirational motivation.

lation. That is, they help their followers recognize problems and ways of solving them. Furthermore, they provide *individualized consideration* by giving followers the support, encouragement, and attention they need to perform their jobs well. Finally, transformational leaders are said to provide *inspirational motivation*. That is, they clearly communicate the importance of the company's mission and rely on symbols (e.g., pins and slogans) to help focus their efforts.

☞ *Mentorship, as described in Chapter 7, is an important tool in the development of careers.*

Transformational leaders arouse strong emotions and identification with the leader. They also help transform their followers by teaching them, often by serving as mentors.[81] In so doing, transformational leaders seek to encourage followers to "do their own thing." By contrast, charismatic leaders may keep their followers weak and highly dependent on them. A charismatic leader may be the whole show, whereas a transformational leader does a good job of inspiring change in the whole organization. At Avon Products Inc., Andrea Jung is refocusing the company on a new marketing strategy (see the CASE IN POINT for this chapter).[82]

Chairman and CEO of General Electric (GE) Jack Welch is a good example of a transformational leader. Under Welch's leadership, GE has undergone a series of changes with respect to the way it does business.[83] At the individual level, GE has abandoned its highly bureaucratic ways and now does a better job of listening to its employees. Not surprisingly, GE has consistently ranked among the most admired companies in its industry in *Fortune* magazine's annual survey of corporate reputations.[84]

Scientists measure transformational leadership by using a questionnaire known as the Multifactor Leadership Questionnaire (MLQ). In completing this instrument, subordinates answer a series of questions in which they describe the behaviour of their superiors. It consists of items tapping the four aspects of transformational leadership described above. So, for example, agreeing with an item such as "My leader makes me feel proud to be associated with him/her" is taken as an indication of the leader's transformational ways. The more subordinates agree with such statements as they describe the leader in question, the more highly that leader is scored as being transformational.

☞ *These work-related attitudes are described more fully in Chapter 6.*

Using this questionnaire, researchers have found that transformational leaders tend to be very effective in making their organizations successful. For example, in a recent study, Kohl, Steers, and Terborg gave the MLQ to teachers in various secondary schools in Singapore and asked them to complete it with their school principals in mind.[85] They found that the more highly transformational the principals were described using the MLQ, the more the teachers engaged in organizational citizenship behaviour, the more they were satisfied with their jobs, and the more strongly they were committed to their organizations. The principals' transformational leadership scores also predicted how well the schools' students performed, although this connection was much weaker. Likewise, additional research has shown managers at FedEx who are rated by their subordinates as being highly transformational tend to be higher performers and are recognized by their superiors as being highly promotable.[86] These and other studies suggest that the benefits of being a transformational leader may be considerable.

With this in mind, it certainly would be useful to consider ways in which people might transform their organizations through their leadership. We have summarized several key guidelines in Table 13-4. Although you may find it easier to understand than to carry out some of these suggestions, the evidence regarding the effectiveness of transformational leadership suggests that the effort may be worthwhile.

Leading Teams: Special Considerations

When most people think of leaders, they tend to think of individuals who make strategic decisions on behalf of followers, who are responsible for carrying them out. In many of today's organizations, however, where the movement toward *self-managed teams* predominates, it is less likely than ever that leaders are responsible for getting others to implement their orders to help fulfill their visions. Instead, team leaders may be called upon to provide special resources to groups empowered to implement their own missions in their own ways. They don't call all the shots but help subordinates take responsibility for their own work. This

☞ *The use of self-managed work teams, as described in Chapter 8, is growing in popularity in today's organizations.*

TABLE 13-4 **Guidelines for Becoming a Transformational Leader**

Being a transformational leader is not easy, but following the suggestions outlined here may help leaders transform and revitalize their organizations.

Source: Based on suggestions by Yukl, 1994; see Note 13.

Suggestion	Explanation
Develop a vision that is both clear and highly appealing to followers.	A clear vision will guide followers toward achieving organizational goals and make them feel good about doing so.
Articulate a strategy for bringing that vision to life.	Don't present an elaborate plan; rather, state the best path toward achieving the mission.
State your vision clearly and promote it to others.	Visions must not only be made clear but also compelling, such as by using anecdotes.
Show confidence and optimism about your vision.	If a leader lacks confidence about success, followers will not try very hard to achieve that vision.
Express confidence in followers' capacity to carry out the strategy.	Followers must believe that they are capable of implementing a leader's vision. Leaders should build followers' self-confidence.
Build confidence by recognizing small accomplishments toward the goal.	If a group experiences early success, it will be motivated to continue working hard.
Celebrate successes and accomplishments.	Formal or informal ceremonies are useful for celebrating success, thereby building optimism and commitment.
Take dramatic action to symbolize key organizational values.	Visions are reinforced by things leaders do to symbolize them. For example, one leader demonstrated concern for quality by destroying work that was not up to standards.
Set an example; actions speak louder than words.	Leaders serve as role models. If they want followers to make sacrifices, for example, they should do so themselves.

suggests that the role of team leader is clearly very different than the traditional "command and control" leadership role we have been discussing.[87] With this in mind, here are a few guidelines that may be followed to achieve success as a team leader.

- First, instead of directing people, team leaders work at *building trust and inspiring teamwork.* One way this can be done is by encouraging interaction among all members of the team as well as between the team and its customers and suppliers.

- Second, instead of focusing simply on training individuals, effective team leaders concentrate on *expanding team capabilities.* In this connection, team leaders function primarily as coaches, providing all members with the skills needed to perform the task, removing barriers that might interfere with task success, and finding the necessary resources required to get the job done.

- Third, instead of one-on-one managing, team leaders attempt to *create a team identity.* In other words, leaders must help teams understand their missions and recognize what they're doing to help fulfill them.

- Fourth, although traditional leaders have worked at preventing conflict between individuals, team leaders are encouraged to *make the most of team differences.* Without doubt, it is a considerable challenge to meld a diverse group of individuals into a highly committed and productive team, but doing so is important.

- Fifth, unlike traditional leaders who simply react to change, team leaders should *foresee and influence change.* To the extent that leaders recognize that change is inevitable (a point we will emphasize more fully in Chapter 16), they may be better prepared to make the various adaptations required.

In conclusion, leading teams is a far cry from leading individuals in the traditional directive (or even a participative) manner. The special nature of teams makes the leader's job very different. Although appreciating these differences is easy, making the appropriate adjustments may be extremely challenging—especially for individuals who are well practised in the ways of traditional leadership.

Contingency Theories of Leader Effectiveness

☞ *In Chapter 1 we describe the general nature of the* contingency approach *to the study of organizational behaviour. These theories are representative of this orientation.*

contingency theories (of leadership) Any of several theories which recognize that certain styles of leadership are more effective in some situations than others.

That leadership is a complex process should be obvious by now. It involves intricate social relationships and is affected by a wide range of factors. Given all these complications, you may wonder why so many researchers focus so much of their time and energy on attempting to understand all of its intricacies. The answer, of course, is that effective leadership is an essential ingredient in organizational success. With effective leadership organizations can grow, prosper, and compete. Without it, many simply cannot survive. Recognition of this basic point lies behind several modern theories of leadership collectively referred to as **contingency theories** of leader effectiveness.

As will soon be clear, these theories differ sharply in their content, terminology, and scope. Yet, all are linked by two common themes. First, all adopt a *contingency approach*—they recognize that there is no single preferred style of leadership, and that the key task of organizational behaviour researchers is determining which leadership styles will prove most effective under which specific conditions. Second, all are concerned with the issue of *leader effectiveness*. They seek to identify the conditions and factors that determine whether, and to what degree, leaders will enhance the performance and satisfaction of their subordinates. Yukl has identified several theories in this category.[88] Among these are five that we will describe here: *LPC contingency theory, situational leadership theory, path-goal theory, normative decision theory,* and the *substitutes for leadership* framework.

LPC Contingency Theory: Matching Leaders and Tasks

Leadership does not occur in a social or environmental vacuum. Rather, leaders attempt to exert their influence on group members within the context of specific situations. Since these can vary greatly along many different dimensions, it is reasonable to expect that no single style or approach to leadership will always be best. Rather, as we have noted, the most effective strategy will probably vary from one situation to another.

LPC contingency theory Fiedler's theory suggesting that leader effectiveness is determined both by characteristics of leaders (their LPC scores) and by the degree to which the situation encountered gives leaders control over their subordinates.

LPC Short for "esteem for least preferred coworker"—a personality variable distinguishing between individuals with respect to their concern for people (high LPC) and their concern for production (low LPC).

Essentials of the theory.   Acceptance of this fact lies at the core of the **LPC contingency theory** developed by Fiedler.[89] The *contingency* aspect of the theory is certainly appropriate, for its central assumption is that a leader's contribution to successful performance by his or her group is determined both by the leader's traits and by various features of the situation. To understand leader effectiveness fully, both types of factors must be considered.

With respect to characteristics possessed by leaders, Fiedler identifies *esteem (liking) for least preferred coworker* (**LPC** for short) as most important. This refers to a leader's tendency to evaluate in a favourable or unfavourable manner the person with whom she or he has found it most difficult to work. Leaders who perceive this person in negative terms (low LPC leaders) are primarily concerned with attaining successful task performance. In contrast, those who perceive their least preferred coworker in a positive light (high LPC leaders) are mainly concerned with establishing good relations with subordinates. (As you can see, this dimension is related to two aspects of leader behaviour described previously: initiating structure and showing consideration.) It is important to note that Fiedler considers LPC to be fixed—an aspect of an individual's leadership style that cannot be changed. As we will explain below, this has important implications for applying the theory so as to improve leader effectiveness.

Which type of leader—low LPC or high LPC—is more effective? Fiedler's answer is that it depends. And what it depends on is several situational factors. Specifically, Fiedler suggests that whether low LPC or high LPC leaders are more effective depends on the degree to which the leader has *situational control*—that is, the extent to which conditions provide leaders with control over their subordinates. This, in turn, is determined by three factors: (1) the nature of the leader's relations with group members (the extent to which he or she enjoys their support and loyalty), (2) the degree of structure in the task being performed (the extent to which task goals and subordinates' roles are clearly defined), and (3) the leader's position power (his or her ability to enforce compliance by subordinates). Combining these three factors, the leader's situational control can range from very high (positive relations with group members, a highly structured task, high position power) to very low (negative relations, an unstructured task, low position power).

To return to the central question: When are different types of leaders most effective? Fiedler suggests that low LPC leaders (ones who are task-oriented) are superior to high LPC leaders (ones who are relations- or people-oriented) when situational control is either very low or very high. In contrast, high LPC leaders have an edge when situational control falls within the moderate range (refer to Figure 13-8).

The reasoning behind these predictions is as follows: Under conditions of low situational control, groups need considerable guidance and direction to accomplish their tasks. Since low LPC leaders are more likely to provide structure than high LPC leaders, they usually will be superior in such cases. Similarly, low LPC leaders are also superior under conditions that offer the leader a high degree of situational control. Here, low LPC leaders realize that conditions are very good and that successful task performance is virtually assured. As a result, they turn their attention to improving relations with subordinates and often adopt a relaxed, "hands-off" style. Subordinates appreciate such treatment, and performance and morale are both enhanced. In contrast, high LPC leaders, feeling that they already enjoy good relations with their subordinates, may shift their attention to task performance. Their attempts to provide guidance may then be perceived by subordinates as needless meddling, with the result that performance is impaired.

Turning to situations offering the leader moderate situational control, conditions are mixed, and attention to good interpersonal relations is often needed. High LPC leaders, with their interest in people, often have an important advantage in such cases. In contrast, low LPC leaders, who tend to focus on task performance, may become even more autocratic and directive. The negative reactions of subordinates to such behaviours may then have detrimental effects on performance.

FIGURE 13-8 LPC Contingency Theory: An Overview

Fiedler's *LPC contingency theory* predicts that low LPC leaders (ones who are primarily task-oriented) will be more effective than high LPC leaders (ones who are primarily people-oriented) when situational control is either very low or very high. However, the opposite is true when situational control is moderate.

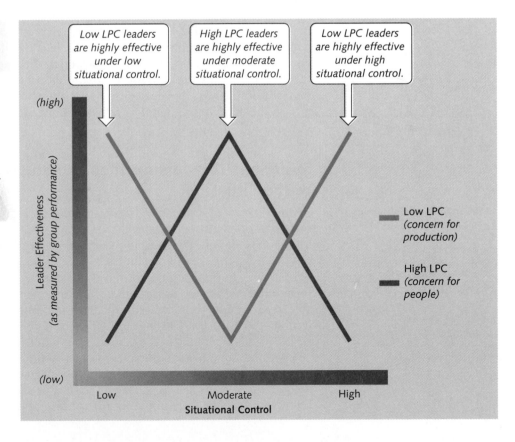

Research status of the theory. Where any scientific theory is concerned, the ultimate question must be: How does it fare when put to actual test? For the contingency theory, the answer appears to be "moderately well." One review of more than 170 studies undertaken to test various aspects of Fiedler's theory indicates that most obtained at least some positive results.[90] Although the results of many studies are encouraging and lend support to the theory (particularly laboratory studies), not all findings have been consistent with it.[91] In particular, field investigations (carried out with existing groups operating in a wide range of contexts) generally have not been as favourable.[92]

Such investigations have sometimes yielded results contrary to what contingency theory would predict. In addition, the theory has been criticized on several important grounds. For example, a degree of ambiguity exists with respect to classifying specific situations along the dimension of situational control. Unless situations can be accurately classified as very low, low, moderate, and so on in this regard, predictions concerning leader effectiveness are difficult to make. Similarly, some critics have questioned the adequacy of the questionnaire used to assess leaders' standing on the LPC dimension. In particular, the reliability of this measure does not seem to be as high as that of other widely used tests of personality.[93] Thus, although LPC contingency theory has added to our understanding of leadership effectiveness, several questions about its accuracy remain.

Applying the theory. Despite the fact that research testing LPC contingency theory has yielded mixed results, practitioners have found it to be quite useful when it comes to suggesting ways of enhancing leader effectiveness. Because the theory assumes that certain kinds of leaders are most effective in certain kinds of situations and that leadership style is fixed, the best way to enhance effectiveness is to fit the right kind of leaders to the situations they face.

This involves completing questionnaires that can be used to assess both the LPC score of the leader and the amount of control he or she faces in the situation. Then, using these indexes, a match can be made such that leaders are put into the situations that best suit their leadership styles—a technique known as **leader match**.[94] This approach also focuses on ways of changing the situational control variables—leader-member relations, task structure, and leader position power—when it is impractical to change leaders. For example, a low LPC leader should be moved to a job in which situational control is either extremely high or extremely low, or alternatively, the situation should be changed (such as by altering relations between leaders and group members, or raising or lowering the leader's position power) so as to increase or decrease the amount of situational control encountered. Several companies, including Sears, have used the leader-match approach with some success. In fact, studies have found that the approach is effective—on at least some occasions—in improving group effectiveness.[95]

Situational Leadership Theory: Adjusting Leadership Style to the Situation

Another theory of leadership, Hersey and Blanchard's **situational leadership theory**, is considered a contingency theory because it focuses on the best leadership style for a given situation.[96] Specifically, Hersey and Blanchard concentrate on the *maturity* of followers—that is, their readiness to take responsibility for their own behaviour. This includes both their job knowledge and skills, as well as their willingness to work without taking direction from others. Effective leaders are, according to this theory, able to adjust their styles to accommodate their followers' needs for guidance and direction—*task behaviour*—as well as their needs for emotional support—*relationship behaviour*. As shown in Figure 13-9, these two dimensions are independent.

By combining high and low levels of each dimension, four different types of situations are identified, each of which is associated with a leadership style that is most effective. Starting in the lower-left corner of Figure 13-9 are situations in which followers need very little in the way of emotional hand-holding and guidance with

☛ *As you recall from Chapter 4, it is essential that all personality measures be highly reliable.*

leader match The practice of matching leaders (based on their LPC scores) to the groups whose situations best match those in which they are expected to be most effective (according to LPC contingency theory).

situational leadership theory A theory suggesting that the most effective style of leadership—either delegating, participating, selling, or telling—depends on the extent to which followers require guidance, direction, and emotional support.

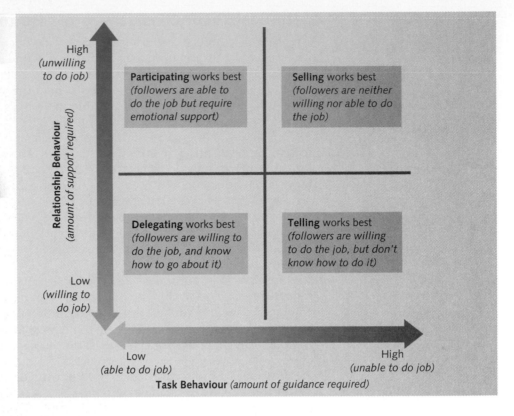

FIGURE 13-9 Situational Leadership Theory: Its Basic Dimensions

Hersey and Blanchard's *situational leadership theory* specifies that the most appropriate leadership style depends on the amount of emotional support required (i.e., followers' willingness to do the job) in conjunction with the amount of guidance required (i.e., followers' capacity to do the job).

High
(unwilling to do job)

Relationship Behaviour *(amount of support required)*

Participating works best
(followers are able to do the job but require emotional support)

Selling works best
(followers are neither willing nor able to do the job)

Delegating works best
(followers are willing to do the job, and know how to go about it)

Telling works best
(followers are willing to do the job, but don't know how to do it)

Low
(willing to do job)

Low
(able to do job)

High
(unable to do job)

Task Behaviour *(amount of guidance required)*

respect to how to do their jobs. In this situation, *delegating* is the best way to treat followers—that is, turning over to followers the responsibility for making and implementing decisions. Then, in the upper-left corner of the diagram is a situation in which followers are able but unwilling to do their jobs, and require high amounts of supportive behaviour to motivate them. A *participating* style of leadership works well in this situation because it allows followers to share their ideas, enhancing their desire to perform. In the next situation followers are unable and unwilling to do their jobs, and require both task direction and emotional support. The style known as *selling* is most appropriate here. This involves explaining decisions and providing opportunities for clarification. Finally, in the lower-right corner are situations in which followers are unable but willing to take responsibility for their actions. They are motivated, but lack the appropriate skills.

The practice of *telling* followers what to do is most useful in such situations—that is, giving them specific instructions and closely supervising their work.

According to this conceptualization, leaders must be able to (1) diagnose the situations they face, (2) identify the appropriate behavioural style, and then (3) implement that response. Because the situations leaders face may change all the time, leaders must constantly reassess them, paying special attention to their followers' needs for guidance and emotional support. To the extent that they do so, they are likely to be effective.

Because situational leadership theory is quite new, little evidence about it currently exists. The handful of studies that have been conducted to test the theory generally have been supportive, although not comprehensive.[97, 98] Still, practitioners have found the approach to be quite useful. In fact, it has been widely used to train leaders in such corporate giants as Xerox, Mobil Oil, and Caterpillar.[99]

Path-Goal Theory: Leaders as Guides to Valued Goals

Suppose you conducted an informal survey in which you asked 100 people to indicate what they expect from their leaders. What kind of answers would you receive? Although they would vary greatly, one common theme you might uncover would be, "I expect my leader to *help*—to assist me in reaching goals I feel are important." This basic idea plays a central role in House's **path-goal theory** of leadership.[100] In general terms, the theory contends that subordinates will react favourably to a leader only to the extent that they perceive this person as helping them progress toward various goals by clarifying actual paths to such rewards. That is, effective leaders clarify for followers what they need to do to get from where they are to where they should be, and to help them do so. More specifically, the theory contends that actions by a leader that clarify the nature of tasks and reduce or eliminate obstacles will increase perceptions on the part of subordinates that working hard will lead to good performance and that good performance, in turn, will be recognized and rewarded. Under such conditions, House suggests employee motivation and satisfaction will be enhanced.

How, precisely, can leaders best accomplish these tasks? The answer, as in other modern views of leadership, is, "It depends." (In fact, that's how you can tell it is a contingency theory.) And what it depends on is a complex interaction between key aspects of *leader behaviour* and certain *contingency factors*. With respect to leader behaviour, path-goal theory suggests that leaders can adopt four basic styles:

1. *Instrumental* (directive): an approach focused on providing specific guidance, establishing work schedules and rules

2. *Supportive*: a style focused on establishing good relations with subordinates and satisfying their needs

3. *Participative*: a pattern in which the leader consults with subordinates, permitting them to participate in decisions

4. *Achievement-oriented*: an approach in which the leader sets challenging goals and seeks improvements in performance

According to the theory, these styles are not mutually exclusive; in fact, the same leader can adopt them at different times and in different situations. Indeed, showing such flexibility is one important aspect of an effective leader.

Which of these contrasting styles is best for maximizing subordinates' satisfaction and motivation? The answer depends on two contingency factors. First, the style of choice is strongly affected by several *characteristics of subordinates*. For example, if followers are high in ability, an instrumental style of leadership may be unnecessary; instead, a less structured, supportive approach may be preferable. On the other hand, if subordinates are low in ability, the opposite may be true; people with poor ability need considerable guidance to help them attain their goals. Similarly, people high in need for affiliation (that is, those desiring close, friendly ties with others) may strongly prefer a supportive or participative style of leadership. Those high in the need for achievement may strongly prefer an achievement-oriented leader.

Second, the most effective leadership style also depends on several *aspects of the work environment*. For example, path-goal theory predicts that when tasks are unstructured and nonroutine, an instrumental approach by the leader may be best; much clarification and guidance are needed. However, when tasks are structured and highly routine, such leadership may actually get in the way of good performance and may be resented by subordinates who think the leader is engaging in unnecessary meddling. (See Figure 13-10 for an overview of all these aspects of path-goal theory.)

Path-goal theory has been subjected to empirical testing in several studies.[101] In general, results have been consistent with major predictions derived from the theory, although not uniformly so. Thus, at present, path-goal theory appears to be another framework offering valuable insights into leadership and the many factors that determine the degree to which individual leaders are successful in this role.

path-goal theory A theory of leadership suggesting that subordinates will be motivated by a leader only to the extent they perceive this individual as helping them to attain valued goals.

☛ Path-goal theory *is an extension of* expectancy theory, *described as a theory of motivation in Chapter 5.*

FIGURE 13-10 Path-Goal
Theory: An Overview

According to *path-goal theory*, perceptions among employees that leaders are helping them reach valued goals enhance both employees' motivation and job satisfaction. Such perceptions, in turn, are encouraged when a leader's style is consistent with the needs and characteristics of subordinates (e.g., their level of experience) and aspects of the work environment (e.g., the requirements of the tasks being performed).

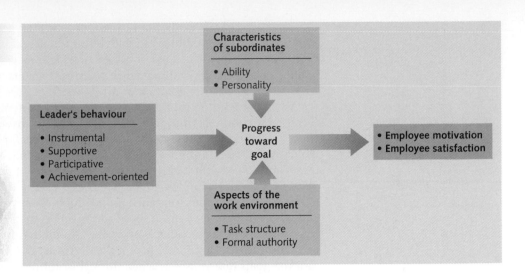

Normative Decision Theory: The Right Time for Employee Participation

As we discussed in Chapter 10, one of the major tasks performed by leaders is making decisions. Leaders who make good decisions will be more effective in the long run than leaders who make bad ones. But, how should they go about making decisions? Specifically, how much participation should leaders invite from subordinates? As we noted earlier, participation in decision making is an important variable in many organizational settings—one with implications for job satisfaction, stress, and productivity. Thus, the manner in which leaders handle this issue can be crucial in determining their effectiveness.

But how much participation in decisions by subordinates should leaders allow? Perhaps the most useful answer to this question is provided by the **normative decision theory** developed by Vroom and Yetton.[102] After careful study of available evidence, these researchers concluded that leaders often adopt one of five distinct methods for reaching decisions. These are summarized in Table 13-5, and as you can see, they cover the entire range—from decisions made solely by the leader in a totally autocratic manner through ones that are fully participative.

Are any of these approaches strongly preferable to the others? Vroom and Yetton claim that the answer is *no*. Just as there is no single best style of leadership, there is no single best strategy for making decisions. Each pattern offers its own mixture of benefits and costs. For example, decisions reached through participative means stand a better chance of gaining support and acceptance among subordinates. However, such decisions require a great deal of time—often more time than a leader or organization can afford. Similarly, decisions reached autocratically (by the leader alone) can be made

normative decision theory A theory of leader effectiveness focusing primarily on strategies for choosing the most effective approach to making decisions.

TABLE 13-5 Potential Strategies for Making Decisions

According to Vroom and Yetton, leaders making decisions often adopt one of the five basic strategies described here.

Source: Based on suggestions from Vroom & Yetton, 1973; see Note 102.

Decision Strategy	Description
AI (autocratic)	Leader solves problem or makes decision unilaterally, using available information.
AII (autocratic)	Leader obtains necessary information from subordinates but then makes decision unilaterally.
CI (consultative)	Leader shares the problem with subordinates individually, but then makes decision unilaterally.
CII (consultative)	Leader shares problem with subordinates in group meeting but then makes decision unilaterally.
GII (group decision)	Leader shares problem with subordinates in a group meeting; decision is reached through discussion to consensus.

more rapidly and efficiently. But such an approach can generate resentment among followers and encounter difficulties with respect to actual implementation. According to Vroom and Yetton, then, a major task faced by leaders is selecting the specific decision-making approach that will maximize potential benefits but minimize potential costs. How can this be done? Again, they offer specific suggestions.

Vroom and Yetton propose that leaders should attempt to select the best approach (or at least eliminate ones that are not useful) by answering several basic questions about the situation. These relate primarily to the *quality of the decision*—the extent to which it will affect important group processes such as communication or production—and to *acceptance of the decision*—the degree of commitment among subordinates needed for its implementation. For example, with respect to decision quality, a leader should ask questions such as: Is a high-quality decision required? Do I have enough information to make such a decision? Is the problem well structured? With respect to decision acceptance, he or she should ask: Is it crucial for effective implementation that subordinates accept the decision? Do subordinates share the organizational goals that will be reached through solution of this problem?

According to normative decision theory, answering such questions, and applying specific rules such as those shown in Table 13-6, eliminate some of the potential approaches to reaching a given decision. Those that remain constitute a feasible set that can, potentially, be used to reach the necessary decision.

To simplify this process, Vroom and Yetton recommend using a decision tree such as the one shown in Figure 13-11. To apply this diagram, a manager begins on the left side and responds, in turn, to the questions listed under each letter (A, B, C, and so on). As the manager replies to each question, the set of feasible approaches narrows. For example, imagine that the manager's answers are as follows:

- Question A: Yes—a high-quality decision is needed.
- Question B: No—the leader does not have sufficient information to make a high-quality decision alone.
- Question C: No—the problem is not structured.
- Question D: Yes—acceptance by subordinates is crucial to implementation.
- Question E: No—if the leader makes the decision alone, it may not be accepted by subordinates.

TABLE 13-6 Decision Rules in Normative Decision Theory

By applying the rules shown here, leaders can eliminate decision-making strategies that are likely to prove ineffective in a given situation and select those likely to be most effective.

RULES DESIGNED TO PROTECT DECISION QUALITY

Leader Information Rule	If the quality of the decision is important and you do not have enough information or expertise to solve the problem alone, eliminate an autocratic style.
Goal Congruence Rule	If the quality of the decision is important and subordinates are not likely to make the right decision, rule out the highly participative style.
Unstructured Problem Rule	If the quality of the decision is important but you lack sufficient information and expertise, and the problem is unstructured, eliminate the autocratic leadership styles.

RULES DESIGNED TO PROTECT DECISION ACCEPTANCE

Acceptance Rule	If acceptance by subordinates is crucial for effective implementation, eliminate the autocratic styles.
Conflict Rule	If acceptance by subordinates is crucial for effective implementation, and they hold conflicting opinions over the means of achieving some objective, eliminate autocratic styles.
Fairness Rule	If the quality of the decision is unimportant but acceptance is important, use the most participatory style.
Acceptance Priority Rule	If acceptance is critical and not certain to result from autocratic decisions, and if subordinates are not motivated to achieve the organization's goals, use a highly participative style.

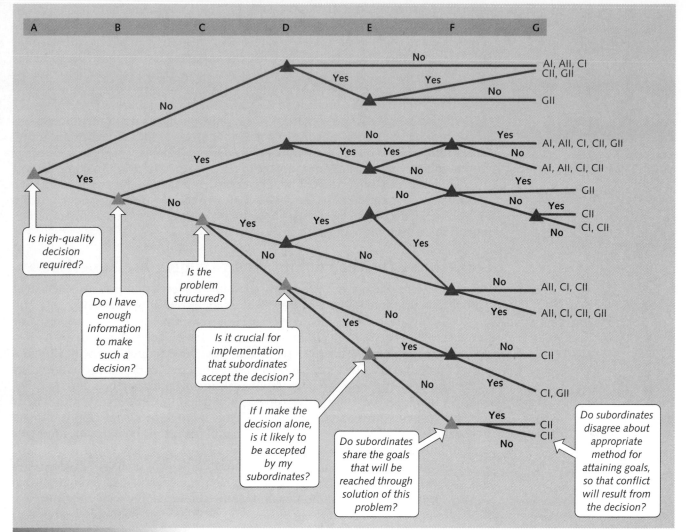

FIGURE 13-11 Normative Decision Theory: An Example

By answering the questions listed here and tracing a path through this decision tree, leaders can identify the most effective approaches to making decisions in a specific situation. Note: The path suggested by the answers to questions A through G (see pages 420–421) is shown by the light-coloured triangles.

(Source: Based on suggestions by Vroom & Yetton, 1973; see Note 103.)

☞ *In Chapter 1 we described the characteristics of a good theory.*

- Question F: No—subordinates do not share organizational goals.
- Question G: Yes—conflict among subordinates is likely to result from the decision.

As you can see, these replies lead to the conclusion that only one decision-making approach is feasible: full participation by subordinates. (The path leading to this conclusion is shown by the light-coloured triangles in Figure 13-11.) Of course, different answers to any of the seven key questions would have led to different conclusions.

The Vroom and Yetton model is highly appealing because it takes full account of the importance of subordinates' participation in decisions and offers leaders clear guidance for choosing among various methods for reaching decisions. As with any theory, though, the key question remains: Is it valid? Are its suggestions concerning the most effective style of decision making under various conditions really accurate? The results of several studies designed to test the model have been encouraging.

For example, it has been found that practising managers rate their own past decisions as more successful when they are based on procedures falling within the set of feasible options identified by the model than when they fall outside this set of methods.[103] Similarly, when small groups reach decisions through methods falling within the feasible set identified by the model, these decisions are judged to be more effective by outside raters than when they are made using other methods.[104] However, all studies have not supported the theory. For example, studies have found that the most effective path is based on considerations that go beyond the model, such as differences in the perspectives of leaders and subordinates and the personal skills or traits of leaders.[105] Such findings have led to the modification of the theory in recent years.[106] The latest version of the theory is more complex: Instead of seven contingency questions there are twelve, and instead of answering questions with a simple "yes" or "no," there are now five response options. This revised model is so highly complex that a computer program is used instead of a decision tree to help find the most appropriate leadership style. Preliminary evidence suggests that the resulting theory is more valid than the original, although it is far too complex to present here.

Whether we're talking about the more sophisticated version or the original version of normative decision theory, it is clear that this formulation makes an important contribution to our understanding of leadership. Insofar as there is widespread current interest in allowing subordinates to participate in decision making, normative decision theory is useful because it gives leaders clear guidance as to when such a move may be expected to improve task performance. Despite this guidance, leaders will be ineffective at consulting subordinates unless they are willing to participate in the decision-making process.

Substitutes for Leadership: When Leaders Are Superfluous

Throughout this chapter, we have emphasized that leaders are important. Their style, actions, and degree of effectiveness all exert major effects on subordinates and, ultimately, on organizations. In many cases, this is certainly true. Yet, almost everyone has observed or been part of groups in which the designated leaders actually had little influence—groups in which these people were mere figureheads with little impact on subordinates. One explanation for such situations involves the characteristics of the leaders in question: They are simply weak and unsuited for their jobs. Another, and in some ways more intriguing, possibility is that in some contexts, other factors may actually substitute for a leader's influence, making it superfluous, or neutralize the effects of the leader's influence. Kerr and Jermier propose this idea formally in their **substitutes for leadership** framework.[107]

According to this conceptualization, leadership may be irrelevant because various factors make it impossible for leaders to have any effect on subordinates—that is, they *neutralize* the effects of leadership. For example, people who are indifferent to the rewards a leader controls are unlikely to be influenced by those rewards. As a result, the leader's influence is likely to be negated. Leadership also may be irrelevant because conditions make a leader's influence unnecessary. That is, various factors *substitute for* leadership. For example, leadership may be superfluous when individuals have a highly professional orientation and find their work to be intrinsically satisfying. When the leader's impact is either neutralized or substituted for by various conditions, his or her impact is limited, at best.

Specifically, many different variables can produce such effects. Thus, we may ask: Under what conditions are leaders expected to have limited impact on task performance? The answers fall into three different categories. First, leadership may be unnecessary because of various individual characteristics. For example, a high level of knowledge, commitment, or experience on the part of subordinates may make it unnecessary for anyone to tell them what to do or how to proceed. Second, leadership may be unnecessary because jobs themselves may be structured in ways that make direction and influence from a leader redundant. For example, highly routine jobs require little direction, and jobs that are highly interesting also require little in the way of outside leadership stimulation. Third, various characteristics of organizations may make leadership unnecessary. For example, various work norms and strong feelings of cohesion among employees may directly affect job performance and render the presence of a leader unnecessary. Similarly, the technology associated with certain jobs may strongly determine the decisions and actions of people performing them, and so leave little room for input from a leader.

Evidence for these assertions has been obtained in several recent studies.[108] For example, in a recent investigation Podsakoff, Niehoff, MacKenzie, and Williams examined the work performance and attitudes of a broad sample of workers (includ-

substitutes for leadership The view that high levels of skill among subordinates or certain features of technology and organizational structure sometimes serve as substitutes for leaders, rendering their guidance or influence superfluous.

ing building service employees, administrative and clerical employees, and managers) who completed scales measuring their perceptions of the extent to which various leadership behaviours and substitutes for leadership were exhibited on their jobs.[109] Consistent with the theory, they found that job performance and attitudes were more strongly associated with the various substitutes than with the leadership behaviours themselves.

If leaders are superfluous in many situations, why has this fact often been overlooked? One possibility, suggested by Meindl and Ehrlich, is that we have a strong tendency to *romanticize* leadership—to perceive it as more important and more closely linked to performance in many contexts than it actually is.[110] To test this suggestion, they presented MBA students with detailed financial information about an imaginary firm, including a paragraph describing the firm's key operating strengths. The content of this paragraph was varied, so that four different groups of subjects received four different versions. These attributed the firm's performance either to its top-level management team, the quality of its employees, changing patterns of consumer needs and preferences, or federal regulatory policies, respectively.

After reading one of these paragraphs and examining other information about the firm, subjects rated two aspects of its overall performance: profitability and risk. Meindl and Ehrlich reasoned that because of the tendency to overestimate the importance of leadership, subjects would rate the firm more favourably when its performance was attributed to top-level management than when it was attributed to any of the other factors. According to the results of the study, this was precisely what occurred. The imaginary company was rated as higher in profitability and lower in risk when subjects had read the leadership-based paragraph than when they had read any of the others.

These findings, plus others obtained by the same researchers, help explain why leaders are often viewed as important and necessary even when, to a large degree, they are superfluous. Note: This in no way implies that leaders are usually unimportant. On the contrary, they often do play a key role in work groups and organizations. However, because this is not always so, their necessity should never be taken for granted.

SUMMARY AND REVIEW

Leadership: Some Basic Issues

Leadership is the process whereby one individual influences other group members toward the attainment of defined group or organizational goals. **Leaders** generally use noncoercive forms of influence and are influenced, in turn, by their followers. Whereas *leaders* create the group's or organization's mission and outline the strategy for attaining it, *managers* are responsible for implementing that mission. In practice, however, many leaders are also responsible for managerial tasks. Thus, although there is a distinction between leaders and managers, it is often blurred in practice.

Leader Traits and Behaviours

Early efforts to identify key traits that set leaders apart from other people—the **great person theory**—generally failed. However, recent evidence suggests that leaders do, in fact, differ from followers in certain respects. They are higher in leadership motivation, drive, honesty, self-confidence, and several other traits. In addition, successful leaders appear to

be high in *flexibility*—the ability to adapt their style to the followers' needs and to the requirements of specific situations.

Leaders differ greatly in their style or approach to leadership. One key dimension involves the extent to which leaders are *directive* or *permissive* toward subordinates—to the extent to which they tell subordinates how to do their jobs. Another involves the extent to which they are *autocratic* or *democratic* in their decision making—to the extent to which they permit subordinates to make decisions. Leaders also vary along two other key dimensions: concern with, and efforts to attain, successful task performance (**initiating structure**) and concern with maintaining favourable personal relations with subordinates (**consideration**). **Grid training** focuses on efforts to improve managers' concern for people and their concern for production by training them in communication skills and planning skills.

Leaders and Followers

Several approaches to leadership focus on the relationships between leaders and their followers. Graen's **leader-**

member exchange (LMX) model specifies that leaders favour members of some groups—referred to as *in-groups*—more than others—referred to as *out-groups*. As a result, in-groups perform better than out-groups.

The **attributional approach** focuses on leaders' attributions of followers' performance—that is, its underlying causes. When leaders perceive that their subordinates' poor performance is caused by internal factors, they react by helping them to improve. However, when poor performance is attributed to external sources, leaders direct their attention toward changing aspects of the work environment believed to be responsible for the poor performance.

Some leaders—known as **charismatic** leaders—exert profound effects on the beliefs, perceptions, and actions of their followers. Such leaders have a special relationship with their followers, in which they can inspire exceptionally high levels of performance, loyalty, and enthusiasm. Charismatic leaders tend to have high amounts of self-confidence, present a clearly articulated vision, behave in extraordinary ways, are recognized as change agents, and are sensitive to the environmental constraints they face. Although many leaders use their charisma for beneficial purposes, others do not.

Transformational leaders are also very charismatic, but they also do things that transform and revitalize their organizations. They provide intellectual stimulation, individualized consideration, and inspirational motivation. Transformational leaders tend to be very effective.

Special considerations are involved when it comes to leading self-managed teams. Notably, instead of directing people, team leaders should work at building trust and inspiring teamwork, expanding team capabilities, creating a team identity, making the most of differences between team members, and foreseeing and influencing change.

Contingency Theories of Leader Effectiveness

Contingency theories of leadership assume that there is no one best style of leadership and that the most effective style of leadership depends on the specific conditions or situations faced. For example, Fiedler's **LPC contingency theory** suggests that both a leader's characteristics and situational factors are crucial. Task-oriented leaders (termed *low LPC leaders*) are more effective than people-oriented leaders (termed *high LPC leaders*) under conditions in which the leader has either high or low control over the group in question. In contrast, people-oriented leaders are more effective under conditions where the leader has moderate control.

The **situational leadership theory** proposed by Hersey and Blanchard suggests that the most effective style of leadership—either delegating, participating, selling, or telling—depends on the extent to which followers require guidance, direction, and emotional support. Effective leaders are required to diagnose the situations they face and implement the appropriate behavioural style for that situation.

House's **path-goal theory** of leadership suggests that leaders' behaviour will be accepted by subordinates and will enhance their motivation only to the extent that it helps them progress toward valued goals and provides guidance or clarification not already present in work settings.

Vroom and Yetton's **normative decision theory** focuses on decision making as a key determinant of leader effectiveness. According to this theory, different situations call for different styles of decision making (e.g., autocratic, consultative, participative) by leaders. Decisions about the most appropriate style of decision making for a given situation are made on the basis of answers to questions regarding the quality of the decision required and the degree to which it is important for followers to accept and be committed to the decisions made. Complex decision trees are used to guide managers to the most appropriate styles of leadership.

Finally, the **substitutes for leadership** approach suggests that leaders are unnecessary in situations in which other factors can have just as much influence. For example, leaders are superfluous when (1) subordinates have exceptionally high levels of knowledge and commitment, (2) jobs are highly structured and routine, and (3) the technology used strongly determines individuals' behaviour.

CASE PREVIEW QUESTIONS FOR DISCUSSION

1. In what way do you think Maureen Kempston Darkes' legal training has influenced her leadership style?
2. In your opinion, do male and female leaders have different leadership styles?
3. Discuss the difference between the leadership style of Maureen Kempston Darkes and the stereotype of leadership in the auto industry.

CHAPTER QUESTIONS FOR DISCUSSION

1. What are the major differences between leaders, dictators, and managers?
2. It has often been said that "great leaders are born, not made." Do you agree? If so, why? If not, why?
3. Argue for or against the following statement: "The best leaders encourage participation from their subordinates."
4. In your experience, do most leaders have a small in-group? If so, what are the effects of this clique on other group members?
5. Explain how the process of attribution is involved in organizational leadership.
6. Consider all the people who have been prime minister of Canada during your lifetime. Which of these (if any) would you describe as charismatic? Which of these (if any) would you describe as transformational? Why?
7. Concern for people and concern for production are two recurring themes in the study of leadership. Describe the way they manifest themselves in various theories of leadership.

When Will Avon Call a Woman CEO?

The president and COO of Avon Products Inc., Toronto-born Andrea Jung, has everything. "A high-powered job. Designer clothes. Stock options." In addition to all this she has a husband (Michael Gould, CEO of Bloomingdale's), two children, and the Father's Day/Mother's Day Council named her a Mother of the year in 1997.[111]

Jung has her work cut out for her as she strives to achieve the company's goal of becoming "the Coca-Cola of the beauty industry."[112] She seems to be well on her way with a 32 percent increase in sales and a 43 percent increase in profits since she took the reins.

There is no question in the minds of Avon employees about Jung's vision for the company. Avon Canada's vice-president of marketing describes Jung as "tenacious" when it comes to the potential of Avon, despite the resistance she has encountered from some.[113]

Jung was originally a contender for Avon's top job. When James Preston retired, there was a widespread belief in the business community that a woman would be his successor. Preston had made a significant contribution to the advancement of women at Avon and it was expected that one of the group of women he had recruited into senior management positions would succeed him.

The pundits were wrong. Duracell's Charles Perrin was appointed to succeed Preston. Jung, who appeared to be the runner-up in the race, became president. The reason given for not hiring the front-running female Avon executives was that they did not have the main qualification the Board required: "experience running a company or a major operating division."[114] As one observer explained, people had their hearts set on a woman taking charge at Avon. "When people fall in love with an idea and it doesn't happen, they feel jilted."[115]

The person who was generally thought to be Jung's rival was Montrealer Christina Gold, who had long been regarded Avon's heir-apparent.[116] Gold's star plummeted when she turned down a position as manager of operations in countries outside North America in favour of a job focusing on direct-selling practices. While she felt this would be a move up, Avon's Board saw it as an indication that she was opting out of the running for the coveted promotion.[117]

Christina Gold and Andrea Jung have very different leadership styles. "Ms. Gold, a loyal [Avon] insider with simple tastes and down-home charm, is beloved from the corporate powers on down to the Avon ladies.... Ms. Jung, who favors Chanel suits, is an effervescent leader who has spent her career in high-end retailing."[118]

While the company has had a long reliance on direct selling, its focus was shifting to Internet and store-based retail efforts. This shift in strategy was inspired by Jung, who once worked for Gold. " 'She has a unique combination of left-brain, right-brain—creativity and business,' says Donna Karan, who put Jung on her own board."[119]

Andrea Jung has expressed exasperation with the focus the media has taken on her promotion. "'They missed the story,' Jung says today of the media response. 'It wasn't about one job. It was about me at age 39 becoming the first president in the company's history. It was exceptional at my age to be rewarded in this way.' "[120]

Critical Thinking Questions

1. Why was Andrea Jung chosen over Christina Gold and other candidates in the leadership race at Avon?

2. Discuss the dilemma facing women at Avon who want to move into the role of CEO.

3. (a) Should the next CEO at Avon be a woman? Explain.

   (b) Do you think Andrea Jung should be the next CEO at Avon? Why?

SKILLS PORTFOLIO

Experiencing Organizational Behaviour

Determining Your Leadership Style

As noted on pp. 416–417, *situational leadership theory* identifies four basic leadership styles. To be able to identify and enact the most appropriate style of leadership in any given situation, it is first useful to understand the style to which you are most predisposed. This exercise will help you gain such insight into your own leadership style.

Directions

Below are eight hypothetical situations in which you have to make a decision affecting you and members of your work group. For each, indicate which of the following actions you are most likely to take by writing the letter corresponding to that action in the space provided.

    A. Let the members of the group decide themselves what to do.

    B. Ask the members of the group what to do but make the final decision yourself.

C. Make the decision yourself but explain your reasons.

D. Make the decision yourself, telling the group exactly what to do.

____**1.** In the face of financial pressures, you are forced to make budget cuts for your unit. Where do you cut?

____**2.** To meet an impending deadline, someone in your secretarial pool will have to work late one evening to finish typing an important report. Who will it be?

____**3.** As coach of a company softball team, you are required to trim your squad to 25 players from 30 currently on the roster. Who goes?

____**4.** Employees in your department have to schedule their summer vacations so as to keep the office appropriately staffed. Who decides first?

____**5.** As chair of the social committee, you are responsible for determining the theme for the company ball. How do you do so?

____**6.** You have an opportunity to buy or rent an important piece of equipment for your company. After gathering all the facts, how do you make the choice?

____**7.** The office is being redecorated. How do you decide on the colour scheme?

____**8.** Along with your associates you are taking a visiting dignitary to dinner. How do you decide what restaurant to go to?

Scoring

1. Count the number of situations to which you responded by marking A. This is your *delegating* score.

2. Count the number of situations to which you responded by marking B. This is your *participating* score.

3. Count the number of situations to which you responded by marking C. This is your *selling* score.

4. Count the number of situations to which you responded by marking D. This is your *telling* score.

Questions for Discussion

1. Based on this questionnaire, what was your most predominant leadership style? Is this consistent with what you would have predicted in advance?

2. According to situational leadership theory, in what kinds of situations would this style be most appropriate? Have you ever found yourself in such a situation, and if so, how well did you do?

3. Do you think that it would be possible for you to change this style if needed?

4. To what extent were your responses to this questionnaire affected by the nature of the situations described? In other words, would you have opted for different decisions in different situations?

Working in Groups | Identifying Great Leaders in All Walks of Life

A useful way to understand the *great person theory* is to identify those individuals who may be considered great leaders and then to consider what it is that makes them so great. This exercise is designed to guide a class in this activity.

Directions

1. Divide the class into four equal-sized groups, arranging each in a semicircle.

2. In the open part of the semicircle, one group member—the recorder—should stand at a flip chart, ready to write down the group's responses.

3. The members of each group should identify the five most effective leaders they can think of—living or dead, real or fictional—in one of the following fields: business, sports, politics/government, humanitarian endeavours. One group should cover each of these domains. If more than five names come up, the group should vote on the five best answers. The recorder should write down the names as they are identified.

4. Examining the list, group members should identify the traits and characteristics that the people on the list have in common but that distinguish them from others who are not on the list. In other words, what is it that makes these people so special? The recorder should write down the answers.

5. One person from each group should be selected to present his or her group's responses to members of the class. This should include both the names, and the underlying characteristics.

Questions for Discussion

1. How did the traits identified in this exercise compare to the ones described in this chapter as important determinants of leadership? Were they similar or different? Why?
2. To what extent were the traits identified in the various groups different or similar? In other words, were different characteristics associated with success in different walks of life? Or were the ingredients for success more universal?
3. Were there some traits identified that you found surprising, or were they all expected?
4. Is it possible to change the traits identified in this exercise, or are they immutable?

TAKE IT TO THE NET

Prentice Hall

We invite you to visit the *Greenberg/Baron/Sales/Owen Companion Website* at *www.prenticehall.ca/greenberg* for this chapter's Internet resources.

Keith Kocho: Visionary, Missionary and Master Storyteller

Keith Kocho is a new breed of leader in a new breed of business. Energetic, creative, unfettered by traditional structures of any kind, he is keeping Digital Renaissance on the cutting edge of digital media development. It may be his equal enthusiasm for Dr. Seuss and Immanuel Kant that allows him to think "out of the box." Whatever the muse, Kocho's inspiration is infectious and it is golden. Digital Renaissance grew 486 percent between 1995 and 1998![1]

"He's the figurehead. The visionary. He does a lot of travelling, spreading the gospel of the company, dealing with clients in various capacities. And he's involved in a lot of industry-type committees," says one admiring staff member. Keith Kocho refers to these activities as his "missionary marketing."[2] When others saw the computer as a "simple data device," he predicted its coming of age as a "the communications medium of choice for business and consumer communications."[3] With evangelistic zeal, he says: "On the Internet we can all be storytellers. . . . Let's connect Canadians of every age, race, religion, and gender to each other and to the rest of the planet."[4]

"*Everything* is about storytelling," Keith Kocho tells his staff members at an early morning meeting. "It's putting a compelling message around what would otherwise be a bunch of bullet points on a slide. It's the stuff that actually gets *inside* people and makes them think."[5] For Kocho, the company's mission is to help his clients tell their stories. Digital Renaissance's home page on the World Wide Web speaks directly to potential new clients: "You have a story to tell. A storyteller is a person with a message and an audience to reach; a storyteller is a business with a product and a market to reach. We can help you tell your story by extending it with technology."[6]

By 1999, not only had Keith Kocho helped many a client tell its own story, but he had also helped his whole fledgling digital media industry to tell its story. As chair of the Digital Media Champion Group (DMCG), an Ontario-based association of digital media representatives formed in 1997, he urged business and government to work closely together to nurture the multimedia industry. In DMCG's report, *Playing To Win*, he urged "Let's work together towards a unified vision."[7]

Kocho's accomplishments have not gone unrecognized. The Business Development Bank of Canada awarded him the Young Entrepreneur of the Year Award in 1997 for his courage to move beyond traditional business thought to create Digital Renaissance ". . . as an organic, fluid organization with strong corporate ethics and a non-hierarchical management system . . . ." In its Website biography of Kocho, the Business Development Bank lists his efforts on Boards of Directors, e.g., ITAC, government committees, and pro bono community pro-

jects. "He was always a believer in the potential of unconventional thought in overcoming obstacles."[8]

Kocho's casual style of dress ". . . belies his impressive knowledge of both the technical and design sides of his business—he has the confidence of one who has pitched to a lot of suits, and brainstormed many a creative meeting on the shop floor." His expertise earned him a spot in *Marketing Magazine*'s "100 most influential communications professionals in Canada" in March 1996. Since his graduation from Ryerson in 1990, he has spent a substantial amount of time developing his skills in ". . . the cultural and design sides of media and in the technology world." He believes that this technological expertise is essential to his working relationship with his colleagues at Digital Renaissance. "I think that's the way I've been able to maintain the respect of the troops here," he says. "I have a lot of hands-on knowledge." He also emphasizes that he has to work constantly to stay up to date with developments in technology so he can communicate with those inside and outside his company. He even reads technical manuals![9]

By 7:00 A.M., Kocho and Scout regularly arrive at the office. After spending a short time in the on-site gymnasium, he glances through some newspapers.[10] Kocho describes his life at Digital Renaissance as "like being on *ER* [the television hospital show]" since he is constantly on call. He makes himself available to meet the priorities of everyone else at Digital Renaissance. This can make it difficult for him to plan his own schedule. He says that he manages to get everything done by working weekends and, basically, by giving up his life to the business.[11] Kocho says he is making a more concerted effort to break away from "wall-to-wall meetings" to find some time for his other "passions" such as hiking, wildlife photography, and canoeing.[12]

Discussion Questions

1. Describe Kocho's leadership style. Given what you have learned about Digital Renaissance in this multi-part cumulative case, do you think Kocho's leadership style is a good fit for this stage in the company's growth? Please explain your answer.

2. What are some of the "substitutes for leadership" available to the staff at Digital Renaissance?

3. What power bases does Kocho have at his disposal? Which bases does he use most often to influence the staff at Digital Renaissance?

4. In what way do you expect the challenges of leading Digital Renaissance to change over the next five to ten years?

Richard Branson: The Fearless CEO

Richard Branson is a modern-day knight riding off to take on giants—and winning. Branson's "giants" are mega businesses he takes on in their own market niche. Branson "says the Virgin brand is irreverent, eager to take on the Establishment, and dedicated to service. He believes that the occasional failure doesn't hurt, as long as Virgin is perceived to be fighting the good fight." From music retailing to clubs, hotels, publishing, and airlines, Branson's company, Virgin Group, is taking on all sectors. His goal is for Virgin to be a "total life company" providing commodities in all sectors. And now Branson has set his sights on Canada.

Branson's style has been described as "free spirited, innovative, irreverent." His daredevil feats are legendary. In 1986 he crossed the Atlantic in record time in his boat, "Virgin Atlantic Challenger II." Not satisfied to cross the ocean by surface conveyance, he set another record as the first hot-air balloonist to cross the Atlantic. In 1991 he ballooned across the Pacific Ocean, another record-breaking feat.

Branson has been an entrepreneur since his student days. In 1968, at the age of 18, he started his first business, *Student* magazine. The forerunner of the current Virgin Group was Virgin mail-order, started in 1970, and was followed in 1971 by the first Virgin record store on Oxford Street in London. Branson built the music business into a major production operation. From there, Branson started moving into other areas of communication, such as videos and broadcasting, and, eventually, expanded into retail and property development. Virgin Atlantic Airways was started in 1984 and has expanding routes around the world. In all, Virgin Group employs more than 15 000 people in 22 countries.

Branson's approach is straightforward. "We look at markets where things have been done the same way for a long time, and we ask whether we can do anything differently." One way he tries to do this is by emphasizing his people orientation. "The main thing we look for in our employees is people skills," says Branson. Branson looks at his job as "empowering people and helping people to get up and go and then leave them to it." He says he is "good at delegating" and depends on the managers of each of his companies to look after day-to-day operations, leaving his relatively small head-office staff to look for new giants to slay—or at least to stress out a bit.

Branson's P. T. Barnum style is closely tied into Virgin's image. His willingness to dress up (he wore a wedding gown to boost Virgin Bridal) and his daring feats contribute to his celebrity status. In 1997 and 1998 he was named Britain's best business leader in a KPMG survey. Some wonder if he might, in time, become Lord Mayor of London. With such reliance on his personality, others ask the inevitable question of what happens to Virgin after Branson. His reply is simple, and practical, "When artists die, their products sell for twice or three times as much." He hopes the same may be true for businesses.

Video Case Discussion Questions

1. **a)** Describe Richard Branson as a leader.
   b) Describe Richard Branson as a manager.
2. **a)** How effective is Branson's leadership style?
   b) What criteria did you use in 2a?
3. Describe Richard Branson's power bases.
4. Discuss Branson's answer to the question about what happens to Virgin after he leaves.

CBC Source: Richard Branson Interview *Venture* #613 (October 20, 1996).

Video Sources: Flynn, J., Zellner, W., Light, L., Weber, J. (1998, October 26). Then came Branson. *Business Week*, pp. 116–120 (quote, p. 118); Virgin: Richard Branson, www/virgin.com/richard_branson.html; Virgin: Corporate History, www.virgin.com/history.html; Carnoy, D. (1998, April). Richard Branson. *Success, 45*, pp. 62, 86 (quotes p. 62); Flynn, J., Zellner, W., Light, L., Weber, J. (1998, October 26). Then came Branson. *Business Week*, pp. 116–120 (quote p. 120).

CHAPTER 14

The Work Environment:
Culture and Technology

LEARNING OBJECTIVES

After reading this chapter you should be able to:

1. Define *organizational culture* and describe the role it plays in organizational functioning.

2. Distinguish between *dominant cultures* and *subcultures*, and the various types of organizational cultures that may exist within organizations.

3. Identify various mechanisms by which organizational culture is created.

4. Describe and give examples of various techniques used to transmit organizational culture.

5. Summarize the effects of organizational culture on both organizational and individual performance.

6. Explain why and how organizational culture is likely to change.

7. Identify the four major types of technology identified by Perrow.

8. Define and give examples of *automation* and explain how people are affected by the use of automation in the organizations within which they work.

9. Describe how *technology* can be used in organizations for purposes of assisting people with disabilities, monitoring job performance, improving the quality of customer service, and improving environmental quality.

The Clash of the Retailing Titans

What do you get when you combine two retail chains, one British and the other American, each with its own established ways of operating? This was the question when the venerable British department store Marks and Spencer acquired the American men's clothier Brooks Brothers, as part of its global expansion strategy. Marks and Spencer has stores around the world (see Figure 14-1), including retail outlets in Canada from St. John's to Victoria. Marks and Spencer's acquisition of Brooks Brothers was a major move and the lesson in the takeover was clear: Things don't always go smoothly when you combine two companies with an (Atlantic) ocean of differences between them.[1]

Both stores have always been highly committed to offering attentive customer service and impeccable goods, but that's where the similarity ended. Brooks Brothers' strong suit was manufacturing fine quality traditional men's clothing, whereas Marks and Spencer had always purchased its broad inventory from a variety of suppliers. Marks and Spencer also used carefully implemented management systems (e.g., cost control and inventory management procedures), which it soon imposed on the more loosely managed Brooks Brothers. At Marks and Spencer sales staff are paid in a manner that takes into account overall store performance, an incentive to work together as a team. By contrast, Brooks Brothers employees had always been rewarded based on their own performance, with salespeople working like individual entrepreneurs—that was, until a management team from London arrived in the United States and introduced the team approach. Their lesson: What is good for the store is also good for the individual employee. The Americans grumbled, at first, and turnover resulted.

Beyond these basic differences, working together was made difficult by even the most mundane aspects of everyday communication. Marks and Spencer executives were more formal than their American counterparts at Brooks Brothers. The Americans tended to keep their office doors open and walk around, but the Marks and Spencer bosses usually sat behind closed doors and wrote memos. Employees from each company recognized what the other had to offer but felt uneasy in their quest for the common ground.

After about three years, Brooks Brothers employees came to recognize that the Marks and Spencer folks were interested in working *with* them, as opposed to simply imposing their ways on them. It helped greatly for Brooks Brothers managers to spend time at the parent company's headquarters where they could be exposed to the company philosophy on a firsthand basis and learn its ways of doing things. To further demonstrate the seriousness of Marks and Spencer's investment in Brooks Brothers, it appointed to its board of directors an individual in charge of North American operations.

Although the Americans may have felt imposed upon by their new parent company, at least initially, they soon recognized that Marks and Spencer was a successful retailer that knew what it was doing. But you cannot blame them for feeling insecure. Before being acquired by Marks and Spencer, Brooks Brothers had undergone two changes of ownership in as many years—the most recent owner being unfamiliar with the world of retailing. As Brooks Brothers employees recognized that they were, in many ways, "rescued" by Marks and Spencer, they came to accept its ways.[2]

Figure 14-1 Marks and Spencer Store Symbolizes the Formality of Its Culture

Marks and Spencer's flagship store on Oxford Street near Marble Arch is a tourist attraction in London, England. It stands as a symbol of the company's formal and carefully implemented management systems—management systems at first resented by its American acquisition, the more loosely managed Brooks Brothers.[3]

The difficulties that Marks and Spencer and Brooks Brothers associates had in dealing with each other stemmed from their companies' different approaches to conducting business. These were fundamental differences in the shared beliefs, expectations, and core values of people in the organization—collectively referred to as *organizational culture*.[4] An organization's culture can be so deeply imbedded within the way it operates that its effects can be quite profound. In the case of Marks and Spencer, culture was reinforced by over a century's worth of successful business experience. Likewise, other companies—such as CIBC, Husky Injection Molding Systems (see the CASE PREVIEW for Chapter 5), Roots Canada (see the CASE IN POINT for Chapter 1), McDonald's, and the Walt Disney Company—have exceptionally strong and effective cultures that have been credited for contributing to their success. Consider, for example, Intel, the leading developer of computer chips. A large part of its success has been linked to an organizational culture in which people are encouraged to work together and share resources as needed. To help bring people together, just about everyone works in cubicles so that they are readily accessible to others, even CEO Andy Grove.[5]

Although the effects of organizational culture can be quite profound, it would be misleading to suggest that culture operates in a vacuum. Indeed, whereas culture influences organizations from inside, the external environments within which organizations operate also have considerable impact on their functioning. For example, economists tell us how economic forces affect corporate performance, lawyers consider the impact of legal rulings and governmental regulations, and marketers investigate the effects of competition and product demand. Specialists in organizational behavior are also sensitive to the effects of the external environmental forces acting on organizations, particularly the use of *technology*—that is, the organization's methods for transforming raw materials (whether physical entities, such as iron ore, or abstract ones, such as ideas) into various goods or services.[6]

Because these two aspects of the work environment, culture and technology, are so vital to organizational functioning, they will be the focus of this chapter.[7] Specifically, we will begin by describing the basic nature of organizational culture, including the role it plays in organizations. Then, we will describe the processes through which organizational culture is formed and maintained. Next, we will review the effects of organizational culture on individual and organizational functioning and examine when and how culture is subject to change. Following this, we will shift our attention to technology. In this regard, we will examine the role of technology in organizations, focusing especially on the way people respond to automation. Finally, we will review various ways technology is used today to improve both the quality of employees' work lives and the effectiveness of organizational functioning.

Organizational Culture: Its Basic Nature

To understand organizational culture more fully, we will begin by exploring three very fundamental issues. First, we will formally define organizational culture. Second, we will examine the role that culture plays in organizations. Finally, we will consider a key issue relevant to understanding culture: whether there is only one or many different cultures operating within organizations.

Organizational Culture: A Definition

Anyone who has worked in several different organizations knows that each is unique. Even organizations concerned with the same activities or that provide similar products or services can be very different places in which to work.

It's tempting to speculate that because people have different personalities, the organizations in which they work are likely to be different from each other as well. However, when you consider that entire organizations are often so consistently different from each other, it's apparent that there's more involved than simply differences in the personalities of the employees. In fact, in many organizations, employees are a constantly changing cast of characters—old ones frequently leave and new ones join. Despite such shifts, however, the organizations themselves alter slowly, if at all. In fact, it is often the new employees who change rather than their organizations. In a sense, then, organizations have a stable existence of their own, quite apart from the unique combination of people of which they are composed at any given time.

What accounts for such stability? To a great extent, the answer involves the impact of **organizational culture**—a cognitive framework consisting of attitudes, values, behavioural norms, and expectations shared by organization members.[8] Once established, these beliefs, expectancies, and values tend to be relatively stable and exert strong influences on organizations and those working in them.

At the root of any organization's culture is a set of core characteristics that are collectively valued by members of an organization. Recent research by Chatman and Jehn has shown that seven elements of organizational culture may be used to describe organizations.[9] These are as follows:

1. *Innovation:* the extent to which people are expected to be creative, and generate new ideas. For example, Nortel Networks (see CASE PREVIEW for Chapter 3), Bombardier Inc., Newbridge Networks Corp., and Ballard Power Systems Inc. are Canadian companies noted for their innovation.[10]

2. *Stability:* valuing a stable, predictable, rule-oriented environment. For example, the Bank of Canada is generally perceived to be very conservative.

3. *Orientation toward people:* being fair, supportive, and showing respect for individuals' rights. As defined in this way, Husky Injection Molding Systems (see the CASE PREVIEW for Chapter 5), Dofasco, and Magna International Inc. have been recognized as having highly "people-oriented" cultures.[11]

4. *Results-orientation:* the strength of its concern for achieving desired results. Bombardier Inc., Nortel, BCE Inc., Magna International, and Barrick Gold are all respected high performers.[12]

5. *Easygoingness:* the extent to which the work atmosphere is relaxed and laid back. Roots Canada projects such an easygoing image (see CASE IN POINT for Chapter 1).

6. *Attention to detail:* concern for being analytical and precise. For example, one employee of Merck, the world's largest maker of prescription drugs, recognized the importance of precision in the company's work: "Here we make drugs and there's no room for error."[13]

7. *Collaborative orientation:* emphasis on working in teams, as opposed to individually. Companies in which there is a great deal of research and development work, such as 3M Canada Inc. and Newbridge Networks Corp.,[14] tend to have cultures that emphasize a collaborative orientation.

As these examples suggest, different sets of core values are reflected in the cultures of different organizations. Testing this idea, Chatman and Jehn compared 15 companies in four different industries with respect to these seven aspects of organizational culture. Their results suggest that there were similarities between the cultures of companies within the same industries. Specifically, they found that the companies studied had cultures that were more similar to each other when they were in the same industry than when they were in different industries. For example, consulting firms had cultures that were more similar to each other than they were to other types of companies, such as accounting firms. The researchers also found connections between culture and various industry characteristics. In general, companies had cultures that were in keeping with the kind of work they did. For example, consulting firms had cultures that were more innovative and more people-oriented than did the postal service. These results suggest that organizational culture is not only a key factor in distinguishing between individual companies, but between entire industries.

organizational culture A cognitive framework consisting of attitudes, values, behavioural norms, and expectations shared by organization members.

Newbridge Networks Corp.
www.newbridge.com

Ballard Power Systems Inc.
www.ballard.com

Culture's Role in Organizations

As you read about the various cultural values that make organizations special, it probably strikes you that culture is an intangible force, but one with far-reaching consequences. Indeed, culture plays several important roles in organizations. Most obviously, an organization's culture provides a *sense of identity* for its members. The more clearly an organization's shared perceptions and values are defined, the more strongly people can associate themselves with their organization's mission and feel a vital part of it.

A second important function of culture is generating *commitment to the organization's mission*. Sometimes it's difficult for people to go beyond thinking of their own interests: How will this affect me? However, when there is a strong, overarching culture, people feel that they are part of that larger, well-defined whole and involved in the entire organization's work. Bigger than any one individual's interests, culture reminds people of what their organization is all about.

A third important function of culture is that it serves to *clarify and reinforce standards of behaviour*. While this is essential for newcomers, it is also beneficial for seasoned veterans. In essence, culture guides employees' words and deeds, making it clear what they should do or say in a given situation. In this sense, it provides stability to behaviour, both with respect to what one individual might do at different times, but also what different individuals may do at the same time. For example, in a company with a culture that strongly supports customer satisfaction, employees will have clear guidance as to how they are expected to behave: doing whatever it takes to please the customer (a topic we will discuss in more detail later in this chapter). By serving these three important roles, it is clear that culture is an important force influencing behaviour in organizations (for a summary, see Figure 14-2).

☛ In Chapter 6 we discuss the idea of commitment to one's organization.

FIGURE 14-2 The Basic Functions of Organizational Culture

Organizational culture serves the three major functions summarized here.

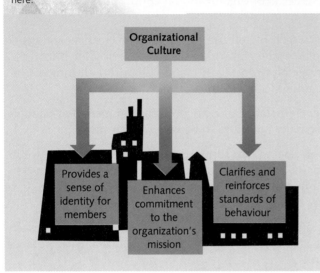

Cultures within Organizations: One or Many?

☛ A parallel can be drawn between organizational subcultures and national subcultures, as discussed in Chapter 2.

Our discussion thus far has implied that each organization has only a single, uniform culture—one set of shared values, beliefs, and expectations. In fact, this is rarely the case. Instead, organizations—particularly large ones—typically have *several* cultures operating within them.[15]

In general, people tend to have more attitudes and values in common with others in their own fields or work units than they do with those in other fields or other parts of the organization. These various groups may be said to have several different **subcultures**—cultures existing within parts of organizations rather than entirely through them. These typically are distinguished with respect to either functional differences (i.e., the type of work done) or geographic distances (i.e., the physical separation between people). For example, the subculture of a university's philosophy department may call for faculty to dress casually, whereas the subculture of the law faculty may dictate dressing more formally. Research suggests that several subcultures based on occupational, professional, or functional divisions usually exist within any large organization.[16]

subcultures Cultures existing within parts of organizations rather than entirely through them. Members of subcultures share values in addition to the core values of their organization as a whole.

dominant culture The overall culture of an organization, reflected by core values that are shared throughout the organization.

This is not to say, however, that there also may not be a **dominant culture**, a distinctive, overarching "personality" of an organization—the kind of culture to which we have been referring. An organization's dominant culture reflects its core values, dominant perceptions that are generally shared throughout the organization. Typically, while members of subcultures may share additional sets of values, they generally also accept the core values of their organizations as a whole (see Figure 14-3).[17] Thus, subcultures should not be thought of as a bunch of totally separate cultures, but rather "mini" cultures operating within a larger, dominant culture.

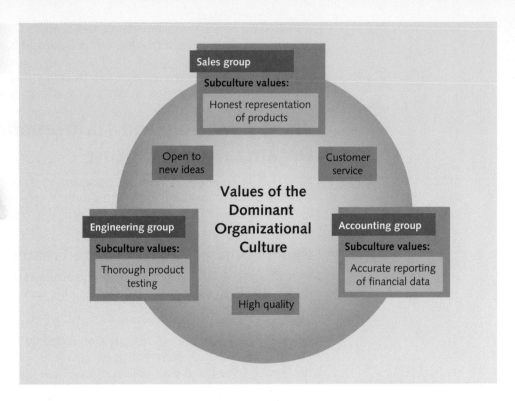

Types of Organizational Culture

Although organizations tend to have their own unique cultures, Sonnenfeld notes that these commonly fall into one of four different categories—the *academy*, the *club*, the *baseball team*, and the *fortress*.[18]

1. **Academy:** Think of an organization that hires lots of new college graduates and gives them the special training they need to do a wide variety of jobs. An organization that provides opportunities for people to master many different jobs and to move from one to the next is known as an *academy*. Examples include Nortel (see CASE PREVIEW for Chapter 3), Canadian Tire Acceptance Limited, Coca-Cola, General Motors, IBM, and Procter & Gamble.

2. **Club:** As you probably know from experience, some organizations are highly concerned with getting people to fit in and be loyal. Such an organization is called a *club*. In a club, one's age and experience are highly valued. Various government agencies, including the military, are clubs.

3. **Baseball team:** If you think about your favourite professional baseball team, you can probably identify stars who are very talented and highly paid but who are willing to go to another team if they are offered a better deal. Many organizations are the same way, notably those in high-tech fields (e.g., software development firms and biotech companies), and professional fields (e.g., investment banking, law, and accounting). People in such organizations tend to be entrepreneurs who take risks and are handsomely rewarded for their successes.

4. **Fortress:** Imagine an organization that is facing hard times, such as a large retailer or a forest products company. Its main preoccupation is not inventiveness, like the baseball team, but something more basic—survival. For those who enjoy the challenges of seeing a company turn around, and who don't mind the lack of job security, a fortress may be a stimulating place to work.

As you might imagine, not all organizations fit perfectly into these four different types. One reason is simply that organizations may have a blend of cultures operating at the same time. Another reason is that organizations tend to change over time and may be in transition. For example, Apple Computer appears to have started life as a baseball team, attracting top programmers and engineers who launched the company. Then, as it matured, it became an academy. With reports of Apple's decline it may have become more of a fortress.[19] As the push for turnaround builds at the company, Apple may yet return to its earlier baseball team or academy status.

The Formation and Maintenance of Organizational Culture

Now that we have described what organizational culture is and how it operates, we are prepared to consider two more important issues: how culture is initially created and how it is sustained—that is, what keeps it going once it is created.

How Is Organizational Culture Created?

Why do many individuals within an organization share basic attitudes, values, and expectations? Several factors contribute to this state of affairs and hence to the emergence of organizational culture.

Company founders.   First, organizational culture may be traced, at least in part, to the *founders of the company*.[20] These individuals often possess dynamic personalities, strong values, and clear visions of how their organizations should operate. Since they are on the scene first and play a key role in hiring initial staff, their attitudes and values are readily transmitted to new employees. The result: These views become the accepted ones in the organization, and persist long after the founders are no longer on the scene. For example, workaholic Ted Rogers, lying in a hospital bed three days after having heart surgery in 1992, was on the phone with his office. He expects the same dedication from his employees.[21] Ray Kroc founded the McDonald's restaurant chain on the values of good food at a good value served in clean, family-oriented surroundings—key cultural values that persist today. Likewise, although he's no longer with us, Walt Disney's wholesome family values are still cherished at the company that bears his name—in large part because employees ask themselves, "What would Walt think?"[22] These individuals' values continue to permeate their entire companies and are central parts of their dominant cultures.

Organizational experience.   Second, organizational culture often develops out of an organization's *experience with the external environment*.[23] Every organization must find a niche for itself in its industry and in the marketplace. As it struggles to do so in its early days, it may find that some values and practices work better than others. For example, one company may determine that delivering defect-free products is its unique market niche; by doing so, it can build a core of customers who prefer it to competing businesses. As a result, a deep, shared commitment to high quality may become part of the organization's culture. In contrast, another company may find that selling products of moderate quality, but at attractive prices, works best. The result: A dominant value centring on *price leadership* takes shape. In these and countless other ways, an organization's culture is shaped by its interaction with the external environment.

Internal interaction.   Third, organizational culture develops out of *contact between groups of individuals within an organization*. To a large extent, culture involves shared interpretations of events and actions on the part of organization members.[24] In short, organizational culture reflects the fact that people assign similar meaning to various events and actions—that they come to perceive the key aspects of the world, those relevant to the organization's work, in a similar manner. But does repeated interaction between organization members actually lead them to share perceptions or interpretations of the external world?

A study conducted by Rentsch provides direct evidence for this view.[25] In this investigation, members of an accounting firm were first interviewed and asked to de-

☞ *The underlying perceptual processes involved in interpreting events and behaviour are discussed in connection with our treatment of social perception in Chapter 3.*

scribe their organization—what events take place in it, why these events occur, and so on. On the basis of these interviews, 15 frequently occurring events were identified (e.g., account executives allocate billable work to team members; staff and partners are to be reviewed every six months), as were nine sets of adjectives to describe them (e.g., professional/nonprofessional, stressful/ relaxed). Participants then completed questionnaires in which they indicated the extent to which the 15 events were similar to one another and rated each event in terms of the nine adjective dimensions. They also indicated the extent to which they, personally, interacted with all other members of the organization. This last set of data was used to identify various *interaction groups*—groups of people within the organization who interacted regularly with one another. Rentsch's major predictions were straightforward: People belonging to the same interaction groups would perceive organizational events in a similar manner to a greater extent than people belonging to different interaction groups. In other words, people who interacted with one another on a regular basis would come to perceive key aspects of their working world in similar terms, whereas those who did not interact regularly would come to perceive the same events differently. Results offered strong support for these predictions (see Figure 14-4).

These findings suggest that shared meanings or interpretations—a key ingredient in organizational culture—derive, at least in part, from shared experiences and from the experience of working together. Moreover, this same process seems to play a role in the development of organizational subcultures, as groups of employees who usually work together develop views somewhat different from those of other groups of employees about what is happening in their company and of the meaning of such events.

There are several practical applications of these findings. First, because different groups within an organization have somewhat different cultures, interventions designed to change job performance or work-related attitudes through shifts in culture should be customized for each important group.[26] Second, if shared expectations and values are desired across an organization, steps should be taken to increase contact and interaction between various groups. Finally, Rentsch's findings point to the fact that sometimes, seemingly small events can carry big messages. For example, one of the events described most frequently by members of the organization studied was, "Partners sometimes play golf in the afternoon." Senior partners in the company were shocked to discover that this activity, which they viewed as relatively trivial, received so much attention from others. In retrospect, however, they realized that it conveyed important meanings to other employees—meanings such as "Only senior partners have any privileges around here," or "Whatever people say, status is really

FIGURE 14-4 Organizational Culture as Shared Meanings

Organizational members who interacted with one another on a regular basis came to share interpretations of organizational events. Those who did not interact with one another did not share such interpretations. According to Rentsch (1991; see Note 25), such shared meanings or interpretations are an important determinant of organizational culture.

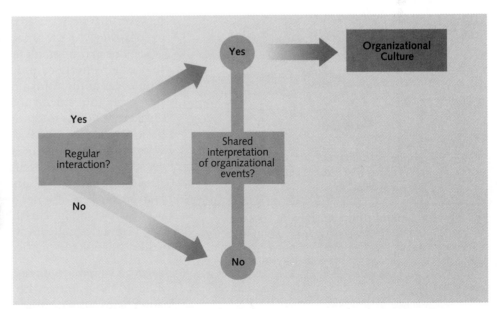

important." We will return to this point in our discussion of efforts to change organizational culture. For now, we simply note that where organizational culture is concerned, actions do indeed "speak louder than words."

Tools for Transmitting Culture

How are cultural values transmitted between people? In other words, how do employees come to learn about their organization's culture? Research has shown that there are several key mechanisms involved, most importantly: *symbols, stories, jargon, ceremonies,* and *statements of principle.*[27]

symbols Material objects that connote meanings extending beyond their intrinsic content.

Symbols: Objects that say more than meets the eye.   First, organizations often rely on **symbols**—material objects that connote meanings that extend beyond their intrinsic content.[28] For example, some companies use impressive buildings to convey the organization's strength and culture. Nortel's Jean Monty is proud of his company's headquarters building, which is designed to encourage innovation and creativity.[29] Other companies rely on slogans such as Dofasco's "Our product is steel, our strength is people." Corporate cars (or even jets!) are also used to convey information about an organization's culture. In some cases, such as the Royal Bank of Canada's John Cleghorn's getting rid of the company jet, the absence of such trappings is an even more powerful cultural symbol (see **THE QUEST FOR QUALITY** in Chapter 13).[30]

☛ *We discuss the use of status symbols in Chapter 8, and the use of power in organizations in Chapter 12.*

Research has shown that symbols are an important vehicle for communicating culture. For example, in an interesting study, Ornstein showed drawings of company reception areas to people and then asked them to evaluate what the companies pictured were like.[31] She found that different types of symbols projected different images of the organizations' likely cultures. For example, firms in which there were lots of plants and flower arrangements were judged to have friendly, person-oriented cultures, whereas those in which waiting areas were adorned with awards and trophies were believed to be highly interested in achieving success. These findings suggest that material symbols are potent tools for sending messages about organizational culture (see Figure 14-5).

"What we're looking for, Ted, is a guy who has pictures of himself with lots of famous people."

FIGURE 14-5 Symbolizing a Culture of Success

If a collection of photos of oneself with successful people symbolize one's own success, then displaying such photos in an organization may be recognized as reflecting the successfulness of the organization. Organizations regularly use such symbols to convey important aspects of their organizational culture.

(Source: Copyright © 1992 by Leo Cullum.)

Stories: "In the old days, we used to . . .".   Organizations also transmit information about culture by virtue of the *stories* that are told in them, both formally and informally.[32] Stories illustrate key aspects of an organization's culture, and telling them can effectively introduce or reaffirm those values to employees.[33] Some of the most effective stories involve recounting *critical incidents*, important events in shaping the company's history.[34] It is important to note, however, that stories need not involve some great event, such as someone who saved the company with a single wise decision but may be small tales that become legends because they so effectively communicate a message. For example, employees at the British confectionery firm, Cadbury, are purposely told stories about the company's founding on Quaker traditions to get them to appreciate and accept the basic Quaker value of hard work.[35] Famous Canadian developer Paul Reichmann is well known for his attention to even the most minute detail. For example, "during the construction phase of Canary Wharf, he spent several hours pouring buckets of water over different marble slabs to see how each would look in the rain. Also, as the story goes, he once kept a design team working all night because he didn't like the look of a particular litter bin."[36]

Jargon: The special language that defines a culture.   Even without telling stories, the everyday language used in companies helps sustain culture. For example, the slang or *jargon*

Canadian Radio-television and Telecommunications Commission
www.crtc.gc.ca

that is used in a company helps its members define their identities as members of an organization. For example, for many years employees at IBM referred to disk drives as "hard files" and circuit boards as "planar boards," terms that defined the insulated nature of their culture.[37] Someone working in telecommunications may be talking about the CRTC (Canadian Radio-television and Telecommunications Commission), or someone in the power industry might refer to AECL (Atomic Energy of Canada Limited), or someone in management development may speak of a "paradigm shift" (a change in thinking and interpreting the world, in this case of management and work).[38] Over time, as organizations—or departments within them—develop unique language to describe their work, their terms, although strange to newcomers, serve as a common factor that brings together individuals belonging to a corporate culture or subculture.

☞ For a discussion of the use of jargon in organizations, see Chapter 9.

Ceremonies: Special events that commemorate corporate values.   Organizations also do a great deal to sustain their cultures by conducting various types of *ceremonies*. Indeed, ceremonies may be seen as celebrations of an organization's basic values and assumptions.[39] Just as a wedding ceremony symbolizes a couple's mutual commitment and a swearing-in ceremony marks the beginning of a new term for a prime minister and Cabinet, various organizational ceremonies also celebrate some important accomplishment. For example, one accounting firm celebrated its move to much better facilities by throwing a party, a celebration signifying that it "has arrived," or "made it to the big time."[40] Such ceremonies convey meaning to people inside and outside the organization. As Deal and Kennedy put it, "Ceremonies are to the culture what the movie is to the script . . . values that are difficult to express in any other way."[41]

☞ Statements of principle are likely to be included within formal codes of ethics, *described in Chapter 2.*

Statements of principle: Defining culture in writing.   A fifth way in which culture is transmitted is via direct *statements of principle*. Some organizations have explicitly written their principles for all to see. For example, Forrest Mars, the founder of the candy company M&M Mars developed his "Five Principles of Mars," which still guide his company today: quality (everyone is responsible for maintaining quality), responsibility (all employees are responsible for their own actions and decisions), mutuality (creating a situation in which everyone can win), efficiency (most of the company's 41 factories operate continuously), and freedom (giving employees opportunities to shape their futures).[42]

Organizational Culture: Its Consequences and Capacity to Change

If you are beginning to think that organizational culture can play an important role in the functioning of organizations, you are right. To make this point explicit, we will now examine the various ways in which organizational culture has been found to affect organizations and the behaviour of individuals in them. Because some of these effects might be undesirable, organizations are sometimes interested in changing their cultures. Accordingly, we will also consider why and how organizational culture might be changed.

The Effects of Organizational Culture

Organizational culture exerts many effects on individuals and organizational processes—some dramatic and others more subtle. Culture generates strong pressures on people to go along, to think and act in ways consistent with the existing culture.[43] Thus, if an organization's culture stresses the importance of product quality and excellent service, its customers will generally find their complaints handled politely and efficiently. If, instead, the organization's culture stresses high output at any cost, customers seeking service may find themselves on a much rockier road. An organization's culture can strongly affect everything from the way employees dress and the amount of time allowed to elapse before meetings begin, to the speed with which people are promoted.

Organizational performance. Turning to the impact of culture on organizational processes, considerable research has focused on the possibility of a link between culture and organizational performance.[44] One view is that in order to influence performance, organizational culture must be strong. In other words, approval or disapproval must be expressed to those who act in ways consistent or inconsistent with the culture, respectively, and there must be widespread agreement on values among organizational members.[45] Only if these conditions prevail, researchers believe, will a link between organizational culture and performance be observed. Some evidence supports this contention. For example, Dennison found that corporations with cultural values favouring participation by employees in activities such as decision making generate a return on investment twice as great as that of corporations lacking this value.[46]

Although it is an intriguing idea that certain types of organizational cultures are better than others, the evidence is not all that compelling.[47] In fact, some of the firms Peters and Waterman classified as having the best cultures, such as Wang Laboratories and Texas Instruments, have suffered serious financial difficulties since their book was published.[48] It makes sense that the financial profitability of a company is linked to so many different factors (e.g., the economy, governmental regulation, the existence of competitors) that a single force alone, even a potent one such as organizational culture, may have only limited impact on a company's financial status. In other words, the idea that some cultures are more strongly associated with successful organizational performance than others must be considered questionable at this time.

Length of employment. This does not mean that organizational culture cannot have considerable effects on individuals' attitudes and performance. Indeed, it appears that people are more willing to work in some types of cultures than others. Demonstrating this idea, Sheridan compared the voluntary survival rates (how long employees stay with the company before resigning) of over 900 new employees at several different public accounting firms over a six-year period.[49] Based on responses to a questionnaire, the cultures of the firms were distinguished between those that primarily emphasized the value of hard work and those that emphasized the value of pleasant interpersonal relationships. As shown in Figure 14-6, survival rates among the new employees differed according to the cultures of the organizations in which they worked. Although voluntary turnover was nonexistent within the first year of employment, differences emerged over time. Specifically, employees survived longer in firms whose cultures stressed pleasant interpersonal relationships than those whose cultures emphasized the value of hard work—14 months longer, on average. Although people stay with jobs for various reasons, it is clear that the nature of the organization's culture is an important consideration.

Person-organization fit. Additional research suggests that to understand the effects of organizational culture, we should consider not just the nature of an organization's culture alone, but also the extent to which the values held by employees match those of their organizations. The better this fit, the more effectively employees should be able to operate on their jobs. To test this idea, O'Reilly, Chatman, and Caldwell conducted a study in which they first asked hundreds of individuals from eight different organizations to complete a questionnaire designed to measure the values of their companies (e.g., orientation toward outcomes or results, attention to detail, innovation, and risk taking).[50] Next, the same participants reported the extent to which similar values were important to them personally. Finally, the researchers assessed how closely individuals' personal values coincided with their organizations' (i.e., *person-organization fit*), and compared this to various attitudinal and behavioural measures over a two-year period (e.g., organizational commitment, job satisfaction, intentions to leave, and records of actual turnover). It was found that the closer the person-organization fit, the more satisfied people were with their jobs, and the less interested they were in quitting. In fact, when participants were divided into groups with relatively high and low person-organization fit, those for whom fit was high were indeed less likely to quit their jobs over a two-year period than those for whom fit was low.

☞ *As we note in Chapter 6, the concept of fit with one's organization is an important determinant of work-related attitudes.*

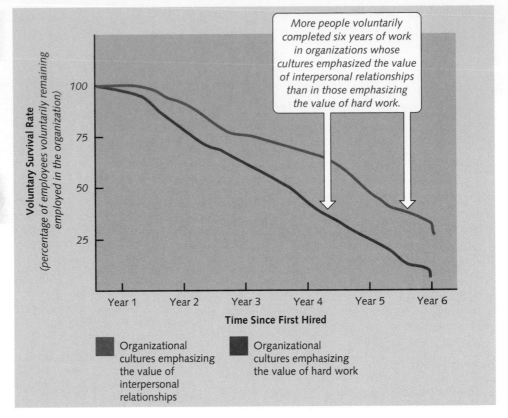

Sheridan examined the voluntary survival rates of new employees of public accounting firms over a six-year period. On average, employees worked longer for firms whose cultures emphasized pleasant interpersonal relationships than those whose cultures emphasized hard work.

(Source: Adapted from Sheridan, 1992; see Note 49.)

These findings have important implications both for individuals and for organizations. First, they suggest that people seeking employment should examine carefully the prevailing culture of an organization before deciding to join it. If they don't, they run the risk of finding themselves in a situation where their own values and those of their company clash. Second, these findings also suggest that organizations should focus on attracting individuals whose values match their own. This involves identifying key aspects of organizational culture, communicating these to prospective employees, and selecting those for whom the person-organization fit is best. Considerable effort may be involved in completing these tasks. Given that high levels of person-organization fit can contribute to commitment, satisfaction, and low rates of turnover among employees, however, the effort appears to be worthwhile. An emerging dimension in the person-environment fit puzzle is spirituality in the workplace. See the **ORGANIZATIONAL TRENDS** feature for a discussion of this important trend.

Why and How Does Organizational Culture Change?

Our earlier comments about the relative stability of organizational culture may have left you wondering about the following questions: If culture tends to be so stable, why and how does it ever change? Why isn't it simply passed from one generation of organizational members to the next in a totally static manner? The basic answer, of course, is that the world in which all organizations operate constantly changes. External events such as shifts in market conditions, new technology, altered government policies, and many other factors change over time, necessitating changes in an organization's mode of doing business—and hence, its culture.

☛ Chapter 16 examines the factors responsible for organizational change.

Composition of the workforce. Over time, the people entering an organization may differ in important ways from those already in it, and these differences may impinge on the existing culture of the organization. For example, people from different ethnic or cultural backgrounds may have contrasting views about various aspects of behaviour at work. For instance, they may hold dissimilar views about

Blending Spirituality into the Workplace Culture: CHOW's Sunrise Ceremony

Increasingly, organizations are recognizing the importance of spirituality in the workplace. Organizational consultant Patrick McNamara says that while interest in spirituality in the workplace is not a new idea, it is only now becoming more of a public phenomenon. "He says the movement is not religious—although many proponents ... are active in an organized religion—but an effort to 'bring more of yourself to work.' That means trying to align personal meaning with corporate needs and to change the way people interact to allow for listening and honesty."[51]

Another leader in the spirituality in the workplace movement is Richard Barrett, author of *A Guide to Liberating Your Soul*. Barrett's approach has a solid foundation in business practice. He believes that "people and companies do well, financially and otherwise, to the degree that their interests match their values."[52] The kind of message that Barrett has brought to the World Bank and elsewhere is receiving increasing acceptance in all kinds of organizations.[53]

For Suzanne Rochon-Burnett this is not a new concept. Rochon-Burnett, who is president and CEO of R. B. Communications, brings her Native cultural and spiritual heritage to her leadership of Welland, Ontario's CHOW radio. At a traditional sunrise cere-

mony (see Figure 14-7) held on a crisp Sunday morning in the fall of 1997, Rochon-Burnett, the first Métis person to obtain a CRTC commercial radio licence, invited the community to celebrate as her organization marked two important milestones. The City of Welland had recognized the station's fortieth anniversary in 1997 by planting a public flower bed in the station's honour. As fall approached, and the city's parks department prepared to dismantle the bed, the sunrise ceremony was held to bid it farewell. It also marked the passage of the AM radio station as CHOW prepared to switch to a new FM frequency.[54]

Aboriginal elder Raymond Gould conducted the ceremony, the first of what is now an annual fall tradition. Participants sprinkled cedar and tobacco on the ceremonial fire. "The two are part of four herbs traditionally used in such ceremonies. The tobacco pays homage to the Creator and the cedar to those present." Among others in the Sacred Circle with Gould and Rochon-Burnett was Larry Hay, a member of the Mohawk nation who serves in the Niagara detachment of the RCMP. During the ceremony, the Speaker of the House of Commons, Gilbert Parent, was awarded the Sacred Eagle Feather. The Eagle Feather is the highest honour given by the people of Canada's First Nations. The Parent family has Ojibway ancestry.

In his words of greeting, Raymond Gould "spoke of the actions [in the ceremony] symbolizing the oneness of all peoples and demonstrating that there were no enemies present."[55]

style of dress, the importance of being on time (or even what constitutes "on time" behaviour), the level of deference one should show to higher-status people, and even what foods should be served in the company cafeteria. In other words, as people with different backgrounds and values enter the workplace, changes in organizational culture may be expected to follow.

An interesting example of this phenomenon may be seen at Ford Motor Company, where increased numbers of women are now employed in positions, such as auto designer, that traditionally have been held by men.[56] Until recently, the prevailing culture of Ford's design teams was insensitive to the idea that women may have special concerns when picking out a car—overlooking the fact that women buy 49 percent of all cars sold today, and influence almost 80 percent of the purchasing decisions. Mimi Vandermolen, a Ford designer responsible for the 1993 Probe, sought to change the subculture of Ford's traditionally male design unit. To do this, not only did she make countless presentations about the needs of women in car design, she even produced a film demonstrating the

[You Be The Consultant]

The owners of a large printing plant are finding that as its workforce diversifies, its organizational culture is changing. They don't know what to make of this, and are becoming concerned about the implications of this for job satisfaction and productivity.

1. How might an organization's culture be influenced by the national culture of its employees?

2. What assurances can you provide that such changes are not, of themselves, threatening to satisfaction and performance? What other determinants of organizational culture may be involved?

FIGURE 14-7 Spirituality: A New Trend in Organizational Culture

Suzanne Rochon-Burnett (third from right), CEO and owner of radio station CHOW and a member of the Canada Council, at the sunrise ceremony marking the radio station's fortieth anniversary and its transition to FM. With Rochon-Burnett in front of the ceremonial fire are (left to right): Romeo Parent (brother of Gilbert Parent, Speaker of the House of Commons), Tony Belcourt, Dave Labbe, Raymond Gould, Larry Hay, and James Latham, a Mohawk from Brantford, Ontario's Six Nations, who performed traditional dances as part of the ceremony.[57]

difficulties women had getting in and out of vehicles. The culture of Ford's design team is now more attuned to the concerns of women than ever. As a result, the Probe was redesigned with such features as upholstery that won't snag pantyhose, glovebox latches that allow for long fingernails, and pedals that are designed at just the right angle for drivers wearing high heels. These small redesigned elements, which make the new Probe friendlier to women, are concrete evidence of changes in a subculture of one large organization.

Mergers and acquisitions.   Another, and even more dramatic, source of cultural change is mergers and acquisitions, events in which one organization purchases or otherwise absorbs another.[58] When this occurs, there is likely to be a careful analysis of the financial and material assets of the acquired organization. However, it is rare that any consideration is given to the acquired organization's culture. This is unfortunate, insofar as there have been several cases in which the merger of two organizations with incompatible cultures leads to serious problems, commonly referred to as *culture clashes*. An example of a culture clash can be seen in our CASE PREVIEW in which the British retailer Marks and Spencer acquired the American clothier Brooks Brothers.

In a recent analysis of culture clashes resulting from organizational mergers, Cartwright and Cooper lament the fact that in too many cases the larger, more powerful, acquiring company attempts to dominate the smaller, acquired company, based on the mistaken belief that it knows best—a situation they liken to a traditional marriage.[59] In such instances, clashes can result when the two merging organizations have certain combinations of cultures. For example, when each is heavily autocratic, neither group will be interested in giving up its ways, resulting in considerable conflict. Similarly, when the dominant culture is highly autocratic and the culture of the acquired organization is highly person-oriented, neither side may see the wisdom of the other's approach.

Rather than jumping into a marriage that may be conflict-ridden, Cartwright and Cooper recommend handling mergers the way it has been done in Japan—by first working collaboratively on a joint venture and merging only after it is clear that the companies' cultures can coexist. In short, just as the marriage of two people requires keen attention to their individual personalities, so too does the marriage of two companies suggest the need to be sensitive to their different organizational cultures.

Planned organizational change. Finally, even if an organization doesn't change by acquiring another, cultural change still may result from other planned changes, such as conscious decisions to alter the internal structure or the basic operations of an organization. Once such decisions are reached, many practices in the company that both reflect and contribute to its culture may change. For example, the company may adopt different criteria for recruiting newcomers or promoting current employees. Similarly, managers may be directed to focus their attention on different goals from those in the past. As these shifts take place, new norms governing preferred or acceptable behaviour emerge, and attitudes and values supporting these norms may take shape. The result may be a considerable shift in existing culture.

A good example of this can be seen in IBM in recent years.[60] In response to staggering losses, IBM realized that one of its problems was that it was heavily bureaucratic, making it difficult for lower-level people to make on-the-spot decisions. As a result, IBM changed the nature of its corporate structure from one in which there was a steep hierarchy with many layers of management to a "delayered" one with far fewer managers. As you might imagine, the newly "rightsized" IBM developed a new corporate culture.[61] Once known for a highly rigid, autocratic culture in which decision making was centralized in the hands of just a few, the reorganized company is now much more open and democratic in its approach than ever before. For another example of a beneficial organizational change that has resulted from changing culture, see **THE QUEST FOR QUALITY** section.

The Quest for Quality

Canadian Companies in Search of a Safety-Conscious Culture

When it comes to job safety, you'd imagine that both company officials and employees are after the same thing. After all, you would think everyone wants a safe place to work. However, when you look at the way people actually behave on the job, you have to wonder how concerned with safety people (and often management) really are. Although company policies and government regulations may dictate the use of various precautionary measures, these may be at odds with organizational norms existing within various subcultures.

For example, the Westray mine in Nova Scotia was described as "a disaster waiting to happen" before the explosion that tragically killed 26 miners. The union representing the Westray workers contended that employees "were threatened with job loss if they refused to take an unsafe job assignment. 'The attitude of their employer and the refusal of the inspectors to intervene gave them few options.' "[62]

On the other side of the safety ledger are companies such as DuPont Canada. When faced with deteriorating safety records after a series of major corporate changes, the company recommitted itself to safety as a central operating principle. This corporate cultural commitment to safety bore fruit and the company's safety record improved.[63] Similarly, the Owens Corning plant in Guelph, Ontario initiated "an integrated safety change process." "Business leaders at the company are convinced that strong safety culture is critical to improvements in safety performance and in maintaining a competitive advantage."

The Power Commission of the City of Saint John, New Brunswick has been described as a "poster company for culture-based safety."[64] The secret of the utility's success is a commitment on the part of its senior management to put people first. The company's human resources and training coordinator identifies the safety initiatives as being mandated by management but indicates that the safety culture is built from the front-line employees up through the organization.[65]

DuPont Canada Inc.
www.dupont.ca

To conclude, it is clear that although organizational culture is generally stable, it is not immutable. In fact, culture often evolves in response to outside forces (e.g., changes in workforce composition) as well as deliberate attempts to change the design of organizations (e.g., through mergers and corporate restructuring). One important outside force that affects culture—and is affected by culture—is *technology*, the topic to which we will now turn.

Technology: Its Role in Organizations

What image comes to mind when you think of technology? The Canadarm? Dr. Roberta Bondar and other Canadian astronauts conducting experiments in space? The latest piece of advanced industrial equipment? Indeed, technology can be all these things—plus more. For all these sophisticated images, the definition of technology is deceptively simple. Specifically, **technology** refers to the physical and mental processes used to transform inputs into usable outputs.[66] Simply put, technology deals with the activities, equipment, and knowledge used to get things done. Although robots, spacecraft, and automated office equipment are examples of technological devices, it is important to note that technology also can take on abstract forms, such as ideas and formulas. Indeed, Procter & Gamble's recipe for a new household detergent is every bit as much an example of technology as the elaborate computer-controlled equipment used to manufacture it.[67]

Technology has been advancing at a staggering pace. In the past decade alone, the compact disc has replaced the phonograph record, word processors have replaced typewriters, and in very many libraries computer terminals have replaced card catalogues. Why are we concerned about these things in the field of OB? The answer is simple: *Technology affects the behaviour of people on the job as well as the effective functioning of organizations.* After all, technology helps individuals work differently (e.g., they may use a teleconference instead of a face-to-face meeting, or they may operate a machine that does the heavy, dangerous work instead of doing that work themselves). It also is used to help companies gain a competitive advantage, such as by finding a more effective and less expensive way to produce products or deliver services.[68] Indeed, staying abreast of the latest technology is often needed just to keep from falling behind the competition (e.g., it's almost impossible to function today without computers and fax machines). In other words, sometimes using technology doesn't give one an advantage; it merely keeps one in the game. Clearly, technology represents a potent external force to which all organizations must be responsive. It is, therefore, not surprising that top management scholars, such as Peter F. Drucker, have asserted that technology holds the key to managing tomorrow's organizations.[69]

We will now turn our attention to the matter of how technology affects individual and organizational functioning. Given how wide-reaching this topic is, it shouldn't be surprising to you that we already have had occasion to describe the effects of technology elsewhere in this book—such as in the contexts of communication and decision making, and that we will do so again later—notably, in connection with organizational structure and design. Here, we will concentrate on the more general aspects of technology. Specifically, we will begin by reviewing the basic dimensions of technology. Following this, we will explore a critical issue involving technology in today's organizations—the way people respond to automation.

Classifying Technology's Basic Dimensions

Although many organizational theorists have described the various types of technologies that exist, the most comprehensive scheme has been suggested by Charles Perrow.[70] This system is useful for categorizing the technologies of both manufacturing and service organizations.

Perrow begins by distinguishing between two basic dimensions. The first is *exceptions*, the degree to which an organization makes use of standard inputs to turn out standard outputs (i.e., makes few exceptions) or encounters many nonroutine situations (i.e., has to make many exceptions in the way it operates). Perrow's

technology The physical and mental processes used to transform inputs into usable outputs.

☞ We will return to the topic of technology in Chapter 15, where we discuss its role in organizational design.

matrix of technologies Perrow's system of categorizing technologies based on two dimensions: *exceptions,* the degree to which an organization makes use of standard inputs to turn out standard outputs; and *problems,* the degree to which the situations encountered are either easy or difficult to analyze.

routine technology Technology involving highly standardized inputs and outputs, and problems that are easy to analyze (e.g., assembly lines and vocational training) (see *matrix of technologies*).

craft technology Technology involving highly standardized inputs and outputs, and problems that are difficult to analyze (e.g., cabinet makers and public schools) (see *matrix of technologies*).

engineering technology Technology involving many exceptions in inputs or outputs and problems which are easy to analyze (e.g., heavy machinery construction and health and fitness clubs).

nonroutine technology Technology involving many exceptions in inputs or outputs, and problems that are difficult to analyze (e.g., research units and psychiatric hospitals).

second dimension is known as *problems*—the degree to which the situations encountered are either easy to analyze, allowing for programmed decisions, or complex and difficult to analyze, requiring nonprogrammed decision making. By dichotomizing both dimensions and overlaying them onto each other, Perrow identified four distinct technological types. The resulting **matrix of technologies** is summarized in Table 14-1.

- The first technological type is known as **routine technology**. It includes operations with highly standardized inputs and outcomes, and problems that are easy to analyze. Examples include assembly-line manufacturing and vocational training, both cases in which the product or service is clearly defined. But, when exceptions occur—such as when new products are to be produced, or new subjects are to be taught—the appropriate reaction is readily apparent.

- Perrow's second technological type, **craft technology**, involves operations in which inputs and outcomes are also standardized, but problems are more difficult to analyze. For example, cabinet makers always use wood and laminated products to create finished furniture products. Similarly, public schools focus their attention on ways of teaching the average student. In either case—such as when a special order is placed, or a student with a learning disability is encountered—the appropriate response is not entirely clear. Organizations of this type are simply not set up to handle exceptional cases where the most appropriate decisions are not clearly specified in advance.

- In contrast, Perrow's final two technological types involve industries that are better prepared to handle exceptions. For example, organizations using **engineering technology**, such as those in heavy machinery construction and health and fitness clubs, expect to encounter many exceptions in inputs or outputs, but these can be dealt with in standardized ways. For example, people come to health and fitness facilities in different physical conditions and with different goals. Some may be trying to lose weight, others may be trying to regain strength and agility after an injury, and still others may be training for a major bodybuilding contest. Although different types, amounts, and difficulty levels of exercise may be dictated on a case-by-case basis, the decision regarding exactly what the client should do to achieve his or her goal is relatively straightforward, and based on preestablished information about the effectiveness of different exercise regimes.

- Other industries also face exceptions but more difficult decisions as well. Such organizations are said to employ **nonroutine technology**. For example, research units, by their very existence, are created to tackle difficult, exceptional situations. Psychiatric hospitals also fit into this category. Not only do they encounter a wide variety of people with unique histories and combinations of mental and physical problems, but the appropriate treatment is not always obvious. Despite widespread advances in psychiatric diagnoses, treatment decisions are extremely complex and far from routine.

TABLE 14-1 Perrow's Matrix of Technologies

By combining two levels of exceptions (few and many) with two levels of problems (easy to analyze and difficult to analyze), Perrow identified the four technological types identified here.

(Source: Perrow, 1967; see Note 70.)

Exceptions	Problems	Technological Type (and Examples)
Few	Easy to analyze	Routine technology (e.g., assembly-line manufacturing, vocational training)
	Difficult to analyze	Craft technology (e.g., cabinet-making, public schools)
Many	Easy to analyze	Engineering technology (e.g., heavy machinery construction, health and fitness club)
	Difficult to analyze	Nonroutine technology (e.g., research unit, psychiatric hospital)

Automation in Today's Organizations

Traditionally, using technology on the job involved the manual or mechanical manipulation of things. People at work used chains and pulleys to help them lift heavy items and manoeuvre them from one place to another. Although work of this type still goes on, today's workplace is making increasing use of **high technology**, an advanced form of technology employing tools that are electronic in nature, usually relying on the use of microprocessor chips. For example, typesetters used to have to move together pieces of metal type on wooden blocks to create plates from which documents were printed. Today, this process goes on invisibly, as compositors simply enter letters onto a keyboard, just as you do word processing at home. Clearly, technology has changed the fundamental nature of work for many people.[71] Some examples of high technology used by today's organizations include:

high technology The kind of technology that is electronic in nature, usually relying on the use of microprocessor chips.

- *Advanced manufacturing technology* (*AMT*): manufacturing in which the various processes are guided by computers

- *Computer-integrated manufacturing* (*CIM*): manufacturing processes that go beyond AMT by using computers to gather information that is used to make decisions about ways in which the manufacturing process needs to be altered

- *Computer-aided design and engineering* (*CAD/CAE*): the processes of using computers to build and simulate the characteristics of products and to test their effectiveness

- *Industrial robotics* (*IR*): computer-controlled machines that manipulate materials and perform complex functions

- *Flexible manufacturing systems*: manufacturing processes relying on computer-controlled machines to produce low volumes of products at costs that rival mass-produced ones

The economics of automation are simple. As competition (frequently from foreign firms) drives prices down, companies are forced to improve quality and reduce labour costs, and so they turn to more efficient modes of operation, **automation**—the process of using machines to perform tasks that might otherwise be done by people. Evidence of automation is all around us. Just think of automated call menuing devices that route your phone calls to the appropriate person (if not to another computer), and automated teller machines that dispense currency. Such equipment has certainly reduced the need for human involvement in many activities. By substituting machines programmed to execute actions faster, more accurately, and more consistently than human beings, today's organizations are seeking the same kinds of increased efficiency that factory owners sought a century ago when they introduced machines driven by steam-powered engines onto their shop floors. Not surprisingly, the growth of automation has been referred to as "the second industrial revolution."[72]

automation The process of using machines to perform tasks that might otherwise be done by people.

Human Responses to Technology

As we've been saying throughout this book, there's more to organizations than money and machines—there's also people. Our examples show that as a result of using high technology in organizations, the kind of work people do is different, as is the nature of the demands on them.[73]

☞ *In Chapter 2 we acknowledge the importance of technology as a determinant of human behaviour in organizations.*

Technology and jobs. One obvious effect is that automation makes people so highly efficient that it eliminates the need for some positions, leading to unemployment. Indeed, the flip side of the effectiveness described above is the human cost: Automation is designed to eliminate jobs, and the more it does so, the more effective it is considered to be. Not surprisingly, many labour unions have been less than enthusiastic about automation despite the fact that it usually allows people to work in safer, cleaner, and healthier conditions while avoiding the tedious and repetitive aspects of many jobs (a dangerous, boring job may be better than none at all). Fearing that automation may make its members obsolete, some labour unions have insisted on agreements with management that prohibit laying off employees or transferring them to lower-paying jobs.[74] Statistics suggest that such fears are not unfounded. Specifically, today's companies are using high-tech tools to get more work out of a smaller workforce than ever before.[75]

Not only might fewer people be needed to do the job, but it is often the case that only those companies that can afford to invest in high-tech equipment will be able to conduct business profitably. As a result, we often see shakeouts in which many smaller companies—and their employees—find themselves casualties of the high-tech revolution. For example, as computer-controlled machines are being used to mill lumber, only a few people are needed to flip switches and monitor logs on video screens. Such mills operate so efficiently that smaller mills—ones that cannot afford the $15 million or more start-up costs—are often driven out of the market and forced to close their doors.[76]

People working with machines. Although some people are being replaced by machines, to be sure, it is frequently the case that people work along *with* machines to help get their jobs done—and better than ever before. The once-popular vision of the workerless factory in which only white-coated technicians walked the floor to check up on the machines, as hoards of displaced factory workers walked the unemployment line has never caught on. More typical is the situation in which people work side by side with robots, each doing what it does best. For example, although robots play a large part in the production of automobiles, such as General Motors' Saturn, company officials acknowledge that the technology only works because of the people.[77] Advanced technology alone won't build a successful car. In the words of the Japanese industrialist, Jaruo Shimada, "Only people give wisdom to the machines."[78] The idea is that people and machines are really complementary aspects of any organization.

If people and machines are to work together as cooperating elements of an organization's technology, however, it is essential that the nature of the work performed by people remain highly motivating. This tends to be a problem in situations in which automation so severely simplifies, or "dumbs down," a job that the worker becomes bored and alienated, leading to lowered quality performance. After all, why should anyone really care about doing a good job when all one has to do is stand around and watch machines doing the job, in the off chance that one will break down?

New jobs and challenges. It would be misleading, however, to imply that automation leaves only routine and boring jobs for people to perform. Indeed, new jobs created by the introduction of robots are often considered more demanding than the old jobs. In the words of one employee describing his response to a robot in his manufacturing plant, "The job now requires more skills. . . . You have to learn how to program the robot and run it . . . The job is more sophisticated."[79]

Indeed, automation, frequently frees people to do more interesting work. For example, the use of automatic teller machines frees human bank tellers to play more of a problem-solving role in dealing with bank customers. Just because opportunities may arise for people to do interesting work, while leaving the boring work to the machinery, doesn't necessarily ensure that this will happen. To make sure, when introducing automation, some companies go out of their way to make the remaining human jobs as involving as possible. For example, at a heavily automated, furniture plant, Westinghouse has an elaborate network of committees and task forces in operation that encourages employees to be highly involved in the facility's decision making.[80] Autonomous work teams have been used in some organizations to ensure that employees keep interested in their jobs when the jobs have changed in response to automation.[81]

In other words, if people don't lose their jobs in response to automation, jobs certainly may change. Automation creates new jobs as growing numbers of people are needed to program and service the high-tech equipment. Thus, automation may be seen as causing a shift in the *kinds* of jobs people do.

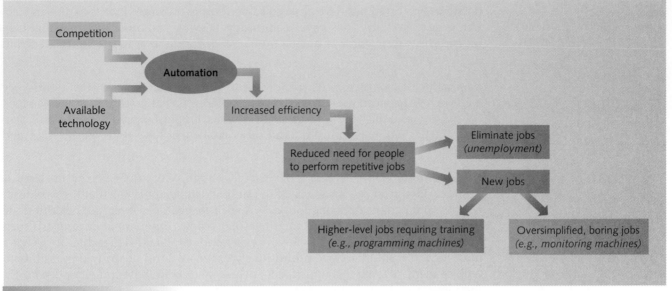

FIGURE 14-8 The Impact of
Automation: A Summary

As summarized here, the economics of automation has a key effect on people in organizations. By making workers so efficient, automation reduces the need for as many people to perform routine jobs. As a result, jobs are either eliminated (leading to unemployment) or changed to new jobs, a few of which may be boring (e.g., monitoring machines) but many of which will be even more challenging (e.g., programming and maintaining the machines).

Changes of this type indicate a need for employee training if automation is to be successful (see Figure 14-8). With this in mind, Chrysler Corporation invested some 900 000 person-hours in training its employees before opening the futuristic factory used to manufacture some of its latest models.[82] Chrysler is not alone in this regard. Many other companies also have been working diligently at upgrading their employees' skills, keeping their skills from becoming obsolete.[83] After all, if a company is going to invest millions in equipment, it certainly ought to make the investment in the people needed to run it.

Using Technology in Modern Organizations

People use technology in various ways while performing many different jobs. In this section of the chapter we will consider several of the latest ways in which technology is being used in organizations today. Specifically, we will focus on four contemporary uses of technology. First, we will describe *assistive technology*—devices that help people with disabilities take advantage of their work skills so they can be fully functioning, productive members of their organizations. Second, we will present a controversial technology that allows company officials to observe—or, some would say, "snoop"—on their employees, a practice known as *computerized performance monitoring*. Third, we present ways in which computer-based technology—often criticized for being cold and impersonal—is being used to improve, and personalize, the quality of *customer service* delivered in today's organizations. Finally, we will discuss the developing trend toward using technology in an environmentally friendly manner, using a process known as *design for disassembly*.

Assistive Technology: Helping People with Disabilities Work Productively

If you've ever seen public telephones with volume controls, elevator signs with floor markings in Braille, and cutaway curbs on sidewalks, you are already familiar with the fact that things can be done to enable people with various physical challenges to function effectively in society. However, these accommodations are just a small part of the picture when it comes to using technology to assist people who have disabilities. In today's organizations technology is widely used to make it possible for skilled people to perform their jobs although they may be challenged by some form of physical or mental condition. (For examples of technological advances used for these purposes,

assistive technology Devices and other solutions that help individuals with physical or mental problems perform the various actions needed to do their jobs.

☞ *The use of assistive technology is helpful in making it possible to further diversify the composition of the workforce, a topic discussed in Chapter 2.*

Canadian Charter of Rights and Freedoms
www.laurentia.com/ccrf-ccdl

refer to Table 14-2.) As a result of this technology, it is possible for people who only a few years ago could not have done so to perform mainstream jobs today. Such technology is referred to as **assistive technology**—devices and other solutions that help individuals with physical or mental problems perform the various actions needed to do their jobs.[84]

Competitive advantages.   There are several good reasons why assistive technology is in such widespread use today. The most obvious is that, to innovate and prosper, companies need the contributions of all workers. Employees who have physical, sensory, intellectual, mental health, and other challenges have skills, knowledge, and talent that benefit organizations.

Demographic imperatives.   A second reason why assistive technology is in such widespread use is because of the simple demographic fact that the workforce is aging and people are living longer.[85] As people get older, even the healthiest are likely to suffer impairments in their hearing, vision, and manual dexterity. If such individuals, who are likely to be highly experienced and knowledgeable, are to leave their jobs, it would likely be prohibitively expensive, and possibly impossible, to replace them. Making the adjustments necessary to help these individuals perform their jobs makes good business sense.

Legal requirements.   The Canadian Charter of Rights and Freedoms guarantees all Canadians equality under the law and freedom from discrimination based on mental or physical disability.[86] In reality, however, employment equity legislation in Canada and in the United States has not necessarily led to an increase in the employment of people who have disabilities. "Bill Chandler, a Finance Department economist, noted the federal government's dismal record of hiring [people who have disabilities] since Canada's Employment Equity Act was passed in 1995." In 1997 only 3.3 percent of Canada's civil servants were people who had disabilities while 6.5 percent of employees in the private sector had disabilities.[87]

In her study of the impact of the Americans with Disabilities Act, Marjorie Baldwin of East Carolina University in Greenville, North Carolina, has expressed her reservations about whether the legislation would live up to the hopes of its proponents. She has identified in the legislation "inadequate provisions for important differences between persons with disabilities."[88] Baldwin's concern highlights the dangers of homogenization. Not all people who are labelled as having a "disability" are the same. Even people who have disabilities in the same area of functioning do not necessarily need the same kind of accommodation or assistive technology.

In examining the kind of support needed by people who have disabilities, Bill Chandler emphasizes the key role played by middle managers.[89] Monica Koeppel's experience at the Department of National Defence (DND) is a dramatic example of

TABLE 14-2 Assistive Technology: Some Examples

Technology can be used to assist people with various disabilities to function effectively on the job. Here are examples of devices—some sophisticated and some simple—applied to this purpose.

(Sources: Tompkins, 1993, see Note 84 Anonymous, 1993, see Note 85.)

Device	Description
Telephone handset amplifier	Mechanism for raising the volume of telephone earpieces, enabling hearing-impaired people to use the telephone.
Voice-activated computer	Software that allows people to input words into a computer by speaking. IBM's "Speech Server" series has a 32 000-word vocabulary, and the capacity to enter 70 words per minute.
Reading machine	Hardware using simulated speech to read to visually impaired people (such as the portable unit introduced by Xerox's Kurzweil Business Unit).
Sight devices	Portable sensory guides and closed-circuit TV monitors with magnification that enable people with visual impairments to navigate their physical environments.
Mouthpicks	Stylus-like tools that quadriplegics can use to operate computers.
Gooseneck telephones	Adjustable telephone headsets that can be used by people with limited physical dexterity.

Department of National Defence
www.cfcsc.dnd.ca

the role of managers in facilitating accommodation. Ms. Koeppel worked as a clerk at DND. She was surprised and concerned when she found that she was expected to answer the phones as part of her job since she felt her hearing impairment would make this task extremely difficult. Her supervisor, recognizing the problem, rearranged her work responsibilities and other staff answered the phones.

When her supervisor was replaced by a person who believed the job description had to be followed to the letter, Ms. Koeppel was required to resume her phone-answering duties. This caused her to have headaches and, eventually, she had to take a leave without pay. Ms. Koeppel filed a complaint with the Canadian Human Rights Commission on the grounds that her employer failed to provide accommodation for her hearing disability. She won the case. The Commission ruled that she had been "a victim of discrimination, and confirmed that an employer has a duty to accommodate [an employee who has a disability], unless it is [un]reasonable to do so due to the hardship involved."[90]

Canadian Human Rights Commission
www.chrc.ca

Computerized Performance Monitoring: Management by Remote Control

One of the most popular uses of technology in the workplace today comes in the form of using computers to collect, store, analyze, and report information about the work people are doing—a practice known as **computerized performance monitoring (CPM)**.[91] As this definition implies, CPM refers to a broad range of procedures that enable supervisors to "look in" on employees doing their jobs. CPM makes it possible for employees' work to be observed and quantified—particularly those who work at computer terminals (e.g., phone sales agents, data entry and word processing personnel, airline reservation agents, and telephone operators). Canadian companies using CPM include Air Canada and Bell Canada.[92] Not all CPM systems are the same. In some, employees are monitored all the time as work is carried out; in others, observation occurs only sometimes, although the software keeps a detailed record of their work.[93] Regardless of differences between systems, all make it possible for job performance to be observed in a constant, unblinking fashion.

computerized performance monitoring (CPM) The practice of using computers to collect, store, analyze, and report information about the work people are doing.

Within the past decade CPM systems have grown in popularity. Recent estimates are that more than 10 million employees are monitored in over 70 000 companies in the United States alone, representing an investment in equipment of over U.S.$1 billion.[94] An increasing number of Canadian companies is adopting the practice, as well.[95] As one California vendor of networking software advertises, their CPM system provides a simple solution to supervisors interested in closely watching many employees at once, all from one convenient spot: "Look in on Sue's computer screen . . . In fact, Sue doesn't even know you're there! Hot key again and off you go on your rounds of the company. Viewing one screen after another, helping some, watching others. All from the comfort of your chair."[96] Clearly, CPM changes the basic nature of the supervisor-subordinate relationship.[97]

Not surprisingly, the use of CPM has been the subject of considerable debate.[98] Some have argued that it represents an invasion of employees' privacy, creates an atmosphere of distrust, and can be a source of work-related stress.[99] Ontario's privacy commissioner has called for tougher legislation to regulate the use of the technique. The commissioner urged that electronic monitoring in the workplace be used in exceptional circumstances only and emphasized that, "Protecting workplace privacy will have a positive impact on the quality of working life, labour productivity and, ultimately, the bottom line."[100] Proponents have countered, however, that CPM makes it possible for supervisors to gather more objective information about performance, providing a valuable source of feedback and information useful for planning training programs and workloads.[101]

Office of the Information and Privacy Commissioner
www.ipc.on.ca

What does the scientific evidence have to say about these arguments? Although there has been only limited research on the effects of CPM, what little work has been done has suggested that to some degree *both* perspectives are correct. For example, research comparing monitored and nonmonitored employees found that monitored employees were, in fact, more productive on simple tasks. However, as we described in

☞ As you may recall from Chapter 8, the impact of CPM on performance may be explained by the process of social facilitation.

Chapter 8, monitoring lowers performance on complex tasks. But, even if performance on simple tasks increases in response to monitoring, CPM also leads people to experience higher levels of stress and lower levels of job satisfaction.[102] Part of the problem seems to be that working in front of video display terminals all day contributes to feelings of isolation and loneliness, unpleasant conditions that are associated with stress.[103]

It is important to note that employees who are monitored with respect to specific aspects of their performance might be expected to work hard to improve those performance measures, even if doing so comes at the expense of other, possibly more important, aspects of performance. For example, Aiello reports an incident in which telephone operators were monitored by supervisors who checked to see that they did not spend longer than 22 seconds on each call.[104] The result: Operators almost always met the standard—but some, as many as 25 percent, admitted that they did so by "cheating." In instances in which customers required more than 22 seconds to help, such as when they had strong accents or hearing impediments, operators simply disconnected such callers so they could be rewarded for meeting the goal. Even those who didn't take such drastic measures lamented that they could not take the time to be as pleasant and friendly as they wanted.

Not only do employees dislike being monitored, evidence also shows that many supervisors dislike the added workload that comes from having to review constantly incoming data about employees' work performance. The problem is that monitoring raises expectations that supervisors will have to "say something" to employees about their performance, holding them to a standard that their busy schedules may not permit.[105] However, when employee performance appears to be unexpectedly poor, supervisors are able to rely on computerized records of performance as the basis for making accurate assessments of the problem.[106] Under such conditions, supervisors will surely benefit from having accurate information at their disposal to help them diagnose the problem at hand.

To summarize, it appears that although there may be some benefits associated with CPM, there are also some limitations (for a summary, see Figure 14-9). It is important to note that this particular use of technology has a long way to go before it gains widespread acceptance. By creating a whole new dynamic between superiors and subordinates, CPM—like many other new technologies that have been introduced in the workplace—appears threatening. But will it ever be completely accepted? We suspect that the answer resides in how the technique is used—or abused—in

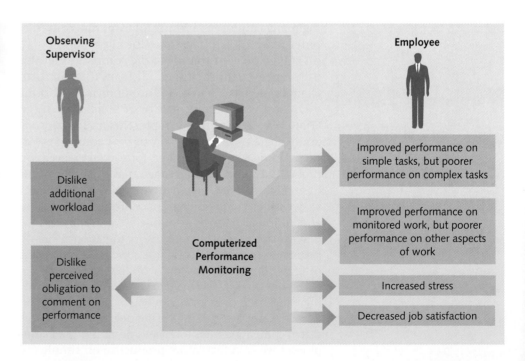

FIGURE 14-9 Computerized Performance Monitoring: A Mixed Bag of Results

Although computerized performance monitoring has been introduced in the hopes of improving employees' work performance, studies have found its impact to be both positive and negative in nature.

practice. If used as a tool to help improve performance, we believe CPM has a valuable role in organizations. However, if it is misused—such as for close surveillance of nonwork activities, such as bathroom trips—such invasions of privacy are sure to be rejected. In conclusion, it is not necessarily the technology itself that is either useful or harmful in practice, but the way in which people use it.

Technological Aids to Customer Service

Have you ever heard someone grumble that the service received today is "not like it was in the good old days"? For the most part, such complaints are well founded. Through the early 1950s, it was not unusual for businesses to provide high levels of courteous, personalized service. You could phone in your order to Mr. Smith's corner store, and his son would deliver your groceries to your table after school, and charge them to your account. You also could go to the corner "service" station, where Gus would pump your gas, clean your windshield, check your oil, and even install a new muffler or set of tires on your car. Today, however, Mr. Smith's place more than likely has given way to a huge, 24-hour supermarket, and Gus has been replaced by a pay-at-the-pump, self-serve operation.

Experts tell us that the depersonalization of service came about as a result of several forces. The automobile led to suburban sprawl, cities grew, and markets expanded. Increasing competition led to reduced profit margins, and the need to standardize goods and services. The result: Mom's diner surely delivered more personalized service than McDonald's, but given its economic disadvantage (e.g., the higher per unit cost of producing on a small scale), it simply couldn't afford to compete. Personal service became a casualty as a result.

Analyzing this state of affairs, Ives and Mason have pointed out that technology is now being used to revitalize customer service.[107] They note that this is occurring in three distinct ways:

1. *Personalizing:* Many of today's organizations are employing technology aimed at *delivering personalized service*. For example, computerized systems are also used to give the most appropriate coupons to shoppers who make certain purchases at their supermarket. Systems are in use in many chains in which in-store coupons are printed on the backs of register receipts (or, in some systems, on separate printers). These coupons are customized to fit the customer's profile of purchases. For example, purchasers of one brand of breakfast cereal may be given a coupon to induce them to try another brand. Or, purchasers of peanut butter may be given coupons for products that might go with it, such as bread or jelly. Although these practices are not "personalized" in the same sense as Mr. Smith taking your grocery order and delivering it to your door, they represent forms of personalization that capitalize on the computer technology available today.

2. *Augmenting:* Technology is being used to help revitalize service by *augmenting service*. This refers to the practice of providing customers with additional support related to the product or service. How can technology be used to help provide "something extra"? Several companies have been fairly ingenious in this regard. Sometimes, the additional service is small—but quite helpful. For example, Hertz pioneered systems by which rental car customers are guided to their vehicles by signs displaying their names, and handheld devices that agents use to check in returned vehicles and print customer receipts on the spot—practices that eliminated check-in and check-out lines. This customer-friendly technology helped Hertz attract considerable business.

3. *Transforming:* Ives and Mason note that technology can help by *transforming business*—that is, developing entirely new practices that better satisfy customers' needs. Specifically, today's advanced computer information systems make it possible for customized goods to be made with almost the same efficiency as standardized goods.

   For example, Benjamin Moore paints uses a photospectrometer to identify the colour of a customer's fabric sample and tell the computer how to match it by appropriately mixing the company's paints. Similarly, Warner Brothers has a system in which customers can order music cassettes containing their favourite songs selected from a menu of available titles.

These examples represent ways in which today's companies are using technology to transform their businesses to provide improved customer service.

Although some technology has led to the depersonalization of service, the above examples make it clear that technology also can be used—and, in fact, *is* being used—to vastly improve customer service.

Environmentally Friendly Technology: Design for Disassembly

Problem: The earth's mineral deposits are rapidly being depleted and landfills are reaching capacity. Believe it or not, 94 percent of materials taken from the earth enter the waste stream only months later.[108] There's no mistaking the fact that the industrialized world has a long history of taking riches from the earth and returning rubbish. Scientists tell us that this cannot go on forever and that if we are to rely on the earth's natural resources in the future, we must conserve them now, using them wisely. Fortunately, a movement is afoot to make manufacturers responsible for taking back their used products and recycling them. Laws across Europe will soon be requiring manufacturers to do this. Already, in Germany, companies are legally responsible for the way their packaging is used, encouraging them not only to recycle, but to come up with ingenious ways to reduce the amount of packaging they use for their products (see Figure 14-10).

The impact of the German legislation has been encouraging: Within the first two years, the "take-back" law has reduced the amount of packaging waste by 4 percent—some 600 million tons. On the heels of this success, companies are moving to reduce the amount of product they waste. One of the most effective processes in this regard is known as **design for disassembly (DFD)**. This is the process of designing and building products so that their parts can be reused several times and then safely disposed of at the end of the product's life. What this boils down to is fewer parts, fewer materials, and assembly processes designed with later disassembly in mind.

A good example of DFD can be seen in the manufacturing of automobiles: By the end of this decade, in Europe, some 200 000 cars will be making "return trips." BMW is a leader in this process.[109] It is replacing glue and solder in bumpers with fasteners, making them easier to recycle. Instrument panels are made of polyurethane foam that can be recycled in one piece. Already 80 percent of the weight of a BMW comes from recycled parts, and the company hopes to get this figure up to 95 percent. But it is not only cars that are prime candidates for DFD. Computers, telephones, and engines are also commonly designed with disassembly in mind.

Although you might not know it, if you've ever used one of Kodak's Fun Saver 35 cameras (with camera and film in a single "disposable" package), you have used a product that was designed for disassembly. But, it wasn't always that way. The first such products were simply tossed away. That was, until 1990 when Kodak was taken to task by environmentalists for putting hundreds of thousands of used cameras into landfills. Today, however, these cameras are designed so that they can be returned to Kodak by film processors, where the plastic is ground up and remoulded into new parts, and the guts of the camera—the moving parts and electronics—are reused up to ten times.

Kodak is not alone among North American companies using DFD. Xerox also has been using recycled parts in its copiers, as has Hewlett-Packard in its DeskJet printers. As you might imagine, the motivation for doing so is "green," no matter what you mean by it. Whether by "green" you're talking about preserving the environment or making money, the result is the same: After retooling costs, companies find themselves saving money by using recycled parts. The Kodak Fun Saver 35 flash camera is the company's most profitable product. And Xerox has been saving about U.S.$500 million a year by remanufacturing and recycling parts. The bottom line: DFD is helping companies save both money and the earth's natural environment at the same time.

design for disassembly (DFD)
The process of designing and building products so that their parts can be reused several times and then safely disposed of at the end of the product's life.

FIGURE 14-10 Recycling Packaging: It's the Law in Germany

German law requires retailers, like this hardware store in Münster, to collect for recycling the packaging materials in which items are sold. Manufacturers are attempting to eliminate such waste by repackaging their merchandise in creative ways.

SUMMARY AND REVIEW

Organizational Culture: Its Basic Nature

Organizational culture is a cognitive framework consisting of attitudes, values, behavioural norms, and expectations shared by organization members. It serves several different functions, including providing members with a sense of identity, generating commitment to the organization's mission, and clarifying and reinforcing standards of behaviour.

Typically, organizations consist of both a **dominant culture**, reflecting the organization's overall values, and various **subcultures**, separate cultures existing within selected parts of the dominant culture. Four main types of organizational culture are the *academy,* the *club,* the *baseball team,* and the *fortress.*

The Formation and Maintenance of Organizational Culture

The emergence of organizational culture can be traced to several different factors. Among these are the influence of founders, the organization's experiences with the external environment, and contact between various people within the organization. Culture is transmitted via various mechanisms, including: **symbols,** *stories, jargon, ceremonies,* and *statements of principle* (including *codes of ethics*).

Organizational Culture: Its Consequences and Capacity to Change

Although it is popularly believed that certain types of organizational culture are associated with more successful organizational performance, scientific evidence does not support this claim. However, the voluntary turnover of in-

dividuals is related to organizational culture: People remain employed longer in cultures that stress pleasant interpersonal relationships than those emphasizing hard work. Turnover is also lower among individuals whose personal values more closely match those of the organizations in which they are employed than those for whom personal and organizational values are less closely matched.

Organizational culture is likely to change due to a variety of factors. Among these are changes in the composition of the workforce (over time, different people bring different values into the organization), mergers and acquisitions (adjustments have to be made to accommodate the "marriage" between companies), and planned change (deliberate decisions to alter the organization's structure or its basic operations).

The Role of Technology in Organizations

Technology refers to the physical and mental processes used to transform inputs into usable outputs. According to Perrow's **matrix of technologies,** four different classes of technology may be identified: **routine technology, craft technology, engineering technology,** and **nonroutine technology**.

Today's organizations frequently rely on the use of such **high technology** tools as **automation**—the process of using machines to perform tasks that might otherwise be done by people. Not only is automation extremely expensive to employ, but it sometimes also leads to high levels of unemployment. When people remain employed in automated work environments, their work is typically either extremely dull (e.g., monitoring machines that do all the work) or highly challenging and involving a great deal of training (e.g., programming and maintaining the machines). Economic competition is making the shift to automation a reality in a growing number of manufacturing and service organizations.

Modern Uses of Technology

Technology is used in many different ways in today's organizations. For example, **assistive technology** focuses on the task of helping people with disabilities perform their jobs. Such efforts are stimulated both by law and economic forces.

Computerized performance monitoring (CPM) is used to observe and record the performance of employees, particularly those working at computer terminals. Although this practice may lead to performance improvement, it is also highly stress-provoking, and generally disliked by employees. Technology is also frequently used to improve customer service. Computers are being used in various ways to deliver not only more personalized service but also to add new and improved services to those currently performed.

Finally, technology known as **design for disassembly** is being used to allow products to be reused, and waste to be reduced, thereby preserving the physical environment.

CASE PREVIEW QUESTIONS FOR DISCUSSION

1. Imagine you were a Brooks Brothers employee during the merger with Marks and Spencer. How do you think your day-to-day work would be affected by the shift from an individual to a team reward system?

2. Discuss the differences in expectations held for frontline managers in the more "loosely managed" Brooks Brothers versus the "carefully" managed Marks and Spencer.

3. Think about an organization for which you have worked. How would the full-time employees of this organization have reacted to such a dramatic change in work environment as the one described in the case?

CHAPTER QUESTIONS FOR DISCUSSION

1. Characterize the culture of any organization with which you may be familiar by describing the core characteristics collectively valued by its members. Would you consider it an academy, club, baseball team, or fortress?

2. Suppose you are founding a new company. Describe how you might either intentionally or unintentionally affect its culture. How might your influences linger within the organization long after you have left it?

3. What kinds of events might be responsible for the changing of organizational culture? Explain why these events are likely to be so influential.

4. Select a major business close to where you live. Then, using Perrow's system for classifying technology, categorize the types of technology employed by this company.

5. It may be said that automation may lead to unemployment on the one hand and new opportunities for employment, on the other. Explain this apparent contradiction.

6. Describe how technology can be used to improve: (a) work opportunities for people with physical disabilities, (b) the quality of customer service delivered, and (c) the quality of the physical environment.

7. Do you think the practice of computerized performance monitoring (CPM) is ethical? Why or why not? What benefits and costs may be expected from using CPM?

CASE IN POINT

Putting the "Service" Back into United Parcel Service

When you've been in business almost 90 years, it's understandable that you might begin to feel comfortable and set in your ways. This is the position in which United Parcel Service (UPS) found itself only a few years ago—a situation that kept growth flat during the late 1980s and early 1990s, while some aggressive competitors, notably Roadway Package Systems (RPS) and Airborne Express, were increasing volume by 30 to 40 percent.

One of UPS's problems was that its pricing and service policies were highly rigid. This "we-know-what's best" approach prevailed at UPS for many years. That was until 1990, when Kent C. "Oz" Nelson, UPS's CEO, overhauled the com-☞

pany's underlying philosophy, transforming it from an aloof and rigid approach to a highly flexible one. This "velvet revolution," as UPS insiders referred to it, reflects a whole new way of doing business. For example, Kodak found service with UPS so difficult that it almost stopped using it. Now, however, UPS has a full-time service representative in place at Kodak who helps reduce shipping expenses. "It's an entirely different company," says a Kodak official, who has increased its business with UPS by 15 percent—shipping some 50 000 packages a week.

Although UPS saved Kodak from defecting to the competition, the highly aggressive RPS was successful in luring away some UPS customers with volume pricing and innovative ways of tracing and billing shipments. UPS has been a longtime believer in a single-price formula. "We'd always prided ourselves on saying your grandmother paid the same price General Motors did," says Nelson. Now, however, GM gets a break, but granny doesn't. Since 1991, UPS's commercial rates grew only 3.4 percent a year, while average residential rates have jumped 11.4 percent per year.

To ensure that UPS's corporate customers remained satisfied—and loyal—Nelson appointed a panel of senior executives to study the company's problems. With this in mind, 25 000 UPS customers were interviewed to find out what new services they required. From this effort a new three-day guaranteed delivery service was introduced in February 1993—a product for customers who wanted assured delivery but who didn't need overnight or second-day deliveries, and who were attracted by the 20 percent lower price. Other changes merely required suspending rigid policies. For example, although customers used to be told when they had to have their packages ready, high-volume shippers can now get customized pickup and delivery times.

Listening to its customers, UPS also invested heavily—some U.S.$2 billion from 1991 to 1993 alone—in the latest technology needed to pinpoint all shipments in the system. Drivers now carry computerized clipboards on which the signatures of receiving parties are stored in digital form. Using cellular phones inside their familiar brown trucks, drivers transmit delivery information back to the company's central computers. If you call about your package, UPS can tell you where it is. Although Federal Express customers were used to this service for some time, the stodgier UPS was behind the times when it came to using the latest technology to improve its tracking service.

When the giant decided to take on Canada, it may have expected the invasion to be easier than it turned out to be. Since its arrival in Canada in 1975, UPS has poured hundreds of millions of dollars into the operation. In 1993, UPS passed on the chance to buy the Canadian courier, Purolator. Canada Post picked up the option, a move UPS did not appreciate. In the same year, UPS Canada Ltd. of Mississauga closed over one-third of its outlets and laid off five percent of its workers. In its effort to cut costs and improve efficiency, UPS announced in January 1995 that it would be moving 900 of its Canadian positions to New Brunswick, where it had installed sophisticated telephone operations. This move was consistent with UPS's ongoing commitment to high-tech communications and tracking.

The company's Canadian operations have grown. UPS employs 5900 people in Canada and has air gateways in Vancouver, Calgary, Winnipeg, Hamilton, and at Mirabel Airport in Quebec.[110]

The fact that people commonly talk about "FedExing," instead of "UPS-ing" their shipments suggests that UPS may have lost the undisputed dominance in the delivery business it had only a decade ago. But, with the changes it has made, it is apparent that "Big Brown," as it is often called, will keep on delivering—and profitably.[111]

Critical Thinking Questions

1. In what ways has UPS's organizational culture changed? What factors stimulated these changes?

2. What barriers would you imagine UPS faced in changing as it did?

3. How has UPS used technology to improve its customer service?

Canada Post
www.canadapost.ca

SKILLS PORTFOLIO

Experiencing Organizational Behaviour

What Is Your Customer Service Orientation?

As noted on pp. 453–454, technology can be used to enhance the quality of an organization's customer service. However, so long as people are still involved in the process, no technology, however sophisticated, will be able to counter the effects of having a poor attitude toward customer service. In fact, the cultures of various organizations can be distinguished with respect to their customer service orientations (see the CASE IN POINT about UPS). The following exercise is designed to help you understand your own orientation toward customer service.

Directions

Answer each of the following questions as honestly as possible by using the following scale:

1 = not at all
2 = slightly
3 = moderately
4 = greatly
5 = extremely

In general, to what extent . . .

_____ **1.** Do your customers think of you as being honest and sincere?
_____ **2.** Would your customers think of you as being reliable?
_____ **3.** Would your customers choose to deal with you if they could deal with someone else who does the same thing?
_____ **4.** Do your clients believe you take their best interests into consideration?
_____ **5.** Do you handle customers' complaints in a satisfactory fashion?
_____ **6.** Do you enjoy solving your customers' problems?
_____ **7.** Are you considered a good source of information about the products or industry you represent?
_____ **8.** Do you receive positive comments from your customers?
_____ **9.** Are you interested in your customers getting the best possible deal?
_____**10.** Do you want your customers to be pleased that they have been dealing with you?

Scoring

Add your individual responses to these ten questions. They will range from 10 through 50. Higher scores, particularly over 42, reflect higher degrees of self-perceived customer service orientation.

Questions for Discussion

1. What did this questionnaire tell you about your customer service orientation?
2. Do you think other people would rate you the same way?
3. How might an organization's culture influence your customer service orientation?
4. How might technology be used to enhance your approach to customer service?

Working in Groups

Assessing Organizational Culture

Assessing the culture of an organization is typically done by administering a questionnaire to large numbers of people working within an organization and then averaging together all their answers. This simple questionnaire is designed to assess only a single aspect of culture—concern for people. (Of course, more complex questionnaires would address several additional aspects of organizational culture.) By administering this questionnaire to people, you can learn about the cultures of their organizations.

Procedure

1. Divide the class into teams of three students each.
2. Secure permission to administer a questionnaire to workers in a local company. It may help to use an organization in which one of the students works or has connections. Be sure to explain what you are doing and to get your permission in writing. (Check with your instructor about any further requirements involved in doing so at your school.)
3. Each team should pay a visit to the participating organizations and ask for volunteers to complete the questionnaire. So as not to disturb work performance, it is helpful to do this during lunch breaks. Be sure to identify yourselves and explain what the questionnaire is all about. Mention also that you have permission to do this and show the letter of permission to anyone who is interested in seeing it. It is important to assure anonymity by not asking participants to put their names on the questionnaires. You are representing your school, so be friendly and professional at all times.
4. Reproduce multiple copies of the following questionnaire and ask the employees to complete it.

This questionnaire asks you to report your feelings about the organization in which you work. Consider each question carefully, and respond frankly by using the following rating scale:

1 = strongly agree
2 = agree
3 = neither agree nor disagree
4 = disagree
5 = strongly disagree

_____ **1.** My boss is concerned about how I feel about my work.
_____ **2.** The people I work with are truly interested in my ideas about things.
_____ **3.** We believe in giving the best possible service to our customers.
_____ **4.** My coworkers are likely to give me a hand when I need it.
_____ **5.** Whenever possible, we get together to socialize outside the job.
_____ **6.** My boss does not misrepresent things when talking to us.
_____ **7.** The suggestions I make are taken seriously.
_____ **8.** When one of us has a birthday, the others all pitch in for a gift.
_____ **9.** Top management treats us with dignity and respect.
_____ **10.** When I'm having trouble with a job, my boss is likely to help without making me feel bad.

5. As you collect the questionnaire from the people completing it, ask them what their job is. If they do not mind telling you, write this down on the questionnaire.
6. After all teams are finished collecting data, they should score the questionnaires as described below and discuss their experiences with the class.

Scoring

1. Compute each person's average score by adding up his or her responses and dividing by 10 (or the actual number they completed). The higher the score, the more the respondent believes that the culture of his or her organization values concern for the well-being of people. Lower scores reflect less of a concern for people permeating the culture of the organization.
2. Compute average scores within each organization, and within groups of people performing similar jobs.

Questions for Discussion

1. What did you think of this experience? Were the people generally cooperative?
2. What connections, if any, did the class find between the culture of the organizations studied and the type of companies they were? How did these compare to relationships described in this text?
3. Did people holding similar jobs perceive their organizational cultures in a similar manner?
4. What additional dimensions of culture may have been included in the questionnaire? What would questions measuring these factors look like?

TAKE IT TO THE NET

Prentice Hall
COMPANION WEBSITE

We invite you to visit the *Greenberg/Baron/Sales/Owen Companion Website* at *www.prenticehall.ca/greenberg* for this chapter's Internet resources.

CHAPTER 15

Organizational Structure and Design

LEARNING OBJECTIVES

After reading this chapter you should be able to:

1. Explain the basic characteristics of organizational structure revealed in an organizational chart (*hierarchy of authority*, *division of labour*, *span of control*, *line versus staff*, and *decentralization*).

2. Describe different approaches to departmentalization—*functional organizations*, *product organizations*, *matrix organizations* and the *boundaryless organization*.

3. Distinguish between *classical* and *neoclassical* approaches to organizational design.

4. Describe how an organization's design is influenced by the environment within which it operates.

5. Distinguish between *mechanistic organizations* and *organic organizations* and describe the conditions under which each is most appropriate.

6. Describe the five organizational forms identified by Mintzberg: *simple structure*, *machine bureaucracy*, *professional bureaucracy*, *divisional structure*, and *adhocracy*.

7. Characterize two forms of intraorganizational design—*conglomerates* and *strategic alliances*.

8. Describe the relationship between organizational design and structure identified in the Woodward studies and the Aston studies.

9. Explain the implications of interdependence on organizational structure.

CASE PREVIEW

Nova Reconfigures Itself

" It's absolutely critically important that you understand the business environment you're operating in. You have to face reality. Don't talk yourself into seeing a world that's much rosier than the one you actually live in." This firm grip on corporate reality spurred NOVA Corp.'s vice-chairman and CEO,[1] Ted Newall, to split his company in two (see Figure 15-1).

In the fall of 1997, NOVA announced that its chemicals and pipeline divisions would separate. While he had wanted to keep the two divisions together longer to strengthen them before the separation, Newall acknowledged the pressure emanating from shareholders and initiated the split as a way to increase value for shareholders.[2]

Analysts praised the move citing the reticence of investors to buy into conglomerates. "NOVA has really been running with one hand tied behind its back in the last several years because investors penalized them for being a conglomerate," said David Silver, an analyst with Credit Suisse First Boston Corp.[3] The divorce settlement included shareholders' receiving one share in each new company for each of their NOVA Corp. shares.[4]

Shortly after the announcement of the NOVA split, the pipelines division announced its betrothal to TransCanada PipeLines Limited. In what was billed as a "merger of equals," this union resulted in the creation of the continent's fourth-largest energy services firm. Newall was very enthusiastic about the union. "Two companies—both born in the 1950s—are being reborn for the new century. We are witnessing the birth of a major Canadian company with remarkable strengths and a commanding presence in global energy. This will build a much stronger platform to create value for shareholders."

The merger plan included provision for half of the members of the new boards of directors for the new energy services company (TransCanada and NOVA pipelines) and the new independent chemicals company to come from TransCanada and the other half from NOVA. Newall was made chairman of the newly merged company.[5] The new entity is expected to save $150 million in annual capital and operating costs.[6]

NOVA and TransCanada PipeLines went into this arrangement believing that the merged company would be in a better position to provide less expensive gas transmission service for their customers. They emphasized that "The new organization will offer flexible, low-cost, competitive gas transmission services from the Western Canada sedimentary basin."[7]

TransCanada Pipelines Limited
www.transcanada.com

FIGURE 15-1 Executive's Decision Enhances Shareholder Value

In 1997, NOVA Corp.'s former vice-chairman and CEO, Ted Newall, made a difficult but strategically important decision to create two independent companies from NOVA's divisions. Its pipeline operation later merged with TransCanada PipeLines Limited. The company's chemicals operation became an independent enterprise.[8]

A s this case illustrates, through careful environmental analysis, NOVA found a way to increase value for its shareholders and clarify the market niche for each of its operations: the pipeline division and the chemicals division. The merger with TransCanada PipeLines allowed the company's pipeline division to position itself for economies of scale and a broader market base. At the heart of these major changes in organizational structure was the drive to attract investors by responding to a market that was shying away from conglomerates. NOVA's situation raises the question of how companies organize themselves (and reorganize as conditions change) to achieve their goals.

OB researchers and theorists have provided considerable insight into this matter by studying what is called *organizational structure*—the way individuals and groups are arranged with respect to the tasks they perform—and *organizational design*—the process of coordinating these structural elements in the most effective manner. As you probably suspect, finding the best way to structure and design organizations is not a simple matter, and NOVA's approach may not work well for all organizations. However, insofar as understanding the structure and design of organizations is essential to appreciate their functioning fully, organizational scientists have devoted considerable energy to this topic. We will describe these efforts in this chapter.

To begin, we will identify the basic building blocks of organizations, which can be depicted by the *organizational chart*, a useful pictorial way of showing key features of organizational structure. Following this, we will examine how these structural elements can be most effectively combined into productive organizational designs. Finally, we will discuss the role of technology as a cause—and a consequence—of organizational design. In so doing, we will be highlighting some basic facts regarding the role of the environment on organizational design.

Organizational Structure: The Basic Dimensions of Organizations

Think about how a simple house is constructed. It is composed of a wooden frame positioned atop a concrete slab covered by a roof and siding materials. Within this basic structure are separate systems operating to provide electricity, water, and telephone services. Similarly, the structure of the human body is composed of a skeleton surrounded by various systems of organs, muscle, and tissue serving bodily functions such as respiration, digestion, and the like. Although you may not have thought about it much, we can also identify the structure of an organization in a similar fashion.

Consider, for example, the college or university you attend. It is probably composed of various groupings of people and departments working together to serve special functions. Individuals and groups are dedicated to tasks such as teaching, providing financial services, maintaining the physical facilities, and so on. Of course, within each group, even more distinctions can be found between the jobs people perform. For example, it's unlikely that the instructor for your organizational behaviour course is also teaching seventeenth-century French literature. You also can distinguish between the various tasks and functions people perform in other organizations. In other words, an organization is not a haphazard collection of people, but a meaningful combination of groups and individuals working together purposefully to meet the goals of the organization.[9] The term **organizational structure** refers to the formal configuration between individuals and groups with respect to the allocation of tasks, responsibilities, and authority within organizations.[10]

Strictly speaking, one cannot see the structure of an organization; it is an abstract concept. However, the connections between various clusters of functions of which an organization is composed can be represented in the form of a diagram known as an **organizational chart**. In other words, an organizational chart can be considered a representation of an organization's internal structure (see Figure 15-2). As you might imagine, organizational charts may be recognized as useful tools for avoiding confusion within organizations regarding how various tasks or functions are interrelated. By carefully studying organizational charts, we can learn about some of the basic elements of organizational structure. With this in mind, we will now turn our attention to the five basic dimensions of organizational structure that can be revealed by organizational charts.

Organizational charts provide information about the various tasks performed within an organization and the formal lines of authority between them. For example, look at the chart depicting part of a hypothetical manufacturing organization shown in Figure 15-3. Each box represents a specific job, and the lines connecting

organizational structure The formal configuration between individuals and groups with respect to the allocation of tasks, responsibilities, and authorities within organizations.

organizational chart A diagram representing the connections between the various departments within an organization; a graphic representation of organizational structure.

☞ As noted in Chapter 9, organizational charts *are also used to trace the formal flow of communication within organizations.*

"I reported to the vice president of finance until someone discovered it wasn't a dotted line at all... just some spilled coffee."

FIGURE 15-2 The Organizational Chart: A Valuable Guide to Organizational Structure

Organizational charts provide useful information about the interrelationships between various organizational units and the basic structural elements of organizations.

(Source: Copyright © 1995 by Mark Litzler.)

hierarchy of authority A configuration of the reporting relationships within organizations; that is, who reports to whom.

☞ For an extended discussion of the trend toward downsizing organizations, see Chapters 2 and 16.

division of labour The process of dividing the many tasks performed within an organization into specialized jobs.

☞ We say "in theory" because, as noted in Chapter 5, if jobs are too narrow in scope, people may lose their motivation to work at a high level and performance may suffer.

them reflect the formally prescribed lines of communication between the individuals performing those jobs. To specialists in organizational structure, however, such diagrams reveal a great deal more.

Hierarchy of Authority: Up and Down the Organizational Ladder

In particular, the organizational chart also provides information about who reports to whom—what is known as **hierarchy of authority**. The diagram reveals which particular lower-level employees are required to report to which particular individuals immediately above them in the organizational hierarchy. In our hypothetical example in Figure 15-3, the various regional salespeople (at the bottom of the hierarchy and the bottom of the diagram) report to their respective regional sales directors, who report to the vice-president of sales, who reports to the president, who reports to the chief executive officer, who reports to the members of the board of directors. As we trace these reporting relationships, we work our way up the organization's hierarchy. In this case, the organization has six levels. Organizations may have many levels, in which case their structure is considered *tall*, or only a few, in which case their structure is considered *flat*.

In recent years, a great deal has appeared in the news about organizations restructuring their workforces by flattening them out.[11] Although it has not been uncommon for large companies to lay off people in low-level assembly-line jobs, these days middle managers and executives, long believed to be secure in their positions, find themselves unemployed as companies "downsize," "rightsize," "delayer," or "retrench" by eliminating entire layers of organizational structure.[12] In the 1990s millions of people have lost their jobs due to the flattening of organizational hierarchies[13] (see **THE ETHICS ANGLE** for a good news story about victims of downsizing). The underlying assumption behind all these cutbacks is that fewer layers reduce waste and enable people to make better decisions (by moving them closer to the problems at hand), thereby leading to greater profitability. In general, most management experts claim that although some hierarchy is necessary, too many layers of hierarchy can be hazardous to a company's bottom line.[14]

Division of Labour: Carving Up the Jobs Done

The standard organizational chart makes clear that the many tasks to be performed within an organization are divided into specialized jobs, a process known as the **division of labour**. The more that tasks are divided into separate jobs, the more those jobs are *specialized* and the narrower the range of activities that job incumbents are required to perform. In theory, the fewer tasks a person performs, the better he or she may be expected to perform them, freeing others to perform the tasks that they perform best. Taken together, an entire organization is composed of people performing a collection of specialized jobs. This is probably the most obvious feature of an organization that can be observed from the organizational chart.

As you might imagine, the degree to which employees perform specialized jobs is likely to depend on the size of the organization. The larger the organization, the more the opportunities for specialization are likely to exist. For example, an individual working in a large advertising agency may get to specialize in a highly narrow field, such as writing jingles for radio and TV spots for automobiles. By contrast, someone working at a much smaller agency may be required to do all writing of print and broadcast ads in addition to helping out with the artwork and meeting with the

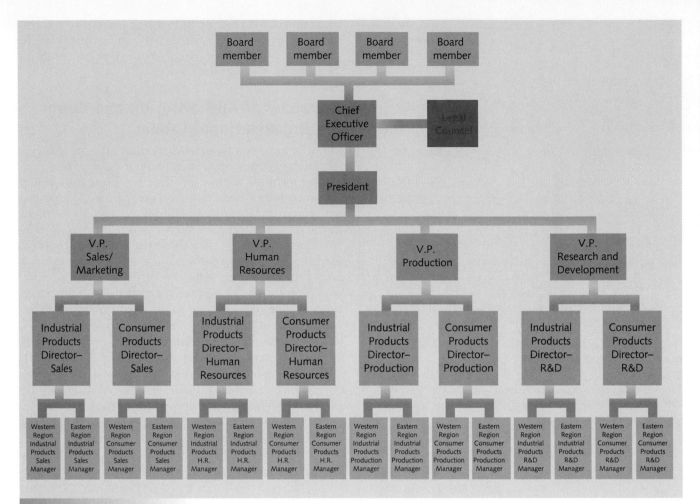

FIGURE 15-3 Organizational Chart of a Hypothetical Manufacturing Firm

An organizational chart, such as this one, identifies pictorially the various functions performed within an organization and the lines of authority between people performing those functions.

clients. Obviously, the larger company might be expected to reap the benefits of efficiently using the talents of its employees (a natural result of an extensive division of labour). As companies downsize, however, many managerial jobs become less specialized. For example, at General Electric, quite a few middle-management positions have been eliminated in recent years. As a consequence, the remaining managers must perform a wider variety of jobs, making their own jobs less specialized.[15] You can see this relationship in our summary in Table 15-1.

Span of Control: Breadth of Responsibility

Over how many individuals should a manager have responsibility? The earliest management theorists and practitioners alike addressed this question.[16] When you look at an organizational chart, the number of people formally required to report to each individual manager is immediately clear. This number constitutes what is known as a manager's **span of control**. Those responsible for many individuals are said to have a *wide* span of control, whereas those responsible for fewer are said to have a *narrow* span of control. In our organizational chart in Figure 15-3, the CEO is responsible for only the

span of control The number of subordinates in an organization who are supervised by managers.

TABLE 15-1 Division of Labour: A Summary

Low and high levels of division of labour can be characterized with respect to the dimensions shown here.

Dimension	Division of Labour	
	Low	High
Degree of specialization	General tasks	Highly specialized tasks
Typical organizational size	Small	Large
Economic efficiency	Inefficient	Highly efficient

Doing Business with a Conscience

Sometimes, being ethical means going beyond simply doing what's acceptable, by doing what's good for others. Indeed, small acts of kindness and generosity can make the world a better place to live. And, if you've been victimized by downsizing, you need all the kindness and generosity you can get. Alan Rappaport, owner of Julius Klein Cleaners, in New York City, was sensitive to this, and in January of 1992, he did something about it.[17] He offered free dry cleaning of one suit or one dress per week for anyone who was unemployed (and could prove it by showing documents from the local unemployment office). Rappaport's reasoning was simple: People who look their best while interviewing are likely to find employment. This was his small way of helping curb the unemployment problem that was so serious in the early 1990s.

Over 100 customers took advantage of Rappaport's offer. Importantly, his generosity was infectious. Soon, other cleaning establishments in the tri-state area "pressed on" and "followed suit." Some customers even gave donations to Rappaport to support his program. Rappaport also has found that his generosity has helped him pick up several new paying customers—individuals from the community who wish to reinforce his generosity by supporting his business.

Alan Rappaport and others who share his spirit lead the way toward a stronger community. Harry Rosen, who has clothing stores across Canada as well as in the U.S. and Japan, is lending a hand with the Raising the Roof campaign (see Figure 15-4). This national charity focuses on "finding long-term solutions to the growing problem of homelessness."[18] Rosen's support of the charity helps raise the organization's profile among potential contributors. Further, Aquilium Software Corp. of Charlottetown found another way to contribute to worthwhile causes. The company issued three-year warrants to a camp for children who have cancer and to a church restoration fund. A warrant is an opportunity to buy a share of stock in the future at a currently determined price. While the company is not yet profitable, as it grows, the warrants could be an effective "rainy day fund" for the two organizations. Since the warrants do not cost the company, they provide a way for small organizations to contribute to charitable causes.[19]

Aquilium Software Corporation
www.aquilium.com

FIGURE 15-4 Businesses Make Charitable Contributions in Unique Ways

Harry Rosen wears a toque to show his support for Raising the Roof, a charitable organization that works to address homelessness in Canada. Donald Murphy, a winner of many *Marketing Magazine* awards, came up with this idea. (see THE ETHICS ANGLE).[20]

actions of the president, giving this individual a narrower span of control than the president himself or herself, who has a span of control of five individuals. Sometimes, when organization leaders are concerned that they do not have enough control over lower-level employees, they restructure their organizations so that managers have responsibility over smaller numbers of subordinates. This is the case at the Royal Bank of Canada, where a team of top managers recently recommended that area managers reduce the number of branches under their control to between seven and twelve.[21]

When a manager's span of control is wide, the organization itself tends to have a flat hierarchy. In contrast, when a manager's span of control is narrow, the organization itself tends to have a tall hierarchy. This is demonstrated in Figure 15-5. The diagram at the top shows a *tall* organization—one in which there are many layers in the hierarchy and the span of control is relatively narrow (i.e., the number of people supervised is low). By contrast, the diagram at the bottom of Figure 15-5 shows a *flat* organization—one in which there are only a few levels in the hierarchy and the span of control is relatively wide. Note that both organizations depicted here have the same number of positions, but these are arranged differently.

The organizational chart may not reflect perfectly a manager's actual span of control. Other factors not immediately forthcoming from the chart itself may be involved. For example, managers may have additional responsibilities that do not appear on the chart—notably, assignments on various committees. Moreover, some subordinates (e.g., new people to the job) might require more attention than others. Also, the degree of supervisory control needed may increase (e.g., when jobs change) or decrease (e.g., when subordinates become more proficient). In fact, it is not readily possible to specify the "ideal" span of control that should be sought.

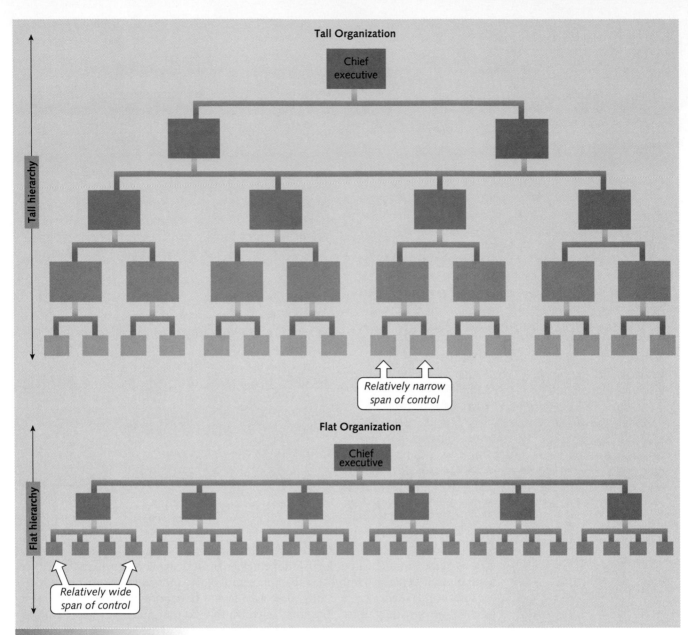

Tall Organization

Chief executive

Tall hierarchy

Relatively narrow span of control

Flat Organization

Chief executive

Flat hierarchy

Relatively wide span of control

FIGURE 15-5 Tall versus Flat Organizations: A Comparison

In *tall* organizations, the hierarchy has many layers and managers have a narrow span of control (i.e., they are responsible for few subordinates). However, in *flat* organizations the hierarchy has few layers and managers have a wide span of control (i.e., they are responsible for many subordinates). Each of the organizations depicted has 31 members, although each one is structured differently.

line positions Positions in organizations in which people can make decisions related to doing its basic work.

Instead, it makes better sense to consider what form of organization is best suited to various purposes. For example, because supervisors in a military unit must have tight control over subordinates and get them to respond quickly and precisely, a narrow span of control is likely to be effective. As a result, military organizations tend to be extremely tall. In contrast, people working in a research and development lab must have an open exchange of ideas and typically require little managerial guidance to be successful. Units of this type tend to have very flat structures.

Line versus Staff Positions: Decision Makers versus Advisers

The organizational chart shown in Figure 15-3 reveals an additional distinction that deserves to be highlighted—that between *line positions* and *staff positions*. People occupying **line positions** (e.g., the various vice-presidents and managers) have decision-making power. However, the individual shown in the dark-coloured box—the legal counsel—cannot make decisions but provides advice and recommendations to be used by the line managers. Such an individual may be said to occupy a

staff position. For example, a corporate attorney may help corporate officials decide whether a certain product name can be used without infringing on copyright restrictions. In many of today's organizations, human resources managers may be seen as occupying staff positions because they may provide specialized services regarding testing and interviewing procedures as well as information about the latest laws on personnel discrimination. However, the ultimate decisions on personnel selection might be made by more senior managers in specialized areas—that is, line managers.

Differences between line and staff personnel are not unusual. Such differences may be conflict-arousing, or even may be used to create intentional sources of conflict. For example, when Harold Green was the CEO of ITT, staff specialists in the areas of planning and strategy were regularly brought in from headquarters to challenge the decisions made by line managers in an attempt to "keep them on their toes."[22] Sociologists have noted that staff managers tend to be younger, better educated, and more committed to their fields than to the organizations employing them.[23] Line managers might feel more committed not only because of the greater opportunities they have to exercise decisions, but also because they are more likely to perceive themselves as part of a company rather than as an independent specialist (whose identity lies primarily within his or her specialty area).

Decentralization: Delegating Power Downward

During the first half of the twentieth century, as companies grew larger and larger, they shifted power and authority into the hands of a few upper-echelon administrators—executives whose decisions influenced the many people below them in the organizational hierarchy. In fact, it was during the 1920s that Alfred P. Sloan Jr., then the president of General Motors, introduced the notion of a "central office," the place where a few individuals made policy decisions for the entire company.[24] As part of Sloan's plan, decisions regarding the day-to-day operation of the company were pushed lower and lower down the organizational hierarchy, allowing those individuals who were most affected to make the decisions. This process of delegating power from higher to lower levels within organizations is known as **decentralization**. It is the opposite, of course, of *centralization*, the tendency for just a few powerful individuals or groups to hold most of the decision-making power.

Recent years have seen a marked trend toward greater decentralization. As a result, organizational charts will likely show fewer staff positions, as decision-making authority is pushed down the hierarchy. Many organizations have moved toward decentralization to promote managerial efficiency and to improve employee satisfaction (the result of giving people greater opportunities to take responsibility for their own actions). For example, Cara Operations Limited, which runs food services including Harvey's, Swiss Chalet, and Beaver Foods, includes a commitment to decentralization in its corporate mission statement.[25] In recent years large numbers of jobs have been lost at the Canadian Broadcasting Corporation, 3M, and Kodak as their companies have decentralized.[26]

Decentralization is not always an ideal step for organizations to take. In fact, for some types of jobs, it actually may be a serious hindrance to productivity. Consider production-oriented positions, like assembly-line jobs. In a classic study, Lawrence and Lorsh found that decentralization improved the performance on some jobs—notably, the work of employees in a research lab—but interfered with the performance of people doing more routine, assembly-line jobs.[27] These findings make sense once you consider that people working in research and development positions are likely to enjoy the autonomy to make decisions that decentralization allows, whereas people working on production jobs are likely to be less interested in taking responsibility for decisions and may enjoy not having to take such responsibility. With this in mind, many of today's companies heavily involved in research and development—including parts of Hewlett-Packard, Intel Corporation, Philips Electronics, and Corel Corp.—have more decentralized designs.[28]

In contrast, under some conditions, such as when only a few individuals are in a position to judge what's best for the company, highly centralized authority makes

☞ We discuss centralization in the process of decision making in Chapter 10 and the bases of social power in Chapter 12.

3M
www.3m.com

☞ In Chapter 5—when describing growth need strength *as a moderator of the job characteristics model*—we discuss the idea that people differ in the extent to which they may seek responsibility for making decisions on the job.

TABLE 15-2 Decentralization: Benefits When Low and When High	Low decentralization (High centralization)	High decentralization (Low centralization)
Various benefits are associated with low decentralization (high centralization) and high decentralization (low centralization) within organizations.	Eliminates the additional responsibility not desired by people performing routine jobs	Can eliminate levels of management, making a leaner organization
	Permits crucial decisions to be made by individuals who have the "big picture"	Promotes greater opportunities for decisions to be made by people closest to problems

the most sense. For example, at Delta Airlines, CEO Ronald W. Allen must personally approve every expenditure over $5000 (except jet fuel).[29] By so doing, he can very carefully monitor the company's expenses and keep it afloat during difficult times. Despite the possible benefits likely to result from relieving Allen of these chores, he believes that it is necessary to enforce tightly the decisions made at times when the margin for error is small. Another example of when centralization makes sense is illustrated by Petro-Canada, which cut hundreds of jobs including positions in information services that were dedicated to specific functional areas within the organization. Instead, the company created one information services unit to serve the entire corporation. This move made information services a company-wide responsibility while eliminating duplication and the filtering of information through layers of management.[30] Table 15-2 summarizes the benefits of both centralization and decentralization.

The five elements of structure described thus far—hierarchy of authority, division of labour, span of control, line versus staff positions, and decentralization—are the building blocks of organizational structure. They represent key dimensions along which organizations differ.

Departmentalization: Ways of Structuring Organizations

Thus far, we have been talking about "the" organizational chart of an organization. Typically, such charts, like the one shown in Figure 15-3, divide the organization according to the various functions performed. However, as we will explain in this section, this is only one option. Organizations can be divided up not only by function, but also by product or market, and by a special blend of function and product or market known as the matrix form. We will now take a closer look at these various ways of breaking up organizations into coherent units—that is, the process of **departmentalization**.

departmentalization The process of breaking up organizations into coherent units.

Functional Organizations: Departmentalization by Task

Because it is the form organizations usually take when they are first created, and because it is how we usually think of organizations, the **functional organization** can be considered the most basic approach to departmentalization. Essentially, functional organizations departmentalize individuals according to the nature of the functions they perform, with people who perform similar functions assigned to the same department. For example, a manufacturing company might consist of separate departments devoted to basic functions such as production, sales, research and development, and accounting (see Figure 15-6).

functional organization The type of departmentalization based on the activities or functions performed (e.g., sales, finance).

Naturally, as organizations grow and become more complex, additional departments are added or deleted as the need arises. As certain functions become centralized, resources can be saved by avoiding duplication of effort, resulting in a higher level of efficiency. Not only does this form of organizational structure take advantage of economies of scale (by allowing employees performing the same jobs to share facilities and by not duplicating functions), but in addition it allows individuals to

FIGURE 15-6 Functional Organization of a Typical Manufacturing Firm

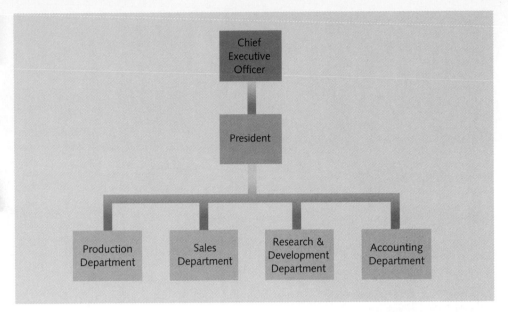

Functional organizations are ones in which departments are formed on the basis of common functions performed. In the hypothetical manufacturing firm shown in this simplified organizational chart, four typical functional departments are identified. In specific organizations the actual functions may differ.

specialize, thereby performing only those tasks at which they are most expert. The result is a highly skilled workforce, a direct benefit to the organization.

Partly offsetting these advantages, however, are several potential limitations. The most important of these stems from the fact that functional organizational structures encourage separate units to develop their own narrow perspectives and to lose sight of overall organizational goals. For example, in a manufacturing company, an engineer might see the company's problems in terms of the reliability of its products and fail to consider other key factors, such as market trends, overseas competition, and so on. Such narrow-mindedness is the inevitable result of functional specialization—the downside of people seeing the company's operations through a narrow lens. A related problem is that functional structures discourage innovation because they channel individual efforts toward narrow, functional areas and do not encourage coordination and cross-fertilization of ideas between areas. As a result, functional organizations are slow to respond to the challenges and opportunities they face from the environment (such as the need for new products and services). In summary, although functional organizations are certainly logical in nature and have proven useful in many contexts, they are by no means the perfect way to departmentalize people in organizations.

Product Organizations: Departmentalization by Type of Output

Organizations—at least successful ones—do not stand still; they constantly change in size and scope. As they develop new products and seek new customers, they might find that a functional structure doesn't work as well as it once did. Manufacturing a wide range of products using a variety of different methods, for example, might put a strain on a manufacturing division of a functional organization. Similarly, keeping track of the varied tax requirements for different types of business (e.g., restaurants, farms, real estate, manufacturing) might pose quite a challenge for a single financial division of a company. In response to such strains, a **product organization** might be created. This type of departmentalization creates self-contained divisions, each of which is responsible for everything to do with a certain product or group of products. (For a look at the structure of a product organization, see Figure 15-7.)

When organizations are departmentalized by products, separate divisions are established, each of which is devoted to a certain product or group of products. Each unit contains all the resources needed to develop, manufacture, and sell its products. The organization is composed of separate divisions, operating independently, the heads of which report to top management. Although some functions might be

product organization The type of departmentalization based on the products (or product lines) produced.

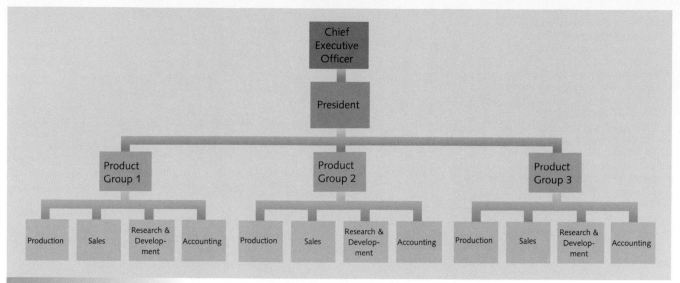

FIGURE 15-7 A Hypothetical Product Organization

In a *product organization*, separate units are established to handle different products or product lines. Each of these divisions contains all of the departments necessary for operating as an independent unit.

centralized within the parent company (e.g., human resource management or legal staff), on a day-to-day basis each division operates autonomously as a separate company or, as accountants call them, "cost centres" of their own.

Consider, for example, how separate divisions of Bombardier are devoted to manufacturing passenger rail vehicles, snowmobiles, aircraft, and the like.[31] The managers of each division can devote their energies to one particular business. Product organizations may be beneficial from a marketing perspective as well. Consider the example of Honda's 1987 introduction of its line of luxury cars, Acura.[32] By creating a separate division, with the cars manufactured in separate plants and sold by a separate network of dealers, the company made its higher-priced cars look special and avoided making its less expensive cars look less appealing by putting them together with superior products on the same showroom floors.

This is not to say that product organizations do not have limitations. Indeed, they have several drawbacks. The most obvious of these is the loss of economies of scale stemming from the duplication of various departments within operating units. For example, if each unit carries out its own research and development functions, the need for costly equipment, facilities, and personnel may be multiplied. Another problem associated with product designs involves the organization's ability to attract and retain talented employees. Since each department within operating units is necessarily smaller than a single combined one would be, opportunities for advancement and career development may suffer. This, in turn, may pose a serious problem with respect to the long-term retention of talented employees. Finally, problems of coordination across product lines may arise. In fact, in extreme cases, actions taken by one operating division may have adverse effects on the outcomes of one or more others.

A clear example of such problems was provided by Hewlett-Packard, a major international manufacturer of computers, printers, and scientific test equipment. During most of its history, Hewlett-Packard adopted a product design. It consisted of scores of small, largely autonomous divisions, each concerned with producing (and selling) certain products. As it grew in size and complexity, the company found itself in an increasingly untenable situation in which sales representatives from different divisions sometimes attempted to sell different lines of equipment, often to be used for the same basic purposes, to the same customers. To deal with such problems, top management at Hewlett-Packard decided to restructure the company into sectors based largely on the markets they served (such as business customers, and scientific and manufacturing customers). In short, Hewlett-Packard switched from a fairly traditional product organization to an internal structure driven by market considerations.[33] Although it's too soon to determine whether the effects of this reorganization will be as positive as top management hopes, initial results, at least, are promising.

The Hewlett-Packard case points out a particular variation on the basic theme of market departmentalization. Self-contained operating units can also be established on the basis of specific geographic regions or territories, and even customers rather than different products. So, for example, a large retail chain might develop separate divisions for different regions of the country, or for different customer bases. Similarly, a large record company (itself likely a division of a larger entertainment company) may establish independent divisions (each with its own labels) to sign, develop, produce, and promote recordings of interest to people in different markets (e.g., children, classical, Latin, pop). By departmentalizing in this fashion, a company can give artists the attention they would expect from a smaller company, and the specialization and economies of scale they would expect from a large company. Regardless of the exact basis for departmentalizing—be it product, region, market, or customer group—the basic rationale remains the same: Divide the organization's operations in a way that enhances efficiency.

Matrix Organizations: Departmentalization by Both Function and Product

When the aerospace industry was first developing, the U.S. government demanded that a single manager in each company be assigned to each of its projects so that it was immediately clear who was responsible for the progress of each project. In response to this requirement, TRW established a "project leader" for each project, someone who shared authority with the leaders of the existing functional departments.[34] This temporary arrangement later evolved into what is called a **matrix organization**, the type of organization in which an employee is required to report to both a functional (or division) manager and the manager of a specific project (or product). In essence, they developed a complex type of organizational structure that combines both the function and product forms of departmentalization.[35] To better understand matrix organizations, let's take a closer look at the organizational chart shown in Figure 15-8.

matrix organization The type of departmentalization in which a product or project form is superimposed on a functional form.

FIGURE 15-8 A Typical Matrix Organization

In a *matrix organization*, a product structure is superimposed on a basic functional structure. This results in a dual system of authority in which some managers report to two bosses—a project (or product) manager, and a functional (departmental) manager.

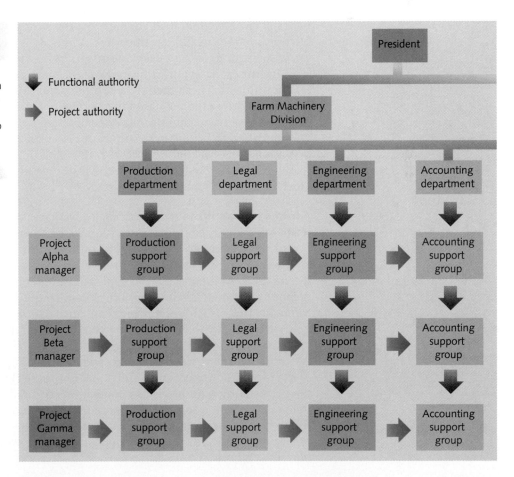

Major roles in matrix organizations. Many employees in matrix organizations have two bosses (or, more technically, they are under *dual authority*). One line of authority, shown by the vertical axes on Figure 15-8, is *functional*, managed by vice-presidents in charge of various functional areas. The other, shown by the horizontal axes, is *product* (or it may be a specific project or temporary business), managed by specific individuals in charge of certain products (or projects).

In matrix designs, there are three major roles. First, there is the *top leader*—the individual who has authority over both lines (the one based on function and the one based on product or project). It is this individual's task to enhance coordination between functional and product managers and to maintain an appropriate balance of power between them. Second, there are the *matrix bosses*—people who head functional departments or specific projects. Since neither functional managers nor project managers have complete authority over subordinates, they must work together to assure that their efforts mesh rather than conflict. In addition, they must agree on issues such as promotions and raises for specific people working under their joint authority. Finally, there are *two-boss managers*—people who must report to both product and functional managers and attempt to balance the demands of each.

Types of matrix designs. Not all organizations using the matrix structure do so on a permanent basis. Several partial, or temporary, types of matrix design have been identified.[36] First, the *temporary overlay* is a form of matrix structure in which projects are crossed with functions on a special, short-term basis. This is in contrast to a *permanent overlay*, in which project teams are kept going after each project is completed. Finally, there are *mature matrix organizations*, those in which both the functional lines and the product lines are permanent and equally strong within the organization.

With a matrix organization that has been in effect for over 20 years, Dow Corning is an example of a mature matrix organization.[37] At this company, each functional representative reports to the leaders of his or her own department, while also contributing to the design and operation of the particular product line for which he or she is responsible. Because people working in this fashion have two bosses, they must have sufficient freedom to attain their objectives. As you might imagine, a fair amount of coordination, flexibility, openness, and trust is essential for such a program to work, suggesting that not everyone adapts well to such a system.

Organizations are most likely to adopt matrix designs when they confront certain conditions. These include a complex and uncertain environment (one with frequent changes) and the need for economies of scale in the use of internal resources. Specifically, a matrix approach is often adopted by organizations with several product lines that do not possess sufficient resources to establish fully self-contained operating units (or that do not wish to create them permanently). Some companies that have adopted this structure, at least on a trial basis, are TRW Systems Group, Liberty Mutual Insurance, and Citibank.[38]

Advantages and disadvantages. Key advantages offered by matrix designs have already been suggested by our discussion so far.[39] First, they permit flexible use of an organization's human resources. Individuals within functional departments can be assigned to specific products or projects as the need arises and then return to their regular duties when this task is completed. Second, matrix designs offer medium-sized organizations an efficient means of responding quickly to a changing, unstable environment. Third, such designs often enhance communication among managers; indeed, they literally force matrix bosses to discuss and agree on many matters.

Disadvantages of such designs include the frustration and stress faced by two-boss managers in reporting to two different supervisors, the danger that one of the two authority systems (functional or product) will overwhelm the other, and the consistently high levels of cooperation required from the people involved for the organization to succeed.[40] In situations where organizations must stretch their financial and human resources to meet challenges from the external environment or take advantage of new opportunities, however, matrix designs can often play a useful role.

☛ *As we noted in Chapter 11, cooperation is sometimes far easier to imagine than to achieve.*

The Boundaryless Organization: A New Corporate Architecture

You hear it all the time: Someone is asked to do something but responds defiantly, saying, "It's not my job." As uncooperative as this may seem, such a comment may make a great deal of sense when it comes to the traditional kind of organizational structures we've been describing—ones with layers of carefully connected boxes neatly stacked atop each other in hierarchical fashion. The advantage of these types of organizations is that they clearly define the roles of managers and employees. Everyone knows precisely what he or she is supposed to do. The problem with such arrangements, however, is that they are inflexible. As a result, they do not lend themselves to the rapidly changing conditions in which today's organizations operate.

boundaryless organization An organization in which chains of command are eliminated, spans of control are unlimited, and rigid departments give way to empowered teams.

Sensitive to this limitation Jack Welch, CEO of General Electric, proposed the **boundaryless organization**. This is an organization in which chains of command are eliminated, spans of control are unlimited, and rigid departments give way to empowered teams. Replacing rigid distinctions between people are fluid, intentionally ambiguous and ill-defined roles. Welch's vision was that GE would operate like a family grocery store (albeit a U.S.$60 billion one)—one in which the barriers within the company that separate employees from each other and that separate the company from its customers and suppliers would be eliminated.[41] The idea is that such barriers inhibit creativity, waste time, smother dreams, and generally slow things down. Welch has referred to organizational boundaries as "speed bumps that slow down the enterprise."[42] Although GE has not yet become the completely boundaryless organization Welch envisioned, it has made significant strides toward breaking down boundaries.

So too have other organizations. As an example, consider the way Chrysler went about making its successful small car, the Neon.[43] In 1990 Robert P. Marcell, head of Chrysler's small-car engineering group, assembled a team of 600 engineers, 289 suppliers, and buses full of blue-collar workers. Together they developed the inexpensive new car in a speedy 42 months and on-budget at U.S.$1.3 billion. Instead of working sequentially using separate specialists in design, manufacturing, and marketing, as typically occurs, members of Marcell's team worked concurrently on several tasks. People from different areas, such as engineering, marketing, purchasing, and finance worked together with assembly-line workers, suppliers, and consumers to coordinate their efforts. In other words, the traditional boundaries that separate people (both inside and outside the organization) were eliminated. As a result, the team was able to work quickly, unhindered by the usual restrictions imposed by their narrow roles.

For boundaryless organizations to function effectively, they must meet many of the same requirements as successful teams. For example, there must be high levels of trust between all parties concerned. Also, everyone involved must have such high levels of skill that they can operate without much, if any, managerial guidance. Insofar as the elimination of boundaries weakens traditional managerial power bases, some executives may find it difficult to give up their authority, leading to political behaviour. However, to the extent that the elimination of boundaries leverages the talents of all employees, such limitations are worth striving to overcome.

☛ *For a discussion of the factors that contribute to the success of teams, see Chapter 8.*

The boundaryless organizations we have been describing involve breaking down both internal and external barriers. As a result, they are sometimes referred to as *barrier-free organizations*. However, there are variations of the boundaryless organization involving only the elimination of external boundaries.[44] These are known as *modular organizations* and *virtual organizations*. Although the key aspects of both types of organizations have been described earlier in this text (see Chapter 2), they deserve to be reiterated here for purposes of identifying them as specific forms of boundaryless organizations.

modular organization An organization that surrounds itself with a network of other organizations to which it regularly outsources non-core functions.

Modular organizations. As we described in Chapter 2, many of today's organizations outsource noncore functions to other companies while retaining full strategic control over their core business. Such companies may be thought of as having a central hub surrounded by networks of outside specialists that can be added or subtracted as needed. As such, they are referred to as **modular organizations**.[45]

As a case in point, you surely recognize Nike and Reebok as major designers and marketers of athletic shoes. However, you probably didn't realize that Nike's production facilities are limited, and that Reebok doesn't even have any plants of its own. Both organizations contract all their manufacturing to companies in countries such as Taiwan and South Korea where labour costs are low. In so doing, not only can they avoid making major investments in facilities, but they can concentrate on what they do best—tapping the changing tastes of their customers. While doing this, their suppliers can focus on rapidly retooling to make the new products.[46] Similarly, such popular computer companies as Dell and Gateway buy computer components made by other companies and perform only the final assembly themselves (as ordered by customers). These apparel and computer companies are both examples of modular organizations.

Toyota, one of the world's most successful automakers, has taken the modular form to the extreme. Its network of 230 suppliers (two of which are owned by Toyota itself) do just about everything the company needs, from making moulds for machine parts, to general contracting.[47] The key to the success of this arrangement is Toyota's very close ties to its suppliers—providing assurances that they will meet its stringent quality standards. Of course, companies that outsource any proprietary work (e.g., high-tech breakthroughs) must be assured that their trade secrets will not be compromised.

Virtual organizations.   Another approach to the boundaryless organization is the **virtual organization**. You will recall from Chapter 2 that such an organization is composed of a continually evolving network of companies (e.g., suppliers and customers) that are linked together to share skills, costs, and access to markets. They form a partnership to capitalize on their existing skills, pursuing common objectives. Then, after these objectives have been met, they disband.[48] Unlike modular organizations, which maintain close control over the companies to which they outsource, virtual organizations give up some control and become part of a new organization, at least for a while.

Corning, the giant glass and ceramics manufacturer, is a good example of a company that builds upon itself by developing partnerships with other companies (including Siemens, the German electronics firm, and Vitro, the large glass manufacturer from Mexico). In fact, Corning officials see their company not as a single entity, but as "a network of organizations."[49] Although Corning's alliances tend to be long-lived, most virtual organizations are formed on a limited basis (such as the Rolling Stones' "Voodoo Lounge" Tour described in Chapter 2).

The underlying idea of a virtual organization is that each participating company contributes only its core competencies (i.e., its areas of greatest strength). By several companies mixing and matching the best of what they can offer, a joint product is created that is better than one that any single company could have created alone. Consider, for example, the case of Pixar, the computer-animation company that partnered with Walt Disney Co. to produce the first computer-animated feature-length movie, *Toy Story*. The alliance these companies formed was not a merger but a temporary, task-focused alliance. This was a virtual corporation.[50] By sharing risks, costs, and expertise, many of today's companies are finding the virtual organization to be a highly appealing type of organizational structure.

To summarize, the boundaryless organization is becoming an increasingly popular organizational form. It involves eliminating all internal boundaries (such as those between employees) and external boundaries (such as those between the company and its suppliers). A variation on this organizational form involves eliminating only external boundaries. This occurs in modular organizations (in which secondary aspects of the company's operations are outsourced) and virtual organizations (in which organizations combine forces with others on a temporary basis to form new organizations, usually only briefly). For a summary of these three organizational structures, see Figure 15-9.

virtual organization A highly flexible, temporary organization formed by a group of companies that join forces to exploit a specific opportunity.

☞ *This type of cooperative effort between organizations is discussed in more detail in Chapter 11.*

FIGURE 15-9 The Boundaryless Organization: Various Forms

The true *boundaryless organization* is free of both internal barriers and external barriers. Variants, such as the *modular organization* and the *virtual organization*, eliminate only external barriers. All forms of boundaryless organizations are growing in popularity.

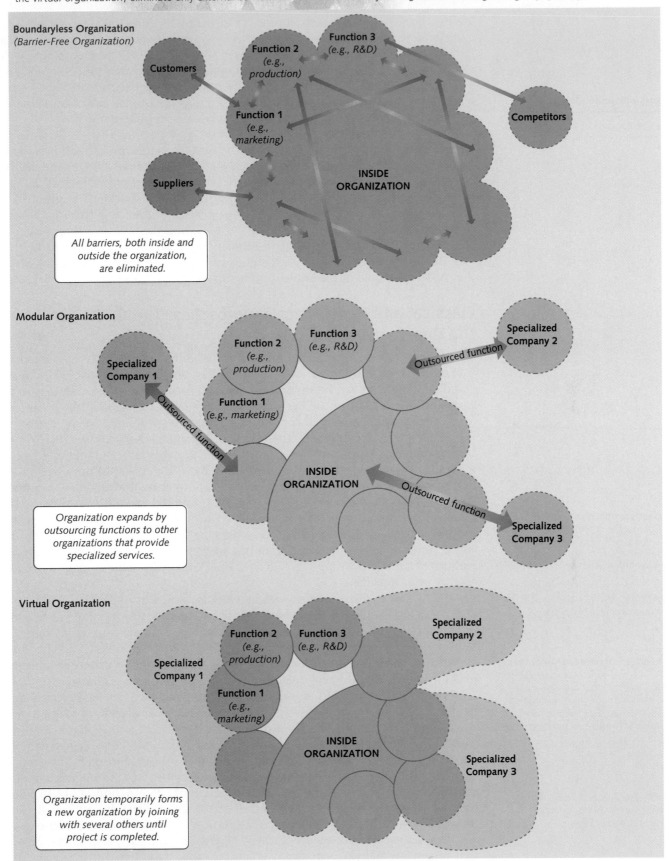

Boundaryless Organization
(Barrier-Free Organization)

Customers

Function 2
(e.g., production)

Function 3
(e.g., R&D)

Competitors

Function 1
(e.g., marketing)

INSIDE ORGANIZATION

Suppliers

All barriers, both inside and outside the organization, are eliminated.

Modular Organization

Specialized Company 1

Function 2
(e.g., production)

Function 3
(e.g., R&D)

Specialized Company 2

Function 1
(e.g., marketing)

Outsourced function

INSIDE ORGANIZATION

Outsourced function

Specialized Company 3

Organization expands by outsourcing functions to other organizations that provide specialized services.

Virtual Organization

Specialized Company 1

Function 2
(e.g., production)

Function 3
(e.g., R&D)

Specialized Company 2

Function 1
(e.g., marketing)

INSIDE ORGANIZATION

Specialized Company 3

Organization temporarily forms a new organization by joining with several others until project is completed.

Organizational Design: Coordinating the Structural Elements of Organizations

We began the first major section of this chapter by likening the structure of an organization to the structure of a house. Now we are prepared to extend that analogy for purposes of introducing the concept of *organizational design*. Just as a house is designed in a particular fashion by combining its structural elements in various ways, so too can an organization be designed by combining its basic elements in certain ways. Accordingly, **organizational design** refers to the process of coordinating the structural elements of organizations in the most appropriate manner.

As you might imagine, this is no easy task. Although we might describe some options that sound neat and rational on the next few pages, in reality this is hardly ever the case. Even the most precisely designed organizations will face the need to change at one time or another, adjusting to the realities of technological changes, political pressures, accidents, and so on. Organizational designs might also be changed purposely in an attempt to improve operating efficiency, such as the promise by some recent Canadian prime ministers to streamline the huge federal bureaucracy. Our point is simple: Because organizations operate within a changing world, their own designs must be capable of changing as well. Those organizations that are either poorly designed or inflexible cannot survive.

Classical and Neoclassical Approaches: The Quest for the One Best Design

The earliest theorists approached the task of designing organizations as a search for "the one best way." Although today we are more attuned to the need to adapt organizational designs to various environmental and social conditions, theorists in the early and middle part of the twentieth century sought to establish the ideal form for all organizations under all conditions—the universal design.

In Chapter 1, we described the efforts of organizational scholars such as Max Weber, Frederick Taylor, and Henri Fayol. These theorists believed that effective organizations were ones that had a formal hierarchy, a clear set of rules, specialization of labour, highly routine tasks, and a highly impersonal working environment. You may recall that Weber referred to this organizational form as a *bureaucracy*. This **classical organizational theory** has fallen into disfavour because it is insensitive to human needs and is not suited to a changing environment. Unfortunately, the "ideal" form of an organization, according to Weber, did not take into account the realities of the world within which it operates. Apparently, what is ideal is not necessarily what is realistic.

In response to these conditions, and with inspiration from the Hawthorne studies, the classical approach to the bureaucratic model gave way to a human relations orientation. Organizational scholars such as McGregor, Argyris, and Likert attempted to improve upon the classical model—which is why their approach is labelled **neoclassical organizational theory**—by arguing that not only is economic effectiveness the goal of an industrial organization, but also employee satisfaction.

Specifically, Douglas McGregor was an organizational theorist who objected to the rigid hierarchy imposed by Weber's bureaucratic form because it was based on negative assumptions about people—primarily that they lacked ambition and wouldn't work unless coerced (the *Theory X* approach).[51] In contrast, McGregor argued that people desire to achieve success by working and that they seek satisfaction by behaving responsibly (the *Theory Y* approach). Another neoclassical theorist, Chris Argyris, expressed similar ideas.[52] Specifically, he argued that managerial domination of organizations blocks basic human needs to express oneself and to accomplish tasks successfully. Such dissatisfaction, he argues, would encourage turnover and lead to poor performance.

Another neoclassical theorist, Rensis Likert, shared these perspectives, arguing that organizational performance is enhanced not by rigidly controlling people's

---

organizational design The process of coordinating the structural elements of an organization in the most appropriate manner.

classical organizational theory Approaches assuming that there is a single best way to design organizations.

☛ We described the Hawthorne studies in detail in Chapter 1.

neoclassical organizational theory An attempt to improve upon the classical organizational theory which argues that not only is economic effectiveness the goal of organizational structure, but also employee satisfaction.

☛ The Theory X and Theory Y philosophies of management are contrasted in Chapter 1.

actions, but by actively promoting their feelings of self-worth and their importance to the organization.[53] An effective organization, Likert proposed, was one in which individuals would have a great opportunity to participate in making organizational decisions—what he called a *System 4 organization*. Doing this, he claimed, would enhance employees' personal sense of worth, motivating them to succeed. Likert called the opposite type of organization *System 1*, the traditional form in which organizational power is distributed in the hands of a few top managers who tell lower-ranking people what to do. (*System 2* and *System 3* are intermediate forms between the System 1 and System 4 extremes.)

The organizational design implications of these neoclassical approaches are clear. In contrast to the classical approach, calling for organizations to be designed with a rigid, tall hierarchy, and with a narrow span of control (allowing managers to maintain close supervision over their subordinates), the neoclassical approach argues for designing organizations with flat hierarchical structures (minimizing managerial control over subordinates) and a high degree of decentralization (encouraging employees to make their own decisions). Indeed, such design features may well serve the underlying neoclassical philosophy.

Like the classical approach, the neoclassical approach also may be faulted on the grounds that it is promoted as "the one best approach" to organizational design. Although the benefits of flat, decentralized designs may be many, to claim that this represents the universally ideal form for all organizations would be naive. In response to this criticism, more contemporary approaches to organizational design have given up on finding the one best way to design organizations in favour of finding designs that are most appropriate to various circumstances and contexts within which organizations operate.

The Contingency Approach: The Impact of Environmental Conditions on Organizational Design

The idea that the best design for an organization depends in part on the nature of the environment in which the organization is operating lies at the heart of the modern **contingency approach** to organizational design. We use the term "contingency" here in a manner similar to the way we used it in our discussion of leadership. But rather than considering the best approach to leadership for a given situation, we are considering the best way to design an organization given certain factors such as the environment within which the organization functions.

contingency approach The approach that recognizes that the best organizational design is the one that best fits with the existing environmental and other conditions.

☞ *The* contingency approach *is described as a general orientation to the study of OB in Chapter 1, and as a specific theory of leadership in Chapter 13.*

The external environment: Its connection to organizational design.   It is widely assumed that the most appropriate type of organizational design depends in part on the organization's *external environment*. In general, the external environment is the sum of all the forces impinging on an organization with which it must deal effectively if it is to survive.[54] These forces include general work conditions, such as the economy, geography, and national resources, as well as the specific task environment within which the company operates—notably, its competitors, customers, workforce, and suppliers.

Let's consider some examples. Banks operate within an environment that is highly influenced by the general economic environment (e.g., interest rates and government regulations) as well as a task environment sensitive to other banks' products (e.g., types of accounts) and services (e.g., service hours, access to account information by computers and/or telephone), the needs of the customer base (e.g., direct deposit for customers), the availability of trained personnel (e.g., individuals suitable for entry-level positions), as well as the existence of suppliers providing goods and services (e.g., automated teller equipment, surveillance equipment, computer workstations) necessary to deliver requisite services. Analogous examples can be found in other industries as well. For example, think about the environmental forces faced by the airlines, the computer industry, and automobile manufacturers. It's easy to recognize the features of their environments that must be taken into account when considering how organizations in these industries could be designed.

Although many features of the environment may be taken into account when considering how an organization should be designed, a classic investigation by Burns and Stalker provides some useful guidance.[55] These scientists interviewed people in 20 industrial organizations in the United Kingdom to determine the relationship between managerial activities and the external environment. In so doing, they distinguished between organizations that operated in highly *stable*, unchanging environments, and those that operated in highly *unstable*, turbulent environments. For example, a rayon company in their sample operated in a highly stable environment: The environmental demands were predictable, people performed the same jobs in the same ways for a long time, and the organization had clearly defined lines of authority that helped get the job done. In contrast, a new electronics development company in their sample operated in a highly turbulent environment: Conditions changed on a daily basis, jobs were not well defined, and no clear organizational structure existed.

Burns and Stalker noted that many of the organizations studied tended to be described in ways that were appropriate for their environments. For example, when the environment is stable, people can do the same tasks repeatedly, allowing them to perform highly specialized jobs. However, in turbulent environments, many different jobs may have to be performed, and such specialization should not be designed into the jobs. Clearly, a strong link exists between the stability of the work environment and the proper organizational form. It was Burns and Stalker's conclusion that two different approaches to management existed and that these are largely based on the degree of stability within the external environment. These two approaches are known as *mechanistic organizations* and *organic organizations*.

Mechanistic versus organic organizations: Designs for stable versus turbulent conditions.

If you've ever worked at a Harvey's, you probably know how highly standardized each step of the most basic operations must be.[56] These steps are highly mechanistic. Organizations can be highly mechanistic when conditions don't change. Although the fast-food industry has changed a great deal in recent years (with the introduction of new, healthier menu items, competitive pricing, and the like), the selling of fries at Harvey's has not changed. The key to using mechanization is the lack of change. If the environment doesn't change, a highly mechanistic organizational form can be very efficient. A **mechanistic organization** exists under stable conditions.

An environment is considered stable whenever there is little or no unexpected change in product, market demands, technology, and the like. Have you ever seen an old-fashioned-looking bottle of Buckley's Mixture (cough syrup)? The Mississauga, Ontario–based W. K. Buckley Ltd. moved into its first factory in 1920 and has been going strong, and tasting strong, ever since. In fact, Buckley's' advertising campaign boasts that it tastes awful but it works.[57] Buckley's' long history, despite its legendary bad taste, suggests that it is operating in a relatively stable environment. As we described earlier, stability affords the luxury of high employee specialization. Without change, people can easily specialize. When change is inevitable, specialization is impractical.

Mechanistic organizations can be characterized in several additional ways (for a summary, see Table 15-3). Not only do mechanistic organizations allow for a high degree of specialization, but they also impose many rules. Authority is vested in a few people located at the top of a hierarchy who give direct orders to their subordinates. Mechanistic organizational designs tend to be most effective under conditions in which the external environment is stable and unchanging.

Now think about high-technology industries, such as those dedicated to computers, aerospace products, and biotechnology. Their environmental conditions are likely to be changing all the time. These industries are so prone to change that as soon as a new way of operating could be introduced into one of them, it would have to be altered. It isn't only technology, however, that makes an environment turbulent. Turbulence also can result from changing market demographics, changing government legislation and regulations, shifts in the global economy, and the like. An **organic organization** is better able to respond effectively to these kinds of turbulence than is a mechanistic organization.

mechanistic organization An organizational structure in which people perform specialized jobs, many rigid rules are imposed, and authority is vested in a few top-ranking officials.

☞ *In Chapter 14 we discuss the impact of the introduction of high-technology into the workplace.*

organic organization An organizational structure in which jobs tend to be very general, there are few rules, and decisions can be made by lower-level employees.

TABLE 15-3 Mechanistic versus Organic Designs: A Summary

Mechanistic and organic designs differ along several key dimensions identified here. These represent extremes; organizations can be relatively organic, relatively mechanistic, or somewhere in between.

Dimension	Structure	
	Mechanistic	Organic
Stability	Change unlikely	Change likely
Specialization	Many specialists	Many generalists
Formal rules	Rigid rules	Considerable flexibility
Authority	Centralized in few top people	Decentralized, diffused throughout the organization

The pure organic form of organization may be characterized in several different ways (see Table 15-3). The degree of job specialization possible is very low; instead, a broad knowledge of many different jobs is required. Very little authority is exercised from the top. Rather, self-control is expected, and an emphasis is placed on co-ordination between peers. As a result, decisions tend to be made in a highly democratic, participative manner. Be aware that the mechanistic and organic types of organizational structure described here are ideal forms. The mechanistic-organic distinction should be thought of as opposite poles along a continuum rather than as completely distinct options for organization. Certainly, organizations may be relatively organic or relatively mechanistic compared with others, but may not be found at either extreme.

Finally, note that research supports the idea that organizational effectiveness is related to the degree to which an organization's structure (mechanistic or organic) is matched to its environment (stable or turbulent). In a classic study, Morse and Lorsch evaluated four departments in a large company—two of which manufactured containers (a relatively stable environment) and two of which dealt with communications research (a highly unstable environment).[58] One department in each pair was evaluated as being more effective than the other. It was found that for the container manufacturing departments, the more effective unit was the one structured in a highly mechanistic form (roles and duties were clearly defined). In contrast, the more effective communications research department was structured in a highly organic fashion (roles and duties were vague). Additionally, the other, less effective departments were structured in the opposite manner (i.e., the less effective manufacturing department was organically structured, and the less effective research department was mechanistically structured) (see Figure 15-10). Taken together, the results made it clear that departments were most effective when their organizational structures fit their environments. This notion of "which design is best under which conditions?" lies at the heart of the modern orientation—the contingency approach—to organizational structure. Rather than specifying *which* structure is best, the contingency approach specifies *when* each type of organizational design is most effective.

Mintzberg's Framework: Five Organizational Forms

Although the distinction between mechanistic and organic designs is important, it is not terribly specific with respect to exactly how organizations should be designed. Filling this void, however, is the work of contemporary organizational theorist, Henry Mintzberg.[59] Specifically, Mintzberg claims that organizations are composed of five basic elements, or groups of individuals, any of which may predominate in an organization. The one that does will determine the most effective design in that situation. The five basic elements are:

1. *The operating core:* employees who perform the basic work related to the organization's product or service. Examples include teachers (in schools) and chefs and waiters (in restaurants).

In a classic study, Morse and Lorsch evaluated the performance of four departments in a large company. The most effective units were ones in which the way the group was structured (mechanistic or organic) matched the most appropriate form for the type of task performed (i.e., organic for research work and mechanistic for manufacturing work).

(Source: Based on suggestions by Morse & Lorsch, 1970; see Note 58.)

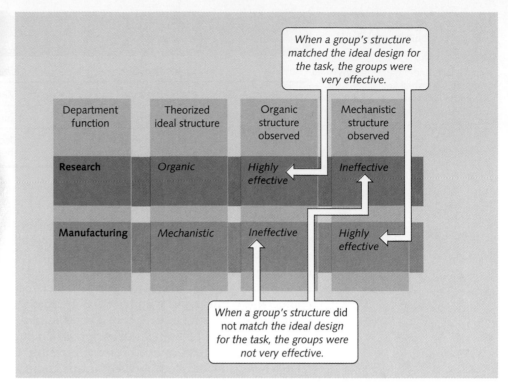

When a group's structure matched the ideal design for the task, the groups were very effective.

Department function	Theorized ideal structure	Organic structure observed	Mechanistic structure observed
Research	*Organic*	*Highly effective*	*Ineffective*
Manufacturing	*Mechanistic*	*Ineffective*	*Highly effective*

When a group's structure did not match the ideal design for the task, the groups were not very effective.

2. **The strategic apex:** top-level executives responsible for running the entire organization. Examples include the entrepreneur who runs her own small business and the general manager of an automobile dealership.

3. **The middle line:** managers who transfer information between the strategic apex and the operating core. Examples include middle managers, such as regional sales managers (who connect top executives with the sales force), and the chair of an academic department in a college or university (an intermediary between the dean and the faculty).

4. **The technostructure:** those specialists responsible for standardizing various aspects of the organization's activities. Examples include accountants, auditors, and computer systems analysts.

5. **The support staff:** individuals who provide indirect support services to the organization. Examples include consultants on technical matters and corporate attorneys.

What organizational designs best fit under conditions in which each of these five groups dominates? Mintzberg has identified five specific designs: *simple structure, machine bureaucracy, professional bureaucracy,* the *divisional structure,* and the *adhocracy* (see summary in Table 15-4).

Simple structure.   Imagine that you open up an antique shop and hire a few people to help you out around the store. You have a small, informal organization in which there is a single individual with the ultimate power. There is little in the way of specialization or formalization, and the overall structure is organic in nature. The hierarchy is quite flat, and all decision-making power is vested in a single individual—you. An organization so described, simple in nature, with the power residing at the strategic apex, is referred to by Mintzberg as having a **simple structure**. As you might imagine, organizations with simple structure can respond quickly to the environment and be very flexible. For example, the chef-owner of a small, independent restaurant can change the menu to suit the changing tastes of customers whenever needed, without first consulting anyone else. The down side of this, how-

simple structure An organization characterized as being small and informal, with a single powerful individual, often the founding entrepreneur, who is in charge of everything.

TABLE 15-4 Mintzberg's Five Organizational Forms: A Summary

Mintzberg has identified five distinct organizational designs, each of which is likely to occur in organizations in which certain groups are in power.

Source: Based on suggestions by Mintzberg, 1983; see Note 59.

Design	Description	Dominant Group	Example
Simple structure	Simple, informal, authority centralized in a single person	Strategic apex	Small, entrepreneurial business
Machine bureaucracy	Highly complex, formal environment with clear lines of authority	Technostructure	Government offices
Professional bureaucracy	Complex, decision-making authority is vested in professionals	Operating core	Universities
Divisional structure	Large, formal organizations with several separate divisions	Middle line	Multidivision businesses such as Bombardier
Adhocracy	Simple, informal, with decentralized authority	Support staff	Software development firm

ever, is that the success or failure of the entire enterprise is dependent on the wisdom and health of the individual in charge. Not surprisingly, organizations with simple structure are risky ventures.

Machine bureaucracy. If you've ever worked for your province's department of motor vehicles, you probably found it to be a very large place, with numerous rules and procedures for employees to follow. The work is highly specialized (e.g., one person gives the tests, and another completes the registration forms), and decision making is concentrated at the top (e.g., you need to get permission from your supervisor to do anything other than exactly what's expected). This type of work environment is highly stable, and does not have to change. An organization so characterized, where power resides with the technostructure, is referred to as a **machine bureaucracy**. Although machine bureaucracies can be highly efficient at performing standardized tasks, they tend to be dehumanizing and very boring for the employees.

Professional bureaucracy. Suppose you are a doctor working at a large city hospital. You are a highly trained specialist with considerable expertise in your field. You don't need to check with anyone else before authorizing a certain medical test or treatment for your patient; you make the decisions as they are needed, when they are needed. At the same time, the environment is highly formal (e.g., there are lots of rules and regulations for you to follow). Of course, you do not work alone; you also require the services of other highly qualified professionals such as nurses and laboratory technicians. Organizations of this type—and these include universities, libraries, and consulting firms as well as hospitals—maintain power with the operating core, and are called **professional bureaucracies**. Such organizations can be highly effective because they allow employees to practise those skills for which they are best qualified. However, sometimes specialists become so overly narrow that they fail to see the "big picture," leading to errors and potential conflict between employees.

Divisional structure. When you think of large organizations, such as Bombardier, General Motors, Du Pont, Xerox, and IBM, the image that comes to mind is probably closest to what Mintzberg describes as **divisional structure**. Such organizations consist of a set of autonomous units coordinated by a central headquarters (i.e., they rely on departmental structure based on products, as described on pages 469–471). In such organizations, because the divisions are autonomous (e.g., a General Motors employee at Buick does not have to consult with another at Chevrolet to do his or her job) division managers (the *middle line* part of Mintzberg's basic elements) have considerable control. Such designs preclude the need for top-level executives to think about the day-to-day operations of their companies and free them to concentrate on larger scale, strategic decisions. At the same time,

machine bureaucracy An organizational form in which work is highly specialized, decision making is concentrated at the top, and the work environment is not prone to change (e.g., a government office).

☞ This is consistent with our discussion of Max Weber's description of bureaucracy in Chapter 1.

professional bureaucracy Organizations (e.g., hospitals and universities) in which there are lots of rules to follow, but employees are highly skilled and free to make decisions on their own.

☞ For a discussion of several other sources of conflict in organizations, see Chapter 11.

divisional structure The form used by many large organizations, in which separate autonomous units are created to deal with entire product lines, freeing top management to focus on larger-scale, strategic decisions.

companies organized into separate divisions frequently tend to have high duplication of effort (e.g., separate order-processing units for each division). Having operated as separate divisions for the past 70 years, General Motors is considered the classic example of divisional structure.[60] Although the company has undergone many changes during this time, it has maintained its divisional structure.

Adhocracy.   After graduating from college, where you spent years learning how to program computers, you take a job at a small software company. Compared to your friends who found positions at large accounting firms, your professional life is much less formal. You work as a member of a team developing a new time-management software product. There are no rules, and schedules are made to be broken. Innovation is the order of the day. You all work together, and although there is someone who is "officially" in charge, you'd never know it. Using Mintzberg's framework, you work for an **adhocracy**—an organization in which power resides with the support staff. Essentially, this is the epitome of the organic structure identified earlier. Specialists coordinate with each other not because of their shared functions (e.g., accounting, manufacturing), but as members of teams working on specific projects.

adhocracy A highly informal, organic organization in which specialists work in teams, coordinating with each other on various projects (e.g., many software development companies).

Interorganizational Designs: Going Beyond the Single Organization

All the organizational designs we have examined thus far have concentrated on the arrangement of units within an organization—what may be termed *intraorganizational designs*. However, sometimes at least some parts of different organizations must operate jointly. To coordinate their efforts on such projects, organizations must create *interorganizational designs*, plans by which two or more organizations come together. Two such designs are commonly found: *conglomerates* and *strategic alliances*.

Conglomerates: Diversified "Megacorporations"

When an organization diversifies by adding an entirely unrelated business or product to its organizational design, it may be said to have formed a **conglomerate**. Some of the world's largest conglomerates may be found in Asia. For example, in Korea, companies such as Samsung and Hyundai produce home electronics, automobiles, textiles, and chemicals in large, unified conglomerates known as *chaebols*.[61] These are all separate companies overseen by the same parent company leadership. In Japan, the same type of arrangement is known as a *keiretsu*.[62] A good example of a keiretsu is the Matsushita Group.[63] This enormous conglomerate consists of a bank (Asahi Bank), a consumer electronics company (Panasonic), and several insurance companies (e.g., Sumitomo Life, Nippon Life). These examples are not meant to suggest that conglomerates are unique to Asia. Indeed, many large Canadian-based corporations, such as Imasco Ltd., Onex, and Power Corp., are also conglomerates.

conglomerate A form of organizational diversification in which an organization (usually a very large, multinational one) adds an entirely unrelated business or product to its organizational design.

Companies form conglomerates for several reasons. First, as an independent business, the parent company can enjoy the benefits of diversification. Thus, as one industry languishes, another may excel, allowing for a stable economic outlook for the parent company. In addition, conglomerates may provide built-in markets and access to supplies, since companies typically support other organizations within the conglomerate. For example, General Motors cars and trucks are fitted with Delco radios, and Ford cars and trucks have engines with Autolite spark plugs, separate companies that are owned by their respective parent companies. In this manner conglomerates can benefit by providing a network of organizations that are dependent on each other for products and services, thereby creating considerable advantages.

In recent years, however, many large conglomerates have been selling off parts of themselves in a move to concentrate on their core business.[64] For example, the giant Korean chaebol, Hyundai (which accounts for 10 percent of Korea's gross national product), has recently dismantled parts of its sprawling corporate structure, selling controlling interests in its heavy manufacturing and shipping companies, and severing all ties with its hotel, insurance, and department store companies.[65] In other words, compared to the 1960s, which was a period of growth for many conglomerates, the 1990s appears to have been a period of decline.

Strategic Alliances: Joining Forces for Mutual Benefit

strategic alliance A type of organizational design in which two or more separate companies combine forces to develop and operate a specific business.

A **strategic alliance** is a type of organizational design in which two or more separate firms join their competitive capabilities to operate a specific business. The goal of a strategic alliance is to provide benefits to each individual organization that could not be attained if they operated separately. Strategic alliances are low-risk ways of diversifying (adding new business operations) and entering new markets. Some companies, such as BCE, GE, and Ford have strategic alliances with many others. Some alliances last only a short time, whereas others have remained in existence for well over 20 years, and are still going strong.[66]

The continuum of alliances. In a recent study of 37 strategic alliances from throughout the world, Kanter and her associates found that three types of cooperative arrangements between organizations could be identified.[67] These may be arranged along a continuum ranging from those alliances that are weak and distant, at one end, to those that are strong and close, at the other end. As shown in Figure 15-11, at the weak end of the continuum are strategic alliances known as **mutual service consortia**. These are arrangements between two similar companies from the same or similar industries to pool their resources to receive a benefit that would be too difficult or expensive for either to obtain alone. Often, the focus is some high-tech capacity, such as an expensive piece of diagnostic equipment that might be shared by two or more local hospitals (e.g., a magnetic-resonance imaging, or MRI unit).

mutual service consortia A type of strategic alliance in which two similar companies from the same or similar industries pool their resources to receive a benefit that would be too difficult or expensive for either to obtain alone.

At the opposite end of the scale are the strongest and closest type of collaborations, referred to as **value-chain partnerships**. These are alliances between companies in different industries that have complementary capabilities. Customer-supplier relationships are a prime example. In such arrangements one company buys necessary goods and services from another so that it can do business. Because each company greatly depends on the other, each party's commitment to their mutual relationship is high. As noted earlier, Toyota has a network of 230 suppliers with whom it regularly does business. The relationship between Toyota and these various companies represents value-chain partnerships.

value-chain partnerships Strategic alliances between companies in different industries that have complementary capabilities.

Between these two extremes are **joint ventures**. These are arrangements in which companies work together to fulfill opportunities that require the capabilities of the other. For example, two companies might enter into a joint venture if one has a valuable technology and the other has the marketing knowledge to help transform that technology into a viable commercial product. For a description of a highly successful joint venture, see THE QUEST FOR QUALITY section.

joint ventures Strategic alliances in which several companies work together to fulfill opportunities that require the capabilities of one another.

FIGURE 15-11 Strategic Alliances: A Continuum of Interorganizational Relationships

The three types of strategic alliances identified here may be distinguished with respect to their location along a continuum ranging from weak and distant to strong and close.

(Source: Based on suggestions by Kanter, 1994; see Note 66.)

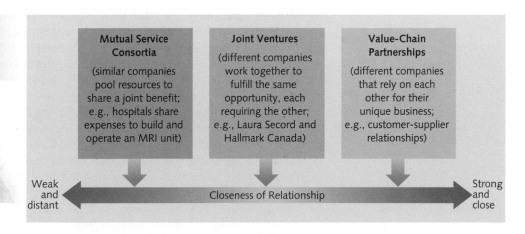

Mutual Service Consortia	Joint Ventures	Value-Chain Partnerships
(similar companies pool resources to share a joint benefit; e.g., hospitals share expenses to build and operate an MRI unit)	(different companies work together to fulfill the same opportunity, each requiring the other; e.g., Laura Secord and Hallmark Canada)	(different companies that rely on each other for their unique business; e.g., customer-supplier relationships)

Weak and distant ← Closeness of Relationship → Strong and close

The Quest for Quality

The Sweet Taste of Success

What do you get when you mix chocolates and greeting cards? Good times? Cavities? Or a thriving alliance?

Just ask Laura Secord Inc. and Hallmark Cards Canada, two retailers who teamed up to expand their markets. Laura Secord President Colleen Fleming and Tanya Boyd-Saffran, Hallmark's VP of marketing administration, oversaw the 1998 roll-out of Laura Secord/Hallmark "combo" stores. There are now 18 outlets across Canada, performing so well that plans call for 30 more.

Industry statistics suggest an alarming 55 percent of alliances and 78 percent of mergers fall apart within three years. What's the secret at Laura Secord/Hallmark? Good planning and constant communication have served their alliance well.

In 1994, both companies went seeking a partner, figuring two retailers could draw more customers than either alone. Each looked for a partner with integrity, long-term vision, brand excellence, and solid financing. From there, says Fleming, "we formed an agreement based on trust, the relationship, and the guarantee the selection criteria allowed."

Now both benefit from each other's strengths. Easter, for instance, is a peak period for chocolate, while Mother's Day is card heaven. Combo stores thus enjoy more peak-traffic periods and sales spillover.

Fleming and Boyd-Saffran stayed in touch every step of the way, from initial idea to prototype stores, testing, and roll-out. Moving ahead required more meetings: updating agreements, redrafting goals, and setting financial limits. Fleming and Boyd-Saffran agree that had they not had open communication and trust from the outset, their success would not have been nearly so sweet.[68]

As our descriptions of these types of alliances illustrate, there are clear benefits to be derived from forming alliances. These primarily come in the form of improved technology, widened markets, and greater economies of scale (e.g., sharing functional operations across organizations). However, as you might imagine, for these benefits to be realized, a high degree of coordination and fit must exist between the parties, each delivering on its promise to the other.

As you might imagine, not all strategic alliances are successful. The CASE IN POINT for this chapter describes the rocky attempted marriage between Volvo and Renault. Similarly, AT&T and Olivetti tried unsuccessfully to work together on manufacturing personal computers. Strong differences in management styles and organizational culture were cited as causes. Clearly, for strategic alliances to work, the companies must not only be able to offer each other something important, but they also must be able to work together to make it happen.

> *Recall our discussion in Chapter 2 of how the global nature of the economy influences the study of organizations.*

Strategic alliances in the global economy. Strategic alliances with companies in nations with transforming economies (such as China and eastern Europe) provide good opportunities for those nations' economies to develop.[69] Given the rapid move toward globalization of the economy, we may expect to see many companies seeking strategic alliances in the future as a means for gaining or maintaining a competitive advantage.[70] Frequently, companies form strategic alliances with foreign firms to gain entry into that country's market (see Figure 15-12). The company in the host country also may benefit by the influx of foreign expertise and capital. For example, Florida's Orlando Helicopter Airway Company and China's Guangdong No. 3 Machine Tools Factory formed a strategic alliance in 1986 to make the first helicopters available in Guangdong Province, China.[71] Such arrangements also may allow for an exchange of technology and manufacturing services. For example, Korea's Daewoo receives technical information and is paid to manufacture automobiles for companies with which it has entered into alliances, such as General Motors, as well as Germany's Opel and Japan's Isuzu and Nissan.[72] Some companies, such as the telecommunications giant MCI, are actively involved in several strategic alliances, including one in Canada and several in New Zealand.[73]

FIGURE 15-12 Strategic Alliances as the Key to Growth in Foreign Markets
These employees of the Korean company Samsung Electronics might not know it, but their CEO, Kim Kwang-Ho is hoping to develop their organization into a global electronics giant by establishing strategic alliances with partners in other countries. With this in mind, Samsung has been building its technological strength and market penetration by partnering with Japanese firms (such as Toshiba and Fujitsu) and American firms (such as AT&T and Motorola).

In addition to the financial incentives (circumventing trade and tariff restrictions) and marketing benefits (access to internal markets) associated with strategic alliances, direct managerial benefits also are associated with extending one company's organizational chart into another's. These benefits primarily come from improved technology and greater economies of scale (e.g., sharing functional operations across organizations). For these benefits to be derived, a high degree of coordination and fit must exist between the parties, each delivering on its promise to the other.

Technology and Organizational Design

Organizations differ tremendously with respect to *technology*—the means by which they transform inputs into outputs. These can vary from the simplest of tools used by single individuals to huge machines and complex, automated equipment. Clearly, the technology employed by a given organization is closely linked to the work it performs and the major tasks it seeks to accomplish. But growing evidence indicates that this relationship, too, is something of a two-way street. Organizations not only choose the technology they will employ; they are also affected by such tools once they are selected.

In short, just as the design of a specific building reflects the activities that take place within it, the structure of many organizations, too, tends to mirror the technologies they employ. In the discussion that follows, we will describe several major studies that point to this conclusion. As you will soon see, these investigations classify technology in contrasting ways and focus on a wide range of issues. Thus, their findings are often difficult to compare in a simple or direct manner. Generally, though, all point to the same basic conclusion: Technology plays an important role in shaping both the design and performance of many organizations.

☞ *You may wish to refer to our more general discussion of technology in Chapter 14.*

Technology and Structure in Manufacturing Companies: The Woodward Studies

Perhaps the best-known study on the effects of technology is one conducted in England during the 1960s by Woodward and her associates.[74] To determine the relationship between various structural characteristics (e.g., span of control, decentralization) and organizational performance (e.g., profitability, market share), these investigators gathered data about 100 manufacturing firms. In keeping with the classical view of management (described on page 476), they initially expected that organizations classified as highly successful would share similar structural characteristics, and those classified as relatively unsuccessful would share other characteristics. Surprisingly, this was not the case. Instead, various aspects of organizational structure appeared to be just as common in successful and unsuccessful companies. Thus, there was little if any support for the accuracy of universal principles of management.

Instead, Woodward and her colleagues found that the organization's success depended on the degree to which it was structured in the most appropriate way given the technology used. Specifically, they compared organizations using each of three different types of technology in popular use at the time. In the first, labelled **small-batch production**, custom work was the norm. Capital equipment (machinery) was not highly mechanized, and the companies involved typically produced small batches of products to meet specific orders from customers. Employees were either skilled or unskilled, depending on the tasks they performed. Firms included in this category made items such as specialized construction equipment or custom-ordered electronic items. Other examples include dressmaking and printing.

Companies in the second category, known as **large-batch** or **mass production**, used basic assembly-line procedures. These organizations typically engaged in long production runs of standardized parts or products. Their output then went into inventory from which orders were filled on a continuous basis. Employees were mainly unskilled or semiskilled, with a sprinkling of research and engineering personnel.

The third category, known as **continuous-process production**, was the most technologically complex. Here, there was no start and no stop to production, which was automated and fully integrated. Employees were skilled workers or engineers. Among the organizations employing such advanced technology were oil refining and chemical companies.

When companies using these various types of technology were compared, important differences were noted. First, as expected, they demonstrated contrasting internal structures. For example, the span of control (of first-level supervisors) and centralization were higher in companies employing mass production than in ones using small-batch or continuous-process technologies. Similarly, chains of command were longest in organizations using continuous-process production, and shortest in those using small-batch methods. In short, the type of technology employed in production appeared to be an important variable in shaping organization structure. As Woodward herself put it, "Different technologies imposed different kinds of demands on individuals and organizations, and those demands had to be met through an appropriate structure."[75]

Perhaps even more important than these findings was the fact that the characteristics distinguishing highly successful from unsuccessful companies also varied with technology. At the low and high ends of the technology dimension described above, an *organic* management approach seemed best; companies showing this strategy were more successful than those demonstrating a *mechanistic* approach. In contrast, in the middle of the technology dimension (mass production), the opposite was true. Here, companies adopting a mechanistic approach tended to be more effective (see Figure 15-13). Another finding was that successful firms tended to have structures suited to their level of technology. Specifically, those with above-average performance showed structural characteristics similar to most other firms using the same type of production methods; in contrast, those with below-average records tended to depart from the median structure shown by companies in the same technology category. In summary, the results of Woodward's study indicated that important links exist between technology and performance.

Additional support for these conclusions was later obtained in several other studies. For example, in a project involving 55 U.S. firms, Zwerman found that organizations employing small-batch or continuous-process technology tended to adopt an organic management approach.[76] Those employing mass production generally showed a mechanistic approach. In general, research has shown that the more

small-batch production A technology in which products are custom-produced in response to specific orders from customers.

large-batch (mass) production Technology based on long production runs of standardized parts or products.

continuous-process production A highly automated form of production that is continuous in nature and highly integrated in terms of component steps and processes.

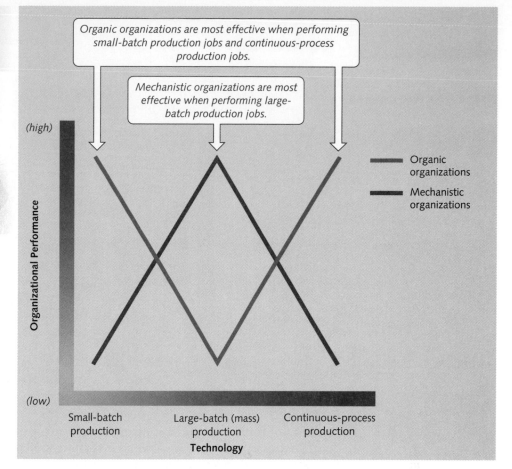

FIGURE 15-13 The Woodward Studies: The Relationship between Technology and Design

In a classic study, Woodward found that organic organizations were most effective when performing small-batch production and continuous-batch production jobs, whereas mechanistic organizations were most effective when performing large-batch production jobs.

(Source: Based on findings by Woodward, 1965; see Note 74.)

Organic organizations are most effective when performing small-batch production jobs and continuous-process production jobs.

Mechanistic organizations are most effective when performing large-batch production jobs.

— Organic organizations

— Mechanistic organizations

(high)

(low)

Organizational Performance

Small-batch production — Large-batch (mass) production — Continuous-process production

Technology

sophisticated the technology used, the greater are the opportunities for organizations to thrive when authority is decentralized (in essence, because the "smart" technology is making the decisions, eliminating the need for some people in the hierarchy).[77] Woodward's findings are valuable because they were among the first that recognized the value of the contemporary, contingency approach to organizational structure.

As you might imagine, we have learned a great deal about organizational design since Woodward's time—if for no other reason than technology has changed so very much. In addition to the three types of technology studied by Woodward, today some organizations produce highly customized, high-performance products in relatively small runs. However, because these products are technologically advanced and complex, they are produced by highly automated, computer-controlled equipment. Moreover, the people involved in their manufacture must often possess a high level of professional or technical knowledge. In short, such companies share some characteristics with the traditional small-batch firms studied by Woodward, but share others with the technologically advanced continuous-process firms at the other end of her continuum.

What type of internal structure do such technical batch organizations demonstrate? Evidence on this issue has been provided by Hull and Collins.[78] These researchers examined the internal structure of 110 separate companies operating in the United States. On the basis of careful examination of their methods of production, Hull and Collins divided these organizations into four categories: traditional batch, technical batch, mass production, and process production. Then they compared the companies' internal structures along several key dimensions (e.g., supervisory span of control, occupational specialization, decentralization, formalization). As the examples in Figure 15-14 show, the types differed in various ways.

Consistent with predictions, organizations classified as traditional batch or technical batch in their methods of production showed contrasting structure in several respects. For example, the traditional batch companies possessed a larger supervisory

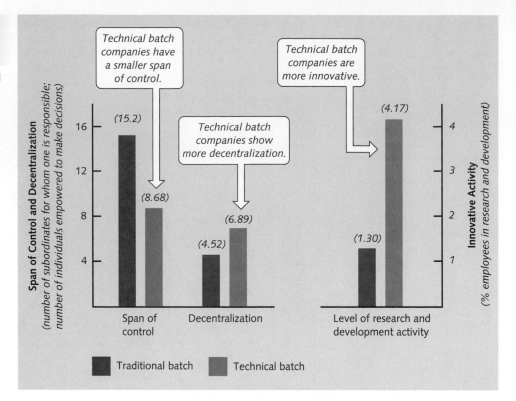

FIGURE 15-14 Technology and Structure: Evidence of Linkages

Organizations employing technical batch technology differ in several respects from those employing traditional batch technology.

(Source: Based on data from Hull & Collins, 1987; see Note 78.)

span of control. In contrast, the technical batch companies showed a greater degree of occupational specialization and more decentralization. Further, and perhaps most important, the technical batch companies showed a much higher level of innovative activity (e.g., a higher percentage of employees involved in research and development activities).

In summary, expanding Woodward's original categories to reflect recent developments in methods of production yielded additional evidence for the powerful impact of technology on internal structure. Additional research along similar lines may help us to sharpen our knowledge of this important relationship still further.

Workflow Integration: The Aston Studies

As the heading of the preceding section suggests, Woodward's project, and several subsequent investigations, focused primarily on the links between technology and structure in manufacturing companies. Thus, as thorough as this work was, it left a basic issue unresolved: Would similar findings be observed in other types of companies as well?

Evidence on this question was provided by another team of British researchers affiliated with the University of Aston.[79] After studying a wide range of both manufacturing and service organizations (e.g., savings banks, insurance companies, department stores), these researchers concluded that technology can be described in terms of three basic characteristics: *automation of equipment*—the extent to which work activities are performed by machines; *workflow rigidity*—the extent to which the sequence of work activities is inflexible; and *specificity of evaluation*—the degree to which work activities can be assessed by specific, quantitative means. Since these three factors appeared to be highly associated, they were combined into a single scale labelled **workflow integration**. The higher an organization's score on this scale, the more likely it was to employ automation, rigid task sequences, and quantitative measurement of its operations. The workflow integration scores obtained by various companies are shown in Table 15-5. As you can see from this table, manufacturing firms generally score higher than those whose primary output is service.

workflow integration A measure of technology that takes account of the degree of automation, workflow rigidity, and specificity of evaluation within an organization.

TABLE 15-5 Workflow Integration in Different Organizations

Manufacturing firms generally score higher on workflow integration than do service organizations (e.g., banks, stores).

Source: Based on data from Hickson, Pugh & Pheysey, 1969; see Note 79.

Organization	Classification (Manufacturing or Service)	Workflow Integration Score
Vehicle manufacturer	Manufacturing	17
Metal goods manufacturer	Manufacturing	14
Tire manufacturer	Manufacturing	12
Printer	Service	11
Local water department	Service	10
Insurance company	Service	7
Savings bank	Service	4
Department stores	Service	2
Chain of retail stores	Service	1

[You Be The Consultant]

Fabricate-It, Inc. is a medium-sized manufacturing company that uses standard assembly lines to produce its products. Its employees tend to be poorly educated and perform monotonous work. Think-It, Inc. is a software design firm that writes customized programs to solve its customers' problems. Its employees tend to be highly educated and perform highly creative work. Both are reconsidering their present organizational designs.

1. What type of organizational design would you imagine would best suit the needs of Fabricate-It? Explain your decision.

2. What type of organizational design would you imagine would best suit the needs of Think-It? Explain your decision.

When workflow integration was related to structural characteristics in the organizations studied, no strong or general links were uncovered. Thus, at first glance, findings seemed contradictory to those reported by Woodward. Closer analysis of the data obtained, however, revealed that technological complexity *was* related to structural features, in at least some ways. For example, as workflow integration increased, so did specialization, standardization, and decentralization of authority. The magnitude of these findings was small, and they seemed to involve mainly those aspects of structure closely connected to actual workflow. Moreover, *size* exerted stronger effects on several aspects of structure than technology.

These findings, plus those obtained in later studies, point to two conclusions. First, although technology does indeed seem to affect the internal structure of organizations, it is only one of several influences. As a result, the so-called *technological imperative*—the view that technology always has a compelling influence on organizational structure—clearly overstates the case.[80] Second, technology probably exerts stronger effects on structure in small organizations, where such characteristics impinge directly on workflow, than in large ones, where structure is complex and often far removed from actual production. In any case, taken as a whole, the findings of the Aston studies can be interpreted as indicating that the impact of technology on organizational structure is not restricted to manufacturing concerns. Under certain conditions, it can be observed in other types of companies as well.

Technology and Interdependence: Thompson's Framework

Another aspect of technology with important implications for organizational structure is **interdependence**. This refers to the extent to which individuals, departments, or units within a given organization depend on each other in accomplishing their tasks. Under conditions of low interdependence, each person, unit, or group can carry out its functions in the absence of assistance or input from others. Under high interdependence, in contrast, such coordination is essential. A framework proposed by Thompson helps clarify the various types of interdependence possible in organizations, and also the implications of this factor for effective structural design.[81]

interdependence The extent to which the units or departments within an organization depend on each other to accomplish tasks.

pooled interdependence A relatively low level of interdependence in which units within an organization operate in a largely independent manner.

sequential interdependence An intermediate level of interdependence in which the output of one unit serves as input for another.

reciprocal interdependence A high level of interdependence in which the output of each unit within an organization serves as the input for others, and vice versa.

The lowest level within this framework is known as **pooled interdependence**. Under such conditions, departments or units are part of an organization, but work does not flow between them. Rather, each carries out its tasks independently. One example of pooled interdependence is provided by the branch stores of a clothing retailer in many large shopping malls. Each contributes to the total earnings of the parent company, but there is little, if any, contact or coordination between them.

The next higher level suggested by Thompson is **sequential interdependence**. Here, the output of one department or subunit becomes the input for another. For example, the marketing department of a food company cannot proceed with promotional campaigns until it receives information about new products from the product development unit. Similarly, in a company that manufactures electronic toys, final assemblers cannot perform their jobs unless they receive a steady supply of component parts from other work units or outside suppliers. Note that in sequential interdependence, information, products, and components flow in one direction. Thus, units farther along the chain of production are dependent on ones that precede them, but the reverse is not true.

The highest level in Thompson's model is known as **reciprocal interdependence**. Here the output of each department or unit serves as the input for other departments or units in a reciprocal fashion. Thus, the output of Department A provides input for Department B, and the output of Department B serves as the input for Department A. An example of such reciprocal interdependence is provided by the operations of the marketing and production departments of many companies. Marketing, through appropriate surveys, may develop a profile of new products or product innovations attractive to potential customers. This serves as input for Production, which considers the feasibility of actually making such products and suggests modifications. The appeal of these modifications is then assessed by Marketing and the results obtained serve as the basis for further planning by Production. This process may be repeated until a plan for product innovations acceptable to both units is devised (see Figure 15-15).

These three forms of interdependence require varying levels of coordination between the units involved. The need for coordination is quite low under conditions of pooled interdependence, since each of the departments involved is relatively independent. Rules and standard operating procedures usually suffice. In contrast, sequential interdependence requires substantially greater coordination. Here, formal meetings and vertical communication are often needed. Finally, reciprocal interdependence calls for concerted efforts at coordination, including many meetings and a high level of horizontal communication.[82]

FIGURE 15-15 Reciprocal Interdependence: An Example

Under conditions of *reciprocal interdependence,* the output of two or more departments serves as the input for each other in a reciprocal fashion.

(Source: Based on suggestions by Thompson, 1967; see Note 81.)

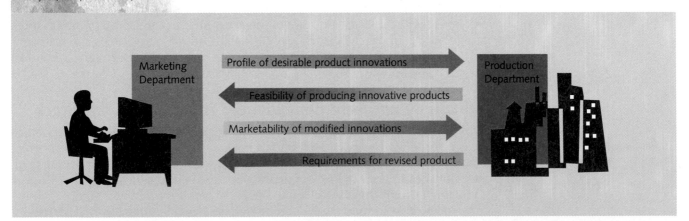

The level of interdependence existing between various units within an organization also has important implications for internal structure. Special attention should be directed in organizational design to departments or units that are reciprocally interdependent. These should be grouped together so that they can engage in continuous, mutual adjustment (e.g., they should be close to each other physically and should fall under the authority of the same person). Further, specific mechanisms for assuring a high degree of coordination between them (e.g., daily meetings, the creation of special liaison positions) should be developed. Although top priority in devising internal structure should be given to reciprocal interdependence, efforts to establish effective communication between units that are sequentially interdependent are important, too. These should have ready access to one another so that workflow between them can proceed in a smooth and orderly manner.

In summary, the kind of work activities performed within an organization, and the specific technologies it employs, often determine the level of interdependence between its various units. Such interdependence, in turn, should be taken into careful account when planning internal structure.

SUMMARY AND REVIEW

Organizational Structure

The formal configuration between individuals and groups with respect to the allocation of tasks, responsibilities, and authority within organizations is known as **organizational structure**, an abstract concept that can be represented by an **organizational chart**. Such diagrams represent five different elemental building blocks of organizational structure: **hierarchy of authority** (a summary of reporting relationships), **division of labour** (the degree to which jobs are specialized), **span of control** (the number of individuals over which a manager has responsibility), **line** versus **staff positions** (jobs permitting direct decision-making power versus jobs in which advice is given), and **decentralization** (the degree to which decisions can be made by lower-ranking employees as opposed to a few higher-ranking individuals).

Departmentalization

Within organizations, groups of people can be combined into departments in various ways. The most popular approach is the **functional organization**, organizations created by combining people in terms of the common functions they perform (e.g., sales, manufacturing). An alternative approach is to departmentalize people by virtue of the specific products for which they are responsible, known as the **product organization**.

Another form of departmentalization combines both of these approaches into a single form known as the **matrix organization**. In such organizations, people have at least two bosses; they are responsible to a superior in charge of the various functions and a superior in charge of the specific product. Employees also may have to answer to high-ranking people responsible for the entire organization, the top leaders.

Following the lead of General Electric, many of today's companies are moving toward **boundaryless organizations** (ones in which chains of command are eliminated, spans of control are unlimited, and rigid departments give way to empowered teams). These involve eliminating all internal boundaries (such as those between employees) and external boundaries (such as those between the company and its suppliers). Variations on this organizational form involve only the elimination of external boundaries. These include the **modular organization** (in which secondary aspects of the company's operations are outsourced) and the **virtual organization** (in which organizations combine forces with others on a temporary basis to form new organizations, usually only briefly).

Organizational Design

The process of coordinating the structural elements of organizations in the most appropriate manner is known as **organizational design**. *Classical organizational theorists* (such as Weber and his notion of bureaucracy) believed that a universally best way to design organizations exists, an approach based on high efficiency. *Neoclassical organizational theorists* (such as McGregor, Argyris, and Likert) also believe that there is one best way to design organizations, although their approach emphasizes the need to pay attention to basic human needs to succeed and express oneself.

In contrast, the **contingency approach** to organizational design is predicated on the belief that the most appropriate way to design organizations depends on the external environments within which they operate. Specifically, a key factor has to do with the degree to which the organization is subject to change: A stable environment is one in which business conditions do not change, whereas a turbulent environment is one in which conditions change rapidly. Research has shown that when conditions are stable, a **mechanistic organization** is effective. A mechanistic organization is one in which people perform specialized jobs, many rigid rules are imposed, and authority is vested in a few top-ranking officials. When conditions are turbulent, an **organic organization** is effective. These are organizations in which jobs tend to be very general, there are few rules, and decisions can be made by low-level employees. The mechanistic and organic forms are pure types, and organizations can be located in-between these two extremes.

Five specific organizational forms have been identified by Mintzberg. Organizations with **simple structure** are small and informal, and have a single powerful individual, often the founding entrepreneur, who is in charge of everything (e.g., a small retail store owned by a sole proprietor). In a **machine bureaucracy** work is highly specialized, decision making is concentrated at the top, and the work environment is not prone to change (e.g., a government office). In **professional bureaucracies**, such as hospitals and universities, there are lots of rules to follow, but employees are highly skilled and free to make decisions on their own. **Divisional structure** characterizes many large organizations (such as Bombardier) in which separate autonomous units are created to deal with entire product lines, freeing top management to focus on larger-scale, strategic decisions. Finally, the **adhocracy** is a highly informal, organic organization in which specialists work in teams, coordinating with each other on various projects (e.g., many software development companies).

Interorganizational Designs

Other organizational designs represent ways of combining more than one organization. Such interorganizational designs include the **conglomerate** (large corporations that diversify by getting involved in unrelated businesses), and the **strategic alliance** (organizations combining forces to operate a specific business). There are three major types of strategic alliances: **mutual service consortia**, **joint ventures**, and **value-chain partnerships**.

Technology as a Factor in Organizational Design

The technology employed by an organization often affects its internal structure. Companies employing **small-batch**, **large-batch (mass) production**, and **continuous-process** technologies often differ with respect to their internal structure. In recent years, companies employing small-batch production coupled with a high-level technology have emerged. The internal characteristics of such companies are different from those of traditional small-batch organizations, which typically employ simpler means of production.

Organizations vary with respect to the level of **interdependence** between departments or other work units. The higher such interdependence, the greater the need for structural components that enhance coordination.

CASE PREVIEW QUESTIONS FOR DISCUSSION

1. Why are investors shying away from conglomerates such as NOVA before the split?
2. Why was the merger a good idea for NOVA?
3. What challenges would a merger of this type bring for each partner?

CHAPTER QUESTIONS FOR DISCUSSION

1. As organizations grow and become more complex, their designs are likely to change. Describe the various ways in which size may influence organizational design. How are these changes likely to influence individuals?

2. Describe the difficulties you believe will result from implementing a matrix organization.

3. Explain various ways in which traditional organizational designs are changing and are expected to change in the future. What problems, if any, do you envision stemming from these trends?

4. What challenges will people face as organizations become increasingly "boundaryless"?

5. Identify contemporary organizations that are relatively mechanistic or relatively organic in nature. To what extent is each characterized by stable or turbulent environments as predicted by the contingency approach to organizational design?

6. Give an example of a specific company you know that fits each of the five organizational forms identified by Mintzberg: *simple structure, machine bureaucracy, professional bureaucracy, divisional structure*, and *adhocracy*. On what grounds does each qualify as an example?

7. Using an example of an organization you know, describe how its prevailing technology is related to its organizational design.

"Do You, Volvo, Take Thee, Renault . . . ?": An Alliance Doomed to Divorce

Although vows may not have been spoken and rice thrown, the 1990 alliance between Volvo and Renault, according to Rick Dowden, president and CEO of Volvo of North America, was "intended to be a marriage."[83] As in the marriage of two people, the marriage of two companies is not taken lightly; each has some idea of what it is looking for in a partner.

Because Volvo manufactures only 400 000 cars a year, and its competitors produce millions, it was looking for a partner to help it stay competitive in the world market. Specifically, it wanted an alliance with a company that understood its business, could complement it, and was not so large that it would dominate the relationship. After its successful joint venture with Renault in the realm of engine manufacturing, Volvo felt comfortable with Renault. And Renault met Volvo's criteria: It was another auto manufacturer, but with strengths in different areas (e.g., Renault is strong in small cars and diesel engines, with developed markets in southern Europe and Latin America, whereas Volvo is strong in larger cars and gasoline technology, with strong markets in northern Europe and North America).

Importantly, the top executives involved, Volvo's then-chairman, Pehr Gellenhammar, and Renault's then-chairman, Raymond Levy, held similar views about what they wanted to do and how they wanted to do it. As Dowden put it, "These were two people who knew and respected each other and had common goals and aspirations for their companies," adding, "if the people don't work together, I don't care how much the numbers seem to work, you won't get that [spirit] of cooperation."[84]

Like most marriages, the decision to formalize the relationship between Renault and Volvo came only after serious consideration of how it would work out. Various groups were formed to study how functions such as product design, research and development, and purchasing would be accomplished. After much careful study, it was concluded that Renault and Volvo would each benefit from the alliance, with enhanced competitiveness and long-term profitability. And so, in February 1990, their alliance was officially announced —an arrangement viewed as permanent. It was one that kept the parties separate in some ways, but brought them together in many others. To create a financial interdependence between the two companies, each bought a large portion of the other's stock.[85]

Despite the mutual buying of stock and other precautions, like many marriages, this one failed. Volvo's board rejected the deal Volvo chairman Pehr Gellenhammar had negotiated with the French automaker. The board learned that the deal would give the French government 65 percent of the new merged company, with the possibility that the Swedish share could be reduced in the future. Gellenhammar subsequently resigned.[86] The major impetus for the split came from Volvo shareholders who were less than enthusiastic about the deal. In 1997 Renault sold its last shares in Volvo.[87] A Volvo spokesperson said the sell-off "would not affect Volvo's industrial cooperation with the French group." The two companies trade component parts and jointly control a French bus manufacturer.[88]

However, this amicable divorce may not be the last word in the Renault-Volvo relationship. With the announcement of the Daimler-Chrysler merger, the European market is said to be at overcapacity and ripe for more mergers. John Buckland, a Daiwa Europe Ltd. analyst, sees the Renault-Volvo relationship as a good bet. "I still think the Renault-Volvo deal is the one that provided the best fit....Maybe now that management has changed, both companies can rekindle the deal."[89]

Critical Thinking Questions

1. Why might Volvo investors have been hesitant about the merger with Renault?

2. Discuss the impact of the huge Daimler-Chrysler merger on the European and world car markets. Why would this merger stimulate others?

3. Do you think Renault and Volvo will "rekindle the deal"? Should they do this? Explain.

SKILLS PORTFOLIO

Experiencing Organizational Behaviour

Which Do You Prefer—Mechanistic or Organic Organizations?

Because mechanistic and organic organizations are so different, it is reasonable to expect that people will tend to prefer one of these organizational forms over the other. This questionnaire is designed to help you identify your own preferences (and, in so doing, to help you learn about the different forms themselves).

Directions

Each of the following questions deals with your preferences for various conditions that may exist where you work. Answer each one by checking the one alternative that best describes your feelings.

1. When I have a job-related decision to make, I usually prefer to:
   ____**a.** make the decision myself.
   ____**b.** have my boss make it for me.
2. I usually find myself more interested in performing:
   ____**a.** a highly narrow, specialized task.
   ____**b.** many different types of tasks.
3. I prefer to work in places in which working conditions:
   ____**a.** change a great deal.
   ____**b.** generally remain the same.
4. When a lot of rules are imposed on me, I generally feel:
   ____**a.** very comfortable.
   ____**b.** very uncomfortable.
5. I believe that governmental regulation of industry is:
   ____**a.** usually best for all.
   ____**b.** rarely good for anyone.

Scoring

1. Give yourself 1 point each time you answered as follows: 1 = b; 2 = a; 3 = b; 4 = a; 5 = a. This score is your preference for *mechanistic organizations*.

2. Subtract this score from 5. This score is your preference for *organic organizations*.

3. Interpret your scores as follows: Higher scores (closer to 5) reflect stronger preferences, and lower scores (closer to 0) reflect weaker preferences.

Questions for Discussion

1. How did you score? That is, which organizational form did you prefer?
2. Think back over the jobs you've had. Have these been in organizations that were mechanistic or organic?
3. Do you think you performed better in organizations whose designs matched your preferences than those in which there was a mismatch?
4. Do you think you were more committed to organizations whose designs matched your preferences than those in which there was a mismatch?

Working in Groups

Comparing Organizational Structure and Design

Given the great deal of material that is written in the popular press about companies these days, it is not too difficult to learn things about key aspects of organizational structure and design. Uncovering and analyzing such information can be a valuable way to learn how work functions are arranged in organizations. This exercise is designed with this objective in mind.

Directions

1. Divide the class into four equal-sized groups and assign to each group one of the following industry types: (a) manufacturing companies, (b) financial institutions, (c) public utilities, and (d) charities.

2. Divide the students within each group into teams of 2 or 3.

3. Members of each team should work together searching their local libraries for books and articles in the popular literature that describe something about the structure and design of any organizations within their assigned industry. (Feel free to focus on any aspects of design and structure described in this chapter. For example, articles may be found on the tendency for some companies to be eliminating middle management.) Computerized databases that allow you to search for stories about companies by name will be very useful.

4. After completing their research, students within the four groups should meet to discuss the structural characteristics of the organizations described by the various teams.
5. Gather as a class to compare the findings of the various groups.

Questions for Discussion

1. What major trends were found with respect to organizational structure and design? For example, were organizations eliminating levels of management?
2. Did you find that there were differences between companies with respect to key aspects of organizational structure and design? For example, were spans of control different at different organizational levels? If so, how?
3. Did the class find structural similarities between companies in various industries and differences between companies in different industries? If so, what were these? For example, were spans of control generally broader in some industries and narrower in others? If so, how do you explain these differences?

TAKE IT TO THE NET

Prentice Hall

We invite you to visit the *Greenberg/Baron/Sales/Owen Companion Website* at *www.prenticehall.ca/greenberg* for this chapter's Internet resources.

CHAPTER 16

Organizational Change and Development

LEARNING OBJECTIVES

After reading this chapter you should be able to:

1. Identify why it is important for organizations to change.

2. Describe the forces behind *organizational change*.

3. Identify the conditions under which organizational change is likely to occur.

4. Explain the major factors making people resistant to organizational change—and some ways of overcoming them.

5. Describe the major techniques of *organizational development*.

6. Evaluate the effectiveness of organizational development efforts.

7. Debate the idea that organizational development is inherently unethical.

Times Certainly Have Changed at Eaton's

"Retailing is like the ocean. It shifts with the tide in and the tide out. It isn't as though you open a store and you're in business for 100 years. You gotta work at it." John Craig Eaton is certainly well aware of the ebbing tides of retail fortunes. In 1996, this heir to one of Canada's oldest department stores faced a tide as low as the Bay of Fundy's—and lower.[1] The Eaton family has held tightly to the reins of the privately owned company for most of its history, with the CEO always being an Eaton relative, the majority direct descendants of the legendary founder, Timothy Eaton (see Figure 16-1).

The early 1990s was a time of great upheaval in retailing. "Big box" stores with warehouse formats were able to keep prices very low. "Category killers" specializing in high volume, focused markets gave customers a wide range of selection within a product category, such as office supplies, home improvement equipment, or toys. Television shopping was also beginning to cut into the trade of traditional retailers. The major threat, of course, was the increase in the number of discount department stores.

In the face of these major environmental changes, Eaton's looked to outside consultants for advice. The company made major investments in technological upgrades, and improved its efficiency in areas such as distribution, which had previously been notoriously slow. Eaton's invested in store renovations in an effort to attract what it saw as its traditional middle- to upper-middle-class market. The company also partnered with Toronto's Ryerson Polytechnic University to start the Eaton School of Retailing, the first degree program in retailing in Canada. Ironically, the focus of the program was on helping "retailers to turn their companies into 'learning organizations' that encourage innovation, education, and information sharing."[2]

However, despite all its best efforts, the pressure of increasing competition—especially from large numbers of new U.S. competitors arriving in Canada—and the recession of the early-to-mid 1990s caused the unthinkable. The once-mighty Eaton's became insolvent. The company sought court protection from its creditors in 1997. One analyst suggested that, in its attempt to save itself during the 1990s slide, the company's repeated pricing shifts, along with its failure to update its operating systems and renovate stores in a timely fashion, left it to compete "more with Zellers and Wal-Mart than with Hudson's Bay. Competing with Wal-Mart from a base of high-cost retail space has been described as inviting the Montreal Canadiens to play at your local rink." The local team would not and did not fare well.[3]

Another analyst has argued that "Eaton's mistake, in retrospect, was in not recognizing and not reacting sooner to the consumer psyche in which price became the predominant factor in most purchase decisions. They introduced the right, long-term marketing strategy at the wrong time."[4]

Figure 16-1 Upheaval Hits Eaton's Hard
The left toe of the statue in the Eaton Centre store in Toronto is worn shiny from the thousands of passersby who have rubbed it for luck. John Craig Eaton may well look to his great-grandfather for inspiration with the fortunes of the Eaton empire in a state of flux.[5]

Eaton's
www.eatons.com

When you picture a large chain of spacious stores packed with merchandise you probably don't think of a business fighting for survival. Yet, in the wake of some rapid change in the Canadian retailing environment, Eaton's is facing a very uncertain future. Whether the company's new strategy to attract a younger market comes as too little and too late, or whether it marks a successful rebirth of Eaton's, one thing is certain: A great deal of *change* has occurred.

The pressure for change in the world of organizations is enormous, and not just at Eaton's. Think of the changes you may have seen in recent years in the way different businesses operate. In some organizations, formal business attire has been traded in for a more casual look, a number of auto dealerships have adopted no-haggle pricing policies, accommodations for people who have disabilities have appeared, just about everything you can imagine has become computerized, and companies are buying up other companies in foreign lands (see Figure 16-2). Clearly, signs of *organizational change* can be found everywhere. Examining both the causes and consequences of change is one of the key missions of this chapter.

Most people have difficulty accepting that they may have to alter their work methods. After all, if you're used to working a certain way, a sudden change can be very unsettling. Fortunately, social scientists have developed various methods, known collectively as *organizational development* techniques, that are designed to implement needed organizational change in a manner that both is acceptable to employees and enhances the effectiveness of the organizations involved.[6] We will examine these techniques and critical issues surrounding them in this chapter. Before doing so, however, we will take a closer look at the process of organizational change by chronicling different forces for change acting on organizations. Then we will explore some major issues involved in the process of organizational change, such as what is changed, when change will occur, why people are resistant to change, and how this resistance may be overcome.

"Today the secret ingredients for Mom's Apple Pie were sold to the Japanese for sixty-eight million dollars."

FIGURE 16-2 Nothing Is Sacred When It Comes to Organizational Change

Change is so much an inevitable part of life in organizations that even some seemingly sacred traditions are not immune.

(Source: Drawing by Ziegler; © 1988 The New Yorker Magazine, Inc.

Organizational Change: An Ongoing Process

A century ago, advances in machine technology made farming so highly efficient that fewer hands were needed to plant and reap the harvest. The displaced labourers fled to nearby cities, seeking jobs in newly opened factories—ironically, taking advantage of opportunities created by some of the same technologies that displaced them from the farm. The economy shifted from agrarian to manufacturing, and the *industrial revolution* was under way. With it came drastic shifts in where people lived, how they worked, how they spent their leisure time, how much money they made, and how they spent it.

Today's business analysts claim that we are currently experiencing *another* industrial revolution—one driven by a new wave of economic and technological forces.[7] As one observer put it, "This workplace revolution . . . may be remembered as a historic event, the Western equivalent of the collapse of communism."[8] Not surprisingly, a great deal of **organizational change** is occurring—that is, planned or unplanned transformations in an organization's structure, technology, and/or people.

Change Is a Global Phenomenon

Interestingly, the forces for organizational change appear to be global in nature. To illustrate this point, consider a study that examined the percentage of Canadian

☛ *For discussions of the ways in which technology influences the way people work, see Chapters 14 and 15.*

organizational change Planned or unplanned transformations in an organization's structure, technology, and/or people.

executives who planned to make changes in a number of areas of their companies' operations within the next three to five years. The results showed that 41 percent of respondents planned to change their international focus, 51 percent planned to make changes in organizational structure, and 59 percent planned to implement changes to "the diversity of their workforce."[9]

A similar study explored the history of change in organizations from 25 countries. When the 12 000 managers who were surveyed were asked to identify the changes they had experienced in the two years preceding the study, respondents reported that major restructuring, mergers, divestitures and acquisitions, reductions in employment, and international expansion had occurred in their organizations. Although some forms of change were more common in some countries than others, organizations in all countries were actively involved in each of these types of change efforts.[10] This evidence suggests that organizational change is occurring throughout the world. Although different forces may be shaping change at different rates in different places, the conclusion is apparent: Change is a universal fact of life for organizations.

The Message Is Clear: Change or Disappear!

It's shocking when you think of all the once well-known companies, or parts of them, that have gone out of business in the past few decades. Even the Consumers' Distributing Catalogue is now just a memory of a bygone era. No organization is immune. Even industry leaders are vulnerable to failure if they do not adapt to changing times.

Fully 62 percent of new ventures fail to last as long as 5 years, and only 2 percent survive for 50 years.[11] Amazingly, however, some Canadian companies have beaten the odds—so soundly, in fact, that they have remained in business for well over 300 years. As you might imagine, these companies have undergone *many* changes during their years of existence. One notable example in Canada is the Hudson's Bay Company, founded in 1670. It has come a long way from its beginnings in fur trading to its current status as the fifth-largest employer in Canada with 70 000 employees and department stores across the country.[12]

In recent years, just about all companies you can think of have made adjustments in the ways they operate, some more pronounced than others. (One example may be seen in our CASE PREVIEW about Eaton's.) The changes that organizations make differ in scope; some are only minor, whereas others are major. Change that is continuous in nature, and involves no major shifts in the way an organization operates, is known as **first-order change**. Changes of this type are apparent in the very deliberate, incremental changes that Toyota has been making in continuously improving the efficiency of its production process.[13] Similarly, a restaurant may be seen as making first-order changes as it gradually adds new items to its menu and gauges their success before completely revamping its concept.

As you might imagine, however, other types of organizational change are far more complex. **Second-order change** is the term used to refer to more radical change, major shifts involving many different levels of the organization and many different aspects of business.[14] Some of the most publicized examples of second-order change in recent years, General Electric, Bell Canada, NOVA (see the CASE PREVIEW for Chapter 15), and CN, have radically altered the way they operate, their culture, the technologies they use, their structure, and the nature of their relations with employees.

The Learning Organization: Benefiting from Change

Peter Senge, director of the Systems Thinking and Organizational Learning program at the Sloan School of Management, Massachusetts Institute of Technology, introduced the concept of organizational learning in *The Fifth Discipline: The Art and Practice of the Learning Organization*. Senge and his followers argue that organizations must in-

first-order change Change that is continuous in nature and involves no major shifts in the way an organization operates.

second-order change Radical change; major shifts involving many different levels of the organization and many different aspects of business.

learning organization An organization that is successful at acquiring, cultivating, and applying knowledge that can be used to help it adapt to change.

vest considerable time, perhaps years, to become a **learning organization**, and that this is not just another fad in management theory. Canadian Tire Acceptance Limited in Welland, Ontario is an example of a company that is striving to become a learning organization—and succeeding.[15] For Senge, the learning organization is "an organization that is continually expanding its capacity to create its future."[16]

Specifically, organizations "learn" by following four basic steps (see summary in Figure 16-3):[17]

1. *Knowledge acquisition*: This is the process by which organizations tap the expertise of their employees to create a pool of knowledge upon which they can draw. For example, professional and technical information can be shared within organizations on a computer network using computer programs known as *groupware*. (These programs enable several people to work together on the same project and have access to the same information.)[18]

2. *Information distribution*: For information to be used as the basis for change, it must be distributed to and understood by those who require it. For example, at a restaurant chain in the United States, employees are connected via a computer network to an electronic bulletin board in which information is posted on-line about sales figures, cost breakdowns, and even customer complaints.[19] By doing this, company officials hope to provide managers and lower-level employees opportunities to benefit from the experiences of others—thereby helping them better understand their own behaviour.

In Canada, Jean Crépin, cofounder and CEO of Norwest Soil Research, instituted **open-book management**, which involves management's sharing financial information with all employees. Crépin made this move in order to galvanize his staff to help the struggling company to survive. Norwest is not the only company to implement open-book management. Amoco Canada, based in Calgary, has also undertaken an open-book management strategy. At Amoco Canada, this approach has included training employees about the connection between their work and the results achieved by the various units of the company.[20]

open-book management An approach that involves management's sharing financial information with all employees.

FIGURE 16-3 Becoming a Learning Organization: Basic Steps

A *learning organization* is one that is successful at acquiring, cultivating, and applying knowledge that helps it adapt to change. Some of the key steps in this process are summarized here.

(Source: Based on suggestions by Huber, 1991; see Note 17.)

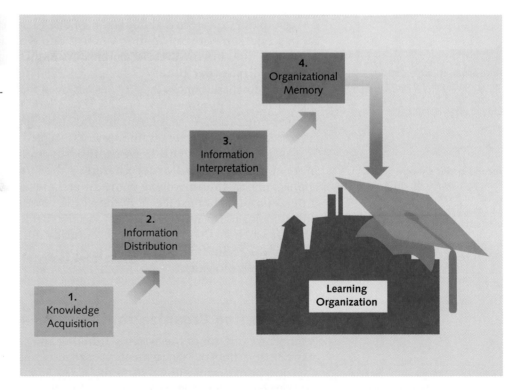

3. **Information interpretation**: For learning to bring effective change, knowledge must be not only thoroughly collected, but also accurately interpreted. With this in mind, organizations are taking steps to ensure that employees can make the best possible use of the information they have gathered. Information technology has proven useful in this regard. For example, at the M. D. Anderson Cancer Center in Houston, systems analysts used software to track their earlier informational sessions to help them draw conclusions about the nature of the software they needed to design for managing their facility.[21] Interpreting their electronic discussions would have been far more difficult without this assistance.

4. **Organizational memory**: This refers to the means by which knowledge from an organization's history is stored so that it can be tapped when needed to initiate change.[22] When people leave an organization, or a part of it, they take with them important lessons of history and knowledge that may be valuable to others. As a result, it is considered important to store the accumulated wisdom of the past in a readily accessible form. Without doing so, present generations will be unable to learn from past generations, providing a distinct disadvantage.

   An example may be seen in the practice of using computerized files to record and keep track of customers' inquiries. Bankers Trust does this in its New York office so that any customer service agent can field a customer's inquiry at a later time, even if the individual who originally helped is out of the office.[23] The idea is that careful records are kept of key experiences so that they may be used as needed in the future. In so doing, the organization is not dependent on the presence—and memory—of any single individual. Rather, key events are made part of "institutional memory."

Chaparral Steel Company
www.chaparralsteel.com

Some companies have turned organizational learning into a competitive advantage. For example, CIBC's Al Flood, the bank's former chairman and CEO, has seen the results of organizational learning. "I ... believe that learning organizations represent a true partnership of mutual advantage between companies and their employees. They are pivotal if we are to seriously address the kind of market realities ... that affect the economic lives of all Canadians."[24] Similarly, Gordon Forward, a former British Columbian who is president and CEO of mini mill Chaparral Steel, is firmly committed to the value of promoting a learning organization that allows for continuous growth and development so his business can lead, rather than follow, industry leaders. Forward and his colleagues dare to challenge themselves. "We constantly chip away the ground we stand on. We have to keep out front all the time."[25]

Senge has identified seven organizational "learning disabilities" that block effective organizational learning. He contends that the remedy lies in the practice of five disciplines concurrently, namely "building shared vision; personal mastery; team learning; mental models; and systems thinking." The crucial skill is the fifth discipline, systems thinking, which challenges organizational members to see the whole organization instead of just its parts.[26]

Most organizations fail to take these steps and cannot be considered learning organizations. They are rather unsystematic about gathering and using information that may facilitate change. However, a growing number of today's organizations are attempting to ensure their long-term viability by taking the steps needed to adapt to a changing world, even if these are dramatic (e.g., redesigning their organizational structure and/or reshaping organizational culture). By collecting and using information, these organizations are learning to make changes that will help them adapt—and survive—in the future.

   Now that we have described the prevalence and importance of change in organizations we will turn our attention to another basic issue: Why do organizations change? In other words, what factors lead organizations to change?

Forces Behind Change in Organizations

If you think about it, it's clear that organizations change either because they want to or because they have to. In our CASE PREVIEW, Eaton's saw the handwriting on the wall and its message was clear: Change or else! Organizations also sometimes confront the need to change because of conditions beyond their control, such as changes in the economy, competition, or government regulations. Of course, companies also change simply because they want to make things better. That is, they believe they can develop a *competitive advantage* if they make changes that put them ahead of their competitors. It is with this in mind that Cognos and Newbridge Networks constantly develop new products (or buy up companies that have already done so).

Essentially, we have been referring to two major classes of forces behind organizational change. These are **planned change**, activities that are intentional, purposive in nature, and designed to fulfill some organizational goals; and **unplanned change**, shifts in organizational activities due to forces that are external in nature, those beyond the organization's control. So that you can appreciate fully the broad scope of factors that influence organizational change, we will describe both planned and unplanned change in organizations (see Figure 16-4).

planned change Activities that are intentional and purposive in nature and designed to fulfill some organizational goals.

unplanned change Shifts in organizational activities due to forces that are external in nature, those beyond the organization's control.

Planned Change

A great deal of organizational change comes from the strategic decision to alter the way an organization does business or the very nature of the business itself. Four examples of planned organizational change can be identified—changes in products or services, changes in organizational size and structure, changes in administrative systems, and the introduction of new technologies.

Vintners Quality Alliance
www.inniskillin.com/vinifera/vqa.html

Changes in products or services. If you can't stand the heat, get out of the kitchen—or get organized and build a sauna. And that is just what the Vintners Quality Alliance (VQA) did with the "heat" from the Free Trade Agreement (FTA). Some wine producers in southern Ontario predicted doom for their industry as a result of the FTA, while others saw it as an opportunity to use the good growing conditions of the Niagara region to move from blended, lower-cost house wines to specialized varietal wines.[28]

The VQA was formed in Ontario in 1988[29] and in British Columbia in 1990.[30] Like other similar appellation of origin systems (which identify the region in which the grapes are grown), the VQA sets quality standards for its members. The gold VQA medallion is awarded only to those wines that perform exceptionally as judged by the VQA tasting panel.[31]

Before the VQA, Canadian wines were regarded as being universally inferior.[32] But with the move to the production of higher-quality wines, the Canadian wine industry has changed its image at home and abroad. Canadian wines are now winning major international awards.[33] The story of the VQA and the success of Canadian wines reflects the foresight and courage of industry leaders in seeking and finding a competitive edge in the face of daunting obstacles.

FIGURE 16-4 Planned Change: Real-Estate Development in Iqaluit

When opportunity knocks, Don Wilson answers. The Calgary-based real-estate developer, president and CEO of Urbco Inc., is headed for Iqaluit. Awaiting his company is the task of building the residential as well as the commercial infrastructure the Baffin Island town needs as the capital of the new Canadian territory, Nunavut. "We're not controlled by the amount of people we have or the money we've got," says Wilson. "We're controlled by opportunity.'"[27]

Changes in organizational size and structure. Just as organizations change their products, services, or administrative systems to stay competitive, so too do they alter the size and basic configurations of their organizational charts—that is, they *restructure*. Many organizations have restructured by completely eliminating parts of themselves that focus on noncore sectors of their business, hiring outside firms to perform these functions instead—that is, by *outsourcing*.[34] Typically, this means reducing the number of employees needed to operate effectively—the practice of *downsizing* the workforce.[35]

☞ Extended discussions of the trends toward downsizing and outsourcing appear in Chapters 2 and 15.

The evidence is clear that downsizing has been occurring on a large-scale basis. "Ask the hundreds of thousands of employees who got severance slips or were forced to take early retirement from such institutional giants as Ontario Hydro, the CBC, Petro-Canada, Bell Canada, IBM, CIBC, and CN." It seems that larger enterprises have been hardest hit by the downsizing epidemic. Statistics Canada figures show that, in the first five years of the 1990s, commercial enterprises under five employees grew at a rate of 3.5 percent in contrast to companies with over 100 employees, which shrank by almost 7 percent.[36]

It is important to note that any gains resulting from layoffs tend to be short-lived. This is because laying off employees merely reduces costs without increasing revenues. Less than half of the companies that lay off workers actually become more profitable. After all, people are needed to produce goods and provide services that can help generate revenue. Not surprisingly, companies tend to replace most of their laid-off workers within two years.[37] The result is a "binge and purge" cycle that does little more than create a great deal of insecurity for company employees.

This leads us to an interesting question: What can companies do to respond to the ever-expanding and contracting demands for employees? Ideally, companies should focus their efforts at anticipating their needs and timing their hiring practices accordingly. However, in today's rapidly changing workplace, this is much easier said than done. Although some layoffs are inevitable, experts have noted that there are several things that management can do to keep its workforce intact—if it just uses a little imagination.[38] For a summary of some of the most widely used alternatives to layoffs, see Table 16-1.

TABLE 16-1 Alternatives to Layoffs

In the face of changing conditions, organizations frequently require fewer employees than they currently have. So as to avoid large-scale layoffs that harm large numbers of employees, several alternative practices are being used.

Source: Based on suggestions by Rosen & Berger, 1991; see Note 38.

Practice	Description	Example
Temporary salary cuts	Reducing the pay of all employees—either by an equal percentage, or in reverse proportion to salary	Intel temporarily cut employees' pay in amounts ranging up to 10% for its highest-paid employees
Layoff rotations	Workers take turns spending time on and off the job	Miners at Climax Molybdenum rotated two weeks on and two weeks off their jobs during a period of decreased demand for steel
Shortened work week	Reducing the number of days worked, with pay reductions to match	Nucor Corp. puts employees on four-day work weeks during slack periods
Flexible employment	Employees get to perform temporary jobs during slow periods	At Worthington Industries, production workers perform maintenance jobs at the factory while their regular services are not required
Early retirement	Offering financial incentives to employees who agree to retire ahead of schedule	Northwest Airlines offered senior flight attendants lump-sum payments of U.S.$20 000 along with fringe benefits
Delaying projects	By delaying the completion of projects, employees nearing retirement could be kept on the payroll	Anheuser Busch kept senior employees on the job by delaying the completion of projects until those individuals were ready to retire
Tin parachutes for employees	Money is put aside to ease transitions should a hostile takeover result in new management which cuts people	Kodak promises severance pay, insurance benefits, and outplacement help to its hourly employees in the event of a takeover
Invite employees back	Hire former employees as conditions improve	Super Value Stores makes an effort to rehire former employees who were laid off during slow periods

Changes in administrative systems. It is not unusual for organizations to plan carefully systematic changes in their policies, reward structure, goals, and management styles. Such changes may stem from a desire to improve efficiency, to change the company's image, or to gain a political power advantage within the organization.[39]

Typically, the pressure to bring about changes in the administration of organizations (e.g., to coordinate activities, set goals and priorities) comes from upper management—that is, from the top down. As an example of this, let's consider the case of Canadian Tire Acceptance Limited (CTAL) in Welland, Ontario. CTAL is the financial service wing of Canadian Tire Corporation. At the start of his tenure, the former president and CEO of CTAL, Jos Wintermans, undertook a massive restructuring of the operation. A consulting group hired by Wintermans to analyze the troubled CTAL operation reported that it was top-heavy with management personnel. Wintermans reported: "They told us we had 11 layers of management when we should have had five.... I hadn't anticipated that it would be that bad—but it was."[40]

This revelation prompted him to examine the match between the abilities of employees and the demands of the job with respect to problem-solving. He started with his vice-presidents. Four were fired. Two other vice-presidential positions were dropped. He said: "This is not the crew that is going to bring this company into the next decade."[41] When managers were given the opportunity to choose whom they wished to keep to build the new company, ten other employees were fired.[42] In the seven years following its restructuring the company tripled its credit card sales.[43]

In contrast, pressure to change the central work of the organization (i.e., the production of goods and services) comes from the technical side of the organization, from the bottom upward.[44] This is the idea behind the **dual-core model** of organizations. Many organizations, especially medium-sized ones, may be characterized by potential conflicts between the administrative and the technical cores—each faction wishing to change the organization according to its own vested interests. Which side usually wins? Research suggests that the answer depends on the design of the organization in question. Organizations that are highly *mechanistic* as opposed to *organic* in their approach (i.e., they are highly formal and centralized) tend to be more successful in introducing administrative changes.[45] The high degree of control wielded by the administrative core paves the way for introducing administrative change.

Introduction of new technologies: From calculators to computers. As described in Chapter 14, advances in technology have produced changes in the way organizations operate. The use of computer technology has been touted as one of the major revolutions occurring in the business world today (see Figure 16-5). Not only are personal computers found in over 23 percent of Canadian homes,[46] but they also are used by people in practically every job you can think of, from agricultural agent to zookeeper.[47] During the earliest years in which computers were used in the workplace, they failed to fulfill the promise of increased productivity that was used to usher them in. Not only was the hardware and software technology too primitive, but also the users were too unprepared. Today, however, this has changed. According to William Wheeler, a consultant at Coopers & Lybrand, "For the first time the computer is an enabler of productivity improvement rather than a cause of lack of productivity.[48]

Even mariners are finding a place for computers. Long gone are the days of total reliance on celestial navigation. Radar too, is being supplanted as navigational king by a Canadian-designed and produced Electronic Chart Precise Integrated Navigation System. This system uses American global positioning satellites to help ships' masters to find their way, even in the thickest fog. Introduced by Offshore Systems International Ltd. of North Vancouver, the system is credited with realizing huge savings with regard to injury and

dual-core model The theory recognizing that changes in the administration of organizations come from upper management (i.e., from the top down), whereas changes in the work performed come from the technical specialists within organizations (i.e., from the bottom up).

☞ A discussion of the distinction between mechanistic and organic organizations appears in Chapter 15.

☞ In Chapter 14 we describe the role of information technology in organizations.

FIGURE 16-5 New Technologies Lead to Success
Alan Hussey, vice-president at Fantom Technologies Inc. in Welland, Ontario, shows off his company's product. The company used 3-D modelling to help it to reduce design cycles from two years to just four months.[49]

damage. Canadian Steamship Lines, based in Montreal, has equipped several of its ships with this high-tech navigational system.[50]

One of the most important sources of information that organizations use as the basis for making changes is information regarding what one's competitors are doing. For a closer look at an intriguing way such information is gathered, see **THE QUEST FOR QUALITY** section.

Unplanned Change

Until now, the forces for change we've discussed represent planned attempts to improve the way organizations operate. However, not all forces for change are deliberate in nature. Indeed, organizations must often be responsive to changes that are unplanned. One of the greatest challenges faced by an organization is its ability to respond to changes from the outside world over which it has little or no control. As the environment changes, organizations must follow suit. In fact, research has shown that organizations that can best adapt to changing conditions tend to survive.[51]

competitive intelligence (CI) The process of gathering information about one's competitors that can be used as the basis for planning organizational change.

We already have identified some major determinants of unplanned organizational change. For example, in Chapter 2, we explained that today's organizations have been forced to adapt to shifts in the demographic makeup of the workplace. They also

---

The Quest for Quality

Competitive Intelligence: Planning Change by Learning about the Competition

Keeping an eye on the competition is a concept that is as familiar to football, hockey, and soccer players as it is to those in business. It is important to know the strengths and weaknesses of your opponents so you can plan your strategy accordingly. And you know they are making the same kind of analysis of you, as well!

This process of systematically gathering information about one's competitors that can be used as a basis for planning organizational change is known as **competitive intelligence (CI)**. CI is a search for clues about what one's competitor is actually doing or considering doing. To stay competitive, some of the biggest companies—especially those in rapidly changing, high-tech fields—engage in CI all the time. In fact, Gary Costley, former president of Kellogg Co. North America, says that managers who don't engage in CI are "incompetent" insofar as it is "irresponsible to not understand your competitors."[52] According to the president of Merlin Global Inc., a CI training firm based in Montreal, "The rules have changed. In business, it's information warfare, and intelligence is a weapons system."[53]

Before you dismiss CI on the grounds that it is unethical, it's important to note that we're not talking about doing anything illegal. Rather, CI efforts usually involve gathering information that is readily available

from sources such as public records. Companies are required to disclose information on their finances, inventories, and compliance with various legal regulations. Documents containing this information are available to anyone, and growing numbers of competitors are availing themselves of them. Valuable information also may be obtained by interviewing people who work for competing companies. It's amazing what employees may tell you without you having to pry it out of them.

Montreal-based flight simulator manufacturer CAE Electronics is just one of the growing number of Canadian firms that are using CI to give them an edge in a competitive market. Employees help CAE to gather intelligence information by posting rumours and tips on competitors on the company's intranet, known as "Marketing Knowledgebase."[54] Bell Canada, Nortel Networks, NOVA Corp and Stentor all employ CI professionals.[55] In 1994, Quebec launched Competitive Intelligence Networks, which, at $7.7 million over five years, has been described as "the most ambitious government-sponsored CI project in North America." Subscribers pay a modest fee to access the service, which distills vast quantities of specialized information into "nuggets" of interest to readers.[56] According to Jonathan Caloff of the University of Ottawa, "CI is taking off."[57]

must be responsive to the growing trend toward globalization. Three additional forces for unplanned change deserve to be mentioned: governmental regulation, economic competition, and performance gaps.

Government regulation. One of the most commonly witnessed unplanned organizational changes results from government regulations. Canadian government activities such as bans on cod and salmon fishing, and the North American Free Trade Agreement (1994) left many businesses scrambling to rethink their operations. In addition, there has been a trend toward deregulation in a variety of sectors, including long-distance telephone systems, airlines, railways, and banking. The increasing privatization of Crown corporations, such as Air Canada, CN, and Petro-Canada, has forced these organizations to undergo massive changes.

Economic competition. It happens every day: Someone builds a better mousetrap—or at least a cheaper one. As a result, companies often must fight to maintain their share of the market, advertise more effectively, and produce products more inexpensively. This kind of economic competition not only forces organizations to change, but also demands that they change effectively if they are to survive.

On some occasions, competition can become so fierce that the parties involved would actually be more effective if they dropped their swords and joined forces. It was this "if you can't beat 'em, join 'em" reasoning that was responsible for the announced alliance between arch rivals IBM and Apple Computer in the summer of 1991, an alliance dubbed "the deal of the decade" by one financial analyst.[58]

Performance gaps. Traditionally, organizations have operated under the philosophy, "If it's not broken, don't fix it." That is, they focused on *performance gaps*, disparities between actual and expected levels of performance. A product line that isn't moving, a vanishing profit margin, a level of sales that isn't up to corporate expectations are examples. Few things force change more effectively than sudden and unexpected information about poor performance.

Historically, organizations have stayed with winning courses of action and changed only in response to failure; in other words, they followed a *win-stay/lose-change rule*. Indeed, several studies have shown that a performance gap is one of the key factors providing an impetus for organizational innovation.[59] Those organizations that are best prepared to mobilize change in response to unexpected downturns are expected to be the ones that succeed.

The Process of Organizational Change: Some Basic Issues

As you might imagine, the process of changing organizations is not haphazard; rather, it proceeds in a well-established, orderly fashion. It is well known, for example, what the targets of organizational change efforts may be, and when organizational change is likely to occur. We will address these basic issues in this section.

Targets of Organizational Change: What Is Changed?

Imagine that you are an engineer responsible for overseeing the maintenance of a large office building. The property manager has noted a dramatic increase in the use of heat in the building, causing operating costs to skyrocket. In other words, a need for change exists—specifically, a reduction in the building's heat usage. You cannot get the power company to lower its rates, so you realize you must bring about changes in the use of heat. But how? One possibility is to rearrange job responsibilities so that only maintenance personnel are permitted to adjust thermostats. Another option is to put timers on all thermostats so that the building temperature is automatically lowered during periods of nonuse. Finally, you consider the idea of putting stickers next to the thermostats, requesting that occupants not adjust them. These three options represent excellent examples of the three potential targets of organizational change we will consider—changes in *organizational structure, technology,* and *people* (see Figure 16-6).

Changes in organizational structure.   In Chapter 15 we described the key characteristics of organizational structure. Here we note that altering the structure of an organization may be a reasonable way of responding to a need for change. In the above example, a structural solution to the heat regulation problem came in the form of reassigning job responsibilities. Indeed, modifying rules, responsibilities, and procedures may be an effective way to manage change. Changing the responsibility for temperature regulation from a highly decentralized system (whereby anyone can make adjustments) to a centralized one (in which only maintenance personnel may do so) is one way of implementing organizational change in response to a problem. This particular structural solution called for changing the power structure (i.e., who was in charge of a particular task).

Different types of structural changes may take other forms.[60] For example, changes can be made in an organization's span of control, altering the number of employees for which supervisors are responsible. Structural changes also may take the form of revising the basis for creating departments—such as from product-based departments to functional departments. Other structural changes may be much simpler, such as clarifying someone's job description or the written policies and procedures followed.

Structural changes are not uncommon in organizations. Consider, for example, some changes reported in recent years at the huge consumer products company Procter & Gamble.[61] In response to growing competition, the company was forced to make a number of changes that streamlined its highly bureaucratic organizational structure. For example, the decision-making process used to be so centralized that many decisions that could have been made at lower levels were being made by top corporate personnel (such as the colour of the cap on the can of decaffeinated instant Folgers coffee!). Now decentralized business teams have been instituted and are permitted to make all the decisions about developing, manufacturing, and marketing products.

FIGURE 16-6 Organizational Change Targets: Structure, Technology, People

To create change in organizations, one can rely on altering organizational structure, technology, and/or people. Changes in any one of these areas may necessitate changes in the others.

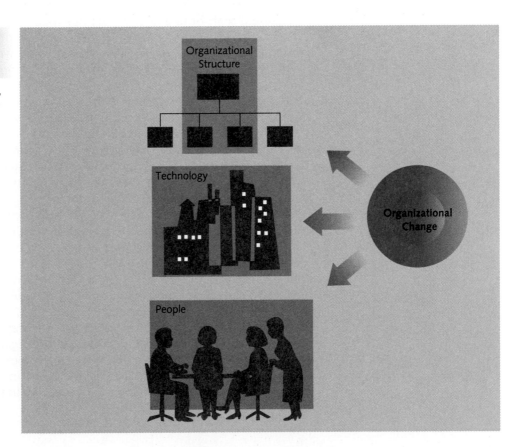

Changes in technology.

In our thermostat example, we noted that one possible solution would be to use thermostats that automatically reduce the building's temperature while it is not in use. This is an example of a technological approach to the need to conserve heat in the building. Placement of regulating devices on the thermostats that would thwart attempts to raise the temperature also would be possible. The thermostats also could be encased in a locked box, or simply removed altogether. A new, modern, energy-efficient furnace could be installed in the building. All of these suggestions represent technological approaches to the need for change.

The underlying idea is that technological improvements can lead to more efficient work. Indeed, if you've ever prepared a term paper on a typewriter, you know how much more efficient it is to do the same job using a word processor. Technological changes may involve a variety of alterations, such as changing the equipment used to do jobs (e.g., robots), substituting microprocessors for less reliable mechanical components (e.g., on airline equipment), or simply using better-designed tools (e.g., hand tools with better grips). Each of these changes may be used to bring about improvements in organizational functioning.

☛ The means by which technology can help enhance the efficiency of work are described in Chapter 14.

Changes in people.

You've probably seen stickers next to light switches in hotels and office buildings asking the occupants to turn off the lights when not in use. These are similar to the suggestion in our opening example to affix signs near thermostats asking occupants to refrain from adjusting the thermostats. Such efforts represent attempts to respond to the needed organizational change by altering the way people behave. The basic assumption is that the effectiveness of organizations is greatly dependent on the behaviour of the people working within them.

As you might imagine, the process of changing people is not easy—indeed, it lies at the core of most of the topics discussed in this book. However, theorists have identified three basic steps that summarize what's involved in the process of changing people.[62,63] The first step is known as *unfreezing*. This refers to the process of recognizing that the current state of affairs is undesirable and in need of change. Realizing that change is needed may be the result of some serious organizational crisis or threat (e.g., a serious financial loss, a strike, or a major lawsuit), or simply becoming aware that current conditions are unacceptable (e.g., antiquated equipment, inadequately trained employees).

In recent years, some executives have gotten employees to accept the need to change while things are still good by creating a sense of urgency. They introduce the idea that there is an impending crisis although conditions are, in fact, currently acceptable—an approach referred to as **doomsday management**.[64] This process effectively unfreezes people, stimulating change before it's too late to do any good. Before rejecting this practice as overly deceptive, consider this analogy. People usually switch to healthier diets only after they've suffered heart attacks, although they may have been able to prevent them altogether had their doctors emphasized the urgency of adapting a healthier lifestyle beforehand.

doomsday management The practice of introducing change by suggesting that an impending crisis is likely.

After unfreezing, *changing* may occur. This step occurs when some planned attempt is made to create a more desirable state for the organization and its members. Change attempts may be quite ambitious (e.g., an organization-wide restructuring) or only minor (e.g., a change in a training program). (A thorough discussion of such planned change techniques will be presented in the next major part of this chapter.)

Finally, *refreezing* occurs when the changes made are incorporated into the employees' thinking and the organization's operations (e.g., mechanisms for rewarding behaviours that maintain the changes are put in place). Hence, the new attitudes and behaviours become a new, enduring aspect of the organizational system. For a summary of these three steps in the individual change process, see Figure 16-7. Despite the simplicity of this model, it does a good job of identifying some of the factors that make people willing to change their behaviour—thereby potentially improving organizational effectiveness.

FIGURE 16-7 **Changing People: Some Basic Steps**

The process of changing people involves the three basic steps outlined here: unfreezing, changing, and refreezing.

(Sources: Based on suggestions by Lewin, 1951; see Note 62; and Schein, 1968; see Note 63.)

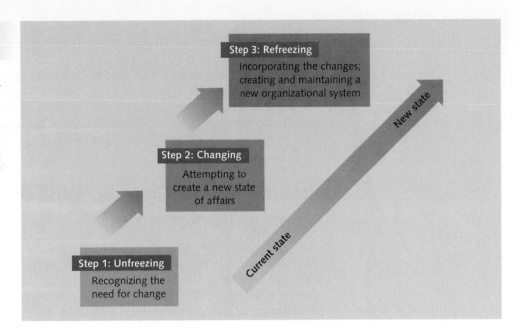

FIGURE 16-8 **Organizational Change: When Will It Occur?**

Whether or not an organizational change will be made depends on people's beliefs regarding the relative benefits and costs of making the change. The benefits are reflected by three considerations reviewed here.

(Source: Based on suggestions by Beer, 1980; see Note 66.

Readiness for Change: When Will Organizational Change Occur?

As you might imagine, there are times when organizations are likely to change, and times during which change is less likely. Even if the need for change is high and resistance to change is low (two important factors), organizational change does not automatically occur. Other factors are involved, and we have summarized some of the key variables in Figure 16-8.[65]

Change is likely to occur when the people involved believe that the benefits associated with making a change outweigh the costs involved. The factors contributing to the benefits of making a change are (1) the amount of dissatisfaction with current conditions, (2) the availability of a desirable alternative, and (3) the existence of a plan for achieving that alternative. Theorists have claimed that these three factors combine multiplicatively to determine the benefits of making a change.[66] Thus, if any one of these factors is very low (or zero), the benefits of making a change, and the likelihood of change itself, are very low (or zero).

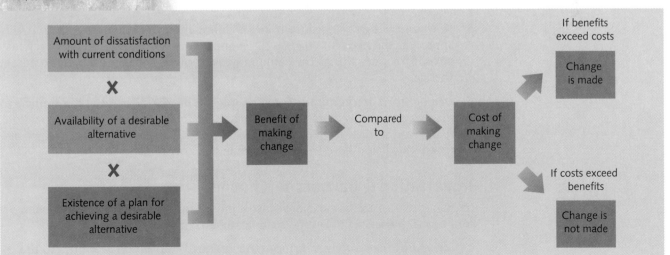

If you think about it, this should make sense to you. After all, people are unlikely to initiate change if they are not at all dissatisfied, or if they don't have any desirable alternative in mind (or any way of attaining that alternative, if they do have one in mind). Of course, for change to occur, the expected benefits must outweigh the likely costs involved (e.g., disruption, uncertainties). Professionals in the field of organizational development pay careful attention to these factors before they attempt to initiate any formal, ambitious organizational change programs. Only when the readiness for change is high will organizational change efforts be successful.

Resistance to Change: Will Organizational Change Be Accepted?

Although people may be unhappy with the current state of affairs confronting them in organizations, they may be afraid that any changes will be potentially disruptive and will only make things worse. Indeed, fear of new conditions is quite real and it creates unwillingness to accept change. Organizational scientists have recognized that **resistance to change** stems from both individual and organizational variables.

resistance to change The tendency for employees to be unwilling to go along with organizational changes, either because of individual fears of the unknown or organizational impediments (such as *structural inertia*).

Individual Barriers to Change

Researchers have noted several key factors that are known to make people resistant to change in organizations.[67] These are as follows.

1. *Economic insecurity:* Because any changes on the job have the potential to threaten one's livelihood—by either loss of job or reduced pay—some resistance to change is inevitable.

2. *Fear of the unknown:* Employees derive a sense of security from doing things the same way, knowing who their coworkers will be and to whom they're supposed to answer from day to day. Disrupting these well-established, comfortable patterns creates unfamiliar conditions, a state of affairs that is often rejected.

3. *Threats to social relationships:* As people continue to work within organizations, they form strong bonds with their coworkers. Many organizational changes (e.g., the reassignment of job responsibilities) threaten the integrity of friendship groups that provide valuable social rewards.

4. *Habit:* Jobs that are well learned and become habitual are easy to perform. The prospect of changing the way jobs are done challenges people to develop new job skills. Doing this is clearly more difficult than continuing to perform the job as it was originally learned.

5. *Failure to recognize need for change:* Unless employees can recognize and fully appreciate the need for changes in organizations, any vested interests they may have in keeping things the same may overpower their willingness to accept change.

6. *Demographic background:* Some people are more predisposed than others to making changes in their organizations. Research has found that organizations that are most likely to change are those in which the executives are younger, better educated, and have less experience in their organization.[68]

Organizational Barriers to Change

Resistance to organizational change also comes from conditions associated with organizations themselves.[69] Several such factors may be identified.

1. *Structural inertia:* Organizations are designed to promote stability. To the extent that employees are carefully selected and trained to perform certain jobs, and rewarded for doing them well, the forces acting on individuals to perform

in certain ways are very powerfully determined—that is, jobs have **structural inertia**.[70] Thus, because jobs are designed to have stability, it is often difficult to overcome the resistance created by the forces that create stability.

2. *Work-group inertia:* Inertia to continue performing jobs in a specified way comes not only from the jobs themselves but also from the social groups within which people work—work-group inertia. Because of the development of strong social norms within groups, potent pressures exist to perform jobs in certain ways. Introducing change disrupts these established normative expectations, leading to formidable resistance.

3. *Threats to existing balance of power:* If changes are made with respect to who's in charge, a shift in the balance of power between individuals and organizational subunits is likely to occur. Those units that now control the resources, have the expertise, and wield the power may fear losing their advantageous positions resulting from any organizational change.

4. *Previously unsuccessful change efforts:* Anyone who has lived through a past disaster understandably may be reluctant to endure another attempt at the same thing. Similarly, groups or entire organizations that have been unsuccessful in introducing change in the past may be cautious about accepting further attempts at introducing change into the system.

5. *Composition of board of directors:* Boards of directors are groups that develop organizational policies. When these bodies are large they tend to make fewer changes than when they are smaller. Furthermore, boards whose members come from diverse specialties are less likely to initiate change than those whose members come from more similar professional backgrounds. In other words, when governing bodies have difficulty agreeing because of their large size or lack of professional accord, these bodies are unlikely to take extreme actions.[71]

Over the past decade, General Electric (GE) has been undergoing a series of widespread changes in its basic strategy, organizational structure, and relationship with employees.[72] In this process, it experienced several of the barriers just identified.[73] For example, GE managers had mastered a set of bureaucratic traditions that made their habits strong and kept them moving straight ahead. The prospect of doing things differently was scary for those who were so strongly entrenched in doing things the "GE way." In particular, the company's interest in globalizing triggered many fears of the unknown. Resistance to change at GE was also strong because it threatened to strip power from those units that traditionally possessed most of it (e.g., the Power Systems and Lighting divisions). Changes also were highly disruptive to GE's "social architecture"; friendship groups were broken up and scattered throughout the company. In all, GE has been a living example of many different barriers to change all rolled into a single company.

Having summarized some of the barriers to organizational change, we will now outline some of the major methods used to overcome this resistance. After all, unless these hurdles can be cleared, any attempts to systematically change organizations may be doomed to failure.

Overcoming Resistance to Organizational Change: Some Guidelines

Because organizational change is inevitable, managers should be sensitive to the barriers to change so that resistance can be overcome. This, of course, is easier said than done. However, several useful approaches have been suggested, and the key ones are summarized here.[74,75]

1. *Shape political dynamics:* In Chapter 12 we described the important role of organizational politics in achieving desired goals. Politics is also involved in getting organizational changes accepted. Politically, resistance to change can be

overcome by winning the support of the most powerful and influential individuals. Doing so builds a critical internal mass of support for change. Demonstrating clearly that key organizational leaders endorse the change is an effective way to get others to go along with it—either because they share the leader's vision or because they fear the leader's retaliation. Either way, the political support will facilitate acceptance of change.

2. *Educate the workforce:* Sometimes, people are reluctant to change because they fear what the future has in store for them. Fears about economic security, for example, may be put to rest by a few reassuring words from power holders. As part of educating employees about what organizational changes may mean for them, top management must show a considerable amount of emotional sensitivity. Doing so makes it possible for the people affected by change to become instrumental in making it work. Some companies have found that simply answering the question "what's in it for me?" can help allay a lot of fears. For example, sales reps in the pharmaceutical industry balked at first when laptop computers were introduced as a means for compiling and transmitting sales reports.[76] Then, once it was explained how this new technology would free them from the cumbersome job of writing weekly sales reports (a task that used to consume much of their weekend time), the computers were not only accepted, but embraced.

3. *Involve employees in the change efforts:* It is well established that people who participate in making a decision tend to be more committed to the outcomes of the decision than are those who are not involved.[77] Accordingly, employees who are involved in responding to unplanned change, or who are made part of the team charged with planning a needed organizational change, may be expected to have very little resistance to change. Organizational changes that are "sprung" on the workforce with little or no warning might be expected to encounter resistance simply as a knee-jerk reaction until employees have a chance to assess how the change affects them.

   In contrast, employees who are involved in the change process are better able to understand the need for change, and are therefore less likely to resist it. Says Duane Hartley, general manager of Hewlett Packard's microwave instruments division, "I don't think people really enjoy change, but if they can participate in it and understand it, it can become a positive [experience] for them."[78]

4. *Reward constructive behaviours:* One rather obvious, and quite successful, mechanism for facilitating organizational change is rewarding people for behaving in the desired fashion. Changing organizational operations may necessitate changing the kinds of behaviours that need to be rewarded by the organization. This is especially critical when an organization is in the transition period of introducing the change. For example, employees who are required to learn to use new equipment should be praised for their successful efforts. Feedback on how well they are doing not only provides a great deal of useful assurance to uncertain employees, but also goes a long way toward shaping the desired behaviour.

☛ *In Chapter 3 we describe how the process of reinforcement is used to bring about desired behaviour in organizations.*

Although these four suggestions may be easier to state than to implement, any effort to follow them will be well rewarded. Given the many forces that make employees resistant to change, managers should keep these guidelines in mind. If organizational change is to be beneficial, all employees must work toward accepting the change rather than using it as a rallying point around which conflict and dissension are focused.

organizational development (OD) A set of social science techniques designed to plan change in organizational work settings for purposes of enhancing the personal development of individuals and improving the effectiveness of organizational functioning.

Organizational Development: The Implementation of Planned Organizational Change

Now that we have shed some light on the basic issues surrounding organizational change, we are ready to look at planned ways of implementing it—collectively known as techniques of **organizational development (OD)**. More formally, we may define organizational development as a set of social science techniques designed to plan and implement change in work settings for purposes of enhancing the personal development of individuals and improving the effectiveness of organizational functioning.[79] By planning organization-wide changes involving people, OD seeks to enhance organizational performance by improving the quality of the work environment and the attitudes and well-being of employees.[80]

Over the years, many different techniques for implementing planned organizational change (referred to as *OD interventions*) have been used by specialists attempting to improve organizational functioning (referred to as *OD practitioners*).[81] All too often, some such techniques are merely managerial fads that do not stand the test of time.[82] However, several well-established OD techniques have been developed over the years, and we will begin this section by summarizing them. Following this, we will examine their effectiveness, addressing the question: Do they work?

All the major methods of organizational development attempt to produce some kind of change in individual employees, work groups, and/or entire organizations. This is the goal of the five well-known OD techniques we will review—*survey feedback, sensitivity training, team building, quality of work life programs*, and *management by objectives*.

Survey Feedback: Inducing Change by Sharing Information

For effective organizational change to occur, employees must understand the organization's current strengths and weaknesses. That's the underlying rationale behind the **survey feedback** method.

survey feedback An OD technique in which questionnaires and interviews are used to collect information about issues of concern to an organization. This information is shared with employees and then used as the basis for planning organizational change.

This technique follows the three steps summarized in Figure 16-9.[83] First, data are collected that provide information about matters of general concern to employees, such as organizational climate, leadership style, and job satisfaction. This may take the form of intensive interviews or structured questionnaires, or both. Because it is important that this information be as unbiased as possible, employees providing feedback should be assured that their responses will be kept confidential. For this reason, this process is usually conducted by outside consultants.

The second step calls for reporting the information obtained back to the employees during small group meetings. Typically, this consists of summarizing the average scores on the attitudes assessed in the survey. Profiles are created of feelings about the organization, its leadership, the work done, and related topics. Discussions also focus on why the scores are as they are, and what problems are revealed by the feedback.

The final step involves analyzing problems dealing with communication, decision making, and other organizational processes to make plans for dealing with them. Such discussions are usually most effective when they are carefully documented and a specific plan of implementation is made, with someone put in charge of carrying it out.

Survey feedback is a widely used organizational development technique.[84] This is not surprising in view of the advantages it offers. It is efficient, allowing a great deal of information to be collected relatively quickly. Also, it is very flexible and can be tailored to the needs of different organizations facing a variety of problems. However, the technique can be no better than the quality of the questionnaire used—

FIGURE 16-9 Survey Feedback: An Overview

The *survey feedback* technique of organizational development follows the three steps outlined here: collecting data, giving feedback, and developing action plans.

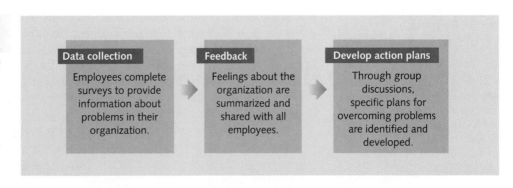

Data collection
Employees complete surveys to provide information about problems in their organization.

Feedback
Feelings about the organization are summarized and shared with all employees.

Develop action plans
Through group discussions, specific plans for overcoming problems are identified and developed.

it must measure the things that really matter to employees. Of course, to derive the maximum benefit from survey feedback, it must have the support of top management. Specifically, the plans developed by the small discussion groups must be capable of being implemented with the full approval of the organization. When these conditions are met, survey feedback can be a very effective OD technique.

Sensitivity Training: Developing Personal Insight

sensitivity training An OD technique that seeks to enhance employees' understanding of their own behaviour and its impact on others.

The method by which small, face-to-face group interaction experiences are used to give people insight into themselves (e.g., who they are, the way others respond to them) is known as **sensitivity training**. Developed in the 1940s, sensitivity training groups (also referred to as *encounter groups, laboratory groups,* or *T-groups*) were among the first organizational development techniques used in organizations (such as Standard Oil and Union Carbide).[85] The rationale behind sensitivity training is that people are usually not completely open and honest with each other, a condition that thwarts insights into oneself and others. However, when people are placed in special situations within which open, honest communication is allowed and encouraged, personal insights may be gained. To do this, small groups (usually about eight to fifteen in number) are created and meet away from the pressures of the job site for several days. An expert trainer (referred to as the *facilitator*) guides the group at all times, helping assure that the proper atmosphere is maintained.

The sessions themselves are completely open with respect to what is discussed. Often, to get the ball rolling, the facilitator will frustrate the group members by not getting involved at all, appearing to be passively goofing off. As members sit around and engage in meaningless chit-chat, they begin to feel angry at the change agent for wasting their time. Once these expressions of anger begin to emerge, the change agent has created the important first step needed to make the session work—he or she has given the group a chance to focus on a current event. At this point, the discussion may be guided into how each of the group members expresses his or her anger toward the others. They are encouraged to continue discussing these themes openly and honestly, and not to hide their true feelings as they would often do on the job. So, for example, if you think someone is relying too much on you, this is the time to say so. Participants are encouraged to respond by giving each other *immediate feedback* to what was said. By doing this, it is reasoned, people will learn more about how they interrelate with others and will become more skilled at interpersonal relations. These are among the major goals of sensitivity groups.

It probably comes as no surprise to you that the effectiveness of sensitivity training is difficult to assess. After all, measuring insight into one's own personality is clearly elusive. Even if interpersonal skills seem to be improved, people will not always be able to transfer successfully their newly learned skills when they leave the artificial training atmosphere and return to their jobs.[86] As a result, sensitivity training tends not to be used extensively by itself for OD purposes. Rather, as we will see, it is often used in conjunction with, or as part of, other OD techniques.

Team Building: Creating Effective Work Groups

team building An OD technique in which employees discuss problems related to their work group's performance. On the basis of these discussions, specific problems are identified and plans for solving them are devised and implemented.

☞ *The important role of teams within organizations is emphasized in Chapter 8.*

The technique of **team building** applies the techniques and rationale of sensitivity training to work groups. The approach attempts to get members of a work group to diagnose how they work together and to plan how this may be improved.[87] Given the importance of group efforts in effective organizational functioning, attempts to improve the effectiveness of work groups are likely to have profound effects on organizations. If one assumes that work groups are the basic building blocks of organizations, it follows that organizational change should emphasize changing groups instead of individuals.[88]

Team building begins when members of a group admit that they have a problem and gather data to provide insight into it. The problems that are identified may

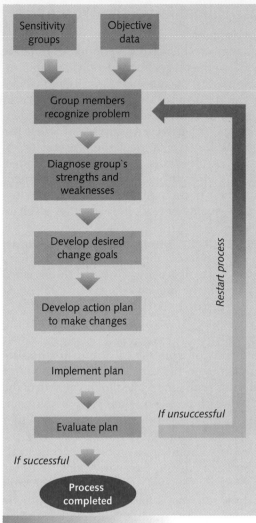

FIGURE 16-10 Team Building: Its Basic Steps

Team building, a popular technique of organizational development, follows the steps outlined here.

☞ *In Chapter 8 we describe work teams and the factors that make them so effective in organizations.*

come from sensitivity training sessions or more objective sources, such as production figures or attitude surveys. These data are then shared, in a *diagnostic session*, to develop a consensus regarding the group's current strengths and weaknesses. From this, a list of desired changes is created, along with some plans for implementing these changes. In other words, an *action plan* is developed—some task-oriented approach to solving the group's problems as diagnosed. Following this step, the plan is carried out, and its progress is evaluated to determine whether the originally identified problems remain. If the problems are solved, the process is completed and the team may stop meeting. If not, the process should be restarted. (See Figure 16-10 for a summary of these steps.)

Work teams have been used effectively to combat a variety of important organizational problems.[89] For these efforts to be successful, however, all group members must participate in the gathering and evaluating of information as well as the planning and implementing of action plans. Input from group members is also especially crucial in evaluating the effectiveness of the team-building program.[90] Keep in mind that because the team-building approach is highly task-oriented, interpersonal problems between group members may be disruptive and need to be neutralized by an outside party. With interpersonal strain out of the way, the stage is set for groups to learn to solve their own problems effectively. However, this does not happen overnight. To be effective, team building should *not* be approached as a onetime exercise undertaken during a few days away from the job. Rather, it should be thought of as an ongoing process that takes several months (or even years) to develop. Given the great impact effective teams can have on organizational functioning, efforts to build effective work teams seem quite worthwhile.

A successful team-building program has been in use at the France-based multinational corporation, Groupe Bull.[91] Instead of using team-building exercises exclusively among top leaders (who presumably have already bought into the company's philosophies), lower-level executives and managers from companies on several different continents are brought together for several two- to three-week sessions in which they try to solve problems of mutual interest.

Some techniques used in team-building exercises for attaining high levels of interpersonal trust are a bit more unorthodox. For example, as part of many team-building exercises, group members are put into highly challenging real-life situations that are metaphors for how they have to pull together to meet challenges on the job. The idea is that by facing these difficult off-the-job challenges successfully, they will develop the skills needed for working together effectively on the job. Group Bull executives so strongly believe in this idea that their team-building exercises have taken them on an adventurous white-water rafting trip in the swirling waters of the river Spey in the mountains of Scotland.[92] Other companies have sent their executives off on such challenges as mountain-climbing expeditions and dogsled trips.[93]

Why the exotic adventures? In theory, learning to work together on navigating the treacherous river while staying afloat can help team members recognize how they interact with each other while navigating the rough waters of international business. But, does it work? Obviously, the effectiveness of such an approach depends on the extent to which participants come away from the experience with the type of insight desired and translate these new-found ideas into meaningful work-related activities. By themselves, some rafting or mountain-climbing expeditions are not likely to make executives become a cohesive team. However, such adventures can be an effective part of an ongoing program of regular team development.

Quality of Work Life Programs: Humanizing the Workplace

When you think of work, do you think of drudgery? Although many people believe these two terms go together naturally, it has grown increasingly popular to improve systematically the quality of life experienced on the job. As more people demand satisfying and personally fulfilling places to work, OD practitioners have attempted systematically to create work conditions that enhance employees' motivation, satisfaction, and commitment—factors that may contribute to high levels of organizational performance. Such efforts are known collectively as **quality of work life (QWL)** programs. Specifically, such programs are ways of increasing organizational output and improving quality by involving employees in the decisions that affect them on their jobs. Typically, QWL programs support highly democratic treatment of employees at all levels and encourage their participation in decision making. Although many approaches to improving the quality of work life exist, they all share a common goal: humanizing the workplace.[94]

quality of work life (QWL) An OD technique designed to improve organizational functioning by humanizing the workplace, making it more democratic, and involving employees in decision making.

One popular approach to improving the quality of work life involves *work restructuring*—the process of changing the way jobs are done to make them more interesting to workers.[95] If this sounds familiar to you, it is because we already discussed several such approaches to redesigning jobs—including *job enlargement*, *job enrichment*, and the *job characteristics model*—in our discussion of motivation in Chapter 5. In the present context, note that such techniques also represent effective ways of improving the quality of work life for employees.

quality circles (QCs) An approach to improving the quality of work life, in which small groups of volunteers meet regularly to identify and solve problems related to the work they perform and the conditions under which they work.

Another approach to improving the quality of work life calls for using **quality circles (QCs)**. These are small groups of volunteers (usually around ten) who meet regularly (usually weekly) to identify and solve problems related to the quality of the work they perform and the conditions under which people do their jobs.[96] An organization may have several QCs operating at once, each dealing with a particular work area about which it has the most expertise. To help them work effectively, the members of the circle usually receive some form of training in problem solving. Large companies such as Westinghouse, Hewlett-Packard, and Eastman Kodak, to name only a few, have included QCs as part of their QWL efforts.[97] Groups have dealt with issues such as how to reduce vandalism, how to create safer and more comfortable working environments, and how to improve product quality. Research has shown that although quality circles are very effective at bringing about short-term improvements in quality of work life (i.e., those lasting up to 18 months), they are less effective at creating more permanent changes.[98]

As you might imagine, a variety of benefits (even if short-term ones) might result from QWL programs. These fall into three major categories.[99] The most direct benefit is usually *increased job satisfaction, organizational commitment, and reduced turnover* among the workforce.[100,101] A second benefit is *increased productivity*. In fact, a recent study comparing the performance of employees who participated in a QC program with a control group (an equivalent group that had not participated in such a program) revealed that in the year following the group involvement, those who had participated received higher job performance ratings and were more likely to get promoted than those who had not participated in the QC program.[102] Related to these first two benefits is a third—namely, *increased organizational effectiveness* (e.g., profitability, goal attainment). Many companies, including industrial giants such as Ford, General Electric, and AT&T, have active QWL programs and are reportedly quite pleased with their results.[103]

Achieving these benefits is not automatic, however. Two major potential pitfalls must be avoided for QWL programs to be successfully implemented. First, both management and labour must cooperate in designing the program. Should any one side believe that the program is really just a method of gaining an advantage over the other, it is doomed to fail. Second, the plans agreed to by all concerned parties must be fully implemented. It is too easy for action plans developed in QWL groups to be forgotten amid the hectic pace of daily activities.[104] It is the responsibility of employees at all levels—from the highest-ranking manager to the lowest-level labourer—to follow through on their part of the plan.

Management by Objectives: Clarifying Organizational Goals

In Chapter 5 we detailed the positive motivational benefits of setting specific goals. As you might imagine, not only individuals, but entire organizations stand to benefit from setting specific goals. For example, an organization may strive to "raise production" and "improve the quality" of its manufactured goods. These goals, noble and well intentioned though they may be, may not be as useful to an organization as more specific ones, such as "increase production of widgets by 15 percent" or "lower the failure rate of widgets by 25 percent." After all, as the old saying goes, "It's usually easier to get somewhere if you know where you're going." Peter Drucker, consulting for General Electric during the early 1950s, was well aware of this idea and is credited with promoting the benefits of specifying clear organizational goals—a technique known as **management by objectives (MBO)**.[105]

The MBO process, summarized in Figure 16-11, consists of three basic steps. First, goals are selected that employees will try to attain to best serve the needs of the organization. The goals should be selected by managers and their subordinates together. The goals must be set mutually rather than be imposed on subordinates by their managers. Further, these goals should be directly measurable and have some time frame attached to them. Goals that cannot be measured (e.g., "make the company better"), or that have no time limits, are useless. As part of this first step, it is crucial that managers and their subordinates work together to plan ways of attaining the goals they have selected—what is known as an *action plan*.

Once goals are set and action plans have been developed, the second step calls for *implementation*—carrying out the plan and regularly assessing its progress. Is the plan working? Are the goals being approximated? Are there any problems being encountered in attempting to meet the goals? Such questions need to be considered while implementing an action plan. If the plan is failing, a midcourse correction may be in order—changing the plan, the way it's carried out, or even the goal itself.

Finally, after monitoring progress toward the goal, the third step may be instituted: *evaluation*—assessing goal attainment. Were the organization's goals reached? If so, what new goals should be set to improve things still further? If not, what new plans can be initiated to help meet the goals? Because the ultimate assessment of the extent to which goals are met helps determine the selection of new goals, MBO is a continuous process.

MBO represents a potentially effective source of planning and implementing strategic change for organizations. Individual efforts designed to meet organizational goals get the individual employee and the organization itself working together toward

management by objectives (MBO) The technique by which managers and their subordinates work together to set and then meet organizational goals.

FIGURE 16-11 Management by Objectives: Developing Organizations through Goal Setting

The organizational development technique of *management by objectives* requires managers and their subordinates to work together on setting and trying to achieve important organizational goals. The basic steps of the process are outlined here.

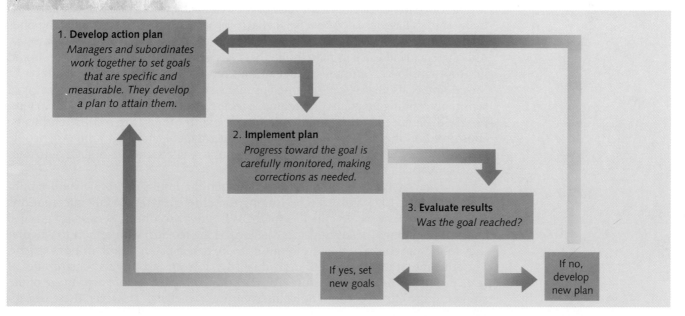

1. **Develop action plan**
Managers and subordinates work together to set goals that are specific and measurable. They develop a plan to attain them.

2. **Implement plan**
Progress toward the goal is carefully monitored, making corrections as needed.

3. **Evaluate results**
Was the goal reached?

If yes, set new goals

If no, develop new plan

common ends. Hence, systemwide change results. Of course, for MBO to work, everyone involved has to buy into it. Because MBO programs typically require a great deal of participation by lower-level employees, top managers must be willing to accept and support the cooperation and involvement of all. Making MBO work also requires a great deal of time—anywhere from three to five years.[106] Hence, MBO may be inappropriate in organizations that do not have the time to commit to making it work.

Despite these considerations, MBO has become one of the most widely used techniques for affecting organizational change in recent years. It not only is used on an ad hoc basis by many organizations, but also constitutes an ingrained element of the organizational culture in some companies, such as Hewlett-Packard and IBM. An MBO program was used effectively by Northwest Airlines in 1989 to help improve various areas of performance in its Atlanta-based crew.[107] The program was reportedly effective in meeting these and other vital goals, thereby helping to improve Northwest's overall safety and performance record. Given the success MBO has experienced, its widespread use is not surprising.[108]

Critical Issues in Organizational Development

No discussion of organizational development would be complete without addressing three very important questions—Do the techniques work, what should be their main focus, and are they ethical? We will now direct our attention to these issues.

The Effectiveness of Organizational Development: Does It Really Work?

Thus far, we have described some of the major techniques used by OD practitioners to improve organizational functioning. As is probably clear, carrying out these techniques requires a considerable amount of time, money, and effort. Accordingly, it is appropriate to ask if the investment in implementing OD interventions is worth it. In other words, does OD really work? Given the growing popularity of OD in organizations, the question is more important than ever.[109]

Research has revealed that the answer is a qualified "yes." In other words, although many studies have revealed beneficial effects associated with OD programs, the findings are far from unanimous. Consider, for example, research on quality circles. Although many researchers have found that QCs help reduce organizational costs and improve employees' attitudes, other studies reported no such beneficial effects.[110] Mixed results also have been obtained in many studies assessing the effectiveness of sensitivity training programs. For example, whereas such programs often lead to temporary differences in the way people interact with others, the results tend to be short-lived on the job and are not related to permanent changes in the way people behave.[111] Thus, whereas OD may have many positive effects, not all desired outcomes may be realized.

A review by Porras and Robertson compared the results of 49 OD studies published between 1975 and 1986.[112] Among the different types of OD interventions studied were those we described: MBO, QWL, survey feedback, sensitivity groups, and team building. The investigators categorized the research with respect to whether they found the effects of the interventions to be beneficial, harmful, or nonexistent. The outcomes studied were both individual (e.g., job satisfaction) and organizational (e.g., profit, productivity) in nature. The results reveal that a sizable percentage of the studies found effects of the various interventions beneficial. However, these beneficial results were not as impressive for individual outcomes (where only 23.55 percent of the studies demonstrated positive effects) as they were for organizational outcomes (where 48.70 percent of the studies found positive effects). Clearly, the benefits of OD techniques are more firmly established with respect to improving organizational functioning than with respect to improving individuals' job attitudes.

We hasten to add that any conclusions about the effectiveness of OD should be qualified in several important ways. First, research has shown that OD interventions tend to be more effective among blue-collar employees than among white-collar employees.[113] Second, it has been found that the beneficial effects of OD can be enhanced by using several techniques instead of just one. Specifically, studies in which four or more OD programs were used together yielded positive findings more frequently than those in which fewer techniques were used.[114] Thus, it appears that the effectiveness of OD efforts can be enhanced by relying not on any one single technique, but rather on a combination of several.[115] Finally, research has shown that the effectiveness of OD techniques depends on the degree of support they receive from top management: The more programs are supported from the top, the more successful they tend to be.[116]

Despite the importance of attempting to evaluate the effectiveness of OD interventions, a great many of them go unevaluated. Although there are undoubtedly many reasons for this, one key factor is the difficulty of assessing change. Because many factors can cause people to behave differently in organizations, and because such behaviours may be difficult to measure, many OD practitioners avoid the problem of measuring change altogether. In a related vein, political pressures to justify OD programs may discourage some OD professionals from honestly and accurately assessing their effectiveness. After all, in doing so, one runs the risk of scientifically demonstrating one's wasted time and money.

In cases where the effects of OD have been studied, however, the research is more often than not conducted in a manner that leaves its conclusions seriously open to question.[117] In particular, it is often very difficult to isolate exactly which aspects of an organizational intervention were responsible for the changes noted. Also, because OD practices are a novelty to most employees, they may have a tendency to produce temporary improvements.[118] In other words, serious questions may be raised about the true effectiveness of organizational development efforts as revealed in existing research. (As noted in the **GLOBALIZATION IN TODAY'S ORGANIZATIONS** section, further limitations may be identified when OD techniques are used in different nations.)

☞ *These temporary improvements may well be due to the Hawthorne effect described in Chapter 1.*

We may conclude that despite some limitations, organizational development is an approach that shows considerable promise in its ability to benefit organizations and the individuals working within them. These benefits notwithstanding, some have raised questions about the ethics of OD practice.

What Should Be the Main Focus of OD: Process or Results?

For the most part, the OD techniques we've described have focused on *how* to get things done (e.g., using certain exercises ranging from simple group discussions to elaborate treks in the wilderness) more so than exactly *what* should be accomplished. Although some general goals are often stated, the emphasis is generally on using the techniques assuming that they will sometime yield benefits. OD *is* by definition results-oriented, and practitioners appear to have become more preoccupied by the processes themselves than by the hopes of achieving any specific results. Indeed, OD activities frequently become management fads; as one company uses a technique, others quickly jump on the bandwagon for fear of not remaining competitive.

Management consultants Robert H. Schaffer and Harvey A. Thomson have countered the process orientation of OD by arguing that successful change programs should begin with results and not with an assortment of activities.[119] They call existing OD programs "corporate rain dances" in that they *may* yield positive results, although not necessarily as a result of the programs themselves. Schaffer and Thomson's prescription calls for using results-driven programs—those that lead to specific, measurable improvements in a short period of time. (If this idea sounds familiar it's

Is OD Universally Effective? Cultural Barriers to Effective OD Interventions

Warren Bennis, an expert in organizational development, recounts an incident in which a large Swiss company terminated an OD program after the company president found that it stressed egalitarian values. It seems that egalitarianism was inconsistent with a key value of the president's Swiss Army training—that authority is based on one's position in an organizational hierarchy.[120] This example raises an interesting question about the extent to which the effectiveness of OD interventions may be dependent upon the national cultures within which the organizations are located.

In analyzing this question, Jaeger relied on the four dimensions of culture identified by Hofstede (described in Chapter 2)—power distance, uncertainty avoidance, individualism-collectivism, and masculinity-femininity.[121] Overall, OD techniques may be understood as placing a low value on power distance (i.e., unequal power is not favoured), a low value on uncertainty avoidance (i.e., ambiguous situations are nonthreatening), a high value on femininity (i.e., willingness to show sensitivity and concern for others' welfare), and a moderate value on individualism (i.e., interest in balancing concern for oneself with concern for one's group). Jaeger reasoned that countries whose national values come closest to this pattern (e.g., Scandinavian nations) may be the most successful in using OD techniques, whereas those that are highly different (e.g., most Latin American nations) may be most unsuccessful.

Because not all OD techniques are alike, Jaeger analyzed specific intervention techniques with respect to their underlying cultural values. For example, MBO, a popular OD technique in Canada and the United States, may have caught on because it promotes the value of willingness to work at attaining high performance. However, because MBO also encourages superiors and subordinates to negotiate freely with each other, the technique has been generally unsuccessful in France, where high power distance between superiors and subordinates is culturally accepted.[122] Following similar reasoning, one may expect the OD technique of survey feedback to be successful in the Southeast Asian nation of Brunei, where the prevailing cultural value is such that problems are unlikely to be confronted openly.[123] These examples illustrate an important point: The effectiveness of OD techniques depends, in part, on the extent to which the values of the technique match the underlying values of the national culture in which it is employed.

Given this, we may conclude that OD practitioners must fully appreciate the cultural norms of the nations where they are operating. Failure to do so not only may make OD interventions unsuccessful, but may even have negative consequences. Therefore, as part of planning an OD intervention, OD practitioners are strongly advised to match carefully the techniques they use to the values of the host culture. The most rigidly held values of a culture should never be challenged by the OD techniques. Remember, those techniques are designed to improve the functioning of the organization *within its culture*. Any techniques that clash with prevailing cultural norms should be avoided.

---

probably because it follows from the basic tenet of goal setting described in Chapter 5—namely, to set *specific* goals. Unfortunately, when applied to MBO programs, sometimes the goals set are far too general to be useful.) A problem noted about OD techniques is that they too often define effort in a general, long-term fashion (e.g., "we're going to be considered to have the best quality production in the industry") as opposed to measurable, short-term goals for improvement (e.g., "by two months from today, we will settle 95 percent of all claims within one week").

As an example of their approach in action, Schaffer and Thomson describe an automotive parts plant plagued by problems of poor quality. The plant superintendent asked the manager on one assembly line to work with the employees and the plant engineers to reduce their most prevalent defect by 30 percent within two months. This goal was met on time, and the effort soon was extended to other assembly lines, where the effects were equally positive. In essence, "The results-driven path strikes out specific targets and matches resources, tools, and action plans to the requirements of reaching those targets. As a consequence, managers know what they are trying to achieve and when it should be done, and how it can be evaluated."[124]

Clearly, Schaffer and Thomson's approach makes good sense. (Indeed, it is founded on one of the best-established principles of OB described in this text.) Their approach, however, does not necessarily make OD techniques obsolete, because these tools are not necessarily designed to have an immediate impact on organizational functioning. In fact, by definition, a *development* tool is meant to have the long-term benefit of developing managerial talent for the long run (as opposed to *training* people to solve immediate problems). If you think of OD as a long-term investment in improving the insight and managerial skills of supervisory personnel, it's difficult to accept Schaffer and Thomson's approach as a substitute for OD. Instead, it appears that *both* long-term (process-oriented) and more immediate (results-oriented) techniques may have their place in the toolbox of today's organizational practitioner. Just as a physician may encourage patients to lead a healthy lifestyle marked by good nutrition and exercise, it would be misleading to condemn this advice simply because it does not also provide relief from an immediate ailment. Here, too, long-term, healthy development is important as well as seeking solutions to immediate problems that present themselves.

Is Organizational Development Inherently Unethical? A Debate

By its very nature, OD applies powerful social science techniques in an attempt to change attitudes and behaviour. From the perspective of a manager attempting to accomplish various goals, such tools may be very useful. However, if you think about it from the perspective of the individual being affected, several ethical issues arise.

For example, it has been argued that OD techniques impose the values of the organization on the individual without taking the individual's own attitudes into account.[125] OD is a very one-sided approach, reflecting the imposition of the more powerful organization on the less powerful individual. A related issue is that the OD process does not provide any free choice on the part of the employees.[126] As a result, it may be seen as *coercive* and *manipulative*. When faced with a "do it, or else" situation, employees tend to have little free choice and are forced to allow themselves to be manipulated, a potentially degrading prospect.

Another issue is that the unequal power relationship between the organization and its employees makes it possible for the true intent of OD techniques to be misrepresented. As an example, imagine that an MBO technique is presented to employees as a means of allowing greater organizational participation, whereas in reality it is used as a means for holding individuals responsible for their poor performance and punishing them as a result. Although such an event might not happen, the potential for abuse of this type does exist, and the potential to misuse the technique—even if not originally intended—might later prove to be too great a temptation.

Despite these considerations, many professionals do not agree that OD is inherently unethical. Such a claim, it has been countered, is to say that the practice of management is itself unethical. After all, the very act of going to work for an organization requires one to submit to the organization's values and the overall values of society at large.[127] One cannot help but face life situations in which others' values are imposed. This is not to say that organizations have the right to impose patently unethical values on people for the purpose of making a profit (e.g., stealing from customers). Indeed, because they have the potential to abuse their power (such as in the MBO example above), organizations have a special obligation to refrain from doing so.

Although abuses of organizational power are all too common, OD itself is not necessarily the culprit. Indeed, like any other tool, OD is not inherently good or evil. Instead, *whether the tool is used for good or evil will depend on the individual using it* (see **THE ETHICS ANGLE**). With this in mind, the ethical use of OD interventions will require that they be supervised by professionals in an organization that places a high value on ethics. To the extent that top management officials embrace ethical values and behave ethically themselves, norms for behaving ethically are likely to develop in organizations. When an organization has a strong ethical culture, it is unlikely

OD Strategies or Psychological Abuse?

At what point do organizational development strategies cross the line between useful tools and techniques of oppression? That question may be more difficult to answer than you may think. At TransAlta, a Calgary-based energy company, the strategies offered by Business Design Associates Inc. (BDA) sounded like just the answer to help the utility to improve operational efficiencies. The California consulting firm was brought in to train TransAlta managers to use its approach to changing employee attitudes. The goal was to make them function more as entrepreneurs rather than simply as employees.[128] However, according to an article in *Western Report,* some of the utility's staff "say this has led to serious personal abuse and motivation techniques that are bizarre and psychologically dangerous."[129] A

former TransAlta employee reported that, "they want to break you down and make you into a new kind of worker, completely dedicated to furthering the company's interests."[130]

The condemnation of the BDA strategy was not unanimous, with 81 TransAlta managers expressing their "support for the direction in which [the company was] moving under [TransAlta president] Ken McCready's leadership...."[131] Nevertheless, when reports of the issues at TransAlta hit the press, the company's president wrote a letter to employees indicating that "As we are learning to do things we have not done in the past we have made some mistakes."[132] McCready assured his staff that the work with BDA would no longer include "personal assessments" conducted in group contexts.[133]

 **TransAlta Corporation**
www.transalta.com

that OD practitioners would even think of misusing their power to harm individuals. The need to develop such a culture has been recognized as a way for organizations to take not only moral leadership in their communities, but financial leadership as well. (For a summary of this debate, see Figure 16-12.)

After considering both sides of this issue, you will probably wish to draw your own conclusions about this matter. The only thing we can be sure about here is that the debate is not settled, and it is likely to remain a key question for years to come. One reason the issue might not be put to rest anytime soon is that executives are becoming increasingly concerned about the importance of ethics in their organizations. Given corporations' ongoing concerns about being competitive, it is also likely that OD interventions will remain popular in the years to come.

FIGURE 16-12 The Ethics of OD: Summary of the Debate

Some have claimed that OD is an inherently unethical practice while others have countered that it is not. The arguments for each side are summarized here.

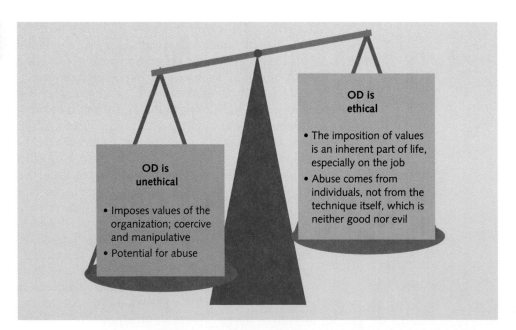

OD is
unethical

• Imposes values of the organization; coercive and manipulative
• Potential for abuse

OD is
ethical

• The imposition of values is an inherent part of life, especially on the job
• Abuse comes from individuals, not from the technique itself, which is neither good nor evil

SUMMARY AND REVIEW

Organizational Change: An Ongoing Process

Organizational change refers to planned or unplanned transformations in an organization's structure, technology, and/or people. It occurs in organizations throughout the world and is required for their long-term survival. The **learning organization** is one that is successful at acquiring, cultivating, and applying knowledge that can be used to help it adapt to change. Organizations learn by acquiring knowledge, distributing information, interpreting information, and taking steps to ensure that this information is stored in memory by the organization.

Forces behind Organizational Change

Changes in organizations may be either planned or unplanned. Planned changes may include changes in products or services, changes in organizational size and structure, changes in administrative systems, and the introduction of new technologies. Unplanned changes include governmental regulation, economic competition, and performance gaps.

The Process of Organizational Change and Resistance to Change

Organizations may change with respect to their organizational structure (responsibilities and procedures used), the technology used on the job, and the people who perform the work. Change is likely to occur whenever the benefits associated with making a change (i.e., dissatisfaction with current conditions, the availability of desirable alternatives, and the existence of a plan for achieving that alternative) outweigh the costs involved.

In general, people are resistant to change because of individual factors (e.g., economic insecurity, fear of the unknown) and organizational factors (e.g., the stability of work groups, threats to the existing balance of power). However, resistance to change can be overcome in several ways, including educating the workforce about the effects of the changes and involving employees in the change process.

Techniques of Organizational Development

Techniques for planning organizational change in order to enhance personal and organizational outcomes are collectively known as **organizational development** practices. For example, **survey feedback** uses questionnaires and/or interviews as the basis for identifying organizational problems, which are then addressed in planning sessions. **Sensitivity training** is a technique in which group discussions are used to enhance interpersonal awareness and reduce interpersonal friction. **Team building** involves using work groups to diagnose and develop specific plans for solving problems with respect to their functioning as a work unit. **Quality of work life** programs attempt to humanize the workplace by involving employees in the decisions affecting them (e.g., through quality circle meetings) and by restructuring the jobs themselves. Finally, **management by objectives** focuses on attempts by managers and their subordinates to work together at setting important organizational goals and developing a plan to help meet them. The rationale underlying all five of these techniques is that they may enhance organizational functioning by involving employees in identifying and solving organizational problems.

Critical Issues in Organizational Development

The effectiveness of most organizational development programs is not systematically assessed in practice, and the few studies that do attempt to measure the success of such programs are not carefully conducted. However, those studies that have systematically evaluated organizational development programs generally find them to be successful in improving organizational functioning and, to a lesser degree, individual satisfaction.

OD, as a whole, has been criticized on the grounds that it focuses too much on processes and not enough on outcomes. However, experts have argued that both orientations are necessary.

Some have argued that OD is unethical for several reasons, most notably because it has the potential to be used for illegitimate purposes. However, others counter that OD is just a tool and that it is people who are at fault for using it inappropriately.

CASE PREVIEW QUESTIONS FOR DISCUSSION

1. Explain why Eaton's had fallen into insolvency by 1997.

2. What efforts did Eaton's make to turn around its fortunes? In your opinion, how successful will Eaton's' management of change be in the long run?

3. If you had been hired by the Eaton family as a change consultant, what would you recommend?

CHAPTER QUESTIONS FOR DISCUSSION

1. Some changes in organizations are unplanned, whereas others are the result of deliberate, planned actions. Give examples of each of these varieties of change and explain their implications for organizational functioning.

2. Suppose you are having difficulty managing a small group of subordinates who work in an office 1500 km away from your home base. What kinds of changes in structure, technology, and people can be implemented to supervise these distant employees more closely?

3. Under what conditions will people be most willing to make changes in organizations? Explain your answer and give an example.

4. Suppose that you are a top executive of a large organization about to undertake an ambitious restructuring involving massive changes in job responsibilities for most employees. Explain why people might be resistant to such changes and what steps could be taken to overcome this resistance.

5. Overall, how effective is organizational development in improving organizational functioning? With respect to what factors does it work or not work?

6. Argue for or against the following statement: "Organizational development is inherently unethical and should not be used."

CASE IN POINT

Browns Shoe Shops Inc.: A Montreal Tradition That Grew

Morton Brownstein has been called the godfather of fashion footware. Now his son hopes to become even more successful by courting the hip young daughters of his father's favourite customers. After nearly 50 years in the business, Morton Brownstein has a clear understanding of his customers. He believes in entertaining his customers. When a woman with 175 pairs of shoes already in her closet walks into the store, she has to be excited by what she sees—enough to make the cash exchange, reasons Brownstein. And that requires his upscale stores to have the right kind of merchandise, window displays, and staff.

He should know. Brownstein heads a shoe dynasty that dots Canada with 40 locations from Vancouver to Montreal, as well as four stores in Chicago and leased departments in Holt Renfrew and The Bay. What is less certain is how his venerable company will fare now that he has stepped down as president and his 48-year-old son and partner, Michael, has taken over. Having worked with his father for more than 25 years, the younger Brownstein is hardly a new face at Browns—but now the fate of the $7-million-a-year business and its 600 staff rests in his hands.

Some changes are definitely in store. While the elder Brownstein cultivated a loyal staff of shoe buyers and a conservative strategy for growth, Michael has spent much of his time as the company's chief women's shoe buyer expanding Browns' well-heeled clientele to include funky fashion victims—more "rave party crowd" than "cocktail circuit." It's a shift that could be vital to Browns' future growth. With the company's having nearly saturated its traditional upper-middle to high-end Canadian market, it will be up to Michael to find new areas for expansion. Building on the inroads he has made already into younger, trendier markets seems an obvious choice. Success in these new areas will also help sustain the company as it begins a planned foray into the U.S., where most Americans associate the name Browns with the National Football League team that used to play in Cleveland.

The Browns chain started in 1938 with one shoe store on Ste-Catherine Street in Montreal. Morton joined the shoe store in 1949, after previously working in his father's other business, a general store. In those early days the business did not have the supporting cast and showcase attractions of today. "There was nothing to it," Morton recalls. But the store's raison d'être changed when it was gutted by fire in 1954. Morton, who had taken over as chief buyer a year earlier, hired an architect from New York to design a new store. "He said, 'What kind of shoe store do you want?' I said, 'What do you mean?'" Morton realized then that Browns was just a shoe store, that it didn't conjure up the classy high-style image consumers would associate with it today. "That fire determined our turnaround and put us on the course that we're on to this day," he says.

The next big change for the company came in 1959, when Morton was about to open Browns' new flagship store in Montreal's Centre Rockland. He wanted an impressive collection for its opening, so he trekked to France, Spain, and Italy. In the process, Browns became one of the first Canadian companies to import European designer labels. "Saying you're from Canada and asking them to ship shoes to Canada —nobody ever heard of that," says Michael. "Not only do you have to be a good shoe buyer, you have to be a pretty powerful character to get them to do that kind of thing."

Today, the younger Brownstein is credited with overhauling the chain's sophisticated image. One glance at any of its storefronts shows his push to attract a younger crowd. Browns has also made its shoes more accessible by selling through two major retailers. Morton struck a lease arrangement to run The Bay's shoe departments in the early 1980s and, six years ago, added a lucrative association with Holt Renfrew when Holt's outgoing president approached him to take over the shoe department for its 11 stores.

Uppermost in the younger Brownstein's mind are plans to build on the company's four-store presence in Chicago with an expansion into New York or Boston. He is also keeping his eye on B2, an experimental shoe store opened in 1996 on Toronto's ultra-hip Queen Street West, as well as a new private label of the same name. Both cater to a funkier, younger crowd—the daughters and sons of Browns' traditional customers, if you will—and their success could do a lot to determine Browns' future growth both here and south of the border. Ultimately, if Michael is to do as well as his father has done, he will have to show that along with learning the shoe business, he has also absorbed some of ☞

his father's management philosophy—something that Morton sums up in a single sentence: "One fella sneezes, everybody has a cold."[134]

Critical Thinking Questions

1. Describe the various forces of change affecting Browns Shoe Shops Inc. over the years.

2. Evaluate Michael Brownstein's various change management techniques and strategies.

3. Put yourself in Michael's position. What extra pressures do you feel as the successor in a family business?

SKILLS PORTFOLIO

Experiencing Organizational Behaviour

Are You Prepared for Downsizing?

As difficult as it may be to confront, downsizing is a way of life in today's restructuring organizations. It is the wise employee who is prepared for this eventuality. If you lose your job to downsizing in your organization, are you ready to move on to another position with only minimum disruption? This exercise will help you tell. (If you currently are not employed, this exercise will sensitize you to the ways you can prepare for the loss of a job you may have someday.)

Directions

Check each of the following statements that applies to you.

____**1.** I keep a record of all my work accomplishments.

____**2.** I keep my résumé ready to go at all times.

____**3.** My communication skills are finely tuned.

____**4.** I keep a notebook full of business and social contacts who would be useful leads in finding a new job.

____**5.** I do whatever I can to be indispensable to my company.

____**6.** I constantly work to further my professional education and training.

____**7.** I try hard to always be pleasant and courteous.

____**8.** I stay abreast of the latest job openings in my field.

____**9.** I regularly read the trade papers in my profession.

Questions for Discussion

1. How many items did you check? The more you checked, the better prepared you are for finding a new job, should you need to do so.

2. In addition to the items on this checklist, what further steps can you take to prepare for the possibility of having to take a new job?

3. Are you concerned that being highly prepared to step into a new position may lower your commitment to your present job (possibly making your need for a new job self-fulfilling)?

Working in Groups

Recognizing Impediments to Change— and How to Overcome Them

To confront the reality of organizational change, one of the most fundamental steps involves recognizing the barriers to change. Then, once these impediments have been identified, consideration can be given to ways of overcoming them. This exercise is designed to help you practise thinking along these lines while working in groups.

Directions

1. Divide the class into groups of approximately six and gather each group into a circle.

2. Each group should consider each of the following situations:

   Situation A: A highly sophisticated e-mail system is being introduced at a large university. It will replace the practice of transmitting memos on paper.

   Situation B: A very popular employee who's been with the company for many years is retiring. He will be replaced by a completely new employee from the outside.

3. For each situation, discuss three major impediments to change.

4. Identify a way of overcoming each of these impediments.

5. Someone from the group should record the answers and present them to the class for a discussion session.

Questions for Discussion

1. For each of the situations, were the impediments to change similar or different?

2. Were the ways of overcoming the impediments similar or different?

3. How might the nature of the situation confronted dictate the types of change barriers confronted and the ease with which these may be overcome?

TAKE IT TO THE NET

We invite you to visit the *Greenberg/Baron/Sales/Owen Companion Website* at *www.prenticehall.ca/greenberg* for this chapter's Internet resources.

CUMULATIVE CASE - PART 6

Digital Renaissance: Leading the Cyber Pack Into the Future

"The Motorcycle Macro Structure," a two-dimensional representation of Digital Renaissance's team-centred organizational structure, bears witness to the company's creative and entrepreneurial spirit. Keith Kocho says the structure, which he identifies as "a hybrid form based on a matrix," has been designed to allow for optimal leverage of the strengths his colleagues bring to the organization.[1]

The organizational structure of Digital Renaissance is horizontal rather than centralized or hierarchical. Instead, As Figure 1 shows, its unique organizational structure consists of three major circles, i.e., a Produce Circle responsible for the development of all products and services, a D.R. Support Circle responsible for all legal, financial, and human resources and information technology to support the other two circles, and a Create Demand Circle. At the core of the three larger circles are three smaller circles namely: the Strategy & Planning Circle, Resources Circle, and Operations Circle. Within each of the three larger circles are two Committees, i.e., the Resources Committee and Operations Committee. If Figure 1 were three dimensional, the layer underneath the surface of each larger circle would resemble a slice of onion with each ring representing a different set of roles: the Create Demand Circle (from the outside layer and moving in towards the centre) consists of account, mar-

keting and product managers, and circle director; the Produce Circle consists of project managers, producer, engineer, developers, artists, instructional designers, usability architects, technical writers, and circle director; and the D.R. Support Circle consists of information technology, human resources, finance, legal, and circle director. Schedulers work closely with the D.R. Support Group. Finally, in each large circle, there are the functional leaders, e.g., marketing leader, instructional design leader and finance leader, among others. To understand the positioning of the functional leaders on our onion-slice view of the chart, picture a line drawn from the centre of the slice (circle director role) straight to the outside.

Project teams are formed by aggregating people who have the right mix of skills to address the challenges faced by each project. A person might be a leader on one project and then become a team member on a project led by a colleague. Everyone at Digital Renaissance is involved in both organizational inputs and organizational outputs. However, some people are closer to the client outputs while others spend more time inputting skills into projects.[2]

Kocho knows that, in his complex high-tech world, no one person can complete a project alone and that no one is perfect. The organization's structure reflects Digital Renaissance's most prized values of autonomy and in-

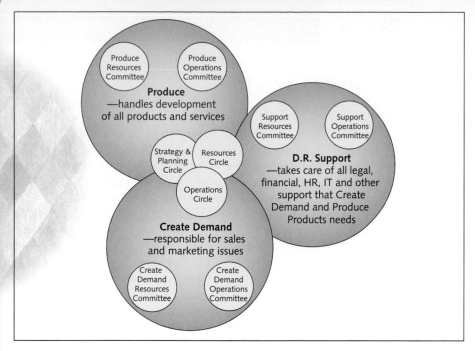

Cumulative Case Figure 1 The Motorcycle Macro Structure

Digital Renaissance's matrix structure, dubbed the "Motorcycle Macro Structure" to acknowledge inspiration received from Harley-Davidson's organizational structure, bears witness to the company's creative and entrepreneurial spirit.

terdependence. Kocho has no interest in what he calls a "culture of blame." In fact, while there is no formal process to reprimand people who make mistakes, the company does have a comprehensive performance management system. Kocho admits he has dismissed, on rare occasions, a couple of people for "gross negligence." He explains that no one is fired for making just one mistake. Instead, he points out that the project teams debrief on the error, rectify it, and chalk it up as yet another valuable learning experience.[3]

As each new wave of growth washes over Digital Renaissance, Kocho keeps a watchful eye on the bigger picture and continually reassesses the company's strategy, structure, and processes. In its earlier days, with far fewer employees, Kocho saw no useful purpose to be served by formal job titles. While this worked extremely well when the company was smaller, Kocho now reports that with the current employee roster at 150 and climbing, he has decided to institute job titles.[4] With all the company's rapid growth, the looser structure is becoming more and more challenging, especially with regard to accountability and decision making. In the end, Kocho says, despite his ideals, he has to be pragmatic to get the job done.[5]

In the late 1990s, Digital Renaissance was beginning to focus more on content areas such as co-producing television programs with companion interactive Websites such as Life Network's *Dish It Out* (www.dish-it-out.com). Described as a "cross-media cooking show" using "media cross-pollination," *Dish It Out* moves beyond passive entertainment to involve Web participants in "strong communities-of-interest."[6]

The community comes full circle with the hosts of *Dish It Out* responding to Web comments on the television show. This kind of integrated production is Kocho's vision of the future: a new-media network. He looks forward to Digital Renaissance's creating its own "'brands, shows, properties' through TV, the Web, and other delivery media."[7] The science fiction novel he's writing, entitled *Rosetta* may well be his first entertainment blockbuster.

True to his roots in the Nexus Generation, Kocho explains that he decided early on to grow Digital Renaissance "not to become a huge megalomaniacal corporation but to pursue the potential of this industry."[8] Perhaps the most inspirational part of Kocho's story is that he has been been able to keep his "social conscience" intact throughout this pursuit. He has reportedly refused to take on two substantial contracts with nuclear weapons manufacturers. "As an industry we're not thinking about the impacts of technology. . . . We're too busy worrying about the bull-market."[9]

For Kocho and others in the newly minted multimedia industry "the next big thing" will be convergence, the melding of various forms of media delivery. And when that day comes, Digital Renaissance will be ready. Until then, the staff at Digital Renaissance will be burning the midnight oil and wearing a path to the beer fridge. Scout will continue to greet visitors in her capacity as chief of security. And the only suit in the building will be the one hanging on the wall—the man's life-sized grey jacket and pants cast in natural concrete, artwork belonging to Creative Lead, Leah Balfe.

Discussion Questions

1. Is the matrix the best organizational structure for Digital Renaissance at this stage in its growth? Explain your answer.

2. How has Digital Renaissance managed to avoid the often-cited disadvantages of the matrix structure?

3. How and why might this company's organizational structure change over the next five years?

4. Would you describe Digital Renaissance as a learning organization? Please explain your answer.

5. What advice would you offer Keith Kocho about managing change at Digital Renaissance?

MacMillan Bloedel: The Axeman Cometh— But Can He Cut It?

MacMillan Bloedel (MacBlo), Canada's forestry giant, has been under siege, especially in the 1990s. For years the company has tried to be everything to everyone in the forestry business. From paper products to building materials, the company has had its hand in producing a wide range of forest products. But analysts contended that this approach went against the grain in the contemporary marketplace. They maintained that the company should become a "pure play," that is a specialist in solid-wood products only, and divest itself of its diversified holdings. This would necessitate a major shift in the company's philosophy and huge restructuring.

As the final year of retiring CEO Bob Finlay's tenure approached, two major investors teamed up to put pressure on the company. The Ontario Teacher's Pension Plan Board and Texas investors Lee and Sid Bass joined forces to purchase 9.5 percent of the company's stock. Shortly after the buy-up, Thomas Taylor, a representative of the Bass–Ontario Teachers' fund partnership, joined MacBlo's Board. With the Bass brothers' reputation as fans of restructuring, the pressure was building for the company to reconsider its position on diversification. Examining MacBlo's position, one analyst suggested: "I would say the corporate culture is what needs to be changed there.... They think the sun rises and sets on MacBlo, and they don't pay attention to what goes on outside of MacBlo."

Late in 1998, things at MacBlo were about to change in a dramatic way. In October 1998, Tom Stephens, formerly of Manville Corp., took over as the company's CEO. The day he arrived he brought with him psychologist Bob Chapman who specializes in assisting companies through the process of restructuring. He also brought a message. " 'Bob and I spent hours and hours and hours having one-on-ones with our people, trying to understand where the company had to be,' says Stephens."

In the end, Stephens told MacBlo employees that the company "was worth more 'dead than alive.' " He dropped the bomb because he believed that employees who felt the sense of crisis were more likely to respond. The crisis was real given the company's heavy losses. Stephens' remedy was to cut 2700 jobs from the company's 13 000-person workforce and to take the company out of paper products completely. This reflects Stephens' belief that "the day when a company can be all things to all markets is over." He explained, "This combination of operational restructuring and portfolio changes builds a platform for future growth and positions us to provide improved returns to our investors."

Stephens' approach has earned him the label "The Axeman" but he hopes he will be remembered more for remedies than for the bitter medicine he had to dole out. Despite the pain of the cuts, MacBlo's unions respect Stephens for his willingness to meet to discuss issues and his installation of a hotline that gives workers the chance to leave direct messages for him. He has a reputation for a willingness to listen to different perspectives.

Whether Stephens' approach will work in the long term remains to be seen. A year after his taking office, the company's profits were up but Stephens remained cautious in his forecasts of the company's earnings.

Video Case Discussion Questions

1. a) What factors in the environment have affected the forestry industry in Canada in the last decade or so?

   b) How has MacMillan Bloedel responded to such factors?

   c) How have other key players in the Canadian forestry industry responded?

2. a) Describe the corporate culture at MacBlo just before Stephens began as CEO.

   b) What impact did MacBlo's culture have on its overall performance?

3. Critique Stephens' strategy for change at MacBlo to date.

CBC Source: MacBlo in Trouble, *Venture* #639 (April 20, 1997).

Video Sources: Waal, P. (1997, August). One damn thing after another. *Canadian Business*, *70*, pp. 46–51, (quote, p. 51); Hunter, J. (1998, February 16). Swinging the axe. *Maclean's Toronto Edition, 111*, p. 38; McCarten, J. (1998, February 11). Renovations at MacBlo lead to staggering 1997 losses. *Canadian Press Newswire*; Gibbon, A. (1998, October 22). MacBlo third-quarter earnings soar. *The Globe and Mail*, p. B1.

NOTES

Chapter 1

1. Staff Writer (1997, November). Boxing match: Meet Randy Powell, Packaging King. *Profiles: the York University Magazine for Alumni and Friends*, www.yorku.ca/profiles/past/nov97/current/dept/gprofile/gprofile3.htm.

2. Staff Writer (1997, July 16). Randy Powell named as president of Second Cup Canada. *Canada Newswire*, www.newswire.ca/releases/July1997/16/c2418.html.

3. See Note 1.

4. Silcoff, Sean (1997, April). The sky's your limit. *Canadian Business*, 58–66.

5. See Notes 1 and 2.

6. See Note 1.

7. See Note 4 (quote, p. 62).

8. Staff Writer (1997, April). Clear visions. *The Financial Post Magazine*, p. 23.

9. See Note 1.

10. See Note 4.

11. See Note 4.

12. Greenberg, J. (Ed.). (1994). *Organizational behavior: The state of the science*. Hillsdale, NJ: Erlbaum.

13. Elden, M., & Chisholm, R. F. (1993). Emerging varieties of action research: Introduction to the special issue. *Human Relations, 46*, 121–142.

14. McGregor, D. (1960). *The human side of enterprise*. New York: McGraw-Hill.

15. Burshtein, Karen (1998, April). Huge cozy building. *The Report on Business Magazine*, pp. 70–71.

16. See Note 15.

17. Katz, D., & Kahn, R. (1978). *The social psychology of organizations*. New York: Wiley.

18. Pennings, J. M. (1992). Structural contingency theory: A reappraisal. In B. M. Staw & L. L. Cummings (Eds.), *Research in organizational behavior* (Vol. 14, pp. 267–310). Greenwich, CT: JAI Press.

19. Jackson, S. E., & Alvarez, E. B. (1992). Working through diversity as a strategic imperative. In S. E. Jackson (Ed.), *Diversity in the workplace* (pp. 13–29). New York: Guilford Press.

20. Mitchell, Alanna (1998, February 18). Face of big cities changing. *The Globe and Mail*, pp. A1, A3.

21. Sloan, Pamela, and Hill, Roger (1995). *Corporate Aboriginal Relations*. Toronto: Hill Sloan Associates Inc., p. ix.

22. Maruyama, M. (1992). Changing dimensions in international business. *Academy of Management Executive*, 6, 88–96.

23. Teagarden, M. B., Von Glinow, M. A., Bowen, D. E., Frayne, C. A., Nason, S., Huo, P., Milliman, J., Arias, M. E., Butler, M. C., Geringer, J. M., Kim, N., Scullion, H., Lowe, K. B., & Drost, E. A. (1995). Toward a theory of comparative management research: An idiographic case study of the best international human resources management project. *Academy of Management Journal, 38,* 1261–1287.

24. Gibb-Clark, Margot (1998, August). Project shapes diversity standards, *The Globe and Mail*, p. B9.

25. Warner, M. (1994). Organizational behavior revisited. *Human Relations, 47,* 1151–1166.

26. Kennedy, C. (1991). *Instant management*. New York: William Morrow.

27. Taylor, F. W. (1947). *Scientific management*. New York: Harper & Row.

28. Drucker, P. F. (1974). *Management: Tasks, responsibilities, practices*. New York: Harper & Row.

29. Münsterberg, H. (1913). *Psychology and industrial efficiency*. New York: Houghton Mifflin.

30. Metcalf, H., & Urwick, L. F. (Eds.). (1942). *Dynamic administration: The collected papers of Mary Parker Follett*. New York: Harper & Row.

31. Bedian, A. (1976, June). Finding the one best way: An appreciation of Frank B. Gilbreth, the father of motion study. *Conference Board Record*, pp. 37–39.

32. Mayo, E. (1933). *The human problems of an industrial civilization*. London: Macmillan.

33. Roethlisberger, F. J., & Dickson, W. J. (1939). *Management and the worker*. Cambridge, MA: Harvard University Press.

34. Baron, R. A., Rea, M. S., & Daniels, S. G. (1992). Lighting as a source of environmentally-generated positive affect in work settings: Impact on cognitive tasks and interpersonal behavior. *Motivation and Emotion, 15*, 1–34.

35. Fayol, H. (1949). *General and industrial management*. London: Pittman.

36. Weber, M. (1921), *Theory of social and economic organization* (A. M. Henderson & T. Parsons, Trans.), London: Oxford University Press.

37. Flexner, S. B. (1976). *I hear America talking*. New York: Van Nostrand Reinhold.

38. Lawrence, P. R. (1987). Historical development of organizational behavior. In J. W. Lorsch (Ed.), *Handbook of organizational behavior* (pp. 1–9). Englewood Cliffs, NJ: Prentice-Hall.

39. Gardner, B., & Moore, G. (1945). *Human relations in Industry*. Homewood, IL: Irwin.

40. See note 39.

41. Webster, Edward C. (1988, January). I/O psychology in Canada: from birth to Couchiching. *Canadian Psychology*, 29, 4–10.

42. Latham, Gary P. (1988, January). The influence of Canadian researchers on organizational psychology. *Canadian Psychology*, 29, 11–17.

43. Cooper, H., & Hedges, L. V. (1994). *The handbook of research synthesis*. New York: Russell Sage Foundation.

44. Van Mannen, J., Dabbs, J. M., Jr., & Faulkner, R. R. (1982). *Varieties of qualitative research*. Beverly Hills, CA: Sage Publications.

45. Greenberg, J., & Folger, R. (1988). *Controversial issues in social research methods*. New York: Springer-Verlag.

46. Eisenhardt, K. M. (1989). Building theories from case study research. *Academy of Management Review*, 14, 532–550.

47. Staff Writer (October, 1993). Happy campers: when they created Roots, Michael Budman and Don Green sold funny shoes, now they sell the Canadian dream. *Toronto Life, 27,* pp. 50–56.

48. Roots Commitment to Social and Environmental Issues, www.209.29.37.194/speed/worldroots1.html.

49. Roots Canada, www.roots.com.

50. Nolan, Stephanie (1998, April 13). Fame, friends, fortune. *Maclean's, 111*, pp. 40–41.

51. See Note 47.

52. See Note 47.

53. See Note 50.

Chapter 2

1. Staff Writer (1996, September 30). The slow burn in Burns Lake. *British Columbia Report, 8*, 20.

2. Staff Writer (1996, September). The new apartheid. *BC Business Magazine, 24*, 36–38.

3. Babine Forest Products, fnfp.gc.ca/sectione/4section/4.10.html.

4. Smith Milway, K. (1995, August 15). Board feat. *The Globe and Mail*, p. B8.

5. See Note 4.

6. See Note 4.

7. Cascio, W. F. (1995). Whither industrial and organizational psychology in a changing world of work? *American Psychologist*, 50, 928–939.

8. See Note 7 (quote, p. 928).

9. Colombo, J. R. (1997). *The 1998 Canadian Global Almanac*. Toronto: Macmillan Canada.

10. See Note 9.

11. Brown, L. R., Kane, H., & Ayres, E. (1994). *Vital signs*. New York: Norton.

12. See Note 11.

13. Lodge, G. C. (1995). *Managing globalization in the age of interdependence*. San Diego, CA: Pfeffer.

14. Staff Writer (1993, September 15). Cross-border investment is high. *Chemical Week*, p. 5.

15. Staff Writer (1998, June 26/July 10). Performance 2000. *Canadian Business*.

16. Ronen, S. (1986). *Comparative multinational management*. New York: Wiley.

17. Staff Writer (1997, November). Fast-track delay could be death knell for free trade. *Financial Post Daily*, 10, p. 14.

18. Durbin, A. (1998, March/April). 10 reasons to kill the MAI. *Canadian Dimension, 32*, 27–29.

19. Huntington, S. P. (1993, summer). The clash of civilizations. *Foreign Affairs*, pp. 22–49.

20. Duerr, M. G. (1986, October). International business management: Its four tasks. *Conference Board Record*, pp. 42–45 (quote, p. 43).

21. Earley, P. C., & Singh, H. (1995). International and intercultural management research: What's next? *Academy of Management Journal, 38*, 327–340.

22. Ogbonna, E. (1993). Managing organizational culture: Fantasy or reality? *Human Resource Management Journal, 3(2)*, 42–54.

23. DeCieri, H., & Dowling, P. J. (1995). Cross-cultural issues in organizational behavior. In C. L. Cooper & D. M. Rousseau (Eds.), *Trends in organizational behavior* (Vol. 2, pp. 127–145). New York: John Wiley & Sons.

24. Hesketh, B., & Bochner, S. (1994). Technological change in a multicultural context: Implications for training and career planning. In H. C. Triandis, M. D. Dunnette, & L. Hough (Eds.), *Handbook of industrial and organizational psychology* (Vol. 4, pp. 190–240). Palo Alto, CA: Consulting Psychologists Press.

25. Janssens, M. (1995). Intercultural interaction: A burden on international managers? *Journal of Organizational Behavior, 16*, 155–167.

26. See Note 23.

27. Hofstede, G. (1980). *Culture's consequences: International differences in work related values*. Beverly Hills, CA: Sage.

28. Carnevale, A. P., & Stone, S. C. (1995). *The American mosaic: An in-depth report on the future of diversity at work*. New York: McGraw-Hill.

29. Staff Writer (1998, January). Molding a nation of immigrants. *Canada and the World Backgrounder, 63*, 4–11 (quote, p. 4).

30. See Note 29 (quote p. 5).

31. See Note 29.

32. Reid, A. (1996). *Shakedown*. Toronto: Doubleday Canada Limited.

33. Carnevale, A. P., & Stone, S. C. (1995). *The American mosaic: An in-depth report on the future of diversity at work*. New York: McGraw-Hill.

34. McCarthy, S. (1998, February 16). Weary traveller plants seed in barren place. *The Globe and Mail*, p. B11.

35. Foot, D. K., & Stoffman, D. (1996). *Boom, Bust & Echo*. Toronto: Macfarlane Walter and Ross.

36. See Note 35.

37. See Note 35.

38. Colombo, J. R. (1997). *The 1998 Canadian Global Almanac*. Toronto: Macmillan Canada.

39. Mitchell, A. (1998, February 18). Face of big cities changing. *The Globe and Mail*, p. A1.

40. See Note 35 (quote, p. 19).

41. See Note 35.

42. Boyett, J. H., & Boyett, J. T. (1995). *Beyond Workplace 2000*. New York: Dutton.

43. See Note 42.

44. Cox, T. C., Jr. (1994). *Cultural diversity in organizations*. San Francisco: Berrett-Kohler.

45. Cohen, A. R., & Gadon, H. (1980). *Alternative work schedules*. Reading, MA: Addison-Wesley.

46. Galen, M., Palmer, A. T., Cuneo, A., & Maremont, M. (1993, June 29). Work & family. *Business Week*, pp. 80–84, 86, 88; Gibb-Clark, M. (1993, June 15). One year in the trenches. *The Globe and Mail*, p. B20; Mark, K. (1993, January–February). Balancing work and family. *Canadian Banker*, pp. 22–24.

47. Olmsted, B., & Smith, S. (1994). *Creating a flexible workplace* (2nd ed.). New York: AMACOM.

48. Meier, L., & Meagher, L. (1993, September). Teaming up to manage. *Working Woman*, pp. 31–32, 108.

49. See Note 47.

50. Gibb-Clark, M. (1998, May 15). Royal Bank scores with flexible work programs. *The Globe and Mail*, p. B23.

51. See Note 9.

52. Akyeampong, E. B. (1997, Spring). Work arrangements: 1995 overview. *Perspectives*, Statistics Canada, catalogue no. 75-001-XPE.

53. Gage, D. N., Gruske, C., and Wheelwright, G. (1997, July). Mobile computing. *InfoWorld Canada, 22*, pp. 29, 31.

54. MacBride-King, J., and Paris, H. (1989, Autumn). Balancing work and family: Canadian organizations and their family-related programs. *Canadian Business Review*, pp. 22–26; Felix, S. (1997, June). Running on empty. *Benefits Canada, 21*, pp. 109, 111+ (quote, p. 109).

55. Shellenbarger, S. (1994, February 6). The aging of America is making "elder care" a big workplace issue. *Wall Street Journal*, p. A1.

56. Felix, S. (1997, June. Running on empty. *Benefits Canada, 21*, pp. 109, 111 and following.

57. Fenn, D. (1993, July). Bottoms up. *Inc.*, pp. 57–60.

58. Martinez, M. N. (1993). Family support makes business sense. *HRMagazine*, pp. 38–43.

59. Workstyle and Lifestyle, www.careermosaic.com/cm/husky2.html, Support: www.husky.on.ca/wortog.htm.

60. See Note 48.

61. Mason, J. C. (1993, July). Working in the family way. *HR Magazine*, pp. 25–28.

62. See Note 61.

63. See Note 48.

64. Zuboff, S. (1988). *In the age of the smart machine*. New York: Basic Books.

65. Bridges, W. (1994). *Job shift: How to prosper in a workplace without jobs*. Reading, MA: Addison-Wesley.

66. See Note 65.

67. Tomasko, R. M. (1990). *Downsizing: Reshaping the corporation for the future*. New York: AMACOM.

68. Hendricks, C. F. (1992). *The rightsizing remedy*. Homewood, IL: Business One Irwin.

69. Tomasko, R. M. (1993). *Rethinking the corporation*, New York: AMACOM.

70. MacIsaac, M. (1994, March 22). New broom sweeps schools. *The Globe and Mail*, p. B22.

71. Conklin, D. W. (1994). *Reengineering to Compete*. Scarborough, Ontario: Prentice Hall Canada Inc.

72. See Note 69.

73. Lusk, A. (1992, May). New business from old clients. *Working Woman*, pp. 26, 28.

74. Bettis, R. A., Bradley, S. P., & Hamel, G. (1992). Outsourcing and industrial decline. *Academy of Management Review, 6*, 7–22.

75. Haapaniemi, P. (1993, winter). Taking care of business. *Solutions*, pp. 6–8, 10–13.

76. See Note 69.

77. Stokes, D. (1998, April 25). Consider the (out)source. *The Financial Post*, p. 31.

78. Fierman, J. (1994, January 24). The contingency workforce. *Fortune*, pp. 30–34, 36.

79. Reid, A. (1996). *Shakedown: How the New Economy is Changing Our Lives*. Toronto: Doubleday Canada Limited (quote, p. 20).

80. See Note 79.

81. Handy, C. (1994). *The age of paradox*. New York: Morrow.

82. Beard, K. M., & Edwards, J. R. (1995). Employees at risk: Contingent work and the psychological experience of contingent workers. In C. L. Cooper & D. M. Rousseau (Eds.), *Trends in organizational behavior* (Vol. 2, pp. 109–126). London: John Wiley & Sons.

83. Bridges, W. (1994, September 19). The end of the job. *Fortune*, pp. 62–64, 68, 72, 74.

84. Nollen, S., & Axel, H. (1995). *The contingent workforce*. New York: AMACOM.

85. Sasseen, J. A., Neff, R., Hattangadi, S., & Sasoni, S. (1994, October 17). The winds of change blow everywhere. *Business Week*, pp. 92, 94.

86. Byrne, J. A., Brandt, R., & Port, O. (1993, February 8). The virtual corporation: The company of the future will be the ultimate in adaptability. *Business Week*, pp. 98–102.

87. Lander, M. (1994, October 10). It's not only rock 'n' roll. *Business Week*, pp. 83–84.

88. O'Connell, S. E. (1996, March). The virtual workplace moves at warp speed. *HR Magazine*, pp. 50–57.

89. Davidow, W. H., & Malone, M. S. (1992). *The virtual corporation*. New York: Harper Business (quote, p. 99).

90. Nankivell, N. (1998, January 29). Alternative work setups win approval. *Financial Post Daily*, 10, p. 21.

91. Hearne, R. (1997, August). First banker in space. *Canadian Business*, 70, p. 15.

92. DuBrin, A. J. (1994). *Contemporary applied management: Skills for managers* (4th ed.). Burr Ridge, IL: Irwin.

93. Walton, M. (1990). *The Demming management method at work*. New York: Perigree.

94. Wood, M. (1992, July 7). A quality teacher gets taut. *The Globe and Mail*, p. B20.

95. McKenna, B. (1992, September 8). Work culture gets shock therapy. *The Globe and Mail*, p. B16.

96. Dodds, D. W. (1992, February). Making it better ... and better. *CMA Management Accounting Magazine*, pp. 16–21.

97. Vido, A. (1993, November). Chrysler and minivans—are we there yet? *CMA Management Accounting Magazine*, pp. 11–16.

98. McCamus, D. R. (1991, December/January). Performance measurement. *CMA Management Accounting Magazine*, pp. 8–10, 12.

99. Church, E. (1998, August 24). Service firms follow the flow to ISO. *The Globe and Mail*, p. B11.

100. ISO 14000 Environmental Management System, www.btii.com/iso14.html.

101. See Note 99.

102. New Brunswick Directory of ISO 9000 Registered Organizations, www.moncton. nbcc.nb.ca/iso9000.

103. Walmsley, A. (1997, October). Six Sigma enigma. *The Globe and Mail Report on Business Magazine*, pp. 56–71, (quote, p. 60).

104. See Note 103.

105. Recipients 96 and Recipients 97, www.nqi.ca/new_web/english/frames/frames.html.

106. Canada Awards for Excellence: Celebrating Canada's Best, www.nqi.ca/new_web/english/frames/frames5.html.

107. See Note 106.

108. Canada Awards for Excellence, www.nqi.ca/new_web/english.frames/frames5.html.

109. See Note 105.

110. Ferrell, O. C., & Fraedrich, J. (1994). *Business ethics: Ethical decision making and cases* (2nd ed.). Boston: Houghton Mifflin.

111. Tannock, B. (1997, October). Barroom creams. *The Globe and Mail Report on Business Magazine*, pp. 44–54.

112. Henderson, V. E. (1992). *What's ethical in business?* New York: McGraw-Hill.

113. Jansen, E., & Von Glinow, M. A. (1985). Ethical ambivalence and organizational reward systems. *Academy of Management Review*, 10, 814–822.

114. Wolfe, D. M. (1988). Is there integrity in the bottom line: Managing obstacles to executive integrity. In S. Srivastava (Ed.), *Executive integrity: The search for high human values in organizational life* (pp. 140–171). San Francisco: Jossey-Bass.

115. Rosen, R. H. (1991). *The healthy company*. New York: Jeremy P. Tarcher/Perigee.

116. See Note 92.

117. Manley, W. W., II. (1991). *Executive's handbook of model business conduct codes*. Englewood Cliffs, NJ: Prentice Hall.

118. Treviño, L. K., & Nelson, K. A. (1995). *Managing business ethics*. New York: Wiley.

119. Tapscott, Don (1998). *Blueprint to the Digital Economy: Creating Wealth in the Era of E- Business*. New York: McGraw-Hill (quote, p. 113).

120. See Note 119.

121. Silcoff, Sean (1997, August). No frills, unbeatable prices: It worked for Wal-Mart. Why can't it work for a bank? *Canadian Business*, 34–42.

122. Menzies, David (1997, December 1). How to launch a bank. *Marketing's Annual Agency Report*, www.marketingmag.ca/Content/45.97/special7.html.

123. See Note 121 (quote p. 34); Blackwell, Richard (1998, May 9). ING chief seeks banking services in post offices. *The Financial Post*, www.ingdirect.ca/ing/press1.html.

124. See Note 122.

125. See Note 122.

126. Leckey, Jane (1998, April). ING Direct Revolutionizes Banking Industry: Branchless Bank Revisits Real Estate Needs. Office Life Canada Online, www.facilitiesnet.com/NS/NS3o8cc.html.

127. Craig, Susanne (1998, June 3). The Web is watching them work. *The Globe and Mail*, p. B27.

128. ING DIRECT Press Release (1998, May 8). New Canadian Tire DIRECT IN-Store Banking Service First of Its Kind, www.ingdirect.ca/ing/press1.html.

129. Silcoff, Sean (1997, August). No frills, unbeatable prices: It worked for Wal-Mart. Why can't it work for a bank? *Canadian Business*, pp. 34–42.

Cumulative Case Part 1

1. Akin, D. (1998, November 13). Kocho stays on the cutting edge with regular visits to 'techie' Santa Fe. *Financial Post*, p. C4.

2. Thompson, Clive. Keith Kocho has seen the future of the Internet and it is television, Internet: 216.13.9.31/shiftonline/html/onlineTOC/6.6/6.6features/kocho1.html.

3. Palmer, Rodney (1995, November). Who To Know: The Digerati. *Shift Magazine*, p. 31.

4. See Note 3.

5. See Note 2.

6. The Interview by Gordon MacLeod, Internet: www.atlarge.net/story_kocho2.html.

7. See Note 2.

8. See Note 2.

9. Rowan, G. (1995, April 10). Renaissance man. *The Globe and Mail Metro Edition*, p. B6.

10. Sheikh, F. (1998, May 4). The Vision Thing. *Marketing Magazine*, pp. 11–12.

11. See Note 9.

12. See Note 2.

13. See Note 2.

14. See Note 2.

15. See Note 10 (quote, pp. 11–12).

16. Digital Renaissance, Internet: www.digital-ren.com/stories/future_stories_q3.htm.

17. Digital Renaissance, Internet: www.digital-ren.com/finder/casestudies_list.asp?i=0.

18. Digital Renaissance, Internet: www.digital-ren.com/press/milestones_press2asp?type=3&page_id=306.

19. See Note 18.

20. See Note 6 (quote, p. 66).

21. See Note 2.

Chapter 3

1. Schofield, John (1997, November). The Nortel job machine. *Maclean's Toronto Edition*, p. 82.

2. See Note 1.

3. Scoffield, Heather (1998, April 15). The cult of the cool company. *The Globe and Mail*, p. B25.

4. See Note 1.

5. Schoffield, Heather (1998, May 27). Nortel leaves employees at home. *The Globe and Mail*, p. B27.

6. See Note 3.

7. Schofield, John (1997, November). The Nortel job machine, *Maclean's Toronto Edition*, 110, pp. 46, 82.

8. Lang, Laura (1996, July). Virtual-Reality Training. *Training and Development*, 50, 7, 9.

9. See Note 8.

10. Schoffield, H. (1998, May 27). Nortel leaves employees at home. *The Globe and Mail*, p. B27.

11. Schiffman, H. R. (1993). *Sensation and perception* (4th ed.). New York: Wiley.

12. Kenny, D. A. (1994). *Interpersonal perception*. New York: Guilford.

13. Weiner, B. (1995). *Judgments of responsibility*. New York: Guilford.

14. Jones, E. E., & McGillis, D. (1976). Correspondent inferences and the attribution cube: A comparative reappraisal. In J. H. Harvey, W. J. Ickes, & R. F. Kidd (Eds.), *New directions in attribution research* (Vol. 1, pp. 389–420). Hillsdale, NJ: Lawrence Erlbaum Associates.

15. Kelley, H. H. (1972). Attribution in social interaction. In E. E. Jones, D. E. Kanous, H. H. Kelley, R. E. Nisbett, S. Valins, & B. Weiner (Eds.), *Attribution:*

Perceiving the causes of behavior (pp. 1–26). Morristown, NJ: General Learning Press.

16. Burger, J. M. (1991). Changes in attribution errors over time: The ephemeral fundamental attribution error. *Social Cognition, 9,* 182–193.

17. Murphy, K. R., Jako, R. A., & Anhalt, R. L. (1993). Nature and consequences of halo error: A critical analysis. *Journal of Applied Psychology, 78,* 218–225.

18. Pulakos, E. D., & Wexley, K. N. (1983). The relationship among perceptual similarity, sex, and performance ratings in manager-subordinate dyads. *Academy of Management Journal, 26,* 129–139.

19. Turban, D. B., & Jones, A. P. (1988). Supervisor-subordinate similarity: Types, effects, and mechanisms. *Journal of Applied Psychology, 73,* 228–234.

20. Dougherty, T. W., Turban, D. B., & Callender, J. C. (1994). Confirming first impressions in the employment interview: A field study of interviewer behavior. *Journal of Applied Psychology, 79,* 659–665.

21. Dearborn, D. C., & Simon, H. A. (1958). Selective perception: A note on the departmental identification of executives. *Sociometry, 21,* 140–144.

22. Waller, M. J., Huber, G. P., & Glick, W. H. (1995). Functional background as a determinant of executives' selective perception. *Academy of Management Journal, 38,* 943–974.

23. Srull, T. K., & Wyer, R. S. (1988). *Advances in social cognition.* Hillsdale, NJ: Lawrence Erlbaum Associates.

24. Mohrman, A. M., Jr., Resnick-West, S. M., & Lawler, E. E., III. (1989). *Designing performance appraisal systems.* San Francisco: Jossey-Bass.

25. Ilgen, D. R., Major, D. A., & Tower, S. L. (1994). The cognitive revolution in organizational behavior. In J. Greenberg (Ed.), *Organizational behavior: The state of the science* (pp. 1–22). Hillsdale, NJ: Lawrence Erlbaum Associates.

26. Hogan, E. A. (1987). Effects of prior expectations on performance ratings: A longitudinal study. *Academy of Management Journal, 30,* 354–368.

27. Wayne, S. J., & Liden, R. C. (1995). Effects of impression management on performance ratings: A longitudinal study. *Academy of Management Journal, 38,* 232–260.

28. Fletcher, C. (1989). Impression management in the selection interview. In R. A. Giacalone & P. Rosenfeld (Eds.), *Impression management in the organization* (pp. 269–282). Hillsdale, NJ: Lawrence Erlbaum Associates.

29. Giacalone, R. A., & Rosenfeld, P. (1989). *Impression management in the organization.* Hillsdale, NJ: Lawrence Erlbaum Associates.

30. Stevens, C. K., & Kristof, A. L. (1995). Making the right impression: A field study of applicant impression management during job interviews. *Journal of Applied Psychology, 80,* 587–606.

31. Garbett. T. (1988). *How to build a corporation's identity and project its image.* Lexington, MA: Lexington Books.

32. Norgate, K. (1997, May 1). Nortel (Northern Telecom) opens new global headquarters. *Nortel News Release.*

33. Gatewood, R. D., Gowan, M. A., & Lautenschlager, G. J. (1993). Corporate image, recruitment image, and initial job choice decisions. *Academy of Management Journal, 36,* 414–427.

34. Bongiorno, L. (1995, April 10). The duller the better: For 1994's annual reports, modesty is a virtue. *Business Week,* p. 44.

35. Jordan, M., & Sullivan, K. (1995, September 8). Saving face: Japanese can rent mourners, relatives, friends, even enemies to buff an image. *Washington Post,* pp. A1, A28.

36. Wick, C. W., & Leon, L. S. (1993). *The learning edge: How smart managers and smart companies stay ahead.* New York: McGraw-Hill.

37. Atkinson, R. C., Herrnstein, R. J., Lindzey, G., & Luce, R. D. (Eds.). (1988). *Stevens' handbook of experimental psychology* (2nd ed.) (Vol. 1, pp. 218–266). New York: Wiley.

38. Skinner, B. F. (1969). *Contingencies of reinforcement.* New York: Appleton-Century-Crofts.

39. Scott, W. E., & Podsakoff, P. M. (1985). *Behavioral principles in the practice of management.* New York: Wiley.

40. Bandura, A. (1986). *Social foundations of thought and action.* Englewood Cliffs, NJ: Prentice Hall.

41. Harrison, J. K. (1992). Individual and combined effects of behavior modeling and the cultural assimilator in cross-cultural management training. *Journal of Applied Psychology, 77,* 962.

42. Goldstein, I. L. (1991). Training in work organizations. In M. D. Dunnette & L. M. Hough (Eds.), *Handbook of industrial and organizational psychology,* (2nd ed.) (Vol. 2, pp. 507–620). Palo Alto, CA: Consulting Psychologists Press.

43. Schnake, M. E. (1986). Vicarious punishment in a work setting. *Journal of Applied Psychology, 71,* 343–345.

44. Sandler, R. (1998, June 15). CBT boosts skills, improves attitude to learning. *Computing Canada, 24,* pp. 30–36.

45. Webster, J., & Martocchio, J. J. (1993). Turning work into play: Implications for microcomputer software training. *Journal of Management, 19,* 127–146.

46. Gist, M. E., Stevens, C. K., & Bavetta, A. G. (1991). Effects of self-efficacy and post-training intervention on the acquisition and maintenance of complex interpersonal skills. *Personnel Psychology, 44,* 837–861.

47. O'Reilly, B. (1993, April 5). How execs learn now. *Fortune,* pp. 52–54, 58.

48. Young, S. (1996, August 20). Banking on learning centres. *The Globe and Mail,* p. C5.

49. Argyris, C. (1991, May–June). Teaching smart people how to learn. *Harvard Business Review, 69*(3), 99–109.

50. Driskell, J. E., Cooper, C., & Moran, A. (1994). Does mental practice enhance performance? *Journal of Applied Psychology, 79,* 481–492.

51. Tracey, B. J., Tannenbaum, S. I., & Kavanaugh, M. J. (1995). Applying trained skills on the job: The importance of the work environment. *Journal of Applied Psychology, 80,* 239–252.

52. Tannenbaum, S. I., & Yukl, G. A. (1992). Training and development in work organizations. *Annual Review of Psychology, 43,* 399–441.

53. Hoffman, R. (1995, April). Ten reasons you should be using 360-feedback. *HRMagazine,* pp. 82–85.

54. Miller, L. (1978). *Behavior management.* New York: Wiley.

55. Smart, T., & Hayes, K. (1995). Look who's showing small fry the ropes. *Business Week Enterprise,* pp. 6–8.

56. Consider a Franchising Opportunity, www.cibc.com/ Small Business/EN231.html.

57. CIBC Aboriginal Banking Team, www.cibc.com/aboriginal/ directory.html#mansask.

58. Brooks, S. S. (1994, April). Noncash ways to compensate employees. *HRMagazine,* pp. 38–43.

59. Staff Writer (1995, April 25). Travel incentives combine business, pleasure. *Financial Post Daily, 8,* p. 23.

60. Lawler, E. O. (1993, April). How MCI wrought a 100-day "miracle," *Business Marketing,* pp. 56–57.

61. Frederiksen, L. W. (1982). *Handbook of organizational behavior management.* New York: Wiley; Cox, K. (1993, March 23). A drifting crew finds an anchor. *The Globe and Mail,* p. B22.

62. Beyer, J., & Trice, H. M. (1984). A field study of the use and perceived effects of discipline in controlling work performance. *Academy of Management Journal, 27,* 743–754.

63. Trahan, W. A., & Steiner, D. D. (1994). Factors affecting supervisors' use of disciplinary actions following poor performance. *Journal of Organizational Behavior, 15,* 129–139.

64. Oberle, R. J. (1978). Administering disciplinary actions, *Personnel Journal, 18*(3), 30–33.

65. Arvey, R. D., & Jones, A. P. (1985). The use of discipline in organizational settings: A framework for future research. In L. L. Cummings & B. M. Staw (Eds.), *Research in organizational behavior* (Vol. 7, pp. 367–408). Greenwich, CT: JAI Press.

66. Kiechell, W., III. (1990, May 7). How to discipline in the modern age. *Fortune,* pp. 179–180 (quote, p. 180).

67. Waller, D. C. (1992, February 28). Tailhook's lightning rod. *Newsweek,* p. 31; Trevino, L. K., & Nelson, K. A. (1995). *Managing business ethics.* New York: John Wiley & Sons.

68. O'Hara, J. (1998, May 25). Rape in the military. *Maclean's,* pp. 15–21 (quote, p. 15).

69. O'Hara, J. (1998, June 1). Speaking out. *Maclean's,* pp. 14–20.

70. O'Hara, J. (1998, May 25). Rape in the military. *Maclean's,* pp. 15–21; O'Hara, J. (1998,

May 25). Breaking ranks. *Maclean's*, p. 24.

71. Arvey, R. E., & Icancevich, J. M. (1980). Punishment in organizations: A review, propositions, and research suggestions. *Academy of Management Review, 5*, 123–132.

72. Trevino, L. K. (1992). The social effects of punishment in organizations: A justice perspective. *Academy of Management Review, 17*, 647–676.

73. Lussier, R. H. (1990, August). A discipline model for increasing performance. *Supervisory Management*, pp. 6–7.

74. Kerr, S. (1975). On the folly of rewarding "A" while hoping for "B." *Academy of Management Journal, 18*, 769–783.

75. Dechant, K., & Viega, J. (1995). More on the folly. *Academy of Management Executive, 9*, 15–16.

76. Browne, Kelvin (1995, May/June). A race for knowledge. *Canadian Banker, 102*, 14–18.

77. See Note 76.

78. See Note 76.

79. LaBarre, Polly (1996). The rush on knowledge. *Industry Week, 245*, 4, (starting p. 53).

80. See Note 79.

81. See Note 79.

82. Pitts, G. (1995, May 30). The vision of Saint Hubert. *The Globe and Mail*, B10.

83. See Note 82.

Chapter 4

1. Staff Writer (1995, August 14). A top cop blazes a gender trail. *Maclean's Toronto Edition, 108*, pp. 20, 22 (quote, p. 20).

2. See Note 1.

3. See Note 1 (quote, p. 22).

4. See Note 1.

5. See Note 1.

6. Portwood, John (1997, May). Force of change. *Chatelaine, 70*, pp. 43–46.

7. See Note 6 (quote, p. 43).

8. See Note 6.

9. See Note 10.

10. Mitchell, Alanna (1996, July 29). Police chief caught in controversies. *The Globe and Mail*, p. A3.

11. See Note 6.

12. See Note 9.

13. See Note 6.

14. See Note 6.

15. Carver, C. S., & Scheier, M. F. (1992). *Perspectives on personality* (2nd ed.). Boston: Allyn & Bacon.

16. Eysenk, M. W. (1994). *Individual differences*. Hillsdale, NJ: Erlbaum.

17. Mischel, W. (1973). Toward a cognitive social learning reconceptualization of personality. *Psychological Review, 80*, 252–283.

18. Friedman, H. W., Tucker, J. S., Tomlinson-Keasey, C., Schwartz, J. E., Wingard, D. L., & Criqui, M. H. (1993). Does childhood personality predict longevity? *Journal of Personality and Social Psychology, 65*, 176–185.

19. Bouchard, T. J., Jr., Lykken, D. T., McGue, M., Segal, N. L., & Tellegen, A. (1990). Sources of human psychological differences: The Minnesota study of twins reared apart. *Science, 250*, 223–228.

20. Osipow, S. H. (1990). Convergence in theories of career choice and development: Review and prospect. *Journal of Vocational Behavior, 36*, 122–131.

21. Caldwell, D. F., & O'Reilly, C. A., III (1990). Measuring person-job fit with a profile-comparison process. *Journal of Applied Psychology, 75*, 648–657.

22. Allport, G. W., & Odbert, H. S. (1936). Trait names: A psycholexical study. *Psychological Monographs, 47*, 211–214.

23. Digman, J. M. (1990). Personality structure: Emergence of the five-factor model. *Annual Review of Psychology, 41*, 417–440.

24. Funder, D. C., & Colvin, C. R. (1991). Explorations in behavioral consistency. Properties of persons, situations, and behavior. *Journal of Personality and Social Psychology, 60*, 773–794.

25. Funder, D. C., & Sneed, C. D. (1993). Behavioral manifestations of personality: An ecological approach to judgmental accuracy. *Journal of Personality and Social Psychology, 64*, 479–490.

26. Tett, R. P., Jackson, D. N., & Rothstein, M. (1991). Personality measures as predictors of job performance: A meta-analytic review. *Personnel Psychology, 44*, 703–741.

27. Cortina, J. M., Doherty, M. L., Schmitt, N., Kaufman, G., & Smith, R. G. (1992). The big five personality factors in the IPI and MMPI: Predictors of police performance. *Personnel Psychology, 44*, 1–26.

28. Barrick, M. R., & Mount, M. K. (1993). Autonomy as a moderator of the relationships between the big five personality dimensions and job performance. *Journal of Applied Psychology, 78*, 111–118.

29. See Note 28.

30. George, J. M., & Brief, A. P. (1992). Feeling good—doing good: A conceptual analysis of the mood at work-organizational spontaneity relationships. *Psychological Bulletin, 112*, 310–329.

31. Isen, A. M., & Baron, R. A. (1992). Positive affect as a factor in organizational behavior. In B. M. Staw & L. L. Cummings (Eds.), *Research in organizational behavior* (Vol. 13, pp. 1–54). Greenwich, CT: JAI Press.

32. Staw, B. M., & Barsade, S. G. (1993). Affect and managerial performance: A test of the sadder-but-wiser vs. happier-and-smarter hypotheses. *Administrative Science Quarterly, 38*, 304–331.

33. George, J. M. (1990). Personality, affect, and behavior in groups. *Journal of Applied Psychology, 75*, 107–116.

34. Friedman, M., & Rosenman, R. H. (1974). *Type A behavior and your heart*. New York: Knopf.

35. Lee, C., Ashford, S. J., & Jamieson, L. F. (1993). The effects of Type A behavior dimensions and optimism on coping strategy, health, and performance. *Journal of Organizational Behavior, 14*, 143–157.

36. Schauabroeck, J., Ganster, D. C., & Kemmerer, B. E. (1994). Job complexity, Type A behavior, and cardiovascular disorder: A prospective study. *Academy of Management Journal, 37*, 426–439.

37. Glass, D. C. (1977). *Behavior patterns, stress, and coronary disease*. Hillsdale, NJ: Erlbaum.

38. Holmes, D. S., McGilley, B. M., & Houston, B. K. (1984). Task-related arousal of Type A and Type B persons: Level of challenge and response specificity. *Journal of Personality and Social Psychology, 46*, 1322–1327.

39. Jamal, M., & Baba, V. V. (1991). Type A behavior, its prevalence and consequences among women nurses: An empirical examination. *Human Relations, 44*, 1213–1228.

40. Lee, M., & Kanungo, R. (1984). *Management of work and personal life*. New York: Praeger.

41. Berman, M., Gladue, B., & Taylor, S. (1993). The effects of hormones, Type A behavior pattern and provocation on aggression in men. *Motivation and Emotion, 17*, 125–138.

42. Baron, R. A. (1989). Personality and organizational conflict: Effects of the Type A behavior pattern and self-monitoring. *Organizational Behavior and Human Decisions Processes, 44*, 281–297.

43. Baron, R. A. , & Neuman, J. H. (Under review). Workplace violence and workplace aggression: Evidence on their relative frequency and potential causes.

44. Lyness, S. A. (1993). Predictors of differences between Type A and B individuals in heart rate and blood pressure reactivity. *Psychological Bulletin, 114*, 266–295.

45. Bateman, T. S., & Crant, J. M. (1993). The proactive component of organizational behavior. *Journal of Organizational Behavior, 14*, 103–118.

46. Crant, J. M. (1995). The proactive personality scale and objective job performance among real estate agents. *Journal of Applied Psychology, 60*, 532–537.

47. Sherman, S. (1995, December 11). Wanted: Company change agents. *Fortune*, 197–198.

48. Wood, R., Bandura, A., & Bailey, T. (1990). Mechanisms governing organizational performance in complex decision-making environments. *Organizational Behavior and Human Decision Processes, 46*, 181–201.

49. Kanger, R., & Kanfer, F. H. (1991). Goals and self-regulation: Applications of theory to work settings. *Advances in Motivation and Achievement, 7*, 287–326.

50. Gist, M. E., & Mitchell, T. R. (1992). Self-efficacy: A theoretical analysis of its determinants and malleability. *Academy of Management Review, 17*, 183–211.

51. Mitchell, T. R., Hopper, H., Daniels, D., George-Falvy, J., & James, L. R. (1994). Predicting self-efficacy and performance during skill acquisition. *Journal*

of *Applied Psychology, 79*, 506–517.

52. Lord, R. G., & Maher, K. J. (1991). Cognitive theory in industrial and organizational psychology. In M. D. Dunnette & L. M. Hough (Eds.), *Handbook of industrial and organizational psychology* (Vol. 2, pp. 1–62). Palo Alto, CA: Consulting Psychologists Press.

53. Snyder, M. (1987). *Public appearance/private realities: The psychology of self-monitoring*. San Francisco: Freeman.

54. Caldwell, D. F., & O'Reilly, C. A., III (1982). Boundary spanning and individual performance: The impact of self-monitoring. *Journal of Applied Psychology, 67*, 124–127.

55. Marshall, A. (1991, February). Hard to pronounce, but it works. *Calgary Herald*, p. C3.

56. Shamir, B. (1986). Self-esteem and the psychological impact of unemployment. *Social Psychology Quarterly, 49*, 61–72.

57. Eden, D., & Aviram, A. (1993). Self-efficacy training to speed reemployment: Helping people to help themselves. *Journal of Applied Psychology, 78*, 352–360.

58. Kilduff, M., & Day, D. V. (1994). Do chameleons get ahead? The effects of self-monitoring on managerial careers. *Academy of Management Journal, 37*, 1047–1060.

59. Rosenbaum, J. E. (1979). Tournament mobility: Career patterns in a corporation. *Administrative Science Quarterly, 24*, 220–241.

60. Sellers, P. (1996, January 15). What exactly is charisma? *Fortune*, 68–72, 74–75.

61. Scandura, T. A. (1992). Mentorship and career mobility: An empirical investigation. *Journal of Organizational Behavior, 13*, 169–174.

62. Turban, D. B., & Dougherty, T. W. (1994). Role of protégé personality in receipt of mentoring and career success. *Academy of Management Journal, 67*, 688–702.

63. Friedman, H. S., & Miller-Herringer, T. (1991). Nonverbal display of emotion in public and private: Self-monitoring, personality, and expressive cues. *Journal of Personality and Social Psychology, 62*, 766–775.

64. Jamieson, D. W., Lydon, J. E., & Zanna, M. P. (1987).

Attitude and activity preference similarity: Different bases of interpersonal attraction for low and high self-monitors. *Journal of Personality and Social Psychology, 53*, 1052–1060.

65. Christie, R., & Geis, F. L. (1970). *Studies in Machiavellianism*. New York: Academic Press.

66. Schultz, C. J., II (1993). Situational and dispositional predictors of performance: A test of the hypothesized Machiavellianism × structure interaction among sales persons. *Journal of Applied Social Psychology, 23*, 478–498.

67. McClelland, D. C. (1985). *Human motivation*. Glenview, IL: Scott, Foresman.

68. Turban, D. B., & Keon, T. L. (1993). Organizational attractiveness: An interactionist perspective. *Journal of Applied Psychology, 78*, 184–193.

69. McClelland, D. C. (1977). Entrepreneurship and management in the years ahead. In C. A. Bramletter (Ed.), *The individual and the future of organizations* (pp. 12–29). Atlanta: Georgia State University.

70. Miller, D., & Droge, C. (1986). Psychological and traditional determinants of structure. *Administrative Science Quarterly, 31*, 539–560.

71. Holpp, L. (1989, October). Achievement motivation and kaizen. *Training and Development Journal*, pp. 53–63.

72. McClelland, D. C., & Boyatzis, R. E. (1982). Leadership motive pattern and long-term success in management. *Journal of Applied Psychology, 67*, 737–743.

73. Totterdell, P., Spelten, E., Smith, L., Barton, J., & Folkard, S. (1995). Recovery from work shifts: How long does it take? *Journal of Applied Psychology, 80*, 43–57.

74. McClelland, D. C. (1961). *The achieving society*. Princeton, NJ: Van Nostrand.

75. Lynn, R. (1991). *The secret of the miracle economy*. London: SAU.

76. Furnham, A., Kirkcaldy, B. D., & Lynn, R. (1994). National attitudes to competitiveness, money, and work among young people: First, second, and third world differences. *Human Relations, 47*, 119–132.

77. de Vos, G. (1968). Achievement and innovation in

culture and personality. In E. Norbeck, D. Price-Williams, & W. McCord (Eds.), *The study of personality: An interdisciplinary appraisal* (pp. 434–478). New York: Holt, Rinehart, and Winston.

78. Imai, M. (1986). *Kaizen: The key to Japan's competitive success*. New York: McGraw-Hill.

79. Guthrie, J. P., Ash, R. A., & Bandapudi, V. (1995). Additional validity evidence for a measure of *morningness. Journal of Applied Psychology, 80*, 186–190.

80. Wallace, B. (1993). Day persons, night persons, and variability in hypnotic susceptibility. *Journal of Personality and Social Psychology, 64*, 827–833.

81. Flynn, J. R. (1987). Massive IQ gains in 14 nations: What IQ tests really measure. *Psychological Bulletin, 101*, 171–191.

82. Sternberg, R. J. (1986). *Intelligence applied*. New York: Harcourt Brace Jovanovich.

83. Goleman, D. (1995) *Emotional intelligence*. New York: Bantam Doubleday

84. Farnham, A. (1996, January 15). Are you smart enough to keep your job? *Fortune*, pp. 34–37, 40, 42, 46, 48.

85. Staff Writer (1996, September 5). Psychological test examines emotional well-being. *Canadian Jewish News, 37*, p. 49.

86. See Note 85.

87. Reed, T. E., & Jensen, A. R. (in press). Conduction velocity in a brain nerve pathway of normal adults correlates with intelligence level. *Intelligence*.

88. Baddeley, A. (1990). *Human memory: Theory and practice*. Boston: Allyn & Bacon.

89. Smith, L. (1995, April 17). Memory: Why you're losing it, how to save it. *Fortune*, pp. 182–192.

90. Hultsch, D. F., & Dixon, R. A. (1990). Learning and memory in aging. In J. E. Birrens & K. W. Schaie (Eds.), *Handbook of the psychology of aging* (3rd ed., pp. 359–374). San Diego: Academic Press.

91. See Note 67.

92. Ibbitson, J. (1996, August 12). New test measures "emotional quotient." *Background in Depth*, www.southam.com/nmc/ waves/depth/psychology/eqi.html.

93. See Note 92.

94. Gibbon, A., and Milner, B. (1995, June 1). Bronfman to shake up MCA. *The Globe and Mail*, p. B1.

95. Bruck, C. (1998, May 11). Bronfman's big deals. *The New Yorker*, pp. 66–77 (quote, p. 66).

96. Milner, B. (1998, June 6). Seagram's top gun shoots for the stars. *The Globe and Mail*, pp. B1, B6.

97. See Note 95.

98. Stevenson, M. (1994, October). Indomitable showman. *Canadian Business*, pp. 23–32.

99. Bruck, C. (1998, May 11). Bronfman's big deals. *The New Yorker*, pp. 66–77.

100. See Note 98.

101. See Note 98 (quote, p. 23).

102. See Note 98.

103. See Note 98 (quote, pp. 25–26).

104. See Note 98.

105. Shapiro, E. (1993, December 22). Bronfman sees stars in Time stake. *The Globe and Mail*, pp. B1, B4.

106. See Note 98 (quote, p. 26).

107. See Note 106.

108. See Note 105.

109. Shapiro, E. (1993, June 4). Act III, Scene I at Seagrams: The Time Warner play. *The Globe and Mail*, pp. B1, B4.

110. Milner, B. (1998, June 6). Seagram's top gun shoots for the stars. *The Globe and Mail*, pp. B1, B6 (quote, p. B1).

Cumulative Case Part 2

1. Livesey, B. (1998, March). Making nice. *The Globe and Mail Report on Business Magazine*, pp. 96–102.

2. Kocho, Keith (1999, January 20). Telephone interview.

3. See Note 2.

4. See Note 2.

5. Staff writer (1995, February). What's up doc? *SI Business, 6*, p. 30.

6. See Note 5.

7. Kelly, T. (1995, May–June). Pacing Multimedia. *EC&I, 9*, pp. 26–29 (quote, p. 28).

8. Crone, G. (1997, December 12). Arthurs-Jones switches focus of core operations. *Financial Post Daily, 10*, p. 25.

9. Staff writer (1995, April 13). CD-ROM technology adds fun to training programs. *Financial Post Daily, 8*, p. 37.

Chapter 5

1. Workstyle and Lifestyle, www.careermosaic.com/cm/husky2.html; Support, www.husky.on.ca/wortog.htm.

2. Opportunity, www.husky.on.ca/wortog.htm.

3. Innes, Eva, Lyon, Jim, and Harris, Jim (1991). *The Financial Post 100 Best Companies to Work for in Canada.* Toronto: HarperCollins Publishers Ltd.

4. Livesey, Bruce (1997, March). Provide and Conquer. *The Globe and Mail Report on Business Magazine,* pp. 34–44.

5. Attraction, www.husky.on.ca/wortog.htm.

6. Overview, www.husky.on.ca/annrep.htm.

7. See Note 4 (quote, p. 39).

8. See Note 5.

9. See Note 4.

10. Communication, www.husky.on.ca/wortog.htm.

11. See Note 4 (quote, p. 44).

12. Staff Writer (1998, July). Top private companies. *The Globe and Mail Report on Business Magazine,* pp. 137–146.

13. See Note 4.

14. See Note 4 (quote, p. 40).

15. Kanfer, R. (1990). Motivational theory and industrial and organizational psychology. In M. D. Dunnette & L. M. Hough (Eds.), *Handbook of industrial and organizational psychology* (2nd ed., Vol. 1, pp. 75–170). Palo Alto, CA: Consulting Psychologists Press.

16. Blau, G. (1993). Operationalizing direction and level of effort and testing their relationships to individual job performance. *Organizational Behavior and Human Decision Processes, 55,* 152–170.

17. Nord, W. R., Brief, A. P., Atieh, J. M., & Doherty, E. M., (1988). Work values and the conduct of organizational behavior. In B. M. Staw & L. L. Cummings (Eds.), *Research in organizational behavior* (Vol. 10, pp. 1–42). Greenwich, CT: JAI Press.

18. "Work still a labor of love." (1981, April 20). *The Columbus Dispatch,* p. 1.

19. Maslow, A. H. (1970). *Motivation and personality* (2nd ed.). New York: Harper & Row.

20. Mudrack, P. E. (1992). 'Work' or 'leisure'? The Protestant work ethic and participation in an employee fitness program. *Journal of*

Organizational Behavior, 13, 81–88.

21. Miller, A., & Springen, K. (1988, October 31). Forget cash, give me the TV. *Newsweek,* p. 58.

22. Porter, L. W. (1961). A study of perceived need satisfaction in bottom and middle management jobs. *Journal of Applied Psychology, 45,* 1–10.

23. Wahba, M. A., & Bridwell, L. G. (1976). Maslow reconsidered: A review of research on the need hierarchy theory. *Organizational Behavior and Human Performance, 15,* 212–240.

24. Alderfer, C. P. (1972). *Existence, relatedness, and growth.* New York: Free Press.

25. Salancik, G. R., & Pfeffer, J. (1977). An examination of need-satisfaction models of job satisfaction. *Administrative Science Quarterly, 22,* 427–456.

26. See Note 4.

27. Miller, A., & Bradburn, E. (1991, July 1). Shape up—or else! *Newsweek,* pp. 42–43.

28. Tully, S. (1995, June 12). America's healthiest companies. *Fortune,* pp. 98–100, 104, 106.

29. Tully, S. (1995, June 12). America's healthiest companies. *Fortune,* pp. 98–100, 104, 106; Waymen, R. (1998, January). Wellness workout. *Benefits Canada, 22,* pp. 24–30.

30. Staff Writer (1996, June). Eureka! *Canadian Business,* pp. 66–69.

31. Leana, C. R., & Feldman, D. C. (1992). *Coping with job loss.* New York: Lexington Books; Staff Writer (1991, August). The right way to handle a closure. *Canadian Business,* pp. 63–65; Marshall, A. (1990, January 20). Petro-Canada leads way in helping layoff victims. *Calgary Herald,* p. G1; Motherwell, C. (1995, March 21). It's tough deciding who stays and who goes. *The Globe and Mail,* p. B12.

32. Schwartz, E. L. (1991, June 17). Hot dogs, roller coasters, and complaints. *Business Week,* p. 27.

33. Jaffe, C. A. (1990, January). Management by fun. *Nation's Business,* pp. 58–60.

34. Kingston, A. (1998, August). Avon's calling. *The Globe and Mail Report on Business Magazine,* pp. 25–36

35. See Note 34 (quote, p. 32).

36. Wood, R. A., & Locke, E. A. (1990). Goal setting and strategy effects on complex tasks. In B. M. Staw & L. L. Cummings (Eds.), *Research in organizational behavior* (Vol. 12, pp. 73–110). Greenwich, CT: JAI Press.

37. Rowan, G. (1998, May 20). High-tech hiatus charges up staff. *The Globe and Mail,* p. B27.

38. Austin, N. K. (1994, March). Why sabbaticals make sense. *Working Woman,* pp. 19, 22, 24.

39. See Note 37.

40. See Note 38 (quote, p. 22).

41. See Note 38 (quote, p. 24).

42. Locke, E. A., & Latham, G. P. (1990). *A theory of goal setting and task performance.* Englewood Cliffs, NJ: Prentice-Hall.

43. Mento, A. J., Locke, E. A., & Klein, H. J. (1992). Relationship of goal level to valence and instrumentality. *Journal of Applied Psychology, 77,* 395–405.

44. Wright, P. M., O'Leary-Kelly, A. M., Cortinak, J. M., Klein, H. J., & Hollenbeck, J. R. (1994). On the meaning and measurement of goal commitment. *Journal of Applied Psychology, 79,* 795–803.

45. Klein, H. J. (1991). Further evidence on the relationship between goal setting and expectancy theories. *Organizational Behavior and Human Decision Processes, 49,* 230–257.

46. Harrison, D. A., & Liska, L. Z. (1994). Promoting regular exercise in organizational fitness programs: Health-related differences in motivational building blocks. *Personnel Psychology, 47,* 47–71.

47. Gellatly, I. R., & Meyer, J. P. (1992). The effects of goal difficulty on physiological arousal, cognition, and task performance. *Journal of Applied Psychology, 77,* 694-704.

48. Wright, P. M. (1992). An examination of the relationships among monetary incentives, goal level, goal commitment, and performance. *Journal of Management, 18,* 677–693.

49. Earley, P. C., & Litucy, T. R. (1991). Delineating goal and efficacy effects: A test of three models. *Journal of Applied Psychology, 76,* 81–98.

50. Latham, G. P., & Lee, T. W. (1986). Goal setting. In E. A. Locke (Ed.), *Generalizing from laboratory to field settings*

(pp. 100–117). Lexington, MA: Lexington Books.

51. Latham, G., & Baldes, J. (1975). The practical significance of Locke's theory of goal setting. *Journal of Applied Psychology, 60,* 122–124.

52. Locke, E. A., & Latham, G. P. (1984). *Goal setting: A motivational technique that works!* Englewood Cliffs, NJ: Prentice-Hall.

53. Wright, P. M., Hollenbeck, J. R., Wolf, S., & McMahan, G. C. (1995). The effects of varying goal difficulty operationalizations on goal setting outcomes and processes. *Organizational Behavior and Human Decision Processes, 61,* 28–43.

54. Bernstein, A. (1991, April 29). How to motivate workers: Don't watch 'em. *Business Week,* p. 56.

55. Stedry, A. C., & Kay, E. (1964). *The effects of goal difficulty on task performance.* General Electric Company, Behavioral Research Service.

56. Latham, G. P., Erez, M., & Locke, E. A. (1988). Resolving scientific disputes by the joint design of crucial experiments by the antagonists: Application to the Erez-Latham dispute regarding participation in goal setting. *Journal of Applied Psychology, 73,* 753–772.

57. Pritchard, R. D., Jones, S. D., Roth, P. L., Stuebing, K. K., & Ekberg, S. E. (1988). Effects of group feedback, goal setting, and incentives on organizational productivity. *Journal of Applied Psychology, 73,* 337–358.

58. Kulik, C. T., & Ambrose, M. L. (1992). Personal and situational determinants of referent choice. *Academy of Management Review, 17,* 212–237.

59. Greenberg, J. (1987). A taxonomy of organizational justice theories. *Academy of Management Review, 12,* 9–22.

60. Adams, J. S. (1965). Inequity in social exchange. In L. Berkowitz (Ed.), *Advances in experimental social psychology* (Vol. 2, pp. 267–299). New York: Academic Press.

61. Greenberg, J. (1989). Cognitive re-evaluation of outcomes in response to underpayment inequity. *Academy of Management Journal, 32,* 174–184.

62. Harder, J. W. (1992). Play for pay: Effects of inequity in a pay-

for-performance context. *Administrative Science Quarterly, 37,* 321–335.

63. Greenberg, J. (1990). Employee theft as a reaction to underpayment inequity: The hidden cost of pay cuts. *Journal of Applied Psychology, 75,* 561–658.

64. Martin, J. E., & Peterson, M. M. (1987). Two-tier wage structures: Implications for equity theory. *Academy of Management Journal, 30,* 297–315.

65. Ross, I. (1985, April 29). Employers win big on the move to two-tier contracts. *Fortune,* pp. 82–92.

66. See Note 65.

67. Lawler, E. E., III. (1967). Secrecy about management compensation: Are there hidden costs? *Organizational Behavior and Human Performance, 2,* 182–189.

68. Greenberg, J. (1990). Looking fair vs. being fair: Managing impressions of organizational justice. In B. M. Staw & L. L. Cummings (Eds.), *Research in organizational behavior,* (Vol. 12, pp. 265–301). Greenwich, CT: JAI Press.

69. Schaubroeck, J., May, D. R., & Brown, F. W. (1994). Procedural justice explanations and employee reactions to economic hardship: A field experiment. *Journal of Applied Psychology, 79,* 455-460.

70. Vroom, V. H. (1964). *Work and motivation.* New York: Wiley.

71. Porter, L. W., & Lawler, E. E., III. (1968). *Managerial attitudes and performance.* Homewood, IL: Irwin.

72. Mitchell, T. R. (1983). Expectancy-value models in organizational psychology. In N. Feather (Ed.), *Expectancy, incentive, and action* (pp. 293–314). Hillsdale, NJ: Lawrence Erlbaum Associates.

73. Nelson, R. (1994). *1001 ways to reward employees.* New York: Workman Publishing Co. Inc., p. 105.

74. "Flexible-benefit plans grow." (1989, March 21) *USA Today,* p. C1.

75. Zippo, M. (1982). Flexible benefits: Just the beginning. *Personnel Journal, 17*(4), 56–58.

76. Ehrenfeld, T. (1993, July). Cashing in. *Inc.,* pp. 69–70.

77. Nelson, R. (1994). *1001 ways to reward employees.* New York: Workman Publishing Co. Inc.; and Human Resources

Development Canada, Bureau of Labour Information (1994). *Workplace Innovations.* Ottawa.

78. Schuster, J. R., & Zingheim, P. K. (1992). *The new pay: Linking employee and organizational performance.* New York: Lexington Books.

79. Jacques, E. (1989). *Requisite organization: The CEO's guide to creative structure and leadership.* Arlington, VA: Cason Hall & Co.

80. Fierman, J. (1994, June 13). The perilous new world of fair pay. *Fortune,* pp. 57, 59, 61, 63.

81. Perry, N. J. (1992, May 4). Talk about pay for performance! *Fortune,* p. 77.

82. Stern, J. M., & Stewart, G. B., III. (1993, June). Pay for performance: Only the theory is easy. *HRMagazine,* pp. 48–49.

83. Griffin, R. W., & McMahan, G. C. (1994). Motivation through job design. In J. Greenberg (Ed.), *Organizational behavior: The state of the science* (pp. 23–44). Hillsdale, NJ: Lawrence Erlbaum Associates.

84. Rigdon, J. E. (1992, May 26). Using lateral moves to spur employees. *Wall Street Journal,* pp. B1, B9.

85. Campion, M. A., & McClelland, C. L. (1991). Interdisciplinary examination of the costs and benefits of enlarged jobs: A job design quasi-experiment. *Journal of Applied Psychology, 76,* 186–198.

86. Byrne, J. A., Bongiorno, L., & Grover, R. (1994, April 25). That eye-popping executive pay: Is anybody worth this much? *Business Week,* pp. 52–56, 58.

87. Crystal, G. S. (1992). *In search of excess: The overcompensation of American executives.* New York: W. W. Norton.

88. Minkin, B. H. (1995). *Future in sight.* New York: Macmillan.

89. Bertin, O. (1998, April 2). Spar CEO's compensation slashed in '97. *The Globe and Mail,* p. B8.

90. Tully, S. (1993, November 1). Your paycheck gets exciting. *Fortune,* pp. 83–84, 88, 95, 98.

91. Campion, M. A., & McClelland, C. L. (1993). Follow-up and extension of the interdisciplinary costs and benefits of enlarged jobs. *Journal of Applied Psychology, 78,* 339–351.

92. Gellenhammar, P. G. (1977). *People at work.* Reading, MA: Addison-Wesley.

93. Luthans, F., & Reif, W. E. (1974). Job enrichment: Long on theory, short on practice. *Organizational Dynamics, 2*(2), 30–43.

94. Steers, R. M., & Spencer, D. G. (1977). The role of achievement motivation in job design. *Journal of Applied Psychology, 62,* 472–479.

95. Goldman, R. B. (1976). *A work experiment: Six Americans in a Swedish plant.* New York: Ford Foundation.

96. Hackman, J. R., & Oldham, G. R. (1980). *Work redesign.* Reading, MA: Addison-Wesley.

97. Graen, G. B., Scandura, T. A., & Graen, M. R. (1986). A field experimental test of the moderating effects of growth need strength on productivity. *Journal of Applied Psychology, 71,* 484–491.

98. Hackman, J. R., & Oldham, G. R. (1976). Motivation through the design of work: Test of a theory. *Organizational Behavior and Human Performance, 16,* 250–279.

99. Johns, G., Xie, J. L., & Fang, Y. (1992). Mediating and moderating effects in job design. *Journal of Management, 18,* 657–676.

100. Orpen, C. (1979). The effects of job enrichment on employee satisfaction, motivation, involvement, and performance: A field experiment. *Human Relations, 32,* 189–217.

101. Ropp, K. (1987, October). Candid conversations. *Personnel Administrator,* p. 49.

102. Hackman, J. R. (1976). Work design. In J. R. Hackman & J. L. Suttle (Eds.), *Improving life at work* (pp. 96–162). Santa Monica, CA: Goodyear.

103. See Note 4.

104. Magnet, M. (1993, May 3). Good news for the service economy. *Fortune,* pp. 46–50, 52.

105. Finegan, J. (1993, July). People power. *Inc.,* pp. 62–63.

106. See Note 105.

107. 100 Years of Ferry Service, www.Marine-atlantic.ca/ introe.html.

108. Cox, T. (1993, March 23). A drifting crew finds an anchor. *The Globe and Mail,* p. B22.

Chapter 6

1. Martinez, M.N. (1995, January). Equality effort sharpens bank's edge. *HRMagazine,* pp. 38- 43.

2. Johanne M. Totta, www.smartbank.ca/bio/totta.htm; The Inside Story, www.smartbank.ca/newsltr/ inside.html.

3. Quarstein, V. A., McAfee, R. B., & Glassman, M. (1992). The situational occurrences theory of job satisfaction. *Human Relations, 45,* 859–873.

4. Hulin, C. L. (1991). Adaptation, persistence, and commitment in organizations. In M. D. Dunnette & L. M. Hough (Eds.), *Handbook of industrial and organizational psychology* (2nd ed.,Vol. 2, pp. 445–506). Palo Alto, CA: Consulting Psychologists Press.

5. Stone, E. F., Stone, D. L., & Dipboye, R. L. (1991). Stigmas in organizations: Race, handicaps, and physical unattractiveness. In K. Kelley (Ed.), *Issues, theory, and research in industrial/organizational psychology* (pp. 385–457). Amsterdam: Elsevier Science Publishers.

6. McGuire, W. J. (1985). Attitudes and attitude change. In G. Lindzey & E. Aronson (Eds.), *Handbook of social psychology* (3rd ed.,Vol. 2, pp. 233–346). New York: Random House.

7. Locke, E. A. (1976). The nature and causes of job satisfaction. In M. D. Dunnette (Ed.), *Handbook of industrial and organizational psychology* (pp. 1297–1350). Chicago: Rand McNally.

8. Thornburg, L. (1992, July). When violence hits business. *HRMagazine,* pp. 40–45.

9. Cordon, Sandra (1997, October 7). Workers underpaid, overworked, stressed: but still satisfied. *Canadian Press Newswire.*

10. Weaver, C. N. (1980). Job satisfaction in the United States in the 1970s. *Journal of Applied Psychology, 65,* 364–367.

11. Eichar, D. M., Brady, E. M., & Fortinsky, R. H. (1991). The job satisfaction of older workers. *Journal of Organizational Behavior, 12,* 609–620.

12. Bedian, A. G., Ferris, G. R., & Kacmar, K. M. (1992). Age, tenure, and job satisfaction: A tale of two perspectives. *Journal of Vocational Behavior, 40,* 33–48.

13. Lambert, S. L. (1991). The combined effect of job and family characteristics on the job satisfaction, job involvement, and intrinsic motivation of men and women workers. *Journal of Organizational Behavior, 12,* 341–363.

14. Staw, B. M., & Ross, J. (1985). Stability in the midst of change: A dispositional approach to job attitudes. *Journal of Applied Psychology*, *70*, 56–77.

15. Gutek, B. A., & Winter, S. J. (1992). Consistency of job satisfaction across situations: Fact or framing artifact? *Journal of Vocational Behavior*, *41*, 61–78.

16. Agho, A. O., Price, J. L., & Mueller, C. W. (1992). Discriminant validity of measures of job satisfaction, positive affectivity and negative affectivity. *Journal of Occupational and Organizational Psychology*, *65*, 185–196.

17. Smith, P. C., Kendall, L. M., & Hulin, C. L. (1969). *The measurement of satisfaction in work and retirement*. Chicago: Rand McNally.

18. Weiss, D. J., Dawis, R. V., England, G. W., & Loftquist, L. H. (1967). *Manual for the Minnesota Satisfaction Questionnaire* (Minnesota Studies on Vocational Rehabilitation, Vol. 22). Minneapolis, MN: Industrial Relations Center, Work Adjustment Project, University of Minnesota.

19. Heneman, H. G., III., & Schwab, D. P. (1985). Pay satisfaction: Its multidimensional nature and measurement. *International Journal of Psychology*, *20*, 129–141.

20. Judge, T. A., & Welbourne, T. M. (1994). A confirmatory investigation of the dimensionality of the Pay Satisfaction Questionnaire. *Journal of Applied Psychology*, *79*, 461–466.

21. Hise, P. (1994, February). The motivational employee-satisfaction questionnaire. *Inc.*, pp. 73–75.

22. Sutton, R. I., & Callahan, A. L. (1987). The stigma of bankruptcy: Spoiled organizational image and its management. *Academy of Management Journal*, *30*, 405–436.

23. Herzberg, F. (1966). *Work and the nature of man*. Cleveland: World.

24. Machungaws, P. D., & Schmitt, N. (1983). Work motivation in a developing country. *Journal of Applied Psychology*, *68*, 31–42.

25. Landy, F. J. (1985). *Psychology of work behavior* (3rd ed.). Homewood, IL: Dorsey.

26. Magnet, M. (1993, May 3). Good news for the service economy. *Fortune*, pp. 46–50, 52.

27. Sundstrom, E. (1986). *Workplaces*. New York: Cambridge University Press.

28. Locke, E. A. (1984). Job satisfaction. In M. Gruenberg & T. Wall (Eds.), *Social psychology and organizational behavior* (pp. 93–117). London: Wiley.

29. McFarlin, D. B., & Rice, R. W. (1992). The role of facet importance as a moderator in job satisfaction processes. *Journal of Organizational Behavior*, *13*, 41–54.

30. Dalton, D. R., & Todor, W. D. (1993). Turnover, transfer, absenteeism: An interdependent perspective. *Journal of Management*, *19*, 193–219.

31. Porter, L. W., & Steers, R. M., (1973). Organizational work and personal factors in employee turnover and absenteeism. *Psychological Bulletin*, *80*, 151–176.

32. Tett, R. P., & Meyer, J. P. (1993). Job satisfaction, organizational commitment, turnover intention, and turnover: Path analyses based on meta-analytic findings. *Personnel Psychology*, *46*, 259–293.

33. Mobley, W. H., Horner S. O., & Hollingsworth, A. T. (1978). An evaluation of precursors of hospital employee turnover. *Journal of Applied Psychology*, *63*, 408–414.

34. Carsten, J. M., & Spector, P. E. (1987). Unemployment, job satisfaction, and employee turnover: A meta-analytic test of the Murchinsky model. *Journal of Applied Psychology*, *72*, 374–381.

35. The dollars and sense of managing absenteeism, www.ehp-ca.com/absent2.html.

36. Iaffaldano, M. T., & Murchinsky, P. M. (1985). Job satisfaction and job performance: A meta-analysis. *Psychological Bulletin*, *97*, 251–273.

37. Porter, L. W., & Lawler, E. E., III. (1968), *Managerial attitudes and performance*. Homewood, IL: Dorsey Press.

38. Magna International Inc. (1996). *Annual Report*, p. 6.

39. See Note 38.

40. Vandenberg, R. J., & Lance, C. E. (1992). Examining the causal order of job satisfaction and organizational commitment. *Journal of Management*, *18*, 153–167.

41. Becker, T. E., & Billings, R. S. (1993). Profiles of commitment: An empirical test. *Journal*

of *Organizational Behavior*, *14*, 177–190.

42. Reichers, A. E. (1985). A review and reconceptualization of organizational commitment. *Academy of Management Review*, *10*, 465–476.

43. Becker, H. S. (1960). Notes on the concept of commitment. *American Journal of Sociology*, *66*, 32–40.

44. Porter, L. W., Steers, R. M., Mowday, R. T., & Boulian, P. V. (1974). Organizational commitment, job satisfaction, and turnover among psychiatric technicians. *Journal of Applied Psychology*, *59*, 603–609.

45. Mathieu, J. E., & Zajoc, D. M. (1990). A review and meta-analysis of the antecedents, correlates, and con-sequences of commitment. *Psychological Bulletin*, *108*, 171–194.

46. Dunham, R. B., Grube, J. A., & Castañeda, M. B. (1994). Organizational commitment: The utility of an integrative definition. *Journal of Applied Psychology*, *79*, 370–380.

47. Meyer, J. P., & Allen, N. J. (1991). A three-component conceptualization of organizational commitment. *Human Resource Management Review*, *1*, 61–89.

48. Hackett, R. D., Boycio, P., & Hausdorf, P. A. (1994). Further assessments of Meyer and Allen's (1991) three-component model of organizational commitment. *Journal of Applied Psychology*, *79*, 15–23.

49. Whitener, E. M., & Waltz, P. M. (1993). Exchange theory determinants of affective and continuance commitment and turnover. *Journal of Vocational Behavior*, *42*, 265–281.

50. Randall, D. M. (1990). The consequences of organizational commitment: A methodological investigation. *Journal of Organizational Behavior*, *11*, 361–378.

51. Somers, M. J. (1995). Organizational commitment, turnover and absenteeism: An examination of direct and interaction effects. *Journal of Organizational Behavior*, *16*, 49–58.

52. Randall, D. M., Fedor, D. P., & Longenecker, C. O. (1990). The behavioral expression of organizational commitment. *Journal of Vocational Behavior*, *36*, 210–224.

53. Van Dyne, L., Graham, J. W., & Dienesch, R. M. (1994). Organizational citizenship behav-

ior: Construct redefinition, measurement, and validation. *Academy of Management Journal*, *37*, 765–802.

54. Romzek, B. S. (1989). Personal consequences of employee commitment. *Academy of Management Journal*, *39*, 641–661.

55. Caldwell, D. F., Chatman, J. A., & O'Reilly, C. A. (1990). Building organizational commitment: A multifirm study. *Journal of Occupational Psychology*, *63*, 245–261.

56. Curry, J. P., Wakefield, D. S., Price, J. L., & Mueller, C. W. (1986). On the causal ordering of job satisfaction and organizational commitment. *Academy of Management Journal*, *29*, 847–858.

57. Rosen, R. H. (1991). *The healthy company*. Los Angeles: Jeremy P. Tarcher (quote, pp. 71–72).

58. Florkowski, G. W., & Schuster, M. H. (1992). Support for profit sharing and organizational commitment: A path analysis. *Human Relations*, *45*, 507–523.

59. Simao, P. (1996, June). Eureka! *Canadian Business*, *69*, pp. 66–69; Barrick Gold Corporation. *Annual Report 1996* (quote, p. 11).

60. Graham, J. W., & Havlick, W. C. (1994). *Mission statements: A guide to the corporate and nonprofit sectors*. New York: Garland.

61. Vancouver, J. B., Milsap, R. E., & Peters, P. A. (1994). Multilevel analysis of organizational goal congruence. *Journal of Applied Psychology*, *79*, 666–679.

62. See Note 42.

63. Stephan, W. G. (1985). Intergroup relations. In G. Lindzey & E. Aronson (Eds.), *Handbook of social psychology* (3rd ed., Vol. 2, pp. 599–658). New York: Random House.

64. Weiner, G. (1993, January). The corporate challenge for racism in Canada. *Canadian Speeches*, pp. 31–33.

65. Staff Writer (1993, July/August). Managing employee diversity: a productivity issue. *Engineering Dimensions*, pp. 18–20.

66. Fernandez, J. P., & Barr, M. (1993). T*he diversity advantage*. New York: Lexington Books.

67. Malone, M. S. (1993, July 18). Translating diversity into

high-tech gains. *New York Times*, p. B2.

68. Yang, C. (1993, June 21). In any language, it's unfair: More immigrants are bringing bias charges against employers. *Business Week*, pp. 110–112.

69. Hawkins, C. (1993, June 28). Denny's: The stain that isn't coming out: Can a pact with the NAACP help it overcome charges of bias? *Business Week*, pp. 98–99.

70. Wells, J. (1997, October 20). Stuck on the ladder, *Maclean's*, pp. 60–64.

71. Solomon, C. M. (1992, July). Keeping hate out of the workplace. *Personnel Journal*, 30–36.

72. Ornstein, S. L., Sankowsky, D. (1994). Overcoming stereotyping and prejudice: A framework and suggestions for learning from groupist comments in the classroom. *Journal of Management Education*, 18, 80–90.

73. Foot, D. K., & Stoffman, D. (1996). *Boom, Bust & Echo*. Toronto: Macfarlane Walter & Ross.

74. Colombo, J. R. (1994). *The 1995 Canadian Global Almanac*. Toronto: Macmillan Canada.

75. Overman, S. (1993, June). Myths hinder hiring of older workers. *HRMagazine*, pp. 51–52.

76. See Note 73; Withers, P. (1998, March). What makes Gen X employees tick? *BC Business Magazine*, pp. 22–28.

77. See Note 76.

78. Hassell, B. L., & Perrewe, P. L. (1995). An examination of beliefs about older workers: Do stereotypes still exist? *Journal of Organizational Behavior*, 16, 457–468.

79. Stone, E. F., Stone, D. L., & Dipboye, R. L. (1991). Stigmas in organizations: Race, handicaps, and physical unattractiveness. In K. Kelley (Ed.), *Issues, theory, and research in industrial/ organizational psychology* (pp. 385–457). Amsterdam: Elsevier Science Publishers.

80. Colombo, J. R. (1997). *The 1998 Canadian Global Almanac*. Toronto: Macmillan Canada (quote p. 142).

81. Yang, C., & Forest, S. A. (1993, April 12). Business has to find a new meaning for "fairness": The Disabilities Act means some workers get special treatment. *Business Week*, p. 72.

82. See Note 81.

83. Martinez, M. N. (1993, June). Recognizing sexual orientation is fair and not costly. *HRMagazine*, pp. 66–68, 70, 72.

84. Williamson, A. D. (1993, July–August). Is this the right time to come out? *Harvard Business Review*, pp. 18–20, 22, 24, 26, 28.

85. See Note 84.

86. See Note 84.

87. Gibb-Clark, M. (1994, June 7). More firms offer same-sex benefits: Change viewed as coming to terms with diversity in the workplace. *The Globe and Mail*, pp. B1, B20; Gibb-Clark, M. (1994, November 30). Bell told to pay same-sex benefits: Arbitrator rules in favour of gay, lesbian employees. *The Globe and Mail*, p. B4; Clark, J. (1993, April). Treating gay couples like spouses. *Report on Business Magazine*, p. 26; Hryciuk, D. (1995, February). Same-sex benefits grow. *Calgary Herald*, p. D5.

88. Skrypnyk, J., & Watanabe, R. (1990, February 23). Tolerance of minorities in Canada. *Calgary Herald*, p. A5.

89. Andiappan, P., Crestohl, M., and Singh, J. (1989). Racial discrimination in employment in Canada. *Relations Industrielles*, 44, pp. 827–849.

90. Spears, J. (1995, May 30). CIBC kicks off diversity month. *Toronto Star*, p. D3.

91. Yang, C. (1993, June 21). In any language, it's unfair: More immigrants are bringing bias charges against employers. *Business Week*, pp. 110–112.

92. Wells, J. (1997, October 20). Stuck on the ladder, *Maclean's*, pp. 60–64.

93. Gibb-Clark, M. (1997, December 10). Women executives say stereotypes keep them out of top jobs. *Canadian Press Newswire*.

94. See Note 93.

95. Brethour, P. (1997, August 25). IBM carves up the market. *The Globe and Mail*, p. B5.

96. Keenan, G., and McFarland, J. (1997, September 27). The boys' club. *The Globe and Mail*, p. B1.

97. Jack, I. (1997, September 10). Magna suit spotlights industry practices. *Financial Post Daily*, p. 1.

98. See Note 96.

99. Maley, Dianne (1997, October 20). Eight Women at the Top (Maureen Kempston Darkes). *Maclean's*, p. 55.

100. Thomas, R. R., Jr. (1992). Managing diversity: A conceptual framework. In S. E. Jackson (Ed.), *Diversity in the workplace* (pp. 306–317). New York: Guilford Press.

101. Murray, K. (1993, August 1). The unfortunate side effects of "diversity training." *New York Times*, pp. E1, E3.

102. Gottfredson, L. S. (1992). Dilemmas in developing diversity programs. In S. E. Jackson (Ed.), *Diversity in the workplace* (pp. 279–305). New York: Guilford Press.

103. Carnevale, A. P., & Stone, S. C. (1995). *The American mosaic*. New York: McGraw-Hill.

104. Battaglia, B. (1992). Skills for managing multicultural teams. *Cultural Diversity at Work*, 4, 4–12.

105. Wright, P., Ferris, S. P., Hiller, J. S., & Kroll, M. (1995). Competitiveness through management of diversity: Effects of stock price valuation. *Academy of Management Journal*, 38, 272–287.

106. Gottfredson, L. S. (1992). Dilemmas in developing diversity programs. In S. E. Jackson (Ed.), *Diversity in the workplace* (pp. 279–305). New York: Guilford Press.

107. Sessa, V. I. (1992). Managing diversity at the Xerox Corporation: Balanced workforce goals and caucus groups. In S. E. Jackson (Ed.), *Diversity in the workplace* (pp. 37–64). New York: Guilford Press.

108. See Note 101.

109. See Note 102.

110. Gardenswartz, L. & Rowe, A. (1994). *The managing diversity survival guide*. Burr Ridge, IL: Irwin.

111. Rynes, S., & Rosen, B. (1995). A field survey of factors affecting the adoption and perceived success of diversity training. *Personnel Psychology*, 48, 247–270.

112. Sloan, Pamela, and Hill, Roger (1995). *Corporate Aboriginal Relations: Best Practice Case Studies*. Toronto: Hill Sloan and Associates Inc.

113. Munk, Nina (1997, March 10). A gallon of milk? That'll be $10, please. *Forbes*, 5, pp. 88–92.

114. See Note 112.

115. See Note 112 (quote, p. 164).

116. Diversity at Work: Sharing the Experience, www.equalopportunity. on.ca/business/lambert.html.

117. See Note 116.

118. Diversity at Work: Sharing the Experience, www.equalopportunity.on.ca/ business/gas.html.

119. See Note 118.

120. Weyerhaeuser Canada Ltd. BC Division Diversity Education Awards, www.parentsguide.com/ awards.weyerhaeuser.html.

121. Nortel Supports the Black Business and Professional Association, www.nortel.com.

122. Phillips, N. (1994). *Managing international teams*. Burr Ridge, IL: Irwin.

Chapter 7

1. Sellers, P. (1995, May 1). So you fail. Now bounce back! *Fortune*, 131, pp. 48–51, 54–55, 58, 62, 64, 66.

2. Greising, David (1998). *I'd Like to Buy the World a Coke: The Life and Leadership of Roberto Goizueta*. New York: John Wiley & Sons (quote, p. 231).

3. See Note 2 (quote, p. 230).

4. See Note 2.

5. Coke marketing chief quits, www.cnnfn.com.

6. See Note 1.

7. See Note 1, p. 49.

8. Quick, J. C., Murphy, L. R., & Hurrell, J. J., Jr. (1992). *Stress and well-being at work*. Washington, DC: American Psychological Association.

9. Cohen, N. (1997, November 29/December 1). The Rise and Fall of Canary Wharf. *Financial Post*, 10, p. 16.

10. Kahn, R. L., & Byosiere, P. (1992). Stress in organizations. In M. D. Dunnette & L. M. Hough (Eds.), *Handbook of industrial and organizational psychology* (2nd ed., Vol. 3., pp. 571–650). Palo Alto, CA: Consulting Psychologists Press.

11. Wanous, J. P. (1992). *Organizational entry: Recruitment, selection, orientation, and socialization*. Reading, MA: Addison-Wesley.

12. Kram, K. E. (1985). *Mentoring at work: Development relationships in organizational life*. Glenview, IL: Scott-Foresman.

13. Ragins, B. R., & Cotton, J. L. (1993). Gender and willingness to mentor in organizations. *Journal of Management*, 34, 939–951.

14. Van Maanen, J., & Schein, E. H. (1991). Toward a theory of organizational socialization. In B. M. Staw (Ed.), *Research in organizational behavior* (Vol. 12, pp. 209–264). Greenwich, CT: JAI Press.

15. Feldman, J. C. (1981). The multiple socialization of organization members. *Academy of Management Review, 6,* 309–318.

16. Fisher, C. D. (1986). Organizational socialization: An integrative review. In G. R. Ferris & K. M. Rowland (Eds.), *Research in personnel and human resources management* (Vol. 4, pp. 101–145). Greenwich, CT: JAI Press.

17. Wanous, J. P., Poland, T. D., Premark, S. L., & Davis, K. S. (1992). The effects of met expectations on newcomer attitudes and behavior: A review and meta-analysis. *Journal of Applied Psychology, 77,* 288–297.

18. Meglino, B. M., DeNisi, A. S., Youngblood, S. A., & Williams, K. J. (1988). Effects of realistic job previews: A comparison using an enhancement and a reduction preview. *Journal of Applied Psychology, 73,* 259–266.

19. Morrison, R. F., & Brantner, T. M. (1992). What enhances or inhibits learning a new job? A basic career issue. *Journal of Applied Psychology, 77,* 926–940.

20. See Note 11.

21. Whitely, W., Dougherty, T. M., & Dreher, G. F. (1991). Relationship of career mentoring and socioeconomic origin to managers' and professionals' early career progress. *Academy of Management Journal, 34,* 331–351.

22. Olian, J., Carroll, S., Giannantonio, D., & Feren, D. (1988). What do protégés look for in a mentor? Results of three experimental studies. *Journal of Vocational Behavior, 33,* 13–37.

23. Turban, D. B., & Dougherty, T. M. (1994). Role of protégé personality in receipt of mentoring and career success. *Academy of Management Journal, 37,* 688–702.

24. Fagenson, E. A. (1992). Mentoring—who needs it? A comparison of protégés' and nonprotégés' need for power, achievement, affiliation, and autonomy. *Journal of Vocational Behavior, 41,* 48–60.

25. Tepper, B. J. (1995). Upward maintenance tactics in supervisory mentoring and nonmentoring relationships. *Academy of Management Journal, 38,* 1191–1205.

26. Kram, K. E. (1983). Phases of the mentor relationship. *Academy of Management Journal, 26,* 608–625.

27. Baron, R. A., & Byrne, D. (In press). *Social psychology* (8th ed.). Boston: Allyn & Bacon.

28. Thomas, D. A. (1993). Racial dynamics in cross-race developmental relationships. *Administrative Science Quarterly, 38,* 169–194.

29. Labich, K. (1995, February 20). Kissing off corporate America. *Fortune,* pp. 44–47, 50, 52.

30. Pierce, C. A. (1995). Attraction in the workplace: An examination of antecedents and consequences of organizational romance. Unpublished Doctoral Dissertation, SUNY - Albany.

31. Holland, J. L. (1985). *Making vocational choices: A theory of vocational personalities and work environments.* Englewood Cliffs, NJ: Prentice-Hall.

32. Meier, S. T. (1991). Vocational behavior, 1988–1990: Vocational choice, decision-making, career development interventions, and assessment. *Journal of Vocational Behavior, 39,* 131–181.

33. Chatman, J. A. (1991). Matching people and organizations: Selection and socialization in public accounting firms. *Administrative Science Quarterly, 36,* 459–484.

34. Judge, T. A., & Bretz, R. D., Jr. (1992). Effects of work values on job choice decisions. *Journal of Applied Psychology, 77,* 261–271.

35. Moss, M. K., & Frieze, I. H. (1993). Job preferences in the anticipatory socialization phase: A comparison of two matching models. *Journal of Vocational Behavior, 42,* 282–297.

36. Cascio, W. F. (1995). *Managing human resources: Productivity, quality of work life, profits* (4th ed.). New York: McGraw-Hill.

37. Stewart, T. A. (1995, March 20). Planning a career in a world without managers. *Fortune,* pp. 72–74, 75, 77, 79.

38. "The 25 hottest careers." (1993, July 6). *Working Woman,* pp. 41–51.

39. Feather, Frank (1997–1998). *Canada's Best Careers Guide: 1997-1998 Edition.* Toronto: Warwick Publishing, p. 77.

40. See Note 39.

41. Campion, M. A., Cheraskin, L., & Stevens, M. J. (1994). Career-related antecedents and outcomes of job rotation. *Academy of Management Journal, 37,* 1518–1542.

42. Goldstein, L. L. (21986). *Training in organizations; needs assessment, development, and evaluation* (2nd ed.). Monterey, CA: Brooks/Cole.

43. See Note 41.

44. Tharenou, P., Latimer, S., & Conroy, D. (1994). How do you make it to the top? An examination of influences on women's and men's managerial advancement. *Academy of Management Journal, 37,* 899–931.

45. Van Velsor, E., & Hughes, M. W. (1990). *Gender differences in the development of managers: How women managers learn from experience.* Technical report no. 145, Center for Creative Leadership, Greensboro, NC.

46. Ohlott, P. J., Ruderman, M. N., & McCauley, C. D. (1994). Gender differences in managers' development job experiences. *Academy of Management Journal, 37,* 46–67.

47. See Note 46.

48. Ross, I. (1997, December 11). Corporate Culture Undercuts Women's Dreams. *The Globe and Mail,* p. B15. Reprinted with permission from the Conference Board of Canada

49. U.S. Department of Labor (1991). *A report on the glass ceiling initiative.* Washington, D.C.: U.S. Department of Labor.

50. See Note 48.

51. Staff Writer (1998, December/January). Study shows CEOs consider women's advancement key factor. *Women in Management, 8,* pp. 1–2.

52. See Note 48.

53. Levinson, D. J. (1986). A conception of adult development. *American Psychologist, 41,* 3–13.

54. See Note 8.

55. Lazarus, R. S., & Folkman, S. (1984). *Stress, appraisal, and coping.* New York: Springer-Verlag.

56. Evans, G. W., & Carrere, S. (1991). Traffic congestion, perceived control, and psycho-physiological stress among urban bus drivers. *Journal of Applied Psychology, 76,* 658–663.

57. Larson, P. (1993, June 14). Counsellors are seeing more stressed-out workers. *Montreal Gazette,* p. F14.

58. Selye, H. (1976). *Stress in health and disease.* Boston: Butterworths.

59. Shaw, J. B., & Riskind, J. H. (1983). Predicting job stress using data from the Position Analysis Questionnaire. *Journal of Applied Psychology, 68,* 253–261.

60. Williams, K. J., Suls, J., Alliger, G. M., Learner, S. M., & Choie, K. W. (1991). Multiple role juggling and daily mood states in working mothers: An experience sampling study. *Journal of Applied Psychology, 76,* 664–674.

61. Williams, K. J., & Alliger, G. M. (1994). Role stressors, mood spillover, and perceptions of work-family conflict in employed parents. *Academy of Management Journal, 37,* 837–868.

62. Newton, T. J., & Keenan, A. (1987). Role stress reexamined: An investigation of role stress predictors. *Organizational Behavior and Human Decision Processes, 40,* 346–368.

63. Thomas, L. T., & Ganster, D. C. (1995). Impact of family-supportive work variables on work-family conflict and strain: A control perspective. *Journal of Applied Psychology, 80,* 6–15.

64. McGrath, J. E. (1987). Stress and behavior in organizations. In M. D. Dunnette (Ed.), *Handbook of industrial and organizational psychology* (pp. 1351–1398). Chicago: Rand McNally.

65. Peterson, M. F., Smith, P. B., et al. (1995). Role conflict, ambiguity, and overload: A 21-nation study. *Academy of Management Journal, 38,* 429–452.

66. Hofstede, G. (1994). Management scientists are human. *Management Science, 40,* 4–13.

67. See Note 65.

68. French, J. R. P., & Caplan, R. D. (1972). Organizational stress and individual strain. In A. J. Morrow (Ed.), *The failure of success* (pp. 68–84). New York: Amacom.

69. McClean, A. A. (1980). *Work stress.* Reading, MA: Addison-Wesley.

70. Doby, V. J., & Caplan, R. D. (1995). Organizational stress as threat to reputation: Effects on anxiety at work and at home. *Academy of Management Journal, 38*, 1105–1123.

71. Canada Labour Code, R.S.C. 1985 (1st Supp.), c. 9, s. 247.1. 2.

72. Gibb-Clark, Margot, (1998, March 31). Harassment tragedy sparks quest for answers. *The Globe and Mail*, p. B13.

73. See Note 72.

74. See Note 72.

75. Baldwin, D. (1992, April). Beating harassment in the workplace. *Canadian Speeches: Issues of the Day*, pp. 51–55.

76. See Note 72.

77. See Note 75.

78. Segal, T., Kelly, K., & Solomon, A. (1992, November 9). Getting serious about sexual harassment. *Business Week*, pp. 78, 82.

79. See Note 72.

80. Baron, R. A. (1994). The physical environment or work settings. Effects on task performance, interpersonal relations, and job satisfaction. In B. M. Staw & L. L. Cummings (Eds.), *Research in organizational behavior*, (Vol. 16, pp. 1–46). Greenwich, CT: JAI Press.

81. Sundstrom, E., Town, J. P., Rice, R. W., Osborn, D. P., & Brill, M. (1994). Office noise, satisfaction, and performance. *Environment and Behavior, 26*, 195–222.

82. Loeb, M. (1996, January 15). What to do if you get fired. *Fortune*, 77–78.

83. See Note 63.

84. Nelson, D. L., & Sutton, C. (1990). Chronic work stress and coping: A longitudinal study and suggested new directions. *Academy of Management Journal, 33*, 659–689.

85. Holmes, T. H., & Rahe, R. H. (1967). Social readjustment rating scale. *Journal of Psychosomatic Research, 11*, 213–218.

86. Holmes, T. H., & Masuda, M. (1974). Life change and illness susceptibility. In B. S. Dohrenwend & B. P. Dohrenwend (Eds.), *Stressful life events: Their nature and effects* (pp. 45–72). New York: Wiley.

87. Lazarus, R. S., & Folkman, S. (1984). *Stress, appraisal, and coping*. New York: Springer-Verlag.

88. Bhagat, R. S., McQuaid, S. J., Lindholm, H., & Segovis, J. (1985). Total life stress: A multi-method validation of the construct and its effects on organizationally valued outcomes and withdrawal behaviors. *Journal of Applied Psychology, 70*, 202–214.

89. See Note 63.

90. Staff Writer (1994, March 23). Worker burnout bad for business employees told. *Toronto Star*, p. A11.

91. Sullivan, S. E., & Bhagat, R. S. (1992). Organizational stress, job satisfaction, and job performance: Where do we go from here? *Journal of Management, 18*, 353–374.

92. Motowidlo, S. J., Packard, H. J., & Manning, M. R. (1986). Occupational stress: Its causes and consequences for job performance. *Journal of Applied Psychology, 71*, 618–629.

93. Baumeister, R. F., & Scher, S. J. (1988). Self-defeating behavior patterns among normal individuals: Review and analysis of common self-destructive tendencies. *Psychological Bulletin, 104*, 3–22.

94. Golombiewski, R. T., Ninzenrider, R. F., & Stevenson, J. G. (1986). *Stress in organizations: Toward a phase model of burnout*. New York: Praeger.

95. Pines, A. M., Aronson, E., & Kafru, D. (1981). *Burn out: From tedium to personal growth*. New York: W. H. Freeman.

96. Gaines, J., & Jermier, J. M. (1983). Emotional exhaustion in high stress organizations. *Academy of Management Journal, 31*, 567–586.

97. Stelzer, J., & Numerof, R. E. (1986). Supervisory leadership and subordinate burnout. *Academy of Management Journal, 31*, 439–446.

98. Frese, M. (1985). Stress at work and psychosomatic complaints: A causal interpretation. *Journal of Applied Psychology, 70*, 214–238.

99. Cohen, S., & Williamson, G. (1991). Stress and infectious disease in humans. *Psychological Bulletin, 109*, 5–24.

100. Kirmeyer, S. L., & Biggers, K. (1988). Environmental demand and demand engendered behavior: An observational analysis of the Type A pattern. *Journal of Personality and Social Psychology, 54*, 997–1005.

101. Schaubroeck, J., Ganster, D. C., & Kemmerer, B. E. (1994). Job complexity, "type A" behavior, and cardiovascular disorder: A prospective study. *Academy of Management Journal, 37*, 426–439.

102. Brown, J. D. (1991). Staying fit and staying well: Physical fitness as a moderator of life stress. *Journal of Personality and Social Psychology, 60*, 555–561.

103. Sobel, D. (1993, May). Outsmarting stress. *Working woman*, pp. 83–84, 101.

104. See Note 102.

105. Benson, H. (1975). *The relaxation response*. New York: William Morrow.

106. Roskies, E. (1987). *Stress management for the healthy Type A*. New York: Guilford.

107. Fierman, J. (1995, February 6). Winning ideas from maverick managers. *Fortune*, pp. 66–68, 70, 74, 78.

108. See Note 62.

109. Gibb-Clark, M. (1998, September 25). Corporate concierges deliver. *The Globe and Mail*, p. B23.

110. Reynolds, S., & Shapiro, D. A. (1991). Stress reduction in transition: Conceptual problems in the design, implementation, and evaluation of worksite stress management inventories. *Human Relations, 44*, 717–733.

111. Quick, J. C., & Quick, J. D. (1984). *Organizational stress and preventive management*. New York: McGraw-Hill.

112. Ramsay, L. (1992, November 21). Firms find assistance schemes work wonders for their workers. *The Financial Post*, p. S16.

113. Philips, S. B., & Mushinki, M. H. (1992). Configuring an employee assistance program to fit the corporation's structure: One company's design. In U. C. Quick, L. R. Murphy, & J. J. Hurrell, Jr. (1992). *Stress and well-being at work* (pp. 317–328). Washington, DC: American Psychological Association.

114. This case was excerpted from Ferguson, J. (1994, April 3). How Ruth Getter cracked a bank's glass ceiling. *Toronto Star*, p. D1. Reprinted with permission, the Toronto Star Syndicate; with additional material from Staff Writer (1996, November 21). JWI gives top honors to TD's chief economist. *Canadian Jewish News, 37*, p. 12.

Cumulative Case Part 3

1. Cukier, W. (1996, September 24). They're hip, hot and happening. *The Globe and Mail*, p. C3.

2. Digital Renaissance Website, Internet: www.digital-ren.com/f_start.htm.

3. Livesey, B. (1998, March). Making Nice. *The Globe and Mail Report on Business Magazine*, p. 98.

4. The Play Ethic. *The Toronto Star*, Internet: www.digital-ren.com/f_start.htm.

5. Thompson, Clive. Keith Kocho has seen the future of the Internet and it is television, 216.13.9.31/shiftonline/html/onlineTOC/6.6/6.6features/kocho1.html.

6. Wah, L. (1998, May). The Power Office. *Management Review*, pp. 11–12.

7. Ross, V. (1998, August 19). Home is where the office is. *The Globe and Mail*, p. C3.

8. Chin, D. (1998, June). Welcome to our new column dedicated to working women. *Flare, 20*, pp. 70, 72.

9. Foot, D. & Stoffman, D. (1996). *Boom, Bust & Echo*. Toronto: Macfarlane Walter & Ross.

10. Bingham, R. (1998, November). Rebels with a Business Plan. *The Globe & Mail Report on Business Magazine*, p. 78.

11. Barnard, R., Cosgrave, D., & Welsh, J. (1998). *Chips & Pop*. Toronto: Malcolm Lester Books (quote, p. 22).

12. See Note 11 (quote, p. 23).

13. See Note 11 (quote, p. 24).

14. See Note 7.

15. Flavelle, Dana (1996, November 11). A New Company Style. *The Toronto Star*, pp. C1, C6.

16. See Note 15 (quote, p. C1).

Chapter 8

1. Southerst, J. (1994, May). Now everyone can be a boss. *Canadian Business*, pp. 48–50.

2. Dorrell, K. (1997, November 24). Breaking down the barriers: Work teams and partnership with union help turn Honeywell plant around. *Plant, 56*, pp. 12–13.

3. See Note 1.

4. Honeywell Company overview, www.honeywell.ca/overview.htm.

5. Honeywell, www.honeywell.ca.

6. See Note 2.

7. See Note 1.

8. See Note 2.

9. See Note 1 (quote, p. 48).

10. See Note 1.

11. Cartwright, D., & Zander, A. (1968). Origins of group dynamics. In D. Cartwright & A. Zander (Eds.), *Group dynamics: Research and theory* (pp. 3–21). New York: Harper & Row.

12. Bettenhausen, K. L. (1991). Five years of groups research: What we have learned and what needs to be addressed. *Journal of Management, 17*, 345–381.

13. Forsyth, D. L. (1983). *An introduction to group dynamics*. Monterey, CA: Brooks/Cole.

14. Long, S. (1984). Early integration in groups: "A group to join and a group to create." *Human Relations, 37*, 311–332.

15. Tuckman, B. W., & Jensen, M. A. (1977). Stages of small group development revisited. *Group and Organization Studies, 2*, 419–427.

16. Gersick, C. J. G. (1988). Time and transition in work teams: Toward a new model of group development. *Academy of Management Journal, 31*, 9–41.

17. Biddle, B. J. (1979). *Role theory: Expectations, identities, and behavior*. New York: Academic Press.

18. Jackson, S. E., & Schuler, R. S. (1985). A meta-analysis and conceptual critique of research on role ambiguity and role conflict in work settings. *Organizational Behavior and Human Decision Processes, 36*, 16–78.

19. Benne, K. D., & Sheats, P. (1948). Functional roles of group members. *Journal of Social Issues, 4*, 41–49.

20. Bales, R. F. (1980). *SYMLOG case study kit*. New York: Free Press.

21. Hackman, J. R. (1992). Group influences on individuals in organizations. In M. D. Dunnette & L. M. Hough (Eds.), *Handbook of industrial and organizational psychology* (2nd ed., Vol. 3, pp. 199–268). Palo Alto, CA: Consulting Psychologists Press.

22. Bettenhausen, K., & Murnighan, J. K. (1985). The emergence of norms in competitive decision-making groups. *Administrative Science Quarterly, 30*, 350–372.

23. Feldman, D. C. (1984). The development and enforcement of group norms. *Academy of Management Review, 9*, 47–53.

24. Wanous, J. P., Reichers, A. E., & Malik, S. D. (1984). Organizational socialization and group development: Toward an integrative perspective. *Academy of Management Review, 9*, 670–683.

25. Watson, T. J., Jr. (1990). *Father son & co.: My life at IBM and beyond*. New York: Bantam.

26. Wilson, S. (1978). *Informal groups: An introduction*. Englewood Cliffs, NJ: Prentice-Hall.

27. Greenberg, J. (1988). Equity and workplace status: A field experiment. *Journal of Applied Psychology, 73*, 606–613.

28. Stryker, S. & Macke, A. S. (1978). Status inconsistency and role conflict. In R. H. Turner, J. Coleman, & R. C. Fox (Eds.), *Annual review of sociology* (Vol. 4, pp. 57–90). Palo Alto, CA: Annual Reviews.

29. Jackson, L. A., & Grabski, S. V. (1988). Perceptions of fair pay and the gender wage gap. *Journal of Applied Social Psychology, 18*, 606–625.

30. Torrance, E. P. (1954). Some consequences of power differences on decision making in permanent and temporary three-man groups. *Research Studies: Washington State College, 22*, 130–140.

31. Greenberg, J. (1976). The role of seating position in group interaction: A review, with applications for group trainers. *Group and Organization Studies, 1*, 310–327.

32. Hare, A. P. (1976). *Handbook of small group research* (2nd ed). New York: Free Press.

33. Aronson, E., & Mills, J. (1959). The effects of severity of initiation on liking for a group. *Journal of Abnormal and Social Psychology, 59*, 177–181.

34. Long, S. (1984). Early integration in groups: "A group to join and a group to create." *Human Relations, 37*, 311–322.

35. Cartwright, D. (1968). The nature of group cohesiveness. In D. Cartwright & A. Zander (Eds.), *Group dynamics: Research and theory* (3rd ed., pp. 91–109). New York: Harper & Row.

36. George, J. M., & Bettenhausen, K. (1990). Understanding prosocial behavior, sales performance, and turnover: A group-level analysis in a service context. *Journal of Applied Psychology 75*, 698–709.

37. Shaw, M. E. (1981). *Group dynamics: The dynamics of small group behavior* (3rd ed.). New York: McGraw-Hill.

38. Janis, I. L.(1982). *Groupthink: Psychological studies of policy decisions and fiascos* (2nd ed.) Boston: Houghton Mifflin.

39. Henderson, J. (1988, June). Groupthink must go. *Policy Options*, p. 21.

40. See Note 39, p. 23.

41. Douglas, T. (1983). *Groups: Understanding people gathered together*. New York: Tavistock.

42. Geen, R. (1989). Alternative conceptualizations of social facilitation. In P. B. Paulus (Ed.), *Psychology of group influence* (2nd ed., pp. 15–51). Hillsdale, NJ: Lawrence Erlbaum Associates.

43. Zajonc, R. B. (1965). Social facilitation. *Science, 149*, 269–274.

44. Zajonc, R. B. (1980). Compresence. In P. B. Paulus (Ed.), *Psychology of group influence* (pp. 35–60). Hillsdale, NJ: Lawrence Erlbaum Associates.

45. Geen, R. B., Thomas, S. L., & Gammill, P. (1988). Effects of evaluation and coaction on state anxiety and anagram performance. *Personality and Individual Differences, 6*, 293–298.

46. Baron, R. S. (1986). Distraction/conflict theory: Progress and problems. In L. Berkowitz (Ed.), *Advances in experimental social psychology* (Vol. 19, pp. 1–40). New York: Academic Press.

47. Aiello, J. R., & Kolb, K. J. (1995). Electronic performance monitoring and social context: Impact on productivity and stress. *Journal of Applied Psychology, 80*, 339–353.

48. Aiello, J. R., & Svec, C. M. (1993). Computer monitoring of work performance: Extending the social facilitation framework to electronic presence. *Journal of Applied Social Psychology, 23*, 537–548.

49. Brahm, E., & Swenerton, D. (1997, December). Mobile tools. *Financial Post Magazine*, pp. 53–74.

50. Koelsch, F. (1995). *The info-media revolution*. New York: McGraw-Hill.

51. Band, W. A. (1994). *Touchstones*. New York: John Wiley & Sons.

52. Minkin, B. H. (1995). *Future insight*. New York: Macmillan.

53. See Note 52.

54. Watson, W. E., Kumar, K., & Michaelsen, K. K. (1993). Cultural diversity's impact on interaction process and performance: Comparing homogeneous and diverse task groups. *Academy of Management Journal, 36*, 590–602.

55. Steiner, I. D. (1972). *Group processes and productivity*. New York: Academic Press.

56. Shepperd, J. A. (1993). Productivity loss in performance groups: A motivation analysis. *Psychological Bulletin, 113*, 67–81.

57. Latané, B., Williams, K., & Harkins, S. (1979). Many hands make light the work: The causes and consequences of social loafing. *Journal of Personality and Social Psychology, 37*, 822–832.

58. Kravitz, D. A., & Martin, B. (1986). Ringelmann rediscovered: The original article. *Journal of Personality and Social Psychology, 50*, 936–941.

59. Karau, S. J., & Williams, K. D. (1993). Social loafing: A meta-analytic review and theoretical integration. *Journal of Personality and Social Psychology, 65*, 681–706.

60. Latané, B., & Nida, S. (1980). Social impact theory and group influence: A social engineering perspective. In P. B. Paulus (Ed.), *Psychology of group influence* (pp. 3–34). Hillsdale, NJ: Lawrence Erlbaum Associates.

61. Weldon, E., & Mustari, E. L. (1988). Felt dispensability in groups of coactors: The effects of shared responsibility and explicit anonymity on cognitive effort. *Organizational Behavior and Human Decision Processes, 41*, 330–351.

62. Earley, P. C. (1993). East meets West meets Mideast: Further explorations of collectivistic and individualistic work groups. *Academy of Management Journal, 36*, 19–348.

63. Nordstrom, R., Lorenzi, P., & Hall, R. V. (1990). A review of public posting of performance feedback in work settings. *Journal of Organizational Behavior Management, 11*, 101–123.

64. Bricker, M. A., Harkins, S. G., & Ostrom, T. M. (1986). Effects of personal involvement: Thought-provoking implications

for social loafing. *Journal of Personality and Social Psychology, 51*, 763–769.

65. George, J. M. (1992). Extrinsic and intrinsic origins of perceived social loafing in organizations. *Academy of Management Journal, 35*, 191–202.

66. Albanese, R., & Van Fleet, D. D. (1985). Rational behavior in groups: The free-riding tendency. *Academy of Management Review, 10*, 244–255.

67. Miles, J. A., & Greenberg, J. (1993). Using punishment threats to attenuate social loafing effects among swimmers. *Organizational Behavior and Human Decision Processes, 56*, 246–265.

68. Katzenbach, J. R., & Smith, D. K. (1993, March–April). The discipline of teams. *Harvard Business Review, 71*(2), 111–120.

69. Harari, O. (1995, October). The dream team. *Management Review*, pp. 29–31.

70. See Note 68.

71. Mohrman, S. A. (1993). Integrating roles and structure in the lateral organization. In J. R. Galbraith & E. E. Lawler, III (Eds.), *Organizing for the future* (pp. 109–141). San Francisco: Jossey-Bass.

72. Tuckman, B. W., & Jensen, M. A. (1977). Stages of small group development revisited. *Group and Organization Studies, 2*, 419–427.

73. Ray, D., & Bronstein, H. (1995). *Teaming up*. New York: McGraw-Hill.

74. Wellins, R. S., Byham, W. C., & Wilson, J. M. (1991). *Empowered teams*. San Francisco: Jossey-Bass.

75. Osburn, J. D., Moran, L., Musselwhite, E., & Zenger, J. H. (1990). *Self-directed work teams*. Burr Ridge, IL: Irwin.

76. Staff Writer (1996, December 14/16). Cashing in on best practices: managing change (Canada's best managed private companies). *Financial Post, 90*, p. 12.

77. Hackman, J. R. (1987). The design of work teams. In J. W. Lorsch (Ed.), *Handbook of organizational behavior* (pp. 315–342). Englewood Cliffs, NJ: Prentice-Hall.

78. See Note 77 (quote, p. 338).

79. Sakus, G. A. (1991, Winter). A strategy for success. *Canadian Business Review, 18*, pp. 37–39.

80. Sheridan, J. H. (1990, October 15). America's best plants. *Industry Week*, pp. 27–64.

81. Hoerr, J. (1989, July 10). The payoff from teamwork. *Business Week*, pp. 56–62.

82. Dumaine, B. (1990, May 7). Who needs a boss? *Fortune*, pp. 52–60.

83. See Note 81.

84. Ilgen, D. R., Major, D. A., Hollenbeck, & Sego, D. J. (1993). Team research in the 1990s. In M. M. Chemers & R. Ayman (Eds.), *Leadership theory and research* (pp. 245–270). San Diego: Academic Press.

85. Lawler, E. E., III, Mohrman, S. A., & Ledford, G. E., Jr. (1992). *Employee involvement and total quality management*. San Francisco: Jossey-Bass.

86. Hackman, J. R. (Ed.) (1990). *Groups that work (and those that don't)*. San Francisco: Jossey-Bass.

87. Manz, C. C., & Sims, *Business without bosses*. New York: John Wiley & Sons.

88. See Note 87.

89. Katzenbach, J. R., & Smith, D. K. (1993). *The wisdom of teams*. Boston: Harvard Business School Press.

90. Wellins, R. S., Byham, W. C., & Wilson, J. M. (1991). *Empowered teams*. San Francisco: Jossey-Bass.

91. Osburn, J. D., Moran, L., Musselwhite, E., & Zenger, J. H. (1990). *Self-directed work teams*. Burr Ridge, IL: Irwin.

92. See Note 87.

93. Pearson, C. A. L. (1992). Autonomous workgroups: An evaluation at an industrial site. *Human Relations, 45*, 905–936.

94. Wall, T. D., Kemp, N. J., Jackson, P. R., & Clegg, C. W. (1986). Outcomes of autonomous workgroups: A long-term field experiment. *Academy of Management Journal, 29*, 280–304.

95. See Note 1.

96. Stern, A. (1993, July 18). Managing by team is not always as easy as it looks. *The New York Times*, p. B14.

97. See Note 96.

98. See Note 96.

99. Pitts, G. (1993, February 16). The cheese plant nobody wanted. *The Globe and Mail*, p. B24.

100. Smith, P. B., Peterson, M. F., & Misumi, J. (1993). Event management and work team effectiveness in Japan, Britain and USA. *Journal of Occupational and Organizational Psychology, 67*, 33–43.

101. Nahavandi, A., & Aranda, E. (1994). Restructuring teams for the re-engineered organization. *Academy of Management Executive, 8*, 58–68.

102. See Note 96.

103. Maginn, M. D. (1994). *Effective teamwork*. Burr Ridge, IL: Business One Irwin.

104. List, W. (1989, October 23). CAW rejects concept of work teams as not in workers' interest. *The Globe and Mail*, p. B3.

105. Payette, S. (1994). Bureau of Labour Information, Human Resources Development Canada. Workplace Innovations Overview—1994, p. 6.

106. Dumaine, B. (1994, September 5). The trouble with teams. *Fortune*, pp. 86–88, 90, 92 (quote, p. 86).

107. See Note 89.

108. Campion, M. A., & Higgs, A. C. (1995, October). Design work teams to increase productivity and satisfaction. *HRMagazine*, pp. 101–102, 104, 107.

109. Campion, M. A., Medsker, & Higgs, A. C. (1993). Relations between work group characteristics and effectiveness: Implications for designing effective work groups. *Personnel Psychology, 46*, 823–850.

110. XEL Communications, Inc.: Why Choose XEL? www.xel.com/businessops/choose_xel.html.

111. Case, J. (1993, September). What the experts forgot to mention. *Inc.*, pp. 66–68, 70, 72, 76, 78.

Chapter 9

1. Lowe, J. (1998). *Jack Welch Speaks: Wisdom from the world's greatest business leader*. New York: John Wiley & Sons, Inc.; Tichy, N., & Sherman, S. (1993). *Control your destiny or someone else will*. New York: Currency Doubleday (quote, p. 4).

2. See Tichy & Sherman, Note 1, p. 5.

3. Slater, R. (1993, October 4). *The new G.E.* Burr Ridge, IL: Richard D. Irwin, p. 214.

4. See Tichy & Sherman, Note 1, p. 201.

5. Larson, P. (1993, October 4). GE mines its employees for ideas in "Work-out" sessions. *Montreal Gazette*, p. F14.

6. See Note 5.

7. See Tichy & Sherman, Note 1, p. 212.

8. See Note 3, p. 231. An interview with J. Braughman, G.E., June 20, 1991.

9. Slater, R. (1999). *Jack Welch and the GE way*. New York: McGraw-Hill, p. 6.

10. Fulk, J. (1993). Social construction of communication technology. *Academy of Management Journal, 36*, 921–950.

11. Scudder, J. N., & Guinan, P. J. (1989). Communication competencies as discriminators of superiors' ratings of employee performance. *Journal of Business Communication, 26*, 217–229.

12. Roberts, K. H. (1984). *Communicating in organizations*. Chicago: Science Research Associates (quote, p. 4).

13. Weick, K. E. (1987). Theorizing about organizational communication. In F. M. Jablin, L. L. Putnam, K. H. Roberts, & L. W. Porter (Eds.), *Handbook of organizational communication* (pp. 97–122). Newbury Park, CA: Sage.

14. Barnard, C. I. (1938). *The functions of the executive*. Cambridge, MA: Harvard University Press.

15. Mintzberg, H. (1973). *The nature of managerial work*. New York: Harper & Row.

16. Baskin, O. W., & Aronoff, C. E. (1980). *Interpersonal communication in organizations*. Santa Monica, CA: Goodyear.

17. Quinn, R. E., Hildebrandt, H. W., Rogers, P. S., & Thompson, M. P. (1991). A competing values framework for analyzing presentational communication in management contexts. *Journal of Business Communication, 28*, 213–232.

18. Lengel, R. H., & Daft, R. L. (1988). The selection of communication media as an executive skill. *Academy of Management Executive, 2*, 225–232.

19. Yates, J., & Orlikowski, W. J. (1992). Genres of organizational communication: A structurational approach to studying communication and media. *Academy of*

Management Review, 17, 299–326.

20. Szwergold, J. (1993, June). Employee newsletters help fill an information gap. Management Review, p. 8.

21. Sibson and Company, Inc. (1989). Compensation planning survey, 1989. Princeton, NJ: Author.

22. Heneman, R. L. (1992). Merit pay. Reading, MA: Addison-Wesley.

23. Killian, C. M. (1993). Effects of a company newsletter on perceptions of procedural justice. Unpublished doctoral dissertation, the Ohio State University, Columbus.

24. Brady, T. (1993, June). Employee handbooks: Contracts or empty promises? Management Review, pp. 33–35.

25. The (handbook) handbook. (1993, November). Inc., pp. 57–64.

26. See Note 25 (quote, p. 64).

27. Level, D. A. (1972). Communication effectiveness: Methods and situation. Journal of Business Communication, 28, 19–25.

28. Klauss, R., & Bass, B. M. (1982). International communication in organizations. New York: Academic Press.

29. Daft, R. L., Lengel, R. H., & Treviño, L. K. (1987). Message equivocality, media selection, and manager performance: Implications for information systems. MIS Quarterly, 11, 355–366.

30. Zuboff, S. (1988). In the age of the smart machine. New York: Basic Books.

31. Ritchie, L. D. (1991). Another turn of the information revolution. Communication Research, 18, 412–427.

32. Piller, C. (1993, July). Bosses with x-ray eyes. Macworld, pp. 118–123.

33. Evans, M. (1998, September 17). Your boss is watching. The Globe and Mail, pp. D1, D4, (quotes, p. D4).

34. Kantrowitz, B., & McKay, B. (1993, December 20). Who holds the key to the e-mailbox? Newsweek, p. 108.

35. See Note 32.

36. Johnson, B. (1988, November–December). Streamlining corporate communications through voice imaging technology. The Professional Communicator, pp. 19–20.

37. See Note 36.

38. Reinsch, N. L., Jr., & Beswick, R. W. (1990). Voice mail versus conventional channels: A cost minimization analysis of individuals' preferences. Academy of Management Journal, 33, 801–816.

39. Malloy, J. T. (1990). Dress for success. New York: Warner Books.

40. Solomon, M. R. (1986, April). Dress for effect. Psychology Today, pp. 20–28.

41. Saporito, B. (1993, September 20). Unsuit yourself: Management goes informal. Fortune, pp. 118–120 (quote, p. 118).

42. Schwartz, G. (1976). Queuing and waiting. Chicago: University of Chicago Press.

43. Greenberg, J. (1989). The organizational waiting game: Time as a status-asserting or status-neutralizing tactic. Basic and Applied Social Psychology, 10, 13–26.

44. Greenberg, J. (1988). Equity and workplace status: A field experiment. Journal of Applied Psychology, 73, 606–613.

45. Zweigenhaft, R. L. (1976). Personal space in the faculty office: Desk placement and student-faculty interaction. Journal of Applied Psychology, 61, 629–632.

46. Greenberg, J. (1976). The role of seating position in group interaction: A review, with applications for group trainers. Group and Organization Studies, 1, 310–327.

47. Capowski, G. S. (1993, June). Designing a corporate identity. Management Review, pp. 37–40.

48. Scully, J. (1987). Odyssey: Pepsi to Apple . . . a journey of adventure, ideas, and the future. New York: Harper & Row.

49. Carstairs, E. (1986, February). No ivory tower for Procter & Gamble. Corporate Design and Reality, pp. 24–30.

50. McCallister, L. (1994). "I wish I'd said that!" How to talk your way out of trouble and into success. New York: Wiley.

51. See Note 50.

52. Kennedy, M. (1998, August 8). New blood boss pledges spirit of openness. The Standard, p. A12.

53. Tannen, D. (1995). Talking 9 to 5. New York: Avon.

54. Tannen, D. (1995, September–October). The power of talk: Who gets heard and why. Harvard Business Review, pp. 138–148.

55. See Note 54 (quote, p. 148).

56. Munter, M. (1993, May–June). Cross-cultural communication for managers. Business Horizons, pp. 75–76.

57. Mellow, C. (1995, August 17). Russia: Making cash from chaos. Fortune, pp. 145–146, 148, 150–151.

58. Shaw, M. E. (1978). Communication networks fourteen years later. In L. Berkowitz (Ed.), Group processes (pp. 351–361). New York: Academic Press.

59. Adler, N. (1991). International dimensions of organizational behavior (2nd ed.). Boston: PWS/Kent.

60. Forsyth, D. R. (1983). An introduction to group dynamics. Monterey, CA: Brooks/Cole.

61. Burgess, R. L. (1968). Communication networks: An experimental reevaluation. Journal of Experimental Social Psychology, 4, 324–327.

62. Harcourt, J., Richerson, V., & Waitterk, M. J. (1991). A national study of middle managers' assessment of organization communication quality. Journal of Business Communication, 28, 348–365.

63. Krackhardt, D., & Hanson, J. R. (1993, July–August). Informal networks: The company behind the chart. Harvard Business Review, pp. 104–111.

64. Zenger, T. R., & Lawrence, B. S. (1989). Organizational demography: The differential effects of age and tenure distributions on technical communication. Academy of Management Journal, 32, 353–376.

65. Ibarra, H. (1992). Homophily and differential returns: Sex differences in network structure and access in an advertising firm. Administrative Science Quarterly, 37, 422–447.

66. Brass, D. J. (1985). Men's and women's networks: A study of interaction patterns and influence in an organization. Academy of Management Journal, 28, 327–343.

67. Krackhardt, D., & Porter, L. W. (1986). The snowball effect: Turnover embedded in communication networks. Journal of Applied Psychology, 71, 50–55.

68. Duncan, J. W. (1984). Perceived humor and social network patterns in a sample of task-oriented groups: A reexamination of prior research. Human Relations, 37, 895–907.

69. Baskin, O. W., & Aronoff, C. E. (1989). Interpersonal communication in organizations. Santa Monica: Goodyear.

70. Walton, E. (1961). How efficient is the grapevine? Personnel, 28, 45–49.

71. Staff Writer (1996, April 25). Anonymous threats bankrupt chocolate company. Canadian Press Newswire.

72. Thibaut, A. M., Calder, B. J., & Sternthal, B. (1981). Using information processing theory to design marketing strategies. Journal of Marketing Research, 18, 73–79.

73. Lesley, E., & Zinn, L. (1993, July 5). The right moves, baby. Business Week, pp. 30–31.

74. Schiller, Z. (1995, September 11). P&G is still having a devil of a time. Business Week, p. 46.

75. See Note 70.

76. Argyris, C. (1974). Behind the front page: Organizational self-renewal in a metropolitan newspaper. San Francisco: Jossey-Bass.

77. Hogarty, D. B. (1993, June). Who goes where? A new look at office design. Management Review, p. 9.

78. Papa, M. J. (1990). Communication network patterns and employee performance with new technology. Communication Research, 17, 344–368.

79. Miller, K. I., Ellis, B. H., Zook, E. G., & Lyles, J. S. (1990). An integrated model of communication, stress, and burnout in the workplace. Communication Research, 17, 300–326.

80. Hawkins, B. L., & Preston, P. (1981). Managerial communication. Santa Monica, CA: Goodyear.

81. Schnake, M. R., Dumler, M. P., Chochran, D. S., & Barnett, T. R. (1990). Effects of differences in superior and subordinate perceptions on superiors' communication practices. Journal of Business Communication, 27, 37–50.

82. Szilagyi, A. (1981). Management and performance. Glenview, IL: Scott, Foresman.

83. Kiechell, W., III. (1986, January 6). No word from on high. Fortune, pp. 19, 26.

84. Coulson, R. (1981) *The termination handbook*. New York: The Free Press.

85. Cropanzano, R., & Greenberg, J. (1997). *International review of industrial and organizational psychology*. London: Wiley.

86. Greenberg, J., Lind, E. A., Scott, K. S., & Welchans, T. D. (1995). *Perceptions of injustice and wrongful termination litigation*. Final report to the National Science Foundation.

87. Walker, C. R., & Guest, R. H. (1952). *The man on the assembly line*. Cambridge, MA: Harvard University Press.

88. Luthans, F., & Larsen, J. K. (1986). How managers really communicate. *Human Relations, 39*, 161–178.

89. Kirmeyer, S. L., & Lin, T. (1987). Social support: Its relationship to observed communication with peers and superiors. *Academy of Management Journal, 30*, 138–151.

90. Read, W. (1962). Upward communication in industrial hierarchies. *Human Relations, 15*, 3–16.

91. Glauser, M. J. (1984). Upward information flow in organizations: Review and conceptual analysis. *Human Relations, 37*, 613–643.

92. Lee, F. (1993). Being polite and keeping MUM: How bad news is communicated in organizational hierarchies. *Journal of Applied Social Psychology, 23*, 1124–1149.

93. Tesser, A., & Rosen, S. (1975). The reluctance to transmit bad news. In L. Berkowitz (Ed.), *Advances in experimental social psychology* (Vol. 8, pp. 192–232). New York: Academic Press.

94. Kiechel, W., III. (1990, June 18). How to escape the echo chamber. *Fortune*, pp. 129–130 (quote, p. 130).

95. Rogers, E. M., & Rogers, A. (1976). *Communication in organizations*. New York: Free Press.

96. Fiol, C. M. (1995). Corporate communications: Comparing executives' private and public statements. *Academy of Management Journal, 38*, 522–536.

97. Alessanddra, T., & Hunksaker, P. (1993). *Communicating at work*. New York: Fireside.

98. Kanter, R. M. (1977). *Men and women of the corporation*. New York: Basic Books.

99. Borman, E. (1982). *Interpersonal communication in the modern organization* (2nd ed.). Englewood Cliffs, NJ: Prentice-Hall.

100. Cantoni, C. J. (1993). *Corporate dandelions*. New York: AMACOM.

101. Rowe, M. P., & Baker, M. (1984, May–June). Are you hearing enough employee concerns? *Harvard Business Review*, pp. 127–135.

102. Burley-Allen, M. (1982). *Listening: The forgotten skill*. New York: John Wiley & Sons.

103 Brownell, J. (1985). A model for listening instructions: Management applications. *ABCA Bulletin, 48*(3), 39–44.

104. Austin, N. K. (1991, March). Why listening's not as easy as it sounds. *Working Woman*, pp. 46–48.

105. See Note 104.

106. Seyper, B. D., Bostrom, R. N., & Seibert, J. H. (1989). Listening, communication abilities, and success at work. *Journal of Business Communication, 26*, 293–303.

107. Penley, L. E., Alexander, E. R., Jernigan, I. E., & Henwood, C. I. (1991). Communication abilities of managers: The relationship to performance. *Journal of Management, 17*, 57–76.

108. Brownell, J. (1990). Perceptions of effective listeners: A management study. *Journal of Business Communication, 27*, 401–415.

109. Nichols, R. G. (1962, winter). Listening is good business. *Management of Personnel Quarterly*, p. 4.

110. See Note 29.

111. McCathrin, Z. (1990, spring). The key to employee communication: Small group meetings. *The Professional Communicator*, pp. 6–7, 10.

112. Vernyi, B. (1987, April 26). Institute aims to boost quality of company suggestion boxes. *Toledo Blade*, p. B2.

113. Taft, W. F. (1985). Bulletin boards, exhibits, hotlines. In C. Reuss & D. Silvis (Eds.), *Inside organizational communication* (2nd ed., pp. 183–189). New York: Longman.

114. Corporate Profile, www.sears.ca/e/profile.htm.

115. Walter, K. (1995, September). Ethics hot lines tap into more than wrongdoing. *HRMagazine*, pp. 79–85.

116. See Note 113.

117. McKeand, P. J. (1990, November). GM division builds a classic system to share internal communication. *Public Relations Journal*, pp. 24–26, 41.

118. Maley, D. (1997, October 20). Eight women at the top. *Maclean's*, p. 55.

119. See Note 118.

120. See Note 118.

Chapter 10

1. Chu, Showwei (1997/8, December/January). Freeze play. *Canadian Business*, pp. 77–78.

2. Staff Writer (1997, September). Some like it cold. *Canadian Business*, pp. 99–103 (quote, p. 100).

3. See Note 2.

4. Crawford, M. G. (1997, June). Covering the bases. *Profit: the Magazine for Canadian Entrepreneurs, 16*, pp. 66–68 (quote, p. 66).

5. See Note 2.

6. See Note 1.

7. Spence, R. (1997). *Secrets of success from Canada's fastest-growing companies*. Toronto: John Wiley & Sons Canada, Ltd., pp. 86–87.

8. See Note 2 (quote, 103).

9. Mintzberg, H. J. (1988). *Mintzberg on management: Inside our strange world of organizations*. New York: Free Press.

10. Allison, S. T., Jordan, A M. R., & Yeatts, C. E. (1992). A cluster-analytic approach toward identifying the structure and content of human decision making. *Human Relations, 45*, 49–72.

11. Harrison, E. F. (1987). *The managerial decision-making process* (3rd ed.). Boston: Houghton Mifflin.

12. Wedley, W. C., & Field, R. H. G. (1984). A predecision support system. *Academy of Management Review, 9*, 696–703.

13. Nutt, P. C. (1993). The formulation process and tactics used in organizational decision making. *Organization Science, 4*, 226–251.

14. Nutt, P. (1984). Types of organizational decision processes. *Administrative Science Quarterly, 29*, 414–450.

15. Cowan, D. A. (1986). Developing a process model of problem recognition. *Academy of Management Review, 11*, 763–776.

16. Dennis, T. L., & Dennis, L. B. (1988). *Microcomputer models for management decision making*. St. Paul, MN: West.

17. Fulk, J., & Boyd, B. (1991). Emerging theories of communication in organizations. *Journal of Management, 17*, 407–446.

18. Sainfort, F. C., Gustafson, D. H., Bosworth, K., & Hawkins, R. P. (1990). Decision support systems effectiveness: Conceptual framework and empirical evaluation. *Organizational Behavior and Human Decision Processes, 45*, 232–252.

19. Stevenson, M. K., Busemeyer, J. R., & Naylor, J. C. (1990). Judgment and decision-making theory. In M. D. Dunnette & L. M. Hough (Eds.), *Handbook of industrial and organizational psychology* (2nd ed., Vol. 1, pp. 283–374). Palo Alto, CA: Consulting Psychologists Press.

20. Rowe, A. J., Boulgaides, J. D., & McGrath, M. R. (1984). *Managerial decision making*. Chicago: Science Research Associates.

21. See Note 20.

22. Adler, N. J. (1991). *International dimensions of organizational behavior*. Boston: PWS-Kent.

23. Roth, K. (1992). Implementing international strategy at the business unit level: The role of managerial decision-making characteristics. *Journal of Management, 18*, 769–789.

24. Hill, C. W., & Jones, G. R. (1989). *Strategic management*. Boston: Houghton Mifflin.

25. See Note 13.

26. Amit, R., & Wernerfelt, B. (1990). Why do firms reduce business risk? *Academy of Management Journal, 33*, 520–533.

27. Provan, K. G. (1982). Interorganizational linkages and influence over decision making. *Academy of Management Journal, 25*, 443–451.

28. Galaskiewicz, J., & Wasserman, S. (1989). Mimetic processes within an interorganizational field: An empirical test. *Administrative Science Quarterly, 34*, 454–479.

29. Parsons, C. K. (1988). Computer technology: Implications for human resources management. In G. R.

Ferris & K. M. Rowland (Eds.), *Research in personnel and human resources management* (Vol. 6, pp. 1–36). Greenwich, CT: JAI Press.

30. Simon, H. A. (1987). Making management decisions: The role of intuition and emotion. *Academy of Management Executive, 1*, 57–64.

31. Kirschenbaum, S. S. (1992). Influence of experience on information-gathering strategies. *Journal of Applied Psychology, 77*, 343–352.

32. Simon, H. (1977). *The new science of management decisions* (2nd ed.). Englewood Cliffs, NJ: Prentice-Hall.

33. Linstone, H. A. (1984). *Multiple perspectives for decision making*. New York: North-Holland.

34. Patterson, J., & Kim, P. (1991). *The day America told the truth*. New York: Plume.

35. Dubrin, A. J. (1994). *Contemporary applied management* (4th ed.). Burr Ridge, IL: Irwin.

36. Simon, H. A. (1979). Rational decision making in organizations. *American Economic Review, 69*, 493–513.

37. March, J. G., & Simon, H. A. (1958). *Organizations*. New York: Wiley.

38. See Note 37.

39. Simon, H. A. (1957). *Models of man*. New York: Wiley.

40. Browning, E. B. (1850/1950). *Sonnets from the Portuguese*. New York: Ratchford and Fulton.

41. Mitchell, T. R., & Beach, L. R. (1990). " . . . Do I love thee? Let me count . . ." Toward an understanding of intuitive and automatic decision making. *Organizational Behavior and Human Decision Processes, 47*, 1–20.

42. Beach, L. R., & Mitchell, T. R. (1990). Image theory: A behavioral theory of image making in organizations. In B. Staw & L. L. Cummings (Eds.), *Research in organizational behavior* (Vol. 12, pp. 1–41). Greenwich, CT: JAI Press.

43. Dunegan, K. J. (1995). Image theory: Testing the role of image compatibility in progress decisions. *Organizational Behavior and Human Decision Processes, 62*, 79–86.

44. Dunegan, K. J. (1993). Framing, cognitive modes, and image theory: Toward an under-

standing of a glass half full. *Journal of Applied Psychology, 78*, 491–503.

45. Gaeth, G. J., & Shanteau, J. (1984). Reducing the influence of irrelevant information on experienced decision makers. *Organizational Behavior and Human Performance, 33*, 263–282.

46. Ginrich, G., & Soli, S. D. (1984). Subjective evaluation and allocation of resources in routine decision making. *Organizational Behavior and Human Performance, 33*, 187–203.

47. Kahneman, D., & Tversky, A. (1984). Choices, values, and frames. *American Psychologist, 39*, 341–350.

48. Highhouse, S., & Yüce, P. (1996). Perspectives, perceptions, and risk-taking behavior. *Organizational Behavior and Human Decision Processes, 65*, 159–167.

49. Frisch, D. (1993). Reasons for framing effects. *Organizational Behavior and Human Decision Processes, 54*, 399–429.

50. Nisbett, R. E., & Ross, L. (1980). *Human inference: Strategies and shortcomings of social judgment*. Englewood Cliffs, NJ: Prentice-Hall.

51. Abelson, R. P., & Levi, A. (1985). Decision-making and decision theory. In G. Lindzey & E. Aronson (Eds.), *Handbook of social psychology* (3rd ed., Vol. 1, pp. 231–309). Reading, MA: Addison-Wesley.

52. Kahneman, D., & Tversky, A. (1973). On the psychology of prediction. *Psychological Review, 80*, 251–273.

53. Gaeth, G. J., & Shanteau, J. (1984). Reducing the influence of irrelevant information on experienced decision makers. *Organizational Behavior and Human Performance, 33*, 187–203.

54. Power, D. J., & Aldag, R. J. (1985). Soelberg's job search and choice model: A clarification, review, and critique. *Academy of Management Review, 10*, 48–58.

55. Soelberg, P. O. (1967). Unprogrammed decision making. *Industrial Management Review, 8*, 19–29.

56. Langer, E., & Schank, R. C. (1994). *Belief, reasoning, and decision making*. Hillsdale, NJ: Lawrence Erlbaum Associates.

57. Conlon, D. E., & Garland, H. (1993). The role of project com-

pletion information in resource allocation decisions. *Academy of Management Journal, 36*, 402–413.

58. Ross, J., & Staw, B. M. (1986). Expo '86: An escalation prototype. *Administrative Science Quarterly, 31*, 274–297.

59. McKay, S. (1994, February). When good people make bad choices. *Canadian Business*, pp. 52–55.

60. Bobocel, D. R., & Meyer, J. P. (1994). Escalating commitment to a failing course of action: Separating the roles of choice and justification. *Journal of Applied Psychology, 79*, 360–363.

61. Staw, B. M. (1981). The escalation of commitment to a course of action. *Academy of Management Review, 6*, 577–587.

62. Whyte, G. (1993). Escalating commitment in individual and group decision making: A prospect theory approach. *Organizational Behavior and Human Decision Processes, 54*, 430–455.

63. Simonson, I., & Staw, B. M. (1992). Deescalation strategies: A comparison of techniques for reducing commitment to losing courses of action. *Journal of Applied Psychology, 77*, 419–426.

64. Garland, H., & Newport, S. (1991). Effects of absolute and relative sunk costs on the decision to persist with a course of action. *Organizational Behavior and Human Decision Processes, 48*, 55–69.

65. Whyte, G. (1991). Diffusion of responsibility: Effects on the escalation tendency. *Journal of Applied Psychology, 76*, 408–415.

66. Heath, C. (1995). Escalation and de-escalation of commitment in response to sunk costs: The role of budgeting in mental accounting. *Organizational Behavior and Human Decision Processes, 62*, 38–54.

67. Tan, H., & Yates, J. F. (1995). Sunk cost effects: The influences of instruction and future return estimates. *Organizational Behavior and Human Decision Processes, 63*, 311–319.

68. Tjosvold, D. (1984). Effects of crisis orientation on managers' approach to controversy in decision making. *Academy of Management Journal, 27*, 130–138.

69. Johnson, R. J. (1984). Conflict avoidance through

acceptable decisions. *Human Relations, 27*, 71–82.

70. Neustadt, R. E., & Fineberg, H. (1978). *The swine flu affair: Decision making on a slippery disease*. Washington, DC: U.S. Department of Health, Education and Welfare.

71. Shull, F. A., Delbecq, A. L., & Cummings, L. L. (1970). *Organizational decision making*. New York: McGraw-Hill.

72. Sonnenberg, F. K. (1994). *Managing with a conscience*. New York: McGraw-Hill.

73. Davis, J. H. (1992). Introduction to the special issue on group decision making. *Organizational Behavior and Human Decision Processes, 52*, 1–2.

74. Delbecq, A. L., Van de Ven, A. H., & Gustafson, D. H. (1975). *Group techniques for program planning*. Glenview, IL: Scott, Foresman.

75. Murninghan, J. K. (1981). Group decision making: What strategies should you use? *Management Review, 25*, 56–62.

76. Hill, G. W. (1982). Group versus individual performance: Are N + 1 heads better than one? *Psychological Bulletin, 91*, 517–539.

77. Wanous, J. P., & Youtz, M. A. (1986). Solution diversity and the quality of group decisions. *Academy of Management Journal, 29*, 149–159.

78. Yetton, P., & Bottger, P. (1983). The relationships among group size, member ability, social decision schemes, and performance. *Organizational Behavior and Human Performance, 32*, 145–149.

79. Michaelsen, L. K., Watson, W. E., & Black, R. H. (1989). A realistic test of individual versus group consensus decision making. *Journal of Applied Psychology, 74*, 834–839.

80. See Note 76.

81. See Note 76.

82. Osborn, A. F. (1957). *Applied imagination*. New York: Scribner's.

83. Bouchard, T. J., Jr., Barsaloux, J., & Drauden, G. (1974). Brainstorming procedure, group size, and sex as determinants of the problem-solving effectiveness of groups and individuals. *Journal of Applied Psychology, 59*, 135–138.

84. Janis, I. L. (1982). *Groupthink: Psychological*

studies of policy decisions and fiascoes (2nd ed.). Boston: Houghton Mifflin.

85. Aldag, R. J., & Fuller, S. R. (1993). Beyond fiasco: A reappraisal of the groupthink phenomenon and a new model of group decision processes. *Psychological Bulletin, 113,* 533–552.

86. Morehead, G., Ference, R., & Neck, C. P. (1991). Group decision fiascoes continue: Space shuttle Challenger and a revised groupthink framework. *Human Relations, 44,* 539–550.

87. Brown-John, L. (1993, August 6). Party politics: Only outsiders get to make real decisions. *Calgary Herald,* p. A5.

88. Janis, I. L. (1988). *Crucial decisions: Leadership in policy making and crisis management.* New York: Free Press.

89. Morehead, G., & Montanari, J. R. (1986). An empirical investigation of the groupthink phenomenon. *Human Relations, 39,* 399–410.

90. Schweiger, D. M., Sandberg, W. R., & Ragan, J. W. (1986). Group approaches for improving strategic decision making: A comparative analysis of dialectical inquiry, devil's advocacy, and consensus. *Academy of Management Journal, 29,* 51–71.

91. Schweiger, D. M., Sandberg, W. R., & Rechner, P. L. (1989). Experiential effects of dialectical inquiry, devil's advocacy, and consensus approaches to strategic decision making. *Academy of Management Journal, 32,* 745–772.

92. Cosier, R. A., & Schwenk, C. R. (1990). Agreement and thinking alike: Ingredients for poor decisions. *Academy of Management Executive, 4,* 69–74.

93. Silcoff, S. (1997, April). The sky's your limit. *Canadian Business, 70,* pp. 58–66 (quote, p. 64).

94. Sloan, A. P., Jr. (1964). *My years with General Motors.* New York: Doubleday.

95. Bottger, P. C., & Yetton, P. W. (1987). Improving group performance by training in individual problem solving. *Journal of Applied Psychology, 72,* 651–657.

96. Dalkey, N. (1969). *The Delphi method: An experimental study of group decisions.* Santa Monica, CA: Rand Corporation.

97. Wiener, E. L. (1993). Crew coordination and training in the ad-

vanced-technology cockpit. In E. L. Wiener, B. G. Kanki, & R. L. Helmreich (Eds.). *Cockpit resource management* (pp. 199–230). San Diego: Academic Press.

98. Kayten, P. J. (1993). The accident investigator's perspective. In E. L. Wiener, B. G. Kanki, & R. L. Helmreich (1993). *Cockpit resource management* (pp. 283–314). San Diego: Academic Press.

99. Lee, A. T. (1991). Aircrew decision-making behavior in hazardous weather avoidance. *Aviation, Space, and Environmental Medicine, 15,* 158–161.

100. Van de Ven, A. H., & Delbecq, A. L. (1971). Nominal versus interacting group processes for committee decision making effectiveness. *Academy of Management Journal, 14,* 203–212.

101. See Note 100.

102. Gustafson, D. H., Shulka, R. K., Delbecq, A., & Walster, W. G. (1973). A comparative study of differences in subjective likelihood estimates made by individuals, interacting groups, Delphi groups, and nominal groups. *Organizational Behavior and Human Performance, 9,* 280–291.

103. Ulshak, F. L., Nathanson, L., & Gillan, P. B. (1981). *Small group problem solving: An aid to organizational effectiveness.* Reading, MA: Addison-Wesley.

104. Harmon, J., Schneer, J. A., & Hoffman, L. R. (1995). Electronic meetings and established decision groups: Audioconferencing effects on performance and structural stability. *Organizational Behavior and Human Decision Processes, 61,* 138–147.

105. Willis, R. E. (1979). A simulation of multiple selection using nominal group procedures. *Management Science, 25,* 171–181.

106. Van de Ven, A. H., & Delbecq, A. L. (1974). The effectiveness of nominal, Delphi, and interacting group decision making processes. *Academy of Management Journal, 17,* 605–621.

107. Stumpf, S. A., Zand, D. E., & Freedman, R. D. (1979). Designing groups for judgmental decisions. *Academy of Management Review, 4,* 589–600.

108. Rogelberg, S. G., Barnes-Farrell, J. L., & Lowe, C. A.

(1992). The stepladder technique: An alternative group structure facilitating effective group decision making. *Journal of Applied Psychology, 77,* 730–737.

109. Segal, H. (1998, August 22). Generation Gap in Quebec Politics. *Financial Post Daily, 11,* p. 19.

Chapter 11

1. This case was excerpted from Parker, J. (1995, January 17). Truce tames chemical warfare. *The Globe and Mail,* p. B32. Reprinted with permission of *The Globe and Mail.*

2. Parker, J. (1995, January 17). Truce tames chemical warfare. *The Globe and Mail,* p. B32.

3. Argyle, M. (1991). *Cooperation: The basis of sociability.* London: Routledge.

4. Deutsch, M. (1990). Sixty years of conflict. *International Journal of Conflict Management, 1,* 237–263.

5. Organ, D. W. (1988). *Organizational citizenship behavior.* Lexington, MA: Lexington Books.

6. Evan, W. M., & Olk, P. (1990). R&D consortia: A new U.S. organizational form. *Sloan Management Review, 31,* 37–46.

7. Thomas, K. W. (1992). Conflict and negotiation processes in organizations. In M. D. Dunnette & L. M. Hough (Eds.), *Handbook of industrial and organizational psychology* (2nd ed., Vol. 3, pp. 651–718). Palo Alto, CA: Consulting Psychologists Press.

8. Baron, R. A. (1995). Workplace aggression and workplace violence: Their nature and scope. Paper presented at the Meetings of the Academy of Management, Vancouver, British Columbia, August, 1995.

9. Spacapan, S., & Oskamp, S. (Eds.). (1992). *Helping and being helped.* Newbury Park, CA: Sage.

10. Stueck, W. (1998, September 4). Image issue lands on grounded pilots. *The Globe and Mail,* p. B21.

11. George, J. T., & Brief, A. P. (1992). Feeling good—doing good: A conceptual analysis of the mood at work-organizational spontaneity relationship. *Psychological Bulletin, 112,* 310–329.

12. See Note 3.

13. See Note 11.

14. Morrison, E. W. (1994). Role definitions and organizational citizenship behavior: The importance of employee's perspective. *Academy of Management Journal, 37,* 1543–1567.

15. Konovsky, M. A., & Pugh, S. D. (1994). Citizenship behavior and social exchange. *Academy of Management Journal, 37,* 656–689.

16. See Note 11.

17. See Note 14.

18. Ball, G. A., Trevino, K. K., & Sims, H. P., Jr. (1994). Just and unjust punishment: Influences on subordinate performance and citizenship. *Academy of Management Journal, 37,* 299–322.

19. Katz, D. (1964). The motivational basis of organizational behavior. *Behavioral Science, 9,* 131–133.

20. See Note 5.

21. Fombrun, C., & Shanley, M. (1990). What's in a name? Reputation building and corporate strategy. *Academy of Management Journal, 33,* 233–258.

22. Near, J. P., & Miceli, M. P. (1985). Organizational dissidence: The case of whistle-blowing. *Journal of Business Ethics, 4,* 1–16.

23. Taylor, P. (1998, August 13). A doctor takes on a drug company. *The Globe and Mail,* pp. A1, A4.

24. See Note 23.

25. Glazer, M. P., & Glazer, P. M. (1989). *The Whistle blowers: Exposing corruption in government and industry.* New York: Basic Books; Stainsbury, M. (1990, June 2). Blowing the whistle and paying the price. *Vancouver Sun,* pp. D1, D8; McHugh, M. (1991, August 26). Blowing the whistle on company can be risky venture. *Financial Post,* p. 2; Staff Writer (1994, November 28). Blowing the whistle. *Maclean's,* p. 41.

26. Millan, L. (1994, June 20). Quebec whistle-blowing case raises need for legislation. *Canadian HR Reporter,* pp. 1–2.

27. Eoin, K. (1998, February 22). MLA wants bill to protect those who speak up. *Canadian Press Newswire;* Staff Writer (1997, August 7). Public service whistle-blowers need legal protection. *Canadian Press Newswire.*

28. Kernaghan, K. (1991). Whistle-blowing in Canadian governments: ethical, political and managerial considerations. *Optimum: The Journal of Public Sector Management*, pp. 34–43.

29. Gibb-Clark, M. (1995, September 21). 'Snitch line' called insult. *The Globe and Mail*, p. B5.

30. See Note 29.

31. Yates, R. E. (1995, July 7). Whistle-blowers pay dearly for heroics. *Chicago Tribune*, pp. 16, 18, 20.

32. Forsyth, D. R. (1983). *An introduction to group dynamics.* Monterey, CA: Brooks/Cole.

33. Ring, P. S., & Van de Ven, A. (1994). Developmental processes of cooperative interorganizational relationships. *Academy of Management Review*, 19, 90–118.

34. Tjosvold, D. (1986). *Working together to get things done.* Lexington, MA: Lexington Books.

35. Gouldner, A. W. (1960). The norm of reciprocity: A preliminary statement. *American Sociological Review*, 25, 161–178.

36. Youngs, G. A., Jr. (1986). Patterns of threat and punishment reciprocity in a conflict setting. *Journal of Personality and Social Psychology*, 51, 541–546.

37. McAllister, D. J. (1995). Affect- and cognition-based trust as foundations for interpersonal cooperation in organizations. *Academy of Management Journal*, 38, 24–59.

38. Smith, K. G., Carrol, S. J., & Ashford, S. J. (1995). Intra- and interorganizational cooperation: Toward a research agenda. *Academy of Management Journal*, 38, 7–23.

39. Korsgaard, M. A., Schweiger, D. M., & Sapienza, H. J. (1995). Building commitment, attachment, and trust in strategic decision-making teams: The role of procedural justice. *Academy of Management Journal*, 38, 60–84.

40. See Note. 37.

41. See Note 39.

42. Knight, G. P., & Dubro, A. F. (1984). Cooperative, competitive, and individualistic social values: An individualized regression and clustering approach. *Journal of Personality and Social Psychology*, 46, 98–105.

43. See Note 42.

44. Hofstede, G. (1980). *Culture's consequences: International differences in work-related value.* Beverly Hills, CA: Sage.

45. Wagner, J. A., III. (1995). Studies on individualism-collectivism: Effects on cooperation in groups. *Academy of Management Journal*, 38, 152–172.

46. Peters, T. J., & Waterman, R. H., Jr. (1982). *In search of excellence: Lessons from America's best-run companies.* New York: Warner Books.

47. Cheng, J. L. (1983). Interdependence and coordination in organizations: A role-system analysis. *Academy of Management Journal*, 26, 156–162.

48. This is excerpted from: Sheppard, R. (1998, March 3). Energy giants learn to trade the right to spew. *The Globe and Mail*, p. B13. Reprinted by permission.

49. See Note 7.

50. Thomas, K. W., & Schmidt, W. H. (1976). A survey of managerial interests with respect to conflict. *Academy of Management Journal*, 10, 315–318.

51. Mamis, R. A. (1994, June). Partner wars: Six true confessions. *Inc.*, 36–42.

52. Walton, R. S., & McKersie, R. B. (1965). *A behavioral theory of labor negotiations: An analysis of a social interaction system.* New York: McGraw-Hill.

53. Thomas, K. W. (1976). Conflict and conflict management. In M. D. Dunnette (Ed.), *Handbook of industrial and organizational psychology* (pp. 889–935). Chicago: Rand McNally.

54. Rahim, M. A. (1983). A measure of styles of handling interpersonal conflict. *Academy of Management Journal*, 26, 368–376.

55. Ting-Toomey, S. (1988). Intercultural conflict styles: A face-negotiation theory. In Y. Kim & W. Gudykunst (Eds.), *Theories in intercultural communication* (pp. 213–235). Newbury Park, CA: Sage.

56. See Note 34.

57. Sprouse, M. (1992). *Sabotage in the American workplace.* San Francisco: Pressure Drop Press.

58. Johnson, T. E., & Rule, B. G. (1986). Mitigating circumstance information, censure, and aggression. *Journal of Personality and Social Psychology*, 50, 537–542.

59. Baron, R. A. (1988). Negative effects of destructive criticism: Impact on conflict, self-efficacy, and task performance. *Journal of Applied Psychology*, 73, 199–207.

60. Baron, R.A. (1990). Countering the effects of destructive criticism: The relative efficacy of four potential interventions. *Journal of Applied Psychology*, 75, 235–245.

61. Pescarella, P. (1993, February 1). 15 ways to win people's trust. *Nation's Business*, pp. 47–51.

62. Levering, R., & Moskowitz, M. (1993). *The 100 best companies to work for in America.* New York: Currency Doubleday.

63. Baron, R. A. (1989). Personality and organizational conflict: Effects of the type A behavior pattern and self-monitoring. *Organizational Behavior and Human Decision Processes*, 44, 281–297.

64. Fodor, E. M. (1976). Group stress, authoritarian style of control and use of power. *Journal of Applied Psychology*, 61, 313–318.

65. Tjosvold, D. (1985). Implications of controversy research for management. *Journal of Management*, 11, 21–37.

66. Robbins, S. P. (1974). *Managing organizational conflict: A nontraditional approach.* Englewood Cliffs, NJ: Prentice-Hall.

67. Schwenk, C. R., & Cosier, R. A. (1980). Effects of the expert, devil's advocate, and dialectical inquiry methods of prediction performance. *Organizational Behavior and Human Decision Processes*, 26, 409–424.

68. Baron, R. A. (in press). Positive effects of conflict: Insights from social cognition. In C. K. W. deDreu & E. Van de Vliert (Eds.), *Conflict escalation and organizational performance.* Thousand Oaks, CA: Sage.

69. Cosier, R. A., & Dalton, D. R. (1990). Positive effects of conflict: A field assessment. *International Journal of Conflict Management*, 1, 81–92.

70. Lewicki, R. J., & Litterer, J. A. (1985). *Negotiation.* Homewood, IL: Irwin.

71. See Note 70.

72. Lewicki, R. J., Weiss, S. E., & Lewin, D. (1992). Models of conflict, negotiation, and third party intervention: A review and synthesis. *Journal of Organizational Behavior*, 13, 209–252.

73. Chertkoff, J. M.., & Baird, S. L. (1971). Applicability of the big lie technique and the last clear chance doctrine to bargaining. *Journal of Personality and Social Psychology*, 20, 298–303.

74. Chertkoff, J. M., & Conley, M. (1967). Opening offer and frequency of concessions as bargaining strategies. *Journal of Personality and Social Psychology*, 7, 181–185.

75. Pinkley, R., & Northcraft, G. B. (1994). Conflict frames of reference: Implications for dispute processes and outcomes. *Academy of Management Journal*, 78, 193–205.

76. Pinkley, R. (1990). Dimensions of conflict frame: Disputant interpretations of conflict. *Journal of Applied Psychology*, 75, 117–126.

77. Huber, V. L., Neale, M. A., & Northcraft, G. G. (1987). Decision bias and personnel selection strategies. *Organizational Behavior and Human Decision Processes*, 40, 136–147.

78. See Note 76.

79. Thompson, L., & Hastie, R. (1990). Social perception in negotiation. *Organizational Behavior and Human Decision Processes*, 47, 98–123.

80. Thompson, L., & Hastie, R. (1990). Judgment tasks and biases in negotiation. In B. H. Sheppard, M. H. Bazerman, & R. J. Lewicki (Eds.), *Research on negotiation in organizations* (Vol. 2, pp. 1077–1092). Greenwich, CT: JAI Press.

81. See Note 80.

82. See Note 52.

83. Tjosvold, D. (1991). *The conflict-positive organization.* Reading, MA: Addison-Wesley.

84. Thomas, K. W. (1992). Conflict and conflict management: Reflections and update. *Journal of Organizational Behavior*, 13, 265–274.

85. Overman, S. (1993). Why grapple with the cloudy elephant? *HR Magazine*, pp. 60–65.

86. See Note 84.

87. Fiske, S. T., & Taylor, S. E. (1991). *Social cognition* (2nd ed.). Reading, MA: Addison-Wesley.

88. Sherif, M., Harvey, O. J., White, B. J., Hood, W. E., & Sherif, C. W. (1961). *Intergroup conflict and cooperation: The Robbers Cave experiment*. Norman, OK: Institute of Group Relations.

89. Tully, S. (1995, February 20). Purchasing's new muscle. *Fortune*, pp. 75–76, 78–79, 82–83.

90. Bergman, B., Howse, J., & Selleck, L. (1993, November 1). Tragic scars. *Maclean's*, pp. 26, 28.

91. Staff Writer (1994, October 26). Warren confessed. *The Globe and Mail*, p. A2; Staff Writer (1993, October 19). Striker charged in death of 9 miners. *Toronto Star*, p. A2.

92. See Note 91.

93. See Note 90.

94. Ramachandran, D. (1998, July 19). Canada ranks high for reported workplace violence. *Canadian Press Newswire*.

95. Brady, M. (1998, January 10). Lawyers as victims. *Financial Post, 91*, pp. 24–25 (quote, p. 25).

96. See Note 95 (quote, p. 24).

97. Staff Writer (1998, July 26). Health professionals warned against increasing violence. *Canadian Press Newswire*.

98. Bjorkqvist, K., Osterman, K., & Lagerspetz, K. M. J. (1994). Sex differences in covert aggression among adults. *Aggressive Behavior, 20*, 27–33.

99. Neuman, J. H., & Baron, R. A. (in press). Aggression in the workplace. In Giacalone, R. A., & Greenberg, J. (Eds.), *Antisocial behavior in organizations*. Thousand Oaks, CA: Sage.

100. Anderson, C. A., Deuser, W. E., & DeNeve, K. M. (1995). Hot temperatures, hostile affect, hostile cognition, and arousal: Tests of a general model of affective aggression. *Personality and Social Psychology Bulletin, 21*, 434–448.

101. Dodge, K. A., Price, J. M., Bachorowski, J. A., & Newman, J. P. (1990). Hostile attributional biases in severely aggressive adolescents. *Journal of Abnormal Psychology, 99*, 385–392.

102. Greenberg, J., & Scott, K. S. (1995). Why do workers bite the hands that feed them?

Employee theft as a social exchange process. In B. M. Staw & L. L. Cummings (Eds.), *Research in organizational behavior* (Vol. 18, pp. 1–46). Greenwich, CT: JAI Press.

103. Baron, R. A. (1994). The physical environment of work settings: Effects in task performance, interpersonal relations, and job satisfaction. In R. M. Staw & L. L. Cummings (Eds.), *Research in organizational behavior* (Vol. 16, pp. 1–46). Greenwich, CT: JAI Press.

104. Baron, R. A., & Neuman, J. H. (1990). Workplace violence and workplace aggression: Evidence on their relative frequency and potential causes. *Aggressive Behavior, 22*, 161–173.

105. Brockner, J., Grover, S., Reed, T., & Dewitt, R. L. (1992). Layoffs, job insecurity, and survivors' work effort: Evidence of an inverted-U relationship. *Academy of Management Journal, 35*, 413–425.

106. Tsui, A., Egan, T., & O'Reilly, C. O., III. (1992). Being different: Relational demography and organizational attachment. *Administrative Science Quarterly, 37*, 549–579.

107. Folger, R., & Skarlicki, D. (1995, August). *A popcorn model of workplace violence*. Paper presented at the meetings of the Academy of Management, Vancouver, British Columbia, Canada.

108. Arvey, R. D., & Jones, A. P. (1985). The use of discipline in organizational settings: A framework for future research. In L. L. Cummings & B. M. Staw (Eds.), *Research in organizational behavior* (Vol. 7, pp. 367–408). Greenwich, CT: JAI Press.

109. Greenberg, J. (1993b). The social side of fairness: Interpersonal and informational classes of justice. In R. Cropanzano (Ed.), *Justice in the workplace: Approaching fairness in human resource management*. Hillsdale, NJ: Lawrence Erlbaum.

110. Mantell, M., & Albrecht, S. (1994). *Ticking bombs: Defusing violence in the workplace*. New York: Irwin.

111. Wolfe, M. (1994, July/August). Dr. Fabrikant's solution. *Saturday Night*, pp. 11–18, 56–59; and Lalonde, M. (1992, August 30). Man who hired Fabrikant says he has no regrets: Background helped land research job at Concordia. *The Montreal Gazette*, p. A3.

112. Kaihla, P. (1992, November). Concordia's trials: savage killings rocked a proud institution already troubled by controversy about the ethics in Engineering. *Maclean's*, pp. 52–55.

113. Adolph, C. (1992, August 5). Teacher's colleagues feared him: Psychiatrist said he just wants attention. *The Montreal Gazette*, pp. A1, A5.

114. See Note 113 (quote, p. A5).

115. Adolph, C. (1992, August 28). We couldn't fire Fabrikant, rector says. *The Montreal Gazette*, p. A1.

116. Staff Writer (1993, August 12). Fabrikant imprisoned for life. *The Globe and Mail*, p. A4.

117. Picard, A. (1993, September 23). Concordia sets up inquiry into murderer's allegations. *The Globe and Mail*, p. A4; Mackie, R. (1994, June 8). Fabrikant complaints supported: research-grant system at universities needs change, report says. *The Globe and Mail*, p. A1; Came, B. (1994, June 20). Publish and perish: A report at Concordia slams the pressures to produce. *Maclean's*, p. 15; Mackie, R. (1994, July 16). Audit backs Fabrikant allegations: Three professors cited agree to leave Concordia. *The Globe and Mail*, p. A4.

118. Young, L. (1998). Workplace violence: beyond the breaking point. *Occupational Health and Safety, 13*, pp. 38–40 (quote, p. 40).

Part 4 Cumulative Case

1. Durrant, Ellen (1998, November 27). E-mail correspondence.

2. Kocho, Keith (1999, January 27). Telephone interview.

3. Flavelle, D. (1996, November 11). A New Company Style. *The Toronto Star*, p. C1.

4. *The Digital Renaissance Development Primer*, Version 3.0 (1997, February), p. 1.

5. Digital Renaissance Website. Project Manager, Internet: www.digital-ren.com/joinus/ job_details.asp?id=9&page_id=200 Creative Lead, Internet: www.digital-ren.com/joinus/job_details.asp?id=26&page_id=200 Functional Lead, Internet: www.digital-ren.com/joinus/job_details.asp?id=18&page_id=200 Technical Lead, Internet: www.digital-ren.com/joinus/job_details.asp?id=27&page-id=200

6. See Note 2.

7. Kocho, Keith (1999, January 20). Telephone interview.

8. See Note 2.

Chapter 12

1. Dabbs, F. (1988, July 5). "Buchaneering" PetroCan chief hasn't changed. *Financial Post*, p. 21.

2. Enchin, H. (1990, November 19). City slicker pushing Ottawa out of oil patch. *The Globe and Mail*, p. B7.

3. See Note 2.

4. McCarthy, S. (1990, October 2). Bill tabled to sell off Petrocan. *Toronto Star*, pp. E1–E2.

5. Motherwell, C. (1991, August 2). Petrocan thrashing in "blood bath" waters. *The Globe and Mail*, pp. B1, B4.

6. Newman, P. C. (1992, February 17). Bill Hopper's blunt and telling prescription. *Maclean's*, p. 38.

7. Hutchinson, B. (1992, April 27). The emperor of Petrocan: A disgruntled Petrocanner attacks his boss's lavish ways. *Western Report*, p. 16.

8. See Note 7.

9. Motherwell, C. (1992, May 6). Investors assail Petrocan bosses: More jobs to go in push to recovery. *The Globe and Mail*, pp. B1, B4.

10. Carlisle, T. (1993, January 30). Why was Hopper given the shove? *The Financial Post*, p. 4.

11. Foster, P. (1992, September). The best friends money can buy. *Canadian Business*, p. 84.

12. Haliechuk, R. (1993, January 30). Firing of PetroCan's Hopper linked to investor discontent. *Toronto Star*, p. C1.

13. See Note 12.

14. Motherwell, C., & Fagan, D. (1993, January 30). Petrocan mum on Hopper firing. *The Globe and Mail*, p. A1.

15. Fotheringham, A. (1993, February 18). Patronage appointments alive and well in Ottawa. *The Financial Post Daily*, p. 15.

16. Hutchinson, B. (1993, February 15). Hopper gets the gate. *Western Report*, p. 23.

17. Cobb, A. T. (1984). An episodic model of power: Toward an integration of theory

and research. *Academy of Management Review, 9*, 482–493.

18. Mayes, B. T., & Allen, R. T. (1977). Toward a definition of organizational politics. *Academy of Management Review, 2*, 672–678.

19. Mintzberg, H. (1983). *Power in and around organizations*. Englewood Cliffs, NJ: Prentice-Hall.

20. Schriesheim, C. A., & Hinkin, T. R. (1990). Influence tactics used by subordinates: A theoretical and empirical analysis and refinement of the Kipnis, Schmidt, and Wilkinson subscales. *Journal of Applied Psychology, 75*, 246–257.

21. Yukl, G., & Tracey, J. B. (1992). Consequences of influence tactics used with subordinates, peers, and the boss. *Journal of Applied Psychology, 77*, 525–535.

22. Yukl, G., Falbe, C. M., & Youn, J. Y. (1993). Patterns of influence behavior for managers. *Group & Organization Management, 18*, 5–28.

23. Falbe, C. M., & Yukl, G. (1992). Consequences for managers of using single influence tactics and combinations of tactics. *Academy of Management Journal, 35*, 638–652.

24. Offermann, L. R. (1990). Power and leadership in organizations. *American Psychologist, 45*, 179–189.

25. Ansari, M. A., & Kapoor, A. (1987). Organizational context and upward influence tactics. *Organizational Behavior and Human Decision Processes, 40*, 39–49.

26. DND, SJ 70–216.

27. Podsakoff, P. M., & Schriesheim, C. A. (1985). Field studies of French and Raven's bases of power: Critique, reanalysis, and suggestions for future research. *Psychological Bulletin, 97*, 387–411.

28. Huber, V. L. (1981). The sources, uses, and conservation of managerial power. *Personnel, 51*(4), 62–67.

29. Kipnis, D., Schmidt, S. M., Swaffin-Smith, C., & Wilkinson, I. (1984, winter). Patterns of managerial influence: Shotgun managers, tacticians, and bystanders. *Organizational Dynamics*, 58–67.

30. Cole, Trevor (1998, July). Canada's 25 most powerful corporate leaders. *The Globe and Mail Report on Business Magazine*, p. 88+. Reprinted with permission.

31. Stewart, T. (1989, November 6). CEOs see clout shifting. *Fortune*, p. 66.

32. Kahn, R. L., Wolfe, D. M., Quinn, R. P., Snoek, J. D., & Rosenthal, R. A. (1964). *Organizational stress: Studies in role conflict and ambiguity*. New York: Wiley.

33. See Note 27.

34. McFarland, J. (1997, December 9). Bullies cling to old ways. *The Globe and Mail*, p. B12.

35. Symonds, W. C., & Siler, J. F. (1991, April 1). CEO disease. *Business Week*, pp. 52–60; Where We Are: Worldwide Locations: www.abbott.com/about/list of locations.htm#Canada.

36. Morris, S. (1990, March 13). Abbott boss's suit points to a trend. *Chicago Tribune*, Business Section, p. 1.

37. O'Brien, D., & Pace, J. (1990). The role of empowerment in social work degree programs for indigenous native people: A critique of one school's experience. *The Canadian Journal of Native Studies*, pp. 1–13.

38. Hogg, D. (1993, May). Power to the people. *CMA Magazine*, pp. 26–29.

39. Ford, R. C., & Fottler, M. D. (1995). Empowerment: A matter of degree. *Academy of Management Executive, 9*, 21–29.

40. Dumaine, B. (1990, May 7). Who needs a boss? *Fortune*, pp. 52–54, 56, 58, 60.

41. Shipper, F., & Manz, C. C. (1991). Employee self-management without formally designated teams: An alternative road to empowerment. *Organizational Dynamics, 20*(3), 48–61.

42. Sherman, J. (1994). *In the rings of Saturn*. New York: Oxford University Press.

43. Dumaine, B. (1993, February 22). The new non-manager managers. *Fortune*, pp. 80–84.

44. Gresov, C., & Stephens, C. (1993). The context of interunit influence attempts. *Administrative Science Quarterly, 38*, 252–276.

45. Pfeffer, J., & Salancik, G. (1978). *The external control of organizations*. New York: Harper & Row.

46. Salancik, G., & Pfeffer, J. (1974). The bases and uses of power in organizational decision-making. *Administrative Science Quarterly, 19*, 453–473.

47. Lawrence, P. R., & Lorsch, J. W. (1967). *Organization and environment*. Cambridge, MA: Harvard University Press.

48. Hickson, D. J., Astley, W. G., Butler, R. J., & Wilson, D. C. (1981). Organization as power. In L. L. Cummings & B. M. Staw (Eds.), *Research in organizational behavior* (Vol. 4, pp. 151–196). Greenwich, CT: JAI Press.

49. Miles, R. H. (1980). *Macro organizational behavior*. Glenview, IL: Scott, Foresman.

50. Saunders, C. S., & Scarmell, R. (1982). Intraorganizational distributions of power: Replication research. *Academy of Management Journal, 25*, 192–200.

51. Hinings, C. R., Hickson, D. J., Pennings, J. M., & Schneck, R. E. (1974). Structural conditions of intraorganizational power. *Academy of Management Journal, 19*, 22–44.

52. See Note 18.

53. Drory, A., & Romm, T. (1990). The definition of organizational politics: A review. *Human Relations, 43*, 1133–1154.

54. Ferris, G. R., & Kacmar, K. M. (1992). Perceptions of organizational politics. *Journal of Management, 18*, 93–116.

55. Mulder, M., de Jong, R. D., Koppelaar, L., & Verhage, J. (1986). Power, situation, and leaders' effectiveness: An organizational field study. *Journal of Applied Psychology, 71*, 566–570.

56. Feldman, S. P. (1988). Secrecy, information, and politics: An essay in organizational decision making. *Human Relations, 41*, 73–90.

57. Greenberg, J. (1990). Looking fair vs. being fair: Managing impressions of organizational justice. In B. M. Staw & L. L. Cummings (Eds.), *Research in organizational behavior* (Vol. 12, pp. 111–157). Greenwich, CT: JAI Press.

58. Ferris, G. R., & King, T. R. (1991). Politics in human resources decisions: A walk on the dark side. *Organizational Dynamics, 20*, 59–71.

59. Boeker, W. (1992). Power and managerial dismissal: Scapegoating at the top. *Administrative Science Quarterly, 37*, 400–421.

60. Cobb, A. T. (1991). Toward the study of organizational coalitions: Participant concerns and activities in a simulated organizational setting. *Human Relations, 44*, 1057–1079.

61. Feldman, S. P. (1988). Secrecy, information, and politics: An essay in organizational decision making. *Human Relations, 41*, 73–90.

62. Liden, R. C., & Mitchell, T. R. (1988). Ingratiatory behaviors in organizational settings. *Academy of Management Review, 13*, 572–587.

63. See Note 19.

64. Sprouse, M. (1992). *Sabotage in the American workplace*. San Francisco: Pressure Drop Press.

65. Madison, D. L., Allen, R. W., Porter, L. W., Renwick, P. A., & Mayes, B. T. (1980). Organizational politics: An exploration of managers perceptions. *Human Relations, 33*, 79–100.

66. Pfeffer, J. (1992). *Managing with power*. Boston: Harvard Business School.

67. See Note 54.

68. Wayne, S. J., & Ferris, G. R. (1990). Influence tactics, affect, and exchange quality in supervisor-subordinate interactions. *Journal of Applied Psychology, 75*, 487–499.

69. See Note 58.

70. Bartol, K. M., & Martin, D. C. (1990). When politics pays: Factors influencing managerial compensation decisions. *Personnel Psychology, 43*, 599–614.

71. Gray, B., & Ariss, S. S. (1985). Politics and strategic change across organizational life cycles. *Academy of Management Review, 10*, 707–723.

72. Hannan, M. T., & Freeman, J. H. (1978). Internal politics of growth and decline. In M. W. Meyer (Ed.), *Environment and organizations* (pp. 177–199). San Francisco: Jossey-Bass.

73. See Note 58.

74. Gandz, J., & Murray, V. V. (1980). The experience of workplace politics. *Academy of Management Journal, 23*, 237–251.

75. Allen, R. W., Madison, D. L., Porter, L. W., Renwick, P. A., & Mayes, B. T. (1979). Organizational politics: Tactics and characteristics of its actors. *California Management Review, 22*, 77–83.

76. See Note 58.

77. See Note 74.

78. Kipnis, D. (1976). *The powerholders*. Chicago: University of Chicago Press.

79. Buchholz, R. A. (1989). *Fundamental concepts and problems in business ethics*. Englewood Cliffs, NJ: Prentice-Hall.

80. Gellerman, S. W. (1986, July–August). Why "good" managers make bad ethical choices. *Harvard Business Review*, pp. 85–90.

81. Velasquez, M., Moberg, D. J., & Cavanaugh, G. F. (1983). Organizational statesmanship and dirty politics: Ethical guidelines for the organizational politician. *Organizational Dynamics*, 11, 65–79.

82. See Note 57.

83. Greenberg, J. (1982). Approaching equity and avoiding inequity in groups and organizations. In J. Greenberg & R. L. Cohen (Eds.), *Equity and justice in social behavior* (pp. 389–435). New York: Academic Press.

84. Commerce Clearing House (1991, June 26). *1991 SHRM/CCH survey*. Chicago: Author.

85. Kumar, P., & Ghadially, R. (1989). Organizational politics and its effects on members of organizations. *Human Relations*, 42, 305–314.

86. Andrews, G. (1994, September). Mistrust, the hidden obstacle to empowerment. *HRMagazine*, pp. 66–68, 70.

87. Hoover, G., Campbell, A., & Spain, P. J. (1994). *Hoover's handbook of American business*. Austin, TX: Reference Press; Vlasic, B., Kerwin, K., Naughton, K., & Woodruff, D. (1995, October 16). Fighting Bob. *Business Week*, pp. 88–90, 92, 95.

88. Press Release: Merger Agreement Signed, www2.chryslercorp.com/daimlerchrysler/index.html.

89. Staff Writer (1998, June 1). People, cultures must mesh in megamerger. *Automotive News*, 71, pp. 42–43 (quote, p. 42).

90. Taylor, Alex (1998, June 8). Gentlemen, start your engines. *Fortune*, 137, pp. 138–146 (quote, p. 140).

Chapter 13

1. Chamberlain, A. (1994, October 2). GM Chief praised as 'tenacious'. *Toronto Star*, p. A10.

2. See Note 1.

3. See Note 1.

4. Staff Writer (1995, July). 25 most powerful CEOs. *Globe and Mail Report on Business Magazine*, p. 65.

5. Fowlie, L. (1994, November 5/7). New GM Canada boss quickly wins the respect of 'car guys'. *The Financial Post*, p. A10.

6. Pritchard, T. (1994, September 24). New GM Canada boss sets her sights on marketing. *The Globe and Mail*, p. B5.

7. See Note 1.

8. See Note 1.

9. See Note 6.

10. Law, A. (1994, October 22). New boss brings reality check to GM. *Toronto Star*, p. J9.

11. See Notes 1, 5, 10, and 12.

12. Posner, M. (1997, December). The 28 billion dollar woman. *Chatelaine*, 70, pp. 70–75 (quote, p. 75).

13. Yukl, G. (1994). *Leadership in organizations* (3rd ed.). Englewood Cliffs, NJ: Prentice-Hall.

14. House, R. J., & Podsakoff, P. M. (1995). Leadership effectiveness: Past perspectives and future directions for research. In J. Greenberg (Ed.), *Organizational behavior: The state of the science* (pp. 45–82). Hillsdale, NJ: Lawrence Erlbaum Associates.

15. Bass, B. M. (1990). *Bass and Stogdill's handbook of leadership* (3rd ed.). New York: Free Press.

16. Bennis, W. G., & Nanus, B. (1985). *Leaders: The strategies for taking charge*. New York: Harper & Row (quote, p. 4).

17. See Note 13.

18. Locke, E. A. (1991). *The essence of leadership*. New York: Lexington Books.

19. Cialdini, R. B. (1988). *Influence* (2nd ed.). Glenview, IL: Scott, Foresman.

20. Kotter, J. P. (1990). *A force for change: How leadership differs from management*. New York: The Free Press.

21. Smith, Vivian (1998, April). Canada's most respected corporations: Money talks. *The Globe and Mail Report On Business Magazine*, pp. 97–100 (quotes, pp. 99 and 100).

22. Geier, J. G. (1969). A trait approach to the study of leadership in small groups. *Journal of Communication, 17*, 316–323.

23. See Note 21.

24. Kingston, A. (1998, April). Stealth Banker. *The Globe and Mail Report on Business Magazine*, pp. 84–94 (quote, p. 88).

25. See Note 24 (quote, p. 92).

26. Staff Writer (1997, November 22/24). Organization Man. *Financial Post*, pp. 14–16.

27. Newman, P. C. (1998, February 2). An unlikely partnership. *Maclean's Toronto Edition*, 111, p. 48.

28. See Note 27.

29. See Note 27.

30. See Note 24.

31. See Note 18.

32. See Note 16.

33. House, R. J., Shane, S. A., & Herold, D. M. (1996). Rumors of the death of dispositional research are vastly exaggerated. *Academy of Management Review, 21*, 203–224.

34. Kirkpatrick, S. A., & Locke, E. A. (1991). Leadership: Do traits matter? *Academy of Management Executive, 5*, 48–60.

35. Lord, R. G., DeVader, C. L., & Alliger, G. M. (1986). A meta-analysis of the relation between personality traits and leadership perceptions: An application of validity generalization procedures. *Journal of Applied Psychology, 61*, 402–410.

36. Zaccaro, S. J., Foti, R. J., & Kenny, D. A. (1991). Self-monitoring and trait-based variance in leadership: An investigation of leader flexibility across multiple group situations. *Journal of Applied Psychology, 76*, 308–315.

37. See Note 34 (quote, p. 58).

38. Muczyk, J. P., & Reimann, B. C. (1987). The case for directive leadership. *Academy of Management Review, 12*, 637–647.

39. Chen, C. C., & Meindl, J. R. (1991). The construction of leadership images in the popular press: The case of Donald Burr and People Express. *Administrative Science Quarterly, 36*, 521–551.

40. Likert, R. (1961). *New patterns in management*. New York: McGraw-Hill.

41. Stogdill, R. M. (1963). *Manual for the leader behavior description questionnaire, form XII*. Columbus, OH: Ohio State University, Bureau of Business Research.

42. Powell, G. N. (1993). *Women and men in management* (2nd ed.). Thousand Oaks, CA: Sage.

43. Eagly, A. H., & Karau, S. J. (1991). Gender and the emergence of leaders: A meta-analysis. *Journal of Personality and Social Psychology, 61*, 685–710.

44. Eagly, A. H., Makhijani, M. G., & Klonsky, B. G. (1992). Gender and the evaluation of leaders: A meta-analysis. *Psychological Bulletin, 108*, 3–22.

45. Melamed, T., & Bosionelos, N. (1992). Gender differences in the personality features of British managers. *Psychological Reports, 72*, 979–986.

46. Weissenberg, P., & Kavanagh, M. H. (1972). The independence of initiating structure and consideration: A review of the evidence. *Personnel Psychology, 25*, 119–130.

47. Vroom, V. H. (1976). Leadership. In M. D. Dunnette (Ed.), *Handbook of industrial-organizational psychology* (pp. 1527–1552). Chicago: Rand-McNally.

48. See Note 16.

49. Blake, R. R., & Mouton, J. J. (1969). *Building a dynamic corporation through grid organizational development*. Reading, MA: Addison-Wesley.

50. Pitcher, P. (1995). *Artists, craftsmen and technocrats: The dreams, realities and illusions of leadership*. Toronto: Stoddart Publishing.

51. Pitcher, P. (1993, Winter). Balancing personality types at the top. *Business Quarterly*, pp. 47–50, 52–57.

52. Graen, G. B., & Wakabayashi, M. (1994). Cross-cultural leadership-making: Bridging American and Japanese diversity for team advantage. In H. C. Triandis, M. D. Dunnette, & L. M. Hough (Eds.) *Handbook of industrial and organizational psychology* (2nd ed., Vol. 4, pp. 415–466). Palo Alto, CA: Consulting Psychologists Press.

53. Phillips, A. S., & Bedian, A. G. (1994). Leader-follower exchange quality: The role of

personal and interpersonal attributes. *Academy of Management Journal, 37,* 990–1001.

54. Dunegan, K. J., Duchon, D., & Uhl-Bien, M. (1992). Examining the link between leader-member exchange and subordinate performance: The role of task analyzability and variety as moderators. *Journal of Management, 18,* 59–76.

55. Duarte, N. T., Goodson, J. R., & Klich, N. R. (1993). How do I like thee? Let me appraise the ways. *Journal of Organizational Behavior, 14,* 239–249.

56. Deluga, R. J., & Perry, J. T. (1991). The relationship of subordinate upward influencing behaviour, satisfaction and perceived superior effectiveness with leader-member exchanges. *Journal of Occupational Psychology, 64,* 239–252.

57. Ferris, G. R. (1985). Role of leadership in the employee withdrawal process: A constructive replication. *Journal of Applied Psychology, 70,* 777–781.

58. Scandura, T. A., & Schriesheim, C. A. (1994). Leader-member exchange and supervisor career mentoring as complementary constructs in leadership research. *Academy of Management Journal, 37,* 1588–1602.

59. Lord, R. G., & Maher, K. (1989). Perceptions in leadership and their implications in organizations. In J. Carroll (Ed.), *Applied social psychology and organizational settings* (Vol. 4, pp. 129–154). Hillsdale, NJ: Erlbaum.

60. Heneman, R. L., Greenberger, D. B., & Anonyuo, C. (1989). Attributions and exchanges: The effects of interpersonal factors on the diagnosis of employee performance. *Academy of Management Journal, 32,* 466–476.

61. Mitchell, T. R., & Wood, R. E. (1980). Supervisors' responses to subordinate poor performance: A test of an attribution model. *Organizational Behavior and Human Performance, 25,* 123–138.

62. Bass, B. M. (1985). *Leadership and performance beyond expectations.* New York: Free Press.

63. Two Corporate VP's Elected at Xerox, www.xerox.com.

64. See Note 26.

65. See Note 24 (quote, p. 86).

66. Staff Writer (1998, October). Then came Branson. *Business Week,* p. 116.

67. Gooding, W. (1997, November). CEO of the Year: Jean Monty. *The Financial Post Magazine,* pp. 224–36.

68. See Note 18.

69. House, R. J., Spangler, W. D., & Woycke, J. (1991). Personality and charisma in the U.S. presidency: A psychological theory of leader effectiveness. *Administrative Science Quarterly, 36,* 364–396.

70. See Note 62.

71. House, R. J. (1977). A 1976 theory of charismatic leadership. In J. G. Hunt & L. L. Larson (Eds.), *Leadership: The cutting edge* (pp. 189–207). Carbondale, IL: Southern Illinois University Press.

72. See Note 71.

73. Conger, J. A. (1991). Inspiring others: The language of leadership. *Academy of Management Executive, 5,* 31–45.

74. House, R. J., Woycke, J., & Fedor, E. M. (1988). Charismatic and noncharismatic leaders: Differences in behavior and effectiveness. In J. A. Conger & R. N. Kanungo (Eds.), *Charismatic leadership* (pp. 122–144). San Francisco: Jossey-Bass.

75. See Note 74.

76. House, R. J., & Howell, J. M. (1992). Personality and charismatic leadership. *Leadership Quarterly, 3(2),* 81–108.

77. Trueheart, C. (1994, October 6). Gun charges brought notoriety to cult in Quebec. www.washingtonpost.com/wp-srv/national/longterm/cult/solar/solar_quebec.htm.

78. Howell, J. M., & Avolio, B. J. (1992). The ethics of charismatic leadership: Submission or liberation? *Academy of Management Executive, 6,* 43–54.

79. See Note 78.

80. See Note 73 (quote, p. 44).

81. See Note 14.

82. Kingston, A. (1998, August). Avon's calling. *The Globe and Mail Report on Business Magazine,* pp. 24–36.

83. Fisher, A. B. (1996, March 6). Corporate reputations. *Fortune,* pp. 90–98.

84. Morris, B. (1995, December 11). The wealth builders. *Fortune,* pp. 80–84, 88, 90, 94.

85. Kohl, W. L., Steers, & Terborg, J. R. (1995). The effects of transformational leadership on teacher attitudes and student performance in Singapore. *Journal of Organizational Behavior, 16,* 319–333.

86. Hater, J. J., & Bass, B. M. (1988). Superiors' evaluations and subordinates' perceptions of transformational and transactional leadership. *Journal of Applied Psychology, 73,* 695–702.

87. Zenger, J. H., Musselwhite, E., Hurson, K., & Perrin, C. (1994). *Leading teams: Mastering the new role.* Homewood, IL: Business One Irwin.

88. See Note 13.

89. Fiedler, F. E. (1978). Contingency model and the leadership process. In L. Berkowitz (Ed.), *Advances in experimental social psychology* (Vol. 11, pp. 60–112). New York: Academic Press.

90. Strube, M. J., & Garcia, J. E. (1981). A meta-analytic investigation of Fiedler's contingency model of leadership effectiveness. *Psychological Bulletin, 90,* 307–321.

91. Schriesheim, C. A., Tepper, B. J., & Terault, L. A. (1994). Least preferred co-worker score, situational control, and leadership effectiveness: A meta-analysis of contingency model performance predictions. *Journal of Applied Psychology, 79,* 561–573.

92. Peters, L. H., Hartke, D. D., & Pohlman, J. T. (1985). Fiedler's contingency theory of leadership: An application of the meta-analytic procedures of Schmidt and Hunter. *Psychological Bulletin, 97,* 274–385.

93. Ashour, A. S. (1973). The contingency model of leadership effectiveness: An evaluation. *Organizational Behavior and Human Performance, 9,* 339–355.

94. Fiedler, F. E., Chemers, M. M., Mahar, L. (1976). *Improving leadership effectiveness: The leader match concept.* New York: Wiley.

95. Fiedler, F. E., Garcia, J. E., Bell, C. H., Chemers, M. M., & Patrick, D. (1984). Increasing mine productivity and safety through management training and organization development: A comparative study. *Basic and Applied Social Psychology, 5,* 1–18.

96. Hersey, P., & Blanchard, K. H. (1988). *Management of organizational behavior.* Englewood Cliffs, NJ: Prentice-Hall.

97. Hambleton, R. K., & Gumpert, R. (1982). The validity of Hersey and Blanchard's theory of leader effectiveness. *Group and Organization Studies, 7,* 225–242.

98. Vecchio, R. P. (1987). Situational leadership theory: An examination of a prescriptive theory. *Journal of Applied Psychology, 72,* 444–451.

99. See Note 98.

100. House, R. J., & Baetz, M. L. (1979). Leadership: Some empirical generalizations and new research directions. In B. M. Staw (Ed.), *Research in organizational behavior* (Vol. 1, pp. 341–424). Greenwich, CT: JAI Press.

101. Milbank, D. (1990, March 5). Managers are sent to "Charm Schools" to discover how to polish up their acts. *Wall Street Journal,* pp. A14, B3.

102. Vroom, V. H., & Yetton, P. W. (1973). *Leadership and decision making.* Pittsburgh: University of Pittsburgh Press.

103. Vroom, V. H., & Jago, A. G. (1978). On the validity of the Vroom-Yetton model. *Journal of Applied Psychology, 63,* 151–162.

104. Field, R. H. (1982). A test of the Vroom-Yetton normative model of leadership. *Journal of Applied Psychology, 67,* 532–537.

105. Heilman, M. E., Hornstein, H. A., Cage, J. H., & Herschlag, J. K. (1984). Reactions to prescribed leader behavior as a function of role perspective: The case of the Vroom-Yetton model. *Journal of Applied Psychology, 69,* 50–60.

106. Vroom, V. H., & Jago, A. G. (1988). *The new leadership: Managing participation in organizations.* Englewood Cliffs, NJ: Prentice-Hall.

107. Kerr, S., & Jermier, J. M. (1978). Substitutes for leadership: Their meaning and measurement. *Organizational Behavior and Human Performance, 22,* 375–403.

108. Sheridan, J. E., Vredenburgh, D. J., & Abelson, M. A. (1984). Contextual model of leadership influence in hospital units. *Academy of Management Journal, 27,* 57–78.

109. Podsakoff, P. M., Niehoff, B. P., MacKenzie, S. B., & Williams, M. L. (1993). Do substitutes for leadership really substitute for leadership? An empirical examination of Kerr and Jermier's situational leadership model. *Organizational Behavior and Human Decision Processes, 54*, 1–44.

110. Meindl, J. R., & Ehrlich, S. B. (1987). The romance of leadership and the evaluation of organizational performance. *Academy of Management Journal, 30*, 91–109.

111. See Note 82 (quote, p. 25).

112. See Note 82 (quote, p. 26).

113. See Note 82.

114. Dugan, I. J. (1998, March 16). Why Avon called a 'non-woman'. *Business Week*, pp. 57–59 (quote, p. 58).

115. See Note 114 (quote, p. 57).

116. See Note 82.

117. See Note 114 (quote p. 59).

118. Gault, Y. (1997, June 2). Avon is calling on its women to fill CEO post. *Crain's New York Business, 13*, pp. 44–46.

119. See Note 118.

120. See Note 82 (quote, p. 36).

Cumulative Case Part 5

1. Thompson, Clive. Keith Kocho has seen the future of the Internet and it is television, Internet: 216.13.9.31/shiftonline/html/onlineTOC/6.6/6.6features/kocho1.html; New Media Leaders, Internet: www.digital_ren.com/press.milestones_press2.asp?type=3&page_id=306.

2. Flavelle, D. (1996, November 11). A New Company Style. *The Toronto Star*, p. C6.

3. Staff writer (1997, November 3). Experiencing a Digital Renaissance. *Maclean's Supplement*, p. 9.

4. Kocho, K. (1998, January 28). cc: The World. *The Financial Post*, p. 16.

5. See Thompson, Clive, Note 1.

6. Welcome to Digital Renaissance, Internet: www.digital-ren.com/main.htm.

7. Digital Media Champion Group: Message from the Chair, Internet: www.multimediator.com/dmcg/chair.html.

8. Keith Kocho, Internet: www.canarie.ca/eng/org/directors/keith_kocho.html.

9. The Interview by Gordon MacLeod, Internet: www.atlarge.net/story_kocho2.html.

10. See Thompson, Clive, Note 1.

11. See Note 9.

12. Sheikh, F. (1998, May 4). The Vision Thing. *Marketing Magazine*, p. 12.

Chapter 14

1. Marks & Spencer: Worldwide Store Directory, www.marks-and-spencer.com/store-directory.

2. Philips, N. (1994). *Managing international teams*. Burr Ridge, IL: Irwin.

3. Marks and Spencer, www.marks-and-spencer.com/marble-arch/.

4. Schneider, B. (1990). *Organizational climate and culture*. San Francisco: Jossey-Bass.

5. Deutschman, A. (1994, October 17). The managing wisdom of high-tech superstars. *Fortune*, pp. 197–198, 200, 202–204, 206.

6. Pennings, J. M., & Buitendam, A. (1987). *New technology as organizational innovation*. Cambridge, MA: Ballinger.

7. Zammuto, R. F. (1992). Gaining advanced manufacturing technologies' benefits: The role of organization design and culture. *Academy of Management Review, 17*, 701–728.

8. Schein, E. H. (1985). *Organizational culture and leadership*. San Francisco: Jossey-Bass.

9. Chatman, J. A., & Jehn, K. A. (1994). Assessing the relationship between industry characteristics and organizational culture: How different can you be? *Academy of Management Journal, 37*, 522–533.

10. Smith, V. (1998, April). Money talks. *The Globe and Mail Report on Business Magazine*, pp. 97–100.

11. See Note 10.

12. See Note 10.

13. Levering, R., & Moskowitz, M. (1993). *The 100 best companies to work for in America*. New York: Currency Doubleday.

14. See Note 10.

15. Martin, J., & Meyerson, D. (1988). Organizational cultures and the denial, channeling, and acknowledgment of ambiguity. In L. R. Pondy, R. J. Boland, Jr., & H. Thomas (Eds.), *Managing ambiguity and change* (pp. 93–125). New York: Wiley.

16. Schein, E. H. (1985). How culture forms, develops, and changes. In R. H. Kilmann, M. J. Saxton, & R. Serpa (Eds.), *Gaining control of corporate culture* (pp. 17–43). San Francisco: Jossey-Bass.

17. Sackmann, S. A. (1992). Cultures and subcultures: Analysis of organizational knowledge. *Administrative Science Quarterly, 37*, 140–161.

18. Sonnenfeld, J. (1988). *The hero's farewell*. New York: Oxford University Press.

19. Rebello, K., Burrows, P., & Sager, I. (1996, February 5). The fall of an American icon. *Business Week*, pp. 34–42.

20. Martin, J., Sitkin, S. B., & Boehm, M. (1985). Founders and the elusiveness of a cultural legacy. In P. J. Frost, L. F. Moore, M. R. Louis, C. C. Lundberg, & J. Martin (Eds.), *Organizational culture* (pp. 99–124). Beverly Hills, CA: Sage.

21. McGuigan, I. (1994, April). Such good friends. *Canadian Business*, pp. 52–59, 63.

22. Dumaine, B. (1990, January 15). Creating a new company culture. *Fortune*, pp. 127–128, 130–131.

23. Schein, E. H. (1985). How culture forms, develops and changes. In R. H. Kilmann, M. J. Saxton, & R. Serpa (Eds.), *Gaining control of corporate culture* (pp. 17–43). San Francisco: Jossey-Bass.

24. Weick, K. E. (1985). The significance of corporate culture. In P. J. Frost, L. F. Moore, M. R. Louis, C. C. Lundberg, & J. Martin (Eds.), *Organizational culture* (pp. 381–390). Beverly Hills, CA: Sage.

25. Rentsch, J. R. (1991). Climate and culture: Interaction and qualitative differences in organizational meanings. *Journal of Applied Psychology, 75*, 668–681.

26. Lundberg, C. C. (1985). On the feasibility of cultural intervention in organizations. In P. J. Frost, L. F. Moore, M. R. Louis, C. C. Lundberg, & J. Martin (Eds.), *Organizational culture* (pp. 169–186). Beverly Hills, CA: Sage.

27. Ott, J. S. (1989). *The organizational culture perspective*. Chicago: Dorsey.

28. Dandridge, T. C. (1985). The life stages of a symbol: When symbols work and when they can't. In P. J. Frost, L. F. Moore, M. R. Louis, C. C. Lundberg, & J. Martin (Eds.), *Organizational culture* (pp. 141–154). Beverly Hills, CA: Sage.

29. Norgate, K. (1997, May 1). Nortel (Northern Telecom) opens new global headquarters. *Nortel News Release*.

30. Newman, P. C. (1998, February 2). An unlikely partnership. *Maclean's Toronto Edition, 111*, p. 48.

31. Ornstein, S. L. (1986). Organizational symbols: A study of their meanings and influences on perceived psychological climate. *Organizational Behavior and Human Decision Processes, 38*, 207–229.

32. Neuhauser, P. C. (1993). *Corporate legends and lore: The power of storytelling as a management tool*. New York: McGraw-Hill.

33. Martin, J. (1982). Stories and scripts in organizational settings. In A. Hastorf, & A. Isen (Eds.), *Cognitive social psychology* (pp. 255–306). New York: Elsevier-North Holland.

34. Gundry, L. K., & Rousseau, D. M. (1994). Critical incidents in communicating culture to newcomers: The meaning is the message. *Human Relations, 47*, 1063–1088.

35. Rowlinson, M., & Hassard, J. (1993). The invention of corporate culture: A history of the histories of Cadbury. *Human Relations, 46*, 299–326.

36. Drohan, M., & Zehr, L. (1995, October 7). Reichmann returns. *The Globe and Mail*, p. B1.

37. Lewis, G. (1993, April 12). One fresh face at IBM may not be enough. *Business Week*, p. 33.

38. Powers, G. (1995, March 22). A guide to re-engineering your paradigm. *The Globe and Mail*, p. A13.

39. See Note 27.

40. See Note 27.

41. Deal, T.E., & Kennedy, A. A. (1982), *Corporate cultures*. Reading, MA: Addison-Wesley (quote, p. 63).

42. Brenner, J. G. (1992, April 19). The world according to planet Mars. *Dallas Morning News*, pp. 1H, 2H, 7H.

43. Hatch, M. J. (1993). The dynamics of organizational culture. *Academy of Management Review, 18,* 657–693.

44. Weiner, Y. (1988). Forms of value systems: A focus on organizational effectiveness and cultural change and maintenance. *Academy of Management Review, 13,* 534–545.

45. Saffold, G. S., III. (1988). Culture traits, strength, and organizational performance: Moving beyond "strong" culture. *Academy of Management Review, 13,* 546–558.

46. Dennison, D. (1984). Bringing corporate culture to the bottom line. *Organizational Dynamics, 13,* 5–22.

47. Siehl, C., & Martin, J. (1988). *Organizational culture: A key to financial performance?* (Research Paper Series No. 998.) Stanford, CA: Stanford University, Graduate School of Business.

48. Hitt, M. A., & Ireland, R. D. (1987). Peters and Waterman revisited: The unended quest for excellence. *Academy of Management Executive, 1,* 91–98.

49. Sheridan, J. E. (1992). Organizational culture and employee retention. *Academy of Management Journal, 35,* 1036–1056.

50. O'Reilly, C. A., III, Chatman, J., & Caldwell, D. F. (1991). People and organizational culture: A profile comparison approach to assessing person-organization fit. *Academy of Management Journal, 34,* 487–516.

51. Church, E. (1998, May 22). Soul surfaces in the office canyons. *The Globe and Mail,* p. B21.

52. Dorsey, D. (1998, August). The new spirit of work. *Fast Company,* pp. 124–134 (quote, p. 126).

53. See Note 52.

54. Staff Writer (1997, October 20). Native sunrise ceremony marks an end of an era for CHOW. *The Tribune,* p. B1.

55. See Note 54.

56. Vandermolen, M. (1992, November). Shifting the corporate culture. *Working Woman,* pp. 25, 28.

57. See Note 54.

58. Walter, G. A. (1985). Culture collisions in mergers and acquisitions. In P. J. Frost, L. F. Moore,

M. R. Louis, C. C. Lundberg, & J. Martin (Eds.), *Organizational culture* (pp. 301–314). Beverly Hills, CA: Sage.

59. Cartwright, S., & Cooper, C. L. (1993). The role of culture compatibility in successful organizational marriage. *Academy of Management Executive, 7,* 57–70.

60. Carroll, P. (1993). *Big blues: The unmaking of IBM.* New York: Crown.

61. Boyett, J. H., Schwartz, S., Osterwise, L., & Bauer, R. (1993). *The quality journey.* New York: Dutton.

62. Certo, S. C., Sales, C.A., and Owen, F. A. (1998). *Modern Management in Canada.* Scarborough, Ontario: Prentice Hall Canada (quote, pp. 369–370).

63. See note 62.

64. Staff writer (1997, January/February). Are you getting your safety message across? *Canadian Occupational Safety, 35,* pp. 18–22.

65. See note 64.

66. Hulin, C. L., & Roznowski, M. (1985). Organizational technologies: Effects on organizations' characteristics and individuals' responses. In L. L. Cummings, & B. M. Staw (Eds.), *Research in organizational behavior* (Vol. 7, pp. 39–86). Greenwich, CT: JAI Press.

67. Krause, T. R. (1991). A behavior-based safety management process. In J. W. Jones, B. D. Steffy, & D. W. Bray (Eds.), *Applying psychology in business* (pp. 813–824). New York: Lexington Books.

68. Rogers, B. (1995, February). Creating a culture of safety. *HRMagzine,* pp. 85–88.

69. Drucker, P. F. (1992). *Managing for the future.* New York: Truman Talley Books/Dutton.

70. Perrow, C. (1967). A framework for the comparative analysis of organizations. *American Sociological Review, 32,* 194–208.

71. Katzell, R. (1994). Contemporary meta-trends in industrial and organizational psychology. In. H. C. Triandis, M. D. Dunnette, & L. M. Hough (Eds.), *Handbook of industrial and organizational psychology* (2nd ed., Vol. 4, pp. 1–89). Palo Alto, CA: Consulting Psychologists Press.

72. Dean, J. W., Yoon, S. J., & Susman, G. I. (1992). Advanced manufacturing technology and

organization structure: Empowerment or subordination? *Organization Science, 3,* 203–229.

73. Weick, K. (1990). Technology as equivoque: Sensemaking in new technologies. In P. S. Goodman, & L. S. Sproull (Eds.), *Technology and organizations* (pp. 1–44). San Francisco: Jossey-Bass.

74. Solomon, J. S. (1987, fall). Union responses to technological change: Protecting the past or looking into the future? *Labor Studies Journal,* pp. 51–65.

75. Farnham, A. (1993, autumn). Making high tech work for you. *Fortune* (Special Issue), p. 1.

76. Bayless, A. (1986, October 16). Technology reshapes North America's lumber plants. *The Wall Street Journal,* p. 6.

77. Sherman, J. (1994). *In the rings of Saturn.* New York: Oxford University Press.

78. Neff, R. (1987, April 20). Getting man and machine to live happily ever after. *Business Week,* pp. 61–63.

79. Argote, L., Goodman, P. S., & Schkade, D. (1983, spring). The human side of robots: How workers react to a robot. *Sloan Management Review,* pp. 31–42.

80. See Note 79.

81. Katzenbach, J. R., & Smith, D. K. (1993). *The wisdom of teams.* Boston: Harvard Business School Press.

82. Valery, N. (1988). Factory of the future. In J. Gibson, J. Ivancevich, & J. Donnelly, Jr. (Eds.), *Organizations close-up* (pp. 274–301). Plano, TX: Business Publications.

83. See Note 75.

84. Tompkins, N. C. (1993, April). Tools that help performance on the job. *HRMagazine,* pp. 84, 87, 89–91.

85. Anonymous (1993, September). New technology and the disabled. *Information Management Forum,* pp. 1, 4.

86. Colombo, J. R. (1997). *The 1998 Canadian Global Almanac.* Toronto: Macmillan Canada.

87. Morris, J. (1998, January 26). Laws promoting employment for disabled still being judged. *Canadian Press Newswire.*

88. See Note 87.

89. See Note 87.

90. Balkin, D. (1998, Spring). Beyond Terry Fox and Tracy Latimer. *Media, 5,* pp. 17–18 (quote, p. 17).

91. U.S. Congress, Office of Technology Assessment (1987). *The electronic supervisor: New technology, new tensions* (OTA-CIT-333). Washington, DC: U.S. Government Printing Office.

92. Baarda, C.W. (1994). *Computerized performance monitoring: Implications for employers, employees, and human resource management.* Kingston, Ontario: Hewson & White Printing (Kingston) Ltd.

93. Aiello, J. R. (1993). Computer-based work monitoring: Electronic surveillance and its effects. *Journal of Applied Social Psychology, 23,* 499–507.

94. See Note 93.

95. See Note 92.

96. Bylinsky, G. (1991, November). How companies spy on employees. *Fortune,* pp. 131–133, 136, 138, 140 (quote, p. 136).

97. Kipnis, D. (1991). The technological perspective. *Psychological Science, 2,* 62–69.

98. Marx, G. T., & Sherizen, S. (1986). Monitoring on the job: How to protect privacy as well as property. *Technology Review, 89,* 62–72.

99. See Note 93.

100. Von Rijn, N. (1993, November 2). Electronic monitoring called threat. *Toronto Star,* p. A8.

101. Kulik, C. T., & Ambrose, M L. (1993). Category-based and feature-based processes in performance appraisal: Integrating visual and computerized sources of performance data. *Journal of Applied Psychology, 78,* 821–830.

102. Irving, R. H., Higgins, C. A., & Safayeni, F. R. (1986). Computerized performance monitoring systems: Use and abuse. *Communications of the ACM, 29,* 794–801.

103. See Note 93.

104. See Note 93.

105. Chalykoff, J., & Kochan, T. A. (1989). Computer-aided monitoring: Its influence on employee satisfaction and turnover. *Personnel Psychology, 40,* 807–834.

106. Fenner, D. B., Lerch, F. J., & Kulik, C. T. (1993). The impact of computerized performance monitoring and prior performance knowledge on perform-

ance evaluation. *Journal of Applied Social Psychology, 23,* 572–601.

107. Ives, B., & Mason, R. O. (1990). Can information technology revitalize your customer service? *Academy of Management Executive, 4,* 52–69.

108. Bylinsky, G. (1996, February 6). Manufacturing for reuse. *Fortune,* pp. 102–104, 108, 110, 112.

109. See Note 108.

110. 1998 News Releases, www.ups.com/canada/news/980619hamilton.html.

111. Freight carriers' technology tune: We've only just begun (1993, June 3). *Purchasing,* p. 37; Fitzgerald, M. (1993, November 29). UPS delivers new bar-code system to public domain. *ComputerWorld,* p. 38; Hawkins, C., & Oster, P. (1993, May 31). After a U-turn, UPS really delivers. *Business Week,* pp. 92–93; Laabs, J. J. (1993, October). Community service helps UPS develop managers. *Personnel Journal,* pp. 90–92, 94, 96, 98; Margolis, N. (1993, March 1). UPS head launched for IS use. *ComputerWorld,* p. 65; Pastore, R. (1993, December 15). A measured success. *CIO,* pp. 40–45.

Chapter 15

1. Jang, B. (1997, November 13). Nova to split in two. *The Globe and Mail,* pp. B1, B14 (quote, p. B1).

2. MacDonald, G., and Ross, I. (1997, November 13). Nova's Newall keeps his cool in big breakup. *The Globe and Mail,* p. B17.

3. See Note 1 (quote, p. B1).

4. Business notes, www.macleans/newsroom112497/bnotes112497.html.

5. Press Release: NOVA and TransCanada announce a merger of equals, creating world class energy services and chemicals companies (1998, January 26), www.nova.ca/press/012698.htm.

6. Merger between NOVA and TransCanada (1998, January 26), www.nova.ca/merger/backgrounder.html.

7. Merger frequently asked questions, www.nova.ca/merger/question.htm (quote, p. 4).

8. See Notes 2, 5.

9. Miller, D. (1987). The genesis of configuration. *Academy of*

Management Review, l2, 686–701.

10. Galbraith, L. R. (1987). Organization design. In J. W. Lorsch (Ed.), *Handbook of organizational behavior* (pp. 343–357). Englewood Cliffs, NJ: Prentice-Hall.

11. Hendricks, C. F. (1992). *The rightsizing remedy.* Homewood, IL: Business One Irwin.

12. Swoboda, F. (1990, May 28–June 3). For unions, maybe bitter was better. *Washington Post National Weekly Edition,* p. 20.

13. Massie, J. (1996, February 26). The downside of downsizing. *Columbus Dispatch,* Section I, pp. 1–2.

14. Lawler, E. E. (1988, summer). Substitutes for hierarchy. *Organizational Dynamics,* pp. 5–6, 15.

15. Speen, K. (1988, September 12). Caught in the middle. *Business Week,* pp. 80–88.

16. Urwick, L. F. (1956). The manager's span of control. *Harvard Business Review, 34(3),* 39–47.

17. Scott, M., & Rothman, H. (1992). *Companies with a conscience.* New York: Birch Lane Press.

18. Staff Writer (1998, March 3). Raising the Roof. *The Globe and Mail,* p. B7; Profile: Harry Rosen, www.acecanada.ca/sprosen.html.

19. Church, E. (1998, February 2). High-tech startup donates a piece of its future. *The Globe and Mail,* p. B11.

20. Staff Writer (1998, March 3). Raising the Roof. *The Globe and Mail,* p. B7.

21. Charan, R. (July–August, 1991). How networks reshape organizations—for results. *Harvard Business Review,* pp. 10–17.

22. Green, H., & Moscow, A. (1984). *Managing.* New York: Doubleday.

23. Dalton, M. (1950). Conflicts between staff and line managerial officers. *American Sociological Review, 15,* 342–351.

24. Chandler, A. (1962). *Strategy and structure.* Cambridge, MA: MIT Press.

25. Cara Operations Limited, *1995 Annual Report.*

26. Staff Writer (1995, November 15). Beatty chops CBC top brass. *Canadian Press*

Newswire; Mitchell, R. (1987, December 14). When Jack Welch takes over: A guide for the newly acquired. *Business Week,* pp. 93–97.

27. Lawrence, P., & Lorsch, J. (1967). *Organization and environment.* Boston: Harvard University.

28. Pitta, J. (1993, April 26). It had to be done and we did it. *Forbes,* pp. 148–152; Staff Writer (1993, June 28). For best results, decentralize R&D. *Business Week,* p. 134; Litchfield, R. (1993, February). Trouble is my business. *Canadian Business,* p. 32.

29. Dumaine, B. (1990, November 5). How to manage in a recession. *Fortune,* pp. 72–75.

30. Staff Writer (1995, May 24). IS jobs to be slashed at Petro-Canada. *Computing Canada, 21,* pp. 1, 6.

31. Company structure, www.bombardier.com/htmen/6_0.htm.

32. Toy, S. (1988, April 25). The Americanization of Honda. *Business Week,* pp. 90–96.

33. Uttal, B. (1985, June 29). Mettle test time for John Young. *Fortune,* pp. 242–244, 248.

34. Mee, J. F. (1964). Matrix organizations. *Business Horizons, 7(2),* 70–72.

35. Bartlett, C. A., & Ghoshal, S. (1990). Matrix management: Not a structure, a frame of mind. *Harvard Business Review, 68(3),* 138–145.

36. Davis, S. M., & Lawrence, P. R. (1977). *Matrix.* Reading, MA: Addison-Wesley.

37. Goggin, W. (1974). How the multidimensional structure works at Dow Corning. *Harvard Business Review, 56(1),* 33–52.

38. See Note 36.

39. Ford, R. C., & Randolph, W. A. (1992). Cross-functional structures: A review and integration of matrix organization and project management. *Journal of Management, 18,* 267–294.

40. See Note 39.

41. GE: Just your average everyday $60 billion family grocery store. (1994, May 2). *Industry Week,* pp. 13–18.

42. Slater, R. (1993). *The new GE.* Homewood, IL: Business One Irwin (quote, p. 257).

43. Woodruff, D., & Miller, K. L. (1993, May 3). Chrysler's Neon: Is this the small car

Detroit couldn't build? *Business Week,* pp. 116–126.

44. Dees, G. D., Rasheed, A. M. A., McLaughlin, K. J., & Priem, R. L. (1995). The new corporate architecture. *Academy of Management Executive, 9,* 7–18.

45. See Note 44.

46. Tully, S. (1993, February 3). The modular corporation. *Fortune,* pp. 106–108, 110.

47. Taylor, A. (1990, November 19). Why Toyota keeps getting better and better and better. *Fortune,* pp. 72–79.

48. Byrne, J. (1993, February 8). The virtual corporation. *Business Week,* pp. 99–103.

49. Sherman, S. (1992, September 21). Are strategic alliances working? *Fortune,* pp. 77–78 (quote, p. 78).

50. Schlender, B. (1995, September 19). Steve Jobs' amazing movie adventure. *Fortune,* pp. 155–156, 160, 164, 172.

51. McGregor, D. (1960). *The human side of enterprise.* New York: McGraw-Hill.

52. Argyris, C. (1964). *Integrating the individual and the organization.* New York: Wiley.

53. Likert, R. (1961). *New patterns of management.* New York: McGraw-Hill.

54. Duncan, R. (1979, winter). What is the right organization structure? *Organizational Dynamics,* pp. 59–69.

55. Burns, T., & Stalker, G. M. (1961). *The management of innovation.* London: Tavistock.

56. Deveney, K. (1986, October 13). Bag those fries, squirt that ketchup, fry that fish. *Business Week,* pp. 57–61.

57. New VP has global focus, www.mhbizlink.com/Content/marketing/1.97/ppl1.html; Marketing Awards for Outdoor Campaigns, www.oaac.com/m_award.htm; Self-Medication Digest, www.ndmac.ca/publicat/smdv2n2.html.

58. Morse, J. J., & Lorsch, J. W. (1970). Beyond Theory Y. *Harvard Business Review, 48(3),* 61–68.

59. Mintzberg, H. (1983). *Structure in fives: Designing effective organizations.* Englewood Cliffs, NJ: Prentice-Hall.

60. Livesay, H. C. (1979). *American made: Men who shaped the American economy.* Boston: Little, Brown.

61. Nakarmi, L., & Einhorn, B. (1993, June 7). Hyundai's gutsy gambit. *Business Week*, p. 48.

62. Gerlach, M. L. (1993). *Alliance capitalism: The social organization of Japanese business*. Berkeley, CA: University of California Press.

63. Miyashita, K., & Russell, D. (1994). *Keiretsu: Inside the Japanese conglomerates*. New York: McGraw Hill.

64. Lubove, S. (1992, December 7). How to grow big yet stay small. *Forbes*, pp. 64–66.

65. See Note 61.

66. Kanter, R. M. (1994, July–August). Collaborative advantage: The art of alliances. *Harvard Business Review*, pp. 96–108.

67. See Note 66.

68. Linklater, K. (1998, April/May). The sweet taste of success. *Profit*, 17, p. 12. Reprinted by permission.

69. Newman, W. H. (1992). Focused joint ventures in transforming economies. *The Executive*, 6, 67–75.

70. Sankar, C. S., Boulton, W. R., Davidson, N. W., & Snyder, C. A. (1995). Building a world-class alliance: The Universal Card-TSYS case. *Academy of Management Executive*, 9, 20–29.

71. Fletcher, N. (1988, December 10). U.S., China form joint venture to manufacture helicopters. *Journal of Commerce*, p. 58.

72. Bransi, B. (1987, January 3). South Korea's carmakers count their blessings. *The Economist*, p. 45.

73. Mason, J. C. (1993, May). Strategic alliances: Partnering for success. *Management Review*, pp. 10–15.

74. Woodward, J. (1965). *Industrial organization: Theory and practice*. London: Oxford University Press.

75. See Note 74 (quote p. 58).

76. Zwerman, W. L. (1970). *New perspectives on organizational theory*. Westport, CT: Greenwood.

77. Huber, G. P. (1990). A theory of the effects of advanced information technologies on organizational design, intelligence, and decision making. *Academy of Management Review*, 15, 47–71.

78. Hull, F. M., & Collins, P. D. (1987). High-technology batch production systems: Woodward's missing type. *Academy of Management Journal*, 30, 786–797.

79. Hickson, D., Pugh, D., & Pheysey, D. (1969). Operations technology and organization structure: An empirical reappraisal. *Administrative Science Quarterly*, 26, 349–377.

80. Singh, J. V. (1986). Technology, size and organization structure: A reexamination of the Okayama study data. *Academy of Management Journal*, 29, 800–812.

81. Thompson, J. D. (1967). *Organizations in action*. New York: McGraw-Hill.

82. Daft, R. L. (1986). *Organizational theory and design* (2nd ed.). St. Paul, MN: West.

83. Mason, J. C. (1993, May). The marriage of Volvo and Renault. *Management Review*, p. 12.

84. See Note 83.

85. Echikson, W. (1993, November, 15). A marriage of necessity. *Fortune*, pp. 129–130.

86. Berman, P. (1994, December 19). Abdication. *Forbes*, p. 198.

87. Frenken, R. (1997, August 28). Renault sells entire Volvo stake, completing divorce. *Bloomberg News*, www.ssnewslink.com.

88. Simonian, H., and McIvor, G. (1997, July 31). Volvo offloads the last of its Renault shares. *Financial Times*, www.ssnewslink.com.

89. Tomesco, F. (1998, May 6). European car mergers seen after Daimler-Chrysler; shares jump. *Bloomberg News*, www.ssnewslink.com.

Chapter 16

1. Johnson, A. (1996, March). Who's minding the store? *Canadian Business*, 69, p. 11.

2. McGugan, I. (1996, March). Eaton's on the brink. *Canadian Business*, 69, pp. 38–73 (quote, p. 44).

3. Thompson, D. N. (1997, Summer). Eaton's and the vulture: A cautionary tale. *Business Quarterly*, 61, pp. 31–39 (quote, p. 35).

4. Fruitman, M. (1997, autumn). Eaton's had right strategy ... at wrong time. *Ivey Business Quarterly*, 62, p. 26.

5. McGugan, I. (1996, March). Eaton's on the brink. *Canadian Business*, 69, pp. 38–73;

McQueen, R. (1998). *The Eatons*. Toronto: Stoddart Publishing Co. Limited.

6. Woodman, R. W. (1989). Organizational change and development: New arenas for inquiry and action. *Journal of Management*, 15, 205–228.

7. Stewart, T. A. (1993, December 13). Welcome to the revolution. *Fortune*, pp. 66–68, 70, 72, 76, 78.

8. Sherman, S. (1993, December 13). How will we live with the tumult? *Fortune*, pp. 123–125.

9. Little, B. (1994, October 31). Companies on the brink of overhaul. *The Globe and Mail*, pp. B1, B2.

10. Kanter, R. M. (1991, May–June). Transcending business boundaries: 12,000 world managers view change. *Harvard Business Review*, pp. 151–164.

11. Nystrom, P. C., & Starbuck, W. H. (1984, spring). To avoid organizational crises, unlearn. *Organizational Dynamics*, 44–60.

12. Staff Writer (1998, July). 50 top employers. *The Globe and Mail Report on Business Magazine*, p. 89; Newman, P. C. (1995). *An illustrated history of the Hudson's Bay Company*. Toronto: The Madison Press Limited.

13. Miller, K. L. (1993, May 17). The factory guru tinkering with Toyota. *Business Week*, pp. 95, 97.

14. Levy, A. (1986). Second-order planned change: Definition and conceptualization. *Organizational Dynamics*, 16(1), 4–20.

15. Vowles, A. (1993, April). Gaining the competitive edge through organizational learning. *CMA—The Management Accounting Magazine*, p. 12.

16. Senge, P. (1990). *The fifth discipline: The art and practice of the learning organization*. New York: Currency Doubleday, p. 14.

17. Huber, G. (1991). Organizational learning: The contributing process and the literatures. *Organization Science*, 2, 88–115.

18. Appleby, C. (1994, January 18). Chicago CIOs take notes. *Information Week*, p. 24; Brennan, L. L., & Rubenstein, A. H. (1995). Applications of groupware in organizational learning. In C. L. Cooper & D. M. Rousseau (Eds.), *Trends in organizational behavior* (Vol. 2, pp. 37–49). New York: Wiley.

19. Serwer, A. (1994, August 8). Lessons from America's fastest growing companies. *Fortune*, pp. 42–60.

20. Certo, S. C., Sales, C., & Owen, F. A. (1998). *Modern Management in Canada*. Scarborough, Ontario: Prentice Hall Canada Inc.

21. Gardner, E. (1993, July 19). At M.D. Anderson, specialists read minds before they write software. *Modern Healthcare*, p. 31.

22. Walsh, J., & Ungson, G. (1991). Organizational memory. *Academy of Management Review*, 16, 57–91.

23. Kirkpatrick, D. (1993, December 27). Groupware goes boom. *Fortune*, pp. 99–106.

24. Flood, A. (1993, December). The learning organization. *Canadian speeches: issues of the day*, pp. 52–57.

25. Luthans, F. (1991, summer). Conversations with Gordon Forward. *Organizational Dynamics*, 20, pp. 63–72; Kantrow, A. M. (1986, May–June). Wide-open management at Chaparral Steel, *Harvard Business Review*, pp. 96–102.

26. See Note 15.

27. Luckow, D. (1998, October). Northern exposure. *Profit*, 17, pp. 97–98.

28. Godfrey, J. (1988, July 18). From plonk to vintage. *Financial Post*, p. 12.

29. Ziraldo, D. J. (1995). *Anatomy of a winery*. Toronto: Key Porter Books, p. 16.

30. Schreiner, J. (1992, March 25). VQA wines go down well. *Financial Post*, p. 10.

31. See Note 29, p. 17.

32. Schreiner, J. (1988, December 5). Yes, there are good Canadian wines. *Financial Post*, p. 17.

33. Strauss, M. (1991, October 12). Bye-bye Baby Duck: Canadian wine makers are determined to change their reputation as producers of plonk. *The Globe and Mail*, p. B18; Foss, K. (1993, May 1). Vintage success. *Financial Times of Canada*, pp. 13–15; Menzies, D. (1994, May). Ontario wines on the rebound. *Food in Canada*, pp. 15–17.

34. Tomasko, R. M. (1993). *Rethinking the corporation*. New York: AMACOM.

35. Tomasko, R. M. (1990). *Downsizing: Reshaping the corporation for the future.* New York: AMACOM.

36. Reid, A. (1996). *Shakedown.* Toronto: Doubleday Canada Limited (quote, pp. 17-18).

37. Downs, A. (1995, October). The truth about layoffs. *Management Review,* pp. 57–61.

38. Rosen, R. H., & Berger, L. (1991). *The healthy company.* New York: Jeremy P. Tarcher/Perigree.

39. Cobb, A. T., & Marguiles, N. (1981). Organizational development: A political perspective. *Academy of Management Review, 6,* 49–59.

40. Ross, A. (1992, May). The long view of leadership. *Canadian Business,* p. 50.

41. See Note 40.

42. See Note 40.

43. Sadlier, D. (1995, August 12). Firm marks credit card sales with a splurge. *The Standard,* p. B3.

44. Daft, R. L. (1982). Bureaucratic versus nonbureaucratic structure and the process of innovation and change. In S. B. Bachrach (Ed.), *Research in the sociology of organizations* (Vol. 1, pp. 56–88). Greenwich, CT: JAI Press.

45. Gaertner, G. H., Gaertner, K. N., & Akinnusi, D. M. (1984). Environment, strategy, and implementation of administrative change: The case of civil service reform. *Academy of Management Journal, 27,* 525–543.

46. Colombo, J. R. (1994). *The 1995 Canadian Global Almanac.* Toronto: Macmillan Canada.

47. Stewart, T. A. (1993, December 13). Welcome to the revolution. *Fortune,* pp. 66–68, 70, 72, 76, 78.

48. See Note 47 (quote, p. 70).

49. Schachter, H. (1998, October). Quantum leaps. *Profit, 17,* pp. 37–47; Lundy, A. (1998, June 29). Filling a vacuum. *The Standard,* p. C1; Staff Writer (1997, January). Iona slashes design cycle time with CAD. *Design Engineering, 43,* p. 23.

50. Williamson, R. (1995, July 18). Cyber seadog. *The Globe and Mail,* p. B10.

51. Singh, J. V., House, R. J., & Tucker, D. J. (1986). Organizational change and mortality. *Administrative Science Quarterly, 31,* 587–611.

52. Ettore, B. (1995, October). Managing competitive intelligence. *Management Review,* pp. 15–19.

53. Crawford, M. G. (1998, February/March). Get smart. *Profit, 17,* pp. 10–11 (quote, p. 10).

54. See Note 53.

55. McBride, H. (1997, July). They snoop to conquer. *Canadian Business, 70,* pp. 45–47.

56. See Note 55 (quote, p. 47).

57. See Note 56.

58. Powell, B., & Stone, J. (1991, July 15). "The deal of the decade." *Newsweek,* p. 40.

59. Wheelen, T. L., & Hunger, J. D. (1989). Strategic management and business policy (3rd ed.). Reading, MA: Addison-Wesley.

60. Glueck, W. F. (1979). *Personnel: A diagnostic approach.* Dallas: Business Publications.

61. Swasy, A. (1993). *Soap opera: The inside story of Procter & Gamble.* New York: Times Books.

62. Lewin, K. (1951). *Field theory in social science.* New York: Harper & Row.

63. Schein, E. H. (1968). Organizational socialization and the profession of management. *Industrial Management Review, 9,* 1–16.

64. Dumaine, B. (1993, June 28). Times are good? Create a crisis. *Fortune,* pp. 123–124, 126, 130.

65. Armenakis, A. A., Harris, S. G., & Mossholder, K. W. (1993). Creating readiness for organizational change. *Human Relations, 46,* 681–703.

66. Beer, M. (1980). *Organizational change and development: A systems view.* Glenview, IL: Scott, Foresman.

67. Nadler, D. A. (1987). The effective management of organizational change. In J. W. Lorsch (Ed.), *Handbook of organizational behavior* (pp. 358–369). Englewood Cliffs, NJ: Prentice-Hall.

68. Wiersma, M. F., & Bantel, K. A. (1992). Top management team demography and corporate strategic change. *Academy of Management Journal, 35,* 91–121.

69. Katz, D., & Kahn, R. L. (1978). *The social psychology of organizations* (2nd ed.). New York: Wiley.

70. Hannan, M. T., & Freeman, J. (1984). Structural inertia and organizational change. *American Sociological Review, 49,* 149–164.

71. Goodstein, J., Gautam, K., & Boeker, W. (1994). The effects of board size and diversity on strategic change. *Strategic Management Journal, 15,* 241–250.

72. Tichy, N. M. (1993). *Control your destiny or someone else will.* New York: Doubleday Currency.

73. Tichy, N. M. (1993, December 13). Revolutionize your company. *Fortune,* pp. 114–115, 118.

74. Kotter, J. P., & Schlesinger, L. A. (1979, March–April). Choosing strategies for change. *Harvard Business Review,* pp. 106–114.

75. See Note 72.

76. Farber, S. (1989, September). When employees ask: "What's in it for me?" *Business Month,* p. 79.

77. Pasmore, W. A., & Fagans, M. R. (1992). Participation, industrial development, and organizational change: A review and synthesis. *Journal of Management, 18,* 375–397.

78. Huey, J. (1993, April 5). Managing in the midst of chaos. *Fortune,* pp. 38–41, 44, 46, 48.

79. Porras, J. I., & Robertson, P. J. (1992). Organization development: Theory, practice, and research. In M. D. Dunnette & L. M. Hough (Eds.), *Handbook of industrial and organizational psychology* (2nd ed., Vol. 3, pp. 719–822). Palo Alto, CA: Consulting Psychologists Press.

80. Sanzgiri, J., & Gottlieb, J. Z. (1992). Philosophic and pragmatic influences on the practice of organization development, 1950–2000. *Organizational Dynamics, 21(2),* 57–69.

81. Huse, E. F., & Cummings, T. G. (1985). Organization development and change (3rd ed.). St. Paul, MN: West.

82. Abrahamson, E. (1991). Managerial fads and fashions: The diffusion and rejection of innovations. *Academy of Management Review, 16,* 586–612.

83. See Note 82.

84. Franklin, J. L. (1978, May–June). Improving the effectiveness of survey feedback. *Personnel,* pp. 11–17.

85. Golombiewski, R. T. (1972). *Reviewing organizations: A laboratory approach to planned change.* Itasca, IL: Peacock.

86. Campbell, J. P., & Dunnette, M. D. (1968). Effectiveness of T-group experiences in managerial training and development. *Psychological Bulletin, 70,* 73–104.

87. See Note 66.

88. See Note 66.

89. Beckhard, R. (1972, summer). Optimizing team building efforts. *Journal of Contemporary Business,* pp. 23–32.

90. Vicars, W. M., & Hartke, D. D. (1984). Evaluating OD evaluations: A status report. *Group and Organization Studies, 9,* 177–188.

91. McClenahen, J. S. (1990, October 15). Not fun in the sun. *Industry Week,* pp. 22–24.

92. See Note 91.

93. Fisher, L. (1992, January 12). The latest word on teamwork? "Mush." *New York Times,* p. B16.

94. Burke, W. W. (1982). *Organization development: Principles and practices.* Boston: Little, Brown.

95. Hackman, J. R., & Oldham, G. R. (1980). *Work redesign.* Reading, MA: Addison-Wesley.

96. Munchus, G. (1983). Employer-employee based quality circles in Japan: Human resource implications for American firms. *Academy of Management Review, 8,* 255–261.

97. Meyer, G. W., & Scott, R. G. (1985, spring). Quality circles: Panacea or Pandora's box? *Organizational Dynamics,* 34–50.

98. Griffin, R. W. (1988). Consequences of quality circles in an industrial setting: A longitudinal assessment. *Academy of Management Journal, 31,* 338–358.

99. Suttle, J. L. (1977). Improving life at work—problems and prospects. In J. R. Hackman & J. L. Suttle (Eds.), *Improving life at work: Behavioral science approaches to organizational change* (pp. 1–29). Santa Monica, CA: Goodyear.

100. Fields, M. W., & Thacker, J. W. (1992). Influence of quality of work life on company and union commitment. *Academy of Management Journal, 35,* 439–450.

101. Buch, K. (1992). Quality circles and employee withdrawal behaviors: A cross-organizational study. *Journal of Applied Behavioral Science, 28,* 62–73.

102. Buch, K., & Spangler, R. (1990). The effects of quality circles on performance and promotions. *Human Relations, 43,* 573–582.

103. Jick, T. D., & Ashkenas, R. N. (1985). Involving employees in productivity and QWL improvements: What OD can learn from the manager's perspective. In D. D. Warrick (Ed.), *Contemporary organization development: Current thinking and applications* (pp. 218–230). Glenview, IL: Scott, Foresman.

104. Deutsch, C. H. (1991, May 26). A revival of the quality circle. *New York Times,* p. E4.

105. Drucker, P. (1954). *The practice of management.* New York: Harper & Row.

106. Kondrasuk, J. N., Flager, K., Morrow, D., & Thompson, R. (1984). The effect of management by objectives on organization results. *Group and Organization Studies, 9,* 531–539.

107. Midas, M. T., Jr., & Devine, T. E. (1991, summer). A look at continuous improvement at Northwest Airlines. *National Productivity Review, 10,* 379–394.

108. Kondrasuk, J. N. (1981). Studies in MBO effectiveness. *Academy of Management Review, 6,* 419–430.

109. French, W. L., Bell, C. H., Jr., & Zawacki, R. A. (1989). *Organization development: Theory, practice, and research* (3rd ed.). Homewood, IL: BPI/Irwin.

110. Steel, R. P., & Shane, G. S. (1986). Evaluation research on quality circles: Technical and analytical implications. *Human Relations, 39,* 449–468.

111. See Note 86.

112. See Note 79.

113. Nicholas, J. M. (1982). The comparative impact of organization development interventions on hard criteria measures. *Academy of Management Review, 7,* 531–542.

114. See Note 95.

115. Neuman, G. A., Edwards, J. E., & Raju, N. S. (1989). Organizational development interventions: A meta-analysis of their effects on satisfaction and other attitudes. *Personnel Psychology, 42,* 461–483.

116. Rodgers, R., Hunter, J. E., & Rogers, D. L. (1993). Influence of top management commitment on management program success. *Journal of Applied Psychology, 78,* 151–155.

117. Roberts, D. R., & Robertson, P. J. (1992). Positive-findings bias, and measuring methodological rigor, in evaluations of organization development. *Journal of Applied Psychology, 6,* 918–925.

118. White, S. E., & Mitchell, T. R. (1976). Organization development: A review of research content and research design. *Academy of Management Review, 1,* 57–73.

119. Schaeffer, R. H. & Thomson, H. H. (1992, January-February). Successful change processes begin with results. *Harvard Business Review,* pp. 80–91.

120. Bennis, W. (1977). Bureaucracy and social change: An anatomy of a training failure. In P. H. Mirvis & D. N. Berg (Eds.), *Failures in organizational development and change: Cases and essays for learning* (pp. 191–215). New York: Wiley.

121. Jaeger, A. M. (1986). Organizational development and national culture: Where's the fit? *Academy of Management Review, 11,* 178–190.

122. Trepo, G. (1973, autumn). Management style *à la française. European Business, 39,* 71–79.

123. Blunt, P. (1988). Cultural consequences for organizational change in a Southeast Asian state: Brunei. *Academy of Management Executive, 2,* 235–240.

124. See Note 119.

125. See Note 119.

126. Cobb, A. T. (1986). Political diagnosis: Applications in organizational development. *Academy of Management Review, 11,* 482–496.

127. White, L. P., & Wotten, K. C. (1983). Ethical dilemmas in various stages of organizational development. *Academy of Management Review, 8,* 690–697.

128. Staff Writer (1995, February 6). TransAlta does damage control on BDA (Business Design Associates). *Western Report, 10,* pp. 18–19; Certo, S. C., Sales, C., & Owen, F. A. (1998). *Modern Management in Canada.* Scarborough, Ontario: Prentice Hall Canada Inc.

129. Staff Writer (1995, February 6). TransAlta does damage control on BDA (Business Design Associates). *Western Report, 10,* pp. 18–19 (quote, p. 18).

130. Certo, S. C., Sales, C., & Owen, F. A. (1998). *Modern Management in Canada.* Scarborough, Ontario: Prentice Hall Canada Inc. (quote, p. 343).

131. See Note 129 (quote p. 18).

132. See Note 129 (quote, p. 18).

133. See Note 129.

134. Chu, S. (1998, January 30). There's no business like shoe business. *Canadian Business, 71,* pp. 46–49. Reprinted by permission.

Cumulative Case Part 6

1. Kocho, Keith (1999, January 20). Telephone interview.

2. Kocho, Keith (1999, January 27). Telephone interview.

3. See Note 1.

4. See Note 1.

5. See Note 1.

6. *Dish It Out* Launches on Life Network and the Internet, Internet: digital-ren.com/press_details.asp?id=114&type=4.

7. Sheikh, F. (1998, May 4). The Vision Thing. *Marketing Magazine,* p. 12.

8. The Interview by Gordon MacLeod, Internet: www.atlarge.net/story_kocho2.html.

9. Palmer, R. (1995, November). Who To Know: The Digerati. *Shift Magazine,* p. 31.

GLOSSARY/SUBJECT INDEX

The page on which the key term is defined is printed in boldface.

A

Abilities, 120
  cognitive, 121–122
  emotional intelligence, 120–121
  intellectual, 120–122
  memory, 121
  physical, 122
  see also Personality
Absenteeism, 43, 175
Academy culture, 435
Accommodation, 200, 349, 451
Achievement motivation, 115–117, 118
  and job enrichment programs, 155
  measurement of, 123
Action
  plan, 515, 517
  research, 4
Adaptability, 189
Additive tasks, 246
Adhocracy, 482
Administrative model, 314
Advanced manufacturing technology (AMT), 447
Affective commitment, 180
Affiliation motivation, 117
Age, 185
  and memory, 121–122
Altruism, 339, 340
Ambiguity, 350, 386
Annual reports, 79–80
Apprenticeship programs, 86
Arbitration, 355–356
Assistive technology, 449–451
Aston studies, 488–489
Attitudes, 167–**168**
  behavioural, 168
  cognitive, 168
  evaluative, 168
  job satisfaction. *See* Job satisfaction
  measurement of, 170–172
  negative, 183–192
  object, 168
  organizational commitment. *See* Organizational commitment
  prejudice. *See* Prejudice
  work-related, 168
Attribution, 68–70
  approach, 408
  causal, 69–70
  concensus, 70
  consistency, 70
  distinctiveness, 70
  faulty, 351
  of responsibility, 69–70
Autocratic leadership style, 402
Automation, 45, 447–449
Autonomy, 156, 159–160
Availability heuristic, 317
Avoidance, 82, 349
Awareness-based diversity training, 188

B

Baby boom generation, 42
Baby bust generation, 185
Bargaining, 353–355
  framing, 354
  perceptions, 354–355
  tactics, 354
  win-win vs. win-lose, 355

Baseball team culture, 435
Baseline audit, 88
Behaviour
  autocratic, 402–403
  causes, 70
  competition, 344
  constructive, 512
  contingent variables, 8–9
  desired, 88
  direction of, 135
  external causes, 70, 75
  extraordinary, 410
  internal causes, 70
  maintaining, 135–136
  organizational. *See* Organizational behaviour
  permissive, 402–403
  prosocial. *See* Prosocial behaviour
  standards of, 434
  undesirable, 94
Behavioural sciences, 3
Benchmarking, 51
Benefits
  cafeteria-style plans, 151
  of group decision making, 321
  same sex, 186
  temporary employees, 47
Benriya, 80
Bias
  in decision making, 318
  favouritism, 407–408
  hostile attributional, 359
  overcoming, 75–76
  political, 389
  qualitative research, 26
  see also Perceptual biases
"Big five" dimensions of personality, 104–105
Board of directors, 511
Boom, Bust and Echo, 42
Bottom-line mentality, 56
Boundary spanning activities, 111–112
Boundaryless organization, 473–475
Bounded
  discretion, 321
  rationality, 314
Brainstorming, 324
Bureaucracy, 14, 476
  machine, 481
  professional, 481
Burnout, 216–217

C

Cafeteria-style benefit plans, 151
Canada Awards for Excellence, 52
Canadian Environmental Protection Act, 343
Canadian mosaic, 40–41
Canardarm, 366
Canary Wharf, 198
Career, 203–**204**
  contracting, 204
  developmental opportunities, 205
  education and training, 205
  and gender, 208–210
  geographic relocations, 204
  goals, 204–205
  health care, 205
  information technology, 205
  job rotation, 207
  lateral moves, 204, 207

  paths, 205–207
  planning, 204–207
  signs of trouble, 207–208
  success. *See* Success
  tracks, 205–207
Case method, 26
Cause-and-effect
  logic of, 22–25
  relationships, 21–22
Centralization, 280
Centralized networks, 280
Chaebols, 482
Change
  adapting to, 499
  administrative systems, 504
  agents, 109, 410
  barriers to, 510–511
  economic competition, 506
  employee involvement in, 512
  first-order, 499
  and globalization, 498–499
  individual barriers to, 510
  information distribution, 500
  information interpretation, 501
  knowledge acquisition, 500
  learning organizations, 499–501
  organizational, 498
  organizational memory, 501
  organizational size, 502–503
  in people, 508
  performance gap, 506
  planned, 502–505
  in products, 502
  readiness, 509–510
  regulatory, 506
  resistance to, 510–512
  second-order, 499
  in services, 502
  structural, 502–503, 507
  survey feedback, 513–514
  targets, 506–508
  technological, 504–505, 508
  unplanned, 502, 505–506
Charisma, 375
Charismatic leaders, 409–410
Chart. *See* Organizational chart
Charter of Rights and Freedoms, 41, 185, 186, 450
Cheaper by the Dozen, 11
Child-care facilities, 44
Circadian rhythm, 117
Classical organizational theory, 14, 476
Client relationships, 159
Closing the Gap, 187, 209
Club culture, 435
Co-op programs, 86
Coalition building, 371
Coalitions, 382
Coercive power, 373
Cognitive
  abilities, 121
  side of intelligence, 120
Cohesiveness, 239–240
Collaboration, 349
Collectivism, 38–39
Commitment
  affective, 180
  bases, 180–181
  continuance, 180
  escalation of, 319–320
  goal, 141–142

normative, 180
organizational. *See* Organizational
commitment
quality of work life programs, 516
to corporate mission, 434
to ethical conduct, 389
to training, 66
and transformational leadership, 412
Communication, 267-268
barriers. *See* Communication barriers
channels of, 268
and coordinated action, 269
cross-cultural differences, 278–279, 280
decoding, 268
downward, 287
electronic media, 272–274
encoding, 268
faulty, 351
feedback, 268–269
formal, 279–283
and gender, 278
horizontal, 289
informal, 283–285
internal vs. external, 290–291
Internet, 273–274
interpersonal facet, 269
MUM effect, 289
networks. *See* Communication networks
noise, 269
nonverbal, 274–276
open door policy, 289
oral. *See* Verbal communication
organizational structure. *See*
Organizational structure
personal communication style, 276–277
process of, 267–269
role of, 269
two-way, 271
upward, 287–289
verbal. *See* Verbal communication
written. *See* Verbal communication
Communication barriers
COMVOC, 291
distortion, 295
effective listening, 292–294
feedback, 295–297
gatekeepers, 294
jargon, 291
KISS principle, 291–292
omission, 295
overload, 294–295
queuing, 294
redundancy, 295
simple language, 291–292
verification, 295
Communication networks, 279
centralization, 280
centralized, 280
decentralized, 280
formal, 279–283
grapevine, 284
informal, 283–285
old-boys network, 283
rumours, 284–285
and task performance, 281–283
varieties of, 279–280
Competition, 344, 349, 350, 399
Competitive intelligence, 505
Competitors, 345
Componential intelligence, 120
Compressed workweeks, 43
Compromise, 349
Computer-aided design and engineering
(CAD/CAE), 447
Computer-based training programs, 86
Computer-integrated manufacturing (CIM), 447
**Computerized performance monitoring,
451**–453
Confirmation candidate, 318
Conflict, 349

ambiguity, 350
cognitive, 353
competition. *See* Competition
cultural differences, 350
distribution, 349–350
distrust, 352
faulty attributions, 351
faulty communication, 351
grudges, 351
inappropriate criticism, 351
integration, 349–350
interpersonal causes, 351–360
management. *See* Conflict management
negative effects, 352–353
organizational causes, 350
positive effects, 353
styles of handling, 349
Conflict management
arbitration, 355–356
bargaining, 353–355
mediation, 355–356
superordinate goals, 356
third party intervention, 355–356
Confrontation meetings, 172
Conglomerate, 482–483
Conscientiousness, 104
Consensus, 70
Consideration, 403
Consistency, 70, 124
Consortium, 348
Consultation, 371
Contextual intelligence, 120
Contingencies of reinforcement, 82
Contingency
approach, 8, 477–479
theories of leadership, 414
Contingent workforce, 47–48
Continuance commitment, 180
Continuous reinforcement, 83
Continuous-process production, 486
Contractual tactics, 202
Control, 17, 25
Convergence hypothesis, 38
Cooperation, 339
benefits, 343
employee interdependence, 347
interorganizational coordination, 347–348
organizational structure, 347
personal orientations, 345–347
reciprocity, 344
reward systems, 347
superordinate goals, 356
trust, 344–345
Cooperators, 346
Core
business, 46, 473–474
competency, 46
Corporate
bullying, 377
hotlines, 295–296
image, 78–80
strategy, 205–206
universities, 86
*Corporate Abuse: How Lean and Mean Robs
People and Profits*, 377
Correlation coefficient, 20
Correlational research, 20
Correlations, 20–21
Correspondent inferences, 68–69
Counternorms, 55
Covictimization, 184
Creative thinking, 323–324
conflict resolution, 355
Creativity, 120
Criterion standard, 88
Criterion-related validity, 124
Critical incident technique, 171
Criticism. *See* Feedback
Cross-functional teams, 252–253
Cultural differences

communication, 278–279, 280
conflict-handling styles, 350
cooperation, 346
decision making, 308–309
organizational development, 520
Cultural homogenization, 35–36
Cultural identity, 35–36
Cultural pluralism, 40
Culture, 36–38
academy, 435
baseball team, 435
club, 435
collectivism, 38–39
collectivist, 309
convergence hypothesis, 38
divergence hypothesis, 38
dominant, 434
feminine, 40
fortress, 435
Hofstede's dimensions of, 38–40
individualism, 38–39
masculine, 40
organizational. *See* Organizational culture
power distance, 39
shock, 37
uncertainty avoidance, 38
Customer service, 453–454

D

Daily hassles, 214–215
Decentralization, 177–178, 467–468
Decentralized networks, 280
Decision making, 304
administrative model, 314
alternative generation, 306
analytical style, 308
analytical model, 305–307
availability heuristic, 317
barriers to effective, 320–321
behavioural style, 308
bounded discretion, 321
choice, 307
conceptual style, 308
confirmation candidate, 318
cultural differences, 308–309
decision-style inventory, 308
directive style, 307–308
empowered, 312
escalation of commitment phenomenon,
319–320
evaluation of solutions, 306
follow-up, 307
formulation, 305
framing, 316–317
groups. *See* Group decision making
groupthink. *See* Groupthink
heuristics, 317–318
image theory, 315–316
implementation, 305, 307
implicit favourite option, 318
objectives, 306
political face-saving pressure, 320
predecision, 306
problem identification, 306
rational-economic model, 313–314
representativeness heuristic, 317
self-justification, 319
style, 307–308
support systems (DSS), 306
time constraints, 320
top-down, 312
types of decisions, 309–312
Decision style, 307
Decision support systems (DSS), 306
Decision-style model, 307–308
Decisions
bounded rationality, 314
certain, 310–312
imperfect, 316–320

and leadership, 420
limitations of, 326
nonprogrammed, 310
probability of outcome, 310
programmed, 309
rational, 312–314
riskiness of, 310–312
satisficing, 314
strategic, 310
uncertain, 310–312
Decoding, 268
Deficiency needs, 138
Delphi technique, 328–330
Demographic trends, 42
Departmentalization, 468–475
Dependent variable, 24
Depersonalization, 216
Design
  for disassembly, 454
  of Experiments, 52
  organizational. *See* Organizational design
Developing nations, 34
Development. *See* Organizational development
Developmental opportunities, 205
Direct tactics, 202
Directorate of Personnel Selection, 15
Disabilities, 185–186, 449–451
Disabilities Act (U.S.), 450
Discipline, 92–95
  communication of reasons, 94
  consistent, 94
  immediate, 93
  maximizing effectiveness of, 93–5
  moderate levels, 93–94
  noncontingent rewards, 94–95
  progressive, 92
  undesirable behaviour, 94
  see also Punishment
Discrimination, 183
  covictimization, 184
  and disabilities, 450–451
  glass ceiling, 184
  see also Diversity; Gender; Minority groups;
  Prejudice; Race; Women
Dissatisfaction, 175–177
Distinction Award (YWCA), 166
Distinctiveness, 70
Distraction-conflict model, 241
Distribution, 349–350
Divergence hypothesis, 38
Diversity, 9, 33
  adaptability, 189
  aging workers, 42
  among Canadian companies, 191–192
  awareness-based training, 188
  cross-cultural understanding, 189
  ethnic. *See* Ethnic diversity
  facilitation skills, 189
  flexibility, 189
  in groups, 244–245
  intercultural communication, 189
  managerial support, 190
  melting pot, 40–41
  mosaic, 40–41
  and prejudice, 184
  and profit, 189–190
  racial. *See* Racial diversity
  in sexual orientation, 186
  skills-based training, 188–189
  support facilities, 44–45
  training, 43, 188–190
  valuing, 41
  workforce, 41–42
  and workplace aggression, 359
Diversity Education Awards, 192
Diversity management programs, 188–190
Division of labour, 14, 463–464
Divisional structure, 481–482
Dominant culture, 434
Doomsday management, 508

Downsizing, 46, 463, 465, 502–503
  see also Restructuring
Drive theory of social facilitation, 241
Dual authority, 472
Dual-core model, 504

E

Economic growth, 118
Economies of scale, 470, 471, 472, 484
Education, 205
Elder-care facilities, 44
Electronic
  mail (e-mail), 273–274
  meeting systems, 331
Emissions trading, 348
Emotional
  intelligence, 120–121
  stability, 105
Empathy, 113, 121
Emphasis on quality, 33
Empire building, 383
Employee
  assistance programs (EAPs), 210, 221
  handbook, 270–271
  withdrawal, 175
Employees
  alignment of interests of, 182
  and change, 508, 512
  and client relationships, 159
  counselling services, 210
  education, 97
  empowerment, 117
  financial security, 139–140
  and goal-setting process, 143
  individualized counselling, 178
  job enrichment programs, 155
  participation, 419–422
  procedural justice, 149
  recognition, 140
  respect for, 130
  social activities for, 140
  termination of, 288–289
  trainers, 205
  treatment, 6
  turnover. *See* Turnover
Employment Equity Act, 450
Employment interview
  impression management, 77–78
  self-promotion, 78
  tactics, 78
Empowered decision making, 312
Empowerment, 117, 377–378
Encoding, 268
Engineering technology, 446
Entry shock, 200
Equalizers, 346
Equitable
  payment, 145
  relationships, 144
Equity theory, 144–149
  equitable payment, 145
  inputs, 145
  outcomes, 145
  overpayment inequity, 145, 147–148
  social comparisons, 144
  underpayment inequity, 145, 147
ERG theory, 138–139
Escalation of commitment phenomenon, 319–320
Esteem needs, 138
Ethics, 33, 54–57
  audit, 57
  bottom-line mentality, 56
  charismatic leaders, 411
  code of, 57
  company initiatives, 296
  counternorms, 55
  decisions, 313
  of downsizing, 465

exploitative mentality, 56
  Madison Avenue mentality, 56
  managerial values, 56
  and organizational development, 521–522
  organizational politics, 386–389
  privacy concerns, 124
  promotion of, 56–57
  punishment, 92
  stonewalling, 55
  test scores, 124
Ethnic diversity, 42, 244–245
Evaluation apprehension, 241
Evening persons, 117–120
Exchange, 371
Executives
  pay-for-performance plans, 154
  performance, 154
  training programs, 86
  women, 166, 184, 187
Exhaustion, 216
Existence needs, 139
Expatriates, 35
Expectancy, 149
Expectancy theory, 149–153
  expectancy, 149
  instrumentality, 149
  valence, 149
Experience
  direct, 110
  and learning, 81
  openness to, 105
  organizational, 436
  sampling, 211
  vicarious, 110
Experienced meaningfulness, 157
Experiential intelligence, 120
Experimental method, 22–25
Expert power, 374, 376
Expertise, 311–312
Exploitative mentality, 56
Extinction, 82

F

Facilitator, 514
Failure, 198
Family-supportive policies, 220
Feedback, 88
  achievement motivation, 116
  brown bag meetings, 297
  and change, 512
  communication, 268–269
  corporate hotlines, 295–296
  employee surveys, 297
  goal attainment, 143–144
  immediate, 514
  inappropriate, 351
  job design, 156, 159
  obtaining, 295–297
  skip-level meetings, 297
  suggestion systems, 295
  survey method, 513–514
  360 degree feedback, 88
Feminine culture, 40
Field studies, 25
The Fifth Discipline: The Art and Practice of the Learning Organization, 499
Financial security, 139–140
First-impression error, 73
First-order change, 499
Fixed
  interval schedules, 83
  ratio schedules, 83
Fixed-sum error, 354
Flexibility, 122, 401
Flexible
  manufacturing systems, 447
  work arrangements, 43–44
Flexplace policies, 44, 49
Flextime programs, 43

Followers, 407–413
Formal groups, 232
Fortress culture, 435
Framing, 316–317, 354
Free ride. *See* Social, loafing
Functional
    authority, 472
    organization, 468–469
Fundamental attribution error, 71

G

Game-playing, 382–384
Gender
    and careers, 208–210
    and communication, 278
    and leadership styles, 404
    and mentoring, 203
    product design, 442–443
    wages, 208
General Management Aptitude Test, 124
Generation X, 185, 226
Generation Y, 185
Glass ceiling, 184, 208–209, 223
Globalization, 33–36
    and change, 498–499
    cross-cultural communication,
        278–279, 280
    cultural homogenization, 35–36
    definition, **35**
    economic interdependence, 35
    international competitiveness, 399
    international trade, 34–35
    multinational corporations, 35
    strategic alliances and, 484–485
Goal commitment, 141–142
Goal-congruence orientation, 179–180
Goal-setting, 140–144
Goals
    acceptable performance, 142–143
    action plan, 517
    assessment of attainment, 517
    career, 204–205
    difficult, 142–143
    effective, 142–144
    feedback, 143–144
    implementation, 517
    management by objectives, 517–518
    and performance, 17–18
    personal, 141–142
    specific, 142
    superordinate, 356
    task, 17
    workers participation in setting, 143
Grapevine, 284
Great person theory, 400–402
Grid training, 405–406
Group decision making, 321–324
    benefits, 321
    brainstorming, 324
    conflict, 321
    defensive avoidance, 327–328
    Delphi technique, 328–330
    drawbacks, 321–322
    electronic meeting systems, 331
    groupthink. *See* Groupthink
    hypervigilance, 327
    improving, 327–328
    vs. individual, 322–324
    intimidation, 322
    nominal group technique, 330–331
    stepladder technique, 331–332
    unconflicted adherence, 327
    unconflicted change, 327
Group dynamics, 230
Group structure, 235–240
Groupism, 184–187
Groups, 5, 230–240
    accountability, 250
    action plan, 515

ad hoc committees, 232
brainstorming, 324
cohesiveness, 239–240, 324–325
command, 232
computerized performance monitoring,
    242–243
conflict, 321–322
and creative thinking, 324
culturally diverse, 244–245
decision making. *See* Group decision
    making
development stages, 233–235
diagnostic session, 515
distraction-conflict model, 241
drive theory of social facilitation, 241
encounter, 514
evaluation apprehension, 241
formal, 232
formation of, 233
friendship, 232
groupthink, 240
improved performance, 327–328
individual performance in, 241–243
inertia, 511
informal, 232
interest, 232
intimidation by leaders, 322
laboratory, 514
membership in, 233
norms, 236–237
power, 378–381
prestige of, 237–239
role, 235
role ambiguity, 235
role differentiation, 235–236
role expectations, 235
role incumbent, 235
self-oriented role, 236
social facilitation, 241–243
social impact theory, 247
social loafing, 246–249
socioemotional role, 236
standing committees, 232
status, 238
structured meeting, 330–331
subgroups, 326
T-groups, 514
task, 232
task forces, 232
task-oriented role, 236
team building, 514–515
teams. *See* Teams
types of, 231–233
videoconferencing, 244
work, 251–252
see also Teams
Groupthink, 240, 325
    avoidance, 326
    and conflict, 353
    devil's advocate, 326
    nature of, 325–326
    second-chance meetings, 326
Growth needs, 138, 139
A Guide to Liberating Your Soul, 442

H

Halo effect, 71–72
Harry Jerome Awards, 192
Hawthorne studies, 11–13, 476
Health
    care, 205
    and personality type, 106–108
    and stress, 217
Herzberg's two-factor theory, 172–173
Heuristics, 317–318
Hierarchy of authority, 463
High technology, 447
High-performance teams, 251
Hofstede's dimensions of culture, 38–40

Horizontal job loading, 153
Hostile attributional bias, 359
Human relations movement, 11–13
Humanagement, 62
HURIER model, 293
Hydrokids, 44
Hypothesis, 18, 20
    convergence, 38
    divergence, 38

I

*I'd Like to Buy the World a Coke: The Life and
    Leadership of Robert Goizueta*, 197
Image theory, 315
Implicit
    favourite, 318
    memory, 121, 122
Impression management, 77
    interviewees, 77–78
    organizations, 78–80
    protégés, 202
    self-monitoring, 113
Incentives, 90
    cafeteria-style benefit plans, 151
    pay-for-performance plans, 152, 154
    profit-sharing plans, 182
    see also Rewards
Incompatibility error, 354
Independent
    contractor, 204
    variable, 24
Individual, 5
    differences. *See* Personal characteristics
Individualism, 38–39
Individualism-collectivism, 346
Individualists, 345
Industrial psychology, 15
Industrial robotics (IR), 447
Informate, 46
Informating, 45
Information
    access to, 381
    in decision making, 311
    distribution, 500
    interpretation, 501
    overload, 294–295
    power, 373
    processing, 120
    reduction of uncertainty, 311
    saturation, 281–282
    shared, 513–514
    technology, 205
Ingratiation, 371
Initiating structure, 403
Initiative, 14
Innovation, 433
Inputs, 145
Inspirational appeal, 371
Instrument conditioning, 81
    see also Operant conditioning
Instrumentality, 149
Integration, 349–350
Intellectual
    abilities, 120–122
    capital, 97
Intelligence, 120–122
    cognitive side of, 120
    competitive, 505
    componential, 120
    contextual, 120
    emotional, 120–121
    experiential, 120
Interactionist perspective, 104
Interdependence, 489–491
Intermittent reinforcement, 83
International Organization for Standardization,
    51–52
International trade, 34–35
International Victimization Survey, 358

Internet, 273–274
Interorganizational coordination, 347–348
Interpersonal relations, and personality type, 108
Interviews
    employment. *See* Employment interview
    job satisfaction, 172
Inventories, 123
Investigator software, 273
IQ tests, 120
Isolation, 212

J

Japan
    achievement motivation, 118
    kaizan, 118
    saving face, 80
Jargon, 291, 438–439
Job characteristics model, 155–158, 516
Job Descriptive Index (JDI), 170
Job design, 153
    autonomy, 156, 159–160
    feedback, 156
    horizontal job loading, 153
    job characteristics model, 155–158, 516
    job enlargement, 153–155, 516
    job enrichment, 155, 516
    and motivation, 158–160
    skill variety, 155
    task identity, 155
    task significance, 155–156
    vertical job loading, 155, 159–160
Job Diagnostic Survey, 158
Job enlargement, 153–155, 181–182, 516
Job enrichment, 155, 516
Job interview. *See* Employment interview
Job performance
    abilities, 150
    communication media sensitivity, 271–272
    monitoring, 243
    vs. motivation, 136, 150
    opportunities to perform, 151
    and personality type, 107–108
    proactive personality trait, 109
    and rewards, 151–152
    role perceptions, 150–151
    and self-monitoring, 111–112
    skills, 150
    and task goals, 17–18
Job rotation, 207
Job satisfaction, 168
    and absenteeism, 175–176
    decentralized power, 177–178
    disposition, 169
    dissatisfaction consequences, 175–177
    employee withdrawal, 175–176
    and equity, 145
    fair pay, 177
    field of interest, 178
    flextime programs, 43
    general, 169
    individualized employee counselling, 178
    Job Descriptive Index (JDI), 170
    Minnesota Satisfaction Questionnaire
        (MSQ), 170
    and organizational culture, 437
    Pay Satisfaction Questionnaire (PSQ), 170
    and productivity, 17
    promotion of, 177–178
    quality supervision, 177
    quality of work life programs, 516
    and supervisory style, 171
    task performance, 176–177
    theories of, 172–174
    and transformational leadership, 412
    and turnover, 175–176
    two-factor theory, 172–173
    and unemployment rates, 176
    value theory, 173–174
Job sharing, 43–44

Jobs, 45
    choosing, 204
    and technology, 447–448
Joint ventures, 483
Judgments, 68–69
    objective factors, 76
    performance appraisals. *See* Performance
    rash, 76
    see also Prejudice; Social perception

K

Kaizen, 118
Keiretsu, 482
Kelley's theory of causal attribution, 70, 71
KISS principle, 291–292
Knowledge
    acquisition, 500
    workers, 48, 130

L

Lab experiments. *See* Experimental method
Large-batch (mass) production, 486
Law of Effect, 81
Leader match, 416
**Leader-member exchange (LMX) model,
    407**–408
Leaders, 398
    as change agents, 410
    charismatic, 409–411
    relationship with followers, 407–408
    team, 412–413
    top, 472
Leadership, 397-398
    achievement-oriented style, 418
    artists, 406
    attribution approach, 408
    autocratic behaviour, 402–403
    cognitive ability, 401
    consideration, 403–405
    contingency theories of effectiveness,
        414–422
    craftsmen, 406
    vs. dictator, 398
    effective, 399
    environmental sensitivity, 410
    esteem for least preferred coworker, 414
    extraordinary behaviour, 410
    flexibility, 401
    great person theory, 400–402
    grid training, 405–406
    individualized consideration, 412
    and influence, 398
    initiating structure, 403–405
    inspirational motivation, 412
    instrumental style, 418
    intellectual stimulation, 412
    leader-member exchange (LMX) model,
        407–408
    LPC contingency theory, 414–416
    vs. managers, 398–399
    motivation, 401
    normative decision theory, 419–422
    participative style, 418
    path-goal theory, 418
    people-oriented, 403–405
    permissive behaviour, 402–403
    price, 436
    production-oriented, 403–405
    romanticizing, 423
    self-confidence, 409
    situational leadership theory, 416–417
    substitutes for, 422–423
    supportive style, 418
    of teams, 412–413
    technocrats, 406
    transformational, 411–412, 413
    vision, 409–410
Leadership motivation pattern (LMP), 117

Learning, 67, **81**
    attention, 85
    baseline audit, 88
    behavioural reproduction, 85
    and change, 81
    competitive advantages of, 501
    corporate universities, 86
    criterion standard, 88, 91
    discipline, 92–95
    experience, 81
    information distribution, 500
    information interpretation, 501
    knowledge acquisition, 500
    observational, 85
    operant conditioning, 81–85
    organization, 499–501
    organizational behaviour management,
        88–91
    organizational memory, 501
    participation, 87
    reinforcer, 88
    repetition, 87
    retention, 85
    rewards, 91
    self-directed, 131
    shaping, 91
    360 degree feedback, 88
    training, 86–88
    transfer of training, 87–88
Legislation
    and change, 506
    employment equity, 450
    German "take back" law, 454
    international trade, 34
    whistle-blowers, 343
Legitimate power, 372
Legitimating, 371
Line positions, 466
Listening, 292–294
Locke's value theory, 173–174
LPC, 414
LPC contingency theory, 414–416

M

Machiavellianism, 113–115
Machine bureaucracy, 481
Madison Avenue mentality, 56
Management
    diverse workforce, 188–190
    doomsday, 508
    effective listening, 293–294
    impression. *See* Impression management
    and need theories, 139–140
    negative views of employees, 6
    by objectives (MOB), 517–518, 520
    open-book, 500
    performance, 161–162
    total quality, 51–52
    and unions. *See* Unions
Managers
    authority of, 14
    definition, 398
    effective performance goals, 142–144
    and equity theory, 147–149
    and expectancy theory, 151–153
    job design guidelines, 158–160
    line vs. staff, 466–467
    middle line, 480
    need for, 205
    project, 206
    two-boss, 472
Masculine culture, 40
Matrix
    bosses, 472
    organization, 471–472
    of technologies, 446
Measurement
    achievement motivation, 123
    confrontation meetings, 172

criterion-related validity, 124
critical incident technique, 171
emotional intelligence, 121
intelligence, 120
internal consistency, 124
interviews, 172
job satisfaction, 170–172
objective tests, 123
and organizational citizenship behaviour, 341
projective tests, 123
questionnaires, 170–171
rating scales, 170–171
reliability of, 123–124
test-retest reliability, 124
validity, 124
Mechanistic organization, 478, 486, 504
Mediation, 355–356
Meditation, 219
Meech Lake Accord, 240, 325
Megacorporations, 482–483
Melting pot, 40–41
Memory, 121–122
and age, 121–122
implicit, 121, 122
organizational, 501
prospective, 121–122
semantic, 121, 122
short-term, 121
working, 121
Mentor, 201
Mentoring, 200–203
cultivation, 202
definition, **201**
formal programs for, 202
formation of, 202
and gender, 203
impression management, 202
initiation, 202
protegé, 201
and race, 203
redefinition, 202
and self-monitoring, 113
separation, 202
and transformational leaders, 412
Mercury Award, 166
Merger, 348, 443–444
Merit-based pay systems, 116
Midlife crisis, 210
Mildly Ill Child/Eldercare program, 44
Minnesota Multiphasic Personality Inventory, 406
Minnesota Satisfaction Questionnaire (MSQ), 170
Minority groups
ethnic diversity, 42
job satisfaction, 169
and prejudice, 186–187
see also Race
Mission statements, 182
Modelling, 85
Modular organizations, 473–474
Monitoring
e-mail, 273
effectiveness of decision, 307
electronic, 273, 451–453
Morning persons, 117–120
Mosaic, 40–41
Motivating potential score (MPS), 158
Motivation, 85, 135
achievement, 115–117
arousal, 135
attainment of desired performance, 151
deficiency needs, 138
direction, 135
equity theory, 144–149
ERG theory, 138–139
esteem needs, 138
expectancy theory, 149–153
goal-setting theory, 140–144
growth needs, 138, 139

inspirational, 412
job design, 153–160
and job performance, 11, 136, 150
leadership, 401
maintaining behaviour, 135–136
multifaceted, 136
need hierarchy theories, 136–139
need theories, 136–140
personalized power, 401
physiological needs, 137
power, 117
quality of work life programs, 516
safety needs, 137–138
self-actualization, 138
social needs, 138
socialized power, 401
Multicultural society, 37
Multiculturalism, 40–41
Multiculturalism Act, 41
Multifactor Leadership Questionnaire, 412
Multigenerational household, 42
Multilateral Agreement on Investment, 35
Multinational corporations (MNCs), 35
Multiple regression, 21
MUM effect, 289
MUT (Multi Unit Transporter), 227
Mutual service consortia, 483

N
National origin, 186–187
Naturalistic observation, 26
Need
for achievement, 115–117
hierarchy theories, 136–139, 233
theories, 136–140
Negative
affectivity, 106
correlation, 20
reinforcement, 82
Negotiation, 353–355
Neo-classical organizational theory, 476–477
Newsletters, 270
Noise, 269
Nominal group technique (NGT), 330–331
Noncontractual tactics, 202
Nonprogrammed decisions, 309
Nonroutine technology, 446
Nonverbal communication, 274–276
appearance, 274–275
organizational space, 275–276
timeliness, 275
Normal science research, 4
Normative
commitment, 180
decision theory, 419–422
Norms, 236–237
North American Free Trade Agreement, 35, 502, 506
Number aptitude, 121

O
OB Mod, 88
Objective tests, 123
Observational learning, 85
Occupational demands, 211
Old-boys network, 283
Open systems, 7
Open-book management, 500
Openness to experience, 105
Operant conditioning, 81–85
avoidance, 82
contingencies of reinforcement, 81–82
continuous reinforcement, 83
extinction, 82
fixed interval schedules, 83
intermittent reinforcement, 83
Law of Effect, 81
negative reinforcement, 82

partial reinforcement, 83
positive reinforcement, 81
punishment, 82
schedules of reinforcement, 83–85
variable interval schedules, 83
variable ratio schedules, 84
Operating core, 479
Oral communication. *See* Verbal communication
Organic organizations, 478–479, 486, 504
Organizational behaviour, 3
applications, 4
classical organizational theory, 14
focus of, 3
history of, 10–16
human relations movement, 11–13
management, 88–91
modification, 88
no "best" approach, 8–9
normative commitment, 180
personality. *See* Personality
and science, 3
scientific management, 10–11
scientific method, 4
Organizational chameleons, 382
Organizational change. *See* Change
Organizational chart, 286–287
communication across, 287–290
decentralization, 467–468
definition, 462–463
division of labour, 463–464
hierarchy of authority, 463
line positions, 466–467
span of control, 464–466
staff positions, 467
Organizational citizenship behaviour (OCB), 340
altruism, 339, 340
civic virtue, 340
conscientiousness, 340
courtesy, 340
determinants, 341
forms of, 340
good sport, 340
and organizational excellence, 341–342
and punishment, 341
transformational leadership, 412
Organizational commitment, 178
affective commitment, 180
bases of commitment, 179–181
commitment profiles, 179
components, 178–181
continuance commitment, 180
employee interests, 182
employee values, 182
enhancing, 181–183
foci of commitment, 179
goal-congruence orientation, 179–180
job enrichment, 181–182
low, 181
profit-sharing plans, 182
recruitment, 182
side-bets orientation, 179
Organizational conflict. *See* Conflict
Organizational culture, 432-433
academy, 435
baseball team, 435
ceremonies, 439
changes in, 441–445
club, 435
collaborative orientation, 433
commitment to corporate mission, 434
company founders, 436
critical incidents, 438
detail-oriented, 433
dominant culture, 434
easygoingness, 433
effects of, 439–441
formation, 436–438
fortress, 435
function of, 434

innovation, 433
internal interaction, 436–437
intervention design, 437
jargon, 438–439
mergers and acquisitions, 443–444
organizational experience, 436
organizational performance, 440
people-oriented, 433
person-organization fit, 440
planned change, 444
results-oriented, 433
sense of identity, 434
stability, 433
standards of behaviour, 434
subculture, 434
symbols, 438
transmission of, 438–439
and turnover, 440
types of, 435–436
workforce composition, 441–444
written principles, 439
Organizational design, 476
adhocracy, 482
Aston studies, 488–489
classical organizational theory, 476
conglomerate, 482–483
contingency approach, 477–479
divisional structure, 481–482
external environment, 477–478
interorganizational, 482–485
joint ventures, 483
machine bureaucracy, 481
middle line, 480
Mintzberg's forms, 479–482
mutual service consortia, 483
neo-classical organizational theory, 476–477
operating core, 479
professional bureaucracies, 481
simple structure, 480–481
stable conditions, 478–479
strategic alliances, 483–485
strategic apex, 480
support staff, 480
technological imperative, 489
technology and, 485–491
technostructure, 480
Thompson's framework, 489–491
turbulent conditions, 478–479
value-chain partnerships, 483
Woodward studies, 485–488
workflow integration, 488–489
Organizational development, 512-513
cultural barriers, 520
effectiveness, 518–519
ethics of, 521–522
interventions, 513
management by objectives, 517–518, 520
practitioners, 513
process orientation, 519–521
quality circles, 516
quality of work life programs, 516
results orientation, 519–521
sensitivity training, 514
survey feedback, 513–514
Organizational effectiveness, 341
Organizational justice, 360
Organizational memory, 501
Organizational politics, 370
access to information, 381
ambiguity, 386
authority games, 383
blame, 382
and change, 511–512
change games, 384
coalitions, 382
connections, 382
ethics, 386–389
games, 382–384
human resource management, 384–385

impressions, 381–382
ingratiation, 382
minimizing effects of, 390
occurrence, 385–386
organizational maturity, 385
power base games, 383
reciprocity, 382
rivalry games, 383–384
scapegoating, 382
support bases, 382
tactical forms, 381–384
timing of action, 384–385
triggers, 384
Organizational socialization, 199
accommodation, 200
encounter stage, 200
entry shock, 200
metamorphosis stage, 200
nature of, 199–200
orientation programs, 200
pre-entry period, 199–200
realistic job previews, 200
Organizational space, 275–276
Organizational structure, 285, 462
boundaryless organization, 473–475
changes in, 507
chart. *See* Organizational chart
and cooperation, 347
decentralization, 467–468
departmentalization, 468–475
downward communication, 287
functional organization, 468–469
horizontal communication, 289
matrix organization, 471–472
modular organizations, 473–474
MUM effect, 289
product organizations, 469–471
technological imperative, 489
temporary overlay, 472
upward communication, 287–289
virtual organizations, 474
Organizations, 5, 7
annual reports, 79–80
barrier-free, 473
boundaryless, 473–475
and change agents, 109
communications role. *See* Communication
corporate image, 78–80
counternorms, 55
divisions within, 469–471
dynamic nature, 7–8
ethical, 54–57
functional, 468–469
global arena, 33–36
impression management, 78–80
intellectual capital. *See* Intellectual
leaner, 45–47
learning, 499–501
matrix, 471–472
mature matrix, 472
mechanistic, 478, 486, 504
mentoring programs, 202
mission statements, 182
modular, 473–474
organic, 478–479, 486, 504
product, 469–471
restructuring, 45–47
stress management, 219–221
virtual, 474
Orientation programs, 200
Outcomes, 145
Outplacement services, 140, 288
Outsourcing, 46, 473–474, 502
Overload, 294-295
Overpayment inequity, 145, 147–148

P

Partial reinforcement, 83
Participant observation, 26

Participation, 87
Pay Satisfaction Questionnaire (PSQ), 170
Pay systems, and job satisfaction, 177
Pay-for-performance plans, 152
Perception, 67
selective, 72–73
see also Social perception
Perceptual biases, 71–74
first-impression error, 73
fundamental attribution error, 71
halo effect, 71–72
overcoming, 75–76
selective perception, 73–74
similar-to-me effect, 72–73
see also Bias
Perceptual speed, 121
Performance
appraisal, 76–77
job. *See* Job performance
management, 161–162
Permissive leadership style, 402
Person-job fit, 104, 108
Personal appeal, 371
Personal characteristics, 102
and cooperation, 344
measurement of, 122–124
see also Personality
Personal communication style, 276–277
Personal power, 373–375
Personal support policies, 45
Personality, 102, **103**
achievement motivation, 115–117, 118
affiliation motivation, 117
agreeableness, 105
"big five" dimensions of, 104–105
conscientiousness, 104
direct experience, 110
emotional stability, 105
evening persons, 117–120
extroversion-introversion, 105
interactionist perspective, 104
and interpersonal relations, 108
leadership motivation pattern, 117
Machiavellianism, 113–115
measurement, 122–1124
morning persons, 117–120
nature of, 102–104
negative affectivity, 106
openness to experience, 105
and performance, 107–108
person-job fit. *See* Person-job fit
person-situation controversy, 103–104
positive affectivity, 106
power motivation, 117
proactive, 108–110
role in organizational behaviour, 102–104
self-efficacy, 110–111
self-monitoring. *See* Self-monitoring
type A behaviour pattern, 106–108, 218, 352
type B behaviour pattern, 106–108, 218, 352
vicarious experience, 110
work-related motives, 115–117
see also Abilities
Personnel, 15
Physical abilities, 122
Physiological needs, 137
Playing To Win, 428
Politics. *See* Organizational politics
Pooled interdependence, 490
Position power, 372
Positive
affectivity, 106
correlation, 20
reinforcement, 81
Power, 115, **370**
charisma, 375
coercive, 373
coercive tactics, 376

corporate bullying, 377
counterpower, 376
distance, 39
empowerment, 377–378
expert, 374, 376
group, 378–381
information, 373
legitimate, 372
motivation, 117
personal, 373–375
politics. *See* Organizational politics
position, 372
rational persuasion, 374
referent, 374
resource-dependency model, 378–379
reward, 372–373
strategic contingencies model, 379–381
subunit, 378–381
use of, 375–376
Predecision, 306
Prediction, 17
Prejudice, 183
adverse affects, 184
age, 185
awareness-based diversity training, 188
cause of friction or conflict, 184
cross-cultural understanding, 189
discrimination, 183
diversity management programs, 188–190
facilitation skills, 189
groupism, 184–187
intercultural communication, 189
national origin, 186–187
physical condition, 185–186
psychological impact, 184
racial, 186–187
sexual orientation, 186
stigmas, 185
women, 187
see also Discrimination; Diversity; Gender;
Minority groups; Race; Women
Pressure, 371
The Prince, 113–114
Privacy
e-mail, 273
electronic monitoring, 451
employee communication, 274
legislation, 451
workplace, 451
Proactive personality, 108–110
Procedural justice, 149
Process innovation. *See* Reengineering
Product
authority, 472
organizations, 469–471
Productivity, 12, 516
Professional bureaucracies, 481
Profit, 189–190
Profit-sharing plans, 182
Programmed decisions, 309
Progressive discipline, 92
Project managers, 206
Projective tests, 123
Prosocial behaviour, 339
organizational citizenship behaviour. *See*
Organizational citizenship   behaviour
organizational spontaneity, 340
whistle-blowing, 342–343
Prospective memory, 121–122
Protegé, 201
Punishment, 82
and organizational citizenship behaviour,
341
progressive, 360
see also Discipline

Q
Qualitative
overload, 212

research, 25–26
underload, 212
Quality
circles, 516
control audits, 51
of work life, 6
revolution, 50–53
of work life programs, 516
Quantitative
overload, 212
underload, 212
Questionnaires, 123, 170–171
commitment bases, 180–181
see also Surveys

R
Race, 186–187
and mentoring, 203
see also Discrimination; Diversity; Minority
groups; Prejudice
Racial diversity, 42, 244–245
Raising the Roof campaign, 465
Random
assignment, 23
basis, 23
Rating scales, 170–171
Rational
decisions, 312–314
economic model, 313–314
persuasion, 371, 374
Realistic job previews, 200
Reciprocal interdependence, 490
Reciprocity, 344, 382
Recognition, 140
Recruitment, ads, 79
Reengineering, 52–53
Referent power, 374
Regulative tactics, 202
Reinforcement
contingencies, 82
continuous, 83
intermittent, 83
negative, 82
organizational behaviour management,
88–91
partial, 83
positive, 81
schedules of, 83–85
shaping, 91
Reinforcer, 90
Relatedness needs, 139
Relaxation training, 219
Reliability, 123–124
Repatriation, 37
Repetition, 87
Representativeness heuristic, 317
Research, 3, 4
correlational, 20
experimental, 22–25
hypothesis, 18, 20
process, 18–19
qualitative, 25–26
random basis, 23
survey, 19–22
Resistance to change, 510
Resource provider, 206
Resource-dependency model, 378–379
Responsibility, 69–70
Restructuring, 502, 504
work, 516
see also Downsizing
Reward power, 372–373
Rewards
constructive behaviour, 512
and cooperation, 347
diversity management, 190
following punishment, 94
non-cash, 152–153
noncontingent, 94

and performance, 151–152
positively valent, 151
team performance, 259, 260
see also Incentives
Rightsizing, 46
Role, 235
ambiguity, 211–212, 235
conflict, 211
differentiation, 235–236
expectations, 235
incumbent, 235
perceptions, 150–151
Routine technology, 446
Rumours, 284–285

S
Safety needs, 137–138
Sandwich generation, 42
Satisfaction. *See* Job satisfaction
Satisficing decisions, 314
Saturation, 281–282
Saving face, 319
Scalar chain of authority, 14
Scapegoat, 382
Scientific
management, 10–11, 153
method, 4
Second-order change, 499
Selective perception, 73–74
Self-actualization, 138
Self-control, 117
Self-efficacy, 110–111
Self-employment, 47
Self-managed work teams, 252
Self-monitoring, 111–113
and career success, 112–113
conflict resolution, 352
impression management, 113
mentoring, 113
and performance, 111–112
potential downside, 113
Self-promotion, 78
Semantic memory, 121, 122
Seniority-based pay systems, 116
Sensitivity training, 514
Sequential interdependence, 490
Sexual
harassment, 212–213
orientation, 186
*Shakedown: How the New Economy is changing
Our Lives*, 47
Shaping, 91
Shared-screen conferencing, 244
Short-term memory, 121
Side-bets orientation, 179
Similar-to-me effect, 72
Simple structure, 480–481
Situational leadership theory, 416–417
Six Sigma, 52
Skills-based diversity training, 188–189
Small-batch production, 486
Social
chameleons, 113
comparisons, 144
facilitation, 241–243
impact theory, 247
influence, 369–372
loafing, 246–249
needs, 138
perception. *See* Social perception
systems, 131
Social perception, 68–70
attribution process, 68–70
bias, 71–76
impression management, 77–78
overcoming bias, 75–76
performance appraisals, 76–77
stereotypes, 74–75
see also Judgments

Socialization, 140
    one-on-one, 200–203
    organizational. *See* Organizational social-
    ization
Span of control, 464, 473, 477
Spatial visualization, 121
Specialization, 14
Stability, 433
Staff position, 467
Statistics Canada
    downsizing, 503
    non-standard work, 47
    V-time option, 44
    visible minority population, 9–10
    women in workforce, 41
Status, 238
    symbols, 238, 438
Stepladder technique, 331–332
Stereotypes, 74–75, 76, 183
    age-based, 185
    conflict and, 353
    diversity management, 190
    sex role, 187
Stigmas, 185
Stonewalling, 55
Strain, 210, 219, 220
Strategic
    alliances, 483–485
    apex, 480
    contingencies model, 379–381
    decisions, 310
Strength, 122
Stress, 210
    burnout, 216–217
    castastrophizing, 219
    cognitive appraisal, 210, 216
    cognitive approaches, 219
    competing demands, 211
    daily hassles, 214–215
    exhaustion, 216
    of failure, 198
    family-supportive practices, 219–220
    and health, 217
    individual differences, 216
    isolation, 212
    lifestyle management, 218
    major life events, 214
    management, 218–221
    management programs, 221
    meditation, 218–219
    occupational demands, 211
    overload, 212
    relaxation, 218–219
    resistance to, 218
    responsibility for others, 212
    role ambiguity, 211–212
    role conflict, 211
    sexual harassment, 212–213
    and task performance, 215–216
    total life stress, 215
    underload, 212
    unpleasant physical working conditions,
    213
    work-family conflicts, 219–220
    work-related causes, 211–213
    worry, 219
Stressors, 198, 210
Structural inertia, 510–512
Structure. *See* Organizational structure
Subcultures, 37, 434
Subgroups, 326
Substitutes for leadership, 422–423
Subunit power, 378–381
Success
    and gender, 208
    and Machiavellianism, 114
    and self-monitoring, 112–113
Suggestion systems, 295
Superordinate goals, 356
Suppliers, 357

Support staff, 480
Survey feedback, 513–514
Surveys, 19–22
    employee, 297
    employee dissatisfaction, 174
Symbols, 438

T

Talent, 206
Task goals. *See* Goals
Task performance
    communication networks, 281–283
    and diverse group composition, 245
    and job satisfaction, 176–177
    and stress, 215–216
Tasks
    additive, 246
    combining, 159
    departmentalization by, 468–469
    experienced meaningfulness, 157
    job characteristics model, 155–157
Team building, 514–515
Team spirit, 50
Teams, 250, 365
    accountability, 250
    authority, 252
    autonomy, 251–252
    building, 254
    co-operation, 257
    co-operation in, 257
    collective work products, 250
    creation of, 253–255
    cross-functional, 252–253
    diversified membership, 259
    duration, 251
    failure of, 257–259
    vs. Groups, 249–251
    high-performance, 251, 259–260
    improvement, 251
    leadership, 412–413
    managers' control, 257
    obstacles, 257–259
    performance, 255–260
    performance conditions, 254
    prework, 254
    purpose, 251
    rewards. *See* Rewards
    self-managed, 229, 251, 252, 378,
    412–413
    size, 259
    spirit, 260
    support, 254, 257
    types of, 251–253
    and unions, 258–259
    work, 251, 515
    see also Groups
Teamwork, 230
Technology, 445
    advanced manufacturing, 447
    advances in, 10, 33, 504–505, 508
    assistive, 449–451
    Aston studies, 488–489
    augmented service, 453
    automation, 447–449
    categorizing, 445–446
    challenges, 448
    computer-aided design and engineering
    (CAD/CAE), 447
    computer-integrated manufacturing (CIM),
    447
    computerized performance monitoring,
    451–453
    continuous-process production, 486
    and customer service, 453–454
    design for disassembly, 454
    engineering, 446
    environmentally friendly, 454
    flexible manufacturing systems, 447
    high, 447, 478

    industrial robotics (IR), 447
    information, 46
    interdependence, 489–491
    and international trade, 34
    and jobs, 447–448
    large-batch (mass) production, 486
    matrix of technologies, 446
    nonroutine, 446
    and organizational design, 487–491
    personalized service, 453
    routine, 446
    small-batch production, 486
    telecommuting, 49
    Thompson's framework, 489–491
    transformation of business, 453–454
    Woodward studies, 485–488
    workflow integration, 488–489
    working with machines, 448
Technostructure, 480
Telecommuting, 44, 49–50
Telework, 44
Termination, 288–289
Test-retest reliability, 124
Thematic Apperception Test, 123
Theory, 17–19
    hypothesis, 18–19
    testing, 18–19
Theory X, 6, 476
Theory Y, 6, 476
Thompson's framework, 489–491
360 degree feedback, 88
Time-and-motion study, 11
Top-down decision making, 312
Total
    life stress, 215
    quality management (TQM), 51–52
Training, 48, 86
    apprenticeship, 86
    careers in, 205
    co-op programs, 86
    commitment to, 66
    computer-based, 86
    continuous, 130
    executive, 86
    grid, 405–406
    listening skills, 294
    relaxation, 219
    sensitivity, 514
    teams, 259
    transfer of, 87–88
    and workplace aggression, 360
Transfer of training, 87–88
Transformational leadership, 411–412, 413
Trends, 10, 15–16
    demographic, 42
    restructuring, 45–48
    virtual corporations, 49
Trust, 344-345
Turnover, 43
    informal communication networks, 283
    and job satisfaction, 175
    and organizational culture, 440
    quality of work life programs, 516
    snowball effect, 283
    and unemployment rates, 176
    voluntary turnover process model,
    175–176
Two-factor theory, 172–173
Two-tier wage structures, 147
Type A behaviour pattern, 106–108, 218, 352
Type B behaviour pattern, 106–108, 218, 352

U

Uncertainty avoidance, 39
Underpayment inequity, 145, 147
Unemployment rates, and employee turnover,
    176
Unions
    and automation, 447–448

communication with management, 299
quality of work life programs, 516
and teams, 258–259
union-management committees, 338
Unity of command, 14

V

V-time programs, 44
Valence, 149
Validity, 124
Value theory, 173–174
Value-chain partnerships, 483
Valuing diversity, 41
Variable
    interval schedules, 83
    ratio schedules, 84
Verbal communication, 269-270
    effectiveness, 271–272
    electronic mail (e-mail), 273–274
    electronic media, 272–274
    employee handbook, 270–271
    media, 270–271
    newsletters, 270
    oral media, 270, 271–272
    video display terminals (VDTs), 273
    voice messaging (voice mail), 274
    written media, 270–272
Vertical job loading, 155, 159–160
Video display terminals (VDTs), 273
Videoconferencing, 244
Violence. *See* Workplace violence
Virtual
    banking, 59–60
    corporation, 49
    organizations, 474
Vocational choices, 204
Voice messaging (voice mail), 274
Voluntary

reduced work time programs, 44
turnover process model, 175–176

W

Wages
    equity theory, 147–149
    gender, 208
    and motivation, 11
    pay freeze, 149
    two-tier wage structures, 147
Western Report, 522
Whistle-blowing, 342–343, 384
Women
    advancement, 166
    developmental opportunities, 208
    discrimination, 184
    flexible work arrangements, 43–44
    glass ceiling. *See* Glass ceiling
    job satisfaction, 169
    job sharing, 44
    as leaders, 404
    managerial positions, 166
    and mentoring, 203
    myths, 166
    prejudice against, 187
    wages, 208
    in workforce, 41
Woodward studies, 485–488
Work
    changing natures of, 9–10
    child-care facilities, 44
    compressed workweeks, 43
    elder-care facilities, 44
    flexible arrangements, 43–44
    flexplace policies. *See* Flexplace policies
    flextime programs, 43
    job sharing, 43–44
    juggling, 211
    non-standard, 47

    part-time, 47
    personal support policies, 45
    psychological need, 6
    quality of life at, 6
    restructuring, 516
    telecommuting. *See* Telecommuting
    telework, 44
    temporary, 47
    voluntary reduced work time (V-time)
        programs, 44
Work-related attitudes, 168
    and organizational culture, 437
Workflow integration, 488–489
Workforce
    aging, 42
    composition, 441–444
    contingent, 47–48
    diversity, 9, 41–42, 188–190, 359
    education of, 512
    healthy, 139
    women in, 41
Working memory, 121
Workplace
    aggression. *See* Workplace aggression
    equality, 166
    flexplace policies. *See* Flexplace policies
    humanizing, 516
    informating of, 46
    violence. *See* Workplace violence
Workplace aggression, 358
    causes, 359
    hostile attributional bias, 359
    prevention, 359–360
Workplace Innovation report 1994, 258–259
Workplace violence, 357
    among professionals, 358
    Workers' Compensation claims, 358
Written communication. *See* Verbal
    communication

NAME INDEX

The page on which a Weblink appears is printed in boldface.

A

Actis, Ron, **299**
Adam, Wilf, 32
Adams, J. Stacy, 145
Aiello, J. R., 242–243, 452, 500
Akers, John, 110
Alderfer, C. P., 138–139
Allen, R. W., 386, 468
Alliger, G. M., 219
Argyris, Chris, 476
Armstrong, Barry, 343
Ash, R. A., 119
Austin, Nancy K., 293
Aviram, A., 112
Avolio, Bruce, **411**

B

Baldes, J., 142
Baldwin, Marjorie, 450
Bandapudi, V., 119
Bar-On, Reuven, **121**
Barnard, Chester, 267
Barnes-Farrell, J. L., 331–332
Baron, R. A., 108, 358
Barrett, Matthew, 59, 166, **375**, 399, 409
Barrett, Richard, 442
Barrick, M. R., 105
Barsade, S. G., 106
Bartol, K. M., 385
Bass, B. M., 271
Bass, Lee, 528
Bass, Sid, 528
Bateman, T. S., 108
Beach, L. R., 315
Beaudoin, Laurent, 399
Beck, Catherine, 209
Becker, T. E., 179
Bennis, Warren, 520
Bertin, Christine, **273**
Billings, R. S., 179
Black, R. H., 322
Blanchard, K. H., 416
Bondar, Roberta, 445
Borger, Annette, 59
Bottger, P. C., 327–328
Bouchard, Lucien, 334
Bouchard, T. J., 324
Boyatzis, R. E., 117
Boyd-Saffran, Tanya, 484
Bradburn, Lenna, 101
Branson, Richard, 410, 429
Bronfman, Edgar Jr., 127–128, **375**
Bronfman, Edgar Sr., 127–128
Brown, F. W., 149
Brownell, J., 293
Browning, Elizabeth Barrett, 315
Brownstein, Michael, 524–525
Brownstein, Morton, 524–525
Buckland, John, 493
Budman, Michael, **28**
Burns, T., 478
Burr, Don, 403

C

Caldwell, D. F., 440
Calkin, Joy, 209

Callender, J.C., 73
Caloff, Jonathan, 505
Campion, M. A., 153, 154
Caplan, R. D., 212
Caron, Marc, 226
Carsten, J. M., 176
Cartwright, S., 443–444
Champy, James, 52
Chandler, Bill, 450
Chapman, Bob, 528
Charest, Jean, 334
Chatman, J. A., 433, 440
Childress, Rusty, 159–160
Clapp, Randy, 171
Clegg, C. W., 256
Cleghorn, John, **375**, 399, 400, 409, 438
Codling, Liz, 49–50
Cohl, Michael, 49
Cohon, George, 400
Collins, Jim, 134
Collins, P. D., 487
Comper, Tony, 166
Conger, Jay, 411
Cook, Libby, 171
Cooper, C. L., 443–444
Cosgrave, Gerald P., 15
Costley, Gary, 505
Coughlin, Paula, 93
Cranston, Lynda, **278**
Crant, J. M., 109–110
Crépin, Jean, 500

D

Daft, R. L., 271
Davis, Russell, 213
Deal, T. E., 439
Delbecq, A. L., 331
Deming, W. Edwards, 51
Denis, Lizzie, 210
Dennison, D., 440
DesRosiers, Dennis, 396
Di Martina, Vittorio, 358
Diefenbaker, John, 366
Diller, Barry, 127
Doby, V. J., 212
Dolida, Roger J., 257
Donnelly, Aldyen, 348
Dougherty, T. W., 73, 113
Dowden, Rick, 492
Drucker, Peter F., 11, 445, 517

E

Earley, P. C., 247
Eaton, Robert J., **392**
Eden, D., 112
Ehrlich, S. B., 423
Elsasser, Al, 51

F

Fabrikant, Valery, **362**
Fawcette, Anne, 397
Fayol, Henri, 14, 476
Feldberg, David, 253
Ferris, Darrell, 66
Ferris, G. R., 382
Ferris, S. P., 189–190
Fiedler, F. E., 414–416

Finlay, Bob, 528
Fiol, C. M., 290
Fleming, Colleen, 209, 484
Flood, Al, **375**, 501
Folger, R., 359–360
Follet, Mary Parker, 11
Foot, David, 42
Forward, Gordon, **501**
Freeman, J. H., 385
Freese, Bob, 160
Furnham, A., 118

G

Gadiesh, Orit, 113
Gagnon, Donald, 151
Galinsky, Ellen, 45
Gandz, J., 385, 386
Ganster, D. C., 219–220
Garrett, Tim, 92
Gartner, Hana, 132
Gates, Bill, 63, 198
Gatewood, R. D., 78–79
Gaunt, Bobbie, 188, 209, **375**
Geddes, Maureen, 212
Gellenhammar, Pehr, 493
George, J. M., 249
Getter, Ruth, 223–224
Gilbreth, Frank, 11
Gilbreth, Lillian, 11
Gilliland, Michael, 171
Glaub, William, **375**
Glick, W. H., 73
Goizueta, Roberto, 197, 334
Gold, Christina, 409, 425
Goleman, Daniel, 120–121
Gordon, Bing, 275
Gould, Michael, 425
Gould, Raymond, 442
Gowan, M. A., 78–79
Graen, G. B., 407
Gray, Ross, 343
Greising, David, 197
Green, Harold, 467
Greenberg, J., 249, 275
Green, Don, **28**
Green, Irwin, 28
Griffin, William E., 296
Grove, Andy, 432
Guthrie, J. P., 119
Gyllenhammar, Pehr, 155
H
Hackman, J. R., 155, 253
Hammer, Michael, 52
Handy, Charles, 47
Haner, Mike, 338
Hannan, M. T., 385
Hargrove, Buzz, 343
Hartley, Duane, 512
Hawking, Stephen, 132
Hay, Larry, 442
Henderson, Jim, 240
Hersey, P., 416
Herzberg, Frederick, 172–173
Hickson, D. J., 380
Hiller, S. J., 189–190
Hofstede, G., 38–40, 520
Hogan, E. A., 76–77
Hopper, Bill, **368**
House, R. J., 410, 418
Howell, Jane, **411**

Huber, G. P., 73
Hull, F. M., 487
Huot, Serge, 266

I

Iacocca, Lee, **392**, 410
Ivany, Terry, 161–162
Ives, B., 453

J

Jackson, P. R., 256
Jaeger, A. M., 520
Jehn, K. A., 433
Jermier, J. M., 422
Jobs, Steven, 377–378
Johnson, David, 410
Jung, Andrea, 412, 425
Jyrkkanen, Jorma, 343

K

Kahneman, D., 316
Kanter, R. M., 291, 483
Kaplan, Mark, 186
Karan, Donna, 425
Katzenbach, John R., 109–110
Kelleher, Herb, 410
Keller, Perry, 62
Kelley, H. H., 70, 71
Kemp, N. J., 256
Kempston Darkes, Maureen, 188, 209, **299**, 343, **375**, 396–**397**
Kennedy, A. A., 439
Kenniff, Patrick, **362**
Keon, T. L., 116
Kerkorian, Kirk, **392**
Kerr, S., 422
King, T. R., 382
Kirkcaldy, B. D., 118
Kirkpatrick, S. A., 401
Klauss, R., 271
Kluge, Holger, 186–187
Kocho, Keith, 62–63, 130–131, 226, 365, 428, 526–527
Koeppel, Monica, 450–451
Kofodimos, Joan, 141
Kohl, W. L., 412
Kotter, J. P., 398
Kovarick, Amy, 62
Krackhardt, D., 283–284
Kramer, Louise, 210
Kreutzer, Jake, 64
Kristof, A. L., 78
Kroc, Ray, 436
Kroll, M., 189–190
Kuhlmann, Arkadi, 59
Kumar, K., 243–244

L

Latham, G. P., 140–142, 142
Laurier, Sir Wilfrid, 40
Lautenschlager, G. J., 78–79
Lawler, E. E., 176–177, 255
Lawrence, P., 467
Lazarus, R. S., 215
Ledford, G. E., 255
Lee, A. T., 329

Lemaire, Laurent, 399
Lengel, R. H., 271
Levy, Raymond, 493
Liden, R. C., 77
Likert, Rensis, 476–477
Locke, E. A., 140–142, 173, 401
Lombard, George, 15
Lorenzo, Frank, 403
Lorsch, J. W., 479
Lorsh, J., 467
Lowe, C. A., 331–332
Lutz, Robert A., 392
Lynn, R., 118

M

McAllister, D. J., 345
McBridge-King, Judith, 187
McCallister, Linda, 277
McCarthy, Kevin, 227
McCauley, C. D., 208
McClelland, C. L., 153, 154
McClelland, D. C., 117, 118
McConnell, Amy, 154
McConnell, Richard, 161–162
McCready, Ken, **522**
MacDonald, Donald, 368
McDonald, Wendy, 41
McGarry, Diane, 409
McGregor, Douglas, 6, 476
Machiavelli, Niccolo, 113–114
MacKenzie, S. B., 422
McKersie, R. B., 355
MacMillan, John, **229**, 257
McNamara, Patrick, 442
Malloy, John T., 275
Manz, C. C., 255–256
Marcell, Robert P., 473
Mars, Forrest, 439
Martell, Rob, 365
Martin, D. C., 385
Maslow, Abraham, 136–137, 233
Mason, R. O., 453
Mathews, Jim, 101
May, D. R., 149
Mayberry, John, 399
Mayo, Elton W., 11–13
Meindl, J. R., 423
Michaelsen, K. K., 244–245
Michaelsen, L. K., 322
Middleton, Deborah, 226
Miles, J. A., 249
Miles, R. H., 380
Minkin, Barry, 154
Mintzberg, Henry, 382–384, 400,
    406, 409, 479–482
Miraglia, Franca, **141**
Misumi, J., 258
Mitchell, T. R., 110, 315, 408
Mobley, W. H., 175–176
Mohrman, S. A., 255
Monty, Jean, 78, **375**, **410**, 438
Moroney, Bill, 273–274
Morse, J. J., 479
Mount, M. K., 105
Muczyk, J. P., 402

Mulroney, Brian, 325, 368
Münsterberg, Hugo, 11
Murray, V. V., 385, 386
Mustari, E. L., 247

N

Nelson, Kent C. "Oz," 456–457
Nelson, Kim, 154
Neuman, J. H., 108, 358
Newall, Ted, 461
Niehoff, B. B., 422
Nininger, Jim, 209
Nixon, Troy, 64

O

Ohlott, P. J., 208
Oldman, G. R., 155
Olivieri, Nancy, **342**
Ookunitani, Kazushi, 80
O'Reilly, C. A., 440
Ornstein, S. L., 438
Orwell, George, 242
Osborn, Alex, 324
Oscapella, Eugene, 124
O'Sullivan, Mark, 51

P

Parent, Gilbert, 442
Parkinson-Marcoux, Dee, 209
Pavlovic, Brenda, **66**
Payton, Holly, 186
Peaples, George, 397
Pearson, C. A. L., 256
Perrin, 425
Perrow, Charles, 445–446
Peters, 440
Peterson, M. F., 211, 258
Peterson, R. B., 399
Petrie, Marilyn, 44
Petrin, Linda, 226
Pfeffer, J., 379
Pitcher, Patricia, **406**–407
Podsakoff, P. M., 422
Porras, J. I., 518
Porter, L. W., 176–177, 179–180,
    283–284
Powell, Randy, **2**, 326
Preston, James, 425
Pura, Vern, 338

R

Rappaport, Alan, 465
Reichman, Paul, 198, 438
Reid, Angus, 47, 169
Reimann, B. C., 402
Reiner, Gary, 52
Rentsch, J. R., 436–437
Ringelmann, Max, 246
Roberts, Mac, 338, 339
Roberts, Malcolm, 50
Robertson, P. J., 518
Rochon-Burnett, Suzanne, 442

Rogelberg, S. G., 331–332
Rogers, Ted, 436
Rolling Stones, 49, 474
Rosen, Harry, 465
Rosen, John, 358
Rosenfeld, Irene, 209
Ross, J., 169
Roth, John, 66, **375**, 399
Ruderman, M. N., 208
Rybiak, Richard, 338

S

St. Onge, Hubert, 97
Salancik, G., 379
Sanko, Bill, 262
Sanson, Geri, 213
Savoie, Ernest J., 181
Sayer, Bob, 244
Schad, Robert, **134**, 159
Schaffer, Robert H., 519–521
Schaubroeck, J., 149
Schnake, M. R., 287
Schoellhorn, Robert, **377**
Schrempp, Jürgen E., 392
Schulich, Seymour, 303
Sculley, John, 276
Semler, Ricardo, 220
Senge, Peter, 499–501
Serruya, Aaron, 303–**304**
Serruya, Michael, 303–**304**
Serruya, Simon, 303–**304**
Sheinin, Rose, **362**
Sheridan, J. E., 440
Shimada, Jaruo, 448
Silverberg, Christine, 101, 102, 115
Sims, 255–256
Skarlicki, D., 359–360
Skinner, B. F., 81
Sloan, Alfred P., 326
Sloan, Alfred P. Jr., 467
Smith, P. B., 258
Smith, Paul, 52
Smye, Marti, 377
Snipe, Wilma, **140**
Spector, P. E., 176
Stalker, G. M., 478
Stanford, Jim, 369
Staw, B. M., 106, 169
Steers, 412
Steiner, D. D., 92
Stephens, Tom, 528
Stephenson, Carol, 209
Stevens, C. K., 78
Stoffman, Daniel, 42
Svec, C. M., 242–243

T

Tannen, Deborah, 278
Taylor, Frederick, 11, 153, 476
Taylor, Kim, 44
Terborg, J. R., 412
Thomas, L. T., 219–220
Thompson, J. D., 489–491
Thomson, Harvey A., 519–521

Tice, Lou, **112**
Tomlinson, Janice, 209
Totta, Johanne M., 166
Trahan, W. A., 92
Trevino, L. K., 271
Trudeau, Pierre, 41
Turban, D. B., 73, 113, 116
Tversky, A., 316

V

Van de Ven, A. H., 331
Vandermolen, Mimi, 442–443
Velasquez, M., 387
Verschuren, Annette, 209
Vince, Theresa, 213
Vroom, V. H., 419–422

W

Walker, Donald, 399
Walker, Frank, 205
Wall, T. D., 256
Waller, M. J., 73
Walton, R. S., 355
Wang, Yang-Hai, **187**
Warren, Roger, 357
Waterman, 440
Watson, W. E., 243–245, 322
Watson, Colin D., **154**, 366
Watson, George, **375**
Watson, Thomas J. Jr., 238
Waye, Brendan, 64
Wayne, S. J., 77
Weber, Max, 14, 476
Welch, Jack, **266**, 412, 473
Weldon, E., 247
Wetmore, John, **187**, 399
Wheeler, William, 504
Whittaker, Sheelagh, 209, 409
Whyte, Glen, 319
Williams, K. J., 211
Williams, M. L., 422
Wilson, Lynton, 399
Wilson, Trevor, **10**
Wintermans, Jos, 501
Wittes, Peggy, 209
Wolfe, Donald M., 56
Wong, Kathy, 28
Wood, R., 110
Wood, R. E., 408
Woodward, J., 485–488
Wright, P., 189–190

Y

Yetton, P. W., 327–328, 419–422

Z

Zajonc, Robert, 241
Zedong, Mao, 398
Zuboff, S., 273
Zwerman, W. L., 486–487
Zyman, Sergio, 197, 198, 219, 334

COMPANY INDEX

The page on which a Weblink appears is printed in boldface.

A

Abbott Laboratories, **377**
Acadie Presse Ltée, 52
AECL. *See* Atomic Energy of Canada Limited
Aetna Canada, **139**
AGT Ltd., 152
Air Canada, **339**, 451, 506
Airborne Express, 456
Alberta College of Physicians and Surgeons, 358
Alberta Human Rights Commission, **213**
Alberta Stock Exchange, 303
Alcan Aluminum Ltd., 35, 140
Alias/Wavefront, **141**
All Purpose Company, 80
Allied Signal, 90
Alphatronix, 160
American Express, 256
American Express Travel Related Services, 190
American Greetings Corp., 153
Amoco Canada, 500
Andersen Consulting, 206, 226
Angus Reid, **169**
Apple Computer, 47, 86, 377, 506
Aquilium Software Corp., **465**
Asahi Bank, 482
Association for Manufacturing Excellence, 262
AT&T, 45, 88, 140, 178, 262, 296, 484, 516
AT&T Bell Labs, 187
AT&T's Phone Stores, 381
Atlantic Canada Opportunities Agency, 227
Atomic Energy of Canada Limited, 439
Autolite, 482
Avon Canada, **140**, 409, 425
Avon Products Inc., 412, 425

B

B. F. Goodrich, 55
Babine Forest Products, 32
Bain & Co., 113
Ballard Power Systems Inc., **433**
Bank of Canada, 433
Bank of Montreal, **43**, 49–50, 166, 375, 399, 400, 409
Institute for Learning, 86
Bank of Montreal Group of Companies, 59
Bankers Trust, 46, 501
Baring Asset Management, 59
Barrick Gold Corp., 139, 182, 433
Bata Shoes, 244
The Bay. *See* Hudson's Bay Company
BC Bearing Engineers Ltd., 41
BCE Inc., 375, 399, **410**, 433, 483
Beaver Foods, 467
Belair Direct, 59
Bell Canada, 143, **186**, 273, 451, 499, 503, 505

Bell Mobility, 57
Benjamin Moore, 453–454
Bethlehem Steel, 11
Bishop's Falls Development Corporation, 227
Black Business and Professional Association, 192
Black Diamond Cheese, 257
Bloomingdale's, 425
BMW, 454
Boeing, 253
Bombardier Inc., **35**, 399, 433, 470, 481
The Boston Co., 219
Bre-X, 54
Brenda Mines, 140
Bresler's Industries Inc., 304
Brice Foods, 304
British Columbia Hydro and Power Authority, 348
Brooks Brothers, 431, 432, 443
Browns Shoe Shops Inc., 524–525
Brunswick Mining and Smelting, 151
Bureau of Labour Information, 259
Burns Lake First Nations, 32
Burns Lake Native Development Corporation, 32
Business Design Associates Inc., 522
Business Development Bank of Canada, 428

C

Cadbury, 438
CAE Electronics, 505
CAE Inc., **505**
Calgary Herald, 102, **325**
Calgary Police Services, 101–102
Cambridge University, 132
Camco, 266
Camco Inc., 52
Campbell Soup, 410
Canada Post, **457**
Canadian Association of Smelter and Allied Workers, 357
Canadian Auto Workers, 233
Canadian Auto Workers (CAW), **258**
Canadian Bar Association, 233
Canadian Blood Services, **278**
Canadian Broadcasting Corporation, 467, **503**
Canadian Human Rights Commission, **451**
Canadian Imperial Bank of Commerce, **43**, 44, 59, 90, 186–187, 375, 432, 501, 503
Leadership Centre, 86
Canadian Industrial Innovation Centre, 227
Canadian Medical Association, 233
Canadian Mental Health Association, **210**
Canadian National Railways, **182**,

499, 503, 506
Canadian Radio-television and Telecommunications Commission, **439**
Canadian Steamship Lines, 505
Canadian Tire Acceptance Ltd., 86, **152**, 435, 500, 504
Canadian Tire Corporation, 59, 504
Canadian Union of Public Employees (CUPE), 233, **358**
Canadian Utilities Ltd., 348
Cangram Inc., 212
Cara Operations Limited, 467
Caribou Systems Corp., **43**
Cascades Inc., 399
Catalyst, 187, 209
Caterpillar, 417
Celestial Seasonings, 56
Chaparral Steel, 378, **501**
Childress Buick Co., 159–160
CHOW radio, 442
Chrysler Canada Ltd., 375, **392**
Chrysler Corporation, 51, 206, 253, 392, 410, 449, 473
Chubb & Son insurance, 203
CIBC. *See* Canadian Imperial Bank of Commerce
Citibank, 472
Clearly Canadian, 46
CN. *See* Canadian National Railways
Coca-Cola, 178, 197, 334, 435
Cognos, 502
Colgate-Palmolive, 203, 252
College of Physicians and Surgeons of Alberta, **358**
Communications, Energy, and Paperworkers Union of Canada, **338**
Competitive Intelligence Networks, 505
Concordia University, **362**
Conference Board of Canada, **176**, 187, 209
Consumers' Distributing, 499
Continental Airlines, 197
Coopers & Lybrand, 190, 504
Coors, 139
Corel Corp., **273**, 467
Corning Glass Works, 152, 159, 255, 474
Cossette Communication Marketing, **6**
CRTC. *See* Canadian Radio-television and Telecommunications Commission
Cynamid Canada, 152

D

Daewoo, 484
Daimler-Benz, 392
DaimlerChrysler AG, 392, 493
Daiwa Europe Ltd., 493
Dalhousie University, **378**
DEC, 190
Delco, 482
Dell, 474

Delta Airlines, 468
Department of National Defence, 450–451
Diamond International, 90
Digital Equipment Corp., 226
Digital Equipment Corporation, 88
Digital Media Champion Group, 428
Digital Renaissance, 62–63, 130–131, 226, 365, 428, 526–527
Disneyland, 178
Dofasco Inc., 399, 433, 438
Dow Chemical Company, 186, 257
Dow Corning, 472
Dow Jones, 203
Drexel Burnham Lambert, 54
Du Pont, 127, **481**
Duke Power Company, 43
Dun & Bradstreet, **47**
DuPont Canada Inc., 141, 444
Duracell, 425

E

E. I. du Pont de Nemours and Company. *See* Du Pont
East Carolina University, 450
Eastman Kodak, 153, 516
Eaton School of Retailing, 497
Eaton's, **497**, 498, 502
École des Hautes Études Commerciales, **406**
Edmonton Oilers Hockey Club, **112**
EdperBrascan Corp., 35
EDS Canada, 409
Electronic Arts, 275
Electronic Messaging Association, 273–274
Enterprise Newfoundland, 227
Epcor Inc., 348
Equitable Life Insurance, 221
Ernst & Young, 51
Expo, '86, 319
Exxon, 140
Exxon Chemical, 193

F

Federal Express, 51, 143, 457, 412, 174
Ford Motor Company, 46, 53, 178, 181–182, 387, 442, 482, 483, 516
Ford Motor Company of Canada Limited, 188, **375**
Fortune magazine, 412
Freport McMoran Copper & Gold Inc., 54

G

Garneau Würstlin Philp Brand Engineering, 59
Gateway, 474
GE Appliances, 331
GE Capital, 90

GEMCo, 348
General Electric Canada, **266**
General Electric Co., 46, 52, 88,
140, 143, 255, 257, 266,
378, 412, 464, 473, 483,
499, 511, 516, 517
General Mills, 154
General Motors, 227, 252, 255,
326, 378, 435, 448, 457,
467, 481, 482, 484
General Motors of Canada Ltd.,
221, **299**, 343, 375, 396, **397**
Giant Food, 147
Globe and Mail Report on Business
Magazine, 130, 396, 400
GM Canada, 188
Greiner Engineering, Inc, 186
Groupe Bull, 515
GTW Corp., 205
Guangdong No. 3 Machine Tools
Factory, 484

H
Halifax, Insurance Co., 59
Hallmark, 53
Hallmark Cards Canada, 484
Hamilton-Wentworth (Ontario)
Regional Police Service, 101
Harvard Business School, 15
Harvey's, 467, 478
Hawthorne Works, 12
Hershey Foods Corporation, 139
Hertz, 453
Hewlett-Packard, 252, 454, 467,
470, 512, 516, 518
Hill Sloan Associates, 10
Holt Renfrew, 524
Honda of America, 90, 92, 470
Honeywell Ltd., **229**, 230, 249, 257
Hospital for Sick Children, **342**
HSN inc., 127
Hudson's Bay Company, 497, 499,
524
Hughes Aircraft Co., 187
Hughes Electronics, 90
Husky Injection Molding Systems,
45, **134**, 139, 159, 432, 433
Husky Oil Ltd., 348
Hydro Quebec, 51
Hyundai, 482

I
I Can't Believe It's Yogurt Ltd., 304
IBM, 50, 110, 140, 152, 178, 238,
435, 438, 481, 503, 506, 518
IBM Canada Ltd., **187**, 399
IBM Credit Corp., 53
IDS, 256
Imasco Ltd., 482
Imperial Oil, **399**
ING Direct, 59–60
Intel Corporation, 432, 467
International Communications
Academy of Arts and
Sciences, 166
International Labour Organization,
208
International Nederlanden Groep
NV, 59
International Organization for
Standardization, 51–52
Isuzu, 484
ITT, 467

J
J. M. Schneider Inc., 51
Java Coast Fine Coffees, 304

Jewish Women International, 224
Jones New York, 197
Julius Klein Cleaners, 465

K
Kellogg Co. North America, 505
Kinko's, 244
Kodak, 53, 90, 178, 454, 457, 467
KPMG, 51, 429
Kraft Canada, **209**

L
L&L Products, 210
Lake Superior Paper Industries, 252
Lancaster Laboratories, 44
Laura Secord Inc., 484
Levi Strauss & Co., 43
Liberty Mutual Insurance, 472
L.L. Bean, 139
London Life, 131
London Life Insurance Co., 186

M
M&M Mars, 439
M. D. Anderson Cancer Center,
501
McCain Foods Ltd., **35**
McDonald's, 86, 141, 285, 432,
436
McDonald's Restaurants of Canada,
400
McDonnell Aircraft Company, 270
McGill University, 15
McGrath Special Committee on
Reform of Canada's Hosue of
Commons, 240
Maclean's, 93
McMaster University, 186
MacMillan Bloedel, 528
Manville Corp., 528
Manville Corporation, 387
Marine Atlantic, 161–162
Maritime Paper Products Limited,
52
Maritime School of Social Work,
378
Marketing Magazine, 428
Marks and Spencer, 431, 432, 443
Marriott Corp., 331
Marriott Hotels, 173, 219
Massachusetts Institute of
Technology, 499
Matsushita Electric industrial
Company, 35, 127
Matsushita Group, 482
Mazda, 46
mbanx, 59
MCI, 484
MCI Communications, **90**
Meloche Monnex, 152
Merck, 433
Merlin Global Inc., 505
Merlin Motors, 51
Metro-Goldwyn-Mayer, 127
Metropolitan Edison, 55
Metropolitan Life Insurance
Company, 221
MHS Inc., **121**
Microsoft, 198
Midvale Steel Company, 11
Ministry of Culture and Citizenship,
184
Ministry of Defence, 93
Mobil Oil, 417
Motorola, 86
Multi-Health Systems. *See* MHS Inc.

N
Nabisco, 88
New Brunswick Hospital
Association, 203
Newbridge Networks, 502
Newbridge Networks Corp., **433**
Nike, 474
Nippon Life, 482
Nissan, 484
NN Life Insurance Co. of Canada, 59
Noranda, 140
Noranda Inc., **244**
Nortel Networks, 43, 57, **66**, 78,
139, 186, 192, 255, 262,
410, 433, 435, 438, 505
North West Company, 191, 192
Northern Telecom Ltd., 365, 375,
399
Northrop/Grumman, 90
Northwest Airlines, 518
Norwest Soil Research, 500
NOVA Corp., 186, 461, 499, 505
Nova Gas Transmission Ltd., 348
Nova Scotia Power Inc., 348
Novacor Chemicals, 53, 140

O
Odetics Inc., 140
Office of the Information and
Privacy Commissioner, **451**
Offshore Systems International Ltd.,
505
Ohio State University, 403
Olivetti, 484
Oneida Canada Limited, 378
Onex, 482
Ontario Hydro, **44**, 213, **319**, 348,
503
Ontario Ministry of the Solicitor
General, 101
Ontario Teacher's Pension Plan
Board, 528
OPEC, 348
Opel, 484
Orlando Helicopter Airway
Company, 484
Owens Corning, 444
Oxford University, 132

P
Pacific Bell, 43
Pacific Institute, 112
Panasonic, 482
Patagonia, 56
Peel Regional Police Service, 101
Pella, 44
People Express Airlines, 403
Pepsi-Cola, 51, 190, 197, 285
PepsiCo, 252, 276
Petro-Canada, 53, 140, 368, **369**,
468, 503, 506
Philips Electronics, 467
Pixar, 474
Placer Dome, 57
Plymouth Tool and Stamping, 378
Polaroid, 219
PolyGram NV, 127
Power Commission of the City of
Saint John, 444
Power Corp., 482
Power Financial Corp., 35
Pratt & Whitney Canada, **252**
Precision Metalcraft, 152
Primerica, 151
Procter & Gamble, 252, 276, 285,
435, 445, 507
Puritan-Bennett Corporation, 257
Purolator, 457

R
Ralston-Purina, 252
Rand Corporation, 328
R.B. Communications, 442
Reebok, 474
Renault, 484, 492–493
*Report on Business. See Globe and
Mail Report on Business*
Magazine
Revenue Canada, 226
Ritz-Carlton, 312
RJR Nabisco, 153
Roadway Package Systems, 456,
457
Robert Simpson Company, 15
Roots Canada, **28**, 432, 433
Royal Bank of Canada, 43, **44**, 59,
90, 375, 399, **400**, 409, 438,
465
Royal Canadian Mounted Police,
273
Ryerson Polytechnic University, 62,
497

S
Saab, 155
Safeway, 176, 177, 178
St. Petersburg Times, 44
Samsung, 482
Sanson & Hunt, 213
SAS Institute, 45
Saskatchewan Power Corp., 348
Saskatoon Chemicals, 339
Saskatoon Chemicals Ltd., 338
S.C. Johnson & Son, Limited, **2**
Sea-Land Service, 159
Seagram Classics Wine Company,
127
Seagram Co. Ltd., 35, 127–128,
375
Sears Canada, 213
Sears, Roebuck and Co., 54, 152,
296
Second Cup Canada, **2**
Semco S/A, 252
ServiceMaster Canada Ltd., **46**
7 Eleven, 197
Shell Canada, 43, 57
Shell Oil, 178
Shoppers Drug Mart Ltd., 186
Siemens, 474
Silicon Graphics Inc., 141
Simon Fraser University, 131
Sloan School of Management, 499
Software Human Resource Council,
66
Solectron Corporation, 184
Southern California Edison
Company, 139
Southwest Airlines, 410
Spar Aerospace Ltd., **154**, 366
Sprint, 86
Standard Oil, 514
Standard Trustco, 343
State University of New York, 411
Stentor, 505
Student magazine, 429
Sumitomo Life, 482
Sun Life Assurance Co. of Canada,
186
Sun Life Assurance Company, 15
Sunnybrook Health Science Centre,
131
Swiss Chalet, 467
Symmetric, 219

T
Taco Bell, 53, 154

TCBY, 303, **304**
Teknion Furniture Systems, 253
Texas Air, 403
Texas Instruments, 251, 440
3M Canada Inc., 433, **467**
Time Warner, 127
Toronto Dominion Bank, 186, 223–224
Toronto Sportsman's Show, 227
Toronto Stock Exchange, 303
Tout Sweet Chocolates, 285
Toyota, 51, 474, 483, 499
TransAlta Corporation, 348, **522**
TransCanada Pipelines Ltd., 375, **461**
The Trinity Group, **10**
TRW Systems Group, 471, 472

U

U. S. Food and Drug Administration, 285
Union Carbide, 53, 514
Union Gas Limited, 43, 192
United Airlines, 147

United Nations Criminal Research Unit, 357
United Parcel Service (UPS), 456–457
Universal Studios, 127
University of Aston, 488
University of Michigan, 403
University of New Brunswick, 52
University of Ottawa, 505
University of Toronto, 15
University of Western Ontario, **411**
UPS Canada Ltd., 457
U.S. Air Force, 143
U.S. Navy, 93
USA Networks, 127

V

Vertically Inclined Rock Gym, 64
Victorian Order of Nurses, **44**
Vintners Quality Alliance, **502**
Virgin Group, 410, 429
Vitro, 474
Volvo, 155, 312, 484, 492–493

W

W. K. Buckley Ltd., 478
Wal-mart, 497
Walt Disney Company, 432, 436, 474
Wang, 140
Wang Laboratories, 440
Warner Brothers, 454
Warner-Lambert, 88
Warner-Lambert Canada Inc., 191
Watts Industries (Canada) Inc., 273
Weldwood of Canada, 32
Wells Fargo Bank, 141
West Fraser Timber Co., 32
Westcoast Energy Group, 348
Western Electric, 12
Western Union Insurance, 59
Westinghouse, 516
Westray, 444
Weyerhaeuser Canada Ltd., 192
Wild Oats Market, 171
Wilton Connor Packaging, 45
WinWhatWhere Corp., 273
W.L. Gore & Associates, 378

Wood Science & Technology Centre, 52
Workspace Dynamics, 226
World Bank, 442

X

XEL Communications, Inc., **260**, 262
Xerox, 43, 44, 46, 141, 190, 252, 417, 454, 481
Xerox Canada, **44**, 51, 409

Y

Yogen Früz World-Wide Inc., 303, **304**
York University, 101
YWCA, 166

Z

Zellers, 497

PHOTO CREDITS